This collection of original articles on offenders with special needs covers all the bases—mental health, medical, special populations, community based treatment, and administration. From legal issues and the role of law enforcement to specific recommendations for special populations like the homeless, incarcerated veterans, and other often overlooked and underserved groups, this volume offers a long overdue contribution to both researchers and practitioners. The *Routledge Handbook on Offenders with Special Needs* is both innovative and thorough in helping the reader to better understand special needs offenders as well as offering insights concerning how to more effectively treat and whenever possible, reintegrate them into their respective communities.

Michael Braswell, Ph.D., Professor Emeritus, Department of Criminal Justice and Criminology, East Tennessee State University

The *Routledge Handbook on Offenders with Special Needs* is a must read for those interested in learning about the various challenges and concerns that impact special needs offenders and the people who care for them. Topics include administration and management, special populations, medical and mental health, and treatment in the community.

Michael Bush, Ph.D., Associate Professor, Department of Political Science, Criminal Justice, and Organizational Leadership, Northern Kentucky University

At long last—a comprehensive resource for academic and criminal justice professionals that addresses the complex and unique needs of a broad range of offenders in need of special care, treatment, and management across the criminal justice system. Drawing on her special advocacy for her brother, Zack, Kimberly Dodson has assembled research that examines all aspects of special offender needs—from unique barriers specific to each need—to emerging, innovative, and evidence-based programs and approaches that offer support for more humane, proactive, and targeted criminal justice policies and practices.

Rosemary L. Gido, Ph.D., Professor Emerita, Department of Criminology, Indiana University of Pennsylvania, Editor, *Women's Mental Health Issues Across the Criminal Justice System*

The average American inmate is nothing close to "average," as the majority of those incarcerated in our prisons and jails have a litany of special needs. Dodson and colleagues provide a thorough examination of these inmates, providing insight into the troubled and frustrating world of men and women whose needs are often not met and challenging the notion that reintegration should be a seamless transition for the thousands reentering society each year. I look forward to using it in my own classroom.

Cathy D. Marcum, Ph.D., Associate Professor, Department of Government and Justice Studies, Appalachian State University

The dispensation of justice in corrections requires individualized treatment. The current movement away from a belief in an ethic of penal harm to an era of penal help among correctional practitioners and scholars also signals the need for compassionate and science-based care for those incarcerated in jails and prisons. In Kimberly Dodson's edited volume, *Routledge Handbook on Offenders with Special Needs*, the authors provide a systematic and valuable delineation of who among these inmates needs specialized care and how it might best be delivered in a manner that is just, appropriate, and befitting a country that professes an evolving sense of decency.

Mary K. Stohr, Ph.D., Professor, Department of Criminal Justice and Criminology, Washington State University

ROUTLEDGE HANDBOOK ON OFFENDERS WITH SPECIAL NEEDS

Current estimates indicate that approximately 2.2 million people are incarcerated in federal, state, and local correctional facilities across the United States. There are another 5 million under community correctional supervision. Many of these individuals fall into the classification of special needs or special populations (e.g., women, juveniles, substance abusers, mentally ill, aging, and chronically or terminally ill offenders). Medical care and treatment costs represent the largest portion of correctional budgets, and estimates suggest that these costs will continue to rise. In the community, probation and parole officers are responsible for helping special needs offenders find appropriate treatment resources. Therefore, it is important to understand the needs of these special populations and how to effectively care for and address their individual concerns.

The *Routledge Handbook on Offenders with Special Needs* is an in-depth examination of offenders with special needs, such as those who are learning-challenged, developmentally disabled, and mentally ill, as well as substance abusers, sex offenders, women, juveniles, and chronically and terminally ill offenders. Areas that previously have been unexamined (or examined in a limited way) are explored. For example, this text carefully examines the treatment of gay, lesbian, bisexual, and transgender offenders, and racial and gender disparities in health care delivery, as well as pregnancy and parenthood behind bars, homelessness, and the incarceration of veterans and immigrants. In addition, the book presents legal and management issues related to the treatment and rehabilitation of special populations in prisons/jails and the community, including police-citizen interactions, diversion through specialty courts, obstacles and challenges related to reentry and reintegration, and the need for the development and implementation of evidence-based criminal justice policies and practices.

This is a key collection for students taking courses in prisons, penology, criminal justice, criminology, and related areas of study, and an essential resource for academics and practitioners working with offenders with special needs.

Kimberly D. Dodson, Ph.D., is an associate professor and criminology program director in the Department of Social and Cultural Sciences at the University of Houston—Clear Lake. She received her Ph.D. in criminology from Indiana University of Pennsylvania. Her research interests include offenders with special needs, correctional policy and program evaluation, and racial and gender inequalities in the criminal justice system. She formerly worked as a criminal investigator for the Greene County Sheriff's Department in Greeneville, Tennessee. Dodson currently serves as the chair of the Academy of Criminal Justice Sciences Minorities and Women Section.

ROUTLEDGE HANDBOOK ON OFFENDERS WITH SPECIAL NEEDS

Edited by Kimberly D. Dodson

LONDON AND NEW YORK

First published 2018 by Routledge

2 Park Square, Milton Park, Abingdon, Oxfordshire OX14 4RN
52 Vanderbilt Avenue, New York, NY 10017

Routledge is an imprint of the Taylor & Francis Group, an informa business

First issued in paperback 2019

Library of Congress Cataloging-in-Publication Data
Names: Dodson, Kimberly D., editor.
Title: Routledge handbook on offenders with special needs / edited by Kimberly D. Dodson.
Description: New York, NY : Routledge, 2018. | Includes bibliographical references and index.
Identifiers: LCCN 2017060137 (print) | LCCN 2018013390 (ebook) | ISBN 9781315626574 (master) | ISBN 9781138648180 (hardback)
Subjects: LCSH: Special needs offenders—United States. | Prisoners—Services for—United States. | Criminal justice, Administration of—United States.
Classification: LCC HV9469 (ebook) | LCC HV9469 .R68 2018 (print) | DDC 364.3087/0973—dc23
LC record available at https://lccn.loc.gov/2017060137

ISBN: 978-1-138-64818-0 (hbk)
ISBN: 978-0-367-81915-6 (pbk)

Typeset in Bembo
by Apex CoVantage, LLC

To the memory of my friend and mentor, Lynnis Jewel Fender, who adopted me as her "protégé" and taught me justice is not just without compassion and mercy.

CONTENTS

CONTRIBUTORS

Cassandra A. Atkin-Plunk, Ph.D., is an assistant professor in the School of Criminology and Criminal Justice at Florida Atlantic University. She received her Ph.D. in criminal justice from Sam Houston State University in Huntsville, Texas. Her research interests span both institutional and community corrections, with an emphasis on contemporary issues in corrections, including problem-solving courts and the reentry and reintegration of offenders. Much of the research she has been involved in focuses on evidence-based practices and program evaluations in an effort to identify what works in corrections.

Laura Barber, M.S., received her degree in criminal justice from the University of North Carolina at Charlotte. Her primary research focus is related to homelessness and recidivism rates.

Alex J. Bishop, Ph.D., is an associate professor and Gerontology Program Coordinator in the Human Development and Family Science Department at Oklahoma State University, Stillwater, Oklahoma. He received his Ph.D. in human development and family studies in 2005 from Iowa State University, Ames, Iowa. His research is focused on measurement, assessment, and identification of underlying attributes of positive and healthy aging for older prisoner inmates. Of particular interest is examining the interplay between religiosity, social support, and forgiveness as mechanisms of physical and mental health for aging-in-prison.

Beverly Blount-Hill, MBA, is a human resource specialist and consultant and formerly worked as a continuous improvement administrator. Her research in sociology includes the stigma of perceived limitations, including discrimination against the aging and others with special needs. She also studies and teaches Christian theology at Canaan Christian Center, especially generational trends in religiosity and methods of Christian evangelism. She currently serves as an advisory board member for the Heritage West Global Biotechnology Research Park, focused on rebuilding parts of Louisville, Kentucky, through sustainable socioeconomic measures.

Kwan-Lamar Blount-Hill, Esq., is a senior research associate at the Research & Evaluation Center at John Jay College of Criminal Justice. He is an adjunct assistant professor at John Jay College and Borough of Manhattan Community College and lectures at Rutgers University School of Criminal Justice. He is an attorney licensed by the New Jersey, Georgia, and South Carolina Bars and previously served as a police officer and firefighter in South Carolina. He is currently completing a doctoral degree in criminal justice at CUNY Graduate Center/John Jay College, where he studies police and legal legitimacy, morality, religion and the law, race and justice, natural resource regulation, and emergency management.

Riane M. Bolin, Ph.D., is an assistant professor in the Department of Criminal Justice at Radford University. She earned her Ph.D. in criminology and criminal justice at the University of South Carolina. Her primary research interests include issues related to juvenile justice and corrections. In 2017, she was awarded the Tony J. Caeti Memorial Award by the Juvenile Justice and Delinquency Section of the Academy of Criminal Justice Sciences. This award recognizes young academics who have made significant contributions to the field of juvenile justice.

Hannah L. Brown, B.A., received her B.A. in psychology from the University of North Texas in 2017. She is currently pursuing a master's degree in criminology at the University of Houston–Clear Lake. Her research interests include attachment and the etiology of crime. It is Brown's goal to become a forensic psychologist by pursuing a doctorate in forensic psychology after the completion of her master's.

Jerrod Brown, Ph.D., is the treatment director for Pathways Counseling Center, Inc. Pathways provides programs and services benefiting individuals impacted by mental illness and addictions. Jerrod is also the founder and CEO of the American Institute for the Advancement of Forensic Studies (AIAFS), and the editor-in-chief of *Forensic Scholars Today* (FST) and the *Journal of Special Populations* (JSP). Jerrod has completed four separate master's degrees and holds graduate certificates in autism spectrum disorder (ASD), other health disabilities (OHD), and traumatic brain injuries (TBI).

LeAnn N. Cabage, Ph.D. candidate, is a lecturer of criminal justice in the Department of Sociology and Criminal Justice at Kennesaw State University. She is a doctoral candidate in the Department of Sociology at Iowa State University. Her research interests include program implementation and evaluation, gender-responsive programming, military veteran populations, and intersectionality. Her research has been published in the *Journal of Offender Rehabilitation* and *Armed Forces and Society*. She previously worked in a group home with at-risk youth with mental health needs. She currently serves as the vice-chair for the Academy of Criminal Justice Sciences Minorities and Women Section.

Andrea Cantora, Ph.D., is an assistant professor in the School of Criminal Justice at the University of Baltimore. She earned her Ph.D. from John Jay College of Criminal Justice, The CUNY. Her primary research interests are focused on issues related to incarceration, prison reentry, and urban crime prevention. Since 2002, Cantora has conducted research in prisons, jails, and community correction settings in New Jersey, New York, and Maryland. She previously worked as a research associate at John Jay's Research and Evaluation Center, and the Vera Institute of Justice's Center on Sentencing and Corrections. Her work has been published in the *Journal of Offender Rehabilitation*, the *Journal of Qualitative Criminal Justice and Criminology*, *Criminal Justice Studies*, and *American Journal of Criminal Justice*.

Lisa M. Carter Ph.D.**,** is an assistant professor in the Criminology Department at Florida Southern College. She also teaches courses for the Women and Gender Studies program at the college. She earned her Ph.D. in criminology at Indiana University of Pennsylvania. Her research interests include female criminality and gender-specific programming, corrections and rehabilitation, reintegration, and death penalty issues. She is the co-editor of the book *Female Offenders and Reentry: Pathways and Barriers to Returning to Society*.

Cody Charette, Ph.D., earned his doctorate from the Psychology, Policy, and Law program of the California School of Forensic Studies at Alliant International University located in Fresno, California. He specializes in threat assessment, deception detection, intelligence analysis, data analysis, and the use of technology for indirect assessment of offenders. He is currently a data analyst for the Fresno Fire Department in Fresno, California.

Janina Cich, M.A., is a retired law enforcement officer with two decades of criminal justice experience. She is an adjunct criminal justice and forensic behavioral health professor and frequent lecturer. Janina conducts crisis intervention training for law enforcement and mental health practitioners focusing on awareness, assessment, intervention, de-escalation techniques, and prevention approaches for mental health populations in the criminal justice systems. She currently serves as the chief operating officer of the American Institute for the Advancement of Forensic Studies (AIAFS).

Aida I. Diaz-La Cilento, Ph.D., is an adjunct instructor of criminal justice and sociology in the Departments of Criminal Justice and Social and Behavioral Sciences at Asnuntuck Community College. In addition to teaching, she is also a licensed professional counselor in the states of Connecticut and Florida. She works as a clinical supervisor with specialized training in trauma in a community mental health clinic serving children and families and adults. She received her Ph.D. in public safety leadership specializing in criminal justice from Capella University. Her research interests include offenders with special needs, prison innovation and reform, and mental health.

Kimberly D. Dodson, Ph.D., is an associate professor and Criminology Program director in the Department of Social and Cultural Sciences at the University of Houston–Clear Lake. She received her Ph.D. in criminology from Indiana University of Pennsylvania. Her research interests include offenders with special needs, correctional policy and program evaluation, and racial and gender inequalities in the criminal justice system. She formerly worked as a criminal investigator for the Greene County Sheriff's Department in Greeneville, Tennessee. She currently serves as the chair of the Academy of Criminal Justice Sciences Minorities and Women Section.

Deborah Eckberg, Ph.D., is a professor of criminal justice at Metropolitan State University (MN). Eckberg has published research spanning a wide variety of topics in journals such as *Race and Justice*, *American Sociologist*, the *Journal of Special Populations*, and the *Journal of Marriage and the Family*. Eckberg earned her bachelor of arts degree from Dartmouth College, and her master of arts and doctorate from the University of Minnesota, all in sociology with an emphasis in criminology.

Bradley D. Edwards, Ed.D., is a senior lecturer in the Department of Criminal Justice and Criminology at East Tennessee State University. His research interests include corrections, restorative justice, corporate misconduct, and policy evaluation. He earned his B.S., M.A, and Ed.D. from East Tennessee State University.

Robert D. Hanser, Ph.D., is the coordinator of the Department of Criminal Justice at the University of Louisiana–Monroe. He is also a past administrator of North Delta Regional Training Academy (NDTRA), where he provided leadership and oversight for police officer and jailer training throughout the northeast region of Louisiana. He is the director of Offender Programming for LaSalle Corrections and is responsible for overseeing inmate reception, drug rehabilitation, and inmate reentry. Lastly, he currently serves on the Louisiana Reentry Advisory Council, a gubernatorial appointment. He likewise is the board president for Freedmen, Inc., a local nonprofit organization that provides reentry assistance for offenders entering society.

Mary E. Harrison Joynt, Ph.D. candidate, is a lecturer in Women and Gender Studies at Iowa State University. She is a doctoral candidate in gerontology with a home department in Human Development and Family Studies. Her research interests are multidisciplinary, covering gender and social inequalities and aging. She has worked with older adults in the Ames community in conjunction with Healthiest Ames to study the effects of exercise on activity level. She received her master's degree in sociology at Iowa State University.

Jeffrey Haun, Psy.D., LP, ABPP, is employed as a forensic psychologist for the Minnesota Department of Human Services. He is also an adjunct assistance professor in the Department of Psychiatry at the University of Minnesota and an adjunct instructor in the Forensic Behavioral Health Program at Concordia University–St. Paul. He is board certified in forensic psychology by the American Board of Professional Psychology.

Sydney M. Kennedy, M.A., earned her M.A. in sociology from the University of Houston–Clear Lake. She also earned her B.S. in psychology from the University of Houston–Clear Lake. Her research interests include offenders with special needs, correctional policy, and serial murder and homicide. Kennedy is a member of the Texas Association Against Sexual Assault and a member of the Academy of Criminal Justice Sciences Minorities and Women Section.

Deborah Koetzle, Ph.D., is an associate professor in the Department of Public Management and the executive officer of the Doctoral Program in Criminal Justice. She earned her doctorate in criminal justice from the University of Cincinnati in 2006. Her research interests center on effective interventions for offenders, problem-solving courts, risk/need assessments, and the use of social media by police departments. She has served as a consultant to local, state, and federal agencies on the topic of assessment, treatment, and quality assurance within both institutional and community-based programs and is currently working with the National Association of Drug Court Professionals to develop empirically based standards for adult drug courts. Her research has appeared in *Justice Quarterly*, *Crime and Delinquency*, and the *Journal of Research in Crime and Delinquency*.

Ryan M. Labrecque, Ph.D., is an assistant professor in the Department of Criminology and Criminal Justice at Portland State University. He received his Ph.D. in criminal justice from the University of Cincinnati. His research focuses on the evaluation of correctional interventions, the effects of prison life, the development of risk and needs assessments for community and institutional corrections settings, and the transfer of knowledge to practitioners and policy makers. Ryan is a former correctional officer and probation officer. His work has appeared in *Criminal Justice Policy Review*; *Journal of Crime and Justice*; *Psychology, Public Policy, and Law*; *Victims and Offenders*; *Violence and Victims*; and most recently *Corrections: Policy, Practice and Research*.

Jodie M. Lawston, Ph.D., is Professor of Women's, Gender, and Sexuality Studies and Faculty Director of Community Engaged Scholarship at California State University San Marcos. She received her Ph.D. in sociology from the University of California, San Diego. Her research interests include the intersections of gender, race, and incarceration, mass incarceration, and immigrant detention and imprisonment.

Margaret E. Leigey, Ph.D., is an associate professor and chair of the Department of Criminology at The College of New Jersey in Ewing, New Jersey. Her research focuses on special populations of offenders including life-sentenced inmates, older inmates, female inmates, and inmates with physical disabilities. In addition to her book *The Forgotten Men: Serving Life without Parole* (2015,

Rutgers University Press), her research has appeared in *The Prison Journal, Journal of Correctional Health Care, Women & Criminal Justice*, and *Drug and Alcohol Dependence*.

Shelley J. Listwan, Ph.D., is an associate professor in the Department of Criminal Justice and Criminology at the University of North Carolina at Charlotte. She earned her Ph.D. from the University of Cincinnati. Her research interests focus on correctional rehabilitation, criminological theory, and victimization in prison. Her work has been published in *Justice Quarterly, International Journal of Offender Therapy and Comparative Criminology, Criminal Justice and Behavior*, and the *Journal of Contemporary Criminology*.

Adam K. Matz, Ph.D., is an assistant professor in the Department of Criminal Justice at the University of North Dakota. He previously worked for the American Probation and Parole Association and received his Ph.D. in Criminology from Indiana University of Pennsylvania. His research interests include community supervision, interagency partnerships, information sharing, and occupational culture. He has been involved in numerous committees, including as an executive counselor for the Academy of Criminal Justice Sciences Corrections Section and as a former vice-chair of the Global Standards Council with the U.S. Department of Justice.

Cedric Michel, Ph.D., is an assistant professor in the Department of Criminology and Criminal Justice at the University of Tampa. He received his doctoral degree from the University of South Florida. His main research interest is the effect of increased public knowledge about crime on attitudes toward it. Such attitudes comprise perceptions of crime seriousness as well as support for punitive criminal justice policies. His research has highlighted racial and gender differences in decreases in public support for the death penalty after exposure to relevant information about capital punishment. Similarly, several of his publications have measured public knowledge about white-collar crime and the effect of increased information on general sentiments toward corporate offenders.

Michael B. Mitchell, B.A., is a master's student and research assistant in the Department of Criminology and Criminal Justice at the University of Texas at Arlington. His research interests include race and crime, families of incarcerated individuals, juvenile justice, and intersectionality. He specifically is interested in exploring how incarceration affects fatherhood among black males and its implications for the black family in the era of mass incarceration. He plans to pursue a Ph.D. in criminal justice and become a college professor.

Jennifer Guriel Myers, Ph.D., is an associate professor of criminal justice and director of the Master's Program in Criminal Justice at Fairmont State University. A licensed clinical psychologist, Myers is also the owner and manager of Mountaineer Psychological Services in Morgantown, West Virginia, where she performs a variety of psychological evaluations for the courts. Myers is a recognized expert in forensic psychology and regularly testifies for local, state, and federal court systems. Prior to her academic work, Myers worked as a psychologist and residential drug abuse program coordinator for the Federal Bureau of Prisons.

Diane Neal, M.S., LPCC, is the executive director of Project Pathfinder, Inc., PPI provides programs and services for problematic and offending sexual behaviors. She has over 25 years working with mental health issues and specializes in sexualized behaviors targeting highest risk and special needs clients. Diane provides consults and training to multifaceted organizations and universities addressing primary prevention and responding to sexual assault. Diane holds multiple certifications in trauma treatment, trauma-informed care, autism spectrum and developmental disorders, sexual offending and healthy sexuality.

Tiffaney Parkman, Ph.D., is a Lecturer in the School of Health and Human Services at the University of Baltimore. She received her Ph.D. from Virginia Polytechnic Institute and State University. Parkman has a love for mental health and taking care of the mentally ill. This love was fostered by her first job after college graduation working in a group home for adults diagnosed with serious mental illnesses. In addition, Parkman has worked as a mental health counselor at a medium-security prison. Her research interests focus on families, prisoner reentry, and the mentally ill.

James R. Patton, Ed.D., is an adjunct associate professor in the Department of Special Education at the University of Texas at Austin. He also is an independent consultant and a former general and special education teacher. Patton's research interests include transition assessment and planning, students with disabilities in higher education, individuals with disabilities in the criminal justice system, and differentiating instruction for students with special needs in inclusive settings. He earned his B.S. from the University of Notre Dame and his M.Ed. and Ed.D. from the University of Virginia.

Jennifer Pealer, Ph.D., is an associate professor in the Department of Criminal Justice and Criminology at East Tennessee State University, where she teaches courses in corrections, juvenile justice, and statistics. Pealer has served as a consultant to many correctional programs throughout the United States by providing training and technical assistance in offender risk/need instruments and effective practices in risk reduction and techniques for changing offending behavior. Jennifer has published articles in the field of correctional rehabilitation and public opinion on crime and correctional issues. She earned her B.A. and M.A. in criminal justice from East Tennessee State University and her Ph.D. in criminal justice from the University of Cincinnati.

Edward A. Polloway, Ed.D., is a Rosel H. Schewel Distinguished Professor of Education at Lynchburg College and the editor of the *Lynchburg College Journal of Special Education*. His research interests are related to policy issues in the fields of intellectual disabilities and learning disabilities and curriculum and methodological issues relative to special education in general. Polloway received his Ed.D. from the University of Virginia.

Elizabeth Quinby, M.A., received her master of arts in counseling and psychological services from Saint Mary's University of Minnesota in 2015. She works as lead event coordinator for the American Institute for the Advancement of Forensic Studies (AIAFS). She is also currently working at Integrity Living Options in Minneapolis as a community supports director, overseeing the creation and implementation of behavior plans and behavior services for individuals with serious and persistent mental illness. Elizabeth is also volunteering with the Innocence Project of Minnesota as a consultant.

Lincoln B. Sloas, Ph.D., is an assistant professor in the School of Criminology and Criminal Justice at Florida Atlantic University. He received his Ph.D. in criminology, law and society from George Mason University. His research interests include evidence-based practices, especially as it applies to the field of corrections, problem-solving courts, and offenders with substance abuse and mental health issues.

Victoria M. Smiegocki is a Ph.D. student in the Department of Justice, Law & Criminology at American University. She currently is also pursuing a secondary major in public policy as well as a certificate program in applied statistics. Her research interests include criminal sentencing disparities, school safety initiatives, policy analysis, and quantitative methods.

Andrew L. Spivak, Ph.D., is associate professor of sociology at the University of Nevada, Las Vegas. A graduate of The University of Oklahoma (Ph.D., 2007), he previously worked in corrections for 10 years. He teaches courses in criminology, penology, demography, research methods, and statistics, supervises a prison casework internship program for students that he developed in partnership with the Nevada Department of Corrections, and is a recipient of several university and state teaching awards. His published scholarship relates to topics including prison recidivism, suicide and violent behavior, juvenile justice processing, tobacco regulation, and residential segregation.

Christine Tartaro, Ph.D., is a professor of criminal justice at Stockton University. She has a Ph.D. in criminal justice from Rutgers University. She has worked as a researcher for the New Jersey Department of Corrections and the Police Foundation and as a research consultant for the New Jersey Juvenile Justice Commission. She does consulting and expert witness work in the area of suicide prevention in custody. Her research interests include new generation jails, suicide in correctional facilities, mental health, and crime prevention.

Aaron Trnka, M.A., LMFT, is the clinical director and CEO of Lighthouse Psychological Services, Inc., a sexual offender program for special needs adult males. He has practiced in the field since 2004. He has specialized in trauma-informed care, is certified in EMDR, and currently directs an adult day treatment program for maladaptive sexual behaviors. Aaron has experience working with children, adults, families, and couples.

Chris Wakefield is a graduate student in sociology at the University of Nevada, Las Vegas. Chris received a bachelor of arts in sociology from Syracuse University with a minor in lesbian, gay, bisexual, and transgender studies. Wakefield's research interests include the medicalization of gender and sexual identity, criminalized sexual identities, and sex offense policy from initial reporting to postrelease control. He is a former intern in the Nevada Department of Corrections, working directly with inmates at a medium-security facility alongside case management staff.

Anthony Wartnik was a trial judge for 34 years, serving as presiding Judge of Juvenile Court, Family Law Court Chief Judge, Dean Emeritus of the Washington Judicial College, Judicial College Board of Trustees chair and the Washington Supreme Court's Judicial Conference Education Committee chair. Wartnik is a nationally and internationally recognized speaker, author, and trainer on issues involving fetal alcohol spectrum disorder and the law and teaches postgraduate courses on forensic mental health and special needs populations at Concordia University, St. Paul, MN.

John H. Weigel, J.D., is a Ph.D. student in the School of Criminal Justice at Texas State University. He earned his juris doctorate from The University of Texas School of Law. Weigel also earned two M.A. degrees, one in history and the other in criminology. He received his B.A. from the University of Texas at Austin. His research interests include correctional policy and historical legal analysis.

FOREWORD

The *Routledge Handbook on Offenders with Special Needs* is a much-needed and timely contribution to our understanding of procedural, social, and criminal justice in the United States. Too often the statistics framing the challenges confronting the criminal justice system are summations of arrest, conviction, and incarceration rates that obscure the everyday reality of professional practice, offending, and victimization. The magnitude of the system and the challenges of trying to achieve justice at the complex intersections of race/ethnicity, gender, class, age, and sexual identity can quickly become overwhelming. Moreover, professionals at each stage of the system are challenged to find solutions within the limits of their agencies to address mental health, atypical neurological function, chemical dependency, trauma, abuse, housing insecurity, family dysfunction, and other unique needs presented by those involved in the criminal justice system. This collection, however, gives hope and provides a path forward in understanding how we may achieve justice through an ethic of care, collaboration, and desire to make meaningful change throughout the criminal justice system.

This *Handbook* illustrates the perils of using the criminal justice system as a first response to the symptoms and public presentations of mental illness, drug addiction, trauma, and poverty. Although police may function as the most readily available to deal with public disorder in most communities, their ultimate power resides within the coercive powers and practices of the criminal justice system and not within the systems of care designed to provide treatment, support, and prevention services such as mental health, medicine, social services, public health, and public education. Likewise, the failure to invest in institutions of care and prevention creates an overreliance on the criminal justice system to respond to emergencies leading to the detrimental consequences of criminalizing mental illness, addiction, and poverty. Therefore, by default rather than by design, the criminal justice system is tasked with the additional responsibility of being the primary provider of mental health, substance abuse treatment, and shelter for the homeless, instead of the systems purposefully designed to deal with such special needs populations. For many people and communities, especially poor communities, the only way to access needed services is to wait until someone breaks the law and enters the criminal justice system. It is time that federal and state legislatures and policy makers begin to understand the human rights crisis this approach creates within our communities and the additional burden it places on the criminal justice system.

As illustrated by the heart-wrenching experiences of editor Kimberly Dodson's family, leading up to her brother Zack's death in prison, families are often overwhelmed by the co-occurring health and justice issues confronting their loved ones. The power of Kim's experiences with her brother is allowing us to observe the emotional turmoil imbedded in the tension between holding

Zack accountable for his unlawful behavior while simultaneously understanding how mental illness (bipolar disorder), atypical neurological function (ADHD), injury (TBI), and substance abuse can culminate in a downward spiral worsened by a criminal justice system ill prepared to deal with such complex issues. Sadly, Zack and his family were subjected to a system that was at best apathetic and at worst criminally responsible for his death. Although Zack's death within the criminal justice system represents a rare event, the experiences of powerlessness experienced by Zack and his family are not unique. Even the well-meaning professionals working within the system are at times held powerless, or even actively sabotaged, in their attempts to understand and to prevent negative outcomes. Unfortunately, failure is often an accepted or unchallenged outcome by many criminal justice systems and made invisible by shifting responsibility for failure from the agency to the individuals passing through the system.

At its core, this volume shows that it is possible to change the outcomes for people like Zack and his family, but it requires purposeful action, in other words professional activism, by leaders across the criminal justice system. If criminal justice professionals are going to be the "gatekeepers" not just to the criminal justice system but also to other needed systems of care, especially mental health and chemical dependency treatment, then it is time that we educate and empower criminal justice professionals to serve as boundary spanners capable of collaborating and interfacing with other systems of care. Without professional advocates employed within the criminal justice system and empowered to divert people with special needs into other systems of care, we automatically default to coercion, control, and punishment instead of accountability, support, and treatment.

The good news is that in the last several decades, researchers and criminal justice professionals have come to understand what works in reforming the criminal justice system to produce positive outcomes for police, courts, and corrections. Advances are being made that acknowledge the need for collaboration and an advanced understanding about how criminal justice personnel may use the coercive power of the state to advance the intentions of helping systems of care to produce positive outcomes for the criminal justice system, communities, families, offenders, and victims. For example, police are mobilizing to create special units to deal with mental health, drug addiction, family violence, homelessness, veterans, and other populations with the intention of diverting special needs populations into other systems equipped to provide appropriate interventions. Courts are developing alternative approaches via therapeutic jurisprudence and problem-solving courts to bring experts together from multiple systems to leverage their resources to hold offenders accountable for their behavior while simultaneously providing support and treatment to address the conditions underlying repeated involvement with the criminal justice system. Corrections is implementing evidence-based practices that support the process of change during incarceration while designing continuums of care that extend into the community to achieve successful reentry and permanent transition out of the criminal justice system. It is clear that successful innovation in criminal justice is being driven by interagency collaboration and the spanning of institutional and interdisciplinary boundaries between agencies and systems.

It is evident that many of the conditions influencing unlawful behavior are greater than any one system can solve independently. Yet we tend to frame the criminal justice system as a "one size fits all" response to solving the multifaceted problems challenging individuals and communities. In general, we still remain politically and philosophically entrenched in the notion that the criminal justice system, through pure determination and hard work, can solve problems independent from the leadership of other systems purposefully designed and positioned to address the needs of individuals destined for the criminal justice system. Such a narrow approach is likely to fail the individuals working within the criminal justice system as well as the victims, families, and communities expecting both justice and positive outcomes.

The timely relevance of the *Routledge Handbook on Offenders with Special Needs* is to bring forth the evidence that innovation within the criminal justice system must be built on collaboration and an ethic of care. The system must move toward understanding the challenges confronting individuals and communities within a human rights framework that is grounded in respecting and protecting the human dignity of all persons. Utilizing a human rights framework promotes a shared responsibility among public institutions to solve problems together versus struggling in isolation, often sabotaging the work of the other, at the ultimate expense of achieving criminal, social, and community justice. The *Handbook* frees the imagination to think about how justice may be achieved through empowering criminal justice professionals to move beyond reactionary strategies within the narrow confines of coercion and punishment to a professional activism that spans institutional boundaries creating the space to pursue meaningful outcomes for all those affected by the criminal justice system.

Faith E. Lutze, Ph.D.
Washington State University

PREFACE

In the United States, approximately 4,500 inmates die annually in state and federal prisons and local jails (Noonan, Rohloff, & Ginder, 2015). In 2001, my brother, Zachary "Zack" Jones, became a part of that national statistic when he died at Northeast Correctional Complex in Mountain City, Tennessee. His death was *the* defining moment of my academic career, and it sent me on a trajectory of research and advocacy for offenders with special needs. Let me explain.

From a young age, Zack was continually in trouble in both school and the community. He did not perform well in school and he was held back in the first and ninth grades. Naturally, he was upset when he realized this meant he was in the same grade as his "little sister." However, Zack was outgoing and funny, people were drawn to his charismatic personality, and no one seemed to notice he was falling behind. He frequently joked around in his classes, and in the eighth grade, one of his teachers awarded him the "Class Turkey" Award (i.e., a small plastic turkey). Zack also had an unpredictable temper and was regularly in the principal's office for fighting with other students, and on one occasion, he physically assaulted a teacher. This latter offense resulted in him being suspended from school.

In hindsight, I believe his behaviors were an attempt to draw attention away from his inability to comprehend his classwork. As he entered high school, school counselors diagnosed him with a learning disability, and my parents hired a personal tutor that he worked with three days a week for nearly two years. However, at this point, Zack was already experimenting with alcohol and drugs, and I believe he was merely going through the motions in an attempt to please our parents. In 1982, we were scheduled to graduate from high school; I did, but Zack did not.

The following year Zack and a friend stole a 5-gallon water bottle from a storage lot at a dentist office. Police apprehended Zack a few moments later and he was charged with petty larceny, which at the time was a felony. His friend ran and was never apprehended or charged with the crime. Zack was sentenced to three years at the Apalachee Correctional Institution, a facility for youthful offenders located in Sneads, Florida. He was 19 years old.

After he completed his sentence, his life became a series of brushes with the law, and he was in and out of jail and prison for a variety of offenses. Typically, his offenses (e.g., public intoxication, driving under the influence, and marijuana possession) were nonviolent and were related to his use of alcohol and/or drugs. I do not mention this to excuse his behavior but to clarify that much of what he did was the result of his addiction. While he was incarcerated, he participated in Alcoholics Anonymous (AA), Narcotics Anonymous (NA), and other self-help groups. However, many of the institutional parole officers and counselors were overworked and simply did not have the time or inclination to help treat Zack's addiction in any real way. Alcohol was a demon he could not conquer.

In 1989, Zack's life took a turn for the worse, and he was charged with two counts of aggravated assault in Sevierville, Tennessee. No one was physically injured during the commission of the crime, but the victims alleged that Zack used a firearm to frighten and intimidate them, although the police never recovered a firearm. Because of his prior criminal history, he was adjudicated as a "career offender," and that, coupled with the seriousness of the offense, resulted in a 15-year prison sentence. He was transferred from the Sevier County Jail to Brushy Mountain Prison in Wartburg, Tennessee, which was the classification center for all inmates in East Tennessee at that time. He was classified as a violent offender and sent to West Tennessee State Penitentiary, a maximum-security facility that he jokingly called "West Tennessee High," for high security. After four years, Zack was reclassified as a medium-security inmate and transferred to Northwest Correctional Complex, where he served two more years of his sentence. At the end of six years, he was reclassified as a minimum-security inmate and sent to Carter County Work Camp in Roan Mountain, Tennessee.

After he served eight years of his sentence, he was granted parole. He was able to secure early release because he had accrued "good time" credits, which Tennessee statute allowed for inmates who worked while they were incarcerated. My family was elated when we brought him home from the prison in the spring of 1997. Sadly, his freedom was short-lived, and he was rearrested just over a year later for driving under the influence, which was a violation of his parole. Zack called me from the Washington County Jail in Jonesborough, Tennessee, that night to let me know he had been arrested. I knew what this meant—he would be returning to prison. I cried most of that night and wondered how I was going to tell our mother.

As expected, in the spring of 1998, the judge ruled that Zack had indeed violated his parole and he was sent back to the Sevier County Jail in Sevierville, Tennessee, where his original crime had been committed and his original sentence was reinstated. Zack was scheduled to be sent back to Brushy Mountain Prison for classification again. However, on June 29, 1998, my mother received a phone call from a jail official who informed her that Zack had fallen backwards and hit his head on the concrete pavement while playing "football" in a recreational area of the jail. He also informed her that Zack was "in real bad shape." Zack was transported via ambulance to the Critical Care Unit (CCU) at the University of Tennessee Hospital in Knoxville, Tennessee.

At the time of his injury, I was working as a deputy sheriff with the Greene County Sheriff's Department in Greeneville, Tennessee. My mother called me at work to let me know about Zack's injury. When I hung up the phone, I yelled out to my sergeant, "I have to go! My brother has been injured and he's been taken to UT hospital!" I did not wait for his response. I ran down the front steps of the sheriff's office, jumped in my cruiser, and drove as fast as I could to my parents' home, which fortunately was less than a mile away.

My parents were waiting on the porch when I arrived, and I yelled to them, "Get in my cruiser! I'll drive you to the hospital!" I did not care that I did not have permission to use my cruiser for personal business. It was an emergency vehicle, and this was an emergency. Once I made it to the interstate, I turned on my blue lights and siren and drove as fast as I could to get to the hospital.

When we arrived at the CCU nurses' desk to ask about the condition of my brother, the nurse asked me, "Are you here to see the inmate?" At that moment, I realized I was still in uniform and she thought I was there to guard him. I replied, "Yes, he's my brother." The look of surprise mixed with embarrassment flashed across her face, but she led us to CCU to see him. He was semi-conscious, his body was flinching, and he was clinching his hands. He was obviously in pain, and a single teardrop rolled out of his left eye and down his cheek. There was dried blood in his hair.

The doctor informed us that Zack had suffered a traumatic brain injury (TBI) that would require surgery to save his life. He asked us if we knew how the injury occurred and my mother relayed the information the jail official had told her, Zack was injured from a fall. The doctor looked puzzled and told us that the trauma to Zack's head was inconsistent with a fall and, in the doctor's opinion, was more likely the result of a severe beating. Over the next few days, inmates from the Sevier County Jail sent letters to my mother alleging that they had witnessed correctional officers beating Zack. However, we were never able to substantiate these claims. The surgery was successful, but Zack remained in a coma for the next two weeks.

While he was still in a coma, the Sevier County Sheriff made the decision to transfer Zack to the Lois M. DeBerry Special Needs Facility (SNF) in Nashville, Tennessee. We were shocked and devastated that the sheriff had made the decision to send him back to prison while he was still in a comatose state. Traveling to DeBerry SNF was a considerable hardship for my family because the facility was over 300 miles away from the town where we lived. In addition, it was a substantial financial burden for my parents because they were on a fixed income. It was especially emotionally and physically taxing on me because I was in the first trimester of my pregnancy with my youngest child, although I had not revealed this to my parents or coworkers. Nevertheless, we pooled our financial and emotional resources to stay near my brother in Nashville because it was important for us to pull together as a family.

When Zack finally woke up, he could not remember our parents, our siblings, his wife, his son, or me. He did not know how to eat, use the bathroom, walk, or talk. He was like infant—learning things for the first time. He was never the same, and the injury had changed him in fundamental ways. The sharp, witty man I had known was gone, and he had been replaced by the child before me. He no longer joked around, teased, or, for that matter, smiled. Through researching his condition, I would learn that his lack of emotional expressiveness was generally known as "flat affect." I also learned that this is a normal consequence for people who suffer TBIs.

After his injury, he was easily manipulated by other inmates, who would talk him into giving away his personal belongings or buying them commissary. Unfortunately, correctional administrators and staff regularly mainstreamed him into general population, where things frequently escalated. Inmates laughed and called him "retard," stole his personal belongings, and assaulted him on numerous occasions. At one point, he was sexually assaulted by three inmates because he refused to give them his shoes. In another instance, one inmate phoned my mother to let her know he was willing "to protect Zack" from other inmates who might try to harm him. In return for his services, he needed my mother to place $50 into his commissary account. He said if she did not send the money he could not be held responsible for what might happen to Zack. Yes, it was extortion, but my mother feared that if she did not comply, Zack would be harmed.

Zack also began having seizures after his injury, and he was prescribed medication for his condition. In 2001, he was transferred to Northeast Correctional Complex in Mountain City, Tennessee. There, he shared a cell with another inmate. Zack requested to be moved on several occasions because his cellmate had threatened him with physical violence. In August 2001, his cellmate heated a coffee pot of water and doused Zack with it as he slept. Zack suffered second and third degree burns to his neck and chest. Once the coffee pot was empty, Zack's cellmate used it as a weapon and repeatedly struck Zack in the head, which left a four-inch gash across his forehead that required stitches. He was temporarily moved to a medical dorm for treatment. When correctional officers questioned the man about why he had assaulted Zack, he replied, "He snores too loud." The man who assaulted him was never charged with a crime. I believe these additional injuries hastened my brother's death.

On August 20, 2001, my mother visited Zack at Northeast Correctional Complex. It was not her usual day to visit, but that day she said she felt compelled to see him. He was late getting to the visitation room that day. He explained that he was not feeling well and that he had attempted to sign up for medical call. He explained to our mother that he was out of his seizure medication, but he did not have the $3 inmate co-pay required for the doctor visit. As a result, he was not seen by medical staff that day.

He brought a deck of cards with him to the visitation room and he asked my mother to play "a couple of hands of rummy." At the time, my mother thought it was odd that he wanted to play rummy because they had not played it since he was a young child. When they finished their second hand of rummy, his eyes rolled backwards, he grabbed his chest, and slid out of his chair onto the floor. My mother jumped up, started screaming and begging for someone, anyone, to help him. According to her, no one rendered medical aid to Zack while he was lying on the floor dying. Later, other inmates wrote to my mother alleging that Zack laid on a gurney in the hallway near the medical unit for approximately 20 minutes before the ambulance arrived to transport him to the local hospital emergency room. During that time, the inmates also alleged that none of the medical staff render any type of medical aid to Zack. Again, we could not confirm these allegations.

My mother believes he died on the floor at the prison, although he was officially declared dead at the Johnson County Community Hospital in Mountain City, Tennessee. A priest at the hospital administered Zack's last rites shortly after his death, with our mother's permission. His autopsy revealed that he died of a massive seizure. He was 39 years old. My mother still puts his turkey on the table every year at Thanksgiving.

In reflecting on his death, I feel I lost him twice—once when he was injured and once when he died. My grief was overwhelming, and I was haunted by questions that had no definitive answers. What really happened the day he was injured? Wasn't his life worth $3? Why did he have to suffer so much and for so long? Why did the parole board deny our request for compassionate release? Why did God let him die? What had his life meant? What was I going to do about it? The answer to this latter question culminates in the writing of the *Routledge Handbook on Offenders with Special Needs*, a journey that was nearly two decades in the making.

The *Routledge Handbook on Offenders with Special Needs* is a comprehensive, in-depth examination of offenders who require special care or management within the criminal justice system. The intent of the handbook is to be an educational resource for criminal justice practitioners and medical and mental health professionals who treat and care for offenders with special needs in both the system and community. Additionally, it is an academic resource for instructors, students, or anyone interested in learning more about the issues related to the treatment offenders with special needs in the criminal justice system.

Although there are several books available on offenders with special needs (see e.g., Aday, 2003; Ashford, Sales, & Reid, 2001; Craig, Lindsay, & Browne, 2010; Fagan & Ax, 2010; Gideon, 2013; Hanser, 2007; Lindsay, Taylor, & Sturmey, 2004; Slate, Buffington-Vollum, & Johnson, 2013; van Wormer, 2010), many focus on one segment of special needs offenders (Aday, 2003; Craig et al., 2010; Fagan & Ax, 2010; Lindsay et al., 2004; Slate et al., 2013; van Wormer, 2010; Young & Reviere, 2006). For example, Craig et al.'s (2010) book examines sex offenders with intellectual disabilities and Aday's (2003) book looks at aging inmates. However, other books have broader coverage and include discussions on a wide range of offenders with special needs (Gideon, 2013; Hanser, 2007). Even so, most of these books tend to limit their discussions to one aspect of the criminal justice system. For instance, Hanser (2007) discusses special needs populations on community corrections and Gideon (2013) focuses on special needs offenders in correctional institutions. The major strength of the *Routledge Handbook on Offenders with Special Needs* is its coverage of a broader range of offenders with special needs and the fact that it examines their experiences across the criminal justice system from arrest to reentry.

The handbook begins with a general discussion of the challenges and obstacles criminal justice practitioners and treatment professionals encounter when working with and treating offenders with special needs in both the criminal justice system and community. Offenders with special needs have diverse medical and mental health needs, and providing adequate treatment and care varies greatly across criminal justice and community settings. In addition, certain populations frequently require special housing considerations because they are vulnerable to mistreatment and abuse. For example, juveniles and lesbian, gay, bisexual, transgender, and queer (LGBTQ) offenders need additional safety and security precautions in many correctional facilities because of their gender identity or sexual orientation, which makes them targets for physical and sexual assault. In response, jail and other correctional officials must implement policies and procedures to prevent or reduce the likelihood of inmate victimization and punish those who victimize others.

The remainder of the handbook consists of four parts that cover administrative and management issues, special populations, medical and mental health issues, and treatment in the community. Part I presents the constitutional and legal issues related to the treatment of offenders with special needs throughout the criminal justice system and in the community. It highlights precedent cases, which represent the rule of law established by a higher court and are subsequently used in deciding similar cases, with the ultimate goal of ensuring prisoners' rights. Part I also includes an examination of specialty courts that address the specific needs of special needs offenders (e.g., mentally ill, drug offenders, and veterans) that allow them to be diverted out of the criminal justice system or avoid incarceration. Two chapters discuss specialized correctional facilities and specialized housing units dedicated to the management and treatment of special needs populations. In a related chapter, we explore the obstacles and barriers to managing and treating these offenders effectively in a jail setting, particularly inadequate staff training and insufficient financial resources.

A significant portion of the handbook is devoted to discussing the specific treatment and management concerns of a variety of special needs offenders who are serving time in jails, prisons, and detention facilities. Specifically, Part II explores individualized issues that relate to women offenders, parenting behind bars, juveniles, LGBTQ offenders, homeless offenders, immigrant prisoners, prison gangs, suicidal prisoners, and death row inmates. Each of these specialized categories of offenders presents criminal justice practitioners and health care professionals with diverse emotional, psychological, physical, and spiritual care and treatment needs.

Part III features an in-depth examination of medical and mental health treatment challenges and obstacles as well as some practical solutions for managing and treating special populations. This section also examines a broad range of special needs offenders, particularly those who present the most pressing safety and security concerns for criminal justice administrators and treatment professionals working throughout the justice system. The topics we cover include mentally ill offenders, substance abuse, offenders with physical disabilities, aging inmates, chronic and terminal illness, intellectually and developmentally disabled offenders, sex offenders with intellectual disabilities, offenders with learning disabilities and special educational needs, and racial, ethnic, and gender health care disparities. Several of these topics are absent from discussions of special needs populations or receive limited attention in the criminal justice literature (see, e.g., chronic and terminal illness, sex offenders with intellectual disabilities, and racial, ethnic, and gender health care disparities). Therefore, we thought it was not only an appropriate but a necessary component of the handbook to include a discussion of these special populations.

The final section of the handbook explores the treatment and management of special needs offenders in the community. We believe it is important to give readers a more complete picture of the experiences of special needs offenders throughout the criminal justice process. To accomplish this goal, as previously noted, we examine the criminal justice process for special needs offenders from arrest to reentry. Therefore, Part IV presents a discussion of policing special needs offenders, treating special needs offenders in the community, and reentry and reintegration. Finally, this section culminates in a discussion of the importance of developing and implementing evidence-based policies and practices in the criminal justice system. As the editor, it is my hope that the *Routledge Handbook on Offenders with Special Needs* will help to facilitate conversations among criminal justice and health care professionals to improve the treatment and care of special needs offenders, and to implement not only empirically supported policies and practices but policies and practices that emphasize care and compassion.

References

Aday, R. H. (2003). *Aging prisoners: Crisis in American corrections.* Westport, CT: Praeger.

Ashford, J. B., Sales, B. D., & Reid, W. H. (2001). *Treating adults and juvenile offenders with special needs.* Washington, DC: American Psychological Association.

Craig, L. A., Lindsay, W. R., & Browne, K. D. (2010). *Assessment and treatment of sexual offenders with intellectual disabilities: A handbook.* Hoboken, NJ: Wiley.

Fagan, T. J., & Ax, R. K. (2010). *Correctional mental health: From theory to best practice.* Thousand Oaks, CA: Sage.

Gideon, L. (2013). *Special needs offenders in correctional institutions.* Thousand Oaks, CA: Sage.

Hanser, R. D. (2007). *Special needs offenders in the community.* Boston, MA: Pearson.

Lindsay, W. R., Taylor, J. T., & Sturmey, P. (2004). *Offenders with developmental disabilities.* Hoboken, NJ: John Wiley & Sons Ltd.

Noonan, M. E., Rohloff, H., & Ginder, S. (2015). *Mortality in local jails and state prisons, 2000–2013.* Washington, DC: U.S. Department of Justice, Bureau of Justice Statistics.

Slate, R., Buffington-Vollum, J., & Johnson, W. W. (2013). *The criminalization of mental illness: Crisis and Opportunity for the justice system.* Durham, NC: Carolina Academic Press.

van Wormer, K. (2010). *Working with female offenders: A gender-sensitive approach.* Hoboken, NJ: Wiley.

Young, V. D., & Reviere, R. (2006). *Women behind bars: Gender and race in U.S. prisons.* Boulder, CO: Lynne Rienner Publishers.

ACKNOWLEDGMENTS

First, thanks to Routledge for the opportunity to serve as the editor of this handbook. It truly has been a labor of love and has allowed me to honor the memory of my brother, Zack, who was an offender with special needs. Thanks to Ellen Boyne, managing editor, for inviting me to work on this project. Thank you for your unwavering support over the years. I owe so much of my professional success to you. Thanks to Dr. Mickey Braswell for encouraging me to edit this handbook and the personal and professional mentorship you have given me. Also, thank you for giving me a platform to honor Zack and for your support of him during his incarceration.

Thanks to LeAnn Cabage for not only agreeing to contribute her expertise to this project but also supporting me personally and professionally. Thank you for the many hours we spent discussing ideas for this project, listening to me read portions of the book aloud, and reading and revising drafts of my writing. This project came together because of you. Thank you to the anonymous reviewers who gave me valuable feedback and suggestions for strengthening the content of this handbook. Thank you to the contributors for lending your time expertise to this project. A special shout out to Dr. Jerrod Brown and Dr. Robert Hanser for contributing multiple chapters to the handbook. Jerrod, thank you for your friendship, encouragement, and support. Rob, thank you for stepping up to ensure the completion of the handbook.

Finally, thanks to my mother, Margaret Hensley Jones, for encouraging me to "write a book about Zack." I know you believe this book will help offenders with special needs by improving their treatment and care in the criminal justice system and that it will be an inducement for justice and treatment professionals to advocate for the humane and ethical treatment of offenders with special needs.

1

CHALLENGES CRIMINAL JUSTICE PRACTITIONERS AND TREATMENT PROFESSIONALS ENCOUNTER WITH SPECIAL NEEDS OFFENDERS

Kimberly D. Dodson

> Mercy benefits the giver of mercy as well as the recipient. It is the act of a reduced punishment that distinguishes mercy from forgiveness. Mercy must also be distinguished from excuse or justification. Mercy assumes that the offender is in a position of powerlessness and need.
>
> —(Misner, 2000, p. 1324)

Introduction

Offenders with special needs are individuals who require special care, treatment, or management within the criminal justice system. Special needs offenders may have a variety of physical or mental disabilities or limitations that include psychological and psychiatric needs, developmental disabilities, social or educational deficiencies, language barriers, deafness or blindness, physical and mental handicaps related to aging, neurological impairments, and chronic and terminal illnesses. Certain physical or medical conditions that require prisoners to receive specialized care or treatment can also result in them being classified as special needs. Pregnant inmates, for instance, require regular gynecological and obstetrical care to monitor the health of both the mother and fetus. Pregnant inmates are more likely to have high-risk pregnancy than nonincarcerated pregnant women because of a lack of prenatal care prior to incarceration, poor nutritional histories, mental illness, substance abuse, and medical conditions, such as hypertension and diabetes (Fogel, 1993; National Commission of Correctional Health Care, 2014).

Medical conditions associated with aging, such as arthritis, osteoporosis, stroke, diabetes, heart disease, Alzheimer's and Parkinson's disease, also require specialized treatment and care. In 1998, the U.S. Supreme Court ruled that the Americans with Disabilities Act (ADA, 1990) applies to inmates in jails and prisons (see *Pennsylvania Department of Corrections v. Yeskey*, 1998). The ADA prohibits discrimination against disabled persons, including those who use walkers, wheelchairs, scooters, or other mobility devices. Jails and prisons are required to construct or retrofit their facilities to be ADA complaint and handicap accessible (Whitehead, Dodson, & Edwards, 2013). For example, wheelchair-bound inmates must have cell doors wide enough for their wheelchairs to fit through and ample room in the cell to maneuver their wheelchairs. Inmates in wheelchairs also need elevated desks, toilets, beds, and handicap ramps to accommodate their physical limitations. Like correctional facilities, police and probation agencies are required to have buildings that are handicap accessible and ADA compliant.

Offenders with mental health diagnoses also have special treatment and management needs. Mentally ill offenders regularly report anxiety disorders (panic disorder and phobias), mood disorders (depression and bipolar disorder), psychotic disorders (schizophrenia), impulse control disorders (kleptomania and pyromania), personality disorders (antisocial personality disorder and obsessive-compulsive personality disorder), and posttraumatic stress disorder (PTSD) (Daniel, 2007; Torrey et al., 2014; Underwood & Washington, 2016). In jails and prisons, mentally ill offenders are typically confined in segregated housing units (SHUs) or solitary confinement cells because they may exhibit bizarre, irritating, or dangerous behavior (Metzner & Fellner, 2010). Additionally, mentally ill inmates are easily manipulated and therefore are more prone to being financially exploited or physically or sexually victimized in the general population (Abramsky & Fellner, 2015; Pittaro, 2015).

Many law enforcement agencies have implemented the use of crisis intervention teams that are trained to respond and assist individuals experiencing a mental health crisis (see Chapter 27 for more about crisis intervention teams). Much of training focuses on increasing disability awareness and reducing officer prejudice or bias. Many police agencies endorse the use of crisis intervention teams as an essential component of improving police response to mentally ill individuals. Likewise, mental health courts have been developed to address the special treatment and care needs of those diagnosed with psychiatric illnesses and disorders. Mental health courts combine court supervision, community mental health treatment, and other support services to reduce the likelihood of criminal offending and improving mental health outcomes for offenders. The use of specialty courts (teen courts, veterans' courts, and drug courts) is designed to divert offenders with special needs out of the criminal justice system.

Offenders may be classified as special needs because they are vulnerable populations. For example, some inmates may be vulnerable because of their sexual orientation or gender identity, and research shows that homosexual and gender nonconforming offenders are more likely than heterosexual and gender conforming offenders to be physically and sexually victimized in jails and prisons (Beck, Berzofsky, & Krebs, 2013). Juveniles are another vulnerable class of offender because their age makes them targets for physical and sexual abuse and exploitation in detention facilities by other offenders (Beck, Cantor, Hartge, & Smith, 2013; Saar, Epstein, Rosenthal, & Vafa, 2015). As a result, these vulnerable inmates may request placement in protective custody or prison staff may place them in administrative segregation[1] for protection. Thirty-five states require that juveniles housed in adult correctional facilities to be sight and sound segregated, while six states (Connecticut, Massachusetts, Missouri, Rhode Island, West Virginia, and Wyoming) strictly prohibit this practice (Office of Juvenile Justice and Delinquency Prevention, 2015).

Inmates may be special needs because they have distinct security or supervision concerns. For example, the nature of some crimes requires special safety and security measures in jails and prisons. Individuals charged with the physical or sexual abuse of a child typically do not fare well in general population because once the word gets out about the nature of the charges, these offenders become targets for verbal abuse and physical violence. Sex offenders and those accused of child abuse often present correctional staff with special safety and security concerns. Like other vulnerable populations, these inmates can request protective custody or correctional officers can administratively segregate them.

As indicated in this introduction, special needs offenders present criminal justice practitioners and health care specialists with a variety of management and treatment needs. The purpose of this chapter is to explore the challenges criminal justice and treatment professionals encounter in treating and managing offenders with special needs. The chapter presents a discussion about the training needs of criminal justice practitioners, including law enforcement officers, court personnel, and correctional officers. The chapter also discusses the inadequacy of training in recognizing and effectively interacting with offenders with special needs. The chapter offers some suggestions for refining training to improve outcomes for criminal justice practitioners and criminal justice-involved special needs offenders. The chapter includes a brief overview of the American Correctional Association Accreditation Standards for jail and prisons and how accreditation improves the operation of correctional facilities and quality of services for inmates. Criminal justice agencies often have limited financial resources that hamper their ability to provide appropriate training for correctional personnel and services to offenders. Therefore, the chapter concludes with a discussion of how limited resources affect the ability to train correctional officers adequately and hinder the delivery of services to offenders with special needs.

Police Response to Special Needs Offenders

Police do not always receive adequate training in recognizing offenders with special needs or how to interact effectively with these individuals. Studies and media accounts document the fact that police have failed to recognize individuals with autism (Bolton & Bolton, 2008), schizophrenia and bipolar disorder (Hause & Melber, 2016; International Association of Chiefs of Police, 2014), posttraumatic stress disorder (Perry & Carter-Long, 2014), developmental and intellectual disabilities, (High, 2016), Down syndrome (Heideman, 2014), cerebral palsy (Perry & Carter-Long, 2014), hypoglycemia (Cizio, 2009), and deafness (Lohr, 2014; Sommerfeldt, 2016). In all of these encounters, police mistook a disability for noncompliance. This is important because one-third to half of all individuals killed by the police have some type of mental or physical disability (Perry & Carter-Long, 2016). These incidents are most likely the result of the police culture that emphasizes compliance and use of force rather than conflict resolution and de-escalation.

Basic Police Recruit School and In-Service Training

Police academy training teaches officers to take control of situations by demanding submission through various compliance techniques. Police officers try to gain compliance with the use of verbal commands. If the person fails to comply with officers' verbal commands, officers will attempt to gain compliance through various physical control techniques. Someone with a mental illness or intellectual disability, because of their impairment or condition, may be unable to comprehend the verbal commands of officers. When officers attempt to restrain people with mental health issues or intellectual disabilities, they may not understand why police are trying to restrict their movements or what they have done wrong. This is the point when offenders with special needs may resist officers' attempts to subdue them, and the situation escalates. Again, officers are trained to gain compliance and they will do so even if it means using deadly force. Loved ones or family members frequently call the police to handle situations involving special needs individuals, particularly when things turn disruptive or violent. It is unlikely that those who call the police for assistance expect their loved one to be killed by police, and these incidents often turn into a public relations nightmare for police agencies (see, e.g., cases reviewed by Heideman, 2014; Lohr, 2014; Perry & Carter-Long, 2016; Sommerfeldt, 2016). Since police are the first point of contact in the criminal justice system, it is imperative that they receive appropriate de-escalation training, especially concerning offenders with mental illness or intellectual disabilities.

Law enforcement officers across the United States must complete annual in-service training to continue their law enforcement certification. Police in-service courses consist of 40 hours of specialized training on law enforcement issues that officers may encounter in the field. Agencies typically allow their officers to choose among a variety of in-service course options, including defense tactics, tactical firearm training, active shooter scenarios, drug interdiction, child abuse investigations, crime scene photography, domestic violence response, human trafficking, racial profiling, and stress management. However, 34 states do not require de-escalation training for law enforcement officers (Gilbert, 2017), and those that do often provide insufficient training. For example, one study of Georgia law enforcement agencies found that in 385 departments out of 582, law enforcement officers had less than one hour of de-escalation training in the previous five years (Gilbert, 2017). These findings led Georgia to mandate one hour of annual de-escalation training for every certified law enforcement officer, which still seems woefully insufficient.

The good news is police chiefs and sheriffs are beginning to recognize that officers under their command need training to respond appropriately to crises, especially those involving individuals with special needs. As a result, many law enforcement agencies are providing crisis intervention and de-escalation training for their officers. For example, the Seattle Police Department (SPD) developed and implemented de-escalation training for all of its officers that the United States Department of Justice (DOJ) endorsed (U.S. DOJ, 2015). Likewise, the Chicago Police Department (CPD) formally adopted a de-escalation policy that states, in part, officers "will not resort to force unless all other reasonable alternatives have been exhausted" (CPD, 2016, p. 2)

De-escalation is a response that allows police officers time to reflect on a situation and to consider options that will increase the chances of resolving a conflict or crisis without the use of force or with minimal force. Utilizing de-escalation techniques at the scene of a crisis reduces the likelihood of injury to the public and police officers. Less use of force by police translates into fewer lawsuits for law enforcement agencies. In the next section, use of force cases involving individuals with special needs are discussed.

Use of Force Involving Special Needs Offenders

Use of force cases tend to garner a significant amount of media attention in the United States. The public is often critical of the conduct of police officers involved in use of force cases, and there are frequently accusations of police using excessive force. The public may be even less tolerant of police use of force against individuals with special needs because acting out may be symptomatic of the condition or diagnosis of the offender rather than deliberate defiance of the police. This is why instituting de-escalation training is so important when dealing with offenders with special needs.

The courts have reviewed numerous cases involving police use of force, including cases concerning offenders with special needs. For example, in 2015, the U.S. Supreme Court granted a *writ of certiorari* in a case involving a mentally ill woman who was shot during a confrontation with the police. The plaintiffs filed a brief claiming that law enforcement officers have no obligation to use crisis de-escalation measures when responding to situations involving seriously mentally ill people who are violent or armed (see *City and County of San Francisco, et al. v. Sheehan*, 2015). The Court dismissed the case without ruling because, as the justices noted, the plaintiffs failed to argue the constitutional question at the center of their case. However, the question remains—what, if any, obligation or duty do the police have to de-escalate situations involving offenders with special needs, especially if they are violent?

To answer this question, we must review *Tennessee v. Garner* (1985), because it is the precedent case governing the use of deadly force by police. The Supreme Court ruled that if an officer has probable cause to believe a suspect poses a serious threat of serious bodily injury or death to officers or others, then the use of deadly force is reasonable under the Fourth Amendment. Although this case does not directly mention special needs offenders, police officers are justified in using deadly force on *anyone* who poses a risk of serious bodily injury or death to officers or others. Police are protected from civil liability because they have qualified immunity. Under qualified immunity, officers are protected from liability unless the officer's conduct goes outside of what he or she should have known was a reasonably protected constitutional right of an individual.

Four years later, the Supreme Court granted a *writ of certiorari* in *Graham v. Connor* (1989). Graham, a diabetic, had his friend drive him to a convenience store for orange juice. The line was long and Graham decided he could not wait so he ran out of the store. Officers witnessed Graham running from the store and stopped him to investigate. Graham's friend tried to explain to police that Graham was having an insulin reaction and needed orange juice. One officer testified that Graham's behavior was erratic so the officer decided to restrain Graham. However, the officer slammed Graham onto the car and denied him his orange juice. Graham sued officers claiming they had use excessive force. The Court held that all claims that police used excessive force—deadly or not—in the course of an investigatory stop, arrest, or other seizure of a free citizen must be analyzed using the Fourth Amendment's objectively reasonable standard. The Court remanded the case to the lower court and directed it to apply the objectively reasonable standard in determining whether the officers used excessive force.

In *Abdullahi v. City of Madison* (2005), police were called to a disturbance involving Jamal Mohamed, who suffered from posttraumatic stress disorder (PTSD). When officers arrived, Mohamed appeared to be disoriented, and he began swinging a belt at a woman officer. Three officers took him to the ground, but they testified that he was squirming and trying to avoid being handcuffed. One of the officers pressed his knee in between Mohamed's shoulder blades and applied pressure to the base of his neck until Mohamed stopped struggling. According to video footage, Mohamed died approximately two and half minutes after being taken to the ground. His autopsy revealed he died of crushing trauma to his neck and chest. His parents filed a lawsuit alleging officers used unreasonable force in subduing their son. The defendant (City of Madison) was granted summary judgment and the lower court ruled there was no evidence officers' actions were objectively unreasonable. The Seventh Circuit Court reversed and remanded the case to the lower court. The justices noted that the testimony of four independent doctors regarding the severity of Mohamed's injuries suggest the use of force may have been objectively unreasonable, but that the lower court would need to make that determination.

Use of force cases, particularly when there is failure to train police officers adequately, increases the chances of civil liability for law enforcement agencies. The Supreme Court decided that liability can be established based on inadequate police training where it can be demonstrated that police administrators exhibited deliberate indifference to the rights of citizens (see *City of Canton, Ohio v. Harris*, 1989). The standard of deliberate indifference can be met when there is an obvious need for more or better training and the constitutional violations are a result of lack of adequate training. Taken together, these cases indicate officers can be held civilly liable for unreasonable use of force, but municipalities and agencies can be civilly liable if they fail to train their officers adequately, including adequate training in the use of force. Departmental general orders (GOs) or standard operating procedures (SOPs) must comport with the most recent Supreme Court decisions. Administrators and officers who act within the bounds of their GOs or SOPs reduce the likelihood of civil liability. Therefore, it is important for law enforcement agencies to consult with the city or county attorney's office or to have a legal advisor on staff to interpret the court decisions and to help police agencies construct policies that are consistent with the most recent court rulings.

Interrogations and False Confessions

Another area of concern for special needs offenders is the methods police use during interrogations. Some interrogation techniques may be problematic because they induce offenders with special needs to confess falsely to crimes they did not commit (Devoy, 2014; Drizin & Leo, 2004). For example, one of the most popular courses for training police interrogators is *The Reid Nine Steps of Interrogations*. Research shows that false confessions are related to two primary causes: manipulative or coercive interrogation techniques and a suspect's vulnerabilities (Gudjonsson & Pearse, 2011). Many scholars and social justice advocates condemn *The Reid Technique* as coercive and outdated (Brean, 2011; Merryman, 2010) (see Box 1.1).

Box 1.1 The Reid Nine Steps of Interrogations

1 **Confrontation**

- The interrogator presents the facts of the case and tells the suspect confidently there is evidence of his or her involvement in the crime.

2 **Theme Development**

- The interrogator creates a story to excuse or justify the suspect's crime.

3 **Handling Denials**

- The interrogator interrupts all denials or stops them before the suspect can speak.

4 **Overcoming Objections**

- Objections are reasoned arguments why he or she could not have committed the crime. It is the job of the interrogator to make the objection appear to be an admission of guilt.

5 **Procurement and Retention of the Suspect's Attention**

- The suspect should be insecure at this point, and the interrogator should capitalize on it. Pretend to be the suspect's ally.

6 **Handling the Suspect's Passive Mood**

- The interrogator should intensify the theme and continue to offer the suspect psychological justifications for the crime.

7 **Alternatives**

- Use two contrasting motives—one that is socially acceptable and one that is morally offensive. The suspect will most likely choose the former.

8 **Bring the Suspect into the Conversation**

- The suspect will choose an alternative that signals the confession is imminent. Introduce a second interrogator to increase the suspect's stress level and desire to admit involvement in the crime.

9 **The Confession**

- Getting a truthful confession is the goal, and the interrogator should have independent, corroborating evidence, such as disclosing key facts of the crime.

Source: John E. Reid & Associates, Inc. (2017)

The Reid Technique is problematic for several reasons, especially when law enforcement officers use it to elicit confessions from offenders with intellectual deficiencies, developmental disabilities, or mental illnesses or impairments. If an individual is in custody and he or she is being questioned by police, the police must advise the individual of his or her Fifth Amendment right to remain silent and Sixth Amendment right to counsel (see *Miranda v. Arizona*, 1966). Police must demonstrate that an individual *knowingly* and *voluntarily* waived his or her *Miranda* rights or the court will toss out any admission or confession obtained unconstitutionally. If police follow the first step of the Reid interrogation, they walk into the interrogation room and confidently announce to the suspect that there is evidence of his or her involvement in the crime. The question is—did the interrogator announce this before or after the suspect waived his or her *Miranda* rights? Clearly, if the interrogator did this prior to *Miranda* it places a considerable amount of pressure on the suspect, and this may be particularly true of individuals with intellectual disabilities or other mental impairments. The court may view this practice as coercive, nullifying the voluntariness of the waiver.

It is highly unlikely that those with intellectual disabilities and mental limitations understand the seriousness of the legal situation they find themselves in, because they do not fully comprehend the legal terms articulated in *Miranda*. In addition, because officers read *Miranda* to suspects, they may feel, since the officers are authority figures, they must not object to the request from police. Research shows that individuals with intellectual disabilities and impairments are easily influenced by and eager to please others (see Davis, 2009). Research also tells us that individuals with intellectual disabilities invariably waive their *Miranda* rights and confess to police without the presence of counsel (Cassell, 1998). Therefore, their waivers are, at best, suspect when one considers the characteristics of their disabilities or disorders.

Steps three and four of the Reid interrogation strategy also are problematic. Step three, for example, encourages police to interrupt the suspect anytime he or she denies involvement in the crime. Step four indicates police are supposed to overcome any objections asserted by the suspect by turning the suspect's statements into admissions of guilt. Again, these tactics are coercive and, as stated earlier, individuals with intellectual disabilities and impairments are easily influenced by and eager to please others. This means special needs offenders are more likely to submit to the authority of interrogators.

In step two, Reid urges police to develop a theme for why the suspect may have committed the crime. Similarly, step seven also encourages police to present the suspect with alternative scenarios that justify the suspect's alleged criminal behavior. Those with intellectual disabilities and impairments are more prone to suggestibility in comparison to those without intellectual disabilities and impairments (Brown, Huntley, Morgan, Dodson, & Cich, 2018; Brown, Mitchell, Wartnik, & Russell, 2015; Watts & Brown, 2016). Put simply, suggestibility is being easily influenced by the suggestions of others, which can lead to confabulation or false confessions.

Confabulation is the recollection and statement of false memories, although the individual relaying the information believes his or her false memories to be true (Brown et al., 2018). In other words, confabulating individuals have no idea they are relaying false or inaccurate information; that is why this condition is also known as "honest lying" (Moscovitch, 1989, p. 139). False memories may include exaggerations of actual events, inserting memories of one event into another place and time, recalling an older memory but believing it happened more recently, filling in memory gaps, or the construction of a new memory of an event or incident that never occurred. If police offer themes about the commission of a crime or justifications for the crime, special needs offenders, because of their suggestibility, are prone to confabulate. Again, these individuals completely believe the information they are communicating is accurate, and they have no intent to deceive. Therefore, there is an increased probability that the police interrogations tactics endorsed in the *Reid Technique* may lead investigators to believe the admissions and/or confessions of suspects with special needs are accurate, when in fact they are false. Although the ninth and final step in the Reid interrogation is to get a "truthful" confession, it is unlikely to happen because of the coercive environment and methods police create and use when questioning suspects, especially suspects with special needs (Kassin, Drizin, Grisso, Gudjonsson, Leo, & Redlich, 2010).

Research demonstrates individuals with fetal alcohol spectrum disorders (FASD) (Brown, 2017), schizophrenia, traumatic brain injuries (TBIs) (Brown et al., 2013) PTSD, and Alzheimer's disease (Attali, De Anna, Dubois, & Dalla Barba, 2008) as well as juveniles (Candel, Merckelbach, Loyen, & Reyskens, 2005; Kassin & Kiechel, 1996) are prone to confabulate. However, researchers also have documented confabulation in people with no apparent brain impairment or disorder or cognitive limitation (Hirstein, 2005). Confabulating individuals have confessed falsely to sexual assault (Drizin & Leo, 2004), gang rape (Leo, 2009), murder (Drizin & Leo, 2004; Gudjonsson, 2017), and serial murder (Drizin & Leo, 2004). Therefore, it is important for police officers and investigators to have extensive training in recognizing offenders with special needs and to avoid coercive interrogation tactics with this population. Law enforcement officers must be extra careful to ensure the constitutional rights of citizens with special needs.

Court Response to Special Needs Offenders

Judges are responsible for ensuring the due process rights of defendants in their courtrooms. The denial of due process "is the failure to observe the fundamental fairness essential to the very concept of justice. To declare a denial of it . . . [the Court] must find that the absence of that fairness fatally infected the trial" (*Lisenba v. California*, 1943, p. 429). Personal bias or prejudice in the trial system or bias created by outside events is one example of a denial of one's right to a fair trial. A biased or partial juror's participation in the jury process also constitutes a denial of one's right to a fair trial. In an effort to increases the likelihood of a fair trial, prosecutors and defense attorneys conduct *voir dire* to eliminate biased or partial jurors from the jury pool. However, it may be more difficult to uncover juror bias in cases involving offenders with special needs. Jurors know it is culturally unacceptable to make disparaging remarks about individuals with special needs, so jurors may go to great lengths to disguise or deny any biases.

Nevertheless, research indicates that jurors do have misconceptions and hold negative stereotypes about special needs offenders. A study conducted by Sabbagh (2011), for instance, shows that jurors believe that individuals with schizophrenia are much more dangerous and violent than individuals without mental illness. Stobbs and Kebbell (2003) found mock-jurors perceive individuals with intellectual disabilities to be honest, but mock-jurors were reluctant to rely solely on the testimony of intellectually disabled individuals.

Research by Cohen (1986) shows that jurors view elderly defendants as more culpable for their crimes because they are old enough to know better and are more familiar with the law than younger defendants. In related research, Feinberg and Khosla (1985) found 50% of the judges in their sample were not particularly sympathetic to elderly defendants. However, jurors appear to be more sympathetic to juveniles with intellectual disabilities than juveniles without intellectual disabilities. Najdowski, Bottoms, and Vargas (2009), for example, found jurors were more likely to believe a juvenile with an intellectual disability was coerced into a confession than a juvenile without an intellectual disability.

Perhaps one of the more troubling research findings is that attractive defendants fare much better in the court system than unattractive defendants. As an example, Gunnell and Ceci (2010) found attractive defendants were more likely to be acquitted of a crime than unattractive defendants. When attractive defendants are convicted of a crime, their sentences are often more lenient than the sentences of unattractive defendants (see DeSantis & Kayson, 1997; Lieberman, 2002). These findings may be particularly problematic for offenders with special needs because they may have outward physical characteristics that others typically rate lower in attractiveness. Research demonstrates that individuals have rated those with mental illness (Boysen, 2017; Farina, Fischer, Sherman, Smith, Groh, & Mermin, 1977) and physical disabilities (Low & Zubir, 2000) as less attractive than individuals without mental illness or physical disabilities.

Studies also suggest that individual differences in speech patterns can affect perceptions of a person's characteristics and ability. Speech disfluency (i.e., stuttering) often leads individuals to assign negative qualities to those who stutter, including nervousness, shyness, self-consciousness, and anxiousness, and they are viewed as withdrawn, fearful, reticent, and guarded (Hurst & Cooper, 1983).

Stuttering also is linked to peer-rejection and bullying in preschool children (Langevin, Kleitman, Packman, & Onslow, 2009), negative hiring decisions, and harassment in the workplace (Mitchell, McMahon, & McKee, 2005). Research also shows that listeners erroneously believe that individuals with speech disorders are more likely to be emotionally disturbed (Bebout & Arthur, 1992).

The bias reported by jurors and others who may be potential jurors against individuals with special needs is a cautionary note for criminal justice practitioners. Offenders with special needs may not receive fair treatment during the criminal justice process because of the misconceptions or misperceptions of those they encounter throughout the system. Unfair treatment is usually not the result of conscious attitudes and beliefs but of unconscious implicit bias. Implicit bias happens when someone shows a bias or discriminates against someone else without being consciously aware of it. Empirical evidence indicates "implicit bias against individuals with disabilities is particularly pronounced in American society" (Larson, 2008, p. 451). Implicit bias distorts a person's perception and later treatment in either a favorable or an unfavorable way. However, implicit bias typically results in negative outcomes for the victim of such bias.

Specialty Courts

Judges and court personnel are often much more responsive to the issues related to special needs offenders than police agencies or corrections officials. For example, the development and implementation of specialty courts continues to grow, and estimates from the Bureau of Justice Statistics indicate there are 3,052 problem-solving or specialty courts currently operating across the United States (Strong & Kyckelhahn, 2016). Drugs courts (55%) are the most commonly utilized specialty courts, followed by mental health courts (11%). Box 1.2 lists examples of the most common specialty courts in the United States.

Specialty courts represent a progressive step forward in addressing the individual needs of a subset of offenders with special concerns or individuals who fall into certain offense categories. Specifically,

Box 1.2 Types of Specialty Courts

- Child protective services courts
- Domestic violence courts
- Drug courts
- Driving while impaired or intoxicated courts
- Fetal alcohol syndrome courts
- Homelessness courts
- Human trafficking courts
- Juvenile courts
- Mental health courts
- Prostitution courts
- Sex offender courts
- Special needs courts
- Substance abuse courts
- Trauma courts
- Tribal wellness
- Veterans' courts

specialty courts attempt to assist low-level offenders suffering from mental health issues, substance abuse problems, social adjustment issues, or co-occurring disorders. The goals of specialty courts are to divert offenders out of jail, reduce the likelihood of recidivism, and successfully reintegrate offenders back into the community.

Specialty court judges supervise preadjudicated and postadjudicated offenders. Preadjudicated offenders are individuals who have charges within the specialty court's jurisdiction. These offenders are typically referred to the court by a judge in consultation with the district attorney's office. A judge from a convicting court transfers postadjudicated offenders to a specialty court, which administers sentencing. Regardless of whether the offender is preadjudicated or postadjudicated, the specialty court will conduct a status hearing to develop and implement an offender treatment or care plan with input from criminal justice and treatment professionals.

Specialty courts are a collaborative effort between court personnel and organizations outside the court system that offer support services to special needs offenders to increase the likelihood that they will successfully graduate from the specialty court. Specialty courts are a team-based approach, and they require the involvement of prosecutors, defense attorneys or public defenders, probation officers, and court-affiliated social workers or case managers. Outside organizational members include substance abuse counselors, mental health providers, and other community-based treatment specialists. A judge is responsible for the oversight of the specialty court, and he or she is the team leader. The team develops and utilizes individualized treatment plans for special needs offenders that offer intensive treatment, interventions, supervision, and community-based services.

Offender participation in a specialty court is voluntary because criminal justice and treatment professionals believe this increases the chance of successful completion. However, critics note that judges may involuntarily admit some offenders to a specialty court, since this may be the only way these offenders will receive the services they need (Frailing, 2016). Judges who oversee specialty courts support their use because they address the specific concerns of offenders with special needs rather than a one-size-fits-all model of treatment (Anchondo, Arreola, & Dominguez, 2016). Successful completion of the specialty court permits judges to expunge the initial crime from the participant's criminal record. Avoiding a criminal record improves the odds of successful reentry and significantly reduces the likelihood of reoffending and relapse (Vallas & Dietrich, 2014).

Corrections Response to Special Needs Offenders

Jails and prisons must adhere to certain legal standards for the treatment and care of special needs inmates or risk inmate litigation. Correctional personnel who commit civil rights violations collectively cost their jurisdictions millions of dollars annually. Jails that fail to meet legal requirements and/or accreditation standards can be decertified, making jail administrators more vulnerable to inmate litigation. Decertification frequently revolves around inadequate medical and mental health care, and state jail inspectors have cited jail administrators for failing to provide continuity of care, which is required "from the time of admission into the jail to inmates' transfer or discharge" (see Nash, 2016, para. 5; see also Satterfield, 2017). Many correctional administrators across the country seek accreditation to avoid decertification and inmate litigation and to improve the standards of training correctional officers receive.

Correctional Officer Certification and Training

Like police, correctional officers do not always receive adequate training in recognizing offenders with special needs or how to respond appropriately to the concerns of this population of offenders. One of the major issues related to training seems to be the number of recommended training hours to become a certified correctional officer is rather minimal. The National Sheriff's Association

(2017) recommends a minimum of 65 hours of training to become a certified jail officer. The American Jail Association (AJA) and the Jail Manager Certification Commission (JMCC) recommends a minimum of 80 hours of training (AJA, 2017).

Some states require a much lower number of training hours to become a correctional officer. For example, Tennessee requires 40 hours of training to become a certified correctional officer in both prisons and jails (Tennessee Department of Commerce and Insurance, 2017). Other states, like Indiana and North Carolina, required 200 and 160 hours of training respectively to become a certified correctional officer (Correctional Officer EDU, 2017; North Carolina Public Safety, 2017). This number of hours translates into one to five weeks of correctional officer academy training, which often does not prepare correctional officers for the situations and individuals they will encounter.

There is a push in jails and prisons to broaden the type of training correctional officers receive. Individuals who complete the National Sheriff's Association (NSA) Jail Officer Certification receive training on offenders with special needs, including inmates with diabetes, epilepsy, psychological disorders, and substance abuse. The training also covers the special medical concerns of women offenders and suicide prevention. The AJA Certified Jail Officer Training is more comprehensive and covers a broader range of special populations and offender concerns. Specifically, it includes training about gangs, juveniles, LGBT offenders, substance abuse, mental illness, communicable diseases, disabilities, foreign nationals, elderly offenders, cultural diversity, special housing, and medical services. However, the quality of the instructional delivery seems somewhat questionable given the NSA's Jail Officer Certification is a correspondence course and the AJA Certified Jail Officer Training is online.

Correctional officers receive little specialized training about how to interact effectively with offenders with psychological disorders and physical disabilities. For example, a sample of correctional officers from the Midwest reported they completed four hours of training in recognizing and responding to offenders with mental illness; however, the training they completed consisted of viewing a four-hour training video (Lombe-Stairwalt, 2015). A study by the National Institute of Corrections (NIC, 2001) found forty states reported that they provided mental health training for correctional officer, but the training was minimal. For example, 10 state prison systems included approximately four hours of mental health training, while 13 states admitted that they provided less than four hours of training. Only seven states reported that they required more than four hours of training (NIC, 2001).

A recent report by Chammah (2015) claims correctional officers at the Estelle Unit in Huntsville, Texas, regularly neglect and abuse inmates with physical disabilities, including blind, deaf, and elderly offenders. Texas Department of Criminal Justice (TDCJ) officials believe "the problems there are the product of poor training, out-of-date infrastructure, understaffing, and weak oversight" (Chammah, 2015, para. 15). Because of this report, the TDCJ Union is pushing for increased training for correctional officers in Texas and to create a process for professional licensure.

Providing comprehensive training for correctional officers in how to identify and communicate effectively with special needs inmates improves the treatment and services inmates receive. Proper training of correctional officers to understand and address the concerns of those with special needs also improves safety for prisoners and officers. Parker (2009) found that 10 hours of mental health training for correctional officers significantly reduced incidents of use of force and inmate-on-staff assaults. The next two sections present a discussion of identifying and assessing offenders with special needs followed by a description of segregated housing units (SHUs) and specialized facilities.

Identification and Assessment of Offenders with Special Needs

States are beginning to implement statutory requirements for identifying offenders with special needs. For instance, the Texas Code of Criminal Procedure requires sheriff's departments to notify a judge or magistrate within 72 hours of admitting an individual they believe to have a mental illness or intellectual disability (see Texas Code of Criminal Procedure § 16.22, 2017). If a judge or magistrate determines an individual may have a mental illness or intellectual disability, a local mental health authority (LMHA) or local intellectual and developmental disability authority (LIDDA) will conduct an assessment. Based on this assessment and other relevant medical history, a judge will make a determination regarding competency to stand trial.

Judges may involuntarily commit a person to a mental health or residential facility for observation and treatment. A person charged with a misdemeanor may be held up to 60 days in a treatment facility, while a person charged with a felony may be held up to 120 days. The primary purpose of the Texas Code of Criminal Procedure § 16.22 is to provide offenders with mental health services and/or medications so they will eventually be competent to stand trial. However, many offenders with intellectual disabilities may never be declared competent to stand trial because of the severity of their conditions.

During the intake process at jails and prisons, correctional staff conduct a preliminary health screening that includes questions about the inmate's mental and physical health. If the inmate reports a history of mental illness or states that he or she is currently experiencing a mental health issue, medical staff will conduct a more in-depth screening. Prisons and jails may lack adequate health care services and have fewer treatment staff than local hospitals or community treatment facilities. Therefore, mental health providers from the community frequently work with jails and prisons to assist with screening inmates with mental illness, especially serious mental health conditions, such as schizophrenia and bipolar disorder.

Special Housing Units and Specialized Facilities

Special populations in jails and prisons are often segregated from the general population and housed in segregated or special housing units (SHUs). Specialized units and facilities should be designed to accommodate the needs of the particular population they house. For example, inmates with physical disabilities may be housed together in units or facilities that have handicap-accessible features and facilitate activities of daily living. Both physically handicapped and elderly offenders may need ramps, handrails in cells and shower areas, and elevated or lowered fixtures. Offenders with serious health conditions may be housed in medical dormitories that allow medical staff to continuously observe and treat these offenders. In addition, specialized units and facilities increase the safety and security of offenders with special care needs.

Most jails and prisons have specialized units in which they house inmates with mental illness. Correctional officers and administrators report the threat of physical violence is the primary reason they segregate mentally ill offenders (see Parker, 2009). However, research shows that offenders with mental illness are not more dangerous or prone to violence than offenders without mental illness (Peterson, Skeem, Kennealy, Bray, & Zvonkovic, 2014). Some state department of corrections facilities report segregating inmates to improve the treatment and care mentally ill prisoners receive. Ohio, for example, made systemic changes to the way it houses and treats offenders with mental illness. Correctional staff screen inmates for mental illness during the intake process, and those identified with serious mental illness, such as schizophrenia and bipolar disorder, receive treatment at a specialized correctional facility (Navasky & O'Connor, 2005).

Other states send all of their special needs offenders to correctional facilities designed to meet the offenders' specific treatment and care needs. In Tennessee, the Lois M. DeBerry Special Needs Facility provides services for inmates recovering from surgery or serious medical conditions, intensive mental health treatment, convalescent health care, and other medical conditions that cannot be treated at other state department of corrections facilities (Tennessee Department of Corrections, 2017). One national survey indicates that approximately 12% of state correctional facilities are designated as specialized (Cropsey, Wexler, Melnick, Taxman, & Young, 2007). To improve the care and treatment offenders with special needs receive, many and jails and prisons seek accreditation through the American Correctional Association (ACA). The next section presents a discussion of accreditation standards for jails and prisons and how these standards improve conditions of confinement and treatment for prisoners with special needs.

Accreditation Standards of Jails and Prisons

ACA accreditation "is intended to improve facility operations through adherence to clear standards relevant to all areas/operations of the facility, including safety, security, order, inmate care, programs, justice, and administration" (ACA, 2017, para. 6). The ACA (2017) notes only 32 states have any form of jail or prison standards, and the majority of these states do not have any mechanism for evaluating adherence to their stated standards. However, if jail or prison administrators seek ACA Accreditation for their facility, the Commission on Accreditation for Corrections (CAC) is the organization responsible for the evaluation of a correctional facility's adherence to the ACA standards.

Accreditation is important because it helps correctional officials to identify and assess weaknesses across the facility. Identifying deficiencies is a starting point for improving standards of care and treatment inmates receive, staff training, and safety and security of staff and inmates, and it reduces the likelihood of inmate litigation. ACA accredited jails and prisons must comply with the ADA requirements of being handicap accessible and usable to the public, and cells and housing units for handicapped inmates must be designed for their use (ACA, 2017). Jails and prisons also must provide the same level of access to rehabilitation and treatment programs for offenders with special needs as inmates without special needs. Library and legal services are required to accommodate blind, deaf, and otherwise physically impaired inmates.

Limited Resources

Criminal justice agencies across the United States struggle to provide training to personnel and to provide appropriate services to offenders because of limited financial resources. Police departments, for instance, can voluntarily pursue accreditation through the Commission on Accreditation for Law Enforcement Agencies (CALEA). Accreditation may be cost prohibitive for many agencies when one considers small law enforcement agencies (1–24 full-time employees) must pay $8,475 and large law enforcement agencies (1,000 or more employees) must pay $19,950 in initial fees (CALEA, 2017). There are additional fees for continued annual accreditation. Likewise, the ACA charges accreditation fees for jails and prisons ranging from $8,100 to $19,500, and additional fees may be assessed at the time of the site visit (Friedmann, 2017). Law enforcement agencies and correctional facilities do not have direct control of their budgets and must seek expense approvals through mayors' offices, city or county commissions, or state and federal legislators. Therefore, the lack of financial resources coupled with bureaucratic hurdles may prevent or reduce the likelihood that agencies will seek accreditation.

A lack of financial resources often leads criminal justice administrators to provide the minimal legal required training to their subordinates. In most states, law enforcement and correctional officers are required to complete academy training and 40 hours of annual in-service training. Minimal training standards may not provide police officers or correctional personnel with the knowledge and skills they need to work with special populations. This means that the amount of training criminal justice practitioners receive may hinder their ability to perform the duties of their jobs effectively.

Mental health and treatment staff in correctional facilities usually have large caseloads, as do probation and parole officers. Large caseloads are often the result of insufficient funding that prevents agencies from hiring a suitable number of employees. Limited resources and inadequate staffing means that practitioners have less time to spend with their clients. As a result, medical and treatment staff may not have the time or resources to treat individuals in their care appropriately. Additionally, treatment staff may misdiagnose or fail to diagnose inmate-patients properly, which increases the likelihood of medical complications for patients. Probation and parole officers may lack the time and resources to supervise their clients adequately and miss signs of relapse or the risk of recidivism.

Conclusion

Criminal justice practitioners and treatment professionals face a variety of challenges when working with offenders with special needs. Training is critical to improving the outcomes for criminal justice-involved offenders, especially those with mental and physical impairments and disabilities. For example, police officers should be trained to identify offenders with special needs so police can respond accordingly. Also, officers must recognize that a failure to comply with police commands may be the result of a mental or physical limitation, not intentional defiance.

The creation of specialty courts is a step in the right direction to focus on the specific treatment needs of special populations. The use of specialty courts is important because it gives offenders with special needs the opportunity to be funneled out of the criminal justice system. When the use of a specialty court is not possible, special needs offenders frequently serve their sentences in jails or prisons. Correctional personnel should receive proper training to address the needs of inmates with physical disabilities or mental disorders.

Accreditation for criminal justice agencies helps to improve the training employees receive and the standard operating procedures of the agencies. Accreditation helps to ensure agencies are using best practices based on the most up-to-date research in the criminal justice field. State and local lawmakers should provide appropriate funding so that criminal justice agencies can better meet their training and accreditation needs. Accreditation and training improve the safety and security of criminal justice practitioners and offenders they encounter, and this may be especially true for offenders with special needs.

Note

1 Administrative segregation, disciplinary segregation, protective custody, restrictive housing, solitary confinement, or "the hole" are synonymous terms.

References

Abdullahi v. City of Madison, 423 F. 3d 763 (2005).

Abramsky, S., & Fellner, J. (2015). *Ill-equipped: U.S. prisons and offenders with mental illness*. New York, NY: Human Rights Watch.

American Correctional Association. (2017). *The history of standards & accreditation*. Retrieved from https://www.aca.org/ACA_Prod_IMIS/ACA_Member/Standards___Accreditation/About_Us/ACA_Member/Standards_and_Accreditation/SAC_AboutUs.aspx?hkey=bdf577fe-be9e-4c22-aa60-dc30dfa3adcb

American Jail Association. (2017). *Certified jail officer*. Hagerstown, MD: American Jail Association. Retrieved from www.americanjail.org/files/CJO%20Handbook%20and%20Application.pdf

Americans with Disabilities Act of 1990, Pub. L. No. 101–336, 104 Stat. 328. (1991).

Anchondo, R. S., Arreola, C. O., & Dominguez, A. (2016). *Specialty courts: Supported and coordinated recovery in the judicial system*. County of El Paso, TX: El Paso County Criminal Court.

Attali, E., De Anna, F., Dubois, B., & Dalla Barba, G. (2008). Confabulation in Alzheimer's disease: Poor encoding and retrieval of over-learned information. *Brain: A Journal of Neurology, 132*(1), 204–212. doi:10.1093/brain/awn241

Bebout, L., & Arthur, B. (1992). Cross-cultural attitudes toward speech disorders. *Journal of Speech and Hearing Research, 35*(1), 45–52.

Beck, A. J., Berzofsky, M., & Krebs, C. (2013). *Sexual victimization in prisons and jails reported by inmates 2011–2012*. Washington, DC: U.S. Department of Justice, Bureau of Justice Statistics.

Beck, A. J., Cantor, D., Hartge, J., & Smith, T. (2013). *Sexual victimization in juvenile facilities reported by youth, 2012*. Washington, DC: U.S. Department of Justice, Bureau of Justice Statistics.

Bolton, M. J., & Bolton, H. A. (2008, November 25). Police and Asperger syndrome: The invisible autistic spectrum disorder. *Law Enforcement Executive Forum, 8*(2), 1–14.

Boysen, G. A. (2017). Stigma toward people with mental illness as potential sexual and romantic partners. *Evolutionary Psychological Science, 3*(3), 212–223. doi:10.1007/s40806-017-0089-5

Brean, J. (2011, November 25). *You're guilty, now confess: False admissions put police's favourite interrogation tactic under scrutiny*. [Web log comment]. Retrieved from http://nationalpost.com/news/canada/youre-guilty-now-confess-false-admissions-put-polices-favourite-interrogation-tactic-under-scrutiny

Brown, J. (2017). Fetal alcohol spectrum disorder and confabulation: A clinical, forensic, and judicial dilemma. *The Journal of Special Populations, 1*(2), 1–11.

Brown, J., Huntley, D., Morgan, S., Dodson, K. D., & Cich, J. (2018). Confabulation: A guide for mental health professionals. *International Journal of Neurology and Neurotheraphy, 4*(2), 1–9.

Brown, J., Long-McGie, J., Oberoi, P., Wartnik, A., Wresh, J., Weinkauf, E., & Falconer, G. (2013). Confabulation: Connections between brain damage, memory, and testimony. *Journal of Law Enforcement, 3*(5), 1–11.

Brown, J., Mitchell, M., Wartnik, A., & Russell, A. (2015). *FASD and the courts: A reference for legal professionals*. Minneapolis, MN: Bench & Bar of Minnesota. Retrieved from http://mnbenchbar.com/2015/11/fasd-and-the-courts/

Candel, I., Merckelbach, H., Loyen, S., & Reyskens, H. (2005). I hit the shift-key and then the computer crashed: Children and false admissions. *Personality and Individual Differences, 38*, 1381–1387.

Cassell, P. G. (1998). Protecting the innocent from false confessions and lost confessions—and from *Miranda*. *Journal of Criminal Law and Criminology, 88*(2), 497–556.

Chammah, M. (2015, January 27). Report: Blind, deaf, disabled inmates abused in Texas prison unit. *The Texas Tribune*. Retrieved from www.texastribune.org/2015/01/27/report-blind-deaf-disabled-inmates-abused-prison/

Chicago Police Department. (2016). *CPD announces draft use of force policy*. Chicago, IL: New Release: Chicago Police Department. Retrieved from https://home.chicagopolice.org/wp-content/uploads/2016/10/07Oct16-CPD-Announces-Draft-Use-of-Force-Policy.pdf

City and County of San Francisco, et al. v. Sheehan, 743 F. 3d, 121, No. 13–1412 (2015).

City of Canton, Ohio v. Harris, 489 U.S. 378 (1989).

Cizio, R. (2009, May 16). Lawsuit against two cities upgraded in light of man's death. *Detroit Herald News*. Retrieved from www.thenewsherald.com/news/detroit-lawsuit-against-two-cities-to-be-upgraded-in-light/article_202015c2-8f5c-5b2e-9023-c5b280583ea5.html

Cohen, L. J. (1986). The role of evidential weight in criminal proof. *Boston University Law Review, 66*, 635–649.

Commission on Accreditation for Law Enforcement Agencies. (2017). *Law enforcement accreditation: The cost*. Retrieved from www.calea.org/content/law-enforcement-accreditation-cost

Correctional Officer EDU. (2017). *Indiana corrections officer job description*. Retrieved from www.correctionalofficeredu.org/indiana/

Cropsey, K. L., Wexler, H. K., Melnick, G., Taxman, F. S., & Young, D. W. (2007). Specialized prisons and services: Results from a national survey. *The Prison Journal, 87*(1), 58–85. doi:10.1177/0032885506299043

Daniel, A. E. (2007). Care of the mentally ill prisons: Challenges and solutions. *The Journal of the American Academy of Psychiatry and the Law, 35*(4), 406–410.

Davis, L. A. (2009). *People with intellectual disability in the criminal justice system: Victims & suspects*. Washington, DC: The Arc.

Department of Justice. (2015). *Justice department applauds adoption of police department-wide tactical de-escalation training program in Seattle*. Washington, DC: U.S. Department of Justice, Office of Public Affairs.

DeSantis, A., & Kayson, W. A. (1997). Defendants' characteristics of attractiveness, race, and sex and sentencing decisions. *Psychological Reports, 81*(2), 679–683. doi:10.2466/pr0.1997.81.2.679

Devoy, P. (2014). The trouble with protecting the vulnerable: Proposals to prevent developmentally disabled individuals from giving involuntary waivers and false confessions. *Hamline Law Review, 37*(2), 252–291.

Drizin, S. A., & Leo, R. A. (2004). The problem of false confessions in the post-DNA world. *North Carolina Law Review, 82*, 891–1007.

Farina, A., Fischer, E. H., Sherman, S., Smith, W., Groh, T., & Mermin, P. (1977). Physical attractiveness ad mental illness. *Journal of Abnormal Psychology, 86*(5), 510–517. doi:10.1037/0021–843X.86.5.510

Feinberg, G., & Khosla, D. (1985, September). Sanctioning elderly delinquents: Judicial responses to misdemeanors committed by senior citizens. *TRIAL*, 46–50.

Fogel, C. I. (1993, January/February). Pregnant inmates: risk factors and pregnancy outcomes. *JOGNN*, 33–39.

Frailing, K. (2016). *The achievements of specialty courts in the United States*. Cambridge, MA: Scholars Strategy Network. Retrieved from www.scholarsstrategynetwork.org/brief/achievements-specialty-courts-united-states

Friedmann, A. (2017, September 23). How the courts view ACA accreditation. *Prison Legal News*. Retrieved from www.prisonlegalnews.org/news/2014/oct/10/how-courts-view-aca-accreditation/

Gilbert, C. (2017, May 5). Not trained to not kill. St. Paul, MN. *APM Reports*. Retrieved from www.apmreports.org/story/2017/05/05/police-de-escalation-training

Graham v. Connor, 490 U.S. 386 (1989).

Gudjonsson, G. H. (2017). Memory distrust syndrome, confabulation and false confession. *Cortex*, *87*, 156–165. doi:10.1016/j.cortex.2016.06.013

Gudjonsson, G. H., & Pearse, J. (2011). Suspect interviews and false confessions. *Current Directions in Psychological Science*, *20*(1), 33–37. doi:10.1177/0963721410396824

Gunnell, J. J., & Ceci, S. J. (2010). When emotionality trumps reason: A study of individual processing style and juror bias. *Behavioral Science & the Law*, *28*(6), 850–877. doi:10.1002/bsl.939

Hause, M., & Melber, A. (2016, March 14). *Half of people killed by police have disability: Report*. Retrieved from www.nbcnews.com/news/us-news/half-people-killed-police-suffer-mental-disability-report-n538371

Heideman, E. (2014, September 8). Police brutality's hidden victims: The disabled. *Daily Beast*. Retrieved from www.thedailybeast.com/police-brutalitys-hidden-victims-the-disabled

High, T. (2016). *The dangers of ignoring mental health and developmental issues: How law enforcement continues to fail the most vulnerable*. Watchung, NJ: Focus for Health. Retrieved from www.focusforhealth.org/mental-health-disability-police-shootings/

Hirstein, W. (2005). *Brain fiction: Self-deception and the riddle of confabulation*. Cambridge, MA: MIT Press.

Hurst, M. I., & Cooper, E. B. (1983). Employer attitudes toward stuttering. *Journal of Fluency Disorders*, *8*(1), 1–12. doi:10.1016/0094-730X(83)90017-7

International Association of Chiefs of Police. (2014). *Improving police response to person affected mental illness*. Alexandria, VA: International Association of Chiefs of Police.

John E. Reid & Associates, Inc. (2017). *Overview of the Reid technique*. Retrieved from www.reid.com/app_ad.html

Kassin, S. M., Drizin, S. A., Grisso, T., Gudjonsson, G. H., Leo, R. A., & Redlich, A. D. (2010). Police-induced confessions: Risk factors and recommendations. *Law and Human Behavior*, *34*, 3–37.

Kassin, S. M., & Kiechel, K. L. (1996). The social psychology of false confessions: Compliance, internalization, and confabulation. *American Psychological Society*, 7(3), 125–128.

Langevin, M., Packman, A., & Onslow, M. (2009). Peer responses to stuttering in the preschool setting. *American Journal of Speech-Language Pathology*, *18*(3), 264–276. doi:10.1044/1058–0360(2009/07–0087)

Larson, D. (2008). Unconsciously regarded as disabled: Implicit bias and the regraded-as prong of the American with Disabilities Act. *UCLA Law Review*, *56*, 451–488.

Leo, R. A. (2009). False confessions: Causes, consequences, and implications. *The Journal of the American Academy of Psychiatry and the Law*, *37*(3), 332–343.

Lieberman, J. D. (2002). Head over the heart or heart over the head? Cognitive experiential self-theory and extralegal heuristics in juror decision making. *Journal of Applied Social Psychology*, *32*(12), 2526–2553. doi:10.1111/j.1559–1816.2002.tb02755.x

Lisenba v. California, 319 U.S. 427 (1943).

Lohr, D. (2014, January 25). Police allegedly beat Pearl Pearson for disobeying orders he could not hear. *HuffPost*. Retrieved from www.huffingtonpost.com/2014/01/15/pearl-pearson-police-brutality_n_4603445.html

Lombe-Stairwalt, J. A. (2015). *Correctional officers' perceptions of rehabilitation and treatment in a jail setting* (Unpublished master's thesis). Western Illinois University, Macomb, IL.

Low, W. Y., & Zubir, T. N. (2000). Sexual issues of the disabled: Implications for public health education. *Asian Pacific Journal of Public Health*, *12* Suppl, S78–S83.

Merryman, B. B. (2010). Arguments against use of the Reid Technique for juvenile interrogations. *Communication Law Review*, *10*(2), 16–29.

Metzner, J. L., & Fellner, J. (2010). Solitary confinement and mental illness in U.S. prisons: A challenge for medical ethics. *Journal of the American Academy of Psychiatry and the Law*, *38*(1), 104–108.

Miranda v. Arizona, 384 U.S. 436 (1966).

Misner, R. L. (2000). A strategy for mercy. *William and Mary Law Review*, *41*(4), 1303–1400.

Mitchell, P. R., McMahon, B. T., & McKee, D. (2005). Speech impairment and workplace discrimination: The national EEOC ADA research project. *Journal of Vocational Rehabilitation*, *23*(3), 163–169.

Moscovitch, M. (1989). Confabulation and the frontal system: Strategic versus associative retrieval n neuropsychological theories of memory. In H. L. Roediger & F. I. M. Craik (Eds.), *Varieties of memory and consciousness: Essays in honour of Endel Tulving* (pp. 133–160). Hillsdale, NY: Lawrence Erlbaum Associates.

Najdowski, C. J., Bottoms, B. L., & Vargas, M. C. (2009). Jurors' perceptions of juvenile defendants: The influence of intellectual disability, abuse history, and confession evidence. *Behavioral Sciences & the Law*, *27*(3), 401–430. doi:10.1002/bsl.873

Nash, J. (2016, June 2). Loudon County Jail decertified. *News-Herald*. Retrieved from www.news-herald.net/news/loudon-county-jail-decertified/article_93072242-516d-559a-8987-897280379cf8.html

Navasky, M., & O'Connor, K. (Producers). (2005). *The new asylums*. [Documentary]. United States: Frontline.
National Commission on Correctional Health Care. (2014). *Women's health care in correctional settings*. Retrieved from www.ncchc.org/women%E2%80%99s-health-care
National Institute of Corrections. (2001). *Provision of mental health care in prisons*. Washington, DC: National Institute of Corrections.
National Sheriff's Association. (2017). *Certified jail officer*. Alexandria, VA: National Sheriff's Association. Retrieved from www.sheriffs.org/global-center-for-public-safety/jail-officer-training-and-certification
North Carolina Public Safety. (2017). *Certified basic training*. Retrieved from www.ncdps.gov/Adult-Corrections/Staff-Development-Training/For-Employees/Certified-Basic-Training
Office of Juvenile Justice and Delinquency Prevention. (2015). *Juvenile justice system structure and process: JJDPA core requirements*. Washington, DC: U.S. Department of Justice, Office of Justice Programs.
Parker, G. F. (2009). Impact of a mental health training course for correctional officers on a special housing unit. *Psychiatric Services*, *60*(5), 640–645.
Pennsylvania Department of Corrections v. Yeskey, 524 U.S. 206 (1998).
Perry, D. M., & Carter-Long, L. (2014, May 6). How misunderstanding disability leads to police violence. *The Atlantic*. Retrieved from www.theatlantic.com/health/archive/2014/05/misunderstanding-disability-leads-to-police-violence/361786/
Perry, D. M., & Carter-Long, L. (2016). *The Ruderman white paper on media coverage of law enforcement use of force and disability*. Newton, MA: Ruderman Family Foundation.
Peterson, J. K., Skeem, J., Kennealy, P., Bray, B., & Zvonkovic, A. (2014). How often and how consistently do symptoms directly precede criminal behavior among offenders with mental illness? *Law and Human Behavior*, *38*(5), 439–449. doi:10.1037/lhb0000075
Pittaro, M. (2015). The challenges of incarcerating mentally ill inmates. *In Public Safety*. Charles Town, WV: American Military University. Retrieved from http://inpublicsafety.com/2015/12/the-challenges-of-incarcerating-mentally-ill-inmates/
Saar, M. S., Epstein, R., Rosenthal, L., & Vafa, Y. (2015). *The sexual abuse to prison pipeline: The girls' story*. Washington, DC: Georgetown University Law Center, Center for Poverty and Inequality.
Sabbagh, M. (2011). Direct and indirect influences of defendant mental illness on jury decision making. *The University of Central Florida Undergraduate Research Journal*, *5*(2), 86–96.
Satterfield, J. (2017, August 7). Federal lawsuits allege lack of proper inmate care at Scott County Jail. *Knoxville News Sentinel*. Retrieve from www.knoxnews.com/story/news/crime/2017/08/07/federal-lawsuits-allege-lack-proper-inmate-care-scott-county-jail/530983001/
Sommerfeldt, C. (2016, August 25). Deaf man shot by N.C. cop was "afraid" of police. *New York Daily News*. Retrieved from www.nydailynews.com/news/national/deaf-man-fatally-shot-n-afraid-police-article-1.2764759
Stobbs, G., & Kebbell, M. R. (2003). Jurors' perception of witnesses with intellectual disabilities and the influence of expert evidence. *Journal of Applied Research in Intellectual Disabilities*, *16*(2), 107–114. doi:10.1046/j.1468-3148.2003.00151.x
Strong, S. M., & Kyckelhahn, T. (2016). *Census of problem-solving courts, 2012*. Washington, DC: U.S. Department of Justice, Bureau of Justice Statistics.
Tennessee Department of Commerce and Insurance. (2017). *Training requirements*. Retrieved from www.tn.gov/commerce/article/tci-training-requirements
Tennessee Department of Correction. (2017). *Lois M. DeBerry special needs facility*. Retrieved from www.tn.gov/correction/article/tdoc-lois-deberry-special-needs-facility
Tennessee v. Garner, 471 U.S. 1 (1985).
Texas Code of Criminal Procedure § 16.22 (2017).
Torrey, E. F., Zdanowicz, M. T., Kennard, A. D., Lamb, H. R., Eslinger, D. F., Biasotti, M. C., & Fuller, D. A. (2014). *The treatment of persons with mental illness in prison and jails: A state survey*. Arlington, VA: Treatment and Advocacy Center.
Underwood, L. A., & Washington, A. (2016). Mentally illness and juvenile offenders. *International Journal of Environmental Research and Public Health*, *13*(2), 228–242. doi:10.3390/ijerph13020228
Vallas, R., & Dietrich, S. (2014). *One strike and you're out: How we can eliminate barriers to economic security and mobility for people with criminal records*. Washington, DC: Center for American Progress.
Watts, E. J., & Brown, J. (2016). Interrogative suggestibility in people with fetal alcohol spectrum disorder (FASD): Neurocognitive and behavioral challenges. *Forensic Scholars Today*, *1*(4), 1–8.
Whitehead, J. T., Dodson, K. D., & Edwards, B. D. (2013). *Corrections: Exploring crime, punishment, and justice in America* (3rd ed.). New York, NY: Routledge.

PART I

Administration and Management Issues

2

CONSTITUTIONAL AND LEGAL ISSUES

Tracing the Legal Landscape from Entry to Release

Kwan-Lamar Blount-Hill and Beverly Blount-Hill

> But though his rights may be diminished by the needs and exigencies of the institutional environment, a prisoner is not wholly stripped of constitutional protections when he is imprisoned for a crime. There is no iron curtain drawn between the Constitution and the prisons of this country.
>
> —(*Wolff v. McDonnell*, 1974, pp. 555–556)

Introduction

In the United States, the reach of the criminal justice process is constant and ubiquitous. As some have noted, it is nearly impossible for the average citizen to keep from running afoul of the myriad of federal, state, county, municipal, and regulatory constraints placed on them (see *United States v. Causey*, 834 F.2d 1179 5th Cir., 1987, Rubin, J., dissenting). To the extent individuals are law abiding, criminological theory suggests this is because of the ever-present and unceasing deterrent effect of criminal statutes. The omnipresence of the criminal justice system in routine life ensures that every citizen will be affected by it in some way—no matter the special circumstances or characteristics of the individual, including race, class, gender, or disability.

An encounter with the criminal justice system brings an individual into a multistep, multilayered process, itself governed by a multitude of legal mandates, differing to some degree depending on the enforcing agency and its jurisdiction. Thus, while acting as a source of coercion to hinder impermissible behavior on the part of citizens, the criminal justice system is itself bound by legal limitations. One might say that understanding the justice system is more about understanding its limits than knowing the substantive provisions of criminal law. The importance of restraining the criminal justice system comes from a recognition of the tremendous power differential between justice officials and those they prosecute and the knowledge of how this can lead to egregiously unfair results when unchecked (see, e.g., the classic case in *Ruffin v. Commonwealth*, 62 Va. 790, 1871).

In the case of citizens with special needs, various legal protections come into play with involvement with the justice system. For instance, such individuals are protected from laws that criminalize inherent physical, developmental, or psychological states (see *Robinson v. California*, 370 U.S. 660, 1962). Special needs may serve as significant factors in judging the appropriateness of a person's handling by the justice system, usually inuring to the benefit of the one with the need. While specific jurisdictions may impose their own restrictions, the most important and far-reaching emanate from the United States Constitution. Once a criminal law is enacted, constitutional requirements regulate appropriate legislative intent and inequitable impacts on certain demographics. Enforcement is further regulated by a number of constitutional injunctions, including rights to equal protection and rights against unreasonable or excessive force. Judicial fora are charged with assuring the competence of those who stand trial, providing for the protection of their legal interests, and determining both the existence of *actus reus* (guilty act) and *mens rea* (guilty mind) before allowing prosecution (Federal Rule of Evidence, Article VI, Rule 601). In punishing crimes, judges must consider the mitigating impact of special conditions and corrections; administrators must see to the equal and fair treatment of those with special needs in such a way that their human dignity is preserved.

Because these areas are tended to most forcefully through constitutional pronouncements, that will be the focus of this chapter. Relevant federal statutes, such as the Americans with Disabilities Act (ADA), also will be addressed. Before beginning there, however, it is necessary to define what is meant by the term *special needs*. In this chapter, special needs refer to a class of physical, developmental, or psycho-neurological conditions, both temporary and long term, that inhibit an individual from functioning as ordinary, given the context, without extraordinary accommodations. These special needs typically arise from two causes—an individual's actual disability or an individual's vulnerability in a specific environmental context.

It is hard to articulate a comprehensive list of these conditions. Disabilities make an individual inherently limited in their ability to perform functions common and necessary in ordinary adult life.[1] Purely physical disabilities may typically refer to limitations arising from the noncognitive bodily features and functions of the individual. Paralysis is one such condition, limiting one's performance of common functions because of immobilized limbs, while sickle cell anemia limits one's functionality because of internal bodily dysfunction. Developmental disabilities arise from quirks in the development of the individual from embryo to adulthood and may encompass strictly physical conditions, such as dwarfism, or cognitive ones, like intellectual disability. Psycho-neurological conditions are those emanating from internal, psychological, and neurological functions, including a number of behavioral and personality disorders.

While the term *special needs* is almost inevitably used to refer to those with disabilities, ordinary people may find themselves requiring special accommodations when placed in extraordinary circumstances. In considering the criminal justice process, incarceration represents the ultimate change in circumstances from normal to extraordinary. In the prison environment, an otherwise average elderly person may be in greater than average danger. Homosexuals or transgender individuals, while functioning normally on the outside, represent another class of individuals with special needs while imprisoned, and women, representative as they are of a small portion of offenders, require segregated facilities with the capacity to address their unique concerns. Juveniles also are a special needs population, both because of their inherent developmental limitations and the legal protections for minors (see *Goss v. Lopez*, 419 U.S. 565, 1975).

These conditions may be inherent or acquired, permanent or temporary. For example, insanity may be a long-term psychological affliction or a temporary bout. Both have legal ramifications for the imposition of criminal sanctions and the type of criminal justice proceedings required (see *Washington v. Harper*, 494 U.S. 210, 1990). On the other hand, the human immunodeficiency virus (HIV) infection and resultant autoimmune deficiency syndrome (AIDS) is an acquired condition, though, once acquired, it can debilitate its host so that major life functions are compromised and special accommodations are required (the Supreme Court recognizes HIV/AIDS as a disability under the ADA).

The case of *Buck v. Bell* (274 U.S. 200, 1927) stands as a stark reminder that the criminal justice system has not always been just or fair for those with special needs. Thus, as the chapter expounds on current legal interpretations of the law regarding special needs individuals, it is important to consider existing gaps and how they might be addressed through both law and policy.

Making Law: Regulating the Impact of Criminal Law on Special Needs Offenders

The criminal justice process begins with the establishment of crimes.[2] Crimes are established in two ways, through (1) judicial decisions and prior case law ("common-law crimes") and (2) statutory enactments. The system of common-law offense comes from the United States' history as a colony of England, having carried over the English tradition of judges being able to establish order through a series of judicial decisions recognizing and punishing those acts deemed *mala in se*, or wrong in and of themselves. These acts were seen as so fundamentally evil that the men intuitively know of their immoral nature and reasonably expect punishment for committing them. John Locke (2015 [original 1690], p. 2, footnote) discussed "natural law," which, he stated, differs from man's positive law in that it "simply arises out of the natures of things," and "is plain and intelligible to all reasonable creatures." After generations of such decisions, a body of judicial opinions comprised the common law, which might be amended in small ways with each new decision. Upon independence, territories in the United States adopted the common law as it was and built upon it largely through formally enacting statutes. Some states and the federal government later abolished use of the common law (see *United States v. Hudson and Goodwin*, 11 U.S. 32, 1812), but other states still permit prosecution based on common-law offenses and others expressly incorporate common-law definitions by reference in their criminal statutes. For example, South Carolina punishes some common-law offenses (see S.C. Code Ann. §16–1–110; §17–19–20), including criminal attempt (§ 16–1–80), assault and battery (§16–8–230(m)), obstruction of justice (§16–8–230(n)), and robbery (§16–11–325). Under this regime, judges were able to formulate protections for those with special needs based on their assessments of due justice and fairness (see *M'Naghten's Case*, UKHL J16, 8 ER 718, 1843, establishing a common-law rule governing the determination of insanity).

Notwithstanding a common-law heritage, today most crimes find their basis in criminal statutes. Statutes are passed by the legislative bodies of government. Federally, in the United States, this involves a bill passing both the House of Representatives and Senate. The several states have either unicameral or bicameral legislatures that enact state statutes, while lower bodies, such as county commissions or city councils, may be empowered to enact criminal ordinances in their jurisdictions.[3] While states are given wide latitude to compose their statutes in whatever way they believe most prudent to safeguard the public welfare (see *Nebbia v. New York*, 291 U.S. 502, 1962), lawmaking is constrained by federal—and usually state—constitutional limits to governmental power. The U.S. Constitution begins to impose boundaries on criminal statutes even at this earliest of points in the governing process.

Generally, legal statutes must bear some "reasonable relation to a proper legislative purpose" (*Nebbia v. New York*, 291 U.S. 502, 537, 1962, p. 539). Even where this is so, those statutes containing some criminal component must "be defined with appropriate definiteness" (*Pierce v. United States*, 314 U.S. 306, 311, 1896, p. 239), have "ascertainable standards of guilt," and be clear enough such that "[m]en of common intelligence cannot be required to guess at the meaning of the enactment" (*Connally v. General Construction Co.*, 269 U.S. 385, 391, 1926, p. 269). Violations of these standards by the federal government constitute a transgression against the Fifth Amendment, which states that no one shall "be deprived of life, liberty, or property, without due process of law." States and their local governments are bound by the Fourteenth Amendment's declaration that, just as with the federal government, "nor shall any State deprive any person of life, liberty, or property, without due process of law."

Laws that are either unreasonable given their stated purpose or that serve no "proper" purpose are unconstitutional and invalid. Either are concerns for special needs populations, which are particularly at-risk of being targeted under unfair legal regimes. The United States Supreme Court's holding in *Mississippi University for Women v. Hogan* (458 U.S. 718, 1982) provides an example of a law that considers gender unjustifiably, considering its stated purpose. In that case, the state argued that a male student was denied admission into a university because the purpose of the school was to serve the educational needs of female students. The Court found that this purpose did not necessitate not admitting male applicants. Admittedly, this case was brought by a defendant asserting discrimination based upon his being male, but the reasoning would apply with equal force to discriminatory situations in the reverse. In the more recent case of *United States v. Windsor*, the Court held "the principle purpose . . . to impose inequality" between heterosexuals and homosexuals was not a legitimate reason to impose upon the fundamental right to marriage (133 S. Ct. 2675, 2696, 2013). Together, these stand for the proposition that, in all areas, including criminal law, statutes must be proper in their stated purpose and related to that purpose, and discrimination on any basis, including against those with unique characteristics or special needs, is invalid and unconstitutional.

Nevertheless, general due process protections are applicable to all citizens and do not speak to legal protections that arise specifically to address the special needs of particular groups or people. However, the Fourteenth Amendment contains the "Equal Protection Clause," often the vehicle used to protect certain classes of individuals. The clause states that no government, state or federal, may "deny to any person within its jurisdiction the equal protection of the laws." This has generally been interpreted to mean that all citizens should be able to avail themselves of the law's protections on an equal basis, that they should be permitted to assert legal rights equitably, and statutes that impose differential treatment or create differential impacts must meet a high bar of justification.

The Supreme Court has created a number of jurisprudential mechanisms for its use in ensuring compliance with the clause. Most importantly, in *Marbury v. Madison* (5 U.S. 137, 1803), the Court established its right to invalidate those federal legislative statutes and executive actions that violate the Constitution. Just a few years later, the Court extended this right to include the invalidation of state statutes and the unconstitutional actions of state executives (*Fletcher v. Peck*, 10 U.S. 87, 1870). Accordingly, the Court has the authority to strike down any laws and official actions that violate the Equal Protection Clause and discriminate against certain classes of people.

Using this power, the Court has gone on to announce the level of scrutiny it will devote to determining when a statute should be struck for unconstitutional inequity. It bases its scrutiny primarily on the class of people being differentiated. There are some classes that, when set apart by law, are presumed to be impermissibly discriminated against; these include racial, ethnic, and religious minorities (see *Adarand Constructors v. Peña*, 515 U.S. 200, 1995). Suspect classes are those "saddled with such disabilities, or subjected to such a history of purposeful unequal treatment, or relegated to such a position of political powerlessness as to command extraordinary protection from the majoritarian political process" (*San Antonio School District v. Rodriguez*, 411 U.S. 1, 1973, p. 28). Laws distinguishing these classes will be subjected to *strict scrutiny* (see *Loving v. Virginia*, 388 U.S. 1, 1967), requiring that they serve a "compelling" government interest and be designed to carefully address that interest in the least burdensome way. While it may be argued that several categories of individuals with special needs meet at least one of these criteria, there has been no explicit recognition of any of these groups as suspect by the Court thus far.

There are some classes of individuals that may be labeled "quasi-suspect." In these cases, the groups are not seen as having been subjected to outright discrimination as invidiously and intensely as those of suspect classes, but they are, nevertheless, seen as vulnerable to discriminatory treatment. Women and, more recently, homosexuals have come to be viewed as quasi-suspect classes (see *United States v. Virginia*, 518 U.S. 515, 1996; *Lawrence v. Texas*, 539 U.S. 558, 2003, respectively). Laws that distinguish gender or sexual orientation must "serve important governmental objectives, and . . . be substantially related to the achievement of those objectives" (*Wengler v. Druggists Mutual Insurance Co.*, 446 U.S. 142, 1980, p. 150). In the criminal justice context, both women and homosexuals, as groups, have a fraught history with justice agencies while also having needs distinct from typical offenders. Thus, where laws or policies are designed specifically for their handling, the *intermediate scrutiny* applied to quasi-suspect classes is relevant. Moreover, some have pointed to the decision in *City of*

Cleburne v. Cleburn Living Center, Inc., (473 U.S. 432, 1985) as directly supporting the application of intermediate scrutiny to laws pertaining to the intellectually disabled.

The Eighth Amendment is another limiting constitutional mandate, prohibiting the imposition of "cruel and unusual punishments." This has, in fact, been the much more common basis upon which those with special needs have gained legal protections peculiar to their conditions. This limits lawmaking in two primary ways: (1) some punishments, by their nature, are sufficiently cruel and unusual as to be unconstitutional on their face;[4] and (2) some punishments are cruel when applied in certain cases. Punishments are typically seen as cruel and unusual in a particular case based either (a) on the offender or (b) the crime being punished. When based on the offender, the unconstitutionality of the criminal sanction is generally based on concerns around culpability and is circumscribed to that case or class of cases. In these cases, the unconstitutionality of the legislated sentences does not vitiate the law's entire penalty scheme. It is more a problem of case-specific sentencing (discussed later) and not one of statutory composition. However, in the case of the latter, the Court has held that punishments must be proportional to the crimes punished and, where they are not, the punishment is unconstitutional when imposed on *anyone* (see *Weems v. United States*, 217 U.S. 349, 1910). In other words, legislatures must ensure that they permit punishments keeping the principle of proportionality in the fore or else the penalty statutes themselves may be overturned.

In the context of individuals with special conditions, disproportionality on this front end comes into play where laws attempt to punish personal characteristics or "statuses." The Supreme Court has roundly decried crimes of these types. In *Robinson v. California*, the Court held that any criminal sanction for the special condition of narcotics addiction would be cruel and unusual (370 U.S. 660, 1962). Going further, in fact, the Court opined that it would hold the same for statutes criminalizing mental illness or venereal disease infection. Notably, however, the Court did legitimate compulsory treatment for addicts and punishing activities that may perpetuate addiction in others. This caveat may be important for other conditions as well, as some have pushed compulsory institutionalization of addicts (Operation Unite, 2015) as well as criminalizing the sexual activities of HIV-positive persons (Centers for Disease Control and Prevention, 2015a).

Law Enforcement: Fairness and Reasonableness for Special Needs Offenders

Generally, state and local empowerment statutes that specifically delineate the power of officers to conduct police work govern law enforcement actions. However, the language of the Fourth Amendment limits all enforcement by officers of federal, state, or local governments or other organizations acting on behalf of the government:

> The right of the people to be secure in their persons, houses, papers, and effects, against unreasonable searches and seizures, shall not be violated, and no Warrants shall issue, but upon probable cause, supported by Oath or affirmation, and particularly describing the place to be searched, and the persons or things to be seized.

For the purposes of the Fourth Amendment, much of the initial work of law enforcement is encompassed in the terms "searches" and "seizures." Of course, the execution of a search warrant is a "search" and confiscation of drugs and paraphernalia is a "seizure," but the Fourth Amendment also considers arrests and uses of force to be seizures of one's body, and investigative stops and protective frisks each represent a seizure and search, respectively.

The Fourth Amendment becomes important for law enforcement encounters with those with special needs mostly over the issue of the "reasonableness" of their actions (see *United States v. Knights*, 534 U.S. 112, 2001). Officers are often placed in situations where they must make split-second, rapid decisions that may lead to life-or-death consequences. Realizing this, the Supreme Court has held that officers' assessments of what actions to take to act in accordance with the law to achieve their mission and protect life and property should be judged by looking to what a reasonable officer would do given the circumstances (*Graham v. Connor*, 490 U.S. 386, 1989). This standard assumes that mistakes and unforeseen consequences may occur, but limits the degree to which officers can escape punishment for blatant recklessness or gross negligence.

Regarding those with special needs, concerns arise when officers are forced to assess the need to physically restrain and detain individuals who may be uncooperative because of psychological or cognitive deficiencies or abnormally given to injury because of physical disabilities. Age also is a major consideration here, where officers need to consider the appropriate levels of force to use in seizing a child or elderly person. Prior Court decisions teach us that carelessly sending officers into the field, without adequate training and policy guidance, will open agencies up to liability should those officers act in ways that harm special needs constituents (see *City of Canton v. Harris*, 489 U.S. 378, 1989).

A narrower consideration arises during one of the few times where a suspect's state of mind becomes important for searches or seizures—consent searches. In most cases, officers have to either have a warrant or, at least, establish probable cause before initiating a search. There are some exceptions, most of which consider the circumstances of the encounter more so than the particular characteristics of the person. Nevertheless, one exception to the necessity of probable cause before searches is when a suspect consents to allow law enforcement to search his or her property. In such cases, the Supreme Court has held that the Fourth Amendment simply requires that the consent be voluntary, absent from explicit or implicit physical or psychological coercion (*Schneckloth v. Bustamonte*, 412 U.S. 218, 1973). In determining whether consent was freely given, courts will not apply as stringent a standard as they would for waivers of Fifth Amendment protections (discussed later), but they do consider the individual characteristics of the person to determine whether officers made her or him believe that she or he had no choice but to consent to the search. A lower bar for coercion thus applies to people who are more suggestable because of psychological or cognitive peculiarities.

Interestingly, while the Fourth Amendment protects against unreasonable measures during seizure or physical detention and the Fifth and Fourteenth Amendments protect against unfair deprivations of life or liberty, the U.S. Supreme Court has made no declarations about the specific contours regarding the duty of care guaranteed to those with special needs. Illustrating the point, the United States Court of Appeals for the District of Columbia Circuit—oft seen as the second highest court in the land (Roberts, 2006)—considered whether it was a "clearly established" constitutional obligation for officers to obtain medical treatment for an individual when taken into their custody ostensibly for his own safety (*Harris v. District of Columbia*, 932 F.2d 10, 1991). In the court's opinion, the exact basis upon which a person is restrained and taken into "custody" is of paramount importance. Previous Supreme Court cases had not addressed whether the medical care of individuals being restrained by officers merely for their own protection, or the safety of officers or the public, as opposed to formal arrest, are officers' responsibility.

It is not clear what responsibilities law enforcement officers owe to individuals not formally the subject of some judicial process when they physically restrain them. Those who may present some indicators of threat to on-scene officers, such as those who may not be responsive to officer commands because of experiencing a hallucinatory episode, having an intellectual disability, or simply being deaf, remain a class with uncertain rights to any threshold duty of care.

While the law does not require officers encountering individuals with special needs to "anticipat[e] the frailties or idiosyncrasies" of the individual (see *Yarborough v. Alvarado*, 541 U.S. 652, 667, 2004), Fifth Amendment protections can be affected by diminished capacities, not the least of which include cognitive limitations. There are two primary inquiries in which an individual's special needs status might have an influence covered by Fifth Amendment constraints: (1) is the individual in custody? and (2) are any statements made by the individual in custody admissible in court?

Particularly, the amendment's protection against self-incrimination requires that, before police may question an individual in custody, the person must be made aware of his or her rights:

> At the outset, if a person in custody is to be subjected to interrogation, he must first be informed in clear and unequivocal terms that he has a right to remain silent. . . . The warning of a right to remain silent must be accompanied by the explanation that anything said can and will be used against the individual in court. . . . [W]e hold than an individual held for interrogation must be clearly informed that he has the right to consult with a lawyer and to have the lawyer with him during interrogation. [I]t is necessary to warn him not only that he has the right to consult with an attorney, but also that, if he is indigent, a lawyer will be appointed to represent him. If the interrogation continues without the presence of an attorney and a statement is taken, a heavy burden rests on the government to demonstrate that the defendant knowingly and intelligently waived his privilege against self-incrimination and his right to retained or appointed counsel.
>
> (*Miranda v. Arizona*, 384 U.S. 436, 1966, pp. 467–475)

Importantly, these rights must be communicated "[a]t the outset" of questioning "if a person is in custody" (*Miranda v. Arizona*, 384 U.S. 436, 1966, p. 467). Determining whether someone is in custody is not as simple as one might think. However, the most succinct annunciation of the applicable test was announced in *California v. Beheler* (463 U.S. 1121, 1983, p. 1125), where the Court stated, "the ultimate inquiry is simply whether there is a formal arrest or restraint on freedom of movement of the degree associated with a formal arrest." The Court has further made clear that this is to be an "objective" test, where "how a reasonable person in the position of the individual being questioned would gauge the breadth of his or her freedom of action" is the core consideration (*Stansbury v. California*, 511 U.S. 318, 1994, p. 323). What should be pointed out, however, is the objectivity here simply means that a neutral fact-finder is able to determine what a reasonable person would perceive if "in the position of the individual," accounting for the totality of the circumstances, "including physical disability, youth, or advanced age" (*Yarborough v. Alvarado*, 541 U.S. 652, 2004, p. 669 O'Connor, J., concurring opinion). Therefore, while a typical adult might not be considered "in custody" in certain circumstances, adding the disadvantage of blindness might rightly affect that determination.

Age has been specifically determined to be an objective factor to consider in determining when a person is in police custody (see *J. D. B. v. North Carolina*, No. 09–11121, 2011). Again, officers are not required to attempt to determine the individual intelligence and competence of minors before questioning them, but the Court has recognized that all minors are limited, to some degree, in their ability to think about long-term negative consequences and are more easily suggestible to pressure from authority figures. When considering what a reasonable person would consider in custody, officers must be concerned about what a reasonable person of the subject's approximate age might consider to be in custody.

It is essential to point out that the reason age may be considered is because of its common impacts across a class of people, impacts that are widely known and apparent, involving a group of individuals readily identifiable. When those needs are neither apparent nor applicable across a broad group, it is more likely the individual will be held to the standard of an ordinarily "reasonable person." Even if an individual suffering from a psychological disturbance subjectively feels he or she is being detained, courts may simply assess this from the perspective of a person in a more typical state of mind.

Nevertheless, whether an individual is "in custody" is only one part of a two-pronged inquiry. Fifth Amendment protections against incrimination arise when a person is taken into custody and subsequently questioned. If such people choose to waive their right to silence or legal counsel and to make statements against their own interests, that waiver must be made "voluntarily, knowingly, and intelligently" (*Miranda v. Arizona*, 384 U.S. 436, 1966, p. 444). Where an individual is incapable of making an informed, judicious decision to confess or offer statements that might lead to prosecutorial evidence, his or her statements would be unavailable for use in a later trial. Moreover, evidence gained from those statements might be regarded as "fruit of the poisonous tree," and; therefore excluded from consideration during prosecution (*Silverthorne Lumber Co. v. United States*, 251 U.S. 385, 1920; see also *Wong Sun v. United States*, 371 U.S. 471, 1963, p. 488).

Law enforcement agents must ensure not only that a person knows of his or her rights, but that the officers themselves do nothing to coerce the suspect when obtaining statements. In short, voluntariness requires that the will of the subject not be "overborne," and that he was in no way coerced or compelled to make incriminating statements (*Lynumn v. Illinois*, 372 U.S. 528, 1963, p. 534). This inquiry requires a consideration both the interrogation method and characteristics of the accused. Intentional manipulation by officers invites more searching scrutiny of officer techniques and increases the likelihood of a finding of coercion (see *Spano v. New York*, 360 U.S. 315, 1959). Special needs become important here to the extent that police interrogators attempt to manipulate the unique disadvantages of the suspect to obtain a confession or fail to account for his peculiarities in ensuring his continued ability to exercise free will (*Fikes v. Alabama*, 352 U.S. 191, 1957). Accordingly, exploitation of a suspect's mental illness makes interrogation coercive (*Blackburn v. Alabama*, 361 U.S. 199, 1960). Likewise, the Court has held that youth makes certain interrogation tactics more coercive than they otherwise would be because of minors' susceptibility to intimidation, which may cause a confession to be involuntary (see *Gallegos v. Colorado*, 370 U.S. 49, 1962; *Haley v. Ohio*, 332 U.S. 596, 1948).

However, in the case of children, it is important that the special condition is apparent and that, in *Blackburn*, the police knew of the special condition and purposely used it to manipulate the individual. Officers are not required to consider the possibility of special needs when the individual is not one of an apparent and well-understood class to proceed with custodial questioning. In *Colorado v. Connelly* (479 U.S. 157, 1986), the Court held that, though the defendant was later determined to suffer from schizophrenia, because the officers had conducted themselves in complete accordance with the law and had no way of knowing the defendant's competence, his confession could be used at trial. It would then be up to a jury to determine how much credibility to give the individual or up to adopted rules of evidence to exclude the testimony (see Fed. Rule Evid. 601).

The Criminal Trial: Concerns Regarding Actus Reus, Mens Rea, and a Fair Trial

Crimes are usually prosecuted based on two sets of facts—those establishing *actus reus* and those proving the requisite *mens rea*. *Actus reus* refers to the actions that comprise a crime; for example, battery typically requires the action of making contact with another where that contact is unsolicited and undesired. *Actus reus* has nothing to do with the state of mind of the offender, however. Most crimes additionally require proof of a "guilty mind," that is *mens rea* or culpability on the part of the offender. In other words, criminal battery usually requires some degree of knowledge that the offender is making unwanted contact with another and, typically, a degree of intention to do so.

Offenders with special needs can present problems on both fronts. Those with physical limitations may be incapable of committing crimes for which they are accused. However, more commonly, special needs come up when prosecutors must consider whether offenders with psychological or cognitive abnormalities have the minimal *mens rea* to convict them for a crime. The Supreme Court has adopted the practice of reading into criminal statutes some degree of criminal intent even when it is not expressly written into a criminal statute (see *Elonis v. United States*, No. 13–983, 2015). Where psychological or cognitive conditions make it impossible for a person to comprehend the wrongness of a criminalized action, jurisdictions usually turn to treating their ailments and separating them from the general public through commitment to psychiatric institutions rather than seek to punish them (see *Clark v. Arizona*, 548 U.S. 735, 2005). However, when this is the case, the offender cannot remain confined after the cessation of his condition and his return to normalcy (see *Foucha v. Louisiana*, 504 U.S. 71, 1992).

Accepting that they may have sufficient culpability to punish them for criminal acts, all states divert legal minors from their traditional systems of justice into separate juvenile justice systems at the point of trial and incarceration (see *Thompson v. Oklahoma*, 487 U.S. 815, 1988). The states may differ as to what they determine a "minor" to be, but all of them make a distinction between the decision making and ultimate guiltiness of children and adults. Just as asylums are supposed to treat and reform the psychologically disturbed, so juvenile justice systems are designed to rehabilitate juvenile offenders rather than to punish them (see *In re Gault*, 387 U.S. 1, 1987). Thus, most juvenile systems have adopted the notion of "individualized justice," by which courts, acting through the paternalistic doctrine of *parens patriae*, purport to act in the best interest of the child to prevent his descent into further criminality. In accord with this difference in focus, juvenile courts often utilize distinct methods from those where adults are prosecuted. For one, the procedures may be relaxed to encourage a more informal and interactive environment. Judges are often more directly engaged in the process. Juvenile parties are often assigned guardians to look after their interests, in addition to their legal counsel. Semantically, the proceedings differ, with the child not being taken into "custody" but rather "under care of" and not adjudicated "criminal" but rather "delinquent."

Still, juveniles are entitled to fundamental due process rights just as adults are. "In our Constitution," Justice Fortas writes in *In re Gault*, "the condition of being a boy does not justify a kangaroo court" (387 U.S. 1, 1987, p. 28). In cases involving juveniles, the offender, his or her legal counsel, and parents must be given appropriate notice of the charges being alleged and the timing of relevant hearings. The minor and his or her parents must be informed of their right to legal counsel. Minors are also entitled to refrain from testifying against themselves during trial and have a right to confront and cross-examine witnesses against them.

A final major concern regarding those with special needs involves the question of competence to stand trial. The Constitution requires that individuals who are being prosecuted be aware enough of the realities of trial to understand the nature of their charges and to be able to assist their counsel in their defense (*Dusky v. United States*, 362 U.S. 402, 1960). In fact, a trial cannot commence unless the individual is competent to understand it—this is why those adjudicated "insane" are committed instead of convicted. Importantly, in the interest of carrying out the function of prosecution, the Supreme Court has ruled that governments may treat psychosis or other disabilities, even where the individual refuses treatment, to bring them to a triable state (*Sell v. United States*, 539 U.S. 166, 2003). The relevant question here is:

> Has the Government, in light of the efficacy, the side effects, the possible alternatives, and the medical appropriateness of a particular course of . . . treatment, shown a need for that treatment sufficiently important to overcome the individual's protected interests in refusing it?
>
> (*Sell v. United States*, 539 U.S. 166, 2003, p. 183)

Unless the treatment is itself harmful, that answer typically will be "yes."

Sentencing and Corrections: Preserving Human Dignity, Avoiding Cruel and Unusual Punishment

Conviction for a crime resulting in imprisonment does not terminate a citizen's claim to his constitutional rights:

> A prisoner retains all the rights of an ordinary citizen except those expressly, or by necessary implication, taken from him by law. While the law does take his liberty and imposes a

> duty of servitude and observance of discipline of his regulation and that of other prisoners, it does not deny his right to personal security against unlawful invasion. When a man possesses a substantial right, the courts will be diligent in finding a way to protect it.
>
> (*Coffin v. Reichard*, 143 F.2d 443, 6th Cir., 1944, p. 445)

The Eighth Amendment is unequivocal in the rights of the incarcerated, declaring, "Excessive bail shall not be required, nor excessive fines imposed, nor cruel and unusual punishments inflicted" (U.S. Const., amend. VIII). Therefore, "the State must respect the human attributes even of those who have committed serious crimes" (*Graham v. Florida*, 130 S.Ct. 2011, 2010, p. 2021). In determining what constitutes cruel and unusual punishment, the U.S. Supreme Court has imposed a *proportionality* standard, whereby a punishment must be proportional to the crime committed and, more importantly, the culpability of the criminal (see *Weems v. United States*, 217 U.S. 349, 1910). An individual's culpability, or guiltiness, depends, in part, on her or his state of mind at the time of the offense and her or his ability to contemplate the wrongfulness and gravity of the act. In the case of those with special needs, state of mind may be impaired by one or more cognitive or psychological disabilities, limiting the degree to which they can be held culpable for their actions.

It is, indeed, difficult to determine whether a punishment is proportionate with a committed offense, and this is, in any case, a subjective judgment. In such cases, the Court draws its decisional cues from "the evolving standards of decency" at the time of its decision (*Trop v. Dulles*, 356 U.S. 86, 1958, p. 101). Current standards of decency are signaled in several sources, among them being the trends in the laws passed by state legislatures, trends in actual practices observed across the states (*Roper v. Simmons*, 543 U.S. 551, 2005), and the judgments of criminal juries (*Thompson v. Oklahoma*, 487 U.S. 815, 1988). To this, the Court also adds its own judgments about what is proper punishment given present societal mores and the culpability that can be assigned to the offender (*Coker v. Georgia*, 433 U.S. 584, 1977; *Thompson v. Oklahoma*, 487 U.S. 815, 1988).

Juveniles are often separated in correctional systems even more strictly than in the judicial systems, universally detained in separate physical spaces, nearly always in separate facilities and geographic locations, with a special set of legal ramifications, and a unique body of law governing their sentencing and correctional experience, all with an entirely different jurisprudential orientation. The reason for this rests in their difference in degree of culpability, which the *Thompson* Court summed most succinctly:

> [L]ess culpability should attach to a crime committed by a juvenile than to a comparable crime by an adult. The basis for this conclusion is too obvious to require extended explanation. Inexperience, less education, and less intelligence make the teenager less able to evaluate the consequences of his or her conduct, while at the same time he or she is much more apt to be motivated by mere emotion or peer pressure than is an adult. The reasons why juveniles are not trusted with the privileges and responsibilities of an adult also explain why their irresponsible conduct is not as morally reprehensible as that of an adult.
>
> (*Thompson v. Oklahoma*, 487 U.S. 815, 1988 p. 835)

In the case of capital punishment, the Court has held that it would be cruel and unusual to sentence the intellectually disabled to death (*Atkins v. Virginia*, 536 U.S. 304, 2002). It has held the same for those who were psychologically disturbed and deemed insane (*Ford v. Wainwright*, 477 U.S. 399, 1986). In both cases, the Court has left states to determine individually what constitutes either condition, but both disabilities trigger legal protections against the imposition of a death penalty. In the case of juveniles, the Court has been even more unequivocal in holding that their execution is unconstitutional and, thus, necessarily foreclosed (*Roper v. Simmons*, 543 U.S. 551, 2005; *Thompson v. Oklahoma*, 487 U.S. 815, 1988). In fact, even life without the possibility of parole, for anything short of homicide, is an unconstitutionally "cruel" punishment when the sentenced is a minor (*Graham v. Florida*, 490 U.S. 386, 1989). The imposition of the death penalty is a vehicle through which society is said to express "moral outrage" and deter the committal of heinous crimes by similarly situated offenders (see *Gregg v. Georgia*, 428 U.S. 153, 183, 1976), yet, in the case of those with diminished capacities for forethought and the suppression of their emotions, both of these ends are moot and state-imposed execution therefore cruel. Some have opined that this line of reasoning portends the extension of death penalty prohibitions for other special classes as well, perhaps a pathway to its ultimate abolition (see Borra, 2005).

As stated earlier, the Fourteenth Amendment mandates, among other things, that state and local governments may not "deprive any person of life, liberty, or property, without due process of the law" (U.S. Const., amend XIV). Due process has been held to encompass two types of concerns: (1) procedural due process, or fairness in the procedures granting governments authority to interfere with one's liberty; and (2) substantive due process, by which the Court determines which rights are inherent to a society guaranteeing due process (see *Mills v. Rogers*, 457 U.S. 291, 1982). Prisoners with special needs may contest due process violations on both these points when prison officials neglect to provide adequate medical care or seek to impose care against one's will.

In *Washington v. Harper* (494 U.S. 210, 1990), the Supreme Court was asked to declare when a prisoner might be administered psychotropic drugs over her or his refusal and against her or his will. Balancing the interests of the prison in the safety of its other inmates, its staff, and the inmate her- or himself, against the interest of an inmate in making her or his own medical decisions, the Court decided that inmates' substantive rights against involuntary invasive medical procedures are limited when "the inmate is dangerous to himself or others and the treatment is in the inmate's medical interest" (*Washington v. Harper*, 494 U.S. 210, 1990, p. 227).

The fact of an abnormality itself can create the special need that the individual be taken under the care of the government, even where involuntary. Several decisions from the Supreme Court have affirmed the state's right to civil commitment of individuals determined to be dangerous and incapable of controlling their actions because of some mental impairment (see *Kansas v. Hendricks*, 521 U.S. 345, 1997). In this case, as with others, the Court has left it to individual states to make the determinations of what qualifies one as being incapable of controlling their own actions—not necessarily a purely medical judgment—provided these determinations follow "proper procedures and evidentiary standards" (*Kansas v. Hendricks*, 521 U.S. 345, 1997, p. 357, citing also *Addington v. Texas*, 441 U.S. 418, 1979).

The Eight Amendment also requires that prisons and correctional facilities provide adequate medical care to their inmates (*Estelle v. Gamble*, 429 U.S. 97, 1976). Importantly, this mandate goes both for "the worst cases," where "such a failure may actually produce physical 'torture or a lingering death'" (quoting *In re Kemmler*, 136 U.S. 436, 447, 1890, p. 103), as well as "less serious cases," where denial of requested care "may result in pain and suffering which no one suggests would serve any penological purpose." This is an important mandate, as many special needs populations are disproportionately housed in local, state, and federal correctional facilities. More than half of all inmates suffered from a mental health issue, approximately half of federal and state prisoners had problems with substance abuse, and the human immunodeficiency virus/acquired immune deficiency syndrome (HIV/AIDS) rate among those in prison is much higher than that of the general population (James & Glaze, 2006).

A facility violates the Constitution when it declines to provide medical care in such a way that shows "deliberate indifference" to the prisoner's need (*Estelle v. Gamble*, 429 U.S. 97, 1976, p. 106). Many claims have been held to fall short of this standard,[5] but it has been the basis of prisoner complaints from several special populations, including aging offenders, narcotics addicts, and those with chronic diseases (Cropsey, Wexler, Melnick, Taxman & Young, 2007). Especially as Eighth Amendment jurisprudence is governed by evolving standards of decency, the argument may be expanded, for instance to include medical care required by prisoners in gender transition, accommodate ever more specialized dietary restrictions, or account for the abundance of non-Judeo-Christian religious traditions with their variant needs.

Just as prison officials may impose care upon someone for safety reasons, the Eighth Amendment also mandates that prison officials have a duty to protect the inmates in their care. Where they show deliberate indifference to dereliction of this duty, they are liable (*Farmer v. Brennan*, 511 U.S. 825, 1994). Certain populations are truly special needs in this regard. Women, while housed in facilities separate from men, are still disproportionately the victims of sexual abuses by prison guards (Piecora, 2014). Gay or transgender inmates also are frequent targets for rape and sexual abuse in prisons by other inmates and staff (Beck, Berzofsky, Caspar, & Krebs, 2014). Very young or older prisoners may be subjected to assault or extortion (Human Rights Watch, 2001; Kerbs & Jolley, 2007). Prisoners with sexually transmitted infections (STIs) often avoid disclosure because of fear of stigma, presenting a special challenge in managing their health and risk to others—for instance, in the case of HIV/AIDS infection (Centers for Disease Control and Prevention, 2015b).

Beyond the Constitution: Federal, State, and Local Practices

The Americans with Disabilities Act of 1990 (ADA) prohibits discrimination based on one's disability (42 U.S.C. § 12182). Its text provides a near comprehensive description of what constitutes special needs, essentially a requirement for "modifications to rules, policies, or practices, the removal of architectural, communication, or transportation barriers, or the provision of auxiliary aids and services" (Public Health and Welfare, 42 U.S.C. § 12131(2)). The ADA covers criminal justice agencies in its application to *public entities*, including federal agencies as well as state and local ones. "Public entities" importantly includes prisons, as declared by a unanimous decision of the Supreme Court (*Pennsylvania Department of Corrections v. Yesky*, 524 U.S. 206, 1998).

Though several Supreme Court decisions of constitutional import preceded the passage of the ADA, its enactment represented a serious change in the legal protection afforded those with special needs arising from recognized disabilities (Krienert, Henderson, & Vandiver, 2003). Instead of having to prove police officers acted "unreasonably" or show that unfair treatment in prison is the result of "deliberate indifference," the ADA provides those with disabilities a vehicle to pursue legal redress through the much easier path of asserting their right to equity with the nondisabled through reasonable accommodation. This extends to the criminal justice arena. For example, under the ADA, prisoners with hearing disabilities and vision impairments are entitled to services and technological aids that place them on par with others in such basic tasks as reading or communicating. Offenders who might suffer with psycho-neurological conditions, such as anxiety, may request psychiatric medications to offer relief from fearfulness, hypersensitivity, social fear, and panic attacks.

Although federal laws often drive actions designed to address the special needs of offenders, for the most part, it still places the execution of these responsibilities in the hands of the official agents of the criminal justice system. The precise determination of what accommodations are reasonable and how they are provided often lie within the discretion of state and local agencies. Corrections departments provide a ready illustration of this fact, where their responses to the wide-ranging needs of those housed in their facilities vary depending on local policy preferences and resources (see Marceau, 2008).

The common response to the mandates of the ADA comes in the form of direct policies incorporating its language. In state of Washington, the state's Department of Corrections (DOC) has enshrined in its policies an ethic of equality and accommodation, where feasible, regarding offenders with disabilities. By policy, the department commits to "ensure the rights of offenders with disabilities are addressed consistent with legitimate penological interest" and make "appropriate accommodation based on barriers to effective participation/use by the offender, facility security and safety, accommodation effectiveness, and cost" and expressly declares it "will not discriminate on the basis of disability when providing services, programs, and activities" (WA DOC 690.400, 2015, p. 2). The department defines disability by reference specifically to federal law, presumably the ADA. The Minnesota Department of Corrections makes similar commitments to its special needs offenders, including requiring housing, program, service, and disciplinary actions affecting an inmate with special needs be cleared by the facility's ADA coordinator (MN DOC Directive 203.250, 2015).

According to the Bureau of Justice Statistics (BJS), as of year 2000, approximately 70 % of state public and private adult correctional facilities tout policies requiring mental health screening of offenders at the time of intake; 89% of them reported that mental health services were provided to inmates who needed them, including such services as "psychiatric assessments (65%), 24-hour mental health care (51%), therapy/counseling by trained mental health professionals (71%) and distribution of psychotropic medications (73%)" (Beck & Maruschak, 2001, p. 1).

Where agencies fail to exercise their discretion properly, however, they have been forced to provide their wards with necessary ADA accommodations through federal enforcement actions. For example, the South Carolina Department of Corrections recently settled with the U.S. Department of Justice (U.S. DOJ, 2013) on an action arising from its practice of segregating HIV-positive inmates from all others without any consideration of their security risk. These inmates were housed in specific dormitories for HIV-positive individuals, dorms that lacked access to many of the services and program offerings of other housing units. Moreover, somewhat shockingly, they were forced to wear clothing and badges that identified their dorm, effectively disclosing their HIV status to staff and other inmates. Using Title II of the ADA, the U.S. DOJ (2013) was able to force the corrections department to implement a new policy prohibiting discrimination against those with special needs, specifically citing HIV as one such disability.

Ultimately, federal law provides an extra-constitutional means to ensure that all special needs offenders are afforded their rights. Still, emerging trends in public and practitioner perceptions have changed the way that individuals with special needs are handled without relying solely on the coercive force of the law. Increasingly, for instance, developmentally disabled offenders are often diverted away from prisons or jails to halfway houses or assisted living homes that can better suit their medical care and needs (Kim, Becker-Cohen, & Serakos, 2015). In addition, while a recent study of police officers in the Southeast revealed lackluster training in how to handle those with special needs, it also found that the majority of those surveyed were "willing to interact" with special needs individuals and that many evinced "positive" attitudes toward them (Eadens, 2016, p. 222).

Conclusion

The task of protecting the rights of special needs offenders can be arduous, complex, and in constant motion, complicated by the countless conditions and circumstances that may constitute *special needs*. The law has had to evolve to recognize and deal with these developments, aided by the continuous evolution of society's sense of "fairness" and "decency." Thus, the constitutional and legal issues that arise regarding the justice system's handling of those with special needs is not separate from but rather reflective of the nation's overarching struggle to afford dignity to all of its citizens in every case and every situation. The great discretion inherent in the criminal justice system means that the law can only provide broad boundaries, only rarely initiating specific fixes. Understanding these issues attunes one into the outer bounds of what is appropriate and tolerable. Within this framework, the continued endeavors of policy makers, researchers and medical practitioners, and advocates, both formal and informal, will be needed to color in the lines and assure that, while often unpleasant, encounters with the criminal justice system for those with special needs are no more onerous than for those without them.

Notes

1 Official definitions of "disability" vary. For example, the federal Americans with Disabilities Act (ADA) of 1990 defines a disability as "(A) a physical or mental impairment that substantially limits one or more major life activities of such [disabled] individual; (B) a record of such impairment; or (C) being regarded as having such an impairment" 42 U.S.C. § 12182. The United Nations' World Health Organization defines the condition as such: "impairments, activity limitations, and participation restrictions. An impairment is a problem in body function or structure; an activity limitation is a difficulty encountered by an individual in executing a task or action; while a participation restriction is a problem experienced by an individual in involvement in life situations" (United Nations World Health Organization, n.d., para. 1).

2 Criminologists have long debated about the proper definition of "crime." However, theorists do not define crime, not if what they are studying are those acts for which a person may incur a state penalty and often do. Legislatures define crime through their enactments; judges, magistrates, prosecutors, police officers perhaps, through interpretation and selective enforcement, define what crime is. Therefore, a good definition of crime is one offered by a critic of its academic utility: "A crime is any act committed in violation of a law that prohibits it and authorizes punishment for its commission" (Wilson & Herrnstein, 1985, p. 22; see also Geis, 2000). Crimes are comprised of two critical elements—proscription and penal punishment—meaning that all crimes, both common law and statutory, can be distinguished from other legislative acts in that they are expressly forbidden and subject to state sanction.

3 Some statutes are written fairly broadly so as to allow executive agencies to promulgate regulations, or rules detailing how they interpret and will enforce criminal statutes. For example, §6 of the Toxic Substances Control Act, which prohibits the import or export of polychlorinated biphenyls (PCBs), is interpreted by the Environmental Protection Agency in 40 C.F.R. § 761.20. There one learns what the agency considers as illegal importation or exportation of the substance.

4 By way of example, in *Wilkerson v. Utah*, the Supreme Court held that Utah's method of execution by firing squad was impermissibly cruel and unusual (99 U.S. 130, 1879).

5 This has led some commentators to call for new standards of evaluating legal complaints regarding prison conditions (see Newman, 1992). For example, Park (2001) proposed applying the same standard of duty that landowners owe to invitees to their properties, namely to protect them from known dangers and any that should have been removed or mitigated had reasonable precautions been taken to ensure the safety of the premises.

References

Adarand Constructors v. Peña, 515 U.S. 200 (1995).

Addington v. Texas, 441 U.S. 418 (1979).

Americans with Disabilities Act of 1990, Pub. L. No. 101–336, 104 Stat. 328 (1991).

Atkins v. Virginia, 536 U.S. 304 (2002).

Beck, A. J., Berzofsky, M., Caspar, R., & Krebs, C. (2014). *Sexual victimization in prisons and jails reported by inmates, 2011–2012 Update*. Washington, DC: United States Department of Justice, Bureau of Justice Statistics.

Beck, A. J., & Maruschak, L. M. (2001). *Mental health treatment in state prisons, 2000*. Washington, DC: U.S. Department of Justice, Bureau of Justice Statistics.

Blackburn v. Alabama, 361 U.S. 199 (1960).

Borra, J. E. (2005). Roper v. Simmons. *Journal of Gender, Social Policy & the Law, 13*(3), 707–715.

Bragdon v. Abbott, 524 U.S. 624 (1998).

Buck v. Bell, 274 U.S. 200 (1927).

California v. Beheler, 463 U.S. 1121, 1125 (1983).

Centers for Disease Control and Prevention. (2015a). *HIV-specific criminal laws*. Retrieved from www.cdc.gov/hiv/policies/law/states/exposure.html

Centers for Disease Control and Prevention. (2015b). *HIV among incarcerated populations*. Retrieved from www.cdc.gov/hiv/group/correctional.html

City of Canton v. Harris, 489 U.S. 378 (1989).

City of Cleburne v. Cleburn Living Center, Inc., 473 US 432 (1985).

Clark v. Arizona, 548 U.S. 735 (2005).

Coffin v. Reichard, 143 F.2d 443, 445 6th Cir. (1944).

Coker v. Georgia, 433 U.S. 584 (1977).

Colorado v. Connelly, 479 U.S. 157 (1986).

Connally v. General Construction Co., 269 U.S. 385 (1926).

Cropsey, K. L., Wexler, H. K., Melnick, G., Taxman, F. S., & Young, D. W. (2007). Specialized prisons and services. *The Prison Journal, 87*(1), 58–85. doi:10.1177/0032885506299043
Dusky v. United States, 362 U.S. 402 (1960).
Eadens, D. M., Cranston-Gingras, A., Dupoux, E., & Eadens, D. W. (2016). Police officer perspectives on intellectual disability. *Policing: An International Journal of Police Strategies & Management, 39*(1), 222–235. doi:10.1046/j.1365-2788.2001.00339.x
Elonis v. United States, No. 13–983 (2015).
Estelle v. Gamble, 429 U.S. 97 (1976).
Federal Rule of Evidence, Article VI, Rule 601. Competency to Testify in General. (Pub. L. 93–595, §1).
Farmer v. Brennan, 511 U.S. 825 (1994).
Fikes v. Alabama, 352 U.S. 191 (1957).
Fletcher v. Peck, 10 U.S. 87 (1870).
Ford v. Wainwright, 477 U.S. 399 (1986).
Foucha v. Louisiana, 504 U.S. 71 (1992).
Gallegos v. Colorado, 370 U.S. 49 (1962).
Geis, G. (2000). On the absence of self-control as the basis for a general theory of crime: A critique. *Theoretical Criminology, 4*(1), 35–53. doi:10.1177/1362480600004001002
Goss v. Lopez, 419 U.S. 565 (1975).
Graham v. Connor, 490 U.S. 386 (1989).
Graham v. Florida, 130 S.Ct. 2011, 2021 (2010).
Gregg v. Georgia, 428 U.S. 153, 183 (1976).
Haley v. Ohio, 332 U.S. 596, (1948).
Harris v. District of Columbia, 932 F.2d 10 (1991).
Human Rights Watch. (2001). *No escape: Male rape in U.S. prisons*. Retrieved from www.hrw.org/legacy/reports/2001/prison/report.html#_1_2
In re Gault, 387 U.S. 1 (1987).
In re Kemmler, 136 U.S. 436, 447 (1890).
James, D. J., & Glaze, L. E. (2006). *Mental health problems of prison and jail inmates*. Washington, DC: U.S. Department of Justice, Bureau of Justice Statistics.
J. D. B. v. North Carolina, No. 09–11121 (2011).
Kansas v. Hendricks, 521 U.S. 345 (1997).
Kerbs, J. J., & Jolley, J. M. (2007). Inmate-on-inmate victimization among older male prisoners. *Crime & Delinquency, 53*(2), 187–218. doi:10.1177/0011128706294119
Kim, K., Becker-Cohen, M., & Serakos, M. (2015). *The processing and treatment of mentally ill persons in the criminal justice system: A scan of practice and background analysis*. Washington, DC: Urban Institute.
Krienert, J. L., Henderson, M. L., & Vandiver, D. M. (2003). Inmates with physical disabilities: Establishing a knowledge base. *Southwest Journal of Criminal Justice, 1*(1), 13–23.
Lawrence v. Texas, 539 U.S. 558 (2003).
Locke, J. (2015). *Second treatise of government*. Retrieved from www.earlymoderntexts.com/assets/pdfs/locke1689a.pdf
Loving v. Virginia, 388 U.S. 1 (1967).
Lynumn v. Illinois, 372 U.S. 528, 534 (1963).
Marbury v. Madison, 5 U.S. 137 (1803).
Marceau, J. F. (2008). Un-incorporating the Bill of Rights: The tension between the fourteenth amendment and the federalism concerns that underlie modern criminal procedure reforms. *The Journal of Criminal Law & Criminology, 98*(4), 1231–1303.
Mills v. Rogers, 457 U.S. 291 (1982).
Minnesota Department of Corrections. (2015). *Division Directive 203.250: Offenders with Disabilities*. Retrieved from www.doc.state.mn.us/DocPolicy2/html/DPW_Display_TOC.asp?Opt=203.250.htm
Miranda v. Arizona, 384 U.S. 436 (1966).
Mississippi University for Women v. Hogan, 458 U.S. 718 (1982).
M'Naghten's Case, UKHL J16, 8 ER 718 (1843).
Nebbia v. New York, 291 U.S. 502 (1962).
Newman, A. (1992). Eighth amendment: Cruel and unusual punishment and conditions cases. *Journal of Criminal Law and Criminology, 82*(4), 979–999.
Operation Unite. (2015). *Casey's law*. Retrieved from http://operationunite.org/treatment/caseys-law/
Park, J. J. (2001). Redefining eighth amendment punishments: A new standard for determining the liability of prison officials for failing to protect inmates from serious harm. *Quinnipiac Law Review, 20*, 407–466.

Pennsylvania Department of Corrections v. Yesky, 524 U.S. 206 (1998).
Piecora, C. (2014). Female inmates and sexual assault. *Jurist*. Retrieved from www.jurist.org/dateline/2014/09/christina-piecora-female-inmates.php
Pierce v. United States, 314 U.S. 306, 311 (1896).
Prohibition of Discrimination by Public Accommodations, 42 U.S.C. § 12182 (1991).
Public Health and Welfare, 42 U.S.C. § 12131(2) (1991).
Roberts, J. G., Jr. (2006). What makes the D. C. circuit different? An historical view. *Virginia Law Review, 92*(3), 375–389.
Robinson v. California, 370 U.S. 660 (1962).
Roper v. Simmons, 543 U.S. 551 (2005).
Ruffin v. Commonwealth, 62 Va. 790 (1871).
San Antonio School District v. Rodriguez, 411 U.S. 1 (1973).
Schneckloth v. Bustamonte, 412 U.S. 218 (1973).
Sell v. United States, 539 U.S. 166 (2003).
Silverthorne Lumber Co. v. United States, 251 U.S. 385 (1920).
Spano v. New York, 360 U.S. 315 (1959).
Stansbury v. California, 511 U.S. 318, 323 (1994).
Thompson v. Oklahoma, 487 U.S. 815 (1988).
Trop v. Dulles, 356 U.S. 86 (1958).
United Nations World Health Organization. (n.d.). *Disabilities*. Retrieved from www.who.int/topics/disabilities/en/
United States v. Causey, 834 F.2d 1179 (5th Cir. 1987).
United States Department of Justice. (2013). *Justice Department settles with South Carolina Department of Corrections to end discrimination against inmates with HIV [Press Release]*. Washington, DC: U.S. Department of Justice, Office of Public Affairs.
United States v. Hudson and Goodwin, 11 U.S. 32 (1812).
United States v. Knights, 534 U.S. 112 (2001).
United States v. Virginia, 518 U.S. 515 (1996).
United States v. Windsor, 133 S. Ct. 2675 (2013).
U.S. Const., amend. XIV
Washington Department of Corrections. (2015). *DOC 690.400: Offenders with disabilities*. Retrieved from http://doc.wa.gov/policies/default.aspx
Washington v. Harper, 494 U.S. 210 (1990).
Wilson, J. Q., & Herrnstein, R. J. (1985). *Crime & human nature: The definitive study of the causes of crime*. New York, NY: The Free Press.
Weems v. United States, 217 U.S. 349 (1910).
Wengler v. Druggists Mutual Insurance Co., 446 U.S. 142 (1980).
Wilkerson v. Utah, 99 U.S. 130 (1879).
Wolff v. McDonnell, 418 U.S. 539 (1974).
Wong Sun v. United States, 371 U.S. 471 (1963).
Yarborough v. Alvarado, 541 U.S. 652 (2004).

3

SPECIALTY COURTS

Funneling Offenders with Special Needs Out of the Criminal Justice System

Cassandra A. Atkin-Plunk and Lincoln B. Sloas

Nevada Supreme Court Justice Michael Douglas notes that "specialty courts are most successful when all of the players in the system work together—district attorneys, defense attorneys, judges, treatment providers, and social service providers."

—(Quast, Mullins, & Kobak-McKown, 2016, para. 20)

Introduction

It is well known that the United States has experienced a substantial increase in the correctional population over the past four decades and that approximately two-thirds of offenders are rearrested within three years of release from prison (Durose, Cooper, & Snyder, 2014). The increase in the correctional population, high recidivism rates, and unique needs of those involved in the criminal justice system has led correctional administrators, policy makers, and researchers to devise alternatives to incarceration that help reduce prison crowding, are resource efficient, and provide treatment services to offenders that may not otherwise be available in an incarcerative setting (Petersilia, Lurigio, & Byrne, 1992). Thus, in the past 30 years, substantial and sustained changes have been made to the way in which the American criminal justice system punishes certain groups of offenders, including offenders with substance abuse issues, mental health problems, and those who have served in the military (Berman & Feinblatt, 2001).

Drawing on various punishment philosophies, but with an overarching goal of holding offenders accountable and providing rehabilitation through effective treatment, specialty courts (also known as problem-solving courts)[1] were designed to provide an alternative to incarceration for specific groups of offenders. Problem-solving courts differ from traditional courts in that they do not simply adjudicate and sentence but also seek to change future behavior and increase community safety through addressing the distinct needs of offenders who are involved in such courts (Berman & Feinblatt, 2001). For example, drug courts seek to reduce drug use of substance-abusing offenders, mental health courts seek to provide mental health treatment to the mentally ill who are involved in the criminal justice system, and veterans' courts seek to address issues stemming from being deployed to a combat or warzone (e.g., posttraumatic stress disorder and drug use). While each problem-solving court addresses different important issues, all have a desire to improve results for victims, offenders, and communities (Berman & Feinblatt, 2001).

In 1997, in response to the growing number of drug courts across the United States, the Bureau of Justice Assistance (BJA, 2004), in collaboration with the National Association for Drug Court

Professionals, outlined 10 key components of drug courts. These components address all aspects of the specialty court model, including the integration of treatment services in a justice system setting, the use of a nonadversarial approach to handling cases and protecting participants' due process rights, early identification and enrollment of participants, monitoring progress through treatment, responding to clients' compliance with court mandates, continued interaction between court participants and judges, program evaluation, interdisciplinary education, and the development of partnerships with community-based organizations (BJA, 2004). Although developed with drug courts in mind, these key components have been adapted by other specialty courts, such as mental health courts and domestic violence courts, which seek to apply the same principles and practices as drug courts (Huddleston & Marlowe, 2011).

The following sections examine three unique problem-solving courts: drug courts, mental health courts, and veterans' treatment courts. Each section begins with an examination of the need for individualized treatment for the offenders of the specific court, a brief history of the development of the specific court, and a review of the research surrounding the effectiveness of each court. Following this is a section on other types of problem-solving courts in existence throughout the United States (e.g., homeless, community, domestic violence, and reentry courts).

Drug Treatment Courts

Forming in 1989 in Miami, Florida, drug courts are a type of voluntary diversionary program that seek to address substance-abusing individuals' needs rather than using punishment practices such as incarceration (Lawrence, 1991). This type of approach is beneficial for substance-abusing offenders for two reasons. First, by diverting them away from jail or prison, drug courts can be used to reduce societal labels or stigmas while addressing the specific needs of substance-abusing offenders. Second, which is often a unique aspect of drug courts, is the dropping of charges if program participants successfully complete (or graduate from) the drug court program (Lawrence, 1991).

Need for Drug Treatment Courts

The 2013 National Survey on Drug Use and Health (NSDUH) reports that 24.6 million Americans aged 12 and older were illicit drug users in the past month (e.g., marijuana, cocaine, and heroin), 136.9 million were consumers of alcohol, and 66.9 million used tobacco products. Nearly 21.6 million were classified as being substance dependent or abusers, where the use of illicit substances and alcohol is a problem interfering with routine life and requiring treatment to address the problem behaviors. Only 2.5 million individuals, however, participated in treatment services, which means, even though substance abuse disorders affect 21.6 million Americans, only 10% are engaged in treatment services. An understanding of why individuals do not seek assistance for their substance abuse problem or why they do not fully benefit from treatment is an understudied area (Green-Hennessy, 2002). This problem holds true for those individuals who are a part of the criminal justice system.

Of particular concern is the growing number of justice-involved individuals who experience substance abuse issues. For example, Belenko and Peugh (2005) suggest upwards of 75% of individuals who come into contact with the criminal justice system have substance abuse issues. Moreover, these individuals tend to experience other issues as well, including mental health problems (Belenko, Lang, & O'Connor, 2003; James & Glaze, 2006; National Institute of Mental Health, 2008; Teplin et al., 2006). Recently, alternatives to incarceration, such as drug courts, have been gaining traction to respond to individuals with substance abuse issues.

Development of Drug Treatment Courts

During the 1980s, the United States proclaimed a "War on Drugs" where harsher penalties were enforced on individuals for drug-related offenses (Wolfe et al., 2004). As a result, incarceration rates began to rise, with the hopes that spending time in jail or prison would deter individuals from future drug-related offenses. In light of such efforts, those affected the most by such policies were individuals with substance abuse addictions (Tyuse & Linhorst, 2005). By spending time in jail or prison, these individuals, once released, experienced an increased rate of recidivism. This occurred for two reasons: (1) the lack of available treatment opportunities while incarcerated; and (2) the stigmatization associated with being a felon, which, in turn limited many opportunities, including employment and housing. Thus, policies on incarceration of individuals with substance abuse issues have produced, if anything, a criminogenic rather than a deterrent effect (Bales & Piquero, 2012; Spohn, Piper, Martin, & Frenzel, 2001).

Specialty courts, such as drug courts, operate under a concept referred to as therapeutic jurisprudence (TJ), which was first developed by Winick (1999) and Wexler (1998). The concept of TJ adheres to the notion that, rather than strictly applying punishment to individuals (e.g., incarceration), the etiology of individuals' substance abuse should be identified and treated (Schneider, 2008). This is similar to some of the 10 key components discussed previously. In drug courts, team members including judges, attorneys, case managers, and the drug court participant work together to develop a treatment modality to diminish both substance abuse and the likelihood of recidivism (Wolfer, 2006). Moreover, research suggests that participants enrolled in drug courts tend to perceive being treated with fairness and respect by judges (Atkin-Plunk & Armstrong, in press). The characteristics of drug courts are somewhat different than what is often demonstrated in traditional criminal courts.

On average, 80–120 individuals participate in each drug court across the United States annually (Bhati, Roman & Chalfin, 2008; Marchand, Waller, & Carey, 2006). Treatment itself does not often occur in the drug court but rather in community-based agencies. These can include both outpatient treatment and inpatient treatment depending on the needs of the individual (Granfield, Eby, & Brewster, 1998; Rempel & Destefano, 2001). One aspect of drug court that is relevant to participants is the use of urine drug screening. The requirements for urine drug screening will vary by participant but decrease as participants are compliant with their conditions and progress through the program (Gottfredson & Exum, 2002; Gottfredson, Najaka, & Kearley, 2003). It is important to note that although drug court's primary focus is to reduce substance abuse and recidivism of its participants, it also does much more. For example, drug court team members can request participants to access services for vocational training and adult education (Peters & Murrin, 2000). When first entering the program, participants will have more frequent contact with the judge to discuss their progress in the program (e.g., compliance with treatment, sanctions/rewards, and if the participant is on track to graduate). As a participant moves through the program, these contacts will become less frequent (Carey, Crumpton, Finigan, & Waller, 2005). Besides the judge, drug court participants will also have frequent contact with other team members including the treatment coordinator (Barton, 2008), district attorney (Porter, 2002), public defender, and corrections officials such as probation officers (Carey et al., 2005).

As mentioned previously, drug courts use TJ as a way to meet the needs of participants coming into the program. Furthermore, a combination of rewards and sanctions are used to monitor individuals' progress while in the program. Drug court participants are rewarded for complying with court mandates and are sanctioned for noncompliance. Rewards can range from verbal praises from the judge (Portillo, Rudes, Viglione, & Nelson, 2013) to tokens, such as gift cards and reducing the amount of urine screenings required (Carey & Marchand, 2005). Sanctions can range from having the drug court participant partake in community service to spending a few days in jail (Carey et al.,

2005; Harrell & Roman, 2001). Although drug courts appear to have value as an alternative to incarceration, it is important to discuss their effectiveness.

Do Drug Treatment Courts Work?

Three important outcomes to discern the effectiveness of drug courts are reducing recidivism, program completion (i.e., graduation), and reducing substance abuse. Peters and Murrin (2000) used a case-controlled match research design to assess the effectiveness of two drug treatment court programs for graduates, nongraduates, and traditional probation supervision individuals. Peters and Murrin (2000) found that both graduates and nongraduates had lower rates of rearrest compared to traditional supervision individuals, with graduates experiencing lower rates of substance abuse compared to both.

In a meta-analysis of drug courts, Wilson, Mitchell, and MacKenzie (2006) discovered drug courts reduced future offending for clients going through the program compared to those going through other correctional programs. In particular, they found that courts that used pre-plea or post-plea models were most effective compared to traditional correctional strategies. Mitchell, Wilson, Eggers, and MacKenzie (2012) supported this general finding, particularly among adult and driving while intoxicated (DWI) drug courts, but they also found that courts using either expungement or dismissal of charges greatly reduced drug recidivism. Recently, Rossman et al. (2011) conducted a multisite quasi-experimental design to examine the efficacy of drug courts as compared to control sites. Examining multiple outcome measures, the authors found that drug courts produced a significant impact in reducing both recidivism and substance use for clients. Additional benefits were detected for psychosocial outcomes, including employment and education, as well as long-term impacts including reducing substance use and arrests once the client had been out of drug court.

Other factors that have been shown to impact drug court completion include race (Dannerbeck, Harris, Sundet, & Lloyd, 2006), untreated mental illness (Webster, Rosen, Krietemeyer, Mateyoke-Scrivner, Staton-Tindall, & Leukefeld, 2006), and having a key drug court team member (i.e., the judge) take on a leadership role for participants (Portillo et al., 2013). For example, Vito and Tewksbury (1998) found when drug court was ran by a black male, black male participants tended to do better, in terms of graduation, compared to their white male counterparts. Webster et al. (2006) note that individuals with mental health issues such as depression experience decreased rates of drug court program completion. Lastly, building a rapport with drug court participants during their duration in the program has been shown to lead to higher rates of completion. For instance, Goldkamp, White, and Robinson (2001) discuss how one drug court produced a 70% completion rate when one judge was on the bench for nearly a decade. Most of the studies discussed to this point comprise an array of quasi-experimental designs which are not considered as rigorous as experimental research, which also lends its support to the effectiveness of drug courts.

Randomized controlled trials (RCTs) are considered to be the gold standard of research designs (Weisburd, Lum, & Petrosino, 2001). With this being said, the research related to drug courts using RCTs is quite promising. Gottfredson and Exum (2002) randomly assigned 235 individuals to either a drug court or nondrug court treatment setting. After a one-year follow-up, Gottfredson and Exum (2002) found almost half of the drug court participants (50%) were arrested for new crimes in comparison to two-thirds of nondrug court participants (66%) who were arrested for new crimes. Finally, for cases that were actually heard in court, 32% of drug court participants were rearrested versus 57% of nondrug court participants.

Deschenes, Turner and Greenwood (1995) conducted an RCT of the Maricopa County, Arizona, drug court program on a sample of probationers convicted of drug possession (n = 630). Probationers were randomly assigned to either a drug court or supervision as usual for a one-year time period.

Although significant differences were not detected between the two groups in terms of new arrests, drug court participants had fewer technical violations and drug charges. Finally, drug court participants completed the program at a rate of 40%. Along with drug courts, there is a significant amount of literature that examines mental health courts—another type of specialty court.

Mental Health Treatment Courts

The first mental health treatment court opened its doors in Broward County, Florida, in 1997 (Rossman et al., 2012). Today there are over 300 mental health treatment courts that operate annually in the United States (Honegger, 2015). The primary goal of mental health treatment courts is to reduce the likelihood of recidivism for individuals with mental health-related issues (Sarteschi, 2013).

Need for Mental Health Treatment Courts

According to a 2006 report from the Bureau of Justice Statistics, roughly 1.26 million individuals incarcerated in the Unites States suffer from mental illness (Glaze & James, 2006). This constitutes about 45% of federal inmates, 56% of state inmates, and 64% of jail inmates. Another 861,000 individuals on probation suffer from some form of mental illness (Sarteschi, 2013). From a policy standpoint, many argue individuals suffering from mental illnesses should be treated by the mental health system rather than confined in prison and jails (Boccaccini, Christy, Poythress, & Kershaw, 2005). As Casey and Rottman (2005) suggest, individuals with mental illness may experience higher rates of recidivism by not having their mental health needs met. The types of mental illness these individuals experience differs from person to person.

Steadman and Veysey (1997) have noted that individuals involved in the criminal justice system have mental health illnesses that include anxiety, antisocial personality disorder, posttraumatic stress disorder (PTSD), and severe depression. Men are more likely to experience antisocial personality compared to women, while being black or Hispanic correlates to an increased likelihood of having schizophrenia compared to whites (National Mental Health Association, 2003). For most of these individuals, treatment services while incarcerated are often insufficient. According to Glaze and James (2006), one-third of individuals in state facilities, a quarter in federal facilities, and roughly 18% in jails receive some type of treatment for their mental health issues. These numbers are quite alarming compared to the percentages of individuals experiencing mental illness. The use of mental health courts has become a means to respond, perhaps more appropriately, to individuals who suffer from mental illness (Honegger, 2015).

Development of Mental Health Treatment Courts

Similar to the key components of drug courts, mental health courts operate under the concept of therapeutic jurisprudence (Winick, 1999; Wexler, 1998). Like drug courts, mental health courts are voluntary in nature, and individuals who are motivated to get help often seek them as an option (Silberberg, Vital, & Brakel, 2001). Mental health courts adhere to a team-based approach which includes a judge, attorneys, and treatment providers. Using treatment providers is a crucial part of mental health court, since responding to the individuals' needs is at the forefront (Casey & Rottman, 2005). In many mental health court jurisdictions, individuals who volunteer for court have to meet other eligibility criteria. For example, most courts will require an individual to have an Axis I diagnosis, which can include major depression, schizophrenia, or panic attacks (Steadman et al., 2005). Besides mental health criteria, mental health courts may also specify types of offenses as eligibility criteria. Boothroyd, Mercado, Poythress, Christy, and Petrila (2005) note the mental health court in Broward County, Florida, will only accept nonviolent individuals. These can include misdemeanors and traffic infractions; however, individuals with criminal charges such as driving under the influence or domestic violence are often excluded. However, some research indicates that some individuals charged with violent crimes will be able to go through felony mental health courts (Walker, Cummings, & Cummings, 2012). Like drug courts, mental health courts see clients more frequently in the beginning and then decrease the need for appearances once individuals move further in the process (Walker, Pann, Shapiro, & Van Hasselt, 2015). Sanctions also are used as a way to reprimand individuals who are not compliant with their obligations. These may include anything from additional hearings to jail time (Redlich, Steadman, Monahan, Petrila, & Griffin, 2006).

Do Mental Health Courts Work?

In a recent systematic review, Honegger (2015) found four outcomes typically examined by researchers of mental health courts, including psychiatric symptoms, connection to behavioral health services, quality of life, and recidivism. As it pertains to psychiatric symptoms, Cosden, Ellens, Schnell, and Yamini-Diouf, (2005), using a global assessment of functioning (GAF), found mental health court participants and non-mental health court participants had similar scores over the assessment period. This led Cosden et al. (2005) also to assess participants using the Behavior and Symptom Identification Scale-32 (BASIS-32) which led to improved psychiatric symptoms scores and quality of life for mental health court participants over non-mental health court participants.

Boothroyd et al. (2003), in a study of connecting individuals to behavioral health services, found that mental health court participants experience nearly a 20% increase in receiving behavioral health services compared to non-mental health court participants. Additionally, the mental health court participants had more access to mental health services compared to non-mental health court participants. This demonstrates the ability of mental health courts to address the needs of participants rather than merely responding with punitive sanctions.

Several studies have been linked to mental health courts demonstrating their ability to reduce recidivism among participants (Frailing, 2010; Henrinckx, Swart, Ama, Dolezal, & King, 2005). For example, Henrinckx et al. (2005) assessed recidivism reduction for a sample of 386 pre-post misdemeanants in mental health court. Benefits for those in the mental health court included everything from increased case management to half of the mental health court participants experiencing a decrease in recidivism. Further, nearly 66% of participants did not experience any new probation violations (Henrinckx et al., 2005). Similarly, Frailing (2010) compared a sample of mental health court participants with a sample of individuals receiving standard treatment practices. Mental health court participants experienced reductions in both incarceration and substance abuse relapse. Therefore, the research on mental health courts results in positive outcomes for participants. We now turn our attention to veterans' treatment courts.

Veterans' Treatment Courts

Veterans' treatment courts are one of the newest problem-solving courts to be established and widely implemented across the United States. As a result of the wars in Afghanistan and Iraq (hereafter post-9/11 wars), drug and mental health court judges began to see an increasing number of veterans coming through their courts with substance abuse and mental health issues (Johnson et al., 2016). Although veterans have high rates of mental illness and alcohol and drug addiction (U.S. Department of Veterans Affairs, 2012; Hawkins, 2010), it is their shared prior military experience and the complex issues encountered by veterans that resulted in the development of veterans' treatment courts throughout the United States (see Chapter 12 for more about veterans).

Need for Veteran Specific Treatment

According to the U.S. Department of Veterans Affairs (2016b), there are over 19.4 million veterans living in the United States, not including active duty military personnel. Of these veterans, approximately 2.6 million are post-9/11 veterans (U.S. Department of Veterans Affairs, 2016a), with an estimated 1.5 million service members who served in or around active combat zones during the post-9/11 wars (Hawkins, 2010). While military experience undeniably has positive benefits (Elder, 1998), a large number of veterans report difficulty readjusting to civilian life and believe that the public cannot relate to the postdeployment struggles encountered by veterans (Pew Research Center, 2011). Readjusting to civilian life is even more difficult for servicemen and -women who experienced a traumatic event while enlisted, served in combat, or were injured or knew someone who was injured or killed (Morin, 2011). As such, there is no doubt that serving in the military and being deployed to active combat zones is difficult and affects the future life experiences of veterans (Bouffard, 2005; Culp, Youstin, Englander, & Lynch, 2013). Upon enlistment, armed service members are quickly institutionalized into the military culture. The norms and viewpoints ingrained in servicemen and women while enlisted (e.g., authoritarian rule, warrior ethos, and structured environment) are difficult, if not impossible, to abandon upon return to civilian life (Ahlin & Douds, 2016; Hollingshead, 1946).

A growing body of empirical research documents the long-lasting effects of military service on veterans (Adams, Corrigan, & Larson, 2012; Institute of Medicine, 2013; Spiro & Settersten, 2012). Of primary concern are the high rates of mental illness, posttraumatic stress disorder (PTSD), traumatic brain injury (TBI), drug addiction, and homelessness experienced by veterans. A study of Operation Enduring Freedom (OEF) and Operation Iraqi Freedom (OIF) veterans found that almost two in five were diagnosed with a mental health disorder, including PTSD and depression (Seal et al., 2009). Moreover, studies have found that upwards of 35% of soldiers and Marines returning from combat in Iraq or Afghanistan met the criteria for alcohol misuse (Hoge et al., 2004). Additionally, veterans are overrepresented in the homeless population, making up 11% of the adult homeless population (U.S. Department of Housing and Urban Development, 2015) while only accounting for 8% of the total adult population (U.S. Department of Veterans Affairs, 2016b). These concerns are not unique to post-9/11 veterans, as veterans from prior war eras (e.g., World War II and the Korean and Vietnam wars) faced similar postdeployment issues. However, the public, medical, and academic communities are paying closer attention to veterans' postdeployment needs (Sayer, Carlson, & Frazier, 2014).

According to the most recent comprehensive statistics, in 2011–2012, an estimated 181,500 veterans were incarcerated in jails and state and federal prison facilities across the United States (Bronson, Carson, Noonan, & Berzofsky, 2015). Veterans incarcerated in prison are significantly more likely compared to nonveteran prisoners to have mental health disorders (48% versus 36%, respectively) and have been diagnosed with PTSD (23% versus 11%, respectively), with similar trends occurring for those incarcerated in local jails. Veterans also are more likely to be serving time for a violent offense (64%) compared to nonveterans (48%) (Bronson et al., 2015). Although many nonveteran justice-involved individuals suffer from mental illness, drug addiction, and homelessness, as the previous statistics indicate, it is the shared experiences among military veterans that create an environment conducive for veterans' treatment courts, and it is the chief motivator for seeking treatment (Ahlin & Douds, 2016).

Development of Veterans' Treatment Courts

As the correctional population steadily increased between 1980 and 2010 (Glaze, 2011), the number of veterans incarcerated in state and federal prisons also increased, albeit at a slower rate than nonveterans (Bronson et al., 2015). Unlike previous wars, the public has paid more attention to the issues and challenges encountered by post-9/11 veterans upon return from deployment to civilian life (Sayer et al., 2014). The first veterans' treatment court was implemented in Anchorage, Alaska, in 2004 (Hawkins, 2010), but its existence was not widely known until Judge Robert Russell implemented a similar court in Buffalo, New York, in 2008 (Johnson et al., 2016).

The development of veterans' treatment courts stemmed from the large number of veterans involved in the criminal justice system, particularly those who were involved in drug and mental health courts (Russell, 2009a). The number of veterans' treatment courts operating throughout the United States has grown tremendously in recent years, from just 24 operating in 2010 to over 300 operating in 2014 (Johnson et al., 2016). Based on the drug and mental health court models, veterans' treatment courts provide an alternative to incarceration for veterans of foreign wars who become involved in the criminal justice system, typically because of drug use and/or mental health issues (Lucas & Hanrahan, 2016; Russell, 2009a). Veterans' treatment courts draw on various punishment philosophies but have overarching goals of holding offenders accountable and providing rehabilitation through effective treatment (Russell, 2009a). Veterans' treatment courts typically target offenders convicted of felony and misdemeanor nonviolent crimes but for which the underlying cause of their criminal behavior is drug use or mental health problems (Russell, 2009a). Some newer veterans' treatment courts, however, allow individuals convicted of violent offenses to participate in the court (Holbrook & Anderson, 2011; Johnson et al., 2016). Ultimately, individual veterans' treatment courts determine which offenses are eligible to be heard, with some courts excluding charges with mandatory sentences, child sexual assault felonies, and/or drug manufacturing charges (Holbrook & Anderson, 2011).

Similar to other problem-solving courts, veterans' treatment courts typically adopt key components to guide the operation of the court. These elements represent a combination of the key components of drug courts and mental health courts, such as the use of a nonadversarial approach to handling cases that includes the involvement of the judge, prosecutor, defense attorney, supervision officer, veterans' administration, and community-based organizations, all of which come together to provide intensive treatment and rehabilitation, typically in lieu of incarceration. Veterans' treatment courts are also characterized by ongoing judicial interaction between the veteran and the judge, who at times is a veteran as well (Russell, 2009a). Additionally, veterans' treatment courts are designed to be less punitive and more healing and restorative than traditional courts while still holding offenders accountable for their actions (Baldwin & Rukus, 2015).

While veterans' treatment courts on the surface may resemble drug and mental health courts, they are unique. Veterans' treatment courts take into account the distinctive characteristics and camaraderie of military personnel and veterans. According to Judge Russell (2009a), "veterans court allows for veterans to go through the treatment court process with people who are similarly situated and have common past experiences and needs" (p. 364). Mentoring is another integral component of veterans' treatment courts, where non-justice-involved veterans provide social support to court participants and assist the participants in setting goals and problem solving (Holbrook & Anderson, 2011; Johnson et al., 2016; Russell, 2009a, 2009b). In a national survey of over 300 veterans' treatment courts, Johnson and colleagues (2016) report that 65% of courts offered mentoring by veteran volunteers to court participants.

Do Veterans' Treatment Courts Work?

While the use of veterans' treatment courts has expanded in recent years, research on the effectiveness of these courts is underexplored. The few studies that have been conducted are either anecdotal in nature (Russell, 2009a, 2009b) or limited in scope (Holbrook & Anderson, 2011; Johnson, Stolar, Wu, Coonan, & Graham, 2015; Knudsen & Wingenfeld, 2016; Slattery, Dugger, Lamb, & Williams,

2013). Judge Robert Russell (2009a) provides anecdotal evidence of the success of the Buffalo Veterans Treatment Court in New York. Specifically, in a one-year follow-up of the court's inception, no participants or graduates recidivated. Additionally, in a descriptive study of 11 veterans' courts across the country, Holbrook and Anderson (2011) examined the success of 59 graduates from these courts. Of the 59 court graduates, only one reoffended following graduation (Holbrook & Anderson, 2011). Another study examined factors predictive of arrests for a group of 100 participants of a veterans' treatment court in Harris County, Texas (Johnson et al., 2015). Although Johnson and colleagues (2015) did not report the number of participants who recidivated, results suggest that court participants who spent fewer days in the court program, had a prior opioid misuse diagnosis, and were unsuccessfully discharged were more likely to be rearrested.

Beyond a focus on reduction in recidivism, studies have examined other positive benefits resulting from participation in a veterans' treatment court. According to Russell (2009a), participants and graduates of the Buffalo Veterans' Treatment Court experienced positive life changes, including reuniting with family and friends, having stable employment and a place to live, remaining drug free, and successfully managing their mental health issues. Participants also experienced a positive change in their attitude, including "a renewed sense of hope, pride, accomplishment, motivation, and confidence in their ability to continue to face challenges and better their lives" (Russell, 2009a, p. 370). Slattery and colleagues (2013), in an exploratory study of veterans' court participants in Colorado Springs, Colorado, found that veterans enrolled in the court experienced improvements in mental health and lower substance use over time, including improvements in PTSD and depression symptoms and severity and a reduction in the use of alcohol and all illegal substances. Knudsen and Wingenfeld (2016) report similar findings with respect to positive outcomes (e.g., reduction in PTSD, depression, and substance abuse) and improvements in quality of life (e.g., family relations, emotional well-being, sleep, energy, social connectedness, and social functioning) for veterans' treatment court participants from a large urban area. Even though previous examinations of the effectiveness of veterans' courts are limited in scope and methodology, which reduces the generalizability of findings, the limited evidence seems to favor the continued use of veterans' courts and provides a foundation for future evaluative research.

Other Specialty Courts

In addition to drug, mental health, and veterans' courts, local jurisdictions across the United States have developed other problem-solving courts to address specific subsets of the population that come in contact with the criminal justice system. As seen in Table 3.1, an estimated 4,000 distinct

Table 3.1 Problem-solving Courts throughout the United States

Type of Specialized Court	*Location and Year First Developed*	*Estimated Number in Operation*
Drug	Miami Dade, FL (1989)	1,540[a]
Homeless	San Diego, CA (1999)	25[b]
Community	Manhattan, NY (1993)	25[b]
Gun	Providence, RI (1994)	6[b]
DWI	Dona Ana County, NM (1995)	262[a]
Domestic violence	Brooklyn, NY (1996)	206[b]
Mental health	Broward County, FL (1997)	350[c]
Reentry	Harlem, NY (2001)	26[a]
Gambling	Amherst, NY (2001)	1[b]
Veterans' treatment	Anchorage, AK (2004)	272[a]

(*Continued*)

Table 3.1 (Continued)

Type of Specialized Court	*Location and Year First Developed*	*Estimated Number in Operation*
Sex offender	Oswego County, NY (2005)	9[d]
Prostitution	New York, NY (2013)	8[b]
Other specialized courts[e]	–	over 1,500[ab]
Total		over 4,000

a Data retrieved from the National Institute of Justice (2016). Numbers current as of December 2014.
b Data retrieved from Huddleston and Marlowe (2011). Numbers current as of December 2009.
c Data retrieved from Honegger (2015). Numbers current as of October 2015.
d Data retrieved from NYcourts.gov (2016) and Parkinson (2016). Numbers current as of January 2016.
e Other specialized courts include family treatment, juvenile, truancy, and tribal courts.

problem-solving courts exist throughout the United States. These specialized courts include, but are not limited to, homeless courts, domestic violence courts, reentry courts, prostitution courts, DWI courts, gambling courts, gun courts, tribal courts, and truancy courts.

Unlike drug and mental health courts, limited research has been conducted on the effectiveness of these other problem-solving courts. The research that does exist demonstrates that newer problem-solving courts tend to be based on the drug court model, with many centering their principles and practices around the 10 key components of drug courts (Huddleston & Marlowe, 2011). Table 3.1 provides a list of the variety of problem-solving courts in operation throughout the United States, the location and year of first development, and the approximate number in operation. It is important to keep in mind when examining Table 3.1 that there is no online repository for problem-solving courts. Thus, the number of problem-solving courts in operation throughout the United States is a rough approximation and is only as current as the most current organizational and research data available. Following is a brief description of the purpose and development of other problem-solving courts currently in operation throughout the United States.

Homeless Courts

The first homeless court was implemented in 1989 in San Diego County, California, to address the needs of the local homeless veteran population. Since then, other homeless courts have taken hold in cities across the United States and have expanded to serve other homeless populations, including nonveterans and battered and homeless women (Binder, 2002). Homeless courts address the needs of homeless defendants who have been charged with minor misdemeanor offenses and/or who have outstanding warrants, typically related to quality of life citations, public disturbance citations, and other issues related to homelessness (Binder, 2002; see Chapter 11 for more on homeless offenders). One feature that distinguishes many homeless courts from other problem-solving courts is that they will resolve outstanding warrants, with some also processing new offenses (Kerry & Pennell, 2001).

Homeless courts not only seek to resolve past citations and outstanding warrants of homeless individuals, they also seek to end the homelessness cycle. Many factors contribute to the homelessness cycle, including the fact that homeless individuals tend to have frequent contact with the police, receive multiple citations during those contacts, and fear attending court because of their inability to pay their citation fines (Binder, 2002). Homeless courts address these issues by providing access to housing and other social services, such as mental health and substance abuse treatment, life skills and literacy classes, and vocational training, in lieu of fines and incarceration (Huddleston & Marlowe, 2011). To date, only one descriptive study of a homeless court exists. This study, of the San Diego Homeless Court, reports high levels of resolved cases, improved access to the courts, and reduced fear of law enforcement among court participants (Kerry & Pennell, 2001).

Community Courts

Unlike other problem-solving courts that address the specialized needs of specific offenders, community courts seek to address quality of life crimes, such as vandalism, petty theft, public intoxication, abandoned property, and low-level drug possession, which tend to be committed in localized areas within a community (Berman & Feinblatt, 2001; Huddleston, & Marlowe, 2011). One defining feature of community courts is their location. Typically, community courts focus on one neighborhood and are centrally located in relation to that neighborhood, as opposed to being located in large downtown courthouses (Lang, 2011; Lee et al., 2013). The first community court was implemented in 1993 in Manhattan, New York, as a way to address low-level crimes committed in and around Times Square. As of 2009, approximately 25 community courts operate throughout the United States (Huddleston & Marlowe, 2011).

Community courts emerged as an extension of the "broken windows theory" of crime and community policing initiatives that took hold in the late 1980s (Lee et al., 2013; see Wilson & Kelling, 1982 for a detailed discussion of broken windows theory). The concept of community courts stems from the belief that neighborhoods face their own unique minor crime problems, and if these minor problems can be addressed, quality of life within these communities can be enhanced. Community courts seek not only to hold offenders accountable for their actions but to transform the neighborhoods in which they are located (Lee et al., 2013). Offenders who partake in community courts can be required to participate in restorative justice programs, community service, and/or individualized social services, such as drug and mental health treatment. Moreover, community courts emphasize partnerships with various stakeholders throughout the community, including residents, store owners, schools, religious institutions, and other community groups. Overall, these courts bring individuals from the community together to determine the best approach for creating long-lasting solutions in their community (Lang, 2011).

Domestic Violence Courts

Domestic violence courts are comprised of a specialized caseload of offenders who either have pled guilty to domestic violence charges or have charges pending against them for crimes such as intimate partner violence, elder abuse, child abuse, or violence between other relatives (Labriola, Bradley, O'Sullivan, Rempel, & Moore, 2009). The first felony domestic violence court opened in 1996 in Brooklyn, New York (Newmark, Rempel, Diffily, & Kane, 2001), and as of 2009, 338 domestic violence courts had been identified throughout the United States (Labriola et al., 2009). Domestic violence courts emerged in the United States as a response to the considerable increase in domestic violence cases that were coming before the courts. This rise in domestic violence cases was due in part to several factors, including the feminist movement, which argued for the recognition of domestic violence as a crime instead of just a family matter; the 1994 Violence Against Women Act, which established pro-arrest laws for perpetrators of domestic violence; and stricter law enforcement and prosecution of those who engage in domestic violence (Labriola et al., 2009).

Similar to other problem-solving courts, domestic violence courts utilize a therapeutic, nonadversarial approach to managing cases, present a coordinated effort between judges, staff, and treatment personnel to provide access to effective treatment, and hold offenders accountable for their actions through frequent interactions between participants and judges (Ostrom, 2003). Additionally, domestic violence courts have been created throughout the United States with many goals in mind, including providing services and safety for victims, holding offenders accountable, providing treatment for offenders, and reducing recidivism. Domestic violence courts seek to coordinate their responses with all parties involved (e.g., judges, probation officers, prosecutors, victim services organizations, treatment providers, and victims) and, through the training of domestic violence court personnel, seek to make informed decisions regarding the necessary actions in managing the dynamics of domestic violence (Labriola et al., 2009).

Despite the fact that domestic violence courts have been in existence for 20 years, relatively few studies examine the effectiveness of domestic violence courts (Labriola et al., 2009). However, a common theme that emerges in the examination of domestic violence courts is the requirement of domestic violence court participants to participate in a batterer intervention program (BIP). While limited research focuses on the impact of completing a BIP as part of participation in a domestic violence court, Petrucci (2010) is cautiously optimistic regarding the impact of such treatment. Nevertheless, the current literature is mixed regarding whether domestic violence courts are effective at reducing future domestic violence. Some studies found a reduction in recidivism, specifically arrests for domestic violence, among court participants (Gover, MacDonald, & Alpert, 2003; Harrell, Schaffer, DeStefano, & Castro, 2006; Petrucci, 2010); while others found no reduction in recidivism (Harrell, Newmark, Visher, & Castro, 2007; Newmark et al., 2001) and an increase in probation revocation rates (Harrell et al., 2006).

Reentry Courts

Reentry courts are designed to assist with the reintegration of ex-offenders as they return to the community from a term of incarceration in local, state, or federal institutions. Reentry courts assist returning citizens with finding employment, securing housing, reconnecting with family, and remaining drug and crime free (Huddleston & Marlowe, 2011), while holding them accountable for their actions in the community through formalized hearings and judicial involvement. Reentry case management services typically begin before an offender is released from jail or prison and will continue until the offender successfully graduates from the reentry court program. The reentry court model requires the use of a collaborative approach between the prison system, judicial system, community corrections, and other community-based partners.

The first reentry court was established in 2001 in Harlem, New York. Since then, over two dozen reentry courts have appeared in jurisdictions across the United States. These reentry courts can take various forms, such as reentry drug courts, which focus solely on drug-addicted returning offenders and utilize the drug court model. Reentry courts also exist at the federal level and serve offenders released from the U.S. Bureau of Prisons (i.e., federal prison system) into the custody of the U.S. Probation Office with oversight by the U.S. District Courts and U.S. Attorney's Office (Huddleston & Marlowe, 2011). Regardless of the type of reentry court, all have the overarching goal of reducing recidivism of parolees.

Conclusion

Each of the specialty courts discussed in this chapter share a similar goal in providing a more therapeutic, rather than a punitive, approach to handling individuals' cases; however, they each have their own unique aspects as well. For example, drug courts seek to reduce individuals' substance abuse and mental health courts seek to alleviate individuals' mental health issues, whereas veterans' courts seek to address the same issues while considering individuals' time in service. What is important for each of these specialty courts is the focus on addressing the unique set of needs individuals present with. The research on specialty courts indicates they are promising (e.g., drug courts, mental health courts, and veterans' courts); however, more research should be conducted on other specialty courts (e.g., homeless courts, community courts and reentry courts) to determine their effectiveness. In light of the favorable research regarding specialty courts and the focus of lawmakers to reduce spending and alleviate the growing correctional population, it appears as if the use of specialty courts as a way to address the needs of specific subsets of offenders will continue to grow in use within the American criminal justice system.

For drug courts and mental health courts, the body of experimental research allows us to draw more generalizable conclusions in terms of the efficacy of such courts. For others, such as veterans' courts and the other courts discussed, more research is needed. It is the task of researchers to provide more in-depth analyses of these courts to move beyond mere descriptions and to be able to draw more robust conclusions about their effectiveness. The value added can be beneficial for policy makers, by implementing practices that are shown to be beneficial, while at the same time assisting individuals who are struggling with certain aspects of their life to become productive in society.

Note

1 Throughout this chapter, we use the terms specialty court and problem-solving court interchangeably.

References

Adams, R. S., Corrigan, J. D., & Larson, M. J. (2012). Alcohol use after combat-acquired traumatic brain injury: What we know and do not know. *Journal of Social Work Practice in Addictions, 12*(1), 28–51. doi:10–1080/1533256X.2012647580

Ahlin, E. M., & Douds, A. S. (2016). Military socialization: A motivating factor for seeking treatment in a veterans' treatment court. *American Journal of Criminal Justice, 41*(1), 83–96. doi:10.1007/s12103-015-9332-4

Atkin-Plunk, C. A., & Armstrong, G. S. (in press). An examination of the impact of drug court clients' perceptions of procedural justice on graduation rates and recidivism. *Journal of Offender Rehabilitation*. doi:10.1080/10509674.2016.1229712

Baldwin, J. M., & Rukus, J. (2015). Healing the wounds: An examination of veterans' treatment courts in the context of restorative justice. *Criminal Justice Policy Review, 26*(2), 183–207. doi:10.1177/0887403413520002

Bales, W. D., & Piquero, A. R. (2012). Assessing the impact of imprisonment on recidivism. *Journal of Experimental Criminology, 8*(1), 71–101. doi:10.1007/s11292-011-9139-3

Barton, G. (2008). *Wicomico County adult drug treatment court (circuit court) process evaluation*. Portland, OR: NPC Research.

Belenko, S., Lang, M., & O'Connor, L. (2003). Self-reported psychiatric treatment needs among felony drug offenders. *Journal of Contemporary Criminal Justice, 19*(1), 9–29. doi:10.1177/1043986202239740

Belenko, S., & Peugh, J. (2005). Estimating drug treatment needs among state prison inmates. *Drug and Alcohol Dependence*, 77(3), 269–281. doi:10.1016/j.drugalcdep.2004.08.023

Berman, G., & Feinblatt, J. (2001). Problem-solving courts: A brief primer. *Law & Policy, 23*(2), 125–140. doi:10.1111/1467-9930.00107

Bhati, A. S., Roman, J. K., & Chalfin, A. (2008). *To treat or not to treat: Evidence on the prospects of expanding treatment to drug-involved offenders*. Washington, DC: Urban Institute Justice Policy Center.

Binder, S. R. (2002). *The homeless court program: Taking the court to the street*. Washington, DC: American Bar Association.

Boccaccini, M. T., Christy, A., Poythress, N., & Kershaw, D. (2005). Rediversion in two postbooking jail diversion programs in Florida. *Psychiatric Services, 56*(7), 835–839. doi:10.1176/appi.ps.56.7.835

Boothroyd, R. A., Poythress, N. G., McGaha, A., & Petrila, J. (2003). The Broward mental health court: Process, outcomes, and service utilization. *International Journal of Law and Psychiatry, 26*(1), 55–71. doi:10.1016/S0160-2527(02)00203-0

Boothroyd, R. A., Mercado, C. C., Poythress, N. G., Christy, A., & Petrila, J. (2005). Clinical outcomes of defendants in mental health court. *Psychiatric Services, 56*(7), 829–834. doi:10.1176/appi.ps.56.7.829

Bouffard, L. A. (2005). The military as a bridging environment in criminal careers: Differential outcomes of the military experience. *Armed Forces & Society, 31*(2), 273–295. doi:10.1177/0095327X0503100206

Bronson, J., Carson, E. A., Noonan, M., & Berzofsky, M. (2015). *Veterans in prison and jail, 2011–2012*. Washington, DC: U.S. Department of Justice, Bureau of Justice Statistics.

Bureau of Justice Assistance. (2004). *Defining drug courts: The key components*. Washington, DC: U.S. Department of Justice, Bureau of Justice Assistance.

Carey, S. M., Crumpton, D., Finigan, M. M. W., & Waller, M. (2005). *California drug courts: A methodology for determining costs and benefits*. Portland, OR: NPC Research.

Carey, S., & Marchand, G. (2005). *Marion County adult drug court outcome evaluation final Report*. Portland, OR: NPC Research.

Casey, P. M., & Rottman, D. B. (2005). Problem-solving courts: Models and trends. *Justice System Journal, 26*(1), 35–56. doi:10.1080/0098261X.2005.10767737

Cosden, M., Ellens, J., Schnell, J., & Yamini-Diouf, Y. (2005). Efficacy of a mental health treatment court with assertive community treatment. *Behavioral Sciences & The Law, 23*(2), 199–214. doi:10.1002/bsl.638

Culp, R., Youstin, T. J., Englander, K., & Lynch, J. (2013). From war to prison: Examining the relationship between military service and criminal activity. *Justice Quarterly, 30*(4), 651–680. doi:10.1080/07418825.2011.615755

Dannerbeck, A., Harris, G., Sundet, P., & Lloyd, K. (2006). Understanding and responding to racial differences in drug court outcomes. *Journal of Ethnicity in Substance Abuse, 5*(2), 1–22. doi:10.1300/J233v05n02_01

Deschenes, E. P., Turner, S., & Greenwood, P. W. (1995). Drug court or probation? An experimental evaluation of Maricopa County's Drug Court. *Justice System Journal, 18*(1), 55–73. doi:10.1080/23277556.1995.10871222

Durose, M. R., Cooper, A. D., & Snyder, H. N. (2014). *Recidivism of prisoners released in 30 states in 2005: Patterns from 2005 to 2010*. Washington, DC: U.S. Department of Justice, Bureau of Justice Statistics.

Elder, G. H. (1998). The life course as developmental theory. *Child Development, 69*(1), 1–12. doi:10.1111/j.1467-8624.1998.tb06128.x

Frailing, K. (2010). How mental health courts function: Outcomes and observations. *International Journal of Law and Psychiatry, 33*(4), 207–213. doi:10.1016/j.ijlp.2010.06.001

Glaze, L. E., & James, D. J. (2006). *Mental health problems of prison and jail inmates*. Washington, DC: U.S. Department of Justice, Bureau of Justice Statistics.

Glaze, L. E. (2011). *Correctional populations in the United States, 2010*. Washington, DC: U.S. Department of Justice, Bureau of Justice Statistics.

Goldkamp, J. S., White, M. D., & Robinson, J. B. (2001). Do drug courts work? Getting inside the drug court black box. *Journal of Drug Issues, 31*(1), 27–72. doi:10.1177/002204260103100104

Gottfredson, D. C., & Exum, M. L. (2002). The Baltimore City drug treatment court: One-year results from a randomized study. *Journal of Research in Crime and Delinquency, 39*(3), 337–356. doi:10.1177/002242780203900304

Gottfredson, D. C., Najaka, S. S., & Kearley, B. (2003). Effectiveness of drug treatment courts: Evidence from a randomized trial. *Criminology & Public Policy, 2*(2), 171–196. doi:10.1111/j.1745-9133.2003.tb00117.x

Gover, A. R., MacDonald, J. M., & Alpert, G. P. (2003). Combating domestic violence: Findings from an evaluation of a local domestic violence court. *Criminology and Public Policy, 3*(1), 109–132. doi:10.1111/j.1745-9133.2003.tb00028.x

Granfield, R., Eby, C., & Brewster, T. (1998). An examination of the Denver Drug Court: The impact of a treatment-oriented drug-offender system. *Law & Policy, 20*(2), 183–202. doi:10.1111/1467-9930.00047

Green-Hennessy, S. (2002). Factors associated with receipt of behavioral health services among persons with substance dependence. *Psychiatric Services, 53*(12), 1592–1598. doi:10.1176/appi.ps.53.12.1592

Harrell, A., Newmark, L., Visher, C., & Castro, J. (2007). *Final report on the evaluation of the Judicial Oversight Demonstration (Volume 1): The impact of the JOD in Dorchester and Washtnaw County*. Washington, DC: Urban Institute.

Harrell, A., & Roman, J. (2001). Reducing drug use and crime among offenders: The impact of graduated sanctions. *Journal of Drug Issues, 31*(1), 207–231. doi:10.1177/002204260103100111

Harrell, A., Schaffer, M., DeStefano, C., & Castro, J. (2006). *The evaluation of Milwaukee's Judicial Oversight Demonstration*. Washington, DC: Urban Institute Justice Policy Center.

Hawkins, M. D. (2010). Coming home: Accommodating the special needs of military veterans to the criminal justice system. *Ohio State Journal of Criminal Law*, 7(563), 563–573.

Henrinckx, H. A., Swart, S. C., Ama, S. M., Dolezal, C. D., & King, S. (2005). Rearrest and linkage to mental health services among clients of the Clark County Mental Health Court Program. *Psychiatric Services, 56*(7), 853–857. doi:10.1176/appi.ps.56.7.853

Hoge, C. W., Castro, C. A., Messer, S. C., McGurk, D., Cotting, D. I., & Koffman, R. L. (2004). Combat duty in Iraq and Afghanistan, mental health problems, and barriers to care. *New England Journal of Medicine, 351*(1), 13–22. doi:10.1056/NEJMoa040603

Holbrook, J. G., & Anderson, S. (2011). Veterans courts: Early outcomes and key indicators for success. *Widener Law School Legal Studies Research Paper No. 11–25*. Retrieved from http://papers.ssrn.com/sol3/papers.cfm?abstract_id=1912655

Hollingshead, A. R. (1946). Adjustment to military life. *The American Journal of Sociology, 51*(5), 439–447. doi:10.1086/219855

Honegger, L. N. (2015). Does the evidence support the case for mental health courts? A review of the literature. *Law and Human Behavior, 39*(5), 478–488. doi:10.1037/lhb0000141

Huddleston, C. W., & Marlowe, D. B. (2011). *Painting the current picture: A national report on drug courts and other problem-solving court programs in the United States*. Washington, DC: National Drug Court Institute.

Institute of Medicine. (2013). *Returning home from Iraq and Afghanistan: Preliminary assessment of readjustment needs of veterans, service members, and their families*. Washington, DC: The National Academies Press.

James, D. J., & Glaze, L. E. (2006). *Mental health problems of prisons and jail inmates*. Washington, DC: U.S. Department of Justice, Bureau of Justice Statistics.

Johnson, R. S., Stolar, A. G., McGuire, J. F., Clark, S., Coonan, L. A., Hausknecht, P., & Graham, D. P. (2016). US veterans' court programs: An inventory and analysis of national survey data. *Community Mental Health Journal, 52*(2), 180–186. doi:10.1007/s10597-015-9972-3

Johnson, R. S., Stolar, A. G, Wu, E., Coonan, L. A., & Graham, D. P. (2015). An analysis of successful outcomes and associated contributing factors in veterans' court. *Bulletin of the Menninger Clinic, 79*(2), 166–173. doi:10.1521/bumc.2015.79.2.166

Kerry, N., & Pennell, S. (2001). *San Diego homeless court program: A process and impact evaluation*. San Diego, CA: San Diego Association of Governments.

Knudsen, K. J., & Wingenfeld, S. (2016). A specialized treatment court for veterans with trauma exposure: Implications for the field. *Community Mental Health Journal, 52*(2), 127–135. doi:10.1007/s10597-015-9845-9

Labriola, M., Bradley, S., O'Sullivan, C. S., Rempel, M., & Moore, S. (2009). *A national portrait of domestic violence courts*. New York, NY: Center for Court Innovation.

Lang, J. (2011). *What is a community court? How the model is being adapted across the United States*. New York, NY: Center for Court Innovation.

Lawrence, R. (1991). Reexamining community corrections models. *Crime and Delinquency, 37*(4), 449–464. doi: 10.1177/0011128791037004003

Lee, C. G., Cheesman, F., Rottman, D., Swaner, R., Lambson, S., Rempel, M., & Curtis, R. (2013). *A community court grows in Brooklyn: A comprehensive evaluation of the Red Hook Community Justice Center*. Williamsburg, VA: National Center for State Courts.

Lucas, P. A., & Hanrahan, K. J. (2016). No soldier left behind: The veterans court solution. *International Journal of Law and Psychiatry, 45*, 52–59. doi:10.1016/j.ijlp.2016.02.010

Marchand, G., Waller, M., & Carey, S. M. (2006). *Barry County Adult Drug Court outcome and cost evaluation*. Portland, OR: NPC Research.

Mitchell, O., Wilson, D. B., Eggers, A., & MacKenzie, D. L. (2012). Assessing the effectiveness of drug courts on recidivism: A meta-analytic review of traditional and non-traditional drug courts. *Journal of Criminal Justice, 40*(1), 60–71. doi:10.1016/j.jcrimjus.2011.11.009

Morin, R. (2011). *The difficult transition from military to civilian life*. Washington, DC: Pew Research Center.

National Institute of Justice. (2016). *Drug courts*. Washington, DC: Department of Justice, National Institute of Justice. Retrieved from www.nij.gov/topics/courts/drug-courts/pages/welcome.aspx

National Survey on Drug Use and Health. (2013). *Results from the 2013 National survey on drug use and health: Summary of National findings*. Washington, DC: U.S. Department of Health and Human Services.

National Institute of Mental Health. (2008). *Statistics*. Washington, DC: National Institute of Mental Health. Retrieved from http://www.nimh.nih.gov/health/topics/statistics/index.html

National Mental Health Association. (2003). *Jail diversion for people with mental illness: Developing supportive community coalitions*. Delmar, NY: The TAPA Center for Jail Diversion.

Newmark, L., Rempel, M., Diffily, K., & Kane, K. M. (2001). *Specialized felony domestic violence courts: Lessons on implementation and impacts from the Kings County experience*. Washington, DC: Urban Institute.

NYcourts.gov. (2016). *Sex offense courts*. Retrieved from www.nycourts.gov/courts/problem_solving/so/home.shtml

Ostrom, B. J. (2003). Domestic violence courts. *Criminology & Public Policy, 3*(1), 105–108. doi:10.1111/j.1745-9133.2003.tb00027.x

Parkinson, P. (2016). Specialist prosecution units and courts: A review of the literature. *Sydney Law School Legal Studies Research Paper No. 16/26*. Retrieved from http://ssrn.com/abstract=2756305

Peters, R. H., & Murrin, M. R. (2000). Effectiveness of treatment-based drug courts in reducing criminal recidivism. *Criminal Justice and Behavior, 27*(1), 72–96. doi:10.1177/0093854800027001005

Petersilia, J., Lurigio, A. J., & Byrne, J. M. (1992). Introduction: The emergence of intermediate sanctions. In J. M. Byrne, A. J. Lurigio, & J. Petersilia (Eds.), *Smart sentencing: The emergence of intermediate sanctions* (pp. ix–xv). Newbury Park, CA: Sage Publications, Inc.

Petrucci, C. J. (2010). A descriptive study of a California domestic violence court: Program completion and recidivism. *Victims and Offenders, 5*(2), 130–160. doi:10.1080/15564880903423037

Pew Research Center. (2011). *The military-civilian gap: War and sacrifice in the Post-9/11 era*. Washington, DC: Pew Social and Demographic Trends.

Porter, R., Vera Institute of Justice, & United States of America. (2002). *Supervised treatment in the criminal court: A process evaluation of the Manhattan Misdemeanor Drug Court.* New York, NY: Vera Institute of Justice.

Portillo, S., Rudes, D. S., Viglione, J., & Nelson, M. (2013). Front-stage stars and backstage producers: The role of judges in problem-solving courts. *Victims & Offenders, 8*(1), 1–22. doi:10.1080/15564886.2012.685220

Quast, T., Mullins, J., & Kobak-McKown, M. (2016, December 15). Editorial: Specialty courts tailor justice to match the crime. *Elko Daily Free Press.* Retrieved from http://elkodaily.com/news/opinion/editorial/editorial-specialty-courts-tailor-justice-to-match-the-crime/article_dc709184-a78f-5744-bf26–38ed088c0588.html

Redlich, A. D., Steadman, H. J., Monahan, J., Petrila, J., & Griffin, P. A. (2006). The second generation of mental health courts. *Psychology, Public Policy, and Law, 11*(4), 527–538. doi:10.1037/1076–8971.11.4.527

Rempel, M., & Destefano, C. D. (2001). Predictors of engagement in court-mandated treatment: Findings at the Brooklyn Treatment Court, 1996–2000. *Journal of Offender Rehabilitation, 33*(4), 87–124. doi:10.1300/J076v33n04_06

Rossman, S. B., Rempel, M., Roman, J. K., Zweig, J. M., Lindquist, C. H., Green, M., . . . Farole Jr, D. J. (2011). *The multi-site adult drug court evaluation: The impact of drug courts.* Washington, DC: The Urban Institute.

Rossman, S. B., Willison, J. B., Mallik-Kane, K., Kim, K., Debus-Sherrill, S., & Downey, P. M. (2012). *Criminal justice interventions for offenders with mental illness: Evaluation of mental health courts in Bronx and Brooklyn, New York: Final report.* Washington, DC: Urban Institute.

Russell, R. T. (2009a). Veterans' treatment courts: A proactive approach. *New England Journal on Criminal and Civil Confinement, 35*(2), 357–372.

Russell, R. T. (2009b). Veterans' treatment courts developing throughout the nation. *Future Trends in State Courts 2009.* Williamsburg, VA: National Center for State Courts. Retrieved from www.ncsc.org/sitecore/content/microsites/future-trends-2013/home/Monthly-Trends-Articles/Veterans-Treatment-Courts.aspx

Sarteschi, C. M. (2013). Mentally ill offenders involved with the US criminal justice system: A synthesis. *Sage Open, 3*(3), 1–11. doi:10.1177/2158244013497029

Sayer, N. A., Carlson, K. F., & Frazier, P. A. (2014). Reintegration challenges in U.S. service members and veterans following combat deployment. *Social Issues and Policy Review, 8*(1), 33–73. doi:10.1111/sipr.12001

Schneider, R. D. (2008). Mental health courts. *Wiley Encyclopedia of Forensic Science.* doi:10.1002/9780470061589.fsa285

Seal, K. H., Metzler, T. J., Gima, K. S., Bertenthal, D., Maguen, S., & Marmar, C. R. (2009). Trends and risk factors for mental health diagnoses among Iraq and Afghanistan veterans using Department of Veterans Affairs health care, 2002–2008. *American Journal of Public Health, 99*(9), 1651–1658. doi:10.2105/AJPH.2008.150284

Silberberg, J. M., Vital, T. L., & Brakel, S. J. (2001). Breaking down barriers to mandated outpatient treatment for mentally ill offenders. *Psychiatric Annals, 31*(7), 433–440. doi:10.3928/0048-5713-20010701-07

Slattery, M., Dugger, M. T., Lamb, T. A., & Williams, L. (2013). Catch, treat, and release: Veteran treatment courts address the challenges of returning home. *Substance Use & Misuse, 48*(10), 922–932. doi:10.3109/10826084.2013.797468

Spiro, A., & Settersten, R. A. Jr. (2012). Long-term implications of military service for later-life health and well-being. *Research in Human Development, 9*(3), 183–190. doi:10.1080/15427609.2012.705551

Spohn, C., Piper, R. K., Martin, T., & Frenzel, E. D. (2001). Drug courts and recidivism: The results of an evaluation using two comparison groups and multiple indicators of recidivism. *Journal of Drug Issues, 31*(1), 149–176. doi:10.1177/002204260103100109

Steadman, H. J., & Veysey, B. M. (1997). *Providing services for jail inmates with mental disorders.* Washington, DC: U.S. Department of Justice, Office of Justice Programs, National Institute of Justice.

Steadman, H. J., Redlich, A. D., Griffin, P., Petrila, J., & Monahan, J. (2005). From referral to disposition: Case processing in seven mental health courts. *Behavioral Sciences & The Law, 23*(2), 215–226. doi:10.1002/bsl.641

Teplin, L. A., Abram, K. M., McClelland, G. M., Mericle, A. A., Dulcan, M. K., & Washburn, J. J. (2006). *Psychiatric disorders of youth in detention.* U.S. Department of Justice, Office of Justice Programs, Office of Juvenile Justice and Delinquency Prevention.

Tyuse, S. W., & Linhorst, D. M. (2005). Drug courts and mental health courts: Implications for social work. *Health & Social Work, 30*(3), 233–240. doi:10.1093/hsw/30.3.233

United States Department of Housing and Urban Development. (2015). *The 2015 annual homeless assessment report (AHAR) to Congress.* Washington, DC: Office of Community Planning and Development. Retrieved from www.hudexchange.info/resources/documents/2015-AHAR-Part-1.pdf

United States Department of Veterans Affairs. (2012). *Profile of sheltered homeless veterans for fiscal years 2009 and 2010.* Washington, DC: Office of Policy and Planning.

United States Department of Veterans Affairs. (2016a). *Profile of post-9/11 veterans: 2014.* Washington, DC: National Center for Veterans Analysis and Statistics. Retrieved from: www.va.gov/vetdata/docs/SpecialReports/Post_911_Veterans_Profile_2014.pdf

United States Department of Veterans Affairs. (2016b). *Profile of veterans: 2014: Data from the American Community Survey*. Washington, DC: National Center for Veterans Analysis and Statistics. Retrieved from www.va.gov/vetdata/docs/SpecialReports/Profile_of_Veterans_2014.pdf

Vito, G. F., & Tewksbury, R. A. (1998). Impact of treatment: The Jefferson County (Kentucky) Drug Court Program. *Federal Probation, 62*(2), 46–51.

Walker, L. E., Pann, J. M., Shapiro, D. L., & Van Hasselt, V. B. (2015). *Best practice for the mentally ill in the criminal justice system*. New York, NY: Springer.

Walker, L. E., Cummings, D. M., & Cummings, N. A. (2012). *Our broken family court system*. New York, NY: Ithaca Press.

Webster, J. M., Rosen, P. J., Krietemeyer, J., Mateyoke-Scrivner, A., Staton-Tindall, M., & Leukefeld, C. (2006). Gender, mental health, and treatment motivation in a drug court setting. *Journal of Psychoactive Drugs, 38*(4), 441–448. doi:10.1080/02791072.2006.10400583

Weisburd, D., Lum, C. M., & Petrosino, A. (2001). Does research design affect study outcomes in criminal justice?. *The Annals of the American Academy of Political and Social Science, 578*(1), 50–70. doi:10.1177/000271620157800104

Wexler, D. B. (1998). Therapeutic jurisprudence forum: Practicing therapeutic jurisprudence: Psychological soft spots and strategies. *Revista Juridica UPR, 67*, 317–1121.

Wilson, D. B., Mitchell, O., & MacKenzie, D. L. (2006). A systematic review of drug court effects on recidivism. *Journal of Experimental Criminology, 2*(4), 459–487. doi:10.1007/s11292-006-9019-4

Wilson, J. Q., & Kelling, G. L. (1982). Broken windows: The police and neighborhood safety. *The Atlantic*. Retrieved from www.theatlantic.com/magazine/archive/1982/03/broken-windows/304465/

Winick, B. J. (1999). Redefining the role of the criminal defense lawyer at plea bargaining and sentencing: A therapeutic jurisprudence/preventive law model. *Psychology, Public Policy, and Law, 5*(4), 1034–1083. doi:10.1037/1076-8971.5.4.1034

Wolfe, S. M., Sasich, L. D., Lurie, P., Hope, R. E., Barbehenn, E., Knapp, D. E., . . . Ku, D. B. (2004). *Worst pills, best pills: A consumer guide to avoid drug-induced death or illness*. New York, NY: Pocket Books.

Wolfer, L. (2006). Graduates speak: A qualitative exploration of drug court graduates' views of the strengths and weaknesses of the program. *Contemporary Drug Problems, 33*(2), 303–320. doi:10.1177/009145090603300206

4

SPECIAL NEEDS CORRECTIONAL AND COMMUNITY FACILITIES

Designing for Inmates with Special Needs

John H. Weigel and Sydney M. Kennedy

> We got to explore our incarcerated prisoners and what occurs in their lives, and how they are able to search for redemption and also to search for a deepening of their own compassion, which hopefully moves toward love.
>
> —(Forest Whitaker, as cited in NPR Staff, 2011, para. 6)

Introduction

The issue of how to address confinement requirements of special needs offenders often confounds corrections officials. They know from their training and experience there are offenders who are in special populations and who require additional time, staff, facilities, and resources. Correctional officials also know they will have additional concerns related to staffing and staff turnover for the officers that guard members of these populations (Stinchcomb & Leip, 2013). However, they are often unsure how to meet the needs of the special populations while at the same time ensuring the safety and stability of the broader inmate population. Wise managers further realize time spent on the issues of the few subtracts from the total time available to address the needs of the many. In addition, the public perception and public debates engendered by special needs inmates are significant and important, because without input from the policy makers, courts can and will intervene, as will be shown in many of the examples cited herein.

When the issue of special management in corrections comes up, questions quickly arise. Can special needs inmates be safely housed in the general population? Most trends in the corrections field point in the direction of separate facilities (Curtin, 2007). If these inmates are best served by segregation into their own institution, what type of institutions need be constructed? Can other public or private facilities be utilized as they are or retrofitted to house special needs offenders? What are the budgetary requirements for these inmates? Can sufficient additional resources be found to meet these needs? Even if state and federal resources are available, is there any political will to spend money on inmates, who are often unsympathetic, maligned, or reviled? This chapter will attempt to address some of those questions by addressing four special needs populations. The chapter also will discuss the facilities that have been and will be constructed or repurposed to house offenders in these four populations.

The first population is the death row population. Neither the state nor the federal government houses any death row offenders in facilities that are not on the grounds of the main prison. In other words, there are no "death row only" prisons. The discussion in this chapter will focus on states with larger death row populations that house those inmates in separate buildings on the prison grounds. States with death row populations that are either so small or so large that condemned inmates are housed with offenders who are not sentenced to die will not be covered. The second population consists of offenders with chronic and serious medical needs that cannot be served within a traditional correctional institution. Infirmaries or clinics that are present in nearly every prison in the United States will not be discussed. Instead of discussing the "prison hospital," this section will shed light on those facilities that might best be referred to as "hospital prisons." The use and repurposing of facilities that were not initially constructed as prisons also will be addressed in this section. Third, this chapter will discuss prison hospice programs that are run separately from the prison hospital or infirmary.

Many facilities provide hospice-type services within their medical units, but there are some institutions that maintain separate hospice programs that are run by separate staff who manage inmate volunteers who work with dying inmates as a distinct group. Finally, the chapter will conclude with a discussion about segregated institutions for mentally ill offenders, who are often known by the public at large as the "criminally insane." Again, this chapter will not focus on mental health treatment services, treatment, or programs within the main institution. It will instead focus its attention on those facilities that are constructed specifically or used exclusively for the mentally ill offender.

Death Row

Death row as we know it is a fairly modern concept. Until the beginning of the Warren Court era in 1953, executions were carried out by the states, by the federal government, and by the United States military quickly and with little fanfare. The time between sentence and legal execution was often measured in months, if not weeks. This does not include extralegal lynchings or deaths occurring during actual or alleged escapes. Therefore, there was no acute need to think about funding and maintaining extensive and expensive facilities on prison grounds to house death row inmates for long periods of time.

Corrections officials across the country at the unit, state, and federal level must operate in the current environment where housing inmates for years, if not decades, under sentence of death is not uncommon. Thirty-one states have capital punishment statutes on the books (Death Penalty Information Center, 2017a). That total number rises to 32 if New Mexico is included. New Mexico abolished the death penalty but plans to execute two offenders sentenced under their now repealed statute (Death Penalty Information Center, 2017a). In each jurisdiction, capital appeals often go through several types of appellate review at both the state and federal level. The federal government and the United States Armed Forces also have death penalty statutes, but death sentences in those courts are not reviewed by the states.

The federal government houses its death row inmates at USP Terre Haute in Indiana. Five inmates on federal death row are held at other facilities, most notably Dzokhar Tsarnaev, the Boston Marathon bomber who is held at the "supermax" USP Florence in Colorado, and Lisa Montgomery, the only woman on federal death row, who is held at the Federal Medical Detention Center–Carswell, in Fort Worth, Texas (Trigg, 2017). The U.S. military houses its death row at the U.S. Disciplinary Barracks at Fort Leavenworth, Kansas. There are no women under sentence of death by the military.

Each state that plans to carry out executions creates and promulgates extensive execution protocols that regulate the actions to be taken as an execution nears (Montana Department of Corrections, 2013). For corrections officials tasked with housing the offenders under sentence of death, the process that moves them from trial to execution often strains limited budgets and resources. In other words, execution dates are set and then often stayed by the courts or the executive branch. Scheduling several execution dates over many years forces corrections officials to repeat the procedures in the protocol each time an execution is scheduled. Those constraints and complications are in addition to the routine issues presented by housing, feeding, and securing inmates under near or actual solitary confinement conditions for long periods. The death row facilities in three states, namely Louisiana, Mississippi, and Texas, will be discussed in this chapter, as an example of the conditions found in other institutions throughout the United States.

In Louisiana, death row is found at the Louisiana State Penitentiary, known throughout the world as Angola (Compa, Kappel, & Montagnes, 2014). Louisiana has 75 inmates on death row as of March 31, making it the 10th largest death row in the United States (NAACP Legal Defense and Educational Fund, 2017). The 75 inmates include one black woman, who is housed at the Louisiana Correctional Institution for Women in St. Gabriel (Death Penalty Information Center, 2017c). Her living conditions will not be discussed here, as she is housed with other female offenders who are not sentenced to death. Executions in Louisiana have slowly ground to a halt. In fact, the last inmate executed in Louisiana was Gerald Bordelon, who was put to death on January 7, 2010, after waiving his appeals. Louisiana has not executed an offender who did not waive his appeals since 2002 (NAACP Legal Defense and Educational Fund, 2017).

None of the inmates on death row in Louisiana is allowed to work. Contact visits, even with attorneys, are severely limited. The death house facility was built in 2007. Since then, macabre "tours" of death row have been conducted, where the most notorious inmates are put on display for dignitaries (Compa et al., 2014). Angola can be less regimented in its management style than other institutions. An example of this is demonstrated in the construction of the unit itself. Unlike many death cells built after the construction of Pelican Bay State Prison in California in 1990, the death cells in Louisiana do not have solid steel doors with Plexiglas panes in them. They were instead built with uncovered iron bars (Compa et al., 2014).

This construction creates a management issue for corrections officers in Louisiana on two fronts. First, open bars give ample opportunity for inmates to communicate and pass messages, sometimes known as "kites," to one another. They can also pass contraband. The second issue involves spitting or throwing objects or bodily fluids at officers. However, death row inmates are generally better behaved than general population inmates, both because most are trying to maintain good conduct to increase their chances for clemency and because the death row population tends to skew older than general population inmates do.

A more routinized but problematic system can be found at the Mississippi State Penitentiary at Parchman, built in 1903 and colloquially known as Parchman Farm. The facility is widely known for famous inmates, such as Huddie William Ledbetter, better known as the folk and blues singer Leadbelly. The recent history of Mississippi death row has been just as noteworthy (Winter & Hanlon, 2008). Mississippi currently has 47 inmates on death row, leaving it tied with Oklahoma for the 14th largest death row population in the United States (Mississippi Department of Corrections, 2017). One female death row inmate is held at Central Mississippi Correctional Facility (CMCF) in Pearl, Mississippi (Mississippi Department of Corrections, 2017).

Until 2010, Mississippi's death row population was held in Unit 32, one of many buildings spread across the 20,000 acres of Delta farmland that comprises Parchman. Beginning in 2002, The American Civil Liberties Union (ACLU) began an investigation of the conditions of the death row inmates on Unit 32, where death row inmates were held along with HIV-positive offenders, persistent prison rule breakers, and mentally ill offenders. The findings of the investigation led to repeated lawsuits against the Mississippi Department of Corrections (MDOC) (Winter & Hanlon, 2008). The unit had persistent plumbing problems. Wastewater from one cell would back up into other cells. There also were persistent roof leaks, mosquitoes, and no air conditioning in the unit, where temperatures reach well over 100 degrees. Based on the intervention of the federal district court and the Fifth Circuit Court of Appeals, Unit 32 was eventually shut down in 2010.

Death row in Mississippi has been in the news again for similar problems. In 2015, a settlement was reached between the MDOC and the McArthur Justice Clinic at the University of Mississippi School of Law. Since then, teams of law students have worked on compliance monitoring for that settlement, which alleged similar problems with the housing unit where the death row inmates were relocated (The University of Mississippi School of Law, 2017).

These problems in Mississippi support the need for extensive planning and resource allocation for death row prisoner populations. The time from sentence to execution exceeded 10 years for all but two of the executions carried out in 2017. Thus, the death row inmate population is a population with distinct, long-term needs. Resources at the public policy level need to be dedicated to a population that will be in the correctional system in the United States for decades to come. Along with the long-term housing of death row inmates, another issue to consider with the death row population is the possibility of escape. To discuss that, we turn to Texas, one of the few states where inmates have escaped from death row. In fact, Texas has had escapes from its death row twice, once in 1934 and the last time in 1999.

The 1934 escape involved Raymond Hamilton and Joe Palmer, two members of the Clyde Barrow gang who had confederates bribe a guard to sneak guns into the Huntsville Unit, nicknamed "the Walls," in downtown Huntsville, Texas. A number of inmates not on death row stormed the death house to release Hamilton and Palmer. Both individuals were quickly recaptured and executed in the electric chair on May 10, 1935 (Tolson, 2007). The 1998 escape involved Martin Gurule and six other inmates who cut through a fence in the outdoor recreation yard surrounding the Ellis Unit before climbing onto a rooftop and scaling their way down. The seven had used pillows and blankets to create dummies of themselves to convince guards they were still in their cells. All of the inmates except Gurule were recaptured on prison grounds. Gurule was found drowned in a swamp near the prison one week later.

That escape, along with the negative publicity that surrounded it, is one of the reasons that Texas' death row was relocated for a second time. The first move occurred in 1965, when death row was moved from Walls to the Ellis Unit. In 1999, death row was moved from the Ellis Unit just outside of Huntsville to the Polunsky Unit in Livingston, Texas, 45 minutes away, where it remains today. This distance adds an additional layer of security concerns and complications to each of Texas' frequent executions, as the condemned inmate must be transferred secretly from the Polunsky Unit to the Walls Unit in the hours leading up to his execution.

A brief look at the Texas death row population shows three alarming facts. Since the death penalty was reauthorized by the United States Supreme Court in 1976, Texas alone has conducted 544 of the 1,463 executions in the United States, or just over 38% of them (NAACP Legal Defense and Educational Fund, 2017). Second, 233 inmates are currently under sentence of death in Texas, which makes Texas the third largest death row in the United States, behind only California and Florida (NAACP Legal Defense and Educational Fund, 2017).

As discussed previously, moving the death row inmates to the Polunsky Unit created a logistical concern, transporting the individual from the Polunsky Unit to the Walls Unit for the execution. Thus, one of the considerations policy makers should consider when building new facilities for death row inmates is the logistical challenge involved in moving an entire death row population from the old facility to the new one. They also should consider if the inmate will need to be transported to a different facility for the execution to occur.

New research suggests death row inmates do not require segregated confinement because they are not any more violent than inmates in the general population (Cunningham, Reidy, & Sorenson, 2016). According to the authors, "CP [capital punishment] inmates, as a class, do not require segregated, solitary, highly restrictive confinement to prevent serious prison violence" (Cunningham et al., 2016, p. 196). To this end, the Arizona Department of Corrections (ADOC) recently settled

Box 4.1 Faces of Death Row

The Faces of Death Row Tool was created to add transparency to Texas' capital punishment system and includes:

- Filters for race, age, sex, and years spent on death row
- Brief summaries detailing the crime for which the inmate was convicted
- County information for where the conviction took place
- Inmate identification photos

Source: McCullough and Hasson (2017)

a lawsuit filed by condemned inmate Scott Nordstrom about the housing conditions on death row there. In the settlement, the ADOC agreed to make individualized determinations of the housing requirements of each individual inmate rather than classify them all at the highest level because they are condemned (Death Penalty Information Center, 2017b). Box 4.1 presents information about the Faces of Death Row Tool use by Texas in capital punishment cases.

Chronic Medical Needs

While death row populations may be effectively "mainlined," the same cannot be said for those inmates with persistent, chronic medical conditions. The constant care they require and their vulnerability to predation by other inmates makes segregating them almost mandatory. This is to say nothing of the fact many of these inmate-patients have communicable diseases such as HIV, hepatitis, herpes, tuberculosis, and pneumonia. Uncontrolled communicable diseases in a prison setting can quickly result in required closure of a facility for reasons of quarantine. It is already common for many states to suspend visitation and limit the traffic in and out of the prison if there are suspected disease outbreaks within the facility. (Texas Department of Criminal Justice, 2017).

According to a 2013 study by the Urban Institute, between 9 and 30 cents of every dollar spent on corrections in this country is spent on inmate health care (Schaenman, Davies, Jordan, & Chakaborty, 2013). According to a survey of medical services to inmates by Cropsey, Wexler, Melnick, Taxman, and Young (2008), better care is provided to inmates with chronic medical needs in facilities that are specially designed for such inmates than by the prison hospital. It is believed the reason for this lies in the generally smaller population at those facilities and the particular training that staff members at those facilities possess. However, there is a concern among the states about opening such facilities since the population of inmates with special medical needs is not fixed and is hard to predict over time, although the trend line in this population indicates further increases.

One facility that has been meeting the needs of this particular inmate population for some time is the Lois M. DeBerry Special Needs Facility in Tennessee. The facility opened in 1992 and has the capacity to house up to 854 male offenders, "with a turnover of 250 beds per month and the majority of these offenders have significant needs" (Tennessee Department of Correction, 2017, para 5). The mission of the DeBerry Special Needs Facility is "to provide acute, sub-acute, long-term acute, chronic and palliative health care that is high-quality, safe, integrative, efficient, and ethical, in a safe and secure environment" (Tennessee Department of Correction, 2017, para. 5). Another interesting fact is the facility also occasionally holds pretrial detainees from county jails who have acute medical needs. Recently, for example, a defendant who was injured in a car accident after fleeing from the police was held at DeBerry (Satterfield, 2017).

However, the maintenance and operation of the facility has not been without its challenges, specifically in the area of staffing. In 2015, after a change in shift allocation for corrections officers from a traditional 40-hour workweek to a 28-day schedule where overtime would be paid for all hours in excess of 212, the turnover rate for staff at the facility, which already was among the highest in the state, only increased. The officers and the corrections union opposed the change because with the regular workweek schedule it was easier for the officers to schedule family commitments and other part-time employment to supplement their incomes. Under the 28-day schedule, if a particular officer had not worked the maximum 212 hours in the past 28 days, he or she could and often would be assigned back-to-back shifts. This was stressful to the officers and caused shortages (Wilemon, 2015).

Even with the staffing issues, DeBerry has facilitated innovative programs in the area of education. In its *Inside Out Think Tank* (see Box 4.2), students from nearby Western Kentucky University come to the DeBerry Facility to meet with inmates at the facility, who also are enrolled in criminology courses like the students who are visiting them. This program is modeled on one began by Lori Pompa at Temple University in 2007. Another program designed to establish outreach to the inner-city is called *Teach the Teachers*. In that program, education students at WKU come in to talk to the inmates at DeBerry to gain an understanding on how to connect with inner-city youth (Mason, 2013).

Another facility that was unique at the time of its opening was the Rocky Hill Skilled Nursing Facility in Rocky Hill, Connecticut. From its name, it does not sound like a prison at all. However, it was specifically contracted by the state of Connecticut to hold elderly and sick prisoners who would be paroled there. An immediate backlash followed, and the facility had problems even getting a license to open because the Rocky Hill community sued to keep it from accepting inmates. That suit ultimately failed. The suit was ultimately a fight about "not in my back yard." The question remains whether we as criminal justice practitioners and as members of society are comfortable with inmates in the bed across the room from grandma.

Once the issue of location was resolved, the next issue that befell the facility was predictably about funding. This fight was concerned with whether inmate-patients would be entitled to Medicaid funding, and more presciently for the private facility, would the facility be entitled to reimbursement from Medicaid for the services they provided. When the legislature approved the contract with Secure Care Options, LLC, to run the facility, they believed they would not be entitled to Medicaid funding since they were in secure wards and would not be allowed to leave them. The fact the individuals were not free to leave the facility made the legislature consider them still prisoners and thus not entitled to Medicaid funding because according to federal law, Medicaid funding cannot be used for prisoners. It was on this basis that the contract with the facility was approved, because the legislature believed that by being classified as prisoners in the nursing home, they would not be costing

Box 4.2 Inside Out Components

- Examining social issues through "the prism of prison"
- Entering into dialogue, into public discourse, across many forms of difference
- Recognizing the power of education as a vehicle for transformation and a catalyst of social change
- Creating spaces of liberation, developing deeper reservoirs of empathy, civic consciousness, and responsive leadership

Source: The Inside-Out Center (2015, para. 3)

the state money. However, the governor, who administered the Medicaid program through his subordinates, believed they were patients and not prisoners and therefore entitled to Medicaid funding, since Medicaid funding is available to poor people that need extended nursing care. The facility staff took this position as well, and they believed that the federal government would reimburse the facility for the cost for caring for these individuals. Eventually, the federal government did step in and agree to fund the care (Drury, 2013).

This idea of specializing and privatizing the care has been considered by many other states as well. There is a serious question of where the public stands on the issue of elderly prisoners. Do we want elderly prisoners locked up for the full extent of their sentences, even well past the point where they are a danger to recidivate? Or do we instead want them to reside in facilities that are close to or equal to the facilities wherein noncriminal elderly reside? That was the key point that the residents of the town of Rocky Hill made and one that has not been adequately answered in the literature or in the public debate. In the term elderly inmates, which part is more important to society? Are they elderly first or are they inmates first? Do we as a society want to continue to punish them, and if so how much are we willing to pay to do it?

Finally, the third facility that has been caring for inmates with special medical needs since it opened in 1930 is the Medical Center for Federal Prisoners (MCFP). The MCFP, located in Springfield, Missouri, has housed such notable inmates as John Gotti, Joseph Bannano, Vito Genovese, Henri Young, who was featured in the film *Murder in the First*, Robert "Birdman of Alcatraz" Stroud, and Jared Loughner, the mass shooter of Tucson, Arizona. Inmates come to this facility with a wide variety of problems, including communicable diseases, such as hepatitis C. A recent study of prisoners at the facility found that hepatitis C contributes to added cognitive deficits (Umaki & Denney, 2012). This makes these offenders special needs offenders not only because of their persistent medical need, but also because of their mental health.

Another issue that is particularly prevalent with mental health inmates at MCFP Springfield is the issue of forced medication. In other words, can a correctional facility forcibly medicate someone like Jared Loughner to make them "sane enough" to be competent to stand trial? The ethics of forcing someone to take medication to be competent to stand trial for a crime that may put them in prison for the rest of the life, or even subject them to the death penalty, has been hotly debated (McMahon, 2013).

Just because this is a facility with special needs inmates does not mean that it is free from the violence that plagues other institutions. Just this month, Ulysses Jones, Jr., already under a life sentence, was resentenced to life in prison for the murder of another inmate (United States Department of Justice, 2017). So whether the facilities are less than a decade old like Rocky Hill, or more than 80 years old like MCFP Springfield, or somewhere in the middle, like Lois DeBerry Special Needs Facility, the issue of how and where to deal with inmates with persistent medical and mental health issues is not going away any time soon.

Hospice

Prison hospice is a relatively new concept in corrections. While traditional hospice care programs have increased over the last 20 years, prison hospice care programs are a new phenomenon (Meier & Bowman, 2017). However, with more and more inmates serving longer and longer sentences, hospice programs will be needed in increasing numbers of prisons and jails throughout the United States. From an institutional perspective, most prison hospices are run within the existing prison hospital or infirmary setting, though some programs, such as the one at the Iowa State Penitentiary at Fort Madison, have a dedicated space. This is a wing off a unit within the larger prison that is dedicated to offenders with special chronic medical needs. Volunteers under the supervision of corrections staff run most units, with inmates as the primary day-to-day caregivers.

This institutional distancing accomplishes two purposes. First, it keeps costs down. Inmate labor and volunteers do not in and of themselves take up a great deal of a correctional budget. Second, if care can be provided at the prison, and the need for expensive transportation costs and outside medical costs at trauma centers or emergency rooms can be avoided, the cost savings to the policy makers can be noteworthy. Further, institutional distancing and outside volunteers tend to deflect some if not all of the political blowback that can result from some finding out that inmates are being coddled or cared for in a way that is seemingly more attentive or compassionate that the care received by many elderly patients who are outside the walls and are not convicted felons, especially convicted violent felons.

Hospice or, by its medical term, palliative care, for the prisoner population is gaining more widespread public acceptance as well. Just this year, Baumann and Todaro-Franceschi (2017) published research about the attitudes of graduate nursing students toward palliative care for the inmate population. Gaining the confidence of the medical community is a necessary first step toward increasing acceptance of palliative care programs in prisons. The research showed after hearing a lecture on palliative care programs in prisons, the nursing students' attitudes changed and, according to the authors, "Loeb's presentation provided a reaffirmation of the most basic nursing premise—that all people deserve compassionate care" (Baumann & Todaro-Franceshi, 2017, p. 258).

This need for acceptance by the medical community is necessary, even though other inmates will administer most of the day-to-day care. This is true because of the essential nature of palliative care. Palliative care is not, in the strictest sense, skilled medical care. The goal of medicine is to cure disease. Palliative care is designed not to reverse the disease process but to provide quality end of life care. Any caring person can therefore perform it. Younger inmates serving long sentences themselves are particularly amenable to the kind of training needed to perform palliative care services. This is because younger inmates with long sentences and especially those with sentences of life without parole are acutely aware that one day the tables will be turned, and they will be the cared for and not the caregiver. Their interest in maintaining these programs is therefore both personal and somewhat self-interested.

From a corrections management perspective, the use of palliative care programs has two major benefits to the prison. The first benefit is financial. One palliative care

> program [tested] has demonstrated high patient satisfaction and significantly reduced costs, particularly at the end of life. Compared to usual care, total monthly care for Transitions patients costs between $2,690 less (for patients with dementia) to $4,258 less (for patients with cancer).
>
> (Cassel et al., 2016 as cited in Meier & Bowman, 2017, p. 77)

Since in nearly all cases there are no insurance reimbursements for prisoners, every dollar saved on care for one inmate is a dollar that can be used elsewhere in the budget for that prison.

The second benefit is disciplinary. Prisoners often see work in the hospice as a desirable, if at times menial, job assignment. There are several reasons for this. First, prison hospice work is nearly always done in the prison infirmary. The environmental conditions there are generally considered by inmates to be more favorable than in other types of prison work. There is generally less noise and more freedom of movement in that environment than as a cell house porter or laundry worker. In addition, from a disciplinary perspective a prison job is one of the first privileges that can be threated or taken away in the event of disciplinary infractions by caregivers. In addition, there is a sense of comradery that develops between inmate caregivers and the inmates that are receiving care. Many of the inmates in prison lacked older male role models. Since in nearly all prison environments, older inmates who have already served long sentences are generally more respected than "fresh fish" or new inmates, this allows the cared-for inmate to serve as a kind of mentor or role model for the younger caregiver.

There also is the respect implicit in the work. As a cell house porter, you are only respected enough to push a mop or broom, and only under the watchful eye of guards. As a hospice worker, you interact with nonsecurity corrections staff and are trusted with the care of another human being. Just like a worker in the free world, a sense of respect and recognition for the importance of a person's work increases feelings of satisfaction and lowers depression and concomitantly the risk of antisocial or self-destructive conduct.

Hoffman and Dickinson (2011, p. 249–250) reported that "prison hospices appear to be mindful of the importance of family to the patient, allowing non-incarcerated and incarcerated family members to visit daily or weekly in nearly a third of the programs." This is despite the legitimate institutional concerns that usually bar other visits or even letters from other penal institutions. Hoffman and Dickinson reported that only a few of the units did not allow visits from inmate family members of the hospice patient.

In addition, Cloyes, Berry, Martz, and Supiano (2015) did a study analyzing the medical needs of hospice patients. In most cases, they found them to have significant chronic medical issues before reaching hospice. According to the research, 41% had prior infectious diseases, 28% had prior heart disease, 14% had prior diabetes, 12% had prior lung disease, 11% had prior cancer, and 10% had prior seizures or other neurological disorders. In other words, they were sicker than the average patient in a nonconfined hospice setting was. This further stresses the need for hospice programs in prison and underscores the good work that is being done in them. If inmates without formal medical training can care for the sickest of patients in the toughest of conditions, that points to the sustainability and necessity of prison palliative care programs.

Cloyes et al. (2017) also found emotional benefits and rehabilitative benefits to prisoners who work in prison hospice programs. Specifically, they found inmates who become prison hospice workers receive several tangible benefits for doing so that are translatable to the outside world. First, the prisoners learn real-world hospital skills in a clinical setting. Through the education and training that is provided to them, the inmates learn transferable work skills. Second, the process that is unique to the hospice is the process of sitting vigil. In that process, which is begun when the medical team believes that death will come within the next three days, a series of volunteers, in this case a group of inmates, will remain at a dying inmate-patient's bedside constantly. This is accomplished by rotating out the inmates every four hours. Third, there is the leadership development that occurs when a more experienced inmate volunteer trains a less experienced volunteer. There are significant and transferable intangible rewards that are gained by both the trainer and the trainee as both build self- and peer respect through the process of teaching and learning. Box 4.3 presents the benefits of the hospice program at Angola Prison.

The prison hospice model is not without ethical pitfalls, however. Stensland and Sanders (2016) looked at many of the ethical issues that arise in the prison hospice environment. The first critical

Box 4.3 Hospice Benefits at Angola

- Patients receive specialized care.
- Their families are afforded support and consolation.
- Staff assigned to the program find the work rewarding.
- The prison population gains peace of mind in knowing that hospice is there for them if they need it.
- Inmate volunteers have increased knowledge and self-esteem.
- The institution saves money and gains an improved public image.

Source: Evans, Herzog, and Tillman (2002, p. 558)

ethical issue that the authors analyzed was the prevalence of dementia among patients eligible for or receiving hospice care. Next, the authors noted that the primary function of institutions like

> prisons [is to] serve the purposes of punishing, incapacitating, and rehabilitating individuals who have committed crimes, and these purposes call for a rigid environment focused nearly exclusively on security and public safety. [This does] not readily reflect an environment conducive to dying and EOL [end of life] care provision.
>
> (Stensland & Sanders, 2016, pp. 261–262)

Finally, the authors noted the fundamental mistrust that inmates have for the system that is not present among nonincarcerated hospice patients. A large majority of patients in free-world hospice programs believe that the doctors, the staff, and the volunteers are working in the patient's best interest, even if that best interest is a less stressful and less painful death. The authors noted that, offenders by and large do not make that same assumption about prison staff. The authors go on to argue that "the extreme power imbalance and freedom differential present between dying offenders and those providing the care are not seen in the patient-provider relationship at the community level" (Stansland & Sanders, 2016, p. 262).

Although the debate about the effectiveness and need for prison palliative care programs is far from settled, the research discussed here does tend to show by and large, on the cost-benefit scale, the benefits of prison hospice programs do tend to outweigh their risks, ethical pitfalls, and financial costs. However, that has been true for many prison programs that have been dramatically cut. A prominent example is the large retrenchment in prison higher education programs that came with the termination of eligibility for prisoners to obtain Pell Grants. Even though there were and are many studies that showed then and show now that higher education for prisoners dramatically reduces recidivism rates, with the recidivism rates for some graduate programs in prisons being literally zero, the political will to maintain the Pell Grant program for prisoners was not present.

The same could happen to prison hospice programs. With enough angry letters about murderers being fawned over instead of punished, there could be the political will to cancel these prison palliative care programs in some areas or nationwide, regardless of the physical and emotional benefits to the inmate caregivers or the inmate-patients. The tranquility and even the budget of the institution could be sacrificed on the altar of the politically facile and expedient position of being tough on crime.

Mentally Ill Offenders

The final special needs population this chapter will analyze is the population of those offenders found not guilty because of insanity or guilty but mentally ill and held long term in state-run hospital facilities for the criminally insane. This population does not include those who are held merely for short periods (usually 72-hour commitments) or those who are held for short periods while their competency to stand trial is studied. This analysis does include those who are held for long periods (generally years) because a court has found the person is unlikely to ever become competent to stand trial. These offenders are subject to periodic monitoring by the courts to determine whether there is a reasonable likelihood that competency to stand trial may be established. Throughout this section, the term "criminally insane" will be used, although it can be seen as a colloquial term; it does simply explain a complex inmate population.

From a housing perspective, generally these inmates are held not in a prison infirmary or prison hospital but instead in a facility designed to house offenders with mental illnesses exclusively or in conjunction with those offenders with chronic medical problems. One example of this was discussed in the earlier section on hospital prisons, as the Lois M. DeBerry Special Needs Facility cohouses both inmates with medical issues and those with mental illnesses in the same facility, though generally in different parts of the facility. This cohousing approach is rare. More common are facilities like the Texas State Hospital at Rusk and the California Department of State Hospitals-Atascadero where so-called "forensic" mental patients are held. Although some noncriminal inmates are held at Rusk, the facility, since 1953, has been the main unit for housing the criminally insane in Texas. In 2012, a new secure unit was constructed on the site (Texas Department of State Health Services, 2017).

The population of the criminally insane have special management needs that other inmate populations do not possess. As we saw with hospice patients, many if not most psychiatric inmates manifest extreme levels of distrust for correctional authorities. It is one thing for an inmate to say, as in the case of hospice inmates, that the prison staff does not care about me and does not put my interests first. It is quite another for a schizophrenic inmate to say that the corrections staff are agents of Satan and are actively subverting God's will on Earth.

Normal corrections management practice uses a system of rewards and punishments. Good behavior, educational attainment, or community outreach is rewarded with privileges, such as family visitation, or less restrictive conditions of confinement, such as confinement in a dormitory-type setting rather than in single, isolated cells. Negative behavior results in the withdrawal of privileges and placement in more restrictive conditions of confinement. A typical general population inmate understands this process, and if he wants privileges, he will seek to conform his conduct to the institutional standard to gain them.

This process does not work effectively with mentally ill inmates. If, due to their illness, they cannot connect privileges with good conduct and punishments with bad conduct, they are unable to conform their conduct to the institutional standard. In addition, some inmates with mental illness may actually believe they did conform their conduct to the institutional standard and may react with disbelief, anger, and defensiveness when confronted with the facts.

An example of this process, though not in the institutional sense, was found in the Jared Loughner case. Throughout his trial, Loughner refused to believe that Congresswoman Gabrielle Giffords, his main target of the shooting spree, was not dead. Loughner went so far as to call himself a failure because he was not an assassin, as he wanted to be. The fact that he killed six others, including a sitting federal judge was irrelevant to him (Dobuzinskis, 2012).

A simplistic version of this hypothetical can be envisioned in the corrections context. If an inmate is ordered to be handcuffed to be transported somewhere, and he believes that he has already been handcuffed, he will likely protest or physically resist an officer who attempts to actually place the handcuffs on him. The inmate will not understand what the officers are saying or trying to do and will react negatively toward them for doing it. In those circumstances, the inmate must often be given powerful psychotropic drugs to put the inmate in a more compliant, if less self-aware, state in order to gain compliance. Often, those medicines must be administered by force, which raises ethical concerns about the utilization of treatment for a medical condition, in this case schizophrenia, for a nontherapeutic reason. In this example, the drugs would be given to make the inmate willing to consent to being handcuffed or at least unable to refuse the handcuffs.

Many studies have been conducted about the efficacy of treatment programs for the criminally insane. Morgan, Kroner, Mills, Bauer, and Serna (2013, p. 911) studied the effectiveness of one such program. After testing the program the researchers found that "T tests performed on pre-post SCL-90-R scores indicated statistically significant ($p < .05$) treatment gains for Depression, Anxiety, Hostility, Paranoid Ideation, Psychoticism, symptom severity (GSI), and symptom intensity (PSDI) scales." The researchers then measured the effect sizes of the program on the treatment group. They found that

> Cohen's effect sizes for these scales indicated medium treatment effects for Anxiety, Hostility, Paranoid Ideation, Psychoticism, and symptom severity scales (Cohen's d range = 0.39–0.44)

and moderately large treatment effects for Depression (Cohen's d = 0.71) and symptom intensity (Cohen's d = 0.64) scales.

(Morgan et al., 2013, p. 911)

From a perspective of corrections management, studies like this one are encouraging because they show that effectively designed and implemented treatment programs can reduce psychiatric symptoms in inmates. This is promising because another corrections management issue surrounding long-term criminally insane inmates—the period of their confinement, generally until such time as they are no longer a danger to themselves or others—is much more vague and amorphous than a prisoner serving a traditional, even if indeterminate, sentence.

In a normal indeterminate sentence, if an inmate is sentenced to, for example, 8 1/3 to 25 years for a felony in New York, the inmate knows that once his time served and any earned merit credits for good behavior or achievement are added to the calendar time served, the inmate will be eligible for release. Now, the prisoner may not be optimistic about his chances to gain that release, or even in some cases may be afraid to be released, but at least the inmate understands the process. Many times, inmates familiarize themselves with the process of parole to an extent that they understand the parole laws better than the corrections staff, because they have a vested interest in the outcome of the parole proceeding.

In the case of a criminally insane inmate, the inmate is held until he is either competent to stand trial or until he is deemed no longer a danger to society. This is based on the decisions of a court, after the court receives recommendations from the treating psychiatrist and other members of the treatment team. Many times, the inmate is not given these reports to read, and even if the inmate is given the report, to read the medical and legal terminology may exceed his understanding. Even worse, if a treating physician does not recommend a patient for release, and the judge concurs in that recommendation, the patient is often sent back to the same facility for treatment by the same physician. It is therefore not entirely irrational for that inmate to believe that the psychiatrist is not working in his best interest, since the inmate witnessed the doctor argue for something that may be diametrically opposed to the desires of the inmate. This tension can cause further resistance to treatment, misconduct, management problems, and longer periods of confinement for the inmate. Box 4.4 list the outcomes from the Washington County Jail Special Needs Pods.

For corrections staff in the hospital, this long-term indefinite confinement poses special challenges. If the inmate is resistant to or unable to help in his plan of treatment, no amount of encouragement by staff, doctors, lawyers, or courts will change that fact. This means that "until you are no longer a danger to yourself and others" can. in practice, become a life without parole sentence. This is

Box 4.4 Washington County Jail: Special Needs Pods (SNP) Observed Outcomes

- Medication pass is completed in half the time required prior to creation of SNP.
- Medication compliance has increased by 20%.
- Medical/mental health staff has more efficient access to inmates.
- Valuable medical beds opened up once mentally ill inmates were moved to SNP.
- Suicide watch, incidents and disciplinary reports are consistently decreasing.
- Communication and information sharing increased among staff.
- Centralization of the special needs population has resulted in reductions in length of stay.

Source: Iverson and Colpean (2009, para. 25–30)

true although it would go against both corrections policy and the law for any one of the aforementioned officials to concede that point publicly or privately to the inmate.

Another study that was less encouraging to corrections managers was conducted by Dumont et al. (2012) in Canada. The study looked at the demographic characteristics of inmates that are held in long-term treatment as criminally insane. In that study, "the bivariate analysis performed . . . showed that the participants who were deemed to require a hospital setting were significantly younger than those who were thought to be able to benefit from a residential setting" (Dumont et al., 2012, p. 113). That is a distressing finding for correctional managers. Younger patients needing the most intensive and long-term treatment means that more time and resources will be needed to manage them. Further, the study found that "a larger proportion of participants who were deemed to require a hospital setting had a history of violent criminal behavior" (Dumont et al., 2012, p. 113–114). This suggests, anecdotally, at least, that once an inmate is deemed to need forensic psychiatric care in a facility for the criminally insane, the chances that that inmate will ever reach a point where he no longer requires confined psychiatric care is low.

Even less encouraging was another Canadian study conducted by Salem et al. (2015). It found that "Controlling for sociodemographic, clinical, and criminal variables, survival analysis showed that individuals placed in independent housing following a conditional discharge from the Review Board were 2.5 times more likely to commit a new offense" (Salem et al., 2015, p. 311). That is, when forensic psychiatric patients were released from confinement and allowed to live independently, they were more likely to recidivate than inmates that were released into monitored housing environments.

Worse, those offenders were "nearly three times more likely to commit an offense against a person, and 1.4 times more likely to be readmitted for psychiatric treatment compared with individuals residing in supportive housing" (Salem et al., 2015, p. 311). So not only were the offenders more likely to reoffend, they were more likely to reoffend in the manner in which the public is most afraid. Studies like this one will increase the public policy pressure on officials at all levels of the criminal justice system to scale back the use and applicability of the insanity defense. The findings will further pressure those in the courts and in corrections to keep and house the offenders that are deemed guilty but mentally ill in more restrictive housing settings and for longer periods of time. An already skeptical public will not see results like this one as a recipe for anything other than more walls, cells, and guards.

Conclusion

For these special needs inmates, the need for special care in specialized facilities is essential. The debate surrounding such care often centers around whether these individuals convicted of crimes, some of violent crimes, deserve care and compassion. The debate should be focused on how correctional facilities can increase their security and provide protection for their staff by providing this care and compassion. Any cost associated with dedicate housing for this population far outweighs the potential of housing them in the general population of a correctional facility and risking safety and security. Simply put, outside those on death row, these inmates should not be housed within the general population. Inmates with chronic illnesses need and deserve specialized care that can only adequately be provided by dedicated and trained staff. Those who are facing death also should be provided with end of life care to ease the pain they face. As mentioned previously, there are several benefits to providing hospice care in a prison setting. Mainly, it provides both the inmates that provide the care and those who are dying with a meaningful experience. Lastly, providing separate facilities for those with mental illness increases the safety of the facility and allows for a dedicated staff with additional training in mental health needs to provide care for the individuals.

The four special needs populations studied will continue to consume a disproportionate share of the corrections policy debate and the corrections budget. If anything, the need for more and broader research into these populations is increasingly acute, as the number of inmates in these populations will likely continue to increase dramatically in the foreseeable future.

References

Baumann, S., & Todaro-Franceschi, V. (2017). Graduate students' reflections on elder and end- of-life care for prisoners. *Nursing Science Quarterly*, *30*(3), 253–259. doi:10.1177/0894318417708416

Cassel, J. B., Kerr, K., McClish, D., Skoro, N., Johnson, S., Wanke, C., & Hoefer, D. (2016). Effect of a home-based palliative care program on healthcare use and costs. *Journal of the American Geriatric Society*, *64*(11), 2288–2295. doi:10.1111/jgs.14354

Cloyes, K., Berry, P., Martz, K., & Supiano, K. (2015). Characteristics of prison hospice patients: Medical history, hospice care, and end-of-life symptom prevalence. *Journal of Correctional Health Care*, *21*(3), 298–308. doi:10.1177/1078345815588842

Cloyes, K., Rosenkranz, S., Supiano, K., Berry, P., Routt, M., Llanque, S., & Shannon-Dorcy, K. (2017). Caring to learn and learning to care. *Journal of Correctional Health Care*, *23*(1), 43–55. doi:10.1177/1078345816684833

Compa, E., Kappel, C., & Montagnes, M. (2014). Litigating civil rights on death row: A Louisiana perspective. *Loyola Journal of Public Interest Law*, *15*, 293–317.

Cropsey, K. L., Wexler, H. K., Melnick, G., Taxman, F. S., & Young, D. W. (2008). Specialized prisons and services: Results from a national survey. *The Prison Journal*, *87*(1), 58–85. doi:10.1177/0032885506299043

Cunningham, M., Reidy, T., & Sorensen, J. (2016). Wasted resources and gratuitous suffering: The failure of a security rationale for death row. *Psychology, Public Policy, and Law*, *22*(2), 185–199. doi:10.1037/law0000072

Curtin, T. (2007). The continuing problem of America's aging prison population and the search for a cost-effective and socially acceptable means of addressing it. *The University of Illinois Elder Law Journal*, *15*, 473–502.

Death Penalty Information Center. (2017a). *Facts about the death penalty* [Fact sheet]. Retrieved from https://deathpenaltyinfo.org/documents/FactSheet.pdf

Death Penalty Information Center. (2017b). *In lawsuit settlement, Arizona to end automatic solitary confinement for death-row prisoners*. Retrieved from https://deathpenaltyinfo.org/node/6824

Death Penalty Information Center. (2017c). *Louisiana general information*. Retrieved from https://deathpenaltyinfo.org/louisiana-1

Dobuzinskis, A. (2012, August 9). Jared Lee Loughner calls self a "failure" because Gabrielle Giffords survived shooting. *Huffington Post*. Retrieved from www.huffingtonpost.com/ 2012/08/09/jared-lee-loughner-gabrielle-giffords_n_1762131.html

Drury, D. (2013). Fight over Rocky Hill nursing home hinging of definition of "Prisoner": Whether nursing home occupants qualify for Medicare or Medicaid depends on interpretation. *The Hartford Courant*. Retrieved from http://articles.courant.com/2013-03-20/community/hc-rocky-hill-nursing-home-letter-20130320-1_1_nursing-home-doyle-and-guerrera-medicaid-services

Dumont, M., Dumais, A., Briand, C., Cote, G., Lesage, A., & Dubreucq, J. L. (2012). Clinical characteristics of patients deemed to require long-term hospitalization in a civil or forensic psychiatric setting. *International Journal of Forensic Mental Health*, *11*(2), 110–118. doi:10.1080/14999013.2012.690019

Evans, C., Herzog, R., & Tillman, T. (2002). The Louisiana State Penitentiary: Angola prison hospice. *Journal of Palliative Medicine*, *5*(4), 553–558. doi:10.1089/109662102760269797

Hoffman, H., & Dickinson, G. (2011). Characteristics of prison hospice programs in the United States. *American Journal of Hospice and Palliative Medicine*, *28*(4), 245–252. doi:10.1177/1049909110381884

Iverson, T., & Colpean, R. (2009). Designing for special-needs inmates. *Correctional News*. Retrieved from http://correctionalnews.com/2009/07/29/sign-the-times/

Mason, C. (2013, March 4). "We stay free" WKU students, professor provide help to prisoners at Nashville maximum security facility. *The Daily News*. Retrieved from www.bgdailynews.com/news/we-stay-free/article_d888744c-84f2-11e2-bbdd-0019bb2963f4.htm

McCullough, J., & Hasson, B. (2017, October 27). Faces of death row. *The Texas Tribune*. Retrieved from https://apps.texastribune.org/death-row/

McMahon, S. (2013). It doesn't pass the *Sell* Test: Focusing on "the facts of the individual case" in involuntary medication inquiries. *American Criminal Law Review*, *50*, 387–416.

Meier, D., & Bowman, B. (2017). The changing landscape of palliative care. *Journal of the American Society on Aging*, *41*(1), 74–80.

Mississippi Department of Corrections. (2017). *Current death row facts*. Retrieved from: www.mdoc.ms.gov/Death-Row/Pages/Current-Death-Row-Facts.aspx

Montana Department of Corrections. (2013). *Montana State Prison execution technical manual*. Retrieved from https://deathpenaltyinfo.org/documents/MontanaExecutionProtocol.pdf

Morgan, R., Kroner, D., Mills, J., Bauer, R., & Serna, C. (2013). Treating justice involved persons with mental illness: Preliminary evaluation of a comprehensive treatment program. *Criminal Justice and Behavior, 41*(7), 902–916. doi:10.1177/0093854813508553

NAACP Legal Defense and Educational Fund. (2017). *Death Row, USA*. Retrieved from: www.naacpldf.org/death-row-usa

NPR Staff. (2011, October 19). "Serving life": Facing death, inmates find humanity. *NPR*. Retrieved from www.npr.org/2011/10/19/141505983/serving-life-prisoners-find-humanity-in-face-of-death

Salem, L., Crocker, A. G., Charette, Y., Seto, M. C., Nicholls, T. L., & Côté, G. (2015). Supportive housing and forensic patient outcomes. *Law and Human Behavior, 39*(3), 311–320. doi:10.1037/lhb0000112

Satterfield, J. (2017, June 6). Judge sets $1.35M bond for Oak Ridge cocaine dealer accused in double fatality. *USA Today Network*. Retrieved from www.knoxnews.com/story/ news/crime/2017/06/09/state-wants-keep-murder-suspect-behind-bars/380525001/

Schaenman, P., Davies, E., Jordan, R., & Chakaborty, R. (2013). Opportunities for cost savings in corrections without sacrificing service quality: Inmate health care. *Urban Institute*. Retrieved from www.urban.org/research/publication/opportunities-cost-savings-corrections-without-sacrificing-service-quality-inmate-health-care

Stensland, M., & Sanders, S. (2016). Detained and dying: Ethical issues surrounding end-of-life care in prison. *Journal of Social Work in End-of-Life and Palliative Care, 12*(3), 259–276. doi:10.1080/15524256.2016.1200517

Stinchcomb, J., & Leip, L. (2013). Retaining desirable workers in a less-than-desirable workplace: Perspectives of line staff and jail administrators. *Corrections Compendium, 37*(2), 1–8.

Tennessee Department of Correction. (2017). *Lois M. DeBerry Special Needs Facility*. Retrieved from www.tn.gov/correction/article/tdoc-lois-deberry-special-needs-facility

Texas Department of Criminal Justice. (2017). *Active alerts*. Retrieved from http://tdcj.state.tx.us/alert/index.html

Texas Department of State Health Services. (2017). *About Rusk State Hospital*. Retrieved from http://dshs.texas.gov/mhhospitals/RuskSH/RSH_About.shtm

The Inside-Out Center. (2015). *2014 annual report of the Inside-Out Prison Exchange Program*. Retrieved from www.alexandrialevin.com/portfolio-pdfs/AJLevin_InsideOut _AnnualReport.pdf

The University of Mississippi School of Law. (2017). *MacArthur Justice Center students enforce death row settlement* [News release]. Retrieved from https://law.olemiss.edu/macarthur-justice-center-students-visit-parchman/

Tolson, M. (2007, October 1). Prison escapes: Myth and mayhem. *Houston Chronicle*. Retrieved from www.chron.com/news/houston-texas/article/Prison-escapes-myth-and-mayhem-1588714.php

Trigg, L. (2017, April 29). Time drags on at death row, USP Terre Haute. *Tribune Star*. Retrieved from www.tribstar.com/news/local_news/time-drags-on-at-death-row-usp-terre-haute/article_1735f81a-6c88-5c54-b529-367d940c96c6.html

Umaki, T., & Denney, R. (2012). Neurocognitive deficits associated with the Hepatitis C virus among incarcerated men. *The Clinical Neuropsychologist, 27*(3), 426–436. doi:10.1080/13854046.2012.758315

United States Department of Justice. (2017). *Inmate at federal medical facility convicted of* murder, assault [Press release]. Retrieved from www.justice.gov/usao-wdmo/pr/inmate-federal-medical-facility-convicted-murder-assault

Wilemon, T. (2015, July 6). Nashville prison faces "emergency staffing issues." *The Tennessean*. Retrieved from www.tennessean.com/story/news/2015/07/06/nashville-prison-faces-emergency-staffing-issues/29796129/

Winter, M., & Hanlon, S. (2008). Parchman Farm blues: Pushing for prison reforms at Mississippi State Penitentiary. *Litigation, 35*(1), 1–8.

5

SPECIALIZED OR SEGREGATED HOUSING UNITS

Implementing the Principles of Risk, Needs, and Responsivity

Ryan M. Labrecque

> After extensive study, we have concluded that there are occasions when correctional officials have no choice but to segregate inmates from the general population, typically when it is the only way to ensure the safety of inmates, staff, and the public. But as a matter of policy, **we believe strongly this practice should be used rarely, applied fairly, and subjected to reasonable constraints**.
>
> —(U.S. Department of Justice, 2016, p. 1, emphasis in the original)

Introduction

On any given day, there are approximately 6.9 million adult offenders under some form of correctional supervision in the United States, with more than 2.2 million who are incarcerated in the nation's correctional institutions (Kaeble, Glaze, Tsoutis, & Minton, 2016). Of those incarcerated, nearly 1.6 million (or 70%) are held in state and federal prisons, and almost 750,000 (or 30%) are held in local jails (Kaeble et al., 2016). A 2015 Bureau of Justice Statistics special report estimates that at any given time, about 4% of all prisoners (or 64,000) and 3% of all jail inmates (or 22,500) are held in segregated (or restricted) housing units (Beck, 2015). The Bureau of Justice Statistics report further estimates that nearly 20% of all prisoners (or about 320,000) and 18% of all jail inmates (or about 135,000) spend time in these restrictive settings each year (Beck, 2015).

These estimates are not inconsequential, especially when one considers the ethical, legal, and practical consequences associated with the use of segregated confinement. For one, there is an increasing concern that these settings contribute to physiological and psychological damage of their inhabitants (see Haney, 2012; Kupers, 2008; Lovell, 2008). Numerous reports suggest that segregation may be related to a number of negative mental health problems, including anger, anxiety, cognitive impairment, depression, irritability, lethargy, psychosis, social withdrawal, and suicidal ideation (see Andersen, Sestoft, Lillebaek, Gabrielsen, Hemmingsen, & Kramp, 2000; Grassian, 1983; Haney, 2003, Kupers, 2008; Lanes, 2011; Lovell, 2008). Opponents further characterize the practice of segregated or solitary confinement as a "cruel and unusual punishment," citing a lengthy list of objectionable conditions, including a lack of windows, poor lighting, minimal access to opportunities for exercise, restricted interpersonal contact, removal of privileges, denial of other personal items, and limited therapeutic and programmatic services (Grassian, 1983; Haney, 1997; Scharff-Smith, 2006). Finally, the available empirical research indicates segregation does not reduce institutional levels of violence

(Briggs, Sundt, & Castellano, 2003; Huebner, 2003), institutional misconduct (Labrecque, 2015a; Morris, 2016), or postrelease recidivism (Butler, Steiner, Makarios, & Travis, 2016; Lovell, Johnson, & Cain, 2007; Mears & Bales, 2009). In response to these concerns, there is a growing effort to reduce the use of restrictive housing in jails and prisons throughout the United States (see Frost & Monteiro, 2016).

In 2016, the United States Department of Justice released a report that describes guidelines for correctional agencies to consider in transforming the use of segregated confinement. The authors of this report recommend that institutions use a multidisciplinary staff committee to make segregation placement decisions; confine individuals to segregation based on their individual behavior (e.g., misconduct) rather than their affiliations or status (e.g., gang members; pregnant and postpartum inmates; lesbian, gay, bisexual, transgender, intersex, and gender nonconforming inmates); hold inmates in segregation for the least amount of time necessary, and only as a last resort; and restrict its use for vulnerable populations (i.e., individuals with serious mental illnesses and juveniles). It is important to emphasize that this report and its recommendations support the use of offender rehabilitation strategies in restrictive housing units (see also Smith, 2016).

Several jurisdictions have attempted to incorporate offender services within the context of their segregated housing units in an effort to reduce the subsequent institutional misconduct and postrelease recidivism of its former inhabitants (e.g., Ohio Department of Rehabilitation and Correction, Oregon Department of Corrections, and Washington State Department of Corrections). Other correctional organizations (e.g., The Vera Institute of Justice) also are engaged in similar initiatives to implement rehabilitative programs and services in these settings (see Shames, Wilcox, & Subramanian, 2015). Despite these efforts, to date, few empirical evaluations of the effectiveness of these interventions in achieving these goals exist. The gap in this research knowledge is especially concerning given segregation represents the institutions' most severe sanction, and these units are often described as targeting the "worst of the worst" inmates (e.g., escape risks, gang members, predators, high-profile or notorious inmates) and is known as "a prison's prison" (Johnson, 2006; Shalev, 2009) It remains paradoxical that segregation settings are comprised of those inmates who are in the most need of services to support both short-term compliance with institutional rules and long-term behavioral change, yet these units often deny access to such rehabilitative efforts. It is, therefore, not surprising that the research on the effects of segregation has generally revealed that the setting is not effective in achieving these desired outcomes (see Gendreau & Labrecque, 2016).

Moving forward, it is important that meaningful interventions address the reasons for segregation and to help individuals' transition out of restrictive housing (Smith, 2016). To maximize the effectiveness of these strategies in improving inmate behavioral outcomes, this endeavor should integrate knowledge of "what works" more generally in correctional programming (Andrews & Bonta, 2010; Gendreau, 1996; MacKenzie, 2006). In an effort to aid corrections officials in this task, the current chapter takes an in-depth examination of the inmates housed in segregated housing units. The purpose of this chapter is to present a systematic review of the literature that highlights the need for the development of more effective treatment strategies and interventions that are responsive to the specific risks and needs of this population.

As a prelude to this discussion, the chapter begins with a brief review of the use and function of segregation in the United States (for more detailed information see Labrecque, 2016). The second section summarizes the principles of effective correctional intervention to provide a framework for understanding how correctional programming might best be integrated into these restrictive housing units (see also Smith, 2016). The third section provides a systematic review of the empirical segregation literature and describes what is known about the inmates held in restrictive housing. The fourth section discusses how the information gathered from the current review of the literature could be used to construct a more informed program design in segregated housing units, and the final section concludes with a review of the available evidence on current attempts to implement offender programming in segregation settings and makes some closing remarks.

Segregated Housing Units

Segregation—often referred to as solitary confinement—is used in many jails and prisons across the United States, ranging from minimum to supermaximum security level facilities (Browne, Cambier, & Agha, 2011). Unfortunately, there is no universally agreed upon definition of what constitutes segregated confinement (Butler, Griffin, & Johnson, 2013), nor is there consensus about who should be placed in such living units (Labrecque & Smith, 2013; Riveland, 1999). In practice, these settings are referred to by a variety of names, such as security housing units (SHUs), restricted housing units (RHUs), and intensive management units (IMUs) (see, e.g., the 2016 position statement by the *Journal of Correctional Health Care*). Nevertheless, the conditions in segregated housing units— regardless what they are called—often include intense isolation and absolute control (Shalev, 2008). Inmates held in these settings typically remain in a single cell for up to 23 hours of the day and are further subjected to increased cell restrictions and heightened security procedures (Lanes, 2011). Inmate movement is severely restricted, and all personal contact—even with correctional staff—is minimal (Fellner, 2000). Inmates in segregation units are granted limited access to education, vocation, visitation, recreation, and other services that are available to the general prison population (see also the review by Metcalf et al., 2013). Even medical and mental health services are extremely limited for inmates in these units (Butler, Johnson, & Griffin, 2014).

Correctional institutions use segregation for at least three purposes: responding to serious disciplinary misconduct (i.e., disciplinary segregation), ensuring the order of the facility (i.e., administrative segregation), and protecting the inmate from harm (i.e., protective custody) (see Labrecque, 2016). Disciplinary segregation is a form of punishment for inmates who violate institutional rules (Harrington, 2015), and inmates typically refer to it as "the hole" (National Commission on Correctional Health Care, 2017). Departmental regulations often place limits on the amount of time an inmate may be housed in disciplinary segregation depending on the severity of the misconduct (e.g., 30 days or less). However, if the offender is charged with multiple violations, or if one incurs new violations while in segregation, one's length of stay often can be extended (Metcalf et al., 2013).

Administrative segregation is used for managerial purposes, including as a response to an inmate who demonstrates a chronic inability to adjust to the general population, or when it is believed an inmate's presence in the general population may cause a serious disruption to the orderly operation of the institution (Shalev, 2008). In some systems, inmates are not told the reason for their transfer to administrative segregation, and options for release back to the general inmate population are few (Fellner, 2000). For the inmates considered to be a continued threat to safety and security of the facility, administrative segregation can be imposed for extended periods of time, sometimes multiple years (Mears & Bales, 2010). In rarer cases, some inmates are held in administrative segregation until discharge to the community at the expiration of their sentence (Lovell et al., 2007).

Protective custody is used to separate vulnerable inmates from the general inmate population because of personal physical safety concerns (Harrington, 2015). Inmates in need of such separation often include sex offenders, confidential informants, former law enforcement officers, those with serious medical conditions (e.g., traumatic brain injury) that may make them vulnerable to victimization, and those at risk for self-harm (Wormith, Tellier, & Gendreau, 1988). Although inmates in protective custody are segregated for their own protection, restrictions on human contact and programming are often similar to those inmates held in segregation for disciplinary and administrative purposes (Browne et al., 2011).

Although correctional institutions segregate inmates for many reasons, the differences in living arrangements and privileges granted to those residing in these settings appear to be minimal

(Kurki & Morris, 2001). In short, within a particular segregation unit, inmates held for disciplinary, administrative, or protective custody purposes are generally exposed to the same restrictive conditions and treatment by staff. Furthermore, it remains difficult to separate the literature on the various forms of segregation because researchers tend to study "solitary confinement" generally without carefully distinguishing among types of segregation (Frost & Monteiro, 2016). Therefore, this chapter uses the term "segregation" to refer to the general practice of isolation in restrictive housing units (see Box 5.1). It is fully acknowledged, however, that any effective reformation effort aimed at successfully reintegrating inmates back into the general population should make use of the reason for placement (e.g., the strategy for returning a protective custody inmate to the general population might differ from the plan for reintegrating one who is in segregation for disciplinary purposes).

Policy makers and corrections officials often justify the use of segregation because they believe it increases safety and promotes order throughout the prison system (see Mears, 2013; Mears & Castro, 2006). However, among the number of controversial issues surrounding the use of this practice (e.g., violates prisoners' constitutional rights, contributes to psychological problems, costs considerably more than other housing options) is the contention that segregation increases—rather than decreases—criminal behavior, therefore making prisons and communities less safe (Pizarro, Stenius, & Pratt, 2006; Pizarro, Zgoba, & Haugebrook, 2014). Two quantitative syntheses of the effects of restrictive housing literature find that segregation does not appear to reduce subsequent antisocial or criminal behaviors as intended and may even contribute to increases in deviant outcomes (see Morgan et al., 2016).

Given the majority of the inmates in segregation settings will eventually be released back into the general inmate population and ultimately the community, it is important that justice officials undertake efforts to reduce the probability that these inmates will engage in violence and other forms of antisocial behavior. From a theoretical perspective, the rationale for the present use of segregation in the United States appears to be limited to specific deterrence (Gendreau & Goggin, 2013). That is,

Box 5.1 Segregation of Inmates with Traumatic Brain Injuries

Estimates indicate that between 25–87% of jail and prison inmates report suffering an injury to the head or a traumatic brain injury (TBI) (Curtis, 2012). In comparison, only 8.5% in the community report a history of TBI. TBIs are typically classified as mild, moderate, or severe. Those with a severe TBI are frequently placed in administrative segregation for acting out or violating institutional rules. However, these behaviors are symptomatic of the TBI itself. For example, memory deficits, which frequently accompany a TBI, make it difficult for the inmate to remember rules or follow instructions given by correctional staff. Such behavior may be misinterpreted as deliberate defiance on the part of the inmate, resulting in administrative segregation. In addition, slow verbal responses also may be misinterpreted as uncooperative behavior and increase the likelihood of administrative segregation. Individuals with TBIs are more likely to experience irritability, anger, and impulsivity, all of which may result in acting out irrationally or in a physical way. Again, the symptomology of the TBI is viewed as a disciplinary problem rather than part of the medical condition. The isolation inmates experience in administrative segregation often exacerbates symptoms associated with mental illness, developmental disabilities, and medical conditions such as TBIs (CDC, 2007). Correctional administrators and staff should be trained to recognize and screen inmates for TBIs as well as how to communicate effectively with this inmate population. Correctional administrators and staff should be trained to use behavioral interventions rather than administrative segregation with those suffering from TBIs.

correctional administrators simply attempt to suppress unwanted behavior with segregated confinement as a form of punishment to prevent future institutional rule violations or misconduct. This is unfortunate, because the extensive research on deterrence more generally finds little support for its ability to reduce crime or misconduct (see Gendreau, Goggin, Cullen, & Andrews, 2000; Pratt, Cullen, Blevins, Daigle, & Madensen, 2006). It is time for policy makers and corrections officials to consider alternative options for dealing with difficult inmates that can more effectively ensure institutional safety and promote improved behavior. This chapter explores one such strategy for taking an evidence-based approach toward segregation reform, using theoretical and empirical evidence to inform decisions.

The Principles of Effective Correctional Intervention

Correctional rehabilitation is a planned intervention that targets for change some aspect about the offender and his or her situation that is thought to cause criminality (e.g., attitudes, cognitive processes, personality or mental health, social relationship to others, educational and vocational skills, and employment), and its intention is to make the offender less likely to break the law in the future (Cullen & Gendreau, 2000). Rehabilitation does not include interventions or strategies that attempt to reduce crime by simply teaching offenders "crime does not pay" (i.e., those that rely primarily or exclusively on use of punishment and sanctions to modify offender behavior) (Cullen, Jonson, & Nagin, 2011). There are now more than 100 meta-analyses of the correctional rehabilitation literature, which consistently find that offender treatment is effective under certain conditions (McGuire, 2013; Smith, Gendreau, & Swartz, 2009). More specifically, these effective strategies are referred to as the *principles of effective correctional intervention* (see Andrews & Bonta, 2010 for a detailed review), and this model has taken over as the predominant paradigm for offender rehabilitation (see also Gendreau, 1996; Gendreau, French, & Gionet, 2004; and Smith, 2013).

This theory of offender rehabilitation has three main principles: risk, need, and responsivity (RNR) (Andrews, Bonta, & Hoge, 1990). The *risk principle* asserts criminal behavior is predictable when valid risk assessment tools are used and treatment intensity is matched to level of risk, where higher risk offenders receive more services than lower risk offenders. Research consistently demonstrates that higher risk offenders derive the most benefit from treatment (Andrews & Bonta, 2010; Lowenkamp, Latessa, & Holsinger, 2006). In contrast, participating in intensive services can increase the recidivism rates of lower risk offenders because it disrupts their protective factors and exposes them to higher risk peers (see Lowenkamp, Latessa, & Smith, 2006).

The *need principle* suggests that to reduce recidivism, the dynamic (i.e., changeable) crime-producing risk factors—or criminogenic needs—should be the target of intervention. Several meta-analyses demonstrate there are certain need factors that are predictive of criminal behavior (see Andrews & Bonta, 2010; Bonta, Law, & Hanson, 1998; Gendreau, Little, & Goggin, 1996). These criminogenic needs include: (1) antisocial personality pattern (e.g., aggression, hostility, impulsivity, lack of self-control, poor emotion regulation); (2) antisocial attitudes, values, and beliefs; (3) the presence of antisocial peers and associates; (4) substance abuse; (5) problematic circumstances within family/marital relationships; (6) difficulties within the areas of education and employment; and (7) lack of prosocial leisure and recreational activities. Taken together with criminal history, the first four criminogenic needs identified in this list are referred to as the "Big Four" because these covariates are especially robust predictors of antisocial behavior (Andrews & Bonta, 2010). The most effective treatment programs target criminogenic needs and prioritize these top tier predictors. Andrews and Bonta (2010) report that treatment programs targeting criminogenic needs reduce recidivism by 20% more than programs that do not. Moreover, these meta-analyses also find that other factors have weak predictive validities (e.g., low self-esteem, depression, anxiety, and fear of official punishment) and should therefore not be the primary targets for intervention (see Gendreau et al., 1996). It is important to note that the predictors of institutional misconduct are similar to those of postrelease recidivism (see French & Gendreau, 2006). Therefore, the implementation of effective offender programming in segregation settings may not only have an effect on institutional misconduct but also on postrelease recidivism (Smith, 2016).

The *responsivity principle* describes how to best target criminogenic needs with treatment (i.e., general responsivity). Studies consistently find that cognitive-behavioral interventions are the most effective in reducing criminal behavior. Andrews and Bonta (2010) report that programs using cognitive-behavioral interventions reduce recidivism by 23%, which is much better than the 4% reduction achieved by those programs employing other models of offender treatment (e.g., unstructured, nondirective, and "get tough" approaches). In addition, it is also important to match offenders and treatment strategies in a manner that is most conducive to their learning style, motivation, abilities, and strengths (i.e., specific responsivity) (Andrews & Dowden, 2006). For example, behavioral interventions are more effective with offenders with lower IQ scores as opposed to cognitive strategies (Cullen, Gendreau, Jarjoura, & Wright, 1997). To summarize the RNR model, the risk principle indicates *who* should be treated (i.e., higher risk offenders), the need principle indicates *what* should be targeted (i.e., criminogenic needs), and the responsivity principle determines how treatment strategies should be employed (i.e., cognitive-behavioral interventions that are matched to the learning styles and motivation of offenders).

A growing body of research finds that stronger adherence to the principles of risk, need, and responsivity is associated with more dramatic reductions in recidivism. For example, a 26% reduction in recidivism exists in programs that adhere to all three principles, whereas a 2% increase is noted in programs with no adherence to these principles (Andrews & Bonta, 2010). Further, in a meta-analysis of 33 studies, Gendreau and Keyes (2001) report that "appropriate" programs (i.e., those that targeted criminogenic needs) reduced prison misconduct by approximately 17%. Any correctional administrator interested in improving institutional safety should certainly welcome such a sizable reduction in misconduct. Research also shows these principles are effective for a variety of correctional subpopulations, including female offenders, racial and ethnic minorities, youthful offenders, mentally disordered offenders, and violent and sex offenders (Andrews, Dowden, & Rettinger, 2001; Dowden & Andrews, 2000).

Despite the overwhelming support for the principles of effective correctional intervention, many correctional organizations continue to implement strategies that are ineffective—and may even increase recidivism (Latessa, Cullen, & Gendreau, 2002). These ineffective practices—referred to as *correctional quackery*—disregard the evidence of "what works" and instead rely on common sense, personal experience, and conventional wisdom (Latessa et al., 2002, p. 43). Segregated confinement is a form of correctional quackery because the practice reinforces short-term thinking and primitive solutions to the management of criminal offenders when there are administrative policies, clinical prediction protocols, and treatment programs that can limit its use while maintaining institutional safety and promoting improved behavior (i.e., those that adhere to the RNR principles) (Gendreau & Labrecque, 2016). It is suggested here that the RNR framework can provide a blueprint for how interventions and services should be designed and delivered in restrictive housing units (Smith, 2016). To do so, it is important for correctional agencies to understand the characteristics of the offenders in its segregated housing units. This information can be used to develop more informed and effective treatment strategies.

Inmates in Segregated Housing Units

This section includes a systematic review of the empirical segregation literature. It is the intention of this review to provide guidance to correctional administrators in developing policies and practices that support the use of offender treatment in segregated housing units. It is argued here that such efforts at reforming segregation units may not only help reduce the rates of institutional misconduct and postrelease recidivism but also the need for segregation in the first place. The independent variable in this review includes isolation in a restricted housing unit. To be included in this review, a study had to compare the characteristics of inmates held in segregation settings to those residing in the general prison population. Studies with nonoffender samples, studies that took place in noncustody laboratory settings, and studies that did not include a control group of general population offenders were excluded.

Studies were identified through various techniques. First, through a keyword search using multiple databases: Criminal Justice Abstracts, Criminal Justice Periodical Index, Dissertation Abstracts Online, National Criminal Justice Reference Service, PsycINFO, Social Sciences Index, Sociological Abstracts, and SocINDEX. The specific keywords used in this literature search included "administrative segregation," "solitary confinement," "restrictive housing," and "supermax." Second, the author reviewed relevant journals—issue by issue—to locate any additional studies (i.e., *Canadian Journal of Criminology, Crime & Delinquency, Criminal Justice and Behavior, Criminology*, and *The Prison Journal*). Third, a search was conducted in Google Scholar to locate additional state and national reports that were not discovered through the other methods. Fourth, the annual conference programs for the American Society of Criminology (ASC) and the Academy of Criminal Justice Sciences (ACJS) were examined to find the most current and up-to-date research in this area. Finally, the reference lists from each identified study was used to locate additional studies (i.e., ancestry method).

A total of 16 studies were identified for inclusion in this evidence review. Of the studies reviewed there were four types of offender characteristics compared: (1) demographics, (2) criminal history, (3) institutional behavior, and (4) criminogenic needs. The majority of the included studies were produced after 2000 (75%) and published in peer-reviewed journals (63%). The majority of these studies were conducted in North American correctional institutions (88%), and most involved predominantly adult male offenders (75%).

No other single factor is discussed more often in the segregation literature than mental health (see e.g., Haney, 2009; Kupers, 2008; Lovell, 2008; Scharff-Smith, 2006; Toch, 2003). Major mental illness is associated with aggressive institutional misconduct (Walters & Crawford, 2014), and studies from many different jurisdictions report a higher prevalence of severe mental disorders among segregated populations compared to general inmate populations (e.g., Anderson, Sestoft, Lillebaek, Gabrielsen, & Kramp, 1996; Coid et al., 2003; Helmus, Johnson, & Harris, 2014; Hodgins & Côté, 1991, Lovell et al., 2007; O'Keefe, 2007). Inmates in segregated housing units also display higher levels of mental health symptomology and lower levels of psychological functioning (Zinger, Wichmann, & Andrews, 2001). In addition, there appear to be some psychiatric diagnoses and conditions that are particularly overrepresented in restrictive housing units, including schizophrenia, bipolar disorder, adjustment disorder, depressive disorder, and individuals displaying borderline personality characteristics or delusional thoughts (Anderson et al., 2000; Hodgins & Côté, 1991; O'Keefe, Klebe, Stucker, Sturm, & Leggett, 2010). Finally, segregated inmates are more likely to possess the personality characteristics of impulsivity, hostility, argumentativeness, opinionatedness, and low tolerance for frustration compared to nonsegregated inmates (Lanes, 2011; Suedfeld, Ramirez, Deaton, & Baker-Brown, 1982).

Inmates in segregated housing units possess several other distinguishable demographic characteristics when compared to the general inmate population. One of the strongest personal predictors of institutional infractions is younger age (Gonçalves, Gonçalves, Martins, & Dirkzwager, 2014). The research also shows that gender and race are influential in the prediction of misconduct (Gendreau, Goggin, & Law, 1997; Harer & Steffensmeier, 1996; Walters & Crawford, 2013). Specifically, this literature shows that segregated inmates tend to be younger and are more likely to be a male and a member of an ethnic or racial minority (Mears & Bales, 2009; O'Keefe, 2008; Ward, 2009). Criminal history and past institutional behavior has a long-standing and well-documented relationship with offender behavior (Andrews & Bonta, 2010). In this study, segregated inmates were found to have a more violent criminal record (Helmus et al., 2014; Lovell & Johnson, 2004; Mears & Bales, 2009) and greater juvenile justice involvement (Motiuk & Blanchette, 1997; Thompson & Rubenfeld, 2013). Inmates in segregation settings also have a greater history of engaging in institutional misconduct (Beck, 2015; Lovell et al., 2007; Mears & Bales, 2009) and are more likely to have previously served time in segregation (Butler et al., 2016; Helmus et al., 2014; Motiuk & Blanchette, 1997; O'Keefe, 2007; Thompson & Rubenfeld, 2013).

Prison gangs represent substantial problems for prison administrators and officials (Tachiki, 1995). Research shows gang affiliation often increases one's propensity toward violent behavior beyond the individual risk factors generally attributed to youth and prior criminal history (Griffin & Hepburn, 2006) (see Chapter 14 to learn more about prison gangs). Therefore, it is not surprising that inmates in segregated housing units are more likely to be members of gangs (Butler et al., 2016; Helmus et al., 2014; O'Keefe, 2007), especially when one considers that inmates are often placed in segregation simply for having a known or suspected gang affiliation (see Butler et al., 2013). Actuarial risk assessments (i.e., assessment of the risk of reoffending) have been shown to produce the highest correlations with institutional misbehavior (Gendreau et al., 1997). Accordingly, offender risk assessment scores (e.g., Level of Service Inventory-Revised [LSI-R]) are also higher among inmates in segregation compared to those in the general inmate population (O'Keefe, 2008; Smith, 2006; Thompson & Rubenfeld, 2013; Wichmann & Nafekh, 2001).

In addition, inmates in segregation also possess much greater levels of criminogenic needs. In particular, segregated inmates have more antisocial attitudes and antisocial associates (Helmus et al., 2014; Motiuk & Blanchette, 1997; Thompson & Rubenfeld, 2013). Segregated inmates also have less education and more issues around gaining and maintaining employment (Butler et al., 2016; Helmus et al., 2014; O'Keefe, 2007; 2008; Thompson & Rubenfeld, 2013). Further, segregated inmates have greater substance abuse problems (Coid et al., 2003; Helmus et al., 2014; Hodgins & Côté, 1991; Motiuk & Blanchette, 1997; O'Keefe, 2008; Thompson & Rubenfeld, 2013) and more family and /or marital issues (Motiuk & Blanchette, 1997; Thompson & Rubenfeld, 2013). Finally, segregated inmates display less motivation for treatment and have a lower ability to function successfully in the community (Motiuk & Blanchette, 1997; Thompson & Rubenfeld, 2013).

Implementing RNR in Segregation Housing Units

As previously discussed, there is a well-developed literature on "what works" to reduce offender recidivism: *the principles of effective correctional intervention* (see Andrews & Bonta, 2010). Recall, this philosophy suggests correctional strategies are more effective when they target the criminogenic needs (*need principle*) of higher risk offenders (*risk principle*) with cognitive-behavioral based interventions in a manner that is conducive to their learning style, motivation, abilities, and strengths (*responsivity principle*). Similarly, there is a substantial literature on "what doesn't work" to rehabilitate offenders (see e.g., Sherman, Gottfredson, MacKenzie, Eck, Reuter, & Bushway, 1998; Sherman, Farrington, Welsh, & MacKenzie, 2002; MacKenzie, 2006). The RNR framework provides a guide for how services should be designed and delivered in segregation settings. However, the use of this information to inform policies and practices within restrictive housing units is in the early stages of development (Smith, 2016). This section considers how this information on the inmates in segregation settings drawn in the previous section can be used to assist correctional researchers and administrators in better incorporating the principles of effective correctional intervention in segregated housing units.

This evidence review overwhelmingly finds that inmates held in segregated housing units tend to possess those traits that correlate more highly with antisocial behavior compared to those living in the general offender population. That is, inmates in these restrictive housing units are younger, more likely to be an ethnic or racial minority, have a mental disorder, be a member of a gang, have a more extensive criminal history, have a record of prior misbehavior in the institution, and be rated as high risk to recidivate when compared to the inmates from the general prison population at large (see also Labrecque, 2015b). This is important information because it could help corrections officials proactively identify and treat inmates with greater propensities toward being placed in restrictive housing, in an effort to reduce the need for segregation in the first place.

Recently, Helmus et al. (2014) developed a risk assessment scale—the Risk of Administrative Segregation Tool (RAST)—to predict the probability that an inmate is placed in administrative segregation in the federal Canadian prison system. The RAST includes six static items (i.e., age, prior convictions, prior segregation placements, sentence length, criminal versatility, and prior violence) and was found to be predictively valid (see also Helmus, 2015). In other words, it is an accurate predictor of the risk an inmate poses for institutional violations. The creation of this instrument represents a crucial first step in assisting correctional agencies in better identifying the inmates who are at high risk for placement in segregated housing units. Such information is essential for agencies to develop efforts to divert offenders from such placements. Once high-risk inmates are identified, proactive interventions can be implemented to teach the high-risk offenders the skills that might help avoid being placed in segregation.

This review of the evidence is also important because it shows that inmates in segregation not only differ from those in the general population on demographic and criminal history variables but also in terms of their criminogenic needs. Across every domain examined, the inmates in segregation settings possessed much greater levels of criminogenic needs than those in the general inmate population. This finding has significant treatment implications because it means correctional administrators can use this information to help identify which areas to target with intervention in segregation settings in an attempt to reduce subsequent institutional misbehavior and postrelease recidivism. It is critical that this programming has a solid basis in the RNR principles and targets not only the top-tier predictors of criminal behavior (i.e., antisocial personality, antisocial attitudes, and antisocial peers), but also the domains of personal/emotional, family/marital, substance abuse, and motivation for treatment (Labrecque, 2015b).

Finally, this review of the research also reveals that segregated inmates also possess certain characteristics (e.g., mental illness, gang affiliation) that may create significant barriers to the successful treatment of offenders. Likewise, efforts at incorporating offender rehabilitative strategies in these units must consider these responsivity factors to maximize the probability of their intended effects (Gendreau & Thériault, 2011). For example, inmates suffering from mental health disorders are clearly overrepresented in segregated housing units (Haney, 2003). However, as Gendreau and Labrecque (2016) point out, it is conceivable that some of these inmates might prefer an isolated living arrangement compared to the general inmate population. Although the idea of living in isolation may not be appealing to most offenders, it is possible that there are several desirable aspects of the setting for some inmates with serious mental health disorders, such as more predictability, less stimulation, less social interactions, and fewer requirements (Brown, Cromwell, Filion, Dunn, & Tollefson, 2002). Mentally ill inmates may not only request to be placed in restrictive housing settings but might also engage in behaviors (e.g., rule infractions, acting out) that would result in being placed in disciplinary segregation. Regardless, any effort at reforming the use of, and need for, segregation must adequately address the mental health issues and develop more appropriate alternatives for mentally ill offenders (see Chapter 17 for a detailed discussion of offenders with mental illness).

There is much less empirical information available on female inmates in segregation settings when compared to that of males. However, there may be some reasons to consider that treatment interventions and strategies might need to differ in male and female restrictive housing units. Some argue that correctional policies, which often fail to consider female histories of trauma—such as segregation—fail to recognize that female offenders may become more agitated from the experience and increase their antisocial behaviors as a result (Dell, Fillmore, & Kilty, 2009). It has also been suggested that ill-adapted correctional policies borrowed from models designed for males have often failed to produce substantive equality to which female inmates are entitled (Arbour, 1996). It is worth noting that Labrecque, Smith, and Gendreau (2015) found no differences in the effect of disciplinary segregation on measures of inmate misconduct based on gender; however, it remains possible that providing females with gender-informed services in segregation that are more responsive to their unique needs (e.g., trauma, relationships) might result in better outcomes (e.g., less misconduct, less recidivism).

There is also some evidence that suggests inmates who are released directly from segregation settings to the community may have a higher risk for recidivism compared to those who are reintegrated first to the general inmate population (Lovell et al., 2007). Likewise, there have been many recommendations to develop practices that gradually introduce segregated offenders back into the general population setting before they are returned to the community (U.S. Department of Justice, 2016). To maximize the potential for a successful reentry, offenders should be taught while in segregation to observe and manage problem situations that may arise when they are released (Smith, 2016). The rehearsal of alternative, prosocial behaviors can occur in the treatment group setting using relatively simple scenarios but should eventually require the offender to practice the newly acquired skills in increasingly difficult situations (e.g., in the general population setting; Spiegler, 2016). When an inmate demonstrates a positive behavior, he or she should be rewarded to encourage the recurrence of the prosocial behavior (Gendreau, Listwan, Kuhns, & Exum, 2014). Moreover, the institution should help segregated offenders to prepare relapse prevention plans before their release and require their participation in aftercare and booster sessions (Andrews & Bonta, 2010).

Conclusion

There is an assumption made in the use of segregated confinement that the practice will improve safety and security within the prison system and beyond (Mears, 2013). Restrictive housing units have historically focused on the aspects of isolation and deprivation to modify offender behavior (Scharff-Smith, 2006). Previous research, however, calls into question the conventional wisdom that harsh prison conditions function as an effective deterrent (see Listwan, Sullivan, Agnew, Cullen, & Colvin, 2013; and Gendreau & Labrecque, 2016). Alternatively, there is compelling meta-analytic evidence that suggests offender treatment that adheres to the principles of effective intervention reduces institutional misconduct and postrelease recidivism (Andrews & Bonta, 2010; French & Gendreau, 2006).

In light of these findings, significant attention should be devoted to transforming segregation into a more therapeutic environment (Smith & Schweitzer, 2012). As research indicates better outcomes are achieved when corrections agents are able to balance the dual roles of care and control (Skeem, Eno Louden, Polaschek, & Camp, 2007), correctional officers who work in segregated housing settings should receive additional training on mental illness, substance abuse, and criminogenic needs.

Although these tasks will likely be challenging for many jurisdictions, such efforts will create a context that is more conducive to offender rehabilitation. The reformative strategy should consider the aspects of the correctional climate, the availability of correctional programming and rehabilitative services, access to meaningful social interactions and other activities, and access to privileges, as well as the content of interactions between staff and inmates. Not all institutions will embrace this agenda or these recommendations. Some individuals continue to insist that harsh segregation settings are critical for maintaining the safety and security of correctional institutions (see e.g., Angelone, 1999; Gavora, 1996), and some even suggest these units need to become more restrictive in order to improve these outcomes (see Rogers, 1993). It is unlikely widespread progress will happen in reforming segregation settings until correctional officials are confident that these alternative options will not affect institutional safety and security in a negative way (Labrecque, 2016). The success of this progressive movement in making a lasting difference in how inmates are managed in correctional institutions hinges on the extent to which these rehabilitative efforts are evaluated.

There is some evidence that rehabilitative services can be effectively implemented into segregated housing settings and the tentative results appear promising (see e.g., U.S. Department of Justice, 2016; and Shames et al., 2015). Officials from the Washington Department of Corrections indicate their belief that offender programming in segregation units has been highly effective in transitioning inmates to successfully remain in the general prison population in Washington State (Pacholke & Mullins, 2016). In a 2016 study in the Canadian federal prison system, Talisman also found that segregated inmates who participated in a transitional rehabilitative program were twice as likely to complete other programs and were 1.5 times as likely to remain employed while in custody. Further, Butler, Solomon, and Spohn (2015) report that segregated inmates who participated in a cognitive-behavioral program in three prisons in the Midwestern United States had lower rates of drug and alcohol misconduct. Butler et al. (2015) also found the program had no effect on assaults or other nonviolent misconduct, but note that one of the major shortcomings of the evaluation was that many of the participants were released from restrictive housing before being able to complete the program. Finally, in a study in a prison in the Northeastern United States, Pizarro et al. (2014) found that inmates released from the state's supermax segregation setting who participated in rehabilitative services while incarcerated were less likely to recidivate than those who did not participate in such treatment.

Research supports the use of offender rehabilitative strategies within restrictive housing units. However, the research is methodologically weak and in short supply. This gap in knowledge about the effect of programming in segregated housing is deeply concerning, especially considering the empirical evidence on the effects of segregation finds that it fails to reduce institutional misbehavior and postrelease recidivism. From a pragmatic perspective, it is no longer defensible to support a correctional practice that is ineffective in achieving these desirable effects. As correctional agencies continue to work on transforming the use of segregation, it would be wise for administrators and policy makers to consider incorporating the principles of effective correctional intervention within the context of these units.

References

Andersen, H. S., Sestoft, D., Lillebaek, T. Gabrielsen, G., Hemmingsen, R., & Kramp, P. (2000). A longitudinal study of prisoners on remand: Psychiatric prevalence, incidence and psychopathology in solitary vs. non-solitary confinement. *Acta Psychiatrica Scandinavica, 102*, 19–25. doi:10.1034/j.1600–0447.2000.102001019.x

Andersen, H. S., Sestoft, D., Lillebaek, T., Gabrielsen, G., & Kramp, P. (1996). Prevalence of ICD-10 psychiatric morbidity in random samples of prisoners on remand. *International Journal of Law and Psychiatry, 19*(1), 61–74. doi:10.1016/0160–2527(95)00025–9

Andrews, D. A., & Bonta, J. (2010). *The psychology of criminal conduct* (5th ed.). Cincinnati, OH: Anderson Publishing.

Andrews, D. A., Bonta, J., & Hoge, R. D. (1990). Classification for effective rehabilitation: Rediscovering psychology. *Criminal Justice and Behavior, 17*(1), 19–52. doi:10.1177/0093854890017001004

Andrews, D. A., & Dowden, C. (2006). Risk principle of case classification in correctional treatment: A meta-analytic investigation. *International Journal of Offender Therapy and Comparative Criminology, 50*(1), 88–100. doi:10.1177/0306624X05282556

Andrews, D. A., Dowden, C., & Rettinger, J. (2001). Special populations within corrections. In J. A. Winterdyk (Ed.), *Corrections in Canada: Social reactions to crime* (pp. 170–212). Toronto, Ontario: Prentice Hall.

Angelone, R. (1999). *Why "super-max" prisons work.* Richmond, VA: Virginia Correctional Security Report.

Arbour, L. (1996). *Commission of inquiry into certain events at the Prison for Women in Kingston.* Ottawa, ON: Public Works and Government Services of Canada.

Beck, A. J. (2015). *Use of restrictive housing in U.S. prisons and jails, 2011–12.* Washington, DC: U.S. Department of Justice, Bureau of Justice Statistics.

Bonta, J., Law, M., & Hanson, K. (1998). The prediction of criminal and violent recidivism among mentally disordered offenders: A meta-analysis. *Psychological Bulletin, 123*(2), 123–142. doi:10.1037/0033-2909.123.2.123

Briggs, C. S., Sundt, J. L., & Castellano, T. C. (2003). The effect of supermaximum security prisons on aggregate levels of institutional violence. *Criminology, 41*(4), 1341–1376. doi:10.1111/j.1745-9125.2003tb01022.x
Brown, C., Cromwell, R. L., Filion, D., Dunn, W., & Tollefson, N. (2002). Sensory processing in schizophrenia: Missing and avoiding information. *Schizophrenia Research, 55*(1–2), 187–195. doi:10.1016/S0920-9964(01)00255-9
Browne, A., Cambier, A., & Agha, S. (2011). Prisons within prisons: The use of segregation in the United States. *Federal Sentencing Reporter, 24*(1), 46–49. doi:10.1525/fsr.2011.24.1.46
Butler, H. D., Griffin III, O. H., & Johnson, W. W. (2013). What makes you the "worst of the worst?": An examination of state policies defining supermaximum confinement. *Criminal Justice Policy Review, 24*(6), 676–694. doi:10.1177/0887403412465715
Butler, H. D., Johnson, W. W., & Griffin III, O. H. (2014). The treatment of the mentally ill in supermax facilities: An evaluation of state supermax policies. *Criminal Justice and Behavior, 41*(1), 1338–1353. doi:10.1177/0093854814535082
Butler, H. D., Solomon, S., & Spohn, R. (2015, November). *Programming in restrictive housing: An evaluation of the transformation project.* Presented at the annual meeting of the American Society of Criminology in Washington, DC.
Butler, H. D., Steiner, B., Makarios, M. D., & Travis, L. F. (2016). Assessing the effects of exposure to supermax confinement on offender post-release behaviors. *The Prison Journal, 97*(3), 275–295. doi:10.1177/0032885517703925
Centers for Disease Control and Prevention. (2007). *Traumatic brain injury in prisons and jails: An unrecognized problem.* Washington, DC: Centers for Disease Control and Prevention.
Coid, J., Petruckevitch, A., Bebbington, P., Jenkins, R., Brugha, T., Lewis, G., . . . Singleton, N. (2003). Psychiatric morbidity in prisoners and solitary cellular confinement, I: Disciplinary segregation. *The Journal of Forensic Psychiatry & Psychology, 14*(2), 298–319. doi:10.1080/1478994031000095510
Cullen, F. T., & Gendreau, P. (2000). Assessing correctional rehabilitation: Policy, practice, and prospects. In J. Horney (Ed.), *Criminal Justice 2000, Volume 3: Policies, processes, and decisions of the criminal justice system* (pp. 109–175). Washington, DC: National Institute of Justice.
Cullen, F. T., Gendreau, P., Jarjoura, G. R., & Wright, J. P. (1997). Crime and the bell curve: lessons from intelligent criminology. *Crime & Delinquency, 43*(4), 387–411. doi:10.1177/0011128797043004001
Cullen, F. T., Jonson, C. J., & Nagin, D. S. (2011). Prisons do not reduce recidivism: The high costs of ignoring science. *The Prison Journal, 91*(3), 48S–65S. doi:10.1177/0032885511415224
Curtis, B. B. (2012). Traumatic brain injury: How to assess and manage an often-hidden condition. *Correct Care, 26*(2), 10–12. Chicago, IL: National Commission on Correctional Health Care.
Dell, C. A., Fillmore, C. J., & Kilty, J. M. (2009). Looking back 10 years after the Arbour inquiry: Ideology, policy, practice, and the federal female prisoner. *The Prison Journal, 89*(3), 286–308. doi:10.1177/0032885509339506
Dowden, C., & Andrews, D. A. (2000). Effective correctional treatment and violent reoffending: A meta-analysis. *Canadian Journal of Criminology, 42*(4), 449–467.
Fellner, J. (2000). *Out of sight: Supermaximum security confinement in the United States.* New York, NY: Human Rights Watch.
French, S., & Gendreau, P. (2006). Reducing prison misconducts: What works! *Criminal Justice and Behavior, 33*(2), 185–218. doi:10.1177/0093854805284406
Frost, N. A., & Monteiro, C. E. (2016). *Administrative segregation in prison.* Washington, DC: National Institute of Justice.
Gavora, J. (1996, August 25). Violent offenders should be placed in supermax prisons. *The Washington Post.* Retrieved from www.washingtonpost.com
Gendreau, P. (1996). The principles of effective intervention with offenders. In A. T. Harland (Ed.), *Choosing correctional options that work: Defining the demand and evaluating the supply* (pp. 117–130). Thousand Oaks, CA: Sage.
Gendreau, P., French, S. A., & Gionet, A. (2004). What works (what doesn't work): The principles of effective correctional treatment. *Journal of Community Corrections, 13*, 4–6, 27–30. doi:10.1177/0093854809338545
Gendreau, P., & Goggin, C. E. (2013). Practicing psychology in correctional settings. In I. B. Weiner & R. K. Otto (Eds.), *The handbook of forensic psychology* (4th ed.). Hoboken, NJ: John Wiley & Sons.
Gendreau, P., Goggin, C. E., Cullen, F. T., & Andrews, D. A. (2000). The effects of community sanctions and incarceration on recidivism. *Forum on Corrections Research, 12*, 10–13.
Gendreau, P., Goggin, C. E., & Law, M. A. (1997). Predicting prison misconducts. *Criminal Justice and Behavior, 24*(4), 414–431. doi:10.1177/0093854897024004002
Gendreau, P., & Keyes, D. (2001). Making prisons safer and more humane environments. *Canadian Journal of Criminology, 43*(1), 123–130.
Gendreau, P., & Labrecque, R. M. (2016). The effects of administrative segregation: A lesson in knowledge cumulation. In J. Wooldredge & P. Smith (Eds.), *Oxford handbook on prisons and imprisonment.* Oxford, UK: Oxford University Press.

Gendreau, P., Listwan, S. J., Kuhns, J. B., & Exum, M. L. (2014). Making prisoners accountable: Are contingency management programs the answer? *Criminal Justice and Behavior, 41*(9), 1079–1102. doi:10.1177/0093854814540288

Gendreau, P., Little, T., & Goggin, C. (1996). A meta-analysis of the predictors of adult offender recidivism: What works! *Criminology, 34*(4), 575–608. doi:10.1111/j.1745-9125.1996.tb01220.x

Gendreau, P., & Thériault, Y. (2011). *Bibliotherapy for cynics revisited: Commentary on a one-year longitudinal study of the psychological effects of administrative segregation.* Washington, DC: National Institute of Corrections.

Gonçalves, L. C., Gonçalves, R. A., Martins, C., & Dirkzwager, A. J. E. (2014). Predicting infractions and health care utilization in prison: A meta-analysis. *Criminal Justice and Behavior, 41*(8), 921–942. doi:10.1177/0093854814524402

Grassian, S. (1983). Psychopathological effects of solitary confinement. *American Journal of Psychiatry, 140*(11), 1450–1454. doi:10.1176/ajp.140.11.1450

Griffin, M. L., & Hepburn, J. R. (2006). The effect of gang affiliation on violent misconduct among inmates during the early years of confinement. *Criminal Justice and Behavior, 33*(4), 419–466. doi:10.1177/0093854806288038

Haney, C. (1997). Psychology and the limits of prison pain: Confronting the coming crisis of the eighth amendment law. *Psychology, Public Policy, and Law, 3*(4), 499–588. doi:10.1037/1076-8971.3.4.499

Haney, C. (2003). Mental health issues in long-term solitary and "supermax" confinement. *Crime & Delinquency, 49*(1), 124–156. doi:10.1177/0011128702239239

Haney, C. (2009). The social psychology of isolation: Why solitary confinement is psychologically harmful. *Prison Service Journal, 181*, 12–20.

Haney, C. (2012). *Testimony of Professor Craig Haney to the Senate Judiciary Subcommittee on the Constitution, civil rights, and human rights hearing on solitary confinement.* Retrieved from www.judiciary.senate.gov

Harer, M. D., & Steffensmeier, D. J. (1996). Race and prison violence. *Criminology, 34*(3), 323–355. doi:10.1111/j.1745-9125.1996.tb01210.x

Harrington, M. P. (2015). Methodological challenges to the study and understanding of solitary confinement. *Federal Probation, 79*(3), 45–47.

Helmus, L. (2015). *Developing and validating a risk assessment scale to predict inmate placements in administrative segregation in the Correctional Service of Canada.* Unpublished Ph.D. dissertation, Carleton University, Ottawa, Ontario.

Helmus, L., Johnson, S., & Harris, A. J. R. (2014). *Developing the Risk of Administrative Segregation Tool (RAST) to predict admissions to segregation.* Ottawa, ON: Solicitor General Canada.

Hodgins, S., & Côté, G. (1991). The mental health of penitentiary inmates in isolation. *Canadian Journal of Criminology, 33*, 175–182.

Huebner, B. M. (2003). Administrative determinants of inmate violence: A multilevel analysis. *Journal of Criminal Justice, 31*(2), 107–117. doi:10.1016/S0047-2352(02)00218-0

Johnson, D. E. (2006, June 6). *The new asylums.* [Web log comment]. Retrieved from www.davemsw.com/blog/the_new_asylums/

Kaeble, D., Glaze, L., Tsoutis, A., & Minton, T. (2016). *Correctional populations in the United States, 2014.* Washington, DC: U.S. Department of Justice, Bureau of Justice Statistics.

Kupers, T. A. (2008). What to do with the survivors? Coping with the long-term effects of isolated confinement. *Criminal Justice and Behavior, 35*(8), 1005–1016. doi:10.1177/0093854808318591

Kurki, L., & Morris, N. (2001). The purposes, practices, and problems of supermax prisons. *Crime and Justice, 28*, 385–424. doi:10.1086/652214

Labrecque, R. M. (2015a). *The effect of solitary confinement on institutional misconduct: A longitudinal evaluation.* Washington, DC: National Institute of Justice.

Labrecque, R. M. (2015b, October). *Who ends up in administrative segregation? Predictors and other characteristics.* Paper presented at the National Institute of Justice meeting on the use of administrative segregation in the United States in Arlington, VA.

Labrecque, R. M. (2016). *The use of administrative segregation and its function in the institutional setting.* Washington, DC: National Institute of Justice.

Labrecque, R. M., & Smith, P. (2013). Advancing the study of solitary confinement. In J. Fuhrman & S. Baier (Eds.), *Prisons and prison systems: Practices, types, and challenges* (pp. 57–70). Hauppauge, NY: Nova Science Publishers.

Labrecque, R. M., Smith, P., & Gendreau, P. (2015, November). *Gender-based differences in the effects of solitary confinement on institutional behavior.* Presented at the annual meeting of the American Society of Criminology in Washington, DC.

Lanes, E. C. (2011). Are the "worst of the worst" self-injurious prisoners more likely to end up in long-term maximum-security administrative segregation? *International Journal of Offender Therapy and Comparative Criminology, 55*(7), 1034–1050. doi:10.1177/0306624X10378494

Latessa, E. J., Cullen, F. T., & Gendreau, P. (2002). Beyond correctional quackery: Professionalism and the possibility of effective treatment. *Federal Probation*, *66*(2), 43–49.

Listwan, S. J., Sullivan, C. J., Agnew, R., Cullen, F. T., & Colvin, M. (2013). The pains of imprisonment revisited: The impact of strain on inmate recidivism. *Justice Quarterly*, *30*(1), 144–168. doi:10.1080/07418825.2011.597772

Lovell, D. (2008). Patterns of disturbed behavior in a supermax prison. *Criminal Justice and Behavior*, *35*(8), 985–1004. doi:10.1177/0093854808318584

Lovell, D., & Johnson L. C. (2004). *Felony and violent recidivism among supermax prison inmates in Washington State: A pilot study*. Seattle, WA: University of Washington.

Lovell, D., Johnson, L. C., & Cain, K. C. (2007). Recidivism of supermax prisoners in Washington State. *Crime & Delinquency*, *53*(4), 633–656. doi:10.1177/0011128706296466

Lowenkamp, C. T., Latessa, E. J., & Holsinger, A. M. (2006). The risk principle in action: What have we learned from 13,676 offenders and 97 correctional programs? *Crime & Delinquency*, *52*(1), 77–93. doi:10.1177/0011128705281747

Lowenkamp, C. T., Latessa, E. J., & Smith, P. (2006). Does correctional program quality really matter? The impact of adhering to the principles of effective intervention. *Criminology and Public Policy*, *5*(3), 575–594. doi:10.1111/j.1745-9133.2006.00388.x

MacKenzie, D. L. (2006). *What works in corrections: Reducing the criminal activities of offenders and delinquents*. New York, NY: Cambridge University Press.

McGuire, J. (2013). "What works" to reduce reoffending: 18 years on. In L. A. Craig, L. Dixon, & T. A Gagnon (Eds.), *What works in offender rehabilitation: An evidence-based approach to assessment and treatment* (pp. 20–49). Chichester, UK: Wiley-Blackwell.

Mears, D. P. (2013). Supermax prisons: The policy and the evidence. *Criminology and Public Policy*, *12*(4), 681–719. doi:10.1111/1745-9133.12031

Mears, D. P., & Bales, W. D. (2009). Supermax incarceration and recidivism. *Criminology*, *47*(4), 1131–1166. doi:10.1111/j.1745-9125.2009.00171.x

Mears, D. P., & Bales, W. D. (2010). Supermax housing: Placement, duration, and time to re-entry. *Journal of Criminal Justice*, *38*(4), 545–554. doi:10.1016/j.jcrimjus.2010.04.025

Mears, D. P., & Castro, J. L. (2006). Wardens' views on the wisdom of supermax prisons. *Crime & Delinquency*, *52*(3), 398–431. doi:10.1177/0011128705279484

Metcalf, H., Morgan, J., Oliker-Friedland, S., Resnik, J., Spiegel, J., Tae, H., . . . Holbrook, B. (2013). *Administrative segregation, degrees of isolation, and incarceration: A national overview of state and federal correctional policies*. New Haven, CT: Liman Public Interest Program.

Morgan, R. D., Gendreau, P., Smith, P., Gray, A. L., Labrecque, R. M., MacLean, N., Van Horn, S., . . . Mills, J. F. (2016). Quantitative syntheses of the effects of administrative segregation on inmates' well-being. *Psychology, Public Policy, and the Law*. Advance on-line publication.

Morris, R. G. (2016). Exploring the effect of exposure to short-term solitary confinement among violent prison inmates. *Journal of Quantitative Criminology*, *32*(1), 1–22. doi:10.1007/s10940-015-9250-0

Motiuk, L. L., & Blanchette, K. (1997). Characteristics of administratively segregated offenders in federal corrections. *Canadian Journal of Criminology*, *43*(1), 131–143.

National Commission on Correctional Health Care. (2017). *Segregated inmates*. Chicago, IL: National Commission on Correctional Health Care. Retrieved from www.ncchc.org/spotlight-on-the-standards-26-2

O'Keefe, M. L. (2007). Administrative segregation for mentally ill Inmates. *Journal of Offender Rehabilitation*, *45*(1/2), 149–165. doi:10.1300/J076v45n01_11

O'Keefe, M. L. (2008). Administrative segregation from within: A corrections perspective. *The Prison Journal*, *88*(1), 123–143. doi:10.1177/0032885507310999

O'Keefe, M. L., Klebe, K. J., Stucker, A., Sturm, K., & Leggett, W. (2010). *One year longitudinal study of the psychological effects of administrative segregation*. Colorado Springs, CO: Colorado Department of Corrections.

Pacholke, D., & Mullins, S. F. (2016). *More than emptying beds: A systems approach to segregation reform*. Washington, DC: U.S. Department of Justice, Bureau of Justice Assistance.

Pizarro, J. M., Stenius, V. M. K., & Pratt, T. C. (2006). Supermax prisons: Myths, realities, and the politics of punishment in American society. *Criminal Justice Policy Review*, *17*(1), 6–21. doi:10.1177/0887403405275015

Pizarro, J. M., Zgoba, K. M., & Haugebrook, S. (2014). Supermax and recidivism: An examination of the recidivism covariates among a sample of supermax ex-inmates. *The Prison Journal*, *94*(2), 180–197. doi:10.1177/0032885514524697

Pratt, T. C., Cullen, F. T., Blevins, K. R., Daigle, L. E., & Madensen, T. D. (2006). The empirical status of deterrence theory: A meta-analysis. In F. T. Cullen, J. P. Wright, & K. R. Blevins (Eds.), *Taking stock: The status of criminological theory—advances in criminological theory* (pp. 367–395). New Brunswick, NJ: Transaction Publishers.

Riveland, C. (1999). *Supermax prisons: Overview and general considerations*. Washington, DC: National Institute of Corrections.
Rogers, R. (1993). Solitary confinement. *International Journal of Offender Therapy and Comparative Criminology, 37*(4), 339–349. doi:10.1177/0306624X9303700407
Scharff-Smith, P. (2006). The effects of solitary confinement on prison inmates: A brief history and review of the literature. *Crime and Justice, 34*(1), 441–528. doi:10.1086/500626
Shalev, S. (2008). *A sourcebook on solitary confinement*. London, UK: Mannheim Centre for Criminology.
Shalev, S. (2009). *Supermax: Controlling risk through solitary confinement*. Portland, OR: Willan Publishing.
Shames, A., Wilcox, J., & Subramanian, R. (2015). *Solitary confinement: Common misconceptions and emerging safe alternatives*. New York, NY: VERA Institute of Justice.
Sherman, L. W., Gottfredson, D. C., MacKenzie, D. L., Eck, J., Reuter, P., & Bushway, S. D. (1998). *Preventing crime: What works, what doesn't, what's promising*. Washington, DC: U.S. Department of Justice, National Institute of Justice.
Sherman, L. W., Farrington, D. P., Welsh, B. C., & MacKenzie, D. L. (2002). *Evidence-based crime prevention*. New York, NY: Routledge.
Skeem, J. L., Eno Louden, J., Polaschek, D., & Camp, J. (2007). Assessing relationship quality in mandated community treatment: Blending care with control. *Psychological Assessment, 19*(4), 397–410. doi:10.1037/1040-3590.19.4.397
Smith, P. (2006). *The effects of incarceration on recidivism: A longitudinal examination of program participation and institutional adjustment in federally sentenced adult male offenders*. Unpublished Ph.D. dissertation, University of New Brunswick, Canada.
Smith, P. (2013). The psychology of criminal conduct. In F. T. Cullen & P. Wilcox (Eds.), *The Oxford handbook of criminological theory* (pp. 69–88). New York: Oxford University Press.
Smith, P. (2016). *Toward an understanding of "what works" in segregation: Implementing correctional programming and reentry-focused services in restrictive housing units*. Washington, DC: National Institute of Justice.
Smith, P., Gendreau, P., & Swartz, K. (2009). Validating the principles of effective intervention: A systematic review of the contributions of meta-analysis in the field of corrections. *Victims and Offenders, 4*(2), 148–169. doi:10.1080/15564880802612581
Smith, P., & Schweitzer, M. (2012). The therapeutic prison. *Journal of Contemporary Criminal Justice, 28*(1), 7–22. doi:10.1177/1043986211432201
Spiegler, M. D. (2016). *Contemporary behavior therapy* (6th ed.). Boston, MA: Cengage Learning.
Suedfeld, P., Ramirez, C., Deaton, J., & Baker-Brown, G. (1982). Reactions and attributes of prisoners in solitary confinement. *Criminal Justice and Behavior, 9*(3), 303–340. doi:10.1177/0093854882009003004
Tachiki, S. N. (1995). Indeterminate sentences in supermax prisons based upon alleged gang affiliations: A reexamination of procedural protection and a proposal for greater procedural requirements. *California Law Review, 83*(4), 1117–1149. doi:10.15779/Z386T6P
Thompson, J., & Rubenfeld, S. (2013). *A profile of women in segregation* (Research report R-320). Ottawa, Ontario: Correctional Service of Canada.
Toch, H. (2003). The contemporary relevance of early experiments with supermax reform. *The Prison Journal, 83*(2), 221–228. doi:10.1177/0032885503254414
United States Department of Justice. (2016). *Report and recommendations concerning the use of restrictive housing: Final report*. Washington, DC: U.S. Department of Justice.
Walters, G. D., & Crawford, G. (2013). In and out of prison: Do importation factors predict all forms of misconduct or just the more serious ones? *Journal of Crime and Justice, 41*(6), 407–413. doi:10.1016/j.jcrimjus.2013.08.001
Walters, G. D., & Crawford, G. (2014). Major mental illness and violence history as predictors of institutional misconduct and recidivism: Main and interaction effects. *Law and Human Behavior, 38*(3), 238–247. doi:10.1037/lhb0000058
Ward, D. A. (2009). *Alcatraz: The gangster years*. Berkeley, CA: University of California Press.
Wichmann, C., & Nafekh, M. (2001). Moderating segregation as a means to reintegration. *Forum on Corrections Research, 13*, 31–33.
Wormith, J. S., Tellier, M. C., & Gendreau P. (1988). Characteristics of protective custody offenders in a provincial correctional center. *Canadian Journal of Criminology, 30*, 39–58.
Zinger, I., Wichmann, C., & Andrews, D. A. (2001). The psychological effects of 60 days in administrative segregation. *Canadian Journal of Criminology, 43*(1), 47–83.

6

ADMINISTRATIVE AND TREATMENT ISSUES WHEN JAILING OFFENDERS WITH SPECIAL NEEDS

Negotiating Limited Resources

Jennifer Guriel Myers

> Ensuring that the protection of the human rights of vulnerable prisoners is an integral part of management is not only a requirement of universally accepted standards, but is also the basis of creating an environment that is safe and healthy and a system that works efficiently on the basis of fairness and justice.
>
> —(United Nations Office on Drugs and Crime, 2009, p. 13)

Introduction

The notion of separating those who have violated the rules or laws from the populace has been a method of social control since colonial settlers came to America. The Order of the Plymouth and the Massachusetts Bay Colony Courts ordered the creation of the oldest wooden jail in the Unites States. Barnstable's Old Gaol (pronounced "jail"), now recognized on the National Register of Historic Places, is located in Barnstable, Massachusetts. This wooden room, thought to be built around 1690, was originally attached to a barn and was designed to hold up to six people. The first jail designed with an individual cell structure in the United States was the Walnut Street Jail, opened in Philadelphia in 1776 on the eve of the American Revolution. When the jail, located conspicuously behind what is now known as Independence Hall, opened, prisoners of all ages, races, and genders were housed together in deplorable conditions. Many were transferred from Philadelphia's High Street Jail, constructed around 1718, in response to the adoption of several English laws. In 1790, a new cellblock was added to the Walnut Street Jail. This area, characterized by cells specifically designed to house one prisoner while restricting communication between cells, was the first correctional facility labeled as a penitentiary (from the Latin, *paenitentia*, meaning repentance or remorse) (Seiter, 2014).

The cells of the Walnut Street penitentiary had 9-foot ceilings with one small window, located out of reach and with the capability to open only for airflow, preventing any visual connection to the outside world. Penitentiary inmates were confined to their cells virtually all of the time with little to no access to reading material and little human contact. Eastern State Penitentiary replaced the Walnut Street Jail in 1829 (Seiter, 2014).

Ironically, the Walnut Street Jail was conceptually aimed at implementing a more humane method of punishing those who had committed crimes less serious than homicide. William Penn, fueled by his Quaker values of penitence and submission, inspired the creation and implementation of new laws and correctional facilities even years after his death in 1718. He was outspoken in his position against capital punishment and had once said, "Men must be governed by God or they will be ruled by tyrants" (Higgs, 2010, p. 1). This philosophy was clearly emphasized in the early Philadelphia correctional facilities, as the focus was on solitary confinement, intended to allow inmates time to pray and repent from their sins. The Quakers and other proponents of the Pennsylvania System believed that if offenders were given time to reflect on their behavior, without the distractions of work or communication, then they would come to recognize the wrongfulness of their criminal behavior and offer repentance. This philosophy of punishment became known as the Pennsylvania System.

As jails grew in popularity and the number of offenders requiring confinement multiplied, it became increasingly difficult to provide an environment of solitude. Minton, Ginder, Brumbaugh, Smiley-McDonald, and Rohloff (2015) outline how recent decades have shown significant growth (not withstanding some recent declines from almost emergent legislation targeted toward overcrowding) in both jail and prison populations (Flatow, 2014; Schlanger, 2013). This has been influenced by several factors. First, mandatory minimum sentences, particularly for drug offenses, have led to a serious increase in the incarceration of female offenders and the influx of those who are actively addicted (Pratt, 2009). The political landscape is considered by many to be a contributing factor to the rise in correctional populations via a competitive wrangling of both conservative and liberal politicians (see e.g., Pratt, 2009; Schept, 2013; Wright & Delisi, 2016). Some scholars theorize that liberals have been compelled to support harshly punitive strategies or to endorse carceral growth and expansion in an attempt to keep up with the largely conservative ideas of mandatory minimum sentencing and "get tough on crime" strategies in general (Alexander, 2010; Feldman, Schiraldi, & Ziedenberg, 2001; Gottschalk, 2006). More recently, the Obama administration was both praised and criticized for efforts at reducing jail and prison populations (Robinson, 2015), while private prison stocks have soared under the Trump administration (Sarhan, 2017).

Jails Today

Jail administrators today continue to struggle with many of the same challenges of the early twentieth-century jails. For example, jails tend to be overcrowded, poorly staffed, and lacking in resources to provide adequate medical and mental health care (Ruddell & Mays, 2007). Thus, it seems little meaningful progress has been achieved through jail reform, and the emphasis on improving most American jails has failed to be a political priority. On a more positive note, correctional administrators and social justice advocates continue to push for penal reform, and it is the centerpiece of ongoing discussions about improving correctional policies and practices.

The United States has the highest rate of incarceration among all developed countries, with over 2.2 million adults in jails and prisons (Daniel, 2007). In 2014, the nearly 3,000 local jails located across the United States processed an estimated 11.4 million bookings and held an average of 744,600 inmates per day (Minton & Zeng, 2016). Between 2011 and 2012, there was a reported 131% turnover rate for jail inmates, which means more people come in and out of jail facilities in one day than the standing population (Blades, 2015; DeHart, Lynch, Belknap, Dass-Brailsford, & Green, 2013). The transient nature of jail populations raises several concerns for inmates and staff. For example, the rapid turnover of jail inmates makes keeping track of persons and property a challenge. Whereas prison staff have the luxury of getting to know the behaviors and attitudes of the offenders they interact with every day, jail staff must always be prepared for the unpredictable, by virtue of having little to no information about the arriving inmates. Even those who are housed in a jail setting for a longer period are unlikely to be consistently in contact with the same staff, so observations about inmate behavioral patterns are difficult. Therefore, correctional staff should be particularly vigilant in where they house incoming inmates, because some may be disruptive or violent. Many prisons have a graduated system of classifying inmates, and new arrivals are usually placed in segregated behavioral units. The inmates, through good behavior, can earn their way into general population, where they receive more privileges.

As you have learned throughout this text, prisons are correctional facilities designed for long-term stays by offenders who have committed serious crimes. Typically, those housed in prison have committed a felony offense or offenses and have been sentenced to a term of greater than one year. Prisons usually hold those who have already been adjudicated. Prisons are most commonly under the control of the state or federal government, although private prison facilities have been increasingly utilized in the past 25 years (Mumford, Schanzenbach, & Nunn, 2016). Although these facilities have inmate movement and turnover because of transfers and new admissions, the average stay of an inmate in prison is generally a year or more. As a result, prison populations tend to be far more stable than the dynamic migration seen regularly in jails.

Jails or detention facilities, on the other hand, are institutions designated for shorter-term stays, theoretically housing inmates serving sentences of less than one year. Ironically, jails are arguably the least studied and most misunderstood segment of the criminal justice system, and yet this segment serves as a point of contact for about five times as many individuals as all other correctional components combined (Seiter, 2014). Jail facilities are correctional centers, usually under county or local jurisdictional control, which may house a wide variety of heterogeneous offenders. At the federal level, there are no jails; instead, detention centers serve the purpose of housing a population consistent with what would be found in a jail (Federal Bureau of Prisons Clinical Practice Guidelines, 2014). However, federal inmates are frequently housed at local jails that meet certain Federal Bureau of Prison (FBOP) guidelines. However, jails usually receive offenders directly from the community. Consequently, there is a far greater likelihood that someone coming to jail may be intoxicated, soiled or disheveled, sick or injured, or cognitively or otherwise impaired. Those coming to jail are generally unprepared and may experience shock or disbelief, feel overwhelmed, panicked, or embarrassed by their arrest.

The inmates housed in jails typically fall into one of four categories. Jail inmates may be newly arrested individuals, awaiting arraignment; those on a pretrial detention status; those who have committed misdemeanor offenses and been sentenced to less than one year of incarceration; and those on a holdover status, pending trial or court proceeding or transfer from one facility to another. This latter group may include individuals who have allegedly violated probation, parole, or bail conditions, those who are absconding from court-ordered programs or other community placements, undocumented immigrants, or juveniles who are awaiting transfer to juvenile facilities or adult state prisons.

Classification and Housing

While prison facilities are usually designed for one specific security level (maximum, medium, or minimum), jails and detention facilities must house inmates of all security levels (Seiter, 2014). For example, jail populations may include offenders facing murder charges being housed with a first-time offender charged with driving under the influence (DUI). The mixing of more serious, possibly violent offenders, with first-time and/or nonviolent detainees can create stress and tension for both offenders and staff. Additionally, most jails are designed to accommodate all genders, presenting unique needs of a coed population that would typically not be found in a prison setting.

Housing conditions in jails and detention facilities also vary widely. Some involve large, multiperson holding cells, others dormitory-type units, and many also have more traditional two-person cells. While most jails have some sort of increased supervision cell(s), suitable for monitoring someone in crisis, for example, most have limited spaces, and some are nonexistent. It is imperative for jails to have an area suitable for monitoring an inmate threatening self-harm. Suicide watch cells, as they are commonly known, are spaces inside the health services area but are sometimes little more than holding cells. Often, positive pressure isolation rooms (typically reserved for offenders suspected to have communicable diseases) double as suicide watch cells.

The ruling authorities also differ significantly for jails and prisons. While prisons tend to be overseen by state or federal authorities, jails fall under local control. In many jurisdictions, jails are run by sheriff's departments or city authority. It is estimated that approximately 85% of jail facilities in the United States are under the supervision of sheriffs (National Sheriff's Association, 2017). Unfortunately, while most prison facilities require some sort of extended, academy-like training for their staff, jail personnel frequently receive little or no jail-specific training (American Psychological Association, 2014). Some jail posts are filled as a rotation from a deputy roster. This is notable because deputies and those trained to work in the community do not always have a skill set that transfers easily to a lockdown environment.

Jails are often in close proximity to where an offender was initially arrested. This can present a challenge, because the same facility is likely to be required to house codefendants who must be segregated from one another. However, jail inmates may know one another, even if their cases bear no overlap. Likewise, correctional officers are likely to encounter people they know from the community.

Jail Designs

Historically, jails were designed to confine inmates for relatively short periods of time, so comfort, accessibility, and programming needs were not emphasized. In modern correctional facilities, there have been three distinct approaches to jail design. First-generation jails followed a linear design, with long rows of cells down a corridor, affording minimal observation of inmates confined to their cells. This design, also referred to as intermittent surveillance design, is now obsolete, and its use has been discontinued in most jurisdictions. The next wave of jail designs was the indirect supervision or remote surveillance model. This is also sometimes referred to as podular or second-generation design and was popularized in the 1970s (Whitehead, Dodson, & Edwards, 2013). In this type of facility, inmates are housed in a unit with a separate officer's station. The officer's station is most often comprised of a series of large, protective windows and is on an elevated platform, permitting the officer to observe the entire housing unit. Communication in these units typically occurs via loudspeaker or microphone. Third generation, or direct supervision, jail designs afford maximum supervision and communication by placing an officer directly in the unit with the inmates and without any protective barrier to separate them. The unit has an officer's station including a control panel and communication system. Benefits of the direct supervision model include allowing inmates the freedom to do laundry, use a microwave, and participate in recreational activities. Direct supervision also allows greater monitoring of inmate behavior and improved communication between officers and inmates. This model has resulted in tension reduction and enhanced conflict resolution. The direct supervision model has been approved and is now promoted by both the National Institute of Corrections (NIC) and the American Correctional Academy (ACA).

One of the major advantages of direct supervisions jails is the ability to "facilitate the classification and programming for special types of offenders" (Wald & Dobbs, 2005, p. 499). For example, offenders with intellectual disabilities might be housed together so that correctional staff can offer treatment or care in a more efficient and effective manner. In addition, studies show that direct supervision lowers incidents of violence and increases the satisfaction of staff and inmates (Wald & Dobbs, 2005; Wener, 2006).

Prisoner Litigation

Given the nature of jails, it comes as no surprise that they are one of the most litigious environments for sheriff's department staff (National Sheriff's Association, 2017). Interestingly, jails see far fewer rates of litigation than their prison counterparts (Schlanger, 2003). One explanation for this may be that jail inmates are simply serving shorter sentences and may be less likely to devote their time to litigious pursuits. While prisoners frequently litigate issues of their Eighth Amendment rights (e.g., conditions of confinement and protection against cruel and unusual punishment), jail inmates' lawsuits often center on issues that address their Fifth or Fourteenth Amendment due process rights (Wagner, 2011). It is important to recognize that not all offenders housed in jails have been convicted. Those who are held awaiting trial or adjudication are often referred to as "pretrial detainees." Pretrial detainees, by definition, cannot be punished; punishment is reserved for those already convicted. Consequently, Eighth Amendment issues are not applicable to pretrial detainees. In other words, pretrial detainees may sue the sheriff, jail administrator, and correctional staff under the Fifth and Fourteenth Amendments but not the Eighth Amendment.

When jail inmates bring forth litigation, it often comes in the form of a class action lawsuit. Class action jail lawsuits have been successful in leading to changes in policies and procedures regarding medical and pharmacological treatments, screening and intake procedures, discipline (including use-of-force policies and guidelines for using restraint chairs), use of technologies (e.g., videotaping of incidents and access to telecommunication device for the deaf [TDD] phones), access to education, suicide and general risk assessment, and population caps and demographic distribution issues (Christensen, 2011; Schlanger, 2003).

Arguably, the best-known and most important case regarding jail conditions for pretrial detainees is that of *Bell v. Wolfish* (1979). In this case, inmates housed at the Metropolitan Correctional Center (MCC) in New York City (opened under federal authority in 1975) alleged their constitutional rights were being violated by a number of policies and procedural operations. They held that it should not be permissible for pretrial detainees (i.e., those not yet convicted of any crime) to be subjected to similar standards and practices as those who were imprisoned following a conviction. Their case covered several issues simultaneously. First, they asserted it was a punishment for one pretrial offender to be housed with another in a single cell. Second, they also argued that cell searches (routine "shakedowns") were a violation of privacy for those not convicted and sentenced. Further, those in the *Bell v. Wolfish* case asserted that the practice of body cavity searches was unreasonable for pretrial detainees who had not engaged in disruptive behavior. Finally, the case addressed the policy of restricting the delivery of packages from outside the prison containing food or personal items and/or the receipt of books not coming directly from the publisher. The latter issue is known as the "publisher rule."

The case was appealed all the way to the United States Supreme Court. While the Supreme Court acknowledged the possibility that some pretrial detainees may, in fact, be innocent, it also recognized the necessity of correctional officials to be able to perform their duties for the safety and security of staff and inmates. The Court emphasized that deference should be provided to correctional staff at each facility in order to operate their institution in the safest manner. The Court further held it was not a violation of a jail detainee's rights to be double bunked with another inmate in a single cell. This was precedent setting. As jail populations skyrocketed in the 1980s, double bunking became both a necessity and standard practice for most facilities. The Court also ruled that it was necessary to execute a body cavity searches on detainees to ensure the safety and security of the facility. However, the Court noted that searches cannot be conducted to harass and must be conducted only when there is a legitimate reason to do so. Similarly, the justices held routine cell searches were not a violation of a pretrial detainee's privacy under the Fourth Amendment. Finally, the publisher rule was upheld, and the Court asserted the risk of contraband, extortion, gang-related communication, and escape communication outweighed the rights of inmates to receive materials from those outside the institution. Although the *Bell v. Wolfish* decision applied to pretrial detainees (thus it could reasonably be expected to be adopted in jails), the ruling was considered a defeat for prisoners' rights.

The Supreme Court ruled in *Estelle v. Gamble* (1976) that correctional administrators and personnel could be held civilly liable if they failed to address the serious medical needs of inmates in their custody. It ruled that the legal standard at the center of medical cases would be whether correctional officials acted with "deliberate indifference." Offenders with special needs often are diagnosed with or develop serious medical and/or mental health issues during incarceration. Jail administrators must provide training to correctional staff and medical personnel regarding the proper treatment of inmates with special needs.

Prison litigation is a real concern for jail administrators, and being aware of the legal requirements for meeting the needs of offenders housed in their facilities should be taken seriously, especially the risk of litigation involving special needs offenders. The remainder of this chapter will discuss some of the issues and challenges special needs offenders present for jail administrators and correctional personnel.

Mentally Ill Offenders

Mentally ill offenders present many challenges to an already overburdened jail system. Jails and prisons, sadly, have become the *de facto* mental health facilities in many communities. The number of inmates entering jails who suffer from serious mental illnesses rose an astonishing 48% in the last 10 years. Of these, over 70% were arrested and booked for nonviolent offenses (Architect, 2015; Torrey et al., 2014). Estimates indicate nearly 15% of men and nearly 30% of women entering jails have met diagnostic criteria for significant clinical psychopathology within the 30 days preceding incarceration (Steadman, Osher, Clark-Robbins, Case, & Samuels, 2009). Over half of all incoming inmates reported they had experienced mental health problems. Jail inmates had the highest rates of mental health disorders, with almost two-thirds reporting depression and a quarter showing symptoms of a psychotic disorder (Steadman et al., 2009). Notably, mental illness in an offending population is frequently coupled with other concerns (e.g., drugs or alcohol dependency), commonly refer to as co-occurring disorders.

Correctional and mental health professionals concur that correctional facilities are not optimal for the provision of acute psychiatric care. Despite this, the number of mentally ill inmates being introduced to jail settings continues to grow, necessitating training and revised policy for many facilities to manage and treat mentally ill offenders. The large influx of the mentally ill into jails and prisons is an unintended consequence of the deinstitutionalization movement. Those who suffer with mental illness usually do not have access to the resources they need for the treatment and management of their conditions. All too often, they are relegated to poverty, homelessness, and, ultimately, the criminal justice system. Acutely mentally ill offenders coming into the system burden jails, and most facilities lack adequate mental health staff to treat these offenders. This places a significant burden on jail staff working in these ill-equipped facilities (Ortiz, 2015).

Mentally ill inmates may not be in touch with reality and may fail to appreciate the consequences of their behavior as a result. They may be in a state of psychosis, agitation, despair, or acute anxiety or panic. These conditions could exacerbate their distress or could result in a failure to appreciate the gravity of the situation, both of which could place an inmate at risk for harassment or harm from other inmates. Interacting with mentally ill inmates is frustrating for jail staff, because they may feel helpless because of a lack of proper training (Ortiz, 2015). Trotter and Noonan (2016) indicate that mentally ill individuals typically have a poor sense of personal boundaries and lack self-control, making them a challenge to manage during intake and difficult to house and place with a cellmate. Mentally ill inmates tend to have more adjustment difficulties and commit more disciplinary infractions than do other offenders (see Torrey et al., 2014). However, acting out is often beyond their conscious control and more symptomatic of their underlying mental illness.

Suicidal Inmates

One of the most critical assessments for inmates in jail settings is determining risk for self-harm or suicidal ideation. It is imperative that all inmates entering a jail or detention facility be evaluated as soon as possible, but certainly within the first 24 hours. Ideally, anyone who is being booked into a jail setting should be assessed immediately for thoughts of self-harm and suicidal ideations. In reality, however, jails typically do not have full-time mental health professionals on staff to perform, such assessments. Therefore, it is imperative that all jail staff be trained to identify possible signs of self-harm. Threatening to harm or kill oneself is obvious and easy to identify, but more subtle signs like expressing passive ideas (e.g., "I don't know how much longer I can take this" or "No one would even notice if I disappeared") may be missed or ignored. Engaging in reckless "death wish" behaviors (e.g., purposely crashing a vehicle), commenting about feeling worthless or hopeless, reporting sleep disturbance or significant behavioral change, or presenting as unusually calm and controlled are more nuanced and may be difficult for untrained or undertrained personnel to recognize.

Jail and medical staff should be aware of the risks of isolating inmates who have expressed a desire to harm themselves. Inmates should be double-celled when possible to provide accountability and decrease feelings of isolation. Identifying potential self-harm ideation and risk is not as straightforward as it may seem. Some inmates present as quiet and withdrawn while others may present as animated, loud, and disruptive. Naturally, inmates who are acting out will be most likely to receive staff attention. Sometimes the inmate who is not acting out, however, has the highest potential for self-harm (Noonan, Rohloff, & Ginder, 2015).

It is important to remember each offender should be assessed from his or her perspective, not his or her actual situation or circumstances. Jails are daunting environments that can elicit feelings of fear, panic, and anxiety and can make someone feel out of control. Most suicides are not cases where no options were available. Suicides frequently happen when individuals feel overwhelmed by their situation and, for one reason or another, they are unable to appreciate the range of other options available. For example, inmates who have been in and out of jail several times may seem like a lower risk because they know what to expect. They have the realistic expectations they will not be there forever or this arrest will not define their lives. However, these same individuals may have reached a breaking point in which they feel they are no longer capable of continuing their cycle of criminality and capture. Repeat offenders are most likely to have personality and/or substance use disorders, which can exacerbate thoughts of self-harm and impair rational thinking.

Perhaps even more salient in terms of risk potential are first-time offenders. Those who have never been in trouble may find it impossible to imagine getting through their current situation. In addition, they may be in a state of panic or disbelief and unable to recognize their options rationally. For example, prominent members of the community who have never been in jail may see their situation as dire. They may feel their reputation will never recover or family and friends will never forgive them. These offenders tend to catastrophize their current situation and believe their lives will be ruined by what may be a relatively minor offense. By contrast, repeat offenders typically see the reality of their situation and know the potential consequences and likely punishment for their criminal behavior. However, repeat offenders may experience depression or thoughts of hopelessness because they view themselves as failures for being returned to jail and being unable to get their lives on track.

One prevailing myth surrounding suicide is that asking an individual if he or she is having thoughts of self-harm may actually prompt suicidal thoughts not previously there. Research has shown this is a myth (Faber, 2007). If self-harm is suspected, jail staff should ask an inmate directly and with compassion if he or she is having thoughts of hopelessness or self-harm. If an inmate is at risk for self-harm, then steps should be taken to ensure his or her safety. Typically, inmates who voice intentions to harm themselves are placed on suicide watch. Suicide watch consists of continual monitoring and observation of the inmate to help ensure his or her safety. Any item that the inmate may use to carry out self-harm is removed from the observation cell, and, in extreme cases, even the inmate's clothing will be removed.

In 2007, the World Health Organization and Task Force on Suicide in Prisons published an updated version of its informational and advisory booklet, *Preventing Suicide in Jails and Prisons* (United Nations World Health Organization, 2007). Many jail administrator and correctional staff use this source for guidance to best manage and protect suicidal offenders. Jail administrators and correctional staff should receive intensive training to identify and protect suicidal inmates or those prone to self-harm (Hayes, 2013).

Substance-Abusing Offenders

Those who have substance abuse problems represent another special needs population within the jail system. It comes as no surprise that high numbers of offenders suffer from substance abuse and dependence. This is an especially salient issue in jails because addicted offenders are entering directly from the community. Individuals who are in the midst of active addiction may be intoxicated when they enter a jail facility. Intoxication increases risk of acting out, self-harm, and needing medical attention (Peters, Wexler, & Harry, 2005). It is important that any offender entering a jail system is assessed for intoxication and medically cleared to be placed in the general population.

Those under the influence of drugs or alcohol should be monitored to ensure their safety and to address detoxification needs (Federal Bureau of Prisons Clinical Practice Guidelines, 2014). Unfortunately, there is little support available for those who experience detoxification in jail. Offenders who are addicted to drugs, in particular, are susceptible to serious medical and psychological issues when going through withdrawal. Addicted offenders' needs will differ, depending on the substance to which they are addicted. For example, if someone is an alcoholic, then he or she may experience acute withdrawal symptoms that frequently include delirium tremens (DTs). It is critical for staff to recognize these symptoms, given the potentially lethal nature of this condition. There has been an increase in the number offenders who are addicted to narcotic pain medications, heroin, or other opioids. These offenders are likely to experience withdrawal symptoms that include intense and acute muscular pain, hot or cold sweats, gastrointestinal issues, runny nose, yawning, tearing, irritability, and anxiety. Those addicted to stimulants, like methamphetamine or cocaine, will likely experience symptoms of depression, sleep disruption, and agitation during their withdrawal. Offenders experiencing withdrawal are likely to have physical and psychological symptoms, which will alter their presentation compared to nonaddicted offenders. Individuals experiencing withdrawal may be at higher risk for frequent and intense mood swings and have difficulty adjusting to confinement (Peters & May, 1992). They may not be thinking rationally and can be prone to self-harm, including suicide attempts.

Most jails in the United States do not offer medically assisted therapies to offenders identified as experiencing symptoms of withdrawal from opioids or other drugs. Those that do frequently do not follow evidence-based practice guidelines (Mitchell et al., 2009). Despite the existence of a federal protocol for the medically assisted management of opioid withdrawal for the incarcerated (Federal Bureau of Prisons, 2014), for example, there is no standard or national guidelines provided for jails.

Sex Offenders

Those accused of sexual offenses may be particularly vulnerable in jail. These inmates are arguably the most stigmatized and least tolerated of any offender group. Interestingly, there is little data available on the incidence of problems of sex offenders in prisons and virtually none with regard to jails (Mann, 2016). Nevertheless, there is a widespread consensus that sex offenders, particularly those accused of crimes involving children, are at risk for being harassed, assaulted, and even raped in a correctional setting. The "inmate code of conduct" not only discourages the acceptance of sexual offenders but also encourages open hostility and retaliation. Many whose offense histories are discovered are forced to seek protective custody.

In a jail setting, however, it may be easier for an offender to cover up his or her offense by avoiding answering questions about it. Local media attention and informal communication chains complicate the security and safety of these offenders because their criminal histories are more easily accessible. Research is needed to determine precisely what the most salient adjustment issues are for sex offender in jail settings.

Since sexual offenders are at higher risk for harm, they frequently require additional protections and represent a significant burden to most jail facilities. While a prison may be large enough to allocate a specialized unit for sexual offenders, most jails do not have similar resources. Further, sex offenders are likely to present with comorbid special needs (e.g., depression, suicidal ideation, and substance abuse) which represent additional challenges for jail staff. In addition to preventing a sexual offender from being a target for violence, it is also important to take steps to ensure that these offenders do not perpetrate further sexual acts while in custody.

LGBTI Inmates

Lesbian, gay, bisexual, transgender, and intersex (LGBTI) offenders present a unique set of challenges to correctional staff, because they have higher rates of sexual victimization, far higher than other inmates (Schuster, 2016). Transgender inmates, in particular, have the highest rates of sexual harassment and victimization, and the inappropriate and illegal behavior may be perpetrated by both inmates and correctional staff. The National Inmate Survey is the most reliable data on the rates of victimization of transgender offenders. The data shows that 23% of transgender inmates in jails report experiencing assaultive behavior from another inmate (compared to 24% in prisons). Equally disconcerting was that 23% of transgender jail inmates and 17% of transgender prisoners indicated they had been mistreated by the staff who were assigned to protect them (Murphy, 2016).

Transgender inmates are particularly vulnerable, and their vulnerability may be heightened in jail setting. First, these individuals will be sent to a facility or placed in a housing unit with those of a gender with which they do not they identify. For example, a biologically male inmate who identifies as female will be housed with other male inmates. The offender's gender identity is not usually a consideration for housing. In contrast with this, biologically female inmates who identify as male may feel most comfortable being housed with male offenders. Therefore, housing issues as well as safety concerns for transgender inmates represent significant challenges for jail staff (Peterson, Stephens, Dickey, & Lewis, 1996).

Transgender individuals may be at various stages of identifying themselves as transgender. For example, some inmates may be in the beginning stages of accepting their gender, while others may be receiving hormone replacement therapy and/or undergoing sex reassignment. Transgender individuals who are transitioning may find it difficult to gain the respect of other inmates and correctional personnel, because although the individual has embraced his or her gender identity, others likely ignore or reject it. This is particularly true when it comes time to classify inmates and put them into the jail population. Jails and prisons typically classify inmates according their assigned sex at birth or biological sex rather than their gender identity.

One of the most pressing issues for staff is to protect transgender inmates from other inmates. Misconceptions about transgender individuals frequently occur because of a lack of awareness or understanding of gender dysphoria. This lack of understanding may prompt other inmates to ridicule, harass, or target transgender inmates for physical or sexual violence. In fact, trans-women (male-to-female) are at highest risk of harassment and sexual violence in both jails and prisons (Schuster, 2016). Safety risks should be taken into consideration when housing or making cell assignments. In addition to concerns about other inmates, correctional administrators must be aware of the risks of mistreatment of transgender inmates by staff. All too often, trans-inmates, particularly trans-women, are subjected to frequent pat-downs or strip searches, often resulting in additional stress or trauma. Federal mandates issued in 2012 regarding the individualized assessment and placement of transgender inmates have been largely ignored, and the vast majority of trans-women continue to be housed in male jail and prison populations.

Homosexual male inmates are sometimes targeted and may be at heightened risk of physical and sexual assault. They may be forced into a position of servitude in exchange for protection from such abuse (Rideau, 1979). However, sexually exploitive relationships are more common in prisons than in jails. Female offenders who identify as lesbian often incur ridicule and harassment from staff, especially male correctional officers. Lesbian inmates are prone to domestic violence from their female partners and are at higher risk of sexual assault from both fellow inmates and staff (see Chapter 10 for more about LGBTI offenders).

Juvenile Offenders

The number of juvenile offenders adjudicated as adults and being housed in adult jail facilities has increased over the past three decades. The "get tough on crime" mentality of the 1980s, coupled with the notion of juvenile "superpredators" (see DiLulio, 1995) in the 1990s, escalated the introduction of youthful offenders into adult jails at alarming rates (Fair Punishment Project, 2016).

Most states have some protocol in place allowing youthful offenders to be tried in the adult court system. In several states, a child charged with a crime in adult court may be held in an adult jail while awaiting trial and sent to an adult prison upon conviction. However, jails are constitutionally required to ensure sight and sound separation of juveniles and adult offenders (see the Juvenile Justice and Delinquency Prevention Act, 1974). Deitch, Barstow, Lukens, and Reyna (2009, p. 71) reported, "On a single day in 2008, 7,703 children under age 18 were held in adult local jails and 3,650 in adult state prisons." This is a major concern because juveniles housed in adult correctional facilities are at an increased risk of maladaptive coping strategies, sexual and physical victimization, and suicide (Deitch et al., 2009; Schiraldi & Zeidenberg, 1997).

Recent decisions by the United States Supreme Court have validated the notion that youthful offenders are different and should not be held to the same legal standards as adults. In *Roper v. Simmons* (2005), the Court ruled that children convicted of homicide prior to the age of 18 could not be sentenced to death. Thirty-seven states and the District of Columbia still allow a juvenile to be sentenced to life for committing a nonhomicidal crime. In 2010, this ruling was expanded in *Graham v. Florida* (2010), when the Court declared that sentencing a juvenile to life in prison without the possibility of parole for a nonhomicidal crime is in violation of the Eighth Amendment, constituting cruel and unusual punishment. More recently, the Court decided it was unconstitutional to sentence a juvenile offender to a mandatory sentence of life without the possibility of parole with the *Miller v. Alabama* (2012) ruling. As a result, states had to review parole decisions for inmates whose crime had been committed prior to adulthood. In 2016, this decision was applied retroactively, allowing some 2,000 inmates imprisoned without the possibility of parole for offenses committed prior to their 18th birthdays to be reconsidered according to the *Miller* guidelines (*Montgomery v. Louisiana*, 2016). Each of these decisions is relevant to a discussion of youthful offenders because they recognize the inherent differences in cognitive capability and maturity between youthful and adult offenders (Child Trends Databank, 2012). It will be interesting to see if these changes lead to a reduction in the number of juveniles being housed in adult facilities.

Women Offenders

The incarceration rate of women, juvenile justice placements, and community corrections programs has been increasing steadily for quite some time. In fact, between 1999 and 2013, the female inmate population in jail facilities across the United States increased by 48%, from approximately 68,100 to 100,940 (The Sentencing Project, 2015). In comparison, the male inmate jail population increased by just 17%, from approximately 537,800 to 630,620 (Minton et al., 2015). Since the rate of increase of women entering the criminal justice system is approximately three times the rate of men, jail administrators have had to make adjustments to better equip facilities to meet the unique needs of female offenders. Women in the criminal justice system have higher rates of mental illness, report greater experiences of trauma, and have different patterns of substance abuse than their male counterparts (Peters, Strozier, Murrin, & Kearns, 1997). They also tend to have higher rates of physical illnesses, less outside social support, and greater barriers to independence than male offenders.

High rates of trauma and abuse (e.g., molestation, rape and sexual assault, and domestic violence) are common experiences among female offenders (Hardyman & Van Voorhis, 2004; Minton et al., 2015; Ney, 2014; Ney, Ramirez & Van Dieten, 2012). Many estimates suggest more than half of all justice-involved women have experienced a significant traumatic event, and most have endured more than one. In some studies, up to 98% of women have reported trauma exposure (Green, Miranda, Daroowalla, & Siddique, 2005). Female offenders also report higher rates of sexual abuse by jail staff than do men (Swavola, Riley, & Subramanian, 2016). The exact number of women who have been sexually assaulted by staff during incarceration is unknown, but high numbers of justice-involved women later report being victimized at jail and detention facilities (Swavola et al., 2016).

Women have different pathways to prison than men that are gender specific (Salisbury & Van Voorhis, 2014). For women, criminality is often directly or indirectly related to unhealthy relationships they frequently maintain. Justice-involved women are more likely to be charged as codefendants with a significant other, family member, or friend. Women are more likely to be in a primary caregiving role for their children. Estimates indicate that approximately two-thirds of female offenders are mothers (American Civil Liberties Union [ACLU], 2016). This means women often leave minor children without a suitable guardian when they enter the justice system. This results in high numbers of children of incarcerated women being funneled into foster care and/or the juvenile justice system (ACLU, 2016).

Women can be difficult to manage in a jail setting because of their unique treatment or medical needs (The Sentencing Project, 2015). For example, some women entering jail may be pregnant. Jails often do not have the resources to provide adequate gynecological and obstetrical care. Some jails contract medical providers in the community to deliver medical services to inmates with specialized treatment or medical needs. However, the medical treatment that many incarcerated women receive in jail is substandard and jail administrators have been slow to respond to the medical needs of women under their supervision and care (see Chapter 7 for more on women offenders). The failure to address the medical needs of pregnant women increases the likelihood of inmate litigation (see *Estelle v. Gamble*, 1976).

Aging Offenders

Traditionally, those in jail were often pictured as young, healthy males. We have already mentioned the growing numbers of female offenders, and now the unique characteristics and needs of an aging population will be addressed. The aging population, in prison terms, is typically defined as those over 50–55 years of age (Aday, 2003). This is because incarcerated individuals age at a rate significantly higher than that of the general population. Most of the available data and literature on aging offenders comes from prison research. Mandatory minimum sentences and the underutilization of a variety of release mechanisms (e.g., compassionate release or medical parole) have resulted in more and more inmates growing old in jails and prisons.

There is some debate about whether elderly offenders should be in jails. Aging inmates have the lowest rates of recidivism, and research indicates offenders typically "age out" of criminal behavior (see e.g., Goldstein, 2015; Hirschi & Gottfredson, 1983). Therefore, it is less likely that new crimes will be committed by those over the age of 50. Between 2007 and 2010, the number of inmates over age 65 in state and federal prison systems grew at an alarming 94 times the rate of the general prison population. According to Williams, Goodwin, Baillargeon, Ahalt, and Walter (2012, p. 1152), "From 2000 to 2010, the number of older U.S. prisoners increased 181%, while the overall prison population increased only 17%."

Abner (2016) chronicles how older inmates often present with multiple medical conditions and physical limitations. They may suffer from cognitive impairments that frequently require costly medical care, both inside and outside jail. Medical costs for aging prisoners are up to nine times more than for younger inmates, making them the costliest subset of all prisoners (Williams et al., 2012). The recent rise in the aging offender population, coupled with projections this group will continue to see substantial growth in the coming decade, have led some to suggest that older offenders should have their own wholly separate system of justice (similar to the distinct juvenile justice system) (see e.g., Aday & Krabill, 2006; Maschi, Viola & Sun, 2013).

Although jails are required under the American with Disabilities Act (1990) to make facilities handicap accessible and fitted to accommodate individuals with disabilities, many are noncompliant. Costs may be a major obstacle to ADA compliance, but this does not excuse jail officials for failing to comply, and it may result in litigation. Jails must have handicap ramps, elevated beds and toilets, and handrails to accommodate geriatric and disabled inmates. In addition, elderly inmates are vulnerable to victimization and exploitation because of mental or physical impairments. Jail administrators and staff should be aware of this and adapt the classification of elderly inmates to meet their needs and prevent victimization.

Offenders with Disabilities and Chronic Medical Conditions

According to Bronson, Marsuchak, and Berzofsky (2015), from 2011 to 2012, four in10 local jail inmates reported having at least one disability, with females reporting higher incidences of disabilities (49% females versus 39% of males). Disabilities, for the purposes of this chapter, are defined as deficits substantial enough to cause impairment in hearing, vision, cognitive functioning, ambulation, self-care, or independent living, which includes the ability to navigate daily life schedules, activities, and events without assistance. Those with disabilities often are not immediately accommodated with what they need in jails (BJS survey, 2015). As previously noted, the ADA (1990) requires jails and prisons, just as any other public facilities, to provide "reasonable" accommodations for disabled offenders. Determining what is reasonable inside a jail setting can be tricky because of the need to balance civil liberties and individual rights with safety and security.

Logistical constraints pose a formidable challenge to jail and prison staff. Many older institutions were not built with accessibility for a wheelchair or assistive technologies for the hearing or visually impaired. Screening and processing of those in wheelchairs or with whom communication is difficult can be daunting. Cognitive impairments (e.g., memory impairment, dementia, and intellectual deficits) may not be readily apparent and are difficult to treat effectively in jail. Few correctional personnel can communicate using American Sign Language and may be unfamiliar with the unique needs of those with disabilities. Facilities, unless newly constructed, are usually ill-equipped to provide for disabled offenders adequately.

Binswanger, Krueger, and Steiner (2009) outlined some of the issues associated with the high rates of chronic illness among jail and prison inmates. The biggest obstacle to managing chronically or terminally ill inmates is the cost. Incarcerated offenders have higher rates of hypertension, asthma, arthritis, cancer, hepatitis, and HIV/AIDS than the general population. These conditions often require specialized treatment or medical procedures, which drives up the cost for jails. Once a person is in custody, the jail administrators and personnel are responsible for providing medical and mental health care. If the jail lacks the trained personnel or medical staff, it must contract with medical and mental professionals in the community to provide services to inmates.

Veterans

Veterans represent another special needs population of concern in jail facilities.Veterans often present with high rates of mental health disorders and substance abuse. Most commonly, veteran offenders suffer from depression, posttraumatic stress disorder (PTSD), or anxiety disorders. In fact, fully half of all veterans in jail facilities report they have been diagnosed with a mental health disorder (Bronson, Carson, Noonan, & Bersofsky, 2015). However, many times these disorders are undiagnosed until after a service member has already entered the legal system.Veterans' reintegration to society following combat deployment can be complicated by unemployment, a lack of available treatment resources, and the perception of isolation or estrangement from supportive others.

Veteran inmates may actually have lower rates of conflict within the jail system, in part because other inmates may assume they are trained to defend themselves (Noonan & Mumola, 2007). Especially disconcerting, however, is the fact that veteran inmates are far more likely than their civilian counterparts to commit suicide (U.S. Department ofVeterans Affairs, 2016). As their military training may prepare them to fight another inmate, unfortunately, it may also assist them with choosing or enacting the most lethal approaches to a suicide attempt.

Several states (e.g., Colorado, Florida, Illinois, Maine, Minnesota, Missouri, Pennsylvania, and Texas) have created veterans' treatment courts.Veterans courts allow justice-involved service members be processed through a specialized court designed to address their rehabilitative and treatment needs. These courts have shown excellent early success in terms of reducing recidivism rates and assisting veteran offenders with obtaining employment, housing, and other resources necessary to reduce their risk of reoffending (Knudsen & Wingenfeld, 2015).

Immigrants

Recently, there has been a focus on the costs of housing undocumented immigrants in U.S. jails and prisons. In 2014, $1.87 billion, largely from state budgets, was spent on housing undocumented immigrants in correctional facilities in the U.S. (Gehrke, 2015). Texas, California, and Florida are the hardest hit in preventing illegal entry into the country. Noncitizen offenders are most likely to be incarcerated for immigration, drug, burglary, larceny, and traffic violation charges, with drug offenses accounting for the vast majority of arrests (Gehrke, 2015). However, there is no empirical evidence that suggests undocumented immigrants are more likely to be involved in criminal behavior (see. e.g., Moehlin & Piehl, 2009; Wilson, 2017), and crimes rates are actually lower for undocumented immigrants than native-born citizens (Ghandnoosh & Rover, 2017).

Undocumented immigrants present to jail facilities with some predictable logistical concerns. First, if English is not a first or primary language, then the offender may have difficulty communicating with jail staff. Next, it may be nearly impossible to obtain accurate records for undocumented immigrants. For example, undocumented immigrants cannot obtain a valid driver's license or other forms of identification; therefore, it can be a challenge to identify them accurately when they are brought into the jail. These offenders may have difficulty contacting family or others who could help post bail or offer other types of support (see Chapter 13 to learn more about immigrant prisoners).

Immigration cases fall under federal civil law, and the rights of undocumented immigrants who are charged with criminal offenses are sometimes unclear. Communication problems between state and local jail authorities and federal immigration officers often lead to confusion and make some cases increasingly difficult to prosecute. Some have alleged that undocumented immigrants may actually seek housing in jail to obtain resources and have their basic needs met (Bosworth & Kaufman, 2011) because they do not qualify for government assistance programs (Wilson, 2017). However, this is unlikely given the notorious reputation of immigration detention centers in the United States. For example, Karnes County Residential Center in San Antonio, Texas, has been under investigation for ignoring or disregarding the medical needs of inmates (Hennessy-Fiske, 2015). In addition, there have been allegations of rape by staff and child sexual abuse perpetrated by inmates (Garcia-Ditta, 2016). A correctional officer at Berks County Residential Center in Leesport, Pennsylvania admitted to sexually assaulting a 19-year-old Honduran woman and received a 23-month sentence (Feltz, 2016). Many of these cases are well publicized, so it is unlikely that undocumented immigrants seek out incarceration to meet their needs.

Jail administrators, particularly in ethnically diverse communities, should hire bilingual correctional staff. If this is not possible, jail administrators should consider hiring a reputable translator to facilitate communication between jail staff and immigrant inmates. Many courts employ translators, and in small communities, these individuals work with local jails. Jail administrators are responsible for ensuring the safety and security of all inmates in their custody. In addition, they are responsible for addressing the medical and mental health needs of inmates; therefore, having a translator on retainer not only facilitates communication, it helps to decrease the likelihood of inmate litigation.

Conclusion

As we improve our methods of identifying special needs offenders in jails, it is imperative that we develop and implement policies, procedures, and programs to meet the needs of these individuals while maintaining the safety and security of the institution and protecting society. We must recognize the unique issues and needs of jail populations and not simply attempt to apply prison policy to jail settings. To do this, there must be more research specific to jails and detention settings. Improved screening and early identification of special needs offenders can be cost effective and can improve operations and morale of both staff and inmates. To justify these necessary expenses, however, data must support what is already widely known by correctional administrators and staff.

The first step to effectively managing special needs offenders in jail is the development of efficient policies and procedures for effective screening and classification. If the needs are recognized during admission, accommodations and precautions can be immediately addressed. Unfortunately, programming in jails is severely limited (Collins, 2007; Harlow, 2003). One reason for this is simply the instability of the jail population and the limited time an offender may be present and available for intervention. As such, most programming has to be made accessible via a drop-in or add-on basis, sometimes resulting in a different constellation of participants from one session to the next.

Much of the available programming has been designed for male offenders who do not have special needs. This "one-size-fits-all" approach is generally ineffective for special populations, and research shows targeted approaches are far more effective in reducing recidivism (Daniel, 2007; Mann, 2016; Reed, 2000; Salisbury & Van Voorhis, 2014). Many jails have little to no budget for rehabilitation, and the competing needs for funding and resources leave little in an already strained budgetary culture (Tincher, 2016). Some jails, however, have recognized the long-term benefits and associated cost savings of programming for special needs offenders.

One innovative program, the Special Needs Pod (SNP) program at the Washington County Jail in Hillsboro, Oregon, for example, has demonstrated excellent early success in reducing disruptive incidents, improving the identification and treatment of a variety of medical and mental health disorders, and increasing medication compliance. This unit is staffed by specially trained officers and houses offenders typically considered high risk in the general population because of major mental health disorders, developmental disabilities or physical limitations, a history of emotional problems, a history of head trauma, attempted suicide, or extremely young or geriatric inmates (Colpean & Iverson, 2009). This program has resulted in meaningful reductions in recidivism and assisted offenders with making changes to improve their self-efficacy (Tomasino, Swanson, Nolan, & Shuman, 2001). This approach should be replicated and data collected so that we can establish evidence-based practices specific to jail settings.

References

Abner, C. (2016). Graying prisons: States face challenges of an aging inmate population. *The Council of State Governments*. Retrieved from www.csg.org/knowledgecenter/docs/sn0611GrayingPrisons.pdf

Aday, R. H. (2003). *Aging prisoners: Crisis in American corrections*. Westport, CT: Praeger.

Aday, R. H., & Krabill, J. J. (2006). Aging offenders in the criminal justice system. *Marquette Elder's Advisor, 7*(2), 237–258.

Alexander, M. (2010). *The new Jim Crow: Mass incarceration in the era of color-blindness*. New York, NY: The Free Press.

American Civil Liberties Union. (2016). *Facts about the over-incarceration of women in the United States*. New York, NY: American Civil Liberties Union. Retrieved from www.aclu.org/facts-about-over-incarceration-women-united-states

Americans with Disabilities Act of 1990. (1990). Pub. L. No. 101–336, 104 Stat. 328.

American Psychological Association. (2014). Incarceration nation. *American Psychological Association, 45*(9), 56. Retrieved from www.apa.org/monitor/2014/10/incarceration.aspx

Architect, T. (2015). Designing the modern county jail: Facility design tips for safely and effectively managing a growing mentally ill population. *Corrections One Online*. Retrieved from www.correctionsone.com/facility-design-and-operation/articles/8115045-Designing-the-modern-county-jail/

Bell v. Wolfish, 441 US 520, (1979).

Binswanger, I.A., Krueger, P.M., & Steiner, J.F. (2009). Prevalence of chronic medical conditions among jail and prison inmates in the USA compared with the general population. *Journal of Epidemiology & Community Health, 63*(11), 912–919. doi:10.1136/jech.2009.090662

Bureau of Justice Statistics. (2015). *BJS survey finds 40 percent of prison and jail inmates reported current chronic medical problems*. Washington, DC: U.S. Department of Justice, Bureau of Justice Statistics.

Blades, M. (2015, January 2). U.S. incarceration rate sickening, disgraceful, and far exceeds that of every other nation. *Daily Kos*. Retrieved from www.dailykos.com/story/2015/1/2/1353354/-U-S-incarceration-rate-sickening-disgraceful-and-far-exceeds-that-of-every-other-nation

Bosworth, M., & Kaufman, E. (2011). Foreigners in a carceral age: Immigration and imprisonment in the United States. *Stanford Law & Policy Review, 22*, 429–454.

Bronson, J., Carson, A., Noonan, M., & Berzofsky, M. (2015). Veterans in prison and jail, 2011–2012. *Bureau of Justice Statistics*. Retrieved from www.bjs.gov/index.cfm?ty=pbdetail&iid=5479

Bronson, J., Marsuchak, L., & Berzofsky, M. (2015). *Disabilities among prison and jail inmates, 2011–2012*. Washington, DC: U.S. Department of Justice, Bureau of Justice Statistics, Special Report.

Child Trends Data Bank. (2012, April). *Young adults in jail or prison*. Bethesda, MD: Child Trends. Retrieved from www.childtrends.org/?indicators=young-adults-in-jail-or-prison

Christensen, R. (2011, June 29). *Jail personnel liability and deliberate indifference*. [Blog post]. Law Enforcement Lawyers Blog, Health and Safety Code Section 11550.

Collins, W. C. (2007). *Jails and the constitution: An overview* (2nd ed.). Washington, DC: U.S. Department of Justice, National Institute of Corrections.

Colpean, R., & Iverson, T. (2009, July 29). Designing for special-needs inmates. *Correctional News*. Retrieved from www.correctionalnews.com/articles/2009/07/29/sign-the-times

Daniel, A. (2007). Care of the mentally ill in prisons: Challenges and solutions. *Journal of the American Academy of Psychiatry and the Law, 35*(4), 406–410.

DeHart, D., Lynch, S., Belknap, J., Dass-Brailsford, P., & Green, B. (2013). Life history of models of female offending: The roles of serious mental illness and trauma in women's pathways to jail. *Psychology of Women Quarterly, 38*(1), 138–151. doi:10.1177/0361684313494357

Deitch, M., Barstow, A., Lukens, L., & Reyna, R. (2009). *From time out to hard time: Young children in the adult criminal justice system*. Austin, TX: The University of Texas at Austin, LBJ School of Public Affairs.
DiLulio, J. J. (1995, November 27). The coming off the superpredators. *The Weekly Standard*. Retrieved from www.weeklystandard.com/the-coming-of-the-super-predators/article/8160
Estelle v. Gamble, 429 U.S. 97 (1976).
Faber, B. (2007). Civil liability for jail and prisoner suicide. *Americans for Effective Law Enforcement (AELE) Monthly Law Journal, 2*, 301–310. Retrieved from www.aele.org/law/2007JBFEB/2007-02MLJ301.pdf
Fair Punishment Project. (2016, April 12). *The "superpredator" myth and the rise of JLWOP*. [Web log comment]. Fair Punishment Project. Retrieved from http://fairpunishment.org/the-superpredator-myth-and-the-rise-of-jwlop/
Federal Bureau of Prisons Clinical Practice Guidelines. (2014). *Detoxification of chemically dependent inmates*. Retrieved from www.bop.gov/resources/pdfs/detoxification.pdf
Feldman, L., Schiraldi, V., & Ziedenberg, J. (2001). *Too little too late: President Clinton's prison legacy*. Washington, DC: The Justice Policy Institute.
Feltz, R. (2016, April 23). Immigration facility guard given jail time for sexual assault of detainee. *The Guardian*. Retrieved from www.theguardian.com/us-news/2016/apr/23/immigration-detention-center-guard-sexual-assault-prison
Flatow, N. (2014, September 14). *The United States has the largest prison population in the world—and it's growing*. Retrieved from https://thinkprogress.org/the-united-states-has-the-largest-prison-population-in-the-world-and-its-growing-d4a35bc9652f
Garcia-Ditta, A. (2016, April 14). Despite systemic failures, state moves to license detention centers for child care. *Texas Observer*. Retrieved from www.texasobserver.org/dfps-child-care-licenses-detention/
Gehrke, J. (2015, July 28). Report: U.S. spent $1.87 billion to incarcerate illegal-immigrant criminals in 2014. *National Review*. Retrieved from www.nationalreview.com/article/421673/nearly-2-billion-spent-jailing-illegal- immigrant-criminals-america-2014
Ghandnoosh, N., & Rover, J. (2017). *Immigration and public safety*. Washington, DC: The Sentencing Project.
Goldstein, D. (2015). *Too old to commit crime? Why people age out of crime, and what is could mean for how long we put them away*. New York, NY: The Marshall Project.
Gottschalk, M. (2006). *The prison and the gallows: The politics of mass incarceration in America*. New York, NY: Cambridge University Press.
Graham v. Florida, 560 U.S. 48, (2010).
Green, B., Miranda, J., Daroowalla, A., & Siddique, J. (2005). Trauma exposure, mental health functioning, and program needs of women in jail. *Crime & Delinquency, 51*(1), 133–151. doi:10.1177/0011128704267477
Hardyman, P., & Van Voorhis, P. (2004). *Developing gender-specific classification systems for women offenders*. Washington, DC: U.S. Department of Justice, National Institute of Corrections.
Harlow, C.W. (2003). *Education and correctional populations*. Washington, DC: U.S. Department of Justice, Office of Justice Programs, Special Report.
Hayes, L. M. (2013). Suicide prevention in correctional facilities: Reflections on the next steps. *International Journal of Law and Psychiatry, 36*(3–4), 188–194. doi:1016/j.ijlp.2013.04.010
Hennessy-Fiske, M. (2015, July 27). Immigrants' attorneys say they were 'locked out' of detention centers after raising concerns. *Los Angeles Times*. Retrieved from www.latimes.com/nation/la-na-immigrant-family-detention-20150727-story.html#page=1
Higgs, R. (2010). Consent of the governed? *The Beacon*. Retrieved from http://blog.independent.org/2010/06/01/consent-of-the-governed/
Hirschi, T., & Gottfredson, M. (1983). Age and the explanation of crime. *The American Journal of Sociology, 89*(3), 552–584.
Juvenile Justice and Delinquency Prevention Act, (1974).
Knudsen, K. J., & Wingenfeld, S. (2015). A specialized treatment court for veterans with traumatic exposure: Implications for the field. *Community and Mental Health Journal, 52*(2), 127–135. doi:10.1007/s10597-015-9845-9
Mann, R. (2016). Sex offenders in prison. In Y. Jewkes, J. Bennet, & B. Crewe (Eds.), *Handbook on prisons* (pp. 246–264). New York, NY: Routledge.
Maschi, T., Viola, D., & Sun, F. (2013). The high cost of the international aging prisoner crisis: well-being as the common denominator for action. *The Gerontologist, 53*(4), 543–554.
Miller v. Alabama, 567 U.S. 460 (2012).
Mitchell, S. G., Kelly, S. M., Brown, B. S., Reisinger, H. S., Peterson, J. A., Ruhf, A., . . . Schwartz, R. P. (2009). Incarceration and opioid withdrawal: The experiences of methadone patients and out-of-treatment heroin users. *Journal of Psychoactive Drugs, 41*(2), 145–152. doi:10.1080/02791072.2009.10399907
Minton, T., Ginder, S., Brumbaugh, S., Smiley-McDonald, H., & Rohloff, H. (2015). *Census of jails: Population changes, 1999–2013. Summary report*. Washington, DC: U.S. Department of Justice, Bureau of Justice Statistics.

Minton, T. D., & Zeng, Z. (2016). *Jail inmates in 2015.* Washington, DC: U.S. Department of Justice, Bureau of Justice Statistics.

Moehling, C., & Piehl, A. M. (2009). Immigration, crime, and incarceration in early Twentieth Century America. *Demography, 46*(4), 739–763. doi:10.1353/dem.0.0076

Montgomery v. Louisiana, 136 S. Ct. 718, (2016).

Mumford, M., Schanzenbach, D. W., & Nunn, R. (2016). The economics of private prisons. *Brookings Institute.* Retrieved from www.brookings.edu/research/the-economics-of-private-prisons/

Murphy, T. (2016, February 23). *There are twice as many LGBTQ people in prison as in the general population.* San Francisco, CA: LGBTQ Nation. Retrieved from www.lgbtqnation.com/2016/02/there-are-twice-as-many-lgbtq-people-in-prison-as-in-the-general-population/

National Sheriff's Association. (2017). *Jail resources.* Alexandria, VA: National Association of Jail Operations. Retrieved from www.sheriffs.org/global-center-for-public-safety/jail-resources

Ney, B. (2014, January 8). 10 facts about women in jails. *American Jail Association Magazine.* Retrieved from www.americanjail.org/10-facts-about-women-in-jails/

Ney, B., Ramirez, R., & Van Dieten, M. (2012). Ten truths that matter when working with justice involved women. *National Resource Center on Justice Involved Women*, 1–18.

Noonan, M., & Mumola, C. (2007). *Veterans in state and federal prison, 2004.* Washington, DC: U.S. Department of Justice, Bureau of Justice Statistics.

Noonan, M., Rohloff, H., & Ginder, S. (2015). *Mortality in local jails and state prisons, 2000–2013—statistical tables.* Washington, DC: U.S. Department of Justice, Bureau of Justice Statistics.

Ortiz, N. (2015). Addressing mental illness and medical conditions in county jails. *NACo Why Counties Matter Series, 3*, 1–8. Washington, DC: National Association of Counties. Retrieved from www.naco.org/addressing-mental-illness-and-medical-conditions-county-jails

Peters, R. H., & May, R. I. (1992). Drug treatment services in jails. In C. G. Leukefeld & F. M. Tims (Eds). *Drug abuse treatment in prison and jails.* Rockville, MD: NIDA Research Monograph 118.

Peters, R. H., Strozier, A. L., Murrin, M. R., & Kearns, W. D. (1997). Treatment of substance-abusing jail inmates: Examination of gender differences. *Journal of Substance Abuse Treatment, 14*(4), 339–349. doi:10.1016/S0740-5472(97)00003-2

Peters, R. H., & Wexler, H. K. (2005). *Substance abuse treatment for adults in the criminal justice system.* Rockville, MD: U.S. Department of Health and Human Services, Public Health Service, Substance Abuse and Mental Health Services Administration, Center for Substance Abuse Treatment.

Petersen, M., Stephens, J., Dickey, R., & Lewis, W. (1996). Transsexuals within the prison system: An international survey of correctional services policies. *Behavioral Sciences & the Law, 14*(2), 219–229. doi:10.1002/(SICI)1099-0798(199621)14:2<219::AID-BSL234>3.0.CO;2-N

Pratt, T. C. (2009). *Addicted to incarceration: Corrections policy and the politics of misinformation in the United States.* Thousand Oaks, CA: Sage.

Reid, W. (2000, September). Law and psychiatry: Offenders with special needs. *Journal of Psychiatric Practice*, 280–283.

Rideau, W. (1979, December). Prison: The sexual jungle. *Angolite*, 51–78.

Robinson, P. H. (2015). Obama's get-out-of-jail-free decree. *Faculty Scholarship.* Paper 1568.

Roper v. Simmons, 543 U.S. 551, (2005).

Ruddell, R., & Mays, G. L. (2007). Rural jails: Problematic inmates, overcrowded cells, and cash-strapped counties. *Journal of Criminal Justice, 35*(3), 251–260. doi:10.1016/j.jcrimjus.2007.03.002

Salisbury, E. J., & Van Voorhis, P. (2014). *Correctional counseling and rehabilitation.* New York, NY: Routledge.

Sarhan, A. (2017, February 24). Prison stocks soar as Jeff Sessions okays private jails. *Forbes.* Retrieved from www.forbes.com/sites/adamsarhan/2017/02/24/prison-stocks-soar-under-trump-as-sessions-oks-private-jails-again/#373e64aa10ce

Schept, J. (2013). A lockdown facility with the feel of a small, private college: Liberal politics, jail expansion, and the carceral habitus. *Theoretical Criminology, 17*(1), 71–88. doi:10.1177/1362480612463113

Schlanger, M. (2013). Plata v. Brown and realignment: Jails, prisons, courts, and politics. *Harvard Law Review, 48*(1), 165–215.

Schlanger, M. (2003). Inmate litigation: Results of a national survey. *JLN Exchange*, 1–12. Retrieved from www.law.umich.edu/facultyhome/margoschlanger/Documents/Publications/Inmate_Litigation_Results_National_Survey.pdf

Schiraldi, V., & Zeidenberg, J. (1997). *The risks juveniles face when they are incarcerated with adults.* Washington, DC: The Justice Policy Institute.

Schuster, T. (2016, March 7). PREA and LGBTI rights. *American Jails Magazine, Online.* Retrieved from www.americanjail.org/prea-and-lgbti-rights/

Seiter, R. P. (2014). *Corrections: An introduction* (4th ed.). Upper Saddle River, NJ: Pearson.

Steadman, H. J., Osher, F. C., Robbins, P. C., Case, B. A., & Samuels, S. (2009). Prevalence of serious mental illness among jail inmates. *Psychiatric Services, 60*(6), 761–765. doi:10.1176/ps.2009.60.6.761

Swavola, E., Riley, K., & Subramanian, R. (2016). *Overlooked: Women and jails in an era of reform*. New York, NY: The Vera Institute of Justice.

The Sentencing Project. (2015). *Fact sheet: Incarcerated women and girls*. Washington, DC: The Sentencing Project. Retrieved from www.sentencingproject.org/wp-content/uploads/2016/02/Incarcerated-Women-and-Girls.pdf

Tincher, S. (2016, March 5). Cost of justice: WV counties struggle to balance financial losses—business, government legal news from throughout WV. Ghent, WV. *59 News*. Retrieved from www.statejournal.com/story/31139485/cost-of-justicewv-counties-struggle-to-balance-financial-losses-rising-jail-fees

Tomasino, V., Swanson, A., Nolan, J., & Shuman, H. (2001). The key extended entry program (KEEP): A methadone treatment program for opiate-dependent inmates. *The Mount Sanai Journal of Medicine, 68*(1), 14–20.

Torrey, E. F., Zdanowicz, M. T., Kennard, A. D., Lamb, H. R., Eslinger, D. F., Biasotti, M. C., & Fuller, D. A. (2014). *How many individuals with serious mental illness are in jails and prisons?* Arlington, VA: Treatment and Advocacy Center. Retrieved from www.treatmentadvocacycenter.org/storage/documents/backgrounders/how%20many%20individuals%20with%20serious%20mental%20illness%20are%20in%20jails%20and%20prisons%20final.pdf

Trotter, A., & Noonan, M. (2016, May 3). Medical conditions, mental health problems, disabilities, and mortality among jail inmates. *American Jail Association Magazine*. www.americanjail.org/medical-conditions-mental-health-problems-disabilities-and-mortality-among-jail-inmates/

United Nations Office on Drug Crime. (2009). *Handbook on prisoners with special needs*. New York, NY: United Nations.

United Nations World Health Organization. (2007). *Preventing suicide in jails and prisons*. Geneva, Switzerland: World Health Organization, WHO Document Production Services.

United States Department of Veterans Affairs. (2016). *Suicide among veterans and other Americans, 2011–2014*. Washington, DC: U.S. Department ofVeterans Affairs, Office of Suicide Prevention.

Wagner, D. (2011, June 30). *The duty to protect at the jail*. [Weblog Comment]. Law Enforcement Lawyers Blog. Retrieved from https://lawenforcementlawyers.wordpress.com/2011/06/30/the-duty-to-protect-at-the-jail/

Wald, C. A., & Dobbs, R. R. (2005). Jail design and philosophy. In M. Bosworth (Ed.), *Encyclopedia of prisons & correctional facilities*. Thousand Oaks, CA: Sage.

Wener, R. (2006). Effectiveness of the direct supervision system of correctional design and management: A Review of the literature. *Criminal Justice and Behavior, 33*(3), 392–410. doi:10.1177/0093854806286202

Whitehead, J. T., Dodson, K. D., & Edwards, B. D. (2013). *Corrections: Exploring crime, punishment, and justice in America* (3rd ed.). New York, NY: Routledge.

Williams, B. A., Goodwin, J. S., Baillargeon, J., Ahalt, C., & Walter, L. C. (2012). Addressing the aging crisis in U.S. criminal justice healthcare. *Journal of the American Geriatrics Society, 60*(6), 1150–1156. doi:10.1111/j.1532-5415.2012.03962.x

Wilson, T. (2017). *Do undocumented immigrants overuse government benefits?* Medford, MA: Econofact.

Wright, J. P., & Delisi, M. (2016). *Conservative criminology: A call to restore balance to the social sciences*. New York, NY: Routledge.

PART II

Special Populations

7
WOMEN OFFENDERS
Gender-Responsive Treatment During Incarceration and Reentry

Lisa M. Carter

> Our nation's response to the crisis in drugs, unemployment, under education, mental illness, and the like is not to deal with those social ills but to find a way to control and capture those female prisoners who have no voice in where they live, sleep, or eat.
>
> —(Collins, 1997, p. 12)

Introduction

According to the Bureau of Justice Statistics, over 112,000 women were under the jurisdiction of federal and state correctional authorities in 2014 (Carson, 2013). Women account for roughly 7% of the total population in state and federal prisons (Carson & Sabol, 2012). Typically, women prisoners are young, poor, undereducated, underemployed prior to incarceration, mothers to minor children, and struggle with histories of substance abuse (Belknap, 2015; Bloom, Owen, & Covington, 2003; Comack, 2006; Enos, 2001; Richie, 2001; Sharp, 2014). In examining the ethnic and racial backgrounds of women prisoners, women of color are disproportionally represented among prison populations (Sharp, 2014). Black women are nearly three times and Hispanic women nearly twice as likely to be incarcerated as white women (Belknap, 2015; Carson & Golinelli, 2013; Carson & Sabol, 2012).

Many women prisoners experienced emotional, psychological, physical and sexual abuse and exposure to drug/alcohol abuse as children and during adulthood (Gilfus, 2006; Parillo, 2001). In addition, women prisoners have frequently been involved in abusive romantic relationships as adults. As a result, many women turned to drug use and/or other destructive behaviors to ease their suffering and as a means to deal with their traumatic pasts (Chesney-Lind & Pasko, 2013; Pollock, 2004).

Women are less likely to be incarcerated for violent offenses than men (BJS, 2006a; Bloom et al., 2004; Covington & Bloom, 2006; Gilfus, 2006; Moe & Ferraro, 2006; Petersilia, 2003; Pollock, 2004). Generally, women are sentenced for drug offenses and property crimes—more specifically, nonviolent crimes such as check fraud, forgery, prostitution, shoplifting, and larceny (Alarid & Cromwell, 2006; Bloom et al., 2004; Gilfus, 2006). In 2011, 36% of women sentenced to prison were incarcerated as a result of property crimes, with fraud being the most frequently cited crime (Carson & Golinelli, 2013). For that same year, 18% of women incarcerated in prisons had been sentenced for violent offenses (assault and robbery being the most common crimes) compared to roughly 32% of male inmates (Carson & Golinelli, 2013).

Meeting the Health Care Needs of Incarcerated Women

When discussing the incarceration of women, it is important to examine not only the individual, social, and environmental factors that lead to incarceration but also the experiences and needs women face as prisoners. Women's experiences are gendered; that is, women suffer "the pains of imprisonment" differently than their male counterparts (Hulley, Crewe, & Wright, 2017, p. 1). Therefore, when studying the situations of women prisoners, their concerns, and their treatment needs, correctional administrators, staff, and policy makers should do so based on gender-specific and gender-responsive approaches (Van Voorhis & Salisbury, 2014).

As Menabde (2009, p. v) points out, "Health is a fundamental right, especially for individuals held in the custody of the state." Women prisoners often report serious concerns regarding the state of their physical health. This group of women experience more significant health risks than that of women in the general population for a variety of reasons. Although prison health services are available, the needs of women prisoners often exceed the medical resources in place at a given correctional facility (Aday, 2003).

Gynecological and Obstetrician Needs and Care

Approximately 6% of women entering in correctional facilities in the United States are pregnant (Belknap, 2015; Henriques & Gladwin, 2013). Prior to their incarceration, many of these women are not likely to have received prenatal care and often experience high-risk pregnancies. Economic and social problems such as poor nutrition, substance abuse and addiction, physical and sexual victimization, and other risky lifestyle behaviors complicate the pregnancies of women prisoners. For example, Women who abuse drugs are more likely to deliver premature babies, have babies with low birth weight, and/or have babies who experience fetal distress or suffer neonatal aspiration of meconium. Neonatal complications may also include narcotic withdrawal, neurological problems, postnatal growth deficiency, birth defects, and an increase in neonatal mortality, such as sudden infant death syndrome (Schempf, 2007).

Women prisoners frequently experience complications during labor and delivery. The most serious danger of substance abuse for pregnant women is the increased likelihood of malpresentation of the infant during labor. This is more commonly known as breech birth, and it usually results in the need for a cesarean-section delivery. Cesarean deliveries may result in increased blood loss, organ injury, blood clots, emergency hysterectomy, adverse reactions to anesthesia, postsurgical infection, scar tissue that hinders future deliveries, emotional trauma, and occasionally maternal death. Substance abuse, such as cocaine and opioid use, during pregnancy can lead to other medical complications for mothers, including an increased risk of heart attacks, strokes, seizures, and respiratory failure (Bhuvaneswar, Chang, Epstein, & Stern, 2008).

Health care for pregnant prisoners is often woefully inadequate. For instance, detoxifying pregnant women involves specialized treatment protocols that are largely unavailable in prisons (Whitehead, Dodson, & Edwards, 2013). Since 2005, the U.S. Department of Health and Human Services (2005) has recommended opioid-addicted pregnant women receive methadone replacement as a treatment to avoid withdrawal for both the mother and fetus. Although some state correctional systems (e.g., California) allow for methadone replacement for pregnant prisoners, many do not (McKenzie, Nunn, Zaller, Bazazi, & Rich, 2009). Methadone replacement therapy can be expensive, and many prison administrators may view it as an unnecessary.

Thirty-eight states receive a grade of "D" or lower for their failure to implement adequate health care policies, or any policies at all, regarding the prenatal care of women in prison. A recent study of correctional facilities in the United States found serious deficiencies in the availability and delivery of prenatal care as well (see Box 7.1: Number of States with Inadequate Prenatal Care for Prisoners).

Box 7.1 Number of States with Inadequate Prenatal Care for Prisoners

- Forty-eight states do not offer human immunodeficiency virus (HIV) screening.
- Forty-four states do not make advance arrangements with hospitals for deliveries.
- Forty-three states do not include medical examinations as an element of prenatal care.
- Forty-one states have no provisions for prenatal nutritional counseling and do not offer pregnant prisoners nutritionally appropriate diets.
- Thirty-four states do not screen or treat incarcerated women for high-risk pregnancies.

Source: Rebecca Project for Human Rights (2010)

Shackling pregnant prisoners during labor and delivery is a common practice in the United States, with thirty-two states allowing it (American Civil Liberties Union, 2015). The American Congress of Obstetricians and Gynecologists (ACOG) denounces the shackling of pregnant prisoners because they deem the practice as demeaning and unnecessary. In addition, it poses a safety risk to patients because restraints may impede medical responses to unfolding emergency events during delivery (Dodson, in press). In response to this debate, the Federal Bureau of Prisons (FBOP), the United States Marshals Service (USMS), U.S. Immigration and Customs Enforcement (ICE), and the American Correctional Association (ACA) have limited the use of shackles on pregnant prisoners, particularly during labor and delivery (American Civil Liberties Union, 2015).

Abortion Access

Women prisoners have a constitutional right to an abortion (see *Bryant v. Maffucci*, 1991; *Roe v. Crawford*, 2008), and correctional administrators and staff do not have the authority to impede or prevent a woman from terminating a pregnancy (see *Monmouth County Correctional Institutional Inmates v. Lanzaro*, 1987; *Roe v. Crawford, 2008*). The courts have held that "prisons and jails can, and must, reasonably accommodate a woman's decision to have an abortion" (Kasdan, 2009, p. 3). However, state and local correctional facilities are not required to bear the cost of an abortion, since it is considered an elective procedure. Federal prisons are prohibited from paying for abortions by federal law (What You Should Know, 2017). However, federal prisons can use federal dollars to pay for abortions when the mother's life is in danger if the fetus is carried to term or in the case of rape.

Prison Doulas

Although there is much room for improved delivery of prenatal care, there are correctional systems across the United States that have embraced policies and practices designed to improve the health care services for incarcerated pregnant women. For example, in Washington State, there is a nonprofit organization known as "The Birth Attendants" that coordinate The Prison Doula Project at the Washington Center for Women (Newman, 2007). A doula is a woman who is a professionally trained labor and birth attendant. Doulas provide nonmedical assistance to pregnant women, including physical, emotional, and psychological support during and after delivery. Doula services includes advocating for proper nutrition for pregnant prisoners, assisting pregnant prisoners with the development of a childbirth plan in consultation with an obstetrician, counseling resources to deal with postnatal separation, and placement or custody arrangements for the infant (Dodson, in press). However, some state correctional systems have taken these services one step further and implemented prison nursery programs to address the needs of pregnant prisoners.

Prison Nursery Programs

Eleven states (California, Illinois, Indiana, Ohio, Nebraska, New York, South Dakota, Texas, Washington, West Virginia, and Wyoming) currently offer prison nursery programs that allow infants to remain with their mothers for a limited period of time following birth. Bedford Hills Correctional Facility in Bedford Hills, New York, established the first prison nursery program in 1901 (Yager, 2015). Today, the nursery program at Bedford Hills is a model for other nursery programs, and it describes the criteria for program eligibility and participation. For example, the child must be born while the mother is in state custody, and her criminal record should be clear of violent crimes or a history of child abuse or neglect. In addition, inmates cannot have any violent disciplinary infractions, including inmate-on-staff or inmate-on-inmate assaults. Each state specifies other criteria beyond the general criteria outlined by Bedford Hills. The length of stay and capacity of the programs also varies from state-to-state. The average stay for the correctional facilities is between 12 to 18 months, and program capacity is limited.

The principal purpose of prison nursery programs is to allow infants to remain with their incarcerated mothers for a specified amount of time within the correctional facility in the hopes of creating strong mother-infant bonds or attachments. An increasing number of criminal justice policy makers and correctional administrators recognize that the immediate separation of the infant from his or her mother significantly reduces the likelihood of forming maternal bonds. Mother-infant bonds are important because they improve long-term outcomes for children. For instance, children who form strong bonds with their mothers have fewer occurrences of delinquency, decreased aggression, and an easier time forming strong bonds or attachments to others (Hirschi, 1969). Mothers who form maternal bonds have positive outcomes, too, including greater parental competency, improved mental health, and lower recidivism rates (Borelli Goshin, Joestl, Clark, & Byrne, 2010; Whiteacre, Fritz, & Owen, 2013).

Recently, the Federal Bureau of Prisons (FBOP) established a community residential program called Mothers and Infants Nurturing Together (MINT) for women who are pregnant at the time of incarceration (What You Should Know, 2017). Similar to state-operated prison nursery programs, MINT is a residential reentry center-based program that is designed to encourage mother-infant bonding and parenting skills for low-risk pregnant prisoners. MINT participants learn about prenatal and postnatal programs such as childbirth, coping skills, and parenting classes. In addition, MINT takes a holistic approach to the helping inmates successfully navigate reentry, and it offers a variety of other programs, including substance abuse treatment, physical and sexual abuse counseling, vocational and educational programs, and budgeting classes to accomplish this goal (What You Should Know, 2017). Women are eligible to participate in the MINT program if they are in their last trimester and they have less than five years remaining on their sentence. Once the infant is born, incarcerated mothers are allowed to remain with the child up to three months to bond; however, additional time may be granted in some cases. Mother-participants must designate a guardian for the newborn prior to delivery to ensure appropriate placement for the infant once participants have completed the MINT program.

Motherhood Behind Bars

A primary concern and cause of stress for incarcerated women is their role as mothers. Female prisoners frequently report that a leading concern related to their imprisonment is the well-being of their children. They often note that being away from their children is the hardest and most stressful aspect of serving their sentences (Belknap, 2007; Enos, 2001; Pollock, 2002). Nearly 70% of incarcerated women are mothers to minor children, and prior to incarceration they are typically the sole financial and care provider in the household (Belknap, 2015; Glaze & Muraschak, 2008; Marcus-Mendoza, 2016).

Many women never see their children during their incarceration. For those who are able to maintain contact, visits are likely to be sporadic. Financial difficulties related to transportation and/or geographic distances, elderly caregivers' ability to facilitate trips for visits, and foster care placement are all factors that create barriers to visitation. These experiences are particularly prevalent among women of color and their children because of higher incarceration rates among these groups of women, who lack the resources to maintain regular contact with their children (Mumola, 2000). Minority families experience further difficulties in providing for the resources that enable visits with their incarcerated mothers because of higher rates of poverty and other factors resulting from social, racial, and economic marginalization (Christian & Thomas, 2009).

Incarcerated mothers normally express a desire to resume care for their children postrelease (Glaze & Maruschak, 2008), although long absences from their children make this transition more difficult (Call, 2011). In addition, many women have difficulty reintegrating into the lives of their children (Brown & Bloom, 2009). For instance, mothers report a loss of confidence in their parenting skills that impedes their ability to respond effectively to their children (Poehlmann, 2005). However, many prison nursery programs include parenting classes, which may help mothers improve their parenting skills (see e.g., Carlson, 1998; 2001; 2009; Koch & Tomlin, 2010; Staley 2002; Whiteacre et al., 2013). Mothers who complete parenting programs report increased levels of self-esteem and more confidence in their ability to parent their children (Harm & Thompson, 1997). Mothers also report significant positive changes in their parenting attitudes, including "empathetic awareness of their children's needs, alternatives to corporal punishment, and appropriate family roles and responsibilities" (Harm & Thompson, 1997, p. 135). The Girl Scouts Behind Bars is an organization that helps incarcerated mothers develop parenting skills and is dedicated to keeping mothers and daughters connected (see Box 7.2 for more about Girl Scouts Behind Bars).

Box 7.2 Girl Scouts Behind Bars

The National Institute of Justice (NIJ) created the Girls Scouts Behind Bars (GSBB), and the first chapter was established in Maryland in 1992. It is an unlikely partnership between correctional departments across the United States and the Girls Scouts of the United States of America (GSUSA). The program was established "to respond to the needs of girls whose mothers are incarcerated and perceived inadequacies of in-prison visitation" (Moses, 1995, p. 4). The primary goal of GSBB is "to nurture, and in some cases reestablish, mother-daughter relationships" (GSUSA, 2007, p. 3). GSBB is frequently the only resource low-income mothers can turn to help pay for trips to the prison, especially those located in remote locations. GSBB consists of four components: (1) mother-daughter meetings at a correctional facility, (2) traditional in-the-community troop meetings for the girls, (3) in-prison enrichment activities for the mothers, and (4) support and linking of caregivers and guardians with social services. A three-year evaluation of GSBB found that participation improved the self-esteem of girls, strengthened their relationship with their mothers, and helped them to develop leadership skills. Mothers reported a stronger relationship with their daughters, improved communication, and the ability to encourage their daughters (CSR Incorporated, 2008; see also Grant, 2006 for an evaluation of GSBB).

Dental Care and Services

Inmates experience a greater need regarding oral health and dental treatment than those among the general population. These dental problems include tooth decay, tooth loss, and self-esteem concerns that can be related to oral health needs. According to the Survey of Inmates in State and Federal Correctional Facilities of 2004, roughly half of female prisoners reported having some sort of dental issue at some point during their incarceration (Harner & Riley, 2013). Boyer and colleagues (2002) found that in their study of a sample Iowa prisoners, females averaged 5.5 teeth with decay and had 5.12 missing teeth. This may be compared to females in the general population with 1.5 decayed teeth and 4.7 missing teeth. Various factors may be considered to explain the increased problems related to oral health. For one, availability and affordability of oral health care may be of greater concern to those incarcerated versus the general population.

HIV/AIDS Risks and Treatment

During incarceration, the prevalence of infectious disease and fear of contraction becomes a serious health concern. This is especially true and significant when discussing the prevalence of human immunodeficiency virus infection and acquired immune deficiency syndrome (HIV/AIDS) among inmates. The incarcerated population is more likely to test positive for HIV/AIDS than those living in the general population. Some reports show that these numbers may be up to five times higher when comparing rates of HIV infection (Hammett, Harmon, & Maruschak, 1999; Petersilia, 2003; Richie, 2001).

Inmates create a unique culture inside of correctional facilities to adjust, cope, and adapt to "the deprivations of prison life" (Sykes, 1958, p. 69). Inmates share common attitudes, beliefs, and practices of everyday life on the inside. A characteristic often shared among offenders is their engagement in risky behaviors and attitudes of invincibility. The belief that they will not, or cannot, contract diseases is a common reason why unprotected sex is often practiced (Olivero, 1992; Staton-Tindall, 2007). Homosexual acts, both consensual and nonconsensual, are common and even accepted practices in prison (Hensley, 2002; Olivero, 1992; Pollock-Byrne, 1992). These acts increase the chances for an inmate to become infected with the HIV/AIDS virus and other sexually transmitted infections (STIs).

The risk of HIV/AIDS is greater for prisoners primarily because of higher populations of intravenous drug users and the practice and acceptance of the sex trade for goods and services among the prison culture (Hensley, 2002; Rideau, 2011). Not only are inmates at great risk for contracting the virus, but these risks are also passed onto their families and communities upon their release from incarceration (Robillard, Gallito-Zaparaniuk, Arriola, Kennedy, Hammett, & Braithwaite, 2003). Among female offender populations, HIV/AIDS creates a special concern. Female inmate populations are at greater risk and have a greater rate of infection than their male counterparts (BJS, 2006a; Greenfeld & Snell, 1999; Hammett, Rhodes, & Harmon, 1999; Maruschak, 2009). When comparing the problem across inmate populations by gender, females have showed higher rates of testing positive for HIV than males. By 2008, roughly 2% of women prisoners housed in state and federal prisons were HIV-positive or diagnosed with AIDS (Maruschak, 2009). This is compared to 1.5% of male inmates. In addition, female offenders have rates of infection 15 times greater than women among the general population (DeGroot & CuUvin, 2005). This creates a concern for health care providers within institutional settings and communities in terms of trying to prevent the spread of the disease as well as the associated cost of treatment.

By the end of 2008, nearly 22,000 state and federal inmates had tested positive for HIV or had confirmed cases of AIDS (Maruschak, 2009). Leading causes of infection are sharing drug needles, unprotected sex with multiple partners, relationships with others at risk for HIV/AIDS infection, having sex under the influence of drugs and/or alcohol, and exchanging sex for drugs, money, and other favors (Anderson, Rosay, & Saum, 2002; Belgrave, Corneille, Nasim, Fitzgerald, & Lucas, 2008; Staton-Tindall et al., 2007). Drug use has been an overwhelming contributor to HIV/AIDS infection.

Women often contract the disease from intravenous drug use and engage in sex while under the influence of drugs and alcohol. While under the influence of substances, women may lose their inhibitions and make impaired decisions regarding sexual encounters and their partners. The decisions often end in unprotected sex, increasing the risk of infection of HIV/AIDS and other STIs (Belgrave et al., 2008; Staton-Tindall et al., 2007). As a result, women will need guidance during the reentry process to ensure continuity of care and to prevent the spread of STIs.

Sexual Victimization

Incarcerated women not only experience higher rates of mental health problems than those among the general population and those of their male counterparts, but also higher rates of sexual victimization (James & Glaze, 2006; Sharp, 2003; 2014). According to the Bureau of Justice Statistics (1999), 41% of women in jails and 48% of women prisoners report histories of physical or sexual victimization. Women and girls in U.S. jails, prisons, and immigrant detention centers are extremely vulnerable to sexual assault. Women are more likely than men to be sexually victimized during incarceration, especially by correctional staff (Swavola, Riley, & Subramanian, 2016) (see Box 7.3: Sexual Assault in Immigrant Detention Centers).

Box 7.3 Sexual Assault in Immigrant Detention Centers

Women and girls held at immigration detention centers have made allegations of sexual assault from both inmates and staff. One mother alleges that her 12-year-old daughter was sexually harassed and sexually assaulted by another woman housed at the Karnes County Residential Center in Karnes City, Texas (Garcia-Ditta, 2016). The mother of the victim also alleges that although correctional officials moved her and her daughter to another location within the facility, they never notified her that the case had been closed because of a lack of evidence, and she has filed a lawsuit against the administrators at Karnes. In 2014, the Mexican American Legal Defense and Education Fund (MALDEF) and attorneys from the University of Texas School of Law allege substantial ongoing sexual abuse at Karnes. Women at Karnes recounted stories of being removed from their cells at night to engage in sexual acts, promising immigration assistance in exchange for sexual favors, and groping of women in front of their children (Seville, 2014). A 40-year-old male correctional officer, Daniel Sharkey, at the Berks County Residential Center in Leesport, Pennsylvania, admitted he sexually assaulted a 19-year-old Honduran woman while she was in custody. He initially denied the allegations but evidently pleaded guilty to institutional sexual assault, and he was sentenced to 23 months in prison (Feltz, 2016). In 2017, a watchdog and national advocacy group known as the Community Initiatives for Visiting Immigrants in Confinement (CIVIC) filed a civil rights suit about sexual assault and abuse against immigration detention centers across the United States. CIVIC made a Freedom of Information Act (FOIA) request and discovered that a total of 14,693 complaints of physical and/or sexual abuse had been alleged by detainees against Immigration and Commerce Enforcement (ICE) between January 2010 and July 2016 (Wick, 2017). CIVIC also found that the Office of Inspector General (OIG) received reports of 1,016 complaints of sexual abuse or assault between May 2014 and July 2016, but only 24 of the complaints were investigated by the OIG. The remaining complaints were referred back to ICE for further investigation, and the OIG did not request any follow-up (Wick, 2017). Most of these alleged abuses occur in privately operated facilities.

It is no surprise that a history of sexual abuse is a common cause of the onset of mental health issues and a predictor of female criminality, especially illegal substance abuse. Therapeutic responses to the mental health needs of women, particularly victims of sexual abuse, should be gender-responsive and recognize the gendered pathways of women offenders. For example, a woman's self-identity is often associated with her ability to foster relationships and connections with others (Van Voorhis & Salisbury, 2014). Two key features of healthy relationships include mutuality and empathy (Baker Miller, 1976). Mutuality means that relationships are built on a foundation of "mutual influence and mutual responsiveness" within the relationship (Baker Miller, 1976, p. 26). Empathy refers to the ability to understand another person's thoughts and feelings without surrendering one's self. Sexual abuse typically starts during childhood, and the perpetrators are likely a parent, close relative, guardian, or caregiver. In sexually abusive relationships, mutuality and empathy are absent. This early disruption and trauma associated with fostering close relationships increases the odds that women will have difficulty forming close attachments and/or relationships throughout life.

In prison, mental health professionals should make sure that women receive an accurate mental health diagnoses and treatment information. Women may be prescribed psychotropic medications to address their specific diagnoses and should understand the potential benefits and side effects of these medications. Women who have been victims of sexual abuse frequently have substance abuse histories. Women sexual abuse victims benefit from both individual counseling and group therapy (Bein, 2011; Van Voorhis & Salisbury, 2014). However, any treatment regime should be based on the person's specific therapeutic needs. For women, this means understanding the unique circumstances and gendered experiences that contributed to their incarceration.

Drug Offenses

The "War on Drugs" has had a profound and disproportionate effect on the growth of female incarceration rates over the past several decades (Bloom et al., 2004; Pollock, 2004; Richie, 2001). The Bureau of Justice Statistics (2000) reports that between the years 1990–1998, more than 12,000 women were imprisoned for drug offenses. Since 1992, incarceration rates for women have increased about 7% each year (Chesney-Lind & Pasko, 2004). Increases of the offenses may be attributed to the "War on Drugs" and mandatory minimum sentencing for drug crimes. In 2011, roughly 32% of the female prison population was serving a state sentence for a drug-related crime (Carson & Golinelli, 2013). The significance of this number is even more evident when compared to trends in 1986, when roughly 15% of imprisoned women were incarcerated for drug offenses (Richie, 2001). Because of this, Chesney-Lind and Pasko (2013, p. 140) have suggested the "War on Drugs" has translated into a "War on Women."

Mandatory sentencing laws have led judges to sentence women in the same manner as men who committed the same types of offenses. Women were no longer spared because of their caretaker roles or the secondary roles they may have played in committing a drug offense. In turn, women's prison populations have dramatically increased over the past 20 years and continue to grow at faster rates than men's (Pollock, 2002; Chesney-Lind & Pasko, 2013). After the passage of mandatory sentencing laws in 1986, during the height of the drug war and moral panic over the dangers of crack cocaine, female populations increased by 888% the following decade for drug crimes alone (Hattery & Smith, 2010). Not only did these reforms lead to an increase in numbers, but also sentence lengths became longer and probation, as an optional sentence often vanished for female offenders (Faris & Miller, 2010).

Many of the drug crimes were committed because of women's involvement in drug networks, often involving their intimate partners (Petersilia, 2005). For some women, the only way to distance themselves from these networks would mean ending the relationship. Women may lack self-esteem or independence, especially if there are children involved. Some of these relationships may involve domestic violence, lending an ever-greater aspect of fear of leaving. One report by the BJS (1999) indicates that among female probationers, 40% report abusive relationships in during childhood and/

or adulthood. In contrast, only 9% of male probationers report abusive relationships in childhood and/or adulthood. Estimates show 30–50% of incarcerated women are victims of intimate partner violence (Greenfeld & Snell, 1999).

Many drug and property crimes committed by females may have been economically motivated and act as a means of personal survival or an effort to provide for their families (Belknap, 2007; Chesney-Lind & Pasko, 2013; Covington & Bloom, 2006; Gilfus, 2006; Moe & Ferraro, 2006). With little education and job training, women often turn to theft or larceny as means to support the family financially. However, roles in criminality are often gendered, meaning women play secondary, minor, and subordinate roles when committing offenses in connection with a male counterparts or intimate partners (Chesney-Lind & Rodriguez, 1983; Chesney-Lind & Pasko, 2013). Women's roles in crimes are often committed under a division of labor and within abusive relationships with male partners. Women often report they shoplift and turn over their acquisitions to their male partners, pimps, or fathers (Gilfus, 2006). The men then sell the products and keep the money for themselves, benefitting from female criminality. Women may receive only a small portion of the earnings. Women may also act as lookouts during robberies or prostitute themselves, again for a small portion of the money earned for the act or for drugs. If a man feels that a woman does not produce enough money for her criminal activities, violence often results. Sixteen of the 20 women interviewed in the Gilfus (2006) study report being involved in such relationships.

To illustrate how the "War on Drugs" has affected blacks over the past several decades, drug convictions should be examined. In 1990, blacks constituted roughly 12% of the general population, while 60% of all drug convictions around that time were for those who were black (Parenti, 1999). In 1999, two-thirds of women parolees were minorities; 42% of those women had been incarcerated for drug offenses. This number had increased from 36% in 1990 (Greene & Schiraldi, 2002). Black women are convicted and incarcerated at higher rates when prosecuted for drug crimes than white and Hispanic women (Belknap, 2015; Pasko & Chesney-Lind, 2013; Sharp, 2014). These findings demonstrate women of color have been and continue to be disproportionately affected by drug enforcement policies and practices in the United States.

Treatment for Addiction

Women prisoners experiences higher rates of substance abuse and addiction than those women in the general population. In 2015, roughly 25% of women prisoners in state correctional facilities and nearly 59% in federal facilities were serving sentences for drug offenses (Carson & Anderson, 2016). Common charges included drug use, possession, and drug trafficking. Drug crimes committed by women are typically nonviolent. Often, women who have not been convicted of drug crimes committed crimes that were, in some way, drug related. For example, women may have been convicted of robbery but were under the influence of substances at the time of the offense and have committed economic crimes to support their drug habits (Carter, 2012).

The "War on Drugs" led to harsher sentencing guidelines for drug convictions. Sentences for drug offenders became longer, misdemeanor offenses became felonies, mandatory minimums were put into place, and "Three Strikes" laws required life sentences for some drug offenders (Hattery & Smith, 2010). Over several decades, the increase in the numbers of women charged with drug offenses has been significant because of drug policies. For example, 45% of state and federal inmates are incarcerated for nonviolent drug charges (Hattery & Smith, 2010). Approximately 35% of the offenders released in 1997 were incarcerated for drug offenses. Of those inmates released in 1985, 12% were incarcerated for drug convictions (Beck, 2000). Many of those same offenders were found to have been under the influence of drugs at the time of their arrests, while many admitted to using drugs during the month before committing their crime (Bloom et al., 2004). The BJS (2006b) reported that nearly one-third of state inmates and a quarter of federal inmates committed their crimes while under the influence of drugs.

With increasingly punitive sentences for drug crimes, the "face" of these offenders has changed among those incarcerated. This is especially true for female prisoner populations. Just as the "War on Drugs" policies have rapidly increased the numbers of male populations, changes in female populations have been drastic. Women are twice as likely to be incarcerated for drug crimes as men (Belknap, 2007).

Women who are drug users are more likely to be involved in crime (Merlo & Pollock, 1995). Often, women's crimes are driven by drug use, much more so than their male counterparts'. Research indicates that the majority of incarcerated females have engaged in drug use at some point in their lives. Cotton-Oldenburg Jordan, Martin, and Kupper (1999) reported that 73% of women reported drug use prior to serving time. Bloom et al. (2004) reported that 40% of females in state prisons (versus 32% of males inmates) admitted to being under the influence of drugs at the time they committed their crimes. About half reported they were using alcohol, drugs, or both at the time. This suggests that substance abuse programming is necessary for successful reintegration for a substantial number of women prisoners. In 2004, 40% of substance-abusing state inmates and roughly 45% of federal inmates were reported to have been in a drug treatment program since their admission to prison (BJS, 2006b).

Mental Illness

Mental health illnesses and disorders are especially prevalent among incarcerated female populations. Women prisoners are much more likely than their male counterparts to suffer from mental health issues. In 2005, 73% of females in state prisons and 75% in local jails suffered from symptoms of serious mental illness (e.g., depression, bipolar disorder, and schizophrenia). In comparison, 55% of men in state prisons and 63% in jails suffered from serious mental illness (James & Glaze, 2006). Researchers from BJS (2006b) found that around 24% of inmates in jails, 15% of state inmates, and 10% of federal inmates reported symptoms that indicated a psychotic disorder (i.e., experiencing delusions or hallucinations). Veysey and Bichler-Robertson (2002) reported that nearly 30% of inmates suffered from an anxiety disorder. Common anxiety disorders included social anxiety disorder, posttraumatic stress disorder, panic disorder, and separation anxiety. Rates of serious mental illness are much lower for women in the general population. Specifically, roughly 12% of women in the general population suffer from a diagnosis of serious mental illness (BJS, 2006b).

Bloom and Covington (2009) contend that characteristics often found among incarcerated women's backgrounds may lay the foundation for explaining higher rates of mental health issues. These researchers argue that traumatic life experiences, along with inadequate health services, play dynamic roles in the onset and prevalence of mental health issues for this population of offenders. Unstable lives, inadequate coping mechanisms, and untreated mental disorders carry over to higher rates of offending and eventually incarceration. The end result is higher rates of women suffering from mental illness in correctional facilities.

Despite the seriousness of women prisoners' needs for care, previous research indicates women may not receive adequate health and psychological care during incarceration (Anderson et al., 2002). The women included in this study specifically stated opinions regarding the inadequacies of medical and psychological services provided in prison. If women do not receive the needed counseling and treatment for these mental health and other health-related issues, successful reentry is unlikely. A lack of adequate health care services and medical neglect supports feminist critics' assertion that incarcerated women are "forgotten and invisible" during incarceration (Belknap, 2015, p. 289; see also Gido, 2009, p. 25). Without having their needs met in prison, women will return to society with unaddressed issues. Where they return to may factor into their ability to seek care, knowledge of where to seek services, and any available resources that may assist them with their needs.

Few women receive adequate mental health treatment while in prison. Bloom and Covington (2009) explained that female inmate populations are much more prone to mental health issues, primarily because of traumatic childhood and other life experiences, which often lead to crimes resulting in a prison sentence. Therefore, it is not surprising that depression, anxiety, and counseling for past abuse and victimization are commonly reported psychological needs of women prisoners. Mental health not only represents a major issue for incarcerated women, it often carries over during the reentry process. Issues regarding mental health, history of substance abuse and addiction, and life stressors presented during reentry may place many ex-offenders at a high risk for reoffending and drug or alcohol relapse (Covington, 1998; Seiter & Kadela, 2003).

Correctional Programming for Reentry

Ideally, correctional programming policies are designed to prepare inmates who lack the social, vocational, and educational skills needed to become productive, law-abiding citizens. A portion of this chapter examines female ex-offender's perceptions of the correctional programming they received during their incarceration. Their views of the benefits and shortcomings of treatment and programming are also of concern. Administrators of correctional institutions are partly responsible for providing training and programs inmates will need to ease the burdens they face upon returning to society.

Educational and Vocational Training

Female inmates are often poor and uneducated or undereducated. Many female offenders describe attending schools in poor, urban, inner-city areas where drugs were readily available, teachers failed to notice warning signs of abuse and neglect, and peers were often members of deviant groups (Gilfus, 2006). These factors created difficulty in terms of concentration and academic performance and resulted in many women dropping out of high school. Therefore, many women need to be educated, taught skills and trades that will allow them to be successful in the workforce, and create academic and professional support systems upon their return to society.

Offering General Education Diploma (GED) programs to female inmates may also be necessary for successfully reintegrating back into society. Brewster and Sharp (2002) found evidence to support lower recidivism rates for women completing their GEDs compared to those women who did not. Unfortunately, few prisons offer college degree programs, even though research shows that higher educational attainment is related to lower recidivism rates and successful reentry (Lerman, 2013). Increasing the education levels aids in securing jobs and receiving higher pay.

A 2014 study by the National Center for Education Statistics' (NCES) Program for the International Assessment of Adult Competencies (PIAAC) gives a comprehensive portrait of prisoners' educational history and current desire for services. The PIAAC data shows that prisoners had not received any formal academic program since entering prison, and this is particularly true for women prisoners. Specifically, 47% of women compared to 41% of men reported they had not advanced academically during their current period of incarceration (NCES, 2014).

Many women become involved in criminal activity as a result of a lack of vocational skills, shorter work histories, and overall lower economic status in comparison to men (Greenfeld & Snell, 1999; Richie, 2001). Educational and vocational training provide inmates with life skills that are pertinent to creating family support systems. These opportunities can also aid women in becoming more marketable when seeking employment upon release, which may lead to greater satisfaction and positive attitudes (Greenfeld & Snell, 1999). In addition, research indicates that vocational and educational programs reduce recidivism rates. For example, one study showed that inmates participating in vocational programs were 13% less likely to recidivate once released (Aos, Phipps, Barnoski, & Lieb, 2001). Reduced rates in recidivism can equate to lower correctional spending per inmate and increased production in the community and workforce.

Women are typically less educated prior to incarceration than men (Sharp, Marcus-Mendoza, Bentley, Simpson, & Love, 1999). Many women prisoners are uneducated, with only about 44%

possessing a high school diploma or the equivalent (GED) (Harlow, 2003). This may be the reason why women were more likely than men to request academic programs during a study on coed prisoners (Wilson, 1980), and this continues to be the trend (NCES, 2014).

Women are less likely than men to be employed at the time of their arrest and prior to incarceration (Pollock, 2004). In regard to income, less than 40% of state females prisoners were employed full-time, and about 35% earned less than $600 a month (Richie, 2001). Women often lack employment experience, marketable job skills, and vocational training that can allow them better opportunities to earn incomes that are much above minimum wage pay.

At the times of their arrests, women were generally living in low-income neighborhoods in urban areas. Even after incarceration, many women are likely to return to the same disenfranchised neighborhoods upon their release from jail or prison (Enos, 2001). Without adequate programming, the chances for successful reintegration are hindered. Chances are likely that these environments and situations will allow for or create opportunities to fall back into criminal activities, specifically drug use. These environments often create the structural barriers that lead these women to be incarcerated in the first place (Maher, Dunlap, & Johnson, 2006; Moe & Ferraro, 2006; Morash, 2010).

HIV/AIDS Education

In 1999, as a result of the AIDS epidemic and pressures to implement prevention interventions, the Centers for Disease Control and Prevention (CDCP) published a group of evidenced-based HIV prevention programs known as the Diffusion of Effective Behavioral Interventions (DEBI) (Collins, Whithers, & Braithwaite, 2007). Sisters Informing Sisters about Topics on AIDS (SISTA) was the response for gendered and culturally DEBI for incarcerated females at risk for contracting HIV. The program is a peer-led HIV prevention program targeting heterosexual black women. The primary goal of the SISTA program is to increase knowledge about HIV/AIDS infection and decrease the risky behaviors that contribute to HIV/AIDS infection among black women (see Box 7.4 for more about the core elements of SISTA).

The focus of SISTA is to present gender-specific and culturally relevant information and skills training to this group of women. This has been extremely important because of the growing numbers of women offenders contracting the disease, especially black women (Belgrave et al., 2008; Collins et al., 2007; Staton-Tindall et al., 2007). According to the CDC (2004, 2007), African-American women are much more likely than white women to contract HIV/AIDS, and the primary reason for

Box 7.4 Core Elements of SISTA

- Small group discussions focusing on session objectives, role-playing women's skills acquisitions, and addressing the challenges and joys of being African American;
- Skilled African-American female facilitators;
- Use of cultural and gender-specific materials to enhance pride and self-worth;
- Teach women skills to communicate and negotiate with their partners;
- Instruction on effective and consistent condom use;
- Discussion on cultural barriers to negotiation and using condoms; and
- Emphasis on partner involvement in safe-sex practices.

Source: Collins et al. (2007)

contraction is heterosexual activity. Roughly three-quarters of the women contracted the disease from an infected male partner, while the other (nearly) one-quarter contracted it through contaminated needle exchange (CDC, 2007). Other cultural factors affecting these rates (common throughout the literature) are IV drug use, higher rates of incarceration among African-American men, and unprotected sex because of inconsistent, or lack of, condom use (Anderson et al., 2002; Belgrave et al., 2008).

Through participating in the SISTA project, respondents have been shown to possess greater knowledge pertaining to HIV/AIDS, increase the practice of safe sex through condom use, and improve communication and assertiveness skills (Belgrave et al., 2008; DiClemente & Wingood, 1995). DiClemente and Wingood (1995) indicated that not only were women influenced by the program, but participants' partners were more likely to adapt to condom use and support the attitudes surrounding safe-sex practices.

Trauma and Substance Abuse

Covington (2004; 2003; 2002) and Covington et al. (2006 contend that effective programming for women involved with the criminal justice system must be gender-responsive and developed based on female pathways to criminality. Sexual, physical, and emotional abuse and drug use that follows as a result of these experiences are the leading links to explaining females' involvement in crime. The first step in overcoming abuse as a pathway to crime is to teach women to acknowledge abuse as a form of victimization. For some women, abuse may not be viewed as a serious issue, especially if their early reports were ignored. Sexual abuse may be a cyclical pattern in some families, with little

Box 7.5 Addiction Recovery Treatment Model for Women

The etiology of addiction, especially gender-specific issues related to addiction, including social, physiological, and psychological consequences of addiction and factors related to the onset of addiction:

- Low self-esteem;
- Appearance and overall health and hygiene;
- Eating disorders;
- Race, ethnicity, and cultural issues;
- Gender discrimination and harassment;
- Disability-related issues as applicable;
- Relationships with family and significant others;
- Attachments to unhealthy interpersonal relationships;
- Grief related to the loss of alcohol and other substances, children, family, or partner;
- Isolation related to a lack of social support systems;
- Interpersonal violence, including incest, sexual assault, and other abuse;
- Sexuality, including sexual functioning and sexual orientation;
- Parenting;
- Child care and child custody;
- Employment; and
- Life plan development.

Source: United States Department of Health and Human Services (2014)

intervention when the crime is reported to adults. Therefore, women may accept this as a normative part of intimate relationships.

As a response to trauma, women often turn to illegal drug use as a coping mechanism to alleviate the pain of these experiences. By providing women with programming that allows for them to appropriately address their issues and concerns, women may be better equipped to overcome the struggles related to their abusive pasts. Implementing programs so that women can be capable of understanding and coping with trauma may be beneficial in reducing problems with substance abuse, addiction, and relapse.

The United States Department of Health and Human Services (2014) recommends personalized therapy sessions with prison psychologists specializing in matters dealing with sexual abuse, domestic violence, and substance abuse. Women often find it difficult to discuss these issues in group therapy sessions because of embarrassment or the fear that others are judging them (Carter, 2012). Unfortunately, one-on-one counseling is uncommon during incarceration, and counseling often occurs within a group setting. Recently, the U.S. Department of Health and Human Services SAMHSA's Center for Substance Abuse Treatment (2014) outlined the key issues that should be included in a comprehensive model of treatment for women with substance abuse histories (see Box 7.5: Addiction Recovery Treatment Model for Women).

Conclusion

Women frequently face serious medical problems during incarceration, especially those related to mental health and addiction (Covington & Bloom, 2006; Gido & Dalley, 2009). These problems will often carry over to the reentry process as a result of the unmet needs of women and inadequate health care prior to and during incarceration (Petersilia, 2003; Pollock, 2002). Incarcerated women often have serious medical conditions that require treatment, including pregnancy, sexually transmitted infections, and mental illness.

Access to health care and competent medical personnel in women's prisons and lack of medical care inmates receive during incarceration are serious issues women prisoners face. However, during incarceration women are usually provided with basic medical care and receive prescribed medications needed to treat diseases or mental illnesses, many of which are extremely expensive. Upon release, women will need to find an employer that offers health benefits or find access to social services for their medical needs, treatments, and medications. Access to welfare medical insurance and financial difficulties of meeting the costs of medical needs and uncertainty as to where to seek assistance and resources for their medical needs are likely to be a barrier once leaving prison.

Receiving social welfare insurance or any type of coverage for treatment and medicines is necessary for these women. Public health and reentry programming should coordinate to devise treatment plans for those returning home and suffering from various diseases and mental health diagnoses. As more people are incarcerated, the risk of spreading diseases increase, especially STIs. Because of risky lifestyles prior to incarceration and cramped living quarters and other conditions related to prison living, inmates are susceptible to infectious diseases such as tuberculosis, Hepatitis C, and HIV/AIDS (Petersilia, 2003; Travis & Visher, 2005). Providing more affordable treatment may alleviate the potential risks of spreading the disease in correctional facilities and in the communities where women will return. Addressing the health needs of incarcerated women and those who are returning from prisons not only benefit the inmate population but should also be regarded as addressing a public health matter.

The growing rate of female incarceration makes the needs of this group a pressing issue. Policy and programming are most effective when they are designed to target the social-based causes of female criminality and treat the specific physical, psychological, emotional, and social needs of women. Research indicates policies that are gender-focused will best address the concerns of this population (Chesney-Lind & Pasko, 2013; Van Voorhis & Salisbury, 2014).

References

Aday, R. H. (2003). *Aging prisoners: Crisis in American corrections*. Westport, CT: Praeger.

Alarid, L. F., & Cromwell, P. (Eds.). (2006). *In her own words: Women offenders' views on crime and victimization*. Los Angeles, CA: Roxbury.

American Civil Liberties Union. (2015). *The shackling of pregnant women & girls in U.S. prisons, jails, & youth detention centers*. New York, NY: ACLU Reproductive Freedom Project; ACLU National Prison Project.

Anderson, T. L., Rosay, A. B., & Saum, C. (2002). The impact of drug use and crime involvement on health problems among female offenders. *The Prison Journal, 82*(1), 50–68. doi:10.1177/003288550208200104

Aos, S., Phipps, P., Barnoski, R., & Lieb, R. (2001). *The comparative costs and benefits of programs to reduce crime*. Olympia, WA: Washington State Institute for Public Policy.

Baker Miller, J. (1976). *Toward a new psychology of women*. Boston, MA: Beacon Press.

Beck, A. J. (2000, April). *State and federal prisoners returning to the community: Findings from the Bureau of Justice Statistics*. Paper presented at the First Reentry Courts Initiative Cluster Meeting, Washington, DC.

Bein, K. (2011). *Action, engagement, remembering: Services for adult survivors of child sexual abuse*. National Sexual Assault Coalition, 1–21. Retrieved from www.nsvrc.org/sites/default/files/Publications_RSP_Action-engagement-remembering-services-for-adult-survivors-child-sexual-abuse.pdf

Belgrave, F. Z., Corneille, M., Nasim, A., Fitzgerald, A., & Lucas, V. (2008). An evaluation of an enhanced sister informing sisters about topics on AIDS (SISTA) HIV prevention curriculum: The role of drug education. *Journal of HIV/AIDS & Social Services*, 7(4), 313–327. doi:10.108/15381500802529822

Belknap, J. (2007). *The invisible woman: Gender, crime, and justice* (3rd ed.). Belmont, CA: Thomson Wadsworth.

Belknap, J. (2015). *The invisible woman: Gender, crime, and justice* (4th ed.). Stamford, CT: Cengage Learning.

Bhuvaneswar, C. G., Chang, G., Epstein, L. A., & Stern, T. A. (2008). Cocaine and opioid use during pregnancy: Prevalence and management. *Primary Care Companion to the Journal of Clinical Psychiatry, 10*(1), 59–65. doi:10.4088/PCC.v10n0110

Bloom, B., & Covington, S. (2009). Addressing the mental health needs of women offenders. In R. L. Gido & L. Dalley (Eds.), *Women's mental health issues across the criminal justice system* (pp. 160–176). Upper Saddle River, NJ: Pearson Prentice Hall.

Bloom, B., Owen, B., & Covington, S. (2003). *Gender responsive strategies: Research, practice, and guiding principles for women offenders*. Washington, DC: U.S. Department of Justice. National Institute of Corrections.

Bloom, B., Owen, B., & Covington, S. (2004). Women offenders and the gendered effects of public policy. *Review of Policy Research, 21*(1), 31–48. doi:10.1111/j.1541-1338.2004.00056.x

Borelli, J. L., Goshin, L., Joestl, S., Clark, J., & Byrne, M. W. (2010). Attachment organization in a sample of incarcerated mothers: Distribution of classifications and associations with substance abuse, depressive symptoms, perceptions of parenting competency and social support. *Attachment & Human Development, 12*(4), 355–374. doi:10.1080/14616730903416971

Boyer, E. M., Nielson-Thompson, N. J., & Hill, T. J. (2002). A comparison of dental caries and tooth loss for Iowa prisoners with other prison populations and dentate U.S. adults. *The Journal of Dental Hygiene, 76*(2), 141–150.

Brewster, D. R., & Sharp, S. F. (2002). Educational programs and recidivism in Oklahoma: Another look. *The Prison Journal, 82*(3), 314–334. doi:10.1177/003288550208200302

Brown, M., & Bloom, B. (2009). Reentry and renegotiating motherhood: Maternal identity and success on parole. *Crime & Delinquency, 55*(2), 313–336. doi:10.1177/0011128708330627

Bryant v. Maffucci, 923 F.2d 979 (1991).

Bureau of Justice Statistics. (1999). *Prior abuse reported by inmates and* probationers. Washington, DC: U.S. Department of Justice, Bureau of Justice Statistics.

Bureau of Justice Statistics. (2000). *Incarcerated parents and their children*. Washington, DC: U.S. Department of Justice.

Bureau of Justice Statistics. (2006a). *Factsheet: Women in prison*. Washington, DC: Government Printing Office.

Bureau of Justice Statistics. (2006b). *Special report: Drug use and dependence, state and federal prisoners, 2004*. Washington, DC: U.S. Department of Justice, Bureau of Justice Statistics.

Call, K. D. (2011). *Childcare opinions project: Incarcerated mothers' perceptions of appropriate childcare*. (Unpublished master's thesis, The Ohio State University, Columbus, OH.

Carlson, J. R. (1998). Evaluating the effectiveness of a live-in nursery within a women's prison. *Journal of Offender Rehabilitation, 27*(1/2), 73–85. doi:10.1300/j076v27n01_06

Carlson, J. R. (2001). Prison nursery 2000: A five-year review of the prison nursery at the Nebraska Correctional Center for Women. *Journal of Offender Rehabilitation, 33*(3), 75–97. doi:10.1300/j076v33n03_05
Carlson, J. R. (2009). Prison nurseries: A pathway to crime-free futures. *Corrections Compendium, 34*(1), 17–24.
Carson, E. A., & Anderson, E. (2016). *Prisoners in 2015.* Washington, DC: U.S. Department of Justice, Bureau of Justice Statistics.
Carson, E. A., & Golinelli, D. (2013). *Prisoners in 2012 trends in admissions and releases 1991–2012.* Washington, DC: U.S. Department of Justice, Bureau of Justice Statistics.
Carson, E. A., & Sabol, W. J. (2012). *Prisoners in 2011.* Washington, DC: U.S. Department of Justice, Bureau of Justice Statistics.
Carter, L. (2012). *A qualitative study of reintegration focusing on the perceptions of female ex-offenders returning to society (doctoral dissertation).* ProQuest LLC. (UMI Number: 3522589).
Centers for Disease Control and Prevention. (2004). *HIV/AIDS among African Americans* (Face Sheet). Washington, DC: National Center for HIV, STD, and TB Prevention.
Centers for Disease Control and Prevention. (2007). *HIV/AIDS fact sheet 2007.* Washington, DC: Centers for Disease Control and Prevention.
Chesney-Lind, M., & Pasko, L. (2013). *Girls, women, and crime: Selected readings.* Thousand Oaks, CA: Sage.
Chesney-Lind, M., & Pasko, L. (2004). *The female offender: Girls, women, and* crime. Thousand Oaks, CA: Sage.
Chesney-Lind, M., & Rodriguez, N. (1983). Women under lock and key: A view from the inside. *The Prison Journal, 63*, 47–65. doi:10.1177/003288558306300205
Christian, J., & Thomas, S. (2009). Examining the intersections of race, gender, and mass incarceration. *Journal of Ethnicity in Criminal Justice,* 7(1), 69–84. doi:10.1080/15377930802711797
Collins, C. F. (1997). *The imprisonment of African American women.* Jefferson, NC: MacFarland.
Collins, C. E., Whithers, D. L., & Braithwaite, R. (2007). The saved SISTA project: A faith-based HIV prevention program for black women in addiction. *American Journal of Health Studies, 22*(2), 76–82. doi:10.1.1.562.3227&rep=rep1&type=pdf
Cotton-Oldenburg, N. U., Jordan, B. K., Martin, S. L., & Kupper, L. (1999). Women inmates' risky sex and drug behaviors: Are they related? *American Journal of Drug and Alcohol Abuse, 25*(1), 129–149. doi:10.1081/ADA-100101850
Comack, E. (2006). Coping, resisting, and surviving: Connecting women's law violations to their histories of abuse. In L. F. Alarid & P. Cromwell (Eds.), *In her own words: Women offenders' views on crime and victimization* (pp. 237–245). Los Angeles, CA: Roxbury.
Covington, S. C. (1998). The relational theory of women's psychological development: Implications for the criminal justice system. In R. T. Zaplin (Ed.), *Female offenders: Critical perspectives and effective interventions* (pp. 113–128). Gaithersburg, MD: Aspen.
Covington, S. C. (2002). *Helping women recover: Creating gender-responsive treatment.* (pp. 52–72). In S.L.A. Straussner & S. Brown (Eds.), The handbook of addiction treatment for women. San Francisco, CA: Jossey-Bass.
Convington, S. C. (2003). *Beyond trauma: A healing journey for women.* Center City, MN: Hazelden.
Convington, S. C. (2004). *Voices: A program of self-discovery and empowerment for girls.* Carson City, NV: The Change Companies.
Covington, S. C., & Bloom, B. E. (2006). Gender responsiveness and services in correctional settings. In E. Leeder (Ed.), *Inside and out: Women, prison, and therapy* (pp. 9–33). Binghampton, NY: The Hawthorne Press.
CSR, Incorporated. (2008). *Third-year evaluation of Girl Scouts Beyond Bars: Final report.* Arlington, VA.
DeGroot, A. S., & Cu Uvin, S. (2005, May/June). HIV infection among women in prison: Consideration for care. *Infectious Disease in Corrections Report.* Retrieved from www.idcronline.org.
DiClemente, R. J., & Wingood, G. M. (1995). A randomized controlled trial of an HIV sexual risk reduction intervention for young African-American women. *Journal of the American Medical Association, 27*(16), 1271–1276. doi:10.1001/jama.1995.03530160023028
Dodson, K. D. (in press). Motherhood behind bars. In F. Bernat & K. Frailing (Eds.), *Encyclopedia of women and criminal justice*: Hoboken, NJ: Wiley.
Enos, S. (2001). *Mothering from the inside: Parenting in a women's prison.* New York, NY: State University of New York Press.
Faris, J., & Miller, J. A. (2010). Family matters: Perceptions of fairness among incarcerated mothers. *The Prison Journal, 90*(2), 139–160. doi:10.1177/0032885510361824
Feltz, R. (2016, April 23). Immigration facility guard given jail time for sexual assault of detainee. *The Guardian.* Retrieved from www.theguardian.com/us-news/2016/apr/23/immigration-detention-center-guard-sexual-assault-prison
Garcia-Ditta, A. (2016, May 2). 'She lives in fear' not in El Salvador, but in Texas detention. *Texas Observer.* Retrieved from www.texasobserver.org/sexual-abuse-karnes-immigrant-detention/

Gido, R. L., & Dalley, L. (2009). *Women's mental health issues across the criminal justice system*. Upper Saddle River, NJ: Pearson Prentice Hall.

Gilfus, M. E. (2006). From victims to survivors to offenders: Women's routes of entry and immersion into street crime. In L. F. Alarid & P. Cromwell (Eds.), *In her own words Women offenders' views on crime and victimization* (pp. 5–14). Los Angeles, CA: Roxbury.

Girl Scouts of the United States of America. (2007). *Girl Scouts behind bars and girls scouting in detention centers: Supporting girls, connecting families*. New York, NY: Girl Scouts of the United States of America.

Glaze, L. E., & Maruschak, L. M. (2008). *Parents in prison and their children: Bureau of Justice Statistics Special Report*. Washington, DC: U.S. Department of Justice, Bureau of Justice Statistics.

Grant, D. (2006). Resilience of girls with incarcerated mothers: The impact of girl scouts. *The Prevention Researcher, 13*(2), 11–14.

Greene, J., & Schiraldi, V. (2002). *Cutting correctly: New prison policies for times of fiscal crisis*. Washington, DC: Center for Juvenile and Criminal Justice.

Greenfeld, L., & Snell, T. L. (1999). *Women offenders: Special report*. Washington, DC: U.S. Department of Justice, Government Printing Office.

Hammett, T. M., Harmon, P., & Maruschak, L. M. (1999). *1996–1997 Update: HIV/AIDS, STDs, and TB in correctional facilities*. Washington, DC: U.S. Department of Justice, Government Printing Office.

Hammett, T. M., Rhodes, W., & Harmon, P. (1999). *HIV/AIDS and other infectious diseases among correctional inmates: A public health problem and* opportunity. Paper presented at the 1999 National HIV Prevention Conference, Atlanta, GA.

Harlow, C. (2003). *Education and correctional populations*. Washington, DC: U.S. Department of Justice, Bureau of Justice Statistics.

Harm, N. J., & Thompson, P. J. (1997). Evaluating the effectiveness of parent education for incarcerated mothers. *Journal of Offender Rehabilitation, 24*(3/4), 135–152. doi:10.1300j076v24n03_08

Harner, H. M., & Riley, S. (2013). Factors contributing to poor physical health in incarcerated women. *Journal of Health Care for the Poor and Underserved, 24*(2), 788–801. doi:10.1353/hpu.2013.0059

Hattery, A., & Smith, E. (2010). *Prisoner reentry and social capital: The long road to reintegration*. Lanham, MD: Lexington Books.

Henriques, Z. W., & Gladwin, B. P. (2013). Pregnancy and motherhood behind bars. In L. Gideon (Ed.), *Special needs offenders in correctional institutions* (pp. 83–116). Thousand Oaks, CA: Sage.

Hensley, C. (2002). *Prison sex: Practice & policy*. Boulder, CO: Lynne Rienner Publishers.

Hirschi, T. (1969). *Causes of delinquency*. Berkeley, CA: University of California Press.

Hulley, S., Crewe, B., & Wright, S. (2017). *The gendered pains of imprisonment*. Centre for Crime and Justice Studies. Retrieved from www.crimeandjustice.org.uk/resources/gendered-pains-imprisonment

James, D. J., & Glaze, L. E. (2006). *Mental health problems of prison and jail inmates*. Washington, DC: U.S. Department of Justice, Bureau of Justice Statistics.

Kasdan, D. (2009). Abortion access for incarcerated women: Are constitutional health practices in conflict with constitutional standards? *Viewpoint, 41*(1), 1–4.

Koch, S. M., & Tomlin, A. M. (2010). *Wee Ones Nursery evaluation: Findings from 2008–2009*. Indianapolis, IN: Indiana University School of Medicine.

Lerman, A. E. (2013). *The modern prison paradox: Politics, punishment, and social community*. New York, NY: Cambridge University Press.

Maher, L., Dunlap, E., & Johnson, B. D. (2006). Black women's pathways to involvement in illicit drug distribution and sales. In L. F. Alarid & P. Cromwell (Eds.), *In her own words: Women offenders' views on crime and victimization* (pp. 237–245). Los Angeles, CA: Roxbury.

Marcus-Mendoza, S. (2016). Incarcerated women in the United States. In T. L. Freiburger & C. D. Marcum (Eds.), *Women in the criminal justice system* (pp. 209–222). Boca Raton, FL: CRC Press.

Maruschak, L. M. (2009). *HIV in prisons, 2007–2008*. Washington, DC: U.S. Department of Justice, Bureau of Justice Statistics.

McKenzie, M., Nunn, A., Zaller, N. D., Bazazi, A. R., & Rich, J. D. (2009). Overcoming obstacles to implementing methadone therapy for prisoners: Implications for policy and practice. *Journal of Opioid Management, 5*(4), 219–227. doi:10.1080/02791072.2011.601984

Menabde, N. (2009). *Women's health in prison: Correcting gender inequity in prison health*. Copenhagen, Denmark: World Health Organization.

Merlo, A., & Pollock, J. (1995). *Women, law, and social control*. Boston, MA: Allyn and Bacon.

Moe, A. M., & Ferraro, K. J. (2006). Criminalized mothers: The value and devaluation of parenthood from behind bars. In E. Leeder (Ed.), *Inside and out: Women, prison, and therapy* (pp. 135–164). Binghampton, NY: The Hawthorne Press.

Morash, M. (2010). *Women on probation and parole: A feminist critique of community programs and service*. Boston, MA: Northeastern University Press.

Mumola, C. J. (2000). *Incarcerated parents and their children*. Washington, DC: U.S. Department of Justice, Bureau of Justice Statistics.

Monmouth County Correctional Institutional Inmates v. Lanzaro, 834 F2d 326 (1987).

Moses, M. C. (1995). *Keeping incarcerated mothers and their daughters together: Girl Scouts Behind Bars*. Washington, DC: U.S. Department of Justice, Office of Justice Programs, National Institute of Justice.

National Center for Education Statistics. (2014). *Program for the international assessment of adult competencies*. Washington, DC: U.S. Department of Education.

Newman, A. (2007, August 17). Pregnant behind bars: The Prison Doula Project. Reproductive Health Reality Check. *Rewire*. Retrieved from http://rhrealitycheck.org/article/2007/08/02/pregnant-behind-bars-the-prison-doula-project/

Olivero, J. M. (1992). AIDS in prison: Judicial and administrative dilemmas and strategies. In P. J. Benekos & A.V. Merlo (Eds.), *Corrections: Dilemmas and directions* (pp. 37–55). Cincinnati, OH: Anderson.

Parenti, C. (1999). *Lockdown America: Police and prisons in the age of crisis*. New York: Verso.

Parrillo, K. M., Freeman, R. C., Collier, K., & Young, P. (2001). Association between early sexual abuse and adult HIV-risky sexual behaviors among community-recruited women. *Child Abuse and Neglect, 25*(3), 335–346. doi:10.1016/S0145–213(00)00253–2

Pasko, L., & Chesney-Lind, M. (2013). Incarcerated females: A growing population. In L. Gideon (Ed.). *Special needs offenders in correctional institutions*. (pp. 51–82). Thousand Oaks, CA: Sage.

Petersilia, J. (2003). *When prisoners come home: Parole and prisoner reentry*. New York, NY: Oxford University Press.

Petersilia, J. (2005). From cell to society: Who is returning home? In J. Travis & C. Visher (Eds.), *Prisoner reentry and crime in America* (pp. 15–49). Cambridge, MA: Cambridge University Press.

Poehlmann, J. (2005). Incarcerated mothers' contact with children, perceived family relationships and depressive symptoms. *Journal of Family Psychology, 19*(3), 350–357. doi:10.1037/0893–3200.19.3.350

Pollock-Byrne, J. (1992). Women in prison: Why are their numbers increasing? In P. J. Benekos & A. V. Merlo (Eds.), *Corrections: Dilemmas and directions*. (pp. 79–95). Cincinnati, OH: Anderson.

Pollock, J. (2002). *Women, prison, and crime* (2nd ed.). Belmont, CA: Wadsworth/Thomson Learning.

Pollock, J. (2004). *Prisons and prison life: Costs and consequences*. Los Angeles, CA: Roxbury.

Rebecca Project for Human Rights. (2010). *Motherhood behind bars: A state-by-state report card and analysis of federal policies on conditions for confinement for pregnant and parenting women and the effect on their children*. Washington, DC: The National Women's Law Center.

Richie, B. E. (2001). Challenges incarcerated women face as they return to their communities: Findings from life history interviews. *Crime and Delinquency, 47*(3), 368–389. doi:10.1177/0011128701047003005

Rideau, W. (2011). *In the pace of justice: A story of punishment and deliverance*. New York, NY: Vintage Books.

Robillard, A. G., Gallito-Zaparaniuk, P., Arriola, K. J., Kennedy, S., Hammett, T., & Braithwaite, R. L. (2003). Partners and processes in HIV services for inmates and ex-offenders: Facilitating collaboration and service delivery. *Evaluation Review, 27*(5), 535–562. doi:10.1177/0193841X03255631

Roe v. Crawford, 514 F.3d 789 (2008).

Schempf, A. H. (2007). Illicit drug use and neonatal outcomes: A critical review. *Obstetrical & Gynecological Survey, 62*(11), 749–757. doi:10.1097/01.ogx.0000256562.31774.76

Seiter, R. P., & Kadela, K. R. (2003). Prisoner reentry: What works, what does not, and what is promising. *Crime and Delinquency, 49*(3), 360–388. doi:10.1177/0011128703253761

Seville, L. R. (2014, October 4). Sex abuse alleged at immigrant family detention center in Texas. *NBC News*. Retrieved from www.nbcnews.com/storyline/immigration-border-crisis/sex-abuse-alleged-immigrant-family-detention-center-texas-n217166

Sharp, S. F. (2003). Mothers in prison: Issues in parent-child contact. In S. Sharp (Ed.), *The incarcerated woman: Rehabilitative programming in women's prison* (pp. 151–165). Upper Saddle River, NJ: Prentice Hall.

Sharp, S. F. (2014). *Mean lives, mean laws: Oklahoma's women prisoners*. New Brunswick, NJ: Rutgers University Press.

Sharp, S. F., Marcus-Mendoza, S. T., Bentley, R. G., Simpson, D. B., & Love, S. R. (1999). Gender differences in the impact of incarceration on the children and families of drug offenders. In M. Corsianos & K. Train (Eds.), *Interrogating social justice* (pp. 217–246). Toronto: Canadian Scholar's Press.

Staley, E. M. (2002). *Profile and three-year follow-up of Bedford Hills and Taconic nursery program participants: 1997 and 1998*. New York, NY: New York State Department of Correctional Services, Division of Program Planning, Research and Evaluation, 1–23.

Staton-Tindall, M., Leukefeld, C., Palmer, J., Oser, C., Kaplan, A., Krietemeyer, J., . . . Surrat, H. L. (2007). Relationships and HIV risk among incarcerated women. *The Prison Journal, 87*(1), 143–165. doi:10.1177/0032885506299046

Swavola, E., Riley, K., & Subramanian, R. (2016). *Overlooked: Women and jails in an era of reform*. New York, NY: Vera Institute of Justice.

Sykes. G. M. (1958). *The society of captives: A study of a maximum security prison*. Princeton, NJ: Princeton University Press.

Travis, J., & Visher, C. A. (Eds.). (2005). *Prisoner reentry and crime in America*. Cambridge, MA: Cambridge University Press.

United States Department of Health and Human Services, Substance Abuse and Mental Health Services Administration. (2005). Medication-assisted treatment for opioid addiction during pregnancy. In *Medication-assisted treatment for opioid addiction in opioid treatment programs, TIP 43* (pp. 211–224). Rockville, MD: Substance Abuse and Mental Health Services Administration, Center for Substance Abuse Treatment.

United States Department of Health and Human Services. (2014). *Substance abuse treatment for adults in the criminal justice system, TIP 44* (pp. 1–337). Rockville, MD: Substance Abuse and Mental Health Services Administrations' (SAMHSA) Center for Substance Abuse Treatment.

Van Voorhis, P., & Salisbury, E. J. (2014). *Correctional counseling and rehabilitation*. New York, NY: Routledge.

Veysey, B. M., & Bichler-Robertson, G. (2002). Prevalence estimates of psychiatric disorders in correctional settings in health status of soon-to-be released inmates. *Report to Congress, Volume 2* (pp. 157–166). Chicago, IL: National Commission on Correctional Health.

What You Should Know. (2017). *Female offender programs*. Washington, DC: Federal Bureau of Prisons. Retrieved from http://wysk.lamp.uscourts.gov/ex-offender-suggestions/female-offender-programs-w-y-s-k/

Whiteacre, K., Fritz, S., & Owen, J. (2013). *Assessing outcomes for Wee Ones Nursery at the Indiana women's prison*. Indianapolis, IN: University of Indianapolis Community Research Center.

Whitehead, J. T., Dodson, K. D., & Edwards, B. D. (2013). *Corrections: Exploring crime, punishment, and justice in America* (3rd ed.). New York, NY: Routledge.

Wick, J. (2017, April 11). Sexual assault claims at private immigrant detention centers are rarely investigated. *Laist*. Retrieved from http://laist.com/2017/04/11/sexual_assault_claims_immigrant_detention.php

Wilson, N. K. (1980). Styles of doing time in a co-ed prison: Masculine and feminine alternatives. In J. O. Smykla (Ed.), *Co-ed prison* (pp. 150–171). New York, NY: Human Services Press.

Yager, S. (2015, July/August). Prison born. *The Atlantic*. Retrieve from www.theatlantic.com/magazine/archive/2015/07/prison-born/395297/

8

PARENTING BEHIND BARS

The Experiences of Incarcerated Mothers and Fathers

Michael B. Mitchell, Kimberly D. Dodson, and LeAnn N. Cabage

> Having a parent in prison can have an impact on a child's mental health, social behavior, and educational prospects. The emotional trauma that may occur and the practical difficulties of a disrupted family life can be compounded by the social stigma that children may face [because] of having a parent in prison or jail.
>
> —(Children of Incarcerated Parents, 2017, para. 1)

Introduction

The United States Bureau of Justice Statistics estimates that over 800,000 prisoners are parents of minor children (Glaze & Maruschak, 2008). Incarcerated parents in state and federal correctional facilities report having an estimated 1.6 million children. According to the most recent year of reporting, state and federal prisons held 744,200 fathers and 65,600 mothers. Black children are seven and half times more likely than white children to have a parent in prison. This trend also holds true for Hispanic children, who are two and half times more likely to have a parent in prison than white children (Glaze & Maruschak, 2008).

Estimates indicate "4 in 10 fathers [in prison] are Black, about 3 in 10 [are] White and about 2 in 10 [are] Hispanic" (Glaze & Muraschak, 2008. p. 2). Figures also show that 1.6 million children had a father in prison, and approximately half (46%) are black fathers. The total population of blacks living in the United States is approximately 13%, with black men representing about 48% of the black population (U.S. Census Bureau, 2010; Black Demographics, 2013). Black mothers represent about 28% of all mothers incarcerated in prison, white mothers represent 48%, and Hispanics 17% of all mothers incarcerated in prison (Glaze & Marsuchak, 2008). The disproportionate incarceration of black mothers and fathers has had devastating impact on black families and black communities (Alexander, 2010). These figures suggest that more black children than white children have lived a sizable portion of their lives without one or both parents.

Children are often the hardest hit by parental incarceration. When someone is arrested, it often happens without warning. From a young child's perspective, he or she does not understand why mommy or daddy is gone. If the child is present when the parent is arrested, it may trigger emotional trauma. Older children realize an arrest means their mother or father is in trouble, and they often worry about what will happen to their parents. In addition, children may worry about what the arrest means for them—where will I live or who will take care of me? If the mother or father is the primary source of household income, this often throws the family into a fiscal crisis. Studies also show that children of incarcerated parents are more likely to be depressed, anxious, perform poorly in school, and engage in delinquency (Martin, 2017; Parke & Clarke-Stewart, 2001). To complicate matters, parents are often incarcerated hundreds of miles from home, and children have no control over being able to visit their parents. In short, incarceration represents a significant disruption in the lives of children, and because incarceration disproportionately affects communities of color, it likely compounds the disadvantages these children face.

The purpose of this chapter is to discuss the experiences of incarcerated mothers and fathers. The chapter begins with a general discussion of what motherhood looks like behind bars and some of the key issues incarcerated mothers experience because of being separated from their children. We examine pregnancy in jails and prisons and the need for appropriate obstetrical and gynecological care. We also introduce the reader to prison nursery, parenting, and visitation programs designed to facilitate mother-infant bonds and improve maternal efficacy.

The chapter also includes a discussion of what fatherhood looks like behind bars and the major issues incarcerated fathers face in trying to remain actively involved in their children's lives. We also examine programs designed to help incarcerated fathers improve their parenting skills and stay connected to their children. The chapter includes a discussion of jailed fathers and how incarceration disproportionately affects black and Latino children.

Motherhood Behind Bars

Women represent about 9% of individuals incarcerated in the United States. Women of color are the fastest-growing population, with their imprisonment rate being twice that of white women (Carson, 2014). Estimates also indicate the number of children with a mother in prison has more than doubled in the last two decades. Approximately two-thirds of women behind bars are mothers of minor children, and three-fourths of these women were the principal caregiver of their children prior to incarceration (Glaze & Maruschak, 2008). Therefore, it makes sense that the incarceration of mothers represents a significant disruption to the family unit. The children of incarcerated mothers are most likely to end up in the custody of close family relatives, particularly the maternal grandmother. Custody arrangements are often informal agreements among family members in which the parties try to escape state agency intervention. Incarcerated mothers fear that formal state agency intervention may result in the loss of child custody or the termination of their parental rights. Roughly 11% of children with imprisoned mothers end up in foster care (Glaze & Maruschak, 2008).

About half of incarcerated mothers report that they provided the primary financial support for their minor children while on the outside (Glaze & Maruschak, 2008). Incarceration means that these mothers will not have the financial resources to help care for their children, resulting in a substantial financial burden for family caregivers. Even if incarcerated mothers are employed within the prison, they would likely receive meager wages, most of which range from a low of .25 cents per hour in state prisons to a high of $1.15 per hour in federal prisons (Kovensky, 2014). However, there are mothers in prison who send money home to support their children, although their contributions do little to offset the cost of child care (Leeder, 2012). Unfortunately, public assistance programs like Temporary Assistance for Needy Families (TANF) do not have provisions to support certain types of relative caregivers. For instance, family grants requested through TANF have work eligibility requirements, which means retired individuals do not qualify for assistance. Families that are already feeling the financial burden of the mother's absence often lack the community resources they need to provide adequately for their loved ones.

Incarcerated mothers usually have limited physical contact with their children, and prison visits for many mothers are rare. There are fewer women's prisons at both the state and federal level, which means once a woman has been sentenced, she is frequently incarcerated hundreds of miles from the community where she lived prior to incarceration. As a result, visits are difficult because of the long distances between prison and home. Many families do not have the financial means to travel to the correctional facilities to visit. Caregivers or guardians may be apprehensive to take the children to visit because of concerns about exposing them to a prison environment. In some states, social workers may resist or prohibit such visits because it is disturbing for children to see their mothers in prison. A mother also may not want the children to see her in prison or subject them to the search and admission procedures required for visitation. She may feel guilty or too embarrassed to allow her children to see her in a prison setting. Additionally, visits unavoidably include saying goodbye, which is an experience that is so painful to both mothers and children that many mothers would rather avoid it (Henriques, 1996). In 2008, 58% of a national sample of incarcerated mothers reported no visits, compared to 2% of those surveyed in a similar sample in 1978 who reported no visits (Bloom & Steinhart, 1993; Glaze & Maruschak, 2008). Nonetheless, visitation may be crucial because one of the most significant predictors of family reunification after release is contact during incarceration (Tuerk & Loper, 2014).

Pregnancy in Jails and Prisons

Approximately 4% of women in state prisons and 3% of women under federal correctional supervision are pregnant at the time of admittance, which translates into roughly 10,000 pregnant women being admitted to U.S. prisons annually (Belknap, 2015; Henriques & Gladwin, 2013; Glaze & Maruschak, 2008). Pregnancies among incarcerated women are often high risk because of certain lifestyle and behavioral choices. Many incarcerated women, for instance, have histories of drug use and abuse, which may cause premature delivery, low birth weight, or babies who experience fetal distress or suffer neonatal aspiration of meconium. Neonatal complications may also include narcotic withdrawal, neurological problems, postnatal growth deficiency, birth defects, and an increase in neonatal mortality, such as sudden infant death syndrome (Schempf, 2007).

Women prisoners also may have trouble during labor and delivery. Substance abuse in pregnant women increases likelihood of malpresentation or malpositioning of the infant during labor. This is more commonly known as "breech birth," and it typically requires a delivery by cesarean section. Cesarean deliveries may result in increased blood loss, organ injury, blood clots, emergency hysterectomy, adverse reactions to anesthesia, postsurgical infection, scar tissue that hinders future deliveries, emotional trauma, and, in rare cases, maternal death. Substance abuse, such as cocaine and opioid use, during pregnancy can lead to other medical complications for mothers, including an increased risk of heart attacks, strokes, seizures, and respiratory failure (Bhuvaneswar, Chang, Epstein, & Stern, 2008).

Health care is often woefully inadequate for pregnant women in jails and prisons. For example, detoxifying pregnant women involves specialized treatment protocols that are mostly unavailable in correctional facilities (Whitehead, Dodson, & Edwards, 2013). Since 2004, the U.S. Department of Health and Human Services has recommended opioid-addicted pregnant women receive methadone replacement as a treatment to avoid withdrawal for both the mother and infant. Although some state correctional systems (e.g., California and Rhode Island) allow for methadone replacement for pregnant prisoners, most do not (McKenzie, Nunn, Zaller, Bazazi, & Rich, 2009). Methadone replacement therapy can be costly, and many prison officials may view it as an unnecessary operational expense.

The American Academy of Pediatrics and the American Congress of Obstetricians and Gynecologists (ACOG), both of which are leading U.S. experts in maternal, fetal, and child health care, recommend a minimum standard of care for pregnant incarcerated women and girls (see Box 8.1).

Box 8.1 AAP and ACOG Guidelines for Prenatal Care

Intake

- Assess for pregnancy risk by inquiring about menstrual history, heterosexual activity, and contraceptive use and test for pregnancy as appropriate.

During Pregnancy

- Provide pregnancy counseling and abortion services;
- Provide prenatal care following guidelines of the American Academy of Pediatrics and the American Congress of Obstetrics and Gynecologists;
- Assess for substance abuse and initiate treatment; prompt initiation of opioid-assisted therapy with methadone or buprenorphine is critical for pregnant women who are opioid-dependent;
- Test for and treat HIV/AIDS to prevent perinatal HIV transmission;
- Screen for depression and mental stress during pregnancy and for postpartum depression after delivery and treat as needed;
- Provide dietary supplements to incarcerated pregnant and breastfeeding women;
- Deliver services in a licensed hospital that has the facilities for high-risk pregnancies when available; and
- Provide postpartum contraceptive methods during incarceration.

Source: American Academy of Pediatrics, American College [Congress] of Obstetrics and Gynecologists (2007)

Shackling Pregnant Prisoners

Thirty-two states allow pregnant prisoners to be shackled during childbirth (International Human Rights Clinic, 2013). The ACOG (2011, p. 1) opposes shackling pregnant inmates because it "interferes with the ability of physicians to safely practice medicine and is demeaning and rarely necessary." The National Commission on Correctional Health Care (NCCHC), the American Jail Association (AJA), the American Psychological Association (APA), Human Rights Project for Girls (HRPG), National Council of Juvenile Family Court Judges (NCJFCJ), and the ACOG issued a joint statement condemning the practice of shackling pregnant prisoners because it

> limits the ability of medical care providers to assess and evaluate their patient and increases the likelihood of falls, inability to break a fall, life-threatening embolic complications, and impediments to epidurals, emergency caesarian section, and other emergency obstetrical interventions, which may also affect the fetus.
>
> (NCCHC, 2016, p. 1)

These organizations also point out that a majority of incarcerated women's experiences include domestic and sexual violence, trauma, and mental health problems. As a result, shackling prisoners during labor increases physical, mental, and emotional vulnerability and is essentially retraumatizing these women. Finally, medical authorities report that restraint after childbirth can inhibit a mother's "ability to bond with and safely handle her infant," with possible "negative effects on the infant's health" (NCCHC, 2016, p. 1).

Criminal justice agencies across the country are embracing the recommendations of the NCCHC. Specifically, the Federal Bureau of Prisons (FBOP), the United States Marshals Service (USMS), U.S. Immigration and Customs Enforcement (ICE), and the American Correctional Association (ACA) have limited the use of shackles on pregnant prisoners, particularly during labor and delivery (American Civil Liberties Union, 2015).

Prison Nursery Programs

Parenting programs, including prison nurseries, are not new. Prison nursery programs emerged in early nineteenth-century England, and the concept was later adopted in the United States. By the early 1800s, women were allowed to keep their children with them at the Newgate Gaol in London (Rush, 1991). In the U.S., the history of children being present in correctional facilities dates back to between 1800 and 1840. A report of the prison populations during that time in Maryland, Massachusetts, New York, and Pennsylvania suggested children were among those present (Zemans & Smith, 1946). For example, records from New York's Western House of Refuge at Albion, which operated between 1894 and 1931, showed that babies born in the prison could stay with their mothers up to age 2. The underlying concept of such programs was the mothers should care for the babies after birth because it would make them feel responsible for the child after their release from the institution. Although laws existed to allow children to remain with their mothers after birth, few locations actually implemented this as a practice. For those that did, many of the programs were short-lived. One exception is the Bedford Hills Correctional Facility for Women in New York. The facility opened in 1901, allowing unwed mothers to keep their children until the child's first birthday (Goshin & Byrne, 2009). In 1930, legislation was enacted to continue allowing mothers to keep their babies with them for one year; this remains unchanged today.

Studies of women's prisons show that infants were frequently born behind bars. For instance, a study conducted by Shepard and Zemans (1950) revealed 364 children born to inmates in 37 state correctional institutions in 1947. State laws governing children born to incarcerated mothers varied widely in the United States, according to their study. Twenty of the correctional facilities reported having no law, while 13 indicated there were laws in place. The remaining facilities did not respond to the question (Shepard & Zemans, 1950). Many of the laws did not specify the amount of time an infant or child could remain with their mothers and simply suggested the children should be removed when it was no longer healthy for the children to remain in prison (Baunach, 1985). Thus, the time mothers were allowed to keep their children varied greatly, with many children being taken away almost immediately, although some children remained with their mothers for up to three years (Shepard & Zemans, 1950).

Programs allowing children to remain with their incarcerated mothers continued unrestricted until the 1960s. However, in 1960, federal judges grew wary about the number of children residing at the Federal Correctional Camp at Alderson. Their primary concern was the distance to the nearest prenatal and postnatal care facilities. Two social workers from the Department of Health, Education, and Welfare (DHEW) declared Alderson an unsafe environment for children, essentially ending the practice of allowing infant and mothers to stay together during incarceration (Heffernan, 1993). Nevertheless, as the number of incarcerated women surged in the 1980s there was a call to develop parenting programs, provide special visitation areas, and to reintroduce prison nurseries (Kauffman, 2001; Loper & Tuerk, 2006; Snyder, Carlo, & Coats Mullins, 2001). Today, 11 states offer prison nursery programs (California, Illinois, Indiana, Nebraska, New York, Ohio, South Dakota, Texas, Washington, West Virginia, and Wyoming).

The guidelines for program participation vary across locations, but women who wish to participate in the programs undergo extensive screening, and strict criteria must be met before individuals can participate in a prison nursery program (Dodson, Cabage, Brown, & McMillan, 2017; Cabage, 2016). The infant must be born while the mother is in state custody. The mother's criminal record should be clear of violent crimes. Mothers who wish to participate in a prison nursery program must not have a history of child abuse or neglect (Women's Prison Association, 2009). The length of stay and capacity of the programs also vary from state to state. The average stay for the facilities is between 12 to 18 months, and program capacity ranges from five mother/infant pairs to 29 mother/infant pairs. Table 8.1 presents detailed information pertaining to individual state nursery programs. Wyoming is not included in Table 8.1 because the opening of the facility has been delayed. The exception to the average stay is California, but similar to other community-based programs, the length of stay is greatly increased.

Table 8.1 Nursery Programs by State

Program	*Capacity*	*Length of Stay*	*Criteria*
Community Prisoner Mother Program Prototypes Pomona, California	24 mother/infant pairs	Up to 6 years	✓ Eligible for Minimum Support Facility placement. ✓ Be pregnant or have a child 6 years old or younger. ✓ Cannot have the custody challenged or be declared an unfit parent. ✓ At least 90 days remaining on sentence, but no more than six years. ✓ No prior convictions for violent crimes, arson, or kidnapping. ✓ Cannot have a serious rule violation.
Moms & Babies Program Decatur Correctional Center Decatur, Illinois	5 mother/infant pairs	Up to 24 months	✓ Nonviolent offense. ✓ Within two years of release after giving birth.
Wee Ones Nursery Program Indiana Women's Prison Indianapolis, Indiana	10 mother/infant pairs	Up to 18 months	✓ Give birth while in custody. ✓ Eligible for release by the time the child is 18 months old. ✓ No prior child abuse or violent crime convictions.
Nebraska Correctional Center for Women York, Nebraska	15 mother/infant pairs	18 months; can be extended at staff discretion	✓ Give birth while in custody. ✓ Cannot have a violent criminal record. ✓ No serious mental health concerns. ✓ Complete sentence by the time the child is 18 months old.
Bedford Hills and Taconic Correctional Facility Bedford Hills, New York	29 mother/infant pairs 15 mother/infant pairs	12–18 months	✓ Give birth while in custody. ✓ Cannot have prior record of arson or child abuse. ✓ Several aspects of the woman's past are examined, including who will have custody of the child, history of involvement with child-welfare system, length of sentence, past incarceration, and nature of crime.

(Continued)

Table 8.1 (Continued)

Program	*Capacity*	*Length of Stay*	*Criteria*
Achieving Baby Care (ABC) Success Program Ohio Reformatory for Women Marysville, Ohio	20 mother/infant pairs	Up to 18 months	✓ Give birth while in custody. ✓ Cannot have a violent criminal record. ✓ Attend family training courses. ✓ Adhere to rules. ✓ Be in good mental and physical condition. ✓ Must be serving a sentence of less than 18 months at time of delivery.
South Dakota Women's Prison Pierre, South Dakota	No limit	30 days	✓ Give birth while in custody. ✓ Mother's crime nonviolent in nature.
Texas Baby and Mother Bonding Initiative (BAMBI)	No Limit	12 months: can be extended under special conditions	✓ Give birth while in custody. ✓ Mothers must be screened and approved by the Texas Department of Criminal Justice.
Residential Parenting Program (RPP) Washington Correctional Center for Women Gig Harbor, Washington	20 mother/infant pairs	Up to 36 months	✓ Sentence must be completed within three years of giving birth. ✓ Classified as minimum custody. ✓ Convicted of a nonviolent offense.
KIDS Unite Lakin Correctional Center for Women West Columbia, West Virginia	5 mother/infant pairs	Up to 18 months	✓ Within 18 months of release or parole. ✓ No prior convictions for a sex crime or crime against a child. ✓ Be free of disciplinary write-ups.

Source: Cabage (2016).

Goals and Benefits of Prison Nurseries

The primary goal of prison nursery programs is to allow mothers and infants an opportunity to form attachments or bonds. The importance of forming a secure attachment as an infant has been established in the literature for decades (see e.g., Ainsworth, 1967, Bowlby, 1944; 1969; 1982). The secondary goal is to prevent recidivism. In other words, prison nursery programs are designed to foster strong mother-infant bonds that diminish the likelihood of future offending for the mother-participants. Researchers have evaluated the effectiveness of prison nursery programs to increase mother-infant bonds or secure attachment. As expected, prison nursery participants report greater attachment to their infants than nonparticipant mothers (Berry & Eigenberg, 2003; Borelli, Goshin, Joestl, Clark, & Byrne, 2010; Bruns, 2006; Cassidy et al., 2010). In addition, several studies have examined the effectiveness of prison nursery programs to reduce recidivism. The findings have been positive and indicate that prison nursery participants are less likely to reoffend than nonparticipant incarcerated mothers (see Carlson, 1998, 2001, 2009, Dodson et al., 2017; Koch & Tomlin, 2010; Staley, 2002; Whiteacre, Fritz, & Owen, 2013). Together this body of research indicates that prison nurseries are achieving the program goals of increasing mother-infant bonds and reducing recidivism.

Mothers participating in prison nursery programs in California, Indiana, New York, Ohio, South Dakota, and Washington State are required to participate in parenting skills classes if they wish to remain in the nursery program (Goshin & Byrne, 2009). Parental education is a critical component of prison nursery programs because many incarcerated mothers report they had poor parental role models and perceived their parental efficacy to be inadequate (Howze-Browne, 1989; Newman, Fowler, & Cashin, 2011; Miller, Perryman, Markovitz, Franzen, Cochran, & Brown, 2013). Parenting programs improve parenting skills, parental self-efficacy, and self-esteem (Berry & Eigenberg, 2003; Borelli et al., 2010; Bruns, 2006; Cassidy et al., 2010). Parenting programs also teach mothers how to build healthy family relationships, choose and administer appropriate discipline, and improve communication with their children (Bednarowski, 2014).

Prison nursery programs have positive outcomes for children across their life course. For example, studies show that children who were born to nursery participants develop secure attachment at a similar rate as low-risk infants whose mothers were not incarcerated (Cassidy et al., 2010; Byrne, Goshin, & Joestl, 2010; Goshin, Byrne, Blanchard-Lewis, 2014). Children who spent more time with their mothers in the prison nursery program were more likely to have secure attachments. Byrne et al. (2010) found that 75% of infants who spent more than a year with their mothers were classified as securely attached compared to 43% of infants who spent less than a year with their mothers.

Securely attached children go on to become securely attached adolescents (Byrne et al., 2010). Securely attached adolescents have healthier peer relationships, greater academic success, and better social skills and competency (Moretti & Peled, 2004; Papini & Roggman, 1992). Children and adolescents who have secure attachments are less likely to be anxious and depressed (Papini & Roggman, 1992), targets for bullying (Troy & Sroufe, 1987), and/or delinquent (Hirschi, 1969). Secure attachment also carries into adulthood, and securely attached adults have healthier social relationships (Marušić, Kamenov, Jelić, 2010), dating and marital success (Dinero, Conger, Shaver, Widaman, Larsen-Rife, 2008; Simpson, Collins, & Salvatore, 2012), and academic achievement (Beauchamp, Martineau, Gagnon, 2016). The ability of prison nursery programs to create secure attachments in both mother and infant should influence the decision making of policy makers when considerations are made regarding treatment for pregnant women in the criminal justice system. Policy makers also should consider the impact visitation has for both the parent and the child.

Although Bedford Hills serves as a model for prison programs across the United States, its program has been expanded to include a foster home that is situated near the correctional facility for the children of incarcerated mothers, which is managed by Catholic nuns. The close proximity of the foster home allows the children to visit with their mothers on a frequent and consistent basis. Mothers who participate in this visitation program are more likely to build close relationships with their children, and their participation increases the odds that they will regain custody of their children after release (Parke & Clarke-Stewart, 2001). The prison also runs weeklong day camps for children during the summer months. Children live with volunteer families close to the prison for one week out of the month. The prison schedules activities for the mothers and children and gives them the opportunity to spend free time together. In addition, Bedford Hills has a parenting center that offers a variety of programs and classes to incarcerated mothers in conjunction with the nursery and child visitation programs.

Mothers ineligible to participate in the nursery or visitation programs are still eligible to participate in the parenting programs. *Parenting Inside Out* is a cognitive-behavioral evidence-based intervention for helping mothers to develop parenting skills. As mentioned earlier, many incarcerated mothers did not develop prosocial parenting skills growing up because they lacked appropriate parental role models. *Parenting Inside Out* uses a wide variety of cognitive-behavioral interventions (e.g., self-control and self-motivation, modeling, skills rehearsal, and simulations or role-plays) to teach parenting skills and prosocial parenting behaviors. Mothers completing the program were more likely to use positive parental reinforcement skills and be involved in the lives of their child one year after release from prison. Mothers also were less likely to be rearrested or reincarcerated one year postrelease (Kjellstrand, Cearley, Eddy, Foney, & Martinez, 2012).

Although prison nursery and parenting programs certainly assist incarcerated mothers in providing appropriate care for their infants, many prisons rely on nonprofit organizations to provide support to prison nursery programs. For instance, volunteers from the community frequently serve as doulas for pregnant inmates. Doulas provide pregnancy and childbirth support, including childbirth plans, emotional and physical support during and after labor and delivery, educational information on breastfeeding and newborn care, and placement of the newborn. Other nonprofit community organizations provide additional social support services to pregnant inmates during their incarceration and once they return to the community (see Box 8.2 to learn more about Angel's Wings).

Fatherhood behind Bars

Over the past several years, "fatherlessness" has been declared an epidemic in America by prominent political and social commentators on both sides of the ideological spectrum. The bipartisan rhetorical assault on absent fathers in America has been particularly damaging in the fact that it has contributed to a public consensus of the decline of middle class, heteronormative, ideals of the American family. Unfortunately, these simplistic, nonempirical claims lack context and fail to attribute the impact of federal and state criminal justice policy on the decline of father presence. Mass incarceration has been a major social problem that has profoundly affected a large population of fathers, mostly of color, as well as played a role in redefining the masculine identity (Travis, 2005). Incarcerated fathers already are a marginalized social group; their demographics provide a portrait of social inequality defined by race, class, and gender.

An unprecedented mass experiment in incarceration evolved in the United States over the past 40 years (Clear & Frost, 2014; Clear, 2007). Despite fluctuation in national crime rates, retributive justice has been the go-to response for crime in America. The primary victims of this increased criminalization have been men of color from economically disadvantaged and segregated communities. While the issue of mass incarceration has galvanized academics, policy makers, and the public into strategic action, there has been a paucity of awareness around the fact that over half of imprisoned

Box 8.2 Angel's Wings: Supporting the Forgotten Victims of Crime

Angel's Wings is a nonprofit organization located in Indianapolis, Indiana, created to assist pregnant incarcerated women. Their mission is to promote family preservation by providing alternative residential placement for infants whose mothers are incarcerated, mentors for incarcerated pregnant women, and reentry assistance to ex-offenders for successful reintegration back into the community. In 1999, Wendi Middleton, director and founder of Angel's Wings, worked for Prison Fellowship. She received a phone call about a 19-year-old pregnant prisoner incarcerated in Evansville, Indiana. The young woman wanted to find an organization that was willing to take care of her child while she was incarcerated. At the time, there was no such organization. On February 1, 2000, the young woman gave birth to a daughter she named Angel. Wendi made the decision to step in and care for the infant until her mother's release. Wendi took the infant weekly to visit her mother in prison. Eighteen months after Angel's birth, her mother was released; Wendi and her husband gave the young woman a place to live, helped her get a car and a job and develop a postrelease life plan to help her avoid returning to prison. Wendi knew that there were other incarcerated mothers in need of support and that children were the "forgotten victims of crime" (Angel's Wings, 2017, para. 4). Wendi's experience led her to establish Angel's Wings. Since its inception, Angel's Wings has helped hundreds of women successfully reenter society.

adults are parents. Left behind are the hidden victims of mass incarceration: their children. Consequently, on any given day approximately 1.7 million children in America suffer, often in silence.

While women are the fastest-growing incarcerated population, men continue to reign as the majority population in prison. At midyear 2007, approximately 93% of the U.S. prison population (state and federal) was male, with roughly 92% of incarcerated parents being fathers (Glaze & Maruschak, 2008). This male effect in incarceration rates stem from a change in American punitiveness sparked during the 1970s during President Richard Nixon's "War on Crime" and subsequently carried out aggressively through President Ronald Reagan's "War on Drugs" (Clear & Frost, 2014; Swisher & Waller, 2008; Woldoff & Washington, 2008). While the explosion of the U.S. prison population has mainly affected men, the racial demographics of the incarcerated male population is most startling.

African-American and Hispanic males are disproportionately represented in the U.S. prison population and often possess low educational attainment and previous histories of contact with the criminal justice system, and come from families marked by intergenerational patterns of criminality (Arditti, Smock, & Parkman, 2005; Arditti, 2012). Many of these men are products of communities characterized by racialized spatial containment and depleted political and financial resources (Geller, Garfinkel, & Western, 2011). Mass incarceration, primarily driven by selective enforcement of criminal sanction policies in these urban communities, serves as a constant feeder system into what Michelle Alexander (2010) describes as a permanent undercaste. After imprisonment and release, these men, mostly black, return to ghettos and forever face a life of exclusion, stigma, and legal discrimination (Alexander, 2010).

The funneling of primarily men of color into the prison system has resulted in a realignment of families in disadvantaged communities (Clear, 2007). According to the Bureau of Justice Statistics (BJS), more than 4 in 10 fathers in state and federal prisons were black (Glaze & Maruschak, 2008). Not surprisingly, this has led to the decimation of families and the social ecology of many urban communities, especially large urban areas such as Baltimore, New York City, and Chicago (Alexander, 2010). Arresting and imprisoning men *en masse* creates the opposite effect from intended reasons for punishment. Rather than remove law violators from high crime communities, the hyper-surveillance, racialized enforcement, and mass incarceration of men by the punitive state has severed parent-child bonds, created a "gender imbalance" for marriage-seeking women, and deepened poverty in already impoverished communities (Clear, 2007; Travis, 2005). Simply put, the "male effect" in incarceration has been a significant contributing factor to the disappearing of fathers in American homes and communities.

The demographics of incarcerated fathers reveal several commonalties. Among state inmates, a little over half (54%) are between age 25 to 34, indicating a relatively young population (Glaze & Maruschak, 2008). Many have had a history of contact with the criminal justice system, whether it be police stops, arrests, or previous stints in jail or prison. Often these men encounter the legal apparatus by way of nonviolent, drug-related offenses. State and federal inmates convicted of drug offenses are more likely than those convicted of violent and property offenses to have minor children (Glaze & Maruschak, 2008. p 4). Also, state and federal prisoners with prior criminal histories are more likely those with no previous criminal history to have minor children (Glaze & Maruschak, 2008. p 4).

While fewer than half (46%) of incarcerated fathers resided with their children prior to incarceration, over half report providing financial support to their children (Arditti, 2012). However, an overwhelming proportion of incarcerated fathers lived below the poverty line prior to incarceration, therefore hampering their ability to provide substantial financial support. Furthermore, their brand as a felon hinders their ability more so upon reentry. The absence of fathers from the home, as well as their limited capacity to display fathering roles during incarceration, places a large economic burden on the mother, the usual primary caregiver on the outside (Arditti et al., 2005).

The large concentration of young, minority, fathers in prison has created a gender imbalance, primarily in poor, urban communities. With a higher ratio of women to men, the removal of men because of incarceration provides bleak marriage prospects. Almost half (45%) of incarcerated fathers are unmarried prior to incarceration (Visher, 2013) and, once released, fare even worse socially and financially, therefore lacking the qualities that marriage-seeking women look for. Marriage has been shown to serve as a life turning point for criminally active individuals, and therefore a contributing factor in desistance from crime (Clear, 2007). Another collateral consequence of mass incarceration is that it weakens family functioning and informal social control. In poor, urban communities already ravaged by structural inequalities, the mass incarceration of men makes disadvantaged communities even worse.

Father Involvement in Prison

Despite conventional views about the lack of father involvement and fathering identity in poor, urban communities of color, many of these fathers have a presence in the lives of their children. Incarceration provides a physical barrier to contact; however, fathers in prison maintain several other forms of contact, mainly through mail and phone calls. Unfortunately, fathering is extremely constrained and regulated while behind bars, and incarcerated fathers who desire to maintain a parent-child bond do so under strict limitations and deprivations. Institutional policies, maternal gatekeeping, and economic strains are a few factors that limit or deny incarcerated fathers the opportunity to be involved with their children (Crandall-Williams & McEvoy, 2016). Not surprisingly, the children suffer the most deleterious effects when the parent-child bond is severed or weakened.

Distance may be the most significant barrier to contact between incarcerated fathers and their children. About 62% of state inmates and roughly 84% of federal inmates are housed more than a hundred miles away from their last place of residence (Glaze & Maruschak, 2008). This places a financial burden on children and their caregivers, especially when transportation and lodging are accounted for. Over half of state inmates and nearly half of federal inmates report never having a personal visit with their children, an issue that varies by gender and ethnicity (Hairston, 2007). While face-to-face contact may be the most effective way to maintain strong parent-child ties, distance often denies the opportunity. However, incarcerated fathers utilize other alternatives that allow for contact with their children.

Letters and phone calls are alternative and less restrictive methods in which incarcerated fathers stay in contact with their children. Both methods of contact allow fathers to maintain contact with their children even from a distance; however, problems exist there as well. Letters often take weeks, since they undergo close inspection and screening by correctional personnel. Inmates are prohibited from possessing money in prison and often must rely on financial support from the outside or menial jobs that provide meager wages inside prison. Dependence on spouses becomes problematic because the loss of income from the absent male places an economic burden on the women (Arditti, 2012). Since many of these fathers come from poor families and communities already, forcible separation because of incarceration deepens the financial strain, directly affecting the methods and frequency of contact between incarcerated fathers and their children.

Many incarcerated fathers do want to continue their fathering role, however, one major barrier they often face is maternal gatekeeping (Arditti et al., 2005; Arditti, 2012; Roy & Dyson, 2005). The contact between the incarcerated father and his child sometimes depend on the willingness of his former or current partner, the usual caregiver on the outside during his absence. This phenomenon is often a conflict between the incarcerated father's role and the role of the child's mother in the parenting process (Arditti, 2012). Gatekeeping ultimately proves to be harmful for children because their contact with their father is affected by what Roy and Dyson (2005) call "babymama drama." The climate of the relationship between the incarcerated father and the child's mother is sometimes the predictor of whether he will have some form of contact with his child. Despite the physical and institutional barriers that affect the contact between incarcerated fathers and their children, many are still able to execute their fathering role and maintain parent-child bonds.

The carceral environment can provide a conflict between an incarcerated father's dual identities (Tripp, 2009). Incarcerated fathers undergo an identity transformation often referred to as prisonization, where he accepts a hardened, hypermasculine identity that serves as a survival mechanism throughout the carceral experience (Arditti, 2012). This new prison identity can conflict with the preprison identity, which could affect the parent-child relationship. One aspect of the prisonization process is the suspension of family ties (Tripp, 2009). One immerses oneself into the prison subculture and adopts the mores of the carceral milieu. Family, including children, may not understand the lack of father involvement because of physical and social distance from the predatory, hypermasculine, environment of the prison.

Incarceration interrupts the confirmation process of a father's identity (Dyer, 2005). Because of physical and institutional restraints, preincarceration father identity is nearly impossible to maintain. Intimate forms of affection such as hugs and kisses are prohibited or extremely limited during visitation, if the incarcerated father is permitted to have face-to-face visits. Incarcerated fathers cannot provide the same level of financial support, help with homework, or even discipline their children, which are meaningful ways to enact fatherhood roles. The deprivations of the prison environment prove to be harmful to the parent-child bond and destabilizes the inmate's father identity (Dyer, 2005). While the prison environment hinders father involvement, many fathers remain concerned about their children and share great concern for their livelihood.

Incarcerated fathers worry about their children and want to maintain a presence in their lives; however, prison diminishes the capacity to do so. These fathers often share concern about their children's grades in school, behavior, and general welfare at home. Stressors associated with the inability to be physically present in the lives of their children makes the incarceration experience even harder, which causes some incarcerated fathers to completely shed their fathering role and fully take on the inmate role (Arditti, 2012; Dyer, 2005). Abandoning fathering roles in prison can serve as a strategy that reduces the emotional harm tied to the constraints of the parent-child relationship during incarceration. However, failure to maintain family relationships during incarceration, especially with children, can have detrimental effects postrelease.

Programs for Incarcerated Fathers

Despite the bleak reality of parenting behind bars, successful programs and services for incarcerated fathers do exist. Some local, state, and federal correctional facilities have implemented parenting programs, but space is limited, and the vast majority of incarcerated fathers do not have access to them because of factors such as seriousness of offense and security classification level. Two major parenting programs for justice-system-involved parents that have been utilized across the nation are *Parenting Inside Out* and *Inside Out Dad*. *Parenting Inside Out* is an evidence-based parenting skills training program for parents under correctional supervision. *Parenting Inside Out* includes skills training for both incarcerated mothers and fathers through the prison-parenting program, while the community version is tailored for the needs of parents on probation or parole. Topics covered include problem solving, communication, anger management, child guidance, and more. Many incarcerated fathers often show concern for living up to conventional standards of responsible fathering (Arditti, 2012). As mentioned earlier, many incarcerated fathers come from communities and families of concentrated poverty and histories of intergenerational involvement with the criminal justice system; therefore, many of their fathers were incarcerated as well, resulting in fatherless homes and primarily female-headed households. *Parenting Inside Out* has proven to be an effective program that helps provide a blueprint for justice-involved fathers who may lack the skills necessary for responsible fathering.

Inside Out Dad is a subpart of the National Fatherhood Initiative and the only national evidence-based program designed specifically for incarcerated fathers. *Inside Out Dad* is implemented in over 25 department of corrections facilities, as well as many Federal Bureau of Prisons facilities. Program materials to put one father through the *Inside Out Dad* program cost as little as $60. The program aims to strengthen families of incarcerated fathers, encourage prosocial attitudes, and lower recidivism rates by equipping incarcerated fathers with the training and skills necessary to build strong, healthy, parent-child and family relationships. Maintaining close family relationships is often a factor in desistance from crime, so programs tailored specifically for this subpopulation of parents can be advantageous.

Incarcerated Fathers in Jails

While this chapter has focused primarily on fathers in prison, thousands of fathers linger in local jails everyday across the nation. Jail are reserved for pretrial detainees, people awaiting transfer to prison, and individuals serving a sentence up to one year. Unfortunately, there are no rough estimates of the number of parents incarcerated in local jails; however, the demographics resemble parents in prison. Many fathers in jail are indigent, possess low educational attainment and minority status, and come from economically disadvantaged neighborhoods. One significant distinction between jail and prison is the opportunity to post bail. Many incarcerated individuals in jail are pretrial detainees and often receive a bail amount, or a sum of money that can be paid to be released back into the community until the disposition of their case is decided. However, those that cannot afford to post their bail amount remain in jail for months while having only been accused of a crime.

The bail industry in the United States has served as a tool for the privileged to escape confinement in jail while thousands of poor, minority men and women linger, sometimes for several months, in local jails across the country. Recent social justice advocacy efforts have taken place in recent years to bond out parents that cannot afford to post bail themselves. Two organizations, Southerners on New Ground and Color of Change held a major fundraising drive in 2017 that resulted in them posting bail for 100 mothers for Mother's Day. Acclaimed hip-hop artist Jay Z was inspired by such efforts and publicly criticized America's bail industry while pledging to participate in similar advocacy efforts (see Box 8.3 to learn more about Jay Z's efforts).

Incarcerated Fathers and Their Children

Most incarcerated parents (93%) are fathers, with a large proportion being black and Latino fathers (Travis, 2005; Arditti, 2012; Woldoff & Washington, 2008). The vast majority of Americans fail to

Box 8.3 Jay Z Bails Out Fathers for Father's Day

On June 16, 2017, Shawn Carter, known to many by the stage name Jay Z, wrote an op-ed for *TIME* about the for-profit bail bond industry in the United States and its inhumane practices against poor people of color detained in local jails around the country. Jay Z became obsessed with the injustices of the profitable bail bond industry while producing the docuseries, *Time: The Kalief Browder Story*. Inspired by philanthropic efforts by organizations the month prior for incarcerated mothers, Jay Z set out to support those same organizations by pledging to bail out fathers for Father's Day who could not afford "the due process our democracy promises" (Carter, 2017, para. 5). Jay Z argued that we cannot fix the broken American justice system until we attack the for-profit bail bond industry.

realize, no matter what race or gender, that most inmates are parents (Foster & Hagan, 2009). The mass incarceration of parents in America has resulted in roughly 1.7 million children without one or both parents on any given day. Children of incarcerated parents experience cumulative disadvantages after a parent is removed from the home, and this subpopulation of vulnerable children has special needs that warrant attention from a variety of stakeholders in their communities. The impact of paternal incarceration on children deserves attention because of its common occurrence, especially among African-American children.

The racially disproportionate arrest and incarceration of African Americans has deeply affected their children. About 1 in 9 African-American children have an incarcerated parent (Wakefield & Wildeman, 2014). Wakefield and Wildeman (2014) argue that mass incarceration exacerbates childhood inequality, mainly of youth of color who already experience cumulative risks. Children of incarcerated parents experience several sudden changes once their father is removed from the home. First, if the father lived with them and provided most of the financial support for the family, his removal shifts the entire economic burden onto the mother or other caregiver (Arditti, 2012; Clear, 2007). Then, if the economic burden becomes too great, the child may be sent to live with another relative, usually the maternal grandparents. Trying to adjust to a new living situation can induce anxiety and depression while resulting in behavioral problems at both home and school. Loss of a parent to incarceration is considered an ambiguous loss because the incarcerated parent is living but not accessible (Arditti, 2012).

For children who are given the privilege of having limited access through visitation, they usually realize that the constraints of the carceral environment are not child friendly (Comfort, 2008; Arditti, 2012). Children visiting their incarcerated parent are viewed with close suspicion, are regulated emotionally, and eventually realize that their conduct is a predictor of whether their parent will maintain family visitation privileges. Children, like significant others and spouses, undergo a secondary prisonization process in which the norms and regulations of the carceral environment immerse that environment in the lives of outsiders that encounter the prison (Comfort, 2008). Children of incarcerated parents have been labeled the invisible victims of mass incarceration and unfortunately pay the price for actions and criminal justice policies aimed toward their parents. The racially disparate criminalization of people of color in the United States has a direct effect on their children. Until American citizens, policy makers, and criminal justice officials begin to see inmates as parents, and mass incarceration is dismantled, a large population of children in this country will live in the shadows of the carceral milieu: outside its walls but forever entangled in its web.

Conclusion

It is difficult to negotiate motherhood and fatherhood during incarceration. Incarcerated parents worry about the effects their incarceration has on their children. For example, incarcerated parents fear they will lose their emotional connection to their children, which means these children will have life-long difficulties forming attachments to others. Parents also fear that their children will become involved in the criminal justice system. Incarceration magnifies parental failings and often leads to feelings of shame and guilt for both parents and children.

Correctional administrators recognize the need to repair and maintain family bonds. Therefore, correctional facilities across the United States offer a variety of programs designed to improve parenting skills and to teach incarcerated parents age-appropriate activities for their children. Women's prisons offer nursery programs in the hopes of fostering mother-infant bonds and breaking the cycle of intergenerational criminality. Likewise, the *Inside Out Dad Program* helps incarcerated fathers create and preserve bonds with their children. Parenting programs not only teach incarcerated parents the skills they need to be effective with their children but also significantly reduce the likelihood of reoffending and reincarceration.

References

Ainsworth, M. D. S. (1967). *Infancy in Uganda: Infant care and the growth of love*. Baltimore, MD: The John Hopkins Press.

Alexander, M. (2010). *The new Jim Crow: Mass incarceration in the age of colorblindness*. New York, NY: The New Press.

American Academy of Pediatrics, American College [Congress] of Obstetrics and Gynecologists. (2007). *Guidelines for perinatal care* (6th ed.). Washington, DC: Elk Grove Village.

American Civil Liberties Union. (2015). *ACLU briefing paper: The shackling of pregnant women & girls in U.S. prions, jails, & youth detention centers*. New York, NY: American Civil Liberties Union. Retrieved from www.aclu.org/files/assets/anti-shackling_briefing_paper_stand_alone.pdf

American College [Congress] of Obstetricians and Gynecologists. (2011). *Health care for pregnant and postpartum incarcerated women and adolescent females*. Committee Opinion Number 511. Retrieved from www.acog.org/-/media/Committee-Opinions/Committee-on-Health-Care-for-Underserved-Women/co511.pdf?dmc=1&ts=20170830T0504489748

Angel's Wings. (2017). *Our history*. Indianapolis, IN: Angels' Wings. Retrieved from www.angelswingsinc.org/about-us.html

Arditti, J. A. (2012). *Parental Incarceration and the family: Psychological and social effects of imprisonment on children, parents, and caregivers*. New York, NY: NYU Press.

Arditti, J. A., Smock, S., & Parkman, T. (2005). "It's been hard to be a father": A qualitative exploration of incarcerated fatherhood. *Fathering, 3*, 267–288.

Bednarowski, J. (2014). *Prison parenting programs: Resources for parenting instructors in prisons and jails*. Laurel, MD: Parenting Special Interest Group of the Correctional Education Association.

Belknap, J. (2015). *The invisible woman: Gender, crime, and justice* (4th ed.). Stamford, CT: Cengage Learning.

Berry, P. E., & Eigenberg, H. M. (2003). Role strain and incarcerated mothers: Understanding the process of mothering. *Women & Criminal Justice, 15*(1), 101–119. doi:10.1300/j012v15n01_06

Bhuvaneswar, C. G., Chang, G., Epstein, L. A., & Stern, T. A. (2008). Cocaine and opioid use during pregnancy: Prevalence and management. *Primary Care Companion to the Journal of Clinical Psychiatry, 10*(1), 59–65. doi:10.4088/PCC.v10n0110

Borelli, J. L., Goshin, L., Joestl, S., Clark, J., & Byrne, M. W. (2010). Attachment organization in a sample of incarcerated mothers: Distribution of classifications and associations with substance abuse history, depressive symptoms, perceptions of parenting competency and social support. *Attachment & Human Development, 12*(4), 355–374. doi:10.1080/14616730903416971

Baunach, P. J. (1985). *Mothers in prison*. New Brunswick, NJ: Transaction Books.

Beauchamp, G., Martineau, M., & Gagnon, A. (2016). Examining the link between adult attachment style, employment, and academic achievement in first semester higher education. *Social Psychology of Education, 19*(2), 367–384.

Black Demographics. (2013). *Interesting facts about the African American population*. Retrieved from http://blackdemographics.com/

Bloom, B., & Steinhart, D. (1993). *Why punish the children? A reprisal of the children of incarcerated mothers in America*. San Francisco, CA: National Council on Crime and Delinquency.

Bowlby, J. (1944). *Forty-four juvenile thieves: Their character and home-life*. London: Tavistock Clinic.

Bowlby, J. (1969). *Attachment and loss (Volume 1)*. New York, NY: Basic Books.

Bowlby, J. (1982). Attachment and loss: Retrospect and prospect. *American Journal of Orthopsychiatry, 52*(4), 664–678. doi:10.1111/j.1939-0025.1982.tb01456.x

Bruns, D. A. (2006). Promoting mother-child relationships for incarcerated women and their children. *Infants & Young Children, 19*(4), 308–322. doi:10.1097/00001163-200610000-00004

Byrne, M. W., Goshin, L. S., & Joestl, S. (2010). Intergenerational attachment for infants raised in a prison nursery. *Attachment & Human Development, 12*(4), 375–394. doi:10.1080/14616730903417011

Cabage, L. N. (2016). *Baby don't come back: Female inmate narratives from the inside*. Unpublished manuscript, Iowa State University, Ames, Iowa.

Carlson, J. R. (1998). Evaluating the effectiveness of a live-in nursery within a women's prison. *Journal of Offender Rehabilitation, 27*(1/2), 73–85. doi:10.1300/j076v27n01_06

Carlson, J. R. (2001). Prison nursery 2000: A five-year review of the prison nursery at the Nebraska Correctional Center for Women. *Journal of Offender Rehabilitation, 33*(3), 75–97. doi:10.1300/j076v33n03_05

Carlson, J. R. (2009). Prison nurseries: A pathway to crime-free futures. *Corrections Compendium, 34*(1), 17–24.

Carson, E. A. (2014). *Prisoners in 2013*. Washington, DC: U.S. Department of Justice, Bureau of Justice Statistics.

Carter, S. (2017, June 16). Jay Z: For father's day, I'm taking on the exploitative bail industry. *TIME*. Retrieved from http:// http://time.com/4821547/jay-z-racism-bail-bonds/

Cassidy, J., Ziv, Y., Stupica, B., Sherman, L. J., Butler, H., Karfgin, A., . . . Powell, B. (2010). Enhancing attachment security in the infants of women in a jail diversion program. *Attachment & Human Development, 12*(4), 333–353. doi:10.1080/14616730903416955

Children of Incarcerated Parents. (2017). *Children of incarcerated parents*. Retrieved from http://youth.gov/youth-topics/children-of-incarcerated-parents

Clear, T. (2007). *Imprisoning communities: How mass incarceration makes disadvantaged neighborhoods worse*. New York, NY: Oxford University Press.

Clear, T., & Frost, N. (2014). *The punishment imperative: The rise and failure of mass incarceration in America*. New York, NY: NYU Press.

Comfort, M. (2008). *Doing time together: Love and family in the shadow of the prison*. Chicago, IL: University of Chicago Press.

Crandall-Williams, A., & McEvoy, A. (2016). Fathers on parole: Narratives from the margins. *Journal of Men's Studies, 25*(3), 1–16. doi: 10.1177/1060826516676840

Dinero, R. E., Conger, R. D., Shaver, P. R., Widaman, K. F., & Larsen-Rife, D. (2008). Influence of family origin and adult romantic partners on romantic attachment security. *Journal of Family Psychology, 22*(4), 622–632.

Dodson, K. D., Cabage, L. N., Brown, J., & MacMillan, S. (2017). *Mothering behind bars: Evaluating the effectiveness of prison nursery programs on recidivism reduction*. Manuscript submitted for publication.

Dyer, J. (2005). Prison, fathers, and identity: A theory of how incarceration affects men's paternal identity. *Fathering, 3*(3), 201–219.

Foster, H., & Hagan, J. (2009). The mass incarceration of parents in America: Issues of race/ethnicity, collateral damage to children, and prisoner reentry. *The Annals of the American Academy of Political and Social Science, 163*(1), 179–194. doi:10.1177/0002716208331123

Geller, A., Garfinkel, I., & Western, B. (2011). Paternal incarceration and support for children in fragile families. *Demography, 48*, 25–47. doi:10.1007/s13524-010-0009-9

Glaze, L. E., & Maruschak, L. M. (2008). *Parents in prison and their minor children*. Washington, DC: Bureau of Justice Statistics Special Report.

Goshin, L. S., & Byrne, M. W. (2009). Converging streams of opportunity for prison nursery programs in the United States. *Journal of Offender Rehabilitation, 48*(4), 271–295. doi:10.1080/10509670902848972

Goshin, L. S., Byrne, M. W., & Blanchard-Lewis, B. (2014). Preschool outcomes of children who lived as infants in a prison nursery. *The Prison Journal, 94*(2), 139–158. doi:10.1177/0032885514524692

Hairston, C. (2007). *Focus on children with incarcerated parents: An overview of the research literature*. Retrieved from http://repositories.lib.utexas.edu/bitstream/handle/2152/15158/AECasey_Children_IncParents.pdf?sequence=2

Heffernan, E. (1993). Alderson: The early years. In American Correctional Association (Ed.), *Female offenders: Meeting needs of a neglected population* (pp. 7–11). Laurel, MD: American Correctional Association.

Henriques, Z. W. (1996). Imprisoned mothers and their children: Separation-reunion syndrome dual impact. *Women & Criminal Justice, 8*(1), 77–97. doi:10.1300/J012v08n01_05

Henriques, Z. W., & Gladwin, B. P. (2013). Pregnancy and motherhood behind bars. In L. Gideon (Ed.), *Special needs offenders in correctional institutions* (pp. 83–116). Thousand Oaks, CA: Sage.

Hirschi, T. (1969). *Causes of delinquency*. Berkeley, CA: University of California Press.

Howze-Browne, D. C. (1989). Incarcerated mothers and parenting. *Journal of Family Violence, 4*(2), 211–221.

International Human Rights Clinic. (2013). *Shacking of pregnant prisons in the United States*. Chicago, IL: The University of Chicago. Retrieved from https://ihrclinic.uchicago.edu/page/shackling-pregnant-prisoners-united-states

Kauffman, K. (2001). Mothers in prison. *Corrections Today, 63*(1), 62–65.

Kjellstrand, J., Cearley, J., Eddy, J. M., Foney, D., & Martinez, C. R., Jr. (2012). Characteristics of incarcerated fathers and mothers: Implications for preventive interventions Targeting children and families. *Child Youth Services Review, 34*(12), 2409–2415. doi:10.1016/j.childyouth.2012.08.008

Koch, S. M., & Tomlin, A. M. (2010). *Wee Ones Nursery evaluation: Findings from 2008–2009*. Indianapolis, IN: Indiana University School of Medicine.

Kovensky, J. (2014). It's time to pay prisoners the minimum wage. *New Republic*. Retrieved from https://newrepublic.com/article/119083/prison-labor-equal-rights-wages-incarcerated-help-economy

Leeder, E. J. (2012). *Inside and out: Women, prison, and therapy*. New York, NY: Routledge.

Loper, A. B., & Tuerk, E. H. (2006). Parenting programs for incarcerated parents: Current research and future directions. *Criminal Justice Policy Review, 17*(4), 407–427. doi:10.1177/0887403406292692

Martin, E. (2017). *Hidden consequences: The impact of incarceration on dependent children*. Washington, DC: National Institute of Justice, Office of Justice Programs.

Marušić, I., Kamenov, Z., & Jelić, M. (2010). Personality and attachment to friends. *Društvena istraživanja, 20*(4), 1119–1137. doi:10.5559/di.20.4.10

McKenzie, M., Nunn, A., Zaller, N. D., Bazazi, A. R., & Rich, J. D. (2009). Overcoming obstacles to implementing methadone therapy for prisoners: Implications for policy and practice. *Journal of Opioid Management, 5*(4), 219–227. doi:10.1080/02791072.2011.601984

Miller, A. L., Perryman, J., Markovitz, L., Franzen, S., Cochran, S., & Brown, S. (2013). Strengthening incarcerated families: Evaluating a pilot program for children of incarcerated parents and their caregivers. *Family Relations, 62*(4), 584–596. doi:10.1111/fare.12029

Moretti, M. M., & Peled, M. (2004). Adolescent-parent attachment: Bonds that support healthy development. *Paediatrics Child Health, 9*(8), 551–555.

National Commission on Correctional Health Care. (2016). *Joint statement on the federal role in restricting the use of restraints on incarcerated women and girls during pregnancy, labor, and postpartum recovery*. Retrieved from www.apa.org/about/gr/pi/news/2015/joint-statement.pdf

Newman, C., Fowler, C., & Cashin, A. (2011). *The development of a parenting program for incarcerated mothers in Australia: A review of prison-based parenting programs, 39*(1), 2–11. doi:10.5172/conu.2011.39.1.2

Papini, D. R., & Roggman, L. A. (1992). Adolescent perceived attachment to parents in relation to competence, depression, and anxiety: A longitudinal study. *Journal of Early Adolescence, 12*(4), 420–440. doi:10.1177/0272431692012004005

Parke, R. D., & Clarke-Stewart, K. A. (2001). *From prison to home: The effect of incarceration and reentry on children, families, and communities*. Washington, DC: U.S. Department of Health & Human Services.

Roy, K. M., & Dyson, O. L. (2005). Gatekeeping in context: Babymama drama and the involvement of incarcerated fathers. *Fathering, 3*(3), 289–310.

Rush, B. (1991). *A plan for the punishment of crime*. Philadelphia, PA: Pennsylvania Prison Society.

Schempf, A. H. (2007). Illicit drug use and neonatal outcomes: A critical review. *Obstetrical & Gynecological Survey, 62*(11), 749–757. doi:10.1097/01.ogx.0000256562.31774.76

Shepard, D., & Zemans, E. S. (1950). *Prison babies: A study of some aspects of the care and treatment of pregnant inmates and their infants in training schools, reformatories, and prisons*. Chicago, IL: John Howard Association.

Simpson, J. A., Collins, W. A., & Salvatore, J. E. (2012). The impact of early interpersonal experience on adult romantic relationship functioning: Recent findings from the Minnesota longitudinal study of risk and adaptation. *Current Directions in Psychological Science, 20*(6), 355–359. doi:10.1177/0963721411418468

Snyder, Z. K., Carlo, T. A., & Coats Mullins, M. M. (2001). Parenting from prison: An examination of a children's visitation program at a Women's Correctional Facility. *Marriage & Family Review, 32*(3/4), 33–61. doi:10.1300/j002v32n03_04

Staley, E. M. (2002). *Profile and three-year follow-up of Bedford Hills and Taconic nursery program participants: 1997 and 1998*. New York, NY: New York State Department of Correctional Services, Division of Program Planning, Research and Evaluation, 1–23.

Swisher, R. R., & Waller, M. R. (2008). Confining fatherhood: Incarceration and paternal involvement among nonresident white, African American, and Latino fathers. *Journal of Family Issues, 29*(8), 1067–1088. doi:10.1177/0192513X08316273

Travis, J. (2005). *But they all come back: Facing the challenges of prisoner reentry*. Washington, DC: Urban Institute Press.

Tripp, B. (2009). Fathers in jail: Managing dual identities. *Applied Psychology in Criminal Justice, 5*(1), 26–56.

Troy, M., & Sroufe, L. (1987). Victimization among preschoolers: Role of attachment relationship history. *Child & Adolescent Psychiatry, 26*(2), 166–172. doi:10.1097/00004583-198703000-00007

Tuerk, E. H., & Loper, A. B. (2014). Contact between incarcerated mothers and their children. *Journal of Offender Rehabilitation, 43*(1), 23–43. doi:10.1300/J076v43n01_02

United States Census Bureau. (2010). *Quick facts*. Washington, DC: United States Census Bureau.

Visher, C. A. (2013). Incarcerated fathers: Pathways from prison to home. *Criminal Justice Policy Review, 24*(1), 9–26. doi:10.1177/0887403411418105

Wakefield, S., & Wildeman, C. (2014). *Children of the prison boom: Mass incarceration and the future of American inequality*. New York, NY: Oxford University Press.

Whiteacre, K., Fritz, S., & Owen, J. (2013). *Assessing outcomes for Wee Ones Nursery at the Indiana Women's Prison*. Unpublished report. Community Research Center, University of Indianapolis.

Whitehead, J. T., Dodson, K. D., & Edwards, B. D. (2013). *Corrections: Exploring crime, punishment, and justice in America* (3rd ed.). New York, NY: Routledge.

Woldoff, R. A., & Washington, H. M. (2008). Arrested contact: The criminal justice system, race, and father engagement. *The Prison Journal, 88*(2), 179–206. doi:10.1177/0032885508319154

Women's Prison Association. (2009). *Mothers, infants and imprisonment: A national look at prison nurseries and community-based alternatives*. New York, NY: Women's Prison Association Institute on Women & Criminal Justice.

Zemans, E. S., & Smith, M. N. (1946). *War activities of women and girls in state correctional institutions 1943–1944*. Chicago, IL: Central Howard Association.

9

JUVENILE OFFENDERS

Diverting Youth and Utilizing Evidence-Based Practices

Riane M. Bolin

> It is easy to forget that most children who are incarcerated will be out on the streets in a few years or months. What they learn through the juvenile justice system is likely to influence their behavior later. Their access to appropriate education and vocational training and to mental health services may make all the difference between successful reintegration into society and reoffending.
>
> —(Institute of Medicine and National Research Council, 2001, p. 186)

Introduction

A juvenile offender is an individual below the legal age of criminal responsibility (the youngest age at which an individual can be tried in criminal court) who has committed a violation of the criminal law or committed a status offense. Individual states have varying definitions of the age of criminal responsibility. North Carolina and New York, for example, have set the age of criminal responsibility for delinquent offenses at 16, while Wisconsin and Georgia have determined the appropriate age to be 17 (Griffin, Addie, Adams, & Firestine, 2011). While some variation exists, most states utilize the federal definition, which holds 18 as the age of criminal responsibility. Persons under the age of criminal responsibility are processed in a separate court, the juvenile court, which is designed specifically to address the needs of juvenile offenders.

Juveniles have not always been processed in a separate court. In fact, the first juvenile court was not established until 1899 in Cook County, Illinois (Platt, 1969). Prior to this time, juveniles were largely treated as adults, being held to the same legal standards and receiving the same punishments (Binder, Geis, & Dickson, 2001; Mack, 1909; Simonsen & Gordon, 1982). The development of a separate juvenile court resulted from the growing recognition that juveniles were distinctly different from adults and thus should be treated differently in a court of law (Mennell, 1973; Platt, 1969). Recognizing that juveniles were more malleable than adults, the original court was focused on rehabilitation and treatment as opposed to accountability and punishment (Feld, 1999; Mack, 1909; Platt, 1969; Simonsen & Gordon, 1982) and embraced the doctrine of *parens patriae*. Under the doctrine of *parens patriae* (Latin for "parent of his or her country"), the state has the legal authority to act as sovereign or "parent" to protect those who are unable to protect themselves; this includes minors. Therefore, generally speaking, juveniles have been viewed as a vulnerable population is need of special legal protections and considerations.

However, since the inception of the juvenile justice system there have been two waves of "adultification." The once clear-cut lines between the juvenile and adult systems have merged (Bernard & Kurlychek, 2010). The first wave of adultification, referred to as the due process era, occurred during the 1960s and 1970s (Merlo, Benekos, & Cook, 1999; Vito, Tewskbury, & Wilson, 1998). Responsible for this change was a series of Supreme Court cases, which granted juveniles a number of due process rights not originally afforded to them, such as the right to remain silent, the right to an attorney, and the protection against double jeopardy (*Breed v. Jones*, 1975; *In re Gault*, 1967; *In re Winship*, 1970). The Court's decisions in these cases were largely a result of their waning optimism about the juvenile court's ability to "treat" juveniles (Snyder & Sickmund, 1999).

The second wave of adultification, the "get tough era," resulted from public fear of the rise in juvenile crime, particularly violent crime, during the 1980s and 1990s. In response to the rising crime rates, legislators, both conservative and liberal, implemented a number of policies that moved the focus of the system away from rehabilitation and treatment toward accountability and punishment (Fox, 1996; Merlo et al., 1999; Zimring, 1998). Changes that resulted from the implementation of "get tough" legislation include changes in purpose clauses, the juvenile court process, the available dispositional outcomes, and juvenile court jurisdiction (Snyder & Sickmund, 1999; Torbet & Szymanski, 1998; Torbet & Thomas, 1997). Ultimately, the legislation helped further adultify the juvenile justice system by implementing policies and procedures that were more in line with the criminal justice system than the original conceptualization of the juvenile justice system.

While the goal of treatment was never eliminated, interest in it did wane during these periods, particularly during the "get tough" era. Recently, however, scholars have begun to argue that the pendulum is beginning to shift back toward rehabilitation (Benekos & Merlo, 2008; Bernard & Kurlychek, 2010; Merlo & Benekos, 2010). Such scholars claim that the elimination of the death penalty for juveniles (*Roper v. Simmons*, 2005), declining passage of get tough legislation (Snyder & Sickmund, 2006), and new laws and practices being implemented to reduce harsh punishments for juveniles (Campaign for Youth Justice, 2010; Juvenile Justice Initiative, 2013), along with a more positive public attitude toward juvenile offenders (Applegate & Davis, 2006; Nagin, Piquero, Scott, & Steinberg, 2006; Piquero, Cullen, Unnever, Piquero, & Gordon, 2010), all point to the fact that the juvenile justice system is beginning to return to its original purpose of rehabilitation.

This chapter will focus on some of the interventions and treatment programs that have been developed to rehabilitate juvenile offenders both within the community and within institutions. The chapter will begin with a discussion on diversion programs, a type of intervention that is designed to keep juveniles from being formally processed in the juvenile court. Next, the chapter will discuss three different types of specialty courts—teen courts, substance abuse courts, and mental health courts—that fall under the category of diversion. Following this section, rehabilitation and treatment programs both within correctional facilities and within the community will be discussed, with an emphasis being placed on evidence-based practices. The chapter will conclude with a discussion on future directions for rehabilitation and treatment programs for juvenile offenders.

Juvenile Diversion Programs

Juvenile diversion refers to the process of routing cases that would have otherwise been formally handled by the juvenile court to noncourt institutions (Roberts, 2004; Whitehead, Dodson, & Edwards, 2013; Whitehead & Lab, 1999). The purpose of diversion is to give youth a chance to avoid formal processing and adjudication. Diversion programs have been around since the development of the juvenile court in 1899 (Nejelski, 1976); however, programs were not formalized until the late-1960s, when the juvenile justice population was on the rise and critics were questioning the effectiveness of the system to reduce crime and rehabilitate delinquents (Cocozza et al., 2005; Roberts, 2004).

The 1967 President's Commission on Law Enforcement and the Administration of Justice was instrumental in promoting the implementation of diversion programs. The Commission was critical of the juvenile justice system's ability to rehabilitate youthful offenders and acknowledged the crime-producing effects that formal system intervention had on youth (Whitehead & Lab, 1999). Their recommendation was to limit the use of formal court processing, focusing instead on the use of alternative, nonjudicial dispositional methods to connect youth to appropriate services (President's Commission, 1967). The ultimate goal was to increase the use of nonjudicial interventions while saving formal court processing as a last resort. Following the commission's recommendation, diversion programs, also referred to as youth service bureaus, began to pop up across the country. During the time frame of 1967–1971, the number of diversion programs available in the United States rose from zero to more than 150 (Howlett, 1973).

Diversion programs and the use of such programs continued to expand during the 1970s. To illustrate, in Los Angeles, California, the number of youth referred to diversion programs from 1968–1974 by the Los Angeles County Sherriff's Department rose from 119 to 1,646 (Klein, Teilmann, Styles, Lincoln, & Labin-Rosenweig, 1976). Largely responsible for the sustained expansion of diversion was continued federal support (Cocozza et al., 2005; Roberts, 2004). Of particular importance was the $10 million made available in 1976 by the Office of Juvenile Justice and Delinquency Prevention to help develop diversion programs across the United States (Roberts, 2004). In response to the increased attention given to diversion, researchers began to explore the effectiveness of such programs. While some studies found positive results, such as reducing recidivism (e.g., Klein, 1975; Lipsey, Cordray, & Berger, 1981; Quay & Love, 1977; Regoli, Wilderman, & Pogrebin, 1985), others found negative results of diversion, including net widening (Blomberg, 1983; Palmer & Lewis, 1980), failure to decrease referrals to the juvenile justice system (Lipsey et al., 1981), failure to significantly reduce recidivism (Gensheimer, Mayer, Gottschalk, & Davidson, 1986), and, in some cases, increased recidivism (Lincoln, 1976). The negative research findings in conjunction with the rise in juvenile crime during the late 1980s resulted in a reduced emphasis on diversion. However, within the last two decades, a renewed interest has emerged (Models for Change Juvenile Diversion Workgroup, 2011).

In conjunction with the renewed interest in diversion programs, researchers have once again begun exploring the impact of diversion programs on youth. Within the past five years, three separate meta-analyses have been conducted examining the research findings on the effectiveness of diversion programs and, consistent with prior research, have found mixed results (Schwalbe, Gearing, MacKenzie, Brewer, & Ibrahim, 2012; Wilson & Hoge, 2013; Wong, Boucharad, Gravel, Bouchard, & Morselli, 2016). For example, Schwalbe and colleagues (2012) conducted a meta-analysis using 28 studies published from 1980–2011. Five distinct categories of diversion programs were identified and analyzed independently of one another, including case management/brokered services only, individually oriented treatment, family-based treatment, youth court, and restorative justice to determine whether they were effective in reducing recidivism. Overall, it was found that diversion failed to reduce recidivism significantly. In fact, of the five program types identified, only family treatment was found to reduce recidivism significantly.

Wilson and Hoge's (2013) and Wong et al.'s (2016) meta-analyses, however, found contradictory results, with both studies finding support for the idea that diversion reduces recidivism. Specifically, Wilson and Hoge (2013) examined 45 diversion studies published between 1972 and 2010. They found that participation in a diversion program was more effective in reducing recidivism than traditional judicial interventions. Similar to Schwalbe et al. (2012), Wilson and Hoge (2013) explored whether program type affected recidivism rates. They categorized programs as either caution programs or formal diversion programs. Caution programs were defined as those designed to divert youth out of the system with no additional action, except a formal warning. Formal diversion programs, on the other hand, were described as those typically involving certain conditions, such as admitting guilt or agreeing to program participation. Unlike Schwalbe et al. (2012), both types of programs were found to reduce recidivism significantly.

Most recently, Wong et al. (2016) conducted a meta-analysis focusing specifically on restorative diversion programs. Twenty-one studies published between 1990 and 2013 were included. Consistent with Wilson and Hoge (2013), restorative justice diversion programs were found to have a significant positive effect on reducing recidivism. Explanations have been provided regarding the inconsistent findings of the various research studies. Most notable is the heterogeneous nature of diversion programs (Schwalbe et al., 2012; Wong et al., 2016). When the 1967 President's Commission promoted the use of diversion, it failed to provide an adequate definition of the term, thus leaving it up to program designers and researchers to develop their own meaning (Whitehead & Lab, 1999). Not surprisingly, this resulted in a wide array of programs categorized under the umbrella of diversion. Programs have been found to vary based on a number of different factors including, but not limited to, referral stage, types of services provided, and populations served (Cocozza et al., 2005; Whitehead & Lab, 1999).

The research on diversion is similarly heterogeneous, differing on characteristics such as research design, publication source, and program implementation and monitoring (Schwalbe et al., 2012; Wilson & Hoge, 2013; Wong et al., 2016). The inconsistent nature of both diversion programs and diversion research makes it difficult to assess the impact of diversion on recidivism and other related outcomes adequately. Thus, as noted by Wong et al. (2016, p. 15), there is

> a strong need for more peer reviewed studies using rigorous research designs that document important program and study components that may play a meaningful role (e.g., parental involvement, length of follow-up), as well as programs that target youths of diverse racial/ethnic backgrounds.

Findings from such studies may help eliminate ineffective programs while encouraging the implementation of evidence-based diversion programs.

Specialty Courts

Specialty courts, also referred to as problem-solving or therapeutic courts, represent another way in which the juvenile justice system is attempting to deal with juvenile offenders more effectively (see Chapter 3 for a detailed discussion of specialty courts). Such courts first made their appearance in the U.S. justice system during the 1980s and 1990s. The courts are designed to address specific issues (e.g., truancy, drug use) or populations (e.g., mentally ill, sex offenders) in the juvenile justice system (Ohio Juvenile Justice Association, 2015). The goal is to provide services to youth to help them address the underlying issues that lead them to become court-involved. The problem-solving orientation of specialty courts has been referred to as "therapeutic jurisprudence," as it maintains a focus on justice while also emphasizing treatment and care (Rottman & Casey, 1999, p. 12). The underlying assumption of specialty courts (or therapeutic jurisprudence programs) is that more effective dispositions will result when there is a focus on both the legal issues before the court as well as the individual needs and circumstances of an offender (Sloan & Smykla, 2003).

Drug courts represent the best-known example of specialized courts and, in fact, have been in existence the longest, with the first adult drug court emerging in Dade County, Florida, in 1989 (Belenko, 1990), followed by the establishment of juvenile drug courts in the mid-1990s (Sloan & Smykla, 2003). Since this time, however, a number of different courts have emerged to address the multitude of issues faced by juvenile offenders, such as truancy, mental health, guns, reentry, gangs, domestic violence, and teen courts ("Children at Risk," 2014). The following paragraphs will discuss in detail two of the most prevalent specialty courts utilized within the juvenile justice system today: teen courts and juvenile drug courts.

Teen Courts

According to the National Association of Youth Courts (2016), teen courts, also referred to as peer, youth, or student courts, are specialized diversion programs in which youth sentence their peers for minor delinquent and status offenses. Conflicting accounts exist regarding when the first teen courts were developed. However, it is believed that similar programs have been in operations for over 50 years. Butts, Buck, and Coggeshall (2002), for example, found a report in the *Mansfield News Journal* from 1949 about a youth-operated bicycle court. The court met every Saturday morning to handle minor traffic cases committed by juveniles on bicycles. Others have also located anecdotal reports of teen courts in operation during the 1960s and 1970s (Godwin, 1998). Regardless, the number of teen court programs has been increasing rapidly since the 1990s. From 1991 to 1998, the number of teen courts nationwide expanded from 50 programs to between 400 and 500 programs (Nessel, 1998). As of March 2010, the most recent data available, there are more than 1,050 programs in operation in 49 states and the District of Columbia (National Association of Youth Courts, 2016). The rapid expansion of teen courts is said to be the result of the widely held belief that a peer-led restorative justice model represents an improved alternative to both traditional juvenile court processing and other less formal options (Hiller & Saum, 2014).

Typically, teen courts are offered to young (12–15), first-time, nonviolent offenders, as a voluntary alternative to being formally processed in juvenile court (Butts & Ortiz, 2011). Studies have found that the most common offenses handled include theft, minor assault, alcohol and marijuana possession or use, curfew violations, and disorderly conduct (Butts & Buck, 2000; Rasmussen & Diener, 2005; Smith & Chonody, 2010). While teen courts resemble traditional courts in both the key actors and court processes, they differ in that those responsible for filling those roles are mostly young people. For example, in a teen court, a 16-year-old prosecutor may present charges, a 17-year-old defense attorney may represent the defendant, and the disposition may be decided, depending on the type of model utilized, by a 16-year-old judge or a jury made up of solely of youth.

While the focus of teen courts is to have youth heavily involved in the court process, the extent of their involvement varies based on the type of youth court model in place. Teen courts follow one of four models: (1) the adult judge model; (2) the youth judge model; (3) the youth tribunal; and (4) the peer jury model (Godwin, 1998). In the adult judge model, youth volunteers serve in the roles of attorneys (both prosecution and defense) and jurors. However, adults, typically volunteer attorneys, or judges, serve in the capacity of the judge, ruling on courtroom procedure and clarifying legal terminology. The youth judge model is the same as the adult judge model, differing only in that the role of judge is served by a youth. The youth tribunal model eliminates the use of a peer jury. Youth attorneys present their case directly to youth judges, who then are responsible for determining sanctions. Lastly, the peer jury model eliminates the use of attorneys. Instead, a panel of teen jurors directly questions the defendant and determines appropriate sanctions (Godwin, Heaward, & Spina, 2000). According to the National Youth Court Center (2004), the adult judge model is the most common model used by teen courts, with over half of teen courts in operation utilizing this model. The peer jury model is the next most commonly used (31%), followed by the youth judge model (18%), and the youth tribunal model (10%).

Most teen courts are responsible only for determining the appropriate sanctions for the defendant, as most courts require that the youth admit guilt prior to participation (National Association of Youth Courts, 2016). In fact, according to the National Youth Court Database, 93% of youth court programs have such a requirement. As such, the primary goal of teen courts is to help youth understand the consequences of their actions and hold them accountable through the use of various sanctions (Hiller & Saum, 2014). Vital to the teen court philosophy is the idea that the sanctions imposed should serve to repair some of the harm levied on the victim and the community (Butts et al., 2002, Godwin et al., 2000). Thus, not surprisingly, the most common disposition imposed on defendants is community service. Other common sanctions include oral or written apologies, educational workshops, restitution, and participating in the teen court process as a juror in a subsequent trial (Butts & Buck, 2000; Minor, Wells, Soderstrom, Bingham, & Williamson, 1999; National Association of Youth Courts, 2016).

A number of criminological theories support the belief that the use of young people in the teen court process will be effective in reducing negative behavior. Differential association theory, for example, posits that delinquent behavior is learned through interaction with delinquent peers (Sutherland, 1947). Specifically, by associating with deviant or delinquent others, youth are taught definitions, attitudes, and techniques favorable toward law violation. Teen courts utilize this power of peer influence, but in a more positive manner. By participating in a teen court, youth involved experience pressure from prosocial peers, thus learning new definitions and techniques that encourage law-abiding behavior (Butts et al., 2002; Butts & Ortiz, 2011).

Principles of Braithwaite's (1989) reintegrative shaming theory are also utilized by teen courts to reduce delinquency. Teen courts emphasize restorative justice, with an open dialog procedure concentrating on repairing harms done to the victim and/or community (Fisher, 2007). The process used by teen courts adheres to the ideas of reintegrative shaming by holding the offenders accountable, yet also reintegrating them back into the community through the use a variety of different sanctions aimed at repairing harm (Stickle, Connell, Wilson, & Gottfredson, 2008). It is believed that this reintegrative approach, as opposed to stigmatizing offenders through formal processing, helps reduce the likelihood that the youth will recidivate.

A final theoretical perspective, posited by LoGalbo and Callahan (2001), views the success of teen courts through a procedural justice lens. Research has found that the perception of procedural mechanisms as fair increases individuals' commitment to the law and, in turn, reduces the possibility of recidivating (Mashaw, 1985). Participation in teen courts, LoGalbo and Callahan (2001) argue, enhances youth's knowledge of the legal system, thus influencing their perception of the fairness of the system.

Much research has been conducted exploring whether teen courts are achieving the success suggested by theory and supported by teen court proponents. Such research has produced mixed results. Many studies have found that teen courts are effective in achieving desired outcomes (Forgays, 2008; Garrison, 2001; LoGalbo & Callahan, 2001; Rasmussen, 2004). Specifically, a number of studies have found relatively low postintervention recidivism rates: 12% in Illinois (Rasmussen, 2004), 15% in Delaware (Garrison, 2001), 20% in Florida (Vose & Vannan, 2013), and 25% in New Mexico (Harrison, Maupin, & Mays, 2000; 2001). These studies are limited, though, in that comparison groups were not included. However, studies utilizing comparison groups have found similar positive findings (Butts et al., 2002; Forgays, 2008; Hissong, 1991). Butts et al. (2002), for example, found in their quasi-experimental study of teen courts that in two of the four study sites (i.e., Alaska and Missouri) recidivism rates over a six month follow-up period were significantly lower for teen court participants than that of the comparison group (6% versus 23% and 9% versus 28%, respectively). Recidivism rates from a third site, Arizona, also favored the teen court programs (9% versus 15%), but the difference was not statistically significant.

Positive findings have even held true when focusing on repeat offenders processed in teen courts. Forgays (2008) compared the recidivism rates of repeat adolescent offenders who were processed either through teen court or through a court diversion program. Participants were tracked for a period of three years. In the three years following completion of the program, youth who had participated in the teen court program had significantly lower recidivism rates than those who had participated in the court diversion program (14% versus 31%, 12% versus 25%, and 25% versus 80% for years 1, 2, and 3, respectively).

While many studies have found teen courts to be effective, others have found less promising results (Gase, Schooley, DeFosset, Stoll, & Kuo, 2016). The majority of these studies have found no significant differences when comparing teen court participants to comparison groups. A recent systematic review conducted by Gase et al. (2016) found that, of the 15 studies located that assessed statistical significance of recidivism, 10 found null results (i.e., there was no difference in teen court participants and nonparticipants). In another study, Norris, Twill, and Kim (2011) utilized survival analysis to compare the time to recidivism of teen court participants to a comparison group of regular diversion participants. Survival analysis is a statistical technique that allows researchers to examine the time of occurrence of a particular event; in this case, Norris et al. (2011) used recidivism as the event. Survival curves for both groups were similar, with the comparison group actually having a consistently better survival rate. However, the differences were not found to be statistically significant. Similarly, in the study by Butts et al. (2002) mentioned earlier, one of the sites included in their study, Maryland, found no significant differences in the recidivism rates of teen court participants and the comparison group of nonparticipants (8% versus 4%, respectively).

Studies have not only found that teen courts have a null effect on participants, but some have even found that teen court involvement has a negative impact on participants. Utilizing an experimental design, Stickle et al. (2008) explored the effectiveness of four Maryland teen courts. Participants were randomly assigned to either participate in teen court or be processed by the traditional juvenile court. Official records reviewed following an 18-month follow-up period found that the teen court sample recidivated at a higher rate than the comparison sample (32.1% versus 25.5%, respectively). Further, participants in the teen court group had a higher average number of total arrests than their nonparticipant counterparts (.75 versus .53, respectively).

Many have offered explanations as to why teen courts are not achieving the desired effect. Norris et al. (2011) posit that the effectiveness of teen courts may be limited because of the inclusion of inappropriate participants. They note that teen courts often contribute to "net widening" by capturing minor delinquents who might otherwise have been released with a warning. They also recommend the development of better screening procedures to avoid the inclusion of offenders not suitable for teen court (Norris et al., 2011). Additionally, Stickle et al. (2008) provided a number of explanations for their findings that teen court appeared to be detrimental to participants. One such explanation was that teen courts might not be adequately reintegrating participants into the community. They argue that perhaps the embarrassment of being judged by one's peers causes irreparable harm to the participants, thus alienating them instead of reintegrating them. They also suggest that the labeling that occurs during the traditional processing of juveniles may be just as potent in the teen court. A final explanation offered is that the sanctions used by some teen courts may be responsible for producing negative effects. For example, they point to the use of detention tours as a possible sanction and refer to the research on "Scared Straight" programs which have shown that they are not only ineffective in deterring crime but may actually promote further offending (see Klenowski, Bell, & Dodson, 2010).

Overall, the verdict is still out regarding the effectiveness of teen courts. To date, a meta-analysis has not been conducted, so it is hard to make a single conclusion regarding the effectiveness of teen courts. Partially responsible for the lack of meta-analyses is the wide variation that exists among both teen court models and the studies designed to evaluate them (Gase et al., 2016). Further, of the evaluations that have been conducted, most have not employed rigorous methodologies. Therefore, future research should focus on utilizing stronger research designs and clearly describing the core elements of both the teen court program being evaluated and the comparison condition so that variation can be accounted for in the analyses. The popularity of teen courts is increasing and the number of courts in operation expanding; thus, it is essential that research continue to evaluate programs to demonstrate their effectiveness and to identify best practices (Gase et al., 2016).

Juvenile Drug Courts

Juvenile drug courts are a type of drug court established within and supervised by the juvenile court designed to deal with substance-abusing juvenile offenders and their families through the use of intensive treatment and an array of specialized services focused on mental health, primary care, family, and education (Cooper & Bartlett, 1998; Cooper, 2001). Typically, only juveniles with nonviolent drug or drug-related offenses are eligible for participation in drug court (Sloan & Smykla, 2003). However, this varies across the courts, with some programs allowing more serious offenders to participate, such as those who commit certain assaults while under the influence of a substance (American University, 1998).

As noted earlier, the first juvenile drug courts were developed in the mid-1990s. The establishment of juvenile drug courts was the result of a number of different factors. Largely responsible was the increased number of juvenile drug offenders entering the juvenile court and delaying the system (Roberts, Brophy, & Cooper, 1997; Sloan & Smykla, 2003). To illustrate, the number of delinquency cases involving drug law violations handled by juvenile courts increased 120% between 1986 and 1995 (Stahl, 1998).

Another factor influencing the establishment of juvenile drug courts was the growing belief among many juvenile court practitioners that the conventional way with which the juvenile court handled delinquency cases was ineffective when applied to the problems of juvenile substance-abusing offenders (American University, 1998). Specifically, juvenile court judges found that dealing with substance-abusing juveniles within the traditional court often resulted in extensive waiting lists for treatment, disjointed delivery of services, limited family involvement, and minimal input on the nature and extent of treatment and auxiliary services provided (McGee, Parnham, Merrigan, & Smith, 2000). To help address these concerns, juvenile justice systems across the country began to explore and experiment with adapting adult drug courts to fit the needs of the juvenile justice system and, more specifically, the needs of substance-abusing juveniles. The idea of juvenile drug courts quickly spread, and by 2000, more than 160 juvenile drug courts had been established across the United States (Sloan, Smykla, & Rush, 2004). That number has since more than doubled, with more than 400 being established as of June 30, 2014 (National Drug Court Resource Center, 2014).

While there is a lot of variability among juvenile drug courts on key elements including, but not limited to, target problem, target population, court processing, and the extent of system-wide support (Hiller et al., 2008; Sloan & Smykla, 2003), the courts typically share the following common goals: (1) to provide juveniles with an opportunity to be clean and sober through the immediate use of intervention treatment; (2) to provide constructive support and skills to aid juveniles in resisting future criminal involvement; (3) to provide support to help juveniles succeed in school and develop positive relationships with both their families and within the community; (4) to provide juveniles with skills that will help them to become successful, productive, substance-free and crime-free community members; and (5) to promote accountability of both juvenile offenders and those responsible for providing services (American University, 1998; Cooper, 2001).

To accomplish these goals requires juvenile justice personnel to take on new roles that are distinct from their traditional juvenile court roles. The judge is perhaps the most important actor within juvenile drug courts (Bureau of Justice Assistance, 2003). Judges are not only required to maintain close oversight of each case, both sanctioning violations and rewarding success, but they are also responsible for collaborating with a team of treatment providers, attorneys, and court personnel to help coordinate the most appropriate treatment for each juvenile (Cooper & Bartlett, 1998). The roles of prosecutors and defense attorneys are also transformed from the traditional adversarial relationship to a more collaborative one (Sloan & Smykla, 2003). Prosecutors work closely with defense attorneys (and judges) to help coordinate services that will help the juvenile defendant recover and maintain a substance-free, crime-free life. Because of the collaboration of key court personnel, juvenile drug courts are able to focus solely and purposefully on the treatment and success of substance-abusing juvenile offenders.

Much research has been conducted examining the effectiveness of adult drug courts, consistently finding that such courts are effective in reducing both substance use and recidivism (see Belenko, 1998; Cooper, 1998; Mitchell, Wilson, Eggers, & MacKenzie, 2012; Wilson, Mitchell, & MacKenzie, 2006). However, much less attention has been paid to the effectiveness of juvenile drug courts. Similar to teen courts, the findings regarding juvenile drug courts' ability to reduce negative outcomes have been mixed (Anspach, Ferguson, & Phillips, 2003; Hartmann & Rhineberger, 2003; Henggeler et al., 2006; Hickert, Becker, Próspero, & Moleni, 2011; Koetzle-Shaffer, 2006; Latessa, Shaffer, & Lowenkamp, 2002; O'Connell, Wright, & Clymer, 2003; Rodriguez & Webb, 2004; Shaw & Robinson, 1998; Sullivan, Blair, Latessa, & Sullivan, 2016; Thompson, 2002).

Some studies have found juvenile drug courts to be effective in reducing substance use and recidivism (Henggeler et al., 2006; Hickert et al., 2011; Latessa et al., 2002; Rodriguez & Webb, 2004; Shaw & Robinson, 1998; Thompson, 2002). Shaw and Robinson (1998) conducted one of the first evaluations of juvenile drug courts and found that juvenile drug court participants, both compliant and noncompliant, were less likely to recidivate during the four-month treatment period than a matched group of nontreated misdemeanor juveniles, 21% compared to 30%, respectively. They also found that drug court participants (33%) were less likely to recidivate 12 months after participation in the drug court than the matched group (51%).

Similarly, Hickert et al. (2011) found that juvenile drug court youth had significantly fewer delinquency and criminal offenses postjuvenile drug court completion than a matched group of probationers. Specifically, they compared the two groups at seven different follow-up points, ranging from three months to 30 months, and found that at each follow-up point, youth who participated in drug court had significantly fewer delinquency and criminal offenses. Interestingly, they found that differences between groups grew larger the further removed from treatment, thus indicating that juvenile drug courts have a positive long-term effect on youth.

In contrast, other studies have found that drug courts are ineffective in achieving their desired outcomes of reduced substance use and recidivism (Anspach, Ferguson, & Phillips, 2003; Sullivan, Blair, Latessa, & Sullivan, 2015; Hartmann & Rhineberger, 2003; Koetzle-Shaffer, 2006; O'Connell, Wright, & Clymer, 2003). For example, while Hickert et al. (2011), discussed earlier, found statistically significant differences between drug court participants and probationers in regard to recidivism for delinquent/criminal offenses, no statistically significant differences were found for rearrest of alcohol and other drug offenses at any of the follow-up points. At the last follow-up point (30 months), 43% of juvenile drug court participants had a new alcohol or other drug offense compared to 39% of probationers.

Additionally, studies have not only found a lack of significant differences between juvenile drug court participants and comparison groups, but a recent study found that participants in a juvenile drug court were even more likely to reoffend than their counterparts. Sullivan et al. (2016) explored the effectiveness of nine juvenile drug courts from across the country. Youth who participated in the drug courts were compared to a matched sample of youth who were on probation in the same jurisdiction. The study found that youth who participated in drug courts were more likely to receive a new referral and adjudication compared to youth on probation. Specifically, they found that 60% of drug court youth compared to 49% of comparison youth had a new referral or arrest while in the program or during the follow-up period. Similarly, a larger percentage of drug court youth received a new adjudication or conviction than the comparison group, 45% to 33%, respectively.

Recently, two meta-analyses have been conducted in an attempt to summarize the literature on juvenile drug courts (Mitchell et al., 2012; Stein, Deberard, & Homan, 2013). First, Mitchell et al. (2012) conducted a meta-analysis focusing broadly on the effectiveness of drug courts, including adult, juvenile, and driving while impaired (DWI) courts. Thirty-four studies on juvenile drug courts were included in the analysis. In contrast to the moderate effects of adult drug courts, juvenile drug courts were found to have relatively small but positive effects on recidivism. Similarly, Stein et al. (2013) found in their meta-analysis, which focused specifically on juvenile drug court programs, that those who graduated from teen court had a small but statistically significant reduced likelihood of reoffending.

One explanation for the mediocre findings is the variability of juvenile drug courts. Sloan and Smykla (2003) explored the variability of juvenile drug courts utilizing a national-level survey, which included all juvenile and family drug courts in operation on January 1, 1998. Considerable variability was found across the different drug courts on a number of key dimensions, including program goals, populations targeted, structure, and content of treatment available, and the amount of external agency support and involvement. They therefore argued that when conducting research on juvenile drug courts, it is important to understand and account for each court's unique processes and dimensions. Otherwise, it will not be possible to determine what variables are producing the outcomes. Ultimately, they concluded "that unless researchers, practitioners, and policy makers focus on understanding the process of juvenile drug court and the dimensional variability . . ., it is meaningless to ask whether juvenile drug courts work" (Sloan & Smykla, 2003, p. 359). Future research should focus on exploring differences, focusing specifically on the structure and processes, among drug courts and work to identify what dimensions have an impact on reducing substance use and recidivism. This type of research will help to identify the most effective models for juvenile drug courts so that evidence-based blueprints can be developed to help in the establishment of new and reformation of old programs (Sullivan et al., 2016).

Evidence-Based Practices in Juvenile Corrections

Each year a large number of youth enter the juvenile justice system. In 2013, an estimated 1.1 million juveniles were arrested and processed in juvenile courts across the country (Furdella & Puzzanchera, 2015). Typically, probation is the most serious sanction issued by judges. In 2013, of the 582,800 youth adjudicated delinquent, 64% received a sanction of probation. While probation is the most common sanction ordered, a significant number of youth are placed in residential facilities each year. Also, in 2013, residential placement was ordered for 24% of all adjudicated youth. According to the most recent data available from the 2013 Census of Juveniles in Residential Placement, approximately 54,000 juvenile offenders were in residential placement as of October 23, 2013 (Hockenberry, 2016).

As is apparent, a large number of juveniles still remain under correctional supervision, be it through probation or residential placement, despite the fact that juvenile crimes rates have decreased (Sickmund & Puzzanchera, 2014). Since reducing recidivism is the ultimate goal of the correctional system and funding to support correctional efforts continues to decrease, it is important that correctional agencies focus their resources and efforts on programming that has been shown to be effective in reducing recidivism. In other words, juvenile corrections should work to implement evidence-based practices.

Evidence-based practices are approaches or programs that have been empirically tested and demonstrate measurable positive outcomes (Hoagwood, Burns, Kiser, Ringeisen, & Schoenwald, 2001; Orchowsky, 2014). The origin of the evidence-based practices movement can be attributed to the fields of medicine and public health, "where an initial interest in safety of treatment was eventually joined by an equal interest in the efficacy of treatment" (Orchowsky, 2014, p. 2). The medical movement began with the passage of the Federal Food, Drug, and Cosmetic Act in 1938. The act required that prior to being placed on the market, scientific investigations must be conducted on new drugs to determine their safety. In 1962, the act was amended to include that the efficacy of the drug also must be demonstrated (Orchowsky, 2014).

Despite the growing emphasis on efficacy within the field of medicine, the Office of Technology Assessment reported in 1978 that few procedures that were in use within the medial practice had been shown to be effective with scientific investigation (Office of Technology Assessment, 1978). The medical community responded to this critique by gathering information on effective interventions and disseminating the information to practitioners via clinical practice guidelines (Eddy, 2011; Przybylski, 2008). Today, the medical community remains committed to the use of evidence-based practices, with organizations such as the Cochrane Collaboration, Agency for Healthcare Research and Quality, and the Oxford Centre for Evidence-Based Medicine helping to identify and synthesize the research on effective clinical practices (Eddy, 2011; Orchowsky, 2014).

Within the criminal justice system, interest in evidence-based practices emerged in response to the "nothing works" movement that resulted following Robert Martinson's (1974) infamous claim that nothing works in rehabilitating offenders. Following Martinson's assertion, many researchers set out to rebut the claim, publishing numerous reviews of the literature (see Gendreau & Ross, 1979; Gendreau, 1981). While researchers continued to summarize the literature on what works during the 1980s and 1990s (e.g., Cullen & Gendreau, 1989; Gendreau & Ross, 1987, McGuire, 1995), systematic efforts were not being used to identify effective programs (Orchowsky, 2014). Further, the quality of research studies was not being taken into account when making conclusions regarding effectiveness. However, changes occurred in the mid-1990s when two different entities, the Center for the Study and Prevention of Violence and the United States Congress, became interested in identifying effective criminal justice programs based on studies that had used strong methodological techniques. Many other organizations soon followed suit, and today there are a number of resources available that present information on evidence-based practices, including Crimesolutions.gov, sponsored by the Office of Justice Programs, the Office of Juvenile Justice and Delinquency Preventions Model Programs Guide, and the Blueprints Programs.

With the emergent emphasis on evidence-based practices, a number of juvenile justice agencies across the country have begun to work toward implementing such programs. The following paragraphs will provide a brief overview of a variety of different evidenced-based practices found within juvenile corrections today, focusing specifically on those in community corrections (i.e., probation and parole) and within residential facilities.

Community Setting

A variety of different community-based programs exists within the juvenile justice system to serve juveniles on probation or parole. Research indicates the most effective community-based interventions are those that involve the family in the process and focus on the development of interpersonal skills (Lipsey, Wilson, & Cothern, 2000). Two programs that have been found to be effective in reducing recidivism and other associated outcomes are discussed in detail here.

Functional Family Therapy

Functional Family Therapy (FFT) was one of the first evidence-based practices utilized in the field (Henggeler & Schoenwald, 2011). Founded in the 1970s by Dr. James F. Alexander (Alexander & Parsons, 1973), the program is aimed at youth ages 11–18 struggling with delinquency, substance abuse, violence, or other maladaptive behaviors who are at risk for institutionalization (Mihalic, Fagan, Irwin, Ballard, & Elliott, 2004). The program is designed to be a family- and community-based treatment in which therapists work with the family to improve family communication, problem solving, and support while decreasing dysfunctional patterns of behavior (Alexander & Parsons, 1982). Specific to youth, the model emphasizes decreasing risk factors and increasing protective factors that directly affect them, emphasizing those related to the family.

The program consists of a series of clinical sessions with the family, typically taking place over a three-month period (Mihalic et al., 2004). In mild cases, the family is likely to only meet for 8–10 one-hour sessions; however, for more difficult situations, up to 30 sessions may be required. The intervention occurs in three different phases: (1) engagement and motivation, (2) behavior change, and (3) generalization (Sexton & Alexander, 2000; 2004). The first phase, engagement and motivation, consists of getting the clients involved and having them "buy in" to the program. In this phase, the therapist attempts to gain the trust of the client and get her or him involved in the process. Ultimately, the goal is to encourage participation from all family members and get them to believe that change is possible and things can be different, thus motivating them to participate in making strides toward change. Key to the success of this phase is continuing to reiterate and emphasize that a positive therapeutic experience can result in long-lasting change.

The goal of the behavior change phase is to target and change specific risk behaviors of individuals and families. To accomplish this task, therapists utilize individualized behavior-change interventions such as skills training in family communication, problem solving, effective parenting, and conflict management (Sexton & Alexander, 2000; 2004). The final phase, generalization, involves families taking the skills they have learned and applying them to other aspects of their lives. To encourage and support the long-term change, therapists connect the family with available community agencies and resources (Mihalic et al., 2004).

The FFT program has enjoyed over 25 years of success, with numerous studies finding the program to be effective (Mihalic et al., 2004). As of 2011, six experimental/quasi-experimental studies (Alexander & Parsons, 1973; Barton, Alexander, Waldron, Turner, & Warburton, 1985; Friedman, 1989; Gordon, Arbuthnot, Gustafson, & McGreen, 1988; Sexton & Turner, 2010; Waldron, Slesnick, Turner, Brody, & Peterson, 2001) utilizing a variety of participants, including status offenders, substance abusers, and juvenile offenders, had been published evaluating the effectiveness of the FFT model (Henggeler & Schoenwald, 2011). Overall, the results of these studies, along with others utilizing less rigorous research designs, have found that youth who participate in FFT experience decreased antisocial behavior, reduced levels of reoffending, reductions in emotional and behavioral needs and risk behaviors, and reductions in sibling entry into deviant, high-risk behaviors (Alexander et al., 2000; Barton, Alexander, Waldron, Turner, & Warburton, 1985; Celinska, Furrer, & Cheng, 2013; Henggeler & Sheidow, 2011; Mihalic et al., 2004).

Multisystemic Therapy

Similar to FFT, Multisystemic Therapy (MST) is an intensive family- and community-based intervention targeted toward violent and chronic juvenile offenders aged 12 to 17 who are at risk of out-of-home placement (Henggeler, Schoenwald, Borduin, Rowland, & Cunningham, 2009; Mihalic et al., 2004). The development of MST began during the 1970s with the work of Dr. Scott Henggeler. Henggeler realized through his work with a number of trouble adolescents that to address the behavior of his trouble patients, "he needed to treat the children in the full context of their lives, to see them where they live, went to school, hung out" (Multisystemic Therapy, 2017, para. 2). Therefore, a key element of MST is that the juvenile be treated within the social environment that helped to create the problem behavior (Henggeler & Borduin, 1990). In other words, all social networks that impact juveniles' lives and contribute to their problem behavior, including family, teachers, and peers, should be addressed if positive change is going to occur.

The overarching goal of the program is to alter the adolescent's social environment in a manner that promotes prosocial behavior while decreasing delinquent behavior (Henngeler & Borduin,

1990). To help achieve this goal, a home-based model is typically utilized; however, treatment also may be provided in schools or other community locations. Over the course of approximately four months, juveniles and their families work with a certified MST therapist who conducts intensive family therapy. Specific to youth, therapists work with them and their families to identify the causes of their delinquency and help them identify ways in which they can facilitate change within their environment to help modify and improve their behavior. For parents, the therapist concentrates on empowering them by providing them with the tools needed to help them identify their own individual strengths and eliminate potential barriers to successful parenting. An interesting element of MST is that the family has 24-hour access/seven days per week to an MST therapist (Henggeler & Sheidow, 2011). Thus, if a problem were to arise, the family can call the therapist and instantly begin to assess and deal with the problem.

MST is one of the most consistently validated evidence-based psychosocial treatments (Borduin et al., 1995; Henggeler & Schoenwald, 2011; Henggeler & Sheidow, 2011; Henggeler, Melton, & Smith, 1992; Timmons-Mitchell, Bender, Kishna, & Mitchell, 2006). In their review of the MST literature, Henggeler and Sheidow (2011) located 20 published outcome studies, 18 of which had utilized randomized trails, and found that MST programs were successful in reducing a number of negative outcomes, including substance use, rearrest, out-of-home placement, and incarceration. To illustrate, various program evaluations have found 25–70% reductions in rearrest rates and 47–64% reductions in out-of-home placements (Mihalic et al., 2004). Other positive outcomes that have been identified in the literature include improved family and peer relations and decreased caregiver and youth psychiatric symptoms (Henggeler & Sheidow, 2011).

Institutional Settings

A number of institutional facilities exist for the placement of juvenile offenders, such as group homes, outdoor/boot camps, and correctional facilities. Three general strategies have been identified in the literature that help to improve the effectiveness of out-of-home placement, including focusing on risk factors that can be changed, tailoring programs to meet client needs, and focusing interventions on higher risk youth (The Future of Children, n.d.). This final section will discuss two institutional-based programs, cognitive-behavioral therapy and aggressive replacement training, that have been proven to be successful in achieving desirable outcomes (Greenwood, 2008).

Cognitive-Behavioral Therapy

Many studies have found that youth with antisocial behavior problems have a variety of impaired social-cognitive skills (Crick & Dodge, 1994; de Castro, Verman, Koops, Bosch, & Monshouwer, 2002). Such youth tend to hold hostile attributional biases, misinterpret social cues, and believe more strongly that aggression will lead to positive outcomes (McCart, Priester, Davis, & Azen, 2006). Additionally, studies have found that delinquent youth tend to score lower on cognitive tests than their nondelinquent peers (Henggeler, 1989). Cognitive-behavioral therapy (CBT) was designed to target these cognitive deficiencies in juvenile offenders. By training youth to attend more effectively to social cues, to generate multiple interpretations for others' behavior, and to engage in nonviolent problem-solving strategies, it is believed that youth will be less likely to respond to social situations in an inappropriate manner (McCart et al., 2006).

Cognitive-behavioral therapy programs are generally utilized in secure correctional facilities as they target serious (violent and chronic) juvenile offenders (Mihalic et al., 2004). The programs work intensely with youth to alter their behavior by using a variety of different strategies, including interpersonal cognitive problem solving, social skills training, anger control, critical reasoning, values development, negotiation abilities, and creative thinking. The ultimate goal of the program is to increase offenders' social-cognitive skills to the extent that when they are released, their likelihood of recidivating is reduced (Milkman & Wanber, 2007).

Extensive research has been conducted on CBT programs implemented both within and outside of correctional facilities. Such research has found that CBT programs are effective in reducing both antisocial behavior and recidivism (Bennett & Gibbons, 2000; Garrido & Morales, 2007; Hinshaw & Anderson, 1996; Landenberger & Lipsey, 2005; McCart et al., 2006). For example, Lipsey, Chapman, and Landenberger (2001) conducted a meta-analysis using 14 cognitive-behavioral studies that included both juvenile and adult populations. Recidivism rates for offenders who completed CBT were lower than the comparison group (26% versus 38%, respectively). While the inclusion of adult offenders in the study could be affecting the rates, it is likely that their inclusion is deflating the rate as opposed to inflating it. To explain, when dividing the studies up by effect sizes (statistical estimates), six of the seven studies including juvenile offenders had medium to large effect sizes compared to only two of the 11 adult studies. Landenberger and Lipsey (2005) confirmed the results of Lipsey et al. (2001) in their meta-analysis, finding that 12 months postintervention, those who had received CBT were 1.53 times less likely to recidivate than the comparison group. While this meta-analysis also included both juvenile and adult offenders, no significant differences were found between the two in regard to recidivism.

Aggressive Replacement Training

Aggressive Replacement Training (ART) is a multimodal, psychoeducational intervention developed specifically to address various emotional and social aspects that contribute to aggressive behavior in youth (Glick & Goldstein, 1987). The program was specifically designed by Glick and Goldstein (1987, p. 356) to target "assaultive, hostile adolescents and children who are either institutionalized or pose severe disruptive behaviors in communities." Throughout the program, youth are taught various techniques to control their angry impulses. The ultimate goal of the program is to reduce aggression and violence levels among the youth.

The program consists of three interrelated components—structured learning training, moral education, and anger control training—that occur over a series of 10 weeks (Glick & Goldstein, 1987). Each week, youth attend a one-hour session for each of the separate components. The structured learning training component is implemented with a small number of youth, usually six or eight. Over the course of the class, students are taught a number of skills aimed at changing how they respond to the presentation of negative stimuli, such as dealing with negative emotions (e.g., anger, fear, sadness) and stressful events (e.g., being left out of something, being wrongfully accused of something). Varieties of techniques are used to communicate the information, including modeling, role-playing, performance feedback, and transfer training.

Moral education is "a set of procedures designed to raise the young person's level of fairness, justice, and concern with the needs and rights of others" (Glick & Goldstein, 1987, p. 357). Essentially, this component is intended to increase participants' moral reasoning skills. Within this component, participants learn to reason in a more advanced manner by being presented with a variety of moral dilemmas. The final component, anger control training, helps youth identify their triggers and cues for violence and techniques to control their anger. Each week, youth are required to bring to the session a description of a recent anger-arousing experience. Youth are then trained how to respond to those experiences. The three components combined are designed to improve anger control, reduce aggressive behavior, and promote constructive, prosocial behaviors (Goldstein & Glick, 1994).

Research has consistently found that ART is effective not only in reducing negative outcomes such as problem behavior and recidivism but also in improving social skills and moral reasoning (Buss, 2000; Etscheidt, 1991; Gibbs, Barriga, & Potter, 2001; Goldstein & Glick, 1994; Gundersen & Svartdal, 2006; Mitchell, 2009; Nugent, Bruley, & Allen, 1998; Washington State Institute for Public

Policy, 2004). In 1994, Goldstein and Glick (1994) reviewed a series of efficacy evaluations that had been conducted on ART and concluded that ART appears to be an effective intervention. They noted that the studies reviewed consistently found that ART promotes skills acquisition and performance, improves anger control, decreases the frequency of acting out behaviors, and increases the frequency of constructive, prosocial behaviors. More recently, Gundersen and Svartdal (2006) evaluated the ART program and found significant improvements were made in the area of social skills and moral reasoning, with significant differences being found between ART participants and the control group. Additionally, they found that problem behavior was significantly reduced among the ART participants compared to the comparison group.

Conclusion

Over the past few decades, the juvenile justice system has been slowly moving away from the "get tough" rhetoric of the past and refocusing its efforts on rehabilitation and treatment. Evidence of this shift can be seen when looking at the emergence and increase in the number of programs aimed at diverting youth from the system, reducing the labeling effect of formal processing, and utilizing evidence-based practices. While it is likely that the legislation passed during the "get tough" era will remain on the books for decades to come, it is promising that the aforementioned trends are emerging. Future research should continue to strive to conduct rigorous evaluations of juvenile justice interventions, identifying the conditions under which programs are most successful. Additionally, researchers should work toward developing user-friendly guides similar to those utilized within the medical community that can be easily disseminated to criminal justice practitioners and professionals working within the field. With the collaborative efforts of both researchers and practitioners, the juvenile justice system will return a greater likelihood to its original intent of rehabilitating and reintegrating juvenile offenders.

References

Alexander, J. F., & Parsons, B.V. (1973). Short-term family intervention: A therapy outcome study. *Journal of Consulting and Clinical Psychology, 41*(2), 195–201. doi:10.1037/h0035181

Alexander, J. F., & Parsons, B.V. (1982). *Functional family therapy: Principles and procedures*. Carmel, CA: Brooks & Cole.

Alexander, J. F., Pugh, C., Parsons, B.V., Sexton, T., Barton, C., Bonomo, J., . . . Waldron, H. (2000). Functional family therapy. In D. S. Elliot (Ed.), *Blueprints for violence prevention: Book 3*. Boulder, CO: Center for the Study and Prevention of Violence, Institute of Behavioral Science, University of Colorado.

American University. (1998). *Juvenile and family drug courts: An overview*. Washington, DC: U.S. Department of Justice, Drug Court Clearinghouse.

Anspach, D. F., Ferguson, A. S., & Phillips, L. L. (2003). *Evaluation of Maine's Statewide Juvenile Drug Treatment Court Program: Fourth year outcome evaluation report*. Portland, ME: University of Southern Maine.

Applegate, B. K., & Davis, R. K. (2006). Public views on sentencing juvenile murderers: The impact of offender, offense, and perceived maturity. *Youth Violence and Juvenile Justice, 4*(1), 55–74. doi:10.1177/1541204005282312

Barton, C., Alexander, J. F., Waldron, H., Turner, C. W., & Warburton, J. (1985). Generalizing treatment effects of functional family therapy: Three replications. *The American Journal of Family Therapy, 13*(3), 16–26. doi:10.1080/01926188508251260

Belenko, S. (1990). The impact of drug offenders on the criminal justice system. In R. Weischeit (Ed.), *Drugs, crime, and the criminal justice system* (pp. 27–78). Cincinnati, OH: Anderson Publishing.

Belenko, S. (1998). Research on drug courts: A critical review. *National Drug Court Institute Review, 1*(1), 1–26.

Benekos, P. J., & Merlo, A. V. (2008). Juvenile justice: The legacy of punitive policy. *Youth Violence and Juvenile Justice, 6*(1), 28–46. doi:10.1177/1541204007308423

Bernard, T. J., & Kurlychek, M. C. (2010). *The cycle of juvenile justice* (2nd ed.). New York, NY: Oxford University Press.

Bennett, D. S., & Gibbons, T. A. (2000). Efficacy of child cognitive behavioral interventions for antisocial behavior: A meta-analysis. *Child and Family Behavior Therapy, 22*(1), 1–15. doi:10.1300/J019v22n01_01

Binder, A., Geis, G., & Dickson, B. (2001). *Juvenile delinquency: Historical, cultural and legal perspectives* (3rd ed.). Cincinnati, OH: Anderson.

Blomberg, T. (1983). Diversion's disparate results and unresolved questions: An integrative evaluation perspective. *Journal of Research in Crime and Delinquency, 20*(1), 24–38. doi:10.1177/002242788302000103

Borduin, C. M., Mann, B. J., Cone, L. T., Henggeler, S. W., Fucci, B. R., Blaske, D. M., & Williams, R. A. (1995). Multisystemic treatment of serious juvenile offenders: Long-term prevention of criminality and violence. *Journal of Consulting and Clinical Psychology, 63*(4), 569–578. doi:10.1037/0022-006X.63.4.569

Braithwaite, J. (1989). *Crime, shame, and reintegration*. Cambridge, England: Cambridge University.

Breed v. Jones, 421 U.S. 519 (1975).

Bureau of Justice Assistance. (2003). *Juvenile drug court: Strategies in practice*. Washington, DC: U.S. Department of Justice, Office of Justice Programs, Bureau of Justice Assistance.

Buss, A. H. (2000). *Aggression questionnaire*. Los Angeles, CA: Western Psychological Services.

Butts, J. A., & Buck, J. (2000). *Teen courts: A focus on research*. Washington, DC: Office of Juvenile Justice and Delinquency Prevention.

Butts, J. A., & Ortiz, J. (2011). Teen courts: Do they work and why? *New York State Bar Association Journal, 83*(1), 18–21.

Butts, J. A., Buck, J., & Coggeshall, M. B. (2002). *The impact of teen courts on young offenders*. Washington, DC: Urban Institute.

Campaign for Youth Justice. (2010). *State trends: Legislative victories from 2005 to 2010 removing youth from the adult criminal justice system*. Washington, DC: Campaign for Youth Justice.

Celinska, K., Furrer, S., & Cheng, C. (2013). An outcome-based evaluation of functional family therapy for youth with behavioral problems. *OJJDP Journal of Juvenile Justice, 2*(2), 23–36.

Children at Risk. (2014). *Juvenile specialty courts: An examination of rehabilitative justice in Texas and across the nation*. Houston, TX: Children at Risk.

Cocozza, J. J., Veysey, B. M., Chapin, D. A., Dembo, R., Walters, W., & Farina, S. (2005). Diversion from the juvenile justice system: The Miami-Dade Juvenile Assessment Center Post-Arrest Diversion Program. *Substance Use & Misuse, 40*(7), 935–951. doi:10.1081/JA-200058853

Cooper, C. S. (1998). *1998 Drug court survey: Preliminary findings*. Washington, DC: Drug Court Clearinghouse and Technical Assistance Project, American University.

Cooper, C. S. (2001). *Juvenile drug court programs*. Washington, DC: Office of Juvenile Justice and Delinquency Prevention.

Cooper, C. S., & Bartlett, S. (1998). *Juvenile and family drug courts: Profile of program characteristics and implementation issues*. Washington, DC: Office of Juvenile Justice and Delinquency Prevention.

Crick, N. R., & Dodge, K. A. (1994). A review and reformulation of social information-processing mechanisms in children's social adjustment. *Psychological Bulletin, 115*(1), 74–101. doi:10.1037/0033-2909.115.1.74

Cullen, F., & Gendreau, P. (1989). The effectiveness of correctional rehabilitation. In L. Goodstein & D. L. MacKenzie (Eds.), *The American prison: Issues in research policy* (pp. 23–44). New York: Plenum.

de Castro, B. O., Veerman, J. W., Koops, W., Bosch, J. D., & Monshouwer, H. J. (2002). Hostile attribution of intent and aggressive behavior: A meta-analysis. *Child Development, 73*(3), 916–934. doi:10.1111/1467-8624.00447

Eddy, D. M. (2011). The origins of evidence-based medicine—a personal perspective. *American Medical Association Journal of Ethics, 13*(1), 55–60. doi:10.1001/virtualmentor.2011.13.1.mhst1-1101

Etscheidt, S. (1991). Reducing aggressive behavior and improving self-control. A cognitive-behavioral training program for behaviorally disordered adolescents. *Behavioral Disorders, 16*(2), 107–115.

Feld, B. (1999). *Bad kids: Race and the transformation of the juvenile court*. New York, NY: Oxford University Press.

Fisher, M. (2007). *Youth cases for youth courts: A guide to the typical offenses handled by youth courts*. Chicago, IL: American Bar Association.

Forgays, D. K. (2008). Three years of teen court offender outcomes. *Adolescence, 43*(171), 473–484.

Fox, J. (1996). *Trends in juvenile violence: A report to the United States Attorney General on current and future rates of juvenile offending*. Washington, DC: U.S. Department of Justice, Bureau of Justice Statistics.

Friedman, A. S. (1989). Family therapy vs. parent groups: Effects on adolescent drug abusers. *The American Journal of Family Therapy, 17*(4), 335–347. doi:10.1080/01926188908250780

Furdella, J., & Puzzanchera, C. (2015). *Delinquency cases in juvenile court, 2013*. Washington, DC: Office of Juvenile Justice and Delinquency Prevention.

Garrido, V., & Morales, L. A. (2007). Serious (violent or chronic) juvenile offenders: A systematic review of treatment effectiveness in secure corrections. *Campbell Systematic Reviews* 7. Oslo, Norway: The Campbell Collaboration.

Garrison, A. H. (2001). An evaluation of a Delaware teen court. *Juvenile and Family Court Journal, 52*(3), 11–21. doi:10.1111/j.1755-6988.2001.tb00044.x

Gase, L. N., Schooley, T., DeFosset, A., Stoll, M. A., & Kuo, T. (2016). The impact of teen courts on youth outcomes: A systematic review. *Adolescent Research Review, 1*(1), 51–67. doi:10.1007/s40894-015-0012-x

Gendreau, P. (1981). Treatment in corrections: Martinson was wrong. *Canadian Psychology, 22*(4), 332–338.

Gendreau, P., & Ross, R. R. (1979). Effective correctional treatment: Bibliotherapy for cynics. *Crime & Delinquency, 25*(4), 463–489. doi:10.1177/001112877902500405

Gendreau, P., & Ross, R. R. (1987). Revivification of rehabilitation: Evidence from the 1980s. *Justice Quarterly, 4*(3), 349–407. doi:10.1080/07418828700089411

Gensheimer, L. K., Mayer, J. P., Gottschalk, R., & Davidson, W. S. (1986). Diverting youth from the juvenile justice system: A meta-analysis of intervention efficacy. In S. J. Apter & A. P. Goldstein (Eds.), *Youth violence: Program and prospects* (pp. 39–57). New York: Pergamon Press.

Gibbs, J., Barriga, G., & Potter, G. (2001). *How I think questionnaire*. Champaign, IL: Research Press.

Glick, B., & Goldstein, A. P. (1987). Aggression replacement training. *Journal of Counseling & Development, 65*(7), 356–362. doi:10.1002/j.1556-6676.1987.tb00730.x

Godwin, T. M. (1998). *Peer justice and youth empowerment: An implementation guide for teen court programs*. Lexington, KY: American Probation and Parole Association.

Godwin, T. M., Heaward, M. E., & Spina, T. (2000). *National youth court guidelines*. Lexington, KY: American Probation and Parole Association, National Youth Court Center.

Goldstein, A. P., & Glick, B. (1994). Aggression replacement training: Curriculum and evaluation. *Simulation and Gaming, 25*(1), 9–26. doi:10.1177/1046878194251003

Gordon, D. A., Arbuthnot, J., Gustafson, K. E., & McGreen, P. (1988). Home-based behavioral-system family therapy with disadvantaged juvenile delinquents. *American Journal of Family Therapy, 16*(3), 243–55. doi:10.1080/01926188808250729

Greenwood, P. (2008). Prevention and intervention programs for juvenile offenders. *The Future of Children, 18*(2), 185–210. doi:10.1353/foc.0.0018

Griffin, P., Addie, S., Adams, B., & Firestine, K. (2011). *Trying juveniles as adults: An analysis of state transfer laws and reporting*. Washington, DC: U.S. Department of Justice, Office of Juvenile Justice and Delinquency Prevention.

Gundersen, K. K., & Svartdal, F. (2006). Aggression replacement training in Norway: Outcome evaluation of 11 Norwegian student projects. *Scandinavian Journal of Education Research, 50*(1), 63–81. doi:10.1080/00313830500372059

Harrison, P., Maupin, J. R., & Mays, G. L. (2000). Are teen courts an answer to our juvenile delinquency problems? *Juvenile and Family Court Journal, 51*(4), 27–35. doi:10.1111/j.1755-6988.2000.tb00030.x

Harrison, P., Maupin, J. R., & Mays, G. L. (2001). Teen court: An examination of processes and outcomes. *Crime & Delinquency, 47*(2), 243–264. doi:10.1177/0011128701047002005

Hartmann, D. J., & Rhineberger, G. M. (2003). *Evaluation of the Kalamazoo County Juvenile Drug Treatment Court Program*. Kalamazoo, MI: Western Michigan University, Kercher Center for Social Researcher.

Henggeler, S. W. (1989). Delinquency in adolescence. In A. E. Kazdin (Ed.), *Developmental clinical psychology and psychiatry* (pp. 24–35). Newbury Park: CA: Sage.

Henggeler, S. W., & Borduin, C. M. (1990). *Family therapy and beyond: A multisystemic approach to treating the behavior problems of children and adolescents*. Pacific Grove, CA: Brooks/Cole.

Henggeler, S. W., Halliday-Boykins, C. A., Cunningham, P. B., Randall, J., Shapiro, S. B., & Chapman, J. E. (2006). Juvenile drug court: Enhancing outcomes by integrating evidence-based treatments. *Journal of Consulting and Clinical Psychology, 74*(1), 42–54. doi:10.1037/0022-006X.74.1.42

Henggeler, S. W., Melton, G. B., & Smith, L. A. (1992). Family preservation using multisystemic therapy: An effective alternative to incarcerating serious juvenile offenders. *Journal of Consulting and Clinical Psychology, 60*(6), 953–961. doi:10.1037//0022-006X.60.6.953

Henggeler, S. W., & Schoenwald, S. K. (2011). Evidence-based interventions for juvenile offenders and juvenile justice policies that support them. *Social Policy Report, 25*(1), 1–27.

Henggeler, S. W., Schoenwald, S. K., Borduin, C. M., Rowland, M. D., & Cunningham, P. B. (2009). *Multisystemic therapy for antisocial behavior in children and adolescents* (2nd ed.). New York, NY: Guilford Press.

Henggeler, S. W., & Sheidow, A. J. (2011). Empirically supported family-based treatments for conduct disorder and delinquency in adolescents. *Journal of Marital and Family Therapy, 38*(1), 30–58. doi:10.1111/j.1752-0606.2011.00244.x

Hickert, A. O., Becker, E., Próspero, M., & Moleni, K. (2011). The impact of juvenile drug courts on drug use and criminal behavior. *Journal of Juvenile Justice, 1*(1), 60–77.

Hiller, M. L., & Saum, C. A. (2014). Juvenile drug courts, juvenile mental health courts, and teen courts. In A. R. Roberts, W. T. Church, & D. W. Springer (Eds.). *Juvenile justice source book: Past, present and future* (2nd ed.). New York, NY: Oxford University Press.

Hiller, M. L., Malluche, D., Bryan, V., Dupont, M. L., Martin, B., Abensur, R., . . . Payne, C. (2008). A multisite description of juvenile drug courts: Program models and during-program outcomes. *International Journal of Offender Therapy and Comparative Criminology, 54*(2), 213–235. doi:177/0306624X08327784
Hinshaw, S. P., & Anderson, C. A. (1996). Conduct and oppositional defiant disorders. In E. J. Mash & R. Barkely (Eds.), *Child psychopathology* (pp. 113–152). New York, NY: Guilford Press.
Hissong, R. (1991). Teen court—is it an effective alternative to traditional sanctions? *Journal for Juvenile Justice and Detention Services, 6*, 14–23.
Hoagwood, K., Burns, B. J., Kiser, L., Ringeisen, H., & Schoenwald, S. K. (2001). Evidence-based practice in child and adolescent mental health services. *Psychiatric Services, 52*(9), 1179–1189. doi:10.1176/appi.ps.52.9.1179
Hockenberry, S. (2016). *Juveniles in residential placement, 2013*. Washington, DC: Office of Juvenile Justice and Delinquency Prevention.
Howlett, F. W. (1973). Is the YSB all it's cracked up to be? *Crime & Delinquency, 19*(4), 485–492. doi:10.1177/001112877301900404
Institute of Medicine and National Research Council. (2001). *Juvenile crime, juvenile justice*. Washington, DC: The National Academies Press. doi:10.17226/9747
In re Gault, 387 U.S. 1 (1967).
In re Winship, 397 U.S. 358 (1970).
Juvenile Justice Initiative. (2013). Raise the age. *Juvenile Justice Initiative*. Retrieved from http://jjustice.org/juvenile-justice-issues/raise-the-age/
Klein, M. W. (1975). *Alternative dispositions for juvenile offenders*. Los Angeles, CA: University of Southern California.
Klein, M. W., Teilmann, K. S., Styles, J. A., Lincoln, S. B., & Labin-Rosenweig, S. (1976). The explosion of police diversion programs: Evaluating the structural dimensions of a social fad. In M. W. Klein (Ed.), *The juvenile justice system* (pp. 101–119). Beverly Hills, CA: Sage Publications.
Klenowski, P. M., Bell, K. J., & Dodson, K. D. (2010). An empirical evaluation of juvenile awareness programs in the United States: Can juveniles be "Scared Straight"? *Journal of Offender Rehabilitation, 49*, 254–272. doi:10.1080/10509671003716068
Koetzle-Shaffer, D. (2006). *Reconsidering drug court effectiveness: A meta-analytic review*. Unpublished doctoral dissertation. Cincinnati, OH: University of Cincinnati.
Landenberger, N. A., & Lipsey, M. W. (2005). The positive effects of cognitive-behavioral programs for offenders: A meta-analysis of factors associated with effective treatment. *Journal of Experimental Criminology, 1*(4), 451–476. doi:10.1007/s11292-005-3541-7
Latessa, E. J., Shaffer, D. K., & Lowenkamp, C. (2002). *Outcome evaluation of Ohio's Drug Court efforts*. Cincinnati, OH: University of Cincinnati, Center for Criminal Justice Research.
Lincoln, S. B. (1976). Juvenile referral and recidivism. In R. M. Carter & M. W. Klein (Eds.), *Back on the street: Diversion of juvenile offenders* (pp. 321–328). Englewood Cliffs, NJ: Prentice Hall.
Lipsey, M. W., Chapman, G. L., & Landenberger, N. A. (2001). Cognitive-behavioral programs for offenders. *The Annals of the American Academy of Political and Social Science, 578*(1), 144–157. doi:10.1177/000271620157800109
Lipsey, M. W., Cordray, D. S., & Berger, D. E. (1981). Evaluation of a juvenile diversion program: Using multiple lines of evidence. *Evaluation Research, 5*(3), 283–306. doi:10.1177/0193841X8100500301
Lipsey, M. W., Wilson, D. B., & Cothern, L. (2000). *Effective intervention for serious juvenile offenders*. Washington, DC: Office of Juvenile Justice and Delinquency Prevention.
Logalbo, A., & Callahan, C. (2001). An evaluation of teen court as a juvenile crime diversion program. *Juvenile and Family Court Journal, 52*(2), 1–11. doi:10.1111/j.1755-6988.2001.tb00039.x
Mack, J. W. (1909). The juvenile court. *Harvard Law Review, 23*(2), 104–122.
Martinson, R. (1974). What works? Questions and answers about prison reform. *The Public Interest, 35*, 22–54.
Mashaw, J. L. (1985). *Due process in the administrative state*. New Haven, CT: Yale University Press.
McCart, M. R., Priester, P. E., Davies, W. H., & Azen, R. (2006). Differential effectiveness of behavioral parent-training and cognitive-behavioral therapy for anti-social youth: A meta-analysis. *Journal of Abnormal Child Psychology, 34*(4), 527–543. doi:10.1007/s10802-006-9031-1
McGee, C., Parnham, J., Merrigan, T. T., & Smith, M. (2000). *Applying drug court concepts in the juvenile and family court environments: A primer for judges*. Washington, DC: American University.
McGuire, J. E. (1995). *What works: Reducing reoffending: Guidelines for research and practice*. Oxford: Wiley & Sons.
Mennell, R. M. (1973). *Thorns and thistles: Juvenile delinquents in the United States 1825–1940*. Hanover, NH: University Press of New England.
Merlo, A. V., Benekos, P. J., & Cook, W. J. (1999). The juvenile court at 100 years: Celebration or wake? *Juvenile and Family Court Journal, 50*(1), 1–10.
Merlo, A. V., & Benekos, P. J. (2010). Is punitive juvenile justice policy declining in the United States?: A critique of emergent initiatives. *Youth Justice, 10*(1), 3–24. doi:10.1177/1473225409356740

Mihalic, S., Fagan, A., Irwin, K., Ballard, D., & Elliott, D. (2004). *Blueprints for violence prevention*. Washington, DC: Office of Juvenile Justice and Delinquency Prevention.

Milkman, H., & Wanberg K. (2007). *Cognitive-behavioral treatment: A review and discussion for corrections professionals*. Washington, DC: National Institute of Corrections, U.S. Department of Justice.

Minor, K. I., Wells, J. B., Soderstrom, I. R., Bingham, R., & Williamson, D. (1999). Sentence completion and recidivism among juveniles referred to teen courts. *Crime & Delinquency, 45*(4), 467–480. doi:10.1177/0011128799045004004

Mitchell, C. (2009). *Teaching prosocial skills to antisocial youth: Aggregate evaluation dashboard report*. Sacramento, CA: California Institute of Mental Health.

Mitchell, O., Wilson, D. B., Eggers, A., & MacKenzie, D. L. (2012). Assess the effectiveness of drug courts on recidivism: A meta-analytic review of traditional and non-traditional drug courts. *Journal of Criminal Justice, 40*(1), 60–71. doi:10.1016/j.jcrimjus.2011.11.009

Models for Change Juvenile Diversion Workgroup. (2011). *Juvenile diversion guidebook*. Chicago, IL: MacArthur Foundation.

Multisystemic Therapy. (2017). Our history. *Multisystemic Therapy*. Retrieved from http://mstservices.com/mst-service/our-history

Nagin, D. S., Piquero, A. R., Scott, E. S., & Steinberg, L. (2006). Public preferences for rehabilitation versus incarceration of juvenile offenders: Evidence from a contingent valuation survey. *Criminology and Public Policy, 5*(4), 301–326. doi:10.1111/j.1745-9133.2006.00406.x

National Association of Youth Courts. (2016). *Facts and stats*. National Association of Youth Courts. Retrieved from www.youthcourt.net/?page_id=24

National Drug Court Resource Center. (2014). How many drug courts are there? Drug courts today. *National Drug Court Resource Center*. Retrieved from www.ndcrc.org/content/how-many-drug-courts-are-there.

National Youth Court Center. (2004). *Youth Court Database*. Lexington, KY: American Probation and Parole Association.

Nejelski, P. (1976). Diversion: The promise and the danger. *Crime & Delinquency, 22*(4), 393–410. doi:10.1177/001112877602200401

Nessel, P. A. (1998). *Teen court: A national movement* (Technical Assistance Bulletin, No 17). Chicago, IL: American Bar Association.

Norris, M., Twill, S., & Kim, C. (2011). Smells like teen spirit: Evaluating a Midwestern teen court. *Crime & Delinquency, 57*(2), 199–221. doi:10.1177/0011128709354037

Nugent, W. R., Bruley, C., & Allen, P. (1998). The effects of Aggression Replacement Training on antisocial behavior in a runaway shelter. *Social Work, 8*(6), 637–656. doi:10.1177/104973159800800602

O'Connell, P., Wright, D., & Clymer, B. (2003). *Evaluation of Oklahoma Drug Courts, 1997–2000*. Oklahoma City, OK: Oklahoma Criminal Justice Resource Center.

Office of Technology Assessment. (1978). *Assessing the efficacy and safety of medical technologies*. Washington, DC: Office of Technology Assessment.

Ohio Juvenile Justice Association. (2015). *Juvenile justice fact sheet series: Specialty courts*. Retrieved from www.cdfohio.org/research-library/2015/specialty-courts-fact-sheet-1.pdf

Orchowsky, S. (2014). *An introduction to evidence-based practices*. Washington, DC: Justice Research and Statistics Association.

Palmer, T., & Lewis, R. V. (1980). *An evaluation of juvenile diversion*. Cambridge, MA: Oelgeschlager, Gunn, and Hain Publishers.

Piquero, A. R., Cullen, F. T., Unnever, J. D., Piquero, N. L., & Gordon, J. A. (2010). Never too late: Public optimism about juvenile rehabilitation. *Punishment & Society, 12*(2), 187–207. doi:10.1177/1462474509357379

Platt, A. M. (1969). *The child savers: The invention of delinquency*. Chicago, IL: University of Chicago Press.

President's Commission on Law Enforcement and Administration of Justice. (1967). *Task force report: Juvenile delinquency and youth crime*. Washington, DC: U.S. Government Printing Office.

Przybylski, R. (2008). *What works? Effective recidivism reduction and risk-focused prevention programs*. Denver, CO: Colorado Department of Public Safety.

Quay, H. C., & Love, C. T. (1977). The effect of a juvenile diversion program on rearrests. *Criminal Justice & Behavior, 4*(4), 377–396. doi:10.1177/009385487700400404

Rasmussen, A. (2004). Ten court referrals, sentencing, and subsequent recidivism: Two proportional hazards models and a little speculation. *Crime & Delinquency, 50*(4), 615–635. doi:10.1177/0011128703261616

Rasmussen, A., & Diener, C. I. (2005). A prospective longitudinal study of teen court's impact on offender youths' behavior. *Juvenile and Family Court Journal, 56*(1), 17–32. doi:10.1111/j.1755–6988.2005.tb00100.x

Regoli, R., Wilderman, E., & Pogrebin, M. (1985). Using an alternative evaluation measure for assessing juvenile diversion programs. *Children and Youth Services Review*, 7(1), 21–38. doi:10.1016/0190-7409(85)90037-4

Roberts, A. R. (2004). The emergence and proliferation of juvenile diversion programs. In A. R. Roberts (Ed.), *Juvenile justice sourcebook: Past, present, and future* (pp. 183–195). Oxford: Oxford University Press.

Roberts, M., Brophy, J., & Cooper, C. (1997). *The juvenile drug court movement.* Washington, DC: Office of Juvenile Justice and Delinquency Prevention.

Rodriguez, N., & Webb, V. J. (2004). Multiple measures of juvenile drug court effectiveness: Results of a quasi-experimental design. *Crime and Delinquency, 50*(2), 292–314. doi:10.1177/0011128703254991

Roper v. Simmons, 543 U.S. 551 (2005).

Rottman, D., & Casey, P. (1999). Therapeutic jurisprudence and the emergence of problem-solving courts. *National Institute of Justice Journal, 240*, 12–19.

Schwalbe, C. S., Gearing, R. E., MacKenzie, M. J., Brewer, K. B., & Ibrahim, R. (2012). A meta-analysis of experimental studies of diversion programs for juvenile offenders. *Clinical Psychology Review, 32*(1), 26–33. doi:10.1016/j.cpr.2011.10.002

Sexton, T. L., & Alexander, J. F. (2000). *Functional family therapy.* Washington, DC: Office of Juvenile Justice and Delinquency Prevention.

Sexton, T. L., & Alexander, J. F. (2004). *Functional family therapy clinical training manual.* Washington, DC: Annie E. Casey Foundation.

Sexton, T. L., & Turner, C. W. (2010). The effectiveness of functional family therapy for youth with behavioral problems in a community practice setting. *Journal of Family Psychology, 24*(3), 339–348. doi:10.1037/a0019406

Shaw, M., & Robinson, K. (1998). Summary and analysis of the first juvenile drug court evaluation: The Santa Clara County Drug Treatment Court and the Delaware Juvenile Drug Diversion Program. *National Drug Court Institute Review, 1*, 83–95.

Sickmund, M., & Puzzanchera, C. (2014). *Juvenile offenders and victims: 2014 national report.* Pittsburg, PA: National Center for Juvenile Justice.

Simonsen, C. E., & Gordon, M. S. (1982). *Juvenile justice in America.* New York: Macmillan Publishing Co., Inc.

Sloan, J. J., & Smykla, J. O. (2003). Juvenile drug courts: Understanding the importance of dimensional variability. *Criminal Justice Policy Review, 14*(3), 339–360. doi:10.1177/0887403403253720

Sloan, J. J., Smykla, J. O., & Rush, J. P. (2004). Do juvenile drug courts reduce recidivism?: Outcomes of drug court and an adolescent substance abuse program. *American Journal of Criminal Justice, 29*(1), 95–115. doi:10.1007/BF02885706

Smith, S., & Chonody, J. M. (2010). Peer-driven justice: Development and validation of the Teen Court Peer Influence Scale. *Research on Social Work Practice, 20*(3), 283–292. doi:10.1177/1049731509347857

Snyder, H. N., & Sickmund, M. (2006). *Juvenile justice: A century of change.* Washington, DC: Office of Juvenile Justice and Delinquency Prevention.

Stahl, A. L. (1998). *Delinquency cases in juvenile courts, 1995.* Washington, DC: Office of Juvenile Justice and Delinquency Prevention.

Stein, D. M., Deberard, S., & Homan, K. (2013). Predicting success and failure in juvenile drug treatment court: A meta-analytic review. *Journal of Substance Abuse Treatment, 44*(2), 159–168. doi:10.1016/j.jsat.2012.07.002

Stickle, W. P., Connell, N. M., Wilson, D. M., & Gottfredson, D. (2008). An experimental evaluation of teen courts. *Journal of Experimental Criminology, 4*(2), 137–163. doi:10.1007/s11292-008-9050-8

Sutherland, E. H. (1947). *Principles of criminology* (4th ed.). Philadelphia, PA: Lippincott.

Sullivan, C. J., Blair, L., Latessa, E., & Sullivan, C. C. (2016). Juvenile drug courts and recidivism: Results from a multisite outcome study. *Justice Quarterly, 33*(2), 291–318. doi:10.1080/07418825.2014.908937

The Future of Children. (n.d.). *Best practices in juvenile justice reform.* Princeton, NJ: The Future of Children. Retrieved from www.futureofchildren.org/futureofchildren/publications/highlights/18_02_Highlights.pdf

Thompson, K. (2002). *Statistical summary of North Dakota Juvenile Drug Court—May 2000 to June 2002.* Fargo, ND: North Dakota State University.

Timmons-Mitchell, J., Bender, M. B., Kishna, M. A., & Mitchell, C. C. (2006). An independent effectiveness trial of multisystemic therapy with juvenile justice youth. *Journal of Clinical Child and Adolescent Psychology, 35*(2), 227–236. doi:10.1207/s15374424jccp3502_6

Torbet, P., & Szymanski, L. (1998). *State legislative responses to juvenile crime: 1996–97 update.* Washington, DC: Office of Juvenile Justice and Delinquency Prevention.

Torbet, P., & Thomas, D. (1997). Balanced and restorative justice: Implementing the philosophy. *Pennsylvania Progress, 4*(3), 1–6.

Vito, G. F., Tewskbury, R., & Wilson, D. G. (1998). *The juvenile justice system: Concepts and issues.* Prospect Heights, IL: Waveland Press.

Vose, B., & Vannan, K. (2013). A jury of your peers: Recidivism among teen court participants. *Journal of Juvenile Justice, 3*(1), 97–109.

Waldron, H. B., Slesnick, N., Turner, C. W., Brody, J. L., & Peterson, T. R. (2001) Treatment outcomes for adolescent substance abuse at 4- and 7-month assessments. *Journal of Consulting and Clinical Psychology, 69*(5), 802–813. doi:10.1037/0022-006X.69.5.802

Washington State Institute for Public Policy. (2004). *Outcome evaluation of Washington state's research-based programs for juvenile offenders*. Olympia, WA: Washington State Institute for Public Policy.

Whitehead, J. T., Dodson, K. D., & Edwards, B. D. (2013). *Corrections: Exploring crime, punishment, and justice in America* (3rd ed.). New York, NY: Routledge.

Whitehead, J. T., & Lab, S. P. (1999). Diversion. In *Juvenile justice: An introduction* (3rd ed., pp. 267–286). Cincinnati, OH: Anderson Publishing Co.

Wilson, D. B., Mitchell, O., & MacKenzie, D. L. (2006). A systematic review of drug court effects on recidivism. *Journal of Experimental Criminology, 2*(4), 459–487. doi:10.1007/s11292-006-9019-4

Wilson, H. A., & Hoge, R. D. (2013). The effect of youth diversion programs on recidivism: A meta-analytic review. *Criminal Justice and Behavior, 40*(5), 497–518. doi:10.1177/0093854812451089

Wong, J. S., Boucharad, J., Gravel, J., Bouchard, M., & Morselli, C. (2016). Can at-risk youth be diverted from crime? A meta-analysis of restorative diversion programs. *Criminal Justice and Behavior, 43*(10), 1310–1329. doi:10.1177/0093854816640835

Zimring, F. E. (1998). *American youth violence*. New York, NY: Oxford University Press.

10

LESBIAN, GAY, BISEXUAL, TRANSGENDER, AND QUEER OFFENDERS

Sexual Orientation, Gender Identity, and Incarceration

Chris Wakefield and Andrew L. Spivak

> Jails [and prisons] are traumatizing and often dangerous places, especially for lesbian, gay, bisexual, and transgender people, and anyone who is gender nonconforming. LGBT people are more likely to end up behind bars, and more likely to face abuses behind bars. Being LGBT in a U.S. jail or prison often means daily humiliation, physical and sexual abuse, and fearing it will get worse if you complain.
>
> —(Marksamer & Tobin, 2014, p. 5)

Introduction

Prison administrator and reformers have long been concerned about issues of sexuality in correctional facilities. The contexts of these concerns have varied, from moral prescriptions against homosexual behaviors that have been taboo in western society for centuries to modern concerns about protecting inmates from violence and exploitation (Kunzel, 2008; Propper, 1981). While the sexuality of prisoners can reflect an expression of agency for individuals who have had theirs taken away, sex has generally been treated as a threat to prison order, an automatic violation of consent, and as an illicit form of trade. Consequently, the regulation of sexual acts and those who perform them while incarcerated continues to be a long-running theme in the management of prison systems (Hensley, 2002).

Unsurprisingly, inmates who are not heterosexual or gender normative present dilemmas for correctional administrators. Lesbian, gay, bisexual, transgender, and queer (LGBTQ) inmates are identified as a vulnerable population in prisons because of the higher rates of sexual and physical violence they experience while incarcerated (Beck, Berzofsky, Caspar, & Krebs, 2013; Beck, Rantala, & Rexroat, 2014; Blackburn, Mullings, & Marquart, 2008; National Prison Rape Elimination Committee, 2009). They frequently become the target of other prisoners—particularly in male prison populations—for sexual relationships that blur the lines between consent and exploitation. LGBTQ inmates also can have more complicated medical needs that are beyond the scope of traditional medical training, such as hormone replacement therapy for transgender people. As a result of violence or the fear of violence, access to programming and other services frequently becomes limited to these inmates through excessive use of solitary confinement, extending the time they must remain incarcerated and reducing opportunities for self-improvement (Arkles, 2009; Gruberg, 2013; Sumner & Jenness, 2014). Administrators should be concerned for the behavior of their employees as well, as these inmates experience higher rates of misconduct from officers and other staff (Beck, Rantala, & Rexroat, 2014; Sylvia Rivera Law Project, 2007). As public opinion becomes supportive of LGBTQ identities generally, inmates may become less afraid to express gender or sexual identities besides heterosexuality and gender normativity, leading to greater visibility and higher expectations for administration at all levels to ensure safety and order with appropriate protections and policies.

As with all special needs populations incarcerated today, scholars, activists, and administrators should address the ways in which treatment is unequal between LGBTQ and non-LGBTQ offenders, as well as the effects of seemingly equitable treatments that do not provide equal outcomes for LGBTQ inmates, compared to heterosexual or gender normative inmates. Though this idea invites the critique of "special" or "privileged" treatment by some correctional staff, inmates are often handled differently according to a variety of factors, such as age, racial identity, gang affiliation, offense history, and sentence length. Identifying and addressing the institutional needs unique to LGBTQ inmates is no different.

This chapter will explore the history, conditions, and policies related to lesbian, gay, bisexual, transgender, and queer inmates in state and federal prisons. We begin by discussing key terms and language used to describe LGBTQ inmates appropriately, as well as the pertinent history to put the LGBTQ community and its relationship with law enforcement in greater context. The next section addresses prison demographics and the prevalence of gender nonconformity and sexual orientation. Reviewing key policies that have the greatest impact on LGBTQ inmates, we pay special consideration to transgender inmates and the special challenges of providing them with safe and effective treatment. Finally, the chapter concludes with common criticisms and current best practices for addressing the needs of LGBTQ inmates from a variety of organizations and government agencies, as well as implications for future study.

Who are LGBTQ Offenders? Language, Identity, and Situation

The language used in discussing LGBTQ inmates is worth initial consideration. When we refer to LGBTQ inmates, we mean those who have claimed a specific *identity*. Beginning with identities of sexual orientation, offenders may consider themselves gay, lesbian, and bisexual. Note that these categories are self-defined and not determined by behavior; for example, not all men who have sex with men (MSM) or women who have sex with women (WSW) identify as gay or lesbian. They may identify as straight, bisexual, queer, or a multitude of other terms, the listing of which is beyond the scope of this text. The identity of sexual orientation often involves a connection with culture and a history that extends beyond the individual or the prison environment. Thus, it is fallacious to assume a particular identity based on previous sexual activity, expressions of femininity or masculinity, or other observed characteristics.

Gender identity is generally understood as a separate category from sexual orientation and can include a wide variety of identities, including cisgender, transgender, and other gender nonconforming labels. "Cisgender" is the term used to describe anyone whose biological sex determination at birth matches their gender identity, such as a biological male who identifies as a man. A transgender individuals are those whose gender expression does not align with what might be expected given the biological sex they were identified as at birth. The expectation is that these individuals pursue some level of medical transition, including hormone replacement therapy, counseling, augmentation or reduction of breasts, and, in some cases, surgical modification of the genitals to better align their physiology with their identity. The narratives of the male-to-female (MTF) and female-to-male (FTM) transgender person are only two options. In the LGBTQ community, transgender is often described as an "umbrella" term that encompasses a wide variety of gender variance, including individuals who reject the idea of transition but do not identify with the terms "man" or "woman." A common misconception regarding transgender as a term is that it somehow indicates something about their sexual orientation or preference in partners. Transgender as a term speaks only to gender expression and identity. Often, a trans-identified person will also identify with a sexual orientation of their choice that places themselves in the gender role they view themselves with. For example, a gay trans-man is someone who was identified as female at birth, but who identifies as a man and is attracted to men (GLAAD, 2016).

These definitions represent a broad and inclusive modern cultural history of these topics; however, federal, state, and local agencies may define them more narrowly for policy purposes. The extent to which correctional facilities have policies regarding sexual orientation and gender identity—if they have them at all—is more nuanced and inclusive can impact LGBTQ offenders' risk and safety conditions. Furthermore, if we intend to treat prisoners with some level of respect, understanding and using language appropriately is essential to working with LGBTQ populations regardless of where they are. Special attention, then, should be paid to how both policy and members of staff use language with this population.

Before concluding this discussion of terms, consider two important distinctions. The first addresses the concept of "situational homosexuality." Much has been made of so-called "gay for the stay" or "prison gay" inmates, for whom same-sex sexual behavior only occurs in prison (Buffman, 2004; Eigenberg, 1992; Heffernan, 1972; Ricciardelli, Grills, & Craig, 2016; Sit & Ricciardelli, 2013; Sykes, 1958; Wooden & Parker, 1982; Van Wormer, 1984). The most common explanation for situational homosexuality is referred to as the deprivation model, whereby inmates are deprived of their normal object of desire, so they take same-sex partners as substitutes. Situational homosexuality is an adaptation to deprivation. While the needs of MSM or WSW may be similar to LGBTQ-identified people in some cases, they are not necessarily LGBTQ. Ms or WSWs may be less visible to fellow inmates and staff and may vehemently reject accusations of LGBTQ status for a variety of reasons (Ricciardelli et al., 2016; Sit & Ricciardelli, 2013). They may also be motivated differently when pursuing sex. Some inmates will use sex as a form of control, commodity, or protection and select partners with these goals in mind rather than physical desire (Smith, 2006). Differentiating between these categories can make a difference in effective response to concerns of inmate safety.

The second distinction is between transgender and intersex inmates. Some policies regarding LGBTQ inmates may also be applicable to inmates with an intersex trait. An intersex trait is an ambiguity in the internal or external anatomy that typically denotes biological sex. Another term rising in popularity for intersex traits is "disorders of sex development" (DSD). Over 30 known intersex traits exist. The authors of this text do not intend to equate intersex with LGBTQ, as recent intersex advocacy movements have pointed out that these two groups experience different circumstances and needs regarding their gender identities and social experiences (Davis, 2015; Davis, Dewey, & Murphy, 2016). Nonetheless, intersex offenders can share similar difficulties in prison as those who are LGBTQ, especially transgender inmates. Though this chapter will not address the specific, unique needs of intersex inmates, some limited parallels may be drawn concerning safety and medical needs.

Historical Context

LGBTQ as a social category refers to more than just identity; it also refers to community and culture. To understand the ways in which queer inmates interact with systems of incarceration, they should be conceptualized in a historical context that recognizes decades of resistance to dominant cultural norms and legal prohibitions related to gender and sexuality. Though political support of gay and lesbian legal issues has been on the rise—the United States Supreme Court recently ruled same-sex marriage bans unconstitutional—social and economic discrimination persists at both structural/institutional and individual levels ("Understanding Issues Facing LGBTQ Americans," 2014).

Homosexuality, and the idea that individuals have sexual orientations or identity, is a relatively new phenomenon. It was not until 1886 that the term "homosexuality" was popularized by the early sexologist Krafft-Ebing and his contemporaries to categorize individuals as heterosexual or homosexual (Stryker & Whittle, 2006). This nomenclature was widely adopted by both clinicians and the general population. Homosexual acts and desires were defined through the lens of mental illness requiring treatment. Various legal prohibitions had criminalized same-sex sexual behavior regardless of consent (Mogul, Ritchie, & Whitlock, 2011). Sodomy laws and other vice regulations were a constant threat to anyone engaging in same-sex sexual activity and prevented relationships from being safely revealed in the public sphere.

The precursors of what we now refer to as the LGBTQ community in the United States grew out of the postwar period of the late 1940s and early 1950s, with advocacy organizations protesting discrimination and promoting the idea that gay and lesbian relationships were equivalent to those of heterosexuals. Early activists attempted to portray themselves as fitting social expectations in all ways but their desire, from the civility of their protests to their normative choices in clothing; they succeeded at building networks of LGBTQ people but failed to bring significant political progress to their community (Mogul et al., 2011).

The Stonewall Riots of 1969 are credited with launching a more aggressive campaign for LGBTQ rights. Police raids of bars catering to gay men, lesbians, and gender-bending individuals were common during this time (Guidotto, 2011; Mecca, 2011). One such raid at the Stonewall Inn in Greenwich Village in New York City sparked a riot as some patrons of the bar resisted arrest; patrons and protesters spilled out into the streets and began several days of marching and demonstrating. Generations of LGBTQ people still carry the memory of vice squads and arrests of friends and loved ones for consensual activity or gathering to socialize. The advocacy organizations that grew out of this era viewed the law and the justice system as their main opposition (Mogul et al., 2011).

The appearance of human immunodeficiency virus (HIV) during the 1980s in gay male communities further institutionalized violence and fear toward LGBTQ people. Facing a deadly virus and an executive branch of the United States government reluctant to provide aid, the LGBTQ community created its own organizations, networks, and prevention programs to fight the spread of HIV (Gido, 2002). Again, the community perceived the government, including the president, as having failed them, allowing HIV to kill so many people before taking action precisely because the virus seemed to be affecting LGBTQ communities.

Throughout the 1990s and 2000s, large activist organizations supported LGBTQ initiatives in efforts toward widespread reforms at the local, state, and federal level. In particular, there were efforts for allowing same-sex marriage, decreasing incidents of police brutality, and passing hate crime and equal protections clauses for sexual orientation and gender identity. In 2003, with the U.S. Supreme Court ruling in *Lawrence v. Texas* (2003), sodomy laws that had criminalized consensual sex between LGBTQ people across the country were finally invalidated, many of which were still enshrined in state law (Wardenski, 2005). Increased awareness brought about changes in public opinion, and more LGBTQ people came out publicly to family, friends, and their broader communities.

The present generation of young LGBTQ people may be the first to have grown up in environments that were supportive of claiming an LGBTQ identity and were saved from having to recall the destructive power of an unchecked HIV epidemic. While today's young LGBTQ people expect social acceptance and respect for their identities and civil rights in ways previous generations could not, they still face increased risk of abandonment, abuse, participation in criminal activities, poor relationships with parents, homelessness, and engagement in unsafe sexual behaviors. A national survey of LGBTQ youth conducted by the Human Rights Campaign (2016) found that 26% of LGBTQ youth identified non-accepting families as the most important problem in their life, with bullying and fears regarding their identity coming out behind them. By comparison, non-LGBTQ youth were concerned about classes, careers, and financial pressures. LGBTQ youth were also found to be more likely to feel isolated in their community, twice as likely to be bullied in school, and to be unable to identify adults that they can go to for help. Such factors continue to disadvantage LGBTQ youth, who experience a higher rate of imprisonment than the general population. Transgender individuals in particular have faced reduced opportunities for employment and abandonment by family members, leading some to adapt by engaging in sex work and other illegal behaviors to survive (Sylvia Rivera Law Project, 2007). Researchers have included LGBTQ youth as one group experiencing the "school-to-prison pipeline," where institutional and cultural factors increase the risk of contact with the prison system (Center for American Progress, 2016; Hanssens, Moodie-Mills, Ritchie, Spade, & Vaid, 2014; Mallett, 2016). Meanwhile, older generations of LGBTQ people may be wary of law enforcement and other government agencies after a history of violence, betrayal, and abandonment. When LGBTQ offenders enter prisons or jails, they carry with them a history that affects their choices of interaction with the institution, staff, and other inmates.

LGBTQ Offenders and Prison Sex Research

Research on sexuality in prisons remains underdeveloped, and studies with LGBTQ inmates as the main target population comprise only a fraction of that topic. When issues of inmate sexual orientation or gender identity do surface, they are discussed primarily as risk factors or marginal explanations for some sexual behaviors. Consequently, LGBTQ inmates are often defined by discussions of prison sexuality as opposed to a culturally specific subpopulation with needs across the whole of the incarceration process. Only in the last 10 years have any national statistics been aggregated for nonheterosexual identities in local, state, and federal prison systems (Beck et al., 2013; Dennis, 2014). These data do not provide a thorough picture of sexual and gender identities, especially regarding transgender inmates, for whom a large enough sample has not yet been collected to address appropriately their prevalence or experiences (Shay, 2013). Qualitative and survey data outside of official collection activities have suffered from a variety of weaknesses, including failure to differentiate between consensual and nonconsensual behavior, conflation of identity and situational behaviors, neglect of potential motivations for sexual contact, and assumption of essentialist definitions of identity.

Most data on LGBTQ inmates comes from one of two topics: sexual violence or cultural accounts of sexual behavior. Rape in prison has been a topic of research since the 1960s, with most of the focus being on male prisons (Hensley & Tewksbury, 2002). Most often, gay men and bisexuals come up in this context as victims of assault, whose identity allows them to be regendered by other inmates during situational homosexual encounters. Unfortunately, data is sparse for female prison facilities, providing little information on the potential relationship between sexual identity and experiences of sexual violence (Hensley & Tewksbury, 2002). Research focused on sexual exploitation can compress the nuances of sexual interaction by assuming that inmates are unable to consent or lack agency regarding participation in sexual acts. Thus, acts mutually agreed to for the purpose of exchange, protection, prestige, or pleasure are subsumed under exploitation or victimization. Cultural accounts, in contrast, have tried to explain sexual behaviors by studying the norms and relationship structures that occur in prison environments. Unfortunately, LGBTQ identity is rarely the direct target of these inquiries; instead, they are mentioned only to the extent that is needed to describe larger phenomena, such as prison sexual behavior. As such, most cultural accounts of LGBTQ inmates lack complete narratives of this population's experience with incarceration.

Recent research exploring sexuality in prison has moved decidedly toward a more social constructionist approach (Alarid, 2000; Eigenberg, 1992; Gibson & Hensley, 2013; Tewksbury & West, 2000). Social constructionists do not take for granted the essentialist position that all inmates enter prison with the same identity, desires, or sense of self with which they are released. For example, studies of sexual identity before, during, and after incarceration show that significant numbers of inmates change how they self-report their sexual orientation (Gibson & Hensley, 2013; Hensley,

Tewksbury, & Wright, 2001). A social constructionist approach recognizes that the meaning given to same-sex sexual behavior or categories like gay or bisexual may be altered by the context of the prison or by some level of fluidity of desire. Though taking such an approach complicates our understanding of sexuality in inmates, it also provides additional insight into how these categories are claimed by this population.

Prevalence and Demographics

The first data on nonheterosexual and transgender identity at the national level was first released in the 2007 National Inmate Survey (NIS), an instrument created by the Bureau of Justice Statistics (BJS) in response to the Prison Rape Elimination Act (PREA) (Dennis, 2014). These data, most recently reported for 2011–2012, include individuals housed in state and federal prisons, county jails, military facilities, and immigration detention centers. The main purpose of the NIS is to determine, in accordance with PREA regulations, the extent of sexual victimization that occurs nationally, but it also constitutes the most comprehensive assessment to date of sexual orientation among the incarcerated. In the 2011–2012 NIS, 7.6% of prison and jail inmates (reflecting a projected estimate of 161,600 out of 2.1 million), or about one in 13, self-reported identifying as lesbian, gay, bisexual, or some other sexual orientation (Beck et al., 2013). Table 10.1 shows the nationally estimated number and percentages of inmates identifying with LGB categories across federal and state prisons, as well as county/local jails. Note that the proportion of jail inmates who self-identify as LGB is close the proportion of prison inmates. While juvenile detainees are beyond the scope of this chapter, the 2012 National Survey of Youth in Custody, in a representative sample of 8,707 youth in 326 juvenile detention facilities, found that 12.2% self-identified gay, lesbian, bisexual, or other sexual orientations (Beck, Cantor, Hartge, & Smith, 2013). The higher prevalence of LGB sexual orientations among juveniles as compared to adults may be attributable to greater openness about sexual orientation among younger people.

Though estimating self-identified sexual orientation in the general U.S. population is at least as challenging and imprecise as with prison and jail inmates, national projections using Gallup, the General Social Survey, and the National Survey of Family Growth suggest that 3.4 to 3.8% identify as LGBTQ, making the proportion of LGB persons in prison double that of LGBTQ persons in the United States population overall (Gates & Newport, 2012).

The NIS surveys also asked respondents to identify their gender as male, female, or transgender, thus providing the first national estimate of self-identified transgender inmates. Table 10.2 provides numbers and percentages of gender identities for adult inmates in federal and state prisons, as well as

Table 10.1 Prevalence of Sexual Orientation Self-Identity, National Inmate Survey, 2011–2012[a]

	All Inmates		*Prison Inmates*		*Jail Inmates*	
	Number	*Percent*	*Number*	*Percent*	*Number*	*Percent*
Heterosexual	1,952,500	92.4	1,298,000	92.1	654,500	93.0
Non-heterosexual[b] (Gay, Lesbian, Bisexual, Other)	161,600	7.6	111,500	7.9	50,100	7.0
TOTAL	2,114,100[c]	100	1,409,500	100	704,600	100

a The National Inmate Survey (NIS-3) was conducted by the Bureau of Justice Statistics, administered to a representative sample of 92,449 inmates 18 or older, in 248 federal and state prisons (including ICE and military facilities) and 358 county/local jails (Beck et al., 2013).
b The NIS combines gay, lesbian, bisexual, and other orientations into "Nonheterosexual."
c Numbers of inmates are projected nationally from the representative sample.

Table 10.2 Prevalence of Gender Identities, National Inmate Survey, 2011–2012[a]

	All Inmates		*Prison Inmates*		*Jail Inmates*	
	Number	*Percent*	*Number*	*Percent*	*Number*	*Percent*
Gender Identity						
- Male	1,973,800	91.1	1,345,200	93.1	628,600	87.1
- Female	188,200	8.7	96,600	6.7	91,600	12.7
- Transgender	4,918	0.2	3,209	0.2	1,709	0.2
TOTAL	2,166,918[b]	100	1,445,009	100	721,909	100

a The National Inmate Survey (NIS-3) was conducted by the Bureau of Justice Statistics, administered to a representative sample of 92,449 inmates 18 or older, in 248 federal and state prisons (including ICE and military facilities) and 358 county/local jails (Beck et al., 2013). Figures for transgender inmates are reported in Beck (2014).

b Numbers of inmates are projected nationally from the representative sample.

Table 10.3 Prevalence of Sexual Victimization by Sexual Orientation and Gender Identity, National Inmate Survey (NIS), 2011–2012[a]

	Prison Inmates			*Jail Inmates*		
	Number[b]	*Percent Victims by Other Inmates*	*Percent Victims by Staff*	*Number*[b]	*Percent Victims by Other Inmates*	*Percent Victims by Staff*
Sexual Orientation						
- Heterosexual	1,298,000	1.2*	2.1*	654,500	1.2*	1.7*
- Nonheterosexual[c]	111,500	12.2	5.4	50,100	8.5	4.3
Gender Identity						
- Male	1,345,200	1.7	2.4	628,600	1.4	1.9
- Female	96,600	6.9	2.3	91,600	3.6	1.4
- Transgender	3,209	24.1*	16.7*	1,709	15.8*	18.3*

a The National Inmate Survey (NIS-3) was conducted by the Bureau of Justice Statistics, administered to a representative sample of 92,449 inmates 18 or older, in 248 federal and state prisons (including ICE and military facilities) and 358 county/local jails (Beck et al., 2013). Figures for transgender inmates are reported in Beck (2014).

b Numbers of inmates are projected nationally from the representative sample.

c The NIS combines gay, lesbian, bisexual, and other orientations into "Nonheterosexual."

* Differences between sexual orientation categories and between transgender and nontransgender categories are significant, at alpha < .05.

county/local jails, in the 2011–2012 survey. In both prisons and jails, transgender inmates accounted for just 0.2% of all inmates, or about one in 500 (Beck, 2014). Though this proportion is small, it still represents nearly 5,000 inmates nationwide. Other research has shown that 16% of transgender people in the United States will spend some amount of time in a jail or prison in their lives (Grant et al., 2011).

Growing national concern with sexual violence in prisons was the primary catalyst for data collection on nonheterosexual and transgender identities among inmates. In male prisons, anyone perceived to be gay or bisexual is significantly more likely to be physically or sexually assaulted. Table 10.3 presents the prevalence of sexual victimization among prison and jail inmates from the 2011–2012 NIS. In both prisons and jails, heterosexual inmates were far less likely than LGBs to claim having been sexually victimized by other inmates or by staff (Beck et al., 2013). These differences were even more pronounced for self-reported victimization between transgender and nontransgender inmates (Beck, 2014).

Transgender inmates, often the most visible targets, report higher rates of sexual victimization, nearly one in four at the hands of other inmates and one in six by staff. While the small sample size of transgender inmates in the NIS makes the accuracy of these data uncertain (Shay, 2013), numerous sources employing both qualitative and quantitative methods have pointed to transgender inmates as experiencing higher levels of sexual violence within prisons than other inmates (Hanssens et al., 2014; Marksamer & Tobin, 2014; Okamura, 2011; Schreier Lyseggen, 2015; Smith & Yarussi, 2015; Sylvia Rivera Law Project, 2007). LGBTQ inmates are often housed in facilities where homophobic and transphobic views are commonplace, creating hostile social conditions for all involved (Eigenberg, 2000). Staff are more likely to treat LGBTQ inmates differently, exposing them to unnecessary searches, riskier housing placements, and reacting strongly to physical contact (Iyama, 2012; Lydon, Carrington, Low, Miller, & Yazdy, 2015).

These data only tell a partial story. Public reports of the NIS data are unable to reveal the motivations for sexual activity and do not discuss how consensual and nonconsensual activity can be disaggregated. Critiques have been levied against the NIS and other prison sexuality research for conflating consensual sex with rape, which is not just an issue with research methodology: it highlights the common correctional policy of banning all sexual activity as a solution to the problem of defining consent (Arkles, 2015; Hensley, Struckman-Johnson, & Eigenberg, 2000; Hensley & Tewksbury, 2002; Smith, 2006).

Currently, we cannot determine the level of prostitution, mutually agreed upon protective pairings, consensual relationships or behaviors, or other reasons for same-sex sexual activity. Differentiating the various motives for sexual activity by gendered facilities would be especially informative for women's prisons, which have often been cited as having entirely different social dynamics regarding sex and sexual identity. These motivations represent gray areas that could change the way we understand both prison sex generally and how LGBTQ inmates adapt to incarceration or become coerced into sexual interaction (Smith, 2006). The survey questions inquiring about LGBTQ identities assume, as surveys often must, a widespread understanding of the terms presented to respondents, which may limit expressions outside this framework. The fact that the only source of sexual orientation and identity data is the NIS, a survey designed to estimate the prevalence of sexual victimization, suggests that LGBTQ inmates are only worth identifying in a sexual context. A broader understanding of how LGBTQ identity interacts with prison institutions remains missing in current efforts at representative data collection in the United States.

Prison Culture and LGBTQ Offenders

The prison is not a representative microcosm of society, nor is it merely an institutionalized residence. Those who have resided or worked in a correctional facility can anecdotally confirm researchers' findings that prisons have cultures that create or support many of the social trends observed there (Flanagan, Marquart, & Adams, 1998). Correctional officers, case managers, and administrators must develop some understanding of the norms held by their inmates to protect vulnerable inmates and preserve order in housing units and on the yard. Some special needs populations are identified as such in response to prison culture, often because they are vulnerable to aggression or violating institutional policy. Much of what qualifies LGBTQ inmates as a special needs population stems from the cultural norms of prisons and jails in what is a clearly gendered institution. As LGBTQ inmates often contradict these cultural norms—particularly those around gender—they frequently become the targets of aggression from both fellow inmates and staff. The limited extant research on LGBTQ inmates also skews our view of how they fit into any prison culture. Primarily visible in literature on prison sex, LGBTQ inmates are defined either by the way they engage in sex (assuming they will engage in sex at all) and what their identity means to the maintenance of other inmates' sexual identities. Understanding the research on prison culture as it relates to LGBTQ inmates can be invaluable in designing appropriate policies for prison environments and handling individual inmates.

Men's Prisons

Research on sexuality in prison is most often conducted in facilities for men. The stakes are potentially higher for gay and bisexual men, as well as transgender persons incarcerated there, because of the gendered expectations that serve as foundation for a male prison culture. Men's prisons are "hypermasculine" spaces in which traditional masculine norms are maintained more strictly and with higher overall expectations for qualities including aggressiveness, physical strength, and inclination to physical violence (Arkles, 2009; Eigenberg, 2000; Robinson, 2011). The appearance of sexual prowess is a component of a hypermasculine self-presentation but has no obvious outlet in an all-male prison setting where heterosexuality is an essential norm. Thus, researchers have long adopted the "punk-jocker" model of situational prison homosexuality, in which aggressive "jockers" take younger heterosexual inmates or homosexual inmates ("punks") as targets for sexual aggression (Buffinan, 1972; Knowles, 1999; Sagarin, 1976; Wooden & Parker, 1982). In this perspective, aggressors are immune from accusations of being gay so long as they never give oral sex to or are penetrated by another inmate.

Variations in the vein of the punk-jocker explanations for situational prison homosexuality have also come from outside of academia. Wilbert Rideau, a prisoner incarcerated at the Louisiana State Penitentiary, published his essay entitled *Prison: The Sexual Jungle* in 1979, earning him the prestigious George Polk Award for outstanding journalism. Rideau described homosexual activity as a key component of power relations between inmates and the establishing of a hierarchy based on who victimizes and who is victimized. His work was heralded as a seminal study and first-hand account of a subculture of prison homosexuality (see Box 10.1 for a full summary of his model). Though the punk-jocker model is somewhat outdated and may be presenting an overly coercive view of prison sex, it represents the most common interpretation of sexual relationships in male prisons.

Box 10.1 Abstract from *Prison: The Sexual Jungle*

Status in the inmate subculture is largely established by the homosexual role-aggressors or victims, who desire to establish and reinforce a masculine image, will violently rape newcomers in order to establish their power in contrast to the weakness of the victim. The victim is cast in the role of the subservient woman who must do the bidding of her "man"; victims (generally called "whores," "boygals," or "bitches") are frequently sold by their owners for sex with other inmates. Victims have the benefit of receiving protection from their owners, further confirming their weakness and lack of maleness. In order to keep from becoming enslaved, a newcomer must show that he can resist aggressive advances and meet violence with violence. Assault and killing, with a consequent extension of prison terms, are often the only course for avoiding sexual degradation and enslavement. The administration of many prisons and jails accept the dynamics of the inmate homosexual subculture as a means of establishing social control. The Louisiana State Penitentiary at Angola has reduced forced and violent sexual relationships to a minimum by not tolerating any violent behavior. This approach, combined with conjugal visits, could go a long way in controlling and relieving the need for aggressive status behavior through sexuality. The practice of isolating known homosexuals does little to relieve the situation, since most aggressors are heterosexuals with a need to establish a manly image (Rideau, 1979, p. 51)

Several justifications for engaging in homosexual relationships exist, all of which can apply to a gay or bisexual inmate. Protective pairings are described as arrangements in which the punk develops a sexual relationship to gain protection and influence (Dolovich 2011; Iyama, 2012). Gay inmates, in particular, because of their increasing visibility and expectations for being open about their identities, may seek out pairings for safety or may be coerced into them by aggressors. Alternatively, nonheterosexual inmates may prostitute themselves for resources both legitimate and illicit (Eigenberg, 1992; Hensley et al., 2000). Sexual pleasure, companionship, and self-determination are often forgotten as motivations and remain mostly unexplored (Smith, 2006).

Additionally, transgender inmates, who have only recently become of interest to penologists, are assumed to experience sexual interactions in much the same way as gay men. Few studies exist on transgender women's experiences in male prisons, but there is some data that may suggest they respond and are treated differently than gay men. Depending on the setting and the culture of the facility, some transgender women have preferred to be kept in general population with the inmates most often assumed to be a threat to them (Jenness & Fenstermaker, 2013). In a few anecdotal cases, groups of inmates even banded together to help transgender women in male units, including seeking access to needed medical treatment and protection from others that might attempt to force a sexual relationship (Arkles, 2009). Certainly, transgender inmates still face violence in prisons, and residing in general populations can be risky, but transgender inmates can also build unique relationships as part of all-male tiers that are constructive for the unit.

Women's Prisons

Contrary to the violent narratives in all-male correctional facilities, coercion and aggression are not frequent themes in discussions of same-sex sexual activity for incarcerated women. The few studies that exist on sexuality in women's prisons have focused on consensual or minimally coerced sexual activity and represent some of the earliest general studies on sex among incarcerates (Hensley & Tewksbury, 2002). These early efforts were primarily among juveniles and observed an established set of relations mimicking marriage and family structures. As with men's prisons, researchers originally sought to explain sexual behavior among inmates, not the interactions between identities; however, lesbian women emerge in some of the case studies and interviews of this early work.

The first images of a culture around homosexuality in female prisons reflected "pseudofamily" formation. Women and girls developed friendships and romantic relationships modeled after social institutions, using terms like "marriage," "husband," and "mother" to describe partnerships (Heffernan, 1972; Propper, 1981; Selling, 1931). Juveniles in particular were noted for writing love letters to other girls and even having ceremonies to officiate their affections. Researchers noted different levels for such affections, some being invested in the system only to gain companionship or comfort while others progressed to sexual activity. For still others, same-sex sexual activity was "imported" from the outside. Some scholars borrowed terms from the lesbian community, such as "butch-femme," a performative dynamic between lesbians in which one partner would take a traditionally feminine role while the other would adopt a more masculine role (Ward & Kassebaum, 1965). Though later research tended to use the term "pseudofamily" less, the language of heterosexual relationships has continued to be used in more recent examples.

Inside these narratives, lesbians were often obfuscated under heteronormative descriptions of family structures, as well as a focus on behavior as opposed to identity. The relationships were cultural formations built by the inmates themselves. Whether or not a woman was physically attracted to another woman or identified as a lesbian or bisexual was not necessary knowledge for the system to work, nor did it necessarily change the dynamic itself. We know even less about how transgender men (FTM) might fit into incarcerated populations, for whom no significant qualitative or quantitative data exists to describe their experiences or how prison environments respond to them.

Between incarcerated men and women, the latter have been shown to have significantly less homophobic attitudes, and within incarcerated female populations, younger inmates or inmates who have served longer sentences appear to be less homophobic (Blackburn, Fowler, Mullings, & Marquart, 2011; Hensley, 2000). Race has also been implicated in social attitudes toward LGB persons, with nonwhite inmates being more accepting of same-sex sexual activity in others or participating in it themselves (Hensley, Tewksbury, & Koscheski, 2002).

Correctional Administration and LGBTQ Offenders

Concerns about violence, violation of sex prohibitions, and disruptions to the institutional order of prisons have long motivated administrators and correctional officers to treat LGBTQ inmates differently. Concurrently, shifting social norms outside of prison systems have created the expectation that sexual orientations and gender identities are legitimate categories deserving of respect and equal treatment. The combination of these two factors has made the handling of LGBTQ inmates a delicate and complicated issue. Recently, federal and state legislatures have taken an interest, providing both generic and specific requirements for the management of LGBTQ offenders, but policies between states, or between facilities within states, vary considerably. Nongovernment organizations, activists, and academics have called for reforms to provide better safety and equity in service (Center for American Progress, 2016; Hanssens et al., 2014; Lydon et al., 2015; Marksamer & Tobin, 2014; Sylvia Rivera Law Project, 2007)

One piece of legislation at the federal level is directly responsible for the formation of most of the current policies related to LGBTQ inmates. The Prison Rape Elimination Act (PREA) was passed in 2003 to set guidelines for state and federal agencies regarding the prevention of sexual victimization between inmates and misconduct between inmates and staff members. Compliance with PREA includes conducting mandatory reviews of every inmate as a potential victim or abuser, maintaining special allowances for reporting sexual victimization, and considering vulnerable populations in housing and other policy-making. PREA makes specific references to LGBTQ inmates as a vulnerable population and requires prison facilities to consider the sexual orientation and gender identity of inmates while ensuring access to programs and services. Unfortunately, PREA is far from evenly implemented and oversight and monitoring are scarce. As of the original compliance deadline (May 15, 2015), only 11 state correctional systems had obtained certifications, while an additional 34 gave assurance of intent to pursue compliance (Center for American Progress, 2016). The following section discusses the most frequently cited concerns for LGBTQ inmates and the development of policy surrounding them.

Housing and Violence Issues

As discussed earlier, LGBTQ inmates report disproportionately higher rates of sexual violence than other inmate groups, both at the hands of fellow inmates and from staff. Harassment, sexual misconduct by staff members, physical assault, and sexual assault all constitute clear threats to the safety of this population. With the mandate created by PREA to create a zero-tolerance environment for sexual victimization and every facility's vested interest in decreasing violence between inmates, addressing sexual assault and violence directed at LGBTQ inmates should be built in to current efforts to preserve order and safety.

The most common approach taken to protect LGBTQ inmates has been to modify housing assignments, though most prison facilities have little to no written policy instructing them to do so (Iyama, 2012). In theory, administrative segregation, solitary confinement, protective custody, and other forms of segregation separate potential victims from potential abusers. In many cases, this approach has led to indefinite periods of solitary confinement or otherwise segregating LGBTQ inmates against their will (Arkles, 2009; Gruberg, 2013; Hanssens et al., 2014; Marksamer & Tobin, 2014;. Smith & Yarussi, 2015; Sumner & Jenness, 2014). PREA expressly forbids the use of indefinite solitary confinement as a solution to safeguarding LGBTQ prisoners because of the detrimental effects long residences in solitary can have (Bureau of Justice Assistance [BJA], 2013). Additionally, while solitary confinement decreases the risk of abuse from fellow inmates, it increases the risk of experiencing misconduct from staff members, as well as reducing the likelihood of witnesses to help corroborate mistreatment and discrimination (Arkles, 2009; Iyama, 2012; Sylvia Rivera Law Project, 2007). As a result, some inmates find that solitary confinement does not make them safer—it merely changes the nature and direction of the threat. Segregation policies also severely limit the ability of inmates to access services and programming, which can delay parole eligibility dates and increase time served (Shay, 2013), thus raising the likelihood of inmates' experiencing the abuse such policies attempt to prevent.

A few facilities have attempted to implement special units for LGBTQ inmates, with varying degrees of success. Rikers Island in New York maintained a gay unit for decades until it was closed in 2005 because of security concerns regarding predatory inmates lying to enter the wing. More recently, they have opened a transgender unit specifically for those who identify as MTF. Similarly, in the Los Angeles County Jail, unit K6G (formally known as K11) is a segregated unit for gay men and transgender persons (Dolovich, 2011). Such units do not equate to solitary confinement, as residents can enter into programming, access services, and interact with each other. But residents are kept entirely separate from the rest of the general population, including being given separate time blocks for services. While PREA restricts segregation practices, so-called "gay units" have been allowed when it is shown to be the best way to protect inmates and ensure equal access to services.

Research on K6G has shown that inmates reported little or no sexual assault while in the unit, and those housed within felt safer than in general population (Dolovich, 2011). However, the approach of K6G has not been without criticism. The exclusion of bisexuals meant that some inmates who needed such protection could not get it. Also, K6G inmates wore uniforms with a different color, thereby broadcasting their sexual orientation or gender identity to the rest of the prison. Returning to general population would be extraordinarily unsafe, as they would be identified immediately. Entrance into K6G required an interview with officers who tested them on stereotypically gay information, including local gay clubs, popular culture, and sexual experiences (Robinson, 2011). Inmates that may not fit into the gay community, come from outside the area, are sexually inexperienced, or have remained closeted may not be equipped to pass such an examination, effectively limiting entrants to those who fit into the stereotypes held by the interviewers. Finally, the act of isolating gay and transgender inmates removed the possibility of collaboration and community building between groups of inmates, which have been shown to happen outside of segregated units (Arkles, 2009; Jenness & Fenstermaker, 2013). Overall, the experience of K6G highlights the limitations of segregation, which does not resolve the origins of violence or sexual abuse but merely keeps victims out of immediate arm's reach.

Housing and Transgender Inmates

Safe housing is an important issue for all inmates and is confounded by the presence of transgender inmates. Most prison and jail facilities house inmates based on biological sex (male or female). Transgender inmates complicate the sex/gender binary that staff members rely on to select appropriate housing. A conflict appears for officers at intake immediately: where should a transgender or gender nonconforming person be housed? Needing to know the biological sex of a transgender person for housing assignment has led some staff to force these offenders to confirming genital status by with a strip search (Arkles, 2009; Iyama, 2012; Marksamer & Tobin, 2014; Shay, 2013). Strip searches for this purpose have been banned by PREA as degrading and inhumane (BJA, 2013).

Regardless of gender identity or expression, most transgender inmates are housed in accordance with the markers on their birth certificates (Center for American Progress, 2016). As a result of this practice, only a small percentage of transgender women would be able to house with bio-born women, as birth certificates in most states can only be altered after sex reassignment surgery, a prohibitively expensive procedure that not all transgender women want. Instead, they are housed with men regardless of transition progress or gender identity. As with gay or bisexual men, transgender inmates are commonly placed in solitary confinement for their own safety and, as has been discussed above, to their detriment. PREA recommends that every transgender person be evaluated on a case-by-case basis for the purposes of housing but does not recommend specific criteria for such decisions (BJA, 2013).

Outside of LGBTQ units, some counties and organizations are advocating for housing inmates by gender identity. San Francisco County, for example, recommends that transgender women (MTF) be housed in women's units while transgender men (FTM) be housed as vulnerable males (Scheel & Eustace, 2002). Fears of transgender women who have not had sex reassignment surgery engaging in sexual intercourse with bio-born female prisoners have not been confirmed. Serious concerns remain for transgender men, who may be victimized in the more aggressive environment of the men's prison yard. Housing by gender identity is a rare policy, but one that has the support of LGBTQ activists and organizations. No data exists to evaluate gender identity placement as a policy. Outside of gender identity approaches, some counties have instituted committees that review the cases of transgender inmates, often including community members experienced in dealing with transgender issues (Massachusetts Department of Corrections, 2016; Denver Sheriff's Department, 2012). A team approach creates an environment in which each case can be discussed in detail and provides checks and balances to the decision-making process (Marksamer & Tobin, 2014).

Correctional Staff and LGBTQ Offenders

The concepts of sexual orientation and gender identity remain contentious in the United States, with traditional social norms proscribing same-sex sexual activity and holding gender transition in contempt. Correctional staff may often carry these values into their dealings with LGBTQ inmates; 70% of these inmates report experiencing discrimination and verbal harassment from staff members (Lydon et al., 2015). The effect of negative attitudes can also be indirect. Of the respondents to an independent study of LGBTQ inmates, 76% of those who had been sexually assaulted by another prisoner indicated that prison staff had "intentionally placed them in situations where they would be at high risk of being sexually assaulted" (Lydon et al., 2015, p. 42).

Studies of correctional officers have shown that personal values affect how they interact with inmates. Of particular importance to LGBTQ inmates, correctional officers have a changing definition of rape or assault when a gay inmate is reporting the victimization, implying that some officers believe any sexual contact with a gay inmate to be consensual (Eigenberg, 2000). Staff members may also begin to adopt prison culture norms that place gay men and transgender women in feminine roles, expecting them to be receptive to other inmates' sexual advances. Such attitudes can exacerbate issues of sexual assault reports being documented and investigated in accordance with PREA regulations (BJA, 2013). Additionally, staff are often unaware of current norms regarding the use of gendered pronouns in reference to transgender inmates (Marksamer & Tobin, 2014; Smith, 2006; Sylvia Rivera Law Project, 2007). Referring to a transgender woman as "he" is generally interpreted as a sign of disrespect and can be viewed as transphobic harassment if maintained in spite of requests to use female pronouns. Individual staff members may feel that they should not have to adjust their own behavior for the sake of inmates' sensibilities, but the mental health consequences for these inmates, many of whom regularly suffer derision and harassment, can be significant, and damaging to the stability and productivity of staff-inmate relations.

Services and Medical Care

LGBTQ inmates have a history of being denied services and care in corrections facilities. The use of solitary confinement to protect gay and transgender inmates block many from accessing programming that could shorten prison terms. Even in general population, LGBTQ inmates tend to have less programming available to them (Iyama, 2012). The structure and process of visitation approval and other outside communication similarly become problematic, as many of the intimate connections shared between LGBTQ inmates and their loved ones are not bound by legally recognized relationships. Children, partners, and familial bonds may have no legal status, or even official surname or blood-relation legitimacy. Visitors have also experienced harsh treatment, from limitations or denial regarding inmate contact to, in extreme cases, violence from guards (Center for American Progress, 2016).

Similarly, access to medical and mental health care have been challenging for LGBTQ people, who generally experience difficulty in finding providers who are knowledgeable and sensitive to their specific needs. Expertise in subjects like HIV management is becoming increasingly specialized, and few doctors focus on it, but such expertise can be vital to LGBTQ inmates, who are disproportionately positive. Consistent access to the appropriate antiretrovirals is essential, and prison facilities have sometimes failed to ensure consistency of care (Gido, 2002). Furthermore, selective practices for HIV-positive patients, such as requiring an infirmary appearance for every dose, can reveal their diagnosis to other inmates, putting such patients at risk of assault or harassment by fellow inmates (Lydon et al., 2015).

For those nonheterosexual inmates who engage in sex, access to HIV testing and protection is limited. The risk for contracting HIV is 2.4 times higher for prison inmates than in the general population (Marksamer & Tobin, 2014). As not all sexual contact is consensual, tighter controls on sexual behavior offer scant protection. Most facilities offer testing on intake, but may not do so later. Condoms are rarely available for inmates, though pilot programs in some units have shown almost no misuse by inmates, no increase in overall sexual activity, and an increase in safe sex practices (Butler, Richters, Yap, & Donovan, 2013; Hensley, Tewksbury, & Wright, 2001; Knowles, 1999; May & Williams, 2002; Yap et al., 2007). Though providing condoms and more competent HIV care would benefit all inmates, such policies would disproportionately improve the lives of LGBTQ inmates.

Medical Care Issues for Transgender Inmates

Transgender inmates have additional medical needs that many providers and correctional staff are unprepared to address. Transition services are those medical interventions that allow transgender persons to modify their bodies in response to a diagnosis of gender dysphoria (formerly Gender Identity Disorder [GID]). The most common transition service is hormone replacement therapy (HRT), in which hormone levels in the body are readjusted to match the patient's preferred sex. Hormone levels must be monitored with blood tests and adjusted throughout the process. HRT treatments are then given via injection or daily oral medications. State correctional systems have responded differently to requests for transition services, but few have followed through entirely. Some facilities outright rejected providing services, while others "froze" dosages at prescribed levels on entry (Brown & McDuffie, 2009; Iyama, 2012; Sumner & Jenness, 2014). As of 2015, almost half of states allowed for transgender inmates to continue HRT, and 13 states allow inmates to begin HRT while incarcerated (Routh et al., 2015). In recent years, courts have upheld that denying or freezing HRT treatments—even for those requesting to start them in prison—constitute medical indifference and violates the Eighth Amendment (Smith & Yarussi, 2015). Prisons are required to provide medically necessary treatment, which includes HRT when an inmate experiences clear and consistent gender dysphoria. More controversial is the idea of allowing inmates to receive sex reassignment surgery (SRS) while in prison as part of a gender dysphoria treatment plan. In 2012, the first SRS was approved for an inmate in state prison (Gilbert, 2013). While SRS is not sought by all transgender people, some may see it as the final step in a legitimate, medically necessary transition. The extent to which prisons will make this procedure available to inmates in the future is uncertain.

As with all incarcerated offenders, privacy and respect for identity are important for transgender individuals regardless of the context. Presenting themselves in the attire of their preferred gender, having access to the appropriate toiletries and grooming supplies, and being appropriately gendered by inmates and staff are key components of effective treatment for transgender inmates (Sylvia Rivera Law Project, 2007). Safety in areas where inmates shower and use toiletries is a notorious issue in a prison environment, and especially important for transgender inmates. While these practical concerns may seem small by comparison to medical interventions like HRT, the daily needs that allow transgender inmates to manage their appearance and bodies safely and in ways fitting their gender identity should be understood as part of effective inmate management.

Recommendations and Directions for Future Study

Activists, former inmates, NGOs, and even some aspects of federal, state, and local governments have made recommendations to the broader custodial system regarding LGBTQ offenders in prisons. A complete set of best practices is beyond the scope of this text, and no agency has constructed definitive guidelines for the handling of LGBTQ inmates; however, based on various reports and scholarship on the subject, we have included the recommendations for prisons and jails most supported by current knowledge on the subject.

- **Become PREA compliant:** Most states are not certified complaint with PREA's final regulations (Center for American Progress, 2016). Some of the most egregious and harmful violations suffered by LGBTQ inmates are addressed by this law. Incorporating all PREA recommendations into facility policy and training staff appropriately may have a significant impact on LGBTQ inmates.
- **Support HIV prevention programs:** Making condoms accessible to inmates protects them from contracting harmful diseases. LGBTQ inmates are at an increased risk of contracting HIV and other infections from sexual assaults and consensual sexual activities. Contrary to critics, research shows that providing condoms does not increase sexual activity, just safe sexual activity (Butler et al., 2013; Gido, 2002; Hensley, Tewksbury, & Wright, 2001; May & Williams, 2002; Sylvia Rivera Law Project, 2007; Yap et al., 2007).
- **Create or update policies regarding LGBTQ inmate housing:** Many facilities have no policy related to housing gender nonconforming or nonheterosexual inmates. Others rely on excessive levels of segregation that violate PREA regulations. Housing options should be considered for sexual and gender identity minorities that balance safety with access to resources (Center for American Progress, 2016; Iyama, 2012; Marksamer & Tobin, 2014; Smith & Yarussi, 2015).
- **Ensure equity of service:** LGBTQ inmates are entitled to the same services that other inmates receive at their level of confinement. Access to programming, education, and facility resources should not be lost to ensure safety in most cases (Denver Sheriff's Department, 2012; Hanssens et al., 2014; Scheel & Eustace, 2002; Sylvia Rivera Law Project, 2007).
- **Provide staff training:** Correctional officers, free staff, and administrators should be trained on how to handle special needs populations, including LGBTQ inmates (Center for American Progress, 2016).
- **Provide complete medical care:** Health care providers and mental health providers in prison facilities should be prepared to competently address the particular needs and risks associated

with LGBTQ identities in their facilities, including HIV prevention and transition services like HRT (Center for American Progress, 2016; Marksamer& Tobin, 2014; Massachusetts Department of Corrections, 2016; Smith & Yarussi, 2015; Scheel & Eustace, 2002; Sylvia Rivera Law Project, 2007).

- **Establish written policies regarding LGBTQ inmates**: From intake onward, prison and jail facilities should have detailed, written policies in place outlining how LGBTQ inmates are to be managed. Policies should be updated as needed and should contain input from community members (Center for American Progress, 2016; Denver Sheriff's Department, 2012; Hanssens et al., 2014; Iyama, 2012; Marksamer & Tobin, 2014).
- **Institutionalize respect for gender identity:** All inmates should have access to toiletries, clothes, undergarments, grooming supplies, and other gendered supplies based on their gender identity. Preferred gender pronouns should be recognized by staff. Consideration of gender identity should begin at intake and remain consistent throughout an inmate's prison sentence (Hanssens et al., 2014; Lydon et al., 2015; Sylvia Rivera Law Project, 2007).
- **Reconsider the rationale for banning consensual sex between inmates:** Many jails and prisons ban all sexual activity in response to PREA regulations. Doing so eliminates questions of consent when prosecuting potential assault cases. Some further argue that there can be no consent in a prison environment. However, such policies can also have unintended consequences, such as the criminalization of survival strategies or extending sentences for inmates because of sexual conduct that inflicted no harm on either involved. The decision to maintain or eliminate a ban on all sexual activity between inmates should include both intended and unintended consequences in the decision-making process (Hanssens et al., 2014; Lydon et al., 2015; Smith, 2006; Sylvia Rivera Law Project, 2007).

Conclusion

Unfortunately, the body of literature on LGBTQ offenders is thin, making a strong set of evidence-based practices largely out of reach for current correctional professionals. The Bureau of Justice Statistics does not release data from the NIS outside of summary form, so researchers are presently unable to make more complex inquiries from the results. The questions associated with LGBTQ identity are far from comprehensive and only address a few potential identities, leaving what information we have as partial images of inmate experiences. Furthermore, the focus on sexual victimization obfuscates issues of desire and consensual behavior in prison settings. Any study hoping to address accurately sexual experiences in prison, LGBTQ or otherwise, must include a more nuanced view of sexuality that is not merely coercive. In addition to expanding the survey questions regarding gender identity and sexual orientation, a broader effort to do thorough, valid evaluation research on policies and programs meant to address this population is strongly recommended. Individual or short-term successes can suggest potential best practices, but without effective evaluation research to address outcomes, any sort of consensus on what works with this population generally will remain elusive.

References

Alarid, L. F. (2000). Sexual orientation perspectives of incarcerated bisexual and gay men: The county jail protective custody experience. *The Prison Journal*, *80*(1), 80–95. doi:10.1177/0032885500080001005

Arkles, G. (2009). Safety and solidarity across gender lines: Rethinking segregation of transgender people in detention. *Temple Political & Civil Rights Law Review*, *18*(2), 515–560.

Arkles, G. (2015). Regulating prison sexual violence. *Northeastern University Law Journal*, 7, 69.

Beck, A. J. (2014). *Supplemental tables: Prevalence of sexual victimization among transgender adult inmates*. Washington, DC: U.S. Department of Justice, Bureau of Justice Statistics.

Beck, A. J., Berzofsky, M., Caspar, R., & Krebs, C. (2013). *Sexual victimization in prisons and jails reported by inmates, 2011–2012.* Washington, DC: U.S. Department of Justice, Bureau of Justice Statistics.

Beck, A. J., Cantor, D., Hartge, J., & Smith, T. (2013). *Sexual victimization in juvenile facilities reported by youth, 2012.* Washington, DC: U.S. Department of Justice, Bureau of Justice Statistics.

Beck, A. J., Rantala, R. R., & Rexroat, J. (2014). *Sexual victimization reported by adult correctional authorities, 2009–2011.* Washington, DC: U.S. Department of Justice, Bureau of Justice Statistics.

Blackburn, A. G., Mullings, J. L., & Marquart, J. W. (2008). Sexual assault in prison and beyond toward an understanding of lifetime sexual assault among incarcerated women. *The Prison Journal, 88*(3), 351–377. doi:10.1177/0032885508322443

Blackburn, A. G., Fowler, S. K., Mullings, J. L., & Marquart, J. W. (2011). Too close for comfort: Exploring gender differences in inmate attitudes toward homosexuality in prison. *American Journal of Criminal Justice, 36*(1), 58–72. doi:10.1007/s12103-010-9099-6

Brown, G. R., & McDuffie, E. (2009). Health care policies addressing transgender inmates in prison systems in the United States. *Journal of Correctional Health Care, 15*(4), 1–12. doi:10.1177/1078345809340423

Buffman, P. C. (2004). *Homosexuality in prisons.* Honolulu, HI: University Press of the Pacific.

Bureau of Justice Assistance. (2013). *PREA compliance measures handbook.* Washington, DC: U.S. Department of Justice, Bureau of Justice Assistance.

Butler, T., Richters, J., Yap, L., & Donovan, B. (2013). Condoms for prisoners: No evidence that they increase sex in prison, but they increase safe sex. *Sexually Transmitted Infections, 89*(5), 377–379. doi:10.1136/sextrans-2012-050856

Center for American Progress. (2016). *Unjust: How the broken criminal justice system fails LGBTQ people.* Washington, DC: Center for American Progress.

Davis, G. (2015). *Contesting intersex: The dubious diagnosis.* New York, NY: NYU Press.

Davis, G., Dewey, J. M., & Murphy, E. L. (2016). Giving sex deconstructing intersex and trans medicalization practices. *Gender & Society, 30*(3), 490–514. doi:10.1177/0891243215602102

Dennis, J. P. (2014). The LGBTQ offender. In D. Peterson & V. R. Panfil (Eds.), *Handbook of LGBTQ communities, crime, and justice* (pp. 87–101). New York, NY: Springer.

Denver Sheriff's Department. (2012). *Transgender and gender variant inmates.* Denver, CO: Denver Sheriff.

Dolovich, S. (2011). Strategic segregation in the modern prison. *American Criminal Law Review, 48*(1), 11–22.

Eigenberg, H. M. (1992). Homosexuality in male prisons: Demonstrating the need for a social constructionist approach. *Criminal Justice Review, 17*(2), 219–234. doi:10.1177/073401689201700204

Eigenberg, H. M. (2000). Correctional officers' definitions of rape in male prisons. *Journal of Criminal Justice, 28*(5), 435–449. doi:10.1016/S0047-2352(00)00057-X

Flanagan, T. J., Marquart, J. W., & Adams, K. G. (1998). *Incarcerating criminals: Prisons and jails in social and organizational context.* New York, NY: Oxford University Press.

Gates, G. L., & Newport, F. (2012). Special Report: 3.4% of U.S. Adults Identify as LGBTQ. *Gallup.* Retrieved from www.gallup.com/poll/158066/special-report-adults-identify-LGBTQ.aspx

Grant, J. M., Mottet, L., Tanis, J. E., Harrison, J., Herman, J., & Keisling, M. (2011). *Injustice at every turn: A report of the national transgender discrimination survey.* Washington, DC: National Center for Transgender Equality.

Gibson, L. E., & Hensley, C. (2013). The social construction of sexuality in prison. *The Prison Journal, 93*(3), 355–370. doi:10-1177/0032885513490503

Gido, R. L. (2002). Inmates with HIV/AIDS: A growing concern. In C. Hensley (Ed.), *Prison sex: Practice & policy* (pp. 101–110). Boulder, CO: Lynne Rienner Publishers.

Gilbert, L. V. (2013). Crossing the line: Examining sex reassignment surgery for transsexual prisoners in the wake of Kosilek v. Spencer. *Southern California Review of Law and Social Justice, 23*(1), 29–58.

GLAAD. (2016). *GLAAD media reference guide* (10th ed.). Retrieved from www.glaad.org/sites/default/files/GLAAD-Media-Reference-Guide-Tenth-Edition.pdf

Gruberg, S. (2013). *Dignity denied: LGBTQ immigrants in US immigration detention.* Washington, DC: Center for American Progress. Retrieved from www.americanprogress.org/wp-content/uploads/2013/11/ImmigrationEnforcement.pdf

Guidotto, N. (2011). Looking back: The bathhouse raids in Toronto, 1981. In E. A. Stanley & N. Smith (Eds.), *Captive genders: Trans embodiment and the prison industrial complex* (pp. 69–82). Oakland, CA: AK Press.

Hanssens, C., Moodie-Mills, A. C., Ritchie, A. J., Spade, D., & Vaid, U. (2014). *A roadmap for change: Federal policy recommendations for addressing the criminalization of LGBTQ people and people living with HIV.* New York, NY: Center for Gender & Sexuality Law at Columbia Law School.

Heffernan, E. (1972). *Making it in prison: The square, the cool, and the life.* New York, NY: Wiley Interscience.

Hensley, C. (2000). Attitudes toward homosexuality in a male and female prison: An exploratory study. *The Prison Journal, 80*(4), 434–441. doi:10.1177/0032885500080004008

Hensley, C. (2002). *Prison sex: Practice and policy*. Boulder, CO: Lynne Reinner Publishers.
Hensley, C., Struckman-Johnson, C., & Eigenberg, H. M. (2000). Introduction: The history of prison sex research. *The Prison Journal, 80*(4), 360–367. doi:10.1177/0032885500080004002
Hensley, C., & Tewksbury, R. (2002). Inmate-to-inmate prison sexuality: A review of empirical studies. *Trauma, Violence, & Abuse, 3*(3), 226–243. doi:10.1177/15248380020033005
Hensley, C., Tewksbury, R., & Koscheski, M. (2002). The characteristics and motivations behind female prison sex. *Women & Criminal Justice, 13*(2–3), 125–139. doi:10.1300/J012v13n02_07
Hensley, C., Tewksbury, R., & Wright, J. (2001). Exploring the dynamics of masturbation and consensual same-sex activity within a male maximum security prison. *The Journal of Men's Studies, 10*(1), 59–71. doi:10.3149/jms.1001.59
Human Rights Campaign. (2016). *Growing up LGBTQ in America: HRC Youth Survey report key findings*. Washington, DC: Human Rights Campaign.
Iyama, K. (2012). We have tolled the bell for him: An analysis of the Prison Rape Elimination Act and California's compliance as it applies to transgender inmates. *Tulane Journal of Law and Sexuality, 21*, 23–48.
Jenness, V., & Fenstermaker, S. (2013). Agnes goes to prison: Gender authenticity, transgender inmates in prisons for men, and pursuit of "the real deal." *Gender & Society, 28*(1), 5–31. doi:10.1177/0891243213499446
Knowles, G. J. (1999). Male prison rape: A search for causation and prevention. *The Howard Journal of Criminal Justice, 38*(3), 267–282. doi:10.1111/1468-2311.00132
Kunzel, R. (2008). *Criminal intimacy: Prison and the uneven history of modern American sexuality*. Chicago, IL: University of Chicago Press.
Lawrence v. Texas, 539 U.S. 558 (2003).
Lydon, J., Carrington, K., Low, H., Miller, R., & Yazdy, M. (2015). Coming out of concrete closets: A report on Black & Pink's National LGBTQ Prisoner Survey. Dorchester, MA: Black & Pink.
Mallett, C. A. (2016). The school-to-prison pipeline: Disproportionate impact on vulnerable children and adolescents. *Education and Urban Society, 49*(6), 1–30. doi:10.1177/0013124516644053
Marksamer, J., & Tobin, H. J. (2014). *Standing with LGBTQ prisoners: An advocate's guide to ending abuse and combating imprisonment*. Washington, DC: National Center on Transgender Equality.
Massachusetts Department of Corrections. (2016). *Identification, treatment and correctional management of inmates diagnosed with gender dysphoria*. Retrieved from www.mass.gov/eopss/docs/doc/policies/652.pdf
May, J. P., & Williams Jr., E. L. (2002). Acceptability of condom availability in a US jail. *AIDS Education and Prevention, 14*(5 Suppl), 85–91. doi:10.1521/aeap.14.7.85.23863
Mecca, T. A. (2011). Brushes with lily law. In E. A. Stanley & N. Smith (Eds.), *Captive genders: Trans embodiment and the prison industrial complex* (pp. 63–68). Oakland, CA: AK Press.
Mogul, J. L., Ritchie, A. J., & Whitlock, K. (2011). *Queer (in)justice: The criminalization of LGBTQ people in the United States*. Boston, MA: Beacon Press.
National Prison Rape Elimination Commission. (2009). *National prison rape elimination commission report*. Washington, DC: National Prison Rape Elimination Commission. Retrieved from www.ncjrs.gov/pdffiles1/226680.pdf
Okamura, A. (2011). Equality behind bars: Improving the legal protections of transgender inmates in the California prison systems. *Hastings Race & Poverty Law Journal, 8*, 109.
Propper, A. M. (1981). *Prison homosexuality: Myth and reality*. Toronto, Canada: Lexington Books.
Ricciardelli, R., Grills, S., & Craig, A. (2016). Constructions and negotiations of sexuality in Canadian federal men's prisons. *Journal of Homosexuality, 63*(12), 1–25. doi:10.1080/00918369.2016.1158010
Rideau, W. (1979, November/December). Prison: The sexual jungle. *Angolite*, 51–78.
Robinson, R. K. (2011). Masculinity as prison: Sexual identity, race, and incarceration. *California Law Review, 99*, 1309–1408.
Routh, D., Abess, G., Makin, D., Stohr, M. K., Hemmens, C., & Yoo, J. (2015). Transgender inmates in prisons: A review of applicable statutes and policies. *International Journal of Offender Therapy and Comparative Criminology, 61*(6), 1–22. doi:10.1177/0306624X15603745
Sagarin, E. (1976). Prison homosexuality and its effect on post-prison sexual behavior. *Psychiatry, 39*(3), 245–257. doi:10.1080/00332747.1976.11023894
Scheel, M. D., & Eustace, C. (2002). *Model protocols on the treatment of transgender persons by San Francisco County Jail*. San Francisco: National Lawyers Guild and City and County of San Francisco Human Rights Commission. Retrieved from www.prisonlegalnews.org/media/publications/model_protocols_on_the_treatment_of_transgender_persons_by_san_francisco_county_jail_nlg_and_city_and_county_of_san_francisco_hrc_2002.pdf.pdf
Schreier Lyseggen, K. (Ed.). (2015). *The women of San Quentin: Soul murder of transgender women in male prisons*. Berkeley, CA: SFINX Publishing.

Selling, L. S. (1931). The pseudofamily. *American Journal of Sociology, 37*(2), 247–253.
Shay, G. (2013). PREA's elusive promise: Can DOJ regulations protect LGBTQ incarcerated people. *Loyola Journal of Public Interest Law, 15*, 343.
Sit, V., & Ricciardelli, R. (2013). Constructing and performing sexualities in the penitentiaries attitudes and behaviors among male prisoners. *Criminal Justice Review, 38*(3), 335–353. doi:10.1177/0734016813491965
Smith, B. V. (2006). Rethinking prison sex: Self-expression and safety. *Columbia Journal of Gender and Law, 15*, 1–36.
Smith, B. V., & Yarussi, J. M. (2015). *Policy review and development guide: Lesbian, gay, bisexual, transgender, and intersex persons in custodial settings* (2nd ed.). Washington, DC: National Institute of Corrections.
Stryker, S., & Whittle, S. (Eds.). (2006). *The transgender studies reader*. New York, NY: Routledge.
Sumner, J., & Jenness, V. (2014). Gender integration in sex-segregated US prisons: The paradox of transgender correctional policy. In D. Peterson & V. R. Panfil (Eds.), *Handbook of LGBTQ communities, crime, and justice* (pp. 229–259). New York, NY: Springer.
Sykes, G. M. (1958). *The society of captives: A study of a maximum security prison*. Princeton, NJ: Princeton University Press.
Sylvia Rivera Law Project. (2007). *"Its war in here": A report on the treatment of transgender and intersex people in New York State Men's Prisons*. New York, NY: Sylvia Rivera Law Project. Retrieved from http://srlp.org/files/warinhere.pdf
Tewksbury, R., & West, A. (2000). Research on sex in prison during the late 1980s and early 1990s. *The Prison Journal, 80*(4), 368–378. doi:10.1177/0032885500080004003
Understanding Issues Faced by LGBTQ Americans. (2014). Retrieved from www.LGBTQmap.org/file/understanding-issues-facing-LGBTQ-americans.pdf
Van Wormer, K. (1984). Becoming homosexual in prison: A socialization process. *Criminal Justice Review, 9*(1), 22–27. doi:10.1177/073401688400900104
Ward, D. A., & Kassebaum, G. G. (1965). *Women's prisons*. London, UK: Weidenfeld and Nicolson.
Wardenski, J. J. (2005). A minor exception?: The impact of Lawrence v. Texas on LGBTQ youth. *The Journal of Criminal Law and Criminology (1973–), 95*(4), 1363–1410.
Wooden, W. S., & Parker, J. (1982). *Men behind bars: Sexual exploitation in prison*. New York, NY: De Capo Press.
Yap, L., Butler, T., Richters, J., Kirkwood, K., Grant, L., Saxby, M., & Donovan, B. (2007). Do condoms cause rape and mayhem? The long-term effects of condoms in New South Wales' prisons. *Sexually Transmitted Infections, 83*(3), 219–222. doi:10.1136/sti.2006.022996

11

INCARCERATING THE HOMELESS

Risk Factors and Promising Strategies for Reentry

Shelley J. Listwan, Laura Barber, and Deborah Koetzle

> We know that the unsheltered homeless—especially those living with mental illness and/or addiction—are more likely to be incarcerated, hospitalized or in treatment.
>
> —*Muzzy Rosenblatt, Executive Director, Bowery Residents Committee*
> (Rosenblatt, 2016)

Introduction

Since 1973, the rate of imprisonment has grown from 110 prison inmates per 100,000 United States' residents to 478 (Petersilia, 2003). On any given day, there are 2.2 million individuals incarcerated in prisons and jails across the United States. In addition, it is estimated that over 800,000 people will cycle through local jails per year. Given an estimated 93% of all inmates will eventually return to society (Petersilia, 2003), the successful reintegration of such a vast number of offenders from both jails and prisons is an important challenge.

The failure rates among those reentering the community from prisons and jails are high. Ex-inmates are often mandated to find and maintain housing, become employed, stay free of drugs, and regularly report to their parole officer (Bahr, Harris, Fisher, & Harker, 2010). Violating any of these conditions can, and often does, result in reincarceration. One study found that approximately two-thirds of those who are released from jails and prisons are rearrested within three years, and three-fourths will be rearrested within five years (Durose, Cooper, & Snyder, 2014). Most rearrests occur within the first six months of release (Petersilia, 2000), and this number is especially high for African-American populations (Carson & Gollinelli, 2013).

Individuals returning to the community have a variety of needs, including a lack of permanent housing. Homelessness in general is a pervasive problem in the United States, with the Housing and Urban Development (HUD) estimating that in January 2006, 759,101 individuals were homeless. Of those, 331,000 (44%) were unsheltered, and one-fifth met the federal definition for chronic homelessness (Rickards et al., 2010). The National Alliance to End Homelessness's point-in-time counts estimate that currently over 500,000 Americans are homeless on any given night, and an estimated 1.6 million people access homeless shelters each year (Henry, Cortes, Shivji, & Buck, 2014). Approximately 124,000 homeless people are chronically homeless, which the Department of Housing and Urban Development's defines as "someone who has experienced homelessness for a year or longer, or who has experienced at least four episodes of homelessness in the last three years and has a (physical or mental) disability" (Henry et al., 2014, p. 2). A member of this chronic homeless population is more likely to be male and middle aged, has a substance abuse and mental health problem, and tends to be a frequent user of emergency services, jails, and shelters (Henry et al., 2014; Rickards et al., 2010).

The intersection between homeless and incarceration is clear. Metraux and Culhane (2004) found that in New York City, approximately 11% of released offenders used homeless shelters in the two months following release, and that shelter use increased the risk of recidivism among those studied. A substantial proportion of the jail population identified as homeless as well (McNiel, Binder, & Robinson, 2005). Greenberg and Rosenheck (2008b) found that 15.3% of the jail population was homeless and that "recent homelessness was 7.5 to 11.3 times more common among jail inmates than in the general population" (p. 170). McNiels and colleagues (2005) argue, "jails are de facto assuming responsibility for a population whose needs span multiple service delivery systems" (McNiel et al., 2005, p. 840). A variety of factors contribute to the fact that adult state and federal prisoners have a homeless rate that is four to six times higher than the general population (Greenberg & Rosenheck, 2008a). In particular, the incarcerated homeless are more likely to have mental health and substance abuse problems and be unemployed.

Complex Needs among Homeless and Incarcerated Populations

Studies suggest that certain criminogenic needs increase the risk for recidivism (see Bonta & Andrews, 2007). Although homelessness is not identified as a core criminogenic need identified, we know that it can place the client at greater risk of recidivism through its interaction with these needs. The intersection between homelessness and other important criminogenic needs are discussed next.

Substance Abuse

Over half of those in state and federal prisons admit to using drugs in the month before their offense, and approximately 20% to 30% used drugs at the time of their offense (Mumola & Karberg, 2007). Also, about two-thirds of men and women report active substance abuse in the six months before their incarceration (Mallik-Kane & Visher, 2008). Forty-five percent of federal prisoners and 53% of state prisoners meet the criteria for drug dependence and abuse, according to the DSM-IV (Mumola & Karberg, 2007).

Substance abuse poses a significant challenge for those reentering the community. Released offenders with substance abuse problems are more likely to live with people who pose a risk to their reentry. One-third of men and one-half of women with substance abuse problems were living with former prisoners or individuals with a substance abuse issue as well (Mallik-Kane & Visher, 2008). Prison-based treatment can be effective; offenders who participate in a substance abuse treatment are less likely to return to prison than those who do not (Bahr et al., 2010). However, fewer than 5% of all prison inmates received substance abuse treatment (Petersilia, 2003), and the provision of substance abuse treatment is even less postrelease (Mallik-Kane & Visher, 2008).

Substance abuse results in a number of negative consequences among parolees. Individuals with a preprison substance abuse problem have poorer outcomes with regard to housing, employment, and recidivism. Also, this group is more likely to participate in criminal activity following release and more likely to be reincarcerated than other returning prisoners (Mallik-Kane & Visher, 2008). Individuals who use illegal drugs become "involved in a variety of crimes, such as possession of an illegal substance, possession with intent to distribute, possession of drug paraphernalia, selling of drugs, writing bad checks, and various types of theft and fraud" (Bahr et al., 2010, p. 685). Substance use negatively affects health and family relationships and increases the risk of homelessness (Fries, Fedock, & Kubiak, 2014; Mallik-Kane & Visher, 2008).

In addition to increasing the risk of homelessness, substance abuse increases the risk for adult *first-time* homelessness (Thompson, Wall, Greenstein, Grant, & Hasin, 2013). Drug use both precedes the onset of homelessness and is "independently associated with homelessness" (Shelton, Taylor, Bonner, & van den Bree, 2009, p. 470). One policy that has increased the risk of homelessness among substance abusers is the Public Law 104–121 of 1996, which ended Supplemental Security Income (SSI) benefits to "individuals disabled primarily by a substance-use disorder" (Thompson et al., 2013, p. 285). Another is the Housing Opportunity Extension Act of 1996, which compels public housing organizations to allow their lessors to evict tenants or guests who engage in a drug-related crime (Thompson et al., 2013). Many housing programs require sobriety before placement can occur. However, there is little to no evidence that making clients seek substance abuse treatment or be sober pre-housing helps their ability to maintain or obtain housing (Tsemberis, Gulcur, & Nakae, 2004).

Mental Health

Approximately one in five inmates reports having a mental illness, including schizophrenia/psychosis, major depression, bipolar disorder, and posttraumatic stress disorder (Petersilia, 2000). Homelessness within jail populations has been linked to mental health and substance abuse issues. For example, 22% of homeless individuals in the San Francisco County Jail had a psychiatric diagnosis, and close to 18% had a substance-related disorder, compared to roughly 16% and 12% of the nonhomeless population, respectively (McNiel et al., 2005). This is salient when one considers that approximately 15% of those with mental illness are homeless in a given year compared to 1% of the general population (Slate, Buffington-Vollum, & Johnson, 2013).

The relationship between homelessness and mental illness appears to be reciprocal and persistent in nature. While "having a mental illness places an individual at heightened risk of become homeless . . . being homeless contributes to and exacerbates one's mental illness" (Slate et al., 2013, p. 79). Those with mental illness report higher preprison homelessness rates as well as higher rates of homelessness after incarceration (Mallik-Kane & Visher, 2008).

In addition to being related to homelessness, having mental illness is related to recidivism. At least 80% of offenders returning to incarceration have a chronic physical, mental, and/or substance abuse problem. This issue is even greater for women; over 40% of men and 70% of women were likely to have a mental illness. Other reports indicate that 25% of those returning may have an undiagnosed mental illness (Slate et al., 2013).

Despite the negative consequences of mental illness, very few individuals receive the types of services needed. In 2000, about one in eight state prisoners, or 79% of those mentally ill, received counseling services or therapy. Unfortunately, the medication and counseling that begins in prison is often not continued once they are released (Petersilia, 2003). Only about one-third of ex-offenders with mental illness receive any discharge planning services (Slate et al., 2013). Roughly 75% of probation programs do not have specialized programs for those with a mental illness (Petersilia, 2003). As argued by Slate and colleagues (2013, p. 448),

> discharge protocols that fail to provide a network of support for released offenders with mental illness can only result in the continued recycling of person with mental illnesses through the criminal justice system and needless suffering for these individuals and society.

Employment

Like substance abuse, a lack of employment is also associated with a number of negative consequences, including both recidivism and homelessness. Postrelease employment is significantly associated with successful reintegration while decreasing an ex-offender's chance of recidivism. However, while two-thirds of ex-prisoners report having employment before incarceration, most offenders have difficulty finding a job afterwards (Visher & Kachnowski, 2007). About 75% of ex-offenders remain unemployed up to a year after release (Pager, 2007). "[Although] Congress, various states, and some courts have supported the principle that steps should be taken to integrate ex-offenders back into society, the vast majority of laws legalize employment discrimination based on conviction or arrest records," according to Harris and Keller (2005, p. 11).

Barriers to postrelease employment may be both direct and indirect. Direct barriers are those that are in the various statutes and occupational guidelines, such as public employment positions, which require employers to eliminate candidates with criminal convictions or certain arrest records (Harris & Keller, 2005). Indirect barriers involve the inability to obtain proper documentation for employment. Many offenders and those who are chronically homeless do not have access to their Social Security card, driver's license, or birth certificate (Petersilia, 2003). Many times, these individuals seek jobs on the "spot market," where they are only given temporary or seasonal work instead of permanent employment because of their perceived untrustworthiness (Petersilia, 2003).

Another obstruction to finding employment is the personal bias of employers to hire ex-offenders or homeless. Over 40% of employers stated they would "probably not" or "definitely not" be willing to hire someone with a criminal record, and only 20% indicated that they would definitely or probably hire a person with a criminal record. About 35% stated that it depends on the nature of the crime and applicant (Holzer, Raphael, & Stoll, 2007). For those who answered "probably not" or "definitely not," only 7% hired an ex-offender, 36% of those willing hired an ex-offender, and 24% for those employers who said it depended (Holzer et al., 2007). In another study, 50% of employers were reluctant to consider a competent candidate based merely on the presence of a criminal record (Pager, 2007). The stigma of a criminal record is enough to prevent many employers from hiring or even consider hiring an ex-offender. As noted earlier, employment opportunities are also limited among those who are homeless who lack a phone or address to provide to potential employers.

Age

Age and its impact on homelessness and recidivism is more complex. In general, age is negatively associated with recidivism, but it increases the likelihood of homelessness. Older ex-inmates are the least likely of any group to be reincarcerated upon reentry (Blevins & Blowers, 2014). In fact,

> recidivism rates were inversely related to age at release; the older the person, the lower the rate of recidivism—56.6% of those 25 years of age or younger recidivated compared to 15.3% of those 55 years of age or older.
>
> (Harer, 1995, p. 98)

There are some key differences between the reentering population and those who are chronically homeless. For example, older ex-inmates are less likely to be reincarcerated but are at an increased risk for shelter stays. Specifically, each year of increased age is associated with a 4% increase in shelter stay risk and 3% decreased risk of incarceration (Metraux & Culhane, 2004).

Though age is negatively associated with recidivism, older parolees are more likely to have physical health needs, as they have higher rates of chronic medical issues and a bigger risk of postrelease death (Aday, 2003; Culhane, Kane, & Johnston, 2013; Williams et al., 2010). These conditions can be aggravated by a lack of stable housing. Homelessness aggravates health conditions like respiratory disorders, cardiovascular disease, ulcers, frostbite, hypothermia, skin diseases, diabetes, liver disease, dental disease, seizures, cancer, HIV/AIDS, cognitive impairments, and traumatic injuries (Rickards et al., 2010). One-half of men and two-thirds of women returning from prison reported having been diagnosed with a chronic physical health condition like high blood pressure, hepatitis, asthma, high cholesterol, and arthritis at the time of release (Mallik-Kane & Visher, 2008). Ex-inmates with physical health conditions are less likely to have identified stable housing a month before release (Mallik-Kane & Visher, 2008). Homelessness is associated with a higher incidence of acute and chronic health problems as well as premature mortality, since many homeless individuals are exposed to weather, infections, drugs, and violence while receiving no to little health care (Henwood, Cabassa, Craig, & Padgett, 2013).

Unfortunately, the reentry programs that support older prisoners to find employment or housing are typically reserved only for veterans despite rates of chronic health problems and mental illness being similar between veterans and nonveterans (Williams et al., 2010). While older inmates do receive their prescribed medications during imprisonment, it is normal to be released with only a short supply of medication or none at all, meaning that many go without proper medication for long periods of time after release (Blevins & Blowers, 2014). An important issue for policy makers is that they "understand the difficulties that many older ex-prisoners will face when attempting to obtain healthcare in the community and implement policies that will help ease the transition into the community" (Blevins & Blowers, 2014, p. 18). This influx of older ex-inmates who are also homeless causes additional financial burdens on emergency services and health care institutions. Ending chronic homelessness means assisting people who have one or more severe disabilities, including physical and mental disorders as well as substance or alcohol abuse (Burt, 2003). Traditional shelters have difficulties meeting these needs of the chronically homeless (Lincoln, Plachta-Elliot, & Espejo, 2009), and jails are underequipped to handle the complex needs these individuals possess.

Social Support

The burden of reentry and housing often falls upon families and communities, with evidence suggesting ex-offenders with family support are more successful (Pager, 2007). Strong ties between ex-offenders, their families, and close friends "appear to have a positive impact on post-release success" (Visher & Travis, 2003, p. 99). According to Bahr et al. (2010, p. 685), friends are a "significant predictor of parole success," but a lack of social support can decrease psychological well-being (Listwan, Colvin, Hanley, & Flannery, 2010). Those who participated in enjoyable activities with friends were more likely to succeed during parole periods, whereas those who failed reported fewer friends and increased loneliness (Bahr et al., 2010). Also, those who reported having a partner, being married, being close to parents, and having frequent contact with family members were associated with parole success (Bahr et al., 2010).

While many returning ex-prisoners may have assistance from family members, these family influences can still put the client at risk. Criminal convictions, addiction problems, and a history of homelessness can be common (Mallik-Kane & Visher, 2008). Families with higher levels of conflict are positively related to an ex-offender's postrelease drug use and criminal activity (Mowen & Visher, 2015). Studies of homeless populations confirm this complex relationship. In particular, that homelessness can be preceded by childhood trauma, familial drug use, and family conflict (Mallett, Rosenthal, & Keys, 2005; Martijn & Sharpe, 2006).

Homeless populations can often tax support resources. Families and friends who are willing to provide support for the homeless individual may tire of being asked to provide shelter. As homelessness becomes prolonged, these individuals often begin to replace their previous social networks with other homeless individuals. As noted by Grisby, Baumann, Gregorich, and Roberts-Gray (1990), as individuals replace their social networks they become increasingly acculturated into homelessness. This cycle continues, and those who are chronically homeless are less likely to have supports and more likely to become entrenched into homelessness.

Attending to the factors noted here is key for reducing both homelessness and reincarceration. Although there are a variety of initiatives for the homeless and for those reentering the community, they often do not provide a comprehensive approach to targeting the needs related to housing and the criminogenic needs related to criminal behavior. The next section will outline the various housing strategies and how they may be augmented to improve their effectiveness with reentering populations.

Promising Strategies for Homelessness and Reentry

It is clear that stable housing is an important consideration for successful reentry from either jail or prison, as it provides consistency for day-to-day activities (Lutze, Rosky, & Hamilton, 2014) and provides a platform for physical and mental health (Henwood et al., 2013). Also, a permanent address increases the likelihood of reporting to parole officers and increase the likelihood of obtaining a job or public benefits (Blevins & Blowers, 2014). However, research has shown that providing services for homelessness alone are not effective. In fact, a meta-analysis by Miller and Ngugi (2009) found that simply providing housing to ex-inmates was not sufficient to reduce recidivism rates.

There are a myriad of housing initiatives and programs. Housing initiatives vary throughout the country and can include permanent, transitional, residential, short-term (temporary), or emergency housing. Housing assistance programs can include affordable housing, tenant-based subsidized housing, project-based subsidized housing, and homeless prevention. These initiatives and programs are scarce in availability and have many regulations that restrict occupancy. For example, the public housing authority can deny admission or terminate a lease based on a history of substance use or criminal behavior. Those who owned homes before incarceration are likely to have lost them because of neglect of mortgages while incarcerated (Roman & Travis, 2006). Recently released ex-offenders often do not have the finances to move into private housing, such as an apartment, which usually requires two months' rent as well as a security deposit. Even when people can afford private housing, they may be passed over during the required background or work history checks (Petersilia, 2003). And since certain federal and state policies often keep felons from accessing public housing, many ex-offenders are faced with living in shelters, with friends or acquaintances for short periods of time, or in low-cost hotels located in high-risk communities (Lutze et al., 2014).

Project Greenlight was an "innovative, short-term, prison-based reentry program" (Wilson & Davis, 2006, p. 303). This eight-week reentry program took place at the Queensboro Correctional Facility in New York. This program was created when staff realized that there were a significant number of offenders who would be homeless upon release. They decided to systematically assign and match willing participants to existing, available housing resources (Rodriguez & Brown, 2003). Greenlight aimed to "improve post-release outcomes by (1) incorporating an intensive multimodal treatment regimen during incarceration and (2) providing links to families, community-based service providers, and parole officers after release" (Wilson & Davis, 2006, p. 307).

Project Greenlight addressed issues like employment, education, substance abuse, family issues, and constructive leisure time in a learning environment. Those who participated attended mandatory workshops that concentrated on job readiness, practical skills, and cognitive-behavioral tools. The participants were given volunteer opportunities with on-site job developers, a family counselor, and a community coordinator. This required close partnership with community-based organizations as well as the inmates' families to increase support on the outside (Rodriguez & Brown, 2003).

Project Greenlight was able to secure housing for 63% of those who requested assistance (Rodriguez & Brown, 2003); however, there was no actual follow-up in the community, so rates of success are not fully understood (Wilson & Davis, 2006). However, this project did provide an honest look at an assumption about ex-offenders released to homelessness in terms of the issues that exist with finding and keeping stable housing, including mental illness, employment, and substance abuse. The staff assumed that men who would request their assistance would be truly homeless. They learned that many of those who volunteered had families who had available housing, but the ex-inmates were barred from living with them because of certain restrictive laws and availability of housing (Rodriguez & Brown, 2003). The findings of this project suggest that while short-term programs seem attractive because of low cost and the ability to handle a large number, they were unable to address the numerous needs of ex-offenders.

One promising housing intervention for those with an incarceration history is the supportive housing model. Supportive housing is housing that is permanent and contains social service provisions. The first permanent supportive housing program for the chronically homeless was Pathways' Housing First model. When Housing First was introduced in 1992, it was the first departure from the standard homelessness intervention services, specifically for those with psychiatric and substance use disorders (Greenwood, Stefancic, & Tsemberis, 2013). Housing First programs typically include assessment based targeting of services, assistance in locating rental properties on the private market as well as lease negotiation, housing financial assistance (security deposit, one month's rent, or long-term subsidy), a nonexistent time limit, and a case manager to coordinate services (National Alliance to End Homelessness, 2006). Housing First is a pathway for the homeless and mentally ill to reduce their contact with the court system by increasing both public safety and public health (Somers, Rezansoff, Moniruzzaman, Palepu, & Patterson, 2013). The aim is to help families and chronically homeless individuals by providing quick access to sustainable permanent housing (National Alliance to End Homelessness, 2006).

Housing First was considered a fundamental and profound transformation in homelessness policy for several reasons. First, it changed the order in which homeless adults received housing and services. Under this program, housing was viewed as a human right, not a reward for being sober or completing treatment. Second, this program moved the choices of housing and services from experts to consumers by letting them have the right to choose their housing as well as type, sequence, and intensity of the services they receive. Third, Housing First applied a harm reduction approach to psychiatric and substance abuse treatment. And fourth, it utilized research and evidence-based practices by focusing on rates of homelessness, housing stability, choice, psychiatric symptoms, substance use, and cost effectiveness to deliver services (Greenwood et al., 2013).

Housing First programs have been found to be effective all over the country with different types of chronically homeless individuals. Housing First has achieved residential stability in homeless adults who have mental illnesses, even those with substance abuse disorders (Palepu, Patterson, Moniruzzaman, Frankish, & Somers, 2013; Leff et al., 2009). Finally, Lutze and colleagues (2014) found that reentry programs that utilized a permanent supportive housing model in Washington State reduced new convictions, revocations, and reincarceration.

The Frequent User Systems Engagement (FUSE) initiative is an example of a program relies on a Housing First model. The FUSE model is intended to target high-frequency system users and establishes "permanent supportive housing as a key component of reentry services for persons with recurring experiences of homelessness and criminal justice involvement" that will increase "life outcomes, more efficiently utilize public resources, and likely create cost avoidance in publicly funded crisis care systems, including emergency medical, mental health, and addiction services" (Aidala, McAllister, & Yomogida, 2013, p. 5). The program has been shown to successfully reduce cycling between public systems, days spent in jail, and the use of crisis health services, which in turn reduces the costs for government and society as a whole (Aidala et al., 2013). Frequent users are those with documented repeated episodes of incarceration and homelessness. About three-fourths of frequent users have been incarcerated for drug-related charges, mostly possession. Repeated incarcerations are often associated with low-level misdemeanor charges, such as theft of services, quality of life, and probation or parole violations (Aidala et al., 2013).

The findings for the FUSE initiative in New York suggest significantly reduced costs of public services while maintaining a high rate of housed individuals. Aidala and colleagues (2013) found that after the first 12 months of participating, 91% of those in treatment groups were in stable housing while only 28% of the control group were stably housed, and after the first 24 months, 86% of the treatment group was in stable housing compared to only 42%. Reported recent use of hard drugs was cut in half, and current alcohol and substance use reports are one-third less for participants. The treatment group spent 146.7 days less in shelters than the comparison group, a reduction of 70%. The comparison group spent an average of 8.04 days hospitalized for psychiatric reasons, 4.4 more days than the treatment group. The treatment group scored lower on psychological stress scales and higher on current family and social support. In terms of finances, this intervention reduced the annual costs of inpatient and crisis medical/ behavioral services by $7,308 per individual, and it reduced shelter and jail costs by $8,372 per person (Aidala et al., 2013). The jail outcomes were slightly less impressive, with some reductions achieved among the intervention groups; however, not all of the results were statistically significant between the two groups. As a result of the success in New York, the FUSE initiative has been implemented in a variety of locations throughout the country.

Homelessness and the RNR Model

The philosophy of providing shelter without requiring participation in services makes sense from a housing perspective. In particular, the notion that everyone is entitled to shelter or "housing" as a basic human right is compelling (Thiele, 2002). Moreover, the research noted earlier clearly makes the case for housing as an important foundation that provides the stability many individuals need to before they can work on other issues. However, as noted by Alice Turner (2014), "the elegance of the fundamental principle behind 'Housing First' also risks creating an illusion, wherein agencies and governments might too easily conclude that the entirety of this approach to ending homelessness is merely to begin housing the homeless" (p. 1). Simply providing housing without engaging clients in individualized wraparound treatment services is likely to fall short.

To be effective in reducing recidivism (e.g., jail stays, reincarceration, and rearrest) these initiatives must develop an effective wraparound service-based approach that targets the client's core criminogenic needs. The risk, need, responsivity (RNR) model adopted among many criminal justice agencies provides important lessons that could be incorporated into programs utilizing a Housing First philosophy. The RNR model was developed in the 1990s by researchers in Canada and provides a framework for the assessment and treatment of those involved in the criminal justice system (Bonta & Andrews, 2007). The risk principle suggests that intensive services should be dedicated to moderate and high-risk offenders—that is, to those clients who are higher risk for future criminal behavior. Research supports the risk principle, showing that client risk level in fact does predicts recidivism (Andrews & Dowden, 2006; Andrews et al., 2012; Bonta, Wallace-Capretta, & Rooney, 2000; Bourgon & Armstrong, 2005, Lovins, Lowenkamp, Latessa, & Smith, 2007).

The second principle of the RNR model refers to targeting the criminogenic needs that are highly correlated with criminal behavior. These criminogenic needs are dynamic risk factors that increase the likelihood that an individual will engage in criminal behavior (see Andrews et al., 1990; Gendreau, 1996). Criminogenic needs include pro-criminal values, attitudes, and beliefs, associating with pro-criminal peers, personality factors such as impulsivity, lack of achievement in employment or school, family dysfunction, lack of prosocial leisure activities, and substance abuse. Finally, the responsivity principle has two components. The first component, deemed general responsivity, refers to the treatment modalities that are most effective in changing offending behavior. In particular, cognitive-behavioral treatment is one of the most effective approaches with offender populations, with meta-analyses finding treatment effects in the range of 7–38% (Dowden & Andrews, 1999; Drake, Aos, & Miller, 2009; Landenberger & Lipsey, 2005; Wilson, Gallagher, & MacKenzie, 2000). This modality is particularly effective with the criminogenic needs noted earlier, namely impulsivity, pro-criminal attitudes, and substance abuse. Cognitive theories suggest that those who exhibit pro-criminal decision making and have poor problem-solving and coping skills are more likely to be involved in criminal behavior. Development of these types of programs can increase skill acquisition, coping skills, and social support networks.

Specific responsivity factors can range from individual level characteristics such as motivation and cognitive ability/intelligence to external factors such as homelessness, transportation, and child care. For example, study of reentering violent offenders in Nevada found that many clients were concerned how they would meet the obligations for parole or treatment if they did not have access to transportation and how they would manage to care for their dependents and raise money for a down payment for housing (Listwan, 2009).

In this context, a lack of housing would be considered an important specific responsivity factor. Homelessness is a barrier that must be addressed for individuals to successful participate in treatment services. Chronic homelessness interacts with many criminogenic risk factors to increase the individual's risk of criminal behavior. To maximize their outcomes, housing-based programs should match services to clients that target other important criminogenic needs, especially substance use, criminal thinking patterns, and antisocial peer networks. The challenge for housing programs based on the Housing First philosophy is whether to make these services mandatory. In other words, if the clients do not participate in the services, are they threatened with being removed from their home?

While there is no simple answer to this question, the literature on mandatory treatment among substance abusers provides some important insight. It was once thought that coerced treatment was ineffective and that there was little that the criminal justice system could do to treat addiction unless the client was motivated to change. While it is now clear that coerced treatment can be effective with offenders (see Farabee, Prendergast, & Anglin, 1998; Simpson & Broome, 1998), the client's level of motivation does have the potential to impact the effectiveness of services. For "coerced" treatment to work, the client's motivation level should change during the course of treatment. For many, a major event (such as an arrest) may lead to the client being sent to (rather than choose) a treatment agency. However, it is the responsibility of the staff to meet clients where they are at and increase their motivation to participate. To begin, program staff should assess the client's level of motivation to determine his or her current stage of change (see Miller & Rollnick, 2004). If the individual is resistant to engaging in services, the staff should use techniques such as motivational interviewing. Motivational interviewing includes being nonconfrontational, rolling with resistance, and supporting the client's self-efficacy. Proponents of this approach suggest that the likelihood of sustained behavioral change is greater and longer lasting if we work to decrease client resistance rather than truly coerce him or her (Miller & Rollnick, 2004). This approach is congruent with the Housing First model in that the staff can work on the individual's level of motivation to engage in services after he or she is housed.

Conclusion

Homeless individuals with incarceration histories are a high-risk population with complex needs that require a coordinated and thoughtful cross-system approach. These individuals are at a higher risk for mental illness, substance abuse issues, unemployment, and reincarceration. Homelessness can and does increase the likelihood of recidivism in multifaceted ways that must be addressed through a combination of interventions and initiatives. The "Housing First" approach offers permanent supportive housing without preliminary requirements for rehabilitative participation and/or treatment, in contrast to the "treatment-first" approach, which prioritizes rehabilitative treatment before entering into permanent housing.

While the Housing First initiatives such as FUSE are promising, it is likely that they can increase their impact by utilizing the RNR framework to provide services to clients. In particular, program staff should assess the clients for their risk level and criminogenic need factors. In addition, the client's level of motivation to engage in treatment should be assessed prior to engagement in services. The staff should plan for how to increase the client's level of motivation to engage in services and provide those services throughout. In addition to case management services, the program staff should also provide cognitive-behavioral treatment services to clients or ensure that referral sources are relying on these types of models. Finally, the interventions offered to the clients should be targeted to their needs, and staff should continually update assessment results to respond to the dynamic nature of transitioning away from homelessness and criminality. Only through cross system collaboration can these types of interventions be effective in improving outcomes among the incarcerated homeless.

References

Aday, R. H. (2003). *Aging prisoners: Crisis in American corrections.* Westport, CT: Praeger.

Aidala, A., McAllister, W., & Yomogida, M. (2013). *Returning home initiative—New York City: The frequent users service enhancement project.* Paper presented at the annual meeting of the American Society of Criminology, San Francisco, CA.

Andrews, D. A., & Dowden, C. (2006). Risk principle of case classification in correctional treatment a meta-analytic investigation. *International Journal of Offender Therapy and Comparative Criminology, 50*(1), 88–100. doi:10.1177/0306624X05282556

Andrews, D. A., Guzzo, L., Raynor, P., Rowe, R. C., Rettinger, L. J., Brews, A., & Wormith, J. S. (2012). Are the major risk/need factors predictive of both female and male reoffending? A test with the eight domains of the Level of Service/Case Management Inventory. *International Journal of Offender Therapy and Comparative Criminology, 56*(1), 113–133. doi:10.1177/0306624X10395716

Andrews D, A., Zinger, I., Hoge, R. D., Bonta, J., Gendreau, P., & Cullen, F. T. (1990). Does correctional treatment work? A clinically-relevant and psychologically-informed meta-analysis. *Criminology, 28*(3), 369–404.

Bahr, S. J., Harris, L., Fisher, J. K., & Harker, A. A. (2010). Successful reentry: What differentiates successful and unsuccessful ex-inmates? *International Journal of Offender Therapy and Comparative Criminology, 54*(5), 667–692. doi:10.1177/0306624X09342435

Blevins, K. B., & Blowers, A. N. (2014). Community reentry and aging inmates. (pp. 201–222). In J. J. Kerbs & J. M. Jolley (Eds.), *Senior citizens behind bars: Challenges for the criminal justice system.* Boulder, CO: Lynne Rienner Publishers, Inc.

Bonta, J., & Andrews, D. A. (2007). *Risk-need-responsivity model for offender assessment and rehabilitation* (User Report 2007–06). Ottawa, Ontario: Public Safety Canada.

Bonta, J., Wallace-Capretta, S., & Rooney, J. (2000). Can electronic monitoring make a difference? An evaluation of three Canadian programs. *Crime & Delinquency, 46*(1), 61–75. doi:10.1177/0011128700046001004

Bourgon, G., & Armstrong, B. (2005). Transferring the principles of effective treatment into a "real world" prison setting. *Criminal justice and Behavior, 32*(1), 3–25. doi:10.1177/0093854804270618

Burt, M. R. (2003). Chronic homelessness: Emergence of a public policy. *Fordham Urban Law Journal, 30*(3), 1267–1279.

Carson E. A., & Golinelli, D. (2013). *Prisoners in 2012: Trends in admissions and releases, 1991–2012.* Washington, DC: U.S. Department of Justice, Bureau of Justice Statistics.

Culhane, D. P., Kane, V., & Johnston, M. (2013). Homelessness research: Shaping policy and practice, now and into the future. *American Journal of Public Health, 103*(Suppl 2), 181–182. doi:10.2105/AJPH.2013.301728

Dowden, C., & Andrews, D. A. (1999). What works for female offenders: A meta-analytic review. *Crime & Delinquency, 45*(4), 438–452. doi:10.1177/0011128799045004002

Durose, M. R., Cooper, A. D., & Snyder, H. N. (2014). *Recidivism of prisoners released in 30 states in 2005: Patterns from 2005 to 2010.* Washington, DC: U.S. Department of Justice, Bureau of Justice Statistics.

Drake, E. K., Aos, S., & Miller, M. G. (2009). Evidence-based public policy options to reduce crime and criminal justice costs: Implications in Washington State. *Victims and Offenders, 4*(2), 170–196. doi:10.1080/15564880802612615

Farabee, D., Prendergast, M., & Anglin, M. D. (1998). Effectiveness of coerced treatment for drug-abusing offenders. *Federal Probation, 62*, 3.

Fries, L., Fedock, G., & Kubiak, S. P. (2014). Role of gender, substance use, and serious mental illness in anticipated post jail homelessness. *Social Work Research, 38*(2), 107–116. doi:10.1093/swr/svu014

Gendreau, P. (1996). Offender rehabilitation what we know and what needs to be done. *Criminal Justice and Behavior, 23*(1), 144–161. doi:10.1177/0093854896023001010

Greenberg, G. A., & Rosenheck, R. A. (2008a). Homelessness in the state and federal prison population. *Criminal Behaviour and Mental Health, 18*(2), 88–103. doi:10.1002/cbm.685.

Greenberg, G. A., & Rosenheck, R. A. (2008b). Jail incarceration, homelessness, and mental health: A national study. *Psychiatric Services, 59*(2), 170–177. doi:10.1176/ps.2008.59.2.170

Greenwood, R. M., Stefancic A., & Tsemberis, S. (2013). Pathways housing first for homeless persons with psychiatric disabilities: Program innovation, research, and advocacy. *Journal of Social Issues, 69*(4), 645–663. doi:10.1111/josi.12034

Grisby, C., Baumann, D., Gregorich, S. E., & Roberts-Gray, C. (1990). Disaffiliation to entrenchment: A model for understanding homelessness. *Journal of Social Issues, 46*(4), 141–156. doi:10.1111/j.1540-4560.1990.tb01803.x

Harer, M. D. (1995). Recidivism among federal prisoners released in 1987. *Journal of Correctional Education, 46*, 98–128.

Harris, P. M., & Keller, K. S. (2005). Ex-offenders need not apply: The criminal background check in hiring decisions. *Journal of Contemporary Criminal Justice, 21*(1), 6–30. doi:10.1177/1043986204271678

Henry, M., Cortes, A., Shivji, A., & Buck, K. (2014). *The 2014 Annual Homelessness Assessment Report (AHAR) to congress: Part 1 point in time counts.* Washington, DC: U.S. Department of Housing and Urban Development.

Henwood, B. F., Cabassa, L. J., Craig C. M., & Padgett, D. K. (2013). Permanent supportive housing: Addressing homelessness and health disparities? *American Journal of Public Health, 103*(Suppl 2), S188–S192. doi:10.2105/AJPH.2013.301490

Holzer, H. J., Raphael, S., & Stoll, M. A. (2007). The effect of an applicant's criminal history on employer hiring decisions and screening practices: Evidence from Los Angeles. In S. Bushway, M. Stoll, & D. Weiman (Eds.), *Barriers to reentry? The labor market for released prisoners in post-industrial America* (pp. 117–150). New York, NY: Russell Sage Foundation.

Landenberger, N. A., & Lipsey, M. W. (2005). The positive effects of cognitive-behavioral programs for offenders: A meta-analysis of factors associated with effective treatment. *Journal of Experimental Criminology, 1*(4), 451–476. doi:10.1007/s11292-005-3541-7

Leff, H. S., Chow, C. M., Pepin, R., Conley, J., Allen, I. E., & Seaman, C. A. (2009). Does one size fit all? What we can and can't learn from a meta-analysis of housing models for persons with mental illness. *Psychiatric Services, 60*(4),473–482. doi:10.1176/appi.ps.60.4.473

Lincoln, A. K., Plachta-Elliott, S., & Espejo, D. (2009). Coming in: An examination of people with co-occurring substance use and serious mental illness exiting chronic homelessness. *American Journal of Orthopsychiatry, 79*(2), 236–243. doi:10.1037/a0015624

Listwan, S. J. (2009). Re-entry for serious and violent offenders: An analysis of program retention. *Criminal Justice Policy Review, 20*(2), 154–169. doi:10.1177/0887403408325700

Listwan, S. J., Colvin, M., Hanley, D., & Flannery, D. (2010). Victimization, social support, and psychological well-being: A study of recently released prisoners. *Criminal Justice and Behavior, 37*(10), 1140–1159. doi:10.1177/0093854810376338

Lovins, L. B., Lowenkamp, C. T., Latessa, E. J., & Smith, P. (2007). Application of the risk principle to female offenders. *Journal of Contemporary Criminal Justice, 23*(4), 383–398. doi:10.1177/1043986207309437

Lutze, F. E., Rosky, J. W., & Hamilton, Z. K. (2014). Homelessness and reentry: A multisite outcome evaluation of Washington State's reentry housing program for high risk offenders. *Criminal Justice and Behavior, 41*(4), 471–491. doi:10.1177/0093854813510164

Mallett, S., Rosenthal, D., & Keys, D. (2005). Young people, drug use, and family conflict: Pathways into homelessness. *Journal of Adolescence, 28*(2), 185–199. doi:10.1016/j.adolescence.2005.02.002

Mallik-Kane, K., & Visher, C. A. (2008). *Health and prisoner reentry: How physical, mental, and substance abuse conditions shape the process of reintegration.* Washington, DC: Urban Institute.

Martijn, C., & Sharpe, L. (2006). Pathways to youth homelessness. *Social Science & Medicine, 62*(1), 1–12. doi:10.1016/j.socscimed.2005.05.007

McNiel, D. E., Binder, R. L., & Robinson, J. C. (2005). Incarceration associated with homelessness, mental disorder, and co-occurring substance abuse. *Psychiatric Services, 56*(7), 840–846. doi:10.1176/appi.ps.56.7.840

Metraux, S., & Culhane, D. P. (2004). Homeless shelter use and reincarceration following prison release. *Criminology & Public Policy, 3*(2)139–160. doi:10.1111/j.1745–9133.2004.tb00031.x

Miller, M. G., & Ngugi, I. (2009). *Impacts of housing supports: Persons with mental illness and ex-offenders.* Olympia, WA: Washington State Institute for Public Policy.

Miller, W. R., & Rollnick, S. (2004). Talking oneself into change: Motivational interviewing, stages of change, and therapeutic process. *Journal of Cognitive Psychotherapy, 18*(4), 299–308. doi:10.1891/jcop.18.4.299.64003

Mowen, T. J., & Visher, C. A. (2015). Drug use and crime after incarceration: The role of family support and family conflict. *Justice Quarterly, 32*(2), 337–359. doi:10.1080/07418825.2013.771207

Mumola, C. J., Karberg, J. C., & United States. (2007). *Drug use and dependence, state and federal prisoners, 2004.* Washington, DC: U.S. Department of Justice, Office of Justice Programs, Bureau of Justice Statistics.

National Alliance to End Homelessness. (2006). *How much does the federal government spend on homelessness?* Washington, DC: National Alliance to End Homelessness.

Pager, D. (2007). *Marked: Race, crime, and finding work in an era of mass incarceration* Chicago, IL: University of Chicago Press.
Palepu, A., Patterson, M. L., Moniruzzaman, A., Frankish, J., & Somers, J. (2013). Housing first improves residential stability in homeless adults with concurrent substance dependence and mental disorders. *American Journal of Public Health, 103*(Suppl 2:e30–6), S269–S274. doi:10.2105/AJPH.2013.301628
Petersilia, J., & National Institute of Justice (U.S.). (2000). *When prisoners return to the community: Political, economic, and social consequences.* Washington, DC: U.S. Department of Justice, Office of Justice Programs, National Institute of Justice.
Petersilia, J. (2003). *When prisoners come home: Parole and prisoner reentry.* Oxford: Oxford University Press.
Rickards, L. D., McGraw, S. A., Araki, L., Casey, R. J., High, C. W., Hombs, M. E., & Raysor, R. S. (2010). Collaborative initiative to help end chronic homelessness: Introduction. *The Journal of Behavioral Health Services & Research: Official Publication of the National Council for Community Behavioral Healthcare, 37*(2), 149–166. doi:10.1007/s11414-009-9175-1
Rodriguez, N., & Brown, B. (2003). *Preventing homelessness among people leaving prison: State sentencing and corrections program.* New York, NY: Vera Institute of Justice.
Roman, C. G., & Travis, J. (2006). Where will I sleep tomorrow? Housing, homelessness, and the returning prisoner. *Housing Policy Debate, 17*(2), 389–418. doi:10.1080/10511482.2006.9521574
Rosenblatt, M. (2016, April 1). *The needs of the so-called "service-resistant."* New York, NY: Bowery Residents' Committee.
Shelton, K. H., Taylor, P. J., Bonner, A., & van den Bree, M. (2009). Risk factors for homelessness: Evidence from a population-based study. *Psychiatric Services, 60*(4), 465–472. doi:10.1176/ps.2009.60.4.465
Simpson, D., & Broome, K. M. (1998). Effects of readiness for drug abuse treatment on client retention and assessment of process. *Addiction, 93*(8), 1177–1190. doi:10.1080/09652149835008
Slate, R. N., Buffington-Vollum, J. K., & Johnson, W. W. (2013). *The criminalization of mental illness: Crisis and opportunity for the justice system.* Durham, NC: Carolina Academic Press.
Somers, J. M., Rezansoff, S. N., Moniruzzaman, A., Palepu, A., & Patterson, M. (2013). Housing First reduces re-offending among formerly homeless adults with mental disorders: results of a randomized controlled trial. *PloS ONE, 8*, 9. doi:10.1371/journal.pone.0072946
Thiele, B. (2002). The human right to adequate housing: A tool for promoting and protecting individual and community health. *American Journal of Public Health, 92*(5), 712–715.
Thompson, J. R. G., Wall, M. M., Greenstein, E., Grant, B. F., & Hasin, D. S. (2013). Substance-use disorders and poverty as prospective predictors of first-time homelessness in the United States. *American Journal of Public Health, 103*(Suppl 2), S282–S288. doi:10.2105/AJPH.2013.301302
Tsemberis, S., Gulcur, L., & Nakae, M. (2004). Housing First, consumer choice, and harm reduction for homeless individuals with a dual diagnosis. *American Journal of Public Health, 94*(4), 651–656.
Turner, A. (2014). Beyond housing first: Essential elements of a system planning approach to ending homelessness. *University of Calgary School of Public Policy Research Paper Series*, 7, 1–25. Retrieved from www.housingfirsttoolkit.ca/sites/default/files/beyond-housing-turner.pdf
Visher, C. A., & Kachnowski, V. (2007). Finding work on the outside: Results from the "Returning Home" project in Chicago. In S. D. Bushway, M. A. Stoll, & D. Weiman (Eds.), *Barriers to reentry? The labor market for released prisoners in post-industrial America* (pp. 80–113). New York, NY: Russel Sage Foundation.
Visher, C. A., & Travis, J. (2003). Transitions from prison to community: Understanding individual pathways. *Annual Review of Sociology, 29*, 89–113. doi:10.1146/annurev.soc.29.010202.095931
Williams, B. A., McGuire, J., Lindsay, R. G., Baillargeon, J., Cenzer, I. S., Lee, S. J., & Kushel, M. (2010). Coming home: Health status and homelessness risk of older pre-release prisoners. *Journal of General Internal Medicine, 25*(10), 1038–1044. doi:10.1007/s11606-010-1416-8
Wilson, J. A., & Davis R. C. (2006). Good intentions meet hard realities: An evaluation of the Project Greenlight Reentry Program. *Criminology & Public Policy, 5*(2), 303–338. doi:10.1111/j.1745-9133.2006.00380.x
Wilson, D. B., Gallagher, C. A., & MacKenzie, D. L. (2000). A meta-analysis of corrections-based education, vocation, and work programs for adult offenders. *Journal of Research in Crime and Delinquency, 37*(4), 347–368. doi:10.1177/0022427800037004001

12

INCARCERATED VETERANS

Confronting Military Service Struggles through Treatment and Diversion

LeAnn N. Cabage

> Veterans experience increasing rates of PTSD (11%–20%), traumatic brain injury (20%), and other wounds as deployments increase in quantity, duration, and frequency. Under the burden of their experiences and injuries, many veterans face depression, homelessness, suicide, or substance abuse. These veterans struggle to rejoin civilian society, and criminal justice involvement too often follows.
>
> —(Combined Arms, 2013, para. 4)

Introduction

As of 2014, the U.S. Armed Forces reported the number of veterans at 21.8 million. Approximately 10% of these veterans are women (Risen, 2014). Although the number of veterans represent a small portion of the U.S. citizenry (approximately 7%) and an even smaller percentage of the incarcerated population, many of these individuals have a unique set of needs regarding mental and physical health. This especially holds true for veterans whom experience combat and are direct witness to the loss of both American and enemy lives.

To provide for their well-being, veterans rely on the Department of Veteran Affairs (VA). However, in recent years, the VA has failed to address adequately the needs of these veterans. For incarcerated veterans, the VA discontinues services, and correctional facilities will provide care for the needs of these individuals. However, correctional facilities also frequently fail to address adequately the needs of our nation's veterans. This is especially true for those who find themselves incarcerated in local jails. These facilities simply do not have the resources or monetary support to address the issues veterans face properly.

As noted previously, the incarceration rates of veterans are lower than the incarceration rates of individuals in the general population. However, veterans face a host of issues that make them more susceptible to arrest. Veterans experience homelessness at higher rates than the general population. They also face increased risks of a mental health diagnosis for posttraumatic stress disorder (PTSD) and/or other mental health issues related to traumatic brain injury (TBI). Further, the veteran population is at a greater risk of alcohol and/or drug abuse. The final and perhaps strongest correlate for arrest in the veteran population is the existence of co-occurring disorders (mental health and substance abuse disorders).

To date, veterans constitute approximately 8% of all inmates in state and federal prisons and 7% of all inmates in local jails (U.S. Department of Justice, 2015). The 2015 report indicates a greater percentage of veterans (64%) than nonveterans (48%) are sentenced for violent offenses. They are, however, less likely to have four or more prior arrests. Approximately a quarter of veterans in prison and less than a third of those in jail reported they experienced combat while in the military. In addition, about half of all veterans in prison (48%) and jail (55%) have a mental health diagnosis. This number increases for those veterans who saw combat, with 60% of prison and 67% of jail inmates reporting a mental health diagnosis (U.S. Department of Justice, 2015). An additional concern for addressing the needs of incarcerated veterans is the age at which they are incarcerated. On average, the age of a veteran incarcerated in a jail is 43 years of age. This is 11 years older than nonveterans. Approximately 19% of veterans in jail were age 55 and older. Veterans in prison are an average of 49 years of age, and 33% of those in prison are over the age of 55 (U.S. Department of Justice, 2015).

Veterans incarcerated in prison or jail have a unique set of needs. They are more likely to report a prior mental health diagnosis, more likely to experience homelessness, and more likely to be convicted of a violent offense, and are older on average. These unique needs must be properly addressed if we hope to reduce the number of veterans incarcerated.

This chapter discusses these unique needs veterans face. It examines mental health issues such as PTSD, substance abuse, and homelessness among the veteran population. In addition, a demographic background for those convicted is provided. The chapter concludes with a brief discussion regarding specific programming offered to justice-involved veterans.

Mental Health in the Veteran Population

Veterans returning from war often struggle with PTSD, mental defects related to TBIs, and/or other mental health concerns. However, the percentages of individuals struggling with such diagnoses vary by service era. What does hold consistent across era of service is combat veterans are more likely than noncombat veterans to experience symptoms of PTSD.

Reports on the number of individuals returning from the Operation Enduring Freedom (OEF), Operation Iraqi Freedom (OIF), and Operation New Dawn (OND) wars with PTSD vary. It is possible the prevalence of PTSD among OIF veterans is as high as one in five (Hoge et al., 2004; Seal et al., 2009). Friedman (2004) suggests the percentage may be as high as 35%. The number of OEF veterans with PTSD appears to be similar (Seal et al., 2009). When men and women veterans are compared, women are more likely to screen positive for PTSD and depression than male veterans (Luxton, Skopp, & Maguen, 2010; Skopp et al., 2011; Tanielian et al., 2008).

PTSD rates in the veteran population are linked to aggression. Veterans with a PTSD diagnosis are more likely to exhibit aggressive behaviors than veterans without PTSD or the general public (Beckham et al., 1997; McFall et al., 1999). Further, veterans with PTSD are more likely than veterans without PTSD to express hostility and physical aggression within their intimate relationships (Glenn et al., 2002; Jordan et al., 1992). Jakupcak et al. (2007) provided additional support for the argument. In their examination of 117 Iraq and Afghanistan War combat veterans, they found symptoms of PTSD are correlated with hostility, aggression, and anger. Similar findings are reported for female veterans (Butterfield et al., 2000).

Although PTSD rates are high among veterans, specifically veterans returning from war, they also are affected by other mental health concerns. Seal, Bertenthal, and Miner (2007) examined data pertaining to 103,788 OEF/OIF veterans who sought treatment at a VA health care facility. Of these 103,788 individuals, 25% received a mental health diagnosis. More than half (56%) of those diagnosed with a mental health disorder had two or more distinct mental health diagnoses. This is problematic, because as Hoge et al. (2004) report, only a small percentage of the soldiers and Marines in their study reported receiving help from any mental health professional. Further, "In the military, there are unique factors that contribute to resistance to seeking such help, particularly concern about how a soldier will be perceived by peers and by the leadership" (Hoge et al., 2004, p. 15).

Substance Abuse in the Veteran Population

For veterans returning from war with PTSD, facing the fear of failure and afraid to seek help because of the stigma attached to mental illness within the military, veterans may self-medicate to numb their pain and relieve their thoughts. McFall, Mackay, and Donovan (1992) reported Vietnam era veterans with PTSD experienced more severe drug and alcohol abuse problems. This holds true for Persian Gulf War-era veterans, too (Shipherd, Stafford, & Tanner, 2005).

For Vietnam-era combat veterans, self-medication began with the symptoms of PTSD, and the substance abuse increased as the symptoms of PTSD increased. The individuals reported a preference to self-medicate with alcohol, marijuana, heroin, and benzodiazepines because they treated the symptoms the best (McFall et al., 1992). Brown and Wolfe (1994) further the understanding of the use of drugs and alcohol for self-medication by discussing the types of drugs one may medicate with depending on the symptoms one has. For example, veterans who struggle with avoidance may use drugs (e.g., amphetamines) that stimulate the central nervous system. On the other hand, alcohol may be the medicine of choice for those who have difficulty sleeping or experience irritability and agitation. In an examination of Iraq and Afghanistan war veterans, those who screened positive for PTSD or depression were two times more likely to report alcohol misuse (Jakupcak et al., 2010).

For these individuals, the comorbidity of a PTSD diagnosis and self-medication contributes to additional problems. Veterans who self-medicate may find it difficult to maintain stable employment and find themselves homeless. Facing an untreated mental health diagnosis, addiction, and homelessness, the individual may turn to crime.

Service-Connected Disability and Work in the Veteran Population

The 1990 Americans with Disabilities Act recognizes individuals with a disability face institutional barriers to employment. The act challenged employers to provide reasonable accommodations in an effort to eliminate discrimination against otherwise qualified employees. However, employers have continued to resist providing the reasonable accommodations required by law, thus leaving a number of individuals unemployed (Robert & Harlan, 2006).

The failure to provide reasonable accommodations is particularly relevant to veterans. In addition to other consequences of service, military veterans face a number of disabilities that vary in severity (Prokos & Cabage, 2017). The U.S. Department of Labor (2014) reported approximately 3.2 million veterans (15%) had a service-related disability. Veterans with service-related disabilities are rated on a scale of 0% to 100% by the U.S. Department of Veteran Affairs or the U.S. Department of Defense. Of those with service-related disabilities, 35% reported a disability rating lower than 30%, and approximately 30% had a rating of 60% or higher (U.S. Department of Labor, 2014). The number of OEF/OIF era veterans reporting a service-related disability is 30% (U.S. Department of Labor, 2014).

Individuals with a service-related disability face the same consequences as other individuals with a disability. They face potential loss of earnings and greater economic hardships. Service members with serious injuries face the greatest losses (Heaton, Loughran, & Miller, 2012). For those with less serious injuries, loss of wages was accounted for by military separation, whereas veterans with serious injuries also faced loss of wages from the civilian labor market (Prokos & Cabage, 2017).

The unemployment rate for veterans tends to be slightly higher than the unemployment rate of the general population. An examination of unemployment in the OEF/OIF veteran population in 2013 found 9.6% of women veterans were unemployed compared to 6.8% of nonveterans and 8.8% of men veterans were unemployed compared to 7.5% of nonveterans (U.S. Department of Labor, 2014). It also is important to examine labor force participation rates, as veterans with a service-related disability may no longer be participants in the labor force. Labor force participation rate for veterans with a service-related disability is lower (70.5%) than veterans without a service-related disability

(85.4%) (U.S. Department of Labor, 2014). Further, individuals with a disability rating of 60% or higher are less likely to be in the labor force than those with a disability rating less than 30% (28.9% and 56% in the labor force, respectively) (U.S. Department of Labor, 2014).

Homelessness in the Veteran Population

The rate of homelessness among the veteran population is drastically greater than the rate among the general population. In 2016, approximately 39,471 veterans were homeless (National Alliance to End Homelessness, 2015). Although this represents a decline in the number of homeless veterans, they remain overrepresented in the homeless population.

Traditionally, homeless veterans are male (91%), single (98%), live in the city (76%), and have a mental and/or physical disability (54%). However, as troops have returned from Iraq and Afghanistan, the homeless veteran population has become younger and more likely to be female and heads of households (National Alliance to End Homelessness, 2015). It is likely this trend will continue as more individuals return home from these tours of duty. It also is likely that the number of homeless veterans over the age of 55 will increase in the coming years.

As noted previously, veterans experience homelessness at higher rates than the general population. However, veterans share similar characteristics with the general homeless population. These individuals are most likely from a lower socioeconomic status, have a mental health diagnosis, and/or a history of substance abuse. However, the prevalence of PTSD and TBIs among the veteran populations increases the likelihood of homelessness.

As Metraux et al. (2013) notes, veterans returning from the recent wars in Afghanistan and Iraq (i.e., OEF, OIF, and OND) have increased risks factors that may lead to homelessness. As with other individuals in the homeless population, behavioral and mental health disorders have consistently been identified as risk factors. Although the relationship between PTSD, combat experience, and homelessness has been more tenuous (Rosenheck & Fontana, 1994; Rosenheck, Leda, Frisman, Lam, & Chung, 1996), these factors should not be discounted.

Blackstock, Haskell, Brandt, and Desai (2012) found associations between homelessness and a range of socioeconomic and demographic factors for OEF and OIF veterans. These factors include low educational attainment, being African American, identifying as Hispanic, being unmarried, being enlisted, and located in an urban area. In addition, a veteran's disability rating and various behavioral health diagnoses (e.g., PTSD) contribute to homelessness in the population. Edens, Kasprow, Tsai, and Rosenheck (2011) examined data of all veterans who used VA mental health specialty services in 2009. Their findings support the findings of Blackstock et al. (2012) in the predictive factors of homelessness in the veteran population. Specifically, being male, age 40–64, African American, and an urban dweller, and having an income below $7,000 was predictive of homelessness in the veteran population. A bivariate analysis revealed veterans with a diagnosis of schizophrenia or bipolar disorder, an alcohol or drug addiction, and any personality disorder were more likely to be homeless. It also should be noted, those with an illicit drug addiction were nearly eight times more likely to be homeless, and those with an alcohol addiction were five times more likely to experience homelessness (Edens et al., 2011). In addition, Edens et al. (2011) examined the relationship between service-related disabilities and homelessness. For individuals with a service-connected disability greater than 50%, the factor acted as a protection against homelessness.

In 2012, the U.S. Department of Veterans Affairs examined 310,685 OEF and OIF era veterans that separated from the military between July 1, 2005, and September 30, 2006. These individuals had no prior history of homelessness and had used a VA or Department of Defense (DoD) service since their discharge. The five-year homeless rate was 3.7%, with the highest rates found among women deployed during this era (4%) and the lowest found among men who were not deployed (3.2%) (U.S. Department of Veterans Affairs, 2012). Metraux et al. (2013) utilized the database maintained by the

VA's Office of Inspector General (OIG) to characterize the transition process for individuals that separated from active military duty between July 1, 2005, and September 30, 2006. Their study included 310,685 veterans aged 17 to 64 at time of separation who had no indication of homelessness prior to military service and had used VA or DoD services since separation. Their findings support the findings of the Department ofVeterans Affairs study, with a 3.8% unadjusted five-year incidence rate. When adjusted, the five-year incidence rate becomes 4.9% for men and 4.8% for women (Metraux et al., 2013). The findings indicate homelessness in this population was related to low pay grade (72% of the homeless) and behavioral health disorders (44% of the homeless). They also note connections between TBIs and homelessness.

Women Veterans

Women veterans have the same concerns as men veterans; however, the effects of military service are often more pronounced for women. In addition, women veterans in the OIF, OEF, and OND eras are more likely to have experienced combat than women in previous eras. This experience has created additional problems that women veterans of previous eras may not have experienced.

Although women were not allowed to serve in direct combat positions during the most recent wars, data suggest that roughly three-quarters of women deployed to Iraq have been exposed to one or more combat experiences (Dutra et al., 2010). Zinzow, Grubaugh, Monnier, Suffoletta-Maierle, and Frueh (2007) estimate between 4%–31% of women were exposed to combat. The data pertaining to women veterans of OIF is consistent with studies comprised primarily of men from the same era (Milliken, Auchterlonie, & Hoge, 2007). Beyond the stressors associated with combat, many of the women identified additional stressors associated with leaving their children, family, and friends behind.

Reintegration back into family life and civilian life in general is a challenge for many of the women. They often feel like they now longer know their families or friends. They report feeling unsure how to relate to individuals and often feel uncomfortable discussion their deployments with others. In regard to friends, women veterans reported former friends seemed unavailable. They also feared war had changed them and they could no longer connect with friends as a result.

Women in the military not only face difficulty reintegrating back into society, they often face the possibility of violence directed toward them from men within the military framework. Sadler, Booth, Nielson, and Doebbeling (2000) surveyed 558 women veterans who served in Vietnam and subsequent eras. They reported almost half of the women experienced violence during their time of service. The violence reported included rape (30%), physical assault (35%), or both (16%). Kimerling et al. (2010) suggest 15.1% of women serving during OEF/OIF experienced sexual trauma. National surveys conducted by other researchers report between 13%–30% of women veterans are victims of rape during their service (Coyle, Wolan, and Van Horn, 1996; Hankin et al., 1999; Sadler et al., 2000; Sadler, Booth, Cook, & Doebbeling, 2003). The combination of stressors of experiencing combat situations, coping with absence of family and friends, and the potential or actuality of violence resulted in many of the women experiencing symptoms associated with PTSD.

Experiencing military sexual trauma is linked to higher rates of PTSD in women veterans. Women veterans with a history of military sexual trauma were five to eight times more likely to have a current diagnosis of PTSD, three times more likely to be diagnosed with depressive disorders, and two times more likely to be diagnosed with alcohol abuse disorders when compared to women veterans who did not experience military sexual trauma (Kang, Dalager, Mahan, & Ishii, 2005; Kimerling, Gima, Smith, Street, & Frayne, 2007; Maguen, Luxton, Skopp, & Madden, 2012). Further supporting this claim, Kessler, Sonnega, Bromet, Hughes, and Nelson (1995) argue rape trauma is the most highly correlated with the development of PTSD. Hassija, Jakupcak, Maguen, and Shipherd (2012) found higher rates of PTSD, depressive symptoms, and alcohol abuse in women veterans who reported combat exposure after controlling for other traumatic events across the lifetime. Beyond the diagnosis of PTSD, many of the women fear negative career consequences, having to continue interactions with the perpetrator, and having limited access to outside support (Yaeger, Himmelfarb, Cammack, & Mintz, 2006).

Whether formally diagnosed or not, the symptoms of PTSD have been correlated with lower levels of employment for Vietnam-era male veterans (Smith, Schnurr, & Rosenheck, 2005). Although there is minimal research to indicate the same for females (U.S. Department of Labor, 2014) the trend is consistent. That is, PTSD is often related to unemployment and potentially homelessness in women veterans.

An examination of women veterans of the OEF/OIF era revealed an unemployment rate of 9.6%. This rate is higher than the rate of unemployment of nonveteran women (6.8%). It also is higher than the rate for veteran men from the same era (8.8%) (U.S. Department of Labor, 2014). In addition, women are more likely than men veterans to have a functional limitation or disability (Prokos & Cabage, 2017; Wilmoth, London, & Parker, 2011). Comparing overall general health, women veterans have more physical and mental health problems than women nonveterans. For veteran women, the odds of having any functional limitation/disability are 23% higher than for nonveteran women (Wilmoth et al., 2011). Prokos and Cabage (2017) report women veterans who served between 2001 and 2007 are 27% more likely than nonveteran women to have a functional disability. It is important to understand the role of service-related disabilities because they shape the potential for employment and labor force participation.

A military women veteran is as likely to be employed as she is to be unemployed. However, when disability status is controlled for, women veterans are more likely to be unemployed. Specifically, women veterans who report a service-related disability are 26% more likely to be unemployed than their peers (Prokos & Cabage, 2017). The higher unemployment rates and lower labor force participation rates for these women may translate into homelessness.

Women veterans experience homelessness at three to four times the rate of nonveteran women (Washington et al., 2010). The increase in the likelihood of homelessness in the population is likely the result of their military service. Washington et al. (2010) report being sexually assaulted during military service, being unemployed, being disable, having worse overall health, and screening positive for an anxiety disorder or PTSD as risk factors for women veterans. These findings are further supported by Hamilton, Poza, and Washington (2011). They found five factors that initiated pathways toward homelessness for women veterans: (1) childhood adversity; (2) trauma and/or substance abuse during military service; (3) postmilitary abuse, adversity, and/or relationship termination; (4) postmilitary mental health, substance abuse, and/or medical problems; and (5) unemployment. As discussed previously, veteran women face these problems at a greater rate than veteran men. Therefore, it is especially important to address these needs among women veterans to prevent incarceration or reoffending.

Veteran Incarceration

The research on incarcerated veterans is limited. Research comparing the incarceration rates, type of crime, and length of sentence by gender among veterans is minimal at best. The most recent data estimates 181,500 veterans are incarcerated in state and federal prisons and local jails. These individuals constitute approximately 8% of all inmates. Broken down further, veterans represent 8% of the total prison population and 7% of the total jail population (U.S. Department of Justice, 2015). It should also be noted that from 2001 to 2012, veterans discharged during OEF, OIF, and OND accounted for 13% of veterans in prison and 25% of veterans in jail (U.S. Department of Justice, 2015).

As mentioned previously, PTSD rates and other mental disorders among veterans are higher than the general population. Approximately half of all incarcerated veterans have been told by a mental health profession they have a mental disorder (48% in prison and 55% in jail). Those who saw combat were more likely to be diagnosed with a mental health issue than noncombat veterans (U.S. Department of Justice, 2015).

To understand the dynamics of the incarcerated veteran population, it is important to understand their demographic background and criminal history. This information is summarized from the 2015 U.S. Department of Justice special report discussed here. Information from the 2004 Survey of State and Federal Inmates is included because the demographic information presented in the 2015 report is limited to men. The 2004 data is the most recent data available to the public. The findings from the 2015 report and the 2004 data may differ as a result of the number of individuals included in the analysis and the method in which the data was analyzed.

Demographics

Men veterans are more likely than women veterans to be incarcerated. Men comprise 99% of veterans in prison and 97% of veterans in jail (U.S. Department of Justice, 2015). Veterans comprise 9.1% of state inmates. Approximately 11% of men and 1.5% of women in the sample reported military service (Cabage, 2014). Of the 1,300 men, 19.5% reported seeing combat and 26.7% of the women reported combat experience (Cabage, 2014). At the federal level, veterans comprise 9.3% of the inmates. Two percent of women and 11.9% of men in the federal sample reported prior military service (Cabage, 2014). Men in the federal sample were more likely to have seen combat than women (25.2% and 19.7%, respectively). Women make up a small percentage of the veteran incarceration percentage. Therefore, the information presented from the 2015 U.S. Department of Justice report focuses on incarcerated veteran men. However, the 2004 Survey data include a representation of women veterans.

On average, veterans in prison and jail are older than their nonveteran counterparts. The U.S. Department of Justice (2015) reports the average age of veterans incarcerated in jail is 43 years of age; this is 11 years older than nonveterans. Those incarcerated in a prison average 49 years of age, which is 12 years older than the nonveteran prison inmate. See Figures 12.1 and 12.2 for additional information (adapted from the U.S. Department of Justice, 2015). Broken down into state and federal inmates, the median age of veterans in state custody is 27 and the median age for nonveterans is 35

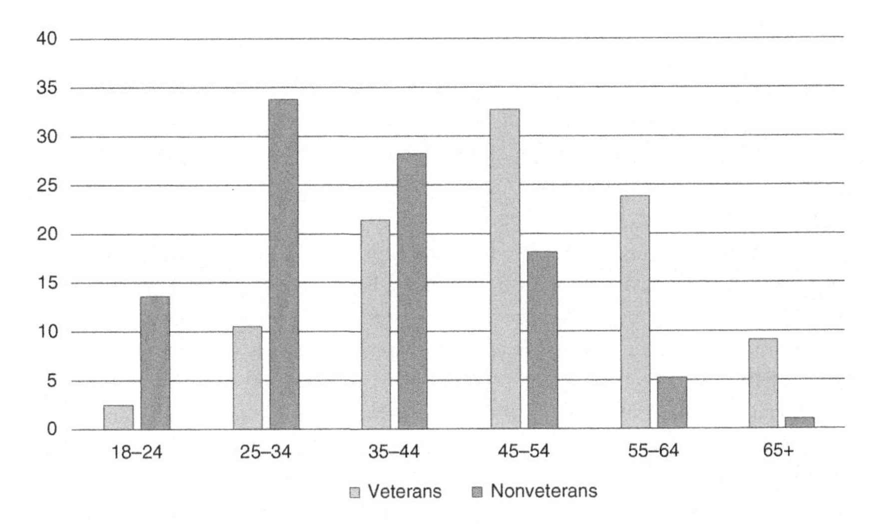

Figure 12.1 Percentage of veterans and nonveterans in prison by age.

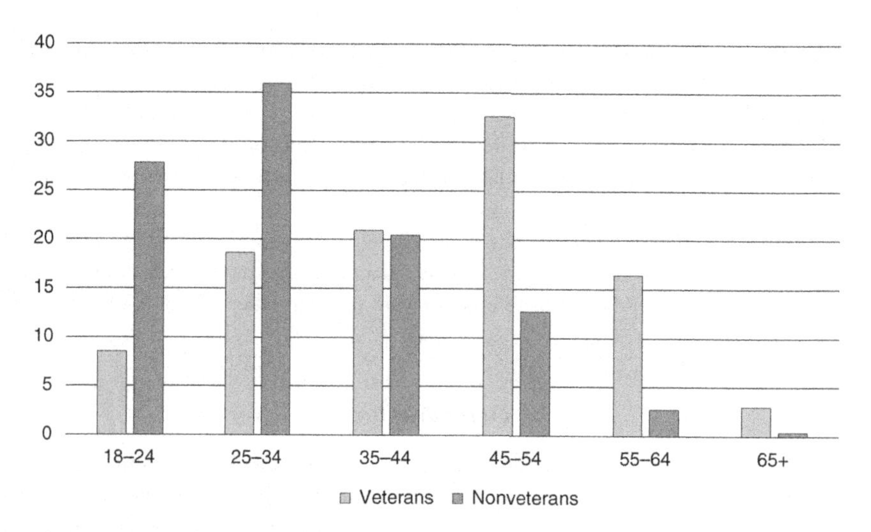

Figure 12.2 Percentage of veterans and nonveterans in jail by age.

(Cabage, 2014). The median age for women veterans (27 years of age) and nonveterans (36 years of age) is similar to that of men (Cabage, 2014). The median age for veteran men in federal custody is 47. The median age for women veterans is 43. Both veteran men and veteran women in federal custody are older than nonveterans.

The majority of incarcerated veterans are between the ages of 45–54, and the majority of nonveterans are between the ages of 25–34.

As with veterans incarcerated in prison, veterans in jail are more likely to be older. The majority of veterans are in the 45–54 age range and the majority of nonveterans are in the 25–34 age range.

The U.S. Department of Justice (2015) report identifies 50% of veterans as white, 27% black, and 11% Hispanic. In the jail setting, non-Hispanic white veterans constitute the majority of the population. Non-Hispanic blacks represented 32% of the population and 11% of the population was Hispanic (U.S. Department of Justice, 2015). See Figures 12.3 and 12.4 for information from the 2004 Survey data that includes women in state prisons and federal custody, respectively.

In the 2004 data, veteran men in state prisons were predominately black, or African American (39.4%). For nonveteran men the predominant race is white (46.3%). Both veteran and nonveteran women are predominately white (Cabage, 2014).

In the federal correctional population, veteran men are predominately white (56.2%), whereas nonveteran men are predominately black (44.3%). The opposite is true for women veterans in federal custody. Veteran women are predominately black (47.4%), and nonveteran women are predominately white (51.2%).

In regard to marriage, veterans incarcerated in both prison and jail were more likely to have been married at some point in their lives than nonveterans. Forty-five percent of veterans in prison and 31% of those in jail reported being divorced (see Figures 12.5 and 12.6). This is higher than the rate of divorce for nonveterans, but this makes sense considering veterans were more likely to have been married in the past.

The 2004 data for state inmates demonstrates a similar pattern to the 2015 data. Veteran men in state prisons were more likely to report being married than nonveteran men. Veteran women also were more likely to report being married than nonveteran women. Both veteran women and men have higher levels of divorce than their nonveteran peers (Cabage, 2014). However, as noted previously, this makes sense as they were more likely to be married in the first place.

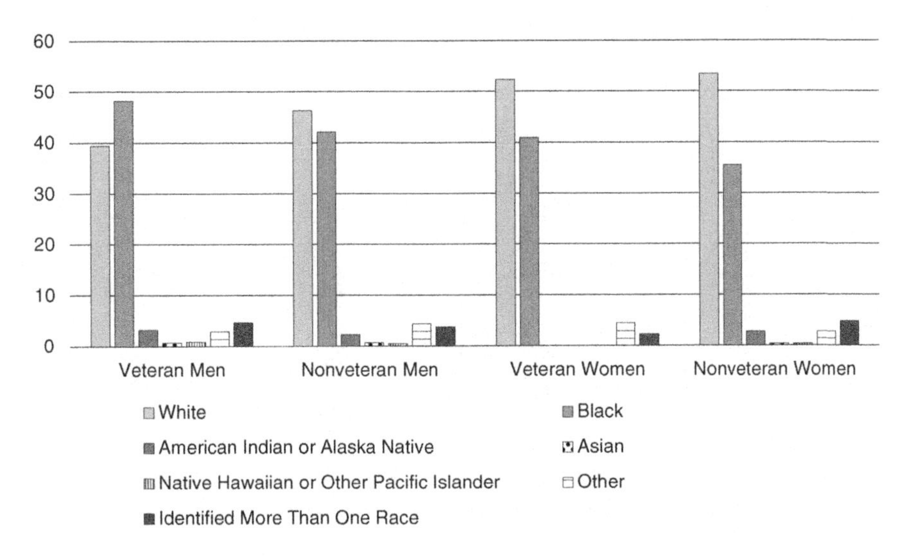

Figure 12.3 Race (percentage) of veterans in state prisons.

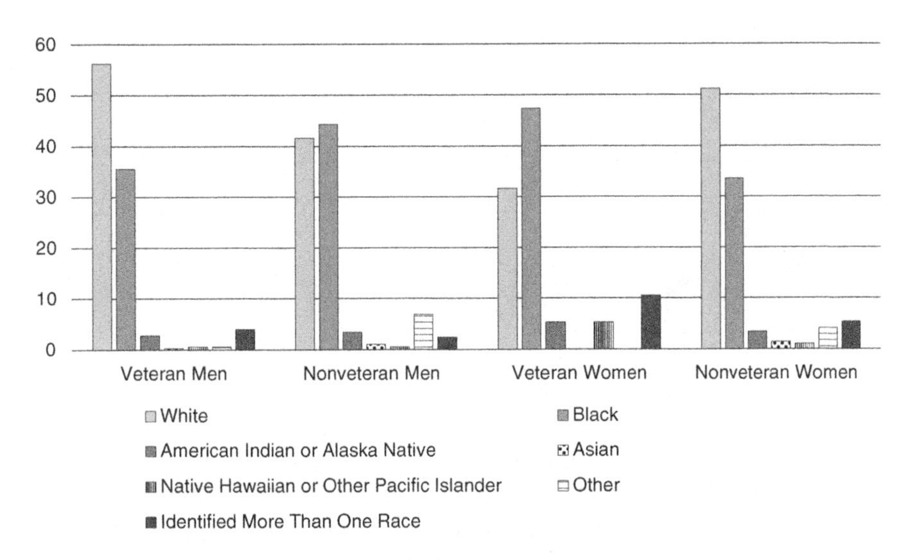

Figure 12.4 Race (percentage) of veterans in federal custody.

At the federal level, veteran men are more likely to be married than nonveterans. However, nonveterans are more likely to be divorced. However, the majority of both veteran and nonveteran men in federal custody reported never being married. For women, the majority of federal inmates reported never being married. Nonveteran women in federal custody were more likely than veteran women to have been both married and divorced (Cabage, 2014).

Veterans reported higher levels of former education than nonveterans (see Figures 12.7 and 12.8). Veterans in prison (20%) and jail (18%) report having a college degree compared to 5% of nonveterans (U.S. Department of Justice, 2015).

The 2004 data is broken down by educational level. Veteran men are more likely than nonveteran men to report having a GED or high school diploma (72% compared to 61.9%). However, the opposite is true for women veterans; women nonveterans are more likely to have a GED or high school

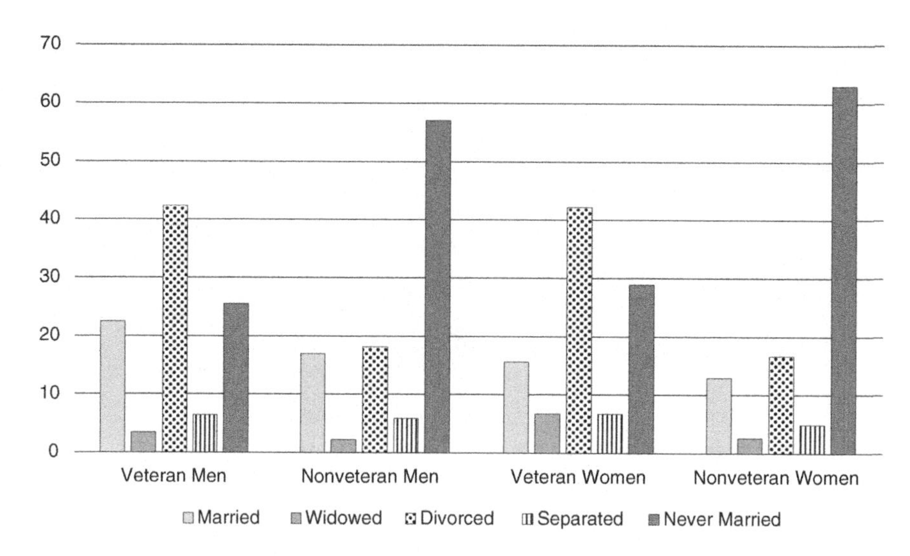

Figure 12.5 Marital status of state respondents by percentage.

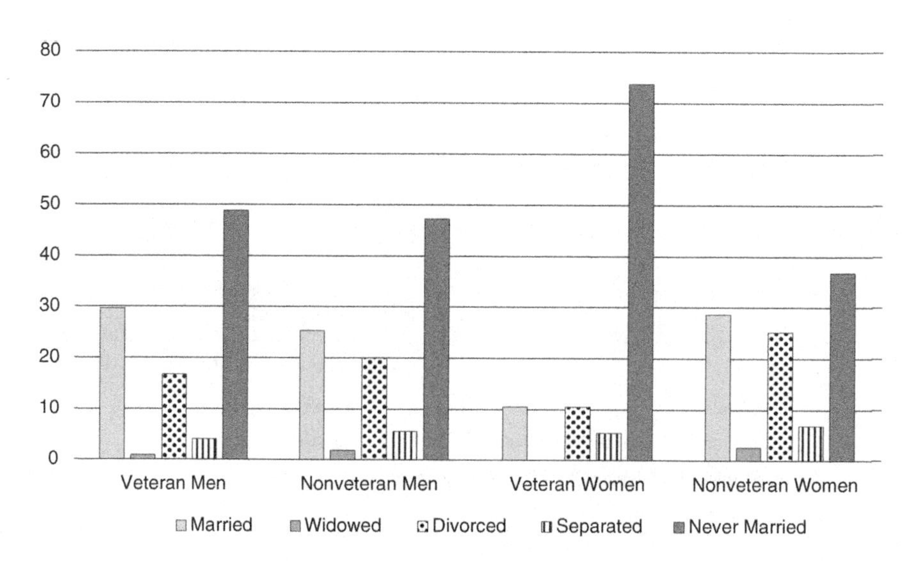

Figure 12.6 Marital status of federal respondents by percentage.

diploma than veteran women (64.3% vs. 51.1%). Veteran men and women both are more likely to have attended college than their nonveteran counterparts (Cabage, 2014).

Nonveteran men in federal custody are more likely to have a high school diploma or GED than veteran men (73.9% vs. 69%). The same applies to women, 75.1% of nonveteran women have a GED or high school diploma, while only 47.4% of veteran women in federal custody have a GED or high school diploma. Nonveteran men and nonveteran women were the most likely to have attended college (Cabage, 2014).

Veteran men and women in state custody are more likely to have been homeless than nonveterans. Approximately 11% of veteran men in state custody reported being homeless and 15.9% of veteran women (Cabage, 2014). Veteran women are the most likely group to have experienced homelessness.

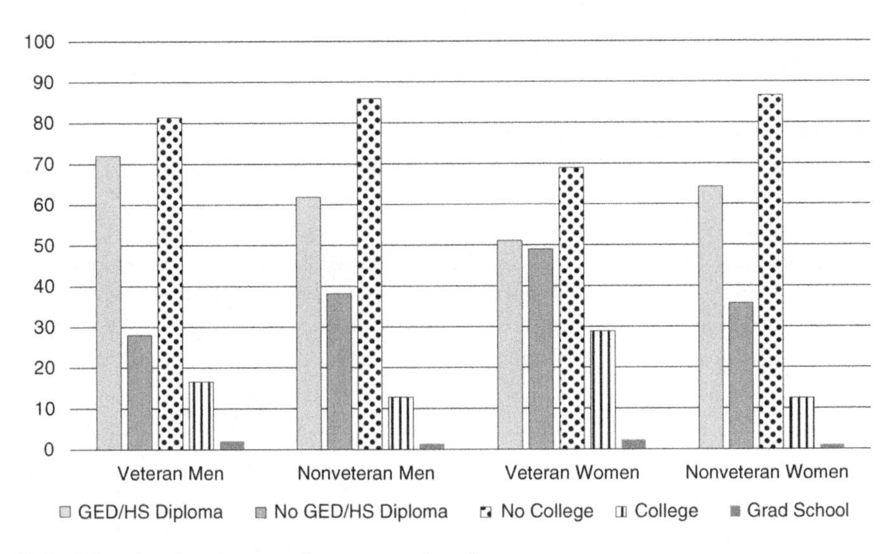

Figure 12.7 Educational attainment of state respondents by percentage.

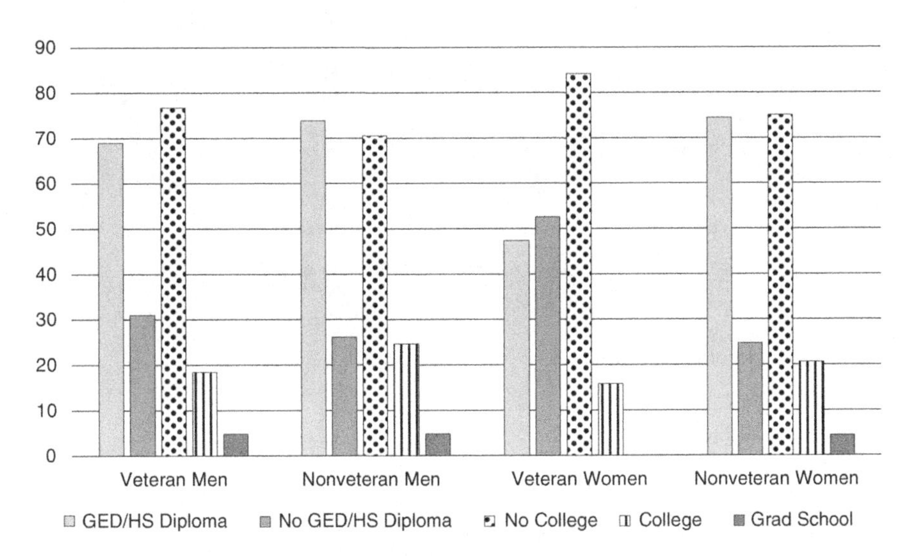

Figure 12.8 Educational attainment of federal respondents by percentage.

For individuals in federal custody, veteran women were the most likely to report being homeless (5.3%). The rate of homelessness for nonveteran women and veteran men in federal custody are similar (3.7% and 3.6% respectively). Nonveteran men are the second most likely group to be homeless (4.5%).

Mental Health and Substance Abuse

Veteran men in state custody (26.4%) are more likely to have been diagnosed with a mental health concern than nonveteran men (17%). Nonveteran women are slightly more likely to have a mental health concern than veteran women in state custody (35.9% compared to 35.6%) (Cabage, 2014). The most common diagnosis for all four groups is a depressive disorder. An examination of PTSD diagnosis reveals veterans are more likely to have a diagnosis than nonveterans in state custody (Cabage, 2014). Women veterans are the most likely to have a diagnosis of PTSD. See Figure 12.9 for additional information on the percentage of mental health diagnoses across all four categories.

In regard to substance use at the time of crime commission, nonveteran men in state custody are more likely to be under the influence of drugs and/or alcohol than veteran men. The same applies to women (Cabage, 2014).

In federal custody, veteran women were more likely than any other group to have a mental health diagnosis (see Figure 12.10). Veteran men were slightly more likely than nonveteran men (24.8% vs. 14.8%). Veteran women also are more likely to have a mental health diagnosis (47.4% vs 35.5%). The most common diagnosis across all groups is a depressive disorder. Focusing on PTSD reveals both nonveteran women and veteran men are more likely to have a diagnosis (Cabage, 2014).

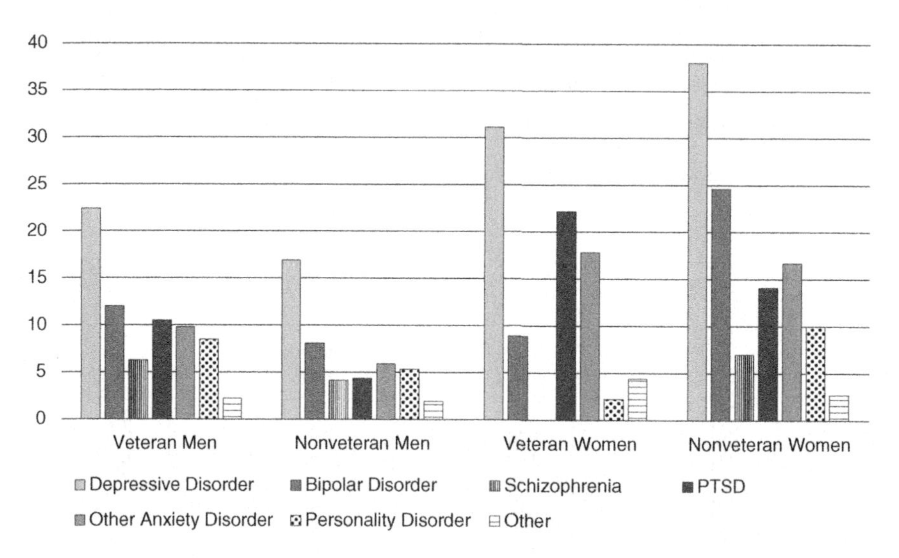

Figure 12.9 Type of mental health diagnosis of state respondents.

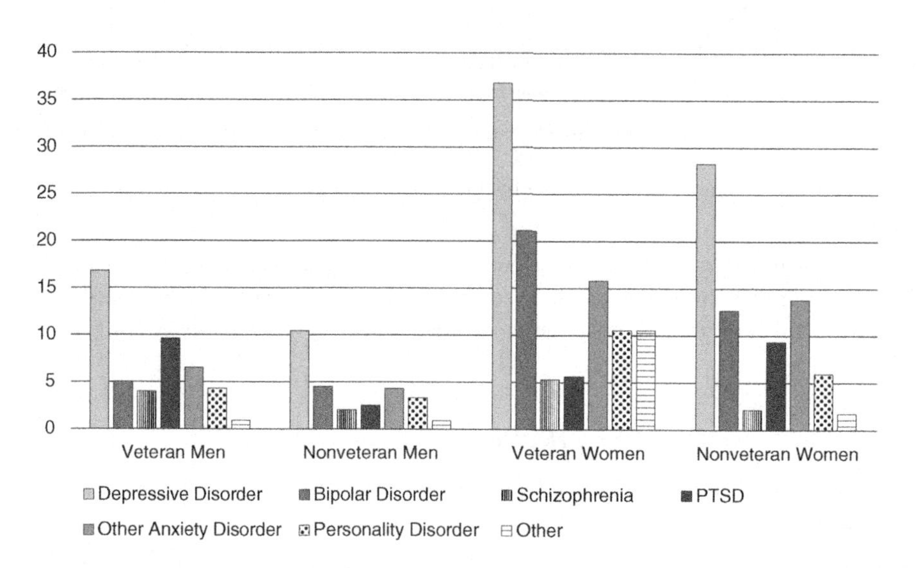

Figure 12.10 Type of mental health diagnosis of federal respondents.

Veteran men in federal custody were slightly more likely to have consumed alcohol at the time the crime was committed. However, nonveteran men were more likely to be under the influence of some type of drug. Veteran women are more likely than nonveteran women to be under the influence of alcohol and/or some type of drug during the commission of the crime.

Criminal History, Offense Type, and Sentence Length

Veterans are less likely to have prior arrests and incarcerations. Approximately 43% of veterans in prison have four or more prior arrests, and 22% have one prior arrest. This is compared to 55% of nonveterans who have four or more prior arrest and 16% of nonveterans with one prior arrest (U.S. Department of Justice, 2015). Despite being less likely to have a prior arrest, veterans are more likely to be convicted of a violent crime. Sixty-four percent of veterans and 52% of nonveterans in prison were sentenced for violent offenses. Veterans also were more likely to be in prison for a violent sexual offense (35% of veterans vs. 23% of nonveterans) (U.S. Department of Justice, 2015). In regard to sentence length, veterans (81%) were more likely to have a sentence of five or more years than nonveterans (77%). Veterans also were more likely to be serving life sentences (U.S. Department of Justice, 2015).

Special Units for Veterans

Veterans who are incarcerated have a unique set of needs that may be best addressed in a specialized setting. The prevalence of PTSD, other mental health problems, and substance abuse among the population increases the propensity of self-harm among the population. As mentioned previously, veterans find it difficult to seek help with these concerns because of the stigma attached. For incarcerated veterans, the stigma is still present and they now have a loss of freedom to cope with. They may feel as if their service to their country has now been depreciated because of their choices and incarceration.

As with any veterans suffering from PTSD, a mental illness, and/or substance abuse, these veterans may benefit from peer support. Specialized units and programs help provide these services. This is especially important for those who carry the burden of war trauma, because discussing the effect of deployment with an individual they feel cannot comprehend may lead to further frustrations and an increased likelihood in suicide (Bullman & Kang, 1994). Therefore, it is essential to create situations in which the veterans feel comfortable and can begin alleviating some of their mental health needs.

In Washington State, veterans are placed in a cellblock organized as a representation of a military unit. The unit is complete with insignia and flag ceremonies. The belief is the unit will allow the veterans to build on the discipline they have from the military to prepare for reentry into the community (Murphy, 2015). Further, grouping the veteran inmates together makes it easier for the state to identify the inmates and help them sign up for VA benefits, services, and job training. However, William Brown (a criminal justice professor at Western Oregon) challenges the success of the program and says, "the real test of the program's success will happen when the inmates are released, when being a veteran with a criminal record isn't the norm" (as cited in Murphy, 2015, para. 19). Brown continues that veterans on the outside are the harshest critics of those who have been caught up in the criminal justice system (Murphy, 2015). If we hope to reintegrate these individuals successfully, we have to change this and harness the support of other veterans to help provide peer support.

A similar unit operates at the Albany County, New York, jail. The sheriff considers the program a success because recidivism rates have been low. Of the 195 veterans released, only 10 have returned (Connor, 2017). In addition to low recidivism rates, problems in the veterans' pod are minimal. There has never been a fight in the pod. This is the same pod that stepped in to assist a correctional officer when he was attacked by an inmate from another wing. Although the evidence suggests this unit is successful in reducing recidivism, additional research should be conducted to determine the success of such units in reducing recidivism and helping veterans with their struggles.

These specialized units are likely effective because of the intensive nature of the units. These individuals are provided with intensive treatment for mental health and substance abuse addiction. These units also are essential in connecting veterans with services from the VA. The veterans incarcerated at the Albany County jail work with a program called *Soldier On*. *Soldier On* collaborated with the jail and provides transitional housing for the veterans as well as provides staff to support the veterans. This is largely paid for by grants from the U.S. Department of Veterans Affairs (Connor, 2017). Florida officials also house their veteran state inmates together. This is done in an effort to expedite the information provided to the veterans related to their benefits. Six months prior to release, the veteran meets with someone from the VA to gather information and to complete his or her application (Alvarez, 2011). These resources become invaluable for the veterans and future success.

Veterans' Courts

Veterans' courts are one of the newest problem-solving court models. As military personnel returned from the Afghanistan and Iraq wars, drug and mental health courts saw an increase in the number of veterans in the given courts (Johnson et al., 2016). While veterans have high rates of mental illness and substance abuse, it is the shared military experience and the complex issues the individuals faced that resulted in the development of veterans' courts in the U.S. These courts give veterans of foreign wars who are entangled in the criminal justice system because of substance abuse or mental health concerns an alternative to incarceration.

Veterans' courts utilize a nonadversarial approach that includes the involvement of the judge, prosecutor, defense attorney, supervision officer, Veteran's Affairs, and community-based organizations. These individuals and organizations come together to provide intensive treatment and rehabilitation for the justice-involved veterans. Although this resembles drug and mental health courts, veterans' courts are unique. They take into account the distinctive characteristics and personalities of military personnel and veterans. This allows the justice-involved veteran to connect with individuals who are similarly situation. Therefore, mentoring is a key component of veterans' courts. The mentoring consists of non-justice-involved veterans providing social support to court participants and assisting the participants in setting goals and problem solving.

Veterans Justice Outreach (VJO) Program

The Veterans Justice Outreach (VJO) Program was designed to avoid the unnecessary criminalization of mental illness within the veteran population. The program seeks to provide eligible justice-involved veterans with access to Veteran Health Administration services. The VJO Program also provides outreach, assessment, and case management for those veterans in the justice system. The VBO Program is essential for the success of veterans' treatment courts as they work to connect veterans with disability compensation, pension benefits, employment, and training.

Conclusion

Veterans are a unique population. They have provided service for their country, but at the same time many pay a large price for doing so. When veterans return home, they may suffer from PTSD, which may lead to substance abuse and homelessness. This also puts these individuals at an increased risk of becoming involved in the criminal justice system.

Approximately 8% of all inmates in state and federal prisons and 7% of inmates in local jails are veterans. These inmates face a unique set of contributing factors to incarceration. A number of veterans are diagnosed with PTSD. This rate is higher for those who experienced combat during their employment. A PTSD diagnosis often leads the individual to self-medicate with alcohol and drugs because of the stigma attached to seeking help. The combination of mental health concerns and substance abuse may then lead to the failure to maintain employment. Loss of employment then means facing potential homelessness. All of this is a risk factor for the general population and criminal justice involvement. As each of these factors increase for the veteran population, they face an increased chance of becoming justice-involved.

The Department of Veterans Affairs offers a number of resources to veterans in an attempt to prevent them from becoming justice-involved. However, not all individuals realize these resources are available to them, and they may find themselves struggling. It is essential for the VA to provide veterans with information related to their benefits and how to apply. For those veterans who become justice-involved, specialized units such as the ones in New York and Florida provide the VA with the opportunity to work directly with the incarcerated individuals to establish what benefits they are eligible for and assist them in applying. The VA also plays a key role in the success of veterans' treatment courts for the same reason. If the justice-involved veterans are informed of what benefits they qualify for and have assistance with completing the necessary paperwork, it is likely they will not return to incarceration. This appears to be the key factor of success for a number of veterans.

Our veterans proudly defended our country and put their lives on the line so we could have the rights we have. We should be doing all we can to provide them with the resources to succeed. Local, state, and federal agencies need to work with the Department of Veterans Affairs to ensure justice-involved veterans understand what benefits they are entitled to and how to apply. This opportunity will likely prevent future offending from these individuals and provide them with a renewed sense of pride.

References

Alvarez, L. (2011, December 11). In Florida, using military discipline to help veterans in prison. *The New York Times*. Retrieved from www.nytimes.com/2011/12/12/us/veterans-in-prison-get-help-in-florida-program.html?mcubz=3

Beckham, J. C., Feldman, M. E., Kirby, A. C., Hertzberg, M. A., & Moore, S. D. (1997). Interpersonal violence and its correlates in Vietnam veterans with chronic posttraumatic stress disorder. *Journal of Clinical Psychology, 53*(8), 859–869. doi:10.1002/(SICI)1097-4679(199712)53:8<859::AID-JCLP11>3.0.CO;2-J

Blackstock, O. J., Haskell, S. G., Brandt, C. A., & Desai, R. A. (2012). Gender and the use of Veterans Health Administration homeless services programs among Iraq/Afghanistan veterans. *Medical Care, 50*(4), 347–352. doi:10.1097/MLR.0b013e318245a738

Brown, P. J., & Wolfe, J. (1994). Substance abuse and post-traumatic stress disorder comorbidity. *Drug and Alcohol Dependence, 35*(1), 51–59.

Bullman, T. A., & Kang, H. K. (1994). Posttraumatic stress disorder and the risk of traumatic deaths among Vietnam veterans. *The Journal of Nervous and Mental Disease, 182*(11), 604–610.

Butterfield, M. I., Forneris, C. A., Feldman, M. E., & Beckham, J. C. (2000). Hostility and functional health status in women veterans with and without posttraumatic stress disorder: A preliminary study. *Journal of Traumatic Stress, 13*(4), 735–741. doi:10.1023/A:1007874620024

Cabage, L. N. (2014). *Incarcerated veterans, their crimes, and length of sentence: A comparison of State and Federal inmates by gender* [Unpublished Manuscript].

Combined Arms. (2013). *Veterans in the criminal justice system*. Retrieved from www.repwavets.org/justice-involved-veterans.html

Connor, T. (2017, February 26). Prisons experiment with cell blocks for military veterans. *NBC News*. Retrieved from www.nbcnews.com/news/us-news/prisons-experiment-cell-blocks-military-veterans-n721306

Coyle, B. S., Wolan, D. L., & Van Horn, A. S. (1996). The prevalence of physical and sexual abuse in women veterans seeking care at a veterans affairs medical center. *Military Medicine, 161*(10), 588–593.

Dutra, L., Grubbs, K., Greene, C., Trego, L. L., McCartin, R. L., Kloezeman, K., & Morland, L. (2010). Women at war: Implications for mental health. *Journal of Trauma & Dissociation, 12*(1), 25–37. doi:10.1080/15299732.2010.496141

Edens, E. L., Kasprow, W., Tsai, J., & Rosenheck, R. A. (2011). Association of substance use and VA service-connected disability benefits with risk of homelessness among veterans. *The American Journal of Addictions, 20*(5), 412–419. doi:10.1111/j.1521-0391.2011.00166.x

Friedman, M. J. (2004). Acknowledging the psychiatric cost of war. *The New England Journal of Medicine, 351*, 75–77. doi:10.1056/NEJMe048129

Glenn, D. M., Beckham, J. C., Feldman, M. E., Kirby, A. C., Hertzberg, M. A., & Moore, S. D. (2002). Violence and hostility among families of Vietnam veterans with combat-related posttraumatic stress disorder. *Violence and Victims, 17*(4), 473–489.

Hamilton, A. B., Poza, I., & Washington, D. L. (2011). "Homelessness and trauma go hand-in-hand": Pathways to homelessness among women veterans. *Women's Health Issues, 21*(S4), S203–209. doi:10.1016/j.whi.2011.04.005

Hankin, C. S., Skinner, K. M., Sullivan, L. M., Miller, D. R., Frayne, S., & Tripp, T. J. (1999). Prevalence of depressive and alcohol abuse symptoms among women VA outpatients who report experiencing sexual assault while in the military. *Journal of Traumatic Stress, 12*(4), 601–612, doi:10.1023/A:1024760900213

Hassija, C. M., Jakupcak, M., Maguen, S., & Shipherd, J. C. (2012). The influence of combat and interpersonal trauma on PTSD, depression, and alcohol misuse in U.S. Gulf War and OEF/OIF women veterans. *Journal of Traumatic Stress, 25*(2), 216–219. doi:10.1002/jts.21686

Heaton, P., Loughran, D. S., & Miller, A. R. (2012). *Compensating wounded warriors: An analysis of injury, labor market earnings, and disability compensation among veterans of the Iraq and Afghanistan wars*. Santa Monica, CA: RAND Corporation.

Hoge, C. W., Castro, C. A., Messer, S. C., McGurk, D., Cotting, D. I., & Koffman, R. L. (2004). Combat duty in Iraq and Afghanistan, mental health problems, and barriers to care. *The New England Journal of Medicine, 351*, 13–22. doi:10.1056NEJMoa040603

Jakupcak, M., Conybeare, D., Phelps, L., Hunt, S., Holmes, H. A., Felker, B., . . . McFall, M. E. (2007). Anger, hostility, and aggression among Iraq and Afghanistan war veterans reporting PTSD and subthreshold PTSD. *Journal of Traumatic Stress, 20*(6), 945–954. doi:10.1002/jts.20258

Jakupcak, M., Tull, M. T., McDermott, M. J., Kaysen, D., Hunt, S., & Simpson, T. (2010). PTSD symptom clusters in relationship to alcohol misuse among Iraq and Afghanistan war veterans seeking post-deployment VA health care. *Addictive Behavior, 35*(9), 840–843. doi:10.1016/j.addbeh.2010.03.023

Johnson, R. S., Stolar, A. G., McGuire, J. F., Clark, S., Coonan, L. A., Hausknecht, P., & Graham, D. P. (2016). US veterans' court programs: An inventory and analysis of national survey data. *Community Mental Health Journal, 52*(2), 180–186. doi:10.1007/s10597-015-9972-3

Jordan, B. K., Marmar, C. R., Fairbank, J. A., Schlenger, W. E., Kulka, R. A., Hough, R. L., & Weiss, D. S. (1992). Problems in families of male Vietnam veterans with posttraumatic stress disorder. *Journal of Consulting and Clinical Psychology, 60*(6), 916–926. doi:10.1037/0022–006X.60.6.916

Kang, H., Dalager, N., Mahan, C., & Ishii, E. (2005). The role of sexual assault on the risk of PTSD among Gulf War veterans. *Annals of Epidemiology, 15*(3), 191–195. doi:10.1016/j.annepidem.2004.05.009

Kessler, R. C., Sonnega, A., Bromet, E., Hughes, M., & Nelson, C. B. (1995). Posttraumatic stress disorder in the national comorbidity survey. *Archives of General Psychiatry, 52*(12), 1048–1060. doi:10.1001/archpsych.1995.03950240066012

Kimerling, R., Gima, K., Smith, M. W., Street, A., & Frayne, S. (2007). The Veterans Health Administration and military sexual trauma. *American Journal of Public Health, 97*(12), 2160–2166. doi:10.2105/AJPH.2006.092999

Kimerling, R., Street, A. E., Pavao, J., Smith, M. W., Cronkite, R. C., Holmes, T. H., & Frayne, S. M. (2010). Military-related sexual trauma among Veterans Health Administration patients returning from Afghanistan and Iraq. *American Journal of Public Health, 100*(8), 1409–1412. doi:10.2105/AJPH.2009.171793

Luxton, D. D., Skopp, N. A., & Maguen, S. (2010). Gender differences in depression and PTSD symptoms following combat exposure. *Depression and Anxiety, 27*(11), 1027–1033. doi:10.1002/da.20730

Maguen, S., Luxton, D. D., Skopp, N. A., & Madden, E. (2012). Gender differences in traumatic experiences and mental health in active duty soldiers redeployed from Iraq and Afghanistan. *Journal of Psychiatric Research, 46*(3), 311–316. doi:10.1016/j.jpsychires.2011.11.007

McFall, M., Fontana, A., Raskind, M., & Rosenheck, R. (1999). Analysis of violent behavior in Vietnam combat veteran psychiatric inpatients with posttraumatic stress disorder. *Journal of Traumatic Stress, 12*(3), 501–517. doi:10.1023/A:1024771121189

McFall, M. E., Mackay, P. W., & Donovan, D. M. (1992). Combat-related posttraumatic stress disorder and severity of substance abuse in Vietnam veterans. *Journal of Studies on Alcohol, 53*(4), 357–363.

Metraux, S., Clegg, L. X., Daigh, J. D., Culhane, D. P., & Kane, V. (2013). Risk factors for becoming homeless among a cohort of veterans who served in the era of the Iraq and Afghanistan conflicts. *American Journal of Public Health, 103*(Supp 2), S255–S261. doi: 10.2105/AJPH.2013.301432

Milliken, C. S., Auchterlonie, J. L., & Hoge, C. W. (2007). Longitudinal assessment of mental health problems among active and reserve component soldiers returning from the Iraq war. *Journal of the American Medical Association, 298*(18), 2141–2148. doi:10.1001/jama.298.18.2141

Murphy, P. (2015, December 7). Prisons experiment with programs to help incarcerated veterans. *NPR*. Retrieved from www.npr.org/2015/12/07/458828465/prisons-experiment-with-programs-to-help-incarcerated-veterans

National Alliance to End Homelessness. (2015). *Veteran homelessness*. Retrieved from https://endhomelessness.org/resource/veteran-homelessness/

Prokos, A., & Cabage, L. N. (2017). Women military veterans, disability, and employment. *Armed Forces & Society, 43*(2), 346–367. doi:10.1177/0095327X15610743

Risen, T. (2014, November 10). Veterans Day data boot camp. *U.S. News & World Report*. Retrieved from www.usnews.com/news/blogs/data-mine/2014/11/10/veterans-day-data-boot-camp

Robert, P. M., & Harlan, S. L. (2006). Mechanisms of disability discrimination in large bureaucratic organizations: Ascriptive inequalities in the workplace. *Sociological Quarterly, 47*(4), 599–630. doi:10.111/j.1533-8525.2006.00060.x

Rosenheck, R. A., & Fontana, A. A. (1994). A model of homelessness among male veterans of the Vietnam War generation. *American Journal of Psychiatry, 151*(3), 421–427. doi:10.1176/ajp.151.3.421

Rosenheck, R. A., Leda, C., Frisman, L. K., Lam, J., & Chung, A. (1996). Homeless veterans. In J. Baumohl (Ed.), *Homelessness in America* (pp. 97–108). Phoenix, AZ: Oryx Press.

Sadler, A. G., Booth, B. M., Cook, B. L., & Doebbeling, B. N. (2003). Factors associated with women's risk of rape in the military environment. *American Journal of Industrial Medicine, 43*, 262–273. doi:10.1002/ajim.10202

Sadler, A. G., Booth, B. M., Nielson, D., & Doebbeling, B. N. (2000). Health-related consequences of physical and sexual violence: Women in the military. *Obstetrics & Gynecology, 96*(3), 473–480.

Seal, K. H., Bertenthal, D., & Miner, C. R. (2007). Bringing the war back home: Mental health disorders among 103,788 US veterans returning from Iraq and Afghanistan seen at Department of Veterans Affairs facilities. *Archives of Internal Medicine, 167*(5), 476–482. doi:10.1001/archinte.167.5.476

Seal, K. H., Metzler, T. J., Gima, K. S., Bertenthal, D., Maguen, S., & Marmar, C. R. (2009). Trends and risk factors for mental health diagnoses among Iraq and Afghanistan veterans using Department of Veterans Affairs health care, 2002–2008. *American Journal of Public Health, 99*(9), 1651–1658. doi:10.2105/AJPH.2008.150284

Shipherd, J. C., Stafford, J., & Tanner, L. R. (2005). Predicting alcohol and drug abuse in Persian Gulf War veterans: What role do PTSD symptoms play? *Addictive Behaviors, 30*, 595–599.

Skopp, N. A., Reger, M. A., Reger, G. M., Mishkind, M., Raskind, M., & Gahm, G. A. (2011). The role of intimate relationships, appraisals of military service, and gender on the development of posttraumatic stress symptoms following Iraq deployment. *Journal of Traumatic Stress, 24*(3), 277–286. doi:10.1002/jts.20632

Smith, M. W., Schnurr, P. P., & Rosenheck, R. A. (2005). Employment outcomes and PTSD symptom severity. *Mental Health Services Research*, 7(2), 89–101.

Tanielian, T. L., Jaycox, L. H., Schell, T. L., Marshall, G. N., Burnam, M. A., Eibner, C., Karney, B. R., Meredith, L. S., Ringel, J. S., & Vaiana, M. E. (2008). *Invisible wounds of war: Summary and recommendations for addressing psychological and cognitive injuries*. Santa Monica, CA: RAND Corporation.

United States Department of Justice, Bureau of Justice Statistics. (2015). *Veterans in prison and jail, 2011–12* (NCJ249144). Washington, DC: U.S. Government Printing Office.

United States Department of Labor. (2014). *Employment situation of veterans-2013* (Publication No. USDL-14-0434). Washington, DC: U.S. Government Printing Office.

United States Department of Veterans Affairs, Office of the Inspector General. (2012). *Incidence of homelessness among veterans and risk factors for becoming homeless in veterans* (Report No. 11–03428–173). Washington, DC: Department of Veterans Affairs, Office of the Inspector General.

Washington, D. L., Yano, E. M., McGuire, J., Hines, V., Lee, M., & Gelberg, L. (2010). Risk factors for homelessness among women veterans. *Journal of Health Care for the Poor and Underserved, 21*(1), 82–91. doi:10.1353/hpu.0.0237

Wilmoth, J. M., London, A. S., & Parker, W. M. (2011). Sex differences in the relationship between military service status and functional limitations and disabilities. *Population Research and Policy Review, 30*(3), 333–354. doi:10.1007/s11113-010-9191-0

Yaeger, D., Himmelfarb, N., Cammack, A., & Mintz, J. (2006). DSM-IV diagnosed posttraumatic stress disorder in women veterans with and without military sexual trauma. *Journal of General Internal Medicine, 21*(S3), S65–69. doi:10.1111/j.1525-1497.2006.00377.x

Zinzow, H. M., Grubaugh, A. L., Monnier, J., Suffoletta-Maierle, S., & Frueh, B. C. (2007). Trauma among female veterans: A critical review. *Trauma, Violence, & Abuse, 8*(4), 384–400. doi:10.1177/1524838007307295

13

IMMIGRANT PRISONERS

Conditions of Confinement and Institutional Abuses

Jodie M. Lawston

Give me your tired, your poor, your huddled masses yearning to breathe free, the wretched refuse of your teeming shore. Send these, the homeless, tempest-tost to me, I lift my lamp beside the golden door!

—Emma Lazarus from *The New Colossus* inscribed at the base of the Statue of Liberty

Introduction

The United States has the highest incarceration rate in the world. With just 5% of the world's population, we house 25% of the world's prisoners (ACLU, 2014). There are currently close to 2.3 million people in prisons, jails, and local correctional facilities, a 500% increase in incarceration rates over the past 40 years (Kaeble, Glaze, Tsoutis, & Minton, 2016; The Sentencing Project, 2015). Much of this increase has been the result of the "War on Drugs" and corresponding changes in sentencing laws—such as the passage of mandatory minimum sentences, which keep drug offenders locked behind bars for longer periods of time—rather than to dramatic changes in crime rates (ACLU, 2014; The Sentencing Project, 2015). These changes in laws have disproportionately affected racial and ethnic minorities, with more than 60% of incarcerated people being of color; black men and women, and Latinos/as, are disproportionately imprisoned across the nation (The Sentencing Project, 2015).

Parallel to the growth in incarceration of people for traditionally defined crimes, such as drug use, a report issued by the ACLU (2014) notes that a recent contributing factor to increased incarceration rates has been the redefinition of immigration violations as criminal offenses. For example,

> Nationwide, more than half of all federal prosecutions initiated in fiscal year 2013 were for unlawfully crossing the border into the United States—an act that has traditionally been treated as a civil offense resulting in deportation, rather than as a criminal act resulting in a federal prison [sentence].
>
> (ACLU, 2014, p. 2)

This ACLU (2014) report notes that U.S. Customs and Border Protection (CBP) now refers more cases than the Federal Bureau of Investigation (FBI) for federal criminal prosecution. In the federal prison system, immigration convictions represent 30% of all federal convictions, second only to drug offenses (which represent 33% of federal convictions) (Light, Lopez, & Gonzalez-Barrera, 2014). The immigrants who are locked up for immigration offenses like unlawfully crossing the border—most of which have long-standing family ties in the U.S.—are incarcerated in Criminal Alien Requirement (CAR) prisons, which will be explored in this chapter. With the redefinition of immigration violations as criminal offenses, Latinos/as are now the largest racial/ethnic group in the federal prison system (Escobar, 2016; Wessler, 2016).

In addition to being locked up in CAR prisons, there are significant numbers of immigrants who are detained in an extensive web of Immigration and Customs Enforcement (ICE) facilities across the nation. Although the Department of Homeland Security (DHS) does not have the authority to hold anybody awaiting trial or serving a criminal sentence, ICE, under the direction of the DHS, detains hundreds of thousands of noncitizens in prisons, jails, and other facilities across the United States.

There is a difference in the terminology used to refer to those confined in CAR prisons and those detained in ICE facilities. Since those held in CAR prisons have been prosecuted for a criminal offense, they are usually referred to as prisoners, while those being held in ICE facilities are referred to as detainees. Those who are detained by ICE include asylum seekers, lawful permanent residents, and individuals with long-standing family ties in the U.S. who may have some sort of relief for obtaining legal status (Dow 2004; Migration and Refugee Services, United States Conference on Catholic Bishops, & The Center for Migration Studies, 2015). Though detainees have not committed a crime, detention is rationalized by the DHS as necessary to ensure that individuals appear for their court hearings or to remove them from the country, if an immigration judge rules so. In some cases, entire families, including children, are imprisoned in detention centers as they await petitions for asylum. Certainly, the decision to place families who are fleeing persecution and dire circumstances and are seeking a better life—into what are essentially prisons—belies the values that the nation holds sacrosanct.

This chapter explores the conditions of confinement for both immigrants, who are increasingly incarcerated in CAR prisons, and immigrants who are locked up in detention facilities. These conditions include emotional, physical, and sexual abuse, limited access to programming, medical neglect, overcrowding, being housed at facilities that are located excessive distances from family and loved ones, and overuse of isolation or segregation. This chapter highlights the abuses that occur inside CAR prisons and immigrant detention centers within a larger climate of punishment and criminalization in the U.S. Moreover, because immigration holds a unique place in our history in forging the values that make our society unique among the nations of the world, the chapter ends with some reflections on what the conditions of confinement mean for our society. The cruelty and indignity with which immigrants—and all prisoners—are treated, arguably, pose a threat to the very integrity of our nation.

The Criminalization of Immigration

The numbers of noncitizen immigrants who are imprisoned in federal facilities has increased significantly over the years. Between 1998 and 2010, for example, immigration offenders accounted for 56% of the increase in federal prison admissions (Light et al., 2014). In 2012 alone, 46% of people sentenced in federal courts did not have U.S. citizenship (Light et al., 2014). The increase in immigration offenses is not the result of immigrants committing more crimes. Rather, this growth has been largely driven by changes in how the federal government deals with immigration. In the absence of any crime, the federal government historically relied on civil enforcement to address undocumented immigration. However, the federal government has increasingly chosen to criminally prosecute what authorities now term "illegal entry or reentry" into the United States (ACLU, 2010). With illegal entry, a person crosses the U.S. border in violation of its immigration laws. Entering the U.S. without being inspected and admitted by an immigration officer is a misdemeanor or, in some instances, a felony, depending on the circumstances (ACLU, 2010). With illegal reentry, an offender has entered or has attempted to enter the U.S. illegally more than once, or he or she has attempted to enter the U.S. after having been deported (Light et al., 2014; Robertson, Beaty, Atkinson, & Libel, 2012). Among the undocumented immigrants sentenced in federal courts, more than two-thirds, or 68%, were convicted of unlawful reentry (Light et al., 2014). Punishment of "unlawful reentry" has largely targeted the U.S.-Mexico border. Wessler (2016) reports that prosecutions for illegal entry and reentry rose from fewer than 4,000 a year at the start of Bill Clinton's presidency to 31,000 in 2004 under former President George W. Bush, to 91,000 in 2013 under former President Obama.

Immigrants apprehended at the U.S.-Mexico border, many of whom are Mexican, have historically been permitted to return voluntarily to Mexico, without any penalty. But unlawful reentry convictions in federal courts, particularly since 2005, are part of a broader effort by the U.S. Border Patrol to curtail repeated attempts to enter the United States and to break the smuggling cycle. As unlawful reentry cases have increased in number, the demographics of sentenced offenders in the Federal Bureau of Prisons (BOP) has changed. Twelve percent of federally sentenced offenders in 1992, as compared to 40% in 2012, were undocumented immigrants, and whereas in 1992 Latinos made up only 23% of sentenced offenders, by 2012 they comprised 48% of sentenced offenders (Light et al., 2014). In 2012, 92% of unlawful reentry offenders were Latino (Light et al., 2014). Most unlawful reentry cases come with a federal prison sentence of approximately two years (Light et al., 2014).

Federal policies, particularly one dubbed "Operation Streamline," rely on the criminal justice system to curtail immigration and have resulted in the criminalization of immigration (ACLU, 2014). The Department of Homeland Security (DHS) and the U.S. Department of Justice (DOJ) instated Operation Streamline in 2005. It has been implemented in every southwest border state except California (ACLU, 2014). Under Operation Streamline, the Department of Homeland Security refers undocumented immigrants to the Department of Justice for federal prosecution, and additionally processes them for deportation (ACLU, 2014). Since the program began, "A rising tide of both misdemeanor and felony immigration prosecutions has strained the resources of federal courts, created serious due process problems, and . . . swelled the flow of immigrants into jails and federal prisons" (ACLU, 2014, p. 22). The ACLU (2014, p. 23) report continues, noting that:

> Nationwide, more than half of all federal criminal prosecutions initiated in fiscal year 2013 were for illegal entry or reentry into the United States. The vast majority of these prosecutions take place in four Operation Streamline jurisdictions, where they dominate federal criminal dockets: in fiscal year 2013, illegal entry and reentry prosecutions accounted for 80% of all federal prosecutions in Arizona and New Mexico, 83% of all federal prosecutions in the Western District of Texas, and a whopping 88% of all federal prosecutions in the Southern District of Texas.

With federal courts overloaded with such cases and increases in the numbers of immigrants who are locked up, the federal government has added what they term "Criminal Alien Requirement" (CAR) prisons to the infrastructure of criminal justice facilities across the nation. Undocumented immigrants who have been federally prosecuted for immigration crimes frequently serve their sentences in CAR prisons until deportation.

Criminal Alien Requirement (CAR) Prisons

Criminal Alien Requirement (CAR) prisons—13 of which currently exist across the nation, housing more than 25,000 people—are facilities that are segregated based on citizenship (ACLU, 2014; Wessler, 2016). According to Wessler (2016), these prisons are "separate but unequal"; they hold only noncitizen male prisoners (immigrant women continue to be housed in BOP facilities) that were prosecuted by the federal government, but they operate *without* the same systems of accountability as other BOP facilities because the CAR facilities are run by private, for-profit companies instead of by the Federal BOP. CAR prisons are low-security facilities with fewer security requirements than medium and maximum facilities run by the BOP (ACLU, 2014).

The ACLU (2014) notes that growth in the number of federal private prisons began in 1999 when the BOP released a call for proposals from private contractors to set up a CAR prison to house up to 7,500 low-security, noncitizen prisoners. Since that first contract, the BOP has expanded its use of CAR prisons. Although the BOP refers to the people in CAR prisons as "criminal aliens," as previously stated, most were convicted of illegal entry or reentry.

The three leading private prison companies that run CAR prisons through contracts with the federal government are the Corrections Corporation of America (CCA), Geo Group, and the Management and Training Corporation (MTC). In 2011, GEO Group reported earnings of $1.61 billion, $640 million of which came from federal contracts (Robertson et al., 2012). Similarly, CCA reported earning $1.74 billion, 43% of which came from the federal government (Robertson et al., 2012). In 2012, CCA, GEO Group, and MTC reported profits of more than $4 billion in revenue (ACLU, 2014). With such high profits, these three corporations have a fiduciary interest in continued expansion of mass incarceration. A CCA annual report to the Securities and Exchange Commission (SEC) states:

> Our growth is generally dependent upon our ability to obtain new contracts to develop and manage new correctional and detention facilities. The demand for our facilities and services could be adversely affected by the relaxation of enforcement efforts, leniency in conviction or parole standards and sentencing practices or through the decriminalization of certain activities that are currently proscribed by criminal laws. For instance, any changes with respect to drugs and controlled substances or illegal immigration could affect the number of persons arrested, convicted, and sentenced, thereby potentially reducing demand for correctional facilities to house them.
>
> (in ACLU, 2014, p. 19)

This focus on profit over humanity—the decision to allow for-profit companies to play a critical role in the criminal justice and immigration systems—has led to gross violations against and abuses of the people within these private prison facilities across the nation. Indeed, since the inexorable imperative for growing profit margins is contingent upon maintaining low operations costs, any expenditures associated with care for the needs of prisoners must be kept as low as possible. The results of the for-profit system, not surprisingly, have been devastating, if not catastrophic, for the well-being of many being held in these facilities.

In addition to the for-profit motive, another contributing factor to the failure of CAR prisons to meet the needs of their detainees is the lack of oversight by the BOP. Open records laws that apply to other federal prisons do not apply to CAR prisons. Since they are privately run, there is little public disclosure about the conditions in these facilities (ACLU, 2014). Nonetheless, in a groundbreaking report that researched five CAR prisons in Texas—Giles W. Dalby Correctional Center in Post, Texas (1,896 prisoners), Big Spring Correctional Center in Big Spring, Texas (3,485 prisoners), Eden Detention Center in Eden, Texas (1,550 prisoners), Reeves County Detention Center in Pecos, Texas (3,636 prisoners), and Willacy County Detention Center in Raymondville, Texas (2,981 prisoners)—the ACLU (2014) uncovered gross neglect and abuses against immigrants. These abuses included emotional abuse, limited access to programming, medical neglect, overcrowding, imprisonment in facilities that are located excessive distances from family and loved ones, and overuse of isolation or segregation. The following sections will explore the ACLU's findings and the conditions of confinement—none of which meet the needs of the imprisoned immigrants.

Emotional Abuse

Similar to the emotional abuse that occurs in state prisons across the nation (Lawston, 2011), private prison guards at CAR prisons in Texas were found to use racial and ethnic slurs against immigrant prisoners (ACLU, 2014). These slurs include the use of terms like "wetback" and "Mexican nigger," which aim to demoralize and dehumanize immigrant prisoners (ACLU, 2014, p. 4). Rather than trying to communicate with the people in their charge, guards were found to degrade them for "failing to speak English in America" (ACLU, 2014, p. 4).

As an example of the emotional abuse endured by immigrants in CAR prisons, in Giles W. Dalby Correctional Facility, a blind prisoner named Emmanuel was often humiliated for his blindness: when he stood in the cafeteria line, a guard holding a barcode reader that is made for scanning prison ID's frequently aimed the reader into Emmanuel's eyes and laughed because he could not see (ACLU, 2014). Emmanuel was also taunted by guards in the recreation area and relied on assistance from other prisoners to move around the facility, since the guards would not help him. In addition, gay and straight prisoners reported that staff use homophobic insults against them, and staff made arbitrary threats of physical violence and disciplinary sanctions against prisoners (ACLU, 2014).

At best, these findings suggest that there is a fundamental misunderstanding by many guards of their roles and responsibilities as overseers of imprisoned people. Such behaviors do not meet the basic human needs of those in the custody of the U.S. government, nor are they fair and humane. Rather, racial slurs and behavior intended to mock and degrade those in their charge, on the part of correctional officers, expresses xenophobia, racial, and heterosexist antipathy, which should have no place in a free democratic society.

Limited Access to Programming

In CAR prisons, research shows that, compared to BOP-operated institutions, there is less access to programming, drug treatment, and education or work opportunities. This is the case even though many of the people locked up in CAR facilities have lived and worked in the United States for significant periods of time. BOP-operated prisons have education, rehabilitation, and work programs, which have been shown to decrease rates of violence in prison, decrease recidivism, and result in higher chances of employment upon release (ACLU, 2014). But immigrants imprisoned in CAR facilities, the BOP argues, are not supposed to return to the U.S. upon release, so any type of programming is seen as unnecessary. As the ACLU (2014) points out, though, many prisoners in CAR facilities do return to the U.S. For example, many have valid asylum claims, the ability to assert derivative citizenship, or other legal rights to remain in the U.S. upon release. In addition, many of the prisoners are located in the U.S., so they return to the U.S. after they serve their time (ACLU, 2014; Romero, 2015; Shueths & Lawston, 2015).

The inability to work in CAR prisons is particularly problematic. In federal prisons, prisoners can work for UNICOR, a government corporation established by Congress to help give prisoners job skills (ACLU, 2014). The jobs pay a meager 12 to 14 cents an hour, but prisoners often use that money for co-pays for medical care, additional food from the commissary, and phone calls to their families (ACLU, 2014). Not only can CAR prisoners not work for the money they need in prison, they are not afforded the opportunity to learn job skills and do not have much, if anything, to do with their time. This can lead to despair and depression for prisoners (Moulton, 2016).

Medical Neglect

Medical understaffing and cost-cutting approaches—so that private prison companies spend less, thereby increasing their profits—is a common practice in CAR prisons. The ACLU (2014) found that immigrant prisoners have limited access to emergency and routine medical care, and little to no access to dental care. Licensed vocational nurses (LVNs), rather than registered nurses (RNs), tend to provide any care that prisoners in CAR prisons may receive. There are significant differences between LVNs and RNs: training to become an LVN takes far less time than training to become an RN. LVNs typically assist RNs in hospitals and are responsible for gathering basic patient information. LVNs also check blood pressure, help patients bathe, and are taught to change dressings (Wessler, 2016). RNs, in contrast, provide evaluations, triage, and substantial medical care (Wessler, 2016). Wessler (2016) notes that BOP-run prisons rarely hire LVNs, because they are too limited in their training. But in CAR prisons, it is not unusual for immigrants to see only LVNs and for doctors to agree with whatever LVNs say (Wessler, 2016). LVNs are cheaper to hire, so CAR prison administrators prefer to hire them. In addition, whereas after hours health care in BOP-run prisons must be provided by RNs and/or EMTs, the same guidelines are not in place for CAR prisons, saving even more money and adding to their shareholders' profit margins.

Wessler (2016) recounts one example of an LVN administering improper care to a prisoner identified as Martin Acosta, who served time for illegal reentry at Reeves County Correctional Center. Acosta began having abdominal pain in the summer of 2010. Over a time period of four and a half months, he went to the medical clinic over 20 times. He saw a doctor once, one month after his complaints began, and otherwise saw nursing staff until the last two weeks of his imprisonment. On 14 visits, he saw only LVNs. Wessler (2016, n.d.) writes:

> Notes in the handwritten medical logs and nursing templates reveal a cascade of missed signs indicating serious illness, said doctors who reviewed the files. The prison medical staff described Acosta as a difficult patient; one thought he was simply trying to obtain a prescription for narcotics. Acosta was sent back to his room with nothing but Maalox nine times. Physicians who reviewed the file said the nurses appear to have missed the larger story of a protracted medical condition.

On one of his many trips for medical help, Acosta reported that he had vomited a dark substance and there was blood in his stool. The LVN took a stool sample, eyeballed it, and did nothing else; a doctor was not called, nor were tests on the stool performed (Wessler, 2016). By the time Acosta finally saw a doctor—four and a half months after he first complained of this illness—he could no longer eat, and a massive tumor was found in his abdomen. Acosta was diagnosed with metastatic stomach cancer and died in January 2011 (Wessler, 2016). Had Acosta received proper medical care, his suffering may have been kept to a minimum and his life, at the very least, prolonged. Acosta is one of at least 137 people in CAR prisons who have died between 1998, the year after the first one opened, and the end of 2014 (Wessler, 2016).

In addition to LVNs who do not have proper medical training, medical treatments in CAR prisons can be inconsistent for prisoners with chronic illnesses like diabetes. The ACLU (2014) found that prescriptions in Texas CAR prisons take weeks to fill or are not filled. A prisoner at Big Spring, for example, reported that he was unable to finish a course of antibiotics because doses were provided to him erratically (ACLU, 2014). Prisoners also reported that they would go weeks without their cholesterol and high blood-pressure pills before their prescriptions were refilled, or they would be put on Tylenol or ibuprofen in place of their prescriptions (ACLU, 2014). For example, staff at Big Spring discontinued one prisoner's medications for diabetes and high cholesterol, and put him on Tylenol (ACLU, 2014). Indeed, in what can only be assumed to be an attempt to save money to increase profits, medical examinations last only a few minutes in CAR prisons, and prisoners report that they are usually just given ibuprofen or Tylenol, no matter their ailment (ACLU, 2014). The erratic behavior in regard to the dispensing of medications extends to mental health care as well. For instance, a prisoner who takes medication for anxiety and depression reported that his prescriptions had been altered and discontinued for two months, resulting in bouts of insomnia and anxiety (ACLU, 2014).

In some cases, prisoners are not informed of their diagnoses of infectious diseases like Hepatitis C and HIV/AIDS. For example, a prisoner named Santiago was diagnosed with Hepatitis C at Eden but was never informed of the diagnosis. It was not until after several visits to the doctor at Willacy, where he was eventually transferred, that he was informed of his diagnosis, and he still failed to receive treatment (ACLU, 2014). In addition, CAR prison staff simply ignore the medical needs of the prisoners, which can result in death. The ACLU (2014) found that at Reeves Correctional Center, after a prisoner started vomiting in the middle of the night, a group of prisoners told the guard who passed through the dorm at 2:00 a.m. that he needed a doctor. The guard did not return until 5:00 a.m., after the man had stopped moving. Medical staff did not arrive to help until 7:00 a.m., when the man looked pale and did not appear to be breathing. This man was pronounced dead three hours later (ACLU, 2014).

Sometimes, the institutions themselves make the people within them sick. In 2011, the Texas Commission on Environmental Quality found that Eden's drinking water contained unacceptable levels of radioactive contamination, which exceeded the level allowed by the Environmental Protection Agency (ACLU, 2014). A notice distributed by the city of Eden stated that people who drink water with a high level of radioactive radium "may have an increased risk of getting cancer" (ACLU, 2014, p. 80). Although signs were eventually posted around Eden to warn of the dangers of drinking the water, prisoners had to purchase bottled water through the prison commissary at 80 cents per bottle. This cost put the purchase of the water out of reach for most men, as they are indigent and are not permitted to work to make any money.

Requests to see a physician can cost money in CAR prisons, whether or not the request is granted. This is money that the vast majority of prisoners do not have. The ACLU (2014) reported on a man named Miguel, incarcerated at Big Spring, who submitted five or six written requests to see a doctor. Each request cost him $2, even when he did not receive an appointment. There is currently no regulation prohibiting staff in CAR prisons from charging for each request for a medical appointment, even if no appointment is actually provided.

It is important to note that many Spanish-speaking prisoners cannot speak with staff because most staff only speak English. At institutions like Reeves, prisoners must submit all medical requests in English (ACLU, 2014). This of course limits Spanish-speaking prisoners. In addition to exacerbating feelings of despair and torment, this type of policy seems to capitalize on the language barrier to prevent immigrant detainees from receiving medical attention, which certainly results in cost savings for the corporation running the facility. It seems reasonable that the CAR prisons should employ bilingual officers and medical staff to facilitate communication and, ultimately, the health care immigrants receive.

There are several reasons health care conditions are so abhorrent in CAR prisons. While the BOP must follow certain regulations in federal facilities, CAR prisons, which are operated by private prison corporations like CCA and GEO Group, have fewer regulations by which to abide. Costs are therefore not as high for health care in CAR prisons, which increases profit margins. The federal government, too, saves money because the BOP does not have to house and care for these prisoners directly (Wessler, 2016).

Overcrowding

In addition to medical atrocities, limited programming, and emotional abuse, immigrant prisoners in CAR institutions endure overcrowded and often squalid living conditions. Private prison contracts for CAR prisons often provide incentives for overcrowding. GEO Group sets a minimum occupancy quota of 90% capacity, and then provides additional per-prisoner payments for up to 115% capacity at Reeves Detention Center (ACLU, 2014). Prisoners therefore live in crowded conditions with no privacy. At Willacy County Correctional Center, for example, most "dormitories" are Kevlar tents that house about 200 to 250 men each (ACLU, 2014). The men sleep in bunk beds that are only spaced a few feet apart. Tents are reportedly dirty, insect-ridden, and can be overrun by raw sewage that overflows through the toilets (ACLU, 2014). Because of this overcrowding, one prisoner reported to the ACLU (2014, p. 84), "Sometimes you can feel the unrest and people start fighting.... There isn't enough space for everybody. We're too crowded."

Excessive Distances from Family and Loved Ones

According to BOP policy, prisoners are to be assigned to a facility that is within 500 miles of their family. But it is assumed that noncitizens will be deported upon release, so proximity to family members is not considered in CAR prisons. Immigrants incarcerated in CAR prisons can be transferred to any CAR prison in the nation, regardless of where their families live. Immigrants incarcerated in CAR prisons also are not permitted to transfer to facilities that are located closer to their families, whereas citizen prisoners in federal prisons are allowed to request such a transfer. It is very difficult for families to travel such long distances to see their loved ones, which means most people housed in CARS prison will not see their families while they are incarcerated. Indeed, the ACLU (2014) identified individuals imprisoned in Texas whose families are located in New York, Florida, or California. The disregard for the family of immigrants, many of whom are citizens, is a failing not only because it causes undue emotional grief for the detainees and their families but also because it seems to bear witness to a system that is cruel rather than fair and is punitive rather restorative.

The Use of Isolation

CAR prisons rely on isolation to punish immigrants incarcerated within them. In isolation, also known as solitary confinement or "segregated housing units" (SHUs), a prisoner spends 22 to 24 hours a day in a cell alone, or with one or two other cellmates if overcrowding is an issue. At the Texas CAR facilities researched by the ACLU (2014), isolation is used to punish people for minor infractions, but it is also used when there is overcrowding and dormitories are full. While in isolation, prisoners cannot use facilities like the library. If recreation is permitted, it is limited to one hour a day, in a "small outdoor cage that is typically 8 to 10 paces wide" (ACLU, 2014, p. 29).

The ACLU (2014) reports that Texas CAR prisons require that they use 10% of their bed space as isolation cells, which is almost double the rate of that found in BOP facilities. The contracts between GEO Group and BOP for Reeves, for example, require that 10% of the facility's contract bed space be for isolation. This requirement means that more than 300 people may be placed in isolation at any time (ACLU, 2014). As a result of overcrowding, three people are often placed in an isolation cell, where two people sleep on beds and one person sleeps on the floor.

Prisoners are regularly sent to isolation for complaints about food and medical care. Mentally ill people also are confined in isolation units, often with no access to medication or treatment for their illnesses. Prisoners report that the SHU is noisy 24 hours a day "with the sounds of other men pounding the walls and doors, screaming, shouting, and crying" (ACLU, 2014, p. 29). This situation has serious consequences and results in the deterioration of the mental health of prisoners. Men confined in CAR isolation units report panic attacks, hallucinations, paranoia, and obsessive or suicidal thoughts (ACLU, 2014), and some have committed suicide. In August 2008, Reyes Garcia Rangel committed suicide at Reeves after prison officials denied him the medication he needed for his bipolar disorder and then isolated him in the SHU without adequate observation or monitoring. A wrongful death suit was recently filed by Rangel's family against Reeves County, the GEO Group, and the Reeves medical contractor (ACLU, 2014).

The American Bar Association's (ABA, 2010) "Standards for the Treatment of Prisoners" calls for the abolition of extreme isolation and requires that all prisoners in segregated housing be supplied with meaningful mental, social, and physical stimulation (see also ACLU, 2014). The ABA argues that isolation should be used sparingly and for the shortest duration possible. BOP policy, too, places limits on when prisoners can be placed in the SHU—including when they pose a threat to themselves or other prisoners or when they violate institutional rules (ACLU, 2014). But neither BOP nor ABA guidelines are followed in CAR prisons. At Willacy, Dalby, and Eden, the ACLU (2014) found that staff regularly send new arrivals to the SHU and leave them there for days or weeks, often because there are not enough beds to house new prisoners in the general population.

Immigrant Detention

There are significant numbers of immigrants who are detained in Immigration and Customs Enforcement (ICE) facilities across the nation, which also contributes to the larger trajectory of mass incarceration in the U.S. In fact, the United States has the world's largest immigrant detention system (Detention Watch Network, 2016). A host of immigrants can be locked up at any one time, including lawful permanent residents, undocumented immigrants, survivors of torture, and asylum seekers. In addition, children, pregnant women, and other vulnerable groups are frequently imprisoned in such facilities.

Many of these detainees are from Central America and have come to the U.S. seeking asylum after they fled inhumane conditions where women and children were raped, abused, and killed (Detention Watch Network, 2016). Eighty-eight percent of detained families have demonstrated to a DHS asylum officer that they have a credible fear of persecution if deported (Detention Watch Network, 2016). Yet they must remain in detention for long periods of time, despite the fact that there is no evidence that they are a danger to society. They are incarcerated while they await a determination of their immigration status or until they are deported (Migration and Refugee Services et al., 2015). According to Detention Watch Network (2016), in 2013, the United States government detained approximately 441,000 immigrants in more than 200 immigration facilities across the country.

Immigrant detention has grown and morphed alongside the larger criminal justice apparatus in the United States. It began in earnest in the 1980s and 1990s. During the "War on Drugs" in the 1980s, Congress amended the Immigration and Naturalization Act for mandatory detention of immigrants with certain criminal convictions, without a hearing or consideration of the immigrants' circumstances (Detention Watch Network, 2016). In 1996, the Antiterrorism and Effective Death Penalty Act (AEDPA) and the Illegal Immigrant Reform and Immigrant Responsibility Act (IIRIRA) expanded mandatory detention in the U.S. to include any noncitizens convicted of petty crimes like shoplifting; those crimes become aggravated felonies in the immigration context, even though they are not considered aggravated felonies in a typical criminal context (Detention Watch Network, 2016; Lawston & Murillo, 2009). Under the Obama administration, the implementation of a detention bed quota and the expansion of deportation programs such as 287(g), the Secure Communities and the Criminal Alien Program, thousands of immigrants were channeled into detention centers (Detention Watch Network, 2016). As the Frontline (2011) episode "Lost in Detention" explains, the Secure Communities program is a "get-tough" policy that has played a crucial role in the nearly 1 million immigrants deported under former President Obama and the burgeoning number of immigrants who have been put into prolonged detention. In 2014, detention expanded when the Obama administration responded to an influx of Central American refugees from Guatemala, Honduras, and El Salvador, who were fleeing violence, by putting entire families into detention (Detention Watch Network, 2016; Migration and Refugee Services et al., 2015). The use and expansion of ICE detention facilities shows no signs of slowing down under the Trump administration (Aguilar, 2017; Schuppe, 2017). Since detainees in ICE facilities are not being charged with crimes, they do not have a right to be represented by legal counsel, so they have little to no access to legal and social services. Few have the right to a bond, so they spend months to years trying to prove they have the right to stay in the U.S. (Detention Watch Network, 2012).

ICE runs the detention system, but as the federal government does with CAR prisons, it subcontracts the majority of detention space to county jails and private prison companies, like CCA and GEO Group. ICE is congressionally mandated to maintain 34,000 detention beds at any given time; no other law enforcement agency operates on a quota system (Detention Watch Network, 2016). This curious mandate from Congress—combined with other policies that provide a steady stream of detainees, and in turn revenue, for private prison companies—is not surprising given that the CCA and GEO Group have spent $25 million to lobby key legislators to obtain prison contracts (Cohen, 2015). Indeed, the private prison industry uses both lobbying and direct campaign contributions to increase profits through political influence (Cohen, 2015).

The conditions in immigrant detention facilities and the failure of these facilities to meet the needs of the people imprisoned within them have been the subject of much media attention in recent years. Like the conditions found in CAR prisons, reports have found medical neglect, unnecessary deaths, and sexual and physical abuse to occur in detention prisons at high rates (Dow, 2004). Adequate medical treatment and mental health care—and access to telephones, legal services, religious services, and library materials—are difficult to come by, and many detainees never receive legal representation. Like those locked up in CAR prisons, detainees are shipped hundreds of miles away to facilities where visits are impossible for family members, and many cannot speak English, so communication with officers is limited (Guzman, 2015). Attorneys and human rights advocates continue to learn of sexual abuse of women detainees, solitary confinement used to punish detainees for complaining about the conditions of their confinement, women forced to give birth in shackles, suicides, government officials pressuring immigrants to give up their legal cases, refusal of family visits, and treatment of severe illnesses with Tylenol, ibuprofen, or Advil (Detention Watch Network, 2016; Migration and Refugee Services et al., 2015).

Most immigrants in ICE detention fear that complaining about their treatment or living conditions will provoke retaliation by guards. This retaliation often comes in the form of being sent to solitary confinement (Heartland Alliance, National Immigrant Justice Center, & Physicians for Human Rights, 2012) or in the form of issues suddenly arising with their immigration cases. Retaliation may also occur in the form of transfers from one detention center to another. For example, in 2015 a group of 27 detained Honduran women who were seeking asylum began a hunger strike that surged to 125 women at T. Don Hutto Detention Center, operated by CCA. The hunger strike was in protest of the conditions of their confinement and prolonged detention without any movement in their cases; the women demanded to be let out on bond. At least two of the women were transferred from the women's facility to an overwhelmingly male facility 200 miles away run by the GEO Group (Democracy Now, 2015). Afraid of retaliation, then, many detainees quietly endure the abuse. As Detention Watch Network (2012, p. 3) poignantly notes, asylum seekers who come to the U.S. seeking protection from persecution are essentially "kept behind bars, denied the medical care they need to recover from physical and emotional trauma, and are subjected to more of the same misery that prompted them to flee their home countries in the first place." The following sections will detail some of the conditions of confinement for those imprisoned in detention facilities.

Emotional Abuse, Medical Neglect, and Poor Sanitation

Like immigrants who are incarcerated in CAR prisons, immigrants imprisoned for detention also are emotionally abused, receive poor medical treatment, and face unhealthy living conditions. At Theo Lacy Detention Center in California, the Baker County, Florida, jail, and the Hudson County, New Jersey, jail, for example, detainees reported being insulted, being cursed and laughed at, and having their clothes and other possessions thrown on the floor by corrections officers (Detention Watch Network, 2012). Racial insults also are not unheard of, as well as sexually charged language around and toward women and lesbian, gay, and transgender detainees.

Immigrants in detention also face some of the same issues with medical care as immigrants in CAR prisons. During the Obama administration, there were 56 deaths in ICE custody, eight of which were clearly identified as resulting from noncompliance with ICE medical standards (ACLU, Detention Watch Network, & National Immigrant Justice Center, 2016). For example, Evalin-Ali Mandza died of a heart attack in Denver Contract Detention Facility, operated by GEO Group, after workers in the facility failed to meet his health care needs in a timely fashion. They failed to place a 911 call, his vital signs failed to be taken, they administered the wrong tests, and other violations in medical protocol occurred (ACLU et al., 2016). Similarly, 39-year-old Roberto Medina-Martinez died at Stewart Detention Center in Georgia in March 2009 of a treatable heart infection. An investigation revealed that the nursing staff failed to refer Medina for timely medical treatment, and the facility physician failed to follow internal oversight procedures (Detention Watch Network, 2012).

Exacerbating poor medical treatment at detention centers is poor sanitation, which is, as previously discussed, typical of CAR prisons as well. At Pinal County Jail in Arizona detainees have reported receiving food on dirty trays, worms in food, bugs and worms in the faucets, dirty laundry, and being overcrowded with 10 other men in one cell and only one toilet (Detention Watch Network, 2012).

Sexual Abuse

In 2000, the Women's Commission for Refugee Women and Children issued a report that exposed widespread verbal, emotional, physical, and sexual abuse in the Krome Service Processing Center in Miami, Florida. Some of the same officers implicated in the abuse were involved in prior abuse cases, yet no disciplinary actions had been taken against them. Sexual abuses ranged from rape and molestation to sexual harassment, with immigrant women living in fear on a daily basis. At least 15 male immigration (then-INS) officers were involved in the sexual abuse, and "Women who cooperated in sexual activities were made false promises of release from detention. Threats of deportation, transfer to county jails, or even death were leveled at women who dared to resist or complain about such abuses"(Women's Commission, 2000, p. 1). Other intimidation tactics, such as yelling at women and the forcing of Muslim women to remove their veils or go without eating, left women vulnerable to these abuses and without recourse.

Human Rights Watch (2010) has since released a report that also documents the risk of sexual abuse of immigrant detainees. In 2010, a guard at T. Don Hutto residential center sexually assaulted several women detainees. In 2008, five women detained at the Port Isabel Processing Center in Texas were assaulted after a guard entered each of their rooms acting as a physician and told each of them to undress as he assaulted them. In 2007, a trafficking victim was sexually assaulted in a Florida jail with which ICE had a contract for immigration bed space. The woman was assaulted by other women at the jail while she was "partially incapacitated" by prescribed sedatives.

Sexual abuse also occurs against transgender women in detention, many of whom have come to the U.S. seeking protection from abuse in their home countries (Human Rights Watch, 2016). In a recent report, Human Rights Watch (2016) documented 28 cases of the sexual assault of transgender women who were held in immigrant detention between 2011 and 2015. More than half were held in men's facilities at some point in their detainment, placing them at high risk for physical and sexual assault. One transgender woman from Honduras, Sara V., was raped by three men at a detention center in Arizona in 2014 after fleeing gang violence in her home country. As she explained to Human Rights Watch (2016, p. 29), when she reported the rape in detention, a guard told her, "You [transgender women] are the ones that cause these problems and always call the men's attention."

Like cisgender women prisoners who have been placed in isolation in retaliation for not having sex with male guards, transgender prisoners are put in isolation as retaliation by guards for merely being transgender. Gloria L., a transgender woman, was put in isolation for four months because a guard said he was "Tired of seeing faggots" (Human Rights Watch, 2016, p. 36). Other transgender detainees are placed in isolation, some argue, for their own safety, particularly if they are in men's detention facilities. They face high rates of sexual violence in men's facilities, both at the hands of male guards and male detainees. However, isolation often causes a great deal of psychological harm. In June 2015, the U.S. government announced a new set of guidelines that prioritized the placing of transgender detainees in facilities that exclusively house other transgender detainees, but Human Rights Watch (2016) notes that an independent oversight mechanism to ensure that this is carried out still does not exist. As a result, transgender detainees continue to be at risk for physical and sexual violence.

Situating Abuses in CAR Prisons and Detention Centers

The abuses that occur inside CAR prisons and immigrant detention centers can be situated within a larger climate of punishment and criminalization in the U.S. Indeed, it is the larger process of criminalization—of people of color, of immigrants, of those deemed "other"—that allows such abuses to occur. Medical neglect, sexual, physical, and emotional abuses, overcrowding, the use of isolation as retaliation or punishment, being locked up in facilities that are located excessive distances away from family or loved ones, and the lack of programming are all issues that can be found in state prisons across the U.S. as well. Much has been written about such abuses in the U.S. prison system (see e.g., Amnesty International, 1999; Human Rights Watch, 1996; Lawston & Lucas, 2011; Price 2015; Sudbury 2005). The treatment of immigrants in CAR prisons and detention centers mirrors the treatment of people in state prisons across the country, who are disproportionately racial and ethnic minorities and poor. Immigration can be seen as part of a criminal justice apparatus that targets the most vulnerable people in society for punishment. Private prison companies like GEO Group and CCA stand to benefit from this ever-expanding criminal justice system, with immigration being the latest addition.

The focus on punishment in prisons and detention facilities and the high rates of abuse that happen with impunity are made possible by a society that dehumanizes those within these facilities and defines them simply as "criminal"—regardless of whether a crime was committed—rather than human beings who are mothers, fathers, sisters, brothers, aunts and uncles, who are often just trying to get by and do the best they can. In a system that commits medical neglect, emotional, physical, and sexual abuse, and other gross violations of human rights against those who are confined within it, it is difficult to imagine how prisoners/detainees might be able to eventually lead productive and healthy lives. Medical needs, legal needs, the need to be close to family and loved ones, the need to live in an environment void of emotional, physical, and sexual abuse, the need to live in clean spaces free of vermin and disease-inducing pathogens, the need to be treated humanely, are rarely met in prisons generally, nor are such needs met in CAR facilities and immigrant detention centers specifically.

Much as groups across the country have fought for prison reform, advocacy groups have made recommendations for reform of the immigration process. Migration and Refugee Services, the United States Conference of Catholic Bishops, and the Center for Migration Studies (2015), for example, have called out immigrant detention facilities as inhumane and unnecessary, and recommend supervised release and case management programs, rather than detention, to address undocumented immigration and asylum claims. Similarly, in its analysis of CAR prisons, the ACLU (2014) recommends that CAR prisons be inspected regularly, with findings made public, and that accountability procedures be put in place so that immigrants are not abused in these facilities. The ACLU (2014) also recommends ending discrimination against prisoners based on citizenship and stopping the expansion of private, for-profit contractors so that companies cannot profit off the warehousing of human beings. But unless humanity is valued over money—unless lawmakers and the media stop vilifying immigrants, people of color, and the poor as "criminal,"—such recommendations will continue to fall on deaf ears and measures that truly make society safe, such as investing in communities, housing, jobs, health care, education, and drug treatment—will not be implemented.

Conclusions

Dostoevsky's (1862 [2004]) oft-cited quote, "The degree of civilization in a society can be judged by entering its prisons," is as resonant today as it was when he wrote it. Even if one believes that the number of immigrants entering the United States should be curtailed—and that so-called "lax immigration policies" pose a threat to the nation—is to a certain degree rendered moot by the pervasive evidence that officers representing our government act with indignity and in a way that is degrading not only to the prisoners and detainees whom they are charged to supervise, but to our society as a whole. The emotional, physical, and sexual abuse and neglect—the torment and indignations that some guards inflict on immigrants—undercuts the very values that they have been charged to uphold. Immigrants seeking to live in a nation that purports to value democracy, equality, freedom, rule of law, fairness, equal opportunity, and all the other values that the nation holds sacrosanct cannot be undermined by cruelty, tyranny, and disregard for those values. Immigrants should not be objects of disdain, nor commodities to produce profits for corporations. Rather, they should bear witness to the noble ideas in the U.S. Constitution, admired by people all over the world, which inspire us all to aspire toward a more perfect union, thus, as the preamble reads, "[securing] the blessings of liberty to ourselves and our posterity."

References

Aguilar, J. (2017, April 14). White house greenlights a new immigration-detention center in Texas. *The Texas Tribune*. Retrieved from www.texastribune.org/2017/04/14/white-house-green-lights-new-immigration-detention-center-texas/

American Bar Association. (2010). *Standards for the treatment of prisoners*. Retrieved from www.americanbar.org/publications/criminal_justice_section_archive/crimjust_standards_treatmentprisoners.html

American Civil Liberties Union. (2010). *Issue brief: Criminalizing undocumented immigrants*. Retrieved from www.aclu.org/files/assets/FINAL_criminalizing_undocumented_immigrants_issue_brief_PUBLIC_VERSION.pdf

American Civil Liberties Union. (2014). *Warehoused and forgotten: Immigrants trapped in our shadow private prison system*. Retrieved from www.aclu.org/sites/default/files/field_document/060614-aclu-car-reportonline.pdf

American Civil Liberties Union, Detention Watch Network, & National Immigrant Justice Center. (2016). *Fatal neglect: How ICE ignores deaths in detention*. Retrieved from www.aclu.org/report/fatal-neglect-how ice-ignores-death-detention

Amnesty International. (1999). *Not part of my sentence: Violations in the human rights of women in custody*. Retrieved from www.amnestyusa.org/node/57783

Cohen, M. (2015). How for-profit prisons have become the biggest lobby no one is talking about: Sen. Marco Rubio is one of the biggest beneficiaries. *The Washington Post*. Retrieved from www.washingtonpost.com/posteverything/wp/2015/04/28/how-for-profit-prisons-have-become-the-biggest-lobby-no-one-is-talking-about/

Democracy Now! (2015). *Exclusive: Detained Honduran women, moved to mostly male Texas prison after hunger strike, speaks out*. Retrieved from www.democracynow.org/2015/11/24/exclusive_detained_honduran_woman_moved_to

Detention Watch Network. (2012). *Executive summary: Expose and close*. Retrieved from www.detentionwatchnetwork.org/pressroom/reports/2012/expose-and-close

Detention Watch Network. (2016). *Immigration detention 101*. Retrieved from www.detentionwatchnetwork.org/issues/detention-101

Dostoyevsky, F. (1862 [2004]). *The house of the dead*. New York, NY: Dover Publications.

Dow, M. (2004). *American gulag: Inside U.S. immigration prisons*. Berkeley, CA: University of California Press.

Escobar, M. (2016). *Captivity beyond prisons: Criminalization experiences of Latina (im)migrants*. Austin, TX: University of Texas Press.

Frontline. (2011). *Lost in detention*. Retrieved from www.pbs.org/wgbh/frontline/film/lost-in-detention/. PBS.org

Guzman, E. (2015). Bringing Pedro home. In A. Shueths & J. Lawston (Eds.), *Living together, living apart: Mixed status families and US immigration policy* (pp. 229–241). Seattle, WA: University of Washington Press.

Heartland Alliance, National Immigrant Justice Center, & Physicians for Human Rights. (2012). *Invisible in isolation: The use of segregation and solitary confinement in immigrant detention*. Retrieved from www.immigrantjustice.org/publications/report-invisible-isolation-use-segregation-and-solitary-confinement-immigration-detenti

Human Rights Watch. (1996). *All too familiar: Sexual abuses of women in state prisons*. Retrieved at www.hrw.org/report/1996/12/01/all-too-familiar/sexual-abuse-women-us-state-prisons

Human Rights Watch. (2010). *Detained and at risk: Sexual abuse and harassment in the United States immigration center*. Retrieved from www.hrw.org/report/2010/08/25/detained-and-risk/sexual-abuse-and-harassment-united-states-immigration-detention

Human Rights Watch. (2016). *Do you see how much I'm suffering here? Abuse against transgender women in U.S. immigration detention*. Retrieved from www.hrw.org/sites/default/files/report_pdf/us0316_web.pdf

Kaeble, D., Glaze, L., Tsoutis, A., & Minton, T. (2016). *Correctional populations in the United States, 2014*. Washington, DC: U.S. Department of Justice, Bureau of Justice Statistics.

Lawston, J. M., & Murillo, R. R. (2009). The discursive figuration of U.S. supremacy in narratives sympathetic to undocumented immigrants. *Social Justice, 36*(2), 38–53.

Lawston, J. M. (2011). From representations to resistance: How the razor wire binds us. In J. M. Lawston & A. E. Lucas (Eds.), *Razor wire women: Prisoners, activists, scholars, and artists* (pp. 1–17). Albany, NY: SUNY Press.

Lawston, J. M., & Lucas, A. E. (2011). *Razor wire women: Prisoners, activists, scholars, and artists*. Albany, NY: SUNY Press.

Light, M. T., Lopez, M. H., & Gonzalez-Barrera, A. (2014). *The rise of federal immigration crimes*. Pew Research Center. Retrieved from www.pewhispanic.org/2014/03/18/the-rise-of-federal-immigration-crimes/

Migration and Refugee Services, United States Conference on Catholic Bishops, & The Center for Migration Studies. (2015). *Unlocking human dignity: A plan to transform the U.S. immigrant detention system*. Retrieved from www.usccb.org/about/migration-and-refugee-services/upload/unlocking-human-dignity.pdf

Moulton, A. D. (2016). No safe haven here: Children and families face trauma in the hands of U.S. immigration. *Unitarian Universalist Service Committee*. Retrieved from www.uusc.org/sites/default/files/no_safe_haven_here_-_children_and_families_face_trauma_in_the_hands_of_u.s._immigration.pdf

Price, J. (2015). *Prisons and social death*. New Brunswick, NJ: Rutgers.

Robertson, A.G., Beaty, R., Atkinson, J., & Libel, B. (2012). Operation streamline: costs and consequences. *Grassroots Leadership*. Retrieved from http://grassrootsleadership.org/sites/default/files/uploads/GRL_Sept2012_Report final.pdf

Romero, M. (2015). Forward. In A. Shueths & J. Lawston (Eds.), *Living together, living apart: Mixed status families and US immigration policy* (pp. xi–xviii). Seattle, WA: University of Washington Press.

Schuppe, J. (2017). Private prisons memo could signal more immigrant lockups. *NBC News*. Retrieved from www.nbcnews.com/news/us-news/private-prisons-memo-could-signal-more-immigrant-lockups-n727641

Shueths, A., & Lawston, J. (2015). Introduction. In A. Shueths & J. Lawston (Eds.), *Living together, living apart: Mixed status families and US immigration policy* (pp. 3–15). Seattle, WA: University of Washington Press.

Sudbury, J. (2005). *Global lockdown: Race, gender, and the prison industrial complex*. New York, NY: Routledge.

The Sentencing Project. (2015). Trends in U.S. corrections. Retrieved from http://sentencingproject.org/wp-content/uploads/2016/01/Trends-in-US-Corrections.pdf

Wessler, S. F. (2016). This man will almost certainly die. *The Nation*. Retrieved from www.thenation.com/article/privatized-immigrant-prison-deaths/

Women's Commission for Refugee Women and Children. (2000). *Behind locked doors: Abuse of refugee women at the Krome Detention Center*. Retrieved from www.womensrefugeecommission.org/press-room/557-sexual-abuse-widespread-at-krome-detention-center-

14

PRISON GANGS

Identification, Management, and Renunciation

Robert D. Hanser

The main reason why inmates affiliate with gangs is for safety. Gangs are a source of safety in a dangerous environment and they regulate social and economic affairs, including the underground economy. Because of their activities, California prisons have fewer chaotic and spontaneous acts of violence.

—David Skarbek, author of *The Social Order of the Underground* (as quoted in Benson, 2015).

Introduction

Prison Gangs and Security Threat Groups, What is the Difference?

The National Gang Crime Research Center (NGCRC) is perhaps one of the best authority sources for research and directives on gangs and gang activity, whether street or institutional. This group has been at the forefront of gang research for over 20 years and provides a wealth of information on gang activity throughout the nation. According to the NGCRC, a prison gang, when defined correctly, consists of a group of three or more persons who recurrently commit crime that is openly known to the group and that operates in a prison. A security threat group (STG), on the other hand, either is a group of three or more persons who engage in repetitive behavior that is a threat or is disruptive to the order of an institution. These threats could be institutional violations resulting in disciplinary action or actual criminal acts. Thus, an STG is always a problem for the prison, but it may not necessarily be an actual gang, particularly if it does not engage in repetitive and recurring criminal acts.

A good example of an STG that is problematic but not considered a gang would be the Self Defense Family (SDF) in the Texas prison system. The SDF consists of a group of inmates who work together to file a variety of lawsuits against prison officials (Knox, 2012). The SDF membership consists mostly of jailhouse lawyers, inmates who are self-taught and have developed substantial proficiency at filing writs for both important and frivolous issues. In this case, the SDF would not be considered a gang, at all, because their activity, while bothersome, is not criminal. In fact, they operate well within the scope of the law (Knox, 2012). Other security threat groups might consist of those aligned with radical religious beliefs or those linked to terrorist ideologies who, by nature of their activities or beliefs, pose a potential threat to the welfare of the prison or persons therein, but whose purpose is not one where the commission of crime is a uniting focal point.

When inmates use the terms "stigged" or "STG'd" they are referring to the process whereby a group has been labeled an STG. In such cases, prisons have specific guidelines that often also entail a certain burden-of-proof requirement that must include recorded incidents of disciplinary infractions, over time, within an institution (Knox, 2012). In most cases, the decision to identify an STG and/or classify a person within the membership of an STG is made by regional or central office administrators who review the reports provided and, provided that the evidence is in order and sufficient, will classify the group as a statewide security threat group throughout the entire prison system.

Despite the clear distinction between prison gangs and security threat groups, it should be mentioned that in modern day corrections, the term STG and prison gang are often used interchangeably. While they are not, technically, the same, many practitioners consider such a distinction to be nothing less than hair-splitting. Thus, the reader should understand that, though this distinction has been provided in this chapter to ensure precision in the use of these terms, the real world of corrections, as well as those who work in that world on a day-to-day basis, may not always honor such razor-fine distinctions between these groups.

Further, when considering prison gangs, it should be mentioned that among practitioners, the notion of prison gangs has developed a type of tradition whereby only those gangs who started within the confines of prison are considered prison gangs. Thus, most prison staff would consider a true prison gang to have developed as a gang that originated within a prison system. Ganges like the Aryan Brotherhood (AB), the Texas Syndicate (TS), and the Black Guerilla Family (BGF) would be considered traditional or purebred prison gangs. These types of organizations engage in a wide variety of activities, including drug smuggling, protection rackets, extortion, and blackmail, as well as violent assault and even murder. In short, they engage in both crimes and rule violations, with criminal activity being varied, organized, and lucrative for the whole in a manner that is similar to organized criminal syndicates.

Despite the fact that most correctional practitioners consider the true or traditional prison gang to be one that originated within a prison system, it is clear that these gangs now operate both within the prison as well as within broader society. Indeed, as various members of these gangs left prison due to fulfilling their sentence, making parole, or early release, their allegiance to persons they had met while doing time did not necessarily end at that point. Rather, many were required to stay in contact with their gang members on the inside by contacting other members on the outside who will wait on their release, sometimes providing support to the inmate's family outside the prison while the gang member is in prison. Naturally, the member of the prison gang, once released and connected with members on the outside, is expected to continue to aid the gang, both in day-to-day affairs and in the commission of criminal activities.

To illustrate this point, consider the activity of the Nuestra Familia, a prison gang that was responsible for a murder spree in southern California in the early part of 2000 (Geniella, 2001; Knox, 2012). The Nuestra Familia is a Latino prison gang based out of northern California. Its nemesis, the Mexican Mafia, is primarily active in southern California. The Nuestra Familia has organized attacks on rival gang members throughout southern California. Indeed, numerous bodies were discovered by law enforcement during the late 1990s, and it was even discovered that plans existed to murder a particularly vigorous prosecutor in Sonoma County, California. Eventually, a pattern in the various homicides linked them to the Nuestra Familia, which made it clear that the gang was active both inside and outside the state's prison system.

Indeed, during the 1990s and from 2000 to the present day, gangs like the Mexican Mafia, the Aryan Brotherhood, and the Barrio Aztecas have become just as formidable in their own ethnic-based regions or communities as they are in prison. This, along with the confluence of street gangs that have permeated prison systems in California, Illinois, New York, Texas, and Florida, has created a blurring of the distinctions between the street gang and the prison gang, making it more a matter of importance for academics rather than that of the world of the offender (Hanser, 2007). Therefore, it would seem that both types of gangs have become cross-pollinated, being operational in both sectors of the criminal world (Hanser, 2007; Hanser, 2016). When referring to the cross-pollination of gangs, the term refers to gangs (whether in the prison or on the street) that have developed sufficient power or influence as to be equally effective regardless of whether their leadership is primarily on the streets or incarcerated. In essence, the leadership continuity remains intact, as do the operations of the gang in both the institution and in the broader community (Hanser, 2007).

Major Prison Gangs in the United States

During the 1950s and 1960s, there was a substantial amount of racial and ethnic bias in prisons. This was true in most all state prison systems, but was particularly pronounced in the southern United States and in the state of California. During the late 1950s, a Chicano gang known as the Mexican Mafia formed (National Gang Intelligence Center, 2009). This gang was drawn from street gang members in various neighborhoods of Los Angeles and, while in San Quentin, began to exercise power over the gambling rackets within that prison. Other gangs soon began to form as a means of opposing the Mexican Mafia. Among the earliest to form were the Black Guerilla Family, the Aryan Brotherhood, La Nuestra Familia, and the Texas Syndicate.

In the paragraphs that follow, a brief overview is provided of several major prison gangs found throughout the United States. As accurately as possible, these gangs are presented in the order in which they developed, following a rough historical timeline. Because the federal government produces accurate resources and data on justice-related topics, information regarding most of these gangs has been obtained from the National Gang Intelligence Center, a think tank of the United States Department of Justice. The following section provides an overview of 13 of the most prevalent prison gangs in the United States. This is a list of the major prison gangs that exist today; however, it is not comprehensive. The history of each gang, criminal activity, and other relevant information is provided. The gangs are presented in the order in which they were formed, starting with the late 1950s and continuing through the early 1990s:

> The Mexican Mafia prison gang, also known as La Eme (Spanish for the letter *M*), was formed in the late 1950s within the California Department of Corrections. It is loosely structured and has strict rules that must be followed by the 200 members. Most members are Mexican-American males who previously belonged to a southern California street gang. The Mexican Mafia is primarily active in the southwestern and Pacific regions of the United States, but its power base is in California. The gang's main source of income is extorting drug distributors outside prison and distributing methamphetamine, cocaine, heroin, and marijuana within prison systems and on the streets. Some members have direct links to Mexican drug traffickers outside of the prison walls. The Mexican Mafia also is involved in other criminal activities, including controlling gambling and homosexual prostitution in prison.

The Black Guerrilla Family (BGF), originally called Black Family or Black Vanguard, is a prison gang founded in San Quentin State Prison, California, in 1966. The gang is highly organized along paramilitary lines, with a supreme leader and central committee. The BGF has an established national charter, code of ethics, and oath of allegiance. BGF members operate primarily in California and Maryland. The gang has 100 to 300 members, most of whom are African-American males. A primary source of income for gang members is cocaine and marijuana distribution. Currently, BGF members obtain such drugs primarily from Nuestra Familia/Norteños members or from local Mexican traffickers. BGF members are involved in other criminal activities, including auto theft, burglary, and drive-by shootings and homicide.

The Aryan Brotherhood (AB) was originally formed in San Quentin in 1967. The AB is highly structured, with two factions—one in the California Department of Corrections (CDC) and the other in the Federal Bureau of Prisons. Most members are Caucasian males, and the gang is active primarily in the southwestern and Pacific regions. Its main source of income is the distribution of cocaine, heroin, marijuana, and methamphetamine within prison systems and on the streets. Some AB members have business relationships with Mexican drug traffickers who smuggle illegal drugs into California for AB distribution. The AB is notoriously violent and is often involved in murder for hire. Although the gang has been historically linked to the California-based prison gang Mexican Mafia (La Eme), tension between AB and La Eme is increasingly evident, as seen in recent fights between Caucasians and Hispanics within CDC.

The Crips are a collection of structured and unstructured gangs that have adopted a common gang culture. The Crips emerged as a major gang presence during the early 1970s. Crips membership is estimated at 30,000 to 35,000; most members are African-American males from the Los Angeles metropolitan area. Large, national-level Crips gangs include 107 Hoover Crips, Insane Gangster Crips, and Rolling 60s Crips. The Crips operate in 221 cities in 41 states and can be found in several state prison systems. The main source of income for the Crips is the street-level distribution of powder cocaine, crack cocaine, marijuana, and PCP. This gang is also involved in other criminal activity, such as assault, auto theft, burglary, and homicide.

The Bloods are an association of structured and unstructured gangs that have adopted a single-gang culture. The original Bloods were formed in the early 1970s to provide protection from the Crips street gang in Los Angeles, California. Large, national-level Bloods gangs include Bounty Hunter Bloods and Crenshaw Mafia Gangsters. Bloods membership is estimated to be 7,000 to 30,000 nationwide; most members are African-American males. Bloods gangs are active in 123 cities in 33 states, and they can be found in several state prison systems. The main source of income for Bloods gangs is street-level distribution of cocaine and marijuana. The gangs also are involved in other criminal activity, including assault, auto theft, burglary, carjacking, drive-by shootings, extortion, homicide, identity fraud, and robbery.

Ñeta is a prison gang that was established in Puerto Rico in the early 1970s and spread to the United States. Ñeta is one of the largest and most violent prison gangs, with about 7,000 members in Puerto Rico and 5,000 in the United States. Ñeta chapters in Puerto Rico exist exclusively inside prisons; once members are released from prison, they are no longer considered part of the gang. In the United States, Ñeta chapters exist inside and outside prisons in 36 cities in nine states, primarily in the Northeast. The gang's main source of income is retail distribution of powder and crack cocaine, heroin, marijuana, and, to a lesser extent, LSD, MDMA, methamphetamine, and PCP. Ñeta members commit assault, auto theft, burglary, drive-by shootings, extortion, home invasion, money laundering, robbery, weapons, and explosives trafficking, as well as witness intimidation.

The Texas Syndicate originated in Folsom Prison during the early 1970s. The Texas Syndicate was formed in response to other prison gangs in the California Department of Corrections, such as the Mexican Mafia and Aryan Brotherhood, which were attempting to prey on native Texas inmates. This gang is composed of predominantly Mexican-American inmates in the Texas Department of Criminal Justice (TDCJ). Though this gang has a rule to accept members who are Latino, it does accept Caucasians into its ranks. The Texas Syndicate has a formal organizational structure and a set of written rules for its members. Since the time of its formation—largely as a means of protection for Texas inmates in the California Department of Corrections—the Texas Syndicate has grown considerably, particularly in Texas.

The Mexikanemi prison gang (also known as Texas Mexican Mafia or Emi) was formed in the early 1980s within the TDCJ. The gang is highly structured and is estimated to have 2,000 members, most of whom are Mexican nationals or Mexican-American males living in Texas at the time of incarceration. Mexikanemi poses a significant drug trafficking threat to communities in the southwestern United States, particularly in Texas. Gang members reportedly traffic multikilogram quantities of powder cocaine, heroin, and methamphetamine; multiton quantities of marijuana; and thousand-tablet quantities of MDMA from Mexico into the United States for distribution inside and outside prison.

The Nazi Low Riders (NLR) evolved in the California Youth Authority, the state agency responsible for the incarceration and parole supervision of juvenile and young adult offenders, in the late 1970s or early 1980s as a gang for white inmates. As prison officials successfully suppressed Aryan Brotherhood activities, the Brotherhood appealed to young incarcerated skinheads, the NLR in particular, to act as middlemen for their criminal operations, allowing the Aryan Brotherhood to keep control of criminal undertakings while adult members were serving time in administrative segregation. Through their connections to the Aryan Brotherhood, the NLR was able to become the principal gang within the Youth Authority and eventually to move into penitentiaries throughout California and across the West Coast. The NLR maintains strong ties to the Aryan Brotherhood and, like the older gang, has become a source of violence and criminal activity in prison. The Aryan Brotherhood still maintains a strong presence in the nation's prison systems, albeit less active, while NLR has also become a major force, viewing itself as superior to all other white gangs and deferring only to the Aryan Brotherhood. Both gangs engage in drug trafficking, extortion, and attacks on inmates and corrections staff.

Barrio Azteca emerged in 1986 in the Coffield Unit of TDCJ by five street gang members from El Paso, Texas. This gang tends to recruit from prior street gang members and is most active in the southwestern region, primarily in correctional facilities in Texas and on the streets of southwestern Texas and southeastern New Mexico. The gang is highly structured and has an estimated membership of 2,000. Most members are Mexican national or Mexican-American males. The gang's main source of income is smuggling heroin, powder cocaine, and marijuana from Mexico into the United States for distribution both inside and outside prisons. Barrio Azteca members also are involved in alien smuggling, arson, assault, auto theft, burglary, extortion, intimidation, kidnapping, robbery, and weapons violations.

Hermanos de Pistoleros Latinos (HPL) is a Hispanic prison gang formed in the TDCJ in the late 1980s. It operates in most prisons and on the streets in many communities in Texas, particularly Laredo. HPL is also active in several cities in Mexico, and its largest contingent in that country is in Nuevo Laredo. The gang is structured and is estimated to have 1,000 members. Members maintain close ties to several Mexican drug trafficking organizations and are involved in trafficking quantities of cocaine and marijuana from Mexico into the United States for distribution.

Tango Blast is one of largest prison/street criminal gangs operating in Texas. Tango Blast's criminal activities include drug trafficking, extortion, kidnapping, sexual assault, and murder. In the late 1990s, Hispanic men incarcerated in federal, state, and local prisons founded Tango Blast for personal protection against violence from traditional prison gangs such as the Aryan Brotherhood, Texas Syndicate, and Texas Mexican Mafia. Tango Blast originally had four city-based chapters in Houston, Austin, Dallas, and Fort Worth. These founding four chapters are collectively known as Puro Tango Blast or the Four Horsemen. From the original four chapters, former Texas inmates established new chapters in El Paso, San Antonio, Corpus Christi, and the Rio Grande Valley. In June 2008, the Houston Police Department estimated that more than 14,000 Tango Blast members were incarcerated in Texas. Tango Blast is difficult to monitor. The gang does not conform to traditional prison/street gang hierarchical rules, either organization or gang rules. Tango Blast is laterally organized, and leaders are elected sporadically to represent the gang in prisons and to lead street gang cells. Corrections officials report that rival traditional prison gangs are now forming alliances to defend themselves against Tango Blast's growing power, exemplifying the significance of Tango Blast.

United Blood Nation is a universal term that is used to identify both West Coast Bloods and United Blood Nation (UBN). The UBN started in 1993 in Rikers Island GMDC (New York) to form protection from the threat posed by Latin Kings and Ñetas, who dominated the prison. While these groups are traditionally distinct entities, both identify themselves by "Blood," often making it hard for law enforcement to distinguish between them. The UBN is a loose confederation of street gangs, or sets, that once were predominantly African American. Membership is estimated to be between 7,000 and 15,000 along the U.S. eastern corridor. The UBN derives its income from street-level distribution of cocaine, heroin, and marijuana; robbery; auto theft; and smuggling drugs to prison inmates.

Gang Management in Corrections

We turn our attention to the means by which prison systems contend with gang members. In doing so, many prison systems must contend with legal filings from inmates who contest and challenge such protocols. The impact is significant on prison systems and administrators, who must ensure that they adhere to policy when classifying inmates as gang members. The reason for these challenges is that inmates, once identified as a gang member, usually will be classified as such throughout the remainder of their contact with the criminal justice system. Further still, they may be restricted from the general population and be required to remain in specialized housing assignments or may be given heightened security. These outcomes are often not considered beneficial to most inmate gang members.

In fact, there are many other potential consequences that inmates might incur who are dubbed "gang members" by prison administrators (Hanser, 2016). Some of the penalties and/or consequences, as well as the reasons for these consequences (Hanser, 2016), are presented as follows:

1. Gang members may be denied the opportunity to have contact visits because contact visits are one way that contraband (drugs, paraphernalia, unauthorized literature, weapons) are brought into the prison. To minimize the likelihood of unauthorized items into the prison, this restriction may be imposed.
2. The frequency of noncontact visits may be reduced. In many cases, these may be reduced because it may not be clear if persons visiting are or are not also gang members. Indeed, some gangs may have multiple family members who are members. In some cases, multiple generations of the same family (i.e., father and son, or even grandfather, father, and son) may be members of the gang. Likewise, it is not uncommon for wives, mothers, and sisters to assist family members who are in a gang.
3. Gang members may not be allowed to participate in many academic activities. This restriction is due to security. Prison staff may place this restriction on gang members to minimize their contact with other inmates throughout the facility. This eliminates both potential contacts with unknown members in general population as well as potential recruiting for new members.
4. Gang members may be denied vocational programming. The reasons for this are identical to those in (3). In addition, some types of vocational programming may require tools or items that, if placed in the wrong hands, can be deadly. Gang members often have a propensity toward violence and should not, therefore, have access to potentially dangerous tools.
5. Denial of emergency absences, such as for a death in the family. This restriction is often because of the likelihood of contact with outside gang members.
6. Inability to participate in good-time awarding programs. This also may be necessary to keep gang members from infiltrating therapeutic communities and other types of prosocial programming. This also minimizes the ability of gangs to recruit from these programs.
7. Denial of potential prison jobs. This restriction is also related to the need to restrict contact between gang members and nongang members.

8 Restricted movement in the prison. This restriction minimizes potential conflict between rival gang members. This restriction, similar to many others, also minimizes the likelihood of gang members recruiting or intimidating nongang members.
9 Placement in administrative segregation. This type of special housing assignment is not punitive but is a housing designation intended to prevent potential disruption of institutional security, including the safety of staff and inmates who may be in danger if a given inmate is allowed to intermingle freely within the general population of the prison.
10 State and local law enforcement are notified when the gang member is released to the community because many prison gang members eventually become linked with other members who were released from prison, thereby becoming active in the surrounding community; it is only prudent to notify officials who are tasked with combatting criminal activity outside of the prison.
11 Parole and conditions of parole can be impacted for released gang members; being in a gang is a rule violation in prisons. Thus, because of this rule violation, gang members may not be eligible for parole. Also, because the granting of parole is often tied to the types of programs that an inmate completes (i.e. education, drug treatment, vocational training, parenting classes, and so forth) and, as noted previously, these individuals may be restricted from these activities, it may be more difficult for them to become eligible for parole.

From the discussion so far, it is clear that offenders who are labeled as gang members in a prison system have numerous potential setbacks. This is precisely why many resist such classifications and hide their membership affiliation. This has led to a number of legal fights between inmates and prison systems, such as the one that is discussed in the subsection that follows. What is important to remember is that, at one time in prison history, gangs were rampant in several prison systems. During this era, prison staff and inmates worked and lived in fear and, until reforms of prison systems were implemented during the 1970s and 1980s, they dominated the day-to-day control of many prisons. In order to keep this from occurring again, regulations against gang affiliation and the consequences given for such membership are a necessity to maintain institutional safety and security for both inmates and staff. We now turn our attention to *Harbin-Bey v. Rutter*, a 2005 case whereby an inmate sought to refute his classification as a gang member by the Michigan prison system.

In 2001, Harbin-Bey, an inmate in the Alger Maximum Correctional Facility in the state of Michigan who was affiliated with the well-known street and prison gang, Vice Lords, sent letters to family and friends about the prison system's policy on security threat groups. It was the opinion of Harbin-Bey that the policy of that state's correctional system infringed on the constitutional rights held by persons in confinement. Harbin-Bey ultimately filed suit on Lyle Rutter, the prison's Security Threat Group (STG) coordinator, as well as other officials of the Michigan correctional system. In particular, Harbin-Bey took issue with his being designated an STG leader without the benefit of a prison disciplinary hearing, claiming this was a violation of his due process of law. Ultimately, in 2005, the Sixth Circuit Court of Appeals held that the STG policies within the state of Michigan's prison system did not violate the constitutional rights of Harbin-Bey and other inmates. Rather, the circuit court stated that, "Identifying, reclassifying, and separating prisoners who are members of groups that engage in planning or committing unlawful acts or acts of misconduct 'targets a core threat to the safety of both prison inmates and officials'" (*Harbin-Bey v. Rutter*, 2005, p. 576). This statement alone is important because it notes that the use of extra security precautions in relation to gang members are both warranted and justified. Further, the need to identify, reclassify, and separate gang offenders was legitimized. While Harbin-Bey may have taken issue with how the process had been implemented (itself found to be an invalid issue), the fact that such processes were utilized were found to be acceptable and appropriate to operating a safe custodial environment. It is with this in mind that we now proceed to discuss issues related to gang management and the maintenance of custodial safety within institutions.

As one might expect, gang management requires a comprehensive policy that specifies legal precedents, procedures, and guidelines, including the verification of gang members. Over the years, most state systems have developed gang intelligence units and have trained correctional staff on gangs and gang activity. In modern times, state and federal corrections may not necessarily distinguish between traditional prison gangs and those that operate both in the prison and in the surrounding community.

When combating prison gangs, the technical aspects, such as the paper classification and procedures needed to investigate gang members, are straightforward. However, the human element is what makes the fight against prison gangs much more difficult. In correctional facilities that do not emphasize professionalism or encourage open communication among security staff and do have a strong underlying prison subculture (both inmate and correctional officer), prison gangs are likely to proliferate. A lack of professionalism, stunted communication, and powerful subcultural norms that are counter to the prison administration serve as the breeding ground for gang development. Further, when selecting correctional staff to serve on gang task forces, the prison administrator must exercise care and remain vigilant. In some cases, an inmate's sibling, cousin, girlfriend, former wives, and companions may be employed within the facility. This is a common tactic used by gangs seeking to infiltrate the correctional system.

Gang Control, Management, and Administrative Segregation

Aside from a prison's physical security features, there are many psychological aspects of controlling gang activity. For instance, the immediate tendency of corrections officials may be to restrict privileges for gang-related inmates. However, as Fleisher (2008) notes, withdrawing incentives or placing these inmates in long-term states of restricted movement can have financial and social consequences for the prison facility. For instance, in Texas, many gang-related inmates are kept in administrative segregation. Administrative segregation is a security status that is intended to keep the assigned inmate from having contact with the general population. It is not punitive in nature, like solitary confinement. This custody status is intended to protect the general population from the inmate in segregation. However, this form of custody is very expensive.

Further, there is a tendency for prison systems that use administrative segregation to house inmates of the same gang in the same area. This prevents them from coming into contact with enemy gang members yet cuts costs that would ensue if they were kept on different cellblocks or dormitories. Nevertheless, doing this replicates the street gang culture, as they are all together but with geographic isolation (i.e., one neighborhood, one gang) where there is one cellblock and one gang. In other words, this can build solidarity for the group. This can also lead to problematic behaviors where inmates exercise power (through the gang rank structure) over a cellblock or dormitory, encouraging security to work with those in power to maintain compliance over the other lower-ranking inmates of that gang. Naturally, this should be avoided because it validates the gang's power and undermines the security staff. Fleisher (2008) notes that other problematic behaviors also can emerge. For instance, gangs may attempt to run cellblocks, "sell" cells on the cell block, or "own" territory on the recreation yard. This simply reinforces their feeling that they have power over the institution. This should be avoided.

Gang Intelligence Units and Gang Management Data

Today's world of corrections is one that is driven more by technology than ever before. Most modern prison facilities have electronic surveillance, improved layout, and staff intelligence-gathering strategies that, during the past two decades, have proven effective in minimizing the activities of prison gangs. According to Fleisher (2008), a key aspect of a comprehensive gang intelligence program is the use of data that is continuously validated. It is important to point out that gang data are of no assistance if they are not well organized and carefully analyzed.

The gang intelligence team should be proficient in the use of database software used by both the prison system as well as the surrounding police agencies. An example of a well-developed gang management data system would be that used at the Rikers Island Prison in New York. The database for this system integrates both prison and police records to ensure that all relevant information on a gang and/or gang member can be accessed. This allows for shared access between agencies, which helps to combat prison gang activity internally as well as street gang activity from members of prison gangs who have been released to the community. As was pointed out in the prior section, circumstances exist where prison gang members are linked to criminal activity on the outside. Shared data between corrections and police help to combat gang operations on both ends of the spectrum. Any good gang data management system will have an effective intelligence and communications network that would accurately indicate how many inmates have gang affiliations, which gangs they are affiliated with, and their status within those gangs. The database should also provide information on which facilities gang members are in and their institutional classification. Further, all of this information can provide the department with data on the proliferation or concentration of any group so that it can forecast where or when a buildup of a particular group could cause problems. Strategic transfers of inmates can assist the agency in controlling the establishment of gang power bases and can ensure that some individuals do not have undue influence over others. In addition, good gang intelligence programs will have developed a digitized imaging program that offers numerous advantages for identifying gang members and their status, behavior, and control. Digitized images should also be made of any tattoos, distinguishing marks, or scars. These images are usually clearer than those obtained by film, and this negates the need for taking additional photographs or for film storage or development. The digitized images can also be entered into a computer and downloaded into the database. This type of process tends to take about two minutes per individual and can produce a permanent record that can be promptly updated, as circumstances require.

Included within the gang intelligence database should also be information on codes and cryptographic writing used by different gangs. Prison gang leaders often order members to engage in various forms of illegal activity through written notes. These notes often are written in code that disguises the true meaning of the message. Indeed, some gangs have very sophisticated forms of cryptography that they change throughout the year as a means of sending and receiving confidential information. Signs, symbols, and coded writings can all have significant meaning in the world of gang operations, both inside prison and in outside operations.

Lastly, gang intelligence units should be multidisciplinary. Consider the New York Unified Intelligence Division (UID) as an example. This division consists of three agencies: the New York City Police Department, the Drug Enforcement Agency (DEA), and the New York State Police. Information gathered inside prison can sometimes provide testimony or information that might help to solve a crime on the outside, once shared. Likewise, police intelligence can tip off correctional staff as to affiliations found to exist among persons on the street that are not known by staff inside the prison. This allows corrections staff to be proactive in separating out gang members and safeguarding against illicit activities within the institution.

Common Themes in Prison Gang Leadership and Organization

Of the research on prison gang leadership and organization, the recent work of Ortiz (2015) seems to be the most comprehensive and accurate. Her work considers both the historical evolution of prison gangs and considers their symbiotic union with street gangs that developed over time. Most importantly, Ortiz (2015) is one of the few researchers to conduct extensive interviews with gang members to get an accurate understanding of how decisions are made. Her research included extensive gang inmate input and integrates academic and practitioner perspectives in a manner that provides a good overview of how leaders are selected and how prison gangs are run.

First, it would be remiss not to mention the seminal work of Sykes (1958) on inmate behavior and prison gang involvement. Ortiz (2015) makes a point to integrate Sykes in her overview and indicates that there is substantial evidence to show that in some cases, prison gangs operate as a form of resistance against their captors and the prison system itself and as a mechanism to endure and cope with the abuses of their captors. In such cases, she notes that gangs operate in either a collectivistic or an individualistic fashion. Collective organization occurs with the gang operates in solidarity against prison officials. On the other hand, gang leadership that operates in an individualistic fashion hold their fellow gang members as objects, similar to pieces on a chessboard, to be moved and manipulated to propel their own individual interests (Ortiz, 2015; Sykes, 1958). Naturally, this individualistic form of leadership tends to develop the least internally motivated members, whereas the collective orientation of leadership holds mutual benefit for the entire gang when coping with prison life. Indeed, Sykes (1958) notes that these types of gangs lead to a reduction in the pains of imprisonment for all inmates. According to Sykes (1958, p. 107):

> A cohesive inmate society provides the prisoner with a meaningful social group with which he can identify himself and which will support him in his battles against the condemners—and thus the prisoner can at least in part escape the fearful isolation of the convicted offender.

Ortiz (2015) goes on to note that leadership within prison gangs may change depending on who comes from the outside and is incarcerated. Indeed, if a gang member on the outside significantly outranks the current leadership in the prison, this can lead to a source of intra-gang disagreement and/or fighting. This type of in-fighting is particularly common for prison gangs run from an individualistic leadership style, as one can imagine.

Another common organization patter for prison gangs, particularly for long-standing prison gangs such as the Mexican Mafia and the Aryan Brotherhood, is the traditional or vertical structure. These gang structures persist through generations of gang membership (for 30, 40, and 50 years or more) and tend to be most frequently studied among researchers. These groups tend to have clear distinctions between core membership and those whose affiliation is on the fringes. Further, these groups will tend to have a broad range of ages among membership (often being intergenerational with members from multiple generations of the same family), with appropriate leadership within each age grouping. The vertical structure tends to engage in a variety of crimes and tends to be the most difficult to counter or suppress.

One other form of prison gang organizational style to be presented in this section is the horizontal structure. In actuality, this type of organization is more common with street gangs rather than prison gangs. This organizational pattern is more common to jails, where street gang members are incarcerated for briefer periods but have alliances based on neighborhoods and are members to independent gangs. This may also be a form of organization in some prison systems where states have gangs with multiple "sets" or groupings throughout a city or the state, such as with the Bloods and Crips in California. To a lesser extent, this type of organization is observed when various prison gangs ally with one another in a war with other opposing gangs.

Prison Gangs as Informal Social Control Mechanisms in Prison

New findings on prison gangs have emerged that would seem to indicate that, at least to some extent, prison gangs serve as a form of informal social order within the prisons. To be clear, this social order has positive benefits for the prison and does not only center on the commission of criminal activities.

Rather, because gangs regulate the behavior of their own members, this provides some degree of order among members and even within the broader nongang general population.

The work of Roth and Skarbek (2014) highlight the role of prison gangs to enforce agreements within the contraband trade of a prison and how they aid in resolving social disputes. In addition, these researchers refer to the informal prison society as a community responsibility system (Blatchford, 2008; Greif, 2006). The community responsibility system is one where members of the group are responsible for the acts committed and the debts incurred by its individual members (Greif, 2006; Roth & Skarbek, 2014). Because of this, it is considered right and proper for the group (the prison gang) to monitor the behavior of its own members, such informal internal governance being lower cost than what official prison security can provide. Further, because members are aware of the "dark figure" of trade and illicit activities—the dark figure being all the illicit activities that occur but are never detected by prison security—they are much more effective in monitoring these activities and keeping peace between parties who trade and traffic (Blatchford, 2008; Greif, 2006).

Consider, also, that most prison gangs have written constitutions, maintain and enforce a lifetime membership requirement, and successfully (meaning without being caught) engage in criminal activity both in the prison and in the broader community (Blatchford, 2008; Skarbek, 2011). The prison gang, therefore, is considered an effective informal governance system that promotes cooperation and trust, and one that aids the illegal contraband market. This is juxtaposed with a formal social control system (i.e., prison security) that, from the inmate's perspective, is unreliable and not helpful to appropriately meeting their needs. Thus, prison gangs form as a means of providing extralegal governance over economic agreements and in social circumstances that are not brought to security staff within a prison (Blatchford, 2008; Greif, 2006; Roth & Skarbek, 2014).

There is one caveat that Roth and Skarbek (2014) note regarding the governing utility of prison gangs—the prison population cannot be too large or too small. These extremes are often troublesome for security. This means that there is an optimal number of prison gang size and an optimal number of gangs within prisons, dependent upon the population dynamics of the prison, the security level of the prison (minimum, medium, maximum security) and the overall population count. Roth and Skarbek (2014) provide very convincing statistical analyses to support this and note that prison wardens would be well served in understanding this balance, in practical terms, rather than attempting to uphold a zero-tolerance approach that is based on ideal terms (Corrections One, 2015; Roth & Skarbek, 2014).

Recruitment into Prison Gangs

In recent years, the impact that gangs have had on correctional systems has diminished. Nevertheless, gang activity does still exist in many prison environments. However, many offenders who are members of prison gangs were initially members of gangs on the outside. Thus, nowadays many gang members in prison are imported from outside the prison as members of a gang that also exists inside the prison.

Despite this fact, recruitment of additional members within the prison is still a chief concern for many prison gang task forces. The survey work of Knox (2012) included an item that inquired as to whether prison administrators believed that inmates at their facility had voluntarily sought out gang membership or had been recruited into a gang while in jail or prison. The results of the survey revealed that nearly 87% of the 125 administrators believed that inmates had voluntarily joined a prison gang or were recruited into a gang while in prison (Knox, 2012, p. 5). Indeed, it was thought that this was a common experience among the prison administrators surveyed.

This is important because it demonstrates the need for anti-gang policies, and it shows that the benefits of gang membership (prestige, money, belonging, protection) are sufficient to risk the potential consequences of joining a gang. In fact, many offenders report that they join a prison gang in an effort to gain power over other inmates and to gain respect from within the prison population. Others may cite that they wish to have the protection of the gang, but this is not a rational used often, because being in a gang usually puts them into a protracted and long-term conflict with other rival gangs.

There are a variety of means by which gangs attempt to persuade offenders to join, aside from the false pretense of protection from other inmates. Financial incentives and support are a common recruitment technique, especially when recruiting indigent inmates. However, for many offenders who join a prison gang, the reason for joining is often the same as for persons on the outside; they join to have a sense of belonging. These offenders may not have many friends or family who come to see them, being estranged from their family who have given up on them while in prison. For these inmates, the gang becomes a new family or structure. The gang becomes a key source of support. This rationale is particularly common among street gangs who attempt to recruit young members in impoverished or crime-ridden communities. The same principle is used with prison gangs, especially when recruiting younger inmates.

Once they are recruited, many offenders realize that gang membership is a double-edged sword. On the one hand, there are benefits, but on the other, there are consequences. For example, they are often asked or required to commit crimes, which can result in an extension of their sentence. Further, even though the gang may refer to itself as a "family," it may ask gang members to engage in a number of actions that require offenders to exploit their families on the outside. Many may be required to do any of the following:

1. The gang member may be required to demand money from his or her family-of-origin on the outside.
2. The gang may harm the new member's family on the outside if the new member does not follow the orders given to him while in prison.
3. The gang may require the new member to "take the heat" for an offense or crime that was committed by a more senior member of the gang.

As one can see, there are some serious issues stemming from gang membership from the gang itself, not to mention the various potential consequences from prison administration for gang association or affiliation. Over time, individuals often want to exit the gang, particularly if their experiences are negative. Naturally, this is a major decision, and it can be a dangerous decision. Thus, most inmates are not able to leave a gang on their own. By the time these individuals get to this point, they are usually more open to working with prison authorities.

Leaving the Prison Gang: An Example Program from Texas

Though difficult, offenders can leave prison gangs, though this is seldom done with the blessing of the gang itself. Rather, most inmates who leave prison gangs are required to denounce their membership and will be required to meet the specifications of structured programs set up within the prison. If they do so, prison authorities will work with these offenders to minimize the risk of retaliation from the prison gang that they seek to escape. One such program exists in the state of Texas, known as the Gang Renouncement and Disassociation (GRAD) process, whereby inmates who agree to renounce their gang membership are required to participate in nine months of activities designed to recondition them to a prosocial and nongang, noncriminal, lifestyle.

To be considered for the program, inmates must first submit a written statement to their STG officer stating their desire to renounce their membership to a particular gang. Afterward, officers conduct a complete investigation of that inmate on their unit to ensure that they truly intend to break their gang ties. Beyond the written letter and the investigation, inmates must meet a variety of other requirements before they are accepted into the program:

1 The individual must have committed no assaults for a period of two years.
2 The candidate cannot have a major disciplinary case for at least one year.
3 The candidate cannot have committed extortion within the past two years.
4 The candidate cannot have a weapons possession case during the past two years.
5 The individual has engaged in no sexual misconduct during the prior two years.
6 The individual must have renounced membership to the prison gang.
7 The offender must not have been involved in any gang activity during the previous two years.
8 The candidate cannot have engaged in any type of escape, staff assault, or hostage situation.

In addition, offenders have to complete a written request, which is reviewed by a committee at the unit level and a then a regional coordinator, before it goes to the statewide administrator. If an inmate is approved for the GRAD program, he is put on a waiting list and, once selected, starts with a cohort of 15 other gang members. Each 16-person cohort includes a mixture of different gang members so that a balance of ethnicity, sentence lengths among participants, demographics, and other characteristics are optimally brought together.

Last, the GRAD program is a nine-month program that is divided into three distinct phases. Phase One lasts for approximately two months and consists primarily of substance abuse classes, completion of the 12-Steps (Alcoholics Anonymous), and chaplaincy videos. The integration of clean living and spirituality is utilized to address both internal and external issues that affect the offender's ability to live a noncriminal lifestyle. Phase Two lasts approximately four months and includes cognitive interventions, anger management, and addictive criminal behavior therapy. This phase addresses many of the contrary belief systems of criminals regarding trust, friendships, responsibility, delayed gratification, and the ability to tolerate stress and frustration in life. Faulty thinking is addressed during this phase as are negative self-talk. The last three months of the GRAD program is Phase Three, which consists of a half-day work schedule (doing laundry, working in the fields, or engaged in food service), with another half-day of classes related to employment interviewing, budgeting, professional conduct, and so forth.

Conclusion

The ability to distinguish between prison gangs and security threat groups is considered more an academic matter than one of practicality. Nevertheless, individuals should understand that a key defining feature of a prison gang is that its purpose is to engage in criminal activity, whereas the purpose of a security threat group may entail other goals that are not necessarily criminal nor in violation of institutional rule. Likewise, the term "prison gang" usually refers to gangs that have their origin within a prison setting, but in modern times, prison gangs sometimes have their birth as a street gang that eventually follows into prison as members are convicted of crimes on the outside but maintain gang membership while serving time on the inside. In addition, gangs with their genesis in prisons have had members released into society, and many of these members maintain their gang affiliation when on the streets. The term cross-pollination refers to this back-and-forth nature of prison and street gang confluence.

There are many reasons for prison gang members to hide their membership, with penalties and consequences from prison security being numerous. In some cases, this has resulted in litigation from inmates who wish to challenge a prison system's attempt to classify them as a gang member. Likewise, this has led to intricate coding of communications, the use of symbols, and other surreptitious forms of communicating day-to-day gang business among members. The evasive and clandestine tactics utilized by gang members make the use of gang intelligence units a necessity as well as effective gang intelligence data systems that provide extensive data that is accessed and inputted by key stakeholder agencies tasked with fighting gangs on the inside and the outside of the prison environment.

In addition, several of the more common and more well-known prison gangs are presented. Characteristics of these gangs, membership, and illicit activities conducted by these gangs are provided. Further still, typical leadership and organizational patterns of prison gangs, the informal governance role that gangs play within the inmate social order, and methods of recruitment, as well as programming for members who wish to exit the gang life, are also discussed. Observing these various dimensions of prison gangs shows the complexities associated with these illicit organizations, their operations, and the impact that they have on both the prison environment and the surrounding community.

References

Benson, Y. (2015). How prison gangs affect inmates. *attn: Justice*. Retrieved from www.attn.com/stories/2602/effects-of-prison-gangs

Blatchford, C. (2008). *The black hand: The bloody rise and redemption of "Boxer" Enriquez, a Mexican mob killer*. New York, NY: William Morrow Paperbacks—Harper Collins.

Corrections One. (2015, March 10). Report suggests prison gangs are "good" for prisons. *CorrectionsOne.com*. Retrieved from www.correctionsone.com/prison-gangs/articles/8420832-Report-suggests-prison-gangs-are-good-for-prisons/

Fleisher, M. S. (2008). Gang management in corrections. In P. M. Carlson & J. S. Garrett (Eds.), *Prison and jail administration: Practice and theory* (2nd ed.). Gaithersburg, MD: Aspen.

Geniella, M. (2001, April 21). Links found to seven Santa Rosa slayings. *The Press Democrat, California*.

Greif, A. (2006). History lesson: The birth of impersonal exchange: The community responsibility system and impartial justice. *Journal of Economic Perspectives*, *20*(2), 221–236. doi:10.1257/jep.20.2.221

Hanser, R. D. (2016). *Introduction to corrections* (2nd ed.). Thousand Oaks, CA: Sage.

Hanser, R. D. (2007). *Special needs offenders*. Upper Saddle River, NJ: Prentice Hall.

Harbin-Bey v. Rutter, 524 F.3d 789 (2005).

Knox, G. W. (2012). *The problem of gangs and security threat groups (STGs) in American prisons and jails today: Recent findings from the 2012 NGCRC National Gang/STG Survey*. Retrieved from www.ngcrc.com/corr2012.html

National Gang Intelligence Center. (2009). *National gang threat assessment 2009: Prison gangs*. Washington, DC: National Gang Intelligence Center.

Orlando-Morningstar, D. (1999). *Prison gangs*. Washington, DC: Federal Judicial Center.

Ortiz, J. M. (2015). The power of place: A comparative analysis of prison and street gangs. *CUNY Academic Works*. Retrieved from http://academicworks.cuny.edu/gc_etds/1081

Roth, G. M., & Skarbek, D. (2014). Prison gangs and the community responsibility system. *The Review of Behavioral Economics*, *1*(3), 223–243. doi:10.1561/105.00000011

Skarbek, D. (2011). Governance and prison gangs. *American Political Science Review*, *105*(4), 702–716.

Sykes, G. M. (1958). *The society of captives: A study of a maximum security prison*. Princeton, NJ: Princeton University Press.

15

SUICIDAL PRISONERS

Identifying Suicide Risk and Implementing Preventative Policies

Christine Tartaro

> Jail environments are conducive to suicidal behavior [because] the inmate is facing a crisis situation. From the inmate's perspective, certain features of the jail environment enhance suicidal behavior: fear of the unknown, distrust of the authoritarian environment, lack of apparent control over the future, isolation from family and significant others, shame of incarceration, and the dehumanizing aspects of incarceration.
>
> —(Hayes, 1995b, p. 2)

Introduction

It is not difficult to see why prisons, jails, and even police lockups would be high-risk locations for suicides and suicide attempts. First, consider the reason why individuals have found themselves detained. They were either caught or reported to have committed a crime. The fact that the crime has come to the attention of the criminal justice system is likely to lead to numerous negative consequences. This initial detention, if prolonged, can lead to loss of a job. It is not uncommon to overhear inmates in booking areas of jails calling friends and relatives to discuss what they should tell the employer about their impending absence. The inmates might be scared to let friends and family know about the incarceration and fear that this will strain relationships. Another possibility is that they may have no one to call and have to be reminded about how this is precisely the type of behavior that has led to their estrangement from family and friends. While we typically think about harm from crime in terms of the impact it has on victims, crime can also be traumatic for offenders. During this initial period of incarceration, the offenders might be haunted by what just happened, especially if a friend or relative was harmed in the process.

The second source of stress may come from fear of the future. Will this incarceration drag out because of an inability to secure pretrial release? Even if the individuals were able to convince their bosses that they will be missing a few days of work because of an illness or family emergency, what will happen if they cannot secure release soon? Will there be a prison term? Will family and friends stand by them during this time? How will this arrest and incarceration affect their reputation in the community?

Third, what about the inmates' immediate surroundings? Incarceration is frightening. Gresham Sykes (1958), in his classic work on the pains of incarceration, noted that one facet of imprisonment that makes it so difficult is the deprivation of security. Throughout incarceration, individuals may face threats to personal safety because of being locked up with other inmates, some of whom might seek to exploit others. While humans' usual reaction to danger is fight or flight, flight is not an option. Inmates must think about the extent to which they will risk their safety and additional incarceration time in an effort to ward off attempts at exploitation.

Fourth, inmates may begin their confinement in a lockup or a jail while intoxicated or under the influence of drugs. According to the James and Glaze (2006), 34% of jail inmates with a mental health problem reported drinking or using drugs at the time of their crime, while 20% of jail inmates without mental health problems also reported being under the influence when the crime was committed. Whether arrested during the commission of the crime or sometime thereafter, jail administrators and police who work near the lockups are frequently faced with supervising intoxicated inmates. This contributes to suicide risk in two ways. First, inmates who are intoxicated have fewer inhibitions and might be more likely to "work up the nerve" to attempt suicide. If inmates are able to get through the period of intoxication without suicide, the hangover, or detox in the case of addicts, can be dangerous. Not only are they likely to feel physically ill, but this might give people the first opportunity in quite some time to assess the state of their lives without the numbing effect of substances.

Finally, and especially for inmates who find themselves incarcerated for long periods of time, the stress and frustration of having the outside world move on can be too much to bear at times. For example, for many inmates spending the holidays in jail or prison exacerbates feelings of loneliness and despair. In addition, bad news from home can lead to sadness and a feeling of helplessness, as inmates know that they will not be released so they can help a child deal with problems, attempt to save a marriage, or comfort or say goodbye to a dying loved one.

Any of the aforementioned challenges might motivate people, even those with good coping skills, to contemplate suicide, even if just for a moment. It can be argued, however, that many who are in jail or prison are there precisely because of their lack of skills to cope with problems in a productive, prosocial manner. Corrections staff members have a responsibility to help maintain the health of inmates (*Estelle v. Gamble*, 1976), and this includes mental health care (*Bowring v. Godwin*, 1977).

Despite the constitutional requirement of health care and the fact that inmates are under more surveillance than the typical person, suicide remains one of the leading causes of death among inmates. This chapter will include an overview of who tends to commit suicide behind bars and how, where, and when these incidents tend to occur. Next, we will discuss the development of suicide prevention practices for inmates over the past 30 to 40 years. Finally, nonincarceration options will be discussed.

The Prevalence of Prisoner Suicide

Suicide is the leading cause of death in jails and juvenile facilities and the fifth most common cause of death in prison (Noonan & Rohloff, 2015). The Bureau of Justice Statistics has been publishing annual reports of inmate mortality since 2000 and found that 4,134 inmates have committed suicide in jails during those years. Thirty-four percent of all jail deaths and 5.5% of prison deaths in the United States in 2013 were attributed to suicide. The 2013 suicide rate in jails, using the average daily population as the denominator, was 46 per 100,000 inmates compared to 40 per 100,000 inmates in 2012 (Noonan & Rohloff, 2015). The overall suicide rate in the general population of the United States in 2013 was 13.4 per 100,000 individuals (Konchanek, Murphy, Xu, & Tejada-Vera, 2016). While the prison suicide rate is slightly higher than this, we must remember that the prison population is mostly male and over the age of 15, while the general population suicide rate is calculated with both males and females and individuals 15 and younger, resulting in a lower overall rate.

The higher frequency of suicides in jails compared to prisons can be attributed to a number of factors. First, jails have transient populations. Jail populations will turn over several times of year, resulting in over 10 million admissions to United States jails each year (Lyman & LoBuglio, 2006). By nature of the constant movement of people in and out of jail, these facilities must work with more people, and that means there are more people who may commit suicide. The lack of transiency in prisons gives the staff an advantage over their jail counterparts in that they have the opportunity to get to know the inmates so they can more easily detect abnormal behavior that may serve as a warning sign of distress. Second, pretrial inmates face greater uncertainty about their futures than prison inmates. Third, as was mentioned earlier, the fact that inmates may enter jail directly from the streets increases the chances of jail inmates being either under the influence of substances or at the beginning phase of a physically and/or psychologically painful withdrawal. Prison inmates, on the other hand, are much more likely to enter the institution sober after being in jail while awaiting sentencing. Fourth, since jail is often inmates' first exposure to incarceration, inmates may be able to work through some of the shock associated with the arrest and entering a facility as a prisoner, so they may be a bit more mentally prepared for incarceration by the time they enter prison.

Who Commits Suicide in Prison and Jail

Patterns of suicide in the general population of the United States are similar to patterns inside correctional facilities in a couple of ways. For instance, in both settings, males are more likely to commit suicide than females. Caucasian individuals inside and outside of custody also are more likely to attempt and commit suicide when compared to African Americans and Hispanics (Kochanek et al., 2016; Noonan & Rohloff, 2015). Across correctional facilities, pretrial or remand inmates tend to be more likely to commit suicide than sentenced inmates (Frottier et al., 2002; Myslimaj & Eglantina, 2016; United Nations World Health Organization, 2007). Among sentenced inmates, those serving life are more likely than others to commit suicide (Borrill, 2002; Couturier, 2001; Reeves & Tamburello, 2014; United Nations World Health Organization, 2007).

Some research on correctional suicides included efforts to identify the "typical" inmate who would take his own life in short-term or long-term incarceration settings (Borrill, 2002; Crighton & Towl, 1997; Hatty & Walker, 1986; Hayes, 1989; Salive, Smith, & Brewer, 1989; Topp, 1979; United Nations World Health Organization, 2007). Researchers have cautioned against using inmate demographic information to attempt to construct a profile of inmates prone to suicide attempts. While the researchers just cited have identified some commonalities among their samples, use of demographic information for suicide profiles typically lead to false positives and false negatives (Pompili et al., 2009). False positives are inmates who will be identified as being suicidal when, in fact, they are not. The allotment of extra supervision and resources provided to false positives may be to the detriment of the false negatives, or inmates who are truly suicidal but did not fit the demographic profile.

There are other inmate characteristics that are better predictors of inmate suicide. Suicide risk factors can be placed into two categories—static and dynamic. Static factors are unable to be changed, but they include important information related to inmates' medical and psychological history. As was noted earlier, gender, race, and legal status (remand or sentenced) and sentence length (lifers) are all risk factors for correctional suicide. Additional static factors are history of substance abuse, history of violence, history of suicide attempts, and prior and current mental health diagnoses (Reeves & Tamburello, 2014). History of nonfatal acts of self-harm, even if there was no suicidal intent, is also a risk factor (Matsumoto et al., 2005). These demographic, legal, and historical characteristics should be part of screening mechanisms, but it is also important to take into account dynamic risk factors at several points in time. Dynamic factors are changeable and include current and recent suicidal ideation and attempts, receipt of bad news from court or home, recent disciplinary charges, and incarceration-related conflicts. Reeves and Tamburello (2014) also suggest that inmate housing assignment needs to be considered as a dynamic risk factor, as type of housing arrangement is associated with correctional suicides. Howells, Hall, and Day (1999) note that inmates' coping abilities are dynamic, and targeting these abilities for intervention may help inmates change their perceptions and response to personal and institutional stressors.

Methods for Committing Suicide While Incarcerated

One area of consistency over the years has been the method that inmates most commonly use to commit suicide—hanging/asphyxiation (Eyland, Corben, & Barton, 1997; Hayes, 2010; Spinellis & Themeli, 1997; Victoria Department of Justice Correctional Services Task Force, 1998; Wobeser, Datema, Bechard, & Ford, 2002). The reason for this is simple—inmates tend to lack access to tools or locations to commit suicide in other ways. The leading form of suicide in the general population of the United States is death by firearm, with 21,334 deaths in 2014 or 6.7 per 100,000 residents (Kochanek et al., 2016). Clearly, this is not an option for incarcerated individuals. While it might be possible to fall off a top tier at a few corrections facilities, most have taken precautions to prevent jumping. Poisonous gas is not available, and death by overdose would require a prolonged period of hoarding pills undetected. Cutting might be available to some inmates, particularly long-term inmates who have accumulated more belongings, but cutting is rarely fatal and is easily detectable during wellness checks. The only conventional method of suicide that remains available to most inmates is asphyxiation or hanging. Inmates only need two things to attempt suicide—something that can be used to fashion a noose and something in the cell to use as a tie-off point. Inmates can, and have, demonstrated that such items as shoelaces, socks, shirts, pants, underwear, and bedsheets can be used to make a noose. While a tie-off point well above the ground is necessary for hanging, anything can be used for asphyxiation as long as an inmate is able to bend forward or backward to tighten the noose and cut off oxygen. This factor presents an additional challenge to corrections staff, as some inmates may be able to position themselves in a sitting or lying position that does not look out of the ordinary to passing officers.

When Suicides Occur

Perhaps the biggest change that has occurred in correctional suicide patterns over the past 30 years is *when* inmates are most likely to commit suicide. Research from the 1970s and 1980s reported over 50% of suicides in jails occurring within the first 48 hours of incarceration (Hayes, 1989). While the initial period of incarceration remains a high-risk time and extra vigilance is still warranted, fewer suicides have occurred upon initial incarceration in the past 10 years. In a follow-up to his earlier work, Hayes (2010) reported that more recent correctional suicides tend to be more temporally distributed than in the past. In a study of suicides in 2005 and 2006, Hayes reported 23% of suicides occurred in the first 24 hours of incarceration, 27% between the first two to 17 days, and then an additional 20% in the first one to four months of incarceration. This is an encouraging sign. Over the past 40 years, suicide in prison and jail has gained much more attention. There have been several articles about correctional suicide not just in the academic publications but also in practitioner magazines, which have helped to raise awareness of the frequency with which suicides occurred upon initial confinement. Additionally, the Bureau of Justice Statistics brought attention to correctional suicide by publishing annual mortality statistics for prisons and jails starting in 2000. Correctional administrations are aware that suicide of an inmate can lead to a lawsuit in state or federal court. It seems that the enhanced awareness has prompted many corrections agencies to be proactive in screening for and addressing suicide risk.

The time around individuals' initial entry into a facility does remain a high-risk period, and it is important to continue to observe inmates during this time. There are also other high-risk times that warrant additional screening and, possibly, supervision. The days leading up to and following a court date can be particularly difficult for inmates (Byrne, Lurigio, & Pimentel, 2009; Hayes, 1996;

Marcus & Alcabes, 1993; United Nations World Health Organization, 2007). Receipt of bad news from home (Hayes, 1996) and stress because of conflict inside the facility (Blaauw, Winkel, & Kerkhof, 2001; Inch, Rowlands, & Soliman, 1995) have also been particularly difficult times for inmates.

Where Suicides Occur

Suicide can only occur if an individual is alone or if there is a bystander with one of three conditions present: (1) the bystander is unable to intervene; (2) the bystander does not recognize there is a problem and need for an intervention; or (3) the bystander simply chooses not to intervene. Given this information, it should not be surprising that suicides are most likely to occur when inmates are alone (British Home Office, 1999; Eyland et al., 1997; Hayes, 1989, 1996; Marcus & Alcabes, 1993). Hayes (2010) found that while only 38% of suicides occurred while an inmate was in a setting that would be considered "isolation," approximately 60% of inmates who committed suicide were assigned to single-occupancy cells at the time of death. In an analysis of suicides in New Jersey state prisons from 2005 through 2011, only one of the 26 deaths involved someone in a double-occupancy cell, and that suicide occurred outside of the cell. All other types of single-cell housing assignments, with the exception of the stabilization unit, where the cells are specifically designed for suicide prevention, had higher rates of suicide than the double-occupancy cells.

There are additional factors associated with inmate location that are related to suicide. Both nonlethal and lethal acts of self-harm tend to be more likely in maximum-security settings (McDonagh & Noel, 2002; Serin, Motiuk, & Wichmann, 2002), disciplinary units, and administrative segregation units (Kaba et al., 2014; Kovasznay, Miraglia, Beer, & Way, 2004; Sanchez, 2013). There are a few possible explanations for this. First, inmates in these units are often housed alone with only periodic staff supervision, thereby presenting them with many opportunities to attempt self-harm and for that harm to turn fatal. Second, inmates in these settings tend to have restricted access to programming and social opportunities that might help refocus them in a more positive direction. Third, their presence in these types of housing units may be a product of their mental illness and/or an inability to cope properly with problems (Lanes, 2011; Reeves & Tamburello, 2014). Lanes (2011) found that Michigan inmates who had a history of self-injury were more likely to have a history of being sent to administrative segregation compared to a randomly selected group of inmates with no history of self-injury.

Suicide Prevention Practices

As previously noted, research has provided us with information about static and dynamic characteristics that impact inmates' risk of suicide, locations where suicides in custody are most likely to occur, high-risk periods when inmates are at greater risk, and the most common technique that inmates use to enact deadly self-harm. This research provides important implications for prevention.

Screening

Screening is a vital component and often the starting point of any correctional suicide prevention program. Hayes (2010) found that 77% of jails and police detention units screen detainees upon intake. It is important, however, to avoid limiting screening to initial entry into a facility. Screening of inmates also should occur during high-risk times to gauge inmates' current state of mind.

There are a number of tools that can be used for screening, but it is recommended that facility staff choose an instrument that has been designed specifically for use with a correctional population. Teplin and Swartz (1989) identified elements of psychometric screening tools that limit their usefulness in the corrections setting. First, some of these tools are long, and understaffed facilities cannot afford to spend the one to two hours per person that a tool such as the Minnesota Multiphasic Personality Inventory (MMPI) requires. Second, the ideal situation would be to have mental health professionals perform every intake screening, but staffing and budget realities rarely allow for that. As a result, administrators and supervisors often have to give the responsibility of screening inmates to corrections officers or civilian employees who lack proper or extensive mental health training. Third, most of the non-correctional-based tests require the respondent to have a minimum of a sixth-grade education, and given the low education and literacy rates among inmates, this is problematic. Fourth, there are validity problems with taking some of the screenings given to nonincarcerated people and using them with incarcerated populations. Specifically, when such screenings are used with inmates, some of the items might be indicative of issues other than mental illness or suicidal ideation. For example, questions about racing thoughts or hallucinations are difficult, as it is hard to untangle the influence of drug abuse on the respondents' answers. Items used to assess paranoia might also be problematic, since inmates who report that they feel like they are being watched are probably correct, in that either corrections staff are currently monitoring them or law enforcement might have had them under surveillance recently. Questions regarding feelings of guilt and shame are also troublesome, as this is already likely a common feeling among inmates and not necessarily an indicator of mental illness or an impending suicide attempt (Veysey, Steadman, Morrissey, Johnsen, & Beckstead, 1998).

Screening instruments that are appropriate for use in a correctional environment should be short and simple enough for a corrections officer or other non-mental health staff member to administer after a brief training (Teplin & Swartz, 1989). The Referral Decision Scale (RDS) was developed specifically for incarcerated populations, but there are concerns about its validity (Veysey et al., 1998). The Brief Jail Mental Health Survey (BJMHS) was written by researchers in response to their concern about the limitations of the RDS. The BJMHS collects information on more current signs of crisis compared to RDS, allowing the BJMHS to include more information about dynamic risk factors. The BJMHS consists of eight items. Studies of the validity of the BJMHS have been somewhat positive (Kroner, Mills, Grazy, & Talbert, 2011; McMullan, 2011; Steadman, Robbins, Islam, & Osher, 2007), but caution should always be exercised in using instruments in new settings as they might not be normed to those populations (Evans, Brinded, Simpson, Frampton, & Mulder, 2010). Other promising tools are the Suicide Probability Scale (36 items), The Suicide Concerns for Offenders in Prison Environment (SCOPE) (28 items), The Suicide Potential Scale (9 items), and the Suicide Checklist (25 items). All have been tested with correctional populations with varying results, although most yield valid measures of suicide risk (Perry, Marandos, Coulton, & Johnson, 2010).[1]

One essential feature of the aforementioned instruments is their brevity. These also are considered screening tools that can be conducted by trained non-mental health staff members as opposed to more thorough clinical assessments that need to be handled by mental health professionals (American Psychiatric Association, 2000; Perry et al., 2010). Inmates who are in crisis or are currently experiencing mental health problems that affect their functioning need to be assessed beyond these brief screenings in two ways: (1) they need to work with a mental health professional, and (2) they need more extensive evaluations. Of course, the ideal scenario would be to provide full evaluations to each inmate, but that is not practical. Instead, a recommended practice is to view the short instruments as screening tools for triage purposes. For example, the Texas Department of Criminal Justice (TDCJ) uses standardized diagnostic interviews to assess inmates for symptoms of psychiatric illness, current suicidal ideation, prior suicidal behavior, unusual behavior, and history of mental health treatment. If, after this screening, staff members believe that inmates require further attention, inmates are referred for a full mental health evaluation with a master's level mental health professional (Baillargeon et al., 2009). The American Psychiatric Association (2000) recommends referring any inmates who are in need of further assessment to a more extensive but still brief mental health assessment with a mental health professional. If this assessment demonstrates the need for a more comprehensive examination, then a comprehensive mental health evaluation should be conducted by a psychiatrist or another appropriately licensed mental health professional. There are times when it might be clinically necessary to skip over the brief mental health assessment and go straight to the comprehensive examination.

It is encouraging that corrections agencies have increased the use of screening over the past 40 years. After finding that 77% of jails and detention centers were screening, Hayes (2010, p. 34) expressed concern, noting

> Thus, although a higher percentage of facilities that sustained inmate suicides had a screening process to identify potentially suicidal behavior at intake, the process was flawed in that most facilities did not verify whether the newly arrived inmate was on suicide precautions during a prior confinement in the jail facility, nor whether the arresting and/or transporting officer(s) believed that the inmate was at risk for suicide.

An essential component to all effective screening practices is communication, not just between the individual inmate and the staff member doing the screening but between staff members themselves and even people external to the correctional facility. There have been instances when the officers transporting people to the jail actually heard suicidal threats or witnessed suicide attempts but failed to relay that information to jail staff (*Jacobs v. West Feliciana Sheriff's Department*, 2000; *Turney v. Waterbury, 2004*; *Wever v. Lincoln County*, 2004). The result is that those detainees were housed without precautions, allowing for easy access to tools for suicide and a lack of supervision to complete it. Just as it is incumbent on law enforcement officers to communicate suicidal threats to corrections personnel, corrections staff members in different departments and different shifts must inform each other about worrisome inmate behavior and the acquisition of any new information about the inmate's recent history (*Snow v. City of Citronelle*, 2005).

Housing and Supervision

The fact that hanging/asphyxiation is the most common type of suicide in prisons and jails does have implications for suicide prevention strategies. Historically, a common way to work with inmates who appeared to be suicidal was to place them in an environment where the suicide would be extremely difficult or impossible to conduct. This usually started with removing from the inmate anything that could be used as a tool for a suicide attempt. Pompili et al. (2009) explain that safer cells are those that have been designed in a manner that prevents inmates from finding any fixtures to use to attach a noose. Specifically, these cells feature covered pipes, modified light fixtures, rounded corners, and safe vents. In addition to cell modifications, some facilities make use of special clothing for suicidal inmates, such as paper gowns or tear-proof smocks.

The aforementioned design changes to cells and clothing do make suicide attempts by hanging or asphyxiation much more challenging, if not impossible. Such cells also tend to be devoid of any personal items, so unless inmates are able to hide and smuggle sharp objects into the cell, almost every conventional method for suicide is removed. All that might be left is the extremely unconventional and painful method of attempting to generate a head injury through banging one's head against a wall. Not only is this painful, but it requires a certain degree of "courage" or lack of inhibition to repeatedly do this. If one does manage to do this multiple times, unconsciousness is likely to set in before inmates could inflict fatal harm.

While these cells do address the immediate threat of a suicide attempt, critics caution against widespread and prolonged use. Eyland et al. (1997) noted that safe cells should only be used when absolutely necessary and not for more than 48 hours. Such cells may be of use during an acute suicidal crisis where an individual is too dangerous to be around others. Power and Moodie (1997) advocated for a balance between risk reduction through control of opportunity for self-harm and the acknowledgement of the importance for inmates to maintain contact with other people. If it is at all possible to keep inmates safe while allowing them to remain in the general population, mental health, or medical unit, where inmates may still access belongings and participate in programming, such a strategy has greater potential to improve inmates' state of mind than isolation in a stripped-down cell (Hayes, 1995a, 1999).

It is important that suicidal inmates remain under *constant* supervision for the duration of the suicidal crisis and any step-down of supervision occur only after a qualified mental health professional assesses the inmates and approves of the adjustment. It is important to understand the lethality of asphyxiation/hanging when discussing the need for inmate supervision. Whether it is being used as an attention-getting suicidal gesture or intended as a suicide attempt, hanging/asphyxiation occurs quickly and is likely to lead to death. In a study of various methods of suicide, Stone (1999) reported that death from this method tends to occur within 5 to 10 minutes. Inmates who attempt hanging or asphyxiation are likely to lose consciousness within the first 30 seconds of blockage of blood flow to the brain. One consciousness is lost, inmates are unable to reverse course and help themselves. Within a few minutes of oxygen deprivation, the vital organs begin to shut down. It is for this reason that periodic health and welfare checks are problematic for suicidal inmates. Even if checks are conducted every 15 minutes, it is still possible to carry out a suicide attempt or have a suicidal gesture turn lethal between checks.

Ideally, suicidal inmates should have one-to-one constant supervision from staff members; however, video surveillance does not count as constant supervision. Closed Caption Television (CCTV) is commonly used inside correctional facilities to enhance surveillance and also to have recordings of incidents. It is tempting to assign officers watching the CCTV monitors several inmates to supervise as well as additional tasks to complete. Hayes (2010) found that four inmates who committed suicide in 2005–2006 did so while under constant observation, including CCTV. An inmate committed suicide in a Rhode Island Correctional facility in 1998 while the institution was using CCTV to monitor multiple inmates simultaneously. The monitoring officers were also tasked with answering phone calls, reviewing reports, and greeting members of the public entering the facility (Hayes, 2004). This led Hayes (2004) to conclude, "CCTV does not *prevent* inmate suicide, it simply *records* a suicide attempt in progress (p. 4, emphasis in original). Pompili et al. (2009) noted that CCTV is helpful to enhance surveillance of blind spots, but when it is used, it should always be supplemented with regular visual inspections. Another drawback to CCTV is that it is impersonal and does nothing to reduce inmates' sense of isolation.

One challenge for facilities managing suicidal inmates is finding the staff members to supply adequate supervision. Some prisons and jails have turned to a resource that is in abundant supply—inmates. In 1992, the Federal Bureau of Prisons (FBOP) used a buddy system consisting of trained inmates to help augment supervision of suicidal inmates. During that year, of the 75,363 hours of suicide watch, 72% of those hours were covered by inmates. For this program, inmates were trained in understanding suicidal behavior, empathetic listening, and other communication techniques. Inmates did not interfere with suicide attempts but summoned staff for assistance instead (Hayes, 1995b). The Victoria Department of Criminal Justice Correctional Services Task Force (1998) describes "buddy cells" as cells that are designed to accommodate two inmates for the purposes of peer support. Inmates may be able to stay in these cells and feel less isolated. If necessary, the facilities also have "Muirhead cells" that are safe cells to be used on a temporary basis for inmates in crisis. Besides the benefit of company and reduced isolation, the buddy cells have the advantage of allowing inmates to keep personal belongings. Inmates who also are able to stay out of isolation wings can retain access to recreation and programming. The United Nations World Health Organization (2000, 2007) recommends that the use of trained inmates should be considered a supplement, but not a complete substitute, for staff supervision. Also, vetting and training of inmates is important, as unsympathetic or malicious inmates placed in the role of buddies could allow a suicide to occur without notifying the staff of the danger.

If suicidal inmates must be housed alone because of security issues, modifications to the physical design of the facility could help to make supervision easier. Cells with full Plexiglas doors should assist officers in proper monitoring. Cells that have blind spots that cannot be viewed from the outside should be avoided. During a suicidal crisis, constant supervision is necessary. Human contact, even if it is with an officer on the other side of a cell door, could help reduce feelings of isolation and provide a safe environment where inmates can continue to wear regular clothing and have bedding (Felthous, 1994). If constant supervision is impossible, then it will be necessary to utilize the suicide-resistant cells and clothing. Even with that, 15-minute checks at staggered intervals are necessary, as some inmates have demonstrated amazing ingenuity when attempting self-harm.

Addressing Inmate Motivation for Suicide

Inmates are typically in situations that an average person would find to be emotionally difficult. Compounding the problem may be the presence of a serious mental illness, substance abuse, and/or a history of poor coping skills. While the use of supervision and safe cells can help inmates to survive a suicidal crisis, efforts should be made to work with inmates to develop more long-term solutions to reduce the chances of an onset of a suicidal crisis. Mental health treatment is necessary for anyone suffering from a serious mental illness. The corrections agencies can also work to develop safer, less stressful correctional environments for the general population as well as special housing sections to inmates whose mental illnesses make it too difficult to manage in the general population.

Mental Health Treatment

Some inmates have had positive experiences with using medication to manage mental illness, while others have yet to try prescription medication or find ones that are effective. For the former group, it may be possible to get information from the inmates themselves about what has worked in the past. Of course, a concern here is inmates' attempts to manipulate the situation to get medications to fuel substance abuse. If working with the inmate is not possible, it is important for the medical and social services staff at the facility to communicate with family members, as they may be able to provide valuable information about inmates' treatment histories. Some jails even allow family to deliver inmates' medication to the facility. While this next recommendation is likely easier for jails than prisons, service providers in the community where the inmate resided before incarceration also might be able to provide valuable information about inmates' treatment history. If the inmates have incarceration histories, then there are likely medical files that could provide information about success or failure of previous prescriptions.

Tartaro and Lester (2009) outlined a five-step crisis intervention process for use with inmates. First, conduct an evaluation to assess the severity of the crisis situation. Second, work to develop a relationship with the inmate in crisis. A theme throughout this chapter has been inmates' feelings of isolation and loneliness. Fostering a relationship with the inmate will reduce those feelings, but it also will help to forge a therapeutic alliance. Inmates should get the sense that the crisis worker is listening, as that will help generate a sense of trust. Third, help the inmates identify their specific problems. Inmates in crisis might find this to be a difficult task, as their thinking might be disorganized. Identification of the problem allows the therapist to help place the problem into perspective. This alone might provide inmates with some relief. At this step, it is important for staff to determine the potential for suicide and then decide on proper housing placement. It is possible that hospitalization might be the best alternative. Fourth, work to assess and mobilize inmates' strengths and resources. People in crisis might not be able to take an objective look at their situation, so they might overlook people who are willing to help. The crisis worker can guide inmates through this process, but it is important for the inmates to do some of the work themselves once the initial confusion and disorganization passes. One obvious challenge is that, with people who are locked away from society, it is more difficult to mobilize resources and support that are on the outside. For example, supporters may live a great distance from the facility, and security procedures limit contact with those on the outside. Fifth, develop an action plan to put the new plan into motion.

Some police and corrections departments are adopting Crisis Intervention Training (CIT) programs to assist staff in working with individuals in crisis. CIT was developed by the Memphis, Tennessee, police department in the wake of a police shooting involving a mentally ill individual and subsequent public outcry. The Memphis CIT model requires staff members to undergo 40 hours of training on appropriate management of the mentally ill. What is particularly helpful about such programs is that they usually involve bringing several different public and private agencies "to the table" to work together and find ways to best use local resources to work with incarcerated and free individuals in crisis. Part of the CIT curriculum involves suicide prevention training, and upon completion, police and corrections agencies that sent officers to the training are able to call on these employees to deescalate situations when individuals are in crisis (Kerle, 2015; see Chapter 27 for more about CIT).

In addition to medication, counseling may be warranted. The extent of the therapy available to inmates is likely to vary based on the setting (prison or jail) and the length of time inmates are expected to be incarcerated. The American Psychiatric Association (APA) (2000) noted that jail inmates with short-term stays are unlikely to receive more than crisis intervention, medication, and brief therapy and education about community resources to address the immediate issue. For inmates who are expected to stay longer in jail or in prison, it might be possible to work on skill building through cognitive-behavioral therapy or other programs. Cognitive-behavioral therapy (CBT) programs address the impact of negative thought patterns on behavior and teach clients how to recognize and stop the counterproductive thought patterns before they lead to problematic behavior (Byrne, Lurigio, & Pimentel, 2009). Dialectical behavior therapy (DBT), a modified form of CBT, has been found to be helpful for inmates diagnosed with borderline personality disorder who are self-harming (Swooger, Walsh, Maisto, & Conner, 2014).

Housing and Treatment

A disturbing practice that has taken hold in correctional facilities has been the use of restrictive housing as a response to negative inmate behavior, regardless of whether a mental illness was involved in the occurrence of such behavior. During the 1990s and early 2000s, administrative segregation became a commonly used tool for corrections administrators wishing to address inmate misconduct. Unfortunately, such an environment can be difficult for all inmates but especially problematic for those already suffering from mental illness. The United States Department of Justice (U.S. DOJ) (2016) recently conducted an investigation of the use of restrictive housing in corrections and found that 31% of inmates who spent time in such housing in the previous 12 months reported suffering serious psychological stress. These inmates are at a greater risk for self-harm while in segregation compared to when they are housed in the general population. In California, while an estimated 5% of the state's inmates were housed in segregation, that 5% made up 69% of the correctional suicides in 2006 (Shames, Wilcox, & Subramanian, 2015). The U.S. DOJ (2016) concluded its report with a recommendation that inmates be housed in the least restrictive setting necessary to maintain the safety of the inmates, staff, and the public; any use of restrictive housing come with a clear plan for how the inmates can return to less restrictive conditions; and correctional systems work to find ways for inmates in restrictive housing to spend more time outside of their cells. The U.S. DOJ also stated its commitment to finding ways of diverting inmates with serious mental illness to mental health treatment programs rather than isolation. At the state level, some departments of correction have been subject to court-ordered changes to how mentally ill inmates are targeted for and treated in segregation (e.g. *D.M. v. Terhune*, 1999; *Jones'el v. Berge*, 2001; *Madrid v. Gomez*, 1995), while others, such as Colorado, sought change through the state legislature (Shames et al., 2015).

These commissions, lawsuits, and new laws and policies have generated some dramatic changes in the way prisons and jails are approaching inmate housing and treatment. Following *Madrid v. Gomez* (1995), California set up a Psychiatric Services Unit (PSU) for inmates who are mentally ill and would have previously been sent right to the security housing unit. Now, the behavior of mentally ill inmates can be addresses in California through medication management and group therapy in a secure setting (King, Steiner, & Breach, 2008). Ohio has developed alternative placements for inmates with serious mental illness who have exhibited serious misconduct and actually has designated mental health correctional facilities to treat inmates in mental health crises (Kowalski, 2016).

One option for states to address the high population of mentally ill individuals in corrections facilities is to set up housing units that allow for more intensive or inpatient-level psychiatric treatment. New York has developed Intermediate Care Units where corrections officers and mental health staff members work together. These units work as "enriched, low-pressure enclaves for prisoners who would otherwise have difficulty dealing with the challenges of prison life" (Toch, 2016, p. 654), and inmates in such units retain access to programs and services offered throughout the facility. The New Jersey Department of Corrections created three new housing units—a Stabilization Unit (SU), Residential Treatment Unit (RTU), and Transitional Care Unit (TCU). The SU holds inmates for several days while they are experiencing an acute mental health crisis. The SU cells are designed to make it difficult or impossible for inmates to commit suicide while housed there. RTUs provide a supportive and structured environment for inmates who are unable to function effectively in the general population. While the hope is that inmates will be able to return to the general population, that may not be possible for some, and those inmates will be able to remain in RTU indefinitely. Inmates who are to transition from the RTU to the general population may be sent to the TCU to help with the transition (*D.M. v. Terhune*, 1999). Specialized housing units have the potential to provide safer environments that will allow inmates in need to receive inpatient-level psychiatric care and avoid victimization by other inmates.

The aforementioned housing options are aimed exclusively at helping those who are already experiencing such serious psychiatric problems that they warrant movement into a special housing area. No matter the type of general population correctional environment, there will likely always be some inmates who are having such a difficult time dealing with a crisis or a mental illness that they will need extra attention and care. For all others, there are ways to make the general population areas of corrections facilities less stressful and possibly reduce the chances of some inmates reaching a crisis point.

During the 1970s, the FBOP introduced a new jail design known as podular direct supervision or new generation jails. These facilities were built with the philosophy that incarceration in jail should do no harm, especially since approximately half of jail inmates have yet to be convicted of the crimes for which they are being held (Nelson & Davis, 1995). New generation jails include a combination of changes to the managerial and supervision philosophy of the institutions as well as a different approach to architecture. Cells are arranged around a dayroom. Unlike more traditional correctional facilities, these units are equipped with fixtures that are more likely to be seen in a college dorm room or community health clinic rather than a jail. The idea is that the jail is seeking to create a more "normal" environment rather than one where bad behavior is expected. Wortley (2002) warned that overreliance on physical barriers to prevent vandalism and other crimes can sometimes generate an environment that almost dares people to misbehave. The idea behind the new generation system is to give inmates a living area with ample access to televisions, phones, and, in some cases, vending machines and a microwave. The second part of the podular direct supervision system is a different managerial philosophy—that staff should be proactive rather than reactive when dealing with inmate misconduct. Corrections officers are placed inside the pods without any physical barriers between themselves and the inmates. They are expected to be trained in communication skills training, be cognizant of when tension is starting to rise, and address minor misconduct so it does not escalate into more serious misconduct. Since the environment includes "carrots" (positive incentives) that can be used as incentives for good behavior, officers have small "sticks" (negative consequences) that they can use, such as suspending television or microwave use. Officers can even make use of peer pressure by threatening to remove an amenity temporarily from everyone if the whole pod does not start to behave.

The introduction of podular direct supervision facilities was met with great skepticism. Since it was first used by the FBOP, local jail administrators attributed the lower levels of violence, vandalism, and suicide to the housing of "soft" inmates awaiting trial for federal white-collar crimes (Nelson & Davis, 1995). California's Contra Costa County Jail was the first nonfederal facility to house inmates in a podular direct supervision facility, and administrators there reported having the same success with violence and suicide reduction as the federal facilities (Gettinger, 1984; Wener, Frazier, & Farbstein, 1993; Zupan, 1991). Direct supervision jails began to appear in counties all over the country, but not all were built and operated in accordance with the original philosophy[2] (Tartaro, 2002; 2006), and these changes were associated with reduced effectiveness in some areas, particularly suicide prevention (Tartaro, 2003; Tartaro & Levy, 2008). While these facilities do hold promise, there needs to consideration for the extent to which administrations deviate from the original plan.

Suicidal Prisoners and Incarceration—Considering other Options

One way to address suicide in incarceration settings is to work on the extent to which we use incarceration. Diversion programs may be useful in moving people who would otherwise head to jail by diverting them into community programs. For people whose cases warrant incarceration, all inmates with the exception of lifers need to address the process of reentry at some point in their incarceration. This can be used as an opportunity to help inmates build the skills they will need to reduce the chances of reincarceration.

Diversion

The idea behind diversion programs is to reduce harm to offenders by limiting their exposure to the criminal justice system while still holding them accountable for their crimes and mandating some type of treatment and/or restitution. The APA identifies two general types of diversion—prebooking and postbooking. Prebooking diversion programs

> involve police and innovative emergency mental health responses that provide alternatives to booking mentally ill people into jail [while postbooking diversion can occur in three different forms:] 1) dismissal of charges in return for agreement for participation in a negotiated set of services; 2) deferred prosecution with requirements for treatment participation; and 3) post-sentence release in which conditions for probation include requirements for mental health services and substance abuse services.
>
> (APA, 2000, p. 29)

Drug courts for substance abusers and pretrial intervention programs for low-level, first-time offenders are perhaps some of the most prominent examples of diversion programs today.

Mental health courts provide jurisdiction options for diverting mentally ill individuals who committed minor offenses that were likely committed because of the defendant's mental illness. Courts vary in terms of the criteria used to allow defendants this option for dealing with criminal charges. Court proceedings are held in a nonadversarial manner, with all participants working in the best interests of the defendants. Defendants who successfully participate in mental health treatment stay out of legal trouble and work with the court to satisfy other court-ordered requirements to graduate from the court. In exchange for successful completion, participants either have their charges dismissed or escape further criminal justice sanctions for that crime. Evaluations of mental health courts have shown that they are promising in terms of recidivism reduction (Burns, Hiday, & Ray, 2013; McNeil & Binder, 2007), but some researchers did not find the courts to improve defendants' clinical status (Boothroyd, Mercado, Poythress, Christy, & Perila, 2005).

Reentry Planning

When diversion is not appropriate and incarceration is necessary, the experience of release back into the community can be a daunting one. It is important to remember that inmates are often incarcerated in part because of their inability to cope adequately with matters in society. To make matters worse, the culture inside prisons and jails is not one that tends to promote prosocial behavior (Sykes, 1958), so those who have spent extended time in a corrections facility are likely to be, at the best, no better prepared for reentry than they were prior to incarceration.

Reentry programs can help prepare all inmates for release from incarceration, but this is especially vital for individuals suffering from mental illness. For example, if inmates have been stabilized on psychotropic medication during incarceration, that stabilization becomes at risk once inmates are released without a way to get medication. Typically, inmates are released directly into the community, and they may not have the financial means to continue their medication and may lack the knowledge to get appropriate mental health help on the outside.

The extent of reentry programs depends on the inmates' incarceration status. Inmates who are expected to be incarcerated in jail for a very short period of time are a difficult group to help. New York's Rikers Island jail has set up a "drop-in" office at courthouses so inmates who are released from court a few hours after incarceration are able to receive information about mental health services, housing, and other benefits available in the community (Barr, 1999). For inmates who will be incarcerated for longer periods of time, Osher, Steadman, and Barr (2003) recommend the assessing, planning, identify, and coordinate (APIC) model for reentry services. Thorough assessment will help staff members identify inmates' needs. Planning involves deciding what treatment services will be needed to address inmates' needs. Next, reentry staff work to identify the community and correctional programs that will be involved in postrelease services. Finally, coordination involves setting up the transition plan so it can be implemented without any gaps in care upon release. The latter is the most critical step in preventing decompensation of one's mental health.

There are several important reentry issues that can be addressed while inmates are still incarcerated. While inmates are still incarcerated, one important step that facility staff can take is to start the process of reactivating benefits. Social Security payments, veterans' benefits, and in most cases Medicaid tend to be terminated upon incarceration. If possible, jails should work with other government agencies to have benefits only suspended upon someone's incarceration (Bazelon Center for Mental Health Law, 2006). For inmates in facilities that have been unable to have the benefits suspended instead of terminated, it is important to start the process of reapplying for these benefits well before inmates are released. Ideally, this process should start two to three months before the expected release date (McVey, 2001). The reestablishment of benefits has important implications for the possibility of inmates succeeding upon reentry. Without the benefits, those who depend on them may be unable to secure housing, purchase food, get psychotropic mediation, or get medical assistance.

Reentry programs vary greatly in their scope, quality, and success (Austin, 2001). The Oklahoma Department of Corrections has been targeting offenders with mental illness who are at high risk of recidivism. The program helps to secure the reactivation of Social Security benefits prior to release, and it also works with inmates on housing options during this time. After release, staff members work with released inmates to help them with their day-to-day needs, such as getting clothing, buying bus passes, and getting some items for housing. Staff also help offenders set up and manage payment plans to take care of fines, fees, and restitution. This is an important component of the program, as failure to pay fines and additional court-ordered financial obligations will likely result in reincarceration. The program has been successful in reducing hospitalizations and recidivism while increasing service engagement and enrollment in Medicaid within 90 days of release from prison (Mann, Bond, & Powitzky, 2011). This program provides a good example of one that provides reentry services not only while inmates are incarcerated but also after they leave custody.

Conclusion

The ideal scenario for criminal justice administrators would be for them to have the option to transfer those suffering from addiction to hospitals and rehabilitation centers and to send inmates who are dealing with serious mental illness or even a temporary, but serious, psychological crisis to a psychiatric hospital. This, however, is not currently possible, nor does it seem that it will be anytime in the near future. The challenge of dealing with suicidal prisoners, many of whom have serious mental health issues, will continue to be an important part of the work of administrators and line staffers who have the most contact with inmates. It is the responsibility of administrators to develop policies and procedures, oversee the training of the staff members, and cultivate a culture that emphasizes the importance of communication between inmates and staff. Part of that culture needs to emphasize the important role that staff members play in looking for signs that individuals might be experiencing mental health issues or having suicidal ideations. There will be times when inmates are unsupervised, and it is possible for someone who is in crisis to go undetected, but overall, sound corrections policies with good screening, proper housing options, and the ability to identify and implement treatment plans can serve to provide an environment where inmate suicide is a rarity.

Notes

1 For a more thorough discussion about the validity of these screens, please see Perry et al. (2010).
2 For a thorough discussion of the philosophy of the new generation jail design, see (Gettinger, 1984).

References

American Psychiatric Association. (2000). *Psychiatric services in jails and prisons* (2nd ed.). Washington, DC: American Psychiatric Association.

Austin, J. (2001). Prisoner reentry: Current trends, practices and issues. *Crime and Delinquency*, *47*(3), 314–334. doi:10.1177/0011128701047003002

Barr, H. (1999). *Prisons and jails: Hospitals of last resort*. New York, NY: The Correctional Association of New York and the Urban Justice Center.

Baillargeon, J., Penn, J. P., Thomas, C. R., Temple, J. R., Baillargeon, G., & Murray, O. J. (2009). Psychiatric disorders and suicide in the nation's largest state prison system. *Journal of the Academy of Psychiatry and the Law*, *37*(2), 188–193.

Bazelon Center for Mental Health Law. (2006). Best practices: Access to benefits for prisoners with mental illnesses. *Jail Suicide/Mental Health Update*, *14*(4), 7–13.

Blaauw, E., Winkel, F. W., & Kerkhof, J. F. M. (2001). Bullying and suicidal behavior in jails. *Criminal Justice and Behavior*, *28*(3), 279–299. doi:10.1177/0093854801028003002

Boothroyd, R. A., Mercado, C. C., Poythress, N. G., Christy, A., & Perila, J. (2005). Clinical outcomes of defendants in mental health court. *Psychiatric Services*, *56*(7), 829–834. doi:10.1176/appi.ps.56.7.829

Borrill, J. (2002). Self-inflicted deaths of prisoners serving life sentences 1988–2001. *British Journal of Forensic Practice*, *4*(4), 30–35. doi:10.1108/14636646200200024

Bowring v. E. Godwin, 551 F.2d 44 (1977).
British Home Office. (1999). *Suicide is everyone's concern*. London, England: Home Office.
Burns, P. J., Hiday, C. A., & Ray, B. (2013). Effectiveness 2 years postexit of a recently established mental health court. *American Behavioral Scientist, 57*(2), 189–208. doi:10.1177/0002764212465416
Byrne, J. M., Lurigio, A., J., & Pimentel, R. (2009). New defendants, new responsibilities: Preventing suicide among alleged sex offenders in the federal pretrial system. *Federal Probation, 73*(2), 40–44.
Couturier, L. (2001). Suicide prevention in a large state department of corrections. *Corrections Today, 63*(5), 90–97.
Crighton, D., & Towl, G. (1997). Self-inflicted deaths in prison in England and Wales. *Issues in Criminological and Legal Psychology, 28*, 12–20.
D. M. v. Terhune, 67 F. Supp, 2d 401 (1999).
Estelle v. Gamble, 429 U.S. 97 (1976).
Evans, C., Brinded, P., Simpson, A., I., Frampton, C., & Mulder, R. T. (2010). Validation of brief screening tools for mental disorders among New Zealand prisoners. *Psychiatric Services, 61*(9), 923–928. doi:10.1176/ps.2010.61.9.923
Eyland, S., Corben, S., & Barton, J. (1997). Suicide prevention in New South Wales correctional centres. *Crisis, 18*(4), 158–164.
Felthous, A. R. (1994). Preventing jailhouse suicides. *Bulletin of the American Academy of Psychiatry and the Law, 22*(4), 477–488.
Frottier, P., Fruhwald, S., Ritter, K., Eher, R., Schwalzler, J., & Bauer, P. (2002). Jailhouse blues revisited. *Social Psychiatry & Psychiatric Epidemiology, 37*(2), 68–73. doi:10.1007/s127-002-8217-7
Gettinger, S. H. (1984). *New generation jails: An innovative approach to an age-old problem*. Longmont, CO: National Institute of Corrections Jails Division.
Hatty, S. E., & Walker, J. R. (1986). *A national study of deaths in Australian prisons*. Canberra, Australia: Australian Institute of Criminology.
Hayes, L. M. (1989). National study of jail suicides: Seven years later. *Psychiatric Quarterly. 60*(1), 7–29. doi:10.1007/BF01064362
Hayes, L. M. (1995a). Prison suicide: An overview and a guide to prevention. *The Prison Journal, 75*(4), 431–457. doi:10.1177/0032855595075004003
Hayes, L. M. (1995b). *Prison suicide: An overview and a guide to prevention*. Washington, DC: U.S. Department of Justice, National Institute of Corrections.
Hayes, L. M. (1996). National and state standards for prison suicide prevention: A report card. *Journal of Correctional Health Care, 3*(1), 5–38. doi:10.1177/107834589600300102
Hayes, L. M. (1999). Suicide in adult correctional facilities: Key ingredients to prevention and overcoming the obstacles. *Journal of Law, Medicine & Ethics, 27*(3), 260–269.
Hayes, L. M. (2004). Use of no-harm contracts and other controversial issues in suicide prevention. *Jail Suicide/Mental Health Update, 12*(2), 1–9.
Hayes, L. M. (2010). *National study of jail suicide: 20 years later*. Washington, DC: U.S. Department of Justice, National Institute of Justice.
Howells, K., Hall, G., & Day, A. (1999). The management of suicide and self-harm in prisons: Recommendations for good practice. *Australian Psychologist, 34*(3), 157–165. doi:10.1080/00050069908257449
Inch, H., Rowlands, P., & Soliman, A. (1995). Deliberate self-harm in a young offender's institution. *Journal of Forensic Psychiatry, 6*(1), 161–171. doi:10.1080/09585189508409882
Jacobs v. West Feliciana Sheriff's Department, 228 F. 3d 388 (2000).
James, D. J., & Glaze, L. E. (2006). *Mental health problems of prison and jail inmates*. Washington, DC: U.S. Department of Justice, Bureau of Justice Statistics.
Jones'el v. Berge, 164 F. Supp. 2d 1096 (2001).
Kaba, F., Lewis, A., Glowa-Kollisch, S., Hadler, J., Lee, D., Alper, H., . . . Venters, H. (2014). Solitary confinement and risk of self-harm among jail inmates. *American Journal of Public Health, 104*(3), 442–447. doi:10.2105/AJPH.2013.301742
Kerle, K. (2015). The mentally ill and crisis intervention teams: Reflections on jails and the U.S. mental health challenge. *The Prison Journal, 96*(1), 153–161. doi:10.1177/0032885515605497
King, K., Steiner, B., & Breach, S. R. (2008). Violence in the supermax: A self-fulfilling prophecy. *The Prison Journal, 88*(1), 144–168. doi:10.1177/0032885507311000
Kochanek, K. D., Murphy, S. L., Xu, J., & Tejada-Vera, B. (2016). *Deaths: Final data for 2014: National Vital Statistics Report*. Washington, DC: Centers for Disease Control and Prevention.
Kovasznay, M. D., Miraglia, R., Beer, R., & Way, B. (2004). Reducing suicides in New York State correctional facilities. *Psychiatric Quarterly, 75*(1), 61–70. doi:10.1023/B:PSAQ.0000007561.83444.a4

Kowalski, B. R. (2016, November). *A closer look at restrictive housing reforms and operational changes in Ohio.* American Society of Criminology Conference, New Orleans, LA.

Kroner, D. G., Mills, J. F., Grazy, A., & Talbert, K. O. N. (2011). Clinical assessment in correctional settings. In Fagan. T. J. & Ax, R. K. (Eds.), *Correctional mental health* (pp. 77–102). Thousand Oaks, CA: Sage.

Lanes, E. C. (2011). Are the worst of the worst self-injurious prisoners more likely to end up in long-term maximum-security administrative segregation? *International Journal of Offender Therapy and Comparative Criminology, 55*(7), 1034–1050. doi:10.1177/0306624X10378494

Lyman, M., & LoBuglio, S. (2006). "Whys and hows" of measuring recidivism. *Jail Reentry Roundtable.* Washington, DC: The Urban Institute.

Madrid v. Gomez, 889 F.Supp. 1146 (1995).

Mann, B., Bond, D., & Powitzky, R. J. (2011). Collaborating for success in interagency correctional mental health reentry. *Corrections Today, 73*(5), 30–33.

Marcus, P., & Alcabes, P. (1993). Characteristics of suicides by inmates in an urban jail. *Hospital and Community Psychiatry, 44*(3), 256–261. doi:10.1176/appi.ps.53.5.574

Matsumoto, T., Yamaguchi, A., Asami, T., Okada, T., Yoshikawa, K., & Hirayasu, Y. (2005). Characteristics of self-cutters among male inmates: Association with bulimia and dissociation. *Psychiatry and Clinical Neurosciences, 59*, 319–326. doi:10.1111/j.1440-1819.2005.01377.x/pdf

McDonagh, D., & Noel, C. (2002). Mental health needs of women offenders: Needs analysis for the development of the intensive intervention strategy. *Forum on Corrections Research, 14*(2), 32–35.

McMullan, E. C. (2011). Seeking medical and psychiatric attention. In L. Gideon & H. E. Sung (Eds.), *Rethinking corrections* (pp. 253–278). Thousand Oaks, CA: Sage.

McNeil, D. E., & Binder, R. L. (2007). Effectiveness of a mental health court in reducing criminal recidivism and violence. *American Journal of Psychiatry, 164*, 1395–1403. doi:10.1176/appi.ajp.2007.06101664

McVey, C. (2001). Coordinating effective health and mental health continuity of care. *Corrections Today, 63*(5), 58–62.

Myslimaj, F., & Eglantina, D. (2016). Suicide attempts and self-inflicting on prison custody and prisons. *Academic Journal of Interdisciplinary Studies, 5*(2), 175–180. doi:10.5901/ajis.2016.v5n2p175

Nelson, W. R., & Davis, R. M. (1995). Podular direct supervision: The first twenty years. *American Jails, 9*(3), 11–22.

Noonan, M., & Rohloff, H. (2015). *Mortality in local jails and state prisons, 2000–2013—Statistical tables.* Washington, DC: U.S. Department of Justice, Bureau of Justice Statistics.

Osher, F., Steadman, H. J., & Barr, H. (2003). A best practice approach to community reentry from jails for inmates with co-occurring disorders: The APIC model. *Crime & Delinquency, 49*(1), 79–96. doi:10.1177/0011128702239237

Perry, A. E., Marandos, R., Coulton, S., & Johnson, M. (2010). Screening tools assessing risk of suicide and self-ham in adult offenders: a systematic review. *International Journal of Offender Therapy and Comparative Criminology, 54*(3), 803–828. doi:10.1.1.833.8504&rep=rep1&type=pdf

Pompili, M., Lester, D., Innamorati, M., Del Casale, A., Girardi, P., Ferracuti, S., & Tatarelli, R. (2009). Preventing suicide in jails and prisons: Suggestions from experience with psychiatric inpatients. *Journal of Forensic Sciences (Wiley-Blackwell), 54*(5), 1155–1162. doi:10.1111/j.1556-4029.2009.01122.x

Power, K. G., & Moodie, E. (1997). Characteristics and management of prisoners at risk of suicide behavior. *Archives of Suicide Research, 3*, 109–123. doi:10.1080/13811119708258262

Reeves, R., & Tamburello, A. (2014). Single cells, segregated housing, and suicide in the New Jersey Department of Corrections. *Journal of the American Academy of Psychiatry & the Law, 42*(4), 484–488.

Salive, M. E., Smith, G. S., & Brewer, T. F. (1989). Suicide mortality in the Maryland state prison system, 1979 through 1987. *Journal of the American Medical Association, 262*, 365–369.

Sanchez, H. G. (2013). Suicide prevention in administrative segregation units: What is missing? *Journal of Correctional Health Care, 19*(2), 93–100. doi:10.1177/1078345812474638

Serin, R. C., Motiuk, L., & Wichmann, C. (2002). An examination of suicide attempts among inmates. *Forum on Corrections Research, 14*(2), 40–42.

Shames, A., Wilcox, J., & Subramanian, R. (2015). *Solitary confinement: Common misconceptions and emerging safe alternatives.* New York, NY: Vera Institute of Justice.

Snow v. City of Citronelle et al., 420 F.3d 1262 (2005).

Spinellis, C. D., & Themeli, O. (1997). Suicide in Greek prisons: 1977 to 1996. *Crisis, 18*(4), 152–156.

Steadman, H. J., Robbins, P. C., Islam, T., & Osher, F. (2007). Revalidating the brief jail mental health screen to increase accuracy for women. *Psychiatric Services, 58*(12), 1598–1601. doi:10.1176/ps.2007.58.12.1598

Stone, G. (1999). *Suicide and attempted suicide.* New York, NY: Carroll and Graf Publishers, Inc.

Swooger, M. T., Walsh, Z., Maisto, S. A., & Conner, K. R. (2014). Reactive and proactive aggression and suicide attempts among criminal offenders. *Criminal Justice & Behavior, 41*(3), 337–344. doi:10.1177/0093854813508764
Sykes, G. (1958). *Society of captives: A study of a maximum security prison*. Princeton, NJ: Princeton University Press.
Tartaro, C. (2002). Examining implementation issues with new generation jails. *Criminal Justice Policy Review, 13*(3), 219–237. doi:10.1177/0887403402133002
Tartaro, C. (2003). Suicide and the jail environment: An evaluation of three types of institutions. *Environment and Behavior, 35*(5), 605–620. doi:10.1177/0013916503254753
Tartaro, C. (2006). Watered down: Partial implementation of the new generation jail philosophy. *The Prison Journal, 86*(3), 284–300. doi:10.1177/0032885506290851
Tartaro, C., & Lester, D. (2009). *Suicide and self-harm in prisons and jails*. Lanham, MD: Lexington Books.
Tartaro, C., & Levy, M. P. (2008). Predictors of suicide in new generation jails. *Justice Research and Policy, 10*(1), 21–37. doi:10.3818/JRP.10.1.2008.21
Teplin, L., & Swartz, J. (1989). Screening for severe mental disorder in jails. *Law and Human Behavior, 13*(1), 1–18.
Toch, H. (2016). Providing sanctuary in New York prisons. *The Prison Journal, 96*(5), 647–660. doi:10.1177/0032885516662606
Topp, D. (1979). Suicide in prison. *British Journal of Psychiatry, 134*, 24–27.
Turney v. Waterbury, 375 F. 3d 756 (2004).
Veysey, B. M., Steadman, H. J., Morrissey, J. P., Johnsen, M., & Beckstead, J. W. (1998). Using the referral decision scale to screen mentally ill jail detainees: Validity and implementation issues. *Law and Human Behavior, 22*(2), 205–215. doi:10.1023/A:1025794104048
United States Department of Justice. (2016). *U.S. Department of Justice report and recommendations concerning the use of restrictive housing*. Washington, DC: U.S. Department of Justice.
United Nations Word Health Organization. (2000). *Preventing suicide: A resource for prison officers*. Geneva, Switzerland: Department of Mental Health, World Health Organization.
United Nations World Health Organization. (2007). *Preventing suicide in jails and prisons*. Geneva, Switzerland: Department of Mental Health and Substance Abuse, World Health Organization.
Victoria Department of Justice Correctional Services Task Force. (1998). *Review of suicides and self-harm in Victorian prisons*. Melbourne, Australia: Victorian Government Printer.
Wener, R., Frazier, F. W., & Farbstein, J. (1993). Direct supervision of correctional institutions. In National Institute of Corrections (Ed.), *Podular, direct supervision jails* (pp. 1–8). Longmont, CO: National Institute of Corrections Jails Division.
Wever v. Lincoln County, 388 F. 3d 601 (2004).
Wobeser, W. L., Datema, J., Bechard, B., & Ford, P. (2002). Causes of death among people in custody in Ontario, 1990–1999. *Canadian Medical Association Journal, 167*(10), 1109–1113.
Wortley, R. (2002). *Situational prison control*. Cambridge, UK: Cambridge University Press.
Zupan, L. L. (1991). *Jails: Reform and the new generation philosophy*. New York, NY: Routledge.

16

DEATH ROW INMATES

Housing and Management Issues

Cedric Michel

> They remove all your property from your cell while an officer sits in front of your cell 24/7 recording everything you do. Staff also performs a "dry run" or "mock execution".... This is when you know ... your death is imminent, easily within reach, you can count it by hours instead of by days.
>
> —William Van Poyck, death row inmate (as quoted in a letter from Death Row Diary, 2013)

Introduction

As of 2017, 30 states in the United States and the federal government retain the death penalty (Death Penalty Information Center, 2017). In the last 10 years, however, a trend toward abolition has begun to emerge, with states repealing their capital punishment statutes almost annually. For example, New Jersey and New York effectively abolished the death penalty in 2007, followed by New Mexico in 2009, Illinois in 2011, Connecticut in 2012, Maryland in 2013, Nebraska in 2015, and Delaware in 2016 (Death Penalty Information Center, 2017). Reasons commonly cited to explain this trend include the incompatibility of such practice with standards of decency shared by modern nations, the lack of a discernible deterrent effect, and the arbitrary and capricious nature of a system accused of disproportionately targeting racial and ethnic minorities, as well as the risk of injustices (Bohm, 2011). The hefty cost of the appeal process is another compelling argument put forth to abolish the death penalty. Though originally designed as a legal safeguard to minimize the risk of executing innocent people, the dual system of collateral review (i.e., at the state and federal level) costs taxpayers anywhere between $2.5 to $5 million per case (Liebman, Fagan, & West, 2000).

Beyond its mere financial impact, this super due process is also quite lengthy. The average prisoner under sentence of death spends over a decade on death row; in some cases, that time often exceeds 20 years (Bohm, 2011). Evidently, such an extended wait paired with solitary confinement (a practice used with death row inmates both for punitive and protective reasons) poses logistic problems for correctional institutions. There are currently about 3,000 death row inmates in the United States (Fins, 2016). The purpose of this chapter is to provide a description of how these individuals are handled and treated once they enter prison and await execution. Topics covered in this chapter include living conditions on death row, housing and management issues, and how the correctional facility provides for inmates' specific needs, as well as various constitutional challenges.

Life on Death Row: Cruel and Unusual Punishment?

Prisoners under sentence of death differ from traditional inmates in many aspects. Because of the extreme severity of both their crime and punishment, they are subject to more intense supervision than inmates sentenced to life without the possibility of parole (LWOP). To this effect, they are housed in individual cells within a separate block, wing, or section commonly known as death row. Over the years, the special treatment reserved for these individuals has raised serious criticism regarding potential human rights violations. More specifically, death penalty abolitionists have argued that inmates' segregation from the rest of the carceral population, extended stay on death row, and lingering uncertainty as to the day of their execution amount to mental cruelty (Bluestone & McGahee, 1962; West, 1975; Johnson, 1979).

In the absence of common standards of prison management, the American Correctional Association (ACA) provides recommendations that state and federal agencies may choose to follow should they seek accreditation. These guidelines are nonetheless superseded by several international standards that uphold the right for prisoners to be free from torture. For example, Article 5 of the United Nations' Universal Declaration of Human Rights (2017) states that no one shall be subjected to torture or to cruel, inhuman or degrading treatment or punishment. Further, Article 10(1) of the International Covenant on Civil and Political Rights (1976, para. 58) states that "All persons deprived of their liberty shall be treated with humanity and with respect for the inherent dignity of the human person." In addition, although nonbinding, the United Nations' Standard Minimum Rules for the Treatment of Prisoners (1955) provide signatory members with guidelines regarding minimum conditions of treatment and management. These safeguards are paramount for the humane treatment of long-term offenders, such as prisoners under sentence of death.

In the United States, the Eighth Amendment protects death row inmates from cruel and unusual punishment. However, whether living conditions on death row actually violate the United States Constitution has been the subject of much controversy. In a series of similar class action lawsuits initiated by death row inmates (e.g., *Chandler v. Crosby*, 2004; *Estelle v. Gamble*, 1976; *Farmer v. Brennan*, 1994; *Gates v. Cook*, 2004; *Lackey v. Texas*, 1995; *Rhodes v. Chapman*, 1981; *Ruiz v. Estelle*, 1980; *Sinclair v. Henderson*, 1971), the Supreme Court and other appellate courts were asked to consider the constitutionality of living conditions described as extremely poor, with inadequate space, sometimes with no natural light, and lack of ventilation and sanitary facilities.

In *Ruiz v. Estelle* (1980), inmate David Ruiz sued the director of the Texas Department of Corrections over what he described as dangerous and degrading living and working conditions, including overcrowding (placing two and even sometimes three prisoners in the same cell), inadequate security (relying on inmates as guards because of understaffing), insufficient health care, exposure to unsafe working conditions, and severe and arbitrary disciplinary measures. Ruiz's individual petition eventually turned into a class action lawsuit. In 1979, the United States District Court for the Eastern District of Texas ruled that the conditions of confinement described by Ruiz indeed constituted cruel and unusual punishment, which resulted in a complete overhaul of the Texas prison system.

In *Rhodes v. Chapman* (1981), however, the Supreme Court held that the Eighth Amendment does not guarantee prisoners comfort but *humane* treatment. Inmates Kelly Chapman and Richard Jaworski, housed in the same cell in an Ohio maximum-security prison, brought a class action lawsuit in Federal District Court against petitioner state officials, complaining that double-celling constituted cruel and unusual punishment. On June 29, 1977, the District Court ruled in favor of the plaintiffs, concluding that although housing two inmates in the same cell was not unconstitutional, the limited amount of square footage and resulting close confinement of cellmates in fact violated their rights. Nevertheless, the Supreme Court reversed the decision, opining that the Constitution does not mandate comfortable prisons and that conditions of confinement, as constituting the punishment at issue, must not involve the wanton and unnecessary infliction of pain, nor may they be grossly disproportionate to the severity of the crime warranting imprisonment (Bohm, 2011, pp. 127–128). This was an extension of the Court's decision in *Estelle v. Gamble* (1976) that only the willful disregard (i.e., deliberate indifference) to inmates' serious medical needs constitutes a violation of their constitutional rights. More specifically, to claim that the Eighth Amendment has been violated, prisoners need to prove: (1) living conditions are so extreme that they pose an unreasonable risk of serious damage to their future health and (2) prison officials acted with a sufficiently culpable state of mind.

In *Farmer v. Brennan* (1994), the Supreme Court nevertheless clarified its position by ruling that the Eighth Amendment demanded that prison officials provide humane conditions of confinement, including adequate food, clothing, shelter, and medical care. Accordingly, each row housing area needs to be well ventilated and adequately heated, with appropriate lighting, and to guarantee inmates basic sanitation. As previously noted, however, the Supreme Court will not recognize constitutional right infringement unless the negligent endangerment of inmates by the correctional facility has been established. Still, whether living conditions on death row—albeit technically legal and thus methodically enforced by staff—pose a serious risk to inmates' physical and mental health remains a hotly debated issue.

Accommodations

In 1994, Amnesty International's special rapporteur, Roy King, provided a thorough description of death row (also known as H-Unit) at the Oklahoma State Penitentiary in McAlester, Oklahoma. The cells he described had one door only and no windows. Food was served to inmates through a flap or bean hole at the bottom of the door. Each cell was designed to house two prisoners. Furnishings included two beds made of poured concrete measuring 80 by 27.5 inches each, a table 26 inches wide and 16 inches deep (inmates had to use their concrete bed as chair), a poured concrete shelf providing less than 3 square feet of storage space, and a stainless-steel combination sink and toilet, as well as a small unbreakable mirror. King brought attention to the lack of a facility for suspending clothes, of a pin board or place to display photographs, a bell to notify officers in case of an emergency (besides a voice-activated intercom system), and lack of natural fresh air ventilation to the cell. King also took issue with the overall lack of space, each cell being 7 feet 7 inches wide by 15 feet 5 inches long by 8 feet 4 inches high for a gross floor area of 116.9 square feet in single occupancy and 58.45 square feet in double occupancy. He calculated three possible measures of net, or unencumbered, space:

> 1) Including the space between the head of the beds and the tables, as well as the central area between the two beds, and between the foot of the beds and the entrance wall; 2) including just the central area between the two beds and the area at the foot of the beds; and 3) counting just the area at the foot of the beds. On the first definition there is 78.08 square feet of unencumbered space in single occupancy or 39.04 square feet each in double occupancy; using the second definition the figures are 71.18 square feet single occupancy or 35.59 square feet double occupancy; and using the third definition, 51.18 square feet single or 25.59 square feet double occupancy.
>
> (King, 1994, pp. 9–10)

Whether such exiguous space can be considered acceptable for a human being—especially one expected to spend years confined to his/her cell—is a matter of interpretation. Still, being exposed to claustrophobic conditions can take a toll on detainees' physical and mental health, an issue to be discussed in a subsequent section.

Sanitation

Articles 12, 13, and 14 of the United Nations Standard Minimum Rules for the Treatment of Prisoners (1955) emphasize the right for inmates to basic hygiene. For example, basic hygiene includes:

- The sanitary installations shall be adequate to enable every prisoner to comply with the needs of nature when necessary and in a clean and decent manner.
- Adequate bathing and shower installations shall be provided so that every prisoner may be enabled and required to have a bath or shower, at a temperature suitable to the climate, as frequently as necessary for general hygiene according to season and geographical region, but at least once a week in a temperate climate.
- All parts of an institution regularly used by prisoners shall be properly maintained and kept scrupulously clean at all times (United Nations Standard Minimum Rules for the Treatment of Prisoners, 1955, pp. 2–3).

In *Gates v. Cook* (2004), however, death row inmates at the Mississippi State Penitentiary in Parchman, Mississippi, complained about severe violations to the abovementioned sanitation guidelines. More specifically, the trial court described the following living conditions on Parchman's death row:

> Inmates have been subjected to cells that were extremely filthy with chipped, peeling paint, dried fecal matter and food encrusted on the walls, ceilings, and bars, as well as water from flooded toilets and rain leaks. Inmates are routinely moved from cell to cell and are forced to clean their new cells that may have been left in horrendous sanitation by the prior occupants, especially if the occupant were mentally ill. Adequate cleaning supplies and equipment are not routinely made available for inmates to clean their cells. These filthy conditions contribute to the infestation of pests and play a role in the mental well-being of inmates.
>
> (Bohm, 2011, p. 128)

The Fifth Circuit Court of Appeals affirmed and required corrections officials to adhere to the following minimum standards: (1) cells should be cleaned before moving new inmates in, and (2) adequate cleaning supplies should be made available to inmates so that they can clean their cell at least once a week.

Laundry

At the same time, the court vacated another injunction regarding inmates' laundry returned foul smelling, which necessitated the inmates to wash their clothes in their cells (see also *Gates v. Cook*, 2004). While the trial court had concluded that prisoners were entitled to laundry that is clean and not foul smelling, the appeals court noted that inmates washing their own clothes were part of prison culture and in no way a form of discipline (Bohm, 2011, p. 129). It also rejected the argument that a correctional institution failing to provide prisoners with laundry detergent was violative of the Eighth Amendment (*Gates v. Cook*, 2004).

Plumbing

In *Sinclair v. Henderson* (1971), petitioner Billy Wayne Sinclair, a death row inmate at the Louisiana State Penitentiary in Angola, Louisiana, complained about inadequate plumbing facilities. The trial court noted that men had to live and eat in cells where toilet facilities leaked and constantly bubbled over and were forced to drink water loaded with rust and be in contact with excessive amounts of bacteria. The appeals court, however, vacated this injunction, based on the warden's promise that the whole plumbing and drainage system would soon be revamped. The issue of outdated and unsanitary plumbing was at the center of the complaint in *Gates v. Cook* (2004). More specifically, the problem of ping-pong toilets was discussed:

> Fecal and other matter flushed by a toilet in one cell will bubble up in the adjoining cell unless the toilets are flushed simultaneously. This has been a problem since the unit opened. Parchman officials have identified the problem as one of calibration, especially if the water is shut off. The toilets must be recalibrated to work properly. Recalibration has helped, but not eliminated, the problem of ping-pong toilets. No one in civilized society should be forced to live under conditions that force exposure to another person's bodily wastes.
>
> (Bohm, 2011, p. 129)

Nevertheless, the appeals court also vacated this injunction, noting that the role of federal courts is not to micromanage state prisons.

Heating and Ventilation

As previously mentioned, keeping death row cells at humanely acceptable temperatures (depending on the state's climate and seasonal changes) is a topic of concern for the judiciary. In *Sinclair v. Henderson* (1971), the court rejected Sinclair's request for cells to be ventilated, pretexting that the warden had promised to redesign the death row unit. The Supreme Court consolidated this rationale with its decision in *Estelle v. Gamble* (1976). Thus, to claim that temperatures are violative of constitutional rights, plaintiffs have to satisfy the aforementioned two-pronged standard and prove (1) they exceed mere discomfort and pose actual health risks, and (2) that the correctional staff knowingly does nothing to prevent it.

In *Gates v. Cook* (2004), inmates also put emphasis of the lack of relief from heat during sweltering summer months:

> The summer temperatures in the Mississippi Delta average in the nineties with high humidity, and Death Row is primarily not an air-conditioned facility. There are industrial type fans in the hallways to help with air circulation, and most inmates have smaller fans. Relief from the heat can be obtained by keeping the windows open in the cell using fans. But keeping the windows open increases the mosquito population in the cells since there are holes in the cell window screens and the screen gauge is not sufficient to keep mosquitoes out. The ambient temperature in the cells is within reasonable limits except during the summer months. The ventilation is inadequate to afford prisoners a minimal level of comfort during the summer months. The probability of heat-related illness is extreme on Death Row, and is dramatically more so for mentally ill inmates who often do not take appropriate behavioral steps to deal with the heat. Also, the medications often given to deal with various medical problems interfere with the body's ability to maintain a normal temperature. The inmates are not afforded extra showers, ice water, or fans if they do not have fans when the heat index is 90 or above. The heat problem extends to all of Death Row and possibly throughout Parchman.
>
> (Bohm, 2011, p. 129)

The appeals court recognized that symptoms of heat-related illness reported among death row inmates belied the Mississippi Department of Corrections' deliberate indifference. Consequently, it affirmed the injunction, but only insofar as it applied to Parchman's death row.

Similarly, in *Chandler v. Crosby* (2004), the Eleventh U.S. Circuit Court of Appeals ruled against a class action lawsuit filed by death row inmates at Union Correctional Institution in Raiford, Florida. Here also, the plaintiffs alleged that the high temperatures in their cells during the summer months paired with an inadequate ventilation system amounted to cruel and unusual punishment under the Eighth Amendment. The court differed, reasoning that at the hottest times of the day, it is cooler in the cells than it is outdoors and that

> the temperatures and ventilation on the unit during the summer months are almost always consistent with reasonable levels of comfort and slight discomfort which are to be expected in a residential setting in Florida in a building that is not air-conditioned.
>
> (Bohm, 2011, p. 130)

Recall that H-Unit at Oklahoma State Penitentiary does not provide death row inmates air conditioning either. The entire facility, however, was built underground, which brings prisoners relief from scorching heat during the summer months. One major tradeoff, though, is the distressing absence of sunlight (Bohm, 2011; Dow, 2002).

Lighting

Living in an environment with poor lighting can be detrimental to one's eyesight. As such, Article 11 of the United Nations Standard Minimum Rules for the Treatment of Prisoners (1955, p. 2) recommends that

> in all places where prisoners are required to live or work, the windows shall be large enough to enable the prisoners to read or work by natural light, and shall be so constructed that they can allow the entrance of fresh air whether or not there is artificial ventilation.

Article 11 further stresses that artificial light shall be provided sufficient for the prisoners to read or work without injury to eyesight (United Nations Standard Minimum Rules for the Treatment of Prisoners, 1955, p. 2).

In *Gates v. Cook* (2004), however, the lighting in the cells was described as grossly inadequate. Twenty foot-candles (i.e., a unit of illuminance or light intensity) has been determined as an appropriate level of lighting for cells in the United States. However, the maximum foot-candles measured on Parchman's death row were 7 or 8, with the typical cell being in the 2–4 foot-candle range. The appellate court recognized that improper lighting impedes sanitation, personal hygiene, and reading and contributes to mental health problems over time. As such, the Supreme Court affirmed the injunction, but again only insofar as it applied to Parchman's death row.

Pest Control

The dilemma of having to choose between scorching heat and pestering bugs was another issue raised by plaintiffs in *Gates v. Cook* (2004):

> The heat problem also exacerbates the problem of pest control. Mosquitoes in Mississippi, and the Delta in particular, are a problem that cannot be eliminated. But the problem must be addressed and the impact lessened, especially with the incidence of West Nile virus, a mosquito-borne disease increasing in Mississippi. Inadequate screening on the cell windows causes the inmates to choose between suffering from the heat or increasing the mosquitoes in their cells. The problems of heat and mosquitoes must be addressed to provide the

> inmates with conditions that would meet minimal constitutional standards. The problem of roaches and other vermin will be met by adhering to the ACA standards and by meeting the sanitation goals the court will set.
>
> (Bohm, 2011, p. 128)

The appeals court affirmed the request to increase efforts at pest control and to have all cell windows repaired and screened with an 18-gauge window screen or better but, once again, only insofar as it applied to Parchman's death row.

Food

Specific alimentary guidelines are contained in Article 20 of the United Nations Standard Minimum Rules for the Treatment of Prisoners (1955, p. 3). More specifically, every prisoner shall be provided by the administration at the usual hours with food of nutritional value adequate for health and strength and of wholesome quality and be well prepared and served. Death row inmates are therefore entitled to food in enough quantities to sustain an average person. To this effect, it should have basic nutritional value. Food on death row is prepared by prison staff, brought to inmates directly to their cell in insulated carts, and inserted in a narrow slot. In an effort to limit access to potentially dangerous items, prisoners have to eat with plastic sporks. They must also eat alone in their cell and are not permitted access to the refectory (i.e., a room used for communal meals).

Meals are served three times a day. In Florida, breakfast is served at 5:00 a.m., lunch between 10:30 a.m.–11:00 a.m., and dinner from 4:00 p.m. to 4:30 p.m. Nevertheless, recent budget cuts have prompted some states to reduce the number of daily meals to only two. In addition, food quality has been the subject of increased scrutiny following numerous complaints by inmates regarding small and cold portions and a lack of healthy options as well as the violation of sanitation standards in kitchens (e.g., tainted meat, evidence of rodent activity, and maggots), which has prompted many prisoners to rely on overpriced and unhealthy snacks purchased at prison commissaries (King, 1994). Part of the plaintiffs' complaint in *Sinclair v. Henderson* (1971) had to do with meals being served in an unsanitary manner, with roaches, worms, human hair, wire, paper clips, and small rocks found in the food. The court nonetheless concluded that the overall food quality was wholesome and that occasional incidents were no proof of intentional harm.

Medical Care

As previously mentioned, the two-pronged requirement to establish Eighth Amendment violation determined by the Supreme Court in *Estelle v. Gamble* (1976) virtually protects detainees from correctional officials' deliberate indifference to serious medical needs. Nevertheless, prisoners have complained that their request for medical or dental treatment was ignored or delayed, even when they were in pain, sometimes on the basis that they were considered already dead men (King, 1994, p. 14). Amnesty International reports the case of Bobby Hill, an inmate at Oklahoma's H-unit who died of a heart attack in June 1993. His cellmate alleged that it took an hour for unit staff to respond despite his banging on the cell door calling for help (King, 1994). One reason why correctional officials might be suspicious of medical requests could be prisoners' desire temporarily to escape monotony and claustrophobia by being transferred to the infirmary despite no actual health condition.

Exercise

The need for adequate medical care on death row is also increased by the lack of adequate physical activity granted to inmates. Article 21 of the United Nations Standard Minimum Rules for the

Treatment of Prisoners (1955, p. 3) specifically addresses the need for inmates to have access to exercise, noting that every prisoner should have at least one hour of suitable exercise in the open air daily if the weather permits and receive physical and recreational training during the period of exercise. As such, installations and equipment should be provided.

Although essential to preserve both physical and mental health, exercise is nonetheless severely restricted for death row inmates. Eighty-one percent of death penalty states allow only one hour or less of physical activity daily, and almost half of them only provide a cage, pen or cell to exercise, which means that, in many cases, inmates are not allowed to enjoy sunshine or fresh air (American Civil Liberties Union, 2013). Moreover, physical fitness equipment is usually limited to a ball. In his report to Amnesty International, King (1994) provided the following description of the exercise yards in Oklahoma State Penitentiary:

> The exercise yards are 23 feet long by 22.75 feet wide, which gives an area of 523.25 square feet. The yards have solid concrete walls which are 18 feet high so that their appearance is essentially that of a cube. Were it not for the fact that the roof is constructed of girders surmounted by square wire mesh giving access to the open air, the exercise yard would give the effect of being another room. Because the walls are solid there is no view of the outside world, except for a square of sky, and no through draught. The only facilities for recreation or physical education provided in the yard are a ball, for playing hand ball, and a permanently fixed bench and weight bar with one set of weights permanently welded to the bar, situated in one corner of the yard. The weight bar cannot be removed from its vertical runners. There is no drinking fountain on the yards.
>
> (King, 1994, p. 10)

The lack of available sports attire and footwear paired with sporadic showers further discourages prisoners from engaging in otherwise healthy cardiovascular activity. The issue of exercise deprivation for death row inmates was brought up in separate court cases. In *Gates v. Cook* (2004), the trial court concluded the following:

> Proper exercise is advantageous for mental health and well-being. The exercise facilities provided are adequate. While, in general, the use of flip-flops is understandable as a security measure, such shoes do not allow effective exercise. The inmates should be given access to sneakers prior to entering the exercise pen and should be given access to water and shade while exercising.
>
> (Bohm, 2011, p. 130)

The appeals court nevertheless opposed the switch to sneakers on the basis that the inmates use shoes to kick other inmates and to throw at correctional staff, and because the flip-flops make escape more difficult. Still, in *Sinclair v. Henderson* (1971), the court found merit in the plaintiff's claim that the lack of exercise facilities for inmates on death row constituted cruel and unusual punishment:

> Inmates on Death Row at Angola are housed in a building separate and apart from the regular dormitories. They live in cells measuring approximately 6 feet by 9 feet. [. . .] During each 24-hour period the inmate is allowed out of this small cell for only 15 minutes. During that time he may go down a closed in corridor to a shower room where he must bathe, wash clothes, and supposedly exercise, all in a matter of 15 minutes. The inmates who testified in this case have been living under this condition for as long as 9 years. Some who did not testify have been there longer than that. [. . .] To be held in solitary confinement does not necessarily mean to be locked up 23 hours and 45 minutes of each day for years

> on end as is being done to the inmates on Death Row at Angola. Solitary confinement as used in the statute simply means separate confinement with only occasional access to any other person and that only as specifically authorized in the statute. Confinement for long periods of time without the opportunity for regular outdoor exercise does, as a matter of law, constitute cruel and unusual punishment in violation of the Eighth Amendment to the United States Constitution.
>
> (*Sinclair v. Henderson*, 1971, pp. 1129–1130)

Isolation

Although each state's department of corrections may set its own directives regarding the handling of prisoners, the American Bar Association nonetheless provides standards recommending that death row inmates should be housed similarly to the general inmate population. Consequently, solitary confinement should only be used for brief periods in cases of discipline, security, or criminal behavior (Susman, 2014). In reality, however, the vast majority of death penalty states in 2016 segregate death row inmates. They are isolated in single cells, spending between 22 and 24 hours a day with little to no human interaction (Bohm, 2011). They stay in their cell all the time except for medical reasons, exercise, social or legal visits, or media interviews. As previously mentioned, death row cells in most death penalty states are roughly the size of an average bathroom, ranging between 36 and 100 square feet with minimum furniture (i.e., a steel bed or concrete slab, and writing table).

Solitary confinement in such an exiguous space coupled with the constant anguish caused by the prospect of execution has been associated with a wide repertoire of both physical and psychological problems. Physical conditions that have been observed include hypersensitivity to external stimuli (Grassian, 1983), lack of impulse control (Miller & Young, 1997), appetite loss and weight loss (Haney, 2003; Korn, 1988), heart palpitations (Haney, 2003), withdrawal (Korn, 1988; Miller & Young, 1997), headaches (Haney, 2003), sleeping disorders (Haney, 2003), dizziness (Haney, 2003), and lower levels of brain function, including a decline in electroencephalogram (EEG) activity after only seven days in solitary confinement (Gendreau, Freedman, Wilde, & Scott, 1972). Similarly, psychological effects comprise perceptual distortions and hallucinations (Haney, 2003; Korn, 1988), increased anxiety and nervousness (Brodsky & Scogin, 1988; Grassian, 1983; Haney, 2003), fears of persecution (Grassian, 1983), severe and chronic depression (Grassian, 1983; Haney, 2003; Miller & Young, 1997), blunting of affect and apathy (Korn, 1988; Miller & Young, 1997), talking to oneself (Brodsky & Scogin, 1988; Haney, 2003), confused thought processes (Brodsky & Scogin; 1988; Haney, 2003), and nightmares (Haney, 2003). Several cases of self-mutilation have been reported (Haney, 2003), and the rates of suicide and suicide attempts also are more prevalent on death row than in other correctional housing units (Holder, 2015).

The Death Row Syndrome

The aforementioned symptoms and disorders are more commonly known as the death row syndrome. Some critics argue the death row syndrome amounts to psychological torture and should therefore be deemed unconstitutional (Bluestone & McGahee, 1962; Johnson, 1979; West, 1975;). In fact, the European Court of Human Rights has declared it cruel and torturous punishment in violation of international human rights law. More specifically, in *Soering v. United Kingdom* (1989), the court ruled that the extradition of a German national to the United States to face charges of capital murder violated Article 3 of the European Convention of Human Rights guaranteeing the right against inhumane and degrading treatment.

According to the American Psychiatric Association (APA), however, there is currently no scientific consensus in the United States as to the existence of the death row syndrome, and the construct is still not included in the Diagnostic and Statistical Manual of Mental Disorders (Harrison & Tamony, 2010). Although the Supreme Court has expressed concerns about the debilitating effects of extended waits on death row (*Foster v. Florida*, 2002; *In re Medley*, 1890; *Knight v. Florida*, 1999; *Lackey v. Texas*, 1995; *Thompson v. McNeil*, 2009), it has not ruled on the constitutionality of these symptoms and disorders but stressed the benefit of time for inmates during their appeal process.

Still, death penalty opponents point out to the methodical dehumanization of death row inmates, a process that they argue purposely tames dangerous offenders and makes them accept the idea of their own death. For example, Johnson (1998) describes life on Oklahoma's Death Row H-unit:

> The peculiar silence of death row stems from the empty and ultimately lifeless regime imposed on the condemned. These offenders, seen as unfit to live in even the prison community, are relegated to this prison within a prison. . . . Typical maximum-security prisoners spend about eight to twelve hours a day in their cells; typically death row inmates spend twenty-two to twenty-four hours a day alone in theirs. Death row prisoners leave their cells to shower (often handcuffed) and to exercise in a restricted area, sometimes fittingly called a recreation cage . . . visits occur under heavy guard, are restricted in frequency and duration, and become increasingly rare as a prisoners' stay on death row continues. . . . Deemed beyond correction, they typically are denied access to meager privileges, amenities, and services available to regular prisoners. . . . With only rare exceptions, condemned prisoners are demoralized by their bleak confinement and defeated by the awesome prospect of death by execution. Worn down in small and almost imperceptible ways, they gradually become less than fully human. At the end, the prisoners are helpless pawns in the modern execution drill. They give in, they give up, and submit: yielding themselves to the execution team and the machinery of death.
>
> (Johnson, 1998, pp. 71–93)

Similarly, in *Gates v. Cook* (2004), the trial court recognized the nefarious psychological effects of isolation on individuals housed on death row:

> At least six severely psychotic prisoners are housed on Death Row, and many more are diagnosed with quantifiable mental health problems. The extremely psychotic prisoners scream at night, throw feces, and generally make life miserable for the other inmates and guards. [. . .] The mental health care afforded the inmates on Death Row is grossly inadequate. The isolation of Death Row, along with the inmates pending sentences of death and the conditions on Death Row are enough to weaken even the strongest individual. [. . .] Moreover, comprehensive mental health evaluations are consistently inadequate. Inmates are also prescribed psychotropic drugs with only sporadic monitoring. This can result in life-threatening situations because of the toxicity of these drugs. Appropriate treatment of mentally ill inmates will in turn help address the issues of excessive noise and sanitation problems caused by severely psychotic inmates.
>
> (*Gates v. Cook*, 2004, pp. 11–12)

The appeals court affirmed that mental health examinations should be given, and inmates diagnosed with psychosis and those with severe mental illnesses should be housed separately.

Supervision and Lack of Privacy

Ironically enough, despite the isolation to which they are subjected, prisoners on death row also suffer from a severe lack of privacy. For example, the staff visits them at least every 15 minutes on an irregular schedule, although problem inmates are visited on a more frequent basis. In some states, inmates are also visited by a custody supervisor or unit manager each shift and inspected at least twice a week by the unit administrator (Reinhart, 2011). Further, stringent physical restrictions are placed on them during the time they spend outside their cell. Article 33 of the United Nations Standard Minimum Rules for the treatment of Prisoners (1955) strictly prohibits the use of chains or irons as restraints. Still, before Connecticut abolished capital punishment, the state department of corrections' directives specified that death row inmates should be:

- Handcuffed behind the back for routine out-of-cell movement, including showers, recreation, social visits, social phone calls, using dayrooms (restraints are removed once the inmate is secured in the area and the process is reversed to return the inmate to his cell);
- Fully restrained in front (handcuffs, leg irons, and tether chain) for professional visits, including attorney, medical, mental health, and related visits and video conferencing, which require staff being secured in an area with the inmate (restraints remain on at all times); and
- Fully restrained behind the back (handcuffs, leg irons, and tether chain) for out-of-unit movement within the facility except when a medical or dental procedure requires full restraints in the front (restraints remain on at all times) (Reinhart, 2011, para. 9).

Distractions

How do prisoners under sentence of death spend all their time? Criminal justice students who visit death row are sometimes surprised by the seemingly comfortable amenities enjoyed by inmates relative to LWOP prisoners housed in maximum-security facilities. For example, despite the small size of the cells, they notice private radios and TV sets that are commonly denied to the population serving life without parole. What they fail to realize is that death row inmates have to pay for extra comfort and entertainment. Despite popular misconceptions, the correctional facility does not provide these items out of compassion, though granting prisoners the possibility to purchase them certainly helps alleviate some of the boredom, solitude, and anxiety experienced on death row. Typically, family and friends are the ones who bear the cost of providing these items to prisoners.

Death row inmates can have personal items for use in their cell, including radios and 13-channel TV but no cable or air conditioning. As previously mentioned, snacks can be purchased at the prison commissary. If they can afford them, prisoners can also have reading materials, including newspapers and magazines, with the exception of pornography. Mail is delivered every day except during holidays and weekends and is commonly opened in an effort to intercept evasion plans, weapons, drugs, and other contraband (Palmer, 2010).

In *Sinclair v. Henderson* (1971), inmates had complained about prison officials improperly censoring correspondence. The court nonetheless vacated the injunction, *de facto* authorizing mail censorship as long as it was not racially motivated. On the other hand, in *Procunier v. Martinez* (1974), the Supreme Court affirmed the right for inmates to send letters without arbitrary and unduly burdensome censorship, unless mail restriction is deemed necessary for safety and/or security reasons. Of course, mail and other privileges can be revoked for disciplinary purposes, and all property can be confiscated from an inmate save for a safety gown and blanket when deemed appropriate.

Visits

Article 37 of the United Nations Standard Minimum Rules for the Treatment of Prisoners (1955, p. 6) states, "prisoners shall be allowed under necessary supervision to communicate with their family and reputable friends at regular intervals, both by correspondence and by receiving visits." Accordingly, visits on death row are allowed but strictly monitored. Sixty-seven percent of death penalty states mandate no contact visitation (American Civil Liberties Union, 2013). Leg and arm constraints are common. Visitors are separated by a glass partition and communicate with inmates via phone. Their conversations can be monitored and recorded. Death row prisoners are allowed up to three visits per week that are limited to one hour each, unless visitors traveled distances exceeding 100 miles. Visitors must be approved and visits scheduled through the unit manager's office. Conjugal visits are not authorized for death row inmates.

These restrictions inevitably have collateral impact on death row inmates' relatives. Family members of prisoners on death row have been reported to experience shame, stigma, fear, and debilitating stress (Hood & Hoyle, 2015) on top of the financial burden resulting from the loss of income when husbands or fathers, who represent the majority of death row inmates, are incarcerated. Moreover, correctional facilities are often located in remote areas away from public transportation routes and often hundreds of miles from loved ones, leaving visitors who cannot afford the travel expenses financially burdened. The humiliation of checks and searches further discourages them from visiting their relatives. Consequently, inmates often complain about receiving fewer visits as time goes by, adding to their psychological distress and overall demoralization of being housed on death row.

Programs

Along with physical exercise and other recreational activities, work, educational and vocational training should provide a welcome relief for prisoners under sentence of death. Article 71 of the United Nations Standard Minimum Rules for the Treatment of Prisoners establishes the following:

- Sufficient work of a useful nature shall be provided to keep prisoners actively employed for a normal working day.
- Vocational training in useful trades shall be provided for prisoners able to profit thereby and especially for young prisoners (1955, p. 11).

Similarly, according to Article 78, "Recreational and cultural activities shall be provided in all institutions for the benefit of the mental and physical health of prisoners" (United Nations Standard Minimum Rules for the Treatment of Prisoners, 1955, p. 12).

Before Connecticut repealed its death penalty statute, its department of corrections had issued the following directives regarding death row programs:

- In-cell classes dealing with choices inmates made and making different choices, handling stressful situations, and interpersonal effectiveness;
- HIV education and support;
- Skill building;
- Religious services and study for various faiths
- Special education and pupil services; and
- Victim-offender dialogue (Reinhart, 2011, para. 16).

In many death penalty states, however, death row inmates are denied access to prison jobs, educational classes, clubs, recreational facilities or treatment programs because of safety concerns and budget constraints (Hood & Hoyle, 2015).

Religious and Spiritual Needs

Religion often provides prisoners with spiritual solace and comfort. This could not be truer of death row inmates, who, in most cases, must abandon any hope of earthly freedom and accept the end of their physical life. Articles 41 and 42 of the United Nations Standard Minimum Rules for the Treatment of Prisoners (1955, p. 6) affirm the right for prisoners to exercise their religion freely. More specifically, an institution containing a sufficient number of inmates of the same religion should appoint a qualified representative of that religion, on a full-time basis if possible. This representative should be allowed to hold regular services and visit prisoners if they choose. In addition, inmates should be allowed to attend religious services and to possess the books of religious observance and instruction of his or her denomination.

In reality, however, a recent survey revealed that 62% of death penalty states offer no religious services, and access to a chaplain or religious advisor is at best infrequent (American Civil Liberties Union, 2013). Evidently, this is also an infringement on the First Amendment, especially for religious minorities (e.g., Buddhists, Muslims, and Jews) whose diet restrictions may be incompatible with standard meals distributed on death row (Palmer, 2010). Nevertheless, under the Religious Freedom Restoration Act (*42 U.S. Code § 2000bb-1*, 1993), the government can deny a person's exercise of religion if the denial is justified by a compelling governmental interest and is shown to be the least restrictive means of serving that compelling interest (Americans for Effective Law Enforcement [AELE], 2007).

Access to Legal Counsel

The United Nations Economic and Social Council (1989) have called on governments to provide prisoners under sentence of death adequate assistance of counsel at every stage of the proceedings, above and beyond the protection afforded in noncapital cases. Death row inmates must therefore be granted full access to their lawyers in complete confidentiality. Similarly, Article 38 of the United Nations Standard Minimum Rules for the Treatment of Prisoners (1955) emphasizes the right for foreign citizens on death row to consult with diplomats from their home countries:

- Prisoners who are foreign nationals shall be allowed reasonable facilities to communicate with the diplomatic and consular representatives of the State to which they belong.
- Prisoners who are nationals of States without diplomatic or consular representation in the country and refugees or stateless persons shall be allowed similar facilities to communicate with the diplomatic representative of the State which takes charge of their interests or any national or international authority whose task it is to protect such persons.

There are currently 138 foreign nationals representing 36 nationalities on U.S. death rows (Warren, 2016). The Optional Protocol to the Vienna Convention on Consular Relations of 1963 requires signatory members to let the United Nation's highest tribunal—the International Court of Justice at The Hague—make the final decision when their citizens claim to have been illegally denied the right to seek consulate assistance when jailed abroad (United Nations Optional Protocol to the Vienna Convention on Consular Relations, 2005). Failing to inform foreign nationals placed under arrest of their rights to confer with their home country's consular officials is actually quite common in the United States. In 2004, the International Court of Justice decided to have state courts review and determine possible Vienna Convention violations in the cases of 51 Mexican nationals on U.S. death rows. In 2006, the U.S. announced its withdrawal from the Optional Protocol to avoid litigation (Bohm, 2011).

Death Watch

After death row inmates have exhausted all their legal appeals and their death warrants have been signed, they are moved into a special security area of the prison known as death watch. There they are placed under 24-hour observation. In Florida, the death watch cell is 12 × 7 × 8.5 feet high. In

Tennessee, the cell has a metal-framed bed with one mattress. There is also a metal desk with a metal stool attached to it, a metal shelf, and a shower, a stainless-steel sink, and toilet. It has a small window that provides a limited view of the prison grounds. The inmate is provided some of the following items:

- Hygiene items such as a tube of toothpaste, a toothbrush, a bar of soap and toilet tissue
- Stationery (12 sheets), 3 stamped envelopes and one pencil that will be in the possession of a correctional officer when not in use
- One set of clothing and one set of undergarments
- Religious materials issued by the chaplain
- Legal documents as requested
- One television outside the cell
- Medication prescribed by the facility's physician and issued and used under direct supervision only
- Not more than one requested newspaper at a time in the cell (Tennessee Department of Corrections, 2016, para. 5).

In most states, a phone is made available so the inmate can make personal and legal calls. Visitation is allowed by the warden but must remain noncontact. Regular meals are served, and inmates can request special food and drink items (coffee, soft drinks, burgers, fries, and ice cream). On the final day before the execution, the inmate may request a special meal. To avoid frivolous demands, however, the total cost of that last meal must not exceed $40. About 30 minutes prior to the scheduled execution, the inmate is escorted into the execution chamber.

Conclusion

This chapter presents several fundamental issues inherent in the housing and managing of prisoners under the sentence of death. These issues are not mutually exclusive. Many inmates will spend decades on death row awaiting execution, and some will die before an execution date is scheduled. For this aging population, frequent access to health care is a vital but costly necessity (Aday, 2003). The many years spent living under squalid conditions further exacerbates the problems death row inmates experience. Budget restrictions may prevent correctional facilities from improving detention standards for prisoners under sentence of death. In the last 40 years, however, the number of class action lawsuits against arguably undignified and dangerous living conditions have been filed, some of which have been successful in challenging the conditions of confinement on death row in several states. While the Supreme Court does not mandate death row inmates be made comfortable, it does require treatment to be humane.

References

Aday, R. H. (2003). *Aging prisoners: Crisis in American corrections.* Westport, CT: Praeger.

American Civil Liberties Union (2013). *A death before dying: Solitary confinement on death row.* Retrieved from www.aclu.org/files/assets/deathbeforedying-report.pdf

Americans for Effective Law Enforcement. (2007). Prison diet. *Legal Issues,* 7, AELE Mo. L. J. 301.

Bluestone, H., & McGahee, C. L. (1962). Reaction to extreme stress: Impending death by execution. *American Journal of Psychiatry, 119*(5), 393–396. doi:10.1176/ajp.119.5.393

Bohm, R. M. (2011). *Deathquest: An introduction to the theory and practice of capital punishment in the United States.* New York, NY: Routledge.

Brodsky, S. L., & Scogin, F. R. (1988). Inmates in protective custody: First data on emotional effects. *Forensic Reports, 1,* 267–280.

Chandler v. Crosby, 379 F.3d 1278 (11th Cir. 2004).

Death Penalty Information Center. (2017). *States with and without the death penalty.* Retrieved from www.deathpenaltyinfo.org/states-and-without-death-penalty

Death Row Diary. (2013, May 23). *Letter May 22, 2013*. [Weblog Comment]. Retrieved from http://deathrow-diary.blogspot.com/

Dow, M. (2002). *Machinery of death: The reality of America's death penalty*. New York, NY: Routledge.

Estelle v. Gamble, 429 U.S. 97, 97 S. Ct. 285, 50 L. Ed. 2d 251 (1976).

Farmer v. Brennan, 511 U.S. 825, 114 S. Ct. 1970, 128 L. Ed. 2d 811 (1994).

Fins, D. (2016). *Death Row U.S.A*. NAACP Legal Defense and Educational Fund, Inc. Retrieved from www.deathpenaltyinfo.org/documents/DRUSAWinter2016.pdf

Foster v. Florida, 537 U.S. 990, 123 S. Ct. 470, 154 L. Ed. 2d 359 (2002).

Gates v. Cook, 376 F.3d 323 (5th Cir. 2004).

Gendreau, P., Freedman, N. L., Wilde, G. J., & Scott, G. D. (1972). Changes in EEG alpha frequency and evoked response latency during solitary confinement. *Journal of Abnormal Psychology*, *79*(1), 54–59. doi:10.1.1.381.2406&rep=rep1&type=pdf

Grassian, S. (1983). Psychopathological effects of solitary confinement. *American Journal of Psychiatry*, *140*(11), 1450–1454. doi:10.1176/ajp.140.11.1450

Haney, C. (2003). Mental health issues in long-term solitary and supermax confinement. *Crime & Delinquency*, *49*(1), 124–156. doi:10.1177/0011128702239239

Harrison, K., & Tamony, A. (2010). Death row phenomenon, death row syndrome and their effect on capital cases in the US. *Internet Journal of Criminology*. Retrieved from www. internetjournalofcriminology.com/Harrison_Tamony_% 20Death_Row_Syndrome% 20_IJC_Nov_2010.pdf

Holder, K. K. (2015). Confined to a concrete cave: The death row torture of Warren Lee Hill. *Elon Law Review*, 7, 591–605.

Hood, R., & Hoyle, C. (2015). *The death penalty: A worldwide perspective*. New York, NY: Oxford.

In re Medley, 134 U.S. 160, 10 S. Ct. 384, 33 L. Ed. 835 (1890).

International Covenant on Civil and Political Rights. (1976). Retrieved from http://www.ohchr.org/en/professionalinterest/pages/ccpr.aspx

Johnson, R. (1979). Under sentence of death: The psychology of death row confinement. *Law and Psychology Review*, *5*, 141–192.

Johnson, R. (1998). *Death work: A study of the modern execution process*. Belmont, CA: Thomson Brooks/Cole Publishing Co.

King, R. D. (1994). *Conditions for death row prisoners in H-unit, Oklahoma State Penitentiary, USA*. New York, NY: Amnesty International.

Knight v. Florida, 528 U.S. 990, 120 S. Ct. 459, 145 L. Ed. 2d 370 (1999).

Korn, R. (1988). The effects of confinement in the high security unit at Lexington. *Social Justice*, *15*(31), 8–19.

Lackey v. Texas, 514 U.S. 1045 (1995).

Liebman, J. S., Fagan, J., & West, V. (2000). A broken system: Error rates in capital cases, 1973 1995. *Columbia Law School, Public Law Research Paper*, *15*, 1–28. doi:10.2139/ssrn.232712

Miller, H. A., & Young, G. R. (1997). Prison segregation: Administrative detention remedy or mental health problem? *Criminal Behaviour and Mental Health*, 7(1), 85–94. doi:10.1002/cbm.146

Palmer, J. W. (2010). *Constitutional rights of prisoners*. New York, NY: Routledge.

Procunier v. Martinez, 416 U.S. 396 (1974).

Reinhart, C. (2011). *Prison conditions for death row and life without parole inmates*. Hartford, CT: Office of Legal Research, OLR Research Report. Retrieved from www.cga.ct.gov/2011/rpt/2011-R-0178.htm

Religious Freedom Restoration Act 42 U.S. Code § 2000bb-1 (1993).

Rhodes v. Chapman, 452 U.S. 337 (1981).

Ruiz v. Estelle, 503 F. Supp. 1265 (S.D. Tex. 1980).

Sinclair v. Henderson, 331 F. Supp. 1123 (E.D. La. 1971).

Soering v United Kingdom, 161 Eur. Ct. H.R. (ser. A) (1989).

Susman, T. (2014). *Reassessing solitary confinement II: The human rights, fiscal, and public safety consequences*. Washington, DC: Statement of the American Bar Association before the Senate Judiciary Subcommittee on the Constitution, Civil Rights, and Human Rights. Retrieved from www.americanbar.org/content/dam/aba/uncategorized/GAO/2014feb25_solitaryconfinements_t.authcheckdam.pdf

Tennessee Department of Corrections. (2016). *Death watch*. Retrieved from www.tn.gov/correction/article/tdoc-death-watch#sthash.K5WS7jxe.dpuf

Thompson v. McNeil, 129 S. Ct. 1299, 556 U.S. 1114, 173 L. Ed. 2d 693 (2009).

United Nations Economic and Social Council. (1989). *Capital punishment and implementation of the safeguards guaranteeing protection of the rights of those facing the death penalty*. New York, NY: United Nations Economic and Social Council, 1–52.

United Nations international covenant on civil and political rights. (1976). New York, NY: United Nations. Retrieved from https://treaties.un.org/doc/publication/unts/volume%20999/volume-999-i-14668-english.pdf

United Nations Optional Protocol to the Vienna Convention on Consular Relations. (2005). *United Nations, Treaty Series*, *596*, 1–30. Vienna, Austria: United Nations.
United Nations standard minimum rules for the treatment of prisoners. (1955). New York, NY: First United Nations Congress. Retrieved from www.unodc.org/pdf/criminal_justice/UN_Standard_Minimum_Rules_for_the_Treatment_of_Prisoners.pdf
United Nations Universal Declaration of Human Rights. (2017). Retrieved from www.ohchr.org/EN/UDHR/Documents/UDHR_Translations/eng.pdf
Warren, M. (2016). *Foreign nationals and the death penalty in the U.S.* Retrieved from www.deathpenaltyinfo.org/foreign-nationals-and-death-penalty-us#Reported-DROW
West, L. J. (1975). Psychiatric reflections on the death penalty. *American Journal of Orthopsychiatry*, *45*(4), 689–700.

PART III

Medical and Mental Health Issues

17

PRISONERS WITH MENTAL ILLNESS

Treatment Challenges and Solutions

Andrea Cantora and Tiffaney Parkman

> Prisons are very ill-equipped to respond to mental health challenges, and there is almost no programing in jails. In prisons there is more programing than in jails but it's not enough and the programs that exist are very hard to get into. There are huge waiting lists to get into these programs and they prioritize those reentering society sooner.
>
> —Lauren-Brooke Eisen, The Brennan Center for Justice (as quoted in Kerr, 2017, para. 8)

Introduction

The issue of treating mentally ill persons within a correctional setting present significant challenges to prisons and jails. Correctional institutions were developed and designed to secure individuals deemed harmful to society. Providing hospital or therapeutic care goes against the very nature of what jails and prisons are designed to do. In many jurisdictions, jails and prisons are often the only resource available for housing mentally ill people who break the law. Over the past several decades, the reduction of mental health services in the community has led to an increase of mentally ill individuals in jails and prisons. As a result, the rate of mental illness among people incarcerated is higher than the rate found in the general population. While incarcerated, people with mental health issues do not always receive the proper treatment to manage the illness. Co-occurring disorders (e.g., a mental health problem and substance abuse) are common, and this makes treating the population even more challenging. The identification and treatment of prisoners with mental illness varies by state. Many states lack the appropriate resources to properly respond to the problem. Correctional officers are often untrained and ill prepared to deal with mentally ill prisoners. The use of disciplinary sanctions, including solitary confinement, are often the response to manage the population. As a result, the lack of appropriate treatment and management may worsen prisoners' symptoms. When released, this population often struggles to function in the community and may end up cycling in and out of jail and prison. This chapter highlights the history of the mentally ill in correctional institutions, the current prevalence of the problem, the range of treatment options available, how correctional workers mange the population, examples of successful programs, and treatment strategies for managing the population once released.

History of Treating the Mentally Ill Prisoner

Since the creation of jails and prisons, people with mental health problems were housed in correctional facilities. In the early 1800s the investigation into the conditions of jails led to the belief that housing mentally ill people in correctional institutions was inhumane. In 1827, Massachusetts became the first state to investigate the conditions of the jails and the high prevalence of mentally ill incarcerated. The effort was led by advocate Louis Dwight, who was the first person to identify the problem in the state's jails. Soon after the investigation of the state's practices, Massachusetts began to change its practice of housing mentally ill people in local jails and prisons and developed the state's first psychiatric hospital (Torrey, Kennard, Eslinger, Lamb, & Pavle, 2010).

Following Dwight's lead, Dorothea Dix was one of the most well know advocates for removing the mentally ill from correctional facilities. Dix argued that the mentally ill prisoners should not be housed in a place where they were not receiving treatment. Dix traveled the country visiting prisons and jails and documented the mistreatment of the mentally ill. She was largely responsible for publicizing the conditions within them and the lack of treatment for the mentally ill. As a result of her investigative and advocacy work, the number of psychiatric hospitals across the country began to increase, therefore decreasing the need to house mentally ill individuals in prison (Torrey, 2014). An 1880 census of mentally ill citizens found that there were approximately 41,000 people in hospitals and psychiatric facilities and less than 400 people in correctional institutions (Torrey et al., 2010). The low number of people with mental illness in jails and prisons continued through the 1960s. The solution for treatment of the seriously mentally ill was the use of state psychiatric hospitals.

In the 1960s, there was a major change in public perception and public health policy. The shift to release patients to the community for treatment was supported by the effectiveness of antipsychotic medications that stabilized people to live independently, as well as a shift in legislation to prevent the involuntary commitment of many mental health patients (Human Rights Watch, 2003). There was a belief that patients in mental hospitals would become institutionalized, and their condition would deteriorate if they remained hospitalized long term. Instead, policy makers decided that releasing them after a short-stay, prescribing them medication, and encouraging them to seek counseling would be more effective (Erickson & Erickson, 2008).

Deinstitutionalization of the 1960s

The closing of state mental hospitals in the 1960s is often referred to as deinstitutionalization. Deinstitutionalization was a massive change in public health policy that resulted in releasing patients into the community to receive mental health treatment. The idea that communities throughout the country were ready to deal with this population was misguided. Many communities were ill prepared to provide treatment, manage medication, and assist with basic living needs. Communities lacked the proper funding and services to treat the amount of people in need. As a result, many people with serious mental health problems did not receive proper care and were unable to live stable lives independently.

The false promise to provide services in the community resulted in not only untreated mental illness but subsequent deviant and criminal behavior. The "criminalization" of the mentally ill became a serious problem, as the new public health response included the arrest, detainment, prosecution, and incarceration of the mentally ill. Jails and prisons were not designed to treat and manage this growing inmate population. Regardless of their readiness, correctional facilities were tasked with housing, managing, and treating the mentally ill.

The closing of mental health hospitals has resulted in a lack of treatment options. Jails become the primary social response because the hospital alternative is often not available. The number of patients receiving inpatient treatment at psychiatric facilities declined from approximately 559,000 in 1955 to 69,000 in 1995 (Felix, Barber, & Lesser, 2001). As of 2004, available bed space at public and private psychiatric hospitals was 100,439. This equates to one bed for every 3,000 citizens (Torrey et al., 2010).

Mentally ill people often cycle between the mental health and criminal justice systems; however, these two systems rarely communicate or coordinate their efforts, leaving people without proper treatment (Lurigio, Fallon & Dincin, 2000), especially a continuity of care. When people leave jail they often do not receive an aftercare plan or referral to mental health treatment. As a result, with the high rate of co-occurring disorders of substance abuse and mental health, mentally ill people leaving jail often relapse back into drug and alcohol abuse. The lack of mental health and substance abuse treatment, along with ongoing substance use, may result in police intervention. Police are rarely trained to deal with mentally ill people and respond by making an arrest (American Psychiatric Association, 2004).

Many argue that this shift in health policy in the 1970s is partially responsible for the increase in incarceration rates in the '80s and '90s. Also responsible for the increase of mentally ill people in prisons and jails was the change in sentencing policy (e.g., federal and state mandatory minimum laws) that targeted nonviolent drug offenders, including those with substance abuse disorders (American Psychiatric Association, 2004). With few mental health resources in the community, law enforcement and the courts do not have many options for alternatives to jail or prison (Human Rights Watch, 2003). Human Rights Watch (2003) reported that mental health providers struggle to get clients into treatment, and it is often not until they commit a crime that treatment becomes available.

Current Statistics and Characteristics of the Mentally Ill Prisoner

Prevalence Rates

Identifying the prevalence of mental health disorders among incarcerated populations is often difficult and inconsistent. There have been national studies conducted by the Bureau of Justice Statistics that rely on self-reporting of mental health status (James & Glaze, 2006) and smaller studies that identify prevalence by use of mental health services (Human Rights Watch, 2003). Most studies conclude an estimated 15–20% of incarcerated people have a serious mental health problem. The most serious mental illnesses are often defined by using the DSM-IV Axis I diagnostic screening to assess for any presence of a serious mental illness within the past month. Serious mental illness includes symptoms of depressive disorder, major depressive disorder, bipolar, schizophrenia, schizoaffective disorder, psychotic disorder, and delusional disorder (Steadman, Osher, Robbins, Case, & Samuels, 2009).

The most recent national study, conducted by the Bureau of Justice Statistics (BJS) (2006), reported that 56% of state prisoners and 64% of jail inmates identified having a mental health problem. BJS defined mental health problem as having a history and/or symptoms of a mental health problem that was treated or diagnosed by a health provider in the past 12 months (James & Glaze, 2006). In their study, James and Glaze (2006) reported that state prisoners were more likely than jail inmates to have used prescribed medication for a mental health issue in the 12 months prior to their incarceration (18% and 14%, respectively) and received therapy from a mental health provider (15% state prisoners versus 10% jail inmates). Common mental health symptoms reported met DSM-IV criteria for mania (43% state prisoners versus 54% jail inmates), major depression (23% state prisoners versus 30% jail inmates), and psychotic disorder (15% state prisoners versus 24% jail inmates). Although state prisoners are more likely to report receiving treatment, as indicated previously, jail inmates experience more mental health symptoms.

In another study, Human Rights Watch (2003) reported the percentage of prisoners at various state departments of corrections who received mental health services while incarcerated in 2003. For example, Pennsylvania reported that 17% of its prison population was receiving mental health services, with Kentucky reporting 15%, California reporting 14%, Texas reporting 12%, and New York reporting 11%. The estimates indicate that the prevalence of mental illness among incarcerated populations is significant.

Types of Mental Health Disorders

The most common types of mental health disorders for people incarcerated include depression, schizophrenia, and bipolar disorder (AbuDagga, Wolfe, Carome, Phatdouang, & Torrey, 2016; American Psychiatric Association, 2004). Additionally, prisoners are frequently diagnosed with personality disorders, especially antisocial personality (Adams & Ferrandino, 2008). Co-occurring (or dual diagnosis) disorders also are common among people incarcerated (see Chapter 19 for more about co-occurring disorders). This usually includes prisoners who have a mental health disorder and a substance abuse problem. For example, the majority of state prisoners (74%) with a mental health problem have a substance abuse problem (James & Glaze, 2006). These co-occurring disorders are more difficult to treat than either one alone because the disorders interact with each other, and individual treatment approaches may be harmful to one of the disorders (Adams & Ferrandino, 2008).

Gender, Race, and Age Differences

Women in state prisons report higher rates of mental health issues than men (73% vs. 55%, respectively) (James & Glaze, 2006). A 2009 jail study found that women have higher rates of serious mental illness than men in jail (31% versus 14.5%, respectively) (Steadman et al., 2009). Co-occurring disorders also are more prevalent among women in prison. Bloom, Owen, and Covington (2003) found that 75% of women with a mental illness also have substance abuse problems. Identifying which problem (mental health or substance abuse) came first is difficult to know (Covington, 2002). In some cases, women may self-medicate to deal with mental health disorders (Grella, Stein, & Greenwell, 2005), or mental health problems may have emerged out of substance use (Covington, 2002). Regardless of which comes first, both factors complicate the ability for treatment providers to adequately address these needs. Similar to the co-occurrence of mental health and substance abuse, a history of victimization also co-occurs with mental health diagnoses. Greenfeld and Snell (1999) report eight out of 10 women in prison with mental health problems also have a history of physical and/or sexual abuse.

When looking at the rates of mental health problems among state prisoners, white inmates are more likely to have mental health problems compared to blacks and Hispanics (62%, 54.7%, and 46%, respectively). Mental illness also varies by age. Younger prisoners (under 24) have the highest rate of mental illness (63% compared to 40% for inmates over 55) (James & Glaze, 2006).

Other Characteristics

Research finds that prisoners with mental health problems also experience higher rates of other personal issues than those without mental health issues. For example, those with mental health problems are more likely to have experienced homelessness, have been physically and/or sexually abused, received public assistance, had a parent abuse drugs and/or alcohol, and had a family member incarcerated (James & Glaze, 2006). The combination of mental illness and other life stressors makes treating this population an even greater challenge.

Prisoners with mental illness are more likely to be incarcerated for violent and property offenses compared to those without mental illness. Additionally, mentally ill prisoners are more likely to have a prior violent offense and, on average, have more prior incarcerations (James & Glaze, 2006). People with mental health issues also are incarcerated longer in prisons (James & Glaze, 2006) and jails (Vera Institute of Justice, 2011) than those without a mental health problem.

Victimization

The correctional setting is considered harmful for people with mental illness. Being admitted into a correctional facility can increase stress and anxiety for people regardless of mental health status. The experience for those with mental health issues can be detrimental to their safety and well-being. Being mixed in with the general prison population can be dangerous for the individual with the mental health problem and for other prisoners and staff. Their symptoms make it difficult to appropriately socialize with other prisoners. Their behavior and interactions may leave them vulnerable to victimization (Carr et al., 2006). For example, in New York State 54% of prisoners receiving mental health treatment reported experiencing physical and/or sexual abuse or had property stolen from them during their incarceration (Correctional Association of New York, 2004).

Suicide

Suicide is one of the main causes of death among jail inmates. The suicide rates for jail inmates is approximately nine to 14 times higher than in the general public. Self-harming and suicidal behaviors often are the result of drug withdrawal, mental illness, and difficulties coping with interactions (Goss, Peterson, Smith, Kalb, & Brodey, 2002). A 2002 study of jail inmates in Washington State found that 77% of the jails' 132 suicide attempts were among inmates with mental illness (Goss et al., 2002). Also in 2002, New York State reported 70% of prisoners who actually completed suicide had a mental illness (Correctional Association of New York, 2004). Box 17.1 presents an example of the health care crisis in California's Correctional System.

Box 17.1 Health Care Crisis in California's Correctional System

The California Department of Corrections and Rehabilitation has had many lawsuits filed against it that question the constitutionality of prison and jail conditions. Many have argued that the severe overcrowding in the state's prisons and jails violate prisoners' Eighth Amendment rights because of the poor living conditions and lack of quality physical and mental health care (Owen & Mobley, 2012; Schlanger, 2013). In 1995, the District Court of California ruled in *Coleman v. Brown* that prisoners with serious mental health issues do not receive adequate care. The state was appointed experts to identify ways to improve the system's mental health services. In 2001, the federal court ruled in *Plata v. Brown* that the state was in violation of prisoners' Eighth Amendment rights because of inadequate health care. Again, the state was appointed experts to improve the conditions of health care. In 2011, after a lengthy legal battle, the courts ruled in *Brown v. Plata* that the state must reduce their prison population to address the harmful living conditions and inadequate health care. As a result, the Public Safety Realignment Act (PSRA) was passed in 2011 to reduce the state's prison population (Owen & Mobley, 2012). The Realignment Act involves several key reduction strategies. The first involves transferring nonviolent state prisoners to county jails; the second strategy shifts parole supervision from the state to the counties; and the third requires parole violators to serve their time in county jails instead of prisons (Schlanger, 2013). If these strategies are successful, the reduction of prison populations should allow the state to improve the mental health and physical health care they provide.

Mismanagement of Mentally Ill Prisoners

People with mental illness need therapeutic settings to deal with their symptoms; unfortunately, correctional facilities are counterproductive to the therapeutic setting (Carr et al., 2006). When mentally ill prisoners are housed with the general prison population, they often become vulnerable to victimization by other prisoners and may experience mistreatment by prison or jail staff. Mentally ill prisoners may struggle to adjust to the prison environment, including following the daily structure and maintaining basic hygiene practices. This population also may fail to understand and/or follow specific orders because of their mental health condition. As a result, they end up violating institutional policy and may face disciplinary action. Research finds that mentally ill prisoners are more likely to be charged with violating institutional rules, to engage in physical or verbal assaults, and to be injured in a fight than those without a mental health problem (James & Glaze, 2006).

The inability to adjust and follow the routine may appear problematic and disruptive to the prison environment. Other prisoners may become frustrated and intolerant to those who fail to adhere to subculture "rules," whereas correctional officers may end up responding with disciplinary sanctions. Correctional officers frequently fail to understand that those with mental illness are most likely not intentionally violating institutional rules rather, their behavior is related to their symptomology. Regardless, prisoners who are noncompliant may be restrained and/or placed in isolation units.

Correctional officers are often not trained to properly deal with mentally ill prisoners. A response may involve using excessive force because they do not know how to manage the erratic behavior of the mentally ill inmate (Erickson & Erickson, 2008). Restraint is often used when mentally ill prisoners are acting aggressive or violent, but it also has been used in situations when prisoners are engaging in nonthreatening behavior, such as urinating in their cell, banging on doors, or using profanity (Human Rights Watch, 2015). Use of force on a mentally ill prisoner can be traumatic and lead to worsening of mental health symptoms (Human Rights Watch, 2015). Excessive use of force is more common in facilities that have a history of violence, have poor physical conditions, are overcrowded, lack rehabilitative programming, have an insufficient number of staff, and do not provide adequate training or salary for staff. Use of force is also more common in segregation units (Human Rights Watch, 2015).

Solitary Confinement

The use of solitary confinement, or segregation, is a constitutional practice used by many correctional facilities as a way to separate prisoners who pose a threat to the institution, to punish misconduct, and to protect vulnerable inmates. Segregation units often house the most aggressive and problematic prisoners but also contain a large number of prisoners who simply are noncompliant or violate minor rules. Inmates with preexisting mental health problems may end up in solitary confinement because prison workers do not always recognize symptoms of mental health and instead respond to deviant/harmful behavior by using punitive sanctions.

The impact of isolation on mental health is a major area of concern. Solitary confinement, especially long-term isolation, affects the mental, emotional, and physical health of those confined to these units (see e.g., Guy, 2016; Metzner & Fellner, 2010; Vallas, 2016). Prisoners with mental health problems are at considerably greater risk of mental deterioration. While it is unconstitutional to house inmates with mental health problems in solitary confinement, these inmates still end up there (Pizarro & Stenius, 2004). For example, a study conducted in New York found that a third of inmates held in segregation units had a mental health problem—including depression, schizophrenia, and bipolar disorder (Correctional Association of New York, 2004).

Mental Health Treatment Availability inside Correctional Facilities

With the influx of mentally ill persons being incarcerated, institutions have struggled with identifying mentally ill persons, employing best practices on how to manage their behaviors and symptoms, and mediating the impact of the prison environment for those suffering mental illnesses (Daniel, 2007; Hills, Siegfried, & Ickowitz, 2004; Kim, Becker-Cohen, & Serakos, 2015; Metzner, Cohen, & Wettstein, 1998).

In 1976, the United States Supreme Court established that prisoners are allowed a minimum level of treatment for medical conditions, including mental health (*Estelle v. Gamble*, 1976). This case highlights provisions in the Eighth Amendment to the Constitution that affords incarcerated individuals to be free from "cruel and unusual punishment" through the "deliberate indifference by prison officials to a prisoner's medical needs" (*Estelle v. Gamble*, 1976, p. 429). In *Bowring v. Godwin* (1977), the right to medical and psychiatric treatment was made not distinguishable, which further acknowledge the state's responsibility to treat mental health disorders. In essence, the law dictates for prison officials that physical and mental illnesses must both be treated with equal care and attention.

With the Supreme Court setting the legal tone for requirements of health care treatment in prisons and jails, the actual application of this law has been more difficult to achieve because prisons have not upheld the legal requirements for mental health care; however, inmates have taken their cases to court and successfully sued prisons for lack of proper mental health treatment (*Coleman v. Brown*, 2013; *Dunn v. Thomas*, 2014; *Dockery et al. v. Epps et al.*, 2013). For instance, in *Dunn v. Thomas* (2014), inmates sued the Alabama Department of Corrections for negligence in addressing their mental and physical health and providing an overcrowded environment that put them at risk for further decompensation of their illnesses. The suit, which was successfully won in court, also described conditions where correctional officers routinely ignored pleas for medical attention even after fights, stabbings, and surgical recovery malfunctions. Despite the fight for just treatment in prisons and jails, the complications of treating the mentally ill in prison are not without legitimate hindrances.

One of the top factors hindering mental health treatment within any correctional system is the burgeoning costs associated with health care in general. As the mentally ill population has increased, so have the financial burdens associated with managing those needs. Mental health treatment, like any chronic illness, is expensive, and the levels of care are broad and multifaceted. The National Association of State Budget Officers presented information that state corrections health care budgets increased 10% annually from 1998–2001 (Kinsella, 2004). Costs associated with mental health are listed as one of the factors for this increase. Specifically, in 1998 states spent between 5–43% of their health care budgets on mental health services (Kinsella, 2004). One reason for this is the rising pharmaceutical costs, which can account for 15–20% annually (Kinsella, 2004). The State Department of Corrections in Georgia, for example, reports spending $6.5 million annually in psychiatric medications alone (Georgia Department of Corrections, 2016). Providing necessary mental health treatment to those who need it most is almost always weighed against strains on the financial budgets of jails and prisons.

In correctional facilities, the financial burden of the mental health bill can determine the level and amount of treatment inmates are able to receive. For instance, state prisons are often supported through state money and/or multiyear contracts to private companies that have a greater opportunity to make adjustments to budgets. Jail facilities are generally supported financially through local funds and may not receive state funds, which could restrict funds needed for treatment. To make the issue of financing more complicated, the privatized prison industry, whose main focus is a for-profit business, must balance caring for inmates with turning a profit. This can be seen in the often debated billion-dollar privatized market that serves to provide health care and mental health services to prisons. A recent article highlights the issue of privatization and how most states contract health services out to protect themselves from the unpredictable and escalating costs of health care (Kutscher, 2013). Kutscher (2013) reports about the way that contracts between prisons and contracted medical providers are designed to yield positive results for the prison (e.g., decreased inmate illness and stable spending on inmates) while yielding a profit for the contracted medical provider. These contracts often come with pharmaceutical formularies that seek to control costs, which often means using cheaper, less effective medications and medical treatments (Kutscher, 2013).

Types of Treatment Offered Inside: Jail vs. Prison

As previously stated, the United States has the largest correctional system in the world. The American Jail Association (2007) reported there are more than 4,500 prison facilities in the United States. In addition, there are 3,096 counties served by 3,163 jails (American Jail Association, 2007). With so many different facilities, public and privatized, understanding the types of treatment offered inside of "lockup" systems can be an arduous task. Both jails and prisons present different treatment options to the mentally ill.

Jails are typically short-term city or county facilities that confine persons who have been arrested, who are awaiting trial, who are convicted of minor offenses, or who are awaiting transport to a state facility (American Jail Association, 2007). Jail management varies across counties (often within the same state) and determines the level of treatment a mentally ill person may receive. Because of the nature of jails, the types of treatment offered are limited because of the amount of time persons are "expected" to be housed there. At a minimum, most jails have procedures for providing mental health screenings upon intake as well as guidelines for suicide prevention. Beyond initial screenings, jails are unlikely to provide any long-term mental health services such as counseling, aftercare planning, or case management. Jails can provide mental health medication, the most important resource for the mentally ill. However, the range of options available and the time frame of medication delivery by a medical professional depends on the management and capabilities of treatment the jail provides. The number of professionals dedicated specifically to the needs of the mentally ill vary by facility, with many jails, particularly in less populated areas, having no full-time dedicated professionals on site to meet the needs of the population.

Additionally, judges can remand individuals to state forensic units for treatment during their time in jail. However, if placements are not available, individuals are returned to jail with the same conditions and symptoms that spurred the recommendation in the first place. One example of this focuses on the Baltimore City Jail in Maryland. Many inmates have been court ordered for mental health treatment and evaluation but remain in jail because there is a lack of space at the state's forensic hospital (Dresser, 2016). As of June 2016, 85 people who were referred for more intensive mental health treatment were waitlisted for spacing at any of the five state mental health facilities and remain untreated in jail (Dresser, 2016).

Once inmates are sent to prisons, their mental health options for treatment appear to increase. Prisons are state or federally operated facilities that confine individuals convicted of long sentences, typically for more than a year. After the determination of *Ruiz v. Estelle* (1980) established lack of health care was a violation of an inmate's constitutional right, every state department of correction had to create some way of identifying and treating the health of all inmates. Every state department of corrections or public safety has classification procedures on identifying prisoners with mental illness and maintains some type of program or facility to treat those who are mentally ill. According to the U.S. Department of Justice, 95% of state adult prisons (public and private) reported providing mental health services to inmates (Beck & Maruschak, 2001). Seventy-eight percent reported evaluating for mental health issues upon processing, 84% stated that they provide therapeutic services by mental health professionals (therapy or counseling), and 83% reported providing psychiatric medications (Beck & Maruschak, 2001). While prisons are providing mental health services, the quality and outcomes of the services have yet to be analyzed. Additionally, many prisons that provide mental health services do so in facilities not designed for mentally ill inmates (Beck & Maruschak, 2001). Courts across the United States often attempt to divert mentally ill offenders away from the criminal justice system (see Box 17.2) because of substandard mental care they receive behind bars and because offenders have better treatment outcomes in the community (see e.g., Frailing, 2010; see Chapter 3 for more on mental health courts).

Classification Systems

Most prisons have classification systems to house inmates in need of mental health services. For example, in Georgia prisons are classified from levels 1 to level 5. A level 1 classified institution has no mental health programs or inmates requiring any mental health services. A level 5 institution is designated as an institution that can house acutely mental disabled inmates. This level is considered hospitalization. While institutions are designated with a level system, so are inmates during classification upon entry into the department of corrections. Inmates diagnosed with a level 3 or higher mental health designation must live in an institution that has a supportive housing unit. According to the Georgia Department of Corrections (2016) website, its services encompasses "individual and group therapy, supportive counseling, psychoeducational services and milieu therapy and psychopharmacology and a staff that includes psychiatrist, psychologists, counselors, nurses and activity therapists."

In Virginia there is one facility designed for the acutely mentally ill population for both men and women. This facility has acute care treatment (ACT) levels (hospitalization), outpatient, and residential treatment for varying prison risk security levels. In 2014, the state of Virginia had 14 psychiatrists to care for 30,000 inmates across the state (Hauseman, 2014). Virginia reports that 15% of their offender population "requires some level of mental health services" (Virginia Department of Corrections, 2010, p. 2). Likewise, in Tennessee inmates with mental illness are treated at one facility, the Lois

Box 17.2 Mental Health Courts

Mental health courts were developed to divert jail inmates with serious mental health problems into community treatment as a way to avoid the formal court process. Mental health courts have popped up all over the country as pilot programs and permanent fixtures in our judicial landscape and have been found to be an important step in keeping the mentally ill out of prisons and jails (McNiel & Binder, 2007). According to Steadman and colleagues (2011), more than 250 mental health courts are in existence throughout the United States. Participation in a mental health court program is voluntary, but criteria for selection varies by state. Some states exclude offenders with felony and/or violent charges, and most require an Axis I diagnosis (i.e., clinical disorders in need of treatment such as bipolar, major depression, schizophrenia, and anxiety disorders). Participants are supervised by the court and required to follow a mental health treatment plan that may include medication compliance, psychiatric hospitalization, outpatient care, case management, and individual and/or group therapy. Steadman and colleagues (2011) evaluated a mental health court program and compared participants to mentally ill offenders who did not go through the court program. They found that participants of the mental health court were significantly less likely to experience a rearrest (49% vs. 58%, respectively). Although mental health courts are considered a "promising" strategy (Crimesolutions.gov, 2015), more research is needed to determine whether mental health courts are effective in other jurisdictions.

M. DeBerry Special Needs Facility, specifically designated for mental health treatment. According to the Tennessee Department of Correction website (TDOC, 2017, para. 3),

> Mental health units are provided for offenders with acute mental health needs. The Mental Health Program is designed to stabilize the offender and move him through a process where the offender takes more responsibility for his behavior and mental health.

In Alabama, more than 3,000 prisoners were receiving some form of mental health treatment as of March 2013. The Alabama Department of Corrections (ADOC) has six psychologists located at six of the state's 15 prisons. Mental health inmates are screened and identified using a classification scale that ranges from level 1, which is used for prisoners with mild mental functioning, to level 6, which is reserved for prisoners who have been committed to a forensic mental hospital (Alabama Department of Corrections, 2013). Despite the increases nationally in mental health populations, the ADOC's expenditure for psychiatric medications decreased by 26% from March 2010 to March 2012. Alabama, like many other states, has distinguished itself for its poor health care practices and outcomes for its prison population. Most recently, in *Dunn v. Thomas* (2014), mentally ill and disabled inmates reported living in deplorable conditions that lacked the necessary and appropriate care for their illnesses. Among them, mentally ill inmates reported physical abuse, extreme punishments in segregation, and a general disregard of their pleas for treatment (*Dunn v. Thomas*, 2014).

Medication Compliance

Mentally ill persons, whether incarcerated or not, will experience a time when they refuse to take their prescribed medications. In the mental health field, it is called a relapse. In prisons and jails, inmates typically relapse because of a refusal to take their medication. A relapse can put mentally ill inmates at risk for self-harm or victimization. Even if inmates refuse medications and decompensate in their illnesses, criminal justice systems are still responsible for protecting individuals in their care from themselves and others. Forcible medication is one way that prisons and jails can intervene in such occurrences. Forcible medication for those in the "free world" is more difficult to secure given the civil rights that each of us carry, unless a person has been found to be a danger to him- or herself or to others. For the confined, this process has been determined via court litigation but is more prominently witnessed in state/federal prisons as opposed to jails. The Supreme Court has ruled, however, that prison administrations can forcibly administer psychiatric medications for inmates deemed a harm to themselves or others as long as the facility has an established administrative protocol (*Washington v. Harper*, 1990). In such cases, prisons can form advisory boards of mental health professionals that can make decisions to involuntarily medicate an inmate prior to an emergency and without an outside court order. The majority of prisons follow the precedent set by *Washington v. Harper* (1990) and have administrative protocols for mentally ill inmates who refuse medications and whose symptoms prevent them from participating in meaningful activities (Torrey, 2014). The remaining states file paperwork for judicial hearings that occur outside of the prison staff administration. In 2014, *The Treatment Advocacy Center* conducted a comprehensive survey report of involuntary medication protocols for each state that highlights which involuntary medication procedure they follow (*Washington v. Harper* model or local judiciary) (Torrey, 2014). Involuntary medication procedures vary across jail locations and throughout the same state, which makes analyzing state practices complicated. Unfortunately, jails often lack the personnel, financing, and skill to carry out such efforts.

An additional obstacle for treatment is the availability of staff to provide critical medication to the inmates. Psychiatric medication dispersal can occur multiple times a day which does not always fit with "prison time." For example, unanticipated events (e.g., lockdowns, random cell/unit searches, prison emergencies) can interrupt "pill call" and prevent inmates from receiving scheduled medications. In prisons with active mental health programs, mentally ill inmates may miss sessions because of institutional infractions that might cause them to be isolated from the prison population (Fellner, 2006; Lamb & Weinberger, 1999; McNiel & Binder, 2007; Metzner, 1993). Taken together, each of these obstacles provide a small glimpse into the issues mentally ill inmates face while receiving treatment in a correctional setting.

Impact of Litigation on Improving Mental Health Care

The law of the land in the United States has ruled in favor of access to mental health treatment for incarcerated individuals. Each state is responsible for providing health care for inmates under its custody. How each state provides health care and the results of those efforts can be seen in the ongoing litigations filed on behalf of mentally ill offenders. The Georgia Department of Corrections is a good example of how a lawsuit may influence a correctional system to change its mental health practices.

In 2002, a class action lawsuit was filed in the U.S. District Court against the Georgia Department of Corrections and staff at Phillip State Prison by a group of mentally ill inmates who reported their Eighth and Fourteenth Amendment rights were being violated through a variety of allegations involving mistreatment, lack of mental health care, improper use of disciplinary segregations, and sexual abuse (*Fluellen et al. v. Wetherington*, 2002). That lawsuit was dismissed because of a procedural mishap, only to be amended and refiled with another inmate as the main plaintiff, with the same allegations (*Ralph v. Adams et al.*, 2004). As the case went through litigation, Phillips State Prison and the Georgia Department of Correction sought to make changes to their mental health programming and mental health units based on the claims filed by the inmates. These changes focused on best practices for prison mental health programs, which consisted of increasing mental health staffing, training correctional officers who worked in the supportive living units, increasing mental health programming, ensuring timely and routine psychiatric appointments, and including mental health staff in the disciplinary process (Metzner, 1993).

One of the significant changes the prison made was to address the issues of abuse and excessive use of force by providing specialized training to correctional officers. All officers who worked in supportive living units (SLU), a specialized housing unit for inmates diagnosed with a mental illness, were formally trained to understand mental illness and how to work with persons exhibiting psychiatric symptoms. Correctional officers who worked in the SLU also were given an increase in pay for working with the specialized population. Additionally, correctional officers are no longer in charge of deciding what type of punishment an inmate might receive for violating institutional policy. This shift in decision making from correctional officer to mental health professional is consistent with best practices as recommended by mental health prison program experts (Metzner, 1993). The new change requires officers to immediately remove an inmate from an unsafe situation and alert the mental health staff within 30 minutes of any action. Mental health counselors and officers work together to ensure that the needs of the inmate are met and that each department is informed about what is occurring with the inmates (particularly those struggling with their symptoms). In addition, mentally ill inmates who break prison rules are interviewed and cleared by a mental health staff person who helps decide what role the mental illness played in the infraction. Mental health staff also provide recommendations for what the punishment should be for the inmate. This multidisciplinary team approach to addressing behavioral issues has improved conditions at the institution.

Another recommendation implemented by the staff at Phillips State Prison was rigorous treatment planning and case management by the mental health counselors. Each inmate is assigned a mental health counselor who designs a treatment plan based on the individual inmate's needs. This plan includes assigning the inmates to psychoeducational and therapeutic groups that fit with their individual needs. Each treatment plan has the input of everyone involved in the inmate's treatment (i.e., psychiatrist, activity therapist, nursing, and correctional officer) and is reviewed every six months. If an inmate is transferred to a new counselor, within a set time frame, a review of the treatment plan is completed by the new counselor. Each inmate, depending on his or her mental health level designation, is seen by their mental health counselor for private sessions either once or twice monthly to provide counseling and to discuss the treatment plan. It is the counselor's responsibility to make sure the inmate sees the psychiatrist as scheduled and during emergencies. To meet the needs of increased programming, all counseling staff are required to develop and run psychoeducational groups.

Upon approaching prison release, all mental health counselors are required to make mental health appointments for the inmates with their local community service board in the county where they will be released. This case management effort is to ensure continuity of care and to provide departing inmates with resources in their community. In Georgia, community service boards are responsible for providing mental health care for each county. When inmates are discharged, they leave the prison with a 30-day supply of medication and an appointment in their community within two weeks of their arrival home. While no data has been analyzed on the effectiveness of this reentry planning, it is a positive action that works to benefit the inmates upon discharge.

Reentry and Community Treatment

Individuals released from prison or jail face a range of barriers that hinder reintegration back into the community. Five key challenges that they face are employability, housing, physical health, mental health, and substance abuse issues. Employability is a crucial hurdle that former prisoners face because of low educational attainment, unemployment history, lack of work experience, and the stigma of having a criminal record. Housing also is challenging to secure because of the lack of affordable housing, laws preventing people from living in public housing, and relationship strain preventing an individual from living with family or friends. Physical and mental health issues, along with substance abuse issues, are additional barriers. Obtaining treatment for these conditions is often a challenge. People who receive treatment on the inside and continue to do so after release are far more likely to be successful in integration than those who do not; however, not everyone with the need for treatment receives it while incarcerated (Travis, Solomon, & Waul, 2001).

Research on mentally ill returning prisoners indicates that this population experiences a greater degree of challenges reintegrating back into the community. In a longitudinal study conducted by the Urban Institute returning prisoners from Ohio and Texas were surveyed on their postprison experiences (Mallik-Kane & Visher, 2008). This report highlighted the issues specific to those with mental health conditions. Of the recently released prisoners surveyed, 19% of men and 45% of women reported a diagnosed mental health condition within three months of their release. About two-thirds of these participants also had a physical health problem, and 7 in 10 reported substance abuse. Within three months of release only 46% of men and 55% of women were receiving mental health treatment. Health insurance was a common barrier to continuing mental health treatment. Only 3 in 10 men and 4 in 10 women reported having health insurance within three months of release. Regardless of health insurance, most participants received some type of health care, with one-third of participants using emergency room services (Mallik-Kane & Visher, 2008).

Returning prisoners with mental illness had greater challenges finding housing than those without mental illness. The challenges may be the result of prior homelessness (see Chapter 11 for more about the incarceration of the homeless). Returning prisoners with mental illness had greater challenges finding employment than those without mental illness. Thirty-six percent of men and 26% of women participants with a mental health issue found work within three months of release. After 10 months of release, the rates increased to 59% for men and 49% for women. Most participants with mental illness were receiving financial support from family or friends (Mallik-Kane & Visher, 2008).

When the mentally ill do receive treatment in the community after prison, they may not respond well to treatment, depending on the severity of their needs. For example, some community providers may not be able to provide the amount of structure needed to manage the person's illness in the community. Resistance to treatment and medication refusal are common barriers to treating this population (American Psychiatric Association, 2004; Torrey et al., 2014). Unaddressed substance abuse also is a barrier to successful treatment and reentry (Mallik-Kane & Visher, 2008; Prendergast, 2009).

The result of many of the barriers discussed is high recidivism rates. Recidivism rates are higher for mentally ill offenders than those without mental illness. Research on mentally ill offenders under community supervision finds they are much more likely to violate parole or probation (Messina, Burdon, Hagopian, & Prendergast, 2004; Prins & Draper, 2009), and return to prison (Casey & Rottman, 2005; Eno Louden, & Skeem, 2011). An examination of homeless shelter users in New York City revealed individuals involved with the mental health system had higher rates of recidivism than those without mental health system involvement (Metraux & Culhane, 2004). To circumvent the barriers to reentry and the high recidivism rates, community-based mental health treatment options grounded in empirical evidence should be utilized.

Assertive Community Treatment (ACT)

One of the most effective community mental health programs is Assertive Community Treatment (ACT). This program was established by the Wisconsin Mendota Mental Health Institute in the 1970s (Phillips et al., 2001). ACT was developed to reduce the arrest and hospitalization among criminal justice-involved people. The idea was to develop a way to help people with mental illness live a stable life in the community (Phillips et al., 2001). ACT provides 24-hour comprehensive and coordinated services to people with serious mental illness. These services include assessment, mental health and drug treatment, health education and care, case management, employment, and education and housing assistance (Case Western Reserve University, 2011). ACT uses a team-based approach to treatment and employs professionals with backgrounds in psychiatry, nursing, substance abuse treatment, and social work. Staff are assigned a small caseload of 10 clients to ensure intensive treatment is provided (Phillips et al., 2001). Research finds ACT greatly reduces psychiatric hospitalizations and increases housing stability more so than other types of case management services (Phillips et al., 2001).

Other Community Treatment Options

There are many other community-based programs for criminal justice-involved clients. The following evidence-based programs and practices are intended to be provided in the community for individuals with mental health and co-occurring disorders (Blandford & Osher, 2013):

- Forensic Assertive Community Treatment (FACT) is a program design based on the ACT model but adapted specifically for people involved in the criminal justice system. This program should target those with mental health issues or co-occurring mental health and substance abuse problems.
- Integrated Mental Health and Substance Abuse Services uses a single service provider as the sole source of providing treatment and recovery services to people with co-occurring mental health and substance abuse conditions.
- Illness Management and Recovery (IMR) is a program that teaches mentally ill persons techniques to reduce the interference of their symptoms on daily functioning.

- Psychopharmacology is used when medication is the appropriate response for people with serious mental health disorders. Use of medication may reduce symptoms of mental health problem by targeting specific brain chemicals.
- Cognitive-behavioral therapy (CBT) is a popular program used with mental health and substance abuse clients. The program focuses on problem solving, decision making, anger management, and other thought processes.
- Modified therapeutic community (MTC) is a program used with people who have co-occurring mental health and substance abuse disorders. This program follows the traditional therapeutic community model but allows for greater flexibility and individualization and is less intense.
- Supported employment gives job opportunities to mentally ill individuals who are able to work, an evidence-based practice that involves job training based on an individuals' skill and ability and matching them with a job appropriate to their skill set.
- Supported housing is a program designed to help mentally ill persons live independently with assistance from case managers and peers. Support services are provided and include crisis intervention, relapse prevention, mental health treatment, substance abuse treatment, and employment assistance.

Conclusion

The public health policy to deinstitutionalize mental health institutions in the United States resulted in an increase of criminalization of that population. Incarceration of the mentally ill has become the new normal in America. The place to receive mental health treatment overwhelmingly became the burden of our local jail or state prison systems. Unfortunately, the role of the criminal justice system has not changed to meet the demands of this population. The need for greater access for the "new mental health system" has a long road ahead to reformation. This reformation starts with the increased availability of treatment services for the mentally ill in the community.

Over the past decade we have seen some shifts in treatment availability and access. The increase in mental health courts in many states has been a positive intervention to divert the mentally ill from the formal criminal justice system. More recently, the 2010 passage of the Patient Protection and Affordable Care Act (ACA) has allowed for criminal justice-involved people to be eligible for mental health and substance abuse services through Medicaid eligibility and other federally subsidized health care programs (Blandford & Osher, 2013). This act was designed to ensure that people with mental health issues get treatment after release from incarceration.

The multiple state lawsuits filed in courts across the country also have resulted in a shift in correctional and public health policy. The unwavering recognition that correctional systems are ill-equipped to address the need of the mentally ill has resulted in the development of a range of best practices. Those practices, discussed in this chapter, are being implemented and evaluated to ensure they work to meet the needs of mentally ill offenders. As more research and evaluations are conducted, many more states will be able to make the necessary changes to improve the delivery of mental health care to criminal justice-involved clients.

References

AbuDagga, A., Wolfe, S., Carome, M., Phatdouang, A., & Torrey, E. F. (2016). *Individuals with serious mental illness in county jails: A survey of jail staff's perspectives*. Washington, DC: Public Citizen's Health Research Group and The Treatment Advocacy Center.

Adams, K., & Ferrandino, J. (2008). Managing mentally ill inmates in prison. *Criminal Justice and Behavior, 35*(8), 913–927. doi:10.1177/0093854808318624

Alabama Department of Corrections. (2013). *Bullock Correctional Facility*. Montgomery, AL: Alabama Department of Corrections Website.

American Jail Association. (2007). *Who's Who in jail management* (5th ed.). Hagerstown, MD: American Jail Association.

American Psychiatric Association. (2004). *Mental illness and the criminal justice system: Redirecting resources toward treatment, not containment.* Arlington, VA: American Psychiatric Association.

Case Western Reserve University. (2011). *Assertive community treatment* [Online]. Cleveland, OH: Case Western Reserve University, Center for Evidence-Based Practices.

Beck, A. J., & Maruschak, L. M. (2001). *Mental health treatment in state prisons, 2000.* Washington, DC: U.S. Department of Justice, Bureau of Justice Statistics.

Blandford, A. M., & Osher, F. (2013). *Guidelines for the successful transition of people with behavioral health disorders from jail and prison.* Delmar, NY: SAMHSA's GAINS Center for Behavioral Health and Justice Transformation.

Bloom, B., Owen, B., & Covington, S. (2003). *Gender-responsive strategies: Research, practice and guiding principles for women offenders.* Washington, DC: U.S. Department of Justice, National Institute of Corrections.

Bowring v. Godwin, 551 F.2d 44 (1977).

Brown v. Plata, 563 U.S. 493 (2011).

Carr, A. W., Rotter, M., Steinbacher, M., Green, D., Dole, T., Garcia-Mansilla, A., Goldberg, S., & Rosenfeld, B. (2006). Structured assessment of correctional adaptation (SACA), a measure of the impact of incarceration of the mentally ill in a therapeutic setting. *International Journal of Offender Therapy and Comparative Criminology, 50*(5), 570–581. doi:10.1177/0306624X06289176

Casey, P. M., & Rottman, D. B. (1995). Problem-solving courts: Models and trends. *Justice System Journal, 26*(1), 35–56. doi:10.1080/0098261X.2005.10767737

Coleman v. Brown, U.S. Dist. E.D. Cal. (1995).

Coleman v. Brown, 938 F.Supp.2d 955 (2013).

Correctional Association of New York. (2004). *Mental health in the house of corrections: A study of mental health care in the New York State prisons.* New York, NY: Correctional Association of New York.

Covington, S. S. (2002). A women's journey home: Challenges for female offenders. In J. Travis & M. Waul (Eds.), *Prisoners once removed.* Washington, DC: The Urban Institute.

Crimesolutions.gov. (2015, March). *Program profile: Mental health courts (multisite).* Washington, DC: U.S. Department of Justice, Office of Justice Programs, National Institute of Justice.

Daniel, A. E. (2007). Care of the mentally ill in prisons: Challenges and solutions. *Journal of American Academy of Psychiatry Law, 35*(4), 406–410.

Dockery et al. v. Epps, 3:13-cv-00326-TSL-JCG (*Epps et al.* 2013)

Dresser, M. (2016, June 8). With psychiatric beds full, mentally ill in Maryland are stuck in jails. *Baltimore Sun.* Baltimore, MD.

Dunn v. Thomas, US Dist. 601 (2014).

Eno Louden, J., & Skeem, J. (2011). Parolees with mental disorder: Toward evidence-based practice. *The Bulletin, 7*(1), 1–9.

Erickson, P. E., & Erickson, S. K. (2008). *Crime, punishment, and mental illness.* New Brunswick, NJ: Rutgers University Press.

Estelle v. Gamble, 429 U.S. 97 (1976).

Felix, A., Barber, C., & Lesser, M. L. (2001). Serving paroled offenders with mental illness who are homeless: Collaboration between the justice and mental health systems. (pp. 11.1–11.11). In G. Landsberg & A. Smiley (Eds.), *Forensic mental health.* Kingston, NJ: Civic Research Institute.

Fellner, J. (2006). A corrections quandary: Mental illness and prison rules. *Harvard Civil Rights—Civil Liberties Law Review, 41*, 391–412.

Fluellen v. Wetherington, N.D. GA (2002).

Frailing, K. (2010). How mental health courts function: Outcomes and observations. *International Journal of Law and Psychiatry, 33*(4), 207–213. doi:10.1016/j.ijlp.2010.06.001

Georgia Department of Corrections. (2016). *Health services.* Atlanta, GA: Georgia Department of Corrections Website.

Goss, J. R., Peterson, K., Smith, L. W., Kalb, K., & Brodey, B. B. (2002). Characteristics of suicide attempts in a large urban jail system with an established suicide prevention program. *Psychiatric Services, 53*(5), 574–579. doi:10.1176/appi.ps.53.5.574

Greenfeld, L. A., & Snell, T. L. (1999). *Women offenders.* Washington, DC: U.S. Department of Justice, Bureau of Justice Statistics.

Grella, C., Stein, J., & Greenwell, L. (2005). Associations among childhood trauma, adolescent problem behaviors, and adverse adult outcomes in substance-abusing women offenders. *Psychology of Addictive Behaviors, 19*(1), 43–53. doi:10.1177/0093854807305150

Guy, A. (2016). *Locked up and locked down: Segregation of inmates with mental illness.* Washington, DC: Amplifying Voices of Inmates with Disabilities Prison Project.

Hauseman, S. (2014, April 8). *Crisis in correctional care: Mental illness*. Roanoke, VA: WVTF, Virginia Public Radio.

Hills, H., Siegfried, C., & Ickowitz, A. (2004). *Effective prison mental health services: Guidelines to expand and improve treatment*. Washington, DC: National Institute of Corrections.

Human Rights Watch. (2015). *Callous and cruel. Use of force against inmates with mental disabilities inside U.S. jails and prisons*. New York, NY: Human Rights Watch.

Human Rights Watch. (2003). *Ill-equipped: U.S. prisons and offenders with mental illness*. New York, NY: Human Rights Watch.

James, D. J., & Glaze, L. E. (2006). *Mental health problems of prison and jail inmates*. Washington, DC: U.S. Department of Justice, Bureau of Justice Statistics.

Kerr, E. (2017, June 22). Majority of U.S. inmates don't get mental health treatment, study finds. *The Daily Beast*. Retrieved from www.thedailybeast.com/majority-of-us-inmates-dont-get-mental-health-treatment-study-finds

Kim, K., Becker-Cohen, M., & Serakos, M. (2015, March). *The processing and treatment of mentally ill persons in the criminal justice system: A scan of practice and background analysis*. Washington, DC: The Urban Institute.

Kinsella, C. (2004). *Correctional health care costs*. Lexington, KY: Council of State Governments.

Kutscher, B. (2013, August 31). Rumble over jailhouse healthcare. *Modern Healthcare (online)*.

Lamb, H. R., & Weinberger, L. E. (1999). Persons with severe mental illness in jails and prisons: A review. *Psychiatric Services, 49*(4), 483–492. doi:10.1002/yd.23320019005

Lurigio, A., Fallon, J., & Dincin, J. (2000). Helping the mentally ill in jails adjust to community life: A description of a post-release ACT and its clients. *International Journal of Offender Therapy and Comparative Criminology, 44*(5), 532–548. doi:10.1177/0306624X00445002

Mallik-Kane, K., & Visher, C. A. (2008). *Health and prisoner reentry: How physical, mental, and substance abuse conditions shape the process of reintegration*. Washington, DC: The Urban Institute.

McNiel, D., & Binder, R. (2007). Effectiveness of a mental health court in reducing criminal recidivism and violence. *American Journal of Psychiatry, 164*(9), 1395–1403. doi:10.1176/appi.ajp.2007.06101664

Messina, N., Burdon, W., Hagopian, G., & Prendergast, M. (2004). One year return to custody rates among co-disordered offenders. *Behavioral Sciences and the Law, 22*(4), 503–518.

Metraux, S., & Culhane, D. P. (2004). Homeless shelter use and reincarceration following prison release. *Criminology & Public Policy, 3*(2), 139–160. doi:10.1111/j.1745-9133.2004.tb00031.x

Metzner, J. (1993). Guidelines for psychiatric services in prisons. *Criminal Behaviour and Mental Health, 3*(4), 252–267. doi:10.1002/cmb.1993.3.4.252

Metzner, J. L., Cohen, F., Grossman, L. S., & Wettstein, R. M. (1998). Treatment in jails and prisons. (pp. 211–264). In Wettstein, R. M. (Ed.), *Treatment of offenders with mental disorders*. New York, NY: The Guilford Press.

Metzner, J. L., & Fellner, J. (2010). Solitary confinements and mental illness in U.S. Prisons: A challenge for medical ethics. *The Journal of the American Academy of Psychiatry and the Law, 38*(1), 104–108.

Owen, B., & Mobley, A. (2012). Realignment in California: Policy and research implications. *Western Criminology Review, 13*(2), 46–52.

Phillips, S. D., Burns, B. J., Edgar, E. R., Mueser, K. T., Linkins, K. W., Rosenheck, R. A., . . . McDonel Herr, E. C. (2001). Moving assertive community treatment into standard practice. *Psychiatric Services, 52*(6), 771–779. doi:10.1176/appi.ps.52.6.771

Pizarro, J., & Stenius, V. (2004). Supermax prisons: Their rise, current practices, and effects on inmates. *The Prison Journal, 84*(2), 248–264. doi:10.1177/0032885504265080

Plata v. Brown, N.D. Cal. (2001).

Prendergast, M. L. (2009). Interventions to promote successful re-entry among drug-abusing parolees. *Addiction Science & Clinical Practice, 5*(1), 4–13.

Prins, S. J., & Draper, L. (2009). *Improving outcomes for people with mental illness under community supervision: A guide to research-informed policy and practice*. New York, NY: Council of State Governments Justice Center.

Ralph v. Adams et al., N.D. GA (2004).

Ruiz v. Estelle, 503 F.Supp. 1265 (1980).

Schlanger, M. (2013). *Plata v. Brown* and realignment: Jails, prisons, courts, and politics. *Harvard Civil Rights-Civil Liberties Law Review, 48*, 165–215.

Steadman, H. J., Redlich, A., Callahan, L., Clark Robbins, P., & Vesselinov, R. (2011). Effect of mental health courts on arrests and jail days: A multisite study. *Archives of General Psychiatry, 68*(2), 167–172.

Steadman, H. J., Osher, F. C., Robbins, P.C., Case, B., & Samuels, S. (2009). Prevalence of serious mental illness among jail inmates. *Psychiatric Services, 60*(6), 761–765. doi:10.1176/ps.2009.60.6.761

Tennessee Department of Correction. (2017). *Lois M. DeBerry Special Needs Facility*. Nashville, TN. Retrieved from www.tn.gov/correction/article/tdoc-lois-deberry-special-needs-facility

Torrey, E. F. (2014, April 8). *The treatment of persons with mental illness in prisons and jails: A state survey*. Arlington, VA: The Treatment Advocacy Center.

Torrey, E. F., Kennard, A. D., Eslinger, D., Lamb, R., & Pavle, J. (2010). *More mentally ill persons are in jails and prisons than hospitals: A survey of the states.* Arlington, VA: The Treatment Advocacy Center.

Torrey, E. F., Zdanowicz, M. T., Kennard, A. D., Lamb, H. R., Eslinger, D. F., Biasotti, M. C., & Fuller, D. A. (2014). *The treatment of persons with mental illness in prisons and jails: A state survey.* Arlington, VA: The Treatment Advocacy Center.

Travis, J., Solomon, A. L., & Waul, M. (2001). *From prison to home: The dimensions and consequences of prisoner reentry.* Washington, DC: Urban Institute Justice Policy Center.

Vallas, R. (2016). *Disabled behind bars: The mass incarceration of people with disabilities in America's jails and prisons.* Washington, DC: Center for American Progress.

Vera Institute of Justice. (2011). *Los Angeles County jail overcrowding reduction project.* New York, NY: Vera Institute of Justice, Center on Sentencing and Corrections.

Virginia Department of Corrections. (2010). *Management information summary annual report year ending June 30, 2010.* Richmond, VA: Virginia Department of Corrections, The Budget Office Division of Administration.

Washington v. Harper, 494 U.S. 210 (1990).

18

SUBSTANCE ABUSE

Screening, Assessment, Planning, and Treatment

Robert D. Hanser

> Addiction is a chronic illness that needs long-term care, much like diabetes or heart disease. It changes the brain, often turning users—including those we love—into people we don't understand, trust or like. While it's tempting to think punishment is the answer, prison alone doesn't teach addicts how to change their thinking and behavior.
>
> —(Sack, 2014, para. 15)

Introduction

When discussing substance abusers as special needs offenders, it is difficult to distinguish this group from the gamut of offenders who are incarcerated or on community supervision. This is because it is estimated that perhaps around 70% or more of all offenders have some type of drug or alcohol issue. Therefore, if the majority of offenders have drug and alcohol problems, this means that it is, in many respects, not a "special need" but is a common need. However, the reason that we refer to substance abusers as special needs offenders has little to do with their numbers but more to do with the specialized knowledge and attention that is required to assist these offenders in contending with their challenges. Indeed, many criminal justice practitioners are not conversant on the various physiological aspects of addiction, which are medically relevant to providing treatment services to substance abusers.

The repeated use of addictive drugs usually, over time, changes the means by which the brain functions (National Institute on Drug Abuse, 2014). These changes affect the brain's natural inhibitory and reward centers, which induces the addicted person to continue drug use despite any health, social, or legal consequences. Further, when substance users attempt to desist from drugs or alcohol, their ability to do so can be easily undermined by stress and/or people and places that are associated with drug use, resulting in relapse. When considering drug or alcohol relapse, there are potential precursors to relapse as risk factors. Risk factors can include pressure from family and friends who continue to use drugs and/or lead a life of crime. In addition, stress and insecurity from friends who are crime prone, a lack of legitimate employment, and the need for housing can all lead to relapse.

From the research, it is clear that the human brain is affected by drug involvement, and this alone makes for long-term considerations in determining the prognosis for special needs offenders. These dynamics are what tend to lead to classifying substance abusers as special needs offenders. In response, research has shown that treatment for drug offenders can be and often is successful. This is especially true if the research is individualized to the unique drugs of choice of the offender and tailored to additional co-occurring disorders as well as life course issues that compromise the offender's recovery and ability to desist from criminal behavior.

American culture is one that is given to a high consumption of drugs, whether they are legal or illegal. The high rate of drug use obviously factors into the rate of criminal behavior, as well. To illustrate this point, consider that in 2010, over 60% of offenders in prison were drug abusers, compared to approximately 15% in the United States population that is not incarcerated (Darke, Torok, Kaye, Ross, & McKetin, 2010). When considering the connection between drug and/or alcohol abuse and criminal activity, three broad issues are evident. First, drug abusers are more likely to commit crime than non-drug abusers. Second, a large number of arrestees have been drinking or using drugs when committing criminal acts. Third, drugs and violence tend to occur together quite frequently (Hanson, Venturelli, & Fleckenstein, 2017).

Other demographics on drug abusers are not always easy to determine. Of those that exist, most are based on either arrests or on admission into detox or treatment programs. Based on data from a 2011 survey from the Substance Abuse and Mental Health Services Administration (SAMHSA), approximately 20% of Caucasians have used cocaine compared with only 10% of African Americans and 10% of Latino Americans. Likewise, higher proportions of Caucasians have used cannabis, OxyContin, and methamphetamine. While crack cocaine is used more frequently by African Americans than for Caucasians, the difference is slight. What is interesting is that while Caucasian Americans are more likely to use illegal drugs, it is the African-American population that is most likely to serve time in prison for drug offenses. Indeed, in 2011, of the 225,242 individuals incarcerated in state prison for drug use, African Americans made up 45% and Caucasians consisted of just 30% (Carson & Golineli, 2012).

Special Needs of Juvenile Substance Abusers

As is commonly understood by most correctional practitioners and scholars alike, juveniles are considered special needs categories of offenders simply because of their age, legal status, and the means by which the juvenile justice system has been developed with the youths' reformation in mind. With this said, studies have shown that, within the youth culture, over 70% of delinquent youth report some type of drug use. Further, nearly half of all juvenile detainees have been found to qualify for a DSM-V diagnosable substance use disorder (Hanson et al., 2017).

Juveniles who first enter the justice system often have a number of comorbid issues that complicate their prognosis for recovery. They tend to experience troubles with school performance, emotional instability, physiological health issues, family discord, and a history of physical neglect and/or sexual abuse (National Institute on Drug Abuse, 2014). These types of issues mean that juveniles frequently experience significant trauma, which requires effective assessment, treatment, case management, and social support. It is important for treatment to be developmentally appropriate and, ideally, gender-specific and responsive (Van Voorhis, 2005).

When juveniles are identified in the justice system as being in need of services, there are a variety of treatment options, some of which may be court-mandated. These include juvenile drug courts, community-based supervision with outpatient counseling (note that outpatient counseling will be discussed in more detail later), juvenile detention, and/or community-based reentry services. Determining the best course of treatment for juveniles often rests on how "deep" they are in the juvenile or criminal justice system.

Families can be an important influence in the recovery process for substance-abusing juveniles. However, treatment professionals should be aware that family influence can be positive (if the family is functional and adequately supervises the juvenile) or negative (if the family is dysfunctional and/or laissez-faire in providing guidance). Indeed, parental substance abuse or criminal involvement, physical or sexual abuse by family members, and lack of parental involvement or supervision are all disruptive to the youth's ability to cope and refrain from further substance abuse. Therefore, the effective treatment of juvenile substance abusers often requires a family-based treatment approach that considers family functioning as well as the potential for the increased involvement of family members.

Special Needs of Female Substance Abusers

As with juvenile offenders, the actual number of female offenders is very small in relation to adult male offenders. Nevertheless, there has been dramatic increase in the proportion of females entering prisons and jails. Indeed, during first decade of this millennia, the rate of growth of the female offender population averaged out to be about three times faster than that of the male offender population (National Institute of Drug Abuse, 2014). Since that time, the female jail population has been the fastest growing correctional population, increasing by an average annual rate of 3.4% annually (Kaeble, Glaze, Tsoutis, & Minton, 2016). Therefore, although women represent a small proportion of the correctional population, their numbers are growing faster than men. The reason that both juveniles and female offenders are considered special needs offenders is because they have "special needs." Women in prison are likely to have a different set of problems and concerns than men, presenting challenges that require gender-specific interventions.

Women in prison who present for treatment have a significantly higher likelihood of having substance abuse problems and co-occurring mental health disorders, such as depression, anxiety, and personality disorders, than do men in prison. Nearly half of all female offenders have histories of physical or sexual abuse, with women in prison having a high likelihood of being a past victim of domestic abuse (Hanser, 2017; National Coalition Against Domestic Violence, 2017; National Institute on Drug Abuse, 2014). Childhood abuse and adult victimization both are strong contributors to long-term drug or alcohol abuse, depression, posttraumatic stress disorder (PTSD), and recidivism (National Institute on Drug Abuse, 2014).

For the most part, it is thought that gender-specific programs are likely to be more effective for female substance abusers behind bars, especially for those with histories of trauma and abuse (Hanser, 2017; National Institute on Drug Abuse, 2014). Indeed, it may well be that within the field of substance abuse treatment, female offenders may need more specialized approaches that also address the underlying trauma that many female addicts seem to carry with them while serving their sentence. One example is eye movement desensitization response (EMDR). EMDR is a form of psychotherapy that stresses the importance of identifying distressing memories and traumatic life experiences and capitalizing on rapid eye movement (REM), which allows patients to reframe such memories and experiences (EMDR Institute, Inc., 2017). For example, a rape victim may experience self-loathing and self-blaming, but through the use of EMDR, the person shifts her beliefs to placing the blame where it belongs—on the perpetrator. Perez-Dandieu, Lenoir, Othily, Tapia, Cassen, and Delile (2015) examined the outcomes of symptoms for both PTSD, addiction severity, and cravings, among seven women in a treatment program in France. During the initial phases of treatment, Perez-Dandieu et al. (2015) found support for EMDR effectiveness in reducing subjective units of distress, PTSD symptoms (using the Psychopathy Check List–Sexual Trauma) as well as early maladaptive schemas. Further, schema therapy was added into the process, craving symptoms and addiction severity symptoms both decreased. These improvements were statistically significant and exceeded results on prior uses of the schema therapy approach, used alone, in prior sessions with these women.

Female offenders are more likely to need medical and mental health services, child care services, and assistance in finding housing and employment. Women with mental health disorders should receive appropriate treatment and case management, including victim services as needed (Hanser, 2017; National Institute on Drug Abuse, 2014). For female offenders with children, parental responsibilities can conflict with their ability to participate in drug treatment. Regaining or retaining custody of their children tends to be a strong motivator for most criminal justice-involved mothers to achieve and maintain sobriety. Treatment programs can improve program retention among female substance abusers by offering child care services and parenting classes (Hanser, 2017).

Special Needs of Substance Abusers with Communicable Diseases

Drug use is often associated with risky behaviors such as unsafe sex practices, needle sharing among intravenous drug users, and poor hygiene practices that can affect the offender's immune system. The criminal lifestyle that many offenders pursue prior to being incarcerated often includes a multiplicity of behaviors that increase the likelihood of contracting HIV, hepatitis, or other types of infectious diseases (National Institute on Drug Abuse, 2017a).

Drugs that are injected are associated with an increased likelihood of contracting HIV/AIDS, hepatitis, and other infectious diseases. The drugs most often used intravenously include heroin, cocaine, and methamphetamine. With heroin use, there is an increased risk of being exposed to HIV, viral hepatitis, and other infections because of contact with infected body fluids from the sharing of injection paraphernalia or unprotected sex with infected individuals. It is important to point out that if drug offenders snort or smoke the drug, this does not necessarily remove the risk of contracting a communicable disease, because people using drugs still frequently engage in risky sexual behaviors.

When considering cocaine use, research has shown that cocaine use actually accelerates the means by which HIV infection spreads throughout the individual's body (National Institute on Drug Abuse, 2017c). This is because cocaine has been found to cause damage to cells that provide immunity to disease and, at the same time, help speed-up the replication of HIV virus cells in the human body. Further, research has found that cocaine use can increase the damage done to various cells in the brain and the spinal cord (the main parts of the nervous system). Lastly, studies have also shown that cocaine aggravates impairment of neurological conditions associated with HIV infection. Symptoms related to cocaine use and communicable diseases often include memory loss, movement problems, and vision impairment.

Methamphetamine use raises the risk of contracting or transmitting HIV and hepatitis B and C—not only for individuals who inject the drug but also for non-intravenous methamphetamine users. As with heroin users, the primary means that communicable diseases are spread among methamphetamine users is through the sharing of contaminated syringes, needles, or other paraphernalia, often referred to as "rigs" among the substance abusers. Regardless of how methamphetamine is taken, it is highly likely to alter inhibitions, so that substance abusers are more prone to engage in risky behaviors. Indeed, meth use is strongly linked to a culture of risky sexual behavior, largely attributed to the fact that methamphetamine and other stimulants increase libido during the initial months of use. Indeed, this combination of intravenous use and sexual risk-taking has resulted in HIV becoming a greater problem among methamphetamine abusers than most other drug users.

Naturally, when one considers drug use and the threat of communicable diseases, the primary concern that most frequently comes to mind is the potential spread of HIV/AIDS within the offender population. This fear is a bona fide one when one considers the prevalence of AIDS is five times higher among prisoners than in the general population. While this proportion of HIV/AIDS in prisons poses a serious threat to inmates in general, research indicates that it poses an increasingly serious threat to female inmates specifically. The rate of infected women remains consistently higher than the rate of their male counterparts, with the most current data, 2010, indicating that women are infected at a rate that is approximately 36% higher than males (Center for Disease Control and Prevention, 2017).

Further, the ways in which women are frequently exposed to HIV/AIDS reflect their lack of information and education related to infection and their propensity to engage in high-risk behavior.

Women are infected through the use of intravenous drug needles and unprotected sex with infected partners. As was discussed earlier, women are more likely to suffer from drug addiction and co-occurring disorders than men, and they tend to use drugs more frequently than men prior to incarceration. This has a direct effect on the likelihood that women will engage in high-risk drug-related behavior (e.g., intravenous drug use and needle sharing), thus increasing their chances of contracting HIV/AIDS. In addition, research shows women are more likely to engage in prostitution in exchange for drugs or money to buy drugs, although many are forced into prostitution before the age of consent (Soroptimist International of the Americas, 2014).

The majority of female offenders with HIV/AIDS enter prison already having the disease. There are, however, inmates, both male and female, who are infected while under correctional supervision. This occurs as a result of engaging in high-risk behaviors while incarcerated. Studies have indicated that inmates transmit HIV/AIDS through sexual activity where inmates participate in both consensual and coerced sex (AVERT, 2017). In addition, inmates engage in illicit intravenous drug use, oftentimes sharing needles, further increasing their risk of HIV/AIDS transmission. Finally, inmates who receive tattoos while in prison increase the possibility of contracting communicable diseases, including HIV/AIDS, because of unsterile needles and inadequate protections against blood-borne transmission.

It is extremely important that offenders with sexually transmitted infections (STIs) are connected with medical programs in the community when they are released. This is for the safety and welfare of society and the infected person. If STIs are left untreated and/or untracked, the entire community is potentially at risk for further infection. It also is important to note that many special needs offenders, particularly those with serious mental health diagnoses, tend to find it challenging to obtain access to health services and adhere to complex treatment protocols following release from prison and jail. One study found that simply helping HIV-infected inmates complete the paperwork required to get their prescriptions filled upon release significantly diminished treatment interruption, although improvement was still needed, since fewer than half had filled their prescriptions within two months of release (National Institute on Drug Abuse, 2014). It is critical that community health, drug treatment, and criminal justice agencies work together to offer education, screening, counseling, prevention, and treatment programs for HIV/AIDS, hepatitis, and other infectious diseases to offenders returning to the community.

Special Needs of Elderly Substance Abusers

When discussing elderly substance abusers, it may help to first identify who is "elderly" and, from there, distinguish between offenders with long-term criminal histories and backgrounds and those who engaged in crime later in life. Typically, offenders are considered elderly once they reach 50 years of age (Aday, 2003). It is important to assess and classify elderly offenders so that one can distinguish between inmates who entered the prison system before age 50 and those who reached that age while in prison. In essence, the data should clearly and prominently note if the offender falls within the category of an elderly first-time offender, a habitual elderly offender, or an offender-turned-elderly-in-prison (Anno, Graham, Lawrence, & Shansky, 2004). This is an important security consideration that most correctional administrators will find useful when running their institution. Once the elderly offender has been appropriately classified and necessary security precautions are resolved, prison staff will then be able to ensure that the needs of these offenders are adequately met.

The rise in numbers of habitual elderly offenders and offenders-turned-elderly-in-prison has to do largely with the advent of "three strikes" felony sentencing in many states (Aday, 2003; Anno et al., 2004). These types of sentences, along with heftier drug sentences, resulted in the graying of the prison population as well as the offender population on community supervision. Indeed, these punitive sentencing measures are associated with the "War on Drugs" of the 1980s and 1990s—during this period, drug-using offenders were locked up at an all-time high, regardless of whether the crime involved violence or any form of drug trafficking (Anno et al., 2004)

Elderly First-Time Offenders

Elderly first-time offenders are those who commit their first offense later in life. It is estimated that approximately 50% of elderly inmates are first-time offenders, incarcerated when they were 60 or older (Aday, 2003; Human Rights Watch, 2012). For these offenders who commit violent crimes, these are usually crimes of passion rather than premeditated crimes. Conflicts in primary relationships appear to increase as social interactions diminish with age. Older first-time offenders often commit their offenses in a spontaneous manner that shows little planning but is instead an emotional reaction to perceived slights or disloyalties. These offenders do not typically view themselves as criminal, per se, but instead see their situation as unique and isolated from their primary identity. Their offenses will usually be directed at a family member because of proximity, if nothing else. Some experience a crisis of one sort or another because of disparity regarding the aging process, and this is also thought to instill a sense of abandonment and resentfulness that may lead to negative forms of coping.

Habitual Elderly Offenders

Habitual elderly offenders have a long history of crime and also have a prior record of imprisonment throughout their lifetime. These offenders are usually able to adjust well to prison life because they have been in and out of the environment throughout a substantial part of their life. Thus, they are well suited and adjusted to prison life. They are also a good source of support for first-time offenders and, if administrators are wise enough to implement this, are able to act as mentors for these offenders. These offenders are quite often thought of as "greyhounds" within the prison facility and command a degree of respect within the prison subculture. While they may cope well with prison life, these offenders typically have substance abuse problems and other chronic issues that make coping with life on the outside difficult. Some of these inmates are not considered violent but instead serve several shorter sentences for lesser types of property crimes and are often considered institutionalized. This is the group most likely to end up as geriatric inmates who die in prison.

Offenders-Turned-Elderly-in-Prison

Offenders-turned-elderly-in-prison have grown old while incarcerated; they have long histories in the system and are the least likely to be discipline problems. Long-term offenders are difficult to place upon release because they have few ties in the community and a limited vocational background from which to earn a living. These offenders are often afraid to leave the prison and go back to the outside world because they have become so institutionalized to the predictable schedule of the prison. When discussing substance abuse characteristics among the elderly, this group is the least likely to meet the characteristics that will be discussed. Rather, they have less access to prescription drugs and alcohol than do other elderly offenders who do not get locked up until later in life. However, even these long-term incarcerated offenders seem to find ways to obtain home-made alcohol within correctional facilities, this becoming their drug of choice in many cases.

Substance Abuse Characteristics among the Elderly

Abuse of alcohol and prescription drugs are two of the fastest growing health issues among persons 60 years of age and older. In fact, in the United States, it is estimated that approximately 2.5 million elderly individuals experience alcohol problems. Also, adults who are 65 and older are taking more prescribed and over-the-counter medications than any other age group in the nation (National Institute on Drug Abuse, 2017c). What is observed in the outside community is that prescription drug interaction with alcohol seems to be the primary presenting drug problem for elderly. While this may not be as relevant to the prison population, these factors most certainly include the elderly offender population that is not locked up but is instead on probation or parole. As was previously noted, those elderly offenders who were incarcerated late in life are also likely to have similar drug use backgrounds as those in the free world.

For the elderly, alcohol consumption can be medically dangerous even if they have not been diagnosed alcoholic. In addition, psychiatric and medical conditions that have not been detected (e.g., dementia, late-onset schizophrenia, cancer, diabetes, and heart disease) can cause, mask, or exacerbate undetected problems among elderly offenders who have substance use disorders. Because alcohol abuse is so prevalent among the elderly population in general and among the elderly offender population in particular, treatment staff should ensure that elderly persons are aware of three physiological changes that affect the way that they are affected by alcohol consumption. First, the elderly have a decrease in body water content over time, and alcohol use can lead to dehydration. Second, elderly persons develop an increased sensitivity and decreased tolerance to alcohol and therefore become intoxicated more easily. Third, there is a decrease in the rate of alcohol metabolism in the gastrointestinal tract with age. With the decreased rate of alcohol metabolizing in the gastrointestinal tract, blood alcohol levels will stay elevated for longer periods of time. This places additional strain on the liver, heart, and even cerebral tissue. This means that alcohol use can worsen any prognosis involving potential heart problems, cirrhosis and other liver diseases, and intestinal bleeding. Further, alcohol almost always contributes to and exacerbates existing rates and severity of depression, anxiety, and other mental health-related diagnoses.

The elderly, including those in prisons as well as those in the community, should be made to understand that mixing alcohol with prescription drugs can have serious health consequences. This is especially true with psychoactive medications such as Xanax, Ativan, Klonopin, and Valium (common forms of benzodiazepines) or codeine, fentanyl, Lortabs, Vicodin, or Demerol (common forms of opioid pain-killing medications). In many cases where elderly are prescribed these medications, they become physiologically dependent and are not aware that they have developed a dependency.

Prison and community corrections treatment providers should make a point to have heightened concern for elderly offenders with previous drinking problems, as this is thought to be the strongest indicator of a late-life alcohol problem, especially among men (Hanson et al., 2017; National Institute on Drug Abuse, 2014). Likewise, mood disorders should be closely tracked, as these often can exacerbate the likelihood of alcohol abuse as well as the likelihood for suicide among the elderly (Curtin, Warner, & Hedegaard, 2016). Indeed, the risk of suicide in alcoholics is 50 to 70% higher than the general population (Curtin et al., 2016). Likewise, contrary to popular belief, suicide occurs most frequently among the elderly, not the young (Curtin et al., 2016). Elderly offenders with substance use problems are more likely than are younger offenders to present with comorbid dual diagnosis. With this in mind, elderly persons with a pre-existing psychiatric disorder are at an increased risk of developing a substance use disorder with their prescribed mental health medications (National Institute of Drug Abuse, 2014).

Delirium and Dementia

Issues with dementia are a common concern when dealing with elderly substance abusers. Indeed, when elderly offenders are initially screened for substance use problems, the cognitive impairments associated with dementia can convolute the process, making it challenging to determine "which is which" when attributing observed symptoms to the correct medical issue (substance use disorder is both a medical and psychological issue, as is dementia). Clinicians conducting these assessments should have sufficient experience with the elderly population to do so effectively, but they often do not. When an elderly offender seems to be incoherent, this is often an indication the offender may have either delirium or dementia. It is especially important for clinicians to distinguish between dementia and delirium, as these can be mistaken for each other by clinicians diagnosing older patients.

Withdrawal from both licit and illicit psychoactive drugs can lead to a state of delirium, especially if a patient is removed suddenly. The National Institute on Drug Abuse (2017a) notes that while delirium is fairly rare and it is reversible, it is nonetheless dangerous to the individual's health and should always be treated as a medical emergency. When screening for delirium, looking for the following signs can be helpful (see Box 18.1).

Dementia, on the other hand, is more a chronic, progressive, and irreversible cognitive impairment (National Institute on Drug Abuse, 2014). The existence of dementia means that it will be difficult to determine if cerebral damage is more because of drinking or drug use or because of the cognitive impairment associated with the dementia. This is largely a result of individuals not being able to relay accurate information regarding their substance use because of severe memory deficits regarding their own activities. Persons with this disorder are also more difficult to get into treatment, and once they are in treatment, this disorder makes them particularly resistant to such treatment. The National Institute on Drug Abuse (2014) notes that the following are common symptoms of dementia among elderly offenders (see Box 18.2).

Substance Abuse Issues, Assessment, and Classification

Many offenders in state and federal prisons are convicted of violating drug laws. In fact, 22.4% of all federal inmates and 32.6% of all state inmates reported being under the influence of drugs or alcohol at the time they committed the offense for which they are incarcerated (Bureau of Justice Statistics, 2015). In addition, more than 83% of all state inmates and more than 73% of all federal inmates reported past drug use, with most of that past drug use occurring during the year prior to their offense (Centers for Disease Control and Prevention, 2003). The problem is compounded by the fact

Box 18.1 Signs of Delirium

1. Disorientation;
2. Impaired attention, concentration, and memory;
3. Anxiety, suspicion, and agitation;
4. Misinterpretation, illusions, or hallucinations; and
5. Delusions, speech abnormalities.

Box 18.2 Signs of Dementia

1. Impairments in short- and long-term memory, abstract thinking, and judgment;
2. Language disorder;
3. Personality change or alteration; and
4. Mood disturbances.

that substance abuse is closely related to recidivism; inmates with prior convictions are significantly more likely than first-time offenders to be regular drug users (Hanser, 2017).

Given the association between injection drug use and HIV/AIDS, detoxification also provides counseling to reduce AIDS-related risk behaviors (McNeese, Springer, & Arnold, 2002). As we have seen, drug abuse elevates the risk of contracting HIV/AIDS and other communicable diseases. This is typically associated with drug abusers who use intravenous drugs and those who engage in risky sexual behaviors, such as when prostitution and drug use are combined. In addition, many cases of mental illness in jails and prisons co-occur with substance abuse disorders. Because an effective screening, assessment, and classification process with the drug-abusing population sets the tone for everything that follows in the treatment process, it is important that we discuss the foundation process to aiding women with addiction problems.

Screening and Placement Criteria

Every form of treatment program involves some sort of screening. According to Myers and Salt (2007), screening serves two major purposes: It attests to the presence of a condition that may go unrecognized if not detected, and it provides data to decide whether a specific treatment program is appropriate for a particular client. In the first use of screening, social, health, and criminal justice workers determine if there are sufficient grounds for referral of an inmate-client to a particular drug or alcohol treatment program. This screening is extremely important because the earlier the intervention takes place, the better the prognosis for the client. Obviously, the odds of reforming a drug experimenter are much better than when treating a chronic user. The second use of screening is to determine a client's appropriateness for a given treatment modality. The discretion in placement should consider the client's individual characteristics and the ability of a given agency to provide the necessary services. For example, fiscal constraints can be a factor despite the fact that the treatment program may be ideal for the client, particularly in a community setting. In any case, it is this use of screening that provides the placement criteria for drug offenders in the criminal justice system.

The initial placement is important for both public safety and treatment-oriented concerns. When examining placement criteria, a match must be made between the severity of the addiction and the level of care needed, which can include medical inpatient care, nonmedical inpatient care, intensive outpatient care, or outpatient care (Hanson et al., 2017). Further, matching the client's profile to a treatment modality is more likely to achieve lasting success, which can translate to the enhanced evaluation of program effectiveness. For example, a client with attention-deficit/hyperactivity disorder (ADHD) might be unsuited for the regimentation of a therapeutic community. Conversely, a person with low self-esteem, insecurities, and a fragile sense of self-worth would not be appropriate for a highly confrontational style of intervention.

Goldberg (2003) notes that several questions should be asked before placing clients in treatment and that these questions should also be considered before treatment begins. According to Goldberg (2003, p. 297), these questions are:

1. Which treatment produces the best outcome for a specific group or person?
2. Do members of certain ethnic or socioeconomic groups respond similarly to certain types of treatment?
3. Is the effectiveness of a specific program linked to age of participants?
4. Do females and males differ in their response to treatment?

The matching of treatment to gender, culture, ethnicity, language, and even sexual identity and orientation has been shown to improve the odds of achieving positive outcomes in a variety of treatment settings for a variety of treatment issues (Goldberg, 2003; National Women's Health Network, 2009).

The utilization of culturally competent programs for various racial/ethnic groups should be particularly addressed given the fact that minorities represent about half of those incarcerated. Goldberg (2003) also points out the importance of addressing issues relevant to female drug offenders, specifically the need for prenatal care and treatment and the need for contact with their children. A high proportion of female offenders on community supervision (72%) are the primary caretakers of children under 18 years of age (Bloom, Owen, & Covington, 2003). Many female offenders may be initially motivated by the desire to reduce drug-related harm to their expected babies or to improve their relationship with and ability to attend to their children. This should not be overlooked, as it can be used to encourage these offenders to complete their treatment, thereby improving their chances for long-term recovery.

The main point is that treatment programming must be effectively matched to the specific inmate-client. Certain groups of inmates may also have needs that are common to that group (e.g., as based on ethnicity, age, or gender), and they may have other, more individualistic factors (e.g., divorce, domestic abuse, or childhood trauma) that may significantly affect their likelihood of success in treatment. In either event, treatment programs must rely on effective screening, assessment, and classification processes for treatment selection for inmate-clients if the treatment is expected to have successful outcomes. However, there is often a widespread tendency to place all inmates into drug treatment because substance abuse issues are so prevalent among the inmate population, with little regard for addressing the underlying issues related to drug and alcohol abuse.

The American Society of Addiction Medicine (ASAM) Criteria

It is important to understand that there are various levels of care in substance abuse treatment that depend on the level of addiction severity. A brief synopsis of each level of care is provided, but it should be noted that these have been modified for the sake of brevity and to simplify the discussion on these standards of care. There are additional characteristics that distinguish these levels of care, especially in the Level III categories. However, providing a simple broad-brush description allows readers to see that categories of treatment exist based on offender criteria, which is intended to align with the specific needs of substance abusers, as demonstrated by their service need. We now turn our attention to the Level I ASAM standard of care.

Level 1: Outpatient Services

This level of care usually entails less than nine hours of therapeutic service per week for adults. For juveniles, this standard consists of anything less than six hours per week of therapy. For both adult and juvenile offenders in this level of substance abuse treatment, therapy consists of a group session that focuses on recovery from addiction and often provides some type of motivational enhancement therapy and/or some type of cognitive-behavioral approach. Treatment planning emphasizes strategies to eliminate "triggers," which are people, places, or things that may induce the individual to relapse. This level of care encompasses organized services that may be delivered in a wide variety of settings.

Level 2: Intensive Outpatient Services (IOP)

Most people familiar with the substance abuse recovery culture simply refer to this as "IOP," without ever really distinguishing between this and routine outpatient services. This is more often true with adult programmers rather than juvenile programmers because intensive outpatient services are more frequently assigned to adults. Regardless, Level II entails nine hours or more of therapy per week (usually done in three-hour groups, three times per week) for adults. For juveniles, intensive outpatient requires six hours or more of therapy per week. This type of therapy addresses what is more commonly known as multidimensional instability by addressing six dimensions of functional recovery (see Box 18.3).

Box 18.3 Six Dimensions of Functional Recovery

Dimension 1: Acute Intoxication and/or Withdrawal Potential

Dimension 1 entails an exploration into the individual's past and present experience with substance use and withdrawal.

Dimension 2: Biomedical Conditions and Complications

Dimension 2 examines biomedical conditions and complications that include an examination of the individual's health history and current physiological fitness and conditioning.

Dimension 3: Emotional, Behavioral, or Cognitive Conditions and Complications

Dimension 3 explores an individual's thoughts, emotions, and mental health issues.

Dimension 4: Readiness to Change

Dimension 4 simply considers the individual's interest and likelihood to commit to making changes in his or her life.

Dimension 5: Relapse, Continued Use, or Continued Problem Potential

Dimension 5 aids the individual in determining triggers for relapse and/or strategizing for the elimination of triggers that can heighten the risk of continued drug use.

Dimension 6: Recovery/Living Environment

Dimension 6 examines features of the individual's total living circumstances, including home/family life, financial issues, and activities in which he or she is involved.

From the point of IOP onward through the higher ASAM levels of care, the six dimensions just provided are a central part of the treatment planning process for persons receiving therapeutic services. If a programmer first enters a residential program or medically assisted program, treatment staff will also integrate these six dimensions into the treatment planning and service delivery process. This will then be utilized later, when the individual does a "step-down" process from residential or inpatient treatment to outpatient treatment. Regardless of where a programmer begins, once they enter treatment levels beyond simple outpatient treatment, these six dimensions are included in the process. This is not to say that these six dimensions are not relevant during routine outpatient services, but it is to infer that as the level of care increases, addressing these six dimensions becomes more integral. Further, Level 2 treatment includes services that are capable of meeting the complex needs of people with substance abuse and co-occurring disorders. Many outpatient programs provide treatment services during the day, before or after work or school, in the evening, and/or on weekends. This is often important for offenders who are on community supervision, as it permits them to maintain employment, family obligations, and other responsibilities while benefitting from therapeutic services. This type of fluid scheduling is also useful for juveniles mandated to treatment, as such programs allow youth to continue attending school and allow them to remain home with families while also getting assistance to overcome the addiction that confronts them.

Level 3.1, 3.3, 3.5 & 3.7: Clinically Managed Low-to-High Intensity Residential Services

These levels of care are combined even though there are nuances and distinctions between them. For the most part, the distinctions have to do with differences in requirements for adults and juveniles (e.g., one might increase time or services for adults, but not juveniles). All of these levels of care provide a 24-hour living support and structure with available trained personnel and offers at least five hours of clinical service a week.

The gamut of the various sections of Level 3 treatment provide treatment that is described as co-occurring capable, co-occurring enhanced, and complexity capable services, which are staffed by designated addiction treatment, mental health, and general medical personnel who provide a range of services in a 24-hour supportive-living environment. When mentioning co-occurring disorders, this entails comorbidity between substance abuse (itself a DSM-V diagnosed disorder) and another mental health disorder. Most often, these disorders include major depression, bipolar depression, substance abuse induced anxiety, generalized anxiety disorder (GAD), schizophrenia, and some personality disorders (e.g., antisocial personality disorder, borderline personality disorder, and paranoid personality disorder (ASPD)). Within medium and close custody institutions, diagnoses of paranoid personality disorder tend to be disproportionately high when compared to the general population. The use of drugs simply compounds the problems these offenders have, both inside and outside penal institutions.

Level 4: Medically Managed Intensive Inpatient Services

Perhaps the primary distinction between Level 4 and other ASAM levels of care is the pervasive presence of bona fide medical staff throughout all aspects of the treatment process. Indeed, Level 4 treatment of care provides 24-hour medical monitoring that includes nursing care and physician contact once per day for those programmers who have unstable outlooks for Dimension 1: Acute Intoxication and/or Withdrawal Potential; Dimension 2: Biomedical Conditions and Complications; and/or Dimension 3: Emotional, Behavioral, or Cognitive Conditions and Complications. In addition to medical assistance, substance abuse and mental health counseling is provided to programmers as an adjunct to the medications that are provided. It is thought that the combination of medications and informed counseling can have a synergistic effect on the programmer's overall outcome.

The Therapeutic Community

Another form of intensive inpatient services is the residential therapeutic community, which may be used either with offenders who are in jail or prison or those who are on community supervision. The therapeutic community operates from a perspective that substance abuse is a disorder that impacts multiple aspects of the whole person. In other words, drug abuse is seen as a symptom of underlying problems in the person's life. This view of recovery aims to change negative patterns of behavior, thinking, and feeling that tend to lead to substance abuse. Most often, this is done through a combination of rewards (reinforcements) and consequences (lack of reinforcement or punishment), where residents hold one another as mutually responsible for their work in recovery. While staff will tend to lead the process and ensure that residents are appropriately working toward the treatment goals of the program, it is the constant immersion within the recovery culture whereby participants hold one another responsible that makes the experience more intense. Naturally, both individual and group counseling are provided by treatment staff, along with a number of psychoeducational courses on a variety of topics that are related to the offender's return to society in a drug-free lifestyle.

Drug Treatment in the Community

There are numerous approaches to assisting substance abuse offenders in the community. Some of these may be mandated, whereas others may be completely voluntary. Next is a discussion of drug courts and other community-based interventions for substance abusers.

Drug Courts and Substance Abuse Offenders

The most common feature of drug courts is the integration of both substance abuse treatment staff and criminal justice professionals such as probation officers, courtroom hearing officers, and caseworkers, who collectively meet and work under a judge. These professionals will meet on a routine basis to discuss the progress of offenders in the program. In addition to the therapeutic element, this type of programming emphasizes strict supervision of offenders, especially during the early stages of participation, along with routine and frequent drug testing. Though these types of programs are considered therapeutic in approach, they are also intended to make case dispositions of drug offenders quicker so as to expedite dockets at the courthouse.

Marlowe (2010) provides one of the best overviews of drug courts and describes the five key components of an effective drug court (see Box 18.4).

Research indicates that drug courts that maintain fidelity to these components are those that tend to be the most successful (Mitchell, Wilson, Eggers, and MacKenzie, 2012). This is particularly true when treatment is focused on high-risk addicted substance abuse offenders. The role of the judge is crucial in a drug court. Judges are free to openly chastise or praise clients for their behavior during the courtroom proceedings. Beyond that, judges may issue court orders requiring that a client attend treatment, submit to urinalysis, seek employment, meet with a probation officer, avoid associations with drug-abusing friends, or any other condition that seems appropriate (McNeese, Springer, & Arnold, 2002). Failure to comply with these judicial requirements or orders may place offenders in contempt of court, in jail, or they may be transferred to a regular criminal court. Judges are provided with continuous feedback on the offender's performance by the other drug court participants. Because of this, there is little room for the offender to evade accountability within the program.

Other Community-Based Treatment

Most substance abuse offenders on probation are placed in outpatient treatment programs (identified as either Level 1: Outpatient Services or Level 2: Intensive Outpatient Services, by ASAM criteria), which most often include individual and group therapy, as well as family therapy and relapse prevention support. An increasing number of drug-free outpatient treatment programs are including case management services as an adjunct to counseling. The basic case management approach is to assist

Box 18.4 Five Key Components of an Effective Drug Court

1. A multidisciplinary team approach;
2. An ongoing schedule of judicial status hearings;
3. Weekly drug testing;
4. Contingent sanctions and incentives; and
5. A standardized regiment of substance abuse treatment.

clients in obtaining needed services in a timely and coordinated manner. The key components of the approach are assessing, planning, linking, monitoring, and advocating for clients within the existing nexus of treatment and social services. Outpatient treatment is the most common form of treatment with substance-abusing offenders. As we discussed earlier, these types of programs are structured treatment settings in which the client participates multiple days throughout the week. This broad category of intensive outpatient treatment may include programs that are more commonly called day treatment or, in a medical setting, partial hospitalization. Offenders who participant in IOPs are allowed to remain living at home, in a therapeutic or long-term residence of some sort, or in apartment dwellings as part of a special program of comprehensive treatment (McNeese, Springer, & Arnold, 2002). All of the components of rehabilitative treatment are usually provided, including counseling (individual, group, and family), treatment planning, crisis management, medication management, client education, and self-help programs.

Self-Help Groups

Self-help groups, also known as 12-step programs, are composed of individuals who meet regularly to stabilize and facilitate their recovery from substance abuse. The best known is Alcoholics Anonymous (AA), in which sobriety is based on fellowship and adhering to the 12 steps of recovery (Hanson et al., 2017). The 12 steps stress faith, confession of wrongdoing, and passivity in the hands of a "higher power." The steps move group members from a statement of powerlessness over drugs and alcohol to a resolution that they will carry the message of help to others and will practice the AA principles in all affairs (see Box 18.5: AA Twelve Steps). In addition to AA, other popular self-help 12-step groups are Narcotics Anonymous, Cocaine Anonymous, and Drugs Anonymous (Hanson et al., 2017). All these organizations operate as stand-alone fellowship programs but are also used as adjuncts to other modalities. Overall, evaluative research has shown these types of interventions to be complimentary to other drug treatment services with a diverse array of clientele.

Box 18.5 AA Twelve Steps

1. We admitted we were powerless over alcohol—that our lives had become unmanageable.
2. Came to believe that a Power greater than ourselves could restore us to sanity.
3. Made a decision to turn our will and our lives over to the care of God *as we understood Him.*
4. Made a searching and fearless moral inventory of ourselves.
5. Admitted to God, to ourselves, and to another human being the exact nature of our wrongs.
6. Were entirely ready to have God remove all these defects of character.
7. Humbly asked Him to remove our shortcomings.
8. Made a list of all persons we had harmed, and became willing to make amends to them all.
9. Made direct amends to such people wherever possible, except when to do so would injure them or others.
10. Continued to take personal inventory, and when we were wrong, promptly admitted it.
11. Sought through prayer and meditation to improve our conscious contact with God as we understood Him, praying only for knowledge of His will for us and the power to carry that out.
12. Having had a spiritual awakening as the result of these steps, we tried to carry this message to alcoholics, and to practice these principles in all our affairs.

Special Needs of Substance Abusers with Co-Occurring Disorders

Closely related to substance use and abuse problems are co-occurring disorders. A co-occurring disorder is a concept used to describe additional diagnoses possessed by an individual, aside from the primary diagnosis of substance abuse. Special needs offenders who are not only suffering from substance abuse issues but also have other psychological or emotional impairments would be considered to have co-occurring disorders. The term "co-occurring disorder" would be the appropriate concept used to describe an offender suffering from substance use in conjunction with some other common diagnosis such as anxiety or depression. In fact, it is the rare case where an offender with substance abuse issues does not also suffer from other psychological or emotional disorders. This is because, for most special needs offenders, substance use is a means of relieving or adapting to life circumstances that are uncomfortable for the individual (Hanser & Mire, 2011). Currently, there is strong movement on behalf of the federal government to address offenders suffering from co-occurring disorders. As previously stated, co-occurring disorders refer to any psychological or emotional disorder that is operating in conjunction with substance abuse. It is important to note that most offenders, once assessed, will meet necessary criteria for dual diagnosis. Dual diagnosis is a term used to describe a phenomenon whereby offenders are suffering from a substance abuse disorder in concert with a mood disorder, anxiety disorder, personality disorder, or a psychotic disorder (Hanser & Mire, 2011). Jail diversion programs have been identified as effective with substance abuse offenders who have co-occurring disorders (Hanser & Mire, 2011). When identified, those offenders who meet the necessary criteria are diverted from jails and placed into comprehensive community service programs aimed at treating the offenders' disorders. The rationale for jail diversion programs rests on the notion that, if offenders suffering from co-occurring disorders are not adequately treated, they will be likely to act in ways that bring them back into contact with the criminal justice system. In other words, if we do not address the co-occurring disorder, then we should expect the offender to relapse and to recidivate, once again ending up in jail or prison (Hanser & Mire, 2011). Currently, most state correctional systems are operating at or above full capacity. Many of the offenders in these systems are offenders who have drug problems coupled with co-occurring disorders. In order to alleviate this problem, we must use all available resources available to treat offenders suffering from co-occurring disorders. This is, perhaps, our greatest means of promoting crime prevention, by reducing the severity of drug and mental health disruptions in the lives of offenders, thereby optimizing their chances of obtaining a productive legal lifestyle. It is common knowledge that recidivism rates are closely related to substance abuse, while rates of recidivism for offenders with co-occurring disorders are even higher. Thus, it simply stands to reason that smart crime prevention policy would include a robust substance abuse and mental health treatment agenda.

Conclusion

Substance abuse issues are common among the offender population. Substance abusers require services that are designed specifically to address addiction and recovery. In addition, different types of offenders are, because of issues specific to their circumstances, in need of drug treatment services that are tailored to and designed for their own specific needs. This approach is required if we are to optimize our treatment services to these offender populations. Further, there are numerous approaches to meeting treatment needs of the substance-abusing offender population. These approaches are usually based on the level of addiction severity of the offender, with the American Society of Addiction Medicine generating specific levels of care based on presenting symptoms of drug users. Aside from the level of care, ranging from detoxification to medically managed intensive inpatient services, there are different types of programming that are available within the criminal justice system, including therapeutic communities, drug courts, and jail diversion programs.

Likewise, it is important to acknowledge and address the plethora of additional disorders that also occur in tandem with substance abuse. These other mental health disorders are important enough to warrant clinical attention in their own right. A failure to address these disorders all but ensures that the individual will relapse and recidivate. If we are to truly lower recidivism and, in the process, lower rates of crime, we must address both these disorders as well as the primary diagnosis of substance use disorder with which these offenders present.

References

Aday, R. H. (2003). *Aging prisoners: Crisis in American corrections*. Westport, CT: Praeger.

Alcoholics Anonymous. (2017). *The twelve steps illustrated*. Retrieved from www.aa.org/assets/en_US/aa-literature/p-55-twelve-steps-illustrated

Anno, B. J., Graham, C., Lawrence, J. E., & Shansky, R. (2004). *Correctional health care: Addressing the needs of elderly, chronically ill, and terminally ill inmates*. Washington, DC: National Institute of Corrections.

AVERT. (2017). *Prisoners, HIV, and AIDS*. Brighton, UK: Averting, HIV, and AIDS.

Bloom, B., Owen, B., & Covington, S. (2003). *Gender-responsive strategies: Research practice and guiding principles for women offenders*. Washington, DC: U.S. Department of Justice, National Institute of Corrections.

Bureau of Justice Statistics. (2015). *Drug offenders in feral prison: Estimates of characteristics based on linked data*. Washington, DC: U.S. Department of Justice, Bureau of Justice Statistics.

Carson, E. A., & Golineli, D. (2012). *Prisoners in 2012: Advance counts*. Washington, DC: Bureau of Justice Statistics.

Center for Disease Control and Prevention. (2003). *Prevention and control of infectious inmates with hepatitis viruses in correctional settings*. MMWR, 52, ((No. RR-1), 1–30. Atlanta, GA: Center for Disease Control and Prevention.

Center for Disease Control and Prevention. (2017). *HIV in the United States: At a glance*. Atlanta, GA: Center for Disease Control and Prevention.

Curtin, S. C., Warner, M., & Hedegaard, H. (2016). *Increase in Suicide in the United States, 1999–2014*. Atlanta, GA: Centers for Disease Control. Retrieved from: www.cdc.gov/nchs/products/databriefs/db241.htm

Darke, S., Torok, M., Kaye, S., Ross, J., & McKetin, R. (2010). Comparative rates of violent crime among regular methamphetamine and opioid users. *Offending and victimization. Addiction, 105*(5), 916–919. doi:10.1111/j.1360-0443.2009.02872.x

EMDR Institute, Inc. (2017). *What is EMDR?* Watsonville, CA: EMDR Institute, Inc. Retrieved from www.emdr.com/what-is-emdr/

Goldberg, R. (2003). *Drugs across the spectrum* (4th ed.). Belmont, CA: Wadsworth.

Hanser, R. D. (2017). *Introduction to corrections* (2nd ed.). Thousand Oaks, CA: Sage Publications.

Hanser, R. D., & Mire, S. (2011). *Correctional counseling*. Upper Saddle River, NJ: Prentice Hall.

Hanson, G. R., Venturelli, P. J., & Fleckenstein, A. E. (2017). *Drugs and society* (13th ed.). Burlington, MA: Jones & Bartlett Learning.

Human Rights Watch. (2012). *Old behind bars: The aging prison population in the United States*. New York, NY: Human Rights Watch.

Kaeble, D., Glaze, L., Tsoutis, A., & Minton, T. (2016). *Correctional populations in the United States, 2014*. Washington, DC: Bureau of Justice Statistics.

Marlowe, D. B. (2010). *Research update on adult drug courts*. Washington, DC: National Association of Drug Court Professionals.

McNeese, C. A., Springer, D. W., & Arnold, E. M. (2002). Treating substance abuse disorders. In J. B. Ashford, B. D. Sales, & W. H. Reid (Ed.), *Treating adult and juvenile offenders with special needs* (pp. 131–170). Washington, DC: American Psychological Association.

Mitchell, O., Wilson, D. B., Eggers, A., & MacKenzie, D. L. (2012). Assessing the effectiveness of drug courts on recidivism: A meta-analytic review of traditional and non-traditional drug courts.) *Journal of Criminal Justice, 40*, 60–71. doi:10.1016/j.crimjus.2011.11.009

Myers, P. L., & Salt, N. R. (2007). *Becoming an addictions counselor: A comprehensive text*. Sudbury, MA: Jones & Bartlett.

National Coalition Against Domestic Violence. (2017). *National Statistics Domestic Violence Fact Sheet*. Denver, CO: National Coalition Against Domestic Violence. Retrieved from http://ncadv.org/images/Domestic%20Violence.pdf

National Institute of Drug Abuse. (2014). *Principles of drug abuse treatment for criminal justice populations—a research-based guide*. Washington, DC: NIDA.

National Institute of Drug Abuse. (2017a). *Health consequences of drug misuse*. Washington, DC: NIDA.

National Institute of Drug Abuse. (2017b). *Misuse of drugs*. Washington, DC: NIDA.

National Institute of Drug Abuse. (2017c). *Why are cocaine users at risk for contracting HIV/AIDS and hepatitis?* Washington, DC: NIDA.

National Women's Health Network. (2009). *Transgender youth: Providing medical treatment for a misunderstood population*. Washington, DC: National Women's Health Network.

Perez-Dandieu, B., Lenoir, H., Othily, E., Tapia, G., Cassen, M., & Delile, J. M. (2015). The impact of eye movement desensitization and reprocessing and schema therapy on addiction severity among a sample of French women suffering from PTSD and SUD. *Drug & Alcohol Dependence*, *146*, e68–e69. doi:10.1016/j.drugalcdep.2014.09.555

Sack, D. (2014, August 14). We can't afford to ignore drug addiction in prison. *The Washington Post*. Retrieved from www.washingtonpost.com/news/to-your-health/wp/2014/08/14/we-cant-afford-to-ignore-drug-addiction-in-prison/?utm_term=.25ae596a5bd9

Soroptimist International of the Americas. (2014). *Prostitution is not a choice: Soroptimist white paper*. Philadelphia, PA: Soroptimist International of the Americas.

Van Voorhis, P. (2005). Classification of women offenders: Gender-responsive approaches to risk/needs assessment. *Community Corrections Report*. *12*(2), 19–20, 26–27. doi:10.1.1.590.9163&rep=rep1&type=pdf

19

OFFENDERS WITH CO-OCCURRING DISORDERS

Mental Health and Substance Abuse Treatment

Jerrod Brown, Jeffrey Haun, and Anthony Wartnik

> The overrepresentation of persons with COD in the justice system is not a new phenomenon, and despite innovative community efforts to divert persons with mental and/or addictive disorders from jail and prison, it remains a significant issue of concern to policy makers, providers, and families. Persons with COD are a heterogeneous group with complex strengths, needs, and risks.
>
> —(Osher, 2013, p. 3)

Introduction

In 2015, approximately 8.9 million American adults met the diagnostic criteria for both mental health and substance use disorders (Substance Abuse and Mental Health Services Administration [SAMHSA], 2015). This combination of diagnoses is commonly referred to as comorbidity, dual diagnosis, or co-occurring disorders (CODs) (Center for Substance Abuse Treatment, 2005a, 2005b). CODs likely have common sources of etiology, risk factors, and short- and long-term outcomes (Scott, Dennis, & Lurigio, 2015), but the classification of CODs requires the independent diagnosis of both a mental health disorder and a substance use disorder (SUD) (Center for Substance Abuse Treatment, 2005a, 2005b; SAMHSA, 2002). Although approximately 20% of adults with a serious mental illness have a co-occurring substance use disorder, over half (55%) of these individuals will go untreated, and only 7.4% will undergo treatment for both of their CODs (SAMHSA, 2015). This is troubling because the symptoms of serious mental illness not only increase the risk of substance use, but substance use can exacerbate the symptoms of serious mental illness and decrease global functioning (Drake, Mueser, Brunette, & McHugo, 2004). The phenomenon of CODs is particularly salient because these individuals often require intensive and expensive treatment and can inflict a substantial financial burden on themselves, family members, and society (Sacks, Melnick, & Grella, 2008).

CODs often come with a complex web of adverse mental health and other long-term outcomes (Ogloff, Talevski, Lemphers, Wood, & Simmons, 2015). Not only are individuals with CODs predisposed to psychosis (e.g., hallucinations and delusions) and mood (e.g., depression and mania) symptoms, but higher rates of self-harm and suicidality has been observed relative to those without CODs (Carrà, Bartoli, Crocamo, Brady, & Clerici, 2014). These comorbid symptoms are often accompanied by lower global functioning and frequent psychiatric hospitalizations

(Peters, Bartoi, & Sherman, 2008). However, the negative outcomes that characterize individuals with CODs are not just psychological and psychiatric in nature. Relative to the general population, individuals with CODs also are more likely to lack adequate social and financial resources and be undereducated, unemployed, and homeless (Mueser, Noordsy, Drake, & Fox, 2003; Peters, Kremling, Bekman, & Caudy, 2012). In total, individuals with CODs are likely to encounter disadvantageous mental, medical, social, and legal conditions (Chan, Dennis, & Funk, 2008; Mueser et al., 2003).

The presence of co-occurring mental health and substance use disorders increases the complexity and difficulty of treatment (Hättenschwiler, Rüesch, & Modestin, 2001). Individuals with CODs are more likely to suffer from recurring episodes of mental illness (e.g., psychosis, mania, and depression) and present with multiple mental health disorders and co-occurring medical issues (e.g., sleep-related problems) than persons without co-occurring disorders (Chan, Dennis, & Funk, 2008; Mueser et al., 2003). Not only do these interconnected symptoms of psychopathology complicate the assessment process, but also the presence of CODs decreases the likelihood of treatment completion, medication compliance, and long-term stability (Dennison, 2005; Peters et al., 2008; Peters, LaVasseur, & Chandler, 2004). To improve the long-term prognosis of individuals with CODs, resource intensive integrated treatment services that address both mental health and substance use issues are necessary (Chandler, Peters, Field, & Juliano-Bult, 2004; Lurigio, 2011; National Institute on Drug Abuse [NDIA], 2010). Unfortunately, because such services are costly and resource intensive, their availability in community and institutional settings is typically limited (Peters, Wexler, & Lurigio, 2015).

Individuals with CODs are disproportionally represented in the U.S. criminal justice system. It has been estimated that as many as half of all offenders serving a sentence within confined settings have a substance use-related disorder (Chandler, Fletcher, & Volkow, 2009; National GAINS Center, 2004). Equally concerning are rates of serious mental illness among offender populations. Relative to noncriminal justice-involved populations, the likelihood of serious mental illness is four to six times greater within jails and three to four times greater in prison (Prins, 2014; Steadman, Osher, Robbins, Case, & Samuels, 2009). This has effectively turned the criminal justice system into the largest mental health provider in the United States. For example, America's largest mental health care facility is the Cook County Jail in Chicago, Illinois (Ford, 2015). Complicating matters, the presence of co-occurring disorders makes it difficult for suspects, defendants, and offenders to navigate the various stages of the criminal justice system (e.g., arrest, interrogation, trial, confinement, and community supervision) (Balyakina et al., 2014; McCabe et al., 2012). Further, offenders with CODs are likely to remain incarcerated for longer periods of time and return to custody after release (Bureau of Justice Statistics, 2006; Council of State Governments, 2012; Houser & Welsh, 2014; Messina, Burdon, Hagopian, & Prendergast, 2004). Exacerbating these issues is the fact that offenders with CODs commonly go undiagnosed or do not receive adequate integrated treatment, which decreases the likelihood of successful reentry (Peters & Petrila, 2004). Going forward, increased collaboration across the criminal justice and mental health systems is necessary to provide offenders with CODs the integrated and seamless care that can ultimately reduce recidivism and improve outcomes for offenders (Ogloff et al., 2015; Ogloff, Davis, Rivers, & Ross, 2007).

The purpose of this chapter is to explore issues related to offenders with co-occurring disorders who are involved in the criminal justice system. Specifically, this chapter will examine relevant empirical research and discuss the impact these disorders have on correctional and forensic settings. In addition, this chapter will present an analysis of the literature pertaining to female and juvenile COD offenders. The chapter will conclude with screening suggestions that are appropriate for offenders with co-occurring disorders and review established intervention strategies.

Exploring the Relationship between Co-occurring Disorders and Crime

The presence of co-occurring disorders may increase the likelihood of an individual to become criminal justice-involved for a variety of reasons, including offending behaviors (Balyakina et al., 2014; Bennett et al., 2011; McCabe et al., 2012; Messina, Burdon, Hagopian, & Prendergast, 2004; Wilson, Draine, Hadley, Metraux, & Evans, 2011). However, the relationship between CODs and crime is less straightforward. This process may be partially explained by both poor policy decisions and mental health symptomatology. An examination of policy decisions can help illuminate the reasons for the disproportionate presence of individuals with CODs in the U.S. criminal justice system. These policy decisions date back to the mid-twentieth century, when mental hospitals were systematically downsized and defunded. Accompanying these fiscal decisions, more restrictive civil commitment criteria was adopted in many places, while community treatment services remained inadequate. As a result, the default mental health care provider became the criminal justice system. Since the 1980s, the "War on Drugs" has exacerbated this issue with mandatory minimum sentences for drug-related crimes, which are often committed by individuals with substance use problems (Osher, 2013).

A wealth of research suggests that serious mental health symptoms (e.g., psychosis, depression, and mania) are weak predictors of violence and other criminal behavior (Short, Thomas, Mullen, & Ogloff, 2013; Skeem, Kennealy, Monahan, Peterson, & Appelbaum, 2016). In contrast, substance use issues are a much stronger risk factor for violent and criminal behavior than serious mental health symptoms (Wright, Gournay, Glorney, & Thornicroft, 2002). The likelihood of such antisocial acts could be increased by acute intoxication, withdrawal symptoms, or long-term dependency issues (Swanson et al., 2008). In the case of intoxication, the consumption of a substance could decrease an individual's inhibitory control, resulting in uncharacteristic behavior such as violence and other criminal behavior (Giancola, 2004). Despite the stronger relationship between substance use and antisocial behavior, some research suggests that the presence of both a serious mental illness and a substance use disorder may interact to render a risk for violence and other criminal behavior that is higher than the risk conferred by either disorder alone (e.g., Elbogen & Johnson, 2009; Fazel, Gulati, Linsell, Geddes, & Grann, 2009; Short et al., 2013). The risk for violence and other criminal behavior may be increased by the presence of other risk factors (e.g., antisocial attitudes, antisocial peers, poor employment, and low educational attainment) that are common among individuals with serious mental illness (Morgan, Fisher, Duan, Mandracchia, & Murray, 2010; Osher, 2013; Skeem, Winter, Kennealy, Louden, & Tatar, 2014). To decrease the persistence of such violent and criminal behavior and prolonged involvement in the criminal justice system, offenders with CODs must be accurately assessed and provided with integrated treatment that addresses their varied and complex symptomatology and treatment needs (Ogloff et al., 2015).

To date, much of the empirical research has focused on the links between CODs and antisocial behavior in incarcerated offenders (e.g., Hartwell, 2004; Smith & Trimboli, 2010). There are at least two areas in need of further exploration before the field can advance. First, much of the research has focused on serious mental illness (e.g., schizophrenia, bipolar disorder, and major depression), but less attention has been paid to the roles of anxiety, posttraumatic stress disorder (PTSD), attention-deficit hyperactivity disorder (ADHD), and personality disorders, all of which are prevalent in criminal justice-involved individuals (Broner, Lattimore, Cowell, & Schlenger, 2002). Second, there has been limited work on the assessment and treatment of CODs in forensic mental health (Ogloff et al., 2015) and community supervision (e.g., probation and parole) settings (Baillargeon et al., 2009). The expansion of research into these realms has the potential to inform treatment that can reduce recidivism.

Correctional Settings

As discussed in detail earlier, offenders are more likely to have mental health and substance use issues than the general population (Soderstrom, 2007). Such difficulties may even be more pronounced in jails (60.5%) than state (49.2%) and federal (39.8%) prisons (James & Glaze, 2006). In light of these estimates and the fact that there were 1,382,418 state prison inmates in 2011 (Carson & Sabol, 2012), over 700,000 prisoners may suffer from a mental health issue of some kind (Blevins & Soderstrom, 2015). The presence of a mental illness with or without an accompanying substance use disorder can complicate the supervision of offenders in both institutional and community settings (Houser & Welsh, 2014; Wood, 2011). With an eye toward offenders with CODs, this section will discuss adjustment to institutional settings, institutional misconduct, assessment and treatment, reentry, and recidivism.

Institutional Adjustment

Offenders with CODs may have a difficult time adjusting to correctional facilities (Fellner, 2007; Gelman, 2007). The capacity to adapt to the policies and social structure of these facilities may be limited by symptoms of mental health and substance use disorders (Houser & Welsh, 2014; O'Keefe & Schnell, 2007) along with underdeveloped coping mechanisms, which are common among offenders with CODs (Spencer & Fallon, 2012). In fact, exposure to living conditions characterized by loss of autonomy and overcrowding frequently exacerbates symptoms of mental illness (American Psychiatric Association, 2004; Fellner, 2007; Gelman, 2007). Further, such situations could precipitate the development of new symptoms of psychotic (i.e., hallucinations and delusions) and mood (i.e., mood swings and mania) disorders (Slate, Buffington-Vollum, & Johnson, 2013). Without proper recognition and treatment, these limitations in the functioning of offenders with CODs can increase the likelihood of victimization by other inmates (e.g., sexual assault) (Blevins & Soderstrom, 2015; Blitz, Wolff, & Shi, 2008).

Institutional Misconduct

Inmates with CODs often have behavioral issues in addition to adjustment problems when incarcerated (Houser & Welsh, 2014). In other instances, inmates with CODs are more likely to engage in institutional misconduct than inmates without CODs (Houser, Belenko, & Brennan, 2012; Slate et al., 2013), including physical aggression toward other inmates and staff members (Felson, Silver, & Remster, 2012; Slate et al., 2013; Wood & Buttaro, 2013). In some instances, mental health and substance use symptoms may be misconstrued as purposeful institutional misconduct by staff members (Houser et al., 2012; Steiner & Wooldredge, 2009). This could include actions such as refusing to leave a cell, self-harming behaviors, poor hygiene, and vandalism (Adams, 1986). Related research conducted by James and Glaze (2006) found that state inmates with mental illness were more likely to engage in institutional misconduct (58% versus 43%) and be injured in a fight (20% versus 10%) than inmates without a mental illness. As such, correctional staff may need to adjust their behavioral expectations of inmates with CODs (Fellner, 2007).

The propensity of inmates with CODs for institutional misconduct places them at a greater risk for punishment and removal from the general population (Fellner, 2007; Spencer & Fallon, 2012). An overreliance on more restrictive placements such as solitary confinement or administrative segregation is commonplace (American Civil Liberties Union of Colorado, 2013; Metzner & Fellner, 2010; Winerip & Schwirtz, 2014). The use of solitary confinement has been linked to trauma and psychological deterioration for all inmates (Beven, 2005). These devastating effects are even more pronounced in inmates with serious mental illness (Arrigo & Bullock, 2008; Smith, 2006). In addition, the worsening and development of new mental health issues is likely, such as hallucinations and self-mutilation caused by the mental stress of isolation (Fellner, 2007). To make matters worse, dense histories of institutional misconduct and placements in segregation decrease the likelihood of a timely release on probation or parole (Slate et al., 2013).

Reentry and Recidivism

Even when released, offenders with CODs are likely to be confronted by persistent difficulties with the criminal justice system (Wood, 2011). The process of reentry for offenders with CODs is likely complicated by maintaining medication access and regular use, finding appropriate treatment services, avoiding substance use relapses, and obtaining adequate housing and employment (Baillargeon, Hoge, & Penn, 2010; Messina et al., 2004; Osher, 2007; Peters & Bekman, 2007). Further, offenders with serious mental illness are less likely to have strong family support systems on which to draw assistance (Feder, 1991). Further complicating matters, offenders with CODs are more likely to have difficulties complying with many of the conditions of community supervision (i.e., probation and parole). Failure to do so can result in revocation of conditional release for technical violations (e.g., missing supervision meetings and failing drug tests). When this is coupled with an elevated risk for violent and other criminal behaviors (National GAINS Center for People with Co-Occurring Disorders in the Justice System, n.d.), offenders with CODs are more likely to be reincarcerated than offenders without CODs (Messina et al., 2004).

Assessment and Treatment

Improved assessment and treatment resources are necessary to address issues with institutional adjustment, institutional misbehavior, and reentry complications (Slate et al., 2013). As it is, many offenders with CODs do not receive adequate assessment and treatment during incarceration or upon reentry (Chandler et al., 2004; Houser & Welsh, 2014; Peters & Bekman, 2007). As a starting point, the American Psychiatric Association ([APA], 2000) and the National Commission on Correctional Health Care (NCCHC, 2014) have called for all inmates to receive standardized mental health assessments during the first week of incarceration (see potential symptoms in Box 19.1). Based on these assessments, inmates with mental health and substance issues should be allocated evidence-based services and treatment. Integrated treatment services in institutions in concert with structured services

Box 19.1 Mental Health Disorder Symptoms

- Feelings of helplessness or hopelessness,
- Loss of interest in daily activities,
- Loss of appetite or weight,
- Sleep disturbances,
- Changes in energy levels,
- Feelings of worthlessness or guilt,
- Concentration problems,
- Anger, rage, or reckless behavior,
- Feelings of euphoria,
- Compulsive behavior,
- Unrealistic or grandiose beliefs,

- Starving, refusing to eat, or binging and purging,
- Feeling extremely irritable or "on edge,"
- Signs of self-injury (e.g., cutting, burns, and scars),
- Rapid speech and racing thoughts,
- Impaired judgment and impulsive behavior,
- Feeling restless and jumpy,
- Racing heart or shortness of breath, and
- Nausea, trembling, or dizziness.

Source: Braude and Miller (2011)

after release into the community may be a powerful option in addressing the needs of offenders with CODs (Houser & Welsh, 2014; Sacks, Sacks, McKendrick, Banks, & Stommel, 2004; Sacks, Chaple, Sacks, McKendrick, & Cleland, 2012). This requires staff with cross-training in both serious mental health and substance use issues (Houser & Welsh, 2014). Nonetheless, providing these costly and intensive services to offenders with CODs will not be an easy task, as this group is likely more difficult to treat in light of pervasive and long-standing struggles with mental health (Peters et al., 2008; Peters et al., 2004). Unfortunately, the last line of defense in providing these assessment and treatment services is the criminal justice system (Blevins & Soderstrom, 2015). However, advancements in assessment and treatment services have the potential to improve institutional adjustment, decrease institutional misconduct, and improve long-term outcomes after reentry into the community, all of which could render important reductions in cost and recidivism (Houser & Welsh, 2014).

Juvenile Offenders

Adolescents with co-occurring mental health and substance use issues are prone to continued involvement in the criminal justice system, as indicated by elevated rates of recidivism (Stewart & Trupin, 2003). For example, Teplin (2001) estimated that as many as two-thirds of adolescents entangled in the criminal justice system have at least one mental health or substance use disorder (Teplin, 2001). Abrantes, Hoffmann, Anton, and Estroff (2004) estimated that over 80% of adolescents involved in the criminal justice system meet the criteria for at least two mood (e.g., depression and bipolar disorder), behavioral (e.g., conduct disorder and oppositional defiant disorder), and substance dependence disorders. Others estimate that 90% of juveniles with co-occurring disorders had a diagnosable mental illness prior to the onset of their substance use issues (Kessler, Chiu, Demler, & Walters, 2005). Further, 50–75% of youth with a substance use disorder also have a comorbid mental illness (Armstrong & Costello, 2002; Chan, Dennis & Funk, 2008; Hawkins, 2009). In light of these observations, the substantial proportion of adolescents with CODs who are involved in the criminal justice system must be prioritized for intervention because symptoms of CODs can worsen, and individuals with CODs often become more entrenched in the criminal justice system (Abrantes, Hoffman, & Anton, 2005; Teplin et al., 2013; Wasserman, McReynolds, Schwalbe, Keating, & Jones, 2010).

The proneness for co-occurring mental illness and substance use disorders during adolescence may be a function of several different neurodevelopmental vulnerabilities (Cicchetti & Rogosch, 2002; Najavits, Gallop, & Weiss, 2006). First, the emergence of CODs could simply stem from the challenges and stresses inherent in transitioning between phases across various developmental domains (e.g., biological, cognitive, and social) (Cicchetti & Rogosch, 2002). Second, many youth suffer from exposure to physical and sexual abuse along with other traumatic experiences that increase the risk of mental illness and substance use (Giaconia et al., 2000; Najavits et al., 2006). Third, higher levels of individual autonomy could create more opportunities for activities such as substance use (Giaconia et al., 2000; Najavits et al., 2006). Lastly, several contextual risk factors such as family members, peers, and neighborhoods can introduce social pressure that increases the likelihood of substance use. An improved understanding of the etiological underpinnings of CODs has the potential to improve identification and inform the development of interventions.

Adolescents with co-occurring disorders place a burdensome demand on treatment providers (Grella, Joshi, & Hser, 2004), particularly in criminal justice settings. When entering treatment, youth with CODs are more likely to present with lower levels of global functioning, denser histories of antisocial behavior, higher levels of antisocial attitudes, and less responsiveness to treatment relative to youth with only a mental health or substance use disorder (Beitchman et al., 2001). As such, these severe needs necessitate comprehensive interventions with a focus on integrated treatment, which are costly and resource intensive (Bender, Springer, & Kim, 2006). Empirical research has found treatment approaches that address antisocial behavior and thinking patterns, family dynamics, peer influences, and school functioning hold the most promise for juveniles (Chassin, 2008). Several intervention programs have shown promise in treating youth with externalizing disorders (e.g., substance abuse and delinquency), including family-based therapies such as multi-systemic therapy (MT), multidimensional family therapy (MFT), and Functional Family Therapy (FFT) (Baldwin, Christian, Berkeljon, Shadish, & Bean, 2012; Von Sydow, Retzlaff, Beher, Haun, & Schweitzer, 2013). These therapeutic frameworks are system-oriented approaches that attempt to modify dysfunctional family patterns that contribute to externalizing disorders (Baldwin et al., 2012; Von Sydow et al., 2013). Such interventions tend to be most effective when delivered in community settings in concert with partnership from the courts (Trupin, 2007; Trupin, Turner, Stewart, & Wood, 2004). If interventions can prevent substance use relapse, the likelihood of antisocial behavior (Trupin, 2007; Trupin et al., 2004) and the development of other mental health issues can be decreased (Chassin, 2008).

Female Offenders

Women are one of the fastest growing populations in the criminal justice system, particularly women of color (Carson & Sabol, 2012; Federal Bureau of Investigation, 2010; Minton, 2012; Pew Center on the States, 2008). This increase in population has inspired research on gender-specific treatment for women in criminal justice settings (Bloom, Owen, Covington, & Raeder, 2002; Chesney-Lind & Pasko, 2013). Some of this research has found that traumatic experiences along with mental health and substance use issues frequently play a stronger role in criminal justice involvement for women than men (Belknap, 2001; Bloom et al., 2002). For example, criminal justice-involved women have higher incidence rates of serious mental illness (Steadman et al., 2009) and substance use (Trestman, Ford, Zhang, & Wiestbrock, 2007) issues than men. Among women in state prisons, it has been estimated over 70% have at least one mental illness diagnosis and over 60% have a documented issue with drug abuse or dependence (James & Glaze, 2006). Further, high rates of co-occurring diagnoses (54%) of serious mental illness and substance use disorders have been observed for incarcerated women in these settings (Abram, Teplin, & McClelland, 2003; Butler, Indig, Allnutt, & Mamoon, 2011; Lynch, Fritch, & Heath, 2012; Houser & Welsh, 2014; James & Glaze, 2006), all of which complicates adjustment to confined settings and community supervision (Houser & Belenko, 2015). Additional research has found that women are more likely to be jailed and imprisoned for drug- and alcohol-related offenses than men (Deschenes, Owen, & Crow, 2006). As such, a substantial number of women involved with the criminal justice system require resource intensive integrated treatment programs for co-occurring mental health and substance use disorders (Blanchette & Brown, 2006; Nowotny, Belknap, Lynch, & DeHart, 2014; Salina, Lesondak, Razzano, & Parenti, 2011).

Criminal justice-involved women often present with an array of risk factors and needs that must be considered when developing an intervention plan. First, women in the criminal justice system are disproportionately likely to have experienced physical and sexual assault (Bloom et al., 2002; Messina & Grella, 2006; Skopp, Edens, & Ruiz, 2007). Such experiences have demonstrated links to later mental illness symptoms and substance use (Bloom et al., 2002; National Institute on Drug Abuse [NIDA], 2008). Second, compared to those not in the system, women involved in the criminal justice system have greater rates of socioeconomic-related difficulty (e.g., poverty, homelessness, unemployment, and lower education) that can affect intervention and supervision (Chandler, 2009). Finally, criminal justice-involved women with CODs are prone to medical issues that may be related to their substance use (e.g. HIV/AIDS) (Belenko, Langley, Crimmins, & Chaple, 2004: Gido & Dalley, 2009). Despite this range of serious risk factors and needs, women in the criminal justice system receive fewer treatment and health services than their male counterparts (Chesney-Lind & Pasko, 2013; Eliason, Taylor, & Williams, 2004).

The varied and nuanced needs of criminal justice-involved women with CODs necessitate the availability of a battery of interventions (Salina et al., 2011). This process begins with a comprehensive assessment, which should take place at the woman's point of entry into the criminal justice system (Lynch et al., 2014). Once assessed and diagnosed, an intervention plan that includes mental health and substance use treatment considerations can be developed. Evidence suggests that the simple reliance on mental health and substance use treatment services that were designed for women without CODs will have limited effectiveness in women with CODs (Houser, Blasko, & Belenko, 2014). Further, plans built around alternatives to incarceration such as diversionary court programs (e.g., mental health and drug courts) and community supervision (i.e., probation and parole) hold promise (Lynch et al., 2014). In light of the prevalence of mental health and substance use issues, criminal justice agencies must make important considerations about the type and intensity of interventions offered to criminal justice-involved women (Belenko & Peugh, 2005; Peters et al., 2008).

Community Reintegration

Offenders with CODs have trouble readjusting to life in the community after release from jail and prison (Hartwell, 2004). Relative to offenders with only mental health or substance use disorders, offenders with CODs are at a greater risk for violence, arrest for new crimes, technical violation of community supervision (e.g., probation and parole), and return to custody (Hartwell, 2004; Messina et al., 2004). For example, in a retrospective investigation of parolees in Texas, Baillargeon and colleagues (2009) found that parolees with CODs were more likely to have their parole revoked because of a violation or a new crime in the first year of placement on parole than parolees with only a mental health or substance use disorder. These startling findings emphasize the need to understand why offenders with CODs are less successful on community supervision.

There are a number of reasons why offenders with CODs are less likely to succeed on community supervision. First, like other offenders reentering society, offenders with CODs often have issues establishing stable access to transportation, housing, and medical benefits. These difficulties may be more common among offenders with CODs, who often have difficulty maintaining a social support network (Epperson et al., 2011; Golzari, Hunt, & Anoshiravani, 2006; Peters et al., 2008). Second, the comorbid presence of mental health and substance use disorders often goes unrecognized or underdiagnosed in the criminal justice system (Peters et al,, 2008). Third, even when offenders with CODs are accurately identified, there are not many treatment programs equipped to deliver integrated treatment for mental health and substance use issues in the criminal justice system (Chandler et al., 2004). This situation may be particularly dire in community supervision agencies (Peters & Bekman, 2007), where the impact on recidivism holds the most promise (Sacks et al., 2004). In light of these barriers to reentry, offenders with CODs are at greater risk for poor treatment outcomes and reincarceration (Baillargeon et al., 2009). Additional assessment and treatment resources are necessary to assist overburdened community supervision agencies in improving the reentry success of offenders with CODs (Wood, 2011).

Screening and Assessment

The screening and assessment of offenders with CODs is a necessary first step in the development of treatment plans and providing services and treatment (Peters et al., 2008; Ruiz, Douglas, Edens, Nikolova, & Lilianfeld, 2012). The importance of this task is highlighted by the high prevalence of individuals with CODs in the criminal justice system (Peters et al., 2008; Sacks & Melnick, 2007). As such, co-occurring mental health and substance use disorders are woefully underdiagnosed in criminal justice settings (Balyakina et al., 2014). To shine light on this issue, this section reviews the current state of assessment options, highlights comorbid symptomatology that complicates any assessment, identifies warning signs that should trigger assessment, and discusses the consequences of inaccurate identification.

A major obstacle in the identification of offenders with CODs is the limited existing options for screening and assessment (Sacks & Melnick, 2007). Although there are independent tools for mental health and substance use issues, few options have been developed for the assessment of both mental health and substance use issues, particularly in criminal justice settings (Osher, Steadman, & Barr, 2003; Sacks & Melnick, 2007). The development of such instruments must overcome at least three issues. First, ensuring both adequate coverage of mental health and substance use problems but reasonable administration time is a delicate balance. The measure must index all important aspects of the intended target construct without incorporating too many items. Second, the reliability and validity of a diagnostic tool must be established in criminal justice settings. It cannot be assumed that a measure validated for use in other settings (e.g., clinical or community populations) will perform similarly in a criminal justice setting. Third, any screening and assessment instruments designed for offenders with CODs should consider the inclusion of context-specific content. This has the potential to better inform the development of treatment plans and ensure the provision of proper services and treatment (Jessup & Dibble, 2011). Once a variety of screening and assessment options have been developed, corrections staff can select the appropriate instrument for their needs based on their purpose and the resource-intensiveness of the instrument.

Besides current limitations in screening and assessment tools, there are a number of difficulties in obtaining accurate information from offenders with CODs during screening and assessment (Chandler et al., 2004; Peters et al., 2008). First, offenders with CODs may be less than forthcoming with information about their mental health and substance use issues. This may be likely when assessment instruments are rather transparent about the issues of interest, particularly when the offender believes disclosure will result in perceived negative consequences. For example, an individual may choose to minimize substance use or psychiatric problems to avoid placement in a treatment program. Second, in contrast, offenders with CODs may feign or exaggerate mental health and substance use issues if they believe this is to their advantage in sentencing or placement. Third, criminal and medical records are often incomplete or inaccurate. For instance, diagnostic information collected in the community may not be available to criminal justice professionals. As such, corrections staff members may have difficulty identifying the underlying issues of offenders with CODs (Peters et al., 2008).

The presentation of comorbid symptomatology, including serious mental illness, pervasive polysubstance use issues, personality disorders, various medical problems, and developmental disabilities, exacerbates the difficulty of screening and assessing offenders with CODs (Peters et al., 2008; Skeem et al., 2014). All of these issues vary in presence and severity across clients. One particularly prevalent issue in offenders with CODs is a history of trauma, which can have a debilitating impact on treatment participation and success when not accounted for by care providers (Hills, Siegfried, &

Ickowitz, 2004). Unfortunately, staff members of criminal justice agencies typically do not have advanced training or experience with trauma-related issues. To address these challenging issues, medical and mental health professionals must adopt a clinical approach that does not rely on any single method of assessment or treatment (Peters et al., 2008).

In criminal justice settings, it may be wise to incorporate the identification of static (unchangeable) and dynamic (changeable) risk factors in any screening and assessment battery. These risk factors typically include antisocial attitudes, thought patterns, peers, and behavioral history (Andrews, Bonta, & Wormith, 2006). This is particularly true of offenders with serious mental illness and CODs (Wilson et al., 2014), in light of emerging research on the role that these factors may play in the criminal behavior of this population (Epperson et al., 2011). Antisocial attitudes, thought patterns and peers may be of particular interest because these dynamic or changeable risk factors can be targeted with interventions (Friendship, Blud, Erikson, Travers, & Thornton, 2003). Failure to account for such criminogenic risk factors may result in ineffective interventions (Skeem et al., 2014).

To combat these identification issues, medical and mental health professionals should be aware of several red flags that can help identify offenders with CODs who may be in need of advanced screening and assessment. This includes several characteristics that may confer risk of developing comorbid mental health and substance use issues. These red flags include basic background characteristics such as gender, poor academic and work performance, and unstable home environment. Antisocial behavior may have had an early onset and resulted in repeated contacts with authorities. Substance use likely begins early, persists across time, and results in several failed treatment attempts. For example, in offenders with CODs, disentangling the presence of any psychiatric symptoms related to substance use from those related to an underlying mental illness is a major issue that exacerbates the difficulties of treating these individuals.

Mental health symptoms may include depression, anxiety, hallucinations, delusions, disorganized thought and speech patterns, impaired coordination and movement, poor judgment, and self-harm (Balyakina et al., 2014; Peters et al., 2008; Ruiz et al., 2012). Impaired memory and cognitive functioning, for example, which are inherent parts of substance use and mental health disorders, often limit the degree that offenders with CODs can be relied upon to self-report information during the diagnostic process, thus further complicating the issue of providing proper treatment. Risk of CODs increases with the presence of more characteristics (Peters et al., 2008).

The maximization of screening and assessment opportunities is imperative because of the consequences that inaccurate identification can have on offenders with CODs. For example, the failure to identify offenders with CODs could result in missed intervention opportunities, the persistence or worsening of psychopathology symptoms, limited treatment participation and completion, adverse effects of inappropriate treatment and medication, and an elevated risk for continued involvement in the criminal justice system (Chandler et al., 2004; Osher et al., 2003). To decrease the likelihood of such consequences, medical and mental health professionals in criminal justice settings should receive advanced and ongoing training in the area of co-occurring mental health and substance use disorders. Training should cover a variety of concepts, including red flags, differential diagnosis, and best practices in screening and assessment (Osher et al., 2003; Peters et al., 2008). The importance of addressing these screening and assessment issues is highlighted by the fact that these activities serve as the backbone of forming treatment plans and allocating interventions to increase the likelihood of individuals receiving adequate treatment and that they may successfully reintegrate into the community (Peters et al., 2008).

Intervention and Treatment Considerations

The costs of constitutionally mandated rights like mental health care have escalated as criminal justice populations continue to rise (*Estelle v. Gamble*, 1976; Pew Center on the States, 2008; *Ruiz v. Estelle*,

1980). Offenders with CODs are an underlying force driving this escalation in costs because they necessitate more treatment services and resources relative to other offenders (Sacks et al., 2008). For example, as many as 80% of state prison inmates who receive substance use treatment present with a co-occurring mental health issue (Sacks et al., 2007; Swartz, 2006). In half of these cases, the mental health issue can be classified as severe (Sacks et al., 2007). Troublingly, the National Comorbidity Survey indicates that less than half of individuals with CODs ever receive treatment for their disorders (Kessler, Petukhova, Sampson, Zaslavsky, & Wittchen, 2012). As such, criminal justice system-wide coordination is needed to ensure that offenders with CODs receive adequate services to address their needs (Koegl, 2008). To this end, this section highlights the importance of integrated substance use and mental health treatment, identifies several promising intervention options, discusses potential treatment barriers, and reviews the importance of individualizing assessment and intervention plans to account for the offender's unique risks and needs.

An integrated mental health and substance use treatment approach is the preferred evidence-based practice for individuals with CODs (Drake et al., 2001; Drake et al., 2004; Mueser et al., 2003). The crux of integrated treatment is that two or more conditions are treated by a single team of providers including psychologists, psychiatrists, social workers, and other human service professionals (Kelly & Daley, 2013; McKee, Harris, & Cormier, 2013). This process is enhanced by improved communication when more and more members of the treatment team work within the same facility (Kelly & Daley, 2013). Services can incorporate an array of one-on-one, group, family, and psychopharmacological treatment components (e.g., cognitive-behavioral therapy, motivational interviewing, and relapse prevention) (Center for Substance Abuse Treatment, 2005a, 2005b; Mueser et al., 2003). Such services can be delivered across custodial and community settings (Center for Substance Abuse Treatment, 2005a, 2005b). Research has established that integrated treatment leads to better long-term outcomes than disaggregated treatment services for individuals with CODs (Kelly & Daley, 2013). Despite the obvious benefits of integrated treatment, such services are costly and rare in the criminal justice system (McFarland & Gabriel, 2004). As a result, an offender with CODs is often required to obtain services from different care providers, which reduces the likelihood of treatment retention and success (Peters et al., 2004).

An integrated treatment approach can incorporate several empirically established interventions. This could include a combination of cognitive-behavioral therapy (CBT), Illness Management and Recovery (IMR), assertive community treatment, and psychopharmacological options (NIDA, 2010; Steadman et al., 2013). In criminal justice settings, such successful interventions for CODs share many key aspects, such as a high degree of structure and supervision, extended inpatient and outpatient care, strategies to increase treatment motivation and engagement, crisis and relapse prevention plans, and mental health and substance use cross-training of staff (Drake et al., 2001; Lurigio, 2011; Peters & Bekman, 2007; Peters et al., 2012). For example, the integrated dual disorder treatment model (IDDT) for substance use issues incorporates many of these key aspects, including mental health care, strategies to increase motivation and engagement, multidisciplinary treatment teams, and a customizable length of treatment services (Kola & Kruszynski, 2010). Integrated treatment programs that incorporate a selection of these diverse interventions on an individualized basis hold promise for offenders with CODs.

Although many of the interventions outlined here can be effective in an integrated treatment framework (Brunette, Mueser, & Drake, 2004; Drake et al., 2004; Dumaine, 2003), the majority of offenders with CODs do not receive adequate treatment for both mental health and substance use issues (National GAINS Center, 2004; Peters et al., 2004; Substance Abuse and Mental Health Services Administration, 2002; Watkins, Burnam, Kung, & Paddock, 2001). These treatment issues are driven at least in part by the institutional management challenges presented by offenders with CODs. However, regardless of criminal justice involvement, Watkins and colleagues (2001) reported that less than 30% of individuals with CODs received adequate treatment within the last year. Other than the limited availability of appropriate treatment options, there are several barriers that preclude offenders with CODs from receiving adequate treatment services (Druss & Mauer, 2010). Foremost among these barriers are administrative and financial obstacles (Drake & Bond, 2010; Padwa, Larkins, Crevecoeur-MacPhail, & Grella, 2013; Sterling, Chi, & Hinman, 2011; Torrey, Tepper, & Greenwold, 2011). Further, the lack of linkages between treatment services in custodial and community settings decreases the likelihood of continuous access to intervention (Taxman, Henderson, & Belenko, 2009). The situation is particularly dire in community settings such as probation and parole, where integrated treatment options are scarce (Chandler et al., 2004; Drake & Green, 2014; Lurigio, 2011). Even when available, intervention options that have the potential to make a difference are often delivered with low fidelity (Chandler, 2009). These issues are further complicated by lower treatment entry rates and underutilization of services among offenders with CODs relative to offenders with only mental illness or substance use issues (Curran et al., 2003; Messina, Burdon, Hagopian, & Prendergast, 2006). Further, offenders with CODs are more likely to present with complicating factors, such as inadequate social and family support, homelessness, and a history of self-harm and other medical issues (Chi, Satre, & Weisner, 2006; SAMHSA, 2015; Watkins et al., 2001). When not accurately identified and treated, inmates with CODs are more likely to exhibit institutional misconduct and poor treatment adherence (Center for Substance Abuse Treatment, 2005b; Houser et al., 2014). These issues that plague access to treatment for offenders with CODs beg for increased efforts to better understand and alleviate barriers to integrated treatment (Priester et al., 2016).

The incorporation of a risk management perspective of assessment may be essential in improving the screening and assessment of offenders with CODs (Koegl, 2008). Specifically, treatment programs in criminal justice settings have been perhaps most effective when incorporating an individualized focus on criminogenic risks and needs. That is, these treatment programs address risk factors that drive an offender's antisocial behavior and build on strengths that protect against antisocial behavior (Andrews & Bonta, 1998; Andrews, Bonta, & Hoge, 1990; Lowenkamp, Latessa, & Smith, 2006). Like traditional risk assessment instruments, risk management tools incorporate relatively static or unchangeable measures of criminal history such as age of first arrest, number and types of arrests, adjustment to correctional programming, and performance on community supervision (Peters et al., 2008). In contrast, risk management instruments also incorporate dynamic or changeable risk factors that can be targeted in treatment. In addition to mental health and substance use symptoms, these dynamic risk factors can include antisocial attitudes, decision making, impulsivity and other aspects of executive control, peer and family relationships, employment and housing stability, and treatment motivation and engagement (Bellack, Bennett, & Gearon, 2007; Peters et al., 2008). Specific risk factors may vary across different subgroups of offenders with CODs, such as gender and age groups. For example, female offenders with CODs may be more likely to have experienced traumatic events and experience resulting symptoms of PTSD (Sacks, 2004). The effectiveness of treatment services can only be enhanced by incorporating interventions tailored to target the individual risks and needs of offenders with CODs.

Several steps can be taken to improve the state of treatment for offenders with CODs. First, corrections agencies should prioritize integrated treatment programs for offenders with CODs. These integrated treatment programs must be composed of interventions with established efficacy in offenders with CODs. Throughout this process, fidelity to treatment programs should be verified throughout and after implementation. Second, more attention must be paid to identifying and addressing the barriers that prevent offenders with CODs from receiving the mental health and substance use treatment services that they need. Third, improved screening and assessment instruments and procedures, particularly those that emphasize individualized risks and needs, may be integral in ensuring that offenders with CODs receive the appropriate services. Together, these three key steps have the potential to decrease the likelihood of serious violence (Sacks et al., 2008) and increase

Box 19.2 Florida Department of Corrections: Programs for Co-Occurring Disorders

Co-Occurring Disorders Residential Therapeutic Community

The Co-Occurring Disorders Residential Therapeutic Community (CDRTC) is a long-term (8–12 months) residential substance abuse program for inmates who have co-occurring substance abuse and mental health disorders. A specialized therapeutic community addresses the inmates' clinical issues through daily specialized groups, which utilize psychological-educational skill development curricula, group and individual counseling, and all other elements of a therapeutic community developed specifically for this population. The Florida Department of Corrections has an eighty (80) bed male unit at Zephyrhills Correctional Institution and a forty (40) bed female unit at Broward Correctional Institution, both of which are funded by a Federal Residential Substance Abuse Treatment (RSAT) for State Prisoners Formula Grant.

Source: Florida Department of Corrections (2016)

the likelihood of successful reentry (Hoge, 2007; Osher et al., 2003) in offenders with co-occurring mental health and substance use disorders.

Conclusion

Offenders with co-occurring mental illness and substance use disorders make up a sizable portion of individuals involved with the U.S. criminal justice system. In this chapter, we have attempted to highlight some of the challenges encountered in the identification, treatment, and management of offenders diagnosed with CODs. It is clear that offenders diagnosed with CODs present with unique needs beyond those experienced by offenders with unitary mental health or substance use problems. Accordingly, it is imperative correctional systems and supervising agencies employ valid methods for identifying offenders with CODs, the results of which should inform intervention and supervision strategies from correctional intake through community supervision.

References

Abram, K. M., Teplin, L. A., & McClelland, G. M. (2003). Comorbidity of severe psychiatric disorders and substance use disorders among women in jail. *The American Journal of Psychiatry*, *160*(5), 1007–1010. doi:10.1176/appi.ajp.160.5.1007

Abrantes, A. M., Hoffmann, N. G., Anton, R. P., & Estroff, T. W. (2004). Identifying co-occurring disorders in juvenile justice populations. *Youth Violence and Juvenile Justice*, *2*(4), 329–341. doi:10.1177/1541204004267781

Abrantes, A. M., Hoffman, N. G., & Anton, R. (2005). Prevalence of co-occurring disorders among juveniles committed to detention centers. *International Journal of Offender Therapy and Comparative Criminology*, *49*(2), 179–193. doi:10.1177/0306624X04269673

Adams, K. (1986). The disciplinary experiences of mentally disordered inmates. *Criminal Justice and Behavior*, *13*(3), 297–316. doi:10.1177/0093854886013003004

American Civil Liberties Union of Colorado. (2013). *Out of sight, out of mind: Colorado's continued warehousing of mentally ill prisoners in solitary confinement*. Denver, CO: American Civil Liberties Union of Colorado.

American Psychiatric Association. (2000). *Diagnostic and statistical manual of mental disorders* (4th ed.). Washington, DC: American Psychiatric Association.

American Psychiatric Association. (2004). *Mental illness and the criminal justice system: Redirecting resources toward treatment, not containment*. Arlington, VA: Resource Document.

Andrews, D. A., & Bonta, J. (1998). *The psychology of criminal conduct* (2nd ed.). Cincinnati, OH: Anderson.

Andrews, D. A., Bonta, J., & Hoge, R. D. (1990). Classification for effective rehabilitation: Rediscovering psychology. *Criminal Justice and Behavior, 17*(5), 19–52. doi:10.1177/0093854890017001004

Andrews, D. A., Bonta, J., & Wormith, S. J. (2006). The recent past and near future of risk and/or need assessment. *Crime & Delinquency, 52*(1), 7–27. doi:10.1177/0011128705281756

Armstrong, T. D., & Costello, E. J. (2002). Community studies on adolescent substance use, abuse, or dependence and psychiatric comorbidity. *Journal of Consulting and Clinical Psychology, 70*(6), 1224–1239. doi:10.1037/0022-006X.70.6.1224

Arrigo, B. A., & Bullock, J. L. (2008). The psychological effects of solitary confinement on prisoners in supermax units: Reviewing what we know and recommending what should change. *International Journal of Offender Therapy and Comparative Criminology, 52*(6), 622–640. doi:10.1177/0306624X07309720

Baillargeon, J., Hoge, S. K., & Penn, J.V. (2010). Addressing the challenge of community reentry among released inmates with serious mental illness. *American Journal of Community Psychology, 46*(3–4), 361–375. doi:10.1007/s10464-010-9345-6

Baillargeon, J., Williams, B. A., Mellow, J., Harzke, A. J., Hoge, S. K., Baillargeon, G., & Greifinger, R. B. (2009). Parole revocation among prison inmates with psychiatric and substance use disorders. *Psychiatric Services, 60*(11), 1516–1521. doi:10.1176/ps.2009.60.11.1516

Baldwin, S. A., Christian, S., Berkeljon, A., Shadish, W. R., & Bean, R. (2012). The effects of family therapies for adolescent delinquency and substance abuse: A meta-analysis. *Journal of Marital and Family Therapy, 38*(1), 281–304. doi:10.1111/j.1752-0606.2011.00248x

Balyakina, E., Mann, C., Ellison, M., Sivernell, R., Fulda, K. G., Sarai, S. K., & Cardarelli, R. (2014). Risk of future offense among probationers with co-occurring substance use and mental health disorders. *Community Mental Health Journal, 50*(3), 288–295. doi:10.1007/s10597-013-9624-4

Beitchman, J., Beitchman, J. H., Adlaf, E. M., Douglas, L., Atkinson, L., Young, A., . . . Wilson, B. (2001). Comorbidity of psychiatric and substance use disorders in late adolescence: A cluster analytic approach. *American Journal of Drug & Alcohol Abuse, 27*(3), 421–440. doi:10.1081/ADA-100104510

Belenko, S., Langley, S., Crimmins, S., & Chaple, M. (2004). HIV risk behaviors, knowledge, and prevention education among offenders under community supervision: A hidden risk group. *AIDS Education and Prevention, 16*(4), 367–385. doi:10.1521/aeap.16.4.367.40394

Belenko, S., & Peugh, J. (2005). Estimating drug treatment needs among state prison inmates. *Drug and Alcohol Dependence, 77*(3), 269–281. doi:10.1016/j.drugalcdep.2004.08.023

Belknap, J. (2001). *The invisible woman: Gender, crime, and justice*. Belmont, CA: Wadsworth.

Bellack, A. S., Bennett, M. E., & Gearon, J. S. (2007). *Behavioral treatment for substance abuse in people with serious and persistent mental illness: A handbook for mental health professionals*. New York, NY: Routledge Press.

Bender, K., Springer, D.W., & Kim, J. S. (2006). Treatment effectiveness with dually diagnosed adolescents: A systematic review. *Brief Treatment and Crisis Intervention, 6*(3), 177–205. doi:10.1093/brief-treatment/mhl001

Bennett, D. J., Ogloff, J. R., Mullen, P. E., Thomas, S. D., Wallace, C., & Short, T. (2011). Schizophrenia disorders, substance abuse and prior offending in a sequential series of 435 homicides. *Acta Psychiatrica Scandinavica, 124*(3), 226–233. doi:10.1111/j.1600-0447.2011.01731.x

Beven, G. E. (2005). Offenders with mental illnesses in maximum-and super maximum-security settings. In C. L. Scott & J. B. Gerbasi (Eds.), *Handbook of correctional mental health*. Arlington, VA: American Psychiatric Publishing, Inc.

Blanchette, K., & Brown, S. L. (2006). *The assessment and treatment of women offenders: An integrative perspective*. Hoboken, NJ: John Wiley & Sons.

Blevins, K. R., & Soderstrom, I. R. (2015). The mental health crisis grows on: A descriptive analysis of DOC systems in America. *Journal of Offender Rehabilitation, 54*(2), 142–160. doi:10.1080/10509674.2015.1009965

Blitz, C. L., Wolff, N., & Shi, J. (2008). Physical victimization in prison: The role of mental illness. *International Journal of Law and Psychiatry, 31*(5), 385–393.

Bloom, B., Owen, B., Covington, S., & Raeder, M. (2002). *Gender responsive strategies: Research, practice, and guiding principles for women offenders*. Washington, DC: U.S. Department of Justice, National Institute of Corrections.

Braude, L., & Miller, N. (2011). *Residential substance abuse treatment (RSAT): Training and technical assistance*. Washington, DC: U.S. Department of Justice, Bureau of Justice Assistance.

Broner, N., Lattimore, P. K., Cowell, A. J., & Schlenger, W. E. (2002). Effects of diversion on adults with co-occurring mental illness and substance use: Outcomes from a national multisite study. *Behavioral Sciences and the Law, 22*(4), 519–541.

Brunette, M. F., Mueser, K. T., & Drake, R. E. (2004). A review of research on residential programs for people with severe mental illness and co-occurring substance use disorders. *Drug and Alcohol Review, 23*(4), 471–481. doi:10.1080/09595230412331324590

Bureau of Justice Statistics. (2006). *Special report: Mental health problems of prison and jail inmates.* Washington, DC: U.S. Department of Justice, Bureau of Justice Statistics.

Butler, T., Indig, D., Allnutt, S., & Mamoon, H. (2011). Co-occurring mental illness and substance use disorder among Australian prisoners. *Drug and Alcohol Review, 30*(2), 188–194. doi:10.1111/j.1465-3362.2010.00216.x

Carrà, G., Bartoli, F., Crocamo, C., Brady, K. T., & Clerici, M. (2014). Attempted suicide in people with co-occurring bipolar and substance use disorders: Systematic review and meta-analysis. *Journal of Affective Disorders, 167*, 125–135. doi:10.1016/j.jad.2014.05.066

Carson, E. A., & Sabol, W. J. (2012). *Prisoners in 2011.* Washington, DC: U.S. Department of Justice, Bureau of Justice Statistics.

Center for Substance Abuse Treatment. (2005a). *Substance abuse treatment for persons with cooccurring disorders: Treatment Improvement Protocol (TIP) series 42* (DHHS Publication No. SMA 05-3922). Rockville, MD: Substance Abuse and Mental Health Services Administration.

Center for Substance Abuse Treatment. (2005b). *Substance abuse treatment for adults in the criminal justice system: Treatment Improvement Protocol (TIP) series 44* (DHHS Publication No. SMA 05-4056). Rockville, MD: Substance Abuse and Mental Health Services Administration.

Chan, Y. F., Dennis, M. L., & Funk, R. L. (2008). Prevalence and comorbidity of major internalizing and externalizing problems among adolescents and adult presenting to substance abuse treatment. *Journal of Substance Abuse Treatment, 34*(1), 14–24. doi:10.1016/j.jsat.2006.12.031

Chandler, D. (2009). Implementation of integrated dual disorders treatment in eight California programs. *American Journal of Psychiatric Rehabilitation, 12*(4), 330–351. doi:10.1010/15487760903248473

Chandler, R., Peters, R., Field, G., & Juliano-Bult, D. (2004). Challenges in implementing evidence-based treatment practices for co-occurring disorders in the criminal justice system. *Behavioral Sciences & the Law, 22*(4), 431–448. doi:10.1002/bsl.598

Chandler, R. K., Fletcher, B. W., & Volkow, N. D. (2009). Treating drug abuse and addiction in the criminal justice system: Improving public health and safety. *Journal of the American Medical Association, 301*(2), 183–190. doi:10.1001/jama.2008.976

Chassin, L. (2008). Juvenile justice and substance use. *Juvenile Justice and Substance Use, 18*(2), 165–183.

Chesney-Lind, M., & Pasko, L. (2013). *Girls, women, and crime: Selected readings.* Thousand Oaks, CA: Sage.

Chi, F. W., Satre, D. D., & Weisner, C. (2006). Chemical dependency patients with cooccurring psychiatric diagnoses: Service Patterns and 1-year outcomes. *Alcoholism: Clinical and Experimental Research, 30*(5), 851–859. doi:10.1111/j.1530-0277.2006.00100.x

Cicchetti, D., & Rogosch, F. A. (2002). A developmental psychopathology perspective on adolescence. *Journal of Consulting and Clinical Psychology, 70*(1), 6–20. doi:10.1007/978-1-4615-4163-9_26

Council of State Governments. (2012). *Adults with behavioral health needs under correctional supervision: A shared framework for reducing recidivism and promoting recovery.* New York, NY: Council of State Governments.

Curran, G. M., Sullivan, G., Williams, K., Han, X., Collins, K., Keys, J., & Kotrla, K. J. (2003). Emergency department use of persons with comorbid psychiatric and substance abuse disorders. *Annals of Emergency Medicine, 41*(5), 659–667. doi:10.1067/mem.2003.154

Dennison, S. J. (2005). Substance use disorders in individuals with co-occurring psychiatric disorders (pp. 904–912). In J. H. Lowinson, P. Ruiz, R. B. Millman, & J. G. Langrod (Eds.), *Substance abuse: A comprehensive textbook* (4th ed.). Philadelphia, PA: Lippincott Williams, & Wilkins.

Deschenes, E. P., Owen, B., & Crow, J. (2006). *Recidivism among female prisoners: Secondary analysis of the 1994 BJS recidivism data set. Final report.* Washington, DC: U.S. Department of Justice, National Institute of Justice.

Drake, R. E., & Bond, G. R. (2010). Implementing integrated mental health and substance abuse services. *Journal of Dual Diagnosis, 6*(3–4), 251–262. doi:10.1080/15504263.2010.540772

Drake, R. E., Essock, S. M., Shaner, A., Carey, K. B., Minkoff, K., Kola, L., . . . Rickards, L. (2001). Implementing dual diagnosis services for clients with severe mental illness. *Psychiatric Services, 52*(4), 469–476. doi:10.1176/appi.ps.52.4.469

Drake, R. E., & Green, A. I. (2014). Developing innovative interventions for people with dual diagnosis. *Journal of Dual Diagnosis, 10*(4), 175–176. doi:10.1080/15504263.2014.969047

Drake, R. E., Mueser, K. T., Brunette, M. F., & McHugo, G. J. (2004). A review of treatments for people with severe mental illnesses and co-occurring substance use disorders. *Psychiatric Rehabilitation Journal, 27*(4), 360–374.

Druss, B. G., & Mauer, B. J. (2010). Health care reform and care at the behavioral health: Primary care interface. *Psychiatric Services, 61*(11), 1087–1092. doi:10.1176/ps.2010.61.11.1087

Dumaine, M. L. (2003). Meta-analysis of interventions with co-occurring disorders of severe mental illness and substance abuse: implications for social work practice. *Research on Social Work Practice, 13*(2), 142–165. doi:10.1177/1049731502250403

Elbogen, E. B., & Johnson, S. D. (2009). The intricate link between violence and mental disorder. *Archives of General Psychiatry, 66*(2), 152–161. doi:10.1001/archgenpsychiatry.2008.537

Eliason, M. J., Taylor, J. Y., & Williams, R. (2004). Physical health of women in prison: Relationship to oppression. *Journal of Correctional Health Care, 10*(2), 175–203. doi:10.1177/107834580301000204

Epperson, M. W., Wolff, N., Morgan, R. D., Fisher, W. H., Frueh, B. C., & Huening, J. (2011). *The next generation of behavioral health and criminal justice interventions: Improving outcomes by improving interventions.* Monograph Series New Brunswick, NJ: Center for Behavioral Health Services & Criminal Justice Research, Rutgers University.

Estelle v. Gamble, 429 U.S. 97, (1976).

Fazel, S., Gulati, G., Linsell, L., Geddes, J., & Grann, M. (2009). Schizophrenia and violence: Systematic review and meta-analysis. *PLOS Medicine, 6*, 1–16. doi:10.1371/journal.pmed.1000120

Feder, L. (1991). A comparison of the community adjustment of mentally ill offenders with those from the general prison population. *Law and Human Behavior, 15*(5), 477–493. doi:10.1007/BF01650290

Federal Bureau of Investigation. (2010). *Crime in the United States 2009. Discussion paper.* Washington, DC: U.S. Department of Justice, Federal Bureau of Investigation.

Fellner, J. (2007, July 19). Keep mentally ill out of solitary confinement. *Huffington Post.* Retrieved from www.hrw.org/news/2007/07/19/keep-mentally-ill-out-solitary-confinement

Felson, R. B., Silver, E., & Remster, B. (2012). Mental disorder and offending in prison. *Criminal Justice and Behavior, 39*(2), 125–143. doi:10.1177/0093854811428565

Florida Department of Corrections. (2016). *Invitation to negotiate (ITN) for in-prison substance abuse treatment services.* Tallahassee, FL: Florida Department of Corrections, Office of Administration, Bureau of Support Services.

Ford, M. (2015, June 8). America's largest mental hospital is a jail. *The Atlantic.* Retrieved from www.atlantic.com/politics/archive/2015/06/americas-largest-mental-hospital-is-a-jail/395012

Friendship, C., Blud, L., Erikson, M., Travers, R., & Thornton, D. (2003). Cognitive-behavioural treatment for imprisoned offenders: An evaluation of HM Prison Service's cognitive skills programmes. *Legal and Criminological Psychology, 8*(1), 103–114. doi:10.1348/135532503762871273

Gelman, D. (2007). Managing inmates with mental health disorders. *Corrections Today*, 22–23.

Giaconia, R. M., Reinherz, H. Z., Hauf, A. C., Paradis, A. D., Wasserman, M. S., & Langhammer, D. M. (2000). Comorbidity of substance use and posttraumatic stress disorders in a community sample of adolescents. *American Journal of Orthopsychiatry, 70*, 253–262.

Giancola, P. R. (2004). Executive functioning and alcohol-related aggression. *Journal of Abnormal Psychology, 113*(4), 541–555. doi:10.1037/0021-843X.113.4.541

Gido, R. L., & Dalley, L. (2009). *Women's mental health issues across the criminal justice system.* Upper Saddle River, NJ: Pearson Prentice Hall.

Golzari, M., Hunt, S. J., & Anoshiravani, A. (2006). The health status of youth in juvenile detention facilities. *Journal of Adolescent Health, 38*(6), 776–782. doi:10.1016/j.jadohealth.2005.06.008

Grella, C. E., Joshi, V., & Hser, Y. I. (2004). Effects of comorbidity on treatment processes and outcomes among adolescents in drug treatment programs. *Journal of Child and Adolescent Substance Abuse, 13*(4), 13–32. doi:10.1300/J029v13n04_02

Hartwell, S. (2004). Triple stigma: Persons with mental illness and substance abuse problems in the criminal justice system. *Criminal Justice Policy Review, 15*(1), 84–99. doi:10.1177/0887403403255064

Hättenschwiler, J., Rüesch, P., & Modestin, J. (2001). Comparison of four groups of substance abusing in-patients with different psychiatric comorbidity. *Acta Psychiatrica Scandinavica, 104*(1), 59–65. doi:10.1034/j.1600-0447.2001.00053.x

Hawkins, E. H. (2009). A tale of two systems: Co-occurring mental health and substance abuse disorders treatment for adolescents. *Annual Review of Psychology, 60*, 197–227. doi:10.1146/annurev.psych.60.110707.163456

Hills, H. A., Siegfried, C., & Ickowitz, A. (2004). *Effective prison mental health services: Guidelines to expand and improve treatment.* Washington, DC: U.S. Department of Justice, National Institute of Corrections.

Hoge, S. K. (2007). Providing transition and outpatient services to the mentally ill released from correctional institutions. In R. B. Greifinger (Ed.), *Public health behind bars: From prisons to communities* (pp. 461–477). New York, NY: Springer.

Houser, K., & Belenko, S. (2015). Disciplinary responses to misconduct among female prison inmates with mental illness, substance use disorders, and co-occurring disorders. *Psychiatric Rehabilitation Journal, 38*, 24–34. doi:10.1037/prj0000110

Houser, K., Belenko, S., & Brennan, P. (2012). The effects of mental health and substance abuse disorders on institutional misconduct among female inmates. *Justice Quarterly, 29*(6), 799–828. doi:10.1080/07418825.2011.641026

Houser, K. A., Blasko, B. L., & Belenko, S. (2014). The effects of treatment exposure on prison misconduct for female prisoners with substance use, mental health, and co-occurring disorders. *Criminal Justice Studies, 27*(1), 43–62. doi:10.1080/1478601X.2013.873204

Houser, K., & Welsh, W. (2014). Examining the association between co-occurring disorders and severeness of misconduct by female prison inmates. *Criminal Justice and Behavior, 41*(5), 650–666. doi:10.1177/0093854814521195

James, D. J., & Glaze, L. E. (2006). *Mental health problems of prison and jail inmates.* Washington, DC: U.S. Department of Justice, Bureau of Justice Statistics.

Jessup, M. A., & Dibble, S. L. (2011). Validity and reliability of the COJAC Screening Tool for co-occurring disorders. *The American Journal on Addictions, 20*(3), 264–270. doi:10.1111/j.1521-0391.2011.00131.x

Kelly, T. M., & Daley, D. C. (2013). Integrated treatment of substance uses and psychiatric disorders. *Social Work in Public Health, 28*(3–4), 388–406. doi:10.1080/19371918.2013.774673

Kessler, R. C., Chiu, W. T., Demler, O., & Walters, E. E. (2005). Prevalence, severity, and comorbidity of 12-month DSM-IV disorders in the National Comorbidity Survey replication. *Archives of General Psychiatry, 62*(6), 617–627. doi:10.1001/archpsyc.62.6.617

Kessler, R. C., Petukhova, M., Sampson, N. A., Zaslavsky, A. M., & Wittchen, H. U. (2012). Twelve-month and lifetime prevalence and lifetime morbid risk of anxiety and mood disorders in the United States. *International Journal of Methods in Psychiatric Research, 21*(3), 169–184. doi:10.1002/mpr.1359

Koegl, C. J. (2008). Prevalence and profile of people with co-occurring mental and substance use disorders within a comprehensive mental health system. *Canadian Journal of Psychiatry, 53*(12), 810–821. doi:10.1177/070674370805301207

Kola, L. A., & Kruszynski, R. (2010). Adapting the integrated dual-disorder treatment model for addiction services. *Alcoholism Treatment Quarterly, 28*(4), 437–450. doi:10.1080/07347324.2010.511067

Lowenkamp, C. T., Latessa, E. J., & Smith, P. (2006). Does correctional program quality really matter? The impact of adhering to the principles of effective intervention. *Criminology and Public Policy, 5*(3), 575–594. doi:10.1111/j.1745-9133.2006.00388.x

Lurigio, A. J. (2011). Co-occurring disorders: Mental health and drug misuse. In C. Leukefeld, T. P. Gullotta, & J. Gregrich (Eds.), *Handbook of evidence-based substance abuse treatment in criminal justice settings* (pp. 279–292). New York, NY: Springer.

Lynch, S. M., DeHart, D. D., Belknap, J. E., Green, B. L., Dass-Brailsford, P., Johnson, K. A., & Whalley, E. (2014). A multisite study of the prevalence of serious mental illness, PTSD, and substance use disorders of women in jail. *Psychiatric Services, 65*(5), 670–674. doi:10.1176/appi.ps.201300172

Lynch, S. M., Fritch, A., & Heath, N. M. (2012). Looking beneath the surface: The nature of incarcerated women's experiences of interpersonal violence, treatment needs, and mental health. *Feminist Criminology,* 7(4), 381–400. doi:10.1177/1557085112439224

McCabe, P. J., Christopher, P. P., Druhn, N., Roy-Bujnowski, K. M., Grudzinskas, A. J., Jr., & Fisher, W. H. (2012). Arrest types and co-occurring disorders in persons with schizophrenia or related psychoses. *The Journal of Behavioral Health Services & Research, 39*(3), 271–284. doi:10.1007/s11414-011-9269-4

McFarland, B. H., & Gabriel, R. M. (2004). Datapoints: Service availability for persons with co-occurring conditions. *Psychiatric Services, 55*(9), 978. doi:10.1176/appi.ps.55.9.978

McKee, S. A., Harris, G. T., & Cormier, C. A. (2013). Implementing residential integrated treatment for co-occurring disorders. *Journal of Dual Diagnosis, 9*(3), 249–259 doi:10.1080/15504263.2013.807073

Messina, N., Burdon, W., Hagopian, G., & Prendergast, M. (2004). One-year return to custody rates among co-disordered offenders. *Behavioral Sciences and the Law, 22*(4), 503–518. doi:10.1002/bsl.600

Messina, N., Burdon, W., Hagopian, G., & Prendergast, M. (2006). Predictors of prison-based treatment outcomes: A comparison of men and women participants. *The American Journal of Drug and Alcohol Abuse, 32*(1), 7–28. doi:10.1080/00952990500328463

Messina, N., & Grella, C. (2006). Childhood trauma and women's health outcomes in a California prison population. *American Journal of Public Health, 96*(10), 1842–1848. doi:10.2105/AJPH.2005.082016

Metzner, J. L., & Fellner, J. (2010). Solitary confinement and mental illness in U.S. prisons: A challenge for medical ethics. *Journal of the American Academy of Psychiatry and the Law, 38*(1), 104–108.

Minton, T. D. (2012). *Jail inmates at midyear 2011—statistical tables.* Washington DC: U.S. Department of Justice, Bureau of Justice Statistics.

Morgan, R. D., Fisher, W. H., Duan, N., Mandracchia, J. T., & Murray, D. (2010). Prevalence of criminal thinking among state prison inmates with serious mental illness. *Law and Human Behavior, 34*(4), 324–336. doi:10.1007/s10979-009-9182-z

Mueser, K. T., Noordsy, D. L., Drake, R. E., & Fox, L. (2003). *Integrated treatment for dual disorders: A guide to effective practice.* New York, NY: Guilford Press.

Najavits, L. M., Gallop, R. J., & Weiss, R. D. (2006). Seeking safety therapy for adolescent girls with PTSD and substance abuse: A randomized controlled trial. *Journal of Behavioral Health Services & Research, 33*(4), 453–463. doi:10.1007/s11414-006-9034-2

National Commission on Correctional Health Care. (2014). *Standards for health services in prisons*. Chicago, IL: National Commission on Correctional Health Care.

National GAINS Center. (2004). *The prevalence of co-occurring mental illness and substance use disorders in jails*. Fact Sheet Series. Delmar, NY: National GAINS Center.

National GAINS Center for People with Co-Occurring Disorders in the Justice System. (n.d.). *Treatment of people with co-occurring disorders in the justice system* [Brochure]. Retrieved from http://gainscenter.samhsa.gov/pdfs/disorders/Treatment.pdf

National Institute on Drug Abuse. (2008, December). *Comorbidity: Addiction and other mental illnesses* (NIH Publication No. 10–5771). Washington, DC: U.S. Department of Health and Human Services.

National Institute on Drug Abuse (NIDA). (2010). *Comorbidity: Addiction and other mental illnesses* (Research Report Series, NIH publication #10–5771). Bethesda, MD: NIDA.

Nowotny, K. M., Belknap, J., Lynch, S., & DeHart, D. (2014). Risk profile and treatment needs of women in jail with co-occurring serious mental illness and substance use disorders. *Women & Health, 54*(8), 781–795. doi: 10.1080/03630242.2014.932892

Ogloff, J., Davis, M., Rivers, G., & Ross, S. (2007). *The identification of mental disorders in the criminal justice system* (Trends & Issues in Crime and Criminal Justice, no. 334. Canberra, Australia: Australian Institute of Criminology.

Ogloff, J. R., Talevski, D., Lemphers, A., Wood, M., & Simmons, M. (2015). Co-occurring mental illness, substance use disorders, and antisocial personality disorder among client of forensic mental health services. *Psychiatric Rehabilitation Journal, 38*(1), 16–23. doi:10.1037/prj0000088

O'Keefe, M. L., & Schnell, M. J. (2007). Offenders with mental illness in the correctional system. *Journal of Offender Rehabilitation, 45*(1–2), 81–104. doi:10.1300/J076v45n01_08

Osher, F. C. (2007, January/February). Short-term strategies to improve reentry of jail populations. *American Jails*, 9–18.

Osher, F. C. (2013). *Integrating mental health and substance abuse services for justice-involved persons with co-occurring disorders*. Retrieved from http://gainscenter.samhsa.gov

Osher, F., Steadman, H. J., & Barr, H. (2003). A best practice approach to community reentry from jails for inmates with co-occurring disorders: The APIC model. *Crime and Delinquency, 49*(1), 79–96. doi:10.1177/0011128702239237

Padwa, H., Larkins, S., Crevecoeur-MacPhail, D. A., & Grella, C. E. (2013). Dual diagnosis capability in mental health and substance use disorder treatment programs. *Journal of Dual Diagnosis, 9*(2), 179–186. doi:10.1080/15504263.2013.778441

Peters, R. H., Bartoi, M. B. G., & Sherman, P. B. (2008). *Screening and assessment of co-occurring disorders in the justice system*. Delmar, NY: CMHS National GAINS Center.

Peters, R. H., & Bekman, N. M. (2007). Treatment and reentry approaches for offenders with co-occurring disorders. In R. B. Greifinger, J. Bick, & J. Goldenson (Eds.), *Public health behind bars: From prisons to communities* (pp. 368–384). New York: Springer.

Peters, R. H., Kremling, J., Bekman, N. M., & Caudy, M. S. (2012). Co-occurring disorders in treatment-based courts: Results of a national survey. *Behavioral Sciences & the Law, 30*(6), 800–820. doi:10.100 10.1002/bsl.20242/bsl.2024

Peters, R. H., LeVasseur, M. E., & Chandler, R. K. (2004). Correctional treatment for co-occurring disorders: Results from a national survey. *Behavioral Science and the Law, 22*(5), 563–584. doi:10.1002/bsl.607

Peters, R., & Petrila, J. (2004). Introduction to this issue: Co-occurring disorders and the criminal justice system. *Behavioral Sciences & the Law, 22*(4), 427–429. doi:10.1002/bsl.833

Peters, R. H., Wexler, H. K., & Lurigio, A. J. (2015). Co-occurring substance use and mental disorders in the criminal justice system: A new frontier of clinical practice and research. *Psychiatric Rehabilitation Journal, 38*(1), 1–6. doi:10.1037/prj0000135

Pew Center on the States. (2008). *One in 100: Behind bars in America 2008*. Retrieved from www.pewcenteronthestates.org/report_detail.aspx? id=35904

Priester, M. A., Browne, T., Iachini, A., Clone, S., DeHart, D., & Seay, K. D. (2016). Treatment access barriers and disparities among individuals with co-occurring mental health and substance use disorders: An integrative literature review. *Journal of Substance Abuse Treatment, 61*, 47–59. doi:10.1016/j.jsat.2015.09.006

Prins, S. J. (2014). Prevalence of mental illnesses in U.S. state prisons: A systematic review. *Psychiatric Services, 65*(7), 862–872. doi:10.1176/appi.ps.201300166

Ruiz, M. A., Douglas, K. S., Edens, J. F., Nikolova, N. L., & Lilienfeld, S. O. (2012). Co-occurring mental health and substance use problems in offenders: Implications for risk assessment. *Psychological Assessment, 24*(1), 77. doi:10.1037/a0024623

Ruiz v. Estelle, 503 F. Supp. 1265 (1980).

Sacks, J. A. (2004). Women with co-occurring substance use and mental disorders (COD) in the criminal justice system: A research review. *Behavior Sciences and the Law, 22*(4), 449–466. doi:10.1002/bsl.597

Sacks, S., Chaple, M., Sacks, J.Y., McKendrick, K., & Cleland, C. M. (2012). Randomized trial of a reentry modified therapeutic community for offenders with co-occurring disorders: Crime outcomes. *Journal of Substance Abuse Treatment, 42*(3), 247–259. doi:10.1016/j.jsat.2011.07.011

Sacks, S., & Melnick, G. (2007). *Brief report: Criminal justice co-occurring disorder screening instrument (CJ-CODSI)*. Washington, DC: National Institute on Drug Abuse, National Institutes of Health.

Sacks, S., Melnick, G., Coen, C., Banks, S., Friedmann, P. D., Grella, C., & Knight, K. (2007). CJDATS co-occurring disorders screening instrument for mental disorders (CODSI-MD): A pilot study. *The Prison Journal, 87*(1), 86–110. doi:10.1177/0032885506299044

Sacks, S., Melnick, G., & Grella, C. E. (2008). Introduction to this issue: Studies of co-occurring disorders in the criminal justice system. *Behavioral Sciences & the Law, 26*(4), 347–349. doi:10.1002/bsl.833

Sacks, S., Sacks, J.Y., McKendrick, K., Banks, S., & Stommel, J. (2004). Modified TC for MICA offenders: Crime outcomes. *Behavioral Sciences & the Law, 22*(4), 477–501. doi:10.1002/bsl.599

Salina, D. D., Lesondak, L. M., Razzano, L. A., & Parenti, B. M. (2011). Addressing unmet needs in incarcerated women with co-occurring disorders. *Journal of Social Service Research, 37*(4), 365–378. doi:10.1080/01488376.2011.582017

Scott, C. K., Dennis, M. L., & Lurigio, A. J. (2015). Comorbidity among female detainees in drug treatment: An exploration of internalizing and externalizing disorders. *Psychiatric Rehabilitation Journal, 38*(1), 35–44. doi:10.1037/prj0000134

Short, T., Thomas, S., Mullen, P., & Ogloff, J. R. (2013). Comparing violence in schizophrenia patients with and without comorbid substance use disorders to community controls. *Acta Psychiatrica Scandinavica, 128*(4), 306–313. doi:10.1111/acps.12066

Skeem, J., Kennealy, P., Monahan, J., Peterson, J., & Appelbaum, P. (2016). Psychosis uncommonly and inconsistently precedes violence among high-risk individuals. *Clinical Psychological Science, 4*(1), 40–49. doi:10.1177/2167702615575879

Skeem, J. L., Winter, E., Kennealy, P. J., Louden, J. E., & Tatar II, J. R. (2014). Offenders with mental illness have criminogenic needs, too: Toward recidivism reduction. *Law and Human Behavior, 38*(3), 212–224. doi:10.1037/lhb0000054

Skopp, N. A., Edens, J. F., & Ruiz, M. A. (2007). Risk factors for institutional misconduct among incarcerated women: An examination of the criterion-related validity of the Personality Assessment Inventory. *Journal of Personality Assessment, 88*(1), 106–117. doi:10.1080/00223890709336841

Slate, R. N., Buffington-Vollum, J. K., & Johnson, W. W. (2013). *The criminalization of mental illness: Crisis and opportunity for the justice system* (2nd ed.). Durham, NC: Carolina Academic Press.

Smith, N., & Trimboli, L. (2010). *Co-morbid substance and non-substance mental health disorders and re-offending among NSW prisoners*. Sydney, Australia: NSW Bureau of Crime Statistics and Research.

Smith, P. S. (2006). The effects of solitary confinement on prison inmates: A brief history and review of the literature. *Crime and Justice, 34*(1), 441–528. doi:10.1086/500626

Soderstrom, I. R. (2007). Mental illness in offender populations: Prevalence, duty, and implications. *Journal of Offender Rehabilitation, 45*(1–2), 1–17. doi:10.1300/J076v45n01_01

Spencer, L. S., & Fallon, C. M. (2012). Today's special needs call for new approaches. *Corrections Today*, 6–8.

Steadman, H. J., Osher, F. C., Robbins, P., Case, B., & Samuels, S. (2009). Prevalence of serious mental illness among jail inmates. *Psychiatric Services, 60*(6), 761–765. doi:10.1176/appi.ps.60.6.761

Steadman, J., Peters, R. H., Carpenter, C., Mueser, K. T., Jaeger, N. D., Gordon, R. B., . . . Noether, C. D. (2013). Six steps to improve your drug court outcomes for adults with co-occurring disorders. National Drug Court Institute and SAMHSA's GAINS Center for Behavioral Health and Justice Transformation. *Drug Court Practitioner Fact Sheet, 8*, 1–28. Alexandria VA: National Drug Court Institute.

Steiner, B., & Wooldredge, J. (2009). Individual and environmental effects on assaults and nonviolent rule breaking by women in prison. *Journal of Research in Crime and Delinquency, 46*(4), 437–467. doi:10.1177/0022427809341936

Sterling, S., Chi, F., & Hinman, A. (2011). Integrating care for people with cooccurring alcohol and other drug, medical, and mental health conditions. *Alcohol Research & Health, 33*(4), 338–349.

Stewart, D. G., & Trupin, E. W. (2003). Clinical utility and policy implications of a statewide mental health screening process for juvenile offenders. *Psychiatric Services, 54*(3), 377–382. doi:10.1176/appi.ps.54.3.377

Substance Abuse and Mental Health Services Administration. (2002). *National and state estimates of the drug abuse treatment gap.* National Household Survey on Drug *Abuse.* Rockville, MD: SAMHSA.
Substance Abuse and Mental Health Services Administration. (2015). *About co-occurring disorders.* Retrieved from http://media.samhsa.gov/co-occurring/
Swanson, J. W., Swartz, M. S., Van Dorn, R. A., Volavka, J., Monahan, J., Stroup, T. S., . . . Lieberman, J. A. (2008). Comparison of antipsychotic medication effects on reducing violence in people with schizophrenia. *The British Journal of Psychiatry, 193*(1), 37–43. doi:10.1192/bjp.bp.107.042630
Swartz, J. A. (2006). A pilot study of co-occurring psychiatric, substance use, and medical disorders among jail detainees in psychiatric treatment. *Offender Substance Abuse Report, 6*, 81–96.
Taxman, F. S., Henderson, C. E., & Belenko, S. (2009). Organizational context, systems change, and adopting treatment delivery systems in the criminal justice system. *Drug and Alcohol Dependence, 103*(Suppl. 1), S1–S6. doi:10.1016/j.drugalcdep.2009.03.003
Teplin, L. A. (2001). *Assessing alcohol, drug, and mental disorders in juvenile detainees.* Washington, DC: U.S. Department of Justice, Office of Justice Programs, Office of Juvenile Justice and Delinquency Prevention.
Teplin, L. A., Abram, K. M., Washburn, J. J., Welty, L. J., Hershfield, J. A., & Dulcan, M. K. (2013). The northwestern juvenile project: Overview. *Juvenile Justice Bulletin, 13*. U.S. Department of Justice, Office of Justice Programs, Office of Juvenile Justice and Delinquency Prevention.
Torrey, W. C., Tepper, M., & Greenwold, J. (2011). Implementing integrated services for adults with co-occurring substance use disorders and psychiatric illness: A research review. *Journal of Dual Diagnosis*, 7(3), 150–161. doi:10.1080/15504263.2011.592769
Trestman, R. L., Ford, J., Zhang, W., & Wiesbrock, V. (2007). Current and lifetime psychiatric illness among inmates not identified as acutely mentally ill at intake in Connecticut's jails. *Journal of the American Academy of Psychiatry and the Law Online, 35*, 490–500.
Trupin, E. (2007). Evidence-based treatment for justice-involved youth. In C. L. Kessler & L. J. Kraus (Eds.), *The mental health needs of young offenders: Forging paths toward reintegration and rehabilitation* (pp. 340–367). Cambridge: Cambridge University Press.
Trupin, E. W., Turner, A. P., Stewart, D. G., & Wood, P. (2004). Transition planning and recidivism among mentally ill juvenile offenders. *Behavioral Sciences & the Law, 22*(4), doi:10.1002/bsl.596
Von Sydow, K., Retzlaff, R., Beher, S., Haun, M. W., & Schweitzer, J. (2013). The efficacy of systemic therapy for childhood and adolescent externalizing disorders: A systematic review of 47 RCT. *Family Process, 52*(4), 576–618. doi:10.1111/famp.12047
Wasserman, G. A., McReynolds, L. S., Schwalbe, C. S., Keating, J. M., & Jones, S. A. (2010). Psychiatric disorder, comorbidity and suicidal behavior in juvenile justice youth. *Criminal Justice and Behavior, 37*(12), 1361–1376. doi:10.1177/0093854810382751
Watkins, K. E., Burnam, A., Kung, F. Y., & Paddock, S. (2001). A national survey of care for persons with co-occurring mental and substance use disorders. *Psychiatric Services, 52*, 1062–1068. doi:10.1176/appi.ps.52.8.1062
Wilson, A. B., Draine, J., Hadley, T., Metraux, S., & Evans, A. (2011). Examining the impact of mental illness and substance use on recidivism in a county jail. *International Journal of Law and Psychiatry, 34*(4), 264–268. doi:10.1016/j.ijlp.2011.07.004
Wilson, A. B., Farkas, K., Ishler, K. J., Gearhart, M., Morgan, R., & Ashe, M. (2014). Criminal thinking styles among people with serious mental illness in jail. *Law and Human Behavior, 38*(6), 592–601. doi:10.1037/lhb0000084
Winerip, M., & Schwirtz, M. (2014). Rikers: Where mental illness meets brutality in jail. *New York Times.* Retrieved from www.nytimes.com/2014/07/14/nyregion/rikers- study inds-prisoners-injuredby-employees.html?_r0
Wood, S. R. (2011). Co-occurring psychiatric and substance dependence disorders as predictors of parolee time to rearrest. *Journal of Offender Rehabilitation, 50*(4), 175–190. doi:10.1080/10509674.2011.571076
Wood, S. R., & Buttaro, A. (2013). Co-occurring severe mental illnesses and substance abuse disorders as predictors of state prison inmate assaults. *Crime & Delinquency, 59*(4), 510–535. doi:10.1177/0011128712470318
Wright, S., Gournay, K., Glorney, E., & Thornicroft, G. (2002). Mental illness, substance abuse, demographics and offending: Dual diagnosis in the suburbs. *The Journal of Forensic Psychiatry, 13*(1), 35–52. doi:10.1080/09585180210123276

20

OFFENDERS WITH PHYSICAL DISABILITIES

Experiences Across the Criminal Justice System

Margaret E. Leigey and Victoria M. Smiegocki

> Offenders with disabilities face disadvantages at various stages of the criminal justice system. They may be indirectly discriminated against in their access to justice, if the special assistance they need is not provided".
>
> —(Atabay, 2009, pp. 44–45)

Introduction

The Americans with Disabilities Act (ADA) of 1990 requires that public facilities, including police stations and courthouses, be accessible to those with disabilities. Title II of the legislation reads:

> Subject to the provisions of this subchapter, no qualified individual with a disability shall, by reason of such disability, be excluded from participation in or be denied the benefits of the services, programs, or activities of a public entity, or be subjected to discrimination by any such entity.
>
> (§ 12132)

In 1998, the United States Supreme Court held in *Pennsylvania Department of Corrections v. Yeskey* that the ADA was applicable to state correctional facilities. Since the Court's decision in this and subsequent cases, there has been increased interest in the criminal justice experiences of offenders with physical disabilities. Interest in this special population also is explained by the overrepresentation of individuals with physical disabilities in the criminal justice system (Bronson, Maruschak, & Berzofsky, 2015) and high-profile cases—for example, South African Olympian Oscar Pistorius.

The ADA defines disability as "a physical or mental impairment that substantially limits one or more major life activities of such individual; a record of such an impairment; or being regarded as having such an impairment" (§ 12102). According to the Bureau of Justice Statistics (BJS), approximately one-third of state and federal inmates and two-fifths of jail inmates in the United States have a disability (Bronson et al., 2015). In terms of the specific disability, about 20% of state and federal inmates and 31% of jail inmates report cognitive impairment (caused by a physical, mental, or emotional issue), approximately 10% report an ambulatory impairment, about 7% report vision impairment, and around 6% report hearing impairment (Bronson et al., 2015). In addition, it is important to note that approximately 16% of jail inmates and 13% of state and federal inmates report multiple disabilities (Bronson et al., 2015). Additional research also indicates that dual disabilities are relatively common. For example, Miller and Vernon (2003) noted that at least 21% of their subsample of 34 deaf sex offenders had IQs that would classify them as borderline intellectual functioning or intellectually disabled (formerly known as mental retardation) (see Diament, 2010). When examining the proportion of inmates with impairment to the proportion in the comparable general population, the prevalence of a visual, auditory, ambulatory, or cognitive disability was significantly higher for incarcerated groups (Bronson et al., 2015).

When disaggregating by sex, age, race/ethnicity, and type of offense, it is apparent that the prevalence of a physical disability is not uniformly distributed. With sex of the inmate, similar percentages of male and female inmates in state and federal prisons have a hearing, vision, or ambulatory impairment; however, a statistically significant higher percentage of female inmates report a cognitive impairment than male inmates, 30% versus 19%, respectively (Bronson et al., 2015). Turning to age, with the exception of cognitive disability, there is a positive correlation between age and a hearing, vision, or ambulatory impairment (Bronson et al., 2015). Inmates above the age of 50 were significantly more likely to report a hearing, vision, or ambulatory impairment than inmates under the age of 24. In fact, as compared to younger inmates, the prevalence of vision impairment is about four times higher for older inmates, about six times higher for hearing impairment, and 16 times higher for ambulatory impairment (Bronson et al., 2015). When looking at race and ethnicity, black and Hispanic inmates were significantly less likely to report a physical disability than white inmates (Bronson et al., 2015). While offenders with physical disabilities commit a variety of crimes, research indicates that deaf individuals are overrepresented in the sex offender population (Miller & Vernon, 2003; Miller, Vernon, & Capella, 2005). For example, Miller and Vernon (2003) noted that "the percentage of the total population of deaf inmates who were convicted sex offenders was a little over four times the percentage of the total population of hearing inmates who were convicted sex offenders" (p. 358).

Offenders with Physical Disabilities and Their Experiences with the Police

As individuals navigate the criminal justice system, they can be confused, unsure, afraid, and frustrated. However, these feelings are undoubtedly magnified for offenders who are blind or visually impaired, deaf or hard of hearing, or who are reliant on wheelchairs or prosthetic legs. The Bill of Rights provides certain protections to criminal suspects, such as the protection against unreasonable search and seizure (Fourth Amendment), self-incrimination and due process (Fifth Amendment), and cruel and unusual punishment (Eighth Amendment). However, there is concern that suspects or offenders with physically disabilities may have these constitutional protections infringed upon, intentionally or not, by criminal justice officials.

The police are usually the first criminal justice actors encountered by suspects. Interaction with police is a critical point in the criminal justice process, as it can have major implications for suspects and their cases. However, police may misinterpret the behaviors of suspects and offenders with physical disabilities. For example, police may erroneously attribute the slurred speech of a suspect to intoxication when in actuality it is the result of a stroke (Toth, 2008). The U.S. Department of Justice (2006, para. 12) provides another example of how misinterpretation could occur when police interact with a deaf citizen:

> An officer yells "freeze" to an individual who is running from an area in which a crime has been reported. The individual, who is deaf, cannot hear the officer and continues to run. The officer mistakenly believes that the individual is fleeing from the scene.

Lack of comprehension is another issue. Vernon and Miller (2005) found that a polygraph agreement required a tenth-grade reading level; however, 80% of deaf offenders in one sample had reading levels below the fifth grade (Miller & Vernon, 2003).

While the ADA requires a "reasonable" accommodation be made for deaf suspects when interacting with police, no automatic right to a sign language interpreter exists (Brunson, 2008), as some justice-involved deaf individuals may believe. When police attempt to communicate with deaf suspects and offenders, they may try to use note writing or lip reading, but problems exist with both of these techniques. Note writing may be an effective means of communication for some deaf suspects, but not for those with low reading levels. Alternatively, with lip reading, "even under ideal conditions, for example, good lighting, face-to-face contact with the speaker, a speaker who articulates clearly, good lipreaders can understand only about five percent of what is said to them" (Vernon & Andrews, 1990, as cited in Vernon, 2009, p. 15).

While sign language interpreters may be the preferred mode of communication, their presence does not ameliorate all issues. Interpreters may lack the proper certification (Brunson, 2008), and evidence suggests that the police have relied on unqualified interpreters for assistance. For example,

> in New York, a deaf woman shot and killed her abusive husband, and had a physical breakdown immediately after (*New York v. Ripic*, 1992). In her hospital room, police attempted to interrogate her by having the child of a deaf neighbor act as an interpreter.
>
> (Miller, 2001, p. 328)

Even among qualified interpreters, disparities in competency could exist, or they could provide legal advice which is prohibited (Brunson, 2008). Deaf suspects with low reading levels may still struggle to comprehend the meaning of complex legal terminology even if it is being correctly translated by an interpreter (Vernon & Miller, 2005). One potential outcome is that deaf offenders may feign understanding when they actually do not (Vernon & Miller, 2005). Interpreters who are meeting a deaf suspect for the first time at a police interrogation may find it difficult to assess the suspect's comprehension level and may look to cues such as inappropriate responses, lack of response, repeating the last sign, or pleasing behaviors (e.g., excessive head nodding or smiling) (Miller & Vernon, 2002). Furthermore, many legal and correctional terms do not have equivalent signs (Vernon & Miller, 2005). For example, no signs exist to distinguish between "correctional officer," "parole officer," and "police officer" (Vernon, 1995). Lastly, the presence of an interpreter in the room may fundamentally alter the interaction as explained by Brunson (2008, p. 78):

> Sign language interpreters are also supposed to be unobtrusive extensions of the focal individual; they are there to facilitate the interaction between a person who is deaf and another party without intervening in or affecting the outcome of the exchange. However, unlike guide dogs and wheelchairs, interpreters are humans; their human agency is a part of the interaction, and their presence often changes the dynamics of the situation.

In sum, issues with communication and comprehension have the potential for deaf suspects or offenders to be more easily coerced by police into confessing or waiving their rights, which could have serious consequences for their cases (Vernon & Miller, 2005). Because of the issues associated with the waiver of rights and police interrogation, it is recommended that the entire interrogation be videotaped and audio-recorded. The recording should include the signing between the defendant and interpreter and the oral communication between the police and interpreter (Vernon & Miller, 2005). Vernon and Miller (2005, p. 287) explained the importance of creating a record:

> Videotape not only provides a record of what the police and suspect said, it is critical in evaluating whether the interpreter transmitted the information accurately and in a way that was understandable to the deaf client. When police interviews are conducted without being

> videotaped, everything that the deaf person signs is hearsay evidence; that is, it is what the interpreter says the deaf person said, not necessarily what was actually said.

These same researchers identified five cases in which videotape evidence helped to determine that *Miranda* warnings were not delivered in a manner in which suspects could comprehend (Vernon & Miller, 2005). It is also important for police to be aware that it can take longer for an interpreter to communicate the information contained in the *Miranda* warnings; one estimate given was between five to six hours (McAlister, 1994).

In addition to deaf suspects, suspects with other types of physical disabilities also face challenges in their interactions with police. Blind suspects may struggle to comprehend nondescriptive commands, for example, if an officer points to an area and directs the suspect to stand over there (USDOJ, 2006). To ensure that visually impaired offenders are knowingly waiving their rights, police officers are required to read documents that require a signature aloud and in their entirety (USDOJ, 2006). Translation of legal documents into Braille is not required, and in fact, may be helpful to only a small percentage of visually impaired individuals, as fewer than one in 10 legally blind Americans read Braille (Rubin, 2009). In communicating legal documents aloud, the suspect is relying on the veracity of the police officer's reading. As with deaf suspects, it is recommended that recordings are made of the police officer's reading of the document to ensure that the document was read accurately and fully and the visually impaired suspect understood the ramifications of signing the document. According to results of the American Community Survey (2014), 24% of visually impaired adults and 22% of adults with an ambulatory disability in the United States do not have a high school diploma (K. Lisa Yan and Hock E. Tan Institute on Employment and Disability, 2016). As such, similar to deaf suspects, some blind suspects and suspects with ambulatory disabilities may struggle to understand complex legal terminology.

Offenders with ambulatory disabilities can also encounter difficulties in their police interactions. The potential exists for police to misinterpret their behavior. For example, the USDOJ (2006, para. 10) provided the following example:

> An officer approaches a vehicle and asks the driver to step out of the car. The driver, who has a mobility disability, reaches behind the seat to retrieve her assistive device for walking. This appears suspicious to the officer. The officer may misinterpret the driver's action and think that she is reaching for a weapon.

This misinterpretation could lead to injury or death for the driver. Injury could also result when police are transporting offenders with ambulatory disabilities. Transport in patrol cars may not be suitable for some suspects with mobility impairment; as such, alternate arrangements may need to be made by police (e.g., a lift-equipped van) (USDOJ, 2006). The USDOJ (2006, para. 24) recommends that officers ask the individual what types of transportation are appropriate and "how to lift or assist him or her in transferring into and out of the vehicle." In *Gorman v. Easley* (2001), a paraplegic prisoner who sustained injuries when he was transported in a van that lacked wheelchair restraints received over $2 million in actual and punitive damages ("Accommodation of Wheelchair-Bound Prisoners," 2009.) When suspects or offenders with physical disabilities are held in police facilities, they must have access to amenities such as a toilet. Law enforcement agencies may need to make structural modifications to make their stations accessible, or they may use alternate accessible facilities. The USDOJ (2006, para. 60) provided the following example:

> A police station in a small town is inaccessible to individuals with mobility disabilities. The department decides that it cannot alter all areas of the station because of insufficient funds. It decides to alter the lobby and restrooms so that the areas the public uses—for filling out

> crime reports, obtaining copies of investigative reports for insurance purposes, or seeking referrals to shelter care—are accessible. Arrangements are made to conduct victim and witness interviews with individuals with disabilities in a private conference room in the local library or other government building, and to use a neighboring department's accessible lock-up for detaining suspects with disabilities.

As will be discussed more fully later, lack of accessibility is a potential violation of both the ADA and the U.S. Constitution and could make the agency vulnerable to litigation.

Offenders with Physical Disabilities and Their Experiences in the Courts

If enough evidence exists against a suspect, the case advances to the courts. At this stage in the process, suspects interact with prosecutors, defense attorneys, judges, and jurors. The Fifth and Fourteenth Amendments require due process in court proceedings. According to Miller (2004, p. 112)

> Due process refers to the court ensuring that a defendant understands the charges against him or her, is able to assist in the development of a defense, can decide which plea to enter, is aware of the implications for his or her position as a defendant, and has an understanding of the roles of the defense, prosecution, and judge.

As in their interactions with the police, offenders with physical disabilities may struggle to comprehend legal terminology or legal documents (Vernon & Miller, 2005). For instance, guilty plea and sentencing hearing documents were found by Vernon and Miller (2001) to be written at a ninth-grade reading level. In extreme cases, if a defendant lacks sufficient understanding of the court proceedings and is unable to assist in his or her defense, the defendant could be declared legally incompetent (Roesch, Zapf, Golding, & Skeem, 2014). Court proceedings could be postponed until legal competency is gained, or the charges could be dismissed (Roesch et al., 2014).

In courthouses and courtrooms, accommodations may need to be made for defendants with physical disabilities. Examples include allowing the defendant to sit in a different location where he or she can hear better, permitting the defendant to use a telecommunication system, or providing a qualified sign interpreter ("Americans with Disabilities—Frequently Asked Questions," 2012). However, even if a qualified sign language interpreter has been appointed by the court, the defendant may still face issues with this accommodation. Deaf offenders have reported that their interpreters have arrived late, left early, or failed to show up to court hearings (Brunson, 2008). This could lead to delays in the case that may require the person to remain in jail for longer periods awaiting trial or sentencing. For blind defendants, accommodations that could be made by the court include:

> providing forms and instructions in Braille, large print or on audiotape; providing assistance at the counter in filling out necessary paperwork; having written materials read out loud in the courtroom; allowing the person to sit closer than usual if they have limited vision; or providing additional lighting.
>
> ("Americans with Disabilities—Frequently Asked Questions," 2012, p. 8)

If a defendant is both blind and deaf, then an interpreter of tactile communication may need to be appointed ("Americans with Disabilities—Frequently Asked Questions," 2012). For defendants with mobility impairment, the ADA stipulates that courthouses and courtrooms must be accessible by constructing wheelchair ramps and accessible restrooms, lowering the height of public information counters, ensuring that aisles are large enough to accommodate wheelchairs, and allowing defendants to sit outside of the witness box when testifying. Assistance animals also are permitted in court ("Americans with Disabilities—Frequently Asked Questions," 2012).

In some cases, a defendant's disability may be used to reduce his or her culpability in the crime committed. For instance, South African Olympian Oscar Pistorius, a double amputee, was convicted of the murder of his girlfriend Reeva Steenkamp and received a prison sentence of six years (Hume, Karimi, & Thompson, 2016). Pistorius's defense team claimed that because of the loss of his legs, Pistorius may have perceived himself to be especially vulnerable to an intruder and would have greater difficulty fleeing the situation (Torchia & Imray, 2014). However, it is unclear to what extent judges and juries take into consideration a defendant's disability when determining guilt and the appropriate punishment. Evidence is mixed. One study conducted in Norway found that physical disability was a mitigating factor in sentencing decisions (Dullum, 2015). In Canada, a judge determined that a jail sentence for a visually impaired defendant convicted of assault and sexual assault would be too harsh because of the lack of appropriate accommodations in the jail; the judge instead imposed a suspended sentence (Koshan, 2013). A higher court later overturned this sentence and ordered a jail term of 90 days and probation for a year instead (Koshan, 2013). In the United States, mock jury research has found that a defendant's physical disability was unrelated to the recommended punishment (Conti & Daley, 2015). In their samples of undergraduate students acting as mock jurors, Conti and Daley (2015) found that defendants with a physically disability received similar sentences as defendants without a physical disability, regardless of the defendant's sex or the crime he or she committed.

Offenders with Physical Disabilities and Their Correctional Experiences

Defendants can be held in jail awaiting trial or sentencing hearing, and if they are convicted and sentenced to a short period of incarceration, they will most likely serve their time in a jail. For defendants who were convicted of felonies and received longer sentences, they likely will be transferred to prison. Heather Gerrard, an ex-offender, described the experience of being deaf in prison as serving "a double sentence" (British Deaf Association, 2016, p. 8). This characterization also extends to inmates with other physical disabilities. Not only does the person have to negotiate the usual "pains of imprisonment" (Sykes, 1958) that accompany incarceration, but he or she also has to contend with the hardships brought about by their physical disabilities. Atabay (2009, p. 45) described the difficulties that inmates with physical disabilities face:

> Prisoners with physical disabilities encounter difficulties in accessing services, complying with rules and participating in prison activities that do not take account of their special needs. Due to architectural barriers, prisoners with mobility impairments may be unable to access dining areas, libraries, sanitary facilities, work, recreation, and visiting rooms. Prisoners with visual disabilities cannot read their own mail unassisted or prison rules and regulations, unless they are provided in Braille. They are unable to use the library, unless taped materials or books in Braille are available. Prisoners with a hearing or speaking disability may be denied interpreters, making it impossible for them to participate in various prison activities, including counselling programmes, as well as their own parole and disciplinary hearings. Prisoners with disabilities can be routinely denied participation in work programmes outside prison, sometimes significantly lengthening their periods of imprisonment.

The Legal Protections for Inmates with Physical Disabilities

The ADA was preceded by two pieces of federal legislation: The Rehabilitation Act of 1973 and The Civil Rights of Institutionalized Persons Act (CRIPA) of 1980. The Rehabilitation Act of 1973 prohibits discrimination by any federal agency, including the Federal Bureau of Prisons (FBOP), and any program that receives federal funding. Conversely, CRIPA allows the federal attorney general to initiate civil action in claims of federal constitutional violations made by individuals in local or state-operated institutions, for example, jails, prisons, and juvenile detention centers, but excludes privately operated facilities. Ten years later, the ADA was passed. To bring a lawsuit under the ADA and/or the Rehabilitation Act, disabled prisoners must show:

> (1) that they are disabled within the meaning of the statutes, (2) that they are "qualified" to participate in the program, and (3) that they are excluded from, are not allowed to benefit from, or have been subjected to discrimination in the program because of their disability.
>
> (American Civil Liberties Union [ACLU] National Prison Project, 2005, p. 3)

With claims involving an infringement of The Rehabilitation Act, the inmate must also show that the defendants are recipients of federal funding. Several exceptions to the ADA exist. For example, "Prison officials are not required to provide accommodations that impose 'undue financial and administrative burdens' or require a 'fundamental alteration in the nature of [the] program'" (ACLU National Prison Project, 2005, p. 4).

There have been several legal challenges to the ADA that have reached the United States Supreme Court. For instance, in *Pennsylvania Department of Corrections v. Yeskey* (1998), the Court held in a unanimous decision that the ADA was applicable to inmates in state prisons. Yeskey was sentenced to serve 18 to 36 months in prison. At sentencing, the judge recommended that Yeskey be admitted into a boot camp program for first-time offenders. If he successfully completed the program, Yeskey would be eligible for release after serving six months. However, Yeskey was refused admission into the program because of a medical history of hypertension. He filed suit against the Pennsylvania Department of Corrections (DOC), alleging that his exclusion from the program violated the ADA. Justice Scalia delivered the unanimous opinion of the Court, writing, "The plain text of Title II of the ADA unambiguously extends to state prison inmates" (*Pennsylvania Department of Corrections v. Yeskey*, 1998, p. 213).

In *Tennessee v. Lane* (2004), the Court again clarified the applicability of the ADA to criminal justice institutions. The case was brought by George Lane and Beverly Jones, both of whom were paraplegics, who claimed that the state was in violation of the ADA because the lack of an elevator in the courthouse made access to the second floor difficult. In its opinion, the majority of the Court noted:

> At his first appearance, Lane crawled up two flights of stairs to get to the courtroom. When Lane returned to the courthouse for a hearing, he refused to crawl again or to be carried by officers to the courtroom; he consequently was arrested and jailed for failure to appear.
>
> (*Tennessee v. Lane*, 2004, p. 514)

In a 5 to 4 decision, the majority of the Court held that individuals were permitted to seek monetary damages against a state for the denial of services because of a disability.

Just three years later, the Court unanimously held in *Goodman v. Georgia* (2006) that an inmate with a disability may seek monetary damages against a state DOC based on a violation of the ADA that was also an independent violation of the Constitution. Goodman alleged that he was prohibited access to certain areas of the prison, sustained injuries, and was denied access to medical treatment, programs, and services (*Goodman v. Georgia*, 2006, p. 155):

> Among his more serious allegations, he claimed that he was confined for 23-to-24 hours per day in a 12-by-3 foot cell in which he could not turn his wheelchair around. He alleged that the lack of accessible facilities rendered him unable to use the toilet and shower

> without assistance, which was often denied. On multiple occasions, he asserted, he had injured himself in attempting to transfer from his wheelchair to the shower or toilet on his own, and, on several other occasions, he had been forced to sit in his own feces and urine while prison officials refused to assist him in cleaning up the waste. He also claimed that he had been denied physical therapy and medical treatment, and denied access to virtually all prison programs and services on account of his disability.

One area that the Court declined to address in its decision was whether monetary damages can be sought when the conduct violates the ADA but not the Constitution (ACLU National Prison Project, 2005).

Other legal avenues that inmates with disabilities have pursued include litigation against a DOC for the conditions of confinement in its prisons and failure to receive adequate medical care, both of which constitute violations of the Eighth Amendment's cruel and unusual punishment clause. In *Ruiz v. Estelle* (1980), the lack of accommodations made to the prison environment and the lack of access to programs for inmates with physical disabilities were cited by inmates as evidence in support of their claim that the conditions in Texas prisons were unconstitutional; the Court agreed. In *Estelle v. Gamble* (1976), the United States Supreme Court held that prison officials, including correctional officers and doctors, could be held liable for failure to respond to an inmate's medical needs.

To be compliant with federal legislation, the DOC may be required to provide a wide variety of aids, accommodations, and equal access to services and programming:

> Examples of auxiliary aids for visually impaired offenders include books on audiotape, in-cell radios, auditory option for written rules, or other text present in prison facilities, and navigational devices, such as walking canes or facilitators. For deaf or hard-of-hearing inmates, examples of auxiliary aids include assistive listening devices, notetakers, interpreters, and closed captioning. For wheelchair users, auxiliary aids include shower chairs, hand rails, wider doors, and ramps for accessibility, and lowered shelves for appliances.
>
> (Kitei & Sales, 2006, p. 31)

However, not all correctional facilities that house inmates with physical disabilities appear to be compliant with the ADA or the Rehabilitation Act. Kitei and Sales (2006) found that some group therapy sessions were scheduled to meet on the third floor of a facility. As such, without functioning elevators or ramps, a wheelchair-bound inmate would be unable to participate in such a program and consequently be denied the service. In addition, they reviewed cases in which architectural barriers posed challenges for offenders with mobility impairment, including lack of access to microwaves and refrigerators, lack of shower chairs and handrails in the shower and toilets, and narrow doorways making entering and exiting cells in a wheelchair difficult. In addition, programming, services, and preferential housing may not be available to inmates with disabilities because they lack the appropriate accommodations. Thus, offenders with physical disabilities may be denied participation in programming that would be helpful to them, accrue good behavior points, or earn privileges (Kitei & Sales, 2006). Evidence suggests that because of the inaccessibility of facilities, jail and prison inmates with a physical disability were more likely to report being injured in an accident during their incarceration than inmates without a physical disability (Maruschak, 2006; Maruschak & Beck, 2001). Finally, inadequate staffing of sign language interpreters poses another issue for deaf inmates. Only 7% of interpreters reported that the facilities where they were employed scheduled interpreters on a 24-hour basis (Miller, 2001). Thus, deaf inmates may not be able to communicate with correctional personnel as often as needed.

Treatment, Programming, and Medical Needs of Inmates with Physical Disabilities

The programming needs of inmates with physical disabilities are profound. According to BJS data, one-half of inmates with a physical disability were homeless at the time of arrest and less than one-third were employed in the month prior to the offense (Maruschak & Beck, 2001). In addition, about one-third had a history of drug abuse, were alcohol dependent, or reported using drugs in the month prior to arrest (Maruschak & Beck, 2001). Participation in educational programs is important, as about one-fourth of adults with a visual impairment and one-fifth of adults with a mobility impairment lack a high school diploma (K. Lisa Yan and Hock E. Tan Institute on Employment and Disability, 2016). Mental health programming is also critical. Specific to deaf inmates, about one-quarter of a sample reported depression or a suicide attempt and almost one-half reported substance abuse (Miller & Vernon, 2003; see Chapter 19 for more on co-occurring disorders). In terms of education, Miller and Vernon (2003) found that four-fifths of their sample of adult deaf inmates had reading, language, and math scores that placed them below a fifth-grade education. Lastly, Vernon and Rich (1997) found that 12 of the 20 deaf male pedophiles in their sample had been victims of sexual abuse.

Despite the clear need for programming, research indicates that few state DOCs provide special programming or aids for this population. In their survey of 36 state DOCS, Long and Sapp (1992) found that no DOC operated a facility that was fully accessible. In terms of programs and environmental features, medical services were the most accessible, followed by access to visitation, access to counseling, religious programming, access to dining facilities, furlough programs, access to recreation and entertainment programs, education, compensated work, shared cells/dormitories, work areas, vocational programs, work release, and single cells. A decade later, in their survey of the accommodations provided to inmates with physical disabilities, Krienert, Henderson, and Vandiver (2003) found that of the 38 state DOCs that responded to their survey, one-third to one-half of state DOCs provided the accommodation for blind or visually impaired inmates, deaf or hearing impaired inmates, or wheelchair-bound inmates. In other words, one-half to two-thirds of state DOCs were not providing the accommodation three years after the *Yeskey* decision. The most commonly provided services to blind inmates were telecommunication devices/text telephones for deaf or hard of hearing inmates (15 state DOCs), Braille material (11 state DOCs), and accessible cells for wheelchair-bound inmates (10 state DOCs).

Housing assignments for inmates with physical disabilities are an important consideration. In their survey, Kreinert et al. (2003) found that only three state DOCs provided specialized housing for blind or visually impaired inmates and one state provided specialized housing for deaf or hearing impaired inmates. Beyond the 10 state DOCS that provided accessible cells for wheelchair-bound inmates, no state DOC reported providing specialized housing for this group. There are several important reasons why inmates with physical disabilities should be placed in specialized housing units. First, it could reduce the potential for verbal, physical, sexual, or economic victimization by other inmates. Second, it could reduce loneliness, as it would allow for inmates with similar physical impairments to socialize with each other. This would be especially true for deaf inmates, who could have other individuals to sign with (Miller, 2002). Third, specialized programming could be developed and implemented that addresses the specific needs of this population. Fourth, medical personnel might find it easier to monitor the health conditions of prisoners if they were all in the same unit. Because of the centralization of services, the prison could potentially reduce its costs and ensure ADA compliance, which would lessen the threat of litigation. However, arguments also exist for mainstreaming inmates with physical disabilities. For example, these inmates may prefer interaction with other inmates (Leigey, 2015). In addition, the housing assignment available to inmates with physical disabilities may be an open dormitory; as such, inmates may dislike the lack of privacy (Leigey, 2015).

A couple of states have implemented programs to address the needs of inmates with physical disabilities. For example, the Ohio Department of Corrections created the Helping Others Together (H.O.T.) program, which provides inmate assistants to help inmates with physical disabilities with daily life activities (Price, 2006). Additionally, the Ohio Department of Corrections offers modified exercise programs (e.g., chair aerobics) for inmates with mobility impairments (Price, 2006). In Texas, the Physically Handicapped Offenders Program (PHOP) helps identify inmates with physical disabilities, evaluate their medical and programming needs, and create individual treatment plans for them (Martin, 2002).

Typically, inmates with special needs, including physical disabilities, are a more expensive population to incarcerate. This is usually because of the increased costs associated with health care. Inmates with physical disabilities may need regular check-ups by prison health care officials to monitor and treat medical conditions. In addition, as the ADA requires the provision of auxiliary aids and services (Schneider & Sales, 2004), inmates with physical disabilities may need to visit medical staff to acquire prosthetic arms and legs, canes, wheelchairs, glasses, and hearing aids. One cost-saving measure that prison administrators may consider is to allow prisoners entering the system to maintain possession of their existing aids. Unless there is a justifiable security concern to ban the current device, such aids should be permitted to alleviate costs to the institution (Atabay, 2009).

The prison infirmary is also responsible for treating the injuries that offenders with physical disabilities sustain. Jail and prison inmates with physical disabilities are more likely to sustain injuries in an accident or in a fight than inmates without physical disabilities (Maruschak, 2006; Maruschak & Beck, 2001). BJS researchers noted other findings that have implications for the health of inmates with disabilities and the corresponding health care required to treat them. For instance, compared to inmates without a disability, jail and prison inmates with a disability were significantly more likely to report serious psychological distress in the past 30 days, significantly more likely to have a co-occurring chronic condition, significantly more likely to report having an infectious disease (e.g., tuberculosis, hepatitis B, hepatitis C, or a sexually transmitted infection) in their lifetimes, and more likely to be obese or morbidly obese (Bronson et al., 2015).

Relationships In and Out of Prison

Maintaining ties to relatives and friends on the outside is important for most inmates. Yet, traditional forms of communication available to inmates (i.e., mail, phones, and visits) pose problems for those with physical disabilities. Inmates with visual impairment might struggle reading mail (Atabay, 2009) or operating regular phones. Inmates with hearing impairment may be unable to speak on regular phones, or if they are seated too far away from visitors in the visiting area, may struggle to lip read or hear what is being said if the noise level in the room is too high. Inmates with mobility impaired may be unable to use the phones if they are placed out of their reach or if the visiting area is not wheelchair accessible (Atabay, 2009; Kitei & Sales, 2006).

During incarceration, the primary group of individuals that inmates are interacting with is other inmates. Inmates with physical disabilities could befriend other inmates who could assist them in performing a variety of daily life activities, such as pushing their wheelchairs, reading their mail aloud to them, carrying their meal trays, or making sure that they are lined up during count times. Instances could exist in which inmates with physical disabilities are given greater respect by other inmates. For example, "depending on culture, canes may be stigmatized as signs of infirmity or valued as icons of power and prestige" (Anderson & Capozzoli, 2011, p. 23). However, some inmates with physical disabilities may feel isolated from other inmates. Deaf inmates who are incarcerated in prisons without other deaf inmates or signers to communicate with could feel especially isolated (Vernon & Miller, 2005). This could lead to mental health issues including depression, self-harm, and suicidal thoughts (Lewis, 2015).

Offenders with physical disabilities can be perceived as being weak or vulnerable (Kitei & Sales, 2006). As a result, other inmates may be reluctant to form relationships with them out of concern that it could increase their likelihood of victimization or stigma (Schneider & Sales, 2004). In addition, because offenders with physical disabilities may need to communicate more regularly with prison staff, they may be perceived as being prison informants, which could make it more difficult for them to form friendships with other inmates (Kitei & Sales, 2006; Miller, 2002). Related to this, "among deaf people, information is often more freely passed on to others than in hearing society, a trait that sometimes earns deaf offenders the title of "'snitch'" (Miller, 2002, p. 90). Other inmates also could be resentful of inmates with physical disabilities because of delays in the prison schedule, for example, lining up for count, meal times, or recreation time (Kitei & Sales, 2006; Schneider & Sales, 2004) or the use of captioning on televisions (Vernon & Miller, 2005).

In terms of inmate-on-inmate victimization, offenders with physical disabilities are at an increased risk of being the victims of physical violence (Schneider & Sales, 2004). Using national-level data, Pare and Logan (2011) found that inmates with the physical disabilities of arthritis/rheumatism, paralysis, or stroke/brain injury were significantly more likely to report a serious victimization than inmates without physical disabilities. National-level data also indicate that inmates with a physical disability were more likely to report sustaining an injury during a fight than inmates without a physical disability. About 4% of federal inmates, 10% of jail inmates, and 12% of state inmates report sustaining an injury during a fight (Maruschak, 2006; Maruschak & Beck, 2001). Anecdotal evidence of the sexual abuse of inmates with physical disabilities also exists (Kitei & Sales, 2006). To reduce victimization, Kitei and Sales (2006, p. 31) recommended that offenders be equipped with "a special device [that] could be attached to their person that, when pushed, could alert guards that they are in danger." In addition, the reduction in the risk of victimization is one of the primary arguments advanced for segregating offenders with physical disabilities, as discussed earlier.

Inmates with physical disabilities also could encounter issues in their interactions with correctional officers. They may have trouble understanding and following orders, and as a result, receive a disciplinary infraction. For example, blind or visually impaired inmates may wander into an unauthorized area, or mobility impaired inmates may struggle to return to their cells on time. Deaf inmates, in particular, may struggle to communicate with correctional officers, as most orders are given verbally. As discussed earlier, relying on lip reading or note writing to relay information to deaf inmates is problematic (Vernon, 2009) because important information may be missed and some deaf inmates may be unable to comprehend notes written on paper. Tapping deaf inmates on their shoulders to get their attention could be misperceived in prison, leading to aggression. Some DOCs have even banned the use of sign language because correctional officers misinterpret the messages as gang signs (Lewis, 2015). Depending on the seriousness of the disciplinary infraction, the penalties could range from loss of privileges (e.g., phone or visitation), removal from work or education programs, to transfer to a more secure area of the institution.

In addition, offenders with physical disabilities may need more time or assistance with completing activities (e.g., showering, eating, or moving around the facilities). Correctional officers may be resentful of inmates with physical disabilities because of the increased time or help required or the presumed intentional violations of rules. Resentment and frustration could lead to correctional officer abuse (Kitei & Sales, 2006; Prison Justice League, 2015). For instance, in *Hucks v. Artuz* (2003), a paraplegic inmate claimed that correctional officers threatened and harassed him, and once, while other correctional officers observed the incident, that an officer forced him out of his wheelchair and onto the ground (Kitei & Sales, 2006). The Prison Justice League (2015) examined correctional officer abuse at the Estelle Unit in Texas. About one-half of the inmates who reported being assaulted by correctional officers had a physical impairment. Inmates with physical disabilities have also reported experiencing correctional officer retaliation for submitting grievances (Kitei & Sales, 2006; Prison Justice League, 2015).

Staff training is crucial for correctional officers so that they are better suited to identify offenders with physical disabilities, avoid writing inmates up for unnecessary disciplinary infractions, and to ensure that the inmates' legal rights are being respected (Atabay, 2009; Prison Justice League, 2015). Correctional officers who abuse inmates should be held accountable and sanctioned in accordance with agency policy and/or state or federal law (Prison Justice League, 2015). Anti-abuse advocates support having correctional officers wear body cameras so that incidents in which force are used could be reviewed (Prison Justice League, 2015).

The Reentry of Inmates with Physical Disabilities

In 2014, approximately 650,000 individuals were released from prisons in the United States (Carson, 2015). Around two-thirds were placed on some form of community supervision (Carson, 2015). An unknown number of individuals released from prison or under community supervision had a physical disability.

Just as incarceration is more challenging for inmates with physical disabilities, it would be expected that the reentry process is more difficult, as disabled offenders negotiate the many challenges of reentry. This population may face a double stigma as they have a prison record and a physical disability. While many ex-offenders struggle to find legitimate employment, those with a physical disability may face even greater adversity as their impairments could prevent them from being able to perform certain types of jobs (Mawhorr, 1997)—for example, physically demanding work or customer service jobs. A lack of education or job experience also limits their employment options. Less than one in three inmates with a physical disability reported being employed in the month prior to arrest (Maruschak & Beck, 2001). While over one-half of inmates with a physical impairment reported receiving some form of government assistance (e.g., disability, Social Security, or veterans' benefits), these funds might not be enough to cover their expenses (Maruschak & Beck, 2001).

Housing is another major barrier to successful reentry because inmates with a physical impairment struggle to maintain stable housing. About one-half of inmates with a physical impairment reported being homeless in the year prior to arrest or at the time of arrest (Maruschak & Beck, 2001). Many ex-offenders lack the financial resources to live independently immediately upon release from prison. As such, they are reliant upon relatives or friends for a place to live. However, depending on the nature of the crime committed (e.g., sexual offense) or the length of incarceration, ex-offenders may no longer have close ties with their outside contacts and may not be able to depend on them for housing. For those ex-offenders who have the financial resources to live independently, there may be limited low-income housing options that are also accessible.

Access to medical care could be another potential issue for ex-offenders with a physical disability, as they may need to have regular check-ups with doctors. However, a lack of income, insurance, or reliable transportation could make it difficult for these individuals to obtain necessary medical care. Without proper medical attention, there is the chance that their physical conditions could worsen. Substance abuse is another major threat to the physical and mental well-being of ex-offenders, including those with a physical disability. Thirty percent of inmates with a physical impairment reported a history of drug abuse, that is, using drugs at least once a week for a month or more: 30% reported using drugs in the month prior to arrest, 36% reported ever using a needle to inject drugs, and 38% were considered to be alcohol dependent (Maruschak & Beck, 2001).

Many released inmates will be reimprisoned, as research indicates that about one-half will return to prison either for a parole or a probation violation or for a new offense within three years of release (Durose, Cooper, & Snyder, 2014). As discussed earlier, comprehension could be an issue, that is, parolees with a physical disability may not understand the conditions of parole and may unknowingly violate them (Vernon, 2010). More research is needed in this area to gain a better understanding the reentry experiences of ex-offenders with a disability, the unique challenges that they face as they reacclimate back to society, and their likelihood of recidivating.

Conclusion

While percentages vary based on sex, age, and race/ethnicity, it is apparent that a sizable number of justice-involved individuals have a visual, auditory, or ambulatory impairment. Research indicates that their experiences in the criminal justice system and interactions with criminal justice actors are fraught with issues. Offenders with a physical disability may be unable to fully communicate with criminal justice personnel or comprehend critical junctures in the criminal justice system. Their actions may be misinterpreted by police, court personnel, or correctional officers. Research indicates that prisons are not universally ADA compliant, and inmates with physical disabilities face additional hardships that compound the normal adversities of prison life. Without proper accommodations, there is a serious concern that their legal and constitutional rights may be infringed upon during police interrogations, court hearings, and imprisonment. Education and training of personnel in police, courts, and corrections is one of the best means to ensure that this population is being treated humanely and in accordance with federal legislation and the Constitution.

References

Accommodation of wheelchair-bound prisoners. (2009). *AELE Monthly Law Journal, 10*, 301–309.

American Civil Liberties Union. (2005). *Legal rights of disabled prisoners*. Washington, DC: American Civil Liberties Union National Prison Project. Retrieved from www.aclu.org/files/images/asset_upload_file735_25737.pdf

American Community Survey. (2014). *2014 Data release new and notable*. Hagerstown, MD: U.S. Census Bureau, U.S. Department of Commerce.

Americans with Disabilities Act of 1990, Pub. L. No. 101–336, 104 Stat. 328 (1991).

Americans With Disabilities Act—Frequently asked questions. (2012). Retrieved from http://courts.mi.gov/Administration/SCAO/OfficesPrograms/Documents/access/ADA%20FAQ%20for%20Trial%20Courts.pdf

Anderson, S. T., & Capozzoli, N. (2011). Walking cane use in prison: A medical and cultural analysis. *Journal of Correctional Health Care, 17*(1), 19–28. doi:10.1177/1078345810385646

Atabay, T. (2009). *Handbook on prisoners with special needs*. Vienna, Switzerland: United Nations Office on Drugs and Crime.

British Deaf Association. (2016). *Throw away the key? How Britain's prisons don't rehabilitate deaf people*. UK: Ministry of Justice.

Bronson, J., Maruschak, L. M., & Berzofsky, M. (2015). *Disabilities among prison and jail inmates, 2011–12* (NCJ 249151). Washington, DC: U.S. Department of Justice, Bureau of Justice Statistics.

Brunson, J. L. (2008). Your case will now be heard: Sign language interpreters as problematic accommodations in legal interactions. *Journal of Deaf Studies and Deaf Education, 13*(1), 77–91. doi:10.1093/deafed/enm032

Carson, E. A. (2015). *Prisoners in 2014* (NCJ 284955). Washington, DC: U.S. Department of Justice, Bureau of Justice Statistics.

Civil Rights of Institutionalized Persons 1980, Pub. L. No. 96–247, 94 Stat. 349 (1980).

Conti, R. P., & Daley, D. J. (2015). Defendant physical disability and sentencing in criminal cases. *Forensic Research & Criminology International Journal, 1*(4), 1–7. doi:10.15406/frcij.2015.01.00022

Diament, M. (2010, October 5). Obama signs bill replacing "mental retardation" with "intellectual disability." *disabilityscoop*. Retrieved from www.disabilityscoop.com/2010/10/05/obama-signs-rosas-law/10547/

Dullum, J. (2015). Sentencing offenders with disabilities. *Scandinavian Journal of Disability Research, 17*(S1), 60–73. doi:10.1080/15017419.2014.998272

Durose, M. R., Cooper, A. D., & Snyder, H. N. (2014). *Recidivism of prisoners released in 30 states in 2005: Patterns from 2005 to 2010* (NCJ 244205). Washington, DC: U.S. Department of Justice, Bureau of Justice Statistics.

Estelle v. Gamble, 429 U.S. 97 (1976).

Goodman v. Georgia, 546 US 151 (2006).

Gorman v. Easley, 257 F. 3d 738 (8th Cir. 2001).

Hucks v. Artuz, 99 Civ. 10420 (S.D.N.Y. 2003).

Hume, T., Karimi, F., & Thompson, N. (2016). Oscar Pistorius sentenced to 6 years in prison for girlfriend's murder. *CNN News*. Retrieved from www.cnn.com/2016/07/06/africa/oscar-pistorius-sentence/

K. Lisa Yan and Hock E. Tan Institute on Employment and Disability. (2016). *Disability statistics*. Retrieved from www.disabilitystatistics.org/reports/acs.cfm?statistic=9

Kitei, N. S., & Sales, B. D. (2006). Physically disabled offenders in prison. In R. J. Morris (Ed.), *Disability research and policy: Current perspectives* (pp. 17–38). Mahwah, NJ: Lawrence Erlbaum Associates, Publisher.

Koshan, J. (2013). *Blind justice? Accommodating offenders with disabilities*. Retrieved from http://ablawg.ca/2013/11/18/blind-justice-accommodating-offenders-with-disabilities/

Krienert, J. L., Henderson, M. L., & Vandiver, D. M. (2003) Inmates with physical disabilities: Establishing a knowledge base. *The Southwest Journal of Criminal Justice*, *1*(1), 13–23.

Leigey, M. E. (2015). *The forgotten men: Serving life without parole*. New Brunswick, NJ: Rutgers University Press.

Lewis, T. A. (2015). Deaf inmates: Communication strategies and legal considerations. *Corrections Today*, 77(3), 44–49.

Long, L. M., & Sapp, A. D. (1992). Programs and facilities for physically disabled inmates in state prisons. *Journal of Offender Rehabilitation*, *18*(1/2), 191–204. doi:10.1300/J076v18n01_09

Martin, K. (2002). Aiding inmates with physical disabilities in Texas. *corrections.com*. Retrieved from www.corrections.com/articles/7948-aiding-inmates-with-physical-disabilities-in-texas

Maruschak, L. M. (2006). *Medical problems of jail inmates*. Washington, DC: U.S. Department of Justice, Bureau of Justice Statistics.

Maruschak, L. M., & Beck, A. J. (2001). *Medical problems of inmates, 1997*. Washington, DC: U.S. Department of Justice, Bureau of Justice Statistics.

Mawhorr, T. L. (1997). Disabled offenders and work release: An exploratory examination. *Criminal Justice Review*, *22*(1), 34–48. doi:10.1177/073401689702200104

McAlister, J. (1994). Deaf and hard-of-hearing criminal defendants: How you gonna get justice if you can't talk to the judge? *Arizona State Law Journal*, *26*, 163–200.

Miller, K. R. (2001). Access to sign language interpreters in the criminal justice system. *American Annals of the Deaf*, *146*(4), 328–330.

Miller, K. R. (2002). Population management strategies for deaf and hard-of-hearing offenders. *Corrections Today*, *64*(7), 90–93,139.

Miller, K. R. (2004). Linguistic diversity in a deaf prison population: Implications for due process. *Journal of Deaf Studies and Deaf Education*, *9*(1), 112–119. doi:10.1093/deafed/enh007

Miller, K. R., & Vernon, M. (2002). Assessing linguistic diversity in deaf criminal suspects. *Sign Language Studies*, *2*(4), 380–390. doi:10.1353/sls.2002.0021

Miller, K. R., & Vernon, M. (2003). Deaf sex offenders in a prison population. *Journal of Deaf Studies and Deaf Education*, *8*(3), 357–362. doi:10.1093/deafed/eng011

Miller, K. R., Vernon, M., & Capella, M. E. (2005). Violent offenders in a deaf prison population. *Journal of Deaf Studies and Deaf Education*, *10*(4), 417–425. doi:10.1093/deafed/eni039

New York v. Ripic, 182 A.D.2d 226 (1992).

Pare, P., & Logan, M. W. (2011). Risks of minor and serious violent victimization in prison: The impact of inmates' mental disorders, physical disabilities, and physical size. *Society & Mental Health*, *1*(2), 106–123. doi:10.1177/2156869311416828

Pennsylvania Department of Corrections v. Yeskey, 524 US 206 (1998).

Price, C. A. (2006). *Aging inmate population study*. Raleigh, NC: North Carolina Department of Corrections, Division of Prisons.

Prison Justice League. (2015). *Cruel & unusual punishment: Excessive use of force at the Estelle Unit*. Austin, TX: Author.

Roesch, R., Zapf, P. A., Golding, S. L., & Skeem, J. L. (2014). *Defining and assessing competency to stand trial*. Retrieved from www.justice.gov/sites/default/files/eoir/legacy/2014/08/15/Defining_and_Assessing_Competency_to_Stand_Trial.pdf

Rubin, B. M. (2009, April 13). Braille report: Few blind people use Braille alphabet, and fewer visually impaired children are learning it than in the 1950s. *Chicago Tribune*. Retrieved from http://articles.chicagotribune.com/2009-04-13/news/0904120130_1_braille-literacy-visually-impaired

Ruiz v. Estelle, 503 F. Supp. 1265 (S.D. Tex. 1980).

Schneider, N. R., & Sales, B. D. (2004). Deaf or hard of hearing inmates in prison. *Disability & Society*, *19*(1), 77–89. doi:10.1080/0968759032000155631

Sykes, G. M. (1958). *The society of captives: A study of a maximum security prison*. Princeton, NJ: Princeton University Press.

Tennessee v. Lane, 541 US 509 (2004).

The Rehabilitation Act of 1973, Pub. L. No. 93–112, 87 Stat. 355 (1973).
Torchia, C., & Imray, G. (2014, May 12). Oscar Pistorius trial: Psychiatrist says anxiety disorder may have contributed to shooting. *Los Angeles Daily News*. Retrieved from www.dailynews.com/general-news/20140512/oscar-pistorius-trial-psychiatrist-says-anxiety-disorder-may-have-contributed-to-shooting
Toth, R. C. (2008). The disabled and physically challenged in the criminal justice system. In R. C. Toth, G. A. Crews, & C. E. Burton (eds.), *In the margins: Special populations and American justice* (pp. 145–176). Upper Saddle River, NJ: Pearson Education, Inc.
United States Department of Justice. (2006). *Commonly asked questions about the Americans With Disabilities Act and law enforcement*. Washington, DC: U.S. Department of Justice, Civil Rights Division, Disability Rights Section.
Vernon, M. (1995). New rights for inmates with hearing loss. *Corrections Today, 57*(2), 140–145.
Vernon, M. (2009). ADA routinely violated by prisons in the case of deaf prisoners. *Prison Legal News, 20*(7), 14–15.
Vernon, M. (2010). The horror of being deaf and in prison. *American Annals of the Deaf, 155*(3), 311–321.
Vernon, M., & Andrews, J. F. (1990). *The psychology of deafness: Understanding deaf and hard of hearing people*. White Plains, NY: Longman Press.
Vernon, M., & Miller, K. R. (2001). Linguistic competence to stand trial: A unique condition in some deaf defendants. *Journal of Interpretation, Millennial Edition, 9*(1), 99–120.
Vernon, M., & Miller, K. R. (2005). Obstacles faced by deaf people in the criminal justice system. *American Annals of the Deaf, 150*(3), 283–291.
Vernon, M., & Rich, S. (1997). *Pedophilia and deafness*. Washington, DC: American Annals of the Deaf.

21

AGING BEHIND BARS

Assessing the Health Care Needs of Graying Prisoners

Mary E. Harrison Joynt and Alex J. Bishop

> Our federal prisons are starting to resemble nursing homes surrounded with razor wire. It makes no sense fiscally, or from the perspective of human compassion, to incarcerate men and women who pose no threat to public safety and have long since paid for their crime.
>
> —Julie Stewart, president and founder of Families Against Mandatory Minimums (as quoted in Horwitz, 2015, para. 9)

Introduction

Despite the decline in overall prison population, over the past three decades, there have been an ever-increasing number of *older* inmates in state and federal prisons in the United States (Kim & Peterson, 2014). Within the federal and state prison system, the proportion of prisoners age 50 and older increased from 12% in 1994 to 17% in 2011. Inmates 65 years of age and older also are projected to increase significantly (Kim & Peterson, 2014). In a report from the U.S. Department of Justice, estimates indicate the older inmate population had increased to over 18% in 2014 (Carson, 2015). The percentage of older prisoners, age 50 and older, is projected to reach 28% by 2019 (Kim & Peterson, 2014). This steady increase is due in large part to an of influx middle-aged "baby boomers" entering prison for the first time under mandatory minimum sentencing laws such as the three strikes law and truth in sentencing (Aday, 2003; Deaton & Aday, 2009; Hayes, Burns, Turnbull, & Shaw, 2012; Koenig, 1995; Maschi, Viola, & Morgen, 2014; Porter, Bushway, Tsao, & Smith, 2016; Williams, Stern, Mellow, Safer, & Greifinger, 2012b). Such policies have created a "graying" of the prison population that introduced a unique set of issues that demand attention and resolution surrounding the cost of caring for an ever-growing population of inmates who are aging-in-place (Chiu, 2010).

The cost of immediate and long-term care of older inmates is an important concern for prison institutions. It costs correctional facilities more to care for older prisoners than their younger counterparts (U.S. Department of Justice [DOJ], 2016b). According to the Federal Bureau of Prisons' (FBOP) 2016 report, aging inmates cost approximately 8% more annually than inmates 49 and younger. Even more alarming, older female inmates, though fewer in numbers, cost considerably more than male inmates in the same age range (Kim & Peterson, 2014). They found, when looking at lifetime per capita health care cost, female inmates cost $92,513, which represents 20% more cost than their male counterparts (Kim & Peterson, 2014). Further, even when adjusting for males serving a life sentence (lifetime cost $305,281), female inmates' lifetime costs are still $55,911 higher

($361,192) (Kim & Peterson, 2014). According to the FBOP (DOJ, 2016c), the overall annual cost for (per capita) federal institutions has been increasing ($23,780 in 2011 to $25,251 in 2014) in lower security prisons. The average cost for an older inmate was estimated at $24,538 per year, and the FBOP (2016c) reported spending a disproportionate amount, 19% of the budget (approximately $881 million), on aging inmates, 50 and older, in 2013.

In response to the increasing rates of incarceration and the cost of care for older prisoners in the United States, a roundtable of 29 national experts was convened at the John Jay College of Criminal Justice in 2011 (Williams et al., 2012b). Nine major areas of concern relative to the maintenance and care aging prisoners were identified (Williams et al., 2012b). These areas included defining who is "old" within the prison system, defining prison-based functional impairment, screening for dementia, identifying the needs of older women prisoners, challenges surrounding release and reentry of older prisoners, improving medical release policies, enhancing palliative care policies, creating uniform policies for geriatric housing units, and uniform training for staff and health care providers for the aging (Rich, Allen, & Williams, 2014). This chapter will explore these areas to explore the impact of aging while in prison.

The chapter will focus on the controversy around defining who is old within the prison setting. The chapter also will discuss age-related functional decline among aging inmates and arguments for and against specialized geriatric prison units. We will provide an overview of dementia and the need for accurate diagnosis and appropriate treatment and caregiving needs of this population. In addition, the chapter will present a discussion of mental health issues (e.g., depression) among older inmates, followed by a discussion of the spiritual needs of those aging in prison. We examine the understudied population of aging female inmates and their unique needs. Finally, the chapter concludes with a discussion about end-of-life care, including hospice care and compassionate release.

Identifying Elderly or "Old" Inmates

The criminal justice literature has yet to come to a consensus on who is "old" or elderly within the prison system. Lack of a definitive age creates many problems, from setting policies to creating protocols that ensure safety for the aging within the prison system. The classification of "old age" for inmates tends to be ambiguous. The designation of who is considered elderly or old is typically a matter of policy. For example, in the United States, old age is chronologically determined by one's designated retirement age (Social Security Administration, 2016). Currently, to retire with full Social Security benefits, one is considered old at 66 years. But, chronological age is far less useful in defining "being old" in prison. Using physical and mental abilities is much more useful in determining and identifying who is an "old" or aging inmate (Aday, 2003). Past literature has varied on the definition of who is old, ranging from 50–65 years of age (Loeb & Dagga, 2006; Williams, 2010; Williams, Goodwin, Baillargeon, Ahalt, & Walter, 2012a). In a 2006 review of literature about aging or older inmates, Loeb and Dagga (2006) found that the age range was 45–65 years of age and older. The National Institute of Corrections defines "old" beginning at age 50 for inmates (Williams et al., 2012a). Beginning in 2007, the U.S. Bureau of Justice defined older inmates within groups (55–59, 60–65, and 65+) (West & Sabol, 2007). As you can see, there are multiple ways to define who is elderly or old, and the differences in age range can be quite large. The lack of uniformity in age definition and range forces states to determine their own definition. This becomes problematic when researchers and policy makers want to learn about those aging in prison and to build cost- and life-saving policies for older inmates.

Because no universal definition has been determined, states have individually determined who is old, which typically ranges between 50 to 70 years of age. The variation in determining who is old is due to the belief that prisoners age at an accelerated rate due to cumulative disadvantage (stress, lack of health care, and drug and alcohol abuse) throughout their life, and research finds these variables vary among the inmate population (Hollenbeak, Schaefer, Penrod, Lob, & Smith, 2015). The majority of the research used the age 50 and above to denote older or aging inmates (Loeb & Dagga, 2006). Williams et al. (2012b, p. 1477) urges the need for a "clear age cutoff" to define older inmates and establish consistency within prison health research. This would allow correctional facilities and policy makers clear guidelines for assessment, interventions, and treatments that targeted the majority of inmates who need specialized care due to aging (Williams et al., 2012b, p. 1478). Also established during the roundtable was an emphasis on the need to measure "age-related vulnerability." Rather than looking at age exclusively, there was a call to focus on function and cognition apart from age, where aging inmates are at considerable more risk of victimization than their younger counterparts.

Age-Related Functional Decline

One normative age-associated limitation among older prisoners involves age-related functional decrements. In a 1992 study, researchers found nearly 42% of the 119 men in their sample age 50 and older had gross physical limitations (Colsher, Wallace, Loeffellolz, & Sales, 1992; Hebert, 1997). Age-related functional decline is defined as a loss of physical and/or mental abilities involved in the aging process. Currently, the FBOP acknowledges that are several areas of concern regarding the care and treatment of older inmates with physical and mental limitations, including a significant lack of staffing to assist aging inmates with limited physical mobility, housing inadequacies that do not fit the needs of aging inmates, lack of programs for aging inmates, and a lack of accessibility for those inmates with declining physical abilities (Carson & Sabol, 2016). Further, there is a need for assistive devices (e.g., walkers, canes, wheelchairs, hearing aids, and corrective eyewear), but often, inmates wait extended periods to be evaluated and have difficulty in receiving the needed devices. It is unclear exactly how many older inmates require the use of assistance devices, but what is known is, as the population of aging prisoners grows, these needs will continue to increase (Carson & Sabol, 2016, Corrections Today, 2012; Whitaker, 2016).

Functional decline has been defined as the period in time when physical and mental capacities are reduced because of the aging process. According to Bernstein and Munoz (2016), functional decline is determined through two common evaluation tools: Activities of Daily Living (ADL) and Instrumental Activities of Daily Living (IADL). The former is explained through an individual's ability to perform such tasks as bathing, toileting, feeding, dressing, and grooming oneself. The latter covers abilities in independent functions of preparing food, doing laundry, and taking medications properly. Declines in functional status progressively inhibit self-care, happen gradually in subtle ways, and may make it difficult for correctional staff and officers to notice aging inmates' functional decline in a timely fashion. For example, the need for reading glasses or hearing aids may not be readily apparent until others begin to see dramatic changes (Stibich, 2015).

When considering functional decline, there are differences between those living in the community and those aging in prison. As previously mentioned, the ADL instrument is an evaluation tool designed to gauge functional decline. Measures of ADL are common for both older individuals living in the community and in prison; however, inmates face tasks that are required and often become increasingly difficult. For example, older inmates must move from their cell to the dining hall, move in and out of a top bunk, hear and acknowledge staff orders, or assume a certain physical position during alarms or inmate counts. These rather simple tasks are often physically taxing for aging prisoners but may go unnoticed by correctional officers and staff. The importance of a uniform list of activities by which staff can begin to identify older inmates' inability to perform daily tasks is needed to provide additional assistance and supervision to inmates near the beginning of their physical decline (Williams et al., 2012b).

Frailty

Although frailty has similar characteristics with functional decline, research has begun to define frailty as a stand-alone syndrome (Fulop et al., 2010). In doing so, recognition and treatment of individuals who are frail is equally important because of an acceleration of cognitive and physical decline. A common definition of frailty is a "physical and functional" decline that coincides with disease, and its presentation includes reduced activity level, slowed walking, loss of dexterity, and weight loss (Fulop et al., 2010, p. 548). The inmates who begin to experience frailty may be aging into a level of care that cannot be met by the standard prison setting. While there are no definitive guidelines that determine when an inmate would need additional care considerations for frailty, the option of more suitable housing becomes the primary focus and concern.

Geriatric Housing in Prison

Correctional administrators and staff express increasing concerns about how to accommodate the physical needs of aging inmates and the inmates' ability to function successfully within prison living arrangements (Bishop & Merton, 2011; Stibich, 2015). In truth, prisons are not designed to house and care for such a large aging inmate population. In one study of housing models for aging inmates, Thivierge-Rikard and Thompson (2016) looked at segregated housing units (SHUs) where older inmates are housed separate from the general population and have separate, more specialized medical facilities, and consolidated housing and housing where older inmates remained in general population. They looked more specifically at the association between mental and physical health service availability for aging inmates in both housing models. Their sample consisted of 918 state facilities. Within these facilities, only 3.9% provided geriatric care. Segregated facilities providing geriatric care were the highest (2%), consolidated housing (1%), and a mixed unit model provided care (1%). The remaining 96% of state facilities provided no geriatric care (Thivierge-Rikard & Thompson, 2016). The authors reported the consolidated housing model was associated with an increase in nongeriatric mental health services. The researchers suggest that the increase prevalence of dementia and depression in older inmates may have facilitated the need for more mental health programs for aging inmates (Thivierge-Rikard & Thompson, 2016).

The physical structure of prison environments poses physical and mental health as well as medical challenges for aging inmates. The design of current correctional facilities is tailored for younger prisoners (Aday, 2003) and creates dangerous obstacles for older and aging inmates. (Corrections Today, 2012). According to West and Sabol (2007), 2% of jailed inmates required the use of a wheelchair, cane, walker, or other device to assist with daily activities. Lack of proper lighting in cells and hallways adds to the complication of mobility and contributes to falls (Human Rights Watch, 2012). Further, excessive noise within the prison creates psychological distress for older inmates (Corrections Today, 2012). The inmates who have already received care for limited mobility and use assistive devices find that the biggest hurdles to mobility come from the actual structure of the prison itself. During an evaluation and inspection of prisons, the FBOP found many aging inmates require the use of wheelchairs, canes, cells located on the first floor, and handicap-accessible facilities (USDOJ, 2016b). Older inmates who require wheelchairs and canes need more space to maneuver. Many older inmates must leave their wheelchairs outside of their cell because of inadequate door width and limited space inside their cell (USDOJ, 2016b).

The physical layout of the building itself presents a barrier for aging-in-place. Stairs and multilevel tiers make it difficult and nearly impossible for aging inmates to navigate and maneuver. Inmates may have little or no access to elevators and/or wheelchair ramps, making it difficult or impossible to attend recreational centers, mental health therapy, and medical treatments (Corrections Today,

2012; USDOJ, 2016b). Moreover, climate is not well controlled and poses other issues for aging inmates, such as exacerbating conditions like asthma, chronic emphysema, and arthritis. Prisons are typically constructed of steel and concrete and often lack proper ventilation. Thus, they can be too cold or too hot depending on weather conditions and/or time of the year (Corrections Today, 2012). Lack of climate control adds to the pain and discomfort of aging inmates, whose muscles and bones continue to deteriorate because of aging (Aday & Krabill, 2011). Additionally, many prisons have separate buildings where the cafeterias, medical facilities, and visitation take place. Snow, inclement weather, uneven pathways, and narrow sidewalks are some of the obstacles older inmates with limitations face when going about their daily routines (USDOJ, 2016b). In response to the growing need for special housing for aging inmates, 13 states have provided specialized elderly units. Aday (2003) provides one of the most comprehensive discussions of needs exclusive to aging inmates, including their unique housing and program needs. There are obvious benefits to having specialized housing or geriatric units for older inmates. Specifically, SHUs have floorplans that are more accessible, are climate controlled to aid in comfort, and provide safety from being victimized by younger, stronger inmates (Marquart, Merianos, & Doucet, 2000).

Support for Integrated Housing

Separate housing for aging inmates has not always been the first choice for older inmates who want to remain connected to the younger population (Aday, 2003). There are many positive aspects to integrated housing, including the ability to maintain bonds with inmates, hold work positions that may not be available in geriatric units, and prevent stress that arises from a transition or move to a separate facility (Aday, 2003). For the aging, it is especially important to maintain ties to family and friends outside the prison; also, contact with family and friends has several important positive effects. Past studies show there is a need to stay connected with family and friends to prevent feelings of isolation (O'Hara et al., 2016). Closeness of relationships helps prevent depression and allows older individuals to pass on life advice to younger generations (Aday, 2003). Older inmates who have the opportunity to transfer to a geriatric unit may decline the offer to remain in general population to maintain bonds inside and outside of the facility. Oftentimes, geriatric facilities are longer distances away from family and friends, and older inmates risk losing those close ties and relationships (Aday, 2003).

Older inmates also have a stabilizing effect on younger inmates. Older inmates often become positive role models, demonstrate better behavior and more compliance with correctional staff, have fewer institutional infractions, and get along with other inmates better than younger inmates. These behaviors are seen as a model for younger inmates to follow. Another argument in favor of integrated housing is the cost of building specialized facilities or housing units. States that do have geriatric units cannot accommodate the number of aging inmates in need of such housing accommodations, and with limited resources, adding such facilities are cost prohibitive. Further, research into the benefits and pitfalls of geriatric housing is needed to determine cost effectiveness, addressing physical and mental needs of the aging, and whether there are better alternatives for addressing this growing population.

Theoretical Applications: Environmental Press Theory

One theory that has been applied to explain the dynamic interaction between the physical and psychological aspects of aging in prison is environmental press theory (Lawton & Nahemow, 1973). This theory examines how older inmates navigate and adapt to the demands of the physical and social nature within prison settings (Aday, 2003). That is, prisoners must adapt to the physical condition of prison. For example, prisoners are required to navigate stairs, climb up and down out of a bunk, and react in a timely manner to staff orders and instructions. Poor eyesight and hearing as well as adjusting to the changing social aspects in prison may become too difficult for older inmates. The amount of environmental press can range from low to high depending on the situations an older inmate is experiencing. Aday (2003) explains that the level of environmental press can be relatively high, for example, when older inmates face a prison where their physical abilities inhibit them from moving from one part of the prison to another in an allotted time. The demands of certain security level prisons add to the environmental press aging inmates may experience. For instance, when older inmates fail to comply in a timely way with the orders of correctional officers or staff, it may result in stress overload and may be viewed as noncompliance by correctional personnel. However, older inmates may experience too little stimulation, becoming bored, which could result in withdrawal, isolation, and depression.

Dementia in Aging Inmates

In addition to physical functioning, mental health decline has been a growing concern for aging inmates (Maschi, Kwak, Ko, & Morrissey, 2012). While prisons' main objective is to provide public safety through the punishment of inmates, recognition, evaluation, and treatment of mental illness of inmates is an essential facet of providing public safety when inmates are released (Jordan, 2011). One major unrecognized and undertreated mental illness facing aging inmates is dementia.

Dementia is defined as a progressive decline in mental ability that severely inhibits everyday living and activities (ALZ.org, 2016). Common symptoms of dementia vary but must include impairment of two core mental functions. Core mental functions include memory, communication/language abilities, focus, reasoning/judgment impairment, and visual perception (ALZ.com, 2016). Other symptoms include aggressive behavior, sleep disturbances, agitation and anxiety, wandering, depressed mood, and repetitive activities (ALZ.org, 2016). According to the World Health Organization (WHO), the total number of people with dementia in 2015 was estimated at 47.5 million worldwide, and by 2030 is expected to increase to 75.6 million.

In the U.S., it is estimated that one in nine older adults has some form of dementia, and 5.1 million Americans of all age groups suffered from Alzheimer's disease (AD) in 2015 (ALZ.org, 2016). Similar increases in cases of dementia will occur within the prison system as well. Currently, there is no one test for diagnosing dementia or AD. Diagnosing dementia and/or Alzheimer's disease is time consuming, costly, and often difficult to pin down because there are multiple reasons for memory loss. For aging inmates, it may be difficult to collect a full medical and mental history. The medical history includes current health status, past illnesses, any diagnosed AD or dementia in family members, diet, alcohol and drug abuse, current prescribed medications, a routine physical exam (blood pressure, heart rate, weight, and pulse), and blood and urine samples (ALZ.org, 2016). Further, during the neurological exam, the specialist is looking for signs of stroke both small and large, brain tumors, fluid on the brain, signs of Parkinson's disease, and illnesses link to memory loss. Mental status is evaluated through numerous testing tools; for example, the mini-mental state exam (MMSE), which is comprised of questions based on everyday mental skills, Mini-Cog, mood assessment, and magnetic resonance imaging (MRI) or computerized tomography (CT) scans that can rule out other issues and conditions and look for head trauma, tumors, and evidence of a stroke (ALZ.org, 2016). These comprehensive exams are most likely outside the reach of most prison facilities, and because these procedures would be considered elective, it is unlikely aging inmates would be taken to a facility where such tests could be performed. In addition, correctional administrators view this as an unnecessary cost (Williams et al., 2012a). Regardless, MRIs and CTs as well as other forms of evaluation and diagnosis are needed to ensure these inmates receive proper medical care.

Diagnosing Dementia in Prison

Among older prisoners, the estimated rate of dementia can range from 1% to 44% (Maschi & Baer, 2012; Williams et al., 2012a). Yet there has been no national study conducted to determine the prevalence of dementia across the U.S. prison population. As previously stated, diagnosis may be hindered by the cost. Specifically, there are typically five areas of testing, including medical history, mental status, neurological examination, physical examination, and brain imaging. Such diagnostic procedures are expensive, and correctional facilities often have limited financial resources. For older adults living in the community, the estimated total cost of dementia and AD for 2015 was $226 billion (Alzheimer's Association, 2015). State prisons face mounting costs in health care for their inmates, and it is well known that older inmates are among the costliest. For example, in 2013, the state of Virginia spent $58 million on inmate health care in offsite facilities costs (Ollove, 2016).

Complete Medical Histories

As noted, there are several components to the accurate diagnosis of dementia or AD, including a thorough medical history, testing of mental status, a complete neurological and physical examination, and blood tests and brain imaging tests to determine the type of mental impairment. The specialists most often sought to diagnose dementia and AD are neurologists specializing in the nervous system and brain, psychiatrists specializing in mood disorders, and psychologists specializing in mental functions and memory testing (ALZ.org, 2016). When considering a comprehensive clinical cognitive assessment for accurate diagnosis, there are several complications for prison systems. First, comprehensive clinical cognitive evaluations are time consuming and require extensive staff training. Training staff to recognize initial signs and determine when to report these issues to medical staff may be difficult in prison settings. For instance, the main purpose of incarceration is punishment, and correctional officers are focused on gaining inmate compliance. However, older inmates may have difficulty complying with orders and instructions from correctional officers because the inmates are exhibiting early signs of dementia. Unfortunately, officers typically miss these early warning signs and mistake the inmate's lack of response or compliance as disobedience (Maschi et al., 2012). Older inmates with dementia will experience diminished reasoning, executive functioning, and altered behaviors that staff and officers may not recognize as illness, and, in turn, older inmates may be written up for disciplinary infractions that result in punishment, typically administrative segregation (Maschi et al., 2012). Sadly, isolation exacerbates dementia symptoms and may cause inmates to act out aggressively or violently (Belluck, 2012).

Future research is needed to develop more cost-effective ways to address the necessary medical evaluation and assessment of inmates for dementia and AD. As a solution, researchers have suggested an annual cognitive screening of all older inmates (turning 55+) during incarceration (Williams et al., 2012b). Screening tools such as the MMSE and the Montreal Cognitive Assessment (MCS) have been utilized for lower socioeconomic status (SES) populations; however, it is still unknown whether they would apply to those living in a prison setting. There is agreement that assessments that take into consideration levels of education and literacy of inmates may prove to be a better tool for screening. Another area that needs to be addressed for inmates living with dementia is housing. While older inmates may need certain accommodations, those with dementia need specialized facilities where supervision and safety are a priority (Williams et al., 2012b).

Caregiving of Dementia and Alzheimer's Disease Diagnosed Patients

Caregivers take on a wide array of duties when caring for someone with dementia/AD. The most common types of care include assisting with instrumental activities of daily living (IADL), providing medications on a proper schedule in the directed amounts, assisting with activities of daily living (ADL), providing supervision for managing behavioral symptoms of dementia/AD (wandering, anxiety, aggression, agitation, and depressive symptoms), making sure proper nursing care is available, finding and maintaining support services, and providing overall care to assist patients throughout the day (Alzheimer's Association, 2015). IADL deal with tasks that require clear cognition, such as household chores, arranging medical appointments, shopping, preparing meals, managing finances, and legal affairs (Alzheimer's Association, 2015). Further, ADL include bathing, grooming, dressing, feeding, assistance in walking, entry and exit from bed, and toileting (Alzheimer's Association, 2015). The toll on a caregiver can be remarkably taxing. Ultimately, older inmates require this extensive care, sometimes around the clock care, costing correctional facilities an annual estimated $93,000 per bed (Osborne Association, 2014). Many state and federal prisons across the U.S. have minimal programs and services that focus on dementia or AD (Maschi et al., 2012). More research is needed to evaluate correctional facilities that house and care for dementia and AD inmates and to determine how to implement evidence-based practices when treating inmates with dementia and AD.

Depression

There are a variety of contributing factors to depression for aging inmates, including entering prison or jail, length of sentence, veteran status, differences between younger and older inmates, and other metal disorders like posttraumatic stress syndrome (PTSD) (Hayes et al., 2012; Kopera-Frye et al., 2013; Maschi & Baer, 2012; Maschi, Morgen, Zgoba, Courtney, & Ristow, 2011; Murdoch, Morris, & Holmes, 2008; O'Hara et al., 2016). Mental well-being represents one of the most important public health issues among aging prisoners (Merten, Bishop, & Williams, 2012). In fact, depression is the most commonly diagnosed mental health problem among older prisoners (Hayes et al., 2012; O'Hara et al., 2016) and is often an underlying cause of some other and more serious health ailments (Kopera-Frye et al., 2013; Murdoch et al., 2008). Early diagnosis and treatment for depression is essential to lowering future health costs among aging prison populations (Maschi & Baer, 2012; Murdoch et al., 2008). However, correctional systems do not have a uniform strategy of mental health management for older inmates (Hayes et al., 2012).

As research continues to look closer at underlying causes of mental illness in older inmates, stress, trauma, and PTSD have all played roles in the increased instances of depression (Maschi et al., 2011; 2014). Maschi et al. (2014) examined 677 older male inmates (50+) and reported that 70% had experienced one or more major life traumas or stressors. Many of these events required legal and or clinical intervention; however, for unknown reasons, many were left unaddressed. Maschi et al. (2014) found a strong mediating effect between trauma and stressful life events and coping resources. Coping resources include physical, cognitive, emotional, spiritual, and social coping skills. Maschi et al. (2014, p. 685) stress the need to address and treat trauma and life stressors, both short and long term, by focusing on coping resources "in the form of individual and social level coping resources, among ethnically diverse older prisoners."

In a 2008 study of older inmates, researchers looked at the underlying causes of depression, most specifically at length of sentence and chronic illness (Murdoch et al., 2008). Of the 121 male inmates age 55 and older who participated, 35 were serving mandatory life sentences, while the remaining 86 were serving indeterminate sentences. Using a modified Geriatric Depression Scale (GDS) to tailor the questions to older inmates who were incarcerated, the measurements were as follows: depression threshold (10 or lower), mild depression (11–20) and severe depression (21–30). The researchers found 49% scored below the threshold, 56% scored at 10, meaning they were bordering on mild depression, 48% of the older inmates scored in the mild depression range (11–20), and 3% scored as severely depressed. Murdoch et al. (2008) reported although they found no association between length of sentence and depression, they did find negative associations between individual chronic health conditions and depression. These negative associations were compounded when there was more than one chronic illness present. The modification to the diagnostic tool was important because the environment in which prisoners live is vastly more hostile and unpredictable than community settings in which most people live.

In a more recent study, O'Hara et al. (2016) looked at 100 older male inmates ages 60–81 who were at the beginning of their incarceration to determine the association between unmet social care and health needs and level of depression. They found that health conditions and treatments were the most common unmet needs (38%), followed closely by psychological distress (34%). Using the Geriatric Depression Scale-15 (GDS-15) they also found a bimodal result for depression, where 55% scored at the cutoff (below 5; 5 indicates the presence of depressive symptoms) and 23% scored above 10, showing symptoms of severe depression. When considering the mental health treatment of older inmates, correctional administrators should make sure staff is properly trained to recognize and treat mental illness at the onset. In doing so, administrators may lower costs over time, improve the inmate's overall well-being, and prevent less disruption within everyday life within the facility.

Limitations

Past research has used multiple depression scales to identify depression in older inmates; however, many of these scales were not developed to assess a population that is incarcerated. The uniqueness of this population makes it imperative to develop a depression scale that targets the qualities and experiences of this group. Creating a tailored geriatric depression scale specifically for older inmates may improve the diagnosis of depression and treatment outcomes. Such scales should reflect the differences between older women and men who are incarcerated and the trauma and life stressors they have experienced. Testing a universal tool for validity and reliability is imperative. Another important limitation is that much of the research on inmate depression is conducted in male prisons. While we do know that female inmates report traumas from childhood (e.g., physical and sexual abuse) and adult trauma (e.g., domestic violence), more focused studies using all-female inmate samples is needed to understand the unique treatment needs of incarcerated women (Aday, 2003; Baidawi & Trotter, 2015). In other words, researchers have highlighted the need to create and implement gender-responsive treatment and programs (Chesney-Lind & Pasko, 2003; Van Voorhis & Salisbury, 2014).

Aging and Spirituality

The benefits of faith-based programming to enhance religiosity and spirituality among older prisoners have been inconclusive (Lonczak, Clifasefi, Marlatt, Blume, & Donovan, 2006). Discrepancies in outcomes have been attributed to the complexity of religiosity, the subjectiveness of religious belief (cultural, social, and behavioral), and defining and measurement of religiosity (Lonczak et al., 2006). In the past, it was shown that religious beliefs, attending religious service and private prayer, meditation, and Bible study were associated with less depression for first-time prison terms among older inmates compared to younger inmates (Koenig, 1995).

More recent research has uncovered various associations between religion and healthy aging among older inmates (Allen et al., 2012; Randall & Bishop, 2013). Religious involvement and spirituality have acted as both a moderator and mediator in the health and well-being of older inmates. For example, Allen et al. (2012) looked at religious coping and depressive symptoms among 94 male inmates ages 45 and above who were residents at the Hamilton Aged and Infirmed Prison located in Hamilton, Alabama. These researchers examined the effects of religiosity and spirituality on physical and mental well-being when considering a desire to die. Using multiple measures (MMSE, Wide Range Achievement Test, functional status items from the Medical Outcomes Survey, Brief Multidimensional Measure of Religiousness and Spirituality, Duke University Religion Index, Hastened

Death Scale-modified, and The Center for Epidemiological Studies Depression Scale [CES-D]), they found that fewer symptoms of depression were found in older inmates with higher levels of positive religious coping and more depressive symptoms in older inmates with higher levels of negative religious coping (Allen et al., 2012). Further, they found older inmates with higher depression scores also desired to hasten death. When including an interaction effect between functional status and negative religious coping, they found hastening desire for death and physical functioning were moderated by negative religious coping for older inmates. In this case, the positive effects of religious involvement buffered the desire to hasten death and increased older inmates' level of well-being.

In a similar study, Randall and Bishop (2013) collected data from 261 male inmates ages 45–82 incarcerated in eight state prisons in Oklahoma. These researchers sought to expand on current research on the associations among religiosity, social provisions, forgiveness, and mental/physical well-being of older inmates. One major finding from their study showed that forgiveness and social provisions are mediators for religiosity and valuation of life for older inmates. They found direct effects between religiosity and valuation of life, where inmates find within themselves an attachment to life. Next, they showed strength of a partial mediated effect of religiosity and valuation of life through forgiveness and social provisions. They urge that inmates may develop and maintain higher self-esteem and a sense of self-worth through increased social resources. In addition, the research shows that through forgiveness, social networks are strengthened and maintained. Other significant indirect effects found were the mediating effects "for religiosity and valuation of life through forgiveness and social provisions" (Randall & Bishop, 2013, p. 57). These paths would indicate that forgiveness of others improves and protects interpersonal relationships. One path in particular was empirically supported; religiosity and social provision through forgiveness of others can be used as an indicator to caseworkers and clinicians that older inmates could benefit from forgiveness therapy intervention for improving mental health and social relationships (Randall & Bishop, 2013). Forgiveness may improve valuation in life, or the degree to which older prisoners achieve a sense of purpose. Forgiveness seems to be further enhanced if the older inmate feels supported by others (Randall & Bishop, 2013).

Aging Women in Prison: Special Concerns

Aging women represent a smaller yet understudied proportion of older prisoners in state and federal correctional systems (Aday & Farney, 2014; Aday & Krabill, 2011; Handtke, Bretschneider, Elger, & Wangmo, 2014). Aday (2003) noted that much of the female inmate population are serving "first-time" long-term sentences for nonviolent crimes. With this increase in female incarceration, the cases of older female inmates with multiple health issues also increase. Much of the aging inmate research has focused on aging male inmates because of the greater number of male inmates compared to female inmates (Aday, 2003; Bishop & Merton, 2011; Maschi et al., 2014; Stibich, 2015). While there are similarities in health-related issues among aging women and men, women face several aspects that are gender specific (Aday & Krabill, 2011; Van Voorhis & Salisbury, 2014). Both male and female inmates share common chronic illnesses (e.g., asthma, emphysema, arthritis, and influenza) but female inmates face reproductive/postmenopausal risks and illness and a higher proportion of debilitating diseases (Aday & Krabill, 2011; Coyle, 2001). These include breast cancer, cervical and uterine cancers, and osteoporosis. A 2006 report on the health of inmates showed that 831 per 10,000 female inmates reported ever having cancer, and of these, 490 per 10,000 previously had or currently had cervical cancer, 110 per 10,000 reported having or had ovarian cancer, and 91 per 10,000 have or had breast cancer (BJS, 2006). Only 108 per 10,000 male inmates reported they have or had any type of cancer (BJS, 2006). These gender-specific illnesses contribute the higher cost of diagnosing and treatment. For example, treatment for older female inmates cost about 20% more in lifetime per capita health care costs than their male counterparts (Kim & Peterson, 2014). Further, older women are at higher risk for common debilitating diseases such as stroke, arthritis, hypertension, diabetes, digestive issues, incontinence, and depression (Aday, 1994; Aday & Krabill, 2011). In addition, female inmates have higher rates of comorbidity than females living in the community.

In a 2014 study, Aday and Farney found that the growth of the "penal harm" movement reverberated into barriers to health care. For example, the inclusion of a medical co-pay, unresponsive prison staff and medical personnel when trying to have medical conditions assessed, and restricting or denial of prescription medications for inmates are just some examples of barriers to health care. The researchers studied 327 older female inmates across seven prisons in the southeastern region of the United States. The age range for the sample was 50–77, with a mean age of 56.4 years of age. Along with demographic information, the researchers used the Hopkins Symptom Checklist, which tests for depression, anxiety, somatization (i.e., medical symptoms with no discernable cause), and interpersonal sensitivity. Further, they included qualitative accounts from older female inmates that exemplified the experiences of these women as they aged within a prison setting. Many of the women in the sample suffer from high/severe levels of depression, anxiety, and interpersonal sensitivity (46%, 43%, and 42%, respectively) (Aday & Farney, 2014). These results may be linked to the preexisting traumas and physical injuries these women experienced preincarceration. The majority of these women described themselves as being in poor health (64%) and that their health has declined within the past two years of incarceration (53%) (Aday & Farney, 2014). In turn, older inmates' accounts of anxiety of dying in prison for fear that prison officials would not respond in time to medical emergencies, declining health, and increased functional impairments add to the daily fear that their health issues will be ignored or neglected. Among the highest reported functional impairments were problems walking independently (88.5%), need for a lower bunkbed (85.8%), and vision problems (8.3%). In addition, a significant number of inmates (4.2%) had comorbid conditions (Aday & Farney, 2014). Along with comorbidity comes chronic pain (Aday & Krabill, 2011). Mistrust between the inmates and prison officials often hinder or prevent health issues from being addressed. Having a lower bunk or request for proper pain management were disregarded as manipulation tactics rather than legitimate health concerns that are addressed and treated in the community on a regular basis. The women in this study found it difficult (at times impossible) to convey to medical staff and prison officials the need for proper pain management (Aday & Farney, 2014).

Mental Health Concerns

Another concern in prison is the high incidence of mental illness among older women inmates (Aday, 2003; Aday & Farney, 2014). It is widely known that female inmates come into the prison system from abusive backgrounds, have lived in poverty, and have abused substances (Aday, 2003; Aday & Farney, 2014, Aday & Krabill, 2011; Reviere & Young, 2004). In a study of older female inmates, Aday and Krabill (2011, p. 52) found "40 percent of state prisoners and 36 percent of federal prisoners report at least one mental health problem," but female inmates show much higher rates of mental health problems at the time of their incarceration. Among older female inmates, depression is most prevalent, and it is more likely when there is comorbidity and lack of social support (Aday & Krabill, 2011).

End-of-Life Care in Prison

When considering aging and end-of-life care in prison, past research has focused on the quality of the dying process and nearing the end of life (Linder & Meyers, 2009; Mezey, Dobler, Mitty, & Brody, 2002), views of dying (Deaton & Aday, 2009), and concerns about dying in prison (Aday, 2006). More recently, researchers have focused their attention on how prison administrations view end-of-life needs among older and dying inmates (Penrod, Loeb, & Smith, 2013).

In an older study, Mezey et al. (2002) examined the experiences of those aging and dying in prison. While individuals living in the community have multiple options at life's end (location, end-of-life directives, comfort, and quality of end-of-life care), less is known about how older and aging inmates prepare for and experience end of life. There appears to be much variation among prisons as to permissibility and appropriateness of care for dying prisoners. For example, end-of-life options may be limited because of availability of end-of-life services (e.g., hospice), the philosophy of wardens and prison administrations, and the officers and supervisors inmates interact with daily (Mezey et al., 2002). Many prisons have small medical units suited to treat illnesses and injuries and are less equipped to treat terminally ill inmates.

Prisoners have less autonomy in end-of-life decisions such as advanced care directives, do not resuscitate (DNR) orders, pain and symptom management, and hospice care (Linder & Meyers, 2009; Mezey et al., 2002). While end-of-life directives can be legally carried out in the prison setting, oftentimes they are disregarded in lieu of administration limits and policies (Mezey et al., 2002). Aging in prison amplifies the possibility that dying in prison may become a reality. Aday (2006) reported a 20.1% increase in natural deaths among older inmates between 1996 and 2001. For inmates, the prospect of dying in prison can conjure feelings of fear, despair, helplessness, and hopelessness. Using the Templer's Death Anxiety Scale (TDAS), Aday (2006) studied 102 older male inmates and the effects of ego integrity (an acceptance of self, both successes and failure) on thoughts of dying. He reported poor health, unsafe environment, and lack of social support were all associated with death anxiety. Aday (2006) also found that the stigma of dying in prison was a large source of death anxiety. Some inmates felt shame and regret when thinking about family members and not being able to ask for forgiveness before dying. Others found solace in religion and spiritual beliefs and that a higher power ultimately had control. Finally, Aday (2006) found that some inmates found the prospect of death as a final escape from the physical and emotional pain of incarceration. In other words, dying inmates frequently see death as a blessing.

Researchers have examined the perspectives of the prison administrators about end-of-life care for prisoners (Penrod et al., 2013). In this qualitative study, Penrod and colleagues (2013) conducted face-to-face interviews of 12 DOCs across the U.S. and found several important themes about how end-of-life care is carried out in prison settings. Administrators were most concerned about treatment versus security, examining end-of-life care treatment on a case-by-case basis rather than systematic treatment protocol, needs of the dying inmate versus public sentiment, and cost. For prison administrators in this study, security was the number one concern. Prison administrators mentioned the desire to learn and possibly incorporate an end-of-life protocol that would not inhibit security. For example, the need to transport an inmate to an outside medical facility and relaxed visitation restrictions pose a certain level of risk, and therefore may require more scrutiny by prison officials.

Many times, requests to waived visitation policies for family members to visit a dying inmate are barred by the DOC superintendent. The lack of system-wide end-of-life care services and the degree to which hierarchical chains of command demand being informed of requests is required make the dying process difficult for inmates. Further, public sentiment may play a role in how end-of-life care is perceived and addressed behind bars. For example, although prison administrators recognize the need for end-of-life care programs like hospice, politically speaking they are acutely aware of how compassionate treatment for inmates, even dying inmates, can be negatively perceived by the public. However, research indicates that end-of-life care was not a substantial burden on the correctional facilities (Penrod et al., 2013). Specifically, much of the care is administered by hospice-trained inmates or by hospice volunteers.

Compassionate Release

One of the solutions to high costs of caring for dying inmates has been to allow them to be released to the community through compassionate release or medical parole laws. Dying inmates must fulfill certain eligibility criteria before they will be considered for compassionate release (see Box 21.1: Criteria for Compassionate Release).

Box 21.1 Criteria for Compassionate Release

- The prisoner is suffering from a terminal illness (i.e., a serious and advanced illness with an end-of-life trajectory).
- A specific prognosis of life expectancy (i.e., a probability of death within a specific time period) is not required.
- The prisoner is suffering from a serious physical or medical condition, suffering from a serious functional or cognitive impairment, or experiencing deteriorating physical or mental health because of the aging process.
- The condition substantially diminishes the ability of the defendant to provide self-care within the environment of a correctional facility and from which he or she is not expected to recover.
- The prisoner is at least 65 years old and is experiencing a serious deterioration in physical or mental health because of the aging process.
- The prisoner has served at least 10 years or 75 percent of his or her term of imprisonment, whichever is less.

Source: U.S. Sentencing Commission (2016)

Unfortunately, these guidelines are not being used by most prisons. In a statement from U.S. Inspector General Michael Horowitz, the lack of utilizing compassionate release in the prison system is resulting in unneeded medical spending for older inmates that have little chance of reoffending (3.5% of nonviolent offenders 65+ and older) (USDOJ, 2016a). He offered two recommendations to alleviate the high costs. First, he urged the FBOP to consider "lowering the age requirement from 65 to 50 and eliminate the minimum 10 years served requirement" (USDOJ, 2016a, p. 5). Citing the vast literature that currently holds the belief that inmates age faster than those in the community, it seemed fitting to acknowledge this rapid aging of prisoners and to benefit from the cost savings compassionate releases represent. Second, he recommended in addition to omitting the 10-year minimum time served requirement, older inmates who had served 75% of their sentence should be eligible for compassionate release (USDOJ, 2016a). Horowitz acknowledged not all inmates 50 years of age or older should be considered for compassionate release. For example, those with violent criminal histories are not typically eligible for compassionate release (USDOJ, 2016a). However, those who are low risk to public safety should be considered for the program. Aday (2003) highlighted potential obstacles to compassionate release long before a program of this kind existed in law. He foresaw the lack of support from nursing homes and aging communities to make available the resources needed to help maintain ex-convicts after release. He also predicted that some families would be unable to support, house, and care for terminally ill relatives that would be released.

Conclusion

Aging inmates face serious medical and mental health-related issues, and correctional facilities are responsible for their treatment and care. Correctional personnel and medical staff working in prisons and jails should be trained to recognize early signs of mental illness and other mental disorders, such as dementia and Alzheimer's disease. Early detection is the key to getting aging inmates the help they need for improved quality of life and to avoid aggressive behavior associated with mental illnesses and disorders. For example, early detection may prevent inmate-on-inmate and inmate-on-staff assaults, because these aging inmates are receiving the treatment they need, including appropriate medications.

Aging women prisoners have gender-specific health concerns that must be addressed during their incarceration. For instance, aging women inmates are often diagnosed with breast and cervical cancer, and therefore are in need of gender-specific medical treatment and care. In addition, aging women are more likely to be diagnosed with a mental health condition than aging men. Research indicates this gender difference in mental health diagnoses is most likely related to differences in childhood trauma (e.g., physical and sexual abuse) and adult trauma (e.g., domestic violence). Medical staff and treatment professionals working in correctional settings should be aware of these differences and provide treatment and care that is gender specific (Van Voorhis & Salisbury, 2014).

Lastly, aging inmates ultimately face terminal illnesses that require correctional personnel to administer end-of-life care. Correctional administrators across the United States are opting to provide hospice programs to address the needs of dying inmates. For example, there are hospice programs at the Mohawk Correctional Facility in Rome, New York; Louisiana State Penitentiary, Angola, Louisiana; and the Michael Unit Hospice, Tennessee Colony, Texas (Neumann, 2016; Nobel, 2015; Texas Department of Criminal Justice, 2017). Hospice is a low-cost option for prisons, because much of the work is carried out by hospice-trained inmate volunteers under the supervision of medical and treatment staff. Aging inmates should receive the same level of treatment and care that they would in the community, and terminally ill inmates should be allowed to die with dignity.

References

Aday, R. H. (1994). Aging in prison: A case study of new elderly offenders. *International Journal of Offender Therapy and Comparative Criminology, 38*, 79–91. doi:10.1177/0306624X9403800108

Aday, R. H. (2003). *Aging prisoners: Crisis in American corrections.* Westport, CT: Praeger Publishers.

Aday, R. H. (2006). Aging prisoners' concerns toward dying in prison. *Omega, 52*(3), 199–216. doi:10.2190/CHTD-YL7T-R1RR-LHMN

Aday, R. H., & Farney, L. (2014). Malign neglect: Assessing older women's health care experiences in prison. *Journal of Bioethical Inquiry, 11*, 359–372. doi:10.1007/s11673-014-9561-0

Aday, R. H., & Krabill, J. J. (2011). *Women aging in prison: A neglected population in the correctional system.* Boulder, CO: Lynne Rienner Publishers Inc.

Allen, R. S., Harris, G. M., Crowther, M. R., Oliver, J. S., Cavanaugh, R., & Phillips, L. L. (2012). Does religiousness and spirituality moderate the relations between physical and mental health among aging prisoners? *Geriatric Psychiatry, 28*(7), 710–717. doi:10.1002/gps.3874

ALZ.org. (2016). *Diagnosis of Alzheimer's disease and dementia.* Retrieved from www.alz.org/alzheimers_disease_diagnosis.asp

Alzheimer's Association. (2015). Alzheimer's disease: Facts and figures. *Alzheimer's & Dementia, 11*(8), 1–88.

Baidawi, S., & Trotter, C. (2015). Psychological distress among older prisoners: A literature review. *Journal of Forensic Social Work, 5*(1–3), 234–275. doi:10.1080/1936928X.2015.1075166

Belluck, P. (2012). Life, with dementia. *The New York Times.* Retrieved from www.nytimes.com/2012/02/26/health/dealing-with-dementia-among-aging-criminals.html

Bernstein, M., & Munoz, N. (2016). *Nutrition for the older adult.* Burlington, MA: Jones & Bartlett Learning.

Bishop, A. J., & Merton, M. J. (2011). Risk of comorbid health impairments among older male inmates. *Journal of Correctional Healthcare, 17*(1), 34–45. doi:10.1177/1078345810385912

Bureau of Justice Statistics. (2006). *Medical problems of jail inmates.* Washington, DC: U.S. Department of Justice, Office of Justice Programs.

Carson, E. A., & Sabol, W. J. (2016). *Aging of the state prison population.* Washington, DC: U.S. Department of Justice, Bureau of Justice Statistics.

Carson, E. A. (2015). *Prisoners in 2014.* Washington, DC: U.S. Department of Justice, Bureau of Justice Statistics.

Chesney-Lind, M., & Pasko, L. (2003). *The female offender: Girls, women, and crime.* Thousand Oaks, CA: Sage.

Chiu, T. (2010). *It's about time: Aging prisoners, increasing costs, and geriatric release.* New York, NY: VERA Institute of Justice. Retrieved from: http://archive.vera.org/sites/default/files/resources/downloads/Its-about-time-aging-prisoners-increasing-costs-and-geriatric-release.pdf

Colsher, P. L., Wallace, R. B., Loeffellolz, P. L., & Sales, M. (1992). Health status of older male prisoners: A comprehensive survey. *American Journal of Public Health, 82*(6), 881–884.

Corrections Today. (2012). *Aging inmates: Correctional issues and initiatives*. Retrieved from www.thefreelibrary.com/Aging+inmates%3a+correctional+issues+and+initiatives.-a0305747639

Coyle, J. M. (2001). *Handbook on women and aging*. Westport, CN: Praeger Publishers.

Deaton, D., & Aday, R. H. (2009). The effect of health and penal harm an aging female prisoners' view of dying in prison. *Omega, 60*(1), 52–70. doi:10.2190/OM.60.1.c

Federal Bureau of Prisons. (2016). *The impact of an aging inmate population of the Federal Bureau of Prisons*. Washington, DC: Office of the Inspector General, U.S. Department of Justice.

Fulop, T., Larbi, A., Witkowski, J. M., McElhanay, J., Loeb, M., Mitnitski, A., & Pawelec, G. (2010). Aging, frailty, and age-related disease. *Biogerontology, 11*, 547–563. doi:10.1007/s10522-010-9287-2

Hayes, A. J., Burns, A., Turnbull, P., & Shaw, J. (2012). The health and social needs of older male prisoners. *International Journal of Geriatric Psychiatry, 27*(11), 1155–1162. doi:10.1002/gps.3761

Handtke, V., Bretschneider, W., Elger, B., & Wangmo, T. (2015). Easily forgotten: Elderly female prisoners. *Journal of Aging Studies, 32*, 1–11. doi:10.1016/j.jaging.2014.10.003

Hebert, R. (1997). Functional decline in old age. *Canadian Medical Association, 157*(8), 1037–1045.

Hollenbeak, C. S., Schaefer, E. W., Penrod, J., Lob, S. J., & Smith, C. A. (2015). Efficiency of health care in state correctional institutions. *Health Services Insights, 8*, 9–15. doi: 10.4137/HSI.S25174

Horwitz, S. (2015). The painful price of aging in prison: Even as harsh sentences are reconsidered, the financial—and human—tolls mount. *The Washington Post*. Retrieved from www.washingtonpost.com/sf/national/2015/05/02/the-painful-price-of-aging-in-prison/?utm_term=.476a698785c1

Human Rights Watch. (2012). *Old behind bars: The aging prison population in the United States*. Retrieved from www.hrw.org/sites/default/files/reports/usprisons0112webwcover_0.pdf

Jordan, M. (2011). The prison setting as a place of enforced residence, it's mental health effects, and the mental healthcare implications. *Health and Place, 17*(5), 1061–1066. doi:10.1016/j.healthplace.2011.06.006

Kim, K., & Peterson, B. (2014). *Aging behind bars: Trends and implications of graying prisoners in the federal prison system*. Urban Institute. Retrieved from www.urban.org/research/publication/aging-behind-bars-trends-and-implications-graying-prisoners-federal-prison-system

Koenig, H. G. (1995). Religion and older men in prison. *International Journal of Geriatric Psychiatry, 10*(3), 219–230. doi:10.1002/gps.930100308

Kopera-Frye, K., Harrison, M. T., Iribarne, J., Dampsey, E., Adams, M., Grabreck, T., . . . Harrison, W. O. (2013). Veterans aging in place behind bars: A structured living program that works. *Psychological Services, 10*(1), 79–86. doi:10.1037/a0031269

Lawton, M. P., & Nahemow, L. (1973). Ecology and the aging process. In C. E. Eisdorfer & P. Lawton (Eds.), *The psychology of adult development and aging* (pp. 660–681). Washington, DC: American Psychological Association.

Linder, J. F., & Meyers, F. J. (2009). Palliative and end-of-life care in correctional settings. *Journal of Social Work in End-of-Life & Palliative Care, 4*, 7–33. doi:10.1080/15524250903173579

Loeb, S. J., & Dagga, A. (2006). Health-related research on older inmates: An integrative review, *Research in Nursing & Health, 29*(6), 556–565. doi:10.1002/nur.20177

Lonczak, H. S., Clifasefi, S. L., Marlatt, G. A., Blume, A. W., & Donovan, D. M. (2006). Religious coping and psychological functioning in a correctional population. *Mental Health, Religion and Culture, 9*(2), 171–192. doi:10.1080/13694670500145713

Marquart, J. W., Merianos, D. E., & Doucet, G. (2000). The heath-related concerns of older prisoners: Implications for policy. *Aging and Society, 20*(1), 79–96. doi:10.1017/S0144686X99007618

Maschi, T., & Baer, J. (2012). The heterogeneity of the world assumptions of older adults in prison: Do differing worldviews have a mental health effect? *Traumatology, 19*(1), 65–72. doi:10.1177/1534765612443294

Maschi, T., Morgen, K., Zgoba, K., Courtney, D., & Ristow, J. (2011). Age, cumulative trauma and stressful life events, and post-traumatic stress symptoms among older adults in prison: Do subjective impressions matter? *The Gerontologist, 51*(5), 675–686. doi:10.1093/geront/gnr074

Maschi, T., Kwak, J., Ko, E., & Morrissey, M. B. (2012). Forget me not: Dementia in prison. *The Gerontologist, 52*(4), 441–451. doi:10.1093/geront/gnr131

Maschi, T., Viola, D., & Morgen, K. (2014). Unraveling trauma and stress, coping resources, and mental well-being among older adults in prison: Empirical evidence linking theory and practice. *The Gerontologist, 54*(5), 857–867. doi:10.1093/geront/gnt069

Merten, M. J., Bishop, A. J., & Williams, A. L. (2012). Prisoner health and valuation of life, loneliness, and depressed mood. *American Journal of Health and Behavior, 36*(2), 275–288. doi:10.5993/AJHB.36.2.12

Mezey, M., Dobler, N. N., Mitty, E., & Brody, A. A. (2002). What impact do setting and transitions have on the quality of life at the end of life and the quality of the dying process. *The Gerontologist, 42*(suppl_3), 54–67. doi:10.1093/geront/42.suppl_3.54

Murdoch, N., Morris, P., & Holmes, C. (2008). Depression in elderly life sentence prisoners. *International Journal of Geriatric Psychiatry, 23*(9), 957–962. doi:10.1002/gps.2017

Neumann, A. (2016, February 16). What dying looks like in America's prisons. *The Atlantic*. Retrieved from www.theatlantic.com/health/archive/2016/02/hospice-care-in-prison/462660/

Nobel, J. (2015, November 12). Hospice in prison? As inmates age, Louisiana's notorious Angola Prison tends to their elderly. *Digital Dying*. Retrieve from www.funeralwise.com/digital-dying/hospice-in-prison-as-inmates-age-louisianas-notorious-angola-prison-tends-to-their-elderly/

O'Hara, K., Forsyth, K., Webb, R., Senior, J., Hayes, A. J., Challis, D., Fazel, S., & Shaw, J. (2016). Links between depressive symptom and unmet health and social care needs among older prisoners. *Age and Aging, 45*(1), 158–163. doi:10.1093/ageing/afv171

Ollove, M. (2016). *Elderly inmates burden state prison*. Washington, DC: Pew Charitable Trust. Retrieved from: www.pewtrusts.org/en/research-and-analysis/blogs/stateline/2016/03/17/elderly-inmates-burden-state-prisons

Osborne Association. (2014). *The high cost of low risk: The crisis of America's aging prison population*. Bronx, NY: Osborne Association.

Penrod, J., Loeb, S. J., & Smith, C. A. (2013). Administrators' perspectives on changing practice in end-of-life care in a state prison system. *Public Health Nursing, 31*(2), 99–108. doi:10.1111/phn.12069

Porter, L. C., Bushway, S. D., Tsao, H., & Smith, H. L. (2016). How the U.S. prison boom has changed the age distribution of the prison population. *Criminology, 54*(1), 30–55. doi:10.1111/1745-9125.12094

Randall, G. K., & Bishop, A. J. (2013). Direct and indirect effects of religiosity on valuation of life through forgiveness and social provisions among older incarcerated men. *The Gerontologist, 53*(1), 51–59. doi:10.1093/geront/gns070

Rich, J. D., Allen, S. A., & Williams, B. A. (2014). The need for higher standards in correctional healthcare to improve public health. *Journal of General Internal Medicine, 30*(4), 503–507. doi:10.1007/s11606-014-3142-0

Reviere, R., & Young, V. D. (2004). Aging behind bars: Health care for older female inmates. *Journal of Women and Aging, 16*(1/2), 55–69. doi: 10.1300/J074v16n01_05

Social Security Administration. (2016). *Retirement age calculator*. Retrieved from www.ssa.gov/planners/retire/ageincrease

Stibich, M. (2015, March 20). What is functional decline: Preventing (or delaying) the loss of basic abilities. *verywell*. Retrieved from www.verywell.com/what-is-functional-decline-2223992

Texas Department of Criminal Justice. (2017). Correctional institutions division-prison. *Texas Department of Criminal Justice*. Retrieved from www.tdcj.state.tx.us/unit_directory/mi.html

Thivierge-Rikard, R. V., & Thompson, M. S. (2016). The association between aging inmate housing management models and non-geriatric health services in state correctional institutions. *Journal of Aging and Social Policy, 19*(4), 39–56. doi:10.1300/J031v19n04_03

U.S. Department of Justice. (2016a). *Compassionate release and the conditions of supervision*. Washington, DC: Office of Inspector General, U.S. Department of Justice.

U.S. Department of Justice. (2016b). *Review of the Federal Bureau of Prisons' monitoring of contract prisons*. Washington, DC: Office of Inspector General, U.S. Department of Justice.

U.S. Department of Justice. (2016c). *The impact of an aging inmate population on the Federal Bureau of Prisons*. Washington, DC: Office of Inspector General, U.S. Department of Justice.

United States Sentencing Commission. (2016). *Amendments to the sentencing guidelines, 2016*. Washington, DC: U.S. Sentencing Commission.

Van Voorhis, P., & Salisbury, E. J. (2014). *Correctional counseling and rehabilitation*. New York, NY: Routledge.

West, H. C., & Sabol, W. J. (2007). *Prisoners in 2007*. Washington, DC: U.S. Department of Justice, Bureau of Justice Statistics.

Williams, B. A., Goodwin, J. S., Baillargeon, J., Ahalt, C. A., & Walter, L. C. (2012a). Addressing the aging crisis in U.S. criminal justice healthcare. *Journal of American Gerontology Society, 60*(6), 1150–1156. doi:10.1111/j.1532-5415.2012.03962.x

Williams, B. A., Stern, M. F., Mellow, J., Safer, M., & Greifinger, R. B. (2012b). Aging in correctional custody: Setting a policy agenda for older prisoner health care. *American Journal of Public Health, 102*(8), 1475–1481. doi:10.2105/AJPH.2012.300704

Williams, J. (2010). Fifty—the new sixty? The health and social care of older prisoners. *Quality and Ageing and Older Adults, 11*(3), 16–24. doi:10.5042/qiaoa.2010.0525

Whitaker, L. (2016). Aging in prison: Life in prison is challenging for anyone. *U.S. Catholic*, 24–29.

22

CHRONIC AND TERMINAL ILLNESS

Providing End-of-Life Care to Dying Prisoners

Kimberly D. Dodson

> Our society has become increasingly aware of the need for good end-of-life care within the community. However, when it comes to end-of-life care in prison, society "is still turning its face from those it punishes."
>
> —(Dubler, 1998, p. 150)

Introduction

As some criminologists so aptly observe, human issues often become criminal justice issues (Whitehead, Braswell, & Gillespie, 2008). End-of-life care is one example of a human issue that has undeniably become a criminal justice issue. Given the fact that the United States is currently on an "incarceration binge" (Irwin & Austin, 1997; Pratt, 2009) and that this trend is likely to continue, we will undoubtedly witness an increase in the number of chronically and terminally ill individuals being admitted to prison. In many prisons, the number of aging and terminally ill prisoners has already increased at an alarming rate (see Abner, 2006; Carson & Sabol, 2016). As a result, the need for end-of-life care has and will continue to be a central issue in many correctional facilities across the country.

Approximately 4,500 prisoners die annually in state and federal correctional facilities and jails (Noonan, Rohloff, & Ginder, 2015). The increasing occurrence of substance abuse and infectious disease, and "get tough" policies such as mandatory minimums, truth-in-sentencing, and three strikes laws are all contributing factors to this trend, and this trend is likely to continue. In an interview, former Warden Burl Cain of the Louisiana State Penitentiary (LSP), Angola, Louisiana, illustrated the seriousness of this growing trend. He estimates that approximately 85% of the inmates currently housed at LSP will die while incarcerated. He states that, "[Angola] prison has become nothing more than an oversized nursing home; it is an 18,000 acre graveyard" (as cited in Whitehead, Dodson, Edwards, 2013, p. 255).

Byock (2002, p. 3) argues that "How we care for the most disadvantaged, frail, elderly, and ill among us is the central social and moral challenge confronting our generation." Prisoners have been described as the "undeserving" (see Conrad, 1982) among us, and many in our society may feel that prisoners are undeserving of forgiveness, mercy, or compassion, even as they die. Dubler (1998, p. 151) argues that "Correctional and medical staff should be helped to regard and treat terminally ill inmates as patients approaching the end of life, not as individuals for whom suffering and dying are yet another appropriate phase of punishment." Cohn (1999, p. 253) acknowledges criminal justice practitioners and medical professionals may "hate the sin" but urges them to "not hate the sinner." In other words, she encourages criminal justice and treatment staff to separate the crime from the criminal. Once they are able to do that, they will have little problem providing for the appropriate and ethical treatment of dying inmates.

Many practitioners and researchers advocate for the needs of dying inmates and fight for them to receive the same level of care as individuals dying in the community (Byock, 2002; Dubler, 2001; Linder & Meyers, 2009; Mahon, 1999; Ratcliff, 2000). However, research indicates that many correctional facilities' end-of-life care services are far below community standards (see e.g., Linder & Meyers, 2009; Schoenly & Knox, 2013). One of the most comprehensive examinations of end-of-life services in prisons was conducted by the Guiding Responsive Action in Corrections at End-of-life (GRACE) Project. The investigators collected data on formal end-of-life care programs within the Federal Bureau of Prisons and 14 state departments of corrections (Ratcliff, 2000; Ratcliff & Craig, 2004). The study concluded that there is a need for continued improvement in end-of-life care for prisoners in the areas of pain and symptom management, family visitation and involvement, advance care planning, training, involvement of inmates as hospice volunteers, and adaptation of the prison environment for "comfort." Likewise, Dubler (1998) claims there is a need to improve the end-of-life care services that inmates receive in the areas of pain and symptom management, palliative care protocols, availability of pharmaceuticals, access to family and friends, and spiritual support. However, many scholars believe the prison environment, because of its focus on punishment, is antithetical to the goals of treatment and care for chronically and terminally ill inmates, which include comfort and compassion.

Peacemaking criminologists reject punishment as the primary goal of prison and believe that criminal justice practitioners should explore "the possibility of mercy and compassion within the framework of justice" (Braswell & Gold, 1998, p. 29). Perhaps nowhere else will we be able to realize the possibility of mercy and compassion more clearly than when considering end-of-life care in prison. Moreover, perhaps nowhere else is peacemaking more applicable than concerning the care of chronically and terminally ill prisoners.

The purpose of this chapter is to explore the treatment of chronically and terminally ill inmates and the process of dying while incarcerated. The chapter begins with a discussion on the legal and professional standards of correctional medical care. The chapter includes a discussion of the factors that are related to death and dying, including aging and infectious disease. In addition, issues related to the medical treatment of terminally ill inmates are discussed, such as coping with dying and death, specialized care facilities, and hospice care. The chapter concludes with a discussion on end-of-life decision making, compassionate release mechanisms, and funeral and burial ceremonies in prison.

Legal and Professional Standards of Correctional Medical Care

In 1972, the American Medical Association (AMA) surveyed the nation's jails and prisons and found that medical services were lacking in three major areas: adequacy, access, and availability (Whitehead et al., 2013). In response, the AMA developed a set of minimum health care standards to address these deficiencies. However, their efforts fell short of their intended goal of reforming medical services within prisons and jails. The issues articulated by the AMA were revisited in *Estelle v. Gamble* (1976, p. 429), in which the United States Supreme Court ruled that "deliberate indifference to the serious medical needs of inmates" was a violation of the Eighth Amendment's ban on "cruel and unusual punishment," and therefore actionable as a civil rights violation under Section 1983 of the United States Constitution. The Court reasoned that because prisoners are wholly dependent on the state for their needs, the state is obligated to provide for the medical needs of prisoners in their care. Both the standards set forth by the AMA and the *Estelle* decision ushered in sweeping changes in the delivery of prison health care services (Whitehead et al., 2013).

The leading authority on correctional health in the United States is the National Commission on Correctional Health Care (NCCHC) The NCCHC sets health care standards for jails, prisons, and juvenile detention facilities. The NCCHC standards include administrative and personnel requirements as well as environmental and preventative health care, routine and emergency health services, and medical-legal issues. Uniform standards across correctional settings are designed to simplify and facilitate the delivery of good medical care. However, in 1980, the United States Supreme Court ruled in *Bell v. Wolfish* (1979) that standards developed by professional associations such as the NCCHC are only advisory in nature and do not necessarily define what is minimally required by correctional officials. Nevertheless, the courts and correctional administrators frequently set health care guidelines in accordance with the standards of the AMA and NCCHC, most often to avoid civil liability.

Other professional health care organizations recognize the importance of developing and requiring adherence to a code of ethics to help ensure the ethical treatment of inmate-patients. For instance, the American Correctional Health Services Association (ACHSA, 2017) has adopted a code of ethics for treating patients within correctional facilities. The ACHSA maintains that the correctional focus of discipline, deterrence, and punishment often runs contrary to the concerns of health care professionals, which include curing, healing, and relieving suffering. Researchers have echoed similar concerns, noting that "punishment and care are generally incompatible" (Dubler & Heyman, 1998, p. 364). For example, Dubler (2001, p. 76) claims that there is a disjuncture between "the goals of medicine—to diagnose, comfort, and cure—and the mandate of corrections—to confine and punish." Even so, the American Correctional Association (ACA) Task Force on Health Care in Corrections also has developed a code of ethics for correctional health care professionals and has issued a mandate that health care services in prison "be consistent with community health care standards" (ACA, 2017; Cohn, 1999, p. 253). However, to date, end-of-life standards of care have not been specifically addressed or evaluated by the ACA or the NCCHC (Cohn, 1999; Whitehead et al., 2013).

The Guiding Response Action for Corrections in End-of-Life (GRACE) Project set forth recommended standards for end-of-life care in prisons. The GRACE Project attempts to promote high-quality hospice and palliative care programs for terminally ill inmates in prisons and jails. The GRACE Project is a collaboration of organizations led by Volunteers of America, a national, nonprofit, spiritually based organization. These standards are designed to "guide correctional professionals in assessing, planning, and improving end-of-life care in correctional settings" (Liebert, 2000, p. 383). Professional organizations such as the ACA and the NCCHC have been encouraged to adopt the GRACE standards, but more importantly, correctional facilities have been encouraged to adopt the GRACE standards, specifically for end-of-life care (Whitehead et al., 2013).

Contributing Factors to Death and Dying Behind Bars

Aging

Within the prison population, the elderly represent the most rapidly expanding class of special needs inmates in the United States (Carson & Sabol, 2016; Roberts, 2015). The combination of longer prison sentences, truth-in-sentencing and "three strikes" legislation, coupled with longer life expectancies, has resulted in an aging inmate population. The presence of this population, with its special needs, is undeniably the result of legislative policy decisions related to crime and punishment. Prisons are dealing with an increased number of elderly and aging prisoners not because of an elderly crime wave but because of changes in sentencing policies. In the not-so-distant past, many prisoners were released before they reached elderly status or paroled when their age reduced their threat to society.

The increased use of incarceration as a means of addressing crime has led to the "graying" of the prison population (Cromwell, 1994; Dubler, 1998; Reimer, 2008). In prison, an offender is considered "elderly" at the chronological age of 50 (Aday, 2003; Dubler, 1998). Prisoners are considered physiologically older as the result of inadequate preventative medical care and the tendency of this population to have histories of high-risk behaviors, such as intravenous drug use, including needle sharing, unprotected sex, and multiple sex partners (Dubler, 1998; Rylander, 2000).

As inmates reach elderly status, correctional health care providers are presented with a variety of treatment dilemmas. These inmates often need treatment for chronic disorders associated with aging, such as cancer, diabetes, heart disease, kidney failure, and Alzheimer's disease. In addition, inmates typically have a high rate of infectious diseases, including human immunodeficiency virus/acquired immunodeficiency syndrome (HIV/AIDS), tuberculosis (TB), and the hepatitis C virus (HCV), and many of these medical conditions and diseases result in a high number of inmate deaths.

Infectious Disease

As previously stated, the rate of infectious diseases such as HIV/AIDS, TB, and HCV is much more prevalent among inmate populations than among the general population (Maruschak, 2015). These diseases pose serious health threats to inmates and have contributed to a significant number of inmate deaths in the United States. In this section, figures on the prevalence of infectious disease are presented, and treatment protocols are discussed.

HIV/AIDS

Human immunodeficiency virus (HIV) is a virus that attacks the immune system, and it seriously hinders the body's ability to fight infection and malignancy. A person with HIV infection is more likely to develop acquired immunodeficiency syndrome (AIDS). AIDS is not a virus but a set of symptoms caused by the HIV virus. AIDS occurs when a person's immune system is too weak to fight off infections and he or she develops defining symptoms and illnesses (AVERT, 2017).

AIDS is a serious health concern in U.S. prisons and jails. The good news is that AIDS-related diagnoses are declining. In 2009, 151 inmates died of AIDS-related causes for every 100,000 state and federally held inmates, but in 2010 that rate was 146 for every 1,000,000 state and federal inmates. In addition, AIDS-related deaths dropped from 94 to 72 between 2009 and 2010 for state and federal inmates. This one-year decline is consistent with an overall downward trend over the past decade. Specifically, AIDS-related deaths declined from 24 deaths per 100,000 inmates in 2001 to 5 per 100,000 in 2010 (Maruschak, 2015).

Male prisoners are more likely to be living with AIDS than female prisoners. Marsuchak (2015) found that at year-end 2010, 18,337 male and 1,756 female prisoners had an AIDS diagnosis. California, Florida, New York, and Texas have the highest prevalence of individuals with HIV/AIDS. To be more precise, these states reported that they housed more than 1,000 inmates with HIV/AIDS, which represents 51% of all state prisoners with HIV/AIDS (Marsuchak, 2015).

Inmates may submit to voluntary screening for infectious diseases like HIV/AIDS during intake; however, medical privacy and confidentiality concerns often reduce the likelihood of screening. Those who are diagnosed with HIV/AIDS should receive counseling about their condition and be presented with the best treatment options available. It is important for seropositive inmates to receive antiretroviral treatment as soon as possible following the diagnosis, and medical staff should monitor seropositive inmates closely to look for side effects of the medications and whether inmates are responding to the treatment.

The spread of HIV/AIDS continues to be a concern for correctional administrators across the United States. Inmates may continue risky behaviors behind bars that may lead to the spread of the infection. For example, inmates frequently use makeshift tattoo guns in prison. If an HIV-positive inmate receives a tattoo and that instrument is used on another inmate, the HIV infection will most likely spread. In addition, many inmates continue to have sex even though they are incarcerated. Having unprotected sex with a seropositive person also increases the likelihood of spreading the infection. In response, correctional facilities across the United States frequently provide condoms and dental dams for inmates to prevent the spread of sexually transmitted infections (STIs) (Talvi, 2007). However, seropositive inmates cannot be segregated from the general population because it is a violation of the ADA's Title II and the Rehabilitation Act's § 504 (1973), which prohibits discrimination based on disability (see *Henderson et al. v. Thomas et al.*, 2013).

Tuberculosis

TB is a contagious infection that typically invades the lungs but can spread to other areas of the body, including the spine and brain. TB is caused by a bacterium known as mycobacterium tuberculosis. It is an air-borne disease, which means if someone has TB and he or she coughs, sneezes, talks, laughs, or sings, tiny droplets of sputum that contain germs are released into the air. If people breathe them in, they are more likely to contract the disease. However, TB is not easy to catch. To contract it, someone typically must have close and repeated contact with an infected person.

According to the Center for Disease Control and Prevention (CDCP, 2014), approximately 16% of federal prisoners and 20% of state prisoners have TB. Estimates also show that 34% of inmates in local jail facilities also have TB. Correctional facilities are environments that are conducive to the spread of communicable diseases. The constant movement of inmates from jails to various prisons, coupled with overcrowding and poor ventilation found in jails and prisons, essentially makes them incubators that enhance the spread of TB.

Inmates should be screened for TB during intake. Those who test positive for TB should be isolated from other inmates to prevent the spread of the disease. Inmates with TB also should wear respiratory protection, and anyone who has come into close contact with the infected person should be screened. TB must be treated with antibiotics, and for optimal recovery, treatment usually lasts about nine months (CDCP, 2014). TB is most serious when it is coupled with other diseases such as HIV/AIDS. Individuals who have HIV/AIDS and contract TB are more likely to die of respiratory complications.

Hepatitis C

Hepatitis C is a serious viral disease that leads to cirrhosis, liver cancer, and in extreme cases liver failure. The CDCP (2013) estimates that one in three people incarcerated in prisons and jails are positive for HCV. People have contracted HCV through needle sharing during drug use, using infected tattoo needles, and having multiple sexual partners. HCV can easily spread through blood, even small amounts that are too small to see (CDCP, 2013). Symptoms of HCV include fatigue, joint pain, belly pain, sore muscles, itchy skin, dark urine, and gray stool.

According to Maurer and Gondles (2015), the exact number of prisoners who are positive for HCV is difficult to pinpoint. Larney et al. (2015) found that between 553,000 and 784,000 inmates in prisons are infected with HCV. The exact number of jail inmates is more difficult to determine because many jails do not screen inmates because of the transient nature of jail populations. A recent survey of prisons (*n* = 43) and large jails (*n* = 23) in the U.S. found "only 11 prisons and 1 jail facility provided routine HCV screening" (Beckwith et al., 2015, p. 69). Although not conclusive, these findings suggest high numbers of inmates with HCV are never diagnosed or receive treatment. It is reasonable to conclude these inmates will return to the community and infect other people.

Several antiviral medications have been successful in treating HCV. When treatment is administered, research shows that medication adherence levels are much higher in correctional settings for several reasons (Hepatitis C Online, 2017). First, the routine of the prison environment increases the odds that inmates will receive their medications at the same time every day, which improves adherence. Second, nursing staff in prisons may be able to monitor patients for side effects and positive response to the treatment. Third, incarcerated individuals have reduced access to alcohol and drugs, which frequently disrupts or derails the treatment in the community. Therefore, if inmates are screened and receive proper treatment, the cure rates could be relatively high.

Coping with Dying and Death

Kübler-Ross has been described as a pioneer in the field of death and dying (see e.g., Kessler, 1997; Maull, 1991; Singh, 1998). No doubt this description is well deserved, given the fact she was among the first physicians to study and document the experiences of dying patients. Kübler-Ross became particularly concerned with understanding the psychology of death and dying and the identification of the coping mechanism utilized by those diagnosed with a terminal illness. According to Kübler-Ross (1969), these coping mechanisms appear in five different stages, including anger, denial and isolation, bargaining, depression, and acceptance.

In Kübler-Ross's (1969) study, denial, or at least partial denial, was the most common coping mechanism used by dying patients. Kübler-Ross (1969, p. 52) explains that "denial functions as a buffer after unexpected shocking news, allows the patient time to collect himself and, with time, mobilize other, less radical defenses." Therefore, denial is generally considered to be a temporary defense mechanism. However, many terminal patients may continue to use some type of denial during various stages of their illness, although sustained denial by any patient is a rarity (Kübler-Ross, 1969).

When denial can no longer be maintained, it often gives way to "feelings of anger, rage, envy, and resentment" (Kübler-Ross, 1969, p. 63). This is the stage in which the dying individual may ask, "Why me?" The patient may be angry and resentful they are ill. When denial and anger are no longer feasible coping strategies, many patients embark upon the bargaining stage. Individuals in this stage may believe that they can "succeed in entering into some sort of an agreement [with God] which may postpone the inevitable happening" (Kübler-Ross, 1969, p. 93). The bargain most patients hope to negotiate is the extension of their lives, and Kübler-Ross (1969, p. 95) notes that many dying patients promise "a life dedicated to God" or "a life in service of the church" in exchange for some additional time. However, when patients realize that the possibility of their lives being extended is unlikely, individuals may simply wish for a few days without physical discomfort or pain.

When the reality of a terminal diagnosis begins to set in, individuals may become depressed. Kübler-Ross (1969) claims that patients actually experience two very distinct types of depression—reactive and preparatory. Reactive depression, also known as situational depression, is a type of depression that occurs in reaction to an external event or circumstance that is shocking or unexpected. Receiving a terminal diagnosis frequently plunges patients into reactive depression. Preparatory depression refers to an overwhelming sense of sadness because of impending or future losses, and this may be heightened for those who are incarcerated. For instance, the knowledge that time has run out to repair damaged relationships or "make things right" may come into focus. For prisoners, the guilt and shame of being locked up often compounds preparatory depression or grief. Acceptance, the final stage, occurs when the patient realizes that death in inevitable and accepts his or her fate.

Nuland (1993) reminds us of the importance of understanding death's perspective from "those who are witnesses to it and felt by those who experience it" (p. xvii). In other words, the experiences of those who are dying and those who work with them are important sources for understanding the dying process in a deeper way. For instance, Aday (2003) studied a sample (n = 102) of aging inmates to determine factors that affected inmates' level of death anxiety. He found that younger inmates (age 50–59) reported a significantly higher level of death anxiety than inmates over the age of 60. He also found respondents who reported lower levels of life satisfaction were more likely to have higher levels of death anxiety. In addition, inmates who reported poor health were more likely to report higher levels of death anxiety. Therefore, improving quality of life may result in lowered death anxiety for aging inmate-patients.

To determine the types of coping mechanisms used by inmates when confronted with the possibility of dying in prison, Aday (2003) included an open-ended question that asked respondents, "Generally, how do you cope with these thoughts of dying in prison?" Like Kübler-Ross (1969), he found respondents used denial as their primary coping mechanism. Specifically, many reported "purposely not thinking about death" or "trying to stay busy" (Aday, 2003, p. 129). Others used acceptance as a coping mechanism, reporting that they "gladly" anticipated death and that death was a "friend that would take them away from their horrible life in prison" (Aday, 2003, p. 129).

Maull (1991), an ex-offender and founder of the National Prison Hospice Association, also attempted to identify the coping mechanisms used by dying inmates. Based on information gathered from inmate-volunteers working in a prison hospice program, he presented the case studies of five terminally ill prisoners. Maull (1991, p. 133) found that inmate-volunteers "regularly report behavior in their patients that resembles the coping mechanisms and patterns observed by Kübler-Ross (1969), Rando (1984), and others." Terminally ill patients vacillate between denial and acceptance. It is important for health care providers to reassure the dying person that everyone copes in different ways when faced with the prospect of dying.

End-of-Life Decisions

When it comes to end-of-life decisions, most health care providers recognize that patient preferences should be honored (Maull, 2006; Mologne, 1999). Research studies have identified a number of salient concerns for both health care providers and patients who are involved in making and administering end-of-life care decisions. The most common concerns include advanced care planning, pain and symptom management, quality of life, and spirituality.

Advance Care Directives

Advance care planning has been identified as one of the most crucial components when making end-of-life decisions. Advance care planning and directives involve a process of communication among patients, their health care providers, their families, and important others regarding the kind of care considered appropriate when the patient can no longer make the decisions (Emanuel, Barry, Stoeckle, Ettelson, & Emanuel, 1991). Advance care planning is designed to help patients organize important personal and legal information and documentation. Some of the information that should be prepared in advance includes health insurance policies, power of attorney for all financial matters, advance care directives and/or power of attorney for care and treatment, and funeral and burial arrangements (Sherman, 2001), although dying inmates are typically concerned with the latter two issues.

Patients at life's end often express the importance of not wanting to be a burden to their families or loved ones. Advance care directives and planning relieve family members and others from the burden of making difficult end-of-life care decisions. In addition, they remove any doubt about what the patient's wishes are and allow the dying patient to have some degree of control over his or her own death. Advance care planning often alleviates death anxiety, which, in turn, helps the dying person to accept his or her prognosis (Brown et al., 2016; Peck, 2009).

Although patients are often advised about advance care directives, such directives are infrequently used (Emanuel et al., 1991), and this may be especially true for prisoners (Andorno, Shaw, & Elger, 2015). Because of their incarceration status, inmates have fewer options available to them to make important end-of-life decisions. In addition, they often do not have the support of family members or friends (Price, 1998). In light of this, inmates may see advance care planning or advance care directives as unnecessary. Nevertheless, state legislators and prison health care administrators have worked together to pass laws requiring that inmate-patients be advised of their "fundamental right to make their own health care decisions, including treatment decisions regarding medications, surgeries, and life-support treatments" (California Prison Health Care Services, 2009, p. 1).

Pain Management

Most physicians in the United Sates have no formal training in end-of-life care (Kelley & Morrison, 2015). As a result, terminally ill patients often suffer unnecessarily because of a lack of appropriate pain management, and their quality of life is significantly reduced. Pain frequently interferes with a peaceful death, which many see as the primary goal of end-of-life care. Therefore, pain management has become the primary focus of physicians and health care staff who treat patients at life's end.

Easely and Elliott (2001) have identified a variety of barriers to pain management. They divide these barriers into two categories: health care provider barriers and patient barriers. Some of the health care provider barriers include an inadequate knowledge of pain management, fear of patient addiction and side effects of medication, poor assessment of pain, and concern about the regulation of controlled substances. Patient barriers include a reluctance to report pain and/or take pain medication, fear that pain means that the disease is getting worse, fear of addiction and side effects of medication, and fear of distracting the physician from treating the underlying disease (Easely & Elliott, 2001).

Pain management may present additional problems within correctional settings. Inmate-patients may be denied medication for pain management for a variety of reasons. Medications are expensive, and correctional facilities incur the cost of medication. Although medical staff cannot legally deny inmates medication based on cost considerations, there may be budget constraints that interfere with the availability of medications. However, medications to alleviate pain and suffering should be available and used in accordance with community standards (Maull, 2006). Additionally, medical staff may believe that inmates are being less than honest about their need for pain medication. This is mostly likely because many prisoners have had long histories of drug abuse prior to their incarceration. Therefore, correctional medical staff may be less likely to dispense pain medication based on this knowledge. Reluctance to dispense medication may mean that prisoners who are experiencing pain will suffer unnecessarily.

Quality of Life

Another primary concern voiced by patients at life's end is "quality of life" (i.e., being able to return to valued life activities) rather than extending life (Huffman, 1999; Rosenfeld, Wenger, & Kagawa-Singer, 2000). Many patients do not want "heroic" or "radical" medical interventions unless it would substantially improve their quality of life. Generally speaking, dying patients identify five major concerns related to quality end-of-life care, including relieving the burden to loved ones, strengthening or repairing relationships with loved ones, adequate pain management, avoiding the prolongation of life, and having a sense of control over the dying process.

Research indicates that avoiding a prolongation of dying is the most frequently cited concern related to quality of life (see e.g., Huffman, 1999). For example, individuals expressed a desire not to be "hooked to machines" or "kept alive" after they could no longer enjoy their lives (Huffman, 1999, p. 2612). However, inmates are rarely concerned with the use of "heroic" interventions; they are more concerned that they are being denied adequate medical care, especially at life's end (Price, 1998). Inmates often do not trust correctional medical care in general, and hospice and other end-of-life care services fall under that umbrella (Price, 1998). They may perceive end-of-life care treatment as the state's attempt to deny life-saving or other more expensive medical treatment options.

Spirituality

Those at life's end also identify the crucial role that spirituality plays in the death experience. Empirical research suggests that terminal ill individuals consider spirituality one of the most important aspects when making end-of-life care decisions (Maull, 2006; Muncy, 1996; Taylor, 1997). Research studies also indicate spiritual distress often increases among individuals who are facing death (Muncy, 1996; O'Connor, 2001; Taylor, 1997). The North American Nursing Diagnosis Association (NANDA, 2017, p. 11) includes "spiritual distress" and "potential for enhanced spiritual well-being" as validated diagnoses. Even so, health care providers frequently avoid discussing spiritual issues with their patients. The primary reason may lie in the fact that most health care professionals are not trained in the spiritual care of the dying (Carpenito, 2000). Additionally, health care providers may be under the erroneous impression that spiritual care is best left up to clergy or other spiritual advisors (Kemp, 2001).

Spiritual distress has been linked to a search for meaning at life's ends. In other words, dying individuals often reflect on what their lives have meant, sometimes called a life review. Those who experience difficulty in finding meaning are more likely to report feeling spiritual distress (Aday, 2003). These individuals may express a sense of hopelessness, which may be exacerbated for someone who is dying in prison. For many inmates, nothing signifies defeat as much as dying behind bars (Brydon, 1991; Price, 1998). Individuals also frequently express the need for forgiveness at the end of life (Kemp, 2001). The desire to be forgiven is also grounded in the spiritual needs of the dying individual (Braswell, Fuller, & Lozoff, 2001; Kemp, 2001). For inmates, forgiveness may prove to be elusive for a number of reasons. Prisoners may find self-forgiveness difficult and may focus on their past mistakes or transgressions. In addition, they may find that others, such as victims, are unable or unwilling to forgive. Therefore, the spiritual needs of inmates may be aggravated by feelings of guilt, regret, and unforgiveness.

It is unclear whether the same factors that affect end-of-life decisions in the community are salient factors in prison. However, there are most certainly other issues that are unique to the prison environment that affect end-of-life care decisions. Security, for example, takes priority in prison. The philosophy of hospice and end-of-life care seems to be the antithesis of security. Health care providers who administer care during life's end advocate for patient autonomy—freedom to make one's own end-of-life decisions. Allowing the patient to make his/her own decisions regarding death affords the dying individual a great deal of control. The idea of inmates, dying or not, having any type of control is a foreign concept to prison administrators and correctional staff. By design, prison takes away freedom and control from the individual. Therefore, issues surrounding security may be one of the greatest obstacles to end-of-life care decisions in prison (Schoenly & Knox, 2013).

Safety is another issue that presents a substantial problem in the prison environment. End-of-life care providers recognize the dying patient's vulnerability, but inmates cannot afford to appear weak and needy (Price, 1998). They may be fearful of being exploited or being preyed upon by other inmates. As a result, inmates may forgo hospice or end-of-life care services because of these personal safety concerns.

End-of-Life Care in Prison

Specialized Care Facilities

Recent reports indicate that many traditional correctional facilities are ill-equipped to deal with chronically and/or terminally ill inmates (Clear, Reisig, Petrosino, & Cole, 2017; Neumann, 2016; Whitehead et al., 2013). As a result, many correctional institutions treat these prisoners in separate facilities that are designed specifically to address their special needs. If an inmate becomes chronically or terminally ill, often he or she is transferred to a specialized care facility within the department of corrections. Some argue that housing special needs inmates in one central location improves the quality of care these inmates receive (Braithwaite, Braithwaite, & Poulson, 1999). For example, the Lois M. DeBerry Special Needs Facility in Nashville, Tennessee, has a 250-bed long-term care facility for chronically and terminally ill inmates. Research indicates that special needs facilities have more resources to care for chronically and terminally ill inmates (Dubler, 2001; Maull, 2006), and they are more likely to receive specialized attention they would not normally receive in a traditional correctional setting.

Not every state has specialized prisons for chronically and terminally ill inmates. As an alternative, many prisons have special wings or segregated housing units on site to treat individuals who are seriously ill (see Chapter 3 to learn more about segregated housing units). For example, the W.J. Estelle Unit in Huntsville, Texas, has a medical facility, including an emergency room, high-tech telemedicine equipment, and full-time medical staff that provide around the clock treatment to patients.

It is important to note that many inmates do not want to be transferred to another correctional facility even if they are terminally ill. Some prisoners may have been incarcerated so long that prison has become their "home" and the other inmates have become their "family." The prospect of being transferred into another facility, to die in an unfamiliar environment surrounded by strangers, is not how these inmates want to die. However, the ultimate decision to transfer an inmate is left up to the prison administrators, not the inmate. Therefore, inmates have little, if any, choice in where they die.

Hospice Care

The absence of an effective medical parole or compassionate release system means that many prisoners will die in correctional institutions and/or long-term care facilities. In lieu of compassionate release, many correctional facilities have implemented hospice care for chronically and terminally ill inmates. Hospice is an "interdisciplinary comfort-oriented care program that allows seriously ill and dying patients to die with dignity and humanity with as little pain as possible in an environment where they have mental and spiritual preparation for the natural process of dying" (National Prison Hospice Association [NPHA], n.d., para. 2).

Although hospice has been established in the community since 1963, it was not until 1991 that hospice was established in prison (NPHA, n.d.). Some may find it surprising to learn that the NPHA was established due largely to the efforts of a former inmate, Fleet Maull. He recognized that end-of-life care is just as important in prison as it is in the community. NPHA is an organization designed to be an educational resource and information sharing network to encourage correctional facilities to implement and administer hospice care.

Cloyes, Rosenkranz, and Berry (2015) conducted a study that included field observations at the Louisiana State Penitentiary Prison Hospice Program and interviewed hospice staff, correctional officers, and inmate-volunteers. They identified five essential components of an effective and sustainable model for hospice programs: "patient centered care, an inmate volunteer model, safety and security, shared values, and teamwork" (Cloyes et al., 2015, p. 390). Dubler and Heyman (2006) also recommend the following (see **Box 22.1**):

Box 22.1 End-of-Life Support

- Palliative care protocols should be in place to ensure that the care team can accurately access the level of physical discomfort and provide effective response.
- The prison formulary should have adequate pharmaceutical interventions available to support pain management.
- Family members and other loved ones should be permitted increased access to the inmate.
- Family members who are not particularly involved should be sought out to support the inmate, if they can, or to make some provisions for burial.
- Chaplains and other spiritual advisors, including inmates, should be permitted increased access to the patient.
- Rituals to commemorate those who have died should be part of the prison culture for terminal care.

Source: Dubler and Heyman (2006, p. 539)

Hospice in prison is a cost-effective health care option for correctional administrators because inmate volunteers are trained to assist nurses in providing care to those who are dying. Inmate-volunteers typically provide companionship and hygiene services to the patients. Medical staff supervise the inmate-volunteers, and there are certain duties inmate-volunteers are not allowed to perform. For example, they do not administer medication to patients because inmates are not allowed to have access to prescriptions, as many medications administered to dying patients are classified as narcotics.

Prior to the implementation of hospice, many inmates often died alone in their prison cells (Cherney, Coyle, & Foley, 1996). Therefore, hospice care is viewed as a more humane treatment alternative regarding the care of terminally ill inmates. Although the use of hospice in U.S. prisons has increased, most terminally ill inmates are currently cared for or die in nonhospice settings (GRACE, 2001; Schoenly & Knox, 2013). The NPHA continues to advocate on behalf of dying inmates and the use of hospice behind bars.

Compassionate Release or Medical Parole

As a result of the growing number of terminally ill inmates and rising medical costs, many states have enacted medical parole laws, also known as "compassionate release" laws, which allow for the early release of terminally ill offenders. Nationally, only five states, Illinois, Massachusetts, South Carolina, South Dakota, and Utah, do not have any legal mechanism for the early release of terminally ill prisoners (Maschi, Kalmanofsky, Westcott, & Pappacena, 2015). The remaining states have a variety of methods for early release that include the reduction of the inmate's sentence by a judge, parole or clemency hearing, administrative release, or even commutation of sentence.

The use of medical parole has not been universally embraced as a solution to addressing the growing number of terminally ill prisoners. For example, many in the public fear that compassionate release will result in the mass release of potentially violent offenders. However, these fears seem unfounded given the fact that very few inmates are actually granted this type of release. Estimates show the number of federal inmates granted compassionate release annually, on average, is two dozen (Human Rights Watch, 2017). Additionally, when an inmate does qualify, his or her release is not guaranteed. The rigorous standards set forth by many states result in some inmates dying while awaiting the release decisions of parole boards or other officials. Given the current "get tough" political climate in the United States, it is likely that compassionate release will continue to be underutilized.

Medical parole is designed to be an early release mechanism for special or medical needs inmates, particularly those who are dying. An examination of legislation across the United States reveals some common themes for medical parole legislation, which include (in **Box 22.2**):

Funeral and Burial Ceremonies

Funerals and burial rituals serve several purposes and address the psychological and emotional needs of those left behind. Funerals provide stability and order in the midst of grief, allow us to celebrate the life of the person who has died, confirm the person has passed on, provide emotional support to survivors and mourners, allow a venue for expressing grief in a positive way, and allow us to say goodbye. As in the community, prisoners need an outlet for their grief and a way to express it appropriately.

In prison, funeral and burial rituals may be especially important because the inmates who are left behind often experience intensified feelings of grief knowing they may face the same fate. Those left behind want to know that the person who died will be remembered and respectfully laid to rest. Many prisoners have lost contact with their families, or their families lack the financial resources to pay for a funeral. Often an inmates' relatives and friends have died while they were incarcerated, leaving no one to accept the body. If this happens, inmates will be buried at the prison in "Potter's graves," that is, burial plots for those too poor to be buried elsewhere.

At the Louisiana State Penitentiary (LSP), inmates are intimately involved in the burial rituals. Specifically, former LSP Warden Burl Cain indicates, "funerals are elaborate affairs, with hand-made coffins pulled to graves by horse-drawn carriages, in rites conducted almost entirely by inmates" (Fields, 2005, para.7). He also notes, "Once a man dies, his sentence is complete and there should be dignity in the passing" (Fields, 2005, para. 21). Likewise, at the Texas State Penitentiary in Huntsville, Texas, also known an as the Huntsville Unit, inmates are involved in the funeral and burial services for those inmates who have died. Allowing inmate-survivors to be a part of the burial ceremonies

Box 22.2 Requirements for Compassionate Release or Medical Parole

- The inmate must have a terminal condition and/or severe physical/medical condition that would significantly reduce the likelihood of committing further crimes.
- Due to the inmate's illness and/or chronic medical condition, he/she no longer presents a substantial danger to society.
- Electronic monitoring for chronically/terminally ill offenders can be used to address public safety concerns.
- Death row inmates and prisoners serving life-without-parole sentences are ineligible for medical release.
- A licensed physician, usually approved by the department of corrections, must certify that the inmate has 12 months or less to live.
- The parole board must require, as a condition of release, that the parolee agree to placement in a hospital, hospice, or other suitable housing accommodation, including his/her family's home.
- The parole board has the option to require a periodic rediagnosis and order a return to custody for any inmate who improves to a point where he/she no longer meets the criteria for release.
- A recommendation for release requires a majority vote by the parole board.
- The governor may approve or deny the recommendation of the parole board.

allows them to honor friends who have passed away and gives them a sense of closure. Inmate participation also allows surviving inmates to witness the respect with which the deceased is laid to rest, which translates into increased respect for prison officials. Dr. Franklin Wilson, an associate professor at Indiana State University, cautions us to remember that, "we are all human and we all have something in common with those buried here. Each of these people, no matter how horrendous the crime, was someone's daughter, son, grandchild, mother, [or] father" (Maly, 2013, para. 16).

Conclusion

As noted at the beginning of this chapter, approximately 4,500 prisoners die while in state, federal, and local custody each year, and this number is expected to grow (Noonan et al., 2015). It is important to keep in mind that the health care provided behind bars must meet the minimum standards of those in the community. Prison officials increase the likelihood of litigation for failing to address the serious medical needs of inmates in their care (see. *Estelle v. Gamble*, 1976).

"Get tough" policies such as mandatory minimums, three strikes laws, and truth-in-sentencing have contributed to the growing number of aging inmates, which in turn has contributed to the increased number of people dying behind bars. In addition, infectious diseases like HIV/AIDS, TB, and HCV are significantly higher in correctional facilities, and many of these inmates will die during incarceration.

Numerous scholars claim that prisons are essentially nursing homes or long-term care facilities (see e.g., Aday, 2003; Ewing, 2015; Maull, 2006; Vestal, 2014). Almost two decades ago, then-Warden Burl Cain stated that "[Angola] prison has become nothing more than an oversized nursing home; it is an 18,000 acre graveyard" (National Institute of Corrections, 2000, interview). Again, this trend shows little evidence of slowing down, which means policy makers and prison administrators need to develop and implement policies and practices to address the needs of this growing population that are effective and humane. The use of specialized care facilities is one such option.

Prison administrators and medical staff need to develop policies to meet the needs of terminally ill inmates, including advance care planning, pain and symptom management, improving quality of life, and providing spiritual guidance at life's end. Those who are dying experience a wide range of feelings about their prognosis, from hopelessness to acceptance. Dying individuals also use a variety of coping mechanisms when faced with the prospect of dying. Prison health care providers should be trained to take a holistic approach to the treatment of dying prisoners that encompasses emotional, psychological, physiological, and spiritual components of care.

Hospice care is seen as one of the most effective and humane health care services that can be provided to dying inmates. Hospice prepares the person for the natural process of dying and helps the person to die with dignity, an experience that most inmates have been denied because of their past criminal behavior. Hospice also is a cost-effective alternative for prisons because inmate-volunteers deliver much of the health care services at no cost to the prison.

Forty-five states currently have some mechanism (compassionate release or medical parole) for the early release of chronically or terminally ill prisoners. However, compassionate release is infrequently used, and many inmates die while their request is under review (Families Against Mandatory Minimums, 2015). Chronically and terminally ill inmates should be released from custody when possible because many of them no longer pose a public safety risk and are unlikely to reoffend. Additionally, under the Affordable Care Act (ACA), prisoners released from custody are eligible for Medicaid coverage (see Public Law 111–148, 2010). Therefore, the early release of seriously and terminally ill prisoners represents a significant cost savings for correctional facilities across the United States.

Finally, funerals and burial ceremonies are frequently carried out in prison. The deceased may not have any living relatives to accept his/her body from the prison. Families may be estranged, unaware of the person's passing, or unwilling to pick up the body. Many families simply lack the financial resources to pay for funeral or burial services for a loved one. As a result, many funeral services occur in prison, and inmates are buried in prison cemeteries. Funeral and burial rituals help survivors honor the deceased, say goodbye, and provide some sense of solace.

References

Abner, C. (2006, November/December). Graying prisons: State face challenges of an aging inmate population. *State News*. Washington, DC: Justice Center, The Council for State Governments.

Aday, R. H. (2003). *Aging prisoners: Crisis in American corrections*. Westport, CT: Praeger.

American Correctional Association. (2017). *ACA code of ethics*. Alexandria, VA: American Correctional Association Task Force on Health Care in Corrections.

American Correctional Health Services Association. (2017). *Mission & Ethics Statement*. Retrieved from www.achsa.org/mission-ethics-statement/

American with Disabilities Title II and the Rehabilitation Act § 504 (1973).

Andorno, R., Shaw, D. M., & Elger, B. (2015). Protecting prisoners' autonomy with advance directives: Ethical dilemmas and policy issues. *Medicine, Health Care, and Philosophy, 18*(1), 33–39. doi:10.1007/s11019-014-9571-z

AVERT. (2017). *What are HIV and AIDS? UK: AVERTing HIV and AIDS*. Retrieved from www.avert.org/about-hiv-aids/what-hiv-aids

Beckwith, C. G., Kurth, A. E., Bazerman, L., Solomon, L. Patry, E., Rich, J. D., & Kuo, I. (2015). Survey of U.S. correctional institutions for routine HCV testing. *American Journal of Public Health, 105*(1), 68–71. doi:10.2105/AJPH.2014.302071

Bell v. Wolfish 441 U.S. 520, (1979).

Braithwaite, R., Braithwaite, K., & Poulson, R. (1999). HIV and TB in prison. In ACA (Ed.), *From AIDS to the internet: Correctional realities* (pp. 1–7). Lanham, MD: American Correctional Association.

Braswell, M. C., Fuller, J., & Lozoff, B. (2001). *Corrections, peacemaking and restorative justice: Individuals and institutions*. New York, NY: Routledge.

Braswell, M.C., & Gold, J. (1998). Peacemaking, justice, and ethics. In M. C. Braswell, B. R. McCarthy, & B. J. McCarthy (Eds.), *Justice, crime and ethics* (3rd ed.). Cincinnati, OH: Anderson.

Brown, A. J., Shen, M. J., Urbauer, D., Taylor, J., Parker, P. A., Carmack, C., . . . Bodurka, D. C. (2016). Room for improvement: An examination of advance care planning documentation among gynecologic oncology patients. *Gynecologic Oncology, 142*(3), 525–530. doi:10.1016/j.ygyno.2016.07.010

Brydon, R. (1991). Remembering prison justice day. In B. Gaucher (Ed.), *The Journal of Prisoners on Prison Anthology (1988–2002)*. Toronto: Canadian Scholars' Press.

Byock, I. R. (2002). Dying well in corrections: Why should we care? *Dying Well*. Retrieved from www.dyingwell.com/jchc02.htm

California Prison Health Care Services. (2009). *Advance directive for health care*. Retrieved from www.cphcs.ca.gov/docs/imspp/IMSPP-v01-ch17A.pdf

Carpenito, L. J. (2000). *Nursing diagnosis: Applications to clinical practice* (7th ed.). Philadelphia, PA: Lippincott.

Carson, E. A., & Sabol., W. J. (2016). *Aging of the state population, 1993–2013*. Washington, DC: U.S. Department of Justice, Bureau of Justice Statistics.

Centers for Disease Control and Prevention. (2013). *Hepatitis C & incarceration*. Washington, DC: U.S. Department of Health and Human Services, Centers for Disease Control and Prevention.

Center for Disease Control and Prevention. (2014). *TB in correctional facilities in the United States*. Washington, DC: Center for Disease Control and Prevention.

Center for Disease Control and Prevention. (2014). *Treatment regimens for latent TB infection (LTBI)*. Washington, DC: Center for Disease Control and Prevention.

Cherney, N. I., Coyle, N., & Foley, K. M. (1996). Guidelines in the care of the dying cancer patients. *Hematology/Oncology Clinics of North America, 10*, 261–286.

Clear, T., Reisig, M. D., Petrosino, C., & Cole, G. F. (2017). *American corrections in brief*. Boston, MA: Cengage.

Cloyes, K. G., Rosenkranz, S. J., & Berry, P. H. (2015). Essential elements of an effective prison hospice program. *American Journal of Hospice and Palliative Medicine, 33*(4), 390–402. doi:10.1177/1049909115574491

Cohn, F. (1999). The ethics of end-of-life care for prison inmates. *Journal of Law, Medicine, & Ethics, 27*(3), 252–259. doi:10.1111/j.1748–720X.1999.tb01459.x

Conrad, J. P. (1982). What do the undeserving deserve? In R. Johnson & H. Toch (Eds.), *The pains of imprisonment*. Prospect heights, IL: Waveland Press, Inc.

Cromwell, P. (1994). The graying of America's prisons. *Overcrowded Times, 6*, 3.

Dubler, N. N. (1998). The collision of confinement and care: End-of-life care in prisons and jails. *Journal of Law, Medicine, & Ethics, 26*(2), 149–156. doi: 0.1111/j.1748-720X.1998.tb01670.x

Dubler, N. N. (2001). Prisoners should receive humane end-of-life care. In M. Wagner (Ed.), *How should prisons treat inmates?* (pp. 71–84). San Diego, CA: Greenhaven Press, Inc.

Dubler, N. N., & Heyman, B. (1998). End-of-life care in prisons and jails. In M. Puisis (Ed.), *Clinical practice in correctional medicine* (pp. 538–544). St Louis, MO: Mosby.

Dubler, N. N., & Heyman, B. (2006). End-of-life care in prisons and jails. In M. Puisis (Ed.), *Clinical practice in correctional medicine* (2nd ed., pp. 538–544). Philadelphia, PA: Mosby Elsevier.

Easely, M. K., & Elliott, S. (2001). Managing pain at the end of life. *Palliative and Supportive Care of Advanced Cancer, 36*(4), 779–794.

Emanuel, L. L., Barry, M. J., Stoeckle, J. D., Ettelson, L. M., & Emanuel, E. J. (1991). Advanced directives for medical care: A case for greater use. *The New England Journal of Medicine, 324*, 889–895. doi:10.1056/NEJM199103283241305

Estelle v. Gamble 429 U.S. 97, (1976).

Ewing, M. (2015). *When prisons need to be more like nursing homes: Finding new ways to treat the growing pool of older, ailing inmates*. New York, NY: The Marshall Project.

Families Against Mandatory Minimums. (2015). *New compassionate release rules: Breaking it down*. Washington, DC: Families Against Mandatory Minimums.

Fields, G. (2005, May 18). As inmates age, a prison carpenter builds more coffins. *The Wall Street Journal*. Retrieved from www.prisonpolicy.org/scans/disturbing/2005/coffins.shtml

Guiding Response Action for Corrections in End-of-Life (GRACE) Project. (2001). *Incarceration of the terminally ill: Current practices in the United States*. Alexandria, VA: A Report of the GRACE Project, Volunteers of America. Retrieved from www.graeprojects.org.

Hepatitis C Online. (2017). *Treatment of hepatitis C in a correctional setting*. Washington, DC: Centers for Disease Control and Prevention.

Henderson et al. v. Thomas et al., 913 F.Supp.2d 1267 (2013).

Huffman, G. B. (1999). Analysis of patients' perspectives on quality care at the end of life. *American Family Physician, 59*(9), 2611–2613.

Human Rights Watch. (2017). *The answer is no: Too little compassionate release in U.S. Federal Prisons*. New York, NY: Human Rights Watch.

Irwin, J., & Austin, J. (1997). *It's about time: America's imprisonment binge* (2nd ed.). New York: Wadsworth.

Kelley, A. S., & Morrison, R. S. (2015). Palliative care for the seriously ill. *The New England Journal of Medicine, 373*, 747–755. doi:10.1056/NEJMra1404684

Kessler, D. (1997). *The needs of the dying: A guide for bringing hope, comfort, and love to life's final chapter*. New York, NY: HarperCollins Publishers, Inc.

Kemp, C. (2001). Spiritual care interventions. In B. R. Ferrell & N. Coyle (Eds.), *Textbook of palliative nursing*. New York, NY: Oxford University Press.

Kübler-Ross, E. (1969). *On death and dying: What the dying have to teach doctors, nurses, clergy, and their own families*. New York, NY: Scribner.

Larney, S., Kopinski, H., Beckwith, C. G., Zaller, N. D., Jarlais D. D., Hagan, H., . . . Degenhadt L. (2015). Incident and prevalence of hepatitis C in prisons and other closed settings: Results of a systematic review and meta-analysis. *Hepatology, 58*(4), 1215–1224. doi:10.1002/hep.26387

Liebert, M. A. (2000). Standards of practice for end-of-life care in correctional settings. *Journal of Palliative Medicine, 3*, 383–388. doi:10.1089/jpm.2000.3.4.383

Linder, J. F., & Meyers, F. J. (2009). Palliative and end-of-life care in correctional settings. *Journal of Social Work in End-of-Life & Palliative Care, 4*, 7–33. doi:10.1080/15524250903173579

Maull, F. W. (2006). Delivery of end-of-life care in the prison setting. In M. Puisis (Ed.), *Clinical practice in correctional medicine* (2nd ed., pp. 529–537). Philadelphia, PA: Mosby Elsevier.

Roberts, S. K. (2015). *Aging in prison: Reducing elder incarceration and promoting public safety*. New York, NY: Center for Justice, Columbia University.

Schoenly, L., & Knox, C. M. (2013). *Essentials of correctional nursing*. New York, NY: Springer.

Mahon, N. B. (1999). Death and dying behind bars—cross-cutting themes and policy imperatives. *Journal of Law, Medicine, & Ethics, 27*(3), 213–215. doi:10.1111/j.1748-720X.1999.tb01454.x

Maly, D. (2013, November 8). Dignity in burials for prisoners and families. *The Texas Tribune*. Retrieved from www.texastribune.org/2013/11/08/prisoners-and-families-burials-dignity/

Maruschak, L. M. (2015). *HIV in prison, 2001–2010*. Washington, DC: U.S. Department of Justice, Bureau of Justice Statistics.

Maschi, T., Kalmanofsky, A., Westcott, K., & Pappacena, L. (2015). *Analysis of United States compassionate and geriatric release: Towards a rights-based response for diverse elders and their families and Communities*. New York, NY: Be the Evidence Press, Fordham University.

Maull, F. W. (1991). *Dying in prison: Sociocultural and psychosocial dynamics*. Springfield, MO: Haworth Press, Inc.

Maurer, K., & Gondles, E. F. (2015). *Hepatitis C in correctional settings: Challenges and opportunities*, *2*(1), 1–20. Alexandria VA: American Correctional Association.

Mologne, M. (1999). A push for better end-of-life care. *AHA News*, *35*, 6.

Muncy, J. F. (1996). Muncy comprehensive spiritual assessment. *American Journal of Hospice & Palliative Care*, *13*(5), 44–45. doi:10.1177/104990919601300515

National Institute of Corrections (Producer). (2000). *Managing the aging and terminally ill inmate*. [NIJ Video Series]. Washington, DC: U.S. Department of Justice.

National Prison Hospice Association. (n.d.). *About NPHA*. Retrieved from https://npha.org/about/

Neumann, A. (2016, February 16). What dying looks like in America's prisons. *The Atlantic*. Retrieved from www.theatlantic.com/health/archive/2016/02/hospice-care-in-prison/462660/

Noonan, M. E., Rohloff, H., & Ginder, S. (2015). *Mortality in local jails and state prisons, 2000–2013*. Washington, DC: U.S. Department of Justice, Bureau of Justice Statistics.

North American Nursing Diagnosis Association. (2017). *NANDA nursing diagnosis list 2015–2017*. Mountain, WI: NANDA International.

Nuland, S. B. (1993). *How we die: Reflections on life's final chapter*. New York, NY: Vintage Books.

O'Connor, C. I. (2001). Characteristics of spirituality, assessment, and prayer in holistic nursing. *Nursing Clinics of North America*, *36*(1), 33–46.

Peck, M. R. (2009). Personal death anxiety and communication about advance care directives among oncology social workers. *Journal of Social Work in End-of-Life & Palliative Care*, *5*(1–2), 49–60. doi:10.1080/15524250903173892

Pratt, T. C. (2009). *Addicted to incarceration: Corrections policy and the politics of misinformation in the United States*. Thousand Oaks, CA: Sage.

Price, C. (1998). *To adopt or adapt? Principles of hospice care in the correctional setting*. Retrieved from www.npha.org

Public Law 111–148, 11th Congress, 2010.

Rando, T. A. (1984). *Grief, dying, and death: Clinical interventions for caregivers*. Champaign, IL: Research Press Company.

Ratcliff, M. (2000). Dying inside the walls. *Journal of Palliative Medicine*, *3*(4), 509–511. doi:10.1089/jpm.2000.3

Ratcliff, M., & Craig, E. (2004). The GRACE project: Guiding end-of-life care in corrections, 1998–2001. *Journal of Palliative Medicine*, 7(2), 373–379. doi:10.1089/109662104773709549

Reimer, G. (2008). The graying of the U.S. prisoner population. *Journal of Correctional Health Care*, *14*(3), 202–208. doi:10.1177/1078345808318123

Rosenfeld, K. E., Wenger, N. S., & Kagawa-Singer, M. (2000). End-of-life decision making: A qualitative study of elderly individuals. *Journal of General Internal Medicine*, *15*, 620–625. doi:10.1046/j.1525-1497.2000.06289.x

Rylander, C. K. (2000). *Public safety and corrections: Develop more effective methods of dealing with special needs inmates*. Retrieved from www.e-texas.org/recommend/ch11/ps04.html

Sherman, D. W. (2001). Patients with acquired immune deficiency syndrome. In B. R. Ferrell & N. Coyle (Eds.), *Textbook of palliative nursing*. New York, NY: Oxford University Press.

Singh, K. D. (1998). *The grace in dying: How we are transformed spiritually as we die*. New York, NY: HarperCollins.

Talvi, S. J. A. (2007). *Women behind bars: The crisis of women in the U.S. prison system*. Emeryville, CA: Seal Press.

Taylor, E. J. (1997). The spiritual and ethical "end-of-life" decisions of cancer survivors. In S. L. Groenwald, M. H. Frogge, M. Goodman, & C. H. Yarbro (Eds.), *Cancer nursing: Principles and practice*. Boston, MA: Jones and Bartlett.

Vestal, C. (2014). For aging inmates, care outside prison walls. *Stateline*. Washington, DC: The Pew Charitable Trusts. Retrieved from www.pewtrusts.org/en/research-and-analysis/blogs/stateline/2014/08/12/for-aging-inmates-care-outside-prison-walls

Whitehead, J. T., Braswell, M. C., & Gillespie, W. (2008). The future of the peacemaking paradigm (pp. 231–250.). In. J. F. Wozniak, M.C. Braswell, R. E. Vogel, & K. R. Blevins, *Transformative justice: Critical peacemaking themes influenced by Richard Quinney*. Lanham, MD: Lexington Books.

Whitehead, J. T., Dodson, K. D., & Edwards, B. D. (2013). *Corrections: Exploring crime, punishment, and justice in America* (3rd ed.). New York, NY: Routledge.

23

OFFENDERS WITH INTELLECTUAL AND DEVELOPMENTAL DISABILITIES

Contact with the Criminal Justice System

James R. Patton and Edward A. Polloway

> People with ID "suffer a number of disadvantages in the Criminal Justice System [CJS], including not understanding information given to them (such as about their rights); being suggestible and acquiescent on interview and in court; and not making wise decisions at crucial points in the CJS."
>
> —(Murphy, n.d., p. 4)

Introduction

The field of intellectual disability (ID) has a long and intriguing history. If one only looks at the terminology used to describe this condition, one can find fascinating information related to how this condition has been studied, conceived, and treated. Given the importance of the topic of "encounters" of individuals with intellectual disability within the criminal justice system, relatively little research has been conducted in this area. At the core of the issue is that many problems may, and often do, arise when persons with ID get involved in the criminal justice system. As Smith, Polloway, Patton, and Beyer (2008, p. 424) advised,

> the criminal justice system is built upon finding justice for persons who are victims of crime and maintaining order in society. While there are protections built into the system to ensure fairness, it is not a system that was developed with a full appreciation of the needs and characteristics of all persons in mind.

This point is particularly appropriate to consider for offenders and victims with ID, who may have difficulty comprehending the various stages of the criminal justice process because of their cognitive impairment.

Significant attention has been directed to persons with ID in recent years (i.e., since 2002), due in great part to the Supreme Court's decision in *Atkins v. Virginia* (2002) that it is cruel and unusual punishment to execute a person with intellectual disabilities. Prior to the legal interest in this topic, only a relatively small number of professionals focused their efforts on the various issues surrounding the interface of individuals with ID and the criminal justice system at either the juvenile or the adult level. It should be noted that individuals with ID can engage the criminal justice system in a variety of ways. The Arc (2014, p. 1), in its position statement on the criminal justice system, pointed out that persons with ID can engage the system as "victims, witnesses, suspects, defendants, or incarcerated individuals."

The intent of this chapter is to summarize what we know about those individuals with ID who do, for whatever reason, encounter law enforcement, judicial, and/or correctional systems. The backdrop of this chapter will be on the U.S. criminal justice system; however, some research and information from other countries will be presented as applicable. The chapter covers six major topics and a number of subtopics related to each of these key topics. The first section is a discussion of the terminology and definition of intellectual disability, including professional and state definitions of ID. Next, we present an overview of persons with ID who encounter the criminal justice system. The third section is a review of the perceptions and misperceptions that the public and professionals within the criminal justice system may have about persons with ID that includes a discussion of stereotypes of individuals with ID. Key features and characteristics of persons with ID also are presented. We also look at the potential problems that this population faces as a function of various phases of the criminal justice system process. The chapter presents an overview of the issues related to the *Atkins* decision on excluding individuals with ID from the death penalty. The chapter concludes with some guidelines that should assist with continuing efforts to address the needs of offenders with ID.

Fundamental Concepts of Intellectual Disability

Intellectual disability is a developmental disorder that originates during the developmental period and is characterized by limitations in various aspects of intellectual functioning (e.g., reasoning) and the performance of certain adaptive behaviors (e.g., home living). This section of the chapter will introduce the terms used to describe this condition and two major professional definitions of ID.

Terminology

The current appropriate terminology to describe this condition is "intellectual disability." However, the use of this term in various professional venues such as legal settings is relatively new. The term that was used in the U.S. for many years was "mental retardation," and as Polloway, Smith, Patton, Lubin, and Antoine (2009) and Bergeron, Floyd and Shands (2008) both reported, 27 states used the term "mental retardation" at the time of their respective studies. This term was replaced, officially and unofficially, by the term "intellectual disability" in recent years (Schalock et al., 2010). Consequently, Polloway, Auguste, Smith, and Peters (2016) found that ID was reported in 42 state guidelines, while mental retardation continued to be used in only three states. The term "intellectual developmental disorder," to which reference is made in the Diagnostic and Statistical Manual of Mental Disorders-5 (DSM-5) (APA, 5th ed., 2013), may also be found in the literature.

The terminology has changed in recent years for two primary reasons. Among experts in the field of intellectual disability, it is believed that the term "intellectual disability" better reflects the nature of the condition and aligns more closely with appropriate responses to the disability. The term "intellectual disability" is also considered less offensive and more consistent with international terminology (Schalock et al., 2010).

The shift to ID (from MR) accelerated with Rosa's Law, federal legislation of the movement to eliminate the "R word" (Polloway, Bouck, Patton, & Lubin, 2017). The Congressional Record provided a synopsis of the rationale for change (as adapted here):

> The term "mental retardation" . . . to describe persons with intellectual disabilities is anachronistic, needlessly insensitive and stigmatizing, and clinically outdated. Terms have gone

> through a steady evolution over the past two centuries, each iteration describing those living with the condition in a pejorative way. . . . "Imbecile," "moron," "idiot," and "feeble-minded" are all terms, which have been used. . . . Each of these terms focused on perceived deficiencies to describe such persons. The most recent term—"mental retardation"—was used to characterize those with cognitive disabilities as having general diminished capacities for cognitive functioning. . . . Within the past 30 years . . . "mental retardation" and "mentally retarded" have also developed into colloquial slurs and pejorative phrases used to demean and insult both persons with and without disabilities. Congress has recognized that these negative attributions toward people with disabilities should not be tolerated. . . . it is also essential that we ensure these persons are provided the respect they deserve as part of our American family. Thus, it is important to revise our terminology in Federal statutes, as appropriate, to further and support the equality of all persons, without regard to disability.
>
> (Rosa's Law, 2010)

Polloway, Patton, and Smith (2015) noted that ID has now been almost universally embraced as the predominant term in clinical settings and the community.

Understanding the different terms that have been used historically in the U.S. and recognizing terms used in other countries is extremely important for making sense of the literature about this population. For instance, the term "learning disability" is the term used in the United Kingdom to refer to intellectual disabilities. In the U.S., the term learning disabilities refers to a different disability and a different set of challenges.

Professional Definitions of ID

The concept, if not the term, of intellectual disability has been recognized for a long time. Specific definitions describing this condition have changed and evolved over the years. The ID concept has consistently been defined around three major components—often referred to as the three prongs of the definition: impairments in intellectual functioning, deficits in adaptive behavior/functioning, and recognition that the condition was present during the developmental period.

The two most commonly referred to definitional sources are the *Intellectual Disability: Definition, Classification, and Systems of Support* manual of the American Association on Intellectual and Developmental Disabilities (AAIDD) (Schalock et al., 2010) and the *Diagnostic and Statistical Manual of Mental Disorders* (DSM-5) of the American Psychiatric Association (APA, 2013). The definitions from both of these sources are provided in Table 23.1. As was noted by Tasse (2015), both definitions focus on the disability as having onset during the developmental period and reflecting difficulties in intellectual functioning and in adaptive behavior deficits in conceptual, practical, and social areas.

Table 23.1 Professional Definitions of ID

Source	*Definition of ID*
American Association on Intellectual and Developmental Disabilities (2010)	Intellectual disability is characterized by significant limitations both in intellectual functioning and adaptive behavior as expressed in conceptual, social, and practical adaptive skills. This disability originates before age 18.
Diagnostic and Statistical Manual of Mental Disorders (5th ed; 2013)	Intellectual disability (intellectual developmental disorder) is a disorder with onset during the developmental period. That includes both intellectual and adaptive functioning deficits in conceptual, social, and practical domains.

Schalock et al. (2010) noted that the AAIDD definition of ID referred to the same persons who earlier would have identified as mentally retarded (see Luckasson et al., 2002), and thus any individual previously diagnosed as the latter (MR) should now be identified as the former (ID). Each of the three key components of both definitions is discussed next.

Prong I: Intellectual Functioning

Intellectual functioning refers to a person's ability to reason, problem solve, use, and understand abstract concepts. In AAIDD's (Schalock et al., 2010, p. 31) manual, intellectual functioning is defined as "general mental ability. It includes reasoning, planning, solving problems, thinking abstractly, comprehending complex ideas, learning quickly, and learning from experience." The APA (2013, p. 33) describes intellectual functioning as "reasoning, problem solving, planning, abstract thinking, judgment, academic learning, and learning from experience."

To meet the criterion of significant limitations in intellectual functioning, a person would have scores on a comprehensive, individually administered, technically sound, and culturally appropriate test of intelligence of approximately two standard deviations below the mean (Watson, 2015). In other words, an individual would have to have an IQ score that is approximately 70, with a standard error of measurement of ±5 points. Thus, a score of 75 would be acceptable for meeting the Prong I criterion (see *Hall v. Florida, 2014* for legal clarification).

While precise cutoff scores have been used in the past—the so-called "bright line" interpretations of ID in which some courts used a strict IQ ceiling—the use of a range of scores is the professionally accepted position and practice. In *Hall v. Florida* (2014), the Supreme Court rejected the use of such a bright line cutoff (Polloway, Patton, & Smith, 2015). In the words of Justice Anthony Kennedy, "intellectual disability is a condition, not a number" (*Hall v. Florida*, 2014, p. 21).

Intellectual functioning assessment also should reflect the Flynn effect (FE). McGrew (2015, p. 156) noted that,

> the Flynn effect is the result of a "softening" of IQ test norms with the passage of time. That is, persons tested today on an IQ test normed many years earlier will obtain artificially inflated IQ test scores, because the older test norms reflect an overall performance that is lower than that of persons in contemporary society.

The FE is generally conceptualized as about three points per decade (or 0.3 points per year) subsequent to the norming of the instrument used (McGrew, 2015).

Prong II: Adaptive Functioning

Adaptive behavior or functioning refers to a person's ability to deal with the everyday demands of life. This component focuses on the practical manifestations of limited intellectual ability. It should be noted that the term "adaptive behavior" is used in the AAIDD manual and the term "adaptive functioning" is used in DSM-5. The terms essentially convey the same concept and, as a result, can be used interchangeably.

In the Schalock et al. (2010, p. 43) manual, adaptive behavior is defined as "the collection of conceptual, social, and practical skills that have been learned and performed by people to function in their everyday lives." The APA (2013, p. 37) described adaptive functioning as "how well a person meets community standards of personal independence and social responsibility, in comparison to others of similar age and sociocultural background."

The contemporary concept of adaptive behavior is based on a tripartite competence model, which gave rise to the identification of the three domains, including conceptual, practical, and social adaptive behavior (Greenspan, 2015a). Contemporary practice requires that an individual show significant deficits in overall adaptive behavior or within conceptual, social, or practical adaptive skills.

A more specific description of what is meant by adaptive functioning can be gleaned from the adaptive domains that have been traditionally associated with the three major areas of conceptual, social, and practical. These adaptive areas, which are described in Table 23.2, are grouped under the three currently used adaptive areas (Patton, 2015).

Adaptive behavior assessment requires the accumulation of information about the individual. This information about adaptive functioning is typically obtained from records, interviews, and the administration of a formal adaptive behavior instrument. According to Olley (2015, p. 189),

> adaptive behavior instruments that are acceptable for diagnostic purposes must meet contemporary standards for standardization, reliability, and validity; . . . have objective wording that focuses on behavior, rather than potential; . . . are administered by someone who has

Table 23.2 Adaptive Functioning Skills

Adaptive Skill	*Characteristic*	*Example*
Conceptual	Communication	Speech, expressive language (speaking), receptive language skills (listening), and use of language in social, practical situations.
	Functional Academics	Ability to use reading, writing, math, and other academic-related skills for everyday purposes (e.g., reading manuals, writing letters, making change or telling time).
Practical	Community Use	Range of skills needed to use services and resources in the community (e.g., shopping, using different types of transportation, accessing services)
	Health	Skills needed to maintain one's ability to stay healthy and to respond to health-related problems when they arise.
	Home Living	Skills needed for everyday living in a home setting (e.g., cooking, cleaning, making repairs, doing chores).
	Safety	Skills needed to display behavior that reflects a concern for and caution about safety in everyday situations.
	Self-Care	Basic skills that are needed to take care of oneself (e.g., eating, bathing, grooming, and other types of hygiene care).
	Self-Direction	Skills associated with being independent and taking control of one's life (e.g., setting goals, making plans, making choices, ability to problem solve, completing tasks).
	Work	skills needed to be successful in various work/job situations (e.g., finding a job, applying and interviewing for a job, performing specific job duties, demonstrating general job skills such as showing up on time and following directions, working with a supervisor, getting along with co-workers).
Social	Leisure	Skills needed to engage in a range of indoor and outdoor recreational activities and other forms of entertainment (e.g., playing sports, understanding the rules of a game, learning how to play a particular sport or activity).
	Social	Skills needed to get along with and interact successfully with other people (e.g., making and keeping friends, helping others, demonstrating age-appropriate skills in a range of social situations, getting along with other individuals).

> known the individual over time and observed him or her across settings;... and require that the person rate the persons with regard to how independently he or she performs each task.

It is essential to point out that AAIDD emphasizes, as one of the key assumptions associated with the definition, that "within an individual, limitations coexist with strengths" (Schalock et al., 2010, p. 1). Therefore, an individual can display some relative areas of strengths in addition to demonstrating significant challenges in everyday functioning. In other words, a person does not have to show significant deficits across all adaptive skill areas to be found to have ID. It also is important to note that, even with relative strengths, a person can still qualify as having deficits in adaptive behavior and meet this criterion of the definition.

Another aspect of adaptive behavior that warrants attention is the emphasis placed on the typical performance rather than optimal performance of adaptive skills. The key feature herein is not can a person perform a given behavior but how well is that behavior performed on a regular basis. Both the AAIDD (2010) and American Psychiatric Association (2013) definitions state that a person only has to show deficits in one of three adaptive behavior domains: conceptual, social, or practical. This fact corroborates the point that an individual does not have to show limitations or deficits in all areas of functioning and that an individual may actually display relative strengths in some areas.

"Significant limitations" in adaptive functioning are defined differently, depending on the assessment technique(s) employed. According to the AAIDD (2010, p. 43), when a formal, standardized, norm-referenced instrument is used,

> significant limitations in adaptive behavior are operationally defined as performance that is approximately two standard deviations below the mean of either (a) one of the following three types of adaptive behavior: conceptual, social, practical; or (b) an overall score on a standardized measure of conceptual, social, and practical skills.

When clinical assessment techniques (informal data collected through collateral interviews) are utilized, "significant limitations" can be identified when the nature of the adaptive deficits has a major impact on the person's functioning that clearly deviates from the standards of personal independence and social responsibility expected of the person's age and cultural group. Furthermore, "significance" is underscored when the information obtained from different sources corroborates these deficits (i.e., convergent validity). The determination that deficits exist or existed should be based on professional judgment that results from training and an extensive experiential background in working with individuals with intellectual disabilities.

Prong III: Developmental Period

The third component of all of the major professional definitions of intellectual disabilities specifies that the onset of this condition must occur during the developmental period. The AAIDD definition (Schalock et al., 2010) requires that the disability be manifested before age 18, which usually means having been labeled as intellectually disabled during that time period, while DSM-5 (APA, 2013) does not specify an exact age range. Polloway et al. (2016), in their study of definitions used in educational settings, noted that 50 states explicitly noted the developmental period as a criterion for this disability. The study also found that 36 states (70.6%) designated an age or range for the developmental period, including 31 that indicated 0–18 or through age 18, and four states (7.8%) stipulating through age 22.

The determination of manifestation during the developmental period becomes challenging when persons (who were not previously identified) are assessed as adults to retrospectively determine whether ID was manifested during the developmental period (that is through age 18) as a basis for adult services and certain criminal justice considerations (Polloway, Patton, & Smith, 2015). Greenspan, Woods, and Switzky (2015) have argued for the consideration of substantial developmental evidence indicating that a clear "continuity of concern" was apparent in such a body of evidence that could be used as a basis for verifying origination during the developmental period.

State Definitions of ID

Many states have enacted legislation that includes definitions of intellectual disability in their penal or criminal code. When a definition of ID is embedded in a state's penal statutes, then this definition will be used in state court proceedings. Often state statutes vary somewhat from the two major professional definitions presented here. This fact may be due to continued use of older definitions or the enactment that differs in wording from the key professional definitions. Some states, such as Texas, have not acted on establishing an up-to-date definition at the state level for use in criminal proceedings. In the case of Texas, the reliance on an older, outdated definition of ID that resides in the Health and Safety Code, along with the use of unscientific criteria referred to as *Briseno* factors, has resulted in the Supreme Court ruling that the use of outdated medical standards regarding intellectual disability to determine whether a person is exempt from execution violates the Eighth Amendment (*Moore v. Texas*, 2017) (for a full discussion of the issues in *Moore v. Texas*, see also Greenspan, 2015a).

The Death Penalty Information Center (DPIC) has a number of resources related to persons with ID. The DPIC maintains a list of definitions of states that still have a death penalty and have specific definitions of ID in their penal codes (DPIC, 2016). The list is in two parts: (1) those states that had definitions in place prior to *Atkins v. Virginia* (2002) and have not changed the definitions; and (2) those states that have changed their definitions of ID since the *Atkins* decision.

Levels of Intellectual Disability

Different levels or subcategories of intellectual disability exist. Historically, different levels of ID (e.g., mild, moderate, severe, and profound) were used to classify individuals; however, in more recent years, less emphasis has been placed on different classification levels of intellectual disability. AAIDD has moved more toward a system that specifies differentiated levels of supports based on various risk factors and level of need. Interestingly, DSM-5 reintroduced this concept of levels by specifying four levels of adaptive functioning: mild, moderate, severe, and profound.

Most individuals with ID fall into the mild range (i.e., have higher IQs, circa 55–70/75) of functioning, although questions have often been raised about the use of the term "mild" as an ID subcategory. Siperstein and Collins (2015) noted that subcategorization by levels had been taking place for 200 years, and the seemingly contradictory concept of mild ID has proven problematic for a significant period of time. Polloway (2006, p. 196) claims that "the mild concept created misconceptions within both the profession and the general population that has had implications for the eligibility of persons for educational and other supports." Regardless of such concerns, "mild" continues to be used widely.

Snell et al. (2009) instead recommended the referent of "people with intellectual disability who have higher IQs." Such an approach is consistent with the contemporary concept of intellectual disability being a spectrum disorder, with persons identified as having mild ID occupying essentially the upper end of the ID spectrum. As Snell and colleagues (2009, p. 222) state, "this group of people with intellectual disability who have higher IQs constitute the large majority of all individuals with intellectual disability."

Individuals who have mild ID typically look very similar to others with whom they may spend time. However, when analyzed more closely, some of their behavior will differ from that of their peers. Snell and colleagues (2009, p. 222) substantiated this point with the following: "Individuals with an intellectual disability who have higher IQs struggle in society. This is true despite the fact that all individuals with intellectual disability typically demonstrate strengths and functioning along with relative limitations."

Individuals with ID and the Criminal Justice System

While much attention has been devoted to the complex situation related to individuals with ID who are charged with capital crimes and whether they qualify to be excluded from execution, many other individuals with ID encounter the criminal justice system in a variety of ways. This section provides a backdrop of the involvement of individuals with ID in the criminal justice system.

Individuals with ID encounter the criminal justice system at both the juvenile and adult levels—whether they are officially identified as ID or not. There are, however, some notable differences between these two levels. Youth with ID who entered the juvenile system and who were previously identified for special education purposes should continue to receive these services while they are in the juvenile setting. There is no such requirement for individuals with ID who were in the adult setting.

Prevalence within the Criminal Justice System

As other chapters in this book note, the prevalence of disability within the criminal justice system is significant (see Chapters 24 and 25). The professional literature has frequently reflected evidence of a possible overrepresentation of persons with ID within the criminal justice system (see e.g., Davis, 2009; Hassan & Gordon, 2003; Newman, Wagner, Cameto, & Knokey, 2009; Petersilia, 2000a, 2000b; Polloway, Patton, Smith, Beyer, & Bailey, 2011; Smith, Polloway, Patton, & Beyer, 2008). While these studies and reports by no means point to a causative relationship between ID and the likelihood of an individual engaging in crime, they do point to the importance of careful attention to the nature of this relationship. Of particular concern is whether persons with ID face special challenges in the criminal justice system because of certain deficits that they may have related to reasoning, thinking, learning, and social interactions, as will be discussed later in the chapter.

Mental health issues and other conditions, such as attention-deficit hyperactivity disorder (ADHD), can be found in many offenders (see also the discussion later on comorbidity). It is also possible for an individual to have more than one disability or condition that can interfere with his or her successful functioning. Most importantly is the reality that many individuals with mild ID may not have been recognized as having ID or may have never been formally identified—either in school or upon entry into the criminal justice system.

At the juvenile level, data on the number of youth with intellectual disability vary somewhat. Rutherford, Bullis, Anderson, and Griller-Clark (2002) estimated that 3.4% of juveniles who were incarcerated had been identified as having ID. This figure is likely to be an underestimate of the percentage of youth in the juvenile system who have ID.

The National Longitudinal Transition Study-2 (Newman et al., 2009) reported the postschool outcomes of student with disabilities across a number of areas. One of the areas studied was encounters with the criminal justice system at some point in the person's life after high school. The study obtained data on the following four dimensions: stopped by the police for reasons other than traffic violations, been arrested, spent a night in jail, and been placed on probation or on parole. The data for young adults with ID is reported in Table 23.3.

Table 23.3 Interactions of Young Adults with ID with the Criminal Justice System

Type of Encounter	*Percentage of Young Adults with ID*
Stopped by police (other than for traffic violation)	31.1%
Arrested	18.4%
Spent night in jail	10.3%
Been on probation or parole	9.5%

Types of Offenses Committed

Persons with ID can commit a range a crimes and can be victims of a range of crimes. As the Arc (2009, p. 2) noted, "research from the mid-80s to the 1990s found that the types of crimes committed range from property crimes, like theft and robbery, to physical and sexual assault. Some have been accused of murder as well."

Public Perceptions and Misconceptions of Persons with ID

Much confusion exists about intellectual disabilities in general and about mild intellectual disability in particular. This confusion is manifest in misperceptions of disability and misconceptions based on restricted stereotypes. Modell and Mak (2008), in their study of law enforcement officers' knowledge of persons with disabilities, found that 56% of this group could not distinguish the difference between physical limitations and cognitive limitations. In addition, they found 82% could not identify the difference between cognitive disabilities and emotional disabilities (see Chapter 27 for more about police interactions with offenders with special needs).

Stereotypes of ID

The lay public often does not understand mild intellectual disability and may likely hold common stereotypes about individuals with intellectual disability. These stereotypes typically may have developed over time because of limited exposure to and experience with this population and as a function of the images of intellectual disabilities that are portrayed in various forms of media. For instance, films such as *I Am Sam* and *Radio* or television shows such as *The Secret Life of an American Teenager* (recurrent character with ID), while not necessarily inaccurate in their depiction of intellectual disability, provide images of individuals who are not at the upper end of the ID spectrum. As Reschly (1990, p. 85) remarked when referencing the misconceptions that people have about individuals who are at the upper end of the spectrum, "the characteristics of the more severely retarded are often mistakenly ascribed to them."

For all practical purposes, the image of an individual with intellectual disability that most people have is often the image of someone with the condition known as Down syndrome. While almost all individuals with Down syndrome (DS) have an intellectual disability, and while there is significant variance in functioning level of persons with DS (see, for example Rynders, Spiker, & Horrobin, 1978; Rynders, 2005; Stancliffe et al., 2012), most individuals in this group do not function at the upper end of the ID spectrum. As a result, this group is not an accurate representation of the individuals who are accused of or have been convicted of a significant crime.

Misconceptions of ID

Given the generalized stereotypes that have arisen and have been perpetuated over time, relatively few persons from the lay public and within various professional communities such as the criminal justice system truly understand the limitations and capabilities of individuals with mild intellectual disability, thus resulting in misconceptions that are limited in scope and often completely inaccurate.

For the most part, the misconceptions are skewed toward deficits. What most people do not know are the capabilities (i.e., relative strengths) that individuals with mild intellectual disability may display. As Siperstein and Collins (2015. p. 26) noted, "if given the opportunity, individuals with ID at the upper end of the spectrum can participate in their communities in ways that far exceed public expectations." They identified and provided research support for some of the behaviors that the public is likely not to associate with individuals with mild intellectual disability. An adapted summary of their findings is provided in Box 23.1.

In addition to the behaviors noted in Box 23.1, other behaviors that exceed typical expectations exist. Some of the more noteworthy behaviors include the ability to:

- demonstrate academic achievement (e.g., reading, writing, and math) at a sixth-grade level (APA, 2013);
- live in housing situations apart from their family without the need of formal agency support (Felce & Perry, 2007); and
- take and pass high school equivalency tests such as the GED (Newman, Madaus, Javitz, 2016).

The major problem that arises, from a criminal justice perspective, is the fact that individuals at the upper end of the ID spectrum may often not be recognized as having ID. As Siperstein and Collins (2015, p. 27) pointed out, "individuals functioning in this range can be difficult to identify as a result of their high levels of adaptive behaviors. Consequently, many go undiagnosed OR misdiagnosed because they do not demonstrate obvious improvements in the skills and behaviors."

This issue is a problem for everyone in the criminal justice system from law enforcement to the judiciary. The need to identify individuals with ID who encounter the criminal justice system is extremely important to ensure that this population is treated in an appropriate fashion. The confusion that is present in recognizing higher functioning persons with ID is usually a focal issue in death penalty cases where the question of ID has been raised. The circumstances surrounding this topic will be covered later in the chapter.

Box 23.1 *Behaviors: Exceeding Public Expectations*

- Attend postsecondary education (Papay & Bambara, 2011);
- Sustain gainful employment in appropriate settings (Jahoda et al., 2009);
- Participate in a variety of community and leisure activities (Dusseljee, Rijken, Cardol, Curgs, & Groenewegen, 2011);
- Drive cars (Dixon & Reddacliff, 2001);
- Have long-term relationships (Siebelink, de Jong, Taal, & Roelvink, 2006);
- Master independent living skills such as using ATMs (Davies, Stock, & Wehmeyer, 2003);
- Cook (Taber-Doughty et al., 2011);
- Make financial decisions (Suto, Clare, Holland, & Watson, 2005);
- Use computers and the internet (Wehmeyer et al., 2006);
- Navigate urban settings (Wright & Wolery, 2011);
- Ride public transportation (Davies, Stock, Holloway, & Wehmeyer, 2010); and
- Live independently with varying levels of support (Bond & Hurst, 2009).

Characteristics and Features of Persons with ID

Individuals with ID comprise a heterogeneous group of people with varying interests, strengths, and challenges. However, certain characteristics are frequently observed in this population and can be noteworthy issues when these individuals encounter the criminal justice system. This section covers three key areas: key characteristics related to the criminal justice system that can be problematic for persons with ID, the overriding need for supports throughout life, and comorbidity.

Problematic Characteristics

Individuals with ID will struggle, to varying degrees, in situations where high levels for reasoning and problem solving are involved. This does not mean that they are totally unable to perform these tasks, as some individuals with mild ID can learn to problem solve in certain situations. Individuals with mild ID can know right from wrong or, in other words, they will know when they have done something they should not have done. Sometimes their social skills are awkward, yet individuals can and do make friends, have romantic relationships, and get married.

Polloway et al. (2017) summarized 11 areas in which persons with ID may struggle within learning-related settings. The 11 areas include attention, metacognition, memory, generalization, learning, motivational considerations, cognitive development, language development, academic development, social-behavioral interactions, and social responding. A more detailed explanation of these characteristics can be found in in Polloway et al. (2017) and Smith, Polloway, Doughty, Patton, and Dowdy (2012).

Siperstein and Collins (2015, p. 26) provided an apt summary of certain key characteristics of persons with mild ID as follows:

> rather than displaying significant general dysfunction, persons with mild ID struggle more with abstract thinking, deficits in planning, problem solving, decision making, social perception, understanding, and judgment. Comparatively, the limitations in mild intellectual disabilities are more subtle, more difficult to detect, and often context-specific.

A number of characteristics that many individuals with mild ID display can, and often will, be challenging for them on a day-to-day basis, whether at school, at work, or in the community. However, if persons with ID encounter the criminal justice system, these characteristics can be particularly problematic and lead to pejorative consequences. Some of the most notable characteristics are listed in Table 23.4. This table is adapted from an original list that was developed by Patton and Keyes (2006) and later refined by Smith, Polloway, Patton, and Beyer (2008).

A particular concern is social vulnerability. Greenspan (2015b) has concluded that there has been increased recognition that gullibility, along with other forms of difficulties related to social competence and thus social vulnerability, may often present as a common problem in persons with ID. Greenspan (2006, 2015b) posited that gullibility is a core characteristic of persons with ID and that they are consequently vulnerable to social manipulation, which can have legal implications. As such, the problems with social vulnerability may provide a partial rationale for the related disproportionately of persons with ID in the criminal justice system, as discussed earlier. In addition, the denial of disability (or "masking") further characterizes some persons within this population and creates potential disadvantages within the system (Patton & Keyes, 2006), which would be consistent with the "cloak of competence" concept in which persons with ID seek to mask their disability (Edgerton, 1967, p. 205).

Table 23.4 Problematic Characteristics of Persons with ID in the Criminal Justice System

Characteristic	*Description*	*Example*
Gullibility	Phenomenon of being duped or lied to and often involving some degree of victimization.	Taking advantage of someone.
Acquiescence	Tendency to give in when under pressure.	Talked into doing things for which one does not understand the consequences. Talked into confessing to a crime that one did not commit.
Naiveté	In experienced, credulous.	Accepts what someone says without question. Does not catch subtlety of situations.
Desire to Please	Interest in pleasing others.	Will do what someone else wants to be accepted. May say what he or she thinks police want to hear.
Concrete Thinking	Inability to understand abstract concepts.	Does not understand *Miranda* rights.
Memory Issues	Difficulty with short-term memory.	Not likely to recognize the seriousness of what he or she is being accused of. Likely to get confused as to the complexities of a crime. Does not remember details of a situation.
Language Problems	Difficulty with receptive and expressive language.	Does not understand what is being said. Cannot articulate what one is thinking or feeling. Cannot respond appropriately to critical questions during an interrogation.
Social Behaviors	Displays certain emotions or feelings.	May display behavior (e.g., laughing) that suggests a lack of remorse at an inappropriate time (e.g., during trial).
Cloak of Competence	Attempt to pass as "normal."	May go to great lengths to deny or hide limitations. May cover for codefendants in an effort to appear strong.

Need for Support

A typical observation associated with individuals with ID is their need for support in their lives. We all use support in varying ways, although most of us may be able to function without them; however, for persons with ID, varying degrees of support are likely to be operative out of necessity. Thompson and colleagues (2009) stressed that the need for support is an ongoing rather that a temporary feature of this population.

The DSM-5 definition of ID emphasizes the concept of supports as well. In reference to meeting Criterion B—deficits in adaptive functioning (i.e., Prong II) of the definition—DSM-5 (2013, p. 38) states:

> Criterion B is met when at least one domain of adaptive functioning—conceptual, social, or practical—is sufficiently impaired that ongoing support is needed . . . for the person

to perform adequately in one or more life settings: school, at work, at home, or in the community.

Another important consideration in assessment relates to an analysis of support needs for persons with ID. While adaptive behavior assessment identifies deficits (and possible strengths) in the person, supports assessment seeks to determine the levels of support are needed for persons to function, particularly within inclusive environments. The *Supports Intensity Scale–Adult Version* (Thompson et al., 2015) and the *Supports Intensity Scale–Children's Version* (Thompson et al., 2016) both reflect the goal of viewing ID as within the context of a supports paradigm.

Comorbidity or Dual Diagnosis

Persons with ID have increased vulnerability to psychiatric or mental health concerns (Siperstein & Collins, 2015). Woods, Freedman, and Derning (2015) concluded that up to 40% of adults with ID may also be clinically diagnosed at some point in time in life with such a disorder. They identified such comorbid disorders as including schizophrenia, mood disorders, and post-traumatic stress disorder, with evidence of 75% of persons reporting at least a single traumatic event in their lifetime and perhaps often related to vulnerability to abuse and exploitation. In addition, individuals with ID may have other comorbid disorders, such as obsessive-compulsive disorder and dementia, with particular concern in early onset Alzheimer's disease. Woods et al. (2015) further observed that such comorbid conditions may be more of standard occurrences than exceptions.

Challenges along and within the Criminal Justice Process

This section is designed to highlight important issues that can arise at various points along the criminal justice system process. The designated phases are clearly part of the adult criminal justice system process; however, most of the phases apply to the juvenile process as well. The process actually begins with some type of initial contact with law enforcement and then continues through a set of adjudication phases. Depending on the outcome of a potential trial or hearing, an individual may have to serve a sentence that often involves some form of incarceration, which can vary from a relatively short sentence to life without parole (LWOP), depending on the offense and sentencing determination. Most individuals with ID who are incarcerated will be released from the system at some point in time and reenter the community after imprisonment.

All of these phases pose challenges for anyone who encounters the system. However, for offenders with ID, unique challenges exist that can result in undesirable and often inappropriate outcomes. Table 23.5 presents a comprehensive list of key issues facing persons with ID who encounter the criminal justice system. The table is organized into eight phases associated with the criminal justice system and separates challenges that are related to characteristics and general behavioral sets of persons with ID from the challenges introduced by those who work in the criminal justice system. The table builds upon the work of Polloway et al. (2011) and Smith et al. (2008) from their previous discussion of many of the challenges noted in Table 23.5.

It is important to acknowledge that, when examining the challenges listed in Table 23.5, the opportunity to apply whatever level of understanding of the subtleties of mild ID thoroughly and thoughtfully in a time of crisis (e.g., initial contact or arrest) is difficult. Nevertheless, it remains critically important that law enforcement that are on the front lines and others within the criminal justice system community who will have contact at a later point have a working understanding of the characteristics and be able to apply this knowledge when needed.

Table 23.5 Challenges for Persons with ID within the Criminal Justice System

Phase within the Criminal Justice System	*Possible Challenges for Persons with ID*
Precontact	*Persons with ID may have:* • insufficient preparation in schools on how to avoid encounters with the law • lack of awareness/education of their legal rights (e.g., the right to attorney, the right to not self-incriminate) • lack of understanding of the *Miranda* warning—a person with ID is not likely to understand this warning without an alternative version being utilized and possibly explained—the *Miranda* warning is written at approximately a seventh-grade reading level—an individual at the high end of the ID continuum is likely to read at a sixth-grade level or below. • vulnerability in being talked into doing something that is not in their best interests • lack of knowledge about the potential repercussions of committing a crime or participating with others in various activities (i.e., naiveté) *Criminal justice system personnel may have:* • lack of understanding of the characteristics and predictable behaviors of persons with ID • lack of understanding that most persons with ID do not look different from others in their communities
Initial Contact /Arrest	*Persons with ID may have:* • confusion typically associated with initial contact • lack of understanding of what is happening • been intimidated during an arrest • emotional reaction to threatening situations *Criminal justice system personnel may have:* • lack of awareness that a person being initially detained has ID—therefore, not taking action to defuse the confusion and provide some sense of stability in a typically chaotic and emotionally charged situation—it is estimated that 75% of persons with ID or other developmental disabilities who are arrested are not identified as having a disability (Petersilia, 2000a)
Intake	*Persons with ID may have:* • confusion about what is happening • discomfort with being taken to an unfamiliar setting (e.g., a jail or detention facility) • continued intimidation • absence of personal support systems being immediately available—i.e., people whom the person with ID knows and who can provide comfort and assistance • absence of law enforcement-provided support systems—i.e., availability of someone knowledgeable about ID being present to provide some level of support—NOTE: a few law enforcement agencies do provide this service *Criminal justice system personnel may have:* • lack of understanding of the characteristics and behaviors of persons with ID—resulting in the person with ID not being directed to a nurse/counselor or other intake-available person for consideration of mental health or other issues (i.e., ID)

(*Continued*)

Table 23.5 (Continued)

Phase within the Criminal Justice System	*Possible Challenges for Persons with ID*
Interrogation	*Persons with ID may have or may be:* • gullible—person with ID not wanting to "rat" on his/her codefendant(s) in an attempt to be a true "friend" • working memory limitations—person with ID not being able to describe what happened accurately or getting facts of what happened mixed up • acquiescence—person with ID will give in to authority figures when under great duress • desire to please—person with ID, in an effort to please those in authority, will say what he/she thinks the person in authority wants to hear • tendency to give a false confession—i.e., being "confused about who is responsible for the crime and 'confess' even though innocent" (Arc, 2009. p. 2). Perske (2008) has documented that persons with ID are very inclined to sign a confession that is not representative of reality *Criminal justice system personnel may have:* • lack of awareness that person being interviewed has ID • not waited for legal or other assistance when it is known that the person being interviewed has ID • use of interrogation tactics that are disadvantageous when used with persons with ID—for detailed discussion of this topic, see Smith et al., 2008)
Pretrial	*Persons with ID may have:* • desire not to be identified, labeled, referred to as ID • "cloak of competence"—person with ID telling his/her legal team, or others, that he/she can do things that, in reality, he/she is not able to perform • receptive language deficits—person with ID may not really understand what is being said to him/her—nodding in approval to the question "do you understand?" does not indicate comprehension of what was said and actual understanding • vulnerability to abuse and mistreatment while being held in jail/detention center *Criminal justice system personnel have or may experience:* • lack of protections that are provided to persons with ID while being jailed/detained and awaiting hearings, trial, and/or placement • lack of understanding/awareness of the limitations and strengths of a person with ID on the part of those involved in direct contact with the person when he/she is in jail or detention • less likelihood that a person with ID will be granted bail, as two key considerations for being granted bail are: having employment and having substantial community ties—both of which may be lacking for a person with ID (Smith et al., 2008) • lack of awareness on the part of the legal team that their client has ID • lack of understanding of the functional impact that ID has on a person's life—it is particularly important for the attorneys in the case to know this information • failure of the legal team to solicit the assistance of professionals who are knowledgeable of ID and can serve in a consulting role for the team (e.g., professionally trained advocate or ID expert) • failure of the legal team to consider the issue of competency to stand trial • failure of the legal team—in a state where the death penalty is a sentencing option in a capital case—to consider investigating and filing an *Atkins* claim—(this issue is discussed later in the chapter)

Phase within the Criminal Justice System	*Possible Challenges for Persons with ID*
Trial/Hearings	*Persons with ID may have*: • lack of remorse shown in a visible manner • lack of interest in what is occurring during proceeding • uncertainty/unsuitability of persons with ID testifying *Criminal justice system personnel may have or experience*: • failure of legal team to present strong mitigation evidence during the sentencing phase of a trial • failure to present adaptive behavior information during the mitigation phase of sentencing • likelihood that a person with ID will receive a longer sentence (McGillivray & Watterman, 2003; Smith et al., 2008) • failure of courts to consider alternative sentencing options for a person with ID—often, as Smith et al. (2008) note: "the communities in which they reside may lack appropriate kinds of community options that ensure subsequent success" (p. 427)
Incarceration (postadjudication)	*Persons with ID may have*: • vulnerability to abuse and mistreatment within juvenile settings or prisons • naiveté—lack of awareness of the "dynamics" of life within walls • serve extended sentences—due to the fact that persons with ID "do not understand or cannot meet steps to reduce time and secure an earlier release (Arc, 2014, p. 2) *Correctional personnel may have*: • lack of separate—and yes, in this case, not inclusionary—settings (i.e., where the risk of abuse/mistreatment is reduced)—persons with ID are at much greater risk within a general population setting • lack of needed medical and physical health services • lack of mental health services (i.e., mental health conditions, substance abuse)
Release/Reintegration	*Persons with ID may have*: • lack of preparedness for reintegration in terms of levels of performance in vocational, educational, behavioral, social areas • uncertainty of what will happen when he/she is released—a certain sense of order or what is known will be disrupted by leaving either a juvenile or adult correctional setting *Correctional personnel may have*: • inadequate education and training opportunities to prepare persons with ID • lack of a "transition" plan for the individual to address the movement from incarceration to the free world

Unique Issues Related to Capital Offenses: Death Penalty

Nowhere has more attention been given to the issue of persons with ID and their involvement in the criminal justice system been more obvious than with the complex issues associated with the death penalty. At the current point in time, 31 states include the death penalty as a sentencing option in capital cases. The death penalty has been banned in 19 states and the District of Columbia (Death Penalty Information Center, 2016). The noteworthy point related to ID is that the United States Supreme Court in 2002 ruled in a 5–4 decision that it was cruel and unusual punishment to execute individuals with ID (see *Atkins v. Virginia*, 2002). This decision triggered a new era of litigation that would focus exclusively at times on the issue of whether an alleged or convicted offender had ID.

Background

The initial case that received significant national attention was *Penry v. Lynaugh* (1989). Penry was convicted of a capital offense and sentenced to execution by the state of Texas, but this case extended over two decades with ongoing federal court review leading to recommendations back to Texas as related to the need to consider "mental retardation" as a mitigating circumstance in sentencing. While the case did not disallow the use of capital punishment for persons with ID, the scrutiny of the process ultimately led to Penry being sentenced to life imprisonment rather than being executed.

Of greater significance was *Atkins v. Virginia* (2002), decided by the U.S. Supreme Court in 2002. The consequence of this decision was that no person diagnosed as having ID could be executed within the United States (Greenspan, 2011). This case has led to litigation whereby a client needs to prove that he or she has ID. This litigation requires a defense team to show that their client has a legitimate claim of ID and, if granted the opportunity to pursue this claim, to demonstrate that their client meets the definition of ID that is used in a particular state—typically in an evidentiary hearing.

The U.S. Supreme Court decision in *Hall v. Florida* (2014) has significant implications for the way in which capital punishment hearings are conducted, especially in instances in which states have adopted "bright line" interpretations of ID. A series of IQ assessments had been administered to Hall over a number of years, as is common with adults within the criminal justice system who are being considered for possible intellectual disability. Although the majority of these assessments resulted in scores that were under the strict 70 IQ ceiling being used at that time in Florida, nevertheless, some of the scores were above 70. Based on the latter finding, Hall's petition had been rejected by the Florida courts, in spite of the other scores and in spite of the adaptive behavior evidence that supported a diagnosis of intellectual disability. The petition made by Hall's attorneys primarily focused on the standard error and the lack of scientific support for the state's use of IQ as an absolute number not subject to broader interpretation.

The Supreme Court in *Hall* rejected the use of the 70 bright line cutoff. Further, it went beyond the defendant's narrow psychometric position and took a broader view of what states may do when considering ID petitions in capital cases, indicating that they were not free to ignore scientific consensus regarding intelligence and the nature and diagnosis of ID. As Justice Kennedy stated, "intellectual disability is a condition, not a number" (*Hall v. Florida*, 2014, p. 21).

Key Issues

A number of key issues can be identified related to individuals with ID when they are involved in capital crimes where the death penalty may be used as a sentence. For this chapter, some of the salient issues can be organized according to the client, the ID determination process, and the judicial proceedings that are associated with this process. Table 23.6 highlights the salient issues that contribute to making the determination of ID in adult clients a complicated process.

Table 23.6 Key Issues Related to the Death Penalty

Focal Area	*Important Issues*
Client	• defendant may never have been identified as ID prior to the time of the crime—not recognized by his/her family—not identified when in school as needing special education • defendant might have been in special education—however, he/she might have been identified under a different disability category—however, he/she might still have ID • defendant is likely to demonstrate strengths that often are misinterpreted as disqualifiers for having ID • cultural and linguistic features must be understood and considered • in all likelihood the defendant will not want to be considered intellectually disabled and will sometimes oppose use of the term and any activity that might suggest that he/she does have this condition • defendant is likely to have experienced unhealthy experiences such as poverty or abuse/neglect in his/her past
ID Determination	• the assessment process, by its very nature, must look retrospectively at the individual • the age of the defendant (i.e., older clients) can be a limiting factor in terms of the availability of people who can speak about knowledgeably him/her (e.g., teachers, former employers) during the developmental period • key records such as special education records may no longer be available, as they are typically destroyed within a specified period of time after the person graduates or leaves school (see Patton, 2015) • determination of adaptive functioning problems may be required at three different points in time: prior to age 18; time of crime; and current (i.e., near the time of the *Atkins* proceedings)
Judicial Proceedings	• various professionals associated with the judicial process do not understand ID • defense team must understand the concepts and implications of ID • testimony from individuals who can explain the day-to-day impact of ID is needed • testimony from individuals who can share real-life stories about the defendant is particularly useful in demonstrating the adaptive functioning of the individual • disposition of the defendant during a hearing or trial can be misinterpreted by a judge or jury • adaptive functioning information can also be helpful to substantiate mitigating factors during the sentencing phase of a trial

Conclusion

Individuals with ID definitely engage with the criminal justice system United States and, in all likelihood, in other parts of the world as well. While this population must conform to the laws and regulations in which all citizens must abide, persons with ID do need to be "handled" in a differential manner. This special handling fundamentally involves a more accurate understanding of this population in terms of their strengths, their needs, their vulnerabilities, and their behaviors.

It is fitting to end this chapter with the position statement on the criminal justice system that was developed by the Arc of the U.S. (2014). We had decided to use this position statement, as shown in Table 23.7, as our concluding points related to this important topic of offenders with intellectual disabilities for two major reasons. First, the position statement summarizes most of the key points

Table 23.7 Position Statement of Arc of the U.S. on the Criminal Justice System

Position	People with intellectual and/or developmental disabilities must receive justice in the criminal justice system, whether as victims, witnesses, suspects, defendants, or incarcerated individuals.
As victims, witnesses, suspects, defendants, or incarcerated individuals, **they must:**	• Be protected by laws and policies that ensure their right to justice and fair treatment; • Be treated fairly by personnel who are knowledgeable and trained about I/DD, including all attorneys (prosecution and defense), judges, law enforcement personnel (including school-based security officers), first responders, forensic evaluators, victim advocates, court personnel, correctional personnel, criminal justice policy makers, and jurors; • Be informed about and have access to appropriate sentencing alternatives to incarceration and be provided the supports and accommodations to enter alternatives; • Receive supports and accommodations to effectively participate in all stages of legal proceedings for which they are competent; • Have necessary supports and accommodations available so that their testimony is heard and fairly considered when they are victims; • Have access to victim supports and compensation as appropriate; • Have access to, and the right to present, expert evaluations and testimony by professionals with training, experience, and expertise in their disability; • Have an advocate, in addition to their lawyer, who has specialized disability-related expertise; • Have their conversations with their advocate covered under, are treated similarly to, attorney-client privilege; and • As a suspect, be protected from harm, self-incrimination, and exploitation at all stages of the investigation and prosecution, including when they are questioned, detained, and incarcerated.
When sentenced, individuals with I/DD **also must:**	• Have available reasonable and appropriate supports, accommodations, treatment, and education, as well as alternatives to sentencing and incarceration that include community-based corrections; and • Have access to well-trained probation and parole officers who treat them fairly based on their individual disability and the need for the supports and accommodations necessary to reenter society, including those that will enable people to re-establish Medicaid waiver services, SSI, housing, education, and job supports.
When death penalty is an issue, individuals with intellectual disability **also must:**	• Continue to be exempt from the death penalty because existing case-by-case determinations of competence to stand trial, criminal responsibility, and mitigating factors at sentencing have proved insufficient to protect the rights of individuals with intellectual disability; • Have access to expert witnesses and professionals who are knowledgeable about, as well as trained and experienced in, intellectual disability and who can accurately determine the presence and effects of intellectual disability; and • Have their intellectual disability determined by state procedures that are accurate and fair. Those state procedures must be consistent with the national standards on making an intellectual disability determination and ensure that people with intellectual disability are not executed.

highlighted in this chapter and serves as a strongly worded reminder of what needs to happen when a person with ID encounters the criminal justice system. Second, this statement contains a cautionary message about the impact and seriousness that this topic has on all of us, and particularly on those whose lives will forever be changed because of their encounter with the criminal justice system.

References

American Association on Intellectual and Developmental Disabilities. (2010). *Intellectual disability: Definition, classification, and systems of supports* (11th ed.). Washington, DC. American Association on Intellectual and Developmental Disabilities.

American Psychiatric Association. (2013). *Diagnostic and statistical manual of mental disorders* (DSM-5; 5th ed.). Washington, DC: American Psychiatric Association.

ARC. (2009). *People with intellectual disabilities in the criminal justice systems: Victims & suspects*. Washington, DC: The Arc.

ARC. (2014). *Position statement: Criminal justice system*. Washington, DC: The Arc.

Atkins v. Virginia, 536 U.S. 304 (2002).

Bergeron, R., Floyd, R. G., & Shands, E. I. (2008). States' eligibility guidelines for mental retardation: An update and consideration of part scores and unreliability of IQs. *Education and Training in Developmental Disabilities, 43*(1), 123–131.

Bond, R. J., & Hurst, J. (2010). How adults with learning disabilities view living independently. *British Journal of Learning Disabilities, 38*(4), 286–292. doi:10.1111/j.1468-3156.2009.00604.x

Davies, D. K., Stock, S. E., & Wehmeyer, M. L. (2003). Utilization of computer technology to facilitate money management by individuals with mental retardation. *Education and Training in Mental Retardation and Developmental Disabilities, 38*(1), 106–112.

Davis, L. A. (2009). *People with intellectual disabilities in the criminal justice system: Victims & suspects*. Washington, DC: The Arc.

Death Penalty Information Center. (2016). *States with and without the death penalty*. Washington, DC: Death Penalty Information Center.

Dixon, R. M., & Reddacliff, C. A. (2001). Family contribution to the vocational lives of vocationally competent young adults with intellectual disabilities. *International Journal of Disability, Development and Education, 48*(2), 193–206. doi:10.1080/10349120120053667

Dusseljee, J. C., Rijken, P. M., Cardol, M., Curfs, L. M., & Groenewegen, P. P. (2011). Participation in daytime activities among people with mild or moderate intellectual disability. *Journal of Intellectual Disability Research, 55*(1), 4–18. doi:10.1111/j.1365-2788.2010.01342

Edgerton, R. (1967). *The cloak of competence: Stigma in the lives of the mentally retarded*. Los Angeles, CA: University of California Press.

Felce, D., & Perry, J. (2007). Living with support in the community. In S. L. Odom, R. H. Horner, M. E. Snell, & J. Blacher (Eds.), *Handbook of developmental disabilities* (pp. 410–428). New York, NY: Guilford Press.

Greenspan, S. (2006). Functional concepts in mental retardation: Finding the natural essence of an artificial category. *Exceptionality, 14*(4), 205–224. doi:10.1207/s15327035ex1404_3

Greenspan, S. (2015a). Briseno factors. In E. A. Polloway (Ed.), *The death penalty and intellectual disability* (pp. 219–231). Washington, DC: American Association on Intellectual and Developmental Disabilities.

Greenspan, S. (2015b). Evolving concepts of adaptive behavior. In E. A. Polloway (Ed.), *The death penalty and intellectual disability* (pp. 173–185). Washington, DC: American Association on Intellectual and Developmental Disabilities.

Greenspan, S. (2011). Homicide defendants with intellectual disabilities: Issues in diagnosis in capital cases. *Exceptionality, 19*(4), 219–237. doi:10.1080/09362835.2011.611086

Greenspan, S., Woods, G. W., & Switzky, H. N. (2015). Age of onset and the developmental period criterion. In E. A. Polloway (Ed.), *The death penalty and intellectual disability* (pp. 77–81). Washington, DC: American Association on Intellectual and Developmental Disabilities.

Hall v Florida, 572 U.S. (2014).

Hassan, S., & Gordon, R. (2003). *Developmental disability, crime, and criminal justice: A literature review* (Criminology Research Centre Occasional Paper #2003-01). Burnaby, CA: Simon Fraser University, Criminology Research Centre.

Jahoda, A., Banks, P., Dagnan, D., Kemp, J., Kerr, W., & Williams, V. (2009). Starting a new job: The social and emotional experience of people with intellectual disabilities. *Journal of Applied Research in Intellectual Disabilities, 22*(5), 421–425. doi:10.1111/j.1468-3148.2009.00497

Luckasson, R., Borthwick-Duffy, S., Buntinx, W. H. E., Coulter, D. L., Craig, E. M., Reeve, A., . . . Tasse, M. J. (2002). *Mental retardation: Definition, classification, and systems of supports* (10th ed.). Washington, DC: American Association of Mental Retardation.

McGillivray, J. A., & Waterman, B. (2011). Knowledge and attitudes of lawyers regarding offenders with intellectual disabilities. *Psychiatry, Psychology, and Law, 10*(1), 244–253.

McGrew, K. S. (2015). Norm obsolescence: The Flynn effect. In E. A. Polloway (Ed.), *The death penalty and intellectual disability* (pp. 155–169). Washington, DC: American Association on Intellectual and Developmental Disabilities.

Modell, S. J., & Mak, S. (2008). A preliminary assessment of police officer's knowledge and perceptions of persons with disabilities. *Intellectual and Developmental Disabilities, 46*(3), 183–189. doi:10.1352/2008.46:183–189

Moore v. Texas, 15–797 (2017).

Murphy, G. (n.d.). *People with learning disabilities and offending behaviours: Prevalence, treatment, risk assessment, and services*. Canterbury: University of Kent. Retrieved from www.kent.ac.uk/tizard/resources/forensicldservices.pdf

Newman, L. A., Madaus, J. W., & Javitz, H. S. (2016). Effect of transition planning on postsecondary support receipt by students with disabilities. *Exceptional Children, 82*(4), 497–514. doi:10.1177/0014402915615884

Newman, L., Wagner, M., Cameto, R., & Knokey, A. (2009). *The post-high school outcomes of youth with disabilities up to 4 years after high school. A report from the National Longitudinal Transition Study-2 (NLTS2)* (NCSER 2009–3017). Washington, DC: U.S. Government Printing Office.

Olley, J. G. (2015). Adaptive behavior instruments. In E. A. Polloway (Ed.), *The death penalty and intellectual disability* (pp. 187–200). Washington, DC: American Association on Intellectual and Developmental Disabilities. Papay, C. K. & Bambara, L. M. (2011). Postsecondary education for transition-age students with intellectual and other developmental disabilities: A national survey. *Education and Training in Autism and Developmental Disabilities, 46*(1), 78-93. Division on Autism and Developmental Disabilities.

Patton, J. R. (2015). Educational records. In E. A. Polloway (Ed.), *The death penalty and intellectual disability* (pp. 293–304). Washington, DC: American Association on Intellectual and Developmental Disabilities.

Patton, J. R., & Keyes, D. (2006). Death penalty issues following Atkins. *Exceptionality, 14*(4), 237–255. doi:10.1207/s15327035ex1404_5

Penry v. Lynaugh, 492 U.S. 302, 335 (1989).

Perske, R. (2008). False confessions from 53 persons with intellectual disabilities: The list keeps growing. *Intellectual and Developmental Disabilities, 46*(6), 468–479.

Petersilia, J. (2000a). *Doing justice? Criminal offenders with developmental disabilities*. Irvine, CA: California Research Center, University of California, Irvine.

Petersilia, J. (2000b). *Doing justice: The criminal justice system and offenders with developmental disabilities*. Irvine, CA: Mental Retardation/Developmental Disabilities Research Center, University of California, Irvine.

Polloway, E. A. (2006). Mild mental retardation: A concept in search of clarity, a population in search of appropriate education and supports, a profession in search of advocacy. *Exceptionality, 14*(4), 183–189. doi:10.1207/s15327035ex1404_1

Polloway, E. A., Auguste, M., Smith, J. D., & Peters, D. (2016). *State guidelines for intellectual disability: A revisitation* [Unpublished Manuscript].

Polloway, E. A., Bouck, E., Patton, J. R., & Lubin, J. (2017). Intellectual and developmental disabilities. In J. M. Kauffman, D. P. Hallahan, & P. Pullen (Eds.), *The handbook of special education* (2nd ed.). London: Routledge.

Polloway, E. A., Patton, J. R., & Smith, J. D. (2015). The death penalty and intellectual disability: An introduction. In E. A. Polloway (Ed.), *The death penalty and intellectual disability* (pp. 3–9). Washington, DC: American Association on Intellectual and Developmental Disabilities.

Polloway, E. A., Patton, J. R., Smith, T., Beyer, J., & Bailey, J. W. (2011). Special challenges for persons with intellectual disabilities within the criminal justice system: An introduction to the special series. *Exceptionality, 19*(4), 211–218. doi:10.1080/09362835.2011.610698

Polloway, E. A., Smith, J. D., Patton, J. R., Lubin, J., & Antoine, K. (2009). State guidelines for intellectual and developmental disabilities and intellectual disabilities: A re-visitation of previous analyses in light of changes in the field. *Education and Training in Developmental Disabilities, 44*(1), 14–24.

Reschly, D. J. (1990). Mild mental retardation: Persistent themes, changing dynamics, and future prospects. In M. C. Wang, M. C. Reynolds, & H. J. Walberg (Eds.), *Special education: Research and practice: Synthesis of findings* (pp. 81–99). New York, NY: Pergamon Press.

Rosa's Law, Pub. L. 111–256 (2010).

Rutherford, R. B., Bullis, M., Anderson, C. W., & Griller-Clark, H. W. (2002). *Youth with disabilities in the corrections system: Prevalence rates and identification issues*. Washington, DC: American Institutes for Research, Center for Effective Collaboration and Practice.

Rynders, J. (2005). Down syndrome: Literacy and socialization in school. *Focus on Exceptional Children, 38*(1), 2–11.

Rynders, J. E., Spiker, D., & Horrobin, J. M. (1978). Underestimating the educability of Down Syndrome children: Examination of methodological problems in recent literature. *American Journal of Mental Deficiency, 82*(5), 440–448.

Schalock, R. L., Borthwick-Duffy, S. A., Bradley, V. J., Buntinx, W. H. E., Coulter, D. L., Craig, E. M., . . . Yeager, M. H. (2010). *Intellectual disability: Definition, classification, and systems of supports* (11th ed.). Washington, DC: AAIDD.

Siebelink, E. M., Jong, M. D., Taal, E., & Roelvink, L. (2006). Sexuality and people with intellectual disabilities: Assessment of knowledge, attitudes, experiences, and needs. *Mental Retardation, 44*(4), 283–294. doi: 10.1352/0047-(2006)44[283:sapwid]2.0.co;2

Siperstein, G., & Collins, M. A. (2015). Intellectual disability. In E. A. Polloway (Ed.), *The death penalty and intellectual disability* (pp. 21–36). Washington, DC: American Association on Intellectual and Developmental Disabilities.

Smith, T. E. C., Polloway, E. A., Doughty, T., Patton, J. R., & Dowdy, C. (2012). *Teaching students with special needs in inclusive settings* (6th ed.). Boston, MA: Allyn & Bacon.

Smith, T., Polloway, E. A., Patton, J. R., & Beyer, J. (2008). Persons with intellectual and developmental disabilities in the criminal justice system and implications for transition planning. *Education and Training in Developmental Disabilities, 43*(4), 421–430.

Snell, M. E., Luckasson, R., Borthwick-Duffy, S., Bradley, V., Buntinx, W. H. E., Coulter, D. L., . . . Yeager, M. H. (2009). The characteristics and needs of people with intellectual disabilities who have higher IQs. *Intellectual and Developmental Disabilities, 47*(3), 220–233. doi:10.1352/1934-9556-47.3.220

Stancliffe, R. J., Lakin, K. C., Larson, S. A., Engler, J., Taub, S., Fortune, J., & Bershadsky, J. (2012). Demographic characteristics, health conditions, and residential service use in adults with down syndrome in 25 U.S. states. *Intellectual and Developmental Disabilities, 50*(2), 92–108. doi:10.1352/1934-9556-50.2.92

Suto, W. M., Clare, I. C., Holland, A. J., & Watson, P. C. (2005). Capacity to make financial decisions among people with mild intellectual disabilities. *Journal of Intellectual Disability Research, 49*(3), 199–209. doi:10.1111/j.1365-2788.2005.00635.x

Tasse, M. (2015). Intellectual disability: A review of its definition and diagnostic criteria. In E. A. Polloway (Ed.), *The death penalty and intellectual disability* (pp. 11–19). Washington, DC: American Association on Intellectual and Developmental Disabilities.

Thompson, J. R., Bradley, V. J., Buntinx, W. H. E., Schalock, R. L. Shogren, K. A., Snell, M. E., . . . Yeager, M. H. (2009). Conceptualizing supports and the support needs of people with intellectual disability. *Intellectual and Developmental Disabilities, 47*(2), 135–146. doi:10.152/1934–9556–47.2.135

Thompson, J. R., Bryant, B. R., Schalock, R. L., Shogren, K. A., Tasse, M. J., Wehmeyer, M. L., . . . Rotholz, D.A. (2015). *The Supports Intensity Scale-Adult version.* Washington, DC: American Association on Intellectual and Developmental Disabilities.

Thompson, J. R., Wehmeyer, M. L., Hughes, C., Shogren, K. A., Seo, H., . . . Tasse, M. J. (2016). *The Supports Intensity Scale-Children's version.* Washington, DC: American Association on Intellectual and Developmental Disabilities.

Watson, D. G. (2015). Intelligence testing. In E. A. Polloway (Ed.), *The death penalty and intellectual disability* (pp. 113–140). Washington, DC: American Association on Intellectual and Developmental Disabilities.

Wehmeyer, M. L., Graner, N., Yeager, D., Lawrence, M. & Davis, A. (2006). Infusing self-determination into 18—21 services for students with intellectual or developmental disabilities: A multistage, multiple component model. *Education and Training in Developmental Disabilities, 41*(1), 3-13. Woods, G. W., Freedman, D. D., & Derning, T. J. (2015). Intellectual disability and comorbid disorders. In E. A. Polloway (Ed.), *The death penalty and intellectual disability* (pp. 279–292). Washington, DC: American Association on Intellectual and Developmental Disabilities.

Wright, T., & Wolery, M. (2011). The effects of instructional interventions related to street crossing and individuals with disabilities. *Research in Developmental Disabilities, 32*(5), 1455–1463. doi:10.1016/j.ridd.2011.03.019

24

SEX OFFENDERS WITH INTELLECTUAL DISABILITIES

Deficits and Risk Factors for Offending

Jerrod Brown, Cody Charette, Aaron Trnka, Diane Neal, and Janina Cich

> Persons with intellectual disabilities and problem sexual behaviors (IDPSB) "who become involved with the criminal justice system experience a variety of disadvantages, including social isolation, greater incidence of mental illness, and higher than average exposure to poverty, . . . and low levels of knowledge about sexuality."
>
> —(Blasingame, Boer, Guidry, Haaven, & Wilson, 2014, p. 5)

Introduction

Formerly known as mental retardation, the diagnosis of intellectual developmental disorders (IDDs) emerged as a part of the American Psychiatric Association's (APA) *Diagnostic and Statistical Manual of Mental Disorders 5th Edition* (DSM-5) in 2013 to improve the classification of intellectual disabilities. IDDs can include a range of cognitive impairments (e.g., short- and long-term memory, learning disabilities, and abstract thinking) across the lifespan. Typically, these cognitive impairments have a deleterious impact on adaptive functioning (e.g., decision making, problem solving, and short- and long-term planning) that make independent living and social responsibilities difficult to manage (APA, 2013). Complicating matters, individuals with IDDs are three to four times more likely than the general population to have comorbid mental problems in the form of autism or mood disorders, developmental impairments resulting in communication difficulties, physical defects in the form of sensory and motor deficiencies, or other medical conditions. In light of the increased difficulty of adequately assessing IDDs, the DSM-5 emphasizes the importance of utilizing clinical assessment and standardized intelligence tests with collateral input from corroborating sources. Symptoms such as impulsivity, eating difficulties, or dysfunctional sleep patterns should be considered across a range of situations and settings (APA, 2013). Without careful integration of information gathered from nuanced assessment techniques, treatment, and case planning, IDDs and other comorbid conditions can increase the probability of negative long-term outcomes. One such consequential negative outcome is involvement with the criminal justice system.

Not only are individuals with IDDs disproportionately more likely to become the victims of crime (Rand & Harrell, 2009), this vulnerable population is also overrepresented in community supervision consisting of the probation and parole systems, county jails, and state prison settings (Lindsay et al., 2004; Murphy & Mason, 2007; Salekin, Olley, & Hedge, 2010). This propensity for criminal justice involvement can be directly linked to the impairments that characterize IDDs. For example, individuals with IDDs may impulsively commit crimes without recognizing the potential consequences or even identifying that their actions were wrong and illegal. Further, individuals with IDDs are prone to social manipulation. As such, peers and other acquaintances may manipulate an individual with IDDs into either committing an illegal act or taking the blame for someone else's illegal actions. Despite this research, proving direct links between IDDs and crime, details on specific types of criminal behavior have been relatively limited. The limited in-depth research is due in large part to disagreement on an acceptable universal definition and the proper assessment of intellectual disabilities (Holland, Clare, & Mukhopadhyay, 2002; Loucks, 2007; McBrien, 2003; Talbot & Riley, 2007).

Individuals with IDDs may be behaviorally prone to sexually offending (Barron, Hassiots, & Banes, 2002). Research in the United Kingdom indicates that 40% to 55% of sexual offenders have at least one diagnosed educational difficulty, which encompasses intellectual difficulties (Almond, Canter, & Salfati, 2006; Dolan, Holloway, Bailey, & Kroll, 1996; Hawkes, Jenkins, & Vizard, 1997). This predisposition to offend sexually is thought to be a result of symptoms associated with IDDs. Specifically, impulsivity and difficulty understanding social cues and norms are both believed to contribute to an inclination for sexual deviance (Lindsay & Michie, 2013). Such direct links are consistent with the counterfeit deviance (CD) hypothesis (Hingsburger, Griffiths & Quinsey, 1991). Counterfeit deviance is defined as behaviors that appear deviant upon initial observation but can be attributed to factors other than deviant sexual arousal. The original researchers contend these behaviors appeared paraphilic but served a function that was not related to paraphilic sexual urges or fantasies. The CD theory asserts that even though individuals with IDDs experience the same sexual urges as the general population, they are typically desexualized by society. In conjunction with the desexualization, many individuals with IDDs are not typically taught how to channel their sexual desires appropriately or what behaviors are acceptable. This lack of education may be driven, at least in part, by concerns about individuals with IDDs participating in procreation. As such, sexual deviance may result from the combination of IDD symptoms and lack of appropriate psychosexual education and outlets.

With the increasing awareness of these issues within the field, there has been a push to use empirical evidence to move beyond the theoretical links between sexual offending behavior and intellectual deficits (Embregts et al., 2010; Keeling & Rose, 2005; Lindsay, 2002a). To this point, much of the research has focused on comparing and contrasting sexual offending behavior between individuals with and without intellectual disabilities (Craig & Hutchinson, 2005; Haaven, Little, & Petre-Miller, 1990; Hayes, 1991; Lindsay, Law, Quinn, Smart, & Smith, 2001). For example, research suggests that offenders with IDDs tend to commit a wide range of sexual offending against a diverse group of victims (Lindsay, 2002a), whereas offenders without IDDs may be more likely to repeat the same sexual offending against a distinct group of victims (Parry & Lindsay, 2003). Consistent with these findings, the victims of sexual offenders with IDDs are more likely to be strangers than the victims of sexual offenders without IDDs (Day, 1994). Considering these findings, researchers have theorized that this difference in offending patterns may be rooted in the pervasive impulsivity and affective dysregulation that often characterizes intellectual disabilities (Ashman & Conway, 1989; Glaser & Deane, 1999; Lane, 1991). Nonetheless, other research has found that sexual offenders both with and without IDDs have high levels of impulsivity and commit a range of criminal behaviors, sexual and nonsexual alike (Fortune & Lambie, 2004; Parry & Lindsay, 2003). These inconsistencies across a multitude of studies may be the result of differences in how intellectual disabilities and sexual behavior are defined, researched, and sampled (Craig & Hutchinson, 2005; Johnston, 2005; Thompson, 2000; Tudway & Darmoody, 2005). As such, it remains difficult to make definitive conclusions about sexual offenders with IDDs (Griffin & Vettor, 2012).

Once involved in the criminal justice system, sexual offenders with IDDs are at a distinct disadvantage in at least three ways. First, among the problems faced by sexual offenders with IDDs is the decreased capacity to comprehend basic legal processes such as police interrogations and legal proceedings and make informed legal decisions, including the waiving of *Miranda* rights or entering a plea (Holland, 2004; Lindsay et al., 2004; Murphy & Mason, 2007). Second, sexual offenders with IDDs are often left to receive the same treatment as sexual offenders without IDDs, which may not be adequately tailored to their complicated symptomology and particular needs (Blasingame et al., 2014; Nezu, Greenberg, & Nezu, 2006). Treatment providers are utilizing the risk-needs-responsivity (RNR) model (Bonta & Andrews, 2007) to ensure a thorough analysis of each client for individualized treatment (see Chapter 5 for more about the RNR model). It would be helpful if this model were adopted in correctional and other forensic settings. Third, a diagnosis of intellectual disabilities often necessitates elevated levels of supervision in custodial and community settings. As a result, sexual offenders with IDDs may be more likely to receive institutional infractions and probation or parole violations (Hodgins, 1992; Law, Lindsay, Quinn, & Smith, 2000; Thompson, 2000). While each of these issues alone would be problematic to deal with, in combination, these disadvantages strongly increase the likelihood of prolonged involvement in the criminal justice system by sexual offenders with IDDs.

As highlighted earlier, some individuals with IDDs may be at an increased risk for sexual offending behaviors relative to the general population. Once arrested, this vulnerable population is less likely to receive the treatment and services that it needs most. This has contributed to the short-term goals of controlling unfavorable behavior, which takes precedence over long-term comprehensive approaches toward medication and treatment, forgoing the use of an array of dynamic assessment tools to identify risk (Fedoroff, Richards, Ranger, & Curry, 2016). As a result, this population is more likely to become entangled, as opposed to moving fluidly, within the criminal justice system.

The aim of this chapter is to increase awareness of the etiology and appropriate treatment of sexual offending behaviors for individuals with IDDs. To this end, the chapter explores prevalence rates of offending among IDD offenders, examines the empirical literature, and documents risk factors for such offenders. It also describes how to reduce recidivism among IDD offenders and then concludes with a discussion of assessment and treatment of IDD offenders.

Prevalence Rates

Over several decades, there has been increasing interest by researchers on sexual offending behaviors by individuals with intellectual disabilities (Hayes, 1991; Lindsay, 2002b; Murphy, Coleman, & Haynes, 1986). To this point, it has been suggested that sexual offending is overrepresented in individuals with intellectual disabilities. However, there is inconsistent evidence to support this claim (Lindsay, Law, & Macleod, 2002). This is due to a large degree because of variation in research findings across studies. Such variation may be attributable to the use of different diagnostic criteria, assessment tools, or populations (Cuskelly, 2004; Fedoroff et al., 2016; MacMillan, Gresham, & Siperstein, 1993; McBrien, 2003). In searching for commonalities between these diverse studies, this section reviews the literature on the prevalence of sexual offending behaviors in individuals with intellectual disabilities.

Individuals with intellectual disabilities are estimated by Scott, Lewis, and McDermott (2006) to make up only 1% to 3% of the U.S. population, but this group accounts for somewhere between 0.6% (according to MacEachron 1979) and 39.6% (according to Holland 1991) of the U.S. criminal justice system population. Other research suggests more conservative estimates, indicating individuals with intellectual disabilities account for 4% to 10% of U.S. inmates (Bowker, 1994; Davis, 2009; Noble & Conley, 1992; Petersilia, 2000). Inconsistent findings across studies also can be found in the international literature. For example, a U.K. study estimated that 1% to 23% of prisoners have borderline intellectual functioning (Herrington, 2009). In contrast, a meta-analysis of data from studies in six countries found that rates of intellectual disabilities among prisoners range from 0% to 2.8% of the population (Fazel, Xenitidis, & Powell, 2008). This body of literature emphasizes that prevalence rates of offending in individuals with intellectual disabilities vary widely as a function of methodology and population.

Similar results have been observed in juveniles. Specifically, a growing body of empirical research indicates that when compared to juveniles without intellectual disabilities, juveniles with intellectual disabilities are disproportionately likely to become enmeshed in the criminal justice system (Frize, Kenny, & Lennings, 2008; Kroll et al., 2002; Rayner, Kelly, & Graham, 2005). Kroll et al. (2002) found that approximately 27% of serious and persistent juvenile offenders scored below 70 on the Wechsler Intelligence Scale for Children 3rd Edition (WISC-III), a standardized measure of intelligence. Similarly, Rayner et al. (2005) found that approximately 32% of serious and persistent juvenile offenders in the United Kingdom scored below 70 on the same standardized measure of intelligence as Kroll. As shown earlier, this inconsistency of prevalence estimates in juveniles is comparable to what findings in adults showed.

Research suggests that somewhere between 10% and 15% of sexual offenses are committed by individuals with intellectual disabilities (Hayes, 2002; Murphy, Coleman, & Haynes, 1983; O'Connor, 1997). Other research has reported that the prevalence of intellectual deficits among individuals who have committed sexual offenses is between 4% and 40% (Gross, 1985; Swanson & Garwick, 1990; Thompson & Brown, 1997; Walker & McCabe, 1973). Although more research is needed in the area of sexual offending among individuals with intellectual disabilities, these findings suggest there is a reason for continued studies of its prevalence.

Despite the growing body of literature, several methodological concerns impede researchers' abilities to make firm conclusions on the prevalence of intellectual disabilities in sexual offenders (Lindsay et al., 2004; Murphy et al., 1983; O'Connor, 1996). On the one hand, sexually offensive behaviors by individuals with intellectual disabilities may go unprosecuted, as these individuals may never be competent enough to stand trial (Davis, 2009). On the other hand, individuals with intellectual disabilities may be more likely to be caught for sexual offending behaviors because many of their offenses are characterized by impulsivity and a lack of planning (Craig & Hutchinson, 2005; Nezu et al., 2006). As such, an inherent observation bias, or preconceived notion of what the researcher will find, could be present in research studies on the sexual offending behaviors of individuals with intellectual disabilities (Craig & Hutchinson, 2005). Going forward, advanced research employing sophisticated methodology is necessary to resolve these quandaries (Keller, 2016).

Clinical and Forensic Considerations

For decades, researchers and clinicians have worked to illuminate the connection between developmental cognitive disorders and sexual offending behaviors (Lindsay, 2011). Specifically, factors such as cognitive processing speed, learning ability, cognitive fluidity, and communication deficits have been shown to increase the likelihood of sexual misbehavior (Craig & Hutchinson, 2005; Day, 1993; Keeling, Beech, & Rose, 2007). At the very least, the presence of an intellectual disorder, a developmental disorder, or both is believed to increase the likelihood of apprehension for sexual misbehavior. These types of disorders are characterized by impulsivity and difficulty with both short- and long-term planning (Wilcox, 2004). One type of offense that individuals with these disorders may be at increased risk for is sexual offending (Walker & McCabe, 1973). Unfortunately, clinical and criminal justice professionals are often ill prepared to provide care and management of sexual offending individuals with these types of disorders (Blasingame et al., 2014; Wheeler, Clare, & Holland, 2014). With all this in mind, the following sections provide overviews of screening and assessment tools, risk assessment tools, and treatment considerations for this vulnerable population.

Screening and Assessment

Assessment, through comprehensive screening, is the necessary first step in developing a case management plan and ensuring adequate treatment of individuals with intellectual and developmental disorders (Bernet & Dulcan, 1999; Keeling et al., 2007). Failure to provide adequate assessment services can result in clients receiving unnecessary treatment that is ineffective or entirely inappropriate. The consequences of such actions can range from an increased risk of future problematic behaviors to a persistent stagnation at the current level (Blasingame et al., 2014). For this reason, it is imperative that clinical and criminal justice professionals are familiar with the challenges of properly screening and assessing this population (Blasingame et al., 2014).

There are two basic areas that require thorough screening and assessment when working with individuals that have intellectual and developmental disorders: intelligence functioning and adaptive functioning (Nezu et al., 2006). Initially, a detailed evaluation of the individual's intelligence and cognitive functioning is necessary. Additional critical information also can be obtained from a systematic and nuanced assessment of the client's adaptive functioning. This refers to the individual's capacity to solve problems, make and execute short- and long-term plans, and perform tasks in daily life. Daily life tasks include independent living skills and self-care. The findings from such an evaluation then play an integral role in clarifying the correct diagnosis and informing all treatment, case management, and legal decisions in the future (Keeling et al., 2007).

Blasingame et al. (2014) identified three key considerations for clinical and criminal justice professionals to keep in mind during this process. First, professionals must factor in the intellectual challenges faced by this population when making assessments. Challenges can range from short- and long-term memory deficits to a broad range of communication deficits in literacy, receptive and expressive language, and social information processing (Basquill, Nezu, Nezu, & Klein, 2004). As such, professionals should avoid an overreliance on verbal forms of communications and introduce diagrams whenever possible. Additionally, complicated verbal communication should be avoided by encouraging simple and concrete language. Second, individuals with these disorders often have lower levels of education, knowledge, and life experience, including appropriate sexual education. Therefore, professionals need to explore carefully client perceptions and understanding of sexual situations without assumptions of normalcy. Because of the wide spectrum of symptoms and disorder presentations, there is no realistic way to define "normal" for this population, as each individual has to define it for him or herself. Third, individuals with intellectual disorders and developmental disorders are often acutely sensitive to environmental factors. Examples of these factors may include sensitivity to loud noises or flashing lights or vulnerability to manipulation by peers or individuals in a position of power. These key considerations should always be taken into account during the screening and assessment process.

Information gathered during intake can be influential in the development of treatment and case plans, but there remains room for improvement. Relative to the research on screening and assessment of sexual offenders in general (e.g. Hanson & Thornton, 2000; Nichols & Molinder, 2000), there has been a dearth of the same research among sexual offenders with intellectual disorders and developmental disorders (Lindsay, Elliot, & Astell, 2004; Nezu, Nezu, & Dudek, 1998; Wilcox, 2004). To address this absence, professionals have had to adapt many of the traditional instruments used with sexual offenders for use with those who have intellectual and developmental disorders (Wilcox, 2004). This is problematic because some of these instruments may not be suitable for use in a subgroup of this variable population (Blasingame et al., 2014). Advancement of the field in this particular area is imperative to maximize the efficacy of interventions (Keller, 2016).

Risk Assessment

In addition to the assessment of basic intellectual functioning and adaptive functioning, sexual offenders with intellectual and developmental disorders require a comprehensive assessment of recidivism risk (Blasingame et al., 2014). Developed for general offenders, this process typically centers on the identification of the client's risk, needs, and responsivity to treatment (Andrews & Bonta, 1998;

Keeling et al., 2007). Instruments that facilitate this process usually include historical information such as the age of the first arrest or a total number of arrests, clinically documented features such as substance use and mental health disorders, personality profiling, such as psychopathy and impulsivity, and contextual environmental factors, such as housing and employment (Wheeler et al., 2014). Careful consideration of information collected during a risk assessment is essential for determining the levels of service required for a client to determine appropriate levels of supervision, case management, and treatment plans (Fedoroff et al., 2016; Hudson, Wales, Bakker, & Ward, 2002; Mikkelsen, 2004; Quinsey, 2004; Turner, 2000).

The assessment of an individual's future antisocial behavior risk typically consists of a number of risk factors. Static or unchangeable risk factors are generally considered unresponsive to treatment, whereas dynamic or changeable risk factors are amenable to treatment (Beech, Friendship, Erikson, & Hanson, 2002; Harkins & Beech, 2007; Harris & Tough, 2004). In the case of sex offenders with intellectual disorders or developmental disorders, static risk factors linked to sexual recidivism include severity of intellectual dysfunction, early onset and history of antisocial behavior, the presence of abuse, and a history of deviant sexual behavior (Day, 1994; Lindsay, Elliot, & Astell, 2004; Embregts et al., 2010; Green, Gray, & Willner, 2002; Lambrick & Glaser, 2004; Lindsay, 2002a). In contrast to static risk factors, dynamic risk factors linked to sexual recidivism in this group include social skill deficits such as communication problems or a lack of empathy, impulsivity, cognitive distortions, self-esteem issues, deviant sexual preoccupations or fantasies, and vulnerability to the influence of others (Caparulo, 1991; Lindsay et al., 2004; Fortune & Lambie, 2004; Lindsay, Olley, Baillie, & Smith, 1999). An emerging topic in dynamic risk assessment of offenders with intellectual disabilities is environmental variables (Boer, Tough, & Haaven, 2004; Fedoroff et al., 2016; Lofthouse et al., 2013). This is particularly salient as these individuals typically rely more strongly upon support systems and mechanisms, including case managers and care providers (Boer, McVilly, & Lambick, 2007; Lindsay et al., 2004; Taylor, Keddie, & Lee, 2003). Continued research in the area of criminogenic dynamic risk factors for this population is critical. These risk factors are considered responsive to treatment and hold the greatest potential to reduce sexual recidivism (Keller, 2016).

Although there is a growing interest in the assessment of sexual recidivism (Boer et al., 2004; Lindsay, 2002b; Linsay et al., 2004; Pouls & Jeandarme, 2014), there is still a limited body of research on those with developmental disorders or intellectual disorders. In a longitudinal study of 52 sexual offenders with intellectual disabilities by Lindsay et al. (2004) the predictive utility of static and dynamic risk factors for sexual recidivism was explored by following participants for approximately three years after release. Of the 15 static factors included in the study, three variables predicted recidivism; a history of violent offending, sexual abuse as a child, and a poor maternal relationship. However, there was little predictive utility of recidivism on the variables of diversity of previous sexual crimes, antisocial peers, or employment history. Additionally, of the 32 dynamic risk factors studied, recidivism was predicted by community supervision and treatment noncompliance, failure to accept responsibility for previous sexual crimes, and antisocial attitudes. Similarly, Quinsey, Book, and Skilling (2004) followed 58 men with intellectual disorders for 16 months. They observed predictive utility in the variables of antisocial attitudes, community supervision, and treatment noncompliance. The importance of accuracy in the assessment process cannot be understated for this complex and often underserved population (Lofthouse et al., 2013).

It is important to keep in mind that these practices were developed for general, nonsexual, offenders rather than sex offenders with the impairments discussed (Keller, 2016). As a result, current risk assessment tools may not incorporate important caveats that are relevant to sex offenders within this population. (Blacker, Beech, Wilcox, & Boer, 2011; Green et al., 2002; Johnston, 2002). Professionals should exercise caution when employing risk assessment instruments not validated or normed for sex offenders with intellectual disorders and developmental disorders (Hocken, Winder, & Grayson, 2013; Lofthouse et al., 2013).

The STATIC-99 has been validated for use with the IDD population to assess for risk. Haaven and colleagues developed the *Assessment of Risk and Manageability of Individuals with Developmental and Intellectual Limitations Who Offend—Sexually* in 2013 (ARMIDILO-S). For assessing individuals who have demonstrated offensive, even criminal, sexual behavior, the ARMIDILO-S has shown promise. The ARMIDILO-S has been proven valid across a range of sex offender groups, including those with IDD. It also has been positively evaluated in qualitative studies as a case management instrument. Blacker et al. (2011) have called for the continued evaluation of the validity of such tools with this population. Research over the past decade has shown that existing risk assessment instruments may require only minor adaptations for use with IDD sexual offenders (Camilleri & Quinsey, 2011). Nonetheless, systematic research is needed to identify differences in risk factors that may exist between sexual offenders who are intellectually or developmentally impaired and the general population of sexual offenders (Boer, Gauthier, Watson, Dorward, & Kolton, 1995; Camilleri & Quinsey, 2011; Keeling et al., 2007). In addition, it is imperative that this research move beyond the realm of violence risk assessment into sexual offending risk assessment (Camilleri & Quinsey, 2011). The merit of this research is enhanced further by how well the information on an individual's risk and needs informs on the level of supervision necessary and the allocation of treatment services (Blasingame et al., 2014; Mikkelsen, 2004; Quinsey, 2004; Turner, 2000).

Intervention and Treatment

Intervention and treatment decisions for sexual offenders with IDD should be guided by each person's individual dynamic risks and needs (Haaven, 2006; Yates, Prescott, & Ward, 2010). As this population is disproportionately likely to suffer from co-occurring mental health problems relative to the general population, treatment and case management planning must be tailored to address the client's problematic sexual behavior along with any other mental health issues (Blasingame et al., 2014). Although more similarities than differences exist for sexual offenders with and without IDD, adjustments must be made to ensure the effectiveness of treatment for sexual offenders with IDD (Blasingame et al., 2014; Coleman & Haaven, 2001). For example, sexual offenders with IDD may require alternative teaching methods to ensure content comprehension and treatment engagement (Murrey, Briggs, & Davis, 1992). Through the use of such methods, sexual offenders with IDD can effectively regulate their inappropriate sexual impulses and behaviors (Blasingame et al., 2014).

Intervention and treatment both need to address a wide range of basic skills for sexual offenders with IDD (Haaven, 2006). Several common skills to target include sexual education, general and sexual self-regulation, and other basic life skills (Blasingame, 2005; Blasingame et al., 2014; Haaven, 2006). Development of skills related to sexual expression and self-regulation come from learning impulse management, avoidance strategies, and cognitive restructuring (Blasingame, 2005; Blasingame et al., 2014; Haaven, 2006; Wilner & Goodey, 2005). These strategies have been shown to decrease the likelihood of sexual recidivism if the origins of the problematic behavior were a lack of skills to fulfill normal sexual impulses (Day, 2001). The central focus must be the development of skills to obtain healthy sexual expression (Day, 2001; Wilson & Burns, 2011). To maximize the impact of these efforts, professionals must work toward increasing the real-world applicability of these skills so that the individual can translate them to community settings outside the context of treatment (Wilson & Burns, 2011).

Treatment of sexual offenders with IDD often requires integrating psychopharmacology with a diverse array of strategies (Miller & Rollnick, 2002; Wilson & Burns, 2011). Traditionally, behavioral conditioning has played a strong role in the treatment of this population. This can range from the use of aversive conditioning to token economies and leveled systems (Blasingame et al., 2014; Wilson & Burns, 2011). Other common aspects include the use of a structured living environment, cognitive-behavioral therapy, ensuring a strong therapeutic alliance, employment of motivational interviewing techniques, role-plays, and relapse prevention plans (Haaven, 2006; Miller & Rollnick, 2002). Haaven et al. (1990) employed a diverse set of therapeutic approaches to maximize participation, ensure comprehension, emphasize role-playing, and develop new social interaction strategies (Haaven, 1993; Haaven & Schlank, 2001; Hordell, Rees, & Robinson, 2001; Wilcox & Leyland 1998; 1999). In recent years, an emerging emphasis has been placed on community engagement during the treatment process. This emphasis ensures that sexual offenders with IDD will be able to interact effectively and appropriately with community members during reentry (Blasingame et al., 2014).

Research has repeatedly shown that the IDD population is vulnerable to suggestibility, confabulation, and manipulation. Therefore, group therapy settings must be supervised to prevent the development of harmful dynamics. Regardless of the specific components employed, the incorporation of a relapse prevention plan is also important when treating sexual offenders with IDD (Boer et al., 1995; Haaven & Coleman, 2000). Care providers must be aware that sexual offenders with IDD benefit most from multifaceted approaches that incorporate components addressing cognitive processes, adaptive behavior, sexual arousal, and interpersonal skills (Nezu et al., 2006).

As highlighted throughout this section, there are important skills that can be targeted by a range of strategies for treating sexual offenders with IDD. However, this does not necessarily mean that the process will be seamless for either the care provider or the client. In point of fact, Lindsay, Hastings, and Beech (2011) summarized that this population "had longer periods of stay in secure hospitals and were more difficult to move onto other establishments" (p. 4). Butwell, Jamieson, Leese, and Taylor (2000) made similar observations, whereby these individuals indeed remained in confinement settings longer and were deprived of moving to a lower security facility. Nonetheless, in total, the research on treatment approaches and outcomes for sexual offenders with IDD is still very limited (Nezu et al., 2006). The existing literature is typically composed of simple program descriptions, case studies, and single subject research designs (Nezu et al., 2006). To move this field forward, systematic research is necessary to elucidate the etiological underpinnings of sexual misbehavior in individuals with IDD and evaluate the most efficacious treatment approach for this highly specialized group (Nezu et al., 2006).

Conclusion

There are many deficits and risk factors that increase the likelihood of criminal sexual offending within the IDD population. With intervention, treatment, and community monitoring, a marked decrease in recidivism has been demonstrated in the research. Both static and dynamic risk factors also have been documented in the empirical literature. Research has strongly indicated that communication and treatment modality must be adapted and individualized for the IDD offender. Empirical validation also suggests adapting treatment and assessments to the subgroups to account for the variability found within this population. Further research is well justified. Clinical observations may be particularly well suited to account for the nuances and subtleties of this challenging population.

References

Almond, L., Canter, D., & Salfati, G. (2006). Youths who sexually harm: A multivariate model of characteristics. *Journal of Sexual Aggression*, *12*(2), 97–114. doi:10.1080/13552600600823605

American Psychiatric Association. (2013). *Diagnostic and statistical manual of mental disorders* (5th ed.). Arlington, VA: American Psychiatric Association.

Andrews, D. A., & Bonta, J. (1998). *The psychology of criminal conduct* (2nd ed.). Cincinnati, OH: Anderson: Publishing Co.

Ashman, A. F., & Conway, R. N. F. (1989). *Cognitive strategies for special education: Process based instruction*. London: Routledge.

Barron, P., Hassiotis, A., & Banes, J. (2002). Offenders with intellectual disability: The size of the problem and therapeutic outcomes. *Journal of Intellectual Disability Research, 46*(6), 454–463. doi:10.1046/j.1365-2788.2002.00432.x

Basquill, M., Nezu, C. M., Nezu, A. M., & Klein, T. L. (2004). Aggression-related hostility bias and social problem-solving deficits in adult males with mental retardation. *American Journal of Mental Retardation, 109*(3), 255–263. doi:10.1352/0895-8017(2004)109<255:AHBASP>2.0.CO;2

Beech, A., Friendship, C., Erikson, M., & Hanson, R. K. (2002). The relationship between static and dynamic risk factors and reconviction in a sample of UK child abusers. *Sexual Abuse: A Journal of Research and Treatment, 14*(2), 155–167. doi:10.1023/A:1014672231744

Bernet, W., & Dulcan, M. K. (1999). Practice parameters for the assessment and treatment of children, adolescents, and adults with mental retardation and comorbid mental disorders. *Child & Adolescent Psychiatry, 38*(12 Supp), 5S–31S. doi:10.1016/S0890-8567(99)80002-1

Blacker, J., Beech, A. R., Wilcox, D. T., & Boer, D. P. (2011). The assessment of dynamic risk and recidivism in a sample of special needs offenders. *Psychology, Crime and Law, 17*(1), 75–92. doi:10.1080/10683160903392376

Blasingame, G. (2005). *Developmentally disabled persons with sexual behavior problems* (2nd ed.). Oklahoma City, OK: Wood 'N' Barnes/Safer Society.

Blasingame, G. D., Boer, D. P., Guidry, L., Haaven, J., & Wilson, R. J. (2014). *Assessment, treatment, and supervision of individuals with intellectual disabilities and problematic sexual behaviors*. Beaverton, OR: Association for the Treatment of Sexual Abusers. Retrieved from www.atsa.com/pdfs/ATSA_IDPSB_packet.pdf

Bonta, J., & Andrews, D. A. (2007). *Risk-need-responsivity model for offender assessment and rehabilitation* (User Report 2007–06). Ottawa, Ontario: Public Safety Canada.

Boer, D. P., Gauthier, C., Watson, D. R., Dorward, J., & Kolton, D. J. C. (1995). *The assessment and treatment of intellectually disabled sex offenders: The Regional Psychiatric Centre (Pacific) "Northstar" treatment and relapse prevention program*. Paper presented at the 1995 Conference on National Sex Offender Strategy, Toronto, Canada. Retrieved from www.csc-scc.gc.ca/005/008/compendium/2000/chap_17-eng.shtml

Boer, D. P., McVilly, K. R., & Lambick, F. (2007). Contextualizing risk in the assessment of intellectually disabled individuals. *Sexual Offender Treatment, 2*(2), 1–4.

Boer, D. P., Tough, S., & Haaven, J. (2004). Assessment of risk manageability of intellectually disabled sex offenders. *Journal of Applied Research in Intellectual Disabilities, 17*(4), 275–283. doi:10.1111/j.1468–3148.2004.00214.x

Bowker, A. (1994, July). Handle with care: Dealing with offenders who are mentally retarded. *FBI Law Enforcement Bulletin*, pp. 12–16.

Butwell, M., Jamieson, E., Leese, M., & Taylor, P. (2000). Trends in special (high security) hospitals: 2: Residency and discharge episodes, 1986–1995. *British Journal of Psychiatry, 176*(3), 260–265. doi:10.1192/bjp.176.3.260

Camilleri, J. A. C., & Quinsey, V. L. (2011). Appraising the risk of sexual and violent recidivism among intellectual disabled offenders. *Psychology, Crime & Law, 17*(1), 59–74. doi:10.1080/10683160903392350

Caparulo, F. (1991). Identifying the developmentally disabled sex offenders. *Sexuality and Disability, 9*(4), 311–322.doi:10.1007/BF01102019

Coleman, E., & Haaven, J. (2001). Assessment & treatment of the intellectually disabled sex offender. In M. S. Carich & S. Mussack (Eds.), *Handbook on sex offender treatment* (pp. 193–209). Brandon, VT: Safer Society Press.

Craig, L.A., & Hutchinson, R. (2005). Sexual offenders with learning disabilities: Risk, recidivism and treatment. *Journal of Sexual Aggression, 11*(3), 289–304. doi:10.1080/13552600500273919

Cuskelly, M. (2004). The evolving construct of intellectual disability: Is everything old new again? *International Journal of Disability Development and Education, 51*(1), 117–122.

Davis, L. (2009). People with intellectual disabilities and sexual offenses. *The Arc*. Retrieved from www.thearc.org/what-we-do/resources/fact-sheets/sexual-offenses

Day, K. (1993). Crime and mental retardation: A review. In: K. Howells & C. R. Hollin (Eds.), *Clinical approaches to the mentally disordered offender* (pp. 48–56). Chichester, UK: John Wiley & Sons.

Day, K. (1994). Male mentally handicapped sex offenders. *British Journal of Psychiatry, 165*(5), 630–639. doi:10.1192/bjp.165.5.630

Day, K. (2001). Treatment and care of mentally retarded offenders. In A. Dosen & K. Day (Eds.), *Treating mental illness and behaviour disorders in children and adults with mental retardation* (pp. 359–389). Washington, DC: American Psychiatric Publishing Inc.

Dolan, M., Holloway, J., Bailey, S., & Kroll, L. (1996). The psychosocial characteristics of juvenile sexual offenders referred to an adolescent forensic service in the UK. *Medical Science and Law, 36*(4), 434–452. doi:10.1177/002580249603600414

Embregts, P., Van Den Bogaard, K., Hendriks, L., Heestermans, M., Schuitemaker, M., & Van Wouwe, H. (2010). Sexual risk assessment for people with intellectual disabilities. *Research in Developmental Disabilities, 31*(3), 760–767. doi:10.1016/j.ridd.2010.01.018

Fazel, S., Xenitidis, K., & Powell, J. (2008). The prevalence of intellectual disabilities among 12,000 prisoners: A systematic review. *International Journal of Law and Psychiatry, 31*(4), 369–373. doi:10.1016/j.ijlp.2008.06.001

Fedoroff, J. P., Richards, D., Ranger, R., & Curry, S. (2016). The predictive validity of common risk assessment tools in men with intellectual disabilities and problematic sexual behaviors. *Research in Developmental Disabilities, 57*, 29–38. doi:10.1016/j.ridd.2016.06.011

Fortune, C., & Lambie, I. (2004). Demographic and abuse characteristics in adolescent male sexual offenders with "special needs." *Journal of Sexual Aggression, 10*(1), 63–84. doi:10.1080/13552600410001667760

Frize, M., Kenny, D., & Lennings, C. (2008). The relationship between intellectual disability, Indigenous status and risk of reoffending in juvenile offenders on community orders. *Journal of Intellectual Disability Research, 52*(6), 510–519. doi:10.1111/j.1365-2788.2008.01058.x

Glaser, W., & Deane, K. (1999). Normalisation in an abnormal world: A study of prisoners with an intellectual disability. *Journal of Offender Therapy and Comparative Criminology, 43*(3), 338–350. doi:10.1177/0306624X99433007

Green, G., Gray, N., & Willner, P. (2002). Factors associated with criminal convictions for sexually inappropriate behavior in men with learning disabilities. *Journal of Forensic Psychiatry, 13*(3), 578–607. doi:10.1080/0958518021000019407

Griffin, H. L., & Vettor, S. (2012). Predicting sexual re-offending in a UK sample of adolescents with intellectual disabilities. *Journal of Sexual Aggression, 18*(1), 64–80. doi:10.1080/13552600.2011.617013

Gross, G. (1985). *Activities of a development disabilities adult offender project*. Olympia, WA: Washington State Developmental Disabilities Planning Council.

Haaven, J. (1993). *An Introduction to the assessment and treatment of intellectually disabled sex offenders*. Orwell, VT: The Safer Society Press.

Haaven, J. (2006). Suggested treatment outline using the Old Me/New Me model. In G. Blasingame (Ed.), *Practical treatment strategies for forensic clients with severe and sexual behavior problems among persons with developmental disabilities* (pp. 85–114). Oklahoma City, OK: Wood 'N' Barnes/Safer Society Press.

Haaven, J. L., & Coleman, E. M. (2000). Treatment of the developmentally disabled sex offender. In D. R. Laws, S. M. Hudson, & T. Ward, (Eds.), *Remaking relapse prevention with sex offenders* (pp. 369–388). Thousand Oaks, CA: Sage Publications.

Haaven, J., Little, R., & Petre-Miller, D. (1990). *Treating intellectually disabled sex offenders: A model residential program*. Orwell, VT: Safer Society Press.

Haaven, J., & Schlank, A. (2001). The challenge of treating the sex offender with developmental disabilities. In A. Schlank (Ed.), *The sexual predator: Vol. 2: Legal issues, clinical issues, and special populations* (pp. 13.1–13.19). Kingston, NJ: Civic Research Institute.

Hanson R. K., & Thornton D. (2000). Improving risk assessments for sex offenders: A comparison of three actuarial scales. *Law and Human Behaviour, 24*(1), 119–136. doi:10.1023/A:1005482921333

Harkins, L., & Beech, A. R. (2007). A review of the factors that can influence the effectiveness of sexual offender treatment: Risk, need, responsivity, and process issues. *Aggression and Violent Behavior, 12*(6), 615–627. doi:10.1016/j.avb.2006.10.006

Harris, A. J. R., & Tough, S. (2004). Should actuarial risk assessments be used with sex offenders who are intellectually disabled? *Journal of Applied Research in Intellectual Disabilities, 17*(4), 235–241. doi:10.1111/j.1468-3148.2004.00211.x

Hawkes, C., Jenkins, J., & Vizard, E. (1997). Roots of sexual violence in children and adolescents. In V. Varma (Ed.), *Violence in children and adolescents* (pp. 84–102). London: Jessica Kingsley.

Hayes, S. (1991). Sex offenders. Australian and New Zealand. *Journal of Developmental Disabilities, 17*(2), 221–227. doi:10.1080/07263869100034441

Hayes, S. C. (2002). Early intervention or early incarceration? Using a screening test for intellectual disability in the criminal justice system. *Journal of Applied Research in Intellectual Disabilities, 15*(2), 120–128. doi:10.1046/j.1468-3148.2002.00113.x

Herrington, V. (2009) Assessing the prevalence of intellectual disability among young male prisoners. *Journal of Intellectual Disability Research, 53*(5), 397–410. doi:10.1111/j.1365-2788.2008.01150.x

Hingsburger, D., Griffiths, D., & Quinsey, V. (1991). Detecting counterfeit deviance: Differentiating sexual deviance from sexual inappropriateness. *The Habilitative Mental Healthcare Newsletter, 10*(9), 51–54.

Hocken, K., Winder, B., & Grayson, A. (2013). Putting responsivity into risk assessment: The use of the Structured Assessment of Risk and Need (SARN) with sexual offenders who have an intellectual disability. *Journal of Intellectual Disabilities and Offending Behaviour, 4*(3/4), 77–89. doi:10.1108/JIDOB-05-2013-0009

Hodgins, S. (1992). Mental disorder, intellectual deficiency, and crime. Evidence from a birth cohort. *Archives of General Psychiatry, 49*(6), 476–482. doi:10.1001/archpsyc.1992.01820060056009

Holland, A. J. (1991). Challenging and offending behavior by adults with developmental disorders. *Australia and New Zealand Journal of Developmental Disabilities, 17*(2), 119–126. doi:10.1080/07263869100034341

Holland, A. J. (2004). Criminal behaviour and developmental disability: An epidemiological perspective. In W. R. Lindsay, J. L. Taylor, & P. Sturmey (Eds.), *Offenders with developmental disabilities* (pp. 23–34). Chichester, UK: John Wiley & Sons.

Holland, T., Clare, I. C., & Mukhopadhyay, T. (2002). Prevalence of "criminal offending" by men and women with intellectual disability and the characteristics of "offenders": Implications for research and service development. *Journal of Intellectual Disability Research, 46*(1), 6–20. doi:10.1046/j.1365-2788.2002.00001.x

Hordell, A., Rees, J., & Robinson, D. (2001). *Sex offender treatment programme for male offenders with learning disabilities*. Northwickshire, UK: North Warwickshire NHS Trust.

Hudson, S. M., Wales, D. S., Bakker, L., & Ward, T. (2002) Dynamic risk factors: The Kia Marama evaluation. *Sexual Abuse: A Journal of Research and Treatment, 14*(2), 103–119. doi:10.1023/A:1014616113997

Johnston, S. J. (2002). Risk assessment in offenders with intellectual disability: The evidence base. *Journal of Intellectual Disability Research, 46*(1), 47–56. doi:10.1046/j.1365-2788.2002.t01-1-00003.x

Johnston, S. (2005). Applicability, reliability, and validity of the Psychopathy checklist-revised in offenders with intellectual disabilities: Some initial findings. *The International Journal of Forensic Mental Health, 4*(2), 207–220. doi:10.1080/14999013.2005.10471225

Keeling, J. A., Beech, A. R., & Rose, J. L. (2007). Assessment of intellectually disabled sexual offenders: The current position. *Aggression and Violent Behavior, 12*(2), 229–241. doi:10.1016/j.avb.2006.08.001

Keeling, J. A., & Rose, J. L. (2005). Relapse prevention with intellectually disabled sex offenders. *Sexual Abuse: Journal of Research and Treatment, 17*(4), 407–423. doi:10.1007/s11194-005-8052-6

Keller, J. (2016). Improving practices of risk assessment and intervention planning for persons with intellectual disabilities who sexually offend. *Journal of Policy and Practice in Intellectual Disabilities, 13*(1), 75–85. doi:10.1111/jppi.12149

Kroll, L., Rothwell, J., Bradley, D., Shah, P., Bailey, S., & Harrington, R. C. (2002). Mental health needs of boys in secure care for serious or persistent offending: A prospective, longitudinal study. *Lancet, 359*(9322), 1975.

Lambrick, F., & Glaser, W. (2004). Sex offenders with an intellectual disability. *Sexual Abuse: A Journal of Research and Treatment, 16*(4), 381–392. doi:1177/107906320401600409

Lane, S. L. (1991). Special offender populations. In G. D. Ryan & S. L. Lane (Eds.), *Juvenile sexual offending: Causes and consequences* (pp. 229–232). Lexington: Lexington Press.

Law, J., Lindsay, W. R., Quinn, K., & Smith, A. H. W. (2000). Outcome evaluation of 161 people with mild intellectual disabilities who have offending or challenging behaviour. *Journal of Intellectual Disability Research, 44*(3/4), 360–361.

Lindsay, W. R. (2002a). Research and literature on sex offenders with intellectual and developmental disabilities. *Journal of Intellectual Disability Research, 46*(1), 74–85. doi:10.1046/j.1365-2788.2002.00006.x

Lindsay, W. R. (2002b). Integration of recent reviews on offenders with intellectual disabilities. *Journal of Applied Research in Intellectual Disabilities, 15*(2), 111–119. doi:10.1046/j.1468-3148.2002.00112.x

Lindsay, W. R. (2011). People with intellectual disability who offend or are involved with the criminal justice system. *Current Opinion in Psychiatry, 24*(5), 377–381. doi:10.1097/YCO.0b013e3283479dc9

Lindsay, W. R., Elliot, S. F., & Astell, A. (2004). Predictors of sexual offence recidivism in offenders with intellectual disabilities. *Journal of Applied Research in Intellectual Disabilities, 17*(4), 299–305. doi:10.1111/j.1468-3148.2004.00217.x

Lindsay, W. R., Hastings, R. P., & Beech, A. R. (2011). Forensic research in offenders with intellectual & developmental disabilities 1: Prevalence and risk assessment. *Psychology, Crime & Law, 17*(1), 3–7. doi:10.1080/1068316X.2011.534913

Lindsay W. R., Law, J., & Macleod F. (2002) Intellectual disabilities and crime. Issues in assessment, intervention, and management. In. A. Needs & G. Towl (Eds.), *Applying psychology to forensic practice*. Oxford: BPS Books/Blackwell Publishing.

Lindsay, W. R., Law, J., Quinn, K., Smart, N., & Smith, A. H. W. (2001). A comparison of physical and sexual abuse histories: Sexual and non-sexual offenders with intellectual disability. *Child Abuse & Neglect, 25*(7), 989–995. doi:10.1016/S0145-2134(01)00251-4

Lindsay, W. R., & Michie, A. M. (2013). Individuals with developmental delay and problematic sexual behaviors. *Current Psychiatry Reports, 15*(4), 1–6. doi:10.1007/s11920-013-0350-y

Lindsay, W. R., Murphy, L., Smith, G., Murphy, D., Edwards, Z., Chittock, C., . . . Young, S. J. (2004). The dynamic risk assessment and management system: An assessment of immediate risk of violence for individuals with offending and challenging behaviour. *Journal of Applied Research in Intellectual Disabilities, 17*(4), 267–274. doi:10.1111/j.1468-3148.2004.00215.x

Lindsay, W. R., Olley, S., Baillie, N., & Smith, A. H. W. (1999). Treatment of adolescent sex offenders with intellectual disabilities. *Mental Retardation, 37*(3), 201–211. doi:10.1352/0047-6765(1999)037<0201:TOASOW>2.0.CO;2

Lofthouse, R. E., Lindsay, W. R., Totsika, V., Hastings, R. P., Boer, D. P., & Haaven, J. L. (2013). Prospective dynamic assessment of risk of sexual reoffending in individuals with an intellectual disability and a history of sexual offending behaviour. *Journal of Applied Research in Intellectual Disabilities, 26*(5), 394–403. doi:10.1111/jar.12029

Loucks N. (2007) *No one knows: Offenders with learning difficulties and learning disabilities—Review of prevalence and associated needs*. London: Prison Reform Trust.

MacEachron, A. E. (1979). Mentally retarded offenders: Prevalence and characteristics. *American Journal of Mental Deficiency, 84*, 165–176.

MacMillan, D. L., Gresham, F. M., & Siperstein, G. N. (1993). Conceptual and psychometric concerns about the 1992 AAMR definition of mental retardation. *American Journal on Mental Retardation, 98*(3), 325–335.

McBrien, J. (2003). The intellectually disabled offender: methodological problems in identification. *Journal of Applied Research in Intellectual Disabilities, 16*(2), 95–105. doi:10.1046/j.1468-3148.2003.00153.x

Mikkelsen, E. J. (2004). Assessment of people with developmental disabilities in the criminal justice system. In W. R. Lindsay, J. L. Taylor, & P. Sturmey (Eds.), *Offenders with developmental disabilities* (pp. 111–130). Chichester, UK: John Wiley & Sons.

Miller, W. R., & Rollnick, S. (2002). *Motivational interviewing* (2nd ed.). New York, NY: Guilford Press.

Murphy, W. D., Coleman, E. M., & Haynes, M. R. (1983). Treatment evaluation issues with the mentally retarded sex offender. In J. G. Greer & I. R. Stuart (Eds.), *The sexual aggressor: Current perspectives on treatment* (pp. 22–41). New York, NY: Van Nostrand Reinhold.

Murphy, W. D., Coleman, E. M., & Haynes, M. R. (1986). Factors related to coercive sexual behaviour in a non-clinical sample of males. *Violence and Victims, 1*(4), 255–278.

Murphy G., & Mason J. (2007). People with intellectual disabilities who are at risk of offending. In N. Bouras & G. Holt (Eds.), *Psychiatric and behavioural disorders in intellectual and developmental disabilities* (pp. 173–201). Cambridge: Cambridge University Press.

Murrey, G. H., Briggs, D., & Davis, C. (1992). Psychopathically disordered, mentally ill and mentally handicapped sex offenders: A comparative study. *Medical Science Law, 32*, 331–336.

Nezu, C. M., Greenberg, J., & Nezu, A. M. (2006). Project STOP: Cognitive behavioral assessment and treatment for sex offenders with intellectual disability. *Journal of Forensic Psychology Practice, 6*(3), 87–103. doi:10. I 300/J I 58v06n03_06

Nezu, C. M., Nezu, A. M., & Dudek, J. A. (1998). A cognitive behavioural model of assessment and treatment for intellectually disabled sexual offenders. *Cognitive and Behavioural Practice, 5*(1), 25–64. doi:10.1016/S1077-7229(98)80020-5

Nichols, H., & Molinder, I. (2000). *Multiphasic Sex Inventory manual-II*. Tacoma, WA: Nichols & Molinder Assessments, Inc.

Noble, J. H. J., & Conley, R. W. (1992). Toward an epidemiology of relevant attributes. In R. W. Conley, R. Luckasson, & G. Bouthilet (Eds.), *The criminal justice system and mental retardation: Defendants and victims* (pp. 17–53). Baltimore, MD: Paul H. Brookes Publishing.

O'Connor, W. (1996). A problem-solving intervention for sex offenders with an intellectual disability. *Journal of Intellectual and Developmental Disability, 21*(3), 219–235. doi:10.1080/13668259600033351

O'Connor, W. (1997). Towards and environmental perspective on intervention for problem sexual behaviour in people with an intellectual disability. *Journal of Applied Research in Intellectual Disabilities, 10*(2), 159–175. doi:10.1111/j.1468-3148.1997.tb00015.x

Parry, C. J., & Lindsay, W. R. (2003). Impulsiveness as a factor in sexual offending by people with mild intellectual disability. *Journal of Intellectual Disability Research, 47*(6), 483–487. doi:10.1046/j.1365-2788.2003.00509.x

Petersilia, J. (2000). *Doing justice? Criminal offenders with developmental disabilities*. Berkeley, CA: California Policy Research Center, University of California.

Pouls, C., & Jeandarme, I. (2014). Psychopathy in offenders with intellectual disabilities: A comparison of the PCL—R and PCL:SV. *International Journal of Forensic Mental Health, 13*(3), 207–216. doi:10.1080/14999013.2014.922138

Quinsey, V. L. (2004). Risk assessment and management in community settings. In W. R. Lindsay, J. L. Taylor, & P. Sturmey (Eds.), *Offenders with developmental disabilities* (pp. 131–142). Chichester, UK: John Wiley & Sons.

Quinsey, V. L., Book, A., & Skilling, T. A. (2004). A follow-up of deinstitutionalized men with intellectual disabilities and histories of antisocial behaviour. *Journal of Applied Research in Intellectual Disabilities, 17*(4), 243–253. doi:10.1111/j.1468-3148.2004.00216.x

Rand, M. R., & Harrell, E. (2009). *Crime against people with disabilities, 2007*. Washington, DC: U.S. Department of Justice, Bureau of Justice Statistics.

Rayner, J., Kelly, T. P., & Graham, F. (2005). Mental health, personality and cognitive problems in persistent adolescent offenders require long-term solutions: A pilot study. *Journal of Forensic Psychiatry and Psychology, 16*(2), 248–262. doi:10.1080/1478994051233130982

Salekin, K. L., Olley, J. G., & Hedge, K. A. (2010). Offenders with intellectual disability: Characteristics, prevalence, and issues in forensic assessment. *Journal of Mental Health Research in Intellectual Disabilities, 3*(2), 97–116. doi:10.1080/19315861003695769

Scott, C. L., Lewis, C. F., & McDermott, B. E. (2006). Dual diagnosis among incarcerated populations: Exception or rule? *Journal of Dual Diagnosis, 3*(1), 33–58.

Swanson, C. K., & Garwick, G. B. (1990). Treatment for low functioning sex offenders: Group therapy and interagency co-ordination. *Mental Retardation, 28*(3), 155–161.

Talbot, J., & Riley, C. (2007). No one knows: offenders with learning difficulties and learning disabilities. *British Journal of Learning Disabilities, 35*(3), 154–161. doi:10.1111/j.1468-3156.2007.00456.x

Taylor, J. L., Keddie, T., & Lee, S. (2003). Working with sex offenders with intellectual disability: Evaluation of an introductory workshop for direct care staff. *Journal of Intellectual Disability Research, 47*(3), 203–209. doi:10.1046/j.1365-2788.2003.00471.x

Thompson, D. J. (2000). Vulnerability, dangerousness and risk: The case of men with learning disabilities who sexually abuse. *Health, Risk & Society, 2*(1), 33–46. doi:10.1080/136985700111431

Thompson, D., & Brown, H. (1997). Men with intellectual disabilities who sexually abuse: A review of the literature. *Journal of Applied Research in Intellectual Disabilities, 10*(2), 140–158. doi:10.1111/j.1468-3148.1997.tb00014.x

Tudway, J. A., & Darmoody, M. (2005). Clinical assessment of adult sexual offenders with learning disabilities. *Journal of Sexual Aggression, 11*(3), 277–288. doi:10.1080/13552600500333796

Turner, S. (2000). Forensic risk assessment in intellectual disabilities: The evidence base and current practice in one English region. *Journal of Applied Research in Intellectual Disabilities, 13*(4), 239–255. doi:10.1046/j.1468-3148.2000.00024.x

Walker, N., & McCabe, S. (1973). *Crime and insanity in England.* Edinburgh: University Press.

Wheeler, J. R., Clare, I. C., & Holland, A. J. (2014). What can social and environmental factors tell us about the risk of offending by people with intellectual disabilities? *Psychology, Crime & Law, 20*(7), 635–658. doi:10.1080/1068316X.2013.854789

Wilcox, D. T. (2004). Treatment of intellectually disabled individuals who have committed sexual offences: A review of the literature. *Journal of Sexual Aggression, 10*(1), 85–100. doi:10.1080/13552600410001670955

Wilcox, D. T., & Leyland, M. (1998). *Group work with learning disabled sex offenders.* Paper Presented for the British Institute of Learning Disabilities. Birmingham, England.

Wilcox, D. T., & Leyland, M. (1999). *Group techniques for working with intellectually disabled sex offenders.* Paper presented for National Organization for Treatment of Abusers Annual Conference, York, England.

Wilner, P., & Goodey, R. (2005). Readiness for cognitive therapy in people with intellectual disabilities. *Journal of Applied Research in Intellectual Disabilities, 19*(1), 67–73. doi:10.1111/j.1468-3148.2005.00279.x

Wilson, R. J., & Burns, M. (2011). *Intellectual disability and problems in sexual behaviour: Assessment, treatment, and promotion of healthy sexuality.* Holyoke, MA: NEARI Press.

Yates, P. M., Prescott, D. S., & Ward, T. (2010). *Applying the good lives and self-regulation models to sex offender treatment: A practical guide for clinicians.* Brandon, VT: Safer Society Press.

25

OFFENDERS WITH LEARNING DISABILITIES AND SPECIAL EDUCATION NEEDS

Applying DEAR and BASE Models

Jerrod Brown, Jeffrey Haun, Elizabeth Quinby, and Deborah Eckberg

> Education and training is vital if individuals with intellectual disability are going to receive equal justice. Children, adolescents, and adults with this disability must learn about the possibility of meeting a police officer, how to protect their rights during encounters with police and how to speak up if they are being victimized.
>
> —(Davis, 2009, p. 3)

Introduction

Offender populations are disproportionately likely to present with a host of special needs relative to the general population. In particular, some of the more common conditions that may present in this population include attention-deficit/hyperactivity disorder (ADHD), autism spectrum disorder (ASD), fetal alcohol spectrum disorder (FASD), intellectual disability (ID), and traumatic brain injury (TBI), all of which will be discussed in detail within this chapter. Further, offenders with these disorders are significantly more likely to have co-occurring disorders (e.g., anxiety, depression, and substance use) and other special needs (e.g., attention, learning, and memory challenges). As such, it is often difficult to identify, supervise, and treat offenders who present with these disorders, especially in the absence of proper identification and awareness on the part of the correctional and forensic professional. A key initial step to alleviating these challenges is improving familiarity with these disorders in professionals working in criminal justice and forensic mental health settings. The behavioral/emotional, adaptive, social, and executive functioning (BASE) model is a promising guide to help professionals understand the complex symptomatology of these disorders. Further, the incorporation of the direct language, engage support system, accommodate needs, and remain patient (DEAR) model may be useful in improving communication with offenders with special needs during interviews, screening and assessments, and other interactions. In light of these benefits, this chapter will review each of the five disorders described earlier, introduce readers to the BASE and DEAR models, and identify potentially useful assessment and treatment strategies.

Attention-Deficit/Hyperactivity Disorder (ADHD)

Attention-deficit/hyperactivity disorder (ADHD) is one of the most common disorders encountered by criminal justice and forensic mental health professionals (Ginsberg, Hirvikoski, & Lindefors,

2010; Usher, Stewart, & Wilton, 2013; Young, Moss, Sedgwick, Fridman, & Hodgkins, 2014). Not only is this disorder characterized by inattention, hyperactivity, and impulsivity, but affective dysregulation, disorganization, and sensation seeking are commonplace (Barkley, 2006; Wender, Ward, Reimherr, & Marchant, 2000). Although these symptoms typically emerge during childhood, they often persist across an individual's life course (Barkley, 2006; Ivanov, Schulz, London, & Newcorn, 2008). Complicating matters, symptoms of ADHD, including poor social adjustment, as well as predictors of ADHD, such as child maltreatment and early behavior problems, may increase the likelihood of criminal behavior (Maggs, Patrick, & Feinstein, 2008; Mohr-Jensen & Steinhausen, 2016). To improve recognition of ADHD in criminal justice and forensic mental health professionals, this section reviews comorbid conditions of ADHD, the prevalence of ADHD, the links between features of ADHD and criminal behavior, and the impact of ADHD on individuals as they interact with and navigate through the criminal justice system.

ADHD has high levels of comorbidity with psychiatric disorders, substance use, and other problems throughout the life course (Belcher, 2014). In children, ADHD often co-occurs with externalizing problems, which can contribute to substance use in adolescence (Crowley, Mikulich, MacDonald, Young, & Zerbe, 1998) and exacerbate rule breaking behaviors that characterize behavioral disorders like conduct disorder (Eisenberg, Hofer, & Vaughn, 2007; Hofvander, Ossowski, Lundström, & Anckarsäter, 2009). When entrenched, such behavioral patterns may contribute to negative attitudes toward authority figures and societal institutions (Pliszka, 1998). As children transition through adolescence into adulthood, the co-occurrence of personality disorders like antisocial personality disorder (Hofvander et al., 2009) and substance use problems (Einarsson, Sigurdsson, Gudjonsson, Newton, & Bragason, 2009; Ginsberg et al., 2010; Rosler, Retz, Yaqoobi, Burg, & Retz-Junginger, 2009; Young, Wells, & Gudjonsson, 2011) may persist. In addition to psychopathology, ADHD is commonly comorbid with neurodevelopmental disorders like dyslexia, which can exacerbate symptoms of psychiatric illnesses (Daderman, Lindgren, & Lidberg, 2004). Finally, individuals with ADHD frequently suffer from other serious problems like poor educational attainment, unstable work history, limited social support systems (Barkley, Guevremont, Anastopoulos, DuPaul, & Shelton, 1993; Biederman et al., 2006; Kessler et al., 2006; Secnik, Swensen, & Lage, 2005; Sobanski, 2006), and risky behavioral patterns (e.g., gambling and unprotected sex) (Nigg, 2006; Pollak et al., 2016). Taken together, these comorbid issues increase the likelihood of negative outcomes and contribute to the difficulty of accurately diagnosing ADHD.

ADHD is still commonly diagnosed among children (Redmond, 2016), with estimated prevalence rates of 5% to 7% (American Psychiatric Association, 2013; Willcutt, 2012) and 4% to 8% (Pliszka, 2007; Simon, Czobor, Balint, Meszaros, & Bitter, 2009; Weiss, Hechtman, Milroy, & Perlman, 1985). Research suggests that symptoms of ADHD persist into adulthood for approximately 60% of these children (Pliszka, 2007; Simon et al., 2009; Weiss et al., 1985). This results in an estimated prevalence rate of somewhere between 2% and 4% in adults (Ginsberg et al., 2010). The estimated prevalence rate of ADHD in correctional settings is substantially greater, such that a large body of research has demonstrated rates of ADHD among offenders ranging from 10% to 50% (Ginsberg et al., 2010; Grieger & Hosser, 2012; Rosler et al., 2009; Usher et al., 2013). In a meta-analysis of 42 studies from across the world, Young and colleagues (2014) found prevalence rates of 30% and 26% in youth and adult offender populations, respectively. Although ADHD prevalence rates have been relatively understudied in all forensic settings, elevated levels are expected in a manner consistent with offenders (Buitelaar & Ferdinand, 2016). Together, these findings highlight the overwhelming presence of ADHD in criminal justice and forensic settings.

Why is ADHD so common in criminal justice and forensic mental health settings? Individuals with ADHD and its diverse array of comorbid symptomatology are at an elevated risk for violating social norms through criminal and other behaviors (Maggs et al., 2008; Mohr-Jensen & Steinhausen, 2016). Specifically, symptoms of impulsivity and hyperactivity in combination with conduct disorder predict later delinquency in children and adolescents (Babinski, Hartsough, & Lambert, 1999; Pardini, Obradovic, & Loeber, 2006). Conversely, the presence of an ADHD diagnosis in the absence of conduct problems is still a significant predictor of criminality (Dalsgaard, Mortensen, Frydenberg, & Thomsen, 2013). The offenses of youth with ADHD tend to be characterized by reactivity, impulsivity, and a lack of planning, which often contributes to an ease of apprehension by authorities (Harpin & Young, 2012). Once apprehended, children with ADHD are over five times more likely to be convicted than youth without mental illness (Dalsgaard et al., 2013). Impulse control can affect various parts of their navigation through the legal process by clouding their ability to think and effectively work through their options for counsel. Further, youth with ADHD are 12 times more likely to be adjudicated delinquent for a violent crime relative to youth without mental illness (Dalsgaard et al., 2013).

After first contact with the criminal justice system, youths with ADHD are more likely to become repeat offenders across the lifespan than youths who have not been diagnosed with ADHD (Young et al., 2015). During incarceration, adult offenders with ADHD are at least six times more likely than offenders without mental illness to commit aggressive acts toward other prisoners, even when controlling for other diagnoses such as antisocial personality disorder (Young et al., 2009). In short, offenders with ADHD are prone to commit more severe offenses and have continued involvement in criminal justice and forensic mental health settings.

Offenders with ADHD present many challenges to criminal justice and forensic mental health professionals before, during, and after adjudication. Initially, offenders with ADHD may exhibit difficulty in coping with arrest as well as comprehending and participating in police interviews and trials. In particular, these legal processes often require sustained attention during activities such as extended and repetitive interrogations and examinations, which can be challenging for individuals with ADHD (Harpin & Young, 2012). Once incarcerated, inmates with ADHD can present a constant challenge to corrections officers through everything from staff-inmate interactions to persistent disruptive and impulsive behavior. Further, inmates with ADHD are disproportionately likely to experience worse outcomes (e.g., institutional infractions, sentence extensions, and victimization) than inmates without ADHD (Gordon, Williams, & Donnelly, 2012; Young et al., 2009). When undiagnosed and/or poorly treated, the risk for problematic externalizing behavior persists, and continued criminal justice involvement increases across the lifespan (Young & Goodwin, 2010).

Criminal justice and forensic mental health professionals have the potential to play an active role in improving this situation. Accurate diagnosis is the necessary first step in identifying ADHD and implementing individualized treatment programs to address this disorder (Olley, Nicholls, & Brink, 2009; Scott, Gignac, Kronfli, Ocana, & Lorberg, 2016; Young et al., 2011). This may be easier said than done, as ADHD is often difficult to diagnose because of the complex web of interconnected co-occurring symptoms that may be present (Mitchell & Shaw, 2011). Early interventions during childhood and adolescence hold the most promise in encouraging prolonged desistance from antisocial behavior (Belcher, 2014). Successful treatment approaches will likely be characterized by all-day symptom suppression through medication in combination with social, family, educational, vocational, and substance use interventions (Belcher, 2014; Burns, 2009; Scott et al., 2016). To maximize impact, treatment programs must be in place prior to release from jail and prison and continue while the offender is on community supervision (e.g., probation and parole) (Belcher, 2014). The importance of improvement through these endeavors is underlined by the fact that criminal behavior in offenders with ADHD has dire economic consequences in the United States: estimates are as high as $2 billion to $4 billion for the criminal behavior of children with ADHD alone (see Fletcher & Wolfe, 2009).

Autism Spectrum Disorder (ASD)

Autism spectrum disorder (ASD) is one of the many disorders confronted by criminal justice and forensic mental health professionals. This developmental disorder consists of cognitive, social, and behavioral symptoms that vary widely by individual in terms of presence and severity. Cognitive symptoms include rigidity of thought patterns, which can contribute to repetitive, obsessive, and disruptive behavior. Further, acute sensitivity to sensory stimulation like touch, smell, and light can profoundly influence the affective and behavioral reactions of individuals with ASD. In combination with these cognitive symptoms, social symptoms often characterized by deficits in communication skills and social etiquette (e.g., trouble reading social cues) are common in ASD (Haskins & Silva, 2006; Murrie, Warren, Kristiansson, & Dietz, 2002; Palermo, 2004). Such limitations in communication skills often lead to social debilitation and isolation. Complicating matters, ASD frequently co-occurs with other psychiatric diagnoses and substance use disorders (Alexander, Chester, Green, Gunaratna, & Hoare, 2015; Freckelton, 2012; Långström, Grann, Ruchkin, Sjöstedt, & Fazel, 2009). Although the vast majority of individuals with ASD never become involved in the criminal justice and forensic mental health systems (Bjørkly, 2009; Browning & Caulfield, 2011; Ghaziuddin, Tsai, Ghaziuddin, 1991; Gómez de la Cuesta, 2010; Mouridsen, 2012), the symptoms of ASD and co-occurring mental health and substance use issues may affect the likelihood of antisocial behavior (Allen et al., 2008; Cashin & Newman, 2009; Freckelton, 2013). To expand awareness of ASD in criminal justice and forensic mental health professionals, this section discusses the prevalence of ASD, the links between ASD and crime, and the impact of ASD in the legal system.

According to the Centers for Disease Control and Prevention (2015), ASD has been diagnosed in approximately one in 68 people. Further, ASD diagnoses are growing by 10–17% annually (National Human Genome Research Institute, 2012), making ASD one of the most rapidly growing developmental disorders in the U.S. (Centers for Disease Control and Prevention, 2015). Less is known about the prevalence rate of ASD in criminal justice and forensic mental health settings (Robinson et al., 2012). Much of this research has been limited to small and unrepresentative samples (Baron-Cohen, 1988; Ghaziuddin et al., 1991; Haskins & Silva, 2006; Kristiansson & Sorman, 2008; Mawson, Grounds, & Tantam, 1985; Mouridsen, Rich, Isager, & Nedergaard, 2008; Schwartz-Watts, 2005). Further, little is known about the how often individuals with ASD go undiagnosed until involvement in the criminal justice and forensic mental health systems. Thus, systematic research on the prevalence of ASD in these settings is necessary to understand the scope and nature of this problem better.

Although prevalence rates have not been clearly established, many researchers have concluded that individuals with ASD may be more likely to commit illegal acts than the general population (Ghaziuddin et al., 1991; Mouridsen, 2012; Petersilia, Foote, Crowell, & National Research Council [U.S.], 2001). In fact, links can be directly drawn from the cognitive symptoms of ASD and risk for criminal behavior. Emotional dysregulation is a common cognitive symptom of ASD that may result in illegal activities. Well established as a risk factor for criminal behavior (Andrews & Bonta, 2010), emotional dysregulation can result in impulsive and aggressive behavior (Rieffe, Camodeca, Pouw, Lange, & Stockmann, 2012). Fixation and obsession is another common ASD symptom that can contribute to criminal charges (Howlin, 2004; Mouridsen et al., 2008; Woodbury-Smith et al., 2005). For example, fixation on a person, object, action, or concept could lead to intentional and unintentional violations of law, such as sexual misconduct and arson (Barry-Walsh & Mullen, 2004; Chen et al., 2003; Silva, Ferrari, & Leong, 2002). Acute sensitivity to sensory stimulation is another common symptom of ASD that may contribute to illegal behavior. During situations characterized by stimuli overload (e.g., bright lights or loud sounds), individuals with ASD are prone to impulsively acting out. If not effectively treated, these cognitive symptoms may result in violence during certain situations (Browning & Caulfield, 2011).

The social symptoms of ASD also influence the likelihood of illegal behavior. Specifically, individuals with ASD often exhibit deficits in communication skills, comprehension of social cues, and social etiquette. These features can contribute to trouble comprehending the nonverbal cues, thoughts, and feelings of other people. As a result, individuals with ASD may engage in inappropriate behaviors (e.g., inappropriate and unwanted sexual behavior) (Freckelton, 2013) that cross legal boundaries without recognizing the gravity of their actions (Haskins & Silva, 2006; Murrie et al., 2002; Palermo, 2004). Alternatively, the social symptoms of ASD increase proneness to peer pressure. Individuals with ASD may be susceptible to pressure to commit illegal actions or persuaded to accept the blame for someone else (Mayes, 2003; White & Schry, 2011). In light of the links between the cognitive and social symptoms of ASD and criminal justice involvement, early and accurate identification along with effective treatment are essential in limiting the role that ASD plays in criminal behavior (Ray, Marks, & Bray-Garretson, 2004; Woodbury-Smith et al., 2010).

The presence of ASD can complicate an individual's participation in the legal system from the point of investigations all the way to supervision in correctional settings. During initial police investigations and interviews, ASD-related deficits in communication and social skills can have a detrimental effect on criminal justice outcomes (Landa, 2000; Tager-Flusberg, Paul, & Lord, 2005). For example, individuals with ASD may respond slowly or not at all to officers' questions during interrogation and attorneys' questions during trial. In other instances, the responses may be blunt, which can then be misinterpreted as inappropriate or callous. Perhaps even more problematic, individuals with ASD are prone to social pressure, which could increase the likelihood of acquiescence and false confessions (Maras & Bowler, 2010; Woodbury-Smith & Dein, 2014). Such false confessions could be the result of pressure from the guilty party (e.g., peer) or simply an attempt to escape the pressure of a stressful situation like a police interrogation (North, Russell, & Gudjonsson, 2008; Woodbury-Smith & Dein, 2014). After conviction, the symptoms of ASD may make it difficult for offenders to adjust to life in custodial settings (e.g., jail and prison) or comply with the requirements of community supervision (e.g., probation and parole) (McAdam, 2012; Robertson & McGillivray, 2015; Underwood, Forrester, Chaplin, & McCarthy, 2013). As a result, criminal justice settings may place offenders with ASD at greater risk for victimization, recidivism, and new forms of psychopathology (e.g., depressive disorders and substance use disorders) and suicidal behavior (McCarthy et al., 2015a; Myers; 2004).

To protect against the risk of ASD symptoms negatively affecting criminal justice outcomes, criminal justice and forensic mental health professionals should be aware of these deficits and receive training in how to interact effectively with individuals who may have ASD (Maras & Bowler, 2010). Critical in this process is improving the identification and assessment of individuals with ASD (Katz & Zemishlany, 2006; Talbot, 2009; Wing, 1997). Early and accurate diagnosis of ASD can help improve how individuals are treated during prosecution as well as after adjudication. In addition to enhanced identification, improvements in treatment and support for offenders with ASD are imperative. For example, Myers (2004) found notable deficits in resources, training, and capacity to treat and support offenders with disorders such as ASD. Addressing these shortcomings is necessary to reduce the likelihood of recidivism and other negative outcomes in individuals with ASD (Kawakami et al., 2012; Lord, 1995; Robinson et al., 2012).

Fetal Alcohol Spectrum Disorders (FASD)

Fetal alcohol spectrum disorder (FASD) is a life course persistent spectrum of disorders common to individuals in criminal justice and forensic mental health settings (MacPherson & Chudly, 2007; Popova, Lange, Bekmuradov, Mihic, & Rehm, 2011). FASD includes fetal alcohol syndrome (FAS), partial fetal alcohol syndrome (pFAS), alcohol-related neurodevelopmental disorder (ARND), and alcohol-related birth defects (ARBD) (Chudley et al., 2005). In the last few years, a new opportunity for diagnosis in the form of Other Specified Neurodevelopmental Disorder (Associated with Prenatal Alcohol Exposure) emerged in the fifth edition of the *Diagnostic and Statistical Manual of Mental Disorders* (DSM-5) (American Psychiatric Association, 2013). Although the presence and severity of symptoms vary by individual, these disorders are generally characterized by cognitive (e.g., executive control, intelligence, and memory), social (e.g., communication skills and social pressure), adaptive (e.g., understanding cause and effect and decision-making ability), and physiological (e.g., skeletal and organ abnormalities symptoms) symptoms (Alloway, Gathercole, Kirkwood, & Elliott, 2009; Bhatara, Loudenberg, & Ellis, 2006; Centers for Disease Control and Prevention, 2014). If not accurately identified and treated, FASD and related psychopathology can increase the risk for antisocial behavior and entanglement in the criminal justice system (Pei, Job, Kully-Martens, & Rasmussen, 2011). To increase familiarity with FASD among criminal justice and forensic mental health professionals, this section reviews the prevalence of FASD, the relationship between FASD and criminal behavior, and the impact of FASD in criminal justice and forensic mental health settings.

The prevalence of FASD in the United States is difficult to estimate. In fact, any prevalence estimates likely underestimate the true prevalence of FASD. This phenomenon is driven by the fact that diagnosis of FASD requires the verification of prenatal alcohol exposure, which is often difficult to obtain, particularly for adults. Nonetheless, a limited body of research has estimated that between 2% and 5% of the general population meets criteria for FASD (May et al., 2009; 2014). Prevalence rates for FASD increases in corrections settings, with estimates suggesting that 10% to 24% of incarcerated offenders experience features of FASD (Fast, Conry, & Loock, 1999; MacPherson & Chudly, 2007). Consistent with these findings, it has been estimated that approximately 60% of adolescents and adults with FASD in the United States have experienced some sort of contact with the criminal justice system (Streissguth, Barr, Kogan, & Bookstein, 1996). In light of these findings, and the fact that these are likely underestimates, there is a strong need for sophisticated research on the prevalence of FASD both in the general population and in criminal justice and forensic mental health settings.

Why might individuals with FASD be prone to antisocial and criminal behavior? The cognitive, social, and adaptive symptoms of FASD can be directly linked to such problematic behavior. First, the cognitive symptoms of FASD include deficits in executive and behavioral control. This tendency for impulsivity can result in illegal behavior (e.g., fights, theft, and sexual misconduct). Second, the social symptoms of FASD include a vulnerability to various forms of social manipulation, including peer pressure. As a result, individuals with FASD may commit antisocial acts in an effort to gain the acceptance and approval of their peers. Alternatively, individuals with FASD may be easily manipulated into taking the blame for the antisocial behavior of others. Third, adaptive deficits, including, difficulty with linking behaviors and consequences, may increase the likelihood of illegal activity. It may be that individuals with FASD do not appreciate the severity of their actions or the potential consequences when engaging in criminal behavior. Although not exhaustive, these examples highlight how easy it is for an individual with FASD to become justice involved.

Once an individual is entangled in the criminal justice system, FASD can have a detrimental impact on an offender's capacity to navigate the legal system. During police interviews and interrogations, the social symptoms of FASD place individuals with the disorder at a disadvantage. Specifically, the vulnerability to social pressures in combination with memory deficits may result in suggestibility and/or confabulation. At worst, the direct impact of these deficits may contribute to false confessions and, ultimately, wrongful convictions. After conviction, the symptoms of FASD can complicate institutional adjustment and contribute to institution misbehavior (Boland, Burrill, Duwyn, & Karp, 1998; MacPherson & Chudley, 2007 Upon release from incarceration, the symptoms of FASD may limit an individual's capacity to meet the expectations of community supervision, which increases his or her likelihood of recidivism. In total, the presence of FASD increases the risk of prolonged involvement in the criminal justice system.

Improving the assessment and diagnosis of FASD is a necessary first step in identification, management, and treatment of individuals with FASD in the criminal justice system. In light of the fact that FASD is overrepresented and underaddressed within criminal justice settings (Fast, Conry, & Loock, 1999; Popova et al., 2011; Streissguth et al., 1996), criminal justice and forensic mental health professionals need to recognize the red flags of FASD (Brown & Singh, 2015; Brown, Wartnik, Connor, & Adler, 2010; McLachlan, Roesch, Viljoen, & Douglas, 2014). When observed, individuals with these red flags should be referred for additional screening and assessment (Boland, Chudley, & Grant, 2002; Fast & Conry, 2009). This assessment process will likely be complex and arduous because of the symptoms of FASD (Burd, Martsolf, & Juelson, 2004; Popova, Lange, Burd, & Rehm, 2015). For example, the social symptoms of FASD include deficits in communications skills that decrease the likelihood of providing accurate self-report information. Further, a proneness to the influence of social pressure and memory deficits may increase the likelihood of an individual complying with an authority figure, even to the point of confabulation. The combination of FASD symptoms and the inherent difficulty of confirming prenatal alcohol exposure continue to make the accurate diagnosis of FASD difficult. Complicating matters, the physical signs of FASD that are present in children (e.g., facial and skeletal abnormalities) are typically not present as the individual ages into adolescence and adulthood (Malbin, 2004; Rasmussen, Horne, & Witol, 2006). As such, the development of improved FASD assessment techniques, instruments, and procedures for use in criminal justice and forensic mental health settings are necessary to enhance the identification of individuals with FASD (Graham, 2014).

Accurate diagnosis is imperative in the development of individualized treatment plans and the allocation of services (Boland et al., 2002; Fast & Conry, 2009). If not identified, offenders with FASD will not receive adequate treatment. As a result, the symptoms of FASD and related secondary disorders will persist and perhaps worsen, particularly in custodial settings such as jail and prison (Boland et al., 2002; Burd, Fast, & Conry, 2010; Cox, Clairmont, & Cox, 2008; Fast & Conry, 2009). Such a downward spiral may contribute to institutional misconduct and continued criminal justice involvement after release from prison. In light of these costly consequences, criminal justice and forensic mental health professionals must take care to ensure that offenders with FASD maintain consistent contact with treatment and social services before, during, and after release from custody (Boland et al., 1998; Brown et al., 2014). The combination of adequate assessment and treatment holds the most promise in assisting offenders with FASD in rehabilitation (Brintnell, Bailey, Sawhney, & Kreftin, 2011; Chartrand & Forbes-Chilibeck, 2003). To this end, an effort to increase awareness and recognition of FASD in criminal justice and forensic mental health professionals is imperative (Boland et al., 1998; Streissguth, 1996).

Intellectual Disabilities

Intellectual disabilities consist of deficits in intellectual functioning that result in limitations of adaptive functioning (e.g., short- and long-term planning, problem solving, and decision making). Individuals with intellectual disabilities may be three to four times as likely as the general population to suffer from comorbid mental disorders (e.g., autism and communication disorders) (Emerson, 2003) and medical conditions (e.g., cerebral palsy and epilepsy) (APA, 2013; Dias, Ware, Kinner, & Lennox, 2013). The overlap of interrelated disorders and conditions complicate the assessment and treatment processes and can foreshadow poor outcomes, such as antisocial behavior, victimization, and suicidal behavior (APA, 2013; Glaser & Deane, 1999; Noble & Conley, 1992). Depending on the extent of impairment and available support systems, individuals with intellectual disabilities may not be able to live independently and often have difficulty with everyday activities including school, work, and social communication (APA, 2013). To draw the attention of criminal justice and forensic mental health professionals to intellectual disabilities, this section reviews the prevalence of intellectual disabilities, identifies the links between intellectual disabilities and criminal behavior, and discusses the significance of intellectual disabilities in the criminal justice system.

A recent meta-analysis of 52 studies found that intellectual disabilities have an estimated prevalence of 10.37 per 1,000 people in developed countries (i.e., about 1.04%) (Maulik, Mascarenhas, Mathers, Dua, & Saxena, 2011). Although researchers have found higher rates of intellectual disabilities in justice-involved individuals, there is a lack of consensus on these prevalence estimates

(Crocker, Mercier, Allaire, & Roy, 2007). Depending on how intellectual disabilities are operationalized, these prevalence estimates can vary greatly from 0.6% (MacEachron, 1979) to 39.6% (Holland, 1991) in criminal justice settings. For example, some research studies have reported prevalence estimates ranging from 4% to 10% for intellectual disabilities in the U.S. and other nations (Bowker, 1994; Davis, 2006; Petersilia, 2000), whereas other prevalence estimates for intellectual disabilities reach as high as 30% in incarcerated settings (Denkowski & Denkowski, 1985; Fazel, Xenitidis, & Powell, 2008; Scheyett, Vaughn, Taloy, & Parish, 2009). In a 2008 systemic literature review of psychiatric surveys involving intellectual disabilities, Fazel et al., (2008) estimated that between 0.5 and 1.5% of incarcerated offenders meet criteria for diagnosis of intellectual disability. The prevalence of intellectual disabilities may be even higher in secure inpatient settings, such as forensic mental health facilities (Salekin, Olley, & Hedge, 2010). Nonetheless, intellectual disabilities may often go unrecognized by criminal justice and forensic mental health professionals, which may contribute to the underestimation of the number of offenders with intellectual disabilities in criminal justice settings. As such, there is a strong need for the systematic assessment of intellectual disabilities in offenders for the sake of public planning and policy purposes (Fazel et al., 2008).

Why might individuals with intellectual disabilities be overrepresented in the criminal justice system? Simply put, intelligence levels are consistently lower in offenders than in the general population. Specifically, the average IQ of an offender is about 10 points lower than that of nonoffending individuals (Diamond, Morris, & Barnes, 2012; Herrnstein & Murray, 1994). For example, Salekin et al. (2010) characterized the intellectual disabilities of offenders as mild, with a typical IQ observed in between 55 and 70. Rather than a direct link between intellectual disabilities and criminal behavior (Holland, 1991), research indicates that a number of risk factors (e.g., income, family structure and support, and mental illness) that commonly co-occur with intellectual disabilities may drive criminal behavior (Crocker & Hodgins, 1997; Farrington, 2000; Lynam, Moffitt, & Stouthamer-Loeber, 1993). When these risk factors are not addressed, individuals with intellectual disabilities may be at greater-than-average risk for criminal behavior such as arson, violence, and sexual offending that may begin at an early age and persist across the life course (Barron, Hassiotis, & Banes, 2004). Indeed, more than one meta-analysis has found that the presence of an intellectual disability increases the risk of both delinquency and recidivism relative to the general population of juveniles (Cottle, Lee, & Heilbrun, 2001; Lipsey & Derzon, 1998). In light of this body of literature, additional research is necessary to disentangle the relationship between intellectual disabilities, comorbid psychopathology and health issues, and criminal behavior (Fogden, Thomas, Daffern, & Ogloff, 2016).

Although some individuals with intellectual disabilities who have engaged in criminal behavior may be shepherded into the social services system (Ali, Ghosh, Strydom, & Hassiotis, 2016), those who become entangled in the criminal justice system may have a difficult time functioning and advocating on behalf of themselves (Salekin et al., 2010). From the earliest point of contact with police, individuals with intellectual disabilities are at risk for difficulty understanding their legal rights and making informed legal decisions. In fact, depending on the nature and severity of the deficit and situational factors, individuals with intellectual disabilities may lack the competency to make these legal decisions (Salekin, Olley, & Hedge, 2010). Individuals with intellectual disabilities may acquiesce to those in a position of authority and are vulnerable to suggestibility and confabulation. This can directly result in false confessions and contribute to wrongful convictions (Ellis & Luckasson, 1985; Everington & Fulero, 1999; Leo & Drizin, 2004; Perske, 2000; 2005). Once convicted, the punishment is often harsher for individuals with intellectual disabilities than for those without such disabilities, simply because individuals with intellectual disabilities struggle to advocate on their own behalf from interrogation to sentencing, even to their own attorneys (Scheyett et al., 2009). Taken together, individuals with intellectual disabilities are at a distinct disadvantage when navigating both criminal investigations and trials.

After sentencing, the disadvantages in the criminal justice system persist for individuals with intellectual disabilities. The presence of intellectual disabilities makes completing basic activities such as filling out paperwork and comprehending rules difficult (McCarthy et al., 2015b). Further, prisoners with intellectual disabilities are vulnerable to bullying, exploitation, and victimization by other inmates, which can initiate new or exacerbate existing psychopathology such as depression and anxiety disorders (McCarthy et al., 2015b; Talbot, 2008). Such difficulties can increase the likelihood of behavioral infractions, which may lead to solitary confinement and extended sentences. The transition to community supervision after release may be just as difficult for offenders with intellectual disabilities (Bhandari, Dooren, Eastgate, Lennox, & Kinne, 2015). The combination of complicated and intensive supervision requirements and a lack of treatment and social support options decrease the likelihood of successful completion of community supervision. As a result, offenders with intellectual disabilities are prone to entering the "revolving door of prison" (Holland & Persson, 2011, p. 7).

To limit the possibility of intellectual disabilities having a deleterious impact on criminal justice outcomes, professionals in criminal justice and forensic mental health settings must be knowledgeable about the diagnosis of intellectual disabilities and their impact on antisocial behavior. The first step in this process requires better recognition, screening, and assessment of intellectual disabilities in these settings (McCarthy et al., 2015b). Assessment of intellectual abilities and adaptive functioning should include instruments that allow for comparisons to the general population rather than prison-based norms (Brodsky & Galloway, 2003; Tassé, 2009). Upon the identification of an intellectual disability, treatment and support services should be identified and allocated to address individual needs. Integral in this process is ensuring continuity of care when transitioning from incarceration to community supervision (Dias et al., 2013). Although therapeutic progress may be difficult to achieve for providers, offenders with intellectual disabilities can and do benefit from quality mental health and social services (Männynsalo, Putkonen, Lindberg, & Kotilainen, 2009).

Traumatic Brain Injury (TBI)

Traumatic brain injury (TBI) is another one of the more common conditions that confront professionals in criminal justice and forensic mental health settings (Schofield et al., 2006). This condition can be described as a change in brain function resulting from an external force (e.g., a blow or jolt to the head) (Menon, Schwab, Wright, & Maas, 2010). The severity of such an incident can vary from "mild," with short-term alterations in brain functioning, to "severe," with long-term consequences in brain functioning and personality. Not only is TBI commonly accompanied by decreased or lost consciousness (Menon et al., 2010) but also by a diverse set of physical (e.g., seizures and sleep-related troubles), cognitive (e.g., deficits in executive control, attention, and memory deficits) (Hawley, 2003; Merbitz, Jain, Good, & Jain, 1995), affective (e.g., emotional dysregulation and mood issues) (Andrews, Rose, & Johnson, 1998; Geraldina et al., 2003; Walker, Hiller, Staton, & Leukefeld, 2003), social (e.g., communication and social skill impairments) (Janusz, Kirkwood, Yeates, & Taylor, 2002), adaptive (e.g., time management, problem-solving, and decision-making issues), and behavioral (e.g., impulsivity) (Bennett & Raymond, 2008; Leon-Carrion & Ramos, 2003; Miller & Donders, 2001) symptoms (Fishbein, Dariotis, Ferguson, & Pickelsimer, 2016; O'Sullivan et al., 2015). Further, the presence of a TBI often co-occurs with substance use issues (Felde, Westermeyer, & Thuras, 2009; Fishbein et al., 2016), and this comorbidity may be more pronounced in criminal justice populations (Walker et al., 2003). As such, TBI may increase the likelihood of involvement in the criminal justice system and complicate participation in the various stages of the criminal justice system (Schofield et al., 2006). In an effort to increase awareness of TBI in criminal justice and forensic mental health professionals, this section discusses the prevalence of TBI, the links between TBI and criminal behavior, and the impact of TBI in the criminal justice system.

TBI is not only the most common type of acquired brain injury (Fleminger & Ponsford, 2005) but also a large-scale public health issue in the United States and across the world (McCrea, 2008). For example, Langlois, Kraus, Zaloshnja, and Miller (2011) estimate that approximately 1.7 million Americans suffer from a TBI each year. Bruns and Hauser (2003) estimate the U.S. annual incidence of TBI is somewhere between 180 and 250 per 100,000. Others estimate the prevalence of TBI as high as 8.5% (Silver, Kramer, Greenwald, & Weissman, 2001). The societal cost of TBI is stunning, with some estimating that TBI leads to over 1 million hospital visits and approximately 50,000 deaths in the U.S. each year (Faul, Xu, Wald, & Coronado, 2010). When shifting focus to criminal justice and forensic mental health settings, these prevalence estimates dramatically escalate for both adolescents and adults (Leon-Carrion & Ramos, 2003; Piccolino & Solberg, 2014; Vaughn, Salas-Wright, DeLisi, & Perron, 2014). TBI has an estimated prevalence of 30% in adolescent offenders (Farrer, Frost, & Hedges, 2013) and 60% in adult offenders (Farrer & Hedges, 2011). This is consistent with a meta-analysis (Shiroma, Ferguson, & Pickelsimer, 2010) that reported prevalence rates of TBI at 64% in male and 70% in female adult offenders. In serious offenders, TBI may be particularly common. For example, Lewis and colleagues (1988) found that each death row inmate in their sample had at least one incident of TBI.

Although the elevated presence of TBI is well established in offenders across developmental groups, it remains difficult to disentangle its relationship to criminal behavior. That being said, research clearly establishes that TBI incidents in childhood and adolescence are associated with higher rates of delinquent behavior (Kelgord, 1968; Williams et al., 2010). Further, a history of TBI increases the likelihood of aggression (Rao et al., 2009; Visscher, van Meijel, Stolker, Wiersma, & Nijman, 2011), including incidents of domestic violence (Cohen, Rosenbaum, Kane, Warnken, & Benjamin, 1999) and other acts of violence (Brewer-Smyth, 2004; Fazel, Lichtenstein, Grann, & Långström, 2011). Memory deficits and uninhibited and impulsive behavior associated with some TBIs may contribute to such behaviors. Not only do these cognitive, personality, and behavioral predispositions increase the likelihood of offending behaviors, but these traits also make it more difficult for offenders with TBI to follow the rules in custodial settings and on community supervision (Merbitz et al., 1995; Shiroma et al., 2010). As such, individuals with TBIs may be more likely to receive disciplinary sanctions in custodial settings than individuals without TBIs (Justice, Young, & Erdberg, 2003; Walker et al., 2003) and recidivate after release into the community (Williams et al., 2010).

Although TBI may play a role in some antisocial behaviors, many of the characteristics (e.g., impulsivity) that increase the likelihood of antisocial behavior also place individuals at risk for TBIs (Miller, 1999). In other words, the same individual differences may result in both TBIs and antisocial behavior. For example, delinquent children and adolescents may suffer TBIs during the commission of antisocial behavior like fighting (Hux, Bond, Skinner, Belau, & Sanger, 1998). In many cases, TBI should not be considered the source of antisocial behavior but instead a complicating factor. These views are consistent with research that found impulsive and aggressive behaviors both result in and are caused by TBI (Dooley, Anderson, Hemphill, & Ohan, 2008). In light of these findings, the relationship between TBI and offending likely varies by individual.

Regardless of the causal sequence in the relationship between offending and TBI, there is an overwhelming presence of offenders with TBI in criminal justice and forensic mental health settings. This is problematic because impairments resultant from TBI can complicate legal processes and correctional supervision. For example, TBI-related impairments may negatively affect an individual's ability to make legal decisions (e.g., confess, waive the right to an attorney, and enter a plea) and to understand court proceedings and assist his or her attorney. Accordingly, referral for evaluation of competency to stand trial should be considered when functional deficits are apparent. Offenders with TBI may also present challenges in custodial (e.g., jail and prison) and community supervision settings (e.g., probation and parole). For example, poor communication skills and attention deficits could lead corrections staff members to misinterpret the behavior of an offender as uncooperative

(Schofield et al., 2006). Alternatively, offenders with TBI may have difficulty remembering and complying with rules (Merbitz et al., 1995). Finally, affective dysregulation may contribute to conflict with other prisoners and staff. In light of these complications, efforts must be made to expand awareness of TBI and its potential impacts in criminal justice settings (Leon-Carrion & Ramos, 2003).

Criminal justice and forensic mental health professionals can play integral roles in improving outcomes for offenders with TBI (Piccolino & Solberg, 2014). First, identifying offenders who may have TBI and referring them for screening and assessment is the necessary first step, although the screening and assessment will not be easy (Colantonio, Stamenova, Abramowitz, Clarke, & Christensen, 2007). The short- and long-term memory deficits that characterize TBI make reliance on self-reported information problematic. To combat this weakness, assessments should incorporate information from collateral sources like the offender's file, family, and friends. Once complete, information gained from assessments is integral in individualizing the treatment plan and interventions for offenders with TBI (Vaughn et al., 2014). In particular, treatment will likely need to address memory loss, attention deficits, affective dysregulation, and disinhibition (Williams et al., 2010). When executed with fidelity, these assessment and treatment services have the potential to improve the likelihood of successful reentry (Leon-Carrion & Ramos, 2003; Williams et al., 2010). If ignored, TBI will continue to have a negative financial impact on the criminal justice and forensic mental health systems (Piccolino & Solberg, 2014).

DEAR and BASE Models

For these reasons, it is important for professionals to be able to call upon a number of different possible models to assist them in working with special needs offenders who present with an array of cognitive, intellectual, and learning challenges. In the next section, we discuss two of those models, the DEAR model and the BASE model, as these two are rooted in approaches shown to produce positive outcomes for these populations.

DEAR Model

The DEAR model is primarily focused on improving communication and intervention approaches. This model may be beneficial in guiding the interactions of criminal justice and forensic mental health professionals with offenders who experience learning, cognitive, and intellectual disabilities. Brown et al. (2014) initially developed this model for use with individuals impacted by FASD based on (a) many years of professional experience and (b) insights gleamed from interviews with numerous caregivers and professionals with advanced knowledge of individuals impacted by various cognitive, intellectual, and learning challenges. Since its inception, the DEAR model has been modified for use with offenders who may have other special needs. Helpful reminders and suggestions from this model may improve outcomes for special needs offenders and are outlined here.

Direct Language

The use of direct language is highly recommended when working with offenders suffering from learning, cognitive, and intellectual disabilities. This is because many of these disorders are characterized by communication issues such as language comprehension and generation deficits. To limit the potential impact of miscommunications, criminal justice and forensic mental health professionals should rely on simple and concrete language and avoid using sarcasm, colloquialisms, and idioms. When asking questions, it is advisable to utilize open-ended questions instead of closed-ended or leading questions (Brown, Haun, Novick Brown, & Zapf, 2016; Dale & Inglis, 2014; Klin & Volkmar, 2000; Whitehouse, Tudway, Look, & Kroese, 2006). This is noteworthy because offenders with special needs may be prone to memory deficits, suggestibility, and confabulation (Mendez & Fras, 2011), all of which can be exacerbated by repetitive and leading questions. In light of these difficulties, verification of any statement from witnesses and other forms of collateral information is imperative to ensure accuracy. Furthermore, criminal justice and forensic mental health professionals should be prepared to receive parroted responses, "I don't know" responses, and responses characterized by "filler" and unusual patterns of speech as the offender tries to process and accurately respond to a question. Throughout any interaction, the conversation should be slow in pace and avoid complications, while the professional consistently verifies the offender's comprehension of the conversation (Close & Walker, 2010).

Engage Support Systems

The engagement of support systems for offenders with special needs suffering from learning, cognitive, and intellectual disorders is integral. These offenders often struggle with problem solving and decision making. As such, these complicated processes often require assistance and guidance from family members, peers, and other members of their social support system (Jones, 2007). To this end, criminal justice and forensic mental health professionals should inquire about the offender's support system (e.g., family members, peers, mentors, and social workers) and verify the presence of adequate legal representation during initial interactions. If the offender is willing to sign a release of information for these individuals, the professional may consider including members of an offender's support system in appointments whenever possible. Even when not present, professionals should seriously consider any concerns that members of the support system have about the treatment of the offender. Further, it may be advisable to meet separately with members of the support system to ensure all concerns are voiced openly and honestly. Throughout this process, professionals may need to ensure that support system members understand the symptomatology of the offender's disorder(s), along with the best ways to maximize the effectiveness of any ongoing interventions (Lamb & Weinberger, 1998).

Accommodate Needs

Criminal justice and forensic mental health professionals must be prepared to accommodate the needs of special needs offenders with learning, cognitive, and intellectual disorders (Browning & Caulfield, 2011; Hayes, 2007, Lamb & Weinberger, 1998). This includes limiting the impact of tendencies toward impulsivity, inattentiveness, and intimidation (Jones, 2007). To this end, ensuring that interview and treatment sessions are an appropriate length for the offender and the removal of distractions are key steps in improving interactions. For example, meetings should take place in quiet rooms with shades drawn. Further, the provision of materials such as fidgets or drawing materials may be useful in easing the nerves of offenders. Professionals should avoid making any physical contact, even something as harmless as a light tap on the shoulder, because special needs offenders can be easily intimidated (Smith & O'Brien, 2004). Throughout this process, criminal justice and forensic mental health professionals should engage an offender's caregivers and support system to help tailor the process to the offender's strengths and needs (Lamb, Weinberger, & Gross, 1999).

Remain Patient

Remaining patient is an important skill for criminal justice and forensic mental health professionals when dealing with offenders with special needs. The varied cognitive, social, and adaptive functioning symptoms of these disorders often render the performance of afflicted offenders as inconsistent. This can complicate and delay the assessment and treatment of these individuals. As mentioned earlier, interpersonal interactions characterized by calmness is an important step in avoiding overwhelming and stressing an offender (Jones, 2007). If interactions become disrupted by threatening, abusive, and otherwise negative language, professionals must remember that these volatile outbursts may simply be driven by the offender's disorder. When developing treatment plans, professionals should ensure the offender's environment and social support enable the intervention.

BASE Model

The primary author of this chapter developed the BASE model. The model is the culmination of (a) his many years of clinical experience and (b) interviews with several caregivers and criminal justice, forensic, and other professionals. Although not exhaustive, this model assists criminal justice and forensic professionals in better understanding the diverse and varied symptomatology of some cognitive, intellectual, and neurobehavioral disorders. Specifically, the model collects tips and reminders that can help augment the supervision, screening and assessment, and treatment of offenders with special needs. It is important to note this is not a one-size-fits-all approach. Instead, the supervision and therapeutic approach must be individualized to the unique risks and needs of each special needs offender, which is where the strength of the BASE model lies.

Offenders with special needs often present with a complicated web of comorbid psychiatric symptoms. This may be even more pronounced among offender populations, a group that typically has a long history of trauma exposure, inaccurate diagnoses, and sometimes inappropriate treatment. To this end, the first author developed the BASE model as a guide designed to help criminal justice and forensic mental health professionals better understand and remember the diverse set of potential symptoms found in some special needs offender populations. Although the BASE model is not exhaustive in scope, the potential utility in this approach lies in helping improve assessment and individualize treatment to the offender rather than a one-size-fits-all approach. This point is particularly salient because each special needs offender has his or her own unique set of symptoms and needs with complicating factors. In this section, we discuss each aspect of the BASE model to improve the recognition (i.e., screening and assessment) and treatment of offenders through increased familiarity with these psychiatric symptoms.

Behavioral/Emotional

Behavioral and emotional symptoms are common among special needs offenders. Perhaps foremost among these symptoms are emotional dysregulation and deficits. This can range from mood swings and extreme emotional episodes (e.g., poor anger management) to an absence of emotions (e.g., fearlessness in dangerous situations). Impulsive and compulsive tendencies also are observed in these disorders. Not only can these tendencies result in self-harm like repeatedly punching, biting, or cutting oneself, but also potentially noncriminal and criminal actions, such as illogical acts of lying or petty theft. Other behavioral manifestations are consistent with attention-deficit/hyperactivity disorder (ADHD), which may include inattentiveness, unusual activity levels, and fidgeting. In combination, these symptoms can make working with special needs offenders somewhat challenging for criminal justice and forensic mental health professionals.

Adaptive

Limitations in adaptive functioning are also common in special needs offenders. Adaptive functioning can be conceptualized as an individual's capacity to employ cognitive (e.g., executive control and memory) and social skills (e.g., communication) to address problems and challenges that arise in everyday situations. Unfortunately, offenders with such impairments often lack the capacity to fulfill these social responsibilities. These limitations affect an individual's daily living skills, threatening their personal independence. In fact, some of these individuals may need to reside with relatives or in assisted living facilities throughout their lifespan. Further, adaptive functioning deficits usually result in low educational attainment and poor occupational functioning. As such, obtaining and keeping adequate employment may be particularly challenging. In light of the varied and pervasive impacts of adaptive functioning deficits across multiple domains, criminal justice and forensic mental health professionals are advised to respond with patience and adjust expectations of offenders with such afflictions.

Social

Social deficits are often present in offenders with special needs. As such, criminal justice and forensic mental health professionals should take time to inquire about an offender's social competency, as many with these disorders behave in a manner characteristic of someone of a much younger chronological age. A key indicator of social deficits is the presence of inappropriate social and sexual behaviors and attention-seeking in person and on social media. Further, offenders with these disorders may be particularly vulnerable to manipulation and suggestion by both friends and strangers, which requires careful consideration in light of the severity and long-ranging impacts of decisions in the criminal justice system. Along these lines, criminal justice and forensic mental health professionals should investigate an offender's interactions with friends. Important points of focus may include naiveté, the presence or lack of close friends, inability to forge friendships, and susceptibility to peer pressure. Forensic mental health professionals must be wary of the influence of others on offenders with these disorders and seek collateral information to corroborate any information elicited from the offender.

Executive Functioning

Finally, yet importantly, executive functioning limitations are common among offenders with special needs. Executive functioning is characterized by executive control, short- and long-term memory, impulse control, and attention span. Limitations in executive functioning can result in the inability to make sound decisions and solve problems. Further, executive functioning deficits can make it difficult to anticipate, plan, and execute the steps necessary to set forth a successful course of action. As such, goal-directed behavior is often a struggle for special needs offenders. Another area limited by executive functioning deficits is reflection, which results in many offenders with these disorders being unable to understand the link between their actions and the resulting consequences. Recognition of these limitations in executive functioning is a first step for criminal justice and forensic mental health professionals to intervene on behalf of offenders with special needs.

Conclusion

In this chapter, we have provided information for criminal justice and forensic mental health professionals about various offender-based special needs populations through an overview of commonly observed disorders involved in the criminal justice system, including attention-deficit/hyperactivity disorder (ADHD), autism spectrum disorder (ASD), fetal alcohol spectrum disorder (FASD), intellectual disability (ID), and traumatic brain injury (TBI). We have discussed the challenges associated with each of these disorders for both the criminal justice and the forensic mental health system. In this discussion, we have also reviewed considerations for screening and intervention and suggested communication techniques and approaches. Each of the disorders discussed in this chapter presents a host of challenges for criminal justice and mental health professionals. While some of the challenges are similar, each disorder is characterized by its own unique difficulties, to which professionals must be sensitive during screening and intervention processes. In addition, it behooves system professionals to create and implement additional and responsive screening tools and intervention techniques, in order to have the most successful possible outcomes while working with these special needs offenders. We suggest some possible approaches, including the DEAR and BASE models, but also challenge researchers to continue to explore additional opportunities for successful interaction and intervention with special needs offenders.

References

Alexander, R. T., Chester, V., Green, F. N., Gunaratna, I., & Hoare, S. (2015). Arson or fire setting in offenders with intellectual disability: Clinical characteristics, forensic histories, and treatment outcomes. *Journal of Intellectual and Developmental Disability, 40*(2), 189–197. doi:10.3109/13668250.2014.998182

Ali, A., Ghosh, S., Strydom, A., & Hassiotis, A. (2016). Prisoners with intellectual disabilities and detention status. Findings from a UK cross sectional study of prisons. *Research in Developmental Disabilities, 53*, 189–197. doi:10.1016/j.ridd.2016.02.004

Allen, D., Evans, C., Hider, A., Hawkins, S., Peckett, H., & Morgan, H. (2008). Offending behavior in adults with Asperger's syndrome. *Journal of Autism and Developmental Disorders, 38*(4), 748–758. doi:10.1007/s10803-007-0442-9

Alloway, T. P., Gathercole, S. E., Kirkwood, H., & Elliott, J. (2009). The cognitive and behavioral characteristics of children with low working memory. *Child Development, 80*(2), 606–621. doi:0.1111/j.1467-8624.2009.01282.x

American Psychiatric Association. (2013). *Diagnostic and statistical manual of mental disorders* (5th ed.). Arlington, VA: American Psychiatric Publishing.

Andrews, D. A., & Bonta, J. (2010). *The psychology of criminal conduct* (5th ed.). New Providence, NJ: Lexis Nexis.

Andrews, T. K., Rose, F. D., & Johnson, D. A. (1998). Social and behavioural effects of traumatic brain injury in children. *Brain Injury, 12*(2), 133–138. doi:10.1080/026990598122755

Babinski, L. M., Hartsough, C. S., & Lambert, N. M. (1999). Childhood conduct problems, hyperactivity-impulsivity, and inattention as predictors of adult criminal activity. *Journal of Child Psychology and Psychiatry, 40*(3), 347–355. doi:10.1111/1469-7610.00452

Barkley, R. A. (2006). *Attention-deficit hyperactivity disorder: A handbook for diagnosis and treatment* (3rd ed.). New York, NY: Guilford Press.

Barkley, R. A., Guevremont, D. C., Anastopoulos, A. D., DuPaul, G. J., & Shelton, T. L. (1993). Driving-related risks and outcomes of attention-deficit hyperactivity disorder in adolescents and young adults: A 3- to 5-year follow-up survey. *Pediatrics, 92*(2), 212–218.

Baron-Cohen, S. (1988). An assessment of violence in a young man with Asperger's syndrome. *Journal of Child Psychology and Psychiatry, 29*(3), 351–360. doi:10.1111/j.1469-7610.1988.tb00723.x

Barron, P., Hassiotis, A., & Banes, J. (2004) Offenders with intellectual disability: A prospective comparative study. *Journal of Intellectual Disability Research, 48*(1), 69–76. doi:10.1111/j.1365-2788.2004.00581.x

Barry-Walsh, J. B., & Mullen, P. E. (2004). Forensic aspects of Asperger's syndrome. *Journal of Forensic Psychiatry & Psychology, 15*(1), 96–107. doi:10.1080/14789940310001638628

Belcher, J. R. (2014). Attention deficit hyperactivity disorder in offenders and the need for early intervention. *International Journal of Offender Therapy and Comparative Criminology, 58*(1), 27–40. doi:10.1177/0306624X12465583

Bennett, T. L., & Raymond, M. J. (2008). The neuropsychology of traumatic brain injury. In A. M. Horton, Jr., & D. Wedding (Eds.), *The neuropsychology handbook* (pp. 535–572). New York, NY: Springer.

Bhandari, A., Dooren, K., Eastgate, G., Lennox, N., & Kinner, S. A. (2015). Comparison of social circumstances, substance use, and substance-related harm in soon-to-be released prisoners with and without intellectual disability. *Journal of Intellectual Disability Research, 59*(6), 571–579. doi:10.1111/jir.12162

Bhatara, V., Loudenberg, R., & Ellis, R. (2006). Association of attention deficit hyperactivity disorder and gestational alcohol exposure: an exploratory study. *Journal of Attention Disorders, 9*(3), 515–522. doi:10.1177/1087054705283880

Biederman, J., Faraone, S.V., Spencer, T. J., Mick, E., Monuteaux, M. C., & Aleardi, M. (2006). Functional impairments in adults with self-report of diagnosed ADHD: A controlled study of 1001 adults in the community. *Journal of Clinical Psychiatry, 67*(4), 524–540.

Bjørkly, S. (2009). Risk and dynamics of violence in Asperger's syndrome: A systematic review of the literature. *Aggression and Violent Behavior, 14*(5), 306–312. doi:10.1016/j.avb.2009.04.003

Boland, J., Burrill, R., Duwyn, M., & Karp, J. (1998). *Fetal alcohol syndrome: Implications for correctional service*. Ottawa: Correctional Services of Canada, Research Branch Corporate Development.

Boland, F. J., Chudley, A. E., & Grant, B. A. (2002). The challenge of fetal alcohol syndrome in adult offender populations. *Forum on Corrections Research, 14*(3). Retrieved from www.csc-scc.gc.ca/research/forum/e143/143s_e.pdf

Bowker, A. (1994). Handle with care: Dealing with offenders who are mentally retarded. *FBI Law Enforcement Bulletin, 63*(7), 12–16.

Brewer-Smyth, K. (2004). Women behind bars: Could neurobiological correlates of past physical and sexual abuse contribute to criminal behavior? *Health Care for Women International, 25*(9), 835–852. doi:10.1080/07399330490517118

Brintnell, S. E., Bailey, P. G., Sawhney, A., & Kreftin, L. (2011). Understanding FASD: Disability and social supports for adult offenders (pp. 233–257). In E. P. Riley, S. Clarren, J. Weinberg, & E. Jonsson (Eds.), *Fetal alcohol spectrum disorder: Management and policy perspectives of FASD*. Germany: Wiley-Blackwell.

Brodsky, S. L., & Galloway, V.A. (2003) Ethical and professional demands for forensic mental health professionals in the post-Atkins era. *Ethics and Behavior, 13*(1), 3–9. doi:10.1207/S15327019EB1201_02

Brown, J., Haun, J., Novick Brown, N., & Zapf, P. (2016). Deleterious effects of fetal alcohol spectrum disorder on competency to stand trial. *The Journal of Special Populations, 1*(1), 1–7.

Brown, J., Oberoi, P., Long-McGie, J., Wartnik, A., Weinkauf, E., & Herrick, S. (2014). Fetal Alcohol Spectrum Disorders (FASD) and confabulation: A review for criminal justice. *Fetal Alcohol Forum, 11*, 40–44.

Brown, J., & Singh, J. (2015, January 7). Fetal Alcohol Spectrum Disorder (FASD): Screening needed in North American criminal justice settings. [E-letter]. *Pediatrics*. Retrieved from http://pediatrics.aappublications.org/content/135/1/e52/reply#pediatrics_el_69147

Brown, N. N., Wartnik, A. P., Connor, P. D., & Adler, R. S. (2010). A proposed model standard for forensic assessment of fetal alcohol spectrum disorders. *The Journal of Psychiatry and Law, 38*(4), 383–418. doi:10.1177/009318531003800403

Browning, A., & Caulfield, L. (2011). The prevalence and treatment of people with Asperger's syndrome in the criminal justice system. *Criminology & Criminal Justice, 11*(2), 165–180. doi:10.1177/1748895811398455

Bruns, J., & Hauser, W. A. (2003). The epidemiology of traumatic brain injury: A review. *Epilepsia, 44*(10), 2–10. doi:10.1046/j.1528-1157.44.s10.3.x

Buitelaar, N. J., & Ferdinand, R. F. (2016). ADHD undetected in criminal adults. *Journal of Attention Disorder, 20*(3), 270–278. doi:10.11177/1087054712466916

Burd, L., Fast, D., & Conry, J. (2010). Fetal alcohol spectrum disorder as a marker for increased risk of involvement with correction systems. *Journal of Psychiatry & Law, 38*(4), 559–584. doi:10.1177/009318531003800408

Burd, L., Martsolf, J. T., & Juelson, T. (2004). Fetal alcohol spectrum disorder in the corrections system: Potential screening strategies. *Journal of FAS International, 2*(1), 1–10.

Burns, K. A. (2009). The top ten reasons to limit prescription of controlled substances in prisons. *Journal of the Academy of Psychiatry and the Law, 37*(1), 50–52.

Cashin, A., & Newman, C. (2009). Autism in the criminal justice detention system: A review of the literature. *Journal Forensic Nurses, 5*(2), 70–75. doi:10.1111/j.1939-3938.2009.01037.x

Centers for Disease Control and Prevention (CDC). (2014). *Facts about ASD*. Washington, DC: Centers for Disease Control and Prevention.

Centers for Disease Control and Prevention. (2015). *Facts about ASD*. Washington, DC: Centers for Disease Control and Prevention.

Chartrand, L. N., & Forbes-Chilibeck, E. M. (2003). The sentencing of offenders with fetal alcohol syndrome. *Health Law Journal, 11*, 35–70.

Chen, P. S., Chen, S. J., Yang, Y. K., Yeh, T. L., Chen, C. C., & Lo, H.Y. (2003). Asperger's disorder: A case report of repeated stealing and the collecting behaviours of an adolescent patient. *Acta Psychiatrica Scandinavica, 107*(1), 73–76. doi:10.1034/j.1600-0447.2003.01354.x

Chudley, A. E., Conry, J., Cook, J. L., Loock, C., Rosales, T., & LeBlanc, N. (2005). Fetal alcohol spectrum disorder: Canadian guidelines for diagnosis. *The Canadian Medical Association Journal, 172*(5), 1–21. doi:10.1503/cmaj.1040302

Close, D. W., & Walker, H. M. (2010). Navigating the criminal justice system for youth and adults with developmental disabilities: Role of the forensic special educator. *The Journal of Behavior Analysis of Offender and Victim Treatment and Prevention, 2*(2), 74–103.

Cohen, R. A., Rosenbaum, A., Kane, R. L., Warnken, W. J., & Benjamin, S. (1999). Neuropsychological correlates of domestic violence. *Violence and Victims, 14*(4), 397–411.

Colantonio, A., Stamenova, V., Abramowitz, C., Clarke, D., & Christensen, B. (2007). Brain injury in a forensic psychiatry population. *Brain Injury, 21*(13–14), 1353–1360. doi:10.1080/02699050701785054

Cottle, C. C., Lee, R. J., & Heilbrun, K. (2001). The prediction of criminal recidivism in juveniles a meta-analysis. *Criminal Justice and Behavior, 28*(3), 367–394. doi:10.1177/0093854801028003005

Cox, L.V., Clairmont, D., & Cox, S. (2008). Knowledge and attitudes of criminal justice professionals in relation to fetal alcohol spectrum disorder. *Canadian Journal of Clinical Pharmacology, 15*(2), 306–313.

Crocker, A. G., & Hodgins, S. (1997). The criminality of noninstitutionalized mentally retarded persons: Evidence from a birth cohort followed to age 30. *Criminal Justice and Behavior, 24*(4), 432–454. doi:10.1177/0093854897024004003

Crocker, A. G., Mercier, C., Allaire, J. F., & Roy, M. E. (2007). Profiles and correlates of aggressive behaviour among adults with intellectual disabilities. *Journal of Intellectual Disabilities, 51*(10), 786–801. doi:10.1111/j.1365-2788.2007.00953.x

Crowley, T. J., Mikulich, S. K., MacDonald, M., Young, S. E., & Zerbe, G. O. (1998). Substance-dependent, conduct-disordered adolescent males: Severity of diagnosis predicts 2-year outcome. *Drug and Alcohol Dependence, 49*(3), 225–237. doi:10.1016/S0376-8716(98)00016-7

Daderman, A. M., Lindgren, M., & Lidberg, L. (2004). The prevalence of AD/HD in a sample of forensic rapists. *Nordic Journal of Psychiatry, 58*(5), 371–381. doi:10.1080/08039480410005936

Dale, C., & Inglis, P. (2014). Caring for vulnerable people: Intellectual disability in the criminal justice system (89–108). In A. Norman & L. Walsh, E. (Eds.), *Nursing in criminal justice services*. Keswick, CA: M&K Publishing.

Dalsgaard, S., Mortensen, P. B., Frydenberg, M., & Thomsen, P. H. (2013). Long-term criminal outcome of children with attention deficit hyperactivity disorder. *Criminal Behaviour and Mental Health, 23*(2), 86–98. doi:10.1002/cbm.1860

Davis, L. A. (2006). *The Arc's justice advocacy guide: An advocate's guide on addicting victims and suspects/defendants with intellectual disabilities*. Silver Spring, MD: The Arc of the United States.

Davis, L. A. (2009). *People with intellectual disabilities in the criminal justice systems: Victims & suspects*. Silver Spring, MD: The Arc of the United States.

Denkowski, G. C., & Denkowski, K. M. (1985). The mentally retarded offender in the state prison system: identification, prevalence, adjustment, and rehabilitation. *Criminal Justice and Behavior, 12*, 55–70. doi:10.1177/0093854885012001005

Diamond, B., Morris, R. G., & Barnes, J. C. (2012). Individual and group IQ predict inmate violence. *Intelligence, 40*(2), 155–122. doi:10.1016/j.intell.2012.01.010

Dias, S., Ware, R., Kinner, S., & Lennox, N. (2013). Co-occurring mental disorder and intellectual disability in a large sample of Australian prisoners. *Australian and New Zealand Journal of Psychiatry, 47*(10), 938–944. doi:10.1177/0004867413492220

Dooley, J. J., Anderson, V., Hemphill, S. A., & Ohan, J. (2008). Aggression after pediatric traumatic brain injury: A theoretical approach. *Brain Injury, 22*(11), 836–846. doi:10.1080/02699050802425444

Einarsson, E., Sigurdsson, J. F., Gudjonsson, G. H., Newton, A. K., & Bragason, O. O. (2009). Screening for attention-deficit hyper-activity disorder and co-morbid mental disorders among prison inmates. *Nordic Journal of Psychiatry, 63*(5), 361–367. doi:10.1080/08039480902759184

Eisenberg, N., Hofer, C., & Vaughn, J. (2007). Effortful control and its socio-emotional consequences. In J. J. Gross (Ed.), *Handbook of emotional regulation* (pp. 287–306). New York, NY: Guilford.

Ellis, J. W., & Luckasson, R. A. (1985). Mentally retarded criminal defendants. *George Washington Law Review, 53*, 414–493.

Emerson, E. (2003). Prevalence of psychiatric disorders in children and adolescents with and without intellectual disability. *Journal of Intellectual Disability Research, 47*(1), 51–58. doi:10.1046/j.1365–2788.2003.00464.x

Everington, C., & Fulero, S. M. (1999). Competence to confess: Measuring understanding and suggestibility of defendants with mental retardation. *Mental Retardation, 37*(3), 212–220. doi:10.1352/0047–6765 (1999)037<0212:CTCMUA>2.0.CO;2

Farrer, T. J., Frost, R. B., & Hedges, D. W. (2013). Prevalence of traumatic brain injury in juvenile offenders: A meta-analysis. *Child Neuropsychology, 19*(3), 225–234. doi:1080/09297049.2011.647901

Farrer, T. J., & Hedges, D. W. (2011). Prevalence of traumatic brain injury in incarcerated groups compared to the general population: A meta-analysis. *Progress in Neuro-Psychopharmacology and Biological Psychiatry, 35*(2), 390–394. doi:10.1016/j.pnpbp.2011.01.007

Farrington, D. P. (2000). Psychosocial causes of offending. In M. G. Gelder, J. J. Lopez-Ibor, & N. Andreasen (Eds.), *New Oxford textbook of psychiatry* (2nd ed., pp. 2029–2036). Oxford: Oxford University Press.

Fast, D. K., & Conry, J. (2009). Fetal alcohol spectrum disorders and the criminal justice system. *Developmental Disabilities Research Review, 15*(3), 250–257. doi:10.1002/ddrr.66

Fast, D. K., Conry, J., & Loock, C. (1999). Identifying fetal alcohol syndrome among youth in the criminal justice system. *Journal of Developmental and Behavioral Pediatrics, 20*(5), 370–372.

Faul, M., Xu, L., Wald, M. M., & Coronado, V. G. (2010). *Traumatic brain injury in the United States: Emergency department visits, hospitalizations and deaths 2002–2006*. Atlanta, GA: Centers for Disease Control and Prevention, National Center for Injury Prevention and Control.

Fazel, S., Lichtenstein, P., Grann, M., & Långström, N. (2011). Risk of violent crime in individuals with epilepsy and traumatic brain injury: A 35-year Swedish population study. *PLoS Medicine, 8*(12), e1001150.

Fazel, S., Xenitidis, K., & Powell, J. (2008). The prevalence of intellectual disabilities among 12000 prisoners: a systematic review. *International Journal of Law & Psychiatry, 31*(4), 369–373. doi:10.1016/j.ijlp.2008.06.001

Felde, A. B., Westermeyer, J., & Thuras, P. (2009). Co-morbid traumatic brain injury and substance use disorder: Childhood predictors and adult correlates. *Brain Injury, 20*(1), 41–49. doi:10.1080/02699050500309718

Fishbein, D., Dariotis, J. K., Ferguson, P. L., & Pickelsimer, E. E. (2016). Relationships between traumatic brain injury and illicit drug use and their association with aggression in inmates. *International Journal of Offender Therapy and Comparative Criminology, 60*(5), 575–597. doi:10.1177/0306624X14554778

Fleminger, S., & Ponsford, J. (2005) Long-term outcome after traumatic brain injury. *British Medical Journal, 17*(331), 1419–1420. doi:10.11136/bmj.331.7530.1419

Fletcher, J., & Wolfe, B. (2009). Long-term consequences of childhood ADHD on criminal activities. *Journal of Mental Health Policy and Economics, 12*(3), 119–138.

Fogden, B. C., Thomas, S. D., Daffern, M., & Ogloff, J. R. (2016). Crime and victimisation in people with intellectual disability: a case linkage study. *BMC Psychiatry, 16*(1), 170. doi:10.1186/s12888-016-0869-7

Freckelton, I. (2012). Expert evidence by mental health professionals: The communication challenge posed by evidence about autism spectrum disorder, brain injuries, and Huntington's disease. *International Journal of Law and Psychiatry, 35*(5–6), 372–379. doi:10.1016/j.ijlp.2012.09.008

Freckelton, I. (2013). Autism spectrum disorder: Forensic issues and challenges for mental health professionals and courts. *Journal of Applied Research in Intellectual Disabilities, 26*(5), 420–434. doi:10.1111/jar.12036

Geraldina, P., Mariarosaria, L., Annarita, A., Susanna, G., Michela, S., Alessandro, D., . . . Enrico, C. (2003). Neuropsychiatric sequelae in TBI: A comparison across different age groups. *Brain Injury, 17*(10), 835–846. doi:10.1080/0269905031000088612

Ghaziuddin, M., Tsai, L., & Ghaziuddin, N. (1991). Brief report: Violence in Asperger syndrome, a critique. *Journal of Autism and Developmental Disorders, 21*(3), 349–354. doi:10.1007/BF02207331

Ginsberg, Y., Hirvikoski, T., & Lindefors, N. (2010). Attention deficit hyperactivity disorder (ADHD) among longer-term prison inmates is a prevalent, persistent, and disabling disorder. *BMC Psychiatry, 10*, 1–13. doi:10.1186/1471–244x-10–112

Glaser, W., & Deane, K. (1999) Normalisation in an abnormal world: A study of prisoners with an intellectual disability. *International Journal of Offender Therapy and Comparative Criminology, 43*(3), 338–356. doi:10.1177/0306624X99433007

Gómez de la Cuesta, G. (2010). A selective review of offending behavior in individuals with autism spectrum disorders. *Journal of Learning Disabilities and Offending Behavior, 1*(2), 47–58. doi:10.5042/jldob.2010.0419

Gordon, V., Williams, D. J., & Donnelly, P. D. (2012). Exploring the relationship between ADHD symptoms and prison breaches of discipline amongst youths in four Scottish prisons. *Public Health, 126*(4), 343–348. doi:10.1016/j.puhe.2012.01.004

Graham, H. (2014). *Fetal alcohol spectrum disorder and inappropriate sexual behavior* (Master's thesis). Laurentian University, Sudbury, Ontario, Canada.

Grieger, L., & Hosser, D. (2012). Attention deficit hyperactivity disorder does not predict criminal recidivism in young adult offenders: Results from a prospective study. *International Journal of Law and Psychiatry, 35*(1), 27–34. doi:10.1016/j.ijlp.2011.11.005

Harpin, V., & Young, S. (2012). The challenge of ADHD and youth offending. *Cutting Edge Psychiatry in Practice, 1*, 138–143.

Haskins, B. G., & Silva, J. A. (2006). Asperger's disorder and criminal behavior: Forensic-psychiatric considerations. *Journal of the American Academy of Psychiatry and the Law, 34*(3), 374–384.

Hawley, C. A. (2003). Reported problems and their resolution following mild, moderate, and severe traumatic brain injury amongst children and adolescents in the UK. *Brain Injury, 17*(2), 105–129. doi:10.1080/0269905021000010131

Hayes, S. (2007). Missing out: Offenders with learning disabilities and the criminal justice system. *British Journal of Learning Disabilities, 35*(3), 146–153. doi: 10.1111/j.1468-3156.2007.00465.x

Herrnstein, R. J., & Murray, C. (1994). *The bell curve: Intelligence and class structure in American life*. New York, NY: Free Press.

Hofvander, B., Ossowski, D., Lundström, S., & Anckarsäter, H. (2009). Continuity of aggressive antisocial behavior from childhood to adulthood: The question of phenotype definition. *International Journal of Law and Psychiatry, 32*(4), 224–234. doi:10.1016/j.ijlp.2009.04.004

Holland, A. J. (1991). Challenging and offending behaviour by adults with developmental disabilities. *Australia and New Zealand Journal of Developmental Disabilities, 17*(2), 119–126.

Holland, S., & Persson, P. (2011). Intellectual disability in the Victorian prison system: Characteristics of prisoners with an intellectual disability released from prison in 2003–2006. *Psychology, Crime & Law, 17*(1), 25–41. doi:10.1080/10683160903392285

Howlin, P. (2004). *Autism and Asperger syndrome: Preparing for adulthood* (2nd ed.). New York, NY: Routledge.

Hux, K., Bond, V., Skinner, S., Belau, D., & Sanger, D. (1998). Parental report of occurrences and consequences of traumatic brain injury among delinquent and non-delinquent youth. *Brain Injury, 12*(8), 667–681. doi:10.1080/026990598122232

Ivanov, L., Schulz, K. P., London, E. D., & Newcorn, J. H. (2008). Inhibitory control deficits in childhood and risk for substance use disorders: A review. *American Journal of Drug and Alcohol Abuse, 34*(3), 239–258. doi:10.1080/00952990802013334

Janusz, J. A., Kirkwood, M. W., Yeates, K. O., & Taylor, H. G. (2002). Social problem-solving skills in children with traumatic brain injury: Long-term outcomes and prediction of social competence. *Child Neuropsychology: A Journal on Normal and Abnormal Development in Childhood and Adolescence, 8*(3), 179–194. doi:10.1076/chin.8.3.179.13499

Jones, J. (2007). Persons with intellectual disabilities in the criminal justice system: Review of issues. *International Journal of Offender Therapy and Comparative Criminology, 51*(6), 723–733. doi:10.1177/0306624X07299343

Justice, J. V., Young, M. H., & Erdberg, P. (2003). Assault in prison and assault in prison psychiatric treatment. *Journal of Forensic Science, 49*(1), 1–9.

Katz, N., & Zemishlany, Z. (2006). Criminal responsibility in Asperger's syndrome. *Israel Journal of Psychiatry and Related Sciences, 43*(3), 166–173.

Kawakami, C., Ohnishi, M., Sugiyamac, T., Someki, F., Nakamurae, K., & Tsujiif, M. (2012). The risk factors for criminal behaviour in high-functioning autism spectrum disorders (HFASDs): A comparison of childhood adversities between individuals with HFASDs who exhibit criminal behaviour and those with HFASD and no criminal histories. *Research in Autism Spectrum Disorders, 6*(2), 949–957. doi:10.1016/j.rasd.2011.12.005

Kelgord, R. E. (1968). Brain damage and delinquency: A question and challenge. *Academic Therapy, 4*(2), 93–99.

Kessler, R. C., Adler, L., Barkley, R., Biederman, J., Conners, C. K., Demler, O., . . . Zaslavsky, A. M. (2006). The prevalence and correlates of adult ADHD in the United States: Results from the National Comorbidity Survey Replication. *American Journal of Psychiatry, 163*(4), 716–723. doi:10.1176/appi.ajp.163.4.716

Klin, A., & Volkmar, F. R. (2000). *Treatment and intervention guidelines for individuals with Asperger syndrome*. Pittsburgh, PA: Learning Disabilities Association of America. Retrieved from www.aspennj.org/pdf/information/articles/aspergers-syndrome-guidelines-for-assesment-and-intervention.pdf

Kristiansson, M., & Sorman, K. (2008). Autism spectrum disorders: Legal and forensic psychiatric aspects and reflections. *Clinical Neuropsychiatry: Journal of Treatment Evaluation, 5*(1), 55–61.

Lamb, H. R., & Weinberger, L. E. (1998). Persons with severe mental illness in jails and prisons: A review. *Psychiatric Services, 49*(4), 482–492.

Lamb, H. R., Weinberger, L. E., & Gross, B. H. (1999). Community treatment of severely mentally ill offenders under the jurisdiction of the criminal justice system: A review. *Psychiatric Services, 50*(7), 907–913. doi:10.1176/ps.50.7.907

Landa, R. (2000). Social language use in Asperger syndrome and high-functioning autism. In A. Kiln, F. V. Volkmar, & S. S. Sparrow (Eds.), *Asperger syndrome* (pp. 125–155). New York, NY: Guilford Press.

Langlois Orman, J. A., Kraus, J. F., Zaloshnja, E., & Miller, T. (2011). Epidemiology. In J. M. Silver, T. W. McAllister, & S. C. Yudofsky (Eds.), *Textbook of traumatic brain injury* (2nd ed.). London, England: American Psychiatric Publishing Inc.

Långström, N., Grann, M., Ruchkin, V., Sjöstedt, G., & Fazel, S. (2009). Risk factors for violent offending in autism spectrum disorder: A national study of hospitalized individuals. *Journal of Interpersonal Violence, 24*(8), 1358–1370. doi:10.1177/0886260508322195

Leo, R. A., & Drizin, S. A. (2004). The problem of false confessions in the post-DNA world. *North Carolina Law Review, 82*, 891–1004.

Leon-Carrion, J., & Ramos, F. J. C. (2003). Blows to the head during development can predispose to violent criminal behaviour: Rehabilitation of consequences of head injury is a measure for crime prevention. *Brain Injury, 17*(3), 207–216. doi:10.1080/0269905021000010249

Lewis, D. O., Pincus, J. H., Bard, B., Richardson, E., Prichep, L. S., Feldman, M., & Yeager, C. (1988). Neuropsychiatric, psychoeducational, and family characteristics of 14 juveniles condemned to death in the United States. *The American Journal of Psychiatry, 145*(5), 584–589. doi:10.1176/ajp.145.5.584

Lipsey, M. W., & Derzon, J. H. (1998). Predictors of violent or serious delinquency in adolescence and early adulthood: A synthesis of longitudinal research. In R. Loeber & D. P. Farrington (Eds.), *Serious and violent juvenile offenders: Risk factors and successful interventions* (pp. 86–105). Thousand Oaks, CA: Sage.

Lord, C. (1995). Follow-up of two-year-olds referred for possible autism. *Journal of Child Psychology and Psychiatry, 36*(8), 1365–1382. doi:10.1111/j.1469-7610.1995.tb01669.x
Lynam, D., Moffitt, T. E., & Stouthamer-Loeber, M. (1993). Explaining the relation between IQ and delinquency: Class, ethnicity, test motivation, school failure, or self-control. *Journal of Abnormal Psychology, 102*(2), 187–196.
MacEachron, A. E. (1979). Mentally retarded offenders: Prevalence and characteristics. *American Journal of Mental Deficiency, 84*, 165–76.
MacPherson, P., & Chudley, A. E. (2007). Fetal Alcohol Spectrum Disorder (FASD): Screening and estimating incidence in an adult correctional population. Presented at the 2nd International Conference on Fetal Alcohol Spectrum Disorder: Research, Policy, and Practice Around the World, Victoria, British Columbia.
Maggs, J. L., Patrick, M. E., & Feinstein, L. (2008). Childhood and adolescent predictors of alcohol use and problems in adolescence. *Addiction, 103*(1), 7–22. doi:10.1111/j.1360-0443.2008.02173.x
Malbin, D.V. (2004). Fetal alcohol spectrum disorder and the role of family court judges in improving outcomes for children and families. *Juvenile and Family Court Journal, 55*(2), 53–63. doi:10.1111/j.1755-6988.2004.tb00161.x
Männynsalo, L., Putkonen, H., Lindberg, N., & Kotilainen, I. (2009). Forensic psychiatric perspective on criminality associated with intellectual disability: A nationwide register-based study. *Journal of Intellectual Disability Research, 53*(3), 279–288. doi:10.1111/j.1365-2788.2008.01125.x
Maras, K., & Bowler, D. (2010). The cognitive interview for eyewitnesses with Autism spectrum disorder. *Journal Autism Developmental Disorders, 40*(11), 1350–1360. doi:10.1007/s10803-010-0997-8
Maulik, P. K., Mascarenhas, M. N., Mathers, C. D., Dua, T., & Saxena, S. (2011). Prevalence of intellectual disability: A meta-analysis of population-based studies. *Research in Developmental Disabilities, 32*(2), 419–436. doi:10.1016/j.ridd.2010.12.018
Mawson, D., Grounds, A., & Tantam, D. (1985). Violence and Asperger's syndrome: A case study. *British Journal of Psychiatry, 147*(5), 566–569. doi:10.1192/bjp.147.5.566
May, P. A., Baete, A., Russo, J., Elliott, A. J., Blankenship, J., Kalberg, W. O., . . . Hoyme, H. E. (2014). Prevalence and characteristics of fetal alcohol spectrum disorders. *Pediatrics, 134*(5), 855–866. doi:10.1542/peds.2013–3319
May, P. A., Gossage, J. P., Kalberg, W. O., Robinson, L. K., Buckley, D., Manning, M., & Hoyme, H. E. (2009). Prevalence and epidemiologic characteristics of FASD from various research methods with an emphasis on recent in-school studies. *Developmental Disabilities Research Review, 15*(3), 176–192. doi:10.1002/ddrr.68
Mayes, T. A. (2003). Persons with autism and criminal justice. *Journal of Positive Behavior Intervention, 5*(2), 92–100. doi:10.1177/10983007030050020401
McAdam, P. (2012). Knowledge and understanding of the autism spectrum amongst prison staff. *Good Autism Practice, 10*(1), 19–25. doi:10.1108/JIDOB-06–2015–0014
McCarthy, J., Chaplin, E., Underwood, L., Forrester, A., Hayward, H., Sabet, J., & Murphy, D. (2015a). Screening and diagnostic assessment of neurodevelopmental disorders in a male prison. *Journal of Intellectual Disabilities and Offending Behaviour, 6*(2), 102–111. doi:10.1108/JIDOB-08-2015-0018
McCarthy, J., Underwood, L., Hayward, H., Chaplin, E., Forrester, A., Mills, R., & Murphy, D. (2015b). Autism spectrum disorder and mental health problems among prisoners. *European Psychiatry, 30*(1), 28–31. doi:10.1016/S0924–9338(15)30674-X
McCrea, M. A. (2008). *Mild traumatic brain injury and postconcussion syndrome*. New York, NY: Oxford University
McLachlan, K., Roesch, R., Viljoen, J. L., & Douglas, K. S. (2014). Evaluating the psycholegal abilities of young offenders with Fetal Alcohol Spectrum Disorder. *Law and Human Behavior, 38*(1), 10–22. doi:10.1037/lhb0000037
Mendez, M. F., & Fras, I. A. (2011). The false memory syndrome: Experimental studies and comparison to confabulations. *Medical Hypotheses, 76*(4), 492–496. doi:10.1016/j.mehy.2010.11.033
Menon, D. K., Schwab, K., Wright, D. W., & Maas, A. I. (2010). Position statement: Definition of traumatic brain injury. *Archives of Physical Medicine and Rehabilitation, 91*(11), 1637–1640. doi:10.1016/j.apmr.2010.05.017
Merbitz, C., Jain, S., Good, G. L., & Jain, A. (1995). Reported head injury and disciplinary rule infractions in prison. *Journal of Offender Rehabilitation, 22*(3–4), 11–19. doi:10.1300/J076v22n03_02
Miller, E. (1999). The neuropsychology of offending. *Psychology, Crime & Law, 5*(4), 297–318. doi:10.1080/10683169908401774
Miller, L. J., & Donders, J. (2001). Subjective symptomatology after traumatic head injury. *Brain Injury, 15*(4), 297–304. doi:10.1080/02699050118115
Mitchell, P., & Shaw, J. (2011). Factors affecting the recognition of mental health problems among adolescent offenders in custody. *Journal of Forensic Psychiatry and Psychology, 22*(3), 381–394. doi:10.1080/14789949.2011.564644

Mohr-Jensen, C., & Steinhausen, H. C. (2016). A meta-analysis and systematic review of the risks associated with childhood attention-deficit hyperactivity disorder on long-term outcome of arrests, convictions, and incarcerations. *Clinical Psychology Review, 48*, 32–42. doi:10.1016/j.cpr.2016.05.002

Mouridsen, S. (2012). Current status of research on autism spectrum disorders and offending. *Research in Autism Spectrum Disorders, 6*(1), 79–86. doi:10.1016/j.rasd.2011.09.003

Mouridsen, S. E., Rich, B., Isager, T., & Nedergaard, N. J. (2008). Pervasive developmental disorders and criminal behavior: A case control study. *International Journal of Offender Therapy and Comparative Criminology, 52*(2), 196–205. doi:10.1177/0306624X07302056

Murrie, D. C., Warren, J. I., Kristiansson, M., & Dietz, P. E. (2002). Asperger's syndrome in forensic settings. *International Journal of Forensic Mental Health, 1*(1), 59–70. doi:10.1080/14999013.2002.10471161

Myers. F. (2004). *On the borderline? People with learning disabilities and/or autistic spectrum disorders in secure, forensic, and other specialist settings*. Scottish Executive Social Research. Retrieved from www.scotland.gov.uk/Publications/2004/06/19505/38853

National Human Genome Research Institute. (2012). *Learning about autism*. Bethesda, MD: National Human Genome Research Institute.

Nigg, J. T. (2006). *What causes ADHD? Understanding what goes wrong and why*. New York, NY: Guilford Press.

Noble, J. H., & Conley, R. W. (1992). Toward an epidemiology of relevant attributes. In R. W. Conley, R. Luckasson, & G. N. Bouthilet (Eds.), *The criminal justice system and mental retardation* (pp. 17–53). Baltimore, MD: Paul Brookes.

North, A. S., Russell, A. J., & Gudjonsson, G. H. (2008). High functioning autism-spectrum disorders: An investigation of psychological vulnerabilities during interrogative interview. *The Journal of Forensic Psychiatry & Psychology, 19*(3), 323–334. doi:10.1080/14789940701871621

Olley, M. C., Nicholls, T. L., & Brink, J. (2009). Mentally ill individuals in limbo: Obstacles and opportunities for providing psychiatric services to corrections inmates with mental illness. *Behavioral Sciences and the Law, 27*(5), 811–831. doi:10.1002/bsl.899

O'Sullivan, J. A., Power, A. J., Mesgarani, N., Rajaram, S., Foxe, J. J., Shinn-Cunningham, B. G., . . . & Lalor, E. C. (2015) Attentional selection in a cocktail party environment can be decoded form single-trial EEG. *Cerebral Cortex, 25*(7), 1697–1706. doi:10.1093/cercor/bht355

Palermo, M. T. (2004). Pervasive developmental disorders, psychiatric comorbidities, and the law. *International Journal of Offender Therapy and Comparative Criminology, 48*(1), 40–48. doi:10.1177/0306624X03257713

Pardini, D., Obradovic, J., & Loeber, R. (2006). Interpersonal callousness, hyperactivity/impulsivity, inattention, and conduct problems as precursors to delinquency persistence in boys: A comparison of three grade-based cohorts. *Journal of Clinical Child and Adolescent Psychology, 35*(1), 46–59. doi:10.1207/s15374424jccp3501_5

Pei, J., Job, J., Kully-Martens, K., & Rasmussen, C. (2011). Executive function and memory in children with fetal alcohol spectrum disorder. *Child Neuropsychology, 17*(3), 290–309. doi:10.1080/09297049.1010.544650

Perske, R. (2000). Deception in the interrogation room: Sometimes tragic for persons with mental retardation and other developmental disabilities. *Mental Retardation, 38*(6), 532–537. doi:10.1352/0047-6765(2000)038<0532:DITIRS>2.0.CO;2

Perske, R. (2005). Search for persons with intellectual disabilities who confessed to serious crimes they did not commit. *Mental Retardation, 43*(1), 58–65. doi:10.1352/0047-6765(2005)43<58:SFPWID>2.0.CO;2

Petersilia, J. (2000). Doing justice? Criminal offenders with developmental disabilities. *CPRC Brief, 12*(4), 1–63. Irvine, CA: California Research Center, University of California, Irvine.

Petersilia, J., Foote, J., Crowell, N. A., & National Research Council (U.S.). (2001). *Crime victims with developmental disabilities: Report of a workshop*. Washington, DC: National Academy Press.

Piccolino, A. L., & Solberg, K. B. (2014). The impact of traumatic brain injury on prison health service and offender management. *Journal of Corrective Health Care, 16*(20), 203–212. doi:10.1177/1078345814530871

Pliszka, S. (2007). Practice parameter for the assessment and treatment of children and adolescents with attention-deficit/hyperactivity disorder. *Journal of the American Academy of Child and Adolescent Psychiatry, 46*(7), 894–921. doi:10.1097/chi.0b013e318054e724

Pliszka, S. R. (1998). Co-morbidity of attention deficit/hyperactivity disorder: An overview. *Journal of Clinical Psychiatry, 59*(Suppl. 7), 50–58.

Pollak, S., Omer-Bendori, S., Even-Tov, E., Lipsman, V., Bareia, T., Ben-Zion, I., & Eldar, A. (2016). Facultative cheating supports the coexistence of diverse quorum-sensing alleles. *Current Issue, 113*(8), 2152–2157. doi:10.1073/pnas.1520615113

Popova, S., Lange, S., Bekmuradov, D., Michic, A., & Rehm, J. (2011). Fetal alcohol spectrum disorder prevalence estimates in correctional systems: A systematic literature review, *Canadian Journal of Public Health, 102*(5), 335–340.

Popova, S., Lange, S., Burd, L., & Rehm, J. (2015). *The burden and economic impact of fetal alcohol spectrum disorder in Canada.* Toronto, Ontario, Canada: Centre for Addiction and Mental Health.
Rao, A.V., Bested, A. C., Beaulne, T. M., Katzman, M. A., Lorio, C., Berardi, J. M., & Logan, A.C. (2009). A randomized, double-blind, placebo-controlled pilot study of a probiotic in emotional symptoms of chronic fatigue syndrome. *Gut Pathogens, 19*(1), 1–19. doi:10.1186/1757-4749-1-6
Rasmussen, C., Horne, K., & Witol, A. (2006). Neurobehavioral functioning in children with fetal alcohol spectrum disorder. *Child Neuropsychology, 12*(6), 453–468. doi:10.1080/09297040600646854
Ray, F., Marks, C., & Bray-Garretson, H. (2004). Challenges to treating adolescents with Asperger's syndrome who are sexually abusive. *Sexual Addiction & Compulsivity, 11*(4), 265–285. doi:10.1080/10720160490900614
Redmond, S. M. (2016). Language impairment in the attention-deficit/hyperactivity disorder context. *Journal of Speech, Language, and Hearing Research, 59*(1), 133–142. doi:10.1044/2015_JSLHR-L-15-0038
Rieffe, C., Camodeca, M., Pouw, L. B., Lange, A. M., & Stockmann, L. (2012). Don't anger me! Bullying, victimization, and emotion dysregulation in young adolescents with ASD. *European Journal of Developmental Psychology, 9*(3), 351–370. doi:10.1080/17405629.2012.680302
Robertson, C. E., & McGillivray, J. A. (2015). Autism behind bars: A review of the research literature and discussion of key issues. *Journal of Forensic Psychiatry and Psychology, 26*(6), 719–736. doi:10.1080/14789949.2015.1062994
Robinson, L., Spencer, M. D., Thomson, L. D., Stanfield, A. C., Owens, D. G., Hall, J., & Johnstone, E. C. (2012). Evaluation of a screening instrument for autism spectrum disorders in prisoners. *Plus One*, 7(5), 1–8. doi:10.1371/journal.pone.0036078
Rosler, M., Retz, W., Yaqoobi, K., Burg, E., & Retz-Junginger, P. (2009). Attention deficit/hyperactivity disorder in female offenders: Prevalence, psychiatric comorbidity and psychosocial implications. *European Archives of Psychiatry and Clinical Neuroscience, 259*(2), 98–105. doi:10.1007/s00406-008-0841-8
Salekin, K. L., Olley, J. G., & Hedge, K. A. (2010). Offenders with intellectual disability: Characteristics, prevalence, and issues in forensic assessment. *Journal of Mental Health Research in Intellectual Disabilities, 3*(2), 97–116. doi:10.1080/19315861003695769
Scheyett, A., Vaughn, J., Taloy, M., & Parish, S. (2009). Are we there yet? Screening processes for intellectual and developmental disabilities in jail settings. *Intellectual and Developmental Disabilities, 47*(1), 13–23. doi:10.1352/2009.47:13–23.
Schofield, P. W., Butler, T. G., Hollis, S. J., Smith, N. E., Lee, S. J., & Kelso, W. M. (2006). Traumatic brain injury among Australian prisoners: Rates, recurrence and sequelae. *Brain Injury, 20*(5), 499–506. doi:10.1080/02699050600664749
Schwartz-Watts, D. M. (2005). Asperger's disorder and murder. *Journal of the American Academy of Psychiatry and Law, 33*(3), 390–393.
Scott, D. A., Gignac, M., Kronfli, R. N., Ocana, A., & Lorberg, G. W. (2016). Expert opinion and recommendations for the management of attention-deficit/hyperactivity disorder in correctional facilities. *Journal of Correctional Health Care, 22*(1), 46–61. doi:10.1177/1078345815618392
Secnik, K., Swensen, A., & Lage, M. J. (2005). Comorbidities and costs of adult patients diagnosed with attention-deficit hyperactivity disorder. *PharmacoEconomics, 23*(1), 93–102. doi:10.2165/00019053-200523010-00008
Shiroma, E. J., Ferguson, P. L., & Pickelsimer, E. E. (2010). Prevalence of traumatic brain injury in an offender population: A meta-analysis. *Journal of Correctional Health Care, 16*(2), 147–159. doi:10.1177/1078345809356538
Silva, J. A., Ferrari, J. A., & Leong, G. B. (2002). The case of Jeffrey Dahmer: Sexual serial homicide from a neuropsychiatric developmental perspective. *Journal of Forensic Science, 47*(6), 1347–1359. doi:10.1520/JFS15574J
Silver, J. M., Kramer, R., Greenwald, S., & Weissman, M. (2001). The association between head injuries and psychiatric disorders: Findings from the New Haven NIMH Epidemiologic Catchment Area Study. *Brain Injury, 15*(11), 935–945. doi:10.1080/02699050110065295
Simon, V., Czobor, P., Balint, S., Meszaros, A., & Bitter, I. (2009). Prevalence and correlates of adult attention-deficit hyperactivity disorder: Meta-analysis. *British Journal of Psychiatry, 194*(3), 204–211. doi:10.1192/bjp.bp.107.048827
Smith, A. H., & O'Brien, G. (2004) Offenders with dual diagnosis. In W. R. Lindsay, J. L. Taylor, & P. Sturmey (Eds.), *Offenders with developmental disabilities* (pp. 241–264). New York, NY: John Wiley & Sons Ltd.
Streissguth, A. P., Barr, H., Kogan, J., & Bookstein, F. L. (1996). Understanding the occurrence of secondary disabilities in clients with fetal alcohol syndrome (FAS) and fetal alcohol effects (FAE). *Final report to the Centers for Disease Control and Prevention, Grant No. R04/CCR008515.* Seattle: University of Washington School of Medicine.
Sobanski, E. (2006). Psychiatric comorbidity in adults with attention-deficit/hyperactivity disorder (ADHD). *European Archives of Psychiatry and Clinical Neuroscience, 256*, i26–i31. doi:10.1007/s00406-006-1004-4

Tager-Flusberg, H., Paul, R., & Lord, C. E. (2005). Language and communication in autism. (pp. 335–364). In F. Volkmar, R. Paul, A. Klin, & D. J. Cohen (Eds.), *Handbook of autism and pervasive developmental disorders: Vol. 1. Diagnosis, development, neurobiology, and behavior* (3rd ed.). New York, NY: Wiley.

Talbot, J. (2008). *Prisoners' voices: Experiences of the criminal justice system by prisoners with learning disabilities and difficulties*. London: Prison Reform Trust.

Talbot, J. (2009). No one knows: Offenders with learning disabilities and learning difficulties. *International Journal of Prisoner Health, 5*(3), 141–152. doi:10.1108/13595474200900004

Tassé, M. J. (2009). Adaptive behavior assessment and the diagnosis of mental retardation in capital cases. *Applied Neuropsychology, 16*(2), 114–123. doi:10.1080/09084280902864451

Underwood, L., Forrester, A., Chaplin, E., & McCarthy, J. (2013). Prisoners with neurodevelopmental disorders. *Journal of Intellectual Disabilities and Offending Behavior, 4*(1–2), 17–23. doi:10.1108/JIDOB-05-2013-0011

Usher, A. M., Stewart, L. A., & Wilton, G. (2013). Attention-deficit hyperactivity disorder in a Canadian prison population. *International Journal of Law and Psychiatry, 36*(3–4), 311–315. doi:10.1016/j.ijlp.2013

Vaughn, M. G., Salas-Wright, C. P., DeLisi, M., & Perron, B. (2014). Correlates of traumatic brain injury among juvenile offenders: A multi-site study. *Criminal Behaviour and Mental Health, 24*(3), 188–203. doi:10.1002/cbm.1900

Visscher, A. J. M., vanMeijel, B., Stolker, J. J., Wiersma, J., & Nijman, H. (2011). Aggressive behaviour of inpatients with acquired brain injury. *Journal of Clinical Nursing, 20*(23–24), 3414–3422. doi:10.1111/j.1365-2702.2011.03800.x

Walker, R., Hiller, M., Staton, M., & Leukefeld, C. G. (2003). Head injury among drug abusers: an indicator of co-occurring problems. *Journal of Psychoactive Drugs, 35*(3), 343–353. doi:10.1080/02791072.2003.10400017

Weiss, G., Hechtman, L., Milroy, T., & Perlman, T. (1985). Psychiatric status of hyperactives as adults: A controlled prospective 15-year follow-up of 63 hyperactive children. *Journal of the American Academy of Child Psychiatry, 24*, 211–220. doi:10.1016/S0002-7138(09)60450-7

Wender, P. H., Ward, M. F., Reimher, F. W., & Marchant, B. K. (2000). ADHD in adults. *Journal of Academic Child and Adolescent Psychiatry, 39*(5), 543. doi:10.1097/00004583-200005000-00001

White, S. W., & Schry, A. R. (2011). Social anxiety in adolescents on the autism spectrum (pp. 183–201). In C. A. Alfano & D. C. Beidel (Eds.), *Social anxiety in adolescents and adults: Translating developmental science into practice*. Washington, DC: American Psychological Association.

Whitehouse, R. M., Tudway, J. A., Look, R., & Kroese, B. S. (2006). Adapting individual psychotherapy for adults with intellectual disabilities: A comparative review of the cognitive-behavioural and psychodynamic literature. *Journal of Applied Research in Intellectual Disabilities, 19*(1), 55–65. doi:10.1111/j.1468-3148.2005.00281.x

Willcutt, E. G. (2012). The prevalence of DSM-IV attention deficit/ hyperactivity disorder: A meta-analytic review. *Neurotherapeutics, 9*(3), 490–499. doi:10.1007/s13311-012-0135-8

Williams, W. H., Mewse, A. J., Tonks, J., Mills, S., Burgess, C. N., & Cordan, G. (2010). Traumatic brain injury in a prison population: Prevalence and risk for re-offending. *Brain Injury, 24*(10), 1184–1188. doi:10.3109/02699052.2010.495697

Wing, L. (1997). Asperger's syndrome: Management requires diagnosis. *Journal of Forensic Psychiatry & Psychology, 8*(2), 253–257. doi:10.1080/09585189708412008

Woodbury-Smith, M. R., Clare, I. C. H., Holland, A. J., Kearns, A., Staufenberg, E., & Watson, P. (2005). A case-control study of offenders with high functioning autistic spectrum disorders. *Journal of Forensic Psychiatry and Psychology, 16*(4), 747–763. doi:10.1080/14789940600589464

Woodbury-Smith, M. R., Clare, I. C. H., Holland, A. J., Watson, P. C., Bambrick, M., Kearns, A., & Staugenberg, E. (2010). Circumscribed interests and "offenders" with autism spectrum disorders: A case-control study. *Journal of Forensic Psychiatry and Psychology, 21*(3), 366–377. doi:10.1080/14789940903426877

Woodbury-Smith, M., & Dein, K. (2014). Autism spectrum disorder (ASD) and unlawful behaviour: Where do we go from here? *Journal of Autism and Developmental Disorders, 44*(11), 2734–2741. doi:10.1007/s10803-014-2216-5

Young, S. J., Adamou, M., Bolea, B., Gudjonsson, G., Muller, U., Pitts, M., . . . Asherson, P. (2011). Identification and management of ADHD in offenders within the criminal justice system: A consensus statement from the UK Adult ADHD network and criminal justice agencies. *BMC Psychiatry, 11*(32), 2–14.

Young, S., & Goodwin, E. (2010). Attention-deficit/hyperactivity disorder in persistent criminal offenders: The need for specialist treatment programs. *Expert Review of Neurotherapeutics, 10*(10), 1497–1500. doi:10.1586/ern.10.142

Young, S., Gudjonsson G. H., Wells, J., Asherson, P., Theobald, D., Oliver, B., . . . Mooney, A. (2009). Attention deficit hyperactivity disorder and critical incidents in a Scottish prison population. *Personality and Individual Differences, 46*(3), 265–269. doi:10.1016/j.paid.2008.10.003

Young, S., Moss, D., Sedgwick, O., Fridman, M., & Hodgkins, P. (2014). A meta-analysis of the prevalence of attention deficit hyperactivity disorder in incarcerated populations. *Psychological Medicine*, *45*(2), 247–258. doi:10.1017/S0033291714000762

Young, S., Sedgwick, O., Fridman, M., Gudjonsson, G., Hodgkins, P., Lantigua, M., & González, R. A. (2015). Co-morbid psychiatric disorders among incarcerated ADHD populations: a meta-analysis. *Psychological Medicine*, *45*(12), 2499–2510. doi:10.1017/S0033291715000598

Young, S., Wells, J., & Gudjonsson, G. H. (2011). Predictors of offending among prisoners: The role of attention-deficit hyperactivity disorder and substance use. *Journal of Psychopharmacology*, *25*(11), 1524–1532. doi:10.1177/0269881110370502

26

FORGOTTEN POPULATIONS

Racial, Ethnic, and Gender Health Care Disparities

Adam K. Matz

> All patients, regardless of race, ethnic origin, gender, nationality, primary language, socioeconomic status, sexual orientation, cultural background, age, disability, or religion, deserve high-quality health care. As our society increasingly becomes racially and ethnically diverse, physicians and other health care professionals need to acknowledge the cultural, informational, and linguistic needs of their patients.
>
> —(American College of Physicians, 2010, p. 3)

Introduction

Inequalities in health care provision, defined as the diagnosis, treatment, and prevention of physical or mental illness or injury, are present within the general population. Blacks and Hispanics from impoverished communities are less likely to have access to and seek out health services than whites (Alegria et al., 2002). There is some empirical evidence that health care disparities exist within correctional facilities, and the quality of care and treatment of racial and ethnic minorities also may be in question (see e.g., Binswanger, Redmond, Steiner, & Hicks, 2012; Nowotny, Rogers, & Boardman, 2017). The criminal justice system disproportionately affects racial and ethnic minorities, which leads to aggregate implications for long-term health outcomes for these individuals (McDonnell, Brookes, & Lurigio, 2014). Criminal justice involvement directly and indirectly influences inmate health and health care and often replicates racial, ethnic, and gender health care disparities that occur in the community (Binswanger et al., 2012). For example, minorities from impoverished communities are less likely to have health insurance and access to preventative care. Formerly incarcerated minorities may be further turned away by perceptions of racism and the stigma associated with a criminal record (Frank, Wang, Nunez-Smith, Lee, & Comfort, 2014). Yet correctional facilities themselves may expose inmates to conditions and infectious diseases at rates much higher than that in the general population.

This chapter examines health care disparities across the criminal justice system, particularly correctional facilities. Specifically, this chapter examines disparities in incarceration for racial and ethnic minorities and the health problems they have when entering the criminal justice system. There is a discussion of the direct and indirect effects of imprisonment on future health outcomes. The chapter also explores the role of probation and parole supervision in promoting offender health care and treatment postrelease. The chapter covers the most pressing health care and treatment issues of justice-involved women, racial and ethnic minorities, and the intersection of both. It concludes with an examination of the organizational approaches to improve the collaboration of criminal justice administrators and community health care providers.

Racial Disparities in Incarceration

A large number of individuals are processed through the criminal justice system. Currently, over 2 million people are incarcerated in jails or prisons, and another 6 million are under community supervision. In the United States, about 12 million adults enter and leave jails annually (McDonnell et al., 2014). Racial and ethnic minorities are disproportionately represented in this correctional population. Most pronounced, blacks comprise 13% of the general population but make up 28% of all arrests and 40% of the incarcerated population (Wang & Green, 2010). Up to 33% of black men will serve time in prison during their lifetime, considerably higher than the 17% for Hispanics and 6% for white men (Binswanger et al., 2012). Not only are minorities overrepresented, but they also are incarcerated for longer sentences than whites (American Civil Liberties Union, 2014). This disparate trend exists in both the adult and juvenile criminal justice systems (Iguichi, Bell, Ramchand, & Fain, 2005). About one of every 100 black male juveniles is in a juvenile residential placement facility, compared to 1 in 200 male Hispanic juveniles and 1 in 500 white male juveniles (Iguichi et al., 2005).

Women of color also are overrepresented in prison populations because of their histories of victimization, especially intimate partner violence (Potter, 2008). For example, one study of a sample (n = 525) of abused women, including women of color, found that nearly half had been coerced into committing crimes by their batterers as "part of a structural sequence of actions in a climate of terror and diminished, violated sense of self" (Loring & Beaudoin, 2000, p. 13). For example, women of color represent two-thirds of women in jail—44% black, 15% Hispanic, and 5% of other racial/ethnic backgrounds; the remaining 36% are white (Swavola, Riley, & Subramanian, 2016).

Sentencing disparities have been fueled largely by the "War on Drugs" from the 1970s and 1980s, and it continues to persist (Hatcher, Toldson, Godette, & Richardson, 2009). Blacks and whites use drugs at similar rates, yet blacks are 13 times more likely to be imprisoned for drug use, and their sentences are typically more punitive (Dumont, Allen, Brockmann, Alexander, & Rich, 2013). Half of the males and over half of females in federal prison, for example, were serving time for drug offenses (Carson, 2015). Because of these racial disparities, black males are more likely to be exposed to the correctional environment and health services associated with correctional entities than other populations. Overrepresentation also exists for Hispanics and Native Americans, though not to the extent of the black population (Hatcher et al., 2009; Kaeble, Glaze, Tsoutis, & Minton, 2016; Tonry, 2011).

Of all Hispanics in the general population, an estimated 1.7%, compared to 4.6% for blacks and 0.7% for Whites, are in jail or prison (Hatcher et al., 2009). Specifically, the Bureau of Justice Statistics (BJS) reports there were 308,700 Hispanic males, accounting for 22% of the state and federal inmate population, but Hispanics represent about 12% of the adult population (Carson, 2015). Native Americans, on the other hand, comprise about 1–2% of the adult population and have not been distinguished from the white population in many of the national prisoner counts. Nor have Native Americans been the focus of many empirical studies on incarceration (see e.g., Willging, Malcoe, Cyr, Zywiak, & Lapham, 2013), despite reports of their overrepresentation in correctional facilities in relatively low-population states such as South Dakota, Montana, and Minnesota ("Native Americans Overrepresented in Prison," 2013). The South Dakota Department of Corrections reports Native Americans represented 29% of their prison population and 38% of juvenile offenders. Compared to 7% of the general population, Montana reports 19% of the male and 33% of its female inmate population is Native American. Minnesota reports 9% of its inmate population is Native American. Finally, in terms of female inmates, black females were up to 4.1 times more likely to be imprisoned than white females in state or federal prison, with an imprisonment rate of 264 per 100,000, which is 160% of the rate of Hispanic female inmates, at 163 per 100,000 (Carson, 2015).

Health Issues of Criminal Justice-Involved Populations

A meta-analysis of 30 studies revealed illicit drug abusers (e.g., heroin, crack, and cocaine) were three to four times more likely to engage in criminal behaviors, not drug related, when compared to non-drug abusers (Bennett, Holloway, & Farrington, 2008; National Institute of Drug Abuse [NIDA], 2014). More specifically, drug users are more likely to be involved in shoplifting, prostitution, burglaries, and robberies. An estimated 85% of jail detainees and 65% of prisoners suffer from drug addiction, seven times the rate of the general population (National Center on Addiction and Substance Abuse [NCASA], 2010). Despite the prevalence, less than 20% of inmates will receive formal addiction treatment while incarcerated (Treatment Research Institute [TRI], 2011).

Jail and prisons have become the *de facto* institutions for assisting individuals with mental health needs. The prevalence of mental illness within institutions is two to three times that of the general population (Hammett, Roberts, & Kennedy, 2001). Adult inmates who are female, white, or elderly, suffer from substance abuse, have developmental disabilities, and are detained within segregated housing units are most likely to suffer from mental illness compared to other inmates (Soderstrom, 2007). Finally, it is estimated anywhere from 13–74% of justice-involved individuals possess a variety of co-occurring medical disorders such as hypertension, arthritis, cancer, hepatitis, and HIV/AIDS (Broner, Lattimore, Cowell, & Schlenger, 2004; Draine, Blank, Kottsieper, & Solomon, 2005; Hall, Golder, Conley, & Sawning, 2013; Shafer, Arthur, & Franczak, 2004; Steadman & Naples, 2005; TRI, 2011).

Impact of Incarceration on Racial Disparities in Health Care

In the past two decades, there has been a growing interest in the intersection between justice and health care organizations (Akers & Lanier, 2009; Akers, Potter, & Hill, 2013; Lanier & Potter, 2010; Lanier, Lucken, & Akers, 2010; Potter, 2002; Potter & Akers, 2010), including the perpetuation and worsening of general population disparities in health care acquisition (Gaiter, Potter, & O'Leary, 2006). The presence of chronic diseases such as hypertension, asthma, hepatitis C, and HIV/AIDS within correctional facilities is higher than that seen in the general population (Frank et al., 2014; Wang & Green, 2010). Unfortunately, individuals often do not get the level of care they need while incarcerated or once released under probation or parole supervision in the community (Frank et al., 2014; Kulkarni, Baldwin, Lightstone, Gelberg, & Diamant, 2010; TRI, 2011).

While health care provision and services within institutions seem to be comparable for all racial groups, the long-term impact of incarceration is disproportionally skewed to leave a lasting impact on impoverished minority communities (Potter, 2002). This is further compounded by the revolving door of American correctional institutions, in which an estimated 600,000 adults and 100,000 juveniles return to the community annually (Petersilia, 2003; Hatcher et al., 2009). The stigma of incarceration has been associated with numerous barriers to successful reentry, including difficulty finding and maintaining stable employment and housing, which makes access to health care access more problematic (Potter, 2002). The inability to locate gainful employment prohibits access to adequate health care insurance coverage.

As a result, the stark growth of punitive sentences and incarceration of the last half-century has significantly affected the lower socioeconomic classes of society, which are disproportionately made up of minorities. Indeed, the likelihood of black imprisonment is over 20% (Massoglia, 2008). Even worse, minorities that fail to obtain a high school diploma possess an even higher likelihood of incarceration, with a rate over 50%. For young blacks, their likelihood of imprisonment rivals that of getting married, suggesting imprisonment borders on becoming a "normal" life event (Pettit,

2012; Pettit & Western, 2004; Western, 2006; 2008). As Western (2008, p. 8) poignantly states, "over a lifetime, about one in five Black men born since 1965 will serve time in prison." Imprisonment jeopardizes employability, leads to lower wages, and reduces marital stability. Specifically, imprisonment of mostly minority, poorly educated, young men is associated with a 30 to 40% decrease in annual earnings, and a criminal record essentially eliminates wage growth potential between the ages of 25 and 35 (Western, 2006). These men often return to their communities averaging less than a tenth-grade education and possessing a history of joblessness and substance abuse (Western, 2008). In addition to issues with reintegration in the workforce, these men also possess increased rates of divorce and separation postrelease (Western, 2006). Though prisoner reentry has received greater emphasis in recent years, Western (2006) notes rehabilitative programming in prisons has actually been reduced in many jurisdictions, including a reported drop in inmate participation in work and education programs from 44% in the 1990s to 25% in the 2000s. Due to overrepresentation, involvement in the criminal justice system has had a more dramatic effect on blacks than whites, including stress-induced health problems and exposure to infectious diseases (Massoglia, 2008). Black-white racial disparities are most dramatic for incarceration but also prevalent in relation to a variety of other social indicators, including unemployment, nonmarital childbearing, infant mortality, and wealth (Western, 2008). Such disparities are further reflected in black health problems and the likelihood of health care provision and access after release (Alegria et al., 2002).

Those exiting institutions often return to their impoverished communities in a worse condition than when they went in. Incarceration lowers the individual's position in the social hierarchy, resulting from stigma, further impacting employment prospects. Indeed, punishment extends beyond the walls of the institution and can have long-term health implications as a result, including primary and secondary stress-related health problems (Massoglia, 2008). Further, the institution increases opportunities for treatment but also exposure to infectious diseases (Farmer, 2002; Travis, Solomon, & Waul, 2001). In general, individuals who are married and employed possess better health, yet for many returning offenders such status will be difficult to obtain (Massoglia, 2008).

Incarceration represents a dramatic and stressful life event and places individuals in an even more disadvantaged social position than when they entered (Massoglia, 2008). These disadvantages can lead to prolonged chronic stress in the form of both primary (i.e., the act of being incarcerated) and secondary stressors (i.e., family, employment, or social stressors experienced after release). Prolonged measures of stress can have a physiological impact that strains the cardiovascular and immune systems of an individual (Massoglia, 2008). These issues can ultimately lead to a host of mental and physical health problems. Incarceration also exposes individuals to infectious diseases at higher rates than what would be experienced in the community. In a given year, over 20% of individuals entering institutions have HIV/AIDS and over 40% are infected with hepatitis C (Massoglia, 2008). Clearly, placement in correctional facilities exposes individuals to a highly infected population, increasing their immediate health risk in addition to other debilitating health implications (Dumont et al., 2013).

In terms of overall health, whites live about six years longer on average than blacks (Massoglia, 2008). Blacks also are likely to spend a greater proportion of their life coping with chronic health conditions. Minority males are five to eight times more likely to be incarcerated than whites with comparable education levels. There are additional correlates that negatively affect health outcomes regardless of race or ethnicity. For example, individuals who engage in illicit drug use and violence increase their risk for health problems and their likelihood of incarceration. Massoglia's (2008) research found families who receive public assistance feel they are in less control of their lives, report prior health problems, and have poorer midlife health. Similar to the finding that prior criminal history is often the strongest predictor of future criminal behavior, the same is true of health. In other words, past health is the strongest predictor of future health.

Incarceration has been found to have a long-lasting impact on physical health of offenders. Incarceration exacerbates social problems for offenders, which further reduces their likelihood of marriage, gainful employment, and education, which are directly related to positive health. Interestingly, the impact of incarceration on health is not significantly different by racial group (i.e., blacks and whites exposed to incarceration are negatively impacted to a similar degree); however, the cumulative effect across the populations as a result of disparate exposure to incarceration makes the overall impact significantly more damaging to minority communities (Massoglia, 2008). Simply put, incarceration exacerbates the health problems associated with poverty and disadvantage, of which minority populations are disproportionately impacted.

The reentry of incarcerated individuals thus leads to negative outcomes regardless of the race of the individual exposed, but because of disproportional representation of minorities in the incarcerated population the cumulative health effects of blacks is greatly jeopardized. Given the likelihood of these individuals to return to impoverished communities, their access to quality health care is even further depreciated. Residing in impoverished minority communities leads to greater likelihood of exposure to incarceration. In turn, incarceration affects employability, which influences access to health insurance and health care.

Further, possessing a criminal record has resulted in reportedly deliberate discrimination from health care providers and workers in the community (Frank et al., 2014; Paradies, 2006; Shavers et al., 2012; Williams & Mohammed, 2009). Criminal history may be identifiable to health care providers by medical histories from correctional health organizations when prisoners are transferred to a community facility or by documentation within the individual's medical record (Frank et al., 2014). Such discrimination increases the likelihood that former offenders will avoid routine physicals, delay needed care, neglect recommendations from health care professionals, and reduce the use of preventative services (Benjamins, 2012; Frank et al., 2014). For example, a study of 172 men released from a state prison found 42% reported a history of criminal record discrimination by health care workers, which was actually higher for whites at 56% compared to minorities at 41% (Frank et al., 2014). Discrimination was reportedly more pronounced for older educated males with lengthier criminal histories. Health care workers also reported more frequent discrimination with former offenders with high emergency department use, but not for primary care.

To summarize, incarceration, which disproportionally affects black males, inhibits access to quality jobs and the health benefits associated with employment, access to adequate housing, benefits such as food stamps, access to military service, financial support for education, voter disenfranchisement, and direct health implications through exposure to a stressful environment, infectious diseases, and other environmental hazards (Iguichi et al., 2005). The possession of a criminal record in addition to these other disadvantages leads to barriers that can hinder the acquisition of health care services in the community for these in-need populations once released or under community supervision (Frank et al., 2014; Lorvick, Comfort, Krebs, & Kral, 2015; Taxman, 2014; Wallace, Eason, & Lindsey, 2015). A national-level study of probationers and parolees found these justice-involved individuals were more likely to receive alcohol and drug treatment and mental health treatment than those not under community supervision (Vaugh, DeLisi, Beaver, Perron, & Abdon, 2012). This finding, however, did not hold true for female probationers and parolees in a more localized sample, implying supervision quality may vary by jurisdiction (Lorvick et al., 2015).

Asthma

In a study of New York City, adults with a history of incarceration were found to be more likely to have asthma than others in the general population but no more likely to have diabetes or hypertension (Wang & Green, 2010). The disproportional representation of blacks in the incarcerated population contributes, in part, to the racial disparity in asthma prevalence as well, even though race was not a key determinant of asthma (Wang & Green, 2010). Interestingly, formerly incarcerated individuals with asthma were also more likely to have an asthma attack or visited the emergency department in the prior year than those who had never been incarcerated. Several sources of asthma that may contribute to the higher rate among formerly incarcerated individuals include higher rates of smoking, drug use, alcohol use, domestic violence, substandard and dilapidated living quarters, socioeconomic status, and adverse prison or jail conditions including poor ventilation and overcrowding (Wang & Green, 2010). While the impact of incarceration on asthma prevalence is similar across races, again the aggregate disproportional representation of blacks in institutions has led to a greater impact on black communities.

Mental Health Disparities

Changes in federal policies from the 1970s and 1980s greatly reduced the funding for community treatment facilities that supported mental illness (Hatcher et al., 2009). These changes ultimately led to the mass closure of mental health institutions and encouraged the criminalization of the mentally ill. An estimated 62% of white inmates, 55% of black inmates, and 46% of Hispanic inmates in state prisons have a mental health diagnosis (Hatcher et al., 2009). Mental illness is more prevalent in jails, and estimates indicate that 71% of whites, 63% of blacks, and 51% of Hispanics have a mental health issue (Hatcher et al., 2009). Overall, over half of all inmates in jails or prisons possess a diagnosable mental illness, which far exceeds the rate in the general population. Mental illness is often accompanied by a myriad of other issues such as alcohol and drug dependence and suicidal or self-destructive behaviors. In addition, mental illness is frequently linked to intimate partner violence, which disproportionately affects women of color (see Barak, Leighton, & Cotton, 2015; Potter, 2008).

Correctional facilities have taken on the role of mental health institutions, yet staff rarely possess specialized training on how to appropriately interact and address inmates with these mental health problems (Chandler, Peters, & Juliano-Bult, 2004). Further, considerable differences in the acquisition of mental health services exist between racial and ethnic groups in the general population (Alegria et al., 2002). Alegria and colleagues (2002) found poor Hispanics possessed lower access to care than poor whites, while nonpoor blacks were also less likely to obtain care than nonpoor whites. Hispanics tended to be younger, less educated, earned less income, were less likely to be married, less likely to have insurance, and more likely to live in the South and West than whites. Further, Hispanics were more likely to report psychiatric issues than both whites and blacks. Blacks were the least likely of the three to report psychiatric problems. Despite this, whites were found to be more likely to receive specialized mental health services than Hispanics. In fact, Hispanics were even less likely to receive specialty care than blacks.

Mental health service access of Hispanics and Latinos is influenced, much like other minorities' access to health care, by poverty status, acculturation (i.e., English proficiency, nativity, and years in U.S.), national origin, and insurance status (Alegria et al., 2002). Clearly the mix of poverty and minority status places an individual at higher risk of reduced access to mental health services, as well as specialty care, which can be further complicated by factors such as geographic location. Nonpoor rural populations are less likely to receive specialty care than poor urban populations.

Several reasons have been identified to explain why Hispanics may avoid mental health services (Alegria et al., 2002). First, non-English-speaking Hispanics are less likely to seek support than more fluent English speaking Hispanics. Hispanics have also shown self-reliance is a strong cultural element of their communities, which may contribute to less mental health service use. Second, the poor communities in which a large proportion of Hispanics live often have considerably fewer behavioral health options than other affluent, predominantly white, communities. Finally, Hispanics may be turned away by prior negative experiences with lower-quality mental health care providers (Alegria et al., 2002). By comparison, blacks are less likely to use mental health services because of limited financial resources and a pervading mistrust of the health care system that is linked to past mistreatment and perceived racism (Diala et al., 2000). Unfortunately, more recent research finds access to mental health services and health care access in general for blacks and Hispanics/Latinos have not improved in relation to whites, while adjusting for rate of need, and still remains a salient issue (Cook, 2007; Cook, McGuire, & Miranda, 2007; Cook et al., 2014).

One appropriate intervention found to be effective for mental health needs with formerly incarcerated populations is the Assertive Community Treatment (ACT) program. The program utilizes individualized service provided by a team of psychiatrists, nurses, substance abuse specialists, social workers, and case managers. The caseload ratio is small, at 1:10, with direct support available 24 hours a day and assistance in housing, employment, education, transportation, family support, substance abuse treatment, and self-sufficiency through cognitive-behavioral programming (Hatcher et al., 2009). The program can be effective for returning minority populations but must be integrated with all aspects of the individual's life and promote a problem-solving orientation. The key is providing or developing the necessary client support network, especially difficult in communities in which services are sparse. Hatcher and colleagues (2009) note the importance of primary care providers' knowledge and cultural aptitude of mental health needs in black communities, as well as the need for greater coordination with correctional entities. Cultural sensitivity is essential to establishing rapport when working with special populations, including Hispanics and Native Americans as well (see, e.g., Cobb, Mowatt, Matz, & Mullins, 2011).

HIV/AIDS and Other Infectious Diseases

Human immunodeficiency virus/acquired immunodeficiency syndrome (HIV/AIDS) is a particularly prevalent problem among black men, with rates indicating that black men are nine times more likely than whites to be diagnosed with HIV/AIDS (Blankenship, Smoyer, Bray, & Mattocks, 2005; Centers for Disease Control and Prevention, 2017a). Despite comprising roughly 13% of the general population, blacks represent up to 39% of all HIV/AIDS cases in correctional facilities (Blankenship et al., 2005), and blacks are more likely to die of HIV/AIDS complications in prison (Maruschak, 2015). Sexual contact has been the primary means of HIV/AIDS infection, followed by injection drug use. Yet studies on sexually risky behavior and injection drug use have shown blacks are not engaging in risky behaviors any more than whites (see Blankenship et al., 2005; Taylor et al., 2012). In fact, evidence has tended to show the contrary; whites display more risky sexual and drug use behaviors (Blankenship et al., 2005; Taylor et al., 2012). As a result, many have come to believe the mass imprisonment of minorities may be the source of HIV/AIDS disparities. The confined environment of the prison and jail setting itself makes it a high-risk setting for the transmission of HIV/AIDS as result of the high prevalence of HIV/AIDS among the incarcerated population and high-risk sexual behaviors that occur (exact rates are unknown, but several studies estimate 20% of men experience some form of sexual contact while imprisoned) (Blankenship et al., 2005). Estimates of 20–26% of the people in the U.S. with HIV are within correctional institutions. Further, even though the risk behaviors of blacks and whites are similar within institutions, the disproportional representation of blacks leads to larger negative outcomes for this population. Countries such as Switzerland, Germany, and Spain have experienced some success with reducing HIV/AIDS risk through prison needle exchange programs without endangering staff or prisoners or increasing drug use (Blankenship et al., 2005). Laws in New York and California require correctional administrators to make condoms available to prisoners in an effort to reduce rates of HIV infection.

Further, upon release, the impact of low employment prospects and a lack of social support may contribute to risky drug use behaviors such as the sharing of syringes (Blankenship et al., 2005). Interestingly, placement on probation or parole supervision, in which drug use is prohibited, has discouraged offenders from using syringe exchange programs, invariably increasing their risk to HIV/AIDS (Blankenship et al., 2005). Further, the prohibition to interact with peers may lead offenders to seek out other new or formerly incarcerated individuals, a population with a potentially greater risk of transmitting HIV/AIDS.

Though indirect, the removal of large numbers of black adult males from impoverished communities has also lead to a misbalanced ratio of men and women. This flux in the community population inadvertently promotes greater exposure to multiple partners, which furthers the potential spread of HIV/AIDS (Adimora & Schoenbach, 2005; Potter, 2002). This is in addition to other negative residual influences on communities rendered by mass incarceration, including, for example, the strains placed on youth with incarcerated parents (Nichols, Loper, & Meyer, 2016).

Somewhat perplexing, one study found few justice-involved women received HIV testing in a correctional setting, with most being tested at community-based agencies afterwards (Lorvick et al., 2015). That said, regardless of race, female offenders are more likely to receive probation than be incarcerated compared to their male counterparts for similar crimes (Doerner & Demuth, 2014). Female probationers, as well as parolees, are likely to return to the same disadvantaged communities as the male offenders, associated with abject poverty, substandard housing, and poor employment opportunities (Lorvick et al., 2015). Further, these communities are more likely to present opportunities for drug use and risky sexual behaviors (Belenko, Langley, Crimmins, & Chaple, 2004). Though sexual contact is the primary means of contracting HIV/AIDS, research demonstrates that people who inject drugs are 28 times more likely to contract HIV/AIDS (AVERT, 2017). However, black women account for 66% of all injection drug use cases of HIV/AIDS among women; the number is 60% for black men among men (Centers for Disease Control and Prevention, 2017b). Recall, the exact prevalence of HIV/AIDS transmission while incarcerated is not clear because of a lack of records on inmate sexual contact and illicit drug use in institutions. Some have argued that illicit drug use within prisons is notably fraught with risk, but its prevalence is largely unknown.

Mortality

Despite the negative long-term effects of incarceration on health, research has shown the mortality rate for the incarcerated population is similar across race and considerably lower for blacks within correctional facilities than blacks in the general population. Specifically, the mortality rate for imprisoned blacks was 57% lower than that of blacks in the general population (Dumont et al., 2013). Alternatively, the mortality rate for imprisoned whites was 10% higher than whites in the general population. Simply put, blacks are less likely to die in prison than on the outside. As such, correctional facilities essentially provide a measure of protection from immediate death, despite having poor health implications otherwise.

Ex-offenders have been found to be 13 times more likely to die in the first two weeks after release for prison, indicating the protective factor of imprisonment immediately disappears after release, stressing the importance of comprehensive reentry efforts to improve desistance and health outcomes. Substance abusers are especially vulnerable to dying the first two weeks after release because they resume their former drug use.

Gender Disparities in Health Care

Women are more likely to be under community supervision than confined in an institution, over 80% of the estimated 1.25 million women under some form of correctional control (Lorvick et al., 2015). Women's health care needs have been largely neglected, although there has been more attention given to women's health care needs over the last three decades (Van Voorhis & Salisbury, 2014), especially when women began outpacing the growth rate of men involved in the justice system (Braithwaite, Treadwell, & Arriola, 2005; Hoskins, 2004; McGurrin, 1993). Women have special medical and mental health issues, and correctional and treatment staff must make sure their care is gender-responsive (Van Voorhis & Salisbury, 2014).

Women commonly commit drug-related crime, which represents up to 59% of the offenses committed by incarcerated women (Binswanger et al., 2010; Lorvick et al., 2015; Golder et al., 2014), many who are obviously drug addicted. To fund their addictions, women frequently rely on prostitution, theft, and assisting in drug dealing (Braithwaite et al., 2005). In a comparison of substance-abusing women under probation or parole supervision versus women not involved in the justice system, Lorvick and colleagues (2015) found no differences in their likelihood of receiving health services (e.g., drug treatment, job counseling, mental health care, and health insurance) in the community. That said, women under probation or parole supervision were found to possess greater social vulnerabilities such as homelessness, physical and sexual assault, and drug use than other women, which contributed to poorer health overall (Lorvick et al., 2015). These results indicate that, given their rates of access to health care and services do not differ from women in the general population, correctional supervision agencies are, in relation to these studies, not substantively improving these women's access to health and employment opportunities (Bahr, Harris, Fisher, & Harker Armstrong, 2010; Lorvick et al., 2015). In addition, research suggests that the stigma of a criminal record can also make accessing health care services in the community more difficult and further impact health disparities by irrevocably damaging social networks, negatively affecting employment opportunities, and reducing economic stability (van Olphen, Eliason, Freudenberg, & Barnes, 2009).

Women are the head of single-parent households and the primary care provider for their children. About two-thirds of incarcerated women have dependent children at the time of their incarceration, with about 1.3 million children in the United States having an incarcerated mother (Braithwaite et al., 2005; Epstein, 2014). Estimates show that 48% of all incarcerated mothers in the United States are white, 28% are black, and 17% are Hispanic (Glaze & Maruschak, 2010).

As Young and Smith (2000, p. 132) state, "The life circumstances and needs of families affected by maternal incarceration cannot be adequately understood without attending to the impact of race, class, and gender oppression." However, both correctional administrators and health care providers have generally overlooked the reproductive health needs and psychosocial impact of losing the female heads of households, especially in communities of color (Hoskins, 2004; Whitehead, Dodson, & Edwards, 2013; Young & Reviere, 2006). Females in prison complain about the lack of regular gynecological and breast examinations and argue their medical concerns have largely been dismissed (Hoskins, 2004; Mignon, 2016). Access to screening and treatment for cervical and breast cancer, STDs, and gynecologic conditions (e.g., abnormal bleeding, menopause) are needed for this population. Compared to men, women tend to be less disruptive but require greater personal care and assistance with family responsibilities (Hoskins, 2004; Mignon, 2016). Hoskins (2004) reported that while 90% of federal and state facilities provide routine screening, this figure was less than 50% for local jails. Screening for conditions such as gonorrhea and chlamydia are reportedly rare occurrences. Too often facilities are reactive, conducting assessments only in the event that a medical issue arises when presented with clinical symptoms or through physical examinations. This lack of screening places community members at greater risk, as infected women are unaware, untreated, and subsequently released.

In addition, 5–10% of women entering an institution are pregnant (Braithwaite et al., 2005; Grubb & del Carmen, 2016; Hoskins, 2004; Johnson, 2011). Correctional responses to the needs of pregnant women have been historically abysmal, including shackling women during birth and frequent separation from the newborn shortly after birth, a time of great importance for maternal-child attachment (Barkauskas et al., 2002; Grubb & del Carmen, 2016; McGurrin, 1993; Shaw, Downe, & Kingdon, 2015; Wismont, 2000). Compared to pregnancies outside of correctional institutions, incarcerated pregnant women are more likely to experience problems such as inadequate prenatal examination, poor emotional support, and increased rates of cesarean deliveries (Wismont, 2000). However, a study in New York State demonstrated prenatal care in institutions with improved nutritional care and health care support can be effective in countering the negative lifestyles of incarcerated women (i.e., drug abuse) (Barkauskas et al., 2002), suggesting positive influences can be realized. Further, the Indiana Women's Prison Wee Ones Nursery (WON) program noted slightly lower rates of new arrests and new admissions to the prison within the first year of release when compared to women of incarcerated births prior to the program (Whiteacre, Fritz, & Owen, 2013). The incarcerated mothers reported higher perceptions of self-esteem, were more likely to retain custody of their newborn, and possessed slightly higher measures of parent-child attachment. Jbara (2012) reiterates the importance of the parent-child bond and the negative consequences for children that can result from a break in their relationship in the formative years, including development delays, inability to connect with others, and greater criminal propensity later in life. Nursery programs, like educational programs and other services provided to inmates, have at times been viewed negatively by the public as an undeserving benefit granted to a convicted criminal. Fortunately, state governments have viewed the preservation of the family as outweighing the retributive aims of incarceration (Jbara, 2012). Grubb and del Carmen's (2016) legal review also highlights California, New Hampshire, New Mexico, and Pennsylvania for possessing the most progressive and comprehensive treatment of pregnant inmates, suggesting they serve as models for other state statutes and regulations. Yet the long-term outcomes of incarcerated births remain unknown (for a comprehensive review of the literature, see Shaw et al., 2015).

In terms of mothers entering correctional facilities, black and Hispanic women are likely to have more children under their care than white women, further complicating their parental needs. Up to 64% of incarcerated mothers report serving as the primary caregiver for their children prior to their incarceration (Scudder, McNeil, Chengappa, & Costello, 2014). Their removal, therefore, is associated with greater disruption to the family unit and negative consequences for their children, such as placement in foster care or heightened behavioral issues (Hoffman, Byrd, & Kightlinger, 2010; Scudder et al., 2014).

A variety of parenting programs are in use in correctional institutions across the U.S., but only 27% of incarcerated mothers report participating (Scudder et al., 2014). In addition, there is no standardization to these programs, and their curriculum is largely defined and implemented independently at the local level. Programs include parenting discussion groups, support groups, or therapeutic visitation programs. Scudder and colleagues (2014) note few of these programs include a combination of classroom instruction with an applied component in which parenting skills are practiced and observed. Of those programs evaluated, most lacked an adequate control group for comparison, leading to tenuous conclusions. Parent-Child Interaction Therapy (PCIT), however, represents an example of an evidence-based intervention shown to enhance parenting practices and to be effective with children ages 2–7 demonstrating behavioral problems (Scudder et al., 2014). However, an attempt to transfer such a training program to correctional facilities was met with only partial implementation, lacking the practice component (i.e., actual observation of parent and child interactions) of the intervention known to lead to more substantial improvements in parenting. To maximize effectiveness, future programs must be implemented with greater fidelity and include actual parent-child observation, not merely classroom instruction or role play.

Women on probation and parole supervision also have been found to be at a higher risk for HIV and cervical cancer (Adams et al., 2011; Belenko et al., 2004). Drug abuse exposes women to a variety of infectious diseases, including HIV and other sexually transmitted infections (STIs) (Shannon et al., 2008). Like justice-involved minority men, justice-involved women (comprised of a disproportionate number of blacks, Hispanics, or other minority groups) often suffer from poverty, substandard housing, and poor employment prospects, which are associated with health problems that drive health disparities in the general population (Hoskins, 2004). Additionally, incarcerated women have higher rates of psychiatric disorders than incarcerated men (Braithwaite et al., 2005; Varney, 2014).

Because women represent a much smaller population in prison in comparison to men, women of different classification and security levels are more likely to be classified together (Braithwaite et al., 2005). It is well known that classifying high-risk offenders with low-risk offenders increases the likelihood of criminal reoffending among low-risk offenders postrelease (Looman, Dickie, & Abracen, 2005). Also, the small number of incarcerated females often results in females being assigned to a single correctional institution within the state, which may be long distances from their native community and lead to further isolation from family and peer social support networks, contributing negatively to their mental and social health.

The Intersection of Justice and Health

Attempts to integrate and improve communication and information sharing between health and justice agencies have only recently gained traction, often stalled by inflated fears of privacy violations (Matz, 2013; 2015; TRI, 2011). However, the coordination of pertinent information between correctional organizations and health organizations in the community represents an opportunity to more proactively reach a population of impoverished minorities with distinct health needs. Yet incarceration itself introduces new problems, with often serious health implications (Dumont et al., 2013). On the one hand, incarceration can lead to improved health and reduced mortality rates, but on the other hand, it can also perpetuate and exacerbate racial and gender health disparities in the community over the long term.

While *Rhodes v. Chapman* (1981) created some ambiguity in the extent of its application, a minimum level of health care is constitutionally guaranteed to inmates under *Estelle v. Gamble* (1976) (see Goldberg, 2016; Wright, 2008). There is little doubt the capacity of health care in institutions has matured substantially from the early 1970s. As Wright (2008, p. 31) notes of that era, "in some jails the only care available was first aid, and even that was not available everywhere." Nonetheless, while incarceration is a negative life course event, it presents an opportunity to engage minorities in improved disease prevention and treatment, which can potentially reduce the health care disparities observed in the community (Wang & Green, 2010). However, the quality of care can still vary considerably across correctional settings (Binswanger et al., 2010). The best models for achieving long-term health care success (i.e., continuity of care) involve the collaboration and cooperation of health care professionals in correctional facilities and community organizations (Wang & Green, 2010). Jails that are located in close proximity to the communities of returning offenders will be more likely to collaborate with community health organizations than those returning from distant prisons, which will require more specialized reentry programming.

If done effectively, transitional treatment services have the potential to improve outcomes for returning offenders, especially for substance abusers and those with mental health needs (Butzin, Martin, & Inciardi, 2005). Intuitively, treatment has the most pronounced impact during an offender's transition back to the community as opposed to treatment solely provided within correctional facilities. Assess, Plan, Identify, and Coordinate (APIC) is a practical tool for correctional institutions and case planning for populations with co-occurring disorders and health needs (Osher, Steadman, & Barr, 2003; see Chapter 18 for more about effecitve programming for substance users).

Because of the disproportionate representation of minorities and women from impoverished communities, correctional institutions and community supervision agencies are vital linkages to health care, housing assistance, treatment, and employment opportunities (Lorvick et al., 2015). Individuals that encounter the justice system are already at risk for poor health (Binswanger et al., 2012). Failure to establish these connections is likely to have a negative long-term impact on offender health, with a pronounced impact on long-term health (Dumont et al., 2013; Dooris, McArt, Hurley, & Baybutt, 2013; Freudenberg, Daniels, Crum, Perkins, & Richie, 2008; Lorvick et al., 2015; Freudenberg, Wilets, Greene, & Richie, 1998).

Binswanger et al. (2010) identified four distinct points in the criminal justice process that represent opportunities to reduce health disparities, including the entry of the system, while incarcerated, while exiting the system and reentering the community, and while under community supervision. Ideally, at entry, health care professionals within the facility should conduct health screening for prevalent issues in incarceration (Ford, Trestman, Wiesbrock, & Zhang, 2009; Hautala, 2015; Primm & Osher, 2005; Prins, Osher, Steadman, Robbins, & Case, 2012; Steadman, Robbins, Islam, & Osher, 2007; Steadman, Scott, Osher, Agnese, & Robbins, 2005). Adequate treatment within the institution must be provided. At exit, coordination with community health providers is essential, as well as reinstatement of insurance and assistance programs. Finally, probation and parole agencies should be aware of the treatment needs of their clientele and provide ongoing support and assistance as a result (Binswanger et al., 2010). Note: For probation agencies located under the judicial branch of government instead of integrated with the state's department of corrections, this may be a more complicated endeavor. One substantial barrier to greater justice-health collaboration in the community, however, is the overtaxed and overworked culture of probation and parole organizations, which suffer from excessive workloads and high caseloads (Taxman, Henderson, & Belenko, 2009).

Finally, the Affordable Care Act (ACA) has expanded Medicaid eligibility to the benefit of impoverished individuals, such as those under probation and parole supervision (Lorvick et al., 2015; McDonnell et al., 2014). Probation and parole agencies are in a position to facilitate greater health care access through assistance for applications for Medicaid under the ACA, granting these populations access to much-needed health insurance. Such assistance, if utilized effectively, can help reduce the disparities and barriers to health care access promulgated by justice system involvement and incarceration (McDonnell et al., 2014).

Conclusion

Incarceration in correctional facilities has short-term benefits for some, such as black males, in the form of reduced mortality, but long-term consequences in terms of poorer health outcomes later in life. While there has been no evidence to suggest disparate health effects or treatment from exposure to correctional institutions, the overrepresentation of minorities among these incarcerated populations and associated health implications further exacerbates aggregate health disparities already present in struggling, disadvantaged communities on the outside. Further, correctional facilities have generally been inadequate in terms of meeting female inmate childrearing needs, where minority overrepresentation also exists. Finally, there has been limited progress in encouraging jail and prison releases to pursue or continue services in the community, where long-term benefits are more likely to be realized. Despite substantial improvements by correctional institutions in providing health care services since *Estelle*, including strong demonstrations of reentry and justice-health initiatives in the last decade, more work must be done.

References

Adams, L. M., Kendall, S., Smith, A., Quigley, E., Stuewig, J. B., & Tangney, J. P. (2011). HIV risk after release from prison: A qualitative study of former inmates. *Journal of Acquired Immune Deficiency Syndromes*, *57*(5), 429–434. doi:10.1097/QAI.0b013e31821e9f41

Adimora, A. A., & Schoenbach, V. J. (2005). Social context, sexual networks, and racial disparities in rates of sexually transmitted infections. *Journal of Infectious Diseases*, *191*(Suppl 1), S115–S122. doi:10.1086/425280

Akers, T. A., & Lanier, M. M. (2009). Epidemiological criminology: Coming full circle. *American Journal of Public Health*, *99*(3), 397–402. doi:10.2105/AJPH.2008.139808

Akers, T. A., Potter, R. H., & Hill, C. V. (2013). *Epidemiological criminology: A public health approach to crime and violence*. San Francisco, CA: Jossey-Bass/Wiley.

Alegria, M., Canino, G., Rios, R., Vera, M., Calderon, J., Rusch, D., & Ortega, A. N. (2002). Inequalities in use of specialty mental health services among latinors, Blacks, and non-Latino whites. *Psychiatric Services, 53*(12), 1547–1555. doi:10.1176/appi.ps.53.12.1547

American Civil Liberties Union. (2014). *Recial disparities in sentencing: Haering on reports of racism in the justice system of the United States*. Washington, DC: American Civil Liberties Union.

American College Physicians. (2010). *Racial and ethnic disparities in health care, updated 2010*. Washington, DC: American College Physicians.

AVERT. (2017). *People who injects drugs, HIV and AIDS*. United Kingdom: AVERT. Retrieved from www.avert.org/professionals/hiv-social-issues/key-affected-populations/people-inject-drugs

Bahr, S. J., Harris, L., Fisher, J. K., & Harker Armstrong, A. (2010). Successful reentry: What differentiates successful and unsuccessful parolees? *International Journal of Offender Therapy and Comparative Criminology, 54*(5), 667–692. doi:10.1177/0306624X09342435

Barak, G., Leighton, P., & Cotton, A. (2015). *Class, race, and gender & crime: the social relaity of justice in America*. Lanham, MD: Rowman & Littlefield.

Barkauskas, V., Pimlott, S., & Kane-Low, L. (2002). Health outcomes of a community based program for pregnant women offenders and their infants. *Journal of Nurse Midwifery, 47*(5), 371–379. doi:10.1016/S1526-9523(02)00279-9

Belenko, S., Langley, S., Crimmins, S., & Chaple, M. (2004). HIV risk behaviors, knowledge, and prevention education among offenders under community supervision: A hidden risk group. *AIDS Education and Prevention, 16*(4), 367–385. doi:10.1521/aeap.16.4.367.40394

Benjamins, M. R. (2012). Race/ethnic discrimination and preventative service utilization in a sample of whites, blacks, Mexicans, and Puerto Ricans. *Medical Care, 50*(10), 870–876. doi:10.1097/MLR.0b013e31825a8c63

Bennett, T., Holloway, K., & Farrington, D. (2008). The statistical association between drug misuse and crime: A meta-analysis. *Aggression and Violent Behavior, 13*(2), 107–118. doi:10.1016/j.avb.2008.02.001

Binswanger, I. A., Merrill, J. O., Krueger, P. M., White, M. C., Booth, R. E., & Elmore, J. G. (2010). Gender differences in chronic medical, psychiatric, and substance-dependence disorders in jail inmates. *American Journal of Public Health, 100*(3), 476–482. doi:10.2105/AJPH.2008.149591

Binswanger, I. A., Redmond, N., Steiner, J. F., & Hicks, L. S. (2012). Health disparities and the criminal justice system: An agenda for further research and action. *Journal of Urban Health: Bulletin of the New York Academy of Medicine, 89*(1), 98–107. doi:10.1007/s11524-011-9614-1

Blankenship, K. M., Smoyer, A. B., Bray, S. J., & Mattocks, K. (2005). Black-white disparities in HIV/AIDS: The role of drug policy and the corrections system. *Journal of Health Care for the Poor and Underserved, 16*(4), 140–156. doi:10.1353/hpu.2005.0110

Braithwaite, R. L., Treadwell, H. M., & Arriola, K. R. (2005). Health disparities and incarcerated women: A population ignored. *American Journal of Public Health, 95*(10), 1679–1681. doi:10.2105/AJPH.98.Supplement_1.S173

Broner, N., Lattimore, P. K., Cowell, A. J., & Schlenger, W. E. (2004). Effects of diversion on adults with co-occurring mental illness and substance use: Outcomes from a national multi-site study. *Behavioral Sciences and Law, 22*(4), 519–541. doi:10.1002/bsl.605

Butzin, C. A., Martin, S. S., & Inciardi, J. A. (2005). Treatment during transition from prison to community and subsequent illicit drug use. *Journal of Substance Abuse Treatment, 28*(4), 351–358. doi:10.1016/j.jsat.2005.02.009

Carson, E. A. (2015). *Prisoners in 2014*. Washington, DC: U.S. Department of Justice, Office of Justice Programs, Bureau of Justice Statistics.

Centers for Disease Control and Prevention. (2017a). *HIV among Blacks*. Washington, DC: Centers for Disease Control and Prevention

Centers for Disease Control and Prevention. (2017b). *HIV among women*. Washington, DC: Centers for Disease Control and Prevention.

Chandler, R. K., Peters, R. H., & Juliano-Bult, D. (2004). Challenges in implementing evidence-based treatment practices for co-occurring disorders in the criminal justice system. *Behavioral Sciences and the Law, 22*(4), 431–448. doi:10.1002/bsl.598

Cobb, K. A., Mowatt, M. A., Matz, A. K., & Mullins, T. (2011). *A desktop guide for tribal probation personnel: The screening and assessment process*. Lexington, KY: Council of State Governments, American Probation and Parole Association.

Cook, B. L. (2007). Effect of Medicaid managed care on racial disparities in health care. *Health Services Research, 42*(1), 124–145. doi:10.1111/j.1475-6773.2006.00611.x

Cook, B. L., McGuire, T., & Miranda, J. (2007). Measuring trends in mental health care disparities, 2000–2004. *Psychiatric Services, 58*(12), 1533–1540. doi:10.1176/ps.2007.58.12.1533

Cook, B. L., Zuvekas, S. H., Carson, N., Wayne, G. F., Vesper, A., & McGuire, T. G. (2014). Assessing racial/ethnic disparities in treatment across episodes of mental health care. *Health Services Research, 49*(1), 206–229. doi:10.1111/1475-6773.12095

Diala, C., Muntaner, C., Walrath, C., Nickerson, K. J., LaVeist, T. A., & Leaf, P. J. (2000). Racial differences in attitudes toward professional mental health care and in the use of services. *American Journal of Orthopsychiatry, 70*(4), 455–464. doi:10.1037/h0087736

Doerner, J. K., & Demuth, S. (2014). Gender and sentencing in the federal courts: Are women treated more leniently? *Criminal Justice Policy Review, 25*(2), 242–269. doi:10.1177/0887403412466877

Dooris, M., McArt, D., Hurley, M. A., & Baybutt, M. (2013). Probation as a setting for building well-being through integrated service provision: Evaluating an offender health trainer service. *Perspect Public Health, 133*(4), 199–206. doi:10.1177/1757913913486036

Draine, J., Blank, A., Kottsieper, P., & Solomon, P. (2005). Contrasting jail diversion and in-jail services for mental illness and substance abuse: Do they serve the same clients? *Behavioral Sciences and the Law, 23*(2), 171–181. doi:10.1002/bsl.637

Dumont, D. M., Allen, S. A., Brockmann, B. W., Alexander, N. E., & Rich, J. D. (2013). Incarceration, community health, and racial disparities. *Journal of Health Care for the Poor and Underserved, 24*(1), 78–88. doi:10.1353/hpu.2013.0000

Epstein, R. (2014). What is justice? Re-imaging penal policy. *The Howard League for Penal Reform*, 1–18. Retrieved from http://howardleague.org/wp-content/uploads/2016/04/HLWP_3_2014.pdf

Estelle v. Gamble, 429 U.S. 97 (1976).

Farmer, P. (2002). The house of the dead: Tuberculosis and incarceration. In M. Mauer & M. Chesney-Lind (Eds.), *Invisible punishment: The collateral consequences of mass imprisonment* (pp. 239–257). New York, NY: New York Press.

Ford, J. D., Trestman, R. L., Wiesbrock, V. H., & Zhang, W. (2009). Validation of a brief screening instrument for identifying psychiatric disorders among newly incarcerated adults. *Psychiatric Services, 60*(6), 842–846. doi:10.1176/ps.2009.60.6.842

Frank, J. W., Wang, E. A., Nunez-Smith, M., Lee, H., & Comfort, M. (2014). Discrimination based on criminal record and healthcare utilization among men recently released from prison: A descriptive study. *Health and Justice, 2*, 6–13. doi:10.1186/2194-7899-2-6

Freudenberg, N., Daniels, J., Crum, M., Perkins, T., & Richie, B. E. (2008). Coming home from jail: The social and health consequences of community reentry for women, male adolscents, and their families and communities. *American Journal of Public Health, 98*(9), S191–S202. doi:10.2105/AJPH.98.Supplement_1.S191

Freudenberg, N., Wilets, I., Greene, M. B., & Richie, B. E. (1998). Linking women in jail to community services: Factors associated with rearrest and retention of drug-using women following release from jail. *Journal of American Medical Women's Association, 53*(2), 89–93.

Gaiter, J. L., Potter, R. H., & O'Leary, A. (2006). Disproportionate rates of incarceration contribute to health disparities. *American Journal of Public Health, 96*(7), 1148–1149. doi:10.2105/AJPH.2006.086561

Glaze, L. E., & Marsuchak, L. M. (2010). *Parents in prison and their minor children*. Washington, DC: U.S. Department of Justice, Bureau of Justice Statistics.

Goldberg, R. C. (2016). The antidotes to the doube standard: Protecting the healthcare rights of mentally ill inmates by blurring the line between *Estelle* and *Youngberg*. *Yale Journal of Health Policy, Law, and Ethics, 16*(1), 111–145.

Golder, S., Hall, M. T., Logan, T. K., Higgins, G. E., Dishon, A., Renn, T., & Winham, K. M. (2014). Substance use among victimized women on probation and parole. *Substance Use and Misuse, 49*(4), 435–447. doi:10.3109/10826084.2013.844164

Grubb, L. M., & del Carmen, R. V. (2016). An analysis of court decisions, statutes, and administrative regulations related to pregnant inmates. *The Prison Journal, 96*(3), 355–391. doi:10.1177/0032885516635088

Hall, M. T., Golder, S., Conley, C. L., & Sawning, S. (2013). Designing programming and interventions for women in the criminal justice system. *American Journal of Criminal Justice, 38*(1), 27–50. doi:10.1007/s12103-012-9158-2

Hammett, T. M., Roberts, C., & Kennedy, S. (2001). Health-related issues in prisoner reentry. *Crime & Delinquency, 47*(3), 390–409. doi:10.1177/0011128701047003006

Hatcher, S. S., Toldson, I. A., Godette, D. C., & Richardson, Jr., J. B. (2009). Mental health, substance abuse, and HIV disparities in correctional settings: Practice and policy implications for Blacks. *Journal of Health Care for the Poor and Underserved, 20*(2), S6-S16. doi:10.1353/hpu.0.0154

Hautala, M. (2015). In the shadow of Sandra Bland: The importance of mental health screening in U.S. jails. *Texas Journal on Civil Liberties & Civil Rights, 21*(1), 89–126.

Hoffman, H. C., Byrd, A. L., & Kightlinger, A. M. (2010). Prison programs and services for incarcerated parents and their underage children: Results from a national survey of correctional facilities. *The Prison Journal, 90*(4), 397–416. doi:10.1177/0032885510382087

Hoskins, I. A. (2004). A guest editorial: Women's health care in correctional facilities: A lost colony. *Obstetrical and Gynecological Survey, 59*(4), 234–236.

Iguichi, M. Y., Bell, J., Ramchand, R. N., & Fain, T. (2005). How criminal system racial disparities may translate into health disparities. *Journal of Health Care for the Poor and Underserved, 16*(4), 48–56. doi:10.1353/hpu.2005.0114

Jbara, A. E. (2012). The price they pay: Protecting the mother-child relationship throug the use of prison nurseries and residential parenting programs. *Indiana Law Journal, 87*(4), 1825–1845.

Johnson, A. (2011). Access to elective abortions for female prisoners under the Eighth and Fourteenth Amendments. *American Journal of Law & Medicine, 37*, 652–683.

Kaeble, D., Glaze, L., Tsoutis, A., & Minton, T. (2016). *Correctional populations in the United States, 2014.* Washington, DC: U.S. Department of Justice, Bureau of Justice Statistics.

Kulkarni, S. P., Baldwin, S., Lightstone, A. S., Gelberg, L., & Diamant, A. L. (2010). Is incarceration a contributor to health disparities? Access to care of formerly incarcerated adults. *Journal of Community Health, 35*(3), 268–274. doi:10.1007/s10900-010-9234-9

Lanier, M. M., & Potter, R. H. (2010). The current status of inmates living with HIV/AIDS. In R. Muraskin (Ed.), *Key correctional issues* (2nd ed., pp. 140–162). Upper Saddle River, NJ: Prentice Hall.

Lanier, M. M., Lucken, K., & Akers, T. A. (2010). Further need for epidemiological criminology. In R. Muraskin (Ed.), *Key correitonal issues* (2nd ed., pp. 163–174). Upper Saddle River, NJ: Prentice Hall.

Looman, J., Dickie, I., & Abracen, J. (2005). Responsivity issues in the treatment of sexual offenders. *Trauma, Violence, & Abuse, 6*(4), 330–353. doi:10.1177/1524838005280857

Loring, M., & Beaudoin, P. (2000). Battered women as coerced victim-perpetrators. *Journal of Emotional Abuse, 2*(1), 3–14. doi: 10.1300/J135v02n01_02

Lorvick, J., Comfort, M. L., Krebs, C. P., & Kral, A. H. (2015). Health service use and social vulnerability in a community-based sample of women on probation and parole, 2011–2013. *Health and Justice, 3*, 13–18. doi:10.1186/s40352-015-0024-4

Maruschak, L. M. (2015). *HIV in prisons, 2001–2010.* Washinton, DC: U.S. Department of Justice, Bureau of Justice Statistics.

Massoglia, M. (2008). Incarceration, health, and racial disparities in health. *Law & Society Review, 42*(2), 275–306.

Matz, A. K. (2015). A note on HIPAA and 42 CFR Part 2: Dispelling the myths about justice-health information sharing. *The Journal of the American Probation and Parole Association: Perspectives, 39*(1), 22–27.

Matz, A. K. (2013). Leveraging technology to enhance corrections-health/human service information sharing and offender reentry. In E. Waltermaurer & T. A. Akers (Eds.), *Epidemiological criminology: Theory to practice* (pp. 187–196). New York: Routledge.

McDonnell, M., Brookes, L., & Lurigio, A. J. (2014). The promise of healthcare reform in transforming services for jail releases and other criminal justice populations. *Health and Justice, 2*, 9–18. doi:10.1186/2194-7899-2-9

McGurrin, M. C. (1993). Pregnant inmates' right to health care. *New England Journal on Criminal and Civil Confinement, 20*(1), 163–194.

Mignon, S. (2016). A questão da saúde nas mulheres encarceradas nos Estados Unidos. *Ciência & Saúde Coletiva, 21*(7), 2051–2059. doi: 10.1590/1413–81232015217.05302016

National Center on Addiction and Substance Abuse. (2010). *Behind bars II: Substance abuse and America's prison population.* New York, NY: Columbia University.

National Institute on Drug Abuse. (2014), *Principles of drug abuse treatment for criminal justice populations: A research-based guide.* Bethesda, MD: National Institute on Drug Abuse.

Native Americans overrepresented in prison: Problems with tribal police cited. (2013, April). *Prison Legal News.* Retrieved from www.prisonlegalnews.org/news/2013/apr/15/native-americans-overrepresented-in-prison-problems-with-tribal-police-cited/

Nichols, E., Loper, A., & Meyer, J. (2016). Promoting educational resiliency in youth with incarcerated parents: The impact of parental incarceration, school characteristics, and connectedneess on school outcomes. *Journal of Youth and Adolescence, 45*(6), 1090–1109. doi:10.1007/s10964-015-0337-6

Nowotny, K. M., Rogers, R. G., & Boardman, J. D. (2017). Racial disparities in health condictions among prisoners compared with the general population. *Population Health, 3*, 487–496. doi:10.1016/j.ssmph.2017.05.011

Osher, F., Steadman, H. J., & Barr, H. (2003). A best practice approach to community reentry from jails for inmates with co-occurring disorders: The APIC model. *Crime and Delinquency, 49*(1), 79–96. doi:10.1177/0011128702239237

Paradies, Y. (2006). A systematic review of empirical research on self-reported racism and health. *International Journal of Epidemiology, 35*(4), 888–901. doi:10.1093/ije/dyl056

Petersilia, J. (2003). *When prisoners come home: Parole and prisoner reentry*. New York, NY: Oxford University Press.

Pettit, B. (2012). *Invisible men: Mass incarceration and the myth of Black progress*. New York, NY: Russell Sage Foundation.

Pettit, B., & Western, B. (2004). Mass imprisonment and the life course: Race and class inequality in U.S. incarceration. *American Sociological Review, 69*(2), 151–169. doi:10.1177/000312240406900201

Potter, H. (2008). *Battle cries: Black women and intinmate partner abuse*. New York, NY: New Yourk University Press.

Potter, R. H. (2002). Guest editor comments: Corrections, health care, and public health. *The Prison Journal, 82*(1), 5–7. doi:10.1177/003288550208200101

Potter, R. H., & Akers, T. A. (2010). Improving the health of minority communities through probation-public health collaborations: An application of the epidemiological criminology framework. *Journal of Offender Rehabilitation, 49*(8), 595–609. doi:10.1080/10509674.2010.519674

Primm, A. B., & Osher, F. C. (2005). Race and ethnicity, mental health services and cultural competence in the criminal justice system: Are we ready to change? *Community Mental Health Journal, 41*(5), 557–569. doi:10.1007/s10597-005-6361-3

Prins, S. J., Osher, F. C., Steadman, H. J., Robbins, P. C., & Case, B. (2012). Exploring racial disparities in the brief jail mental health screen. *Criminal Justice and Behavior, 39*(5), 635–645. doi:10.1177/0093854811435776

Rhodes v. Chapman, 452 U.S. 337 (1981).

Scudder, A. T., McNeil, C. B., Chengappa, K., & Costello, A. H. (2014). Evaluation of an existing parenting class within a women's state correctional facility and a parenting class modeled from Parent-Child Interaction Therapy. *Children and Youth Services Review, 46*, 238–247. doi:10.1016/j.childyouth.2014.08.015

Shafer, M. S., Arthur, B., & Franczak, M. J. (2004). An analysis of post-booking jail diversion programming for persons with co-occurring disorders. *Behavioral Sciences and the Law, 22*(6), 771–785. doi:10.1002/bsl.603

Shannon, K., Rusch, M., Morgan, R., Oleson, M., Kerr, T., & Tyndall, M. W. (2008). HIV and HCV prevalence and gender-specific risk profiles of crack cocaine smokers and dual users of injection drugs. *Substance Use and Misuse, 43*(3–4), 521–534. doi:10.1080/10826080701772355

Shavers, V. L., Fagan, P., Jones, D., Klein, W. M., Boyington, J., Moten, C., & Rorie, E.. (2012). The state of research on racial/ethnic discrimination in the receipt of health care. *American Journal of Public Health, 102*(5), 953–966. doi:10.2105/AJPH.2012.300773

Shaw, J., Downe, S., & Kingdon, C. (2015). Systematic mixed-methods review of interventions, outcomes and experiences for imprisoned pregnant women. *Journal of Advanced Nursing, 71*(7), 1451–1463. doi:10.1111/jan.12605

Soderstrom, I. R. (2007). Mental illness in offender populations: Prevalence, duty and implications. In D. Phillips (Ed.), *Mental health issues in the criminal justice system*. Binghamton, NY: Haworth Press.

Steadman, H. J., & Naples, M. (2005). Assessing the effectiveness of jail diversion programs for persons with serious mental illness and co-occurring substance use disorders. *Behavioral Sciences and the Law, 23*(2), 163–170. doi:10.1002/bsl.640

Steadman, H. J., Robbins, P. C., Islam, T., & Osher, F. C. (2007). Revalidating the brief jail mental health screen to increase accuracy for women. *Psychiatric Services, 58*(12), 1598–1601. doi:10.1176/ps.2007.58.12.1598

Steadman, H. J., Scott, J. E., Osher, F., Agnese, T. K., & Robbins, P. C. (2005). Validation of the brief jail mental health screen. *Psychiatric Services, 56*(7), 816–822. doi:10.1176/appi.ps.56.7.816

Swavola, E., Riley, K., & Subramanian, R. (2016). *Overlooked: Women and jails in an era of reform*. New York, NY: Vera Institute of Justice.

Taylor, B. S., Chiasson, M. A., Scheinmann, R., Hirschfield, S., Humberstone, M., Remien, R. H., . . . Wong, T. (2012). Results from two online surveys comparing sexual risk behaviors in Hispanic, Black, and White Men who have sex with men. *AIDS Behavior, 16*(3), 644–652. doi:10.1007/s10461-011-9983-1

Taxman, F. S. (2014). Building effective service delivery mechanisms for justice-involved individuals: An under-researched area. *Health and Justice, 2*, 2–15. doi:10.1186/2194-7899-2-2

Taxman, F. S., Henderson, C. E., & Belenko, S. (2009). Organizational context, systems change, and adopting treatment delivery systems in the criminal justice system. *Drug and Alcohol Dependence, 103*(S), S1–S6. doi:10.1016/j.drugalcdep.2009.03.003

Tonry, M. (2011). *Punishing race: A continuing American dilemma*. New York, NY: Oxford University Press.

Travis, J., Solomon, A. L., & Waul, M. (2001). *From prison to home: The dimensions and consequences of prisoner reentry*. Washington, DC: The Urban Institute.

Treatment Research Institute. (2011). *Increasing effective communication between criminal justice and treatment settings using health information technology*. Philadelphia, PA: Treatment Research Institute.

van Olphen, J., Eliason, M. J., Freudenberg, N., & Barnes, M. (2009). Nowhere to go: How stigma limits the options of female drug users after release from jail. *Substance Abuse Treatment, Prevention, and Policy, 4*, 10. doi:10.1186/1747-597X-4-10

Van Voorhis, P., & Salisbury, E. J. (2014). *Correctional counseling and rehabilitation.* New York, NY: Routledge.

Varney, S. (2014, May 15). By the numbers: Mentaial illness behind bars. *Kaiser Health News, PBS Newshour.* Retrieved from www.pbs.org/newshour/updates/numbers-mental-illness-behind-bars/

Vaugh, M., DeLisi, M., Beaver, K., Perron, B. E., & Abdon, A. (2012). Toward a criminal justice epidemiology: Behavioral and physical health of probationers and parolees in the United States. *Journal of Criminal Justice, 40*(3), 165–173. doi:10.1016/j.jcrimjus.2012.03.001

Wallace, D., Eason, J. M., & Lindsey, A. M. (2015). The influence of incarceration and re-entry on the availability of health care organizations in Arkansas. *Health and Justice, 3*, 3–14. doi:1186/s40352-015-0016-4

Wang, E. A., & Green, J. (2010). Incarceration as a key variable in racial disparities of asthma prevalence. *BMC Public Health, 10*, 290–299. doi:10.1186/1471-2458-10-290

Western, B. (2006). *Punishment and inequality in American.* New York, NY: Russell Sage Foundation.

Western, B. (2008). *From prison to work: A proposal for a national prisoner reentry program.* Washington, DC: The Brookings Institution. Retrieved from http://scholar.harvard.edu/files/brucewestern/files/12_prison_to_work_western.pdf

Whiteacre, K., Fritz, S., & Owen, J. (2013). *Assessing outcomes for Wee Ones Nursery at the Indiana Women's Prison.* Indianapolis, IN: University of Indianapolis, Community Research Center.

Whitehead, J. T., Dodson, K. D., & Edwards, B. D. (2013). *Corrections: Exploring crime, punishment, and justice in America* (3rd ed.). New York, NY: Routledge.

Willging, C. E., Malcoe, L. H., Cyr, S. S., Zywiak, W. H., & Lapham, S. C. (2013). Behavioral health and social correlates of reincarceration among Hispanic, Native American, and White rural women. *Psychiatric Services, 64*(6), 590–593. doi:10.1176/appi.ps.201200120

Williams, D. R., & Mohammed, S. A. (2009). Discrimination and racial disparities in health: Evidence and needed research. *Journal of Behavioral Medicine, 32*(1), 20–47. doi:10.1007/s10865-008-9185-0

Wismont, J. M. (2000). The lived pregnancy experience of women in prison. *Journal of Midwifery & Women's Health, 45*(4), 292–300. doi:10.1016/S1526-9523(00)00034-9

Wright, L. N. (2008). Health care in prison thirty years after *Estelle v. Gamble*. *Journal of Correctional Health Care, 14*(1), 31–35. doi:10.1177/1078345807309618

Young, D., & Smith, C. J. (2000). When moms are incarcerated: The needs of children, mothers, and caregivers. *Families in Society: The Journal of Contemporary Human Services, 81*(2), 130–141. doi:10.1606/1044-3894.1007

Young, V. D., & Reviere, R. (2006). *Women behind bars: Gender and race in U.S. prisons.* Boulder, CO: Lynne Rienner Publishers, Inc.

PART IV

Treatment in the Community

27

POLICING SPECIAL NEEDS OFFENDERS

Implementing Training to Improve Police-Citizen Encounters

Bradley D. Edwards and Jennifer Pealer

> Given the prevalence of mental illness in police shootings, reducing encounters between on-duty law enforcement and individuals with the most severe psychiatric diseases may represent the single most immediate, practical strategy for reducing fatal police shootings in the United States.
>
> —(Fuller, Lamb, Biasotti, & Snook, 2015, p. 5)

Introduction

In August 2016, a North Carolina state trooper fatally shot Daniel Harris, a 29-year-old deaf man, following an altercation originating from Harris's failure to immediately pull over for a traffic stop. Harris was apparently afraid of police because of a series of previous misunderstandings during encounters with police (Stack, 2016). Just a month earlier, police officers in North Miami shot and wounded an autistic man's caregiver, Charles Kinsey, while Kinsey lay on the ground with both hands up. Prior to police arriving on the scene, Kinsey was trying to assist the autistic man, who had decided to sit in the middle of a road cross-legged while playing with a toy truck. Misunderstanding the autistic man's refusal to comply with instructions to lie on the ground as a threat, even though Kinsey attempted to explain the situation, the officer discharged his firearm, accidently shooting Kinsey in the leg (Alvarado, Miller, & Berman, 2016).

The type of incidents described are all too common as police officers interact with suspects who have physical disabilities or find themselves as the first responders in disturbances involving those with developmental disorders or mental illnesses. Police officers responding to calls must resolve these problems while simultaneously considering the safety of the individual, family members, bystanders, and themselves (Thompson, Reuland & Souweine, 2003). This is an unenviable task that police officers are expected to handle correctly every time. Failure to do so can result in the needless loss of life, loss of the officer's job, legal liability, and/or negative publicity, which could strain the public's support of the police and increase the confrontational nature of future law enforcement interactions.

The Americans with Disabilities Act (ADA) prohibits discrimination against individuals with disabilities in all areas of life. This includes interactions with police officers and the criminal justice system. Police officers who either (1) mistakenly arrest offenders whose actions are the result of their disability rather than a violation of the law or who (2) fail to provide a reasonable accommodation for an offender's disability can be in violation of the ADA (Brodin, 2005; Osborn, 2008). An exception to these requirements exists when the offender endangers the public's safety. Unfortunately, the lack of police training can unintentionally and unnecessarily lead to the situation escalating to the point where the suspect might create a danger to the public or the officer (Osborn, 2008). Thus, even a legally justified arrest or use of force might be one that could have been prevented.

The public attention received when officers use excessive force with mentally ill or other special needs suspects creates the public misperception that police are routinely involved in violent interactions with these populations. In fact, injuries to either the suspect or the officer during these calls are rare events (Kerr, Morabito, & Watson, 2010). Many police officers are hard-working, honest professionals who try to make the best decisions possible in a given situation. The key to improving outcomes to these situations is effective training paired with effective community services. In the sections that follow, we discuss the treatment of special needs offenders by police officers and the training available to help ensure that interactions between police officers and offenders with special needs occur in an ethical, legal, and effective manner. This chapter will focus on policing interactions with individuals who suffer from hearing loss or deafness, intellectual disabilities, and mental illness.

Hearing Loss and Deafness

Approximately 15% of adults in the United States report some sort of hearing loss (Blackwell, Lucas, & Clark, 2012). This is a diverse group of individuals who report symptoms ranging from "a little trouble hearing" to those who are deaf. Most scholarly attention regarding criminal behavior of hearing impaired individuals has focused on those with profound hearing loss or deafness. These individuals have varying degrees of education and ability to read or speak a language (Vernon & Miller, 2005). Many who are born deaf or lose their hearing at young ages experience particular difficulty in educational attainment and communication skills. Some evidence also suggests that profound hearing loss can also be a risk factor for developmental disabilities such as autism and intellectual disability (Szymanski, Brice, Lam, & Hotto, 2012). Unfortunately, evidence also suggests that deaf individuals are overrepresented in the criminal justice system (Vernon & Greenberg, 1999). Specifically, deaf inmates have been shown to be incarcerated for violent and sexual offenses at rates higher than those without hearing problems (Miller & Vernon, 2003; Miller, Vernon, & Capella, 2005; Williamson & Grubb, 2015).

Developmental Disabilities

The prevalence of developmental disabilities such as autism, cerebral palsy, and intellectual disability has increased over time (Boyle et al., 2011). Research related to the prevalence of criminal behavior by individuals with developmental disabilities has been limited by various methodological issues. For example, variations in defining and assessing intellectual disability (ID), paired with the prevalence of police officers who come into contact with individuals with ID but do not make an arrest, make it difficult to determine how many individuals with ID commit crimes (Holland, Clare, & Mukhopadhyay, 2002; Jones, 2007; Lindsay, Hastings, Griffiths, & Hayes, 2007). As with the hearing impaired, the best available data originates from surveys of jail and prison populations. Approximately 31% of jail inmates report having some sort of cognitive disability (Bronson & Berzofsky, 2015). Most intellectually disabled offenders who have formally entered the criminal justice system seem to be individuals with mild disability who are not easily recognizable or distinguishable from nondisabled offenders (Salekin, Olley, & Hedge, 2010). Comparing a group of juvenile offenders with and without intellectual disabilities, Asscher, van der Put, and Stams (2012) found that the disability did not serve as a risk factor in terms of the total volume of criminal offenses. However, the juveniles with ID had more problems with attitude, aggression, and skills such as situational perception and dealing with others. Consequently, the intellectually disabled juveniles were more likely to commit crimes against persons than the juveniles without ID.

Aside from intellectual disability, most research dedicated to examining whether developmentally disabled individuals are at increased risk for criminal activity has focused on autism spectrum disorders. Taken as a whole, there is no conclusive evidence of increased criminal activity by autistic individuals compared to the general population (Maras, Mulcahy, & Crane, 2015; Mouridsen, 2012). However, it is also important to note that many autistic individuals also have mental illness, substance abuse disorder, or intellectual disability. Presence of these comorbidities may increase the likelihood of violence among autistic individuals (Brown et al., 2016a; 2016b; Gunasekaran & Chaplin, 2012; Långström, Grann, Ruchkin, Sjöstedt, & Fazel, 2009). Police also may be called to investigate reports of autistic individuals displaying suspicious behavior such as looking into the windows of homes, attempting to enter strangers' swimming pools, or playing on playground equipment with young children (Debbaudt, 2002).

Mentally Ill Offenders

Cutbacks in state funding of mental health services means that police are increasingly coming into contact with mentally ill individuals (Santos & Goode, 2014). The majority of these encounters involve situations where the suspect has either committed a low-level crime or has exhibited nuisance type behavior for which a relative or concerned citizen seeks police intervention (Engel & Silver, 2001; Fisher et al., 2006; Reuland, Schwarzfeld, & Draper, 2009; Thompson et al., 2003). Many of these suspects are "frequent fliers" whom police interact with on a regular basis (Akins, Burkhardt, & Lanfear, 2016). This seemingly never-ending cycle of interactions could increase the frustration and cynicism among police officers, who may see any disposition as merely a temporary solution to solving the immediate issue. However, this also underscores the importance of police developing a positive rapport with mentally ill persons in their communities and ultimately working toward resolutions which might make a lasting difference.

Despite the fact that most encounters with mentally ill persons involve relatively minor infractions and low levels of risk to officers, police must still be diligent when interacting with more serious offenders who suffer from mental impairment. One study involving a large cohort of mentally ill patients found that nearly 14% of the cohort was arrested at least once for serious violent crimes (e.g., murder, rape, and robbery) over a 10-year time frame (Fisher et al., 2006). Indeed, mental illness can be a risk factor for increased violent behavior, especially when combined with substance use (Elbogen & Johnson, 2009; Van Dorn, Volavka, & Johnson, 2012). Mentally disoriented offenders also have been found to be more likely to possess a weapon and to be disrespectful, resist, or assault police officers (Engel & Silver, 2001; Johnson, 2011; Novak & Engel, 2005). The Federal Bureau of Investigation (FBI, 2014) reported that 1,499 police officers were assaulted in 2014 while responding to calls involving persons with a mental illness. Criminal behavior committed by mentally ill offenders is rarely motivated by their illness; nor is their offense often caused by their symptoms (Peterson, Skeem, Kennealy, Bray, & Zvonkovic, 2014). The lack of obvious connection between criminal activity and mental illness illustrates the difficulty that both dispatchers and police officers might have in correctly identifying calls involving mentally ill offenders and responding accordingly.

Individuals with special needs such as hearing loss, intellectual disabilities, and mental illness are involved in the criminal justice system as both victims and offenders. Furthermore, in many jurisdictions police officers are the first responders on the scene and must interact with the individuals either as victims, offenders, or witnesses. The interactions may become problematic for a few reasons. First, the individual may not be able to communicate or verbalize to the police officer who arrives on the scene. Relatedly, police officers must communicate with the special needs individuals. The individual may not be able to hear or cognitively process what the police officer is communicating. Lastly, the behaviors of the special needs individual may be interpreted as defiance or opposition by the officers. These reasons may escalate the situation as both parties become frustrated by the lack of communication and understanding.

Police Officer Response

Police officers are increasingly likely to serve as a first responder to situations where a mentally ill, developmentally disabled, or hearing impaired individual has committed a criminal offense or is exhibiting unusual behavior. These individuals may be uncooperative or confused when approached by officers. Thus, police officers may believe that an individual is disobeying their commands when the person is actually unable to comply because of his or her disability (Police Executive Research Forum, 2012). Nonetheless, as the first point of contact with these suspects, the actions taken by law enforcement are critical to achieve a successful resolution while ensuring the due process rights of the suspect are maintained and that the situation does not escalate unnecessarily. It is important for officers to identify the presence of the disability to respond appropriately. Nevertheless, the nature of these situations creates a high risk for a misunderstanding. For example, Murgado (2013) describes a situation where he, as a rookie police officer, almost shot a man who he feared was reaching for a gun. In fact, the man was reaching for a laminated card explaining that he was deaf, a mute, and which contained directions for obtaining an emergency contact for assistance. The United States Department of Justice (DOJ) has published a list of suggestions for officers communicating with people who are deaf or hard of hearing with the hope of reducing miscommunications and misunderstandings (see Box 27.1).

The first step in determining an evidence-based police response to special needs suspects is to clearly understand the nature of these interactions. Most scholarly attention to policing special needs offenders has examined the role of law enforcement in responding to calls of mentally ill suspects. As a result of their role as first responders to calls for service involving those with mental illness, police have essentially become the "gatekeepers" of both the mental health and criminal justice systems. Their resolution to a call will help determine whether the individual receives mental health treatment or is formally processed by the criminal justice system. Police officers typically have a range of formal or informal options available in handling these situations (Teplin, 2000). Obviously, these

Box 27.1 Communicating with Deaf or Hearing Impaired Individuals

Police can utilize the following suggestions to improve communication with hearing impaired individuals:

- Speech supplemented by gestures and visual aids;
- A pad and pencil or word processor can be used to exchange written notes;
- A teletypewriter can be used to exchange messages over the telephone;
- An assistive listening system or device to amplify sound;
- A sign language interpreter can be used when speaking with someone who knows sign language; and/or
- An oral interpreter can be used when speaking with a person who has been trained to speech read.

Adapted from: U.S. Department of Justice, Civil Rights Division (2006). Communicating with people who are deaf or hard of hearing: ADA guide for law enforcement officers discretionary decisions can be critically important for the suspect's welfare as well as the public's safety. However, it is important to understand that police officers make decisions that reflect a broader organizational culture. For example, officers often feel pressure to handle a call quickly so that they can return to service. This urgency can cause serious ramifications, such as making an unnecessary arrest or being reluctant to call for mental health professional services (Hoover, 2007). As discussed next, officers who fail to dedicate adequate time handling a call involving a mentally ill person might also unintentionally increase the likelihood of the situation escalating to the point of requiring an arrest and/or use of force.

Arresting Mentally Ill Suspects

It is unclear whether mentally ill suspects are at greater risk of being arrested compared to suspects who are not mentally impaired. Based upon their training and experience, police officers often differentiate mental disturbance calls based on the level of perceived threat and existence of substance use (Watson, Swartz, Bohrman, Kriegel, & Draine, 2014). A combination of situational and officer characteristics determines the presence of a threat or the perceived seriousness of a crime. For example, Green (1997) found that younger officers were more likely to engage those with a mental illness, whereas more experienced officers were more likely to either ignore or take no official action against those perceived to have a mental illness. Markowitz and Watson (2015) found that officers who were combat veterans were more sympathetic to a domestic disturbance involving an offender showing signs of depression, substance use, and posttraumatic stress disorder (PTSD). However, other situational factors such as the presence of an injury or the suspect's lack of compliance were given even greater consideration when determining a proper resolution.

One of the classic studies specifically focused on police interactions with mentally ill suspects was Teplin's (1984) analysis of 1,382 police-citizen encounters that were observed by fieldworkers trained in identifying signs of mental impairment. Teplin found that the probability of being arrested was nearly 20% greater for suspects exhibiting signs of mental disorientation compared to those who showed no signs of mental disorientation. Mental disorientation increased the probability of arrest for nearly every category of crime and was independent of whether the police officer actually recognized the symptoms of mental disorder. This led to the suggestion that the mentally ill were being criminalized because of their status rather than the offenses that they might commit. Subsequent research has challenged Teplin's (1984) finding of an increased risk of arrest among mentally ill suspects. In fact, more recent research suggests that having a mental illness can actually substantially reduce one's likelihood of arrest. Even among studies which have found mentally ill suspects to be more likely to exhibit behavior that might be perceived as a danger to police officers (e.g., verbal aggression, possession of a weapon, or resistance to officers), officers have been found to make an arrest less often than among similar suspects without a mental illness (Engel & Silver, 2001; Novak & Engel, 2005).

Wood, Watson, and Fulambarker (2017) describe encounters with mentally ill suspects as often occurring in a "gray zone" where no easy solutions are available. These cases often occur when a family member, business owner, or citizen makes a complaint about a situation where a crime has not been committed and the legal justification for hospitalization has not been met. In these situations, police officers often must use their best judgment regarding a proper disposition. King and Dunn (2004) even discussed anecdotal evidence regarding the practice of "dumping" troublesome persons, including those with mental disorders, out of that officer's jurisdiction and releasing them on their own recognizance. This is obviously not an ideal resolution to a call for service but might be a symptom of an officer's lack of training regarding mentally ill suspects. In a survey of over 100 police departments in Pennsylvania, Ruiz and Miller (2004) found that over half of the departments did not have guidelines for the management of mentally ill suspects. Thus, it is not surprising that only a slight majority (53%) of officers in these departments felt qualified to manage situations involving mentally ill persons.

Police Use of Force

With the increased media attention given to police shootings in the United States (McLaughlin, 2015), there is perhaps no more pressing issue surrounding the policing profession than use of force. Much of this national attention has been given to police use of force while interacting with racial minorities. Unfortunately, less focus is given to the fact that many of these high-profile African-American victims of police violence also suffered from a mental disability (Perry & Carter-Long, 2016). Officers are trained to use force on a suspect who is causing imminent danger to the officer or the community. Alternatively, they may use force and/or physical restraint to gain compliance with lawful instructions. However, failure to recognize mental illnesses or developmental disabilities can lead to unfortunate and even deadly outcomes. As mentioned before, individuals with developmental disabilities may not understand the inappropriate nature of their actions or behavior and may subsequently fail to comply with or even understand the officer's instructions. Officers should not interpret this as a reason for increased force (Debbaudt, 2002). Indeed, physical force or restraint of any kind increases the risk of positional or aspirational asphyxiation (Pollack, 2016), and therefore should be used only as a last resort to prevent harm (see Box 27.2).

Accurate data on the frequency of force against suspects with mental illness are difficult to obtain, as the federal government does not yet maintain an accurate listing of these incidents. The best available data originates from media outlets that have developed databases from public records and news reports. These records do not specifically mention the presence of physical disabilities such as hearing impairment, nor do they include a classification for developmental disabilities. However, these reports do estimate that between 26–50% of suspects shot and killed by police each year suffer from a mental illness (Bouchard, 2012; Swaine, Laughland, & Lartey, 2015). To provide some perspective, the National Alliance on Mental Illness (NAMI, 2016) suggests that approximately 18.5% of adults experience some form of mental illness in a given year.

Box 27.2 Guidelines for Physical Restraint of IDD Persons to Reduce Asphyxiation Risk

1. Avoid placing restrained persons in a horizontal position. If absolutely necessary, it is best to place them on their side with their back supported.
2. Avoid placing additional pressure on the person's back or chest while being restrained.
3. Make sure you can see the person's face while restrained, being attentive to signs of breathing difficulty, change in color, or facial expressions that indicate distress.
4. Monitor the person's ability to breathe continuously while restrained.
5. Try to help the person remain calm while restrained.
6. If the person has difficulty breathing, release the person from the restraint and move to an upright position.
7. Minimize the duration of the restraint.

Adapted from: Tennessee Department of Intellectual and Developmental Disabilities (2015). *IDD and community policing: DIDD services and investigative processes training for Tennessee law enforcement officers*

A casual examination of the statistics provided here might suggest police shootings of mentally ill suspects are disproportionately high compared to the prevalence of mental illness in the United States. However, we must also examine the existence of the legal and situational factors that might contribute to these rates of police force. Generally, research has found that a suspect's mental impairment is unrelated to an officer's use of force (Kaminski, DiGiovanni, & Downs, 2004; Ruiz & Miller, 2004). Some research has found a tentative relationship between mental illness and use of force that disappears when situational factors are examined. For example, Johnson (2011) found that serious physical force (e.g., striking a suspect or using a weapon) was more likely to be used on mentally unstable suspects. However, when situational factors such as suspect resistance were controlled, Johnson found no relationship between mental disorder and police use of force. The increased use of force was determined to be the result of the increased frequency of officer resistance among mentally ill suspects. Recent research also has determined that situational factors such as resistance are more influential to the officers' use of force as well as whether either the suspect or officer is injured than the presence or absence of mental illness (Engel, 2015; Morabito et al., 2012; Morabito & Socia, 2015).

Procedural Justice

It is important to take into account the possible role of police officers' actions in creating the increased likelihood of resistance by mentally ill suspects (Gur, 2010). Specifically, it is possible that officers' increased hostility and disrespect toward mentally ill suspects may, in turn, result in increased resistance toward the officers. Also, officers may unintentionally escalate a situation as they attempt to interact with mentally ill persons using the same tactics as they would with the general population. Increasingly, a procedural justice framework is being used to evaluate citizens' cooperation with the police (Tyler & Huo, 2002). From this perspective, the perceived fairness of a police-suspect interaction is more important than the actual outcome. The perceived fairness of an encounter can be increased by treating the suspect with dignity and respect and allowing the suspect to explain the situation before an action is taken. Using a procedural justice framework among a sample of police-citizen encounters, Dai, Frank, and Sun (2011) found that a negative demeanor by the police officer (e.g., angry tone, attitude of hostility) may provoke citizen disrespect toward the officer. Likewise, allowing citizens to express their opinions or explaining why citizens' requests could not be fulfilled significantly reduced the likelihood of noncompliance.

Watson and Angell (2007) suggested that a procedural justice framework could help evaluate how police officers' behavior may shape mentally ill suspects' cooperation or resistance. Indeed, subsequent interviews (Watson, Angell, Morabito, & Robinson, 2008) of mentally ill suspects showed that encounters in which officers treated the suspect with dignity and respect were viewed positively, even when the suspect was ultimately arrested. Conversely, situations in which officers acted harshly or did not provide an opportunity for suspects to explain their view were evaluated negatively. Later research showed that mentally ill suspects were, in fact, more cooperative with police when they sensed that the police officer was fair (Watson & Angell, 2013). This effect was particularly strong in situations where the offender was most vulnerable, such as a mental health crisis or significant law violation.

Fortunately, it appears that mentally ill suspects often perceive that police officers treat them fairly. In a survey of mentally ill persons, Livingston and colleagues (2014) reported that approximately half of respondents rated their previous contacts with the police as a positive experience. Reflecting on their most recent interactions with police, 88% of respondents reported they were treated humanely, 85% were treated with respect, and 73% reported that they felt free to express themselves. This presents a more positive view of police encounters with mentally ill individuals than is often portrayed in the media and is certainly an encouraging finding. However, there appears to be room for improving these interactions. When asked to provide suggestions for improved communications with police, mentally ill persons repeatedly suggested that officers treat mentally ill patients as human beings, recognize their mental illnesses, and receive special training to help these situations from escalating (Livingston et al., 2014; Watson et al., 2008).

The Police Executive Research Forum (PERF, 2016) suggested the adoption of 30 guiding principles for handling controversial deadly force situations, including those involving individuals with mental illness or developmental disabilities. In many ways, these principles challenge officers to think more critically about the decisions that they make. Among these principles is mandatory police training on de-escalation techniques and a suggestion to make de-escalation the preferred approach in these situations involving suspects with mental illness or disorders. One illustration provided by the forum involves a mentally disoriented man with a knife. Instead of relying on a use of force continuum, which might require use of force while placing the officer in danger of attack, police are encouraged to critically think about whether the man is acting aggressively with the knife or is threatening himself or the officer. Perhaps the officer could move to a safe distance and buy enough time to call in additional resources, which might ultimately lead to the situation being handled without force. De-escalation requires officers to possess or be trained on effective communication skills and an increased police cultural acceptance for buying additional time instead of simply trying to dispose of calls as quickly as possible. However, it is possible that these changes could both reduce officers' use of force and improve officer safety (PERF, 2016).

Police Training Programs

Police departments have developed several strategies for improving encounters with mentally ill persons. Deane and colleagues (1999) classified these strategies as: police-based specialized police response, police-based specialized mental health response, and mental health based specialized mental health response (see Box 27.3). Each of these strategies involves a unique set of procedures. They each share the goal of increasing collaboration between law enforcement and mental health professionals. In one comparison of these strategies, both of the police-based responses were found to have positive outcomes. The department that relied on a mental health based mobile crisis team experienced frustration at persistently slow response times, making the process impractical (Steadman, Deane, Borum, & Morrisey, 2000).

Most police agencies provide at least some training involving mental health issues. Indeed, police training programs have been identified as an essential part of improving police response to mentally ill individuals (Reuland, 2004). Training most often comes in the form of preservice police

Box 27.3 Types of Specialized Law Enforcement Responses to Mental Health Calls

Police-based specialized police response: Sworn officers receive specialized training and refer mental health crisis situations to appropriate mental health services.

Police-based specialized mental health response: Mental health consultants (non-sworn) are hired by the police to respond and provide consultations to responding police officers.

Mental health based specialized mental health response: Community mental health professionals partner with police departments and respond to the scene to serve as a mobile crisis team.

Source: Deane et al. (1999)

academies, in-service training, brief instruction during roll calls, university-based police training courses, and specialized training programs (Jurkanin & Sergevnin, 2007). Training occurring in a law enforcement setting (e.g., police academies, in-service, and roll calls) is most often focused on increasing disability awareness and reducing officer prejudice. Unfortunately, these settings often do not allocate enough time for in-depth analysis of mental health issues (Hails & Borum, 2003; Jurkanin & Sergevnin, 2007). As a result, the police-based specialized police response strategy is emerging as the leading response to improving these interactions.

Crisis Intervention Training

The most common type of specialized police training is the crisis intervention team (CIT) model. This approach seeks to divert mentally ill and developmentally disabled individuals from the criminal justice system by referring those in need to appropriate mental health services. Police officers volunteer for a minimum 40 hours of training where they learn about several mental health-related topics (see Box 27.4), visit local mental health facilities, interact with individuals with mental illnesses, and are taught scenario-based crisis de-escalation techniques.

It is important to stress the voluntary nature of this training. Officers who are forced to participate in this training will not be as vested into dealing with these issues compared to officers who volunteer. Ideally, approximately 20–25% of a department's patrol officers will participate in the CIT training (Dupont et al., 2007). This should allow for dispatchers to have a CIT-trained officer available to respond to mental health crisis situations at all times. Finally, it is important to note that CIT is not merely a training program. A key element of the CIT model is the presence of a designated no-refusal mental health facility capable of providing needed emergency mental health services. For this approach to be effective, the mental health facility should be available 24/7 and offer quick turnaround times for officers who transport individuals to the facility.

Some police departments have reported barriers that prevent full implementation of CIT program. Specifically, some departments cite the lack of an available no-refusal psychiatric facility, insufficient training for dispatchers, and the expense required to implement the program (Compton et al., 2010; Compton, Broussard, Reed, Crisafio, & Watson, 2015). Although the cost of implementing the program can be high, the savings associated with diverting these individuals from the criminal justice system has ultimately been shown to save money and to be most cost-effective in the long run (El-Mallakh, Kiran, & El-Mallakh, 2014). The lack of CIT training for dispatchers can indeed undermine the program, as the dispatchers are responsible for recognizing the possibility of a situation requiring a CIT-trained police officer. Likewise, the lack of collaborative agreements with mental health

Box 27.4 CIT Specialized Knowledge Topic

Clinical Issues	Mental Health Diversity
Medications and Side Effects	Equipment Orientation
Alcohol and Drug Assessment	Policies and Procedures
Co-Occurring Disorders	Personality Disorders
Developmental Disabilities	Posttraumatic Stress Disorder
Family/Consumer Perspective	Legal Aspects of Officer Liability
Suicide Prevention	Community Resources

Source: Dupont, Cochran, & Pillsbury (2007)

services in certain areas can threaten the impact of the CIT program by limiting the police officers' options when handling these calls (Lord, Bjerregaard, Blevins, & Whisman, 2011). One possible way to mitigate this problem is to train a higher percentage of officers in the CIT program to change the department's overall culture related to handling calls involving mentally ill suspects (Watson, Ottati, Draine, & Morabito, 2011).

Many states have created statewide initiatives aimed at coordinating and promoting the development of specialized responses such as CIT. Most often, these initiatives are led by either a law enforcement, mental health, or nonprofit advocacy organization (Reuland, Draper, & Norton, 2012). Advantages of these efforts include the sharing of training resources, expertise, and the increased ability to lobby state legislators for funding. We would expect these efforts at statewide collaboration to continue as these programs continue to gain popularity. We recognize that each jurisdiction is unique and some flexibility is required to account for these individual jurisdictional characteristics. Smaller law enforcement agencies might not have an available psychiatric drop off facility, while larger agencies may need to collaborate with multiple facilities within their cities.

CIT Effectiveness

Officers who have been trained in the CIT program have reported improved knowledge and awareness of mental health issues and de-escalation techniques, as well as an increased level of support for referring those in need to appropriate mental health services (Compton et al., 2014a; Hanafi, Bahora, Demir, & Compton, 2008; Demir, Broussard, Goulding, & Compton, 2009). Improving knowledge and attitudes about mental illness among law enforcement officers who are dispatched to these situations is obviously an important first step. However, it is unclear whether the improved knowledge and attitudes gained during the CIT training persists long term (Compton et al., 2014a; Davidson, 2016).

The CIT program has also been found to positively impact outcomes of police interactions with mentally ill persons. For example, several researchers have found that CIT-trained officers are willing to spend more time on a call involving mentally ill persons and refer a greater proportion of these individuals to an emergency psychiatric facility or community-based mental health agencies compared to their non-CIT trained counterparts (Canada, Angell, & Watson, 2012; Compton et al., 2014b; Hanafi et al., 2008; Teller, Munetz, Gil, & Ritter, 2006; Watson et al., 2010). CIT training also has been found to reduce the level of force used by law enforcement officers as the suspect's demeanor becomes more resistant (Compton et al., 2014b; Morabito et al., 2012).

Interestingly, two studies (Teller et al., 2006; Watson et al., 2010) have found the CIT program to be ineffective at reducing arrest rates. This is particularly important given that a main objective of the CIT program is to divert these individuals from the criminal justice system. However, these findings may not be a result of an ineffective CIT program. For example, Teller et al. (2006) speculate that perhaps dispatchers are sending CIT officers to the most challenging calls involving mentally ill suspects, where officers will have less discretion as to whether to make an arrest. Likewise, Watson et al. (2010) explained that arresting mentally ill individuals was rare among both CIT-trained officers and non-CIT-trained officers, with over half of arrests involving officers serving arrest warrants. Thus, the CIT training might be reducing the arrest rates of mentally ill suspects in situations where the officer has the most discretion regarding a proper resolution.

The Seattle Police Department's implementation of a CIT program provides an example of the possible benefits of the program. In 2011, the U.S. Department of Justice Civil Rights Division (2011)concluded that the department's officers had demonstrated a pattern of excessive force against persons with mental illness or those under the influence of drugs or alcohol. As a result, the department entered into a consent decree requiring improved training and policy in response to crisis events. The department invested significant resources into creating a full-fledged CIT unit. All officers now receive eight hours of basic CIT training, and those who volunteer to become CIT-certified officers receive the recommended 40-hour training. This has had a significant impact on the outcomes of crisis situations in Seattle. A recent evaluation found that for a three-month time frame, the police department had contact with over 2,500 individuals in crisis. Force was used in only 2% of these cases, and only 7.5% of the individuals were arrested (Seattle Police Monitor, 2016). It appears that a properly funded and implemented CIT program could be a significant benefit to many law enforcement departments across the United States and is now considered by some to be the best practices model for guiding appropriate interaction between law enforcement and mentally ill persons (Walker, Pann, Shapiro, & Van Hasselt, 2016).

Police Questioning and Interrogation

A particular area which has received a great deal of scholarly attention is the increased susceptibility of intellectually and developmentally disabled suspects to police questioning. Ericson and Perlman (2001) found significant differences in the understanding of basic legal terminology between mildly developmentally disabled adults compared to nondisabled results. At least 40% of the developmentally disabled participants did not understand legal terms such as "arrest," "trial," "suspect," and "guilty." Similarly, intellectually disabled suspects have been found to have a poor comprehension of their *Miranda* rights and increased susceptibility to suggestive police questioning, which may result in confabulation (Ellis & Luckasson, 1985; Mertz & Brown, 2015; Salseda, Dixon, Fass, Miora, & Leark, 2011). Confabulation "typically occurs when there is a disturbance in one's ability to make new memories and to monitor recollections for accuracy, which suggests possible brain function deficits in memory and executive functioning" (Mertz & Brown, 2015, p. 1). As a result, someone with these deficits who is in police custody may fabricate confessions rather than admit he or she does not recall certain events. In addition, individuals who confabulate are not intentionally lying and actually believe they are accurately relaying information (Brown et al., 2016b). These concerns have led Kassin et al. (2010) to recommend the electronic recording of all interrogations (regardless of disability) and mandated presence of an attorney when officers are interrogating vulnerable populations such as intellectually and developmentally disabled suspects, including those with autism, fetal alcohol spectrum disorder (FASD), traumatic brain injury (TBI), and other neuropsychiatric disorders (Brown, 2017).

Law enforcement must also ensure that hearing impaired individuals adequately comprehend their *Miranda* rights and can effectively communicate with officers during questioning. Providing such an accommodation may be as simple as calling for a sign language interpreter. Interpreter services are not always required in simple transitions (e.g., traffic tickets in which suspects can understand why they are being pulled over) or in situations where the officer's observations allow for an arrest without an interrogation (DOJ, 2006). However, failure to provide an adequate accommodation to ensure that the suspect understands officers' questions either at the crime scene or at the police station could result in a wrongful conviction and/or postconviction appeal (Miller, 2001). Individuals who have experienced hearing loss at a young age may have never heard the language well enough to read or speak effectively. These suspects pose a particular issue for law enforcement, as simply providing an interpreter might not guarantee successful comprehension of the *Miranda* rights or the often complex legal concepts involved in the questioning (Vernon, Raifman, Greenberg, & Monteiro, 2001). Seaborn, Andrews, and Martin (2010) found that deaf adults at the eighth-grade reading level or below were unable to understand the *Miranda* rights even if given in both English and using sign language.

Vernon et al. (2001) provide several suggestions to administering the *Miranda* warning to deaf suspects. First, law enforcement should obtain the services of a qualified interpreter and have the interpreter assess the suspect's communication skills to determine whether or not to proceed with the interview. If the interpreter concludes that a suspect cannot communicate with sign language and/or has difficulty reading and writing, Vernon et al. (2001) recommends that the interview should not proceed without the presence and consent of an attorney. Finally, they advise that the interview is videotaped so that key facial expressions and body language cues can be recorded for further scrutiny of whether the suspect understood the interview.

Conclusion

Given the recent media accounts of police use of force, there has been a renewed interest on police-citizen interactions. While there are plans by the Department of Justice for a national police use of force database, currently the field does not have a comprehensive mechanism for determining the use of force nor the characteristics of the citizens that come into contact with police. Accordingly, to date, we have limited research on the number of police-citizen contacts involving special needs individuals. Regardless of the number of citizens police encounter, the job of a police officer is not only to enforce the law but to protect the public. It is imperative that law enforcement officers receive quality training that provides them with the necessary skills to identify and manage the individuals with special needs.

The Police Executive Research Forum (2016) suggests that of the recent controversial police use of force incidents, the officers in most cases should not be deemed at fault because their actions reflected the available training that they had received. Certainly, any evaluation of the policing of special needs offenders must acknowledge the difficult position in which police officers often find themselves. However, it is also important to remember that individuals with disabilities, particularly mental illness, are more likely to be shot and killed by police than any other group of people (Fuller et al., 2015; Ruderman Family Foundation, 2016).

Skills-based training should be conducted on a yearly basis to ensure that police officers maintain their interaction skills and know when to slow down and switch gears when working with these citizens. Lastly, many times this specialized training requires a police department to partner with outside entities such as mental health professionals. Thus, departments may want to partner with local mental health agencies to provide the training to their officers. Without the proper training, administrative support, and police culture that values ethics and human life above expediency of call disposition, law enforcement officers across the nation will likely continue to be dispatched to calls for which they are ill prepared.

References

Akins, S., Burkhardt, B. C., & Lanfear, C. (2016). Law enforcement response to "frequent fliers": An examination of high-frequency contacts between police and justice-involved persons with mental illness. *Criminal Justice Policy Review*, *27*(1), 97–114. doi:10.1177/00887403414559268

Alvarado, F., Miller, M. E., & Berman, M. (2016, July 21). North Miami police shoot black man who said his hands were raised while he tried to help autistic group-home resident. *The Washington Post*. Retrieved from www.washingtonpost.com/news/morning-mix/wp/2016/07/21/fla-police-shoot-black-man-with-his-hands-up-as-he-tries-to-help-autistic-patient/

Asscher, J., van der Put, C., & Stams, G. J. J. M. (2012). Differences between juvenile offenders with and without intellectual disability in offense type and risk factors. *Research in Developmental Disabilities*, *33*, 1905–1913. doi:10.1016/j.ridd.2012.05.022

Blackwell, D. L., Lucas, J. W., & Clarke, T. C. (2012). *Summary health statistics for U.S. adults: National Health Interview Survey, 2012*. Washington, DC: National Center for Health Statistics.

Bouchard, K. (2012). Across nation, unsettling acceptance when mentally ill in crisis are killed. *Portland Press Herald*. Retrieved from: www.pressherald.com/2012/12/09/shoot-across-nation-a-grim-acceptance-when-mentally-ill-shot-down/

Boyle, C. A., Boulet, S., Schieve, L. A., Cohen, R. A., Blumberg, S. J., Yeargin-Allsopp, M., . . . Kogan, M. D. (2011). Trends in the prevalence of developmental disabilities in US children, 1997–2008. *Pediatrics*, *127*(6), 1034–1042. doi:10.1542/peds.200–2989

Brodin, R. E. (2005). Remedying a particularized form of discrimination: Why disabled plaintiffs can and should bring claims for police misconduct under the Americans with Disabilities Act. *University of Pennsylvania Law Review, 154*, 157–199.

Bronson, J., & Berzofsky, M. (2015). *Disabilities among prison and jail inmates, 2011–12*. Washington, DC: Bureau of Justice Statistics.

Brown, J. (2017). Fetal alcohol spectrum disorder and confabulation: A clinical, forensic, and judicial dilemma. *The Journal of Special Populations, 1*(2), 1–11.

Brown, J., Anderson, G., Cooney-Koss, L., Hastings, B., Pickett, H., Neal, D., . . . Barfknecht, L. (2016a). Autism spectrum disorder and sexually inappropriate behaviors: An introduction for caregivers and professionals. *The Journal of Special Populations, 1*(1), 1–8.

Brown, J., Long-McGie, J., Oberoi, P., Wartnik, A., Wresh, J., Weinkauf, E., & Falconer, G.. (2016b). Confabulation: Connections between brain damage, memory, and testimony. *Journal of Law Enforcement, 3*(5), 1–11.

Canada, K. E., Angell, B., & Watson, A. (2012). Intervening at the entry point: Differences in how CIT trained and non-CIT trained officers describe responding to mental health-related calls. *Community Mental Health Journal, 48*, 746–755. doi:10.1007/s10597-011-9430-9

Compton, M. T., Bakeman, R., Broussard, B., Hankerson-Dyson, D., Husbands, L., Krishan, S., . . . Watson, A. C. (2014a). The police-based crisis intervention team (CIT) model: 1. Effects on officers; knowledge, attitudes, and skills. *Psychiatric Services, 65*(4), 517–522. doi:10.1176/appi.ps.201300107

Compton, M. T., Bakeman, R., Broussard, B., Hankerson-Dyson, D., Husbands, L., Krishan, S., . . . Watson, A. C. (2014b). The police-based crisis intervention team (CIT) model: II. Effects on level of force and resolution, referral, and arrest. *Psychiatric Services, 65*(4), 523–529. doi:10.1176/appi.ps.201300108

Compton, M. T., Broussard, B., Hankerson-Dyson, D., Krishan, S., Stewart, T., Oliva, J. R., & Watson, A. C. (2010). System and policy level challenges to full implementation of the crisis intervention team (CIT) model. *Journal of Police Crisis Negotiations, 10*, 72–85. doi:10.1080/15332581003757347

Compton, M. T., Broussard, B., Reed, T. A., Crisafio, A., & Watson, A. C. (2015). Surveys of police chiefs and sheriffs and of police officers about CIT programs. *Psychiatric Services, 66*(7), 760–763. doi:10.1176/appi.ps.201300451

Dai, M., Frank, J., & Sun, I. (2011). Procedural justice during police-citizen encounters: The effects of process-based policing on citizen compliance and demeanor. *Journal of Criminal Justice, 39*, 159–168. doi:10.1016/j.crimjus.2011.01.004

Davidson, M. L. (2016). A criminal justice system-wide response to mental illness: Evaluating the effectiveness of the Memphis crisis intervention team training curriculum among law enforcement and correctional officers. *Criminal Justice Policy Review, 27*(1), 46–75. doi:10.1177/0887403414554997

Deane, M. W., Steadman, H. J., Borum, R., Veysey, B. M., & Morrissey, J. P. (1999). Emerging partnerships between mental health and law enforcement. *Psychiatric Services, 50*(1), 99–101. doi:10.1176/ps.50.1.99

Debbaudt, D. (2002). *Autism, advocates, and law enforcement professionals: Recognizing and reducing risk situations for people with autism spectrum disorders*. Philadelphia, PA: Jessica Kingsley Publishers.

Demir, B., Broussard, B., Goulding, S. M., & Compton, M. T. (2009). Beliefs about causes of schizophrenia among police officers before and after crisis intervention team training. *Community Mental Health Journal, 45*(5), 385–392. doi:10.1007/s10597-009-9194-7

Dupont, R., Cochran, S., & Pillsbury, S. (2007). *Crisis intervention team core elements*. The University of Memphis School of Urban Affairs and Public Policy. Retrieved from: http://cit.memphis.edu/pdf/CoreElements.pdf

Elbogen, E. B., & Johnson, S. C. (2009). The intricate link between violence and mental disorder: Results from the national epidemiologic survey on alcohol and related conditions. *Archives of General Psychiatry, 66*(2), 152–161. doi:10.1.1.476.7279&rep=rep1&type=pdf

Ellis, J. W., & Luckasson, R. A. (1985). Mentally retarded criminal defendants. *George Washington Law Review, 53*(3–4), 414–492.

El-Mallakh, P. L., Kiran, K., & El-Mallakh, R. S. (2014). Costs and savings associated with implementation of a police crisis intervention team. *Southern Medical Journal, 107*(6), 391–395. doi:10.14423/01.SNJ.0000450721.14787.7d

Engel, R. S., & Silver, E. (2001). Policing mentally disoriented suspects: A reexaminations of the criminalization hypothesis. *Criminology, 39*(2), 225–252.

Engel, R. S. (2015). Police encounters with people with mental illness: Use of force, injuries, and perceptions of dangerousness. *Criminology & Public Policy, 14*(2), 247–251. doi:10.1111/1745-9133.12146

Ericson, K. I., & Perlman, N. B. (2001). Knowledge of legal terminology and court proceedings in adults with developmental disabilities. *Law and Human Behavior, 25*(5), 529–545.

Federal Bureau of Investigation. (2014). *Law enforcement officers killed and assaulted, 2014*. Washington, DC: Department of Justice.

Fisher, W. H., Roy-Bujnowski, K., Grudzinskas, A. J., Clayfield, J. C., Banks, S. M., & Wolff, N. (2006). Patterns and prevalence of arrest in a statewide cohort of mental health care consumers. *Psychiatric Services*, *57*(11), 1623–1628. doi:10.1176/appi.ps.57.11.1623

Fuller, D. A., Lamb, H. R., Biasotti, M., & Snook, J. (2015). *Overlooked in the undercounted: The role of mental illness in fatal law enforcement encounters*. Arlington, VA: The Treatment Advocacy Center, Office of Research & Public Affairs.

Green, T. M. (1997). Police as frontline mental health workers: The decision to arrest or refer to mental health agencies. *International Journal of Law and Psychiatry*, *20*(4), 469–486.

Gunasekaran, S., & Chaplin, E. (2012). Autism spectrum disorders and offending. *Advances in Mental Health and Intellectual Disabilities*, *6*(6), 308–313. doi:10.1108/2044128121

Gur, O. M. (2010). Persons with mental illness in the criminal justice system: Police interventions to prevent violence and criminalization. *Journal of Police Crisis Negotiations*, *10*(1–2), 220–240. doi:10.1080/15332581003799752

Hails, J., & Borum, R. (2003). Police training and specialized approaches to respond to people with mental illnesses. *Crime & Delinquency*, *49*(1), 52–61. doi:10.1177/0011128702239235

Hanafi, S., Bahora, M., Demir, B. N., & Compton, M. T. (2008). Incorporating crisis intervention team (CIT) knowledge and skills into the daily work of police officers: A focus group study. *Community Mental Health Journal*, *44*, 427–432.

Holland, T., Clare, I. C. H., & Mukhopadhyay, T. (2002). Prevalence of criminal offending by men and women with intellectual disability and the characteristics of offenders: Implications for research and service development. *Journal of Intellectual Disability Research*, *46*(Suppl 1), 6–20. doi:10.1046/j.1365-2788.2002.00001.x

Hoover, L. T. (2007). Atypical situations-Atypical responses. In T. J. Jurkanin, L. T. Hoover, & V. A. Sergevnin (Eds.), *Improving police response to persons with mental illness: A progressive approach*. Springfield, IL: Charles C. Thomas.

Johnson, R. R. (2011). Suspect mental disorder and police use of force. *Criminal Justice and Behavior*, *38*(2), 127–145. doi:10.1177/0093854810388160

Jones, J. (2007). Persons with intellectual disabilities in the criminal justice system: Review of issues. *International Journal of Offender Therapy and Comparative Criminology*, *51*(6), 723–733. doi:10.1177/0306624X07299343

Jurkanin, T. J., & Sergevnin, V. A. (2007). Law enforcement training models. In T. J. Jurkanin, L. T. Hoover, & V. A. Sergevnin (Eds.), *Improving police response to persons with mental illness: A progressive approach*. Springfield, IL: Charles C. Thomas.

Kaminski, R., DiGiovanni, C., & Downs, R. (2004). The use of force between the police and persons with impaired judgement. *Police Quarterly*, 7(3), 311–338. doi:10.1177/1098611103253456

Kassin, S. M., Drizin, S. A., Grisso, T., Gudjonsson, G. H., Leo, R. A., & Redlich, A. D. (2010). Police-induced confessions: Risk factors and recommendations. *Law and Human Behavior*, *34*, 3–38. doi:10.1007/s10979-009-9188-6

Kerr, A. N., Morabito, M., & Watson, A. C. (2010). Police encounters, mental illness and injury: An exploratory investigation. *Journal of Police Crisis Negotiation*, *10*, 116–132. doi:10.1080/15332581003757198

King, W. R., & Dunn, T. M. (2004). Dumping: Policing-initiated transjurisdictional transport of troublesome persons. *Police Quarterly*, 7(3), 339–358. doi:10.1177/1098611102250586

Långström, N., Grann, M., Ruchkin, V., Sjöstedt, G., & Fazel, S. (2009). Risk factors for violent offending in autism spectrum disorder: A national study of hospitalized individuals. *Journal of Interpersonal Violence*, *24*(8), 1358–1370. doi:10.1177/0886260508322195

Lindsay, W. R., Hastings, R. P., Griffiths, D. M., & Hayes, S. C. (2007). Trends and challenges in forensic research on offenders with intellectual disability. *Journal of Intellectual & Developmental Disability*, *32*(2), 55–61. doi:10.1080/13668250701378520

Livingston, J. D., Desmarais, S. L., Verdun-Jones, S., Parent, R., Michalak, E., & Brink, J. (2014). Perceptions and experiences of people with mental illness regarding their interactions with police. *International Journal of Law and Psychiatry*, *37*, 334–340. doi:10.1016/j.ijlp.2014.02.003

Lord, V. B., Bjerregaard, B., Blevins, K. R., & Whisman, H. (2011). Factors influencing the response of crisis intervention team-certified law enforcement officers. *Police Quarterly*, *14*(4), 388–406. doi:10.1177/1098611111423743

Maras, K., Mulcahy, S., & Crane, L. (2015). Is autism linked to criminality? *Autism*, *19*(5), 515–516. doi:10.1177/1362361315583411

Markowitz, F. E., & Watson, A. C. (2015). Police response to domestic violence: Situations involving veterans exhibiting signs of mental illness. *Criminology*, *53*(2), 231–252. doi:10.1111/1745-9125.12067

McLaughlin, E. C. (2015, April 21). We're not seeing more policing shootings, just more news coverage. *CNN*. Retrieved from: www.cnn.com/2015/04/20/us/police-brutality-video-social-media-attitudes/

Mertz, C., & Brown, J. (2015). Confabulation: An introduction for psychologists. *Forensic Scholar Today*, *1*(2), 1–2.

Miller, K. R. (2001). Access to sign language interpreters in the criminal justice system. *American Annals of the Deaf*, *146*(4), 328–330.

Miller, K. R., & Vernon, M. (2003). Deaf sex offenders in a prison population. *Journal of Deaf Studies and Deaf Education, 8*(3), 357–362. doi:10.1093/deafed/eng011

Miller, K. R., Vernon, M., & Capella, M. E. (2005). Violent offenders in a deaf prison population. *Journal of Deaf Studies and Deaf Education, 10*(4), 417–425. doi:10.1093/deafed/eni039

Morabito, M. S., Kerr, A. N., Watson, A., Draine, J., Ottati, V., & Angell, B. (2012). Crisis intervention teams and people with mental illness: Exploring the factors that influence the use of force. *Crime & Delinquency, 58*(1), 57–77. doi:10.1177/0011128710372456

Morabito, M. S., & Socia, K. M. (2015). Is dangerousness a myth? Injuries and police encounters with people with mental illness. *Criminology & Public Policy, 14*(2), 253–276. doi:10.1111/1745-9133.12127

Mouridsen, S. E. (2012). Current status of research on autism spectrum disorders and offending. *Research in Autism Spectrum Disorders, 6*(1), 79–86. doi:10.1016/j.rasd.2011.09.003

Murgado, A. (2013, September 20). Departments: Best practices for dealing with the deaf. *Police*. Retrieved from www.policemag.com/channel/careers-training/articles/2013/09/dealing-with-the-deaf.aspx

National Alliance on Mental Illness. (2016). *Mental health by the numbers*. Arlington, VA: National Alliance on Mental Illness.

Novak, K. J., & Engel, R. S. (2005). Disentangling the influence of suspects' demeanor and mental disorder on arrest. *Policing: An International Journal of Police Strategies & Management, 28*(3), 493–512. doi:10.1108/136395 10510614573?journalCode=pijpsm

Osborn, E. H. (2008). What happened to "Paul's Law"?: Insights on advocating for better training and better outcomes in encounters between law enforcement and persons with autism spectrum disorders. *University of Colorado Law Review, 79*, 333–379.

Perry, D. M., & Carter-Long, L. (2016). *The Ruderman white paper on media coverage of law enforcement use of force and disability*. St. Newton, MA: Ruderman Family Foundation.

Peterson, J. K., Skeem, J., Kennedy, P., Bray, B., & Zvonkovic, A. (2014). How often and how consistently do symptoms directly precede criminal behavior among offenders with mental illness? *Law and Human Behavior, 38*(5), 439–449. doi:10.1037lhb0000075

Police Executive Research Forum (PERF). (2012). *An integrated approach to de-escalation and minimizing use of force*. Washington, DC: Police Executive Research Forum.

Police Executive Research Forum (PERF). (2016). *Critical issues in policing series: Guiding principles on use of force*. Washington, DC: Police Executive Research Forum.

Pollack, H. (2016). Better police training: Learning to interact with people living with intellectual or developmental disabilities. *The Washington Monthly, 48*, 6–8.

Reuland, M. (2004). *A guide to implementing police-based diversion programs for people with mental illness*. Delmar, NY: Technical Assistance and Policy Analysis Center for Jail Diversion.

Reuland, M., Draper, L., & Norton, B. (2012). *Statewide law enforcement/mental health efforts: Strategies to support and sustain local initiatives*. New York, NY: Council of State Governments Justice Center.

Reuland, M., Schwarzfeld, M., & Draper, L. (2009). *Law enforcement responses to people with mental illnesses: A guide to research informed policy and practice*. New York, NY: Council of State Governments Justice Center.

Ruderman Family Foundation. (2016). *Media coverage of law enforcement use of force and disability*. Newton, MA: Ruderman Family Foundation.

Ruiz, J., & Miller, C. (2004). An exploratory study of Pennsylvania police officers' perceptions of dangerousness and their ability to manage persons with mental illness. *Police Quarterly*, 7(3), 359–371. doi:10.1177/109861 1103258957?journalCode=pqxa

Salekin, K. L., Olley, J. G., & Hedge, K. A. (2010). Offenders with intellectual disability: Characteristics, prevalence, and issues in forensic assessment. *Journal of Mental Health Research in Intellectual Disabilities, 3*(2), 97–116. doi: 10.1080/19315861003695769

Salseda, L. M., Dixon, D. R., Fass, T., Miora, D., & Leark, R. A. (2011). An evaluation of *Miranda* rights and interrogation in autism spectrum disorders. *Research in Autism Spectrum Disorders, 5*(1), 79–85. doi:10.1016/j.rasd.2010.06.014

Santos, F., & Goode, E. (2014). Police confront rising number of mentally ill suspects. *New York Times*. Retrieved from www.nytimes.com/2014/04/02/us/police-shootings-of-mentally-ill-suspects-are-on-the-upswing.html?_r=0

Seattle Police Monitor. (2016). *Fifth systematic assessment: Crisis intervention*. Retrieved from: https://static1.squarespace.com/static/5425b9f0e4b0d66352331e0e/t/56c3a9cd07eaa0de7b9ebf8b/1455663566554/Fifth+Systemic+Assessment—Crisis+Intervention.pdf

Seaborn, B., Andrews, J. F., & Martin, G. (2010). Deaf adults and comprehension of *Miranda*. *Journal of Forensic Psychology Practice, 10*(2), 107–132. doi:10.1080/15228930903446732

Stack, L. (2016, August 24). N.C. trooper investigated in fatal shooting of deaf motorist. *The New York Times*. Retrieved from www.nytimes.com/2016/08/25/us/nc-trooper-being-investigated-for-shooting-of-deaf-man.html?_r=0

Steadman, H. J., Deane, M. W., Borum, R., & Morrissey, J. P. (2000). Comparing outcomes of major models of police responses to mental health emergencies. *Psychiatric Services, 51*(5), 645–649. doi:10.1176/appi.ps.51.5.645

Swaine, J., Laughland, O., & Lartey, J. (2015). Black Americans killed by police twice as likely to be unarmed as white people. *The Guardian*. Retrieved from: www.theguardian.com/us-news/2015/jun/01/black-americans-killed-by-police-analysis

Szymanski, C. A., Brice, P. J., Lam, K. H., & Hotto, S. A. (2012). Deaf children with autism spectrum disorders. *Journal of Autism and Developmental Disorders, 42*(10), 2027–2037. doi:10.1007/s10803-012-1452-9

Teller, J. L. S., Munetz, M. R., Gil, K. M., & Ritter, C. (2006). Crisis intervention team training for police officers responding to mental disturbance calls. *Psychiatric Services, 57*(2), 232–237. doi:10.1176/appi.ps.57.2.232.

Tennessee Department of Intellectual and Developmental Disabilities (2015). *IDD and community Policing: DIDD services and investigative processes training for Tennessee law enforcement officers*. Retrieved from www.tn.gov/assets/entities/didd/attachments/DIDD_Materials_for_Law_Enforcement.pdf

Teplin, L. A. (1984). Criminalizing mental disorder: The comparative arrest rate of the mentally ill. *American Psychologist, 39*(7), 794–803.

Teplin, L. A. (2000). *Keeping the peace: Police discretion and mentally ill persons*. Washington, DC: Department of Justice.

Thompson, M. D., Reuland, M., & Souweine, D. (2003). Criminal justice/mental health consensus: Improving responses to people with mental illness. *Crime & Delinquency, 49*(1), 30–51. doi:10.1177/0011128702239234

Tyler, T. R., & Huo, Y. J. (2002). *Trust in the law: Encouraging public cooperation with the police and courts*. New York, NY: Russell Sage Foundation.

U.S. Department of Justice, Civil Rights Division. (2006). *Communicating with people who are deaf or hard of hearing: ADA guide for law enforcement officers*. Retrieved from www.ada.gov/lawenfcomm.htm

U.S. Department of Justice, Civil Rights Division. (2011). *Investigation of the Seattle police department*. Retrieved from www.justice.gov/sites/default/files/crt/legacy/2011/12/16/spd_findletter_12-16-11.pdf

Van Dorn, R., Volavka, J., & Johnson, N. (2012). Mental disorder and violence: Is there a relationship beyond substance use? *Social Psychiatry and Psychiatric Epidemiology, 47*(3), 487–503. doi:10.1007/s00127-011-0356-x

Vernon, M., & Greenberg, S. F. (1999). Violence in deaf and hard of hearing people: A review of the literature. *Aggression and Violent Behavior, 4*(3), 259–272. doi:10.1016/S1359-1789(97)00058-X

Vernon, M., & Miller, K. (2005). Obstacles faced by deaf people in the criminal justice system. *American Annals of the Deaf, 150*(3), 283–291. doi:10.1353/aad.2005.0036

Vernon, M., Raifman, L. J., Greenberg, S. F., & Monteiro, B. (2001). Forensic pretrial police interviews of deaf suspects avoiding legal pitfalls. *Journal of Law and Psychiatry, 24*(1), 43–59. doi:10.1016/S0160–2527(99)00031-X

Walker, L. E. A., Pann, J. M., Shapiro, D. L., & Van Hasselt, V. B. (2016). *Best practices for the mentally ill in the criminal justice system*. Retrieved from www.springer.com/us/book/9783319216553

Watson, A. C., & Angell, B. (2007). Applying procedural justice theory to law enforcement's response to persons with mental illness. *Psychiatric Services, 58*(6), 787–793. doi:10.1176/ps.2007.58.6.787

Watson, A. C., & Angell, B. (2013). The role of stigma and uncertainty in moderating the effect of procedural justice on cooperation and resistance in police encounters with persons with mental illness. *Psychology, Public Policy, and Law, 19*(1), 30–39. doi:10.1037/a0027931.

Watson, A. C., Angell, B., Morabito, M. S., & Robinson, N. (2008). Defying negative expectations: Dimensions of fair and respectful treatment by police officers as perceived by people with mental illness. *Administration and Policy in Mental Health and Mental Health Services Research, 35*(6), 449–457. doi:10.1007/s10488-008-0188-5

Watson, A. C., Ottati, V. C., Draine, J., & Morabito, M. (2011). CIT in context: The impact of mental health resource availability and district saturation on call dispositions. *International Journal of Law and Psychiatry, 34*(4), 287–294. doi:10.1016/j.ijlp.2011.07.008

Watson, A. C., Ottati, V. C., Morabito, M., Draine, J., Kerr, A. N., & Angell, B. (2010). Outcomes of police contacts with persons with mental illness: The impact of CIT. *Administration and Policy in Mental Health and Mental Health Services Research, 37*(4), 302–317. doi:10.1007/s10488-009-0236-9

Watson, A. C., Swartz, J., Bohrman, C., Kriegel, L. S., & Draine, J. (2014). Understanding how police officers think about mental/emotional disturbance calls. *International Journal of Law and Psychiatry, 37*(4), 351–358. doi:10.1016/j.ijlp.2014.02.005

Williamson, L. H., & Grubb, A. R. (2015). An analysis of the relationship between being deaf and sexual offending. *Journal of Sexual Aggression, 21*(2), 224–243. doi:10.1080/13552600.2013.842001

Wood, J. D., Watson, A. C., & Fulambarker, A. J. (2017). The "gray zone" of police work during mental health encounters: Findings from an observational study in Chicago. *Police Quarterly, 20*(1), 81–105. doi:10.1177/1098611116658875

28

TREATING OFFENDERS WITH SPECIALIZED NEEDS IN THE COMMUNITY

Constructing Community and Social Support Systems

Aida I. Diaz-La Cilento

> Without proper planning and extensive support in the reentry process ex-offenders will be set up for failure. Effective discharge planning within the prison system not only prepares offenders for success but assists community based programs in the delivery of services by giving a strong understanding of offender needs.
>
> —(Paulson, 2013, p. 14)

Introduction

A vast number of offenders reenter their communities each year after completing a prison or jail sentence. According to the United States Department of Justice Bureau of Justice Statistics (BJS, 2015a), the United States total correctional population as of December 31, 2014, was 6,814,600. Of this total population, 4,708,100 were under community supervision of probation or parole (BJS, 2015a). Probation refers to offenders who are supervised in the community through a probation agency, generally as an alternative to incarceration (BJS, 2015b). Parole refers to offenders who are supervised in the community after serving a prison term (BJS, 2015b). The primary difference between a probationer and a parolee is the type of offense each has committed. Types of offenses are categorized into misdemeanor, felonies, violent, and nonviolent. Typically, probationers have been convicted and sentenced for misdemeanor offenses while parolees have been convicted and sentenced for felony offenses, the latter of which is more serious.

Offenders and ex-offenders are populations that face many challenges after release back into the community. Foremost, the stigma of being formerly incarcerated means these individuals will carry the label of an ex-offender or a criminal, despite completing the sentence assigned to them by a court system. Although there is a negative stigma for offenders in general, Hardcastle, Bartholomew, and Graffam (2011) found more negative attitudes exist toward ex-offenders with a history of violent crimes, felonies, and sexual offenses in comparison to those who have nonviolent crimes, misdemeanors, and no sexual offenses. Despite the negative connotation tied to offenders, the reality is most of these individuals eventually return to live in their communities and face challenges as they try to become successful upon reentry.

Special Needs Classification

Most offenders are categorized as a population with special needs because they could benefit from some form of intensive treatment services. Special needs in the criminal justice system refer to offenders in specific categories such as juveniles, young adults, women, elderly, substance abusers, mentally ill, sex offenders, veterans, and immigrants. Each of these groups has distinct characteristics and needs. Juveniles in the criminal justice system are between the ages of 15–17, and young adults are between the ages of 18–24, according to the National Institute of Justice (2014). This chapter uses the term offenders in the substance abuse population as having an identified problem with alcohol, illicit drugs, or prescribed medications. Mental health includes those offenders with a diagnosed mental illness. Sexual offenders are persons who have committed a sexual act prohibited by law. Veterans are defined as "U.S. military veterans detained by, or under the supervision of the criminal justice system" (Blonigen et al., 2016, p. 813). Lastly, undocumented immigrants are offenders who are in the United States illegally or recognized as non-United States citizens.

Juveniles

Youth who are incarcerated at a young age, according to Clinkinbeard and Zohra (2012), are likely to have faced a number of issues, such as poverty, lack of education, lack of parental involvement, and trauma. Furthermore, there is the risk of juvenile delinquents continuing into the adult system. Therefore, having the options and access to community programs as a source of help for juveniles to avoid the court system may provide a different outcome for their future.

Coping with psychosocial stressors is challenging for most people. For children between the ages of 15–17, they may feel overwhelmed and may not know how to deal with the issues or who to turn to for help. Depending on the severity of the issue, it may contribute to stress, feelings of burden, fear, worries, sadness, or anger and aggression. In addition, it may lead to deviant behavior, lack of school involvement (Ishoy, 2015), development of negative peers, and the use of alcohol or drugs.

For some youth who commit crimes there is the possibility of restorative justice service. This involves a Juvenile Review Board (JRB) instead of the court system. The JRB is composed of a panel of community members who make recommendations for treatment for the offender after hearing the juvenile's version of the story in an informal hearing. The juvenile must acknowledge the committed act, express an interest in repairing the harm to the victim or community, and follow through with the JRB's recommendations. If the juvenile is successful with the recommendations and does not develop new charges or legal involvement, he or she will be cleared of the incident and have no criminal background record. This provides a second chance for juveniles and allows them to receive the services and treatment they may need to be successful and move on to positive things in the community without entering the criminal justice system.

Young Adults

Young adults, when transitioning from a facility to the community, face the challenge of reintegrating to the community and transitioning from adolescent to adulthood. Like all other individuals in the criminal justice system, they too require the support of family, friends, and other professionals. Treatment programs, such as mental health therapy, anger management, social skills, education, and job training can help them improve their lifestyle and stay away from delinquent behaviors.

Elderly

Elderly is defined as age 65 and older (Stal, 2012); however, correctional facilities identify older offenders as age 50 and older. Aday (1994) report older inmates are more likely to develop health problems such as hypertension, diabetes, arthritis, and kidney and heart problems. In addition, this population may have more difficulty adapting to a new environment with small spaces, minimal privacy, and uncomfortable living conditions. These are some of the issues this population may need help with upon release, while in the community.

Women Offenders

The Bureau of Justice Statistics' total correctional population at year-end in 2014 was 6,814,600; of these, 1,251,600 were women. Female offenders face similar and different challenges from the male offenders. During incarceration, they may face different treatment from male officers compared to male offenders. Other stressors may be related to worries of the outside world, such as finances and who is caring for the children, if there are children involved. While in the community some women face gender-related issues such as physical and mental health issues (Ritchie, 2001). In addition, they may seek help with parenting skills and, when there are abusive situations present, domestic violence support. A variety of services are available to female offenders. Some of the more common ones include financial assistance through the welfare system, housing, and life skills programs (Holtfreter & Wattanaporn, 2014).

Substance Abuse

Petersilia (2005) report 73% of prison inmates in the United States used drugs regularly prior to their incarceration. There are numerous programs designed to help individuals with problems with substance abuse. Bahr, Masters, and Taylor (2012) identified the following treatment modalities for those within and outside correctional facilities: cognitive therapy, individual counseling, group counseling, and 12-step programs (p. 159).

There are a variety of substances under the substance abuse category, which include alcohol and a range of drugs. In addition to the treatments mentioned, there is pharmacological treatment such as methadone maintenance, which is designed to treat heroin dependence (Bahr et al., 2012). The pharmacological treatments are designed to control the dosage and enable them to live relatively normal lives (Bahr et al., 2012). Furthermore, these authors found the combination of therapy with pharmacological treatment to be quite useful, according to Bahr et al. (2012).

Mental Health

The issue of mental health is one of significance and recently has been receiving attention in the media and in literature more frequently. Mental health is common among the criminal justice population. Skeem, Manchak, and Peterson (2011) report nearly three out of four jail detainees with a serious mental illness have a co-occurring substance abuse disorder. As a result, because these individuals are eventually released to the community, it is healthy and beneficial for them to seek mental health treatment as soon as possible after release.

Abracen et al. (2013) in a study found over 56% of the studied offender population were diagnosed with a personality disorder; substance abuse disorders were second highest, with alcohol at 37.5% and drugs 39.1%. The findings suggest a need for increased levels of mental health resources in forensic environments to serve the needs of high-risk offenders (Abracen et al., 2013). Furthermore, these authors found a higher likelihood of recidivism among offenders with a mental health diagnosis not in treatment compared to those offenders with a mental health diagnosis in treatment. As a result, offenders with a mental health condition are more likely to succeed in the community if they are receiving and compliant with mental health treatment.

Sexual Offenders

Most sexual offenders in the United States will serve their sentence under community supervision (Hanson, Helmus, & Harris, 2015). Offenders with a history of sexual offense have different treatment and restrictions in the community, depending on the severity of the charges. Offenders with a sexual offense upon release are typically mandated to sexual offender treatment and supervised in the community by a probation or parole officer. In addition to this mandated treatment, the offender may also be mandated to mental health treatment. Although Piche, Mathesius, Lussier, and Schweighofer (2016, p. 13) found "the cause for not seeking treatment was not knowing who to talk to or having no one to talk to," being mandated minimizes this because the officer usually provides the referral directly to the mental health program. For offenders with mandated treatment, it helps provides direct access to some of the community resources.

Veterans

The criminality of veterans after leaving the service or postwar remains a national concern, according to Murray (2014). There are a number of programs specifically for veteran offenders, such as Veterans Justice Outreach (VJO) and Health Care for Reentry Veterans (HCRV). These programs, according to the National Institute of Corrections (NIC, 2015), are designed to help ease the transition from incarceration to the community. Some of the services offered include vocational training and employment opportunities as well as help coping with issues related to incarceration (NIC, 2015). Although there are programs offered through Veterans Affairs, there are also services available in other organizations throughout the community.

Veteran offenders face challenges, as do other individuals incarcerated. Although they are veterans, they are now faced with the additional label of offender. As a result, they too are faced with similar obstacles related to employment, stigma, and mental health. However, in addition to these issues and the incarceration period, they may have additional trauma exposure from military experiences that may require professional services.

Immigrants

Immigrant offenders are usually handled in federal courts. One of the biggest issues non-U.S. citizen's face is the risk of deportation to their country of origin. One of the factors to consider when working with immigrants is cultural sensitivity. There may be many differences in values, beliefs, and services. A language barrier and immigration status may be added stressors they are faced with on a daily basis. Although they may be limited to certain services and treatments, there are resources available to help them with their needs.

Social Consequences of Incarceration

Individuals who spend time confined in a facility, jail, or prison are impacted in a number of ways. Entering the criminal justice system starts prior to being sentenced to a period of time in jail or prison. For some it may be a cycle in the family or community. Other ways they are impacted include stigma, being a product of the system, destruction of support system, and victimization.

Inmates as Products of the System

Many offenders face major obstacles in their transition from prison to the community. Often the offenders/ex-offenders develop negative views about "the system" because they may have been involved in incidents while incarcerated that did not result in an expected outcome. In some cases, offenders may feel they were treated unfairly. These types of situations can contribute to negative attitudes not just for the offender but also family, friends, and other professionals in the field.

Bowman and Travis (2012) found some former inmates believed their potential for success was sabotaged. Others understood that the transition back to the community came with major challenges (Bowman & Travis, 2012). These views came from the feelings that the criminal justice system was overloaded with problems related to overcrowding and unhealthy conditions and treatment (Bowman & Travis, 2012). Nonetheless, offenders become institutionalized, and it is extremely challenging for them to break away from that culture.

Loss of Social Support

Social support refers to the emotional, informational, or practical help that is received from others, such as family and friends (Thoits, 1995). There are many benefits for offenders to receive support from friends, family, and professionals. For example, Duwe and Clark (2011) found that maintaining visits throughout the incarceration period improves behavior while incarcerated and reduces the likelihood of recidivism when returned to the community. This type of support helps offenders stay connected to the outside world and may enhance their quality of life because they may feel someone cares enough about them to go visit.

The incarceration of a loved one not only affects the offender, it also affects family and friends. The incarceration period may be stressful and emotional for the offender as he/she is adapting to his or her new environment. In addition, it may be as stressful and emotional for the family as they adapt to changes and cope with the loss of their loved one. For many, it changes the family dynamics, causes financial struggles, and may lead to mental health conditions such as anxiety and depression.

Visiting someone in a correctional facility may be stressful. For some the stress begins with finding and paying for transportation and arranging for child care. Once at the facility, there is the stress of dealing with the staff that may or may not treat them respectfully. In addition, there is the actual visit, which may come with mixed emotions: happy to see the loved one and heartbroken when the visit ends.

The struggles that come with a loved one being in the criminal justice system may lead to the destruction of support systems. Clone and DeHart (2014) report there are benefits of support networks during the incarceration period. Some of the ways support is shown may include visits in prison, advocating for the offender by calling the facility, caring for children, sending money to the offender, or accepting phone calls. Many of these things come with a variety of obligations: financial, time, and emotional. Although, these are necessary sources of support to assist with a positive and successful reentry, these are also the reasons why support networks may be destroyed, because it may be too much for the family to handle.

In addition, to family and friends, it is beneficial for offenders to take advantage of the programs offered in the facility such as substance abuse treatment, support groups, and anger management, to name a few. Clone and DeHart's (2014) study showed involvement in facilitated groups while incarcerated led to positive and supportive relationships, which helped offenders cope with life and adjusting to the community after they were released.

Stigma

The stigma of being an offender or ex-prisoner can interfere with reintegration. It is easy to believe what is continuously being told. Chui and Cheng (2013) report a person may adjust his or her behaviors to match the internalized negative labels. Offenders may develop shame and negative views of themselves from their choices and actions, without the added stigma of others.

Chui and Cheng's (2013) findings reports it is much more difficult for adolescents than adults to transition from prison to the community. However, it is also difficult for adults to make the transition, especially if they have been incarcerated many years. They may feel lost when they enter a community surrounded by unfamiliar technology along with the likelihood of rejection, discrimination, and perception of inability to change.

The stigma is unlikely to disappear. However, offenders may be able to help themselves while they are incarcerated by participating in advance education and employment skills or trades. These skills may indicate to potential employers an interest to implement positive changes and may provide a path to employment.

Victimization

There have been studies showing a relationship showing victim-offender overlap (Berg, Stewart, Schreck, & Simons, 2012; Zaykowski & Gunter, 2013). Among the many challenges faced when reintegrating into the community is the return to the old neighborhood. Offenders typically return back to live with family or friends in the neighborhoods they may have lived in most of their lives. Offenders leave the neighborhood with a certain status and reputation when they are incarcerated, which may cause them and others who are influenced by them to feel that they are on top of the world. After being incarcerated for years and released, they may assume the neighborhood is exactly the same when they return. This poses many challenges, because although time may feel stilled to them while incarcerated, many changes occur in society.

Berg et al. (2012) describes an urban neighborhood as different from other conventional cultures. Urban neighborhoods have expectations and expected conduct that define their norms (Berg et al., 2012). Upon release offenders often want to make up for lost time and recuperate any losses over time. These losses may include money, property, and reputation. This may lead to the return of a previous lifestyle, which could contribute to the link between victim-offender overlap.

Serving time in prison affects offenders in different ways. Some may use the time to analyze their lives and implement positive change. In these cases, participating in programs the correctional facility has to offer is a wise choice. In addition, seeking positive supports when released to the community is another avenue to help ensure a successful reentry. There are some offenders who may become rebellious and want to resume their "street lifestyle" in a more powerful manner upon release. These individuals may find themselves in the victim-offender overlap and continue the cycle they know as their life. Change is possible, however; it begins with oneself. Therefore, offenders who want to change must reach out and follow through with the resources in place to assist them throughout the reintegration process.

Decision Making

Each choice made comes with some form of thought process and free will, sometimes resulting in positive outcomes and other times not so positive. For individuals serving a sentence, it may have been as a result of breaking the law after making decisions that did not have the best outcomes. While serving a sentence, whether it is incarceration or community supervision, there is a loss of autonomy for the offender. Although the final decisions still lie in the hands of each individual, it comes under the guidance and orders of the agency and officers assigned to work with each offender.

Individuals are usually aware of the decisions they previously made, which has them in their current situation. During the sentence, offenders have minimal decision-making options. It is pretty clear that they have the option of refusing to follow through with the rules and policies but often understand the ramifications this may cause them. As a result, knowing the benefits and risks of each situation typically influences the decisions being made. Therefore, working with offenders/ex-offenders may have a positive outcome if there is time invested in teaching effective decision-making skills.

Effective decision making may have a different outcome for each individual because it is meeting the individual and working on his or her own issue(s). Because we each have distinct perspectives on a variety of situations, the decision and outcome for each individual will be unique to that person. The decision or results may not be the greatest each time, however; it will provide the opportunity to view the situation with a different lens by considering the risk and benefits involved. This may help individuals regain their autonomy and empower them to make their own decisions while providing them with support in their transition.

It is not easy to work with challenging individuals, however; many offenders are accustomed to people giving up on them or treating them different when compared to nonoffenders. Nonetheless, for those who want the help and show interest in investing the time and energy to implementing a positive change to their lives, it is beneficial for them and the community to help support them as they learn and apply making healthy, positive, effective decisions.

Basic Needs

Upon release from a facility, most offenders are discharged in need of the basic daily essentials, such as housing, food, and clothing. During the incarceration period, the state or federal government provides these basic needs, and the individuals may not think or worry about them. However, upon discharge, individuals are faced with the reality that these are all basic needs to survive and they now have to find a way to get these needs met, especially if they do not have support from family or friends. These needs are essential in the transition process and in the ability to succeed.

Housing

Having a place to call home provides a sense of safety, security, and stability. Each year, offenders are released from an institution, and many find themselves homeless. Gunnison and Helfgott (2011) identified homelessness and residential instability as one of the greatest challenges ex-offenders face when they are transitioning to society. The majority of the offenders upon release return to impoverished neighborhoods (Fontaine & Biess, 2012) that are high in crime and unsafe. This poses a huge problem, for the individuals, their families, the community, and social services. Many public housing communities often prohibit individuals with a felony to rent in their property. On the occasions when the apartment is available and the manager will consider renting it, there is a security deposit required, which may be one, two, or three months' rent as a down payment. The property owners may be reluctant to rent to ex-offenders due to past violent offenses, drug activity, sexual offenses, or mental illness.

Another option for housing includes living with family or friends. This too poses a problem because often the family members are on low-income housing or Section-8, which only allows those tenants listed on the lease to live in the apartment and who must be clear of criminal offenses. Lastly, shelters are common places for offenders because they have encountered so many obstacles for living. However, given the high rates of homelessness, shelters are also becoming less available to ex-offenders. This makes it burdensome to the ex-offender to establish safety and trust in their family, community and their own ability to settle down and prepare for a new beginning. Housing stability helps establish a sense of successful reintegration that otherwise may be difficult to attain.

Treating offenders in the community requires the need for services to be in place to assist with the transition process. The Vera Institute of Justice is launching a pilot program to increase the number of housing programs serving the reentry community. According to the Vera Institute of Justice (2016), this program aims to change the admissions policy for individuals involved in the criminal justice system and reduce barriers that impede successful reentry. Programs such as these will be beneficial not only to the offenders reentering society but to the community as a whole.

Food Assistance

One benefit for most released offenders is the ability to receive Supplemental Nutritional Assistance, also known as food stamps. The amount provided is based on family size and need, which helps with the cost of food and may be used in supermarkets or grocery stores. This allows the offender(s) to purchase their own food, and in cases when they have families, helps them contribute to the household. Although the amount received is very helpful, often it is not enough to provide food for the entire month. Therefore, there may be a sense of stress and frustration regarding how to provide for self and/or family. Other options for food include visiting food pantries in a variety of organizations in the community, such as churches or nonprofit agencies.

Clothing

Clothing helps provide a sense and image of personal identity (Droogsma, 2007). Given the many other issues offenders face when they are released to the community, clothing may not appear a critical item. However, for a period of time, while incarcerated, the wardrobe was evident the individual was state or federal property. The first day inmates were incarcerated, they were stripped of their personal belongings and provided a department of correction uniform, which consists of a jumpsuit or tan or striped pants, shirt and white undershirt. Therefore, upon release, this is one of the areas offenders want to change immediately to help them develop their sense of identity and belonging to the community. Obtaining a new wardrobe involves money, which may be difficult if there is a lack of financial resources in the family. According to Smiley and Middlemass (2016), clothing allows for returning individuals to (1) reshape their identity, (2) reaffirm their sense of manhood, and (3) reconnect with their community.

In situations when there are no financial means to purchase new clothing, there are other resources for offenders/ex-offenders to attain clothing for reduced prices or free. In the community there are organizations that help people in need. Some of these may include local churches, thrift shops, and a number of nonprofit organizations. Although not having the means to purchase their own or the latest styles of clothing could lead to some frustration for the offender/ex-offender, these are available resources that may help to provide basic essentials that will not hinder their progress, until the financial situation allows for other options.

Social Support

With the increased number of offenders being released to their communities, it is essential to review the reentry process. Social support, according to Wallace et al. (2016), is vital to ex-offenders' success in the community and their mental health. Many of the offenders identify family and friends as their first system of support when they return back to their communities. In addition to family and friends, there is a need of social and community supports, which are essential in the transition phase and making the process as simple and painless as possible. Relying on a helping hand and extensive services may instill a sense of hope for a better tomorrow. Identifying the problem alone does not solve the issue, therefore; community support and involvement are necessary to implement change.

Family

The definition of family has changed over time, and for some individuals it is no longer considered just blood relatives. The Vera Institute (2016) suggested we think of family in a broad sense to include other supportive members of a person's social network. Ganong and Colemena (2004) estimated that one-third of American children will spend a significant portion of their lives in cohabiting or stepparent families before they become adults. In addition, there are a high number of children living in foster care or group homes who may identify family as those who are involved in their lives at that time and their primary support system. As a result, stepsiblings, friends, neighbors, mentors, teachers, coworkers, and foster parents may also be considered family members.

The Vera Institute (2011) reports family members tend to be there through good times and in bad, including incarceration and community supervision. Therefore, it is beneficial to know who the support networks are and what strengths and resources exist in each family (The Vera Institute, 2016). Throughout incarceration, family relationships are changed and disrupted, and in some cases the relationships come to an end. However, according to Duwe and Clark (2011), family and friends are the most valuable source of support for offenders returning to the community. Upon release to the community, offenders are faced with many responsibilities, including reconstructing their relationships.

Community

It is not uncommon for members of the community to have a negative attitude or perception about offenders or ex-offenders, in part due to stigmas. As a result, Rade, Desmarais, and Mitchell (2016) report ex-offenders often receive differential treatment. This differential treatment may be in the form of denied employment, challenges finding housing, and exclusion from social events. The offenders or ex-offenders that have been found to face the most challenges are those having a history of a sexual offense, compared to those without a sexual offense (Rade, Desmarais, & Mitchell, 2016).

Communities tend to form a special bond among them. Often, they help each other in times of need and support each other in good times and in bad. Eventually, it is possible to develop a sense of family within the community and the neighborhood. As a result, communities have the ability to influence and assist offenders in the reintegration process through their own civic commitment to their communities (Ward, 2009).

When offenders first arrive to their communities, it is not uncommon for them to be welcomed in a variety of ways. Some community members may welcome them warmly, wishing them well and willing to assist in any possible way to help them succeed. Others may be cautious and fearful of how their presence may affect their community. Nonetheless, the manner in which offenders are treated in their community impacts them, their thought process, and how they adapt to the transition of reintegration. Although, it may not be easy, it may benefit the community to have an open mind and provide assistance and guidance, which may help the offender to view and develop a positive attitude about the reintegration process.

Community Supervision

Release to the community after a period of incarceration is a transition period. It requires more than the personal characteristics. It also includes compliance, cooperation, openness, motivation, determination, and support. In addition, the support required for a successful reentry consists of more than friends and family. The added support encompasses a community of systems such as probation, parole, social services, job placement, education, and mental health treatment.

Probation

Probation is a period of time an offender is to be supervised in the community by an officer of the state after being found guilty of a crime. The officers that choose to do this type of work, according to Worrall and Mawby (2014), do it because of a desire to work with people. Like many other professionals, probation officers also have to build a rapport with the offenders for it to be a "good match." This includes developing trust and working directly with the offender as a team. Worrall and Mawby

(2014) found one of the important ties that bind the probation officer and the offender together is "honorable profession" (p. 347).

Relationships of any kind work best if they are a "good fit" for both parties involved. Offenders are assigned a probation officer without the choice of who the individual is or whether or not it is a good fit for each other. Although offenders may express complaints about their assigned officer, it is essential to note that the job of probation officers is a complicated one, in part because they work with people who can be difficult. They work with a population that has numerous differences within it. Some of the differences include age, race, ethnicity, sex, and offense type. One of the easiest ways to begin to develop a good relationship between the probation officer and the offender is to have open communication. This provides clear expectations of the relationship. To avoid misunderstandings of the expectations, it would be beneficial for these to be summarized and repeated back by the offender, then finalized with a signed copy of the agreement by both officer and offender.

The responsibility of probation officers is not just to supervise offenders in the community. Rather, it is similar to that of a counselor. Although they are not working on clinical goals, they are working with the offenders on other types of life goals. Some of these include employment and housing. Probation officers are a support system to their clients, and how the relationship develops over time, including their attitude and willingness to help the client, may contribute to the success or failure of the offender.

Parole

Parole officers supervise offenders in the community after they have served a designated time incarcerated. Like probation officers, parole officers also work directly with the offenders to help lead them to a successful reentry transition to their communities. Parole officers help offenders with a variety of resources; some are mandated programs and others are voluntary. Some of the mandated programs may include substance abuse counseling, mental health therapy, psychiatric medications, job training, or sex offender treatment.

Parole officers also provide supervision in the community. This involves direct contact with the parolee through office visits, home visits, and phone calls. In addition, parole officers may be in contact with the professionals involved in the offender's treatment, such as monitoring attendance to therapy, drug screenings, or in some cases electronic monitoring. Lastly, there may also be contact with family and employers of the offender.

Mental Health Services

Research studies have shown individuals in the criminal justice system to be overrepresented in mental illness when compared to the general population. Due to the high influx of individuals incarcerated with mental illness, the need to have services available in the community at time of release is essential to ensure the best possibility for a successful reentry and less likelihood of recidivism. The services may include case management, mental health, and substance abuse treatment.

Mental health education or training for providers working with offenders with mental illness will be advantageous, not only for personal growth but also for the offenders and the community. White, Saunders, Fisher, and Mellow (2012) report that offenders, when they return to society from jail or prison, often struggle with their same issues. Some of these issues, according to Solomon, Osborne, LoBuglio, Mellow, and Mukamal (2008), include substance abuse and mental illness.

Case Management

Case management provides an assessment of the offender's needs and provides resources in the community. The resources typically include housing, cash and food assistance, medical insurance, transportation, job readiness, and employment. In addition, there is also coordinating care and advocating among a number of service providers to help the individual stay organized and on task with the services needed and treatment recommendations.

Therapy

There are a number of reasons why individuals seek mental health services. Some include depression, anxiety, eating disorders, mood disorder, personality disorders, schizophrenia, trauma, and mental and substance use disorders. Although there are a variety of treatment models that are effective with clients, research has identified cognitive-behavioral therapy (CBT) (Barnes, Hyatt, & Sherman, 2016) and motivational interviewing (MI) to work well with individuals in the criminal justice population. Psychotropic medications are also used to treat symptoms of many mental health disorders. Sometimes treating the individual includes the medications with therapy.

Research has shown cognitive-behavioral therapy (CBT) is successful in helping offenders change their thoughts and implement positive change. CBT can be used to treat people with a range of mental health problems such as anxiety, depression, and grief, as well as help with substance abuse prevention and relapse prevention. This model is based on the idea that our thoughts, feelings, and behaviors are connected to each other. Furthermore, it addresses undesirable behaviors, including criminal activities, by focusing on reforming maladapted and antisocial thought patterns (Barnes et al., 2016).

Motivational interviewing (MI), according to McMurran (2009), has encouraged people to commit to goals for change and is generally used in offender treatment to help facilitate change. McMurran (2009) report three reasons to use MI are (1) to enhance retention and engagement in treatment, (2) to improve motivation for change, and (3) to change behavior. Although these models have been shown to be effective, the actual interest and motivation to change is required from the individual.

Anger management is another reason offenders seek treatment. Although anger is a natural and common emotion, some individuals do not know appropriate ways to express it. It may become a problem when it is experienced too frequently, intensely or in a harmful manner, such as aggression (Reilly & Shopshire, 2012). Attending a treatment program to learn how to manage and appropriately express the anger is beneficial for offenders who have a history of uncontrolled anger, aggression, or violence.

Psychotropic Medications

With correctional institutions being considered the largest of the mental health facilities, it can be assumed there are more than a few of the inmates prescribed psychotropic medications. Therefore, as they transition to the community, continuing their medication would be in their best interest for their mental health. Discharge planning for offenders on these types of medications would be best practice if they had an appointment with a provider in the community. However, the discharge process, as noted by Baillargeon, Hoge, and Penn (2010), may actually include going home with a few weeks' worth of medication and a list of providers in the community for the offender to follow up with on his/her own.

Employment

Attaining employment may be easy for some individuals; however, for most it is not, and it involves a process. There is an array of challenges involved in attaining a job. One of the first things to take note of is that the job market has become very competitive. There are many jobs that require a certain level of advanced education and skill set, while others require a high school education or general educational development (GED) certificate. Some places of employment are willing to hire and train without previous experience; however, these are becoming less over time. These challenges and criteria are the bare minimum for some organizations, and then comes the additional requirement of no criminal record. Finding a job is one of the biggest challenges offenders face when they leave a correctional facility and transition to the community.

Job Readiness

Securing a job is difficult, because offenders typically lack basic skills and have low levels of education and limited work experience (Bender, Cobbina, & McGarrell, 2016). Unfortunately, time is not something that can be recovered. However, learning new skills, advancing one's education and implementing positive changes are all possible. For incarcerated offenders, it is beneficial to attain the GED, college education, or participate in a trade, if possible, while incarcerated. This helps provide the basic work experience or skills that some employers are seeking.

Job readiness is usually offered as a correctional program to offenders prior to their release to the community. In addition, offenders on probation or parole may also have the ability to attend similar programs in the community. Comprehensive vocational interventions, according to Hurry, Brazier, Parker, and Wilson (2006), that focused on job readiness skills, employment development, and job searching, were the most promising in decreasing recidivism. However, the majority of the vocational programs have failed to include a component that helps offenders change career thoughts and attitudes (Vernick & Reardon, 2001), which may limit their effectiveness.

It may be helpful to consider many of the offenders have not worked in a long time or may have never worked. Therefore, educating them on the basic skills such as how to complete a job application—paper and online, as times have changed—and develop a resume, interview skills, proper dress attire, and etiquette in the workplace, may be beneficial to them. In addition, some of the offenders, particularly those who have a history of earning money fast and illegal, may want to know the pay ranges for the variety of jobs they may qualify for. This for them may be an adjustment period because it may require physical labor. Furthermore, it will take them much longer to earn the amount of money they were once accustomed to when they did not work legally.

Employers Willingness to Hire Offenders or Ex-Offenders

As previously noted, finding a job for an offender or ex-offender is not an easy task. Having a criminal background is typically viewed negatively. However, this does not rule out the possibility of offenders or ex-offenders finding a job. Atkin and Armstrong's (2013) findings report more than half (54%) of the employer respondents were willing to hire ex-offenders, and only 14% indicated they disagreed or totally disagreed with the statement (p. 81). The type of offense, violent or nonviolent, may influence that perception to change. According to Atkin and Armstrong (2013), more than 80% of employers expressed an unwillingness to hire an ex-offender who was convicted of a violent offense. Examples of violent offenses include murder, aggravated assault, and rape.

Although having a criminal history affects the types of employment opportunities, attaining a job is possible. Preparation, determination, and motivation will benefit offenders and ex-offenders in the job search. Even more so, their willingness to accept a job offered rather than be selective in their choices will be helpful. Providing guidance and direction of the realistic job opportunities will be of service to this population. A study by Wells (2013) reported the three most common jobs for individuals with a criminal record were: wait staff, customer service representative, and delivery driver. Other job titles included custodian, auto lot attendant, auto parts person, cashier, clerk/shipping, laborer, auto lube, and warehouse accounting. Assistance from the community officer or other job ready agencies are other valuable resources for offenders/ex-offenders seeking employment.

Financial Challenges

Unemployment may be a source of stress for most people in today's economy. For offenders being released to the community, the need to earn money is a necessity to live, support themselves and family, and to be successful in reintegrating into the community. Having a job will play a significant role in offenders becoming law-abiding citizens and not returning to jail or prison.

Many of the offenders may return to the homes of family and friends when they are released to the community. However, this does not eliminate financial obligations of the home, courts, or parole. In the event offenders are transitioned to a halfway house, they are obligated to pay a specified amount each month. In the event this amount is not paid, the offender could be returned to prison. In addition, legal fines or restitution may also be required upon their release. Other forms of expenses include child support and additional bills, such as old or current credit card debt, program fees, doctor visits, medications, and transportation.

Not having one's own money to pay for one's own financial responsibilities may lead to the feeling of burden on others. This could also lead to the development of a negative perception of self and a sense of failure regarding the inability to be financially successful. This negative self-talk may influence the need for illegal activity or criminal behavior and the risk of recidivism.

Recidivism

Reducing the prison population has become a central concern for many states (Duwe & Clark, 2011). According to Sullivan, McDonald, and Thomson (2016), some of the main predictors of recidivism are age at first conviction, offending history, personality, education, employment, mental health, substance abuse, and relationships with family, friends, and community (p. 407). There are a number of factors that influence low recidivism rates. Maintaining social support to individuals during their incarceration has been shown to help keep offenders from recidivism (Duwe & Clark, 2011). Furthermore, an explicit description of the reintegration phase to the family and friends involved may be useful and help them understand what to expect during the process (Davis, Bahr, & Ward, 2012).

To help offenders to become successful members of society, it is necessary to know the predictors of recidivism and also understand the components that help them desist the criminal activity. Davis et al., (2012) identified four elements that help offenders desist from crime: develop openness to change, exposure to circumstances that help them move toward change, develop a changed identity, and view illegal behavior differently. In addition, knowing some personal history of the offender along with a summary of the incarceration period and its impact may provide a clearer perspective, which may be relevant to helping that individual.

Conclusion

The need for increased success in prisoner reentry, according to Hass and Saxon (2012), has become recognized as an urgent and national issue of relevance at the federal level. Offenders are individuals who commit mistakes but are human beings who eventually will return to live in their communities. Although there are some who may have difficulty or are unable to be rehabilitated, many can. Therefore, as a community, it is beneficial to work with them and support them as they aim to be successful in their reintegration to society.

Offenders and ex-offenders too often hear what they did wrong and what they should not do. It is possible they have been exposed to negative comments and feedback prior to being released to the community, and in some cases most of their lives. In many cases, they are expected to fail. However, instead of continuing the negative trend, it may be helpful to provide them with positive feedback, guidance, a sense of direction, and praise when they do something right.

The positive interaction is more likely to provide hope, encouragement, and increase self-esteem. In addition to the basic needs and resources indicated previously, what offenders/ex-offenders need most are acceptance, guidance, and unbiased and nonjudgmental treatment from the community. Second chances and new opportunities are considerations most individuals would like to be granted. Furthermore, if these individuals are not given an opportunity to implement change, how are they and the community expecting to see change in them?

References

Abracen, J., Langton, C. M., Looman, J., Gallo, A., Ferguson, M., Axford, M., & Dickey, R. (2013). Mental health diagnoses and recidivism in paroled offenders. *International Journal of Offender Therapy and Comparative Criminology, 58*(7), 765–779. doi:10.1177/0306624X13485930

Aday, R. H. (1994). Aging in prison: A case study of new elderly offenders. *International Journal of Offender Therapy and Comparative Criminology, 38*(1), 79–91.

Atkin, C., & Armstrong, G. (2013). Does the concentration of parolees in a community affect employer attitudes toward the hiring of ex-offenders? *Criminal Justice Policy Review, 24*(1), 71–93. doi:10.1177/0887403411428005

Bahr, S. J., Masters, A. L., & Taylor, B. M. (2012). What works in substance abuse treatment programs for offenders? *The Prison Journal, 92*(2), 155–174. doi:10.1177/0032885512438836

Baillargeon, J., Hoge, S. K., & Penn, J.V. (2010). Addressing the challenge of community reentry among released inmates with serious mental illness. *American Journal of Community Psychology, 46*(3–4), 361–375. doi:10.1007/s10464-010-9345-6

Barnes, G., Hyatt, J., & Sherman, L. (2016). Even a little bit helps: An implementation and experimental evaluation of cognitive-behavioral therapy for high-risk probationers. *Criminal Justice and Behavior, 44*(4), 1–20. doi:10.1177/0093854816673862

Bender, K., Cobbina, J., & McGarrell, E. (2016). Reentry programming for high-risk offenders: Insights from participants. *International Journal of Offender Therapy and Comparative Criminology, 60*(13), 1479–1508. doi:10.1177/0306624X15578204

Berg, M.T., Stewart, E.A., Schreck, C.J., & Simons, R.L. (2012). The victim-offender overlap in context: Examining the role of neighborhood street culture. *Criminology, 50*(2), 359–390. doi:10.1111/j.1745-9125.2011.00265.x

Blonigen, D., Bui, L., Elbogen, E. B., Blodgett, J. C., Maisel, N.C., Midboe, A. M., . . . Timko, C. (2016). Risk of recidivism among justice-involved veterans: A systematic review of the literature. *Criminal Justice Policy Review, 27*(8), 812–837. doi:10.1177/0887403414562602

Bowman, S. W., & Travis, R. (2012). Prisoner reentry and recidivism according to the formerly incarcerated and reentry service providers: A verbal behavior approach. *The Behavior Analyst Today, 13*(3&4), 9–19. doi:10.1037/h0100726

Bureau of Justice Statistics. (2015a). *Correctional populations in the United States, 2014.* Washington, DC: U.S. Department of Justice, Bureau of Justice Statistics.

Bureau of Justice Statistics. (2015b). *Probation and parole in the United States, 2014.* Washington, DC: U.S. Department of Justice, Bureau of Justice Statistics.

Chui, W. H., & Cheng, K. K. (2013). The mark of an ex-prisoner: Perceived discrimination and self-stigma of young men after prison in Hong Kong. *Deviant Behavior, 34*(8), 671–684. doi:10.1080/01639625.2013.766532

Clinkinbeard, S. C., & Zohra, T. (2012). Expectations, fears, and strategies: Juvenile offender thoughts on a future outside of incarceration. *Youth & Society, 44*(2), 236–257. doi:10.1177/0044118X11398365

Clone, S., & DeHart, D. (2014). Social support networks of incarcerated women: Types of support, sources of support, and implications for reentry. *Journal of Offender Rehabilitation, 53*(7), 503–521. doi:10.1080/10509674.2014.944742

Davis, C., Bahr, S. J., & Ward, C. (2012). The process of offender reintegration: Perceptions of what helps prisoners reenter society. *Criminology & Criminal Justice, 13*(4), 446–469. doi:10.1/1177/1748895812454748

Droogsma, R. A. (2007). Redefining Hijab: American Muslim women's standpoints on veiling. *Journal of Applied Communication Research, 35*(3), 294–319.

Duwe, G., & Clark, V. (2011). Blessed be the social tie that binds: The effects of prison visitation on offender recidivism. *Criminal Justice Policy Review, 24*(3), 271–296. doi:10.1177/0887403411429724

Fontaine, J., & Biess, J. (2012). *Housing as a platform for formerly incarcerated persons.* Washington, DC: Urban Institute.

Ganong, L. H., & Coleman, M. (2004). *Stepfamily relationships: Development, dynamics, and interventions.* New York, NY: Springer. doi:10.1007/978-1-4419-9112-6

Gunnison, E., & Helfgott, J. B. (2011). Factors that hinder offender reentry success: A view from community corrections officers. *International Journal of Offender Therapy and Comparative Criminology*, *55*(2), 287–304. doi:10.1177/0306624X09360661

Hanson, R. K., Helmus, L., & Harris, A. J. R. (2015). A prospective study using stable-2007, static-99r, and static-2002r. *Criminal Justice and Behavior*, *42*(12), 1205–1224. doi:10.1177/0093854815602094

Hass, A.Y., & Saxon, C. E. (2012). From the inside/out: Greene County Jail inmates on restorative reentry. *International Journal of Offender Therapy and Comparative Criminology*, *56*(7), 1037–1062. doi:10.1177/0306624X11418914

Hardcastle, L., Bartholomew, T., & Graffam, J. (2011). Legislative and community support for offender reintegration in Victoria. *Deakin Law Review*, *16*(1), 111–132. doi:10.21153/dlr2011vol16no1art96

Holtfreter, K., & Wattanaporn, W. A. (2014). The transition from prison to community initiative: An examination of gender responsiveness for female offender reentry. *Criminal Justice and Behavior*, *41*(1), 41–57. doi:10.1177/0093854813504406

Hurry, J., Brazier, L., Parker, M., & Wilson, A. (2006). *Rapid evidence assessment of interventions that promote employment for offenders* [Research Report Number 747]. London, UK: Department for Education and Skills.

Ishoy, G. A. (2015). Exploring morality as a mediator of the association between parenting practices and violent and property offending among a sample of juvenile delinquents. *Crime & Delinquency*, *63*(2), 113–136. doi:10.1177/0011128714560810

McMurran, M. (2009). Motivational interviewing with offenders: A systematic review. *Legal and Criminological Psychology*, *14*, 83–100. doi:10.1348/135532508X278326

Murray, E. (2014). Veteran offenders in Cheshire: Making sense of the "noise". *Probation Journal*, *61*(3), 251–264. doi:10.1177/0264550514536756

National Institute of Corrections. (2015). *Justice-involved veterans and employment: A systematic review of barriers and promising strategies and interventions*. Washington, DC: U.S. Department of Justice, National Institute of Justice.

National Institute of Justice. (2014). *Young offenders: What happens and what should happen*. Washington, DC: U.S. Department of Justice, Office of Juvenile Justice and Delinquency Prevention.

Paulson, P. (2013). *The role of community based programs in reducing recidivism in ex-offenders* (Master of Social Work Clinical Research Papers. Paper 247). St. Paul, MN: St. Catherine University.

Petersilia, J. (2005). From cell to society: Who is returning home? In J. Travis & C. Visher (Eds.), *Prison reentry and crime in America* (pp. 15–49). New York, NY: Cambridge University Press.

Piche, L., Mathesius, J., Lussier, P., & Schweighofer, A. (2016). Preventative services for sexual offenders. *Sexual Abuse: A Journal of Research and Treatment*, [Online First]. 1–19. doi:10.1177/1079063216630749

Rade, C., Desmarais, S., & Mitchell, R. (2016). A meta-analysis of public attitudes toward ex-offenders. *Criminal Justice and Behavior*, *43*(9), 1260–1280. doi:10.1177/0093854816655837

Reilly, P. M., & Shopshire, M. S. (2012). *Anger management for substance abuse and mental health clients: A cognitive behavioral therapy manual*. Retrieved from http://store.samhsa.gov/shin/content/SMA12-4213/SMA12-4213.pdf

Ritchie, B. (2001). Challenges incarcerated women face as they return to their communities: Findings from life history interviews. *Crime and Delinquency*, *47*(3), 368–389. doi:10.1177/0011128701047003005

Skeem, J. L., Manchak, S., & Peterson, J. K. (2011). Correctional policy for offenders with mental illness: Creating a new paradigm for recidivism reduction. *Law and Human Behavior*, *35*(2), 110–126. doi:10.1007/s10979-010-9223-7

Smiley, C. J., & Middlemass, K. M. (2016). Clothing makes the man: Impression management and prisoner reentry. *Punishment & Society*, *18*(2), 220–243. doi:10/1177/1462474516636953

Solomon, A., Osborne, J. W. L., LoBuglio, S. F., Mellow, J., & Mukamal, D. A. (2008). *Life after lockup: Improving reentry from jail to the community*. Washington, DC: Urban Institute Justice Policy Center.

Stal, M. (2012). Treatment of older and elderly inmates within prisons. *Journal of Correctional Health Care*, *19*(1), 69–73. doi:10.1177/1078345812458245

Sullivan, T., McDonald, M., & Thomson, S. (2016). Offender case management: Reducing the rate reoffending by Maori. *Australian & New Zealand Journal of Criminology*, *49*(3), 405–421. doi:10.1177/0004865815575398

Thoits, P. A. (1995). Stress, coping, and social support processes: Where are we? What next? *Journal of Health and Social Behavior*, *35*, 53–79.

Vera Institute of Justice. (2016). *Opening doors to public housing: Expanding access for people with conviction histories*. Retrieved from www.vera.org/projects/opening-doors-to-public-housing/overview

Vera Institute of Justice. (2011). *Why ask about family*? Retrieved from www.ywcaworks.org/document.doc?id=171

Vernick, S. H., & Reardon, R. C. (2001). Career development programs in corrections. *Journal of Career Development*, *27*(4), 265–277. doi:10.1177/089484530102700403

Wallace, D., Fahmy, C., Cotton, L., Jimmons, C., McKay, R., Stoffer, S., & Syed, S. (2016). Examining the role of familial support during prison and after release on post-incarceration mental health. *International Journal of Offender Therapy and Comparative Criminology*, *60*(1), 3–20. doi:10.1177/0306624X14548023

Ward, T. (2009). Dignity and human rights in correctional practice. *European Journal of Probation*, *1*(2), 112–127. doi:10.1177/206622030900100204

Wells, L. (2013, July–September). Milwaukee's disregarded population: Out of sight; out of mind. *Sage Open*, 1–13. doi:10.1177/2158244013502491

White, M. D., Saunders, J., Fisher, C., & Mellow, J. (2012). Exploring inmate reentry in a local jail setting: Implications for outreach, service use, and recidivism. *Crime & Delinquency*, *58*(1), 124–146. doi:10.1177/0011128708327033

Worrall, A., & Mawby, R. (2014). Probation worker cultures and relationships with offenders. *Probation Journal*, *61*(4), 346–357. doi:10.1177/0264550514548251

Zaykowski, H., & Gunter, W. D. (2013). Gender differences in victimization risk: Exploring the role of deviant lifestyles. *Violence and Victims*, *28*(2), 341–56. doi:10.1891/0886-6708.28.2.341

29

REENTRY AND REINTEGRATION OF ADULT SPECIAL POPULATIONS

Community Involvement, Police Partnerships, and Reentry Councils

Robert D. Hanser

> If reentry is simply implemented as a "program" for those leaving prison, and nothing more, it will provide us with little else than an opportunity to pick up the damaged pieces that our affinity for punishment has created. However, if we carefully attend to the wide range of concerns that effect reentry, we can substantially reduce the prison population, avoid the damage, and promote reintegration.
>
> —(Rosenthal & Wolf, 2004, p. 5)

Introduction

Before we can discuss offender reentry programs, we must understand what constitutes offender reentry. Some observers note that offender reentry is the natural byproduct of incarceration, because all prisoners who are not sentenced to life in prison or do not die in prison will reenter the community at some point. According to this school of thought, reentry is not a program or legal status but rather a process that most offenders will undergo. A variant on this approach is the concept that offender reentry includes all activities and programming conducted to prepare ex-offenders to return to the community and live as law-abiding citizens (Nunez-Neto, 2008).

Although this broad definition of reentry certainly encompasses all the activities that may impinge on or affect a prisoner's reentry into society, it may be a cumbersome one for the purposes of crafting and evaluating government policies. This has led many in the field to focus on a more narrow and thus more manageable definition of reentry. This more narrow definition has two parts: (1) correctional programs that focus on transitioning to the community, such as prerelease, work release, halfway houses, or other programs specifically aiming at reentry; and (2) programs that initiate some form of treatment, such as substance abuse, life skills, education, or mental health, that is linked to continuity of treatment once the prisoner is released (Nunez-Neto, 2008).

Regardless of the definition utilized, the federal government has provided significant attention to this issue and has an overarching paradigm for reentry service delivery, commonly referred to as the *Roadmap to Reentry*. The *Roadmap to Reentry* identifies five evidence-based principles that guide efforts to improve correctional programs developed for those who will reenter society after being incarcerated. Much like standard discharge planning among therapeutic treatment professionals, the federal government operates on the premise that reentry begins on the first day of incarceration. Likewise, the work of correctional treatment professionals does not end when the individual leaves prison. Rather, correctional efforts should continue from intake, throughout incarceration, and after release. As developed by the U.S. Department of Justice (2016), the five evidence-based principles to optimal reentry efforts are as follows (see Box 29.1):

Box 29.1 Five Evidence-Based Principles to Optimal Reentry

Principle I: Upon incarceration, every inmate should be provided an individualized reentry plan tailored to his or her risk of recidivism and programmatic needs.

Principle II: While incarcerated, each inmate should be provided education, employment training, life skills, substance abuse, mental health, and other programs that target their criminogenic needs and maximize their likelihood of success upon release.

Principle III: While incarcerated, each inmate should be provided the resources and opportunity to build and maintain family relationships, strengthening the support system available to him or her upon release.

Principle IV: During transition back to the community, halfway houses and supervised release programs should ensure individualized continuity of care for returning citizens.

Principle V: Before leaving custody, every person should be provided comprehensive reentry-related information and access to resources necessary to succeed in the community.

Again, this outlook on reentry is similar to the continuity-of-care idea common among medical and mental health professionals. The idea is as offenders continue to progress through their sentence satisfactorily, their level of supervision is less intense and invasive. The continuity-of-care concept gives offenders more effective tools and strategies to avoid criminogenic influences and embrace involvement in prosocial lifestyle choices.

This chapter will focus on reentry programs for offenders who have a variety of special needs. This topic is more complicated than simply discussing general reentry programming for offenders. There are significant issues associated with the successful reentry of special needs offenders. This chapter provides an overview of the reentry and reintegration process. It also applies this process to specific offender populations who have unique and/or complex treatment needs. The chapter concludes with an examination of how reentry programs effectively address special needs offenders and strategies to reduce the likelihood of their future offending.

Special Needs

Proper classification ensures treatment professionals are able to match programs to offenders' specific criminogenic needs. In addition, proper classification optimizes the outcomes for program participants. From a legal and historical context, needs assessment has been pivotal in designing appropriate responses to different types of offenders (e.g., juvenile and intellectually disabled offenders) (Ashford, Sales, & Reed, 2000). However, when we use the term *need*, this implies that the issue involves something that is necessary, not something that is a mere desire or preference. Thus, if the individual does not have this need met, then he or she will experience some form of serious social, psychological, physical, or emotional impairment within his or her daily functioning. Because correctional institutions are liable for legally defensible standards of care for inmates in their custody, they must be prepared to address specialized needs that may emerge among their prison populations.

The needs of offenders can be either subjective or objective. Subjective needs are those that are perceived by offenders to be of importance, while objective needs are those deemed important by correctional professionals. Objective needs typically center on medical or mental health concerns, social functioning, and/or well-being of offenders and primarily correspond to legal standards of care.

Identifying Offenders with Special Needs

Because there are a number of different types of special needs offenders, this section is divided into several subsections as a means of maintaining clarity and distinction between each group. The following overview of special needs offenders is not meant to be exhaustive, nor is it meant to be comprehensive. Rather, this section demonstrates reentry and reintegration are viable for special needs populations.

Offenders with Mental Illness

One group of special needs offenders are those with mental health diagnoses. In many respects, the issues associated with mentally ill offenders have less to do with their threat to the community and more to do with their abnormal behavior. While some individuals with mental illness may act differently, this does not mean these offenders are more prone to violence. Specifically, data collected by the U.S. Department of Health and Human Services (2015, p. 1) indicates:

> Most people with mental illness are not violent and only 3%–5% of violent acts can be attributed to individuals living with a serious mental illness. In fact, people with severe mental illnesses are over 10 times more likely to be victims of violent crime than the general population.

These findings suggest that mentally ill offenders represent a small percentage of the violent criminal population. Society should be concerned more about the violent victimization of individuals with mental illness. In fact, violent victimization of the mentally ill is even more likely to occur behind bars, as the mentally ill are often vulnerable to intimidation and manipulation by other higher functioning inmates (Hanser, 2016).

Individuals with serious mental health disorders, including major depression, schizophrenia, and bipolar disorder, only commit about 7–8% of violent crimes (Peterson, Skeem, Kennealy, & Bray, 2014). In other words, Peterson et al. (2014) found the majority of persons with mental illness are not violent, not criminal, and not dangerous. Rather, it would seem when an individual with mental illness does commit a crime, it is inflated by the media, giving a false perception that there is a connection between crime and mental illness (Peterson et al., 2014).

Elderly Offenders

Another commonly identified group of special needs offender is the elderly offender. Elderly offenders are those who are convicted and are at least 50 years of age. This criterion has been determined based on factors that include the prior lifestyle, medical and mental health, and effects of prior incarceration on the individual's overall functioning. For the nonincarcerated population, 50 years of age seems young to be considered elderly. However, incarceration and the deleterious effects of a criminal lifestyle prematurely age most individuals.

When discussing elderly offenders, there are three categories to consider: the elderly first-time offender, the habitual elderly offender, and the offender who turns elderly in prison. The elderly first-time offender makes up about half of the elderly population. They have a law-abiding past, are usually in prison for some type of spontaneous crime of passion, and do not adjust well to prison life. The habitual elderly offender, on the other hand, has a history of criminal behavior along with stints in and out of jail and prison. These elderly offenders have adjusted to life behind bars. Lastly, the offenders-turned-elderly-in-prison have spent most of their adult life in lockdown and have long criminal histories. In most cases, these offenders are not discipline problems, but they are the least likely to adjust to life outside prison.

According to recent research from the federal Office of the Inspector General (2016), elderly inmates are the most expensive to house because of associated medical costs. However, elderly offenders tend to commit fewer acts of misconduct while in prison and have a lower rate of rearrest once they are released (OIG, 2016). As a result, the federal government has concluded elderly offenders are good candidates for early release programs. It is likely reentry and reintegration initiatives for elderly offenders will increase in future years, particularly as the graying of America occurs, both in widespread society and behind bars.

Women Offenders

The plight of women offenders and the lack of services traditionally afforded to this group of offenders has been well documented in published literature during the past two decades. Most states lack effective gender-specific programming and do not fully consider the health needs of the incarcerated women. Further, the incarceration of women creates collateral damage because large portions of these women are the primary caretakers for their young children. This collateral damage is realized in terms of the trauma and deprivation experienced by the children. Providing adequate care for the children during the mother's absence creates an additional burden on the families and/or society. Further, women offenders are seldom violent and have lower recidivism rates than men. This means that, in general, women offenders are good candidates for reentry and reintegration programs.

Research by Garcia and Ritter (2012) indicates women offenders have specific and identifiable needs (see Box 29.2):

Box 29.2 Gender-Responsive Services

- Services to help with the transition from prison to the community;
- Health care services (including substance abuse and mental health treatment);
- Employment, education and life skills services;
- Intimate partner violence-related services; and
- Child-related services.

These researchers found employment and educational skills were most needed, followed by transition services. These findings indicate similar reentry needs across genders. Women and men need to be able to support themselves in an independent and autonomous manner.

Offenders with Communicable Diseases

Throughout the United States, the inmate population tends to have a much higher prevalence of infectious disease in comparison to the general population. In other words, the rates of sexually transmitted infections (STIs) such as hepatitis B, hepatitis C, and HIV/AIDS are much higher among prisoners. One key reason for this is that many offenders engage in risky behaviors. Among the most commonly cited risky behaviors are needle-sharing drug use and unprotected sex. Further, many of these individuals do not seek preventative medical care in the community.

Given that many offenders engage in risky behaviors prior to being locked up, it is no surprise many enter the prison system with STIs. However, behaviors while incarcerated also exacerbate the likelihood for contracting or aggravating communicable diseases. Jail facilities, rather than prison facilities, may impact the health and welfare of the surrounding community. This is because jail populations are much more transient. The fact that jail inmates routinely re-enter the community after relatively short periods of incarceration (when compared to prison terms) exacerbates the likelihood of infection. Thus, for jail systems, the implementation of STI testing and screening procedures is the best first step in detecting viruses, diseases, and infections before offenders return to the community, where they may infect others. It is important to have a good working relationship between jail and community practitioners. These relationships will reduce the likelihood that infectious diseases are spread from the jail to the community. Jail and community collaboration helps to provide long-term treatment assistance and improve prevention efforts.

When considering programming for communicable diseases, there is a good deal of continuity between what is offered in the facility and in the community. For instance, education about various illnesses, voluntary testing, counseling, and drug-dependence treatment are effective approaches. In some jurisdictions, needle exchange and condom distribution programs are important prevention measures. All of these efforts help to reduce the incidences of infectious diseases, both within the facility and the community. Further, community-based programs can provide follow-up initiatives such as partner notification and free testing for prior sexual partners. Inevitably, offenders who are positive for infectious diseases will be released into the community. Thus, reentry or reintegration initiatives should address the needs of this offender population. At the very least, programs should utilize the following practices and procedures recommended by MacGowan (2009) when offenders are released back into the community (**Box 29.3**):

Box 29.3 Program and Policy Recommendations for Reentry Programs

- Provide a list of available services that provide case management for illnesses and/or diseases contracted by released offenders.
- Provide contact information for various medical outreach programs and/or local health programs that offenders can utilize.
- Provide assistance with making these appointments while in jail or prison or, better yet, provide such an appointment before leaving jail.
- Integrate appointments and case management with community supervision personnel outside the prison who can provide follow-up to ensure that continuity of services is maintained and to hold offenders accountable for maintaining contact.
- Provide medications for offenders who go into treatment or therapy for these illnesses.

It is important to note that these services are recommended because they are valuable reentry tools for offenders. The offering of these services also helps to protect the health and welfare of the broader public, thereby being a public safety feature.

Sex Offenders

Of all the offender groups included in this chapter, the sex offender population is most controversial when considering reentry and reintegration initiatives. This also is probably the most complicated of offender typologies to address because, in reality, there are numerous categories of sex offenders (Holmes & Holmes, 2009; Salter, 2004; Seto, 2007). Further, research has shown that "one-size-fits-all" approaches to the sex offender population are not as effective as those designed with specificity to the sex offender's particular proclivities. Regardless of the complexities involved, it is an absolute certainty that the majority of these offenders will end up back in the community. As a result, ignoring this group is both negligent and impractical. There is substantial research that shows, contrary to public perception, sex offenders are actually a low-risk group for recidivism, especially reoffending that involves sex-based crimes (Hanson et al., 2002; Swinburne, Romine, Miner, Dwyer, & Berg, 2012). This is particularly true for sex offenders who are not classified as sadistic or pedophiles (Holmes & Holmes, 2009; Salter, 2004; Seto, 2007).

From a public safety perspective, it is reasonable to seek both supervision and treatment perspectives that aid sex offenders and minimize the risk of recidivism. Given the challenges associated with sex offenders, it should be obvious whey they have been included as special needs offenders. The fact that this group presents with a wide range of subcategories, and given the majority seem to be low-risk recidivists, reentry and reintegration programs must address the treatment needs of this offender group. Thus, reentry and reintegration for these offenders requires effective coordination between both community supervision and community treatment personnel.

Offenders with Learning/Cognitive Deficits

This group of offenders often present with a variety of learning disabilities and cognitive deficits. Surprisingly, there is little literature on these offenders in the United States. On the other hand, in countries like Canada, Australia, and the United Kingdom, a good deal of research exists (Hanser, 2007). Indeed, it would seem that issues related to offender learning and cognitive disabilities reached a height of interest in the 1990s and early 2000s, but, in the past decade or so, have tapered off in the United States. For the purposes of this chapter, three groups of learning-disabled offenders are discussed. The first are those with cognitive and developmental lags and represent those offenders who simply have lower intellectual quotients (IQs) than the broader population. These individuals are often 7 to 9 points lower on overall IQ deficit (Cowardin, 1998). Though these individuals may have IQs in the normal range, they are in the lower spectrum. This is important when it is understood that a large portion of repeat offenders have lower average IQs than nonrecidivists. Lower than average IQs also help to explain why a large proportion of convicted "three-strike" offenders present with learning disabilities (Cowardin, 1998; Hanser, 2007).

The work of Bronson, Maruschak, and Berzofsky (2015) is one of the few recent sources in the United States that examines disabilities among the incarcerated. Their research clearly distinguishes between cognitive disabilities and mental disorders, as follows:

> A cognitive disability is a broad term used to describe a variety of medical conditions affecting different types of mental tasks, such as problem solving, reading comprehension, attention, and remembering. A cognitive disability is not the same as a mental disorder, although they often co-occur and a mental disorder can be considered a disability as well. Examples of cognitive disabilities include Down syndrome, autism, dementia, attention deficit disorder, learning disorders, intellectual disabilities, or traumatic brain injury. Examples of mental disorders include depression, anxiety disorders, and schizophrenia.
>
> (Bronson et al., 2015, p. 3)

Both learning/cognitive deficits and mental illness should be addressed in reentry and reintegration programs.

Learning-disabled offenders are those with language immaturity. These offenders often have deficits in internal language that is needed to mediate their own actions. This deficit negatively impacts individuals' social awareness, their sense of individual organization, and self-governance. These characteristics are linked to criminality but usually are linked to disorganized and random crimes that are usually not well thought out. In other words, when engaged in crime with other coconspirators, these individuals are more easily manipulated into criminal activity.

Individuals with attention disorders have attention lapses in which the individual is susceptible to outside influence and/or manipulation by others. These individuals tend to have poor internal vigilance and are easy to manipulate into criminal activity. In addition to these attention lapses are acts of impulsivity. In such cases, because of a lack of effective regulatory dialogue, the individual is more prone to take risks, poorly calculating the outcome that is likely to occur. Lastly, it should be pointed out that there is considerable overlap between learning disabilities and attention-deficit problems (Hanser, 2007), thereby further complicating the prognosis for such offenders but at the same time causing specialized responses to be all the more needed.

Drug Offenders

The use of most drugs are illegal, and their use constitutes an offense. In addition, while alcohol may be legal, its use correlates with violent crimes (especially sexual assault) more frequently than any other drug. Thus, offenders with drug and alcohol problems do have specific needs, but it is arguable as to whether this is a commonly needed area of intervention or a genuine special need.

It also should be noted that within this text, an entire chapter is provided that covers substance abuse and special needs offenders (see Chapter 18). Because this chapter comprehensively covers the issue of drugs and alcohol among the offender population, we will avoid the redundancy of discussing it here as a separate issue. Nevertheless, it should be understood that among all of the offender typologies in this chapter, the use of drugs and/or alcohol is a commonplace occurrence. Further, substance abuse issues tend to exacerbate the issues and challenges that impact each of the special needs offender groups discussed. Thus, when providing reentry and reintegration services, the use of substance abuse programming is considered part and parcel to any comprehensive program.

Reentry and Reintegration Issues

Regardless of the specific offender group, all offenders have common needs that must be met if they are to successfully return to the community and avoid criminal behavior. For instance, safe housing is something that must be obtained by offenders who are released to the community. Nevertheless, the housing needs for each offender type may be quite different. For example, female offenders may need housing designed more for a family, as many are the primary caretakers for their children. On the other hand, mentally ill offenders may fare better in a halfway house or in housing with their family of origin. Conversely, sex offenders may not be allowed to be housed with their own family members, depending on the restrictions placed upon them and the dynamics between them and their prior victims. Naturally, if the sex offender victimized other family members, then housing with the family may be prohibited.

In addition, each group may have differing supervision requirements and may need to interface with different agency services. For instance, sex offenders will usually have numerous formal restrictions on their movement within the community, being prohibited from school grounds and other areas where children are likely located. On the other hand, offenders with mental illness and/or cognitive deficits my face informal restrictions from family and friends who wish to keep the offender safe and secure. Naturally, this also may be a situation observed among elderly offenders who need additional care and oversight because of their own potential for accidental self-harm.

Each of these different types of special needs offenders will have numerous needs for services from social service agencies. Offenders with mental illness and those with cognitive and/or learning disabilities will likely be eligible for services from various state and nonprofit organizations that provide medications, psycho-education, tutoring, and/or life skills development. The elderly also will likely qualify for services with state and local elder community programs. Lastly, offenders with children will often have various organizations for children's services with which they are required to contact. Parenting issues and child-welfare programs may provide assistance that helps families navigating the reentry process.

It is important to point out that many religious organizations assist offenders returning to the community. Indeed, many reentry initiatives have their genesis in churches and through church groups who, as volunteers, go into prisons providing spiritual/religious support. Churches and church groups often fill in the gaps in a comprehensive reentry program by providing mentorship, clothing or food assistance, assistance in employment via individual church members, transportation provided by church-going volunteers, and even some financial assistance, depending on the church and/or needs of the offender.

Given the various types of offenders and the diverse array of concerns and considerations that exist for these individuals, there are multiple issues that need to be addressed along with numerous possible approaches, each with their own pros and cons. It is important that these services not be offered in separate and distinct "silos" but that, instead, there should be at least one person who acts as the case manager or coordinator for these services. Often, it is presumed that the community supervision officer will fill this role, in addition to security functions, but this is not really a practical approach, particularly in light of the typical caseload assigned to most probation/parole officers.

The Use of Mentors

Rather than relying on the formal community supervision system to facilitate collaboration and coordination, it is recommended that some type of informal system be in place to aid these offenders. This is precisely why grass roots programs such as faith-based (Dodson, Cabage, & Klenowski, 2011) programs can be so effective; they are not hamstrung by the restrictions and burdens of the typical state agency. These types of organizations are able to provide a personal touch through volunteers who act as mentors, lay counselors, and friends of the person seeking to build his or her life back. This personal touch is perhaps the most important and most difficult resource to procure for offenders, particularly offenders who have additional special needs and challenges.

The ideal mentor is stable and professional. The use of mentors requires that organizations develop standards, training, and some type of volunteer coordination if this approach is to be effective. The Ready4Reentry model is a collection of practices and procedures for faith-based church organizations (FBCO's) that are involved with offender reentry. The practices outlined in the Ready4Reentry (R4R) model were derived from a prior project, Ready4Work (R4W), which was implemented by the Department of Labor in 2003. This was a three-year pilot project designed to address the needs of offenders who were exiting prison but utilizing the services of FBCO's in surrounding communities.

At the close of R4W in August of 2006, the results of the program were encouraging. First, this program had measured success in placing offenders in jobs, and the offenders tended to retain their jobs in the program. Even more surprising is the fact that per participant, the program costs $4,500, compared with costs from $25,000 to $40,000 per year for reincarceration (U.S. Department of Labor, 2007). This alone might be sufficient support for the R4W program (effective job placement and low cost compared to prison). However, analysis of the program also found that only 2.5% of all R4W participants recidivated in state systems after six months, and only 6.9% recidivated after

Box 29.4 Offender Outcomes for Mentoring Programs

- Mentored participants remained in the program longer than those not mentored (10.2 months versus 7.2 months).
- Mentored participants were twice as likely to obtain a job.
- Mentored participants' odds of getting a job the next month increased by 73%.
- Those who met with a mentor were 56% more likely to remain employed than those who did not (U.S. Department of Labor, 2007, p. 3).

one year postrelease (U.S. Department of Labor, 2007). When compared with other federal research on offender recidivism, it was determined that the R4W program experienced recidivism rates much lower than those around the nation, with 5% recidivism at six months and 10.4% after one year of release around the nation (U.S. Department of Labor, 2007). Thus, the program aided in job placement, was less costly than putting offenders back in prison, and had lower recidivism rates than standard justice responses.

What makes these findings even more relevant to this current chapter is that over 60% of the R4W offenders received mentoring as part of their services (U.S. Department of Labor, 2007). Those who met with a mentor had better outcomes than those who did not (see Box 29.4 for offender outcomes).

Tying it All Together with DOJ's Five Evidence-Based Principles

One key feature that will be extremely important in providing reentry and reintegration services to special needs offenders is a connection between prerelease programming in the prison and services provided after release from prison. In other words, institutional parole officers, mentors inside the prison, and others who are familiar with the offender should help with resources outside the prison before the offender is released. In other words, the first three evidence-based principles noted at the beginning of this chapter should be implemented and shared with reentry resources in the community in advance of the offender's release.

For example, Principle I requires that every offender should be provided with an individualized reentry plan that is tailored to the offender's needs. This is no different from how clinical programs begin discharge planning with clients when they first begin a program. Such preliminary planning gets the participant ready and provides time to develop linkages between the prerelease and postrelease programs.

Second, Principle II contends that prior to release, offenders should be provided education, employment training, life skills, substance abuse or mental health services, and other programs that target their criminogenic needs. This is certainly a laudable goal, but if offenders have several years to serve they may receive these programs too early in their sentence or so late in their sentence that the various programs become a virtual mish-mash of programming goals. Rather, it is suggested that programming is provided in the prison facility but that follow-up programming in the community be provided on many of these issues. The ability for the prison culture to undermine treatment outcomes is circumvented when offered in the community. Naturally, links in the content, approach, and implementation should be made between pre- and postrelease programs.

The third principle is that offenders should be provided the resources and opportunity to build and maintain family relationships, strengthening the support system available to them upon release. The building and maintenance of relationships with mentors can and should begin at this point. This is clearly important for most offenders and especially important with special needs offenders. Maintaining these connections on the inside of the prison walls means a smoother transition will be likely when special needs offenders exit prison. This also helps to fill in gaps in the reentry process and to ensure that offenders are not left in a social vacuum shortly after their release.

The fourth principle requires continuity of care when offenders are released to the community, halfway houses, and other postrelease programs. As has been noted before, this is where linkages between prison and postprison programs are important, and this is where the efforts of mentors can prove even more valuable. A mentor who knows the offender prerelease and postrelease can help with the transition from one environment and the other, being a linking-pin between officials on both sides of the prison fence.

Lastly, the fifth principle simply indicates that some type of comprehensive resource listing and access protocol should be made available for offenders who are reentering the community. This is typically provided in most programs. However, certain services will be more critical to some typologies than others will. What is important is that each resource be current and that an actual live person be the key contact with offenders in a reentry program rather than some obscure listing of organizations. This means, again, that a personal touch is required for this to be developed and maintained, all the more demonstrating that reentry is about human contacts made both in the prison and community.

The Need for Data Follow-Up and Multiple Measures of Success

Often, faith-based and nonprofit communities tend to measure success through anecdotes and personal testimony (U.S. Department of Labor, 2007). This is, of course, far less than what should be expected if a program is to be replicated. The importance of verifiable measures of success cannot be overemphasized. Because of this, it is recommended that reentry programs implement both performance and outcome measures that specifically measure how well the five evidence-based principles are utilized in their organization. Measures of number of contacts, services accessed, programs completed, and goals achieved in the reentry plan can all be collected both inside and outside the prison environment. In addition, mentoring programs should be held to the same level of scrutiny. Simply put, mentor programs must develop goals with defined and operationalized outputs and outcomes that can be expressed in terms of quantifiable data.

The use of offender surveys addressing perceptions of continuity of care and their relationships with family, friends, or mentors in the community can identify areas needing improvement or areas where programs excel. Likewise, ambitious programs might seek survey input from community members and employers who have hired offenders in reentry programs, as well as other potential stakeholders (such as police or community supervision personnel), to gain an idea of the perceived effectiveness of these programs. Naturally, any comprehensive evaluation program will need proper methods of data collection throughout every stage of a program to measure accurately the success or failure of a program. Further, data collection must be integrated into the reentry design itself as a program management tool (U.S. Department of Labor, 2007).

The U.S. Department of Labor (2007) points out two key components for any reentry program include (1) tracking recidivism rates and (2) employment data (both placement and retention). However, programs that serve special needs offenders need to focus on multiple aspects of improvement in offender functioning. For example, the mother-child relationship should be measured for women offenders. On the other hand, mentally ill offenders may benefit from screenings of depression, anxiety, or personality disorders. Elderly offenders should be surveyed regarding their ability to access physical facilities. The list simply shows there are a number of features that can be measured, both for process and outcome indicators of reentry effectiveness, for special needs offenders.

Community Involvement, Police Partnerships, and Reentry Councils

The community must be involved in the process of reentry and reintegration. This means that the average citizen must know both the offender and any programs where offenders might benefit. This is important and requires that community supervision agencies, FBCOs, and other grass roots organizations provide aggressive advertisement and community awareness campaigns. This also means that probation and parole agents should visit not just the offender's home but also other homes in the neighborhood to increase the informal social controls and human supervision that are in place.

Likewise, it is important to gain police partnerships, as reasonable, with reentry initiatives. The manner in which jail systems release offenders (as in "prepared for reentry" versus "not being given much support at all") can impact criminal activity and recidivism within the community. This provides a strong argument for more emphasis on community policing approaches as a means of facilitating reentry efforts and reducing recidivism (or future victimization of community members) and as a means of preventative target-hardening of the community environment.

When discussing community policing in the context of reentry programming, Condon (2003) notes that not only will police need to coordinate with citizens, but it also is in the mutual best interests for police and community supervision officers to collaborate routinely. For one, it is commonly known among criminologists and practitioners that recidivism rates of offenders tend to be high. Indeed, there is a select group of offenders who tend to cycle in and out of prison, and these offenders tend to commit the largest proportion of all criminal activity (Hanser, 2016; Travis, Davis, & Lawrence, 2012). Likewise, it is fairly well understood that during the past 10 years or so, police departments have experienced many fiscal challenges, requiring them to do more with less. It is for this reason that Travis et al. (2012) note that police agencies should be active partners in reentry initiatives.

Likewise, for community supervision officers, rising caseloads place an ever-growing burden on individual officers, and any supervisor assistance can make their job much easier. Further, this makes the supervision process much more effective in detecting offender noncompliance (Hanser, 2007). For police, the advantage is in the intensive background tracking that probation departments are able to provide as well as the ability to search homes, persons, and lives of those who are most likely to be repeat problems while they patrol their jurisdictions (Hanser, 2007).

The International Association of Chiefs of Police (IACP, 2005) notes that law enforcement agencies can serve as strategic collaborative partners and resources in offender reentry efforts. Indeed, "partnerships allow law enforcement to pool its resources with a range of stakeholders to respond to the challenges that returning offenders present" (IACP, 2005, p. 3). Further, these partnerships ensure that law enforcement is made aware, on a timely basis, of those offenders who are released and return to their communities. Primary benefits of these partnerships for agencies and communities, as noted by the IACP (2005, p. 3), include the following (**Box 29.5**):

Box 29.5 Benefits of Agency and Community Collaboration

1. A decrease in criminal activity.
2. An increase in perceived improvement in the quality of crime prevention.
3. A reduction in recidivism.
4. An interruption or break in the cycle of generational crime.
5. An increase in stable families.
6. Increased trust between the community and police.
7. Increased access to information, resources, and shared responsibility for ensuring public safety.

These features help to keep public safety in perspective, while at the same time ensuring that police are aware and involved in the multiagency process of recidivism reduction. Further, when police officers are taught crisis intervention training (i.e., the Memphis Model), they gain an understanding of some of the reactions and challenges that may be facing the mentally ill and/or those addicted to substances. Other types of awareness training can be useful to ensure that police have an adequate understanding of the issues involved with other special needs offenders, such as the elderly, those with communicable diseases, and/or female offenders.

Lastly, a quote from the Council of State Governments, perhaps, captures the essence of how both enforcement and service functions might be envisioned when police are involved. Consider the following from the Council of State Governments (2017, p. 2):

> Officers . . . repeatedly encounter and arrest many of these individuals—often shortly after they leave prison or jail. Returning individuals' safe and successful reentry depends on many factors, such as fulfillment of their educational needs, access to mental health and drug treatment, job readiness, connections with family, housing availability, and others that could help them avoid future criminal activity. Law enforcement professionals are uniquely positioned to engage their community policing networks of service providers who can help address these needs. They can also be important partners with institutional and community corrections, enhancing supervision when appropriate.

Police were often overlooked during the initial momentum of the reentry movement. However, during the past 10 years or so, reentry and reintegration programs have seen partnerships emerge between police agencies, faith-based organizations, civic associations, social services agencies, and a wide range of other organizations. The collaborative schemes usually hold the community supervision agency as the leader in addressing crime as a community-based social problem. Therefore, community supervision agencies should be prepared to spearhead any conjoint community actions when supervising special needs offenders.

In providing this leadership role, many local, regional, and state levels of government have created what are often known as reentry councils. Most states have some type of reentry council or task force, and many larger counties have their own reentry councils. Likewise, many larger cities have found it beneficial to develop their own councils, as well. Regardless, all of these tend to consist of a collaboration of partners who meet routinely throughout the year to pool resources and optimize reentry efforts in their area. However, it is the federal government that has established the most clear and distinct version of this collaborative effort.

According to the U.S. Department of Justice (2016), the Federal Interagency Reentry Council brings together 20 agencies that are tasked with the mission of achieving the following:

- Making communities safer by reducing recidivism and victimization,
- Assisting those who return from prison and jail in becoming productive citizens, and
- Saving taxpayer dollars by lowering the direct and collateral costs of incarceration.

A prime focus of the Federal Interagency Reentry Council is to remove barriers to effective reentry. The idea is to provide sufficient groundwork for motivated individuals who have served their sentence so they can gain employment, have stable housing, be available to support their families, and contribute to the surrounding community. Aside from recidivism reduction, the agencies brought together by the Reentry Council seek to improve public health, child welfare, employment outcomes, housing, and other important aspects to offender reintegration (U.S. Department of Justice, 2016). **Box 29.6** is a partial list of offender needs that are specifically cited by the Federal Interagency Reentry Council, which includes (USDOJ, 2016):

Box 29.6 Offender Reentry Needs

1. Employment
2. Collateral Consequences
3. Children of Incarcerated Parents
4. Reservation Communities
5. Education
6. Health Care
7. Child Support
8. Veterans
9. Housing
10. Women and Reentry

Since this is a federal reentry organization, issues related to Native Americans and reservation communities as well as veterans issues were included in this list. This also brings to bear the point that regardless of whether the reentry program is federal, state, local government, a FBCO, or grass roots organization, cultural groups can and should be considered. Likewise, veterans issues related to health care, potential trauma, educational benefits, and so forth should also be included. It would appear that the list of potential needs and services could be quite encompassing, depending on the offender population that is being served.

Conclusion

This chapter has shown that reentry and reintegration of offenders with special needs has received significant attention from local, state, and federal levels of government as well as many religious-based and grass roots level organizations. Indeed, reentry has been a common topic in the field of corrections during the past 10 to 15 years as correctional systems scramble to address their burgeoning prison populations from the prior "prison boom" of the 1990s. Much of the research conducted has led to several evidence-based principles that the federal government and other sources have identified as key to ensure reentry effectiveness and efficiency of resources available.

When considering reentry efforts for special needs offenders, the matter becomes quite complicated because of the diverse array of needs presented. Indeed, different categories of special needs offenders have different priorities that may be distinct from other categories. On the other hand, some special needs offenders may have co-occurring disorders (e.g., an incarcerated mother who has a communicable disease, or perhaps a learning-disabled offender with drug abuse issues), which then creates an overlap in needs and complicates service delivery.

Further, reentry itself is a multifaceted approach. Employment, housing, transportation, health care, help with mental health issues, and so forth often are needed for many who return to the community. The gamut of issues for any reentry program in general, and for one serving special needs offenders in particular, is encompassing and demanding. This means that no one agency or organization is likely to be able to address all the needs required. Thus, the use of collaborative teams have been identified as, perhaps, the most practical and effective approach. While the use of collaboration is important in meeting the multiple needs of offenders, the personal connections would seem to have a profound impact on reentry success. As a result, the use of mentors has been identified as an effective approach in linking the various services together, both prerelease and postrelease. Mentors can help fill in gaps that may be spontaneous and unknown to officials and/or service providers.

However, just as important is the relationship with another person who is law abiding, caring, and prosocial: the exact type of influence that an offender in reentry needs.

These collaborative efforts should not ignore the potential benefits of police involvement. Inevitably, police agencies will come into contact with at least some offenders who are reentry participants. Ensuring that police are involved, educated, and trained on how reentry serves as a form of crime reduction can help to maintain public safety.

Collaborative efforts have led to reentry councils that exist at all levels around the nation. The federal government has developed one such council that brings together multiple federal agencies whose goal is to reduce challenges in providing effective opportunities for offender reentry. The list of issues this council has identified shows there is a commonality of challenges throughout the nation. The key commonality is acknowledging that, to achieve recidivism reduction, gains in financial, emotional, medical, and spiritual functioning will also need to be realized if programs are to be successful. In fact, these corollary areas of interest are perhaps some of the causal elements to crime in the first place. Thus, addressing these specialized needs could be considered a primary form of crime prevention.

References

Ashford, J. B., Sales, B. D., & Reid, W. H. (2000). *Treating adult and juvenile offenders with special needs*. Washington, DC: American Psychological Association.

Bronson, J., Maruschak, L. M., & Berzofsky, M. (2015). *Disabilities among prison and jail inmates, 2011–12*. Washington, DC: U.S. Department of Justice, Bureau of Justice Statistics.

Condon, C. D. (2003). Falling crime rates, rising caseload numbers: Using police-probation partnerships. *Corrections Today, 65*(1), 44–49. Council for State Governments. (2017). *Law enforcement*. Washington, DC: Council for State Governments.

Cowardin, N. (1998). Disorganized crime: Learning disability and the criminal justice system. *Criminal Justice, 13*(2), 11–16.

Dodson, K. D., Cabage, L. N., & Klenowski, P. M. (2011). An evidence-based assessment of faith-based programs: Do faith-based programs "work" to reduce recidivism? *Journal of Offender Rehabilitation, 50*, 367–383.

Garcia, M., & Ritter, N. (2012). *Improving access to services for female offenders returning to the community*. Washington, DC: National Institute of Justice.

Hanser, R. D. (2016). *Introduction to corrections* (2nd ed.). Thousand Oaks, CA: Sage.

Hanser, R. D. (2007). *Special needs offenders*. Upper Saddle River: NJ: Prentice Hall.

Hanson, R. K., Gordon, G. A., Harris, A. J., Marques, J. K., Murphy, W., Quinsey, V. L., & Seto, M. C. (2002). First report of the collaborative outcome data project on the effectiveness of psychological treatment for sex offenders. *Sex Abuse, 14*(2), 169–194.

Holmes, R. M., & Holmes, S. T. (2009). *Profiling violent crimes* (4th ed.). Thousand Oaks, CA: Sage.

International Association of Chiefs of Police (2005). *Building an offender reentry program: A guide for law enforcement*. Washington, DC: U.S. Department of Justice, Bureau of Justice Assistance.

MacGowan, R. J. (2009). *HIV testing implementation guidance for correctional settings*. Atlanta, GA: Centers for Disease Control.

Nunez-Neto, B. (2008). *Offender reentry: Correctional statistics, reintegration into the community, and recidivism*. Washington, DC: Congressional Research Service.

Office of the Inspector General (2016). *The impact of an aging inmate population on the Federal Bureau of Prisons*. Washington, DC: U.S. Department of Justice.

Peterson, J. K., Skeem, J., Kennealy, P., & Bray, B. (2014). How often and how consistently do symptoms directly precede criminal behavior among offenders with mental illness? *Law and Human Behavior, 38*(5), 439–449.

Rosenthal, A., & Wolf, E. (2004). *Unlocking the potential of reentry and reintegration*. Syracuse, NY: Justice Strategies.

Salter, A. (2004). *Predators: Pedophiles, rapists, and other sex offenders*. New York, NY: Basic Books.

Seto, M. C. (2007). *Pedophilia and sexual offending against children: Theory, assessment, and intervention*. Washington, DC: American Psychological Association.

Swinburne, R. E., Romine, M. H., Miner, D. P., Dwyer, M., & Berg D. (2012). Predicting reoffense for community-based sexual offenders: An analysis of 30 years of data. *Sexual Abuse: A Journal of Research and Treatment, 24*(5), 501–514.

Travis, J., Davis, R., & Lawrence, S. (2012). *Exploring the role of the police in prisoner reentry.* Washington, DC: U.S. New Perspectives in Policing Bulletin, U.S. Department of Justice, National Institute of Justice.

United States Department of Health and Human Services (2015). *Mental health myths and facts.* Washington, DC: U.S. Department of Health and Human Services. Retrieved from: www.mentalhealth.gov/basics/myths-facts/

United States Department of Justice. (2016). *Federal interagency reentry council.* Washington, DC: U.S. Department of Justice. Retrieved from www.justice.gov/reentry/federal-interagency-reentry-council

U.S. Department of Labor. (2007). *Ready4Reetry: Prisoner toolkit for faith-based and community organizations.* Washington, DC: U.S. Department of Labor, Center for Faith-Based and Community Initiatives.

30

DEVELOPING AND IMPLEMENTING EVIDENCE-BASED POLICIES AND PRACTICES

Improving Offender Treatment Outcomes

Kimberly D. Dodson, LeAnn N. Cabage, and Hannah L. Brown

> A critical mass of social science evidence has accumulated challenging what had previously been the prevailing notion that "nothing works" in the rehabilitation of offenders. Findings from academic and program evaluation literatures in the fields of psychology, criminal justice, sociology, and public policy suggest that evidence-based interventions . . . can significantly reduce recidivism.
>
> —(Rempel, 2014, p. 1)

Introduction

Throughout this handbook, the authors present in-depth discussions of the rehabilitation and treatment issues related to offenders with special needs. Identifying the treatment and rehabilitation needs of special offender populations is an important first step in developing and implementing effective treatment interventions and rehabilitation programs. Criminal justice practitioners and treatment professionals often need guidance in creating or implementing effective, evidence-based treatments and programs. They may lack the knowledge to adequately address the diverse treatment needs of special populations, and they may be confused about "what works" (Latessa, Listwan, & Koetzle, 2014; Sherman, Farrington, Welsh, & MacKenzie, 2002; Sherman et al., 1998). Therefore, providing policy makers and criminal justice professionals with empirically supported treatment and rehabilitation options is essential to addressing the needs of offenders, reducing the likelihood of civil liability, and preventing future criminal behavior.

The purpose of this chapter is to discuss the importance of developing and implementing evidence-based policies and practices to improve treatment outcomes for offenders with special needs. Therefore, the chapter includes a discussion of criminal justice policies and practices that are empirically supported and show promise for improving the quality of life for special needs offenders and reducing recidivism. In addition, we also discuss treatment interventions and programs that lack empirical support but are mistakenly believed to be effective.

Space does not allow us to present a comprehensive review of the policies and practices related to each type of offender discussed in this handbook. Instead, we focus our policy discussion to a small portion of the special needs offenders represented in this work. We begin with a discussion of women offenders and review their gendered pathways to crime. We also address the need for gender-responsive treatments, risk assessments, and the rehabilitative needs of women offenders. The chapter includes a discussion of juvenile offenders and how "get tough" policies that lacked empirical support negatively affected criminal justice-involved youth, particularly in communities of color. We also offer a review of some of the treatment and rehabilitation programs that are most effective in treating juvenile offenders.

The chapter includes a discussion of the needs and challenges in treating and managing LGBTQ offenders. We offer suggestions for improving the delivery of services to this special class on inmates. The chapter concludes with a discussion of habilitation programs that are designed to teach offenders skills they may lack, such as balancing a household budget and other life skills. We also include a discussion of the questionable practice of using private prisons and punishing offenders using solitary confinement.

Offenders with Special Needs

The development, implementation, and continuation of rehabilitation and treatment programs should be supported by empirical research. There is a growing body of research that sheds light on the effectiveness (or ineffectiveness) of certain programs and policies. In the next sections, we highlight some of the programs and policies that "work" and some that "do not work."

Pathways to Crime: Women Offenders

Many of the scholars that advocate for gender-responsive programming argue the pathways women take to crime must be addressed (Belknap, 2007; Bloom, Owen & Covington, 2003; Koons, Burrow, Morash, & Bynum, 1997; Salisbury & Van Voorhis, 2009; Van Voorhis, Wright, Salisbury, & Bauman, 2010). The pathways perspective recognizes the influence of various biological, psychological, and social realities that are unique to the experience of women and synthesizes them into theoretical trajectories that describe the incarcerated woman. Much of the research shows that women's criminal trajectory is based on factors (1) either not typically seen with men, (2) typically seen with men but in even greater frequency with women, or (3) seen in relatively equal frequency but with distinct personal and social effects for women (see e.g., Belknap & Holsinger, 2006; Chesney-Lind & Shelden, 2004; Farr, 2000; Salisbury & Van Voorhis, 2009).

It also is necessary to understand the intersectionality of women's pathways to crime. Chesney-Lind (2000) addresses the issues of intersectionality of abuse, depression, and drugs for women. Depression and other internalized mood disorders often result from victimization and trauma in the women's lives, and they turn to drug abuse to self-medicate. Additional research suggests the relationship between abuse and runaways is correlated with higher arrest for juvenile girls, although girls and boys run away at approximately the same rate (Chesney-Lind & Shelden, 2004). They argue this disproportionate arrest rate serves as a mechanism for funneling girls into the juvenile justice system, and it may lead to their incarceration if they choose to continue to flee from abusive homes or violate other conditions placed on them by the courts. Additionally, they may be forced to find ways to survive on the streets, including prostitution. Prostitution may lead to drug use and relationships (sometimes violent) with antisocial men who provide for licit or illicit financial needs of women. The factors that affect juvenile girls also affect women offenders in that many attempt to survive on the streets, become involved in prostitution, become involved in relationships with violent or controlling men, and abuse drugs.

Additional work on the pathways perspective reveals how experiences with abuse, substance abuse, poverty, dysfunctional families, and intimate relationships are distributed differentially across women offenders (Daly, 1992; 1994). In her 1992 work, Daly identified five unique pathways of women into the felony court system. The first pathway is that of "harmed and harming." These women experienced abuse or neglect as a child, were often labeled as problem children, acted out frequently, and suffered from substance abuse and/or mental illness. The second is that of the "street" woman. She often fled from abusive homes as a child, became addicted to substances, and was involved in prostitution and other criminal means, which correlates with extensive criminal histories. The third pathway, known as "battered women," is those individuals who enter the criminal justice system as a direct result of the abuse they experience from violent intimate partners. The fourth pathway, the "drug-connected" woman, is one who became addicted to substances in the context of intimate or familial relationships. The final pathway is that of the "other" woman. She is often economically motivated, with no history of abuse, addiction, or violence.

Abuse and victimization play a role in the pathways of both men and women to incarceration; however, it is more substantial for women offenders. Salisbury and Van Voorhis (2009) argue the context of abuse and victimization plays a primary role in the pathways perspective, and child abuse is more salient to the behavior of women offenders. Specifically, girls are more likely to be sexually abused by someone close to them, such as a father, stepfather, or close relative (Browne & Finkelhor, 1986; Faller, 1990). The relationship between the abuser and child results in the abuse being more frequent and occurring over longer periods; this produces both short- and long-term effects (Faller, 1990). These effects often include low self-esteem, shame, depression, substance abuse, and anxiety (Miller, 1988), which are associated with higher levels of criminality in women.

Salisbury and Van Voorhis (2009) go beyond the traditional concept of pathway theory to include a social and human capital perspective as it relates to the pathways women take toward offending. They argue that increasing social, human, and state capital will result in criminal desistance for women offenders. Holtfreter, Reisig, and Morash (2004) found that providing poor women offenders with state capital (i.e., services related to education, health care, housing, and job training) to support their economic needs reduced the odds of recidivism by 83%. Additionally, Reisig, Holtfreter, and Morash (2002) reported more highly educated women have larger social networks and more social support, which is correlated with desistance from crime. Further, research conducted by Giordano, Cernkovich, and Rudolph (2002) suggest high-quality employment and marriages serve as additional control mechanisms from criminal activity.

Gender-Responsive Treatment

Gender-responsive treatments need to focus on the specific pathways women take to crime. Specifically, considering the intersections of substance abuse, violence, sexual abuse, poverty, and work history when deciding which programs to offer incarcerated women may assist in desistance from crime. Gender-responsive treatment consists of policies, programs, and procedures that reflect empirical, gender-specific differences that make management practices and staff procedures more effective when treating women offenders (Bloom, Owen, & Covington, 2003).

Gender-specific treatment addresses the specific needs of women, centering on substance abuse, victimization, mental illness, and self-efficacy. Traditional rehabilitative programming centers on the treatment needs of incarcerated men and ignore the specific treatment needs of incarcerated women. It is important to recognize the differences in men and women in both their pathways to criminality and responses to rehabilitation and treatment (Bloom, Chesney-Lind, & Owen, 1994). Doing so results in better outcomes for women in both institutional and community settings. For example, gender-specific programs result in greater self-efficacy, strengthened parenting skills, fewer institutional infractions, and lower recidivism rates (Van Voorhis & Salisbury, 2014; Van Voorhis et al., 2010). To address the gender-specific needs of incarcerated women, Bloom and Covington (1998) suggest consideration of the following principles when developing gender-specific correctional programming (Box 30.1):

Box 30.1 Principles for Gender-Responsive Correctional Programming

- Equality does not mean sameness; in other words, equality of service delivery is not simply about allowing women access to services traditionally reserved for men—equality must be defined in terms of providing opportunities relevant to each gender. Thus, treatment services may appear very different depending on to whom the service is being delivered;
- Gender-specific programs are not simply "female only" programs that were designed for males;
- Females' sense of self is manifested and develops differently in female specific groups as opposed to coed groups;
- The unique needs and issues (e.g. physical/sexual/emotional victimization, trauma, physical and mental health, pregnancy and parenting) of women and girls should be addressed in a safe, trusting, and supportive women-focused environment;
- Whenever possible, women should be treated in the least restrictive programming environment available. The level of security should depend on both treatment needs and concern for public safety;
- Treatment and services should build on women's strengths/competencies and promote independence and self-reliance; and
- Cultural awareness and sensitivity should be promoted, and the cultural resources and strengths in various communities should be utilized.

Risk Assessments

Risk assessments serve three primary functions in corrections: determining classification level, determining programmatic needs, and predicting risk associated with recidivism. The concept of risk assessments and the benefits associated with them, like many other areas of correctional policy, grew from their use in facilities housing men. In other words, traditional risk assessments ignore the risk factors and needs that are critical for women offenders (Bloom, Owen, & Covington, 2003; Chesney-Lind, 1997; Morash, Bynum, & Koons, 1998). Gender-neutral risk assessments exclude gender-responsive needs pertaining to relationships, depression, parental issues, self-esteem, self-efficacy, trauma, and victimization (Hardyman & Van Voorhis, 2004). These factors are especially important for women because they typically occur at a greater frequency among women than men. In addition, these factors affect women in uniquely personal and social ways that should be reflected in current correctional assessments (Chesney-Lind & Shelden, 2004; Salisbury & Van Voorhis, 2009).

To examine the gender-responsive needs of women offenders, Van Voorhis et al. (2001) developed a gender-responsive assessment for women and tested it at multiple locations. Van Voorhis et al.'s (2001) findings indicate assessments that include victimization and abuse, relationship problems, mental health, substance abuse, self-efficacy, poverty, and parental issues are beneficial for understanding why women offend, especially women who reoffend while on probation or postrelease. Wright, Salisbury, and Van Voorhis (2007) analyzed the importance of gender-responsive needs as they relate to prison misconduct of incarcerated women. Still focusing on the traits identified by Van Voorhis et al. (2001), Wright et al. (2007) identified gender-responsive needs such as experiencing childhood abuse, depression or anxiety, psychosis, and involvement in unsupportive relationships as having high correlation with measures of institutional misconduct (see also Van Voorhis et al., 2010).

Rehabilitative Needs

An analysis of the research indicates there are several factors that affect incarcerated women more frequently than incarcerated men: prior sexual and/or physical abuse (Bloom, 1993; Brett 1993), mental health and drug-related problems related to their experiences of prior abuse (American Correctional Association, 1990; Daly, 1987; LeClair, 1990), unstable employment histories or prolonged unemployment, and having minor children and being the primary caregiver at the time of arrest (Bureau of Justice Statistics, 1991).

Building on these commonalities, Koons et al. (1997) asked various stakeholders to identify factors they believed to be beneficial to incarcerated women. The stakeholders included state-level administrators, institution-level administrators, and program administrators. Focus groups with the incarcerated women allowed for the collection of additional data. State-level administrators identified individualized and structured programs to have the most effect on positive outcomes; institutional-level administrators identified the impact of program staff as the most important; program administrators indicated meeting specific/multiple needs as the most important; and the program participants identified program staff as the most important key to success.

Based on these findings, state and institutional-level administrators and program participants seem to agree on the elements that are part of positive outcomes. The second most influential factor for program participants was the acquisition of skills. This measure was low across the remaining levels of individuals. Although the Koons et al. (1997) study indicated some level of understanding between institutional-level administrators and program participants, the incorporation of programs to meet the needs of incarcerated women is lacking. Further research should focus on the perceptions of incarcerated women and the programs they feel most benefit them. After all, they are the individuals the treatment programs affect the most. They should be the ultimate decision makers in the types of programs they participate in and receive.

Additional research conducted by Morash and Robinson (2002) addressed the attitudes of correctional administrators specifically to family-related programs. Overall, their results indicate parenting programs are in the top five types of programs state-level administrators feel should be expanded. However, overall, if correctional experts saw a need for expanded family programs, it was related to maintaining and supporting the woman's role as mother. This type of attitude serves not to incorporate gender-responsive treatment but rather to offer gender stereotypical programming. Although family programs may be beneficial, programs need to focus on more than the woman's role as a mother. Programs must focus on other relationships within the family, such as how to build and sustain relationships with family members while coping with potential prior abuse.

It is essential for correctional administrators to recognize the differences in men and women offenders and provide gender-responsive treatment programs to assist with rehabilitation. However, at the same time it is important the programs being implemented do more than provide a stereotypical reifying of what it means to be a woman in society. As Bloom and Covington (1998) suggest, the focus on the large number of males in the criminal justice system resulted in the failure to develop diverse options for addressing gender and cultural specific problems of incarcerated women. Gender-specific services (GSS) are primarily concerned with empowering girls and women and improving their quality of lives. Latessa et al. (2014) argues while the goals of GSS are important, risk-need-responsivity (RNR) is focused on recidivism reduction. Treatment and rehabilitation programs based on RNR have overwhelming empirical support and consistently demonstrate they work to reduce recidivism (Latessa et al., 2014). However, researchers suggest integrating the two perspectives to improve the long-term outcomes for women offenders, including lowering recidivism (see. e.g., Hubbard & Matthews, 2008).

Juvenile Offenders

Former President Bill Clinton's 1994 Crime Bill triggered the "get tough" era of punishment in the United States, and this is particularly true concerning juveniles. The work of political scientist John Dilulio, in which he declared urban youth were overwhelming "fatherless, godless, and jobless," and amoral, was embraced by politicians and legislators (Drizin, 2014, para. 4). Dilulio warned these youth were a new generation of criminals the likes of which America had never seen. Dilulio (1995) dubbed them "superpredators." As a result, unprecedented legislation ramping up the criminal penalties for juvenile offenders swept across the country. Mandatory minimum sentences, truth-in-sentencing, trying juveniles as adults, and life without the possibility of parole became the new norms for addressing juvenile crime. Unfortunately, these punitive policies rested on three faulty assumptions: (1) the proportion of juveniles engaging in serious and violent offending were growing at an alarming rate, (2) these juveniles were getting younger and younger, and (3) juveniles were committing more and more crime (Howell, Feld, & Mears, 2012). Of course, none of these assumptions were correct, and "superpredators" never materialized. However, the damage has been done. The "superpredator myth" has been cited as the greatest contributing factor to the adoption of policies in which juveniles were to be treated as adults (Snyder & Sickmund, 2000; 2006).

Scared Straight and Boot Camps

Unfortunately, the "get tough" policies of the 1990s did little to reduce crime, but resulted in an explosion in the number of individuals being admitted to prisons and jails (Pratt, 2008). Confrontational programs based on fear and intimidation were designed to "scare straight" juvenile offenders. However, research tells us that confrontational programs such as boot camps and "Scared Straight" programs do not reduce recidivism (see e.g., Klenowski, Bell, & Dodson, 2011). In fact, research shows these programs often increase the likelihood of reoffending (Klenowski et al., 2011). This finding should not be a surprise when one considers the research on deterrence consistently demonstrates harsh programming does not reduce criminal behavior (Nagin & Pogarsky, 2001; Wright, 2010). Research also shows extralegal consequences such as parental disapproval are more effective for achieving deterrence among juveniles than legal sanctions (Colvin & Pauly, 1983; Gottfredson & Hirschi, 1990; Hirschi, 1969). In other words, the fear of disappointing one's parents is a more salient factor in deterring juvenile delinquency than the prospects of being arrested or going to jail.

As previously mentioned, we have witnessed harsher penalties for juveniles, including an increased use in juvenile transfers or waivers to adult court and longer sentences for certain types of felony offenses. There is little research to suggest that harsher sentencing policies translate into lower rates of recidivism (Jordan, 2011). As a matter of fact, some studies suggest just the opposite—longer confinement seems to increase the risk of recidivism (see e.g., Song & Lieb, 1993).

Bonds and Attachment

We also know that juveniles who are emotionally attached to their parents are less likely to become delinquent (Gottfredson & Hirschi, 1990; Hirschi, 1969). Meta-analytic studies indicate parenting interventions increase secure attachment in children (Wright & Edginton, 2016). Parenting programs behind bars, such as prison nursery and *Inside Outside Dad* programs also are effective in fostering secure attachment between children and parents (Baradon, Fonagy, Bland, Lénárd, & Sleed, 2008; Byrne, Goshin, & Joestl, 2010; Vann, Watson, Pollard, & Badalament, 2011). This body of research shows that early childhood interventions may be the most effective way to reduce the likelihood of juvenile offending.

LGBTQ Prisoners

Education

Every individual has personal biases, but criminal justice professionals must be careful to recognize their biases and treat offenders fairly. One way to combat the potential mistreatment from personal biases is education. Yingling, Cotler, and Hughes (2017) found when nurses receive training on how to interact with LGBT patients, those nurses not only felt more comfortable in these interactions but also were more at ease in obtaining patients' medical histories. While this study does not directly address interactions between LGBTQ populations and correctional officers, education and training has important implications for facilitating appropriate treatment in correctional settings. Research shows that implicit bias and empathy training provide criminal justice and treatment professionals with the essential interpersonal skills needed to treat offenders with respect and dignity.

Access to Medical Treatment

LGBTQ inmates have special medical needs that are not always provided to them during their incarceration. These needs include hormone replacement therapy (HRT) for transgender inmates. Federal prisons are legally required to provide HRT to transgender inmates (*Adams v. Federal Bureau of Prisons et al.*, 2011). According to the Massachusetts District Court, the decision to provide HRT does not hinge on whether an inmate is receiving HRT prior to incarceration. Regardless, federal prisons are mandated to provide HRT to transgender inmates who request it. One way to ensure all prisons are adhering to the ruling of *Adams v. Federal Bureau of Prisons et al.* (2011) is to have a system in which prisons are held accountable through yearly reviews from the Federal Bureau of Prisons (FBOP). This would ensure that transgender inmates are receiving important medical treatments during their incarceration.

Access to HIV screening during incarceration is important for all inmates. However, it may be especially important for LGBTQ inmates because they are more likely to be sexually victimized while incarcerated (Marksamer & Tobin, 2013). Without access to HIV screening during incarceration, LGBTQ inmates may be denied life-saving medical treatment. A study conducted by Macgowan et al. (2009) facilitated rapid HIV testing for over 33,000 inmates across four states to determine the number of undiagnosed HIV cases in U.S. correctional facilities. The researchers identified 269 previously undiagnosed HIV cases. Macgowan et al. (2009) stresses the importance of all inmates having access to rapid HIV testing, whether they report risky sexual behaviors. It also is important to note the rate of acquisition of HIV while incarcerated is three times higher than in the general United States population (Maruschak & Bronson, 2017). In light of this information, action needs to be taken by prison administration to ensure all inmates have access to rapid HIV testing during incarceration to ensure the health of their prison population.

Preventing the Spread of Sexually Transmitted Infections

Inmates are having sex while incarcerated. However, the primary solution to prevent the spread of sexually transmitted infections (STIs) is to ban sexual behavior among inmates. Mahon (1996) conducted focus groups with current and former inmates of New York State correctional facilities and found that without access to latex barriers, inmates attempt to have safe sex by utilizing rubber gloves and plastic wrap. Krienert, Walsh, and Lech (2014) found similar results and explain that the use of these crude alternatives exacerbates the risk of disease transmission. These studies were published eighteen years apart, yet there has been little effort by prison administrators and staff to educate inmates.

Many prison administrators acknowledge that homosexual behavior is a logical consequence of incarceration and the use of condoms is necessary to prevent the spread of STIs. Providing condoms to inmates is controversial, but if one considers it in terms of general population risks, the need for condoms in prisons is self-evident. Most inmates are eventually released back into the community. If inmates have contracted an STI while incarcerated but never received medical care, they are more likely to transmit this infection in the general population (Krienert et al., 2014). Therefore, prison administrations and medical staff need to take a closer look at the costs and benefits of providing condoms to inmates.

Those who oppose condom distribution believe it will lead to increased sexual behavior, including sexual assault. They also fear condom use will lead to an increase in drug use (i.e., inmates will use the condoms to hide drugs anally) or will disrupt prison operations. Research indicates that these fears are unfounded and access to condoms does not interrupt the prison routine, represents no threat to security or operations, does not lead to an increase in sexual activity or drug use, and is accepted by most prisoners and staff once it is introduced (Gido, 2002). It is important to note that condom distribution is not the only solution to preventing the spread of STIs within the prison system. Educational classes that emphasize sexual health and disease prevention can be a valuable resource to inmates, especially for those who have little to no education regarding sexual health. Krienert et al. (2014) found while inmates try to practice safe sex, their methods reflect a rudimentary understanding of safe sex practices in terms of reducing disease transmission. Therefore, providing condoms as well as educational programs to teach inmates about safe sex practices could potentially reduce the transmission of STIs in prisons.

Much of the research on prison sex focuses almost exclusively on male prisoners, and there is little research examining sexual behavior among female prisoners (see for exception Hensley, 2002). Research does tell us that sexual relationships among women prisoners tend to be consensual (Hensley, 2002; The Howard League for Penal Reform, 2014). However, as with other prison policies and practices, the health concerns of women typically lag behind those of men. For example, at the height of the HIV epidemic in the 1990s, New York State provided condoms to inmates at no costs to prevent the spread of HIV and other STIs (see Gido, 2002). Although the distribution of condoms is widespread in the United States, the use of dental dams in female prisons has not happened. A dental dam is a sheet of plastic or latex used to cover the vagina while performing oral sex. Dental dams reduce the risk of STI transmission during oral sex by acting as a barrier to vaginal and anal secretions that contain bacteria and viruses. The practice of allowing condoms in male prisons but not allowing dental dams in female prisons seems unfair to many female inmates. They argue they should receive the same protection as men against STIs and prison policies that do not allow the use of dental dams are discriminatory.

Promising Policies and Programs

Habilitation Programs

A more recent trend in prisons is the introduction of "habilitation" programs. Unlike rehabilitation, which seeks to help offenders relearn prosocial behaviors in the hopes of avoiding future criminality, habilitation suggests that there are certain skill sets and behaviors that offenders never learned, which may hold especially true for special needs offenders. Life skills training programs, for instance, are designed to help offenders improve their decision-making skills. These training programs teach offenders how to identify "thinking errors" through the use of cognitive restructuring strategies. These programs encourage offenders to explore why they choose criminal behavior over law-abiding behavior.

Some of these programs ask offenders to consider why they have chosen a criminal career rather than a legitimate job or why they acted out violently instead of seeking nonviolent resolutions to problems. Other life skills programs that are modeled after the habilitation philosophy include parenting, problem solving, financial literacy, and computer literacy. Life skills programs recognize the need to teach offenders the cognitive and social skills they need to be successful in the community. Early empirical evidence suggest these programs are effective in improving quality of life and reducing recidivism for offenders returning to the community, especially offenders with special needs (Whitehead, Dodson, & Edwards, 2013).

Questionable Practices and Policies

Private Prisons

Private prison corporations like Corrections Corporation of America (CCA) and the GEO Group are the fastest growing organizations that house prisoners for profit. CCA and the GEO Group boast they can dramatically cut costs for states because they have a lower overhead than state-run correctional facilities. One way private prisons attempt to cut costs is to reduce or eliminate the medical services they provide to inmates. This may result in a lower bottom line for private prisons, but it places the inmates in a position of receiving inadequate medical care. This is a particularly troubling situation for offenders with special needs.

Medical expenses represent the number one cost issue for correctional facilities. However, prisoners with special needs, such as mental illness, HIV, and terminal illness may require costly medications or medical interventions. To reduce costs and increase their profit, CCA and GEO Group may place the desires of stockholders above inmates with serious medical issues. Deliberate indifference to the serious medical needs of inmates also can result in inmate lawsuits. Beyond the cuts to health care for prisoners, private prisons also cut benefits to their employees. For instance, private prisons refuse to give employees full-time status, which prevents the employees from receiving insurance and retirement benefits. The unions do not represent correctional officers in these private-run facilities.

Private prison employees receive 58 hours less training than their publicly employed counterparts. A lack of properly trained personnel can place inmates and correctional officers in dangerous situations because there is insufficient training for responding to crisis situations. In addition, turnover results in fewer staff, which could increase the risk of an escape or riot. Private prisons are undeniably less safe than public prisons. Additionally, inadequate training increases the odds that prison administrators will be held liable for failure to train under Section 1983 claims. Given the troublesome issues surrounding the use of private prisons, especially the questionable cost-cutting measures they utilize, we believe the use of private for-profit prisons should be eliminated.

Solitary Confinement

Solitary confinement is a term used in institutional corrections that refers to the isolation or segregation of prisoners from the general population. Solitary confinement, sometimes called administrative segregation, is carried out in restrictive cellblocks, segregated housing units (SHUs, pronounced "shoes"), or supermax facilities. Correctional staff predominantly use solitary confinement as a punitive measure to control disruptive or dangerous inmates. It is a maximum-security classification level that typically involves inmates living in single cells, the reduction or complete elimination of group activities, among inmates, limited contact with other human beings, infrequent outside interaction including infrequent phone calls and noncontact visitation, strengthened measures to control contraband, the use of additional security measures and equipment, and extremely limited access to rehabilitative or educational programs. In addition, solitary confinement is used as a form of protective custody for inmates who represent vulnerable populations (e.g. mentally ill, developmentally disabled, homosexuals, snitches, high-profile offenders, and sex offenders).

There are a number of ethical concerns surrounding the use of solitary confinement. In supermax prisons, for instance, researchers voice concerns about the effects of prolonged solitary confinement on the mental health of prisoners. Literature in the social sciences consistently shows when human beings are subjected to social isolation and reduced environmental stimulation, they may suffer from mental deterioration and in some cases develop symptoms of psychiatric disturbances (see e.g., Grassian, 2006; Guy, 2016; Weir, 2012). These include perceptual distortions, hallucinations, hyperresponsivity to external stimuli, aggressive fantasies, overt paranoia, inability to concentrate, and problems with impulse control. Although the conditions of solitary confinement are relatively extreme, they do not have a uniform effect on all inmates. Occasionally, the solitary environment may actually prove beneficial. A study conducted by the National Institute of Justice suggests that short-term segregation (less than one year) actually showed improved mental functioning, including lower levels of anxiety, depression, hopelessness, hostility/anger control, hypersensitivity, and psychosis.

There also is evidence to suggest that the medical and psychiatric care of segregated inmates is woefully inadequate. In the case of *Madrid v. Gomez* (1995), inmates challenged the conditions of confinement at Pelican Bay State Prison's segregated housing unit (SHU). The medical services at the SHU were chronically deficient, and medical personnel were provided with insufficient training and supervision. Additionally, mental health services were found to be markedly lacking. For example, Pelican Bay failed to offer screening of inmates entering the SHU for psychiatric illness, and as a result, many psychiatrically ill prisoners did not receive proper treatment until they became flagrantly psychotic or suicidal.

Some legal scholars argue the use of solitary confinement is unfair because inmates are not entitled to the same due process rights as individuals facing disciplinary hearings. In *Hewitt v. Helms* (1987), the court held that prisoners have no independent federal constitutional due process liberty interest in remaining free from segregation because it is a type of confinement that prisoners should reasonably anticipate receiving at some point during their incarceration. The absence of due process rights increases the likelihood that correctional staff may arbitrarily subject prisoners to long periods of segregation. California recognizes the potential for such an abuse and, according to the California Code of Regulations, there is a constitutionally protected liberty interest to be free from placement in administrative segregation. One of three situations must be present: (1) the inmate presents an immediate threat to the safety of the inmate or others, (2) the inmate endangers institution security, or (3) the inmate jeopardizes the integrity of an investigation of an alleged serious misconduct or criminal activity.

It is important to note that solitary confinement may be necessary. Within correctional facilities, there are inmates who are particularly vulnerable to victimization. For instance, jailhouse informants (i.e., snitches), if discovered, may be physically assaulted in retaliation for their perceived disloyalty. As a result, they need to be placed in administrative segregation for protection. Likewise, sex offenders represent a class of inmates that may need additional administrative protection. Many offenders find sex crimes to be morally reprehensible and, therefore, are likely to physically assault sex offenders if given the chance.

The use of solitary confinement is certainly warranted to protect correctional staff and inmates from dangerous prisoners. Inmates who have shown a pervasive pattern for acting out violently must be segregated to reduce the likelihood they will injure others. However, the empirical evidence suggest there are serious emotional, social, and psychological consequences of isolation, and this may exacerbate the conditions of inmates with intellectual disabilities or mental illness (Grassian, 2006; Guy, 2016). In addition, solitary confinement increases the odds that isolated inmates will develop mental health issues (Grassian, 2006). Correctional administrators should weigh the safety and security concerns of their prisons against the psychological and emotional harm inmates may suffer as a result of isolation. In terms of the human costs, we believe the use of solitary confinement should be limited.

Conclusion

In this chapter, we discussed policies and practices related to a narrow group of special needs offenders, including women, juveniles, and LGBTQ offenders. These populations of offenders are frequently overlooked in terms of policies and practices that help them negotiate the criminal justice system and provide effective treatment and rehabilitation options. We know that women have gendered pathways to crime, and the treatment responses should be gender responsive. A "one-size-fits-all" model will not adequately address the treatment and rehabilitation needs of women offenders. Juvenile offenders continue to receive harsh punishments, are more likely to be physically and sexually abused while incarcerated, and receive questionable treatment programs, such as Scared Straight. More effective policies show that improving attachment during early childhood will set juveniles up to be successful adults and avoid criminal justice involvement. LGBTQ offenders are vulnerable during incarceration and, like juveniles, are frequently targets of physical and sexual assault. Transgender offenders may have a particularly difficult time acclimating to the prison environment. Prison administrators must provide for the safety and security of transgender offenders as well as appropriate medical treatments, such as HRT.

Some policies and practices lack empirical support or should be reduced or eliminated because they are ethically questionable. The use of for-profit prisons is troubling because of the cost-cutting measures they utilize. Denying inmates medicines or certain medical interventions to reduce costs means for-profit prisons are putting their financial bottom lines ahead of the medical needs of offenders. In the context of this handbook, this practice would undoubtedly harm one's quality of life and/or hasten death. The use of solitary confinement has detrimental social, emotional, and psychological effects on those who are incarcerated, and it exacerbates the conditions of those diagnosed with mental health issues and intellectual challenges. Therefore, the use of solitary confinement should be used only as a final option to control the behavior of those who are incarcerated.

We encourage criminal justice professionals and policy makers to base the development and implementation of treatment and rehabilitation programs on empirical evidence. Criminal justice practitioners and policy makers should reject policies that are retributive because they do not deter criminal behavior but rather increase the likelihood of future criminality. In addition, policies and practices that improve the quality of life for offenders with special needs should be a priority. Finally, as stated in the preface, we hope this handbook will help to facilitate conversations among criminal justice and health care professionals to improve the treatment and care of special needs offenders and to implement not only empirically supported policies and practices but policies and practices that emphasize care and compassion.

References

Adams v. Federal Bureau of Prisons et al., 09–10272JTL (2011).

American Correctional Association. (1990). *The female offender: What does the future hold?* Alexandria, VA: American Correctional Association.

Baradon, T., Fonagy, P., Bland, K., Lénárd, K., & Sleed, M. (2008). New beginnings—an experience-based programme addressing the attachment relationship between mothers and their babies in prisons. *Journal of Child Psychotherapy*, *34*(2), 240–258. doi:10.1080/00754170802208065

Belknap, J. (2007). *The invisible woman: Gender, crime, and justice* (3rd ed.). Belmont, CA: Thompson Wadsworth.

Belknap, J., & Holsinger, K. (2006). The gendered nature of risk factors for delinquency. *Feminist Criminology*, *1*(1), 48–71. doi:10.1177/1557085105282897

Bloom, B. (1993). Incarcerated mothers and their children: Maintaining family ties. In the American Correctional Association (Ed.), *Female offenders: Meeting needs of a neglected population* (pp. 60–68). Laurel, MD: American Correctional Association.

Bloom, B., Chesney-Lind, M., & Owen, B. (1994). *Women in California prisons: Hidden victims of the war on drugs.* San Francisco, CA: Center on Juvenile and Criminal Justice.

Bloom, B. E., & Covington, S. S. (1998, November). *Gender-specific programming for female offenders: What is it and why is it important.* Paper presented at the annual meeting of the American Society of Criminology, Washington, DC.

Bloom, B., Owen, B., & Covington, S. (2003). *Gender-responsive strategies: Research practice and guiding principles for women offenders.* Washington, DC: U.S. Department of Justice, National Institute of Corrections.

Brett, C. (1993). From victim to victimizer. In the American Correctional Association (Ed.), *Female offenders: Meeting needs of a neglected population* (pp. 26–30). Laurel, MD: American Correctional Association.

Browne, A., & Finkelhor, D. (1986). Impact of child sexual abuse: A review of research. *Psychological Bulletin, 99,* 66–77.

Bureau of Justice Statistics. (1991). *Women in prison.* Washington, DC: U.S. Department of Justice.

Byrne, M. W., Goshin, L. S., & Joestl, S. S. (2010). Intergenerational transmission of attachment for infants raised in a prison nursery. *Attachment & Human Development, 12*(4), 375–393. doi:10.1080/14616730903417011

Chesney-Lind, M. (1997). *The female offender: Girls, women, and crime.* Thousand Oaks, CA: Sage.

Chesney-Lind, M. (2000). What to do about girls? Thinking about programs for young women. In M. McMahon (Ed.), *Assessment to assistance: Programs for women in community corrections* (pp. 139–170). Lanham, MD: American Correctional Association.

Chesney-Lind, M., & Shelden, R. G. (2004). *Girls, delinquency, and juvenile justice* (3rd ed.). Belmont, CA: Thompson Wadsworth.

Colvin, M., & Pauly, J. (1983). A critique of criminology: Toward an integrated structural-Marxist theory of delinquency production. *American Journal of Sociology, 89*(3), 513–551.

Daly, K. (1987). *Survey results of the Niantic interviews December 1983 and May 1986.* Mimeo, Yale University.

Daly, K. (1992). Women's pathways to felony court: Feminist theories of lawbreaking and problems of representation. *Southern California Review of Law and Women's Studies, 2,* 11–52.

Daly, K. (1994). *Gender, crime, and punishment.* New Haven, CT: Yale University Press.

Dilulio, J. J. (1995, November 27). The coming of the superpredators. *The Weekly Standard.* Retrieved from www.weeklystandard.com/the-coming-of-the-super-predators/article/8160

Drizin, S. (2014, April 09). The "superpredator" scare revisited. *Huffington Post.* Retrieved from www.huffingtonpost.com/steve-drizin/the-superpredator-scare_b_5113793.html

Faller, K. C. (1990). *Understanding child sexual maltreatment.* Newbury Park, CA: Sage.

Farr, K. A. (2000). Classification for female inmates: Moving forward. *Crime & Delinquency, 46*(1), 3–17. doi:10.1177/0011128700046001001

Gido, R. L. (2002). Inmates with HIV/AIDS: A growing concern. In C. Hensley (Ed.), *Prison sex: Policy and practice.* Boulder, CO: Lynne Reinner.

Giordano, P. C., Cernkovich, S. A., & Rudolph, J. L. (2002). Gender, crime, and desistance: Toward a theory of cognitive transformation. *American Journal of Sociology, 107*(4), 990–1064.

Gottfredson, M. R., & Hirschi, T. (1990). *A general theory of crime.* Stanford, CA: Stanford University Press.

Grassian, S. (2006). Psychiatric effects of solitary confinement. *Washington University Journal of Law & Policy, 22,* 325–383.

Guy, A. (2016, September 8). Locked up and locked down: Segregation of inmates with mental illness.

Hardyman, P. L., & Van Voorhis, P. (2004). *Developing gender-specific classification systems for women offenders.* Washington, DC: U.S. Department of Justice, National Institute of Corrections. Hensley, C. (2002). *Prison sex: Policy and practice.* Boulder, CO: Lynne Rienner.

Hewitt v. Helms, 482 U.S. 755 (1987).

Hirschi, T. (1969). *Cause of delinquency.* Berkeley, CA: The University of California Press.

Holtfreter, K., Reisig, M. D., & Morash, M. (2004). Poverty, state capital, and recidivism among women offenders. *Criminology & Public Policy, 3*(2), 185–208.

Howell, J. C., Feld, B. C., & Mears, D. P. (2012). Young offenders and an effective justice system repose. In R. Loeber & D. P. Farrington (Eds.), *From juvenile delinquency to adult crime: Criminal careers, justice policy and prevention.* Oxford, UK: Oxford University Press.

Hubbard, D. J., & Matthews, B. (2008). Reconciling the difference between the "gender responsive" and the "what works" literature to improve services for girls. *Crime & Delinquency, 54*(2), 225–258. doi:10.1177/0011128706296733

Jordan, K. L. (2011). Juvenile transfer and recidivism: A propensity score matching approach. *Journal of Crime and Justice, 35*(1), 53–67. doi:10.1080/0735648X.2011.632133Klenowski, P. M., Bell, K. J., & Dodson, K. D. (2011). An empirical examination of juvenile awareness programs in the United States: Can juveniles be "Scared Straight"? *Journal of Offender Rehabilitation, 49*, 254–272. doi:10.1080/10509671003716068

Koons, B. A., Burrow, J. D., Morash, M., & Bynum, T. (1997). Expert and offender perceptions of program elements linked to successful outcomes for incarcerated women. *Crime & Delinquency, 43*(4), 512–532. doi:10.1177/0011128797043004007

Krienert, J., Walsh, J., & Lech, L. (2014). Alternatives to abstinence: the practice of (un)safe sex in prison. *Criminal Justice Studies, 27*(4), 387–401. doi:10.1080/1478601X.2014.938740

Latessa, E. J., Listwan, S. J., & Koetzle, D. (2014). *What works (and doesn't) in reducing recidivism*. New York, NY: Routledge.

LeClair, D. (1990). *The incarcerated female offender: Victim or villain?* Boston, MA: Massachusetts Department of Corrections, Research Division.

Madrid v. Gomez, 899 F.Supp. 1146 (1995).

Mahon, N. (1996). New York inmates' HIV risk behaviors: The implications for prevention policy and programs. *American Journal of Public Health, 86*(9), 1211–1215.

Marksamer, J., & Tobin, H. J. (2013). *Standing with LGBT prisoners: An advocate's guide to ending abuse and combating imprisonment*. Washington, DC: National Center of Transgender Equality.

Maruschak, L. M., & Bronson, J. (2017). *HIV in prisons, 2015—statistical tables*. Washington, DC: Bureau of Justice Statistics, Office of Justice Programs.

Macgowan, R., Margolis, A., Richardson-Moore, A., Wang, T., Lalota, M., French, P. T., . . . Griffiths, S. D. (2009). Voluntary rapid human immunodeficiency virus (HIV) testing in jails. *Sexually Transmitted Diseases, 36*(Suppl 2), S9–S13. doi:10.1097/OLQ.0b013e318148b6b1

Miller, J. B. (1988). *Connections, disconnections, and violations* (Work in Progress No. 33). Wellesley, MA: Stone Center, Working Paper Series.

Morash, M., & Robinson, A. L. (2002). Correctional administrators' perspectives on gender arrangements and family-related programming for women offenders. *Marriage & Family Review, 32*(3/4), 83–109. doi:10.1300/J002v32n03_6

Morash, M., Bynum, T. S., & Koons, B. A. (1998). *Women offenders: Programming needs and promising approaches*. Washington, DC: United States Department of Justice, National Institute of Justice.

Nagin, D., & Pogarsky, G. (2001). Integrating celerity, impulsivity, and extralegal sanction threats into a model of general deterrence. *Criminology, 39*(4), 865–892. doi:10.1111/j.1745-9125.2001.tb00943.x

Pratt, T. C. (2008). *Addicted to incarceration: Corrections policy and the politics of misinformation in the United States*. Thousand Oaks, CA: Sage.

Reisig, M. D., Holtfreter, K., & Morash, M. (2002). Social capital among women offenders: Examining distribution of social networks and resources. *Journal of Contemporary Criminal Justice, 18*(2),167–187. doi:10.1177/1043986202018002004

Rempel, M. (2014). *Evidence-based strategies for working with offenders*. Washington, DC: Center for Court Innovation, Bureau of Justice Assistance, U.S. Department of Justice.

Salisbury, E. J., & Van Voorhis, P. (2009). Gendered pathways: An empirical investigation of women probationers' paths to incarceration. *Criminal Justice & Behavior, 36*(6), 541–566. doi:10.1177/0093854809334076

Sherman, L. W., Farrington, D. P., Welsh, B. C., & MacKenzie, D. L. (2002). *Evidence-based crime prevention*. New York, NY: Taylor & Francis.

Sherman, L. W., Gottfredson, D. C., MacKenzie, D. L., Eck, J., Reuter, P., & Bushway, S. (1998). *Preventing crime: What works, what doesn't, what's promising*. Washington, DC: U.S. Department of Justice, National Institute of Justice.

Snyder, H. N., & Sickmund, M. (2000). *Challenging myths*. Washington, DC: U.S. Department of Justice, Office of Juvenile Justice and Delinquency Prevention.

Snyder, H. N., & Sickmund, M. (2006). *Juvenile offenders and victims: 2006 national report*. Washington, DC: U.S. Department of Justice, Office of Justice Programs.

Song, L., & Lieb, R. (1993). *Recidivism: The effects of incarceration and length of time served*. Olympia, WA: Washington State Institute for Public Policy.

The Howard League for Penal Reform. (2014). *Women in prison: Coercive and consensual sex*. London, UK: The Howard League for Penal Reform.

Vann, N., Watson, J., Pollard, T., & Badalament, J. (2011). *Working with dads: Parenting skills development*. Washington, DC: U.S. Department of Health and Human Services, Office of Family Assistance.

Van Voorhis, P., & Salisbury, E. J. (2014). *Correctional counseling and rehabilitation*. New York, NY: Routledge.

Van Voorhis, P., Pealer, J., Spiropoulis, G., & Sutherland, J. (2001). *Validation of offender custody classification and needs assessment systems for women offenders in the Colorado Department of Corrections*. Cincinnati, OH: University of Cincinnati. Van Voorhis, P., Wright, E. M., Salisbury, E., & Bauman, A. (2010). Women's risk factors and their contributions to existing risk/needs assessment: The current status of a gender-responsive supplement. *Criminal Justice & Behavior, 37*(3), 261–288. doi:10.1177/0093854809357442

Weir, K. (2012). Alone in 'the hole': Psychologists probe the mental health effects of solitary confinement. *American Psychological Association*. Retrieved from www.apa.org/monitor/2012/05/solitary.aspx

Whitehead, J. T., Dodson, K. D., & Edwards, B. D. (2013). *Corrections: Exploring crime, punishment, and justice in America* (3rd ed.). New York, NY: Routledge.

Wright, B., & Edginton, E. (2016). Evidence-based parenting interventions to promote secure attachment. *Global Pediatric Health, 3*, 1–14. doi:10.1177/2333794X16661888

Wright, E., Salisbury, E. & Van Voorhis, P. (2007). Predicting the prison misconduct of women offenders: The importance of gender responsive needs. *Journal of Contemporary Criminal Justice, 23*(4), 310–340.

Wright, V. (2010). Deterrence in criminal justice: Evaluating certainty vs. severity of punishment. *The Sentencing Project*. Washington, DC: The Sentencing Project.

Yingling, C. T., Cotler, K., & Hughes, T. L. (2017). Building nurses' capacity to address health inequities: Incorporating lesbian, gay, bisexual and transgender health content in a family nurse practitioner programme. *Journal of Clinical Nursing, 26*(17/18), 2807–2817. doi:10.1111/jocn.13707

INDEX

Page numbers in italic indicate a figure and page numbers in bold indicate a table.

Made in United States
North Haven, CT
22 August 2023

40597349R00307